# The Face of Music

OVER 300 CLOSE-UP PORTRAITS OF MUSIC'S MOST SIGNIFICANT ICONS OF THE 20TH CENTURY COMPLETE WITH THEIR BIOGRAPHIES AND INTERESTING FACTS

DAVID S. THOMPSON

The Face of Music


tellwell

Tellwell Talent
www.tellwell.ca

ISBN
978-0-2288-4940-7 (Hardcover)
978-0-2288-4939-1 (Paperback)

# TABLE OF CONTENTS



NOTES:

1. All biographies are taken directly from www.wikipedia.org.
2. All Internet Browser URL shortcuts i.e. "myportrait.art/davidbowie" only work when entered into your Browser's address field at the top of your Browser as a URL. It DOES NOT work in Google Searches or any other Search Engine.

# FORWARD

Well 11 years ago being institutionalized in psychological hospitals for severe depression and suicidal tendencies I would day dream about my art to escape my reality. Dreaming of having a book of all my art some day and having people loving my art. Well today I finally finished that dream. Thank you all my Facebook friends that have been with me for years now without your encouraging words keeping me going I would never of made it this far. Your comments were better than any antidepressants any doctor could ever of subscribed.

***<u>Mercedes Hernandas Garcia</u>*** is the formost art critic in the *world* on Facebook and I've added just two of her critiques ...Thank you so much Mercedes for appreciating my art!!! You can vist her Facebook Art Page by entering the URL Shortcut in your Internet Browser myportrait.art/ars

MY GOD.....Thank you all...it's been such a path from bed ridden for too many years to the spirit of hope you all give me each and every day ..THANK YOU. ..THANK YOU. ..THANK YOU. ..

Dave's posts have been liked 110,000 times

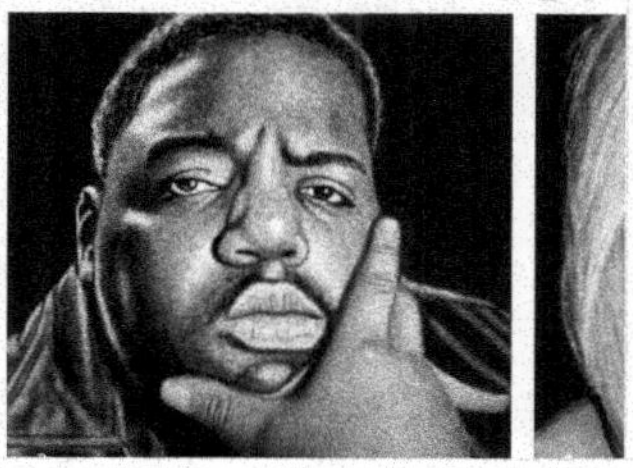

**Tina M. Jorgensen**
You are so very incredibly talented!!

**Sanama Ahmadi**
Dear **Dave Thompson** you are an extraordinary talented and worldwide contemporary visual-artist ,and this is great documentary in the world of documentations and celebrities' ,you not only drawing portrait but attachment the biography of them that the viewers could knowing them and recognize them ,this is huge artistic talented and job . Thanks for being dear **Dave Thompson** ,
27m Like Reply

**Shelly Roxanne Wiseberg**
You are an extremely talented artist and know first hand what it is like living with depression and that art is a way to inspire ourselves when times are tough and wish you only the best in creating from your heart and soul with self expression.

**ReNae Patterson**
Each time I see one of your portraits I just am amazed and totally blown away...you are such an inspiration!! Thanks for sharing!

**L.J. Nogler**
Man, how are you not off the charts yet? Your skill is top notch!

**Iris Estela Medina**
You're a genius... a great artist Dave!!!!! Thank you very much!!!
Automatically Translated

**Nikki Moran**
Ur work....Takes my breath away...Simply Stunning

**Michelle Proctor**
INCREDIBLE GENIUS LEVEL, INTELLECTUAL ARTISTIC ABILITY, WOW!!! I HAVE NEVER SEEN SUCH TALENT,
He looks alive!!!!!!!

**Anne H. Flannery**
Dave, I am so happy that you share these drawings with us. They are just phenomenal!
1m Love Reply

**Mercedes Hernandez Garcia**
I discover myself before such exceptional and great portrait of great musician Johnny Cash, where an impressive and spectacular portrait, our great friend Dave Thompson, reaffirms himself as one of the best artists of the moment! What an exceptional work done to graphite!
Automatically Translated

**Kathy Hoch**
Your talent is exquisite you have been blessed by a higher power!

**Bekah Lynn**
I'm a big fan and I never heard of you before today ... But I will not forget ... You are amazing ...

**Simone Helmus**
Keep making such beautiful art please. I enjoy it very much
4h Like Reply

**Xavier Balzola**
Your work is as good or better than ANYTHING I have ever seen Dave...The Met in New York or ANY salon in New York would be proud to exhibit your work.
12h Love Reply

**Simone Helmus**
Keep making such beautiful art please. I enjoy it very much
4h Like Reply

**Sylvia Brady**
You are truly amazing and inspiring. I love admiring the beautiful art you do.

**Mercedes Hernandez Garcia**
Do you know my friend that I deeply admire the extraordinary exclusive and great creative capacity that you show in every new and great portrait, this time Stevie Ray Vaughan is the protagonist of an extraordinary moment of your unbeatable mastery of drawing!
Like · Reply · See Original (Spanish) · 2d

# ACCOLADES

Some of my accolades and International Art Contest Awards along way...

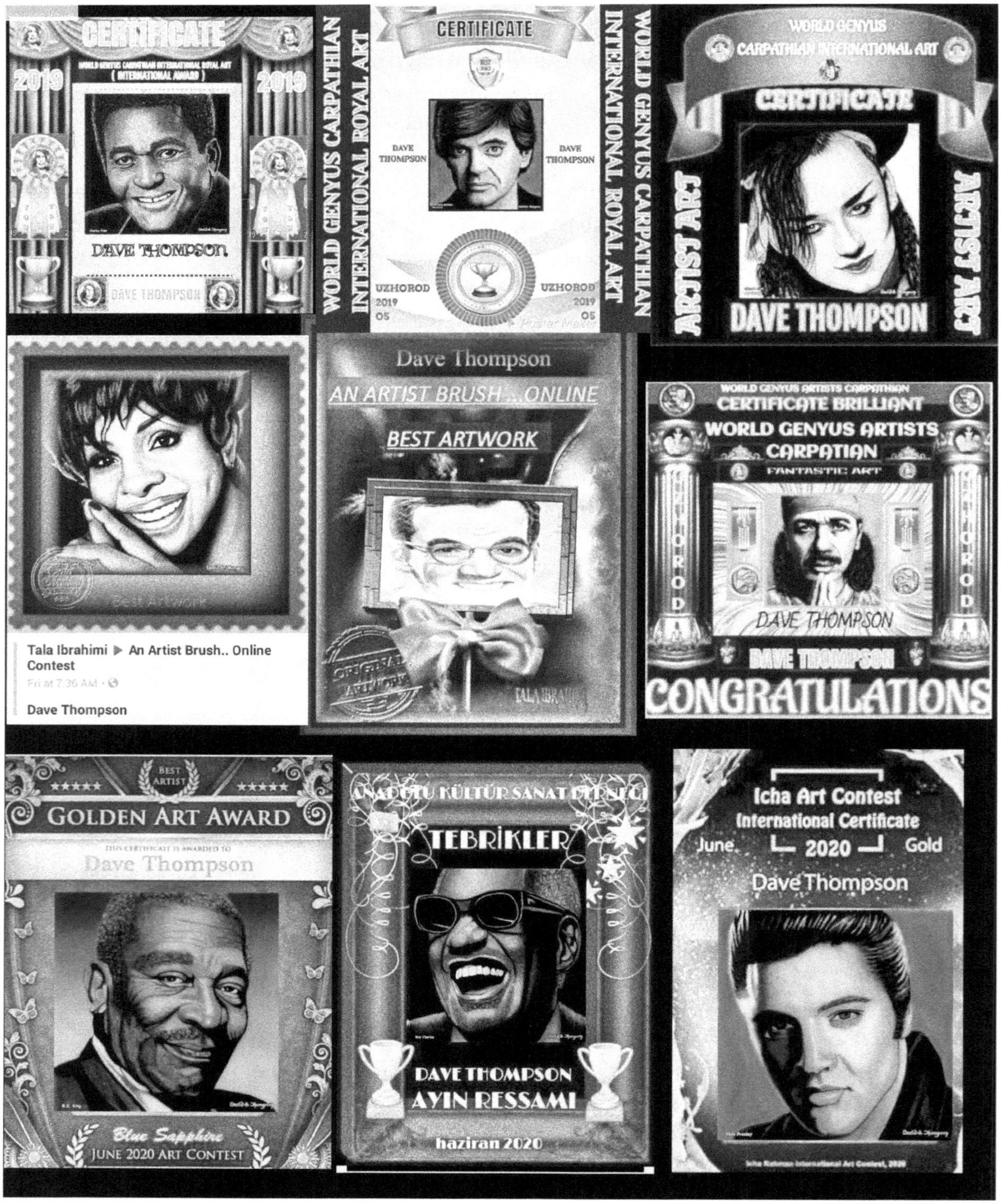

# INTERNATIONAL MAGAZINE COVERS

Some of the International Art Magazines I've been featured on...

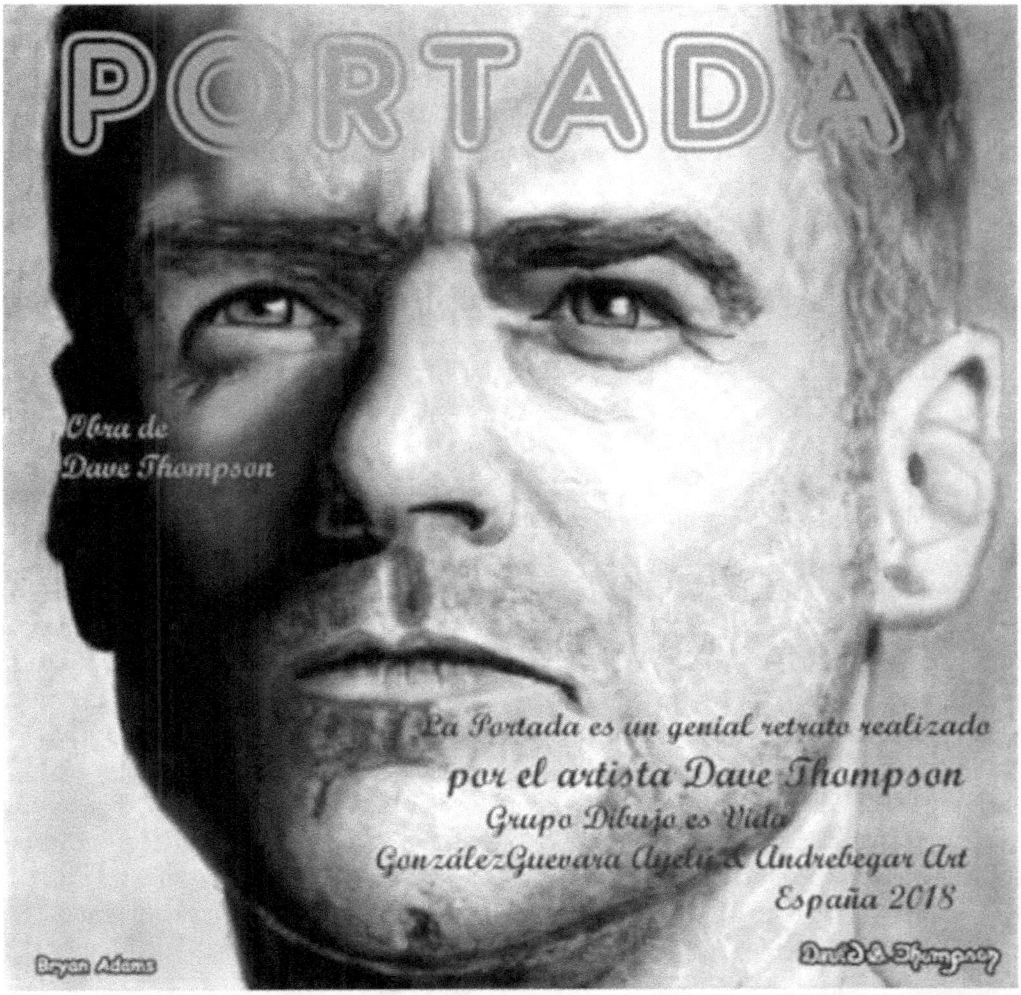


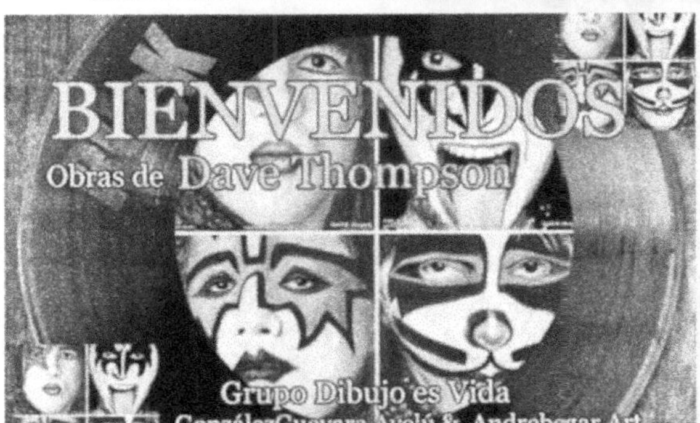


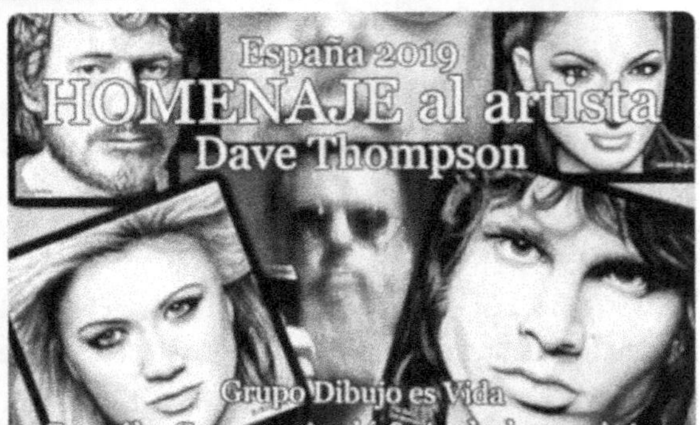

# ABBA

(Total Albums Sold: 350 Million)(Genre: Pop) ABBA are a Swedish pop group formed in Stockholm in 1972 by Agnetha Fältskog, Björn Ulvaeus, Benny Andersson, and Anni-Frid Lyngstad. The group's name is an acronym of the first letters of their first names. They became one of the most commercially successful acts in the history of popular music, topping the charts worldwide from 1974 to 1983. In 1974 ABBA were Sweden's first winner of the Eurovision Song Contest, with the song "Waterloo", which in 2005 was chosen as the best song in the competition's history as part of the 50th anniversary celebration of the contest.During the band's main active years, it consisted of two married couples: Fältskog and Ulvaeus, and Lyngstad and Andersson. With the increase of their popularity, their personal lives suffered, which eventually resulted in the collapse of both marriages. The relationship changes were reflected in the group's music, with latter compositions featuring darker and more introspective lyrics. After ABBA disbanded, Andersson and Ulvaeus achieved success writing music for the stage,while Lyngstad and Fältskog pursued solo careers Ten years after their disbanding, a compilation, ABBA Gold was released, which became a worldwide bestseller. In 1999, ABBA's music was adapted into the successful musical Mamma Mia! that toured worldwide. A film of the same name, released in 2008, became the highest-grossing film in the United Kingdom that year. A sequel, Mamma Mia! Here We Go Again, was released in 2018. That same year it was announced that the band had recorded two new songs after 35 years of being inactive.They are one of the best-selling music artists of all time, with record sales estimated to be 150-385 million records and singles sold worldwide. In 2012, ABBA was ranked eight best selling singles artist in United Kingdom with 11.2 million singles sold. ABBA were the first group from a non-English-speaking country to achieve consistent success in the charts of English-speaking countries, including the United States, United Kingdom, Republic of Ireland, Canada, Australia, New Zealand, The Philippines and South Africa. They are the best-selling Swedish band of all time and one of the best-selling bands originating in continental Europe. ABBA had eight consecutive number-one albums in the UK. The group also enjoyed significant success in Latin America, and recorded a collection of their hit songs in Spanish. The group was inducted into the Rock and Roll Hall of Fame in 2010. In 2015, their song "Dancing Queen" was inducted into the Recording Academy's Grammy Hall of Fame..

# Agatha Faltskog

(Net Worth: $200Million) (Total Albums Sold: 350Million)(Height: 5'-8")

Agnetha Åse Fältskog (born 5 April 1950) is a Swedish singer, songwriter, musician and actress. She achieved success in Sweden after the release of her debut album Agnetha Fältskog in 1968, and reached international stardom as a member of the pop group ABBA, which has sold over 350 million albums and singles worldwide, making them one of the best-selling music artists in history.

After the break-up of ABBA, Fältskog found success with three albums and a leading role in a movie as a solo artist in the 1980s, though she became more solitary in the 1990s, avoiding outside publicity and residing on the Stockholm County island of Ekerö. Fältskog stopped recording music for 16 years until she released a new album in 2004. She returned again in 2013 with A, her highest UK charting solo album to date.

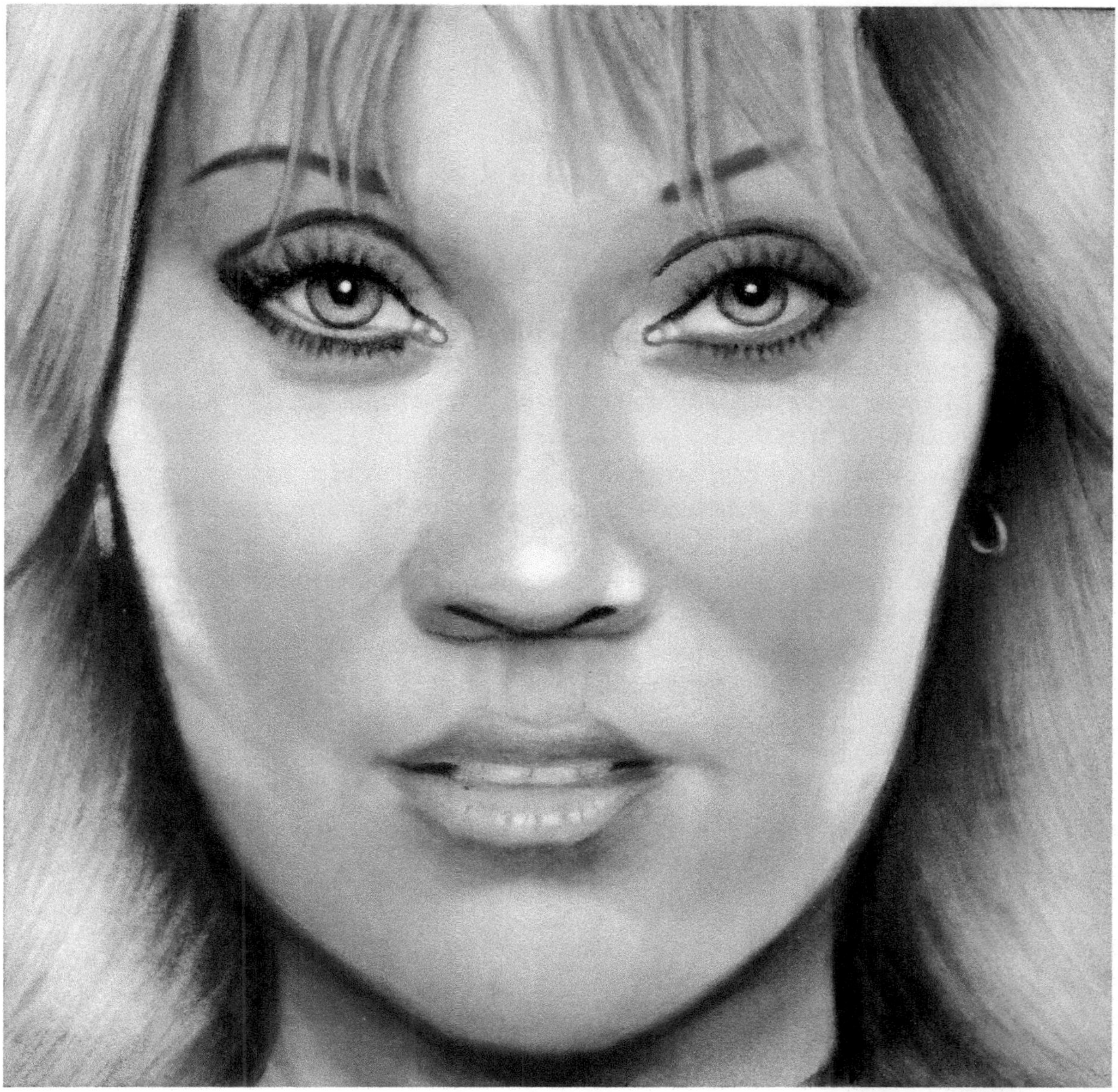

To view how this drawing was masterfully created or to purchase a Limited Edition Framed Artwork of Agnetha Fältskog type into your Internet Browser the URL shortcut ➡ **myportrait.art/agathafaltskog**

To listen to their Greatest Songs type into your Internet Browser the URL shortcut ➡ **radio.surf/abba**

To view all channels on THE FACE OF MUSIC Internet Radio MEGA Station type into your Internet Browser the URL shortcut ➡ **radio.surf/music**

To inquire about purchasing a Limited Edticn NFT of this portrait type into your Internet Browser the URL shortcut ➡ **myartnft.shop/agathafaltskog**

To view all available NFTs type into your Internet Browser the URL shortcut ➡ **myartnft.shop/all**

# AC/DC

(Total Albums Sold: 200 Million)(Genre: Hard Rock) AC/DC are an Australian rock band formed in Sydney in 1973 by Scottish-born brothers Malcolm and Angus Young. Their music has been variously described as hard rock, blues rock, and heavy metal, but the band themselves call it simply "rock and roll". AC/DC underwent several line-up changes before releasing their first album, 1975's High Voltage. Membership subsequently stabilised around the Young brothers, singer Bon Scott, drummer Phil Rudd, and bassist Mark Evans. Evans was fired from the band in 1977 and replaced by Cliff Williams, who has appeared on every AC/DC album since 1978's Powerage. In February 1980, Scott died of acute alcohol poisoning after a night of heavy drinking. The group considered disbanding but elected to stay together, bringing in longtime Geordie vocalist Brian Johnson as Scott's replacement. Later that year, the band released their first album with Johnson, Back in Black, which was dedicated to Scott's memory. The album launched AC/DC to new heights of success and became one of the best selling albums of all time.The band's eighth studio album, For Those About to Rock We Salute You (1981), was their first album to reach number one in the United States. Prior the release of 1983's Flick of the Switch, drummer Rudd left the band and was replaced by Simon Wright, being in turn replaced by Chris Slade in 1989. The band experienced a commercial resurgence in the early nineties with the release of 1990s The Razors Edge. Rudd returned to the band in 1994, replacing Slade and appearing on the band's next five albums. Their fifteenth studio album Black Ice was the second-highest-selling album of 2008, and their biggest chart hit since For Those About to Rock, eventually reaching No.1 worldwide.

- Continued on page 5 -

# Bon Scott

(Net Worth: $10 Million) (Height: 5'-8")

Ronald Belford "Bon" Scott (9 July 1946 – 19 February 1980) was an Australian singer, songwriter and instrumentalist, best known for being the lead vocalist and lyricist of the Australian hard rock band AC/DC from 1974 until his death in 1980.Scott was born in Forfar in Angus, Scotland, and spent his early years in Kirriemuir. He moved to Australia with his family in 1952 at the age of six, living in Melbourne for four years before settling in Fremantle, Western Australia.Scott formed his first band, The Spektors, in 1964 and became the band's drummer and occasional lead vocalist. He performed in several other bands including The Valentines and Fraternity before replacing Dave Evans as the lead singer of AC/DC in 1974 .AC/DC's popularity grew throughout the 1970s, initially in Australia, and then internationally. Their 1979 album Highway to Hell reached the top 20 in the United States, and the band seemed on the verge of a commercial breakthrough. However, on 19 February 1980, Scott died after a night out in London. AC/DC briefly considered disbanding, but the group recruited vocalist Brian Johnson of the British glam rock band Geordie. AC/DC's subsequent album, Back in Black, was released only five months later, and was a tribute to Scott. It went on to become the second-best-selling album in history.In the July 2004 issue of Classic Rock, Scott was rated as number one in a list of the "100 Greatest Frontmen of All Time". Hit Parader ranked Scott as fifth on their 2006 list of the 100 Greatest Heavy Metal Vocalists of all time.

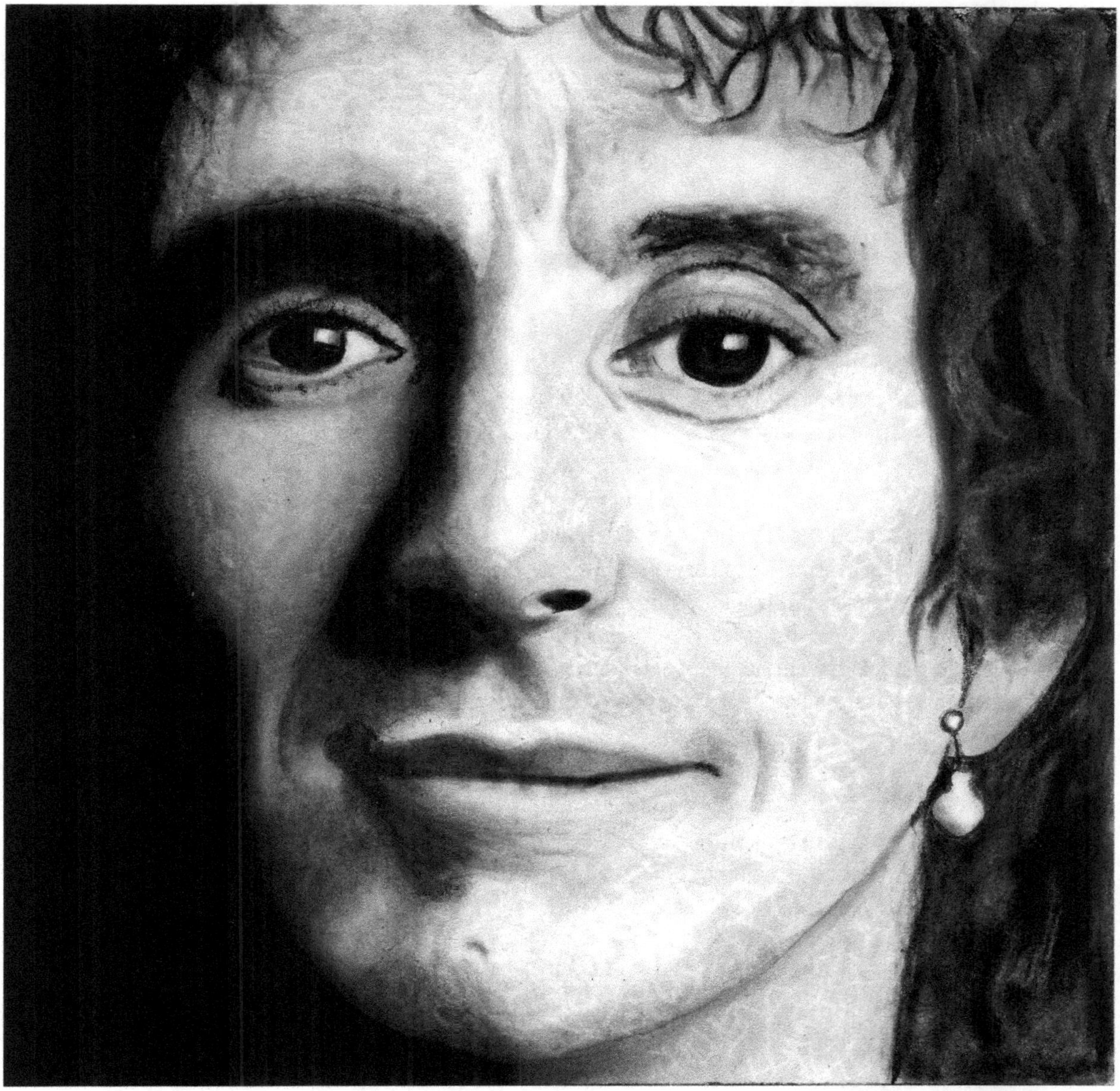

To view how this drawing was masterfully created or to purchase a Limited Edition Framed Artwork of Bon Scott type into your Internet Browser the URL shortcut ➡ **myportrait.art/bonscott**

To listen to AC/DC's Greatest Songs type into your Internet Browser the URL shortcut ➡ **radio.surf/acdc**

To view all channels on THE FACE OF MUSIC Internet Radio MEGA Station type into your Internet Browser the URL shortcut ➡ **radio.surf/music**

To inquire about purchasing a Limited Edtion NFT of this portrait type into your Internet Browser the URL shortcut ➡ **myartnft.shop/bonscott**

To view all available NFTs type into your Internet Browserthe URL shortcut ➡ **myartnft.shop/all**

# AC/DC

-Continued -

The band's line-up remained the same for twenty years, until 2014 with Malcolm Young's retirement due to early-onset dementia (he died in 2017) and Rudd's legal troubles. Malcolm was replaced by his nephew Stevie Young, who debuted on AC/DC's 2014 album Rock or Bust, and on its accompanying tour, previous drummer Chris Slade filled in for Rudd. In 2016, Johnson was advised to stop touring due to worsening hearing loss. Guns N' Roses frontman Axl Rose stepped in as the band's vocalist for the remainder of that year's dates. Long-term bass player and background vocalist Cliff Williams retired from AC/DC at the end of the Rock or Bust tour in 2016 and the group entered a four-year hiatus. A reunion of the Rock or Bust lineup was announced in September 2020 and the band's seventeenth studio album Power Up was released two months later. AC/DC have sold more than 200 million records worldwide, including 75 million albums in the United States, making them the ninth-highest-selling artist in the United States and the 16th-best-selling artist worldwide. Back in Black has sold an estimated 50 million units worldwide, making it the third-highest-selling album by any artist, and the highest-selling album by any band. The album has sold 22 million units in the US where it is the sixth-highest-selling album of all time. AC/DC ranked fourth on VH1's list of the "100 Greatest Artists of Hard Rock" and were named the seventh "Greatest Heavy Metal Band of All Time" by MTV. In 2004, AC/DC ranked No. 72 on the Rolling Stone list of the "100 Greatest Artists of All Time". Producer Rick Rubin, who wrote an essay on the band for the Rolling Stone list, referred to AC/DC as "the greatest rock and roll band of all time". In 2010, VH1 ranked AC/DC number 23 in its list of the "100 Greatest Artists of All Time".

# Brian Johnson

(Net Worth: $90 Million) (Height: 5'-5")

Brian Francis Johnson (born 5 October 1947) is an English singer and songwriter. In 1980, after the death of Bon Scott, he became the third lead singer of the Australian rock band AC/DC. He and the rest of the band were inducted into the Rock and Roll Hall of Fame in 2003. In March 2016, he stepped down from touring on the Rock or Bust World Tour due to hearing problems. He stated in an interview that he "had a pretty good run" in AC/DC and implied that he might not be returning. On September 30, 2020, AC/DC officially confirmed that Johnson along with fellow band mates Phil Rudd and Cliff Williams returned to record the band's 2020 album, Power Up in August 2018.

His first album with AC/DC, Back in Black, became the second best-selling album of all time according to most estimates. The Guardian ranked the successful transition to Johnson at No. 36 on their list of 50 key events in rock music history.

Johnson is known for his distinctive singing voice and strong Geordie accent. In July 2014, he was awarded an honorary degree of Doctor of Music by Northumbria University in the city of Newcastle in recognition of his significant contribution to the music industry.

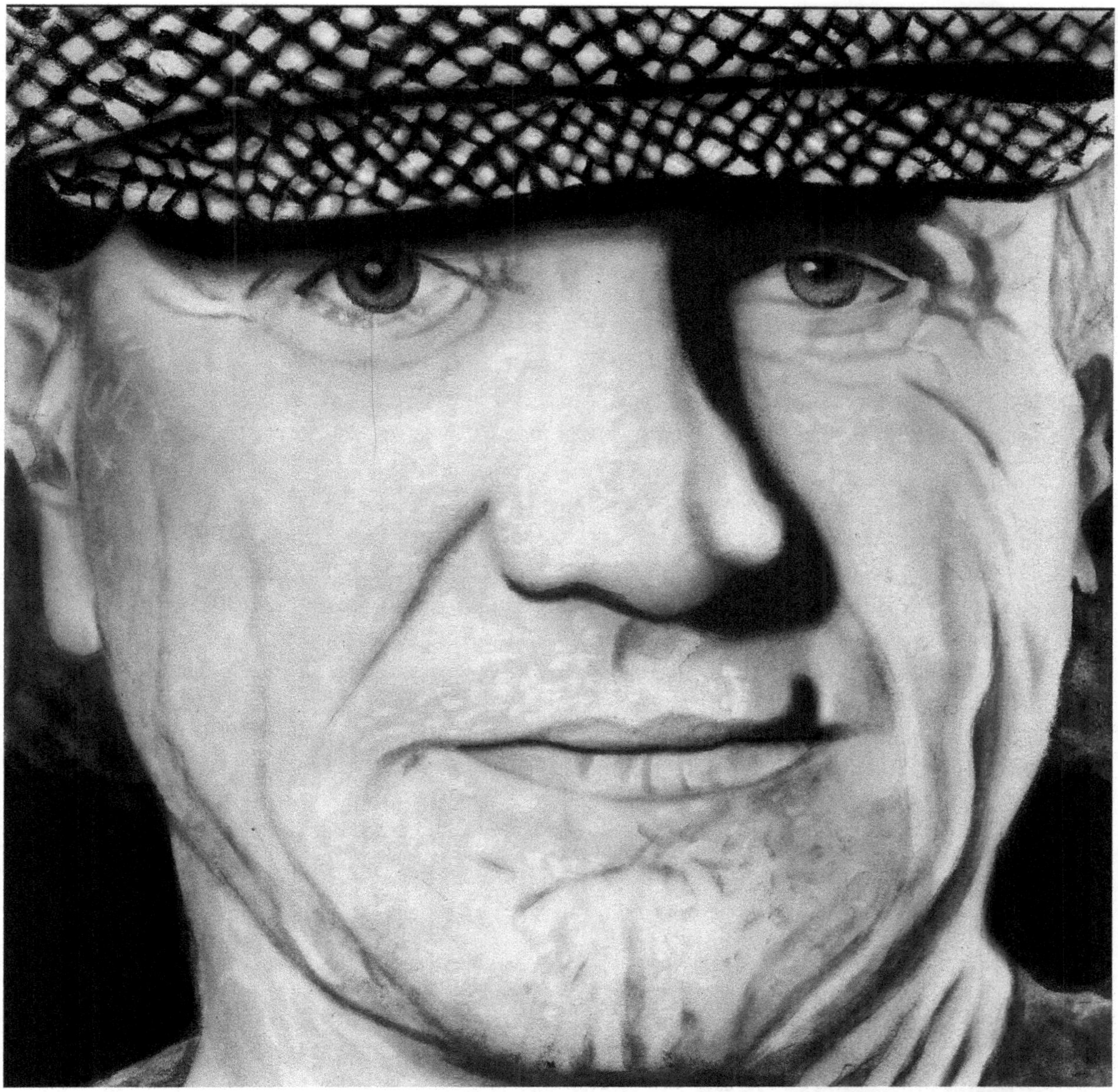

To view how this drawing was masterfully created or to purchase a Limited Edition Framed Artwork of Brian Johnson type into your Internet Browser the URL shortcut ➡ **myportrait.art/brianjohnson**

To listen to AC/DC's Greatest Songs type into your Internet Browser the URL shortcut ➡ **radio.surf/acdc**

To view all channels on THE FACE OF MUSIC Internet Radio MEGA Station type into your Internet Browser the URL shortcut ➡ **radio.surf/music**

To inquire about purchasing a Limited Edtion NFT of this portrait type into your Internet Browser the URL shortcut ➡ **myartnft.shop/brianjohnson**

To view all available NFTs type into your Internet Browser the URL shortcut ➡ **myartnft.shop/all**

# Aerosmith

(Total Albums Sold: 150 Million) (Genre: Classic Rock) Aerosmith is an American rock band formed in Boston in 1970. The group consists of Steven Tyler (lead vocals), Joe Perry (guitar), Tom Hamilton (bass), Joey Kramer (drums) and Brad Whitford (guitar). Their style, which is rooted in blues-based hard rock, has also incorporated elements of pop rock, heavy metal, glam metal, and rhythm and blues, and has inspired many subsequent rock artists. They are sometimes referred to as "the Bad Boys from Boston" and "America's Greatest Rock and Roll Band". The primary songwriting team of Tyler and Perry is often known as the "Toxic Twins".

Aerosmith is the best-selling American hard rock band of all time, having sold more than 150 million records worldwide, including over 70 million records in the United States. With 25 gold, 18 platinum, and 12 multi-platinum albums, they hold the record for the most total certifications by an American group and are tied for the most multi-platinum albums by an American group. They have achieved twenty-one Top 40 hits on the US Hot 100, nine number-one Mainstream Rock hits, four Grammy Awards, six American Music Awards, and ten MTV Video Music Awards. They were inducted into the Rock and Roll Hall of Fame in 2001, and were ranked number 57 and 30, respectively, on Rolling Stone's and VH1's lists of the 100 Greatest Artists of All Time.In 2013, Tyler and Perry were inducted into the Songwriters Hall of Fame, and in 2020, the band received the MusiCares Person of the Year award.merica, and recorded a collection of their hit songs in Spanish. The group was inducted into the Rock and Roll Hall of Fame in 2010. In 2015, their song "Dancing Queen" was inducted into the Recording Academy's Grammy Hall of Fame..

# Steven Tyler

(Net Worth: $150 Million) (Height: 5'-10")

Steven Victor Tallarico (born March 26, 1948), known professionally as Steven Tyler, is an American singer, songwriter, musician, actor, and former television personality. He is best known as the lead singer of the Boston-based rock band Aerosmith, in which he also plays the harmonica, piano, and percussion. He is known as the "Demon of Screamin'" due to his high screams and his wide vocal range. He is also known for his on-stage acrobatics. During his high-energy performances, Tyler usually dresses in bright, colorful outfits with his trademark scarves hanging from his microphone stand.In the 1970s, Tyler rose to prominence as the lead singer of Aerosmith, which released such milestone hard rock albums as Toys in the Attic and Rocks, along with a string of hit singles, including "Dream On", "Sweet Emotion" and "Walk This Way". By the late 1970s and early 1980s, Tyler had a heavy drug and alcohol addiction and the band's popularity waned. In 1986, Tyler completed drug rehabilitation and Aerosmith rose to prominence again when Tyler and Joe Perry joined Run-DMC for a re-make of the classic Aerosmith song "Walk This Way," which became a Top 5 hit. Tyler is included among Rolling Stone's 100 Greatest Singers. He was ranked third on Hit Parader's Top 100 Metal Vocalists of All Time. In 2001, he was inducted into the Rock and Roll Hall of Fame with Aerosmith and in 2013, Tyler and his songwriting partner Joe Perry received the ASCAP Founders Award and were inducted into the Songwriters Hall of Fame.

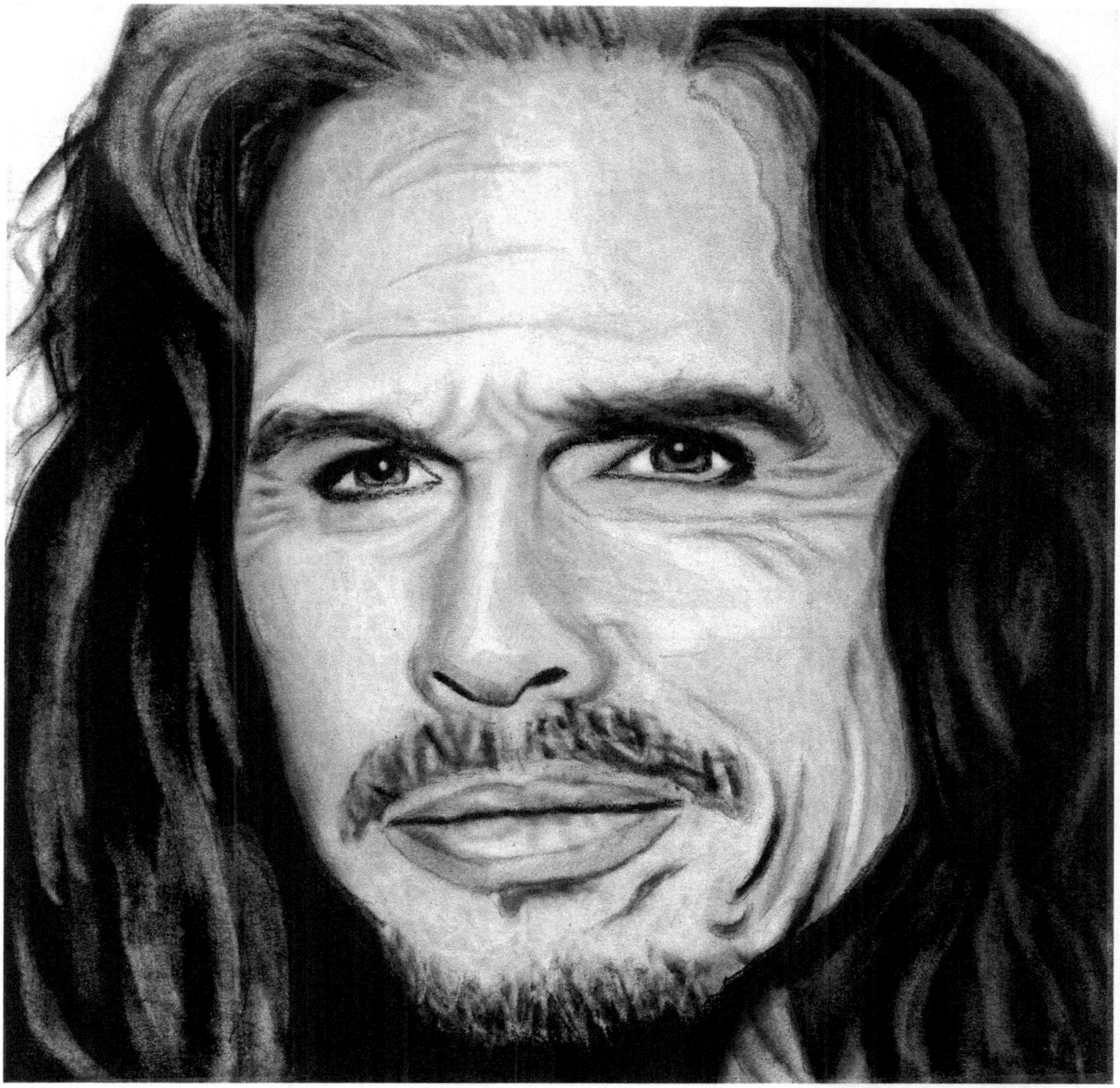

To view how this drawing was masterfully created or to purchase a Limited Edition Framed Artwork of Steven Tyler type into your Internet Browser the URL shortcut ➡ **myportrait.art/steventyler**

To listen to their Greatest Songs type into your Internet Browser the URL shortcut ➡ **radio.surf/aerosmith**

To view all channels on THE FACE OF MUSIC Internet Radio MEGA Station type into your Internet Browser the URL shortcut ➡ **radio.surf/music**

To inquire about purchasing a Limited Edtion NFT of this portrait type into your Internet Browser the URL shortcut ➡ **myartnft.shop/steventyler**

To view all available NFTs type into your Internet Browser the URL shortcut ➡ **myartnft.shop/all**

# Alan Jackson

(Net worth: $ 95 Million)(Total Records Sold: 75+ Million)
(Genre: Country)(Height: 6' - 4")

Alan Eugene Jackson (born October 17, 1958) is an American singer and songwriter. He is known for blending traditional honky-tonk and mainstream country pop sounds (for a style widely regarded as "neotraditional country"), as well as penning many of his own songs. Jackson has recorded 16 studio albums, three greatest hits albums, two Christmas albums, and two gospel albums.

Jackson is one of the best-selling music artists of all-time, having sold over 75 million records worldwide, with 44 million sold in the United States alone. He has had 66 songs appear on the Billboard Hot Country Singles & Tracks chart; of the 66 titles, and six featured singles, 38 have reached the top five and 35 have claimed the number one spot. Out of 15 titles to reach the Billboard Top Country Albums chart, nine have been certified multi-platinum. He is the recipient of two Grammy Awards, 16 CMA Awards, 17 ACM Awards and nominee of multiple other awards. He is a member of the Grand Ole Opry, and was inducted into the Georgia Music Hall of Fame in 2001. He was inducted into the Country Music Hall of Fame in 2017 by Loretta Lynn and into the Nashville Songwriters Hall of Fame in 2018.

Jackson was born to Joseph Eugene "Daddy Gene" Jackson (1927–2000) and Ruth Musick "Mama Ruth" Jackson (1930–2017) in Newnan, Georgia, and has four older sisters. He and his immediate family lived in a small home built around his grandfather's old toolshed. The family is primarily of English descent. His mother lived in the home until she died on January 7, 2017. He began writing music in 1983. Growing up, Jackson
listened primarily to gospel music, until a friend introduced him to Gene Watson, John Anderson, and Hank Williams Jr. Jackson attended the local Elm Street Elementary and Newnan High School, and joined the band, Dixie Steel after graduation. When he was 27, Jackson and his wife of six years, Denise, moved from Newnan to Nashville, Tennessee, where he hoped to pursue music full-time. In 1987, Jackson cut an album titled New Traditional at Doc's Place in Hendersonville, Tennessee, but it is extremely rare and was only released in Japan.nd one of the best-selling bands originating in continental Europe. ABBA had eight consecutive number-one albums in the UK. The group also enjoyed significant success in Latin America, and recorded a collection of their hit songs in Spanish. The group was inducted into the Rock and Roll Hall of Fame in 2010. In 2015, their song "Dancing Queen" was inducted into the Recording Academy's Grammy Hall of Fame..

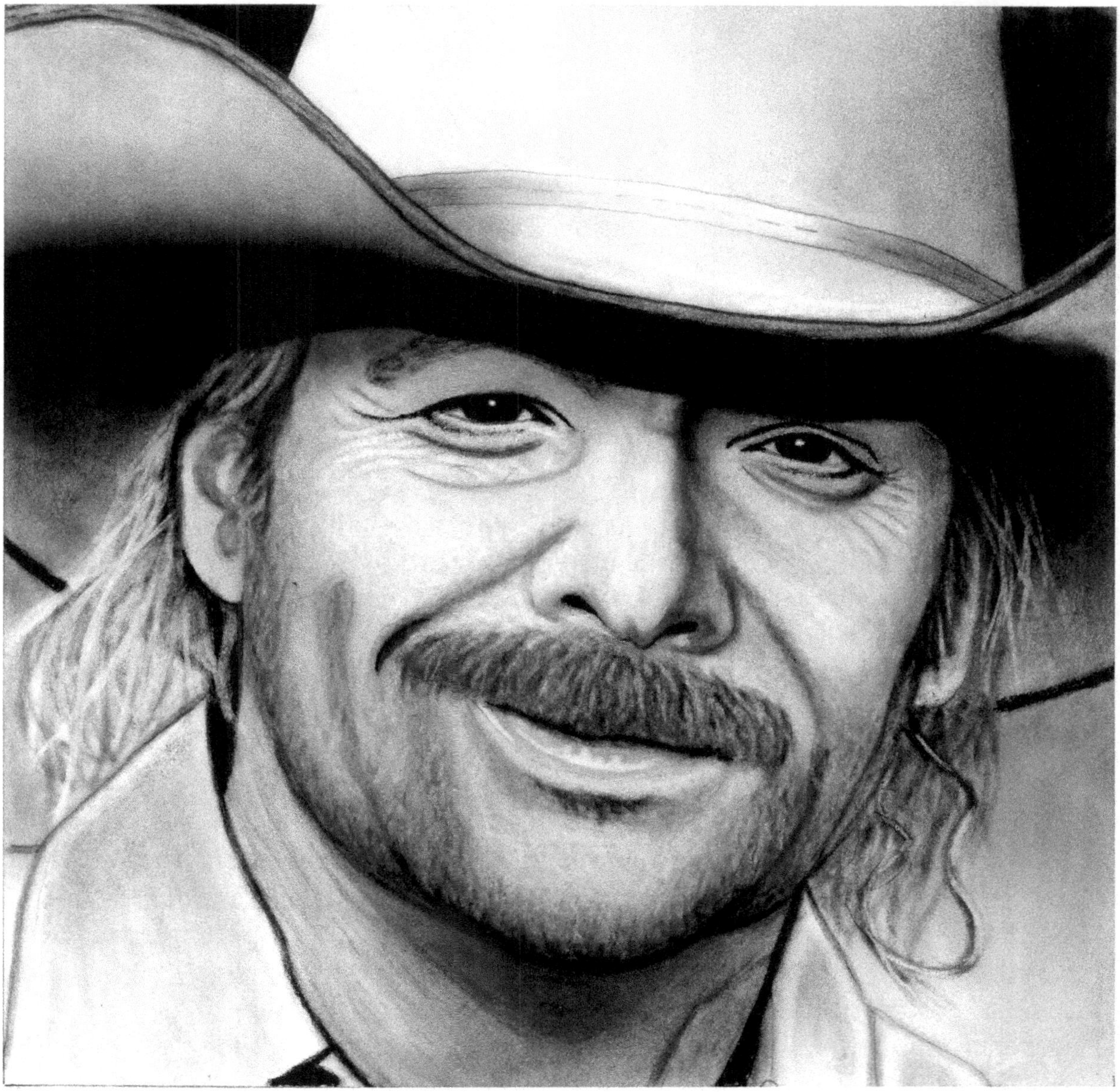

To view how this drawing was masterfully created or to purchase a Limited Edition Framed Artwork of Alan Jackson type into your Internet Browser the URL shortcut ➡ **myportrait.art/alanjackson**

To listen to his Greatest Songs type into your Internet Browser the URL shortcut ➡ **radio.surf/alanjackson**

To view all channels on THE FACE OF MUSIC Internet Radio MEGA Station type into your Internet Browser the URL shortcut ➡ **radio.surf/music**

To inquire about purchasing a Limited Edtion NFT of this portrait type into your Internet Browser the URL shortcut ➡ **myartnft.shop/alanjackson**

To view all available NFTs type into your Internet Browser the URL shortcut ➡ **myartnft.shop/all**

# Alanis Morissette

(Net worth: $ 45 Million)(Total Albums Sold: 33 Million)
(Genre: Alternative / Indie)(Height: 5′ - 4″)

Alanis Nadine Morissette (born June 1, 1974) is a Canadian-American singer-songwriter. Known for her emotive mezzo-soprano voice, Morissette began her career in Canada in the early 1990s with two mildly successful dance-pop albums. Afterward, as part of a recording deal, she moved to Holmby Hills, Los Angeles. In 1995, she released Jagged Little Pill, a more rock-oriented album which sold more than 33 million copies

globally and is her most critically acclaimed work to date. This was made into a rock musical of the same name in 2017, which earned 15 Tony Award nominations including Best Musical. Her follow-up album, Supposed Former Infatuation Junkie, was released in 1998.

Morissette assumed creative control and producing duties for her subsequent studio albums, including Under Rug Swept (2002), So-Called Chaos (2004), Flavors of Entanglement (2008), and Havoc and Bright Lights (2012). Her ninth album, Such Pretty Forks in the Road, was released in 2020. Morissette has sold more than 75 million records worldwide and has been dubbed the "Queen of Alt-Rock Angst" by Rolling Stone

Morissette was born June 1, 1974 at Riverside Hospital of Ottawa in Ottawa, Ontario, Canada to teacher Georgia Mary Ann (née Feuerstein) and high-school principal and French teacher Alan Richard Morissette. She has two brothers: older brother Chad is a business entrepreneur, and twin brother (12 minutes older) Wade is a musician. Her father is of French and Irish descent and her mother has Hungarian and Jewish ancestry. Her parents were teachers in a military school and due to their work often had to move. Between the ages of three and six she lived with her parents in Lahr (Black Forest), Germany.

When she was six years old, she returned to Ottawa and started to play the piano. In 1981, at the age of seven, she began dance lessons. Morissette had a Catholic upbringing. She attended Holy Family Catholic School for elementary school and Immaculata High School for Grades 7 and 8 before completing the rest of her high school at Glebe Collegiate Institute. She appeared on the children's television sketch comedy You Can't Do That on Television for five episodes when she was in junior high school.

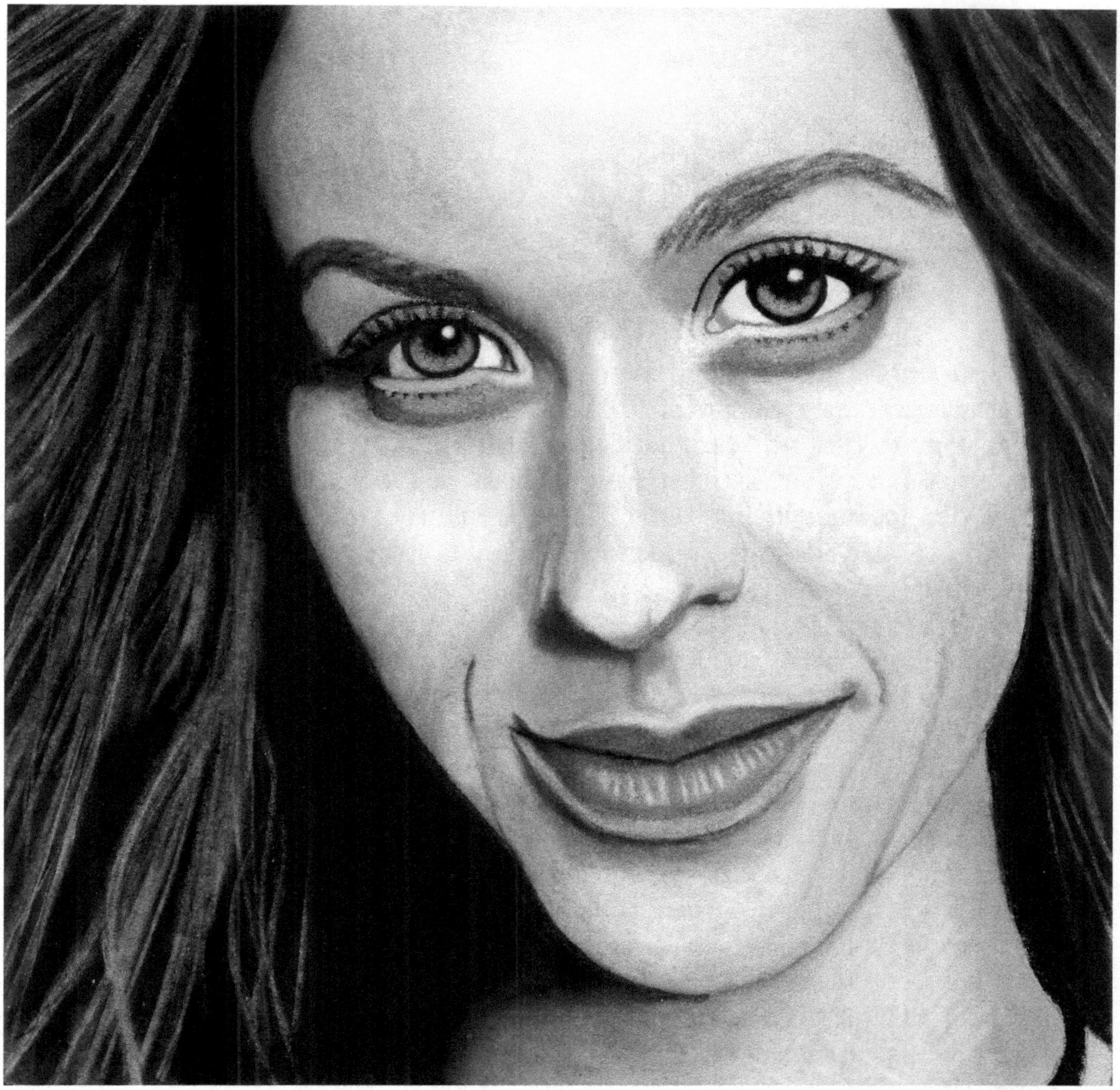

To view how this drawing was masterfully created or to purchase a Limited Edition Framed Artwork of Alanis Morrissette type into your Internet Browser the URL shortcut ➡ **[myportrait.art/alanismorissette**

To listen to her Greatest Songs type into your Internet Browser the URL shortcut
➡ **radio.surf/alanismorissette**

To view all channels on THE FACE OF MUSIC Internet Radio MEGA Station type into your Internet Browser the URL shortcut ➡ **radio.surf/music**

To inquire about purchasing a Limited Edtion NFT of this portrait type into your Internet Browser the URL shortcut ➡ **myartnft.shop/alanismorissette**

To view all available NFTs type into your Internet Browser the URL shortcut ➡ **myartnft.shop/all**

# Alice Cooper

(Net worth: $ 50 Million)(Total Records Sold: 50 Million)
(Genre: Hard Rock)(Height: 5' - 10")

Alice Cooper (born Vincent Damon Furnier, February 4, 1948) is an American singer, songwriter, and actor whose career spans over 50 years. With a raspy voice and a stage show that features numerous props, including pyrotechnics, guillotines, electric chairs, fake blood, reptiles, baby dolls, and dueling swords, Cooper is considered by music journalists and peers to be "The Godfather of Shock Rock". He has drawn equally from horror films, vaudeville, and garage rock to pioneer a macabre and theatrical brand of rock designed to shock audiences.

Originating in Phoenix, Arizona, in 1964, "Alice Cooper" was originally a band with roots extending back to a band called The Earwigs 1964, consisting of Furnier on vocals and harmonica, Glen Buxton on lead guitar, and Dennis Dunaway on bass guitar and background vocals. By 1966, Michael Bruce on rhythm guitar joined the three and Neal Smith was added on drums in 1967. The five named the band band 'Alice Cooper' and released their debut album in 1969 with limited chart success. Following a second album released in 1970, the band into the international music mainstream with the 1971 hit song "I'm Eighteen". The band reached their commercial peak in 1973 with their sixth studio album, Billion Dollar Babies. They broke up in 1975 and Furnier adopted the band's name as both his legal name and his stage name, beginning his solo career with the 1975 concept album Welcome to My Nightmare.Expanding from his Detroit rock roots, Cooper has experimented with a number of musical styles, including art rock, hard rock, heavy metal, new wave, glam metal, and industrial rock. He helped to shape the sound and look of heavy metal, and has been described as the artist who "first introduced horror imagery to rock and roll, and whose stagecraft and showmanship have permanently transformed the genre". He is also known for his wit offstage, with The Rolling Stone Album Guide calling him the world's most "beloved heavy metal entertainer". Away from music, Cooper is a film actor, a golfing celebrity, a restaurateur, and, since 2004, a radio DJ with his classic rock show Nights with Alice Cooper Cooper was born in Detroit, Michigan, the son of Ether Moroni Furnier (1924–1987) and his wife Ella Mae (née McCart; born 1925). He was named after his uncle, Vincent Collier Furnier, and the writer Damon Runyon. His father was an evangelist in The Church of Jesus Christ (Bickertonite) and his paternal grandfather, Thurman Sylvester Furnier, was an apostle (from 1917) in and president (1963–1965) of that church. Cooper was active in his church at ages 11 to 12. Following a series of childhood illnesses, he moved with his family to Phoenix, Arizona, where he attended Cortez High School. In his high school yearbook, his ambition was to be "A million record seller".

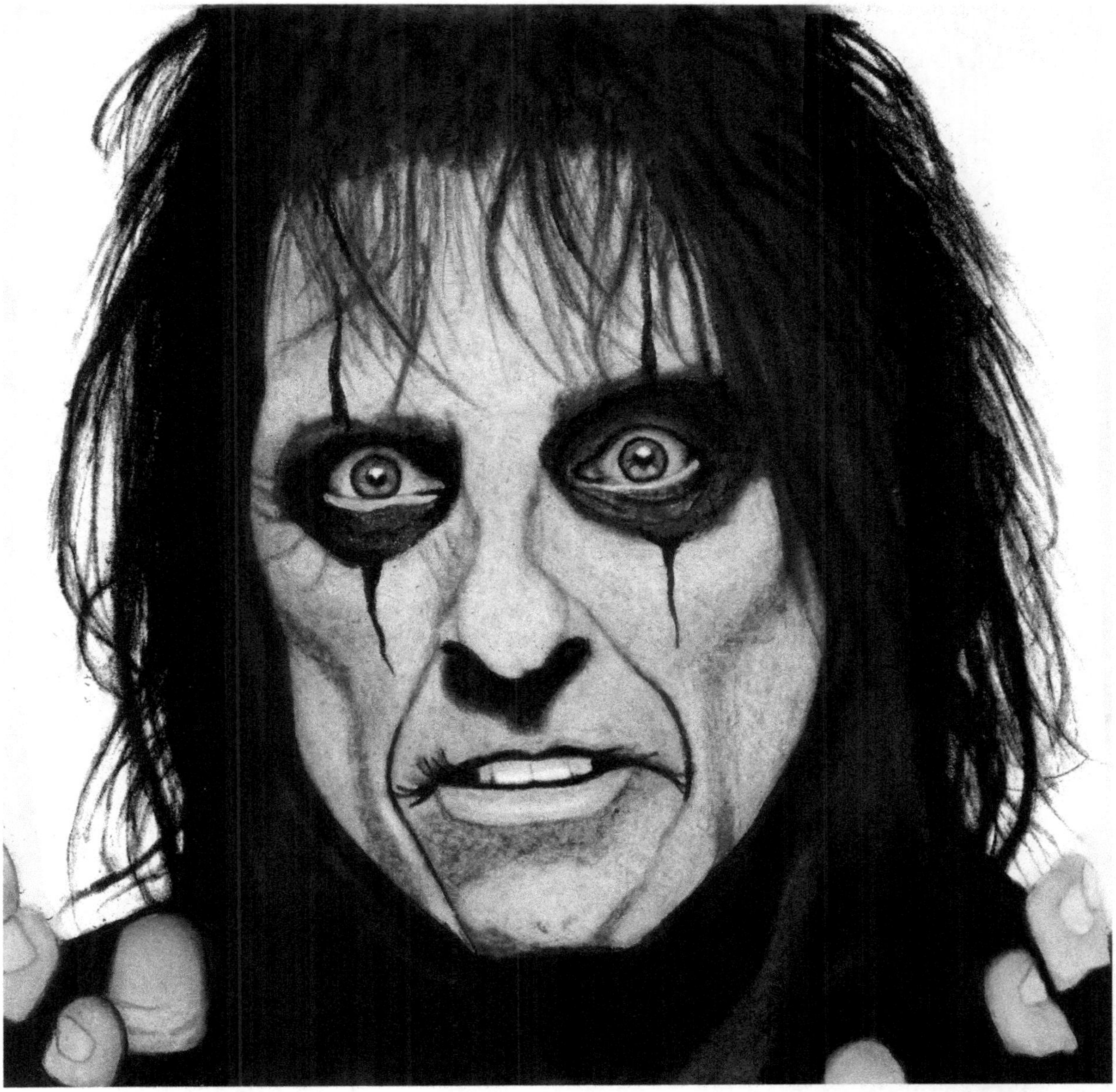

To view how this drawing was masterfully created or to purchase a Limited Edition Framed Artwork of Alice Cooper type into your Internet Browser the URL shortcut ➡ **myportrait.art/alicecooper**

To listen to his Greatest Songs type into your Internet Browser the URL shortcut ➡ **radio.surf/alicecooper**

To view all channels on THE FACE OF MUSIC Internet Radio MEGA Station type into your Internet Browser the URL shortcut ➡ **radio.surf/music**

To inquire about purchasing a Limited Edtion NFT of this portrait type into your Internet Browser the URL shortcut ➡ **myartnft.shop/alicecooper**

To view all available NFTs type into your Internet Browser the URL shortcut ➡ **myartnft.shop/all**

# Alice in Chains

(Total Albums Sold: 30 Million) (Genre: Alternative Rock)

Alice in Chains (often abbreviated as AIC) is an American rock band from Seattle, Washington, formed in 1987 by guitarist and vocalist Jerry Cantrell and drummer Sean Kinney, who later recruited bassist Mike Starr and lead vocalist Layne Staley. Starr was replaced by Mike Inez in 1993. William DuVall joined the band in 2006 as co-lead vocalist and rhythm guitarist, replacing Staley, who died in 2002. The band took its name from Staley's previous group, the glam metal band Alice N' Chains.Often associated with grunge music, Alice in Chains' sound incorporates heavy metal elements. The band is known for its distinctive vocal style, which often included the harmonized vocals between Staley and Cantrell (and later Cantrell and DuVall). Cantrell started to sing lead vocals on the 1992 acoustic EP Sap, and his role continued to grow in the following albums, making Alice in Chains a two-vocal band.Alice in Chains have sold over 30 million records worldwide, and over 14 million records in the US alone. The band has had 18 Top 10 songs on Billboard's Mainstream Rock Tracks chart, 5 No. 1 hits, and received 11 Grammy Award nominations. The band was ranked number 34 on VH1's 100 Greatest Artists of Hard Rock and was ranked as the 15th greatest live band by Hit Parader. Since its formation, Alice in Chains has released six studio albums, three EPs, three live albums, four compilations, two DVDs, 43 music videos, and 32 singles.t success in Latin America, and recorded a collection of their hit songs in Spanish. The group was inducted into the Rock and Roll Hall of Fame in 2010. In 2015, their song "Dancing Queen" was inducted into the Recording Academy's Grammy Hall of Fame..

# Layne Staley

(Net Worth: $5 Million) (Height: 6'-0")

Layne Thomas Staley (born Layne Rutherford Staley; August 22, 1967 – April 5, 2002) was an American musician best known as the original lead singer and co-songwriter of the rock band Alice in Chains, which rose to international fame in the early 1990s as part of Seattle's grunge movement. Staley was known for his distinct vocal style and tenor voice, as well as his harmonizing with guitarist/vocalist Jerry Cantrell. Staley was also a member of the glam metal bands Sleze and Alice N' Chains, and the supergroups Mad Season and Class of '99."Man in the Box", the second single from Alice in Chains' debut album, Facelift (1990), garnered Staley critical recognition for his vocal style. Alice in Chains' EP Jar of Flies (1994), debuted at number one on the Billboard 200, making it Alice in Chains' first record—and the first-ever EP—to top the chart. However, Staley's deteriorating condition due to heroin abuse led him to enter a rehabilitation clinic. He began to work on a side project with several Seattle musicians, Mike McCready of Pearl Jam, Barrett Martin of Screaming Trees and John Baker Saunders of The Walkabouts, which came to be Mad Season, while Alice in Chains went into hiatus.During Alice in Chains' hiatus, reports of Staley's drug addiction began to gain widespread circulation in fan and media communities, in part due to changes in his physical condition brought on by prolonged heroin abuse. On April 10, 1996, the band returned with a performance on MTV Unplugged performance in New York; it was their first concert in two-and-a-half years.From mid-1996 onwards, Staley was out of the public spotlight, never to perform live again. His struggle with depression and addiction for much of his adult life resulted in his death from a speedball overdose on April 5, 2002, at the age of 34. Staley was ranked at No. 27 on Hit Parader's list of "Heavy Metal's All-Time Top 100 Vocalists" in 2006, and at No. 42 on Complex's magazine list of "The 50 Best Lead Singers of All Time" in 2012. Seattle officially declared August 22, 2019 as "Layne Staley Day."

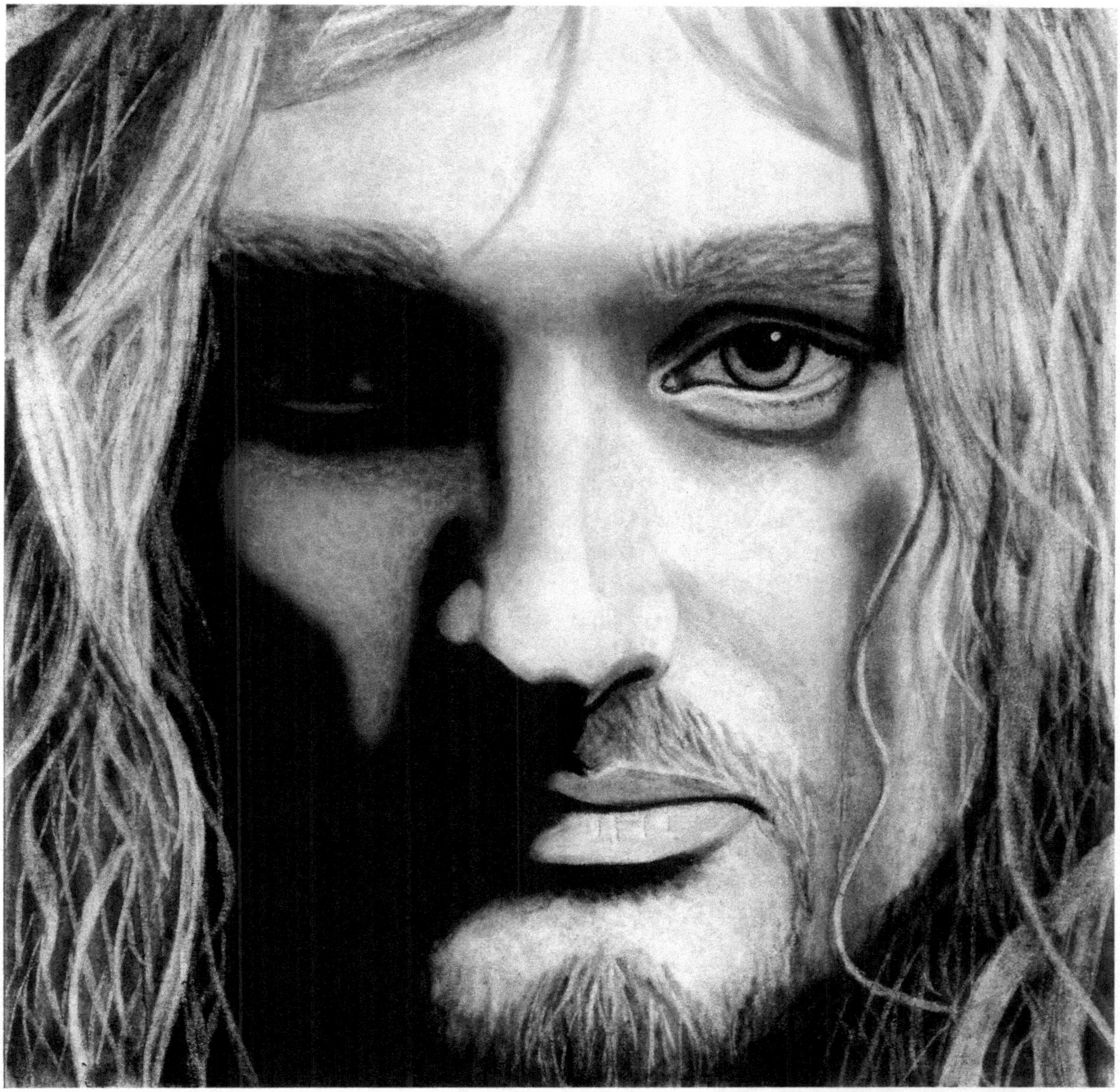

To view how this drawing was masterfully created or to purchase a Limited Edition Framed Artwork of Layne Staley type into your Internet Browser the URL shortcut ➡ **myportrait.art/laynestaley**

To listen to their Greatest Songs type into your Internet Browser the URL shortcut
➡ **radio.surf/aliceinchains**

To view all channels on THE FACE OF MUSIC Internet Radio MEGA Station type into your Internet Browser the URL shortcut ➡ **radio.surf/music**

To inquire about purchasing a Limited Edticn NFT of this portrait type into your Internet Browser the URL shortcut ➡ **myartnft.shop/laynestaley**

To view all available NFTs type into your Internet Browser the URL shortcut ➡ **myartnft.shop/all**

# Allman Brothers Band

(Total Albums Sold: 10+ Million) (Genre: Classic Rock, Southern Rock, Blues Rock)

The Allman Brothers Band were an American rock band formed in Jacksonville, Florida in 1969 by brothers Duane Allman (founder, slide guitar and lead guitar) and Gregg Allman (vocals, keyboards, songwriting), as well as Dickey Betts (lead guitar, vocals, songwriting), Berry Oakley (bass guitar), Butch Trucks (drums), and Jai Johanny "Jaimoe" Johanson (drums). Subsequently based in Macon, Georgia, the band incorporated elements of blues, jazz, and country music, and their live shows featured jam band-style improvisation and instrumentals.The group's first two studio releases, The Allman Brothers Band (1969) and Idlewild South (1970) (both released by Capricorn Records), stalled commercially, but their 1971 live release, At Fillmore East, represented an artistic and commercial breakthrough. The album features extended renderings of their songs "In Memory of Elizabeth Reed" and "Whipping Post", and is considered among the best live albums ever made.Group leader Duane Allman was killed in a motorcycle accident later that year – on October 29, 1971 – and the band dedicated Eat a Peach (1972) to his memory, a dual studio/live album that cemented the band's popularity and featured Gregg Allman's "Melissa" and Dickey Betts's "Blue Sky". Following the motorcycling death of bassist Berry Oakley exactly one year and 13 days later on November 11, 1972, the group recruited keyboardist Chuck Leavell and bassist Lamar Williams for 1973's Brothers and Sisters. This album included Betts's hit single "Ramblin' Man" and instrumental "Jessica". These tunes went on to become classic rock radio staples, and placed the group at the forefront of 1970s rock music. Internal turmoil overtook them soon after; the group dissolved in 1976, reformed briefly at the end of the decade with additional personnel changes, and dissolved again in 1982.The band reformed once more in 1989, releasing a string of new albums and touring heavily. A series of personnel changes in the late 1990s was capped by the departure of Betts. The group found stability during the 2000s with bassist Oteil Burbridge and guitarists Warren Haynes and Derek Trucks (the nephew of their original drummer) and became renowned for their month-long string of shows at New York City's Beacon Theatre each spring. The band retired for good in October 2014 after their final show at the Beacon Theatre.

# Gregg Allman

(Net Worth: $18 Million) (Height: 6'-1")

Gregory LeNoir Allman (December 8, 1947 – May 27, 2017) was an American singer-songwriter and musician. He was known for performing in the Allman Brothers Band. Allman grew up with an interest in rhythm and blues music, and the Allman Brothers Band fused it with rock music, jazz, and country at times. He wrote several of the band's biggest songs, including "Whipping Post", "Melissa", and "Midnight Rider". Allman also had a successful solo career, releasing seven studio albums. He was born and spent much of his childhood in Nashville, Tennessee, before relocating to Daytona Beach, Florida and then Richmond Hill, Georgia. Allman performed with a Hammond organ and guitar, and was recognized for his soulful voice. For his work in music, Allman was referred to as a Southern rock pioneer and received numerous awards, including one Grammy Award; he was inducted into the Rock and Roll Hall of Fame and the Georgia Music Hall of Fame. His distinctive voice placed him in 70th place in the Rolling Stone list of the "100 Greatest Singers of All Time".

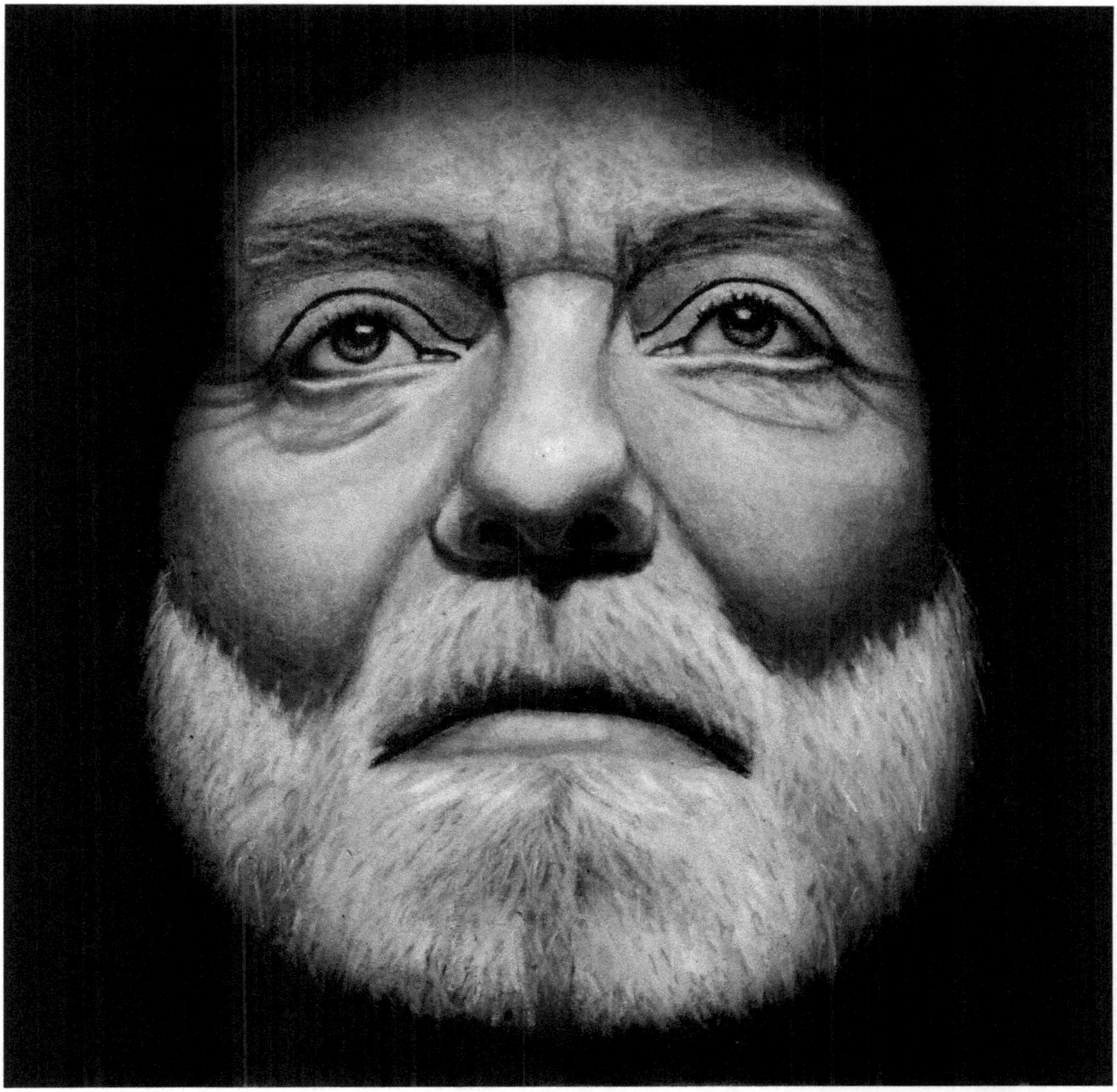

To view how this drawing was masterfully created or to purchase a Limited Edition Framed Artwork of Gregg Allman type into your Internet Browser the URL shortcut ➡ **myportrait.art/greggallman**

To listen to The Allman Brothers Greatest Songs type into your Internet Browser the URL shortcut ➡ **radio.surf/theallmansbrothersband**

To view all channels on THE FACE OF MUSIC Internet Radio MEGA Station type into your Internet Browser the URL shortcut ➡ **radio.surf/music**

To inquire about purchasing a Limited Edtion NFT of this portrait type into your Internet Browser the URL shortcut ➡ **myartnft.shop/greggallman**

To view all available NFTs type into your Internet Browser the URL shortcut ➡ **myartnft.shop/all**

# America

(Total Albums Sold: 5 Million) (Genre: Classic Rock) America is an American rock band that was formed in London in 1970 by Dewey Bunnell, Dan Peek and Gerry Beckley. The trio met as sons of US Air Force personnel stationed in London, where they began performing live. Achieving significant popularity in the 1970s, the trio was famous for its close vocal harmonies and light acoustic folk rock sound. The band released a string of hit albums and singles, many of which found airplay on pop/soft rock stations.The band came together shortly after the members' graduation from high school, and a record deal with Warner Bros. Records followed. Its debut 1971 album, America, included the transatlantic hits "A Horse with No Name" and "I Need You"; Homecoming (1972) included the single "Ventura Highway"; and Hat Trick (1973), a modest success on the charts that fared poorly in sales, included one minor charting song "Muskrat Love". 1974's Holiday featured the hits "Tin Man" and "Lonely People"; and 1975's Hearts generated the number one single "Sister Golden Hair" alongside "Daisy Jane". History: America's Greatest Hits, a compilation of hit singles, was released the same year and was certified multiplatinum in the United States and Australia. Peek left the group in 1977 and their commercial fortunes declined, mdespite a return to the top 10 in 1982 with the single "You Can Do Magic". The band's final Top 40 hit was "The Border", which reached no. 33 on the Billboard Hot 100 in 1983.The group continues to record material and tour with regularity. Its 2007 album Here & Now was a collaboration with a new generation of musicians who credited the band as an influence. America won a Grammy Award for Best New Artist and were nominated for Best Pop Vocal Group at the 15th Annual Grammy Awards in 1973. The group was inducted into the Vocal Group Hall of Fame in 2006 and received a star on the Hollywood Walk of Fame in 2012.

# Dan Peek

(Net Worth: $ 5 Million) (Height: 6'-1")

Daniel Milton Peek (November 1, 1950 – July 24, 2011) was an American musician best known as a member of the folk rock band America from 1970 to 1977, together with Gerry Beckley and Dewey Bunnell. He has been called a "pioneer in contemporary Christian music".

After a brief stint at Old Dominion University in Virginia during 1969, Peek returned from the U.S. back to London. Soon afterwards, the three former London Central High School classmates Peek, Beckley, and Bunnell began making music together. Known for singing the high harmonies, Dan Peek contributed lead and backing vocals, guitars, bass, keyboards, and harmonica to their recordings during his tenure in the band. As a member of America, Peek wrote or co-wrote four Top 100 singles: "Don't Cross the River" (No. 35), "Lonely People" (No. 5), "Woman Tonight" (No. 44), and "Today's the Day" (No. 23), all of which he also sang lead on. "Lonely People" and "Today's the Day" also hit No. 1 on the Billboard AC charts.Peek abused alcohol and other drugs during his time touring with the band and elected to leave shortly after America's February 1977 release of the Harbor album, disenchanted with the travel, recreational drug use and female groupies. In 2004 he released an autobiography about that era entitled An American Band: The America Story which was very difficult for him to write because of the bad memories it brought up.

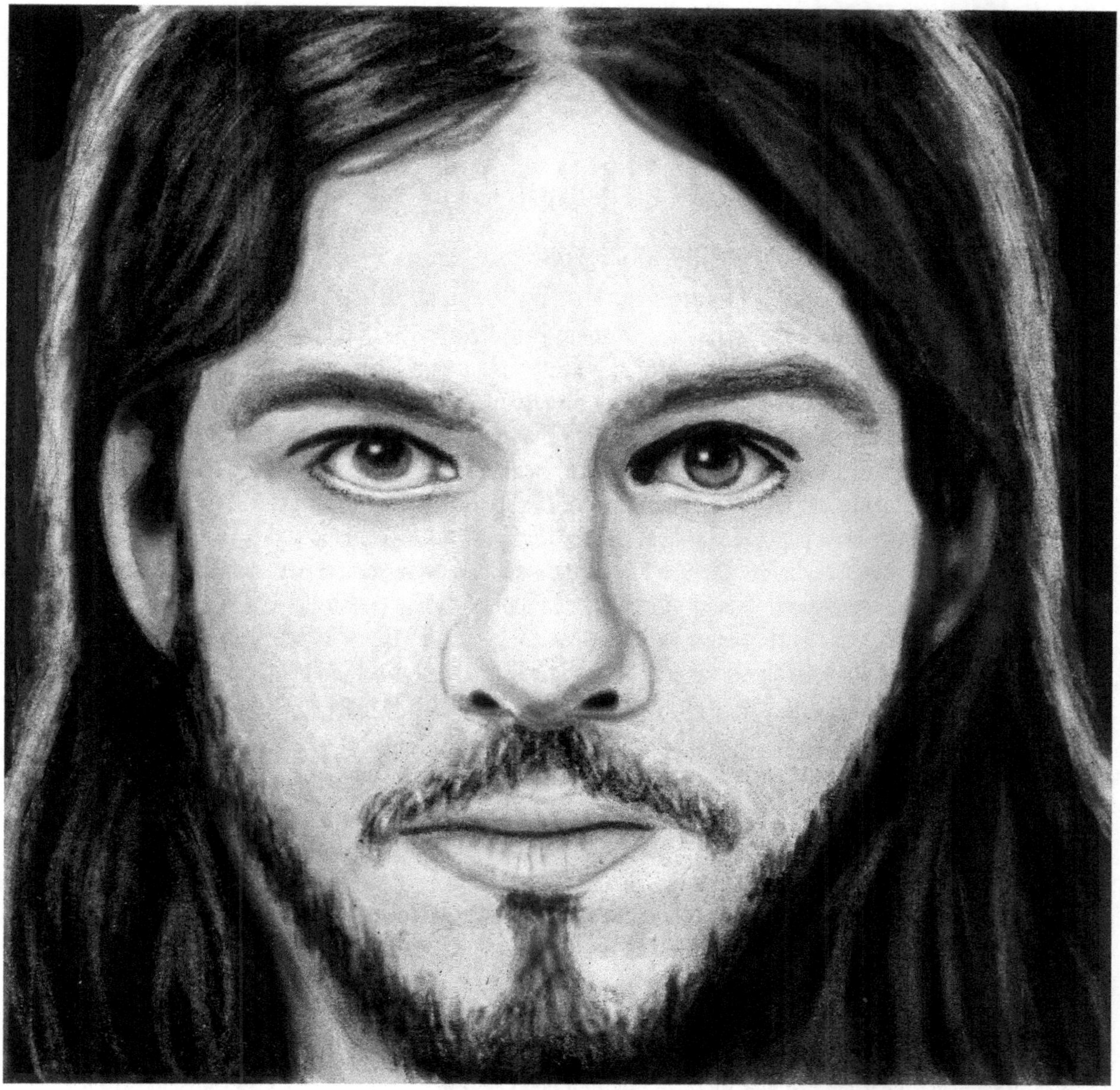

To view how this drawing was masterfully created or to purchase a Limited Edition Framed Artwork of Dan Peek type into your Internet Browser the URL shortcut ➡ **myportrait.art/danpeek**

To listen to their Greatest Songs type into your Internet Browser the URL shortcut ➡ **radio.surf/america**

To view all channels on THE FACE OF MUSIC Internet Radio MEGA Station type into your Internet Browser the URL shortcut ➡ **radio.surf/music**

To inquire about purchasing a Limited Edtion NFT of this portrait type into your Internet Browser the URL shortcut ➡ **myartnft.shop/danpeek**

To view all available NFTs type into your Internet Browser the URL shortcut ➡ **myartnft.shop/all**

# Andrea Bocelli

(Net worth: $ 100 Million)(Total Albums Sold: 80 Million)
(Genre: Operatic Pop)(Height: 6' - 2")

Andrea Bocelli OMRI OMDSM (Italian: [anˈdrɛːa boˈtʃɛlli]; born 22 September 1958) is an Italian opera tenor and multi-instrumentalist. He was diagnosed with congenital glaucoma at 5 months old, and became completely blind at age 12, following a football accident. After performing evenings in piano bars and competing in local singing contests, Bocelli signed his first recording contract with the Sugar Music label. He rose to fame in 1994, winning the preliminary round of the 44th Sanremo Music Festival performing "Miserere", with the highest marks ever recorded in the newcomers section.Since 1982, Bocelli has recorded 15 solo studio albums of both pop and classical music, three greatest hits albums, and nine complete operas, selling over 75 million records worldwide. He has had success as a crossover performer, bringing classical music to the top of international pop charts. His first compilation album, Romanza, is one of the best-selling albums of all time, while Sacred Arias is the biggest selling classical album by any solo artist in history. My Christmas was the best-selling holiday album of 2009 and one of the best-selling holiday albums in the United States.The 2019 album Sì debuted at number one on the UK Albums Chart and US Billboard 200, becoming Bocelli's first number-one album in both countries. His song "Con te partirò", included on his second album Bocelli, is one of the best-selling singles of all time.In 1998, Bocelli was named one of People magazine's 50 Most Beautiful People. He duetted with Celine Dion on the song "The Prayer" for the animated film Quest for Camelot, which won the Golden Globe Award for Best Original Song and was nominated for the Academy Award for Best Original Song. In 1999, he was nominated for Best New Artist at the Grammy Awards. He captured a listing in the Guinness Book of World Records with the release of his classical album Sacred Arias, as he simultaneously held the top three positions on the US Classical Albums charts.Bocelli was born to Alessandro and Edi Bocelli on September 22, 1958. Doctors had advised the couple to abort him, as they predicted that the child would be born with a disability. It was evident at birth that Bocelli had numerous problems with his sight, and he was eventually diagnosed with congenital glaucoma. He has stated that his mother's decision to give birth to him and overrule the doctor's advice was the inspiration for him to oppose abortion.Bocelli grew up on his family's farm where they sold farm machinery and made wine in the small village of La Sterza, a frazione of Lajatico, Tuscany, Italy, about 40 km (25 mi) south of Pisa. His mother and younger brother Alberto still live in the family home; his father died in 2000.Bocelli showed a great passion for music as a young boy. His mother has said that music was the only thing that would comfort him. He started piano lessons at age 6 and later learned to play the flute, saxophone, trumpet, trombone, guitar, and drums. His nanny Oriana gave him the first record of Franco Corelli, and he began to show interest in pursuing the career of a tenor. By age 7, he was able to recognize the famous voices of the time and tried to emulate the great singers.At age 12, Bocelli lost his sight completely following an accident during an association football game. He was hit in the eye playing goalkeeper during a match and suffered a brain hemorrhage. Doctors resorted to leeches in a last-ditch effort to save his sight, but they were unsuccessful and he remained blind.Bocelli also spent time singing during his childhood. He gave his first concert in a small village not far from where he was born. He won his first song competition at age 14 with "'O sole mio" at the Margherita d'Oro in Viareggio. He finished secondary school in 1980, and then studied law at the University of Pisa. To earn money, he performed evenings in piano bars, and it was there that he met his future wife Enrica in 1987. He completed law school and spent one year as a court-appointed lawyer.

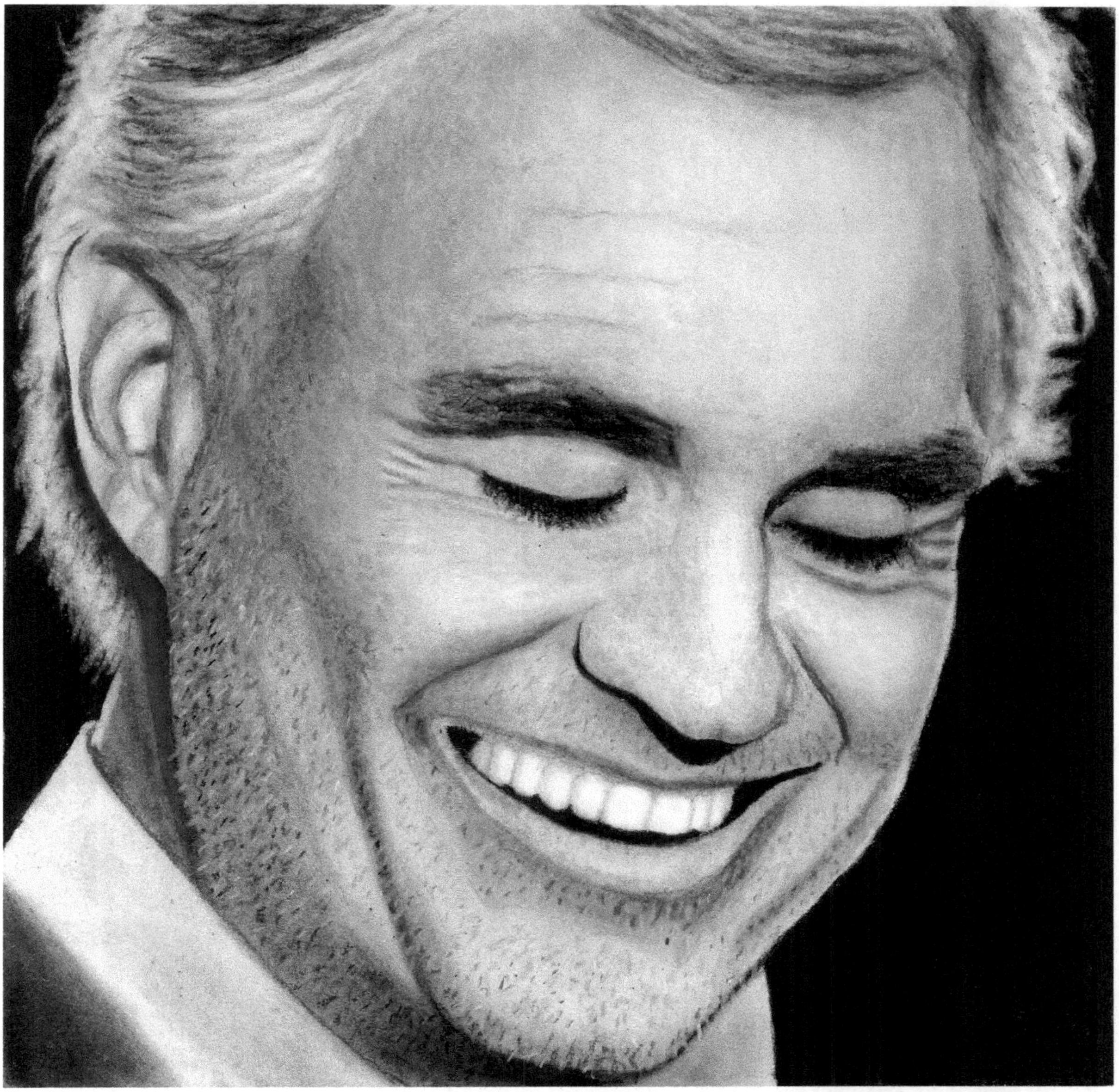

To view how this drawing was masterfully created or to purchase a Limited Edition Framed Artwork of Andrea Bocelli type into your Internet Browser the URL shortcut ➡ **myportrait.art/andreabocelli**

To listen to his Greatest Songs type into your Internet Browser the URL shortcut ➡ **radio.surf/andreabocelli**

To view all channels on THE FACE OF MUSIC Internet Radio MEGA Station type into your Internet Browser the URL shortcut ➡ **radio.surf/music**

To inquire about purchasing a Limited Edition NFT of this portrait type into your Internet Browser the URL shortcut ➡ **myartnft.shop/andreabocelli**

To view all available NFTs type into your Internet Browser the URL shortcut ➡ **myartnft.shop/all**

# Andy Williams

(Net worth: $ 45 Million)(Total Records Sold: 100+ Million)
(Genre: Traditional Pop / Easy Listening)(Height: 5' - 6")

Howard Andrew Williams (December 3, 1927 – September 25, 2012) was an American singer. He recorded 43 albums in his career, of which 15 have been gold-certified and 3 platinum-certified. He was also nominated for six Grammy Awards. He hosted The Andy Williams Show, a television variety show, from 1962 to 1971 along with numerous TV specials. The Andy Williams Show won three Emmy awards. The Moon River Theatre in Branson, Missouri, is named after the song for which he is best known—Johnny Mercer and Henry Mancini's "Moon River". He sold more than 100 million records worldwide, including more than 10 million certified units in the United States.Williams was active in the music industry for over 70 years until his death in 2012.Williams had three older brothers—Bob, Don, and Dick Williams. His first performance was in a children's choir at the local Presbyterian church. He and his brothers formed the Williams Brothers quartet in late 1938, and they performed on radio in the Midwest, first at WHO, in Des Moines, Iowa, and later at WLS in Chicago, and WLW, in Cincinnati.Moving to Los Angeles in 1943, the Williams Brothers sang with Bing Crosby on his 1944 hit record "Swinging on a Star". They appeared in four musical films: Janie (1944), Kansas City Kitty (1944), Something in the Wind (1947) and Ladies' Man (1947).The Williams Brothers were signed by Metro-Goldwyn-Mayer to appear in Anchors Aweigh and Ziegfeld Follies (1945), but before they went before the cameras the oldest brother, Bob, was drafted into military service and the group's contract was canceled. Kay Thompson, a former radio star who was now head of the vocal department at MGM, had a nose for talent and hired the remaining three Williams brothers to sing in her large choir on many soundtracks for MGM films, including The Harvey Girls (1946). When Bob completed his military service, Kay hired all four brothers to sing on the soundtrack to Good News (1947).By then, Thompson was tired of working behind the scenes at MGM, so with the four Williams boys as her backup singers and dancers, she formed a nightclub act, Kay Thompson and the Williams Brothers. They made their debut in Las Vegas in 1947 and became an overnight sensation. Within a year, they were the highest-paid nightclub act in the world, breaking records wherever they appeared.Williams revealed in his memoir Moon River and Me that he and Thompson became romantically involved while on tour despite the age difference (he was 19 and she was 38). The act broke up in 1949 but reunited for another hugely successful tour from the fall of 1951 through the summer of 1953. After that, the four brothers went their separate ways. A complete itinerary of both tours is listed on the Kay Thompson biography website.Williams and Thompson, however, remained very close, both personally and professionally. She mentored his emergence as a solo singing star. She coached him, wrote his arrangements, and composed many songs that he recorded, including his 1958 Top 20 hit "Promise Me, Love" and, later, "Kay Thompson's Jingle Bells" on his 1964 No. 1 The Andy Williams Christmas Album. Using her contacts in the business, Thompson helped Williams land his breakthrough television gig as a featured singer for two and a half years on Tonight Starring Steve Allen: it helped that the producer of the series, Bill Harbach, was Kay's former aide de camp. Thompson also got Williams his breakthrough recording contract with Cadence Records, whose owner, Archie Bleyer, had gotten early career breaks because of Kay and owed her a favor. Meanwhile, Williams sang backup on many of Thompson's recordings through the 1950s, including her Top 40 hit Eloise, based on her bestselling books about the mischievous little girl who lives at the Plaza Hotel in New York.Williams in a William Morris publicity photo, 1960Thompson also served as a creative consultant and vocal arranger on Williams's three summer replacement network television series in 1957, 1958, and 1959. In the summer of 1961, Thompson traveled with Williams and coached him throughout his starring role in a summer stock tour of the musical Pal Joey. Their personal and professional relationship finally ended in 1962, when Williams met and married Claudine Longet and Thompson moved to Rome.

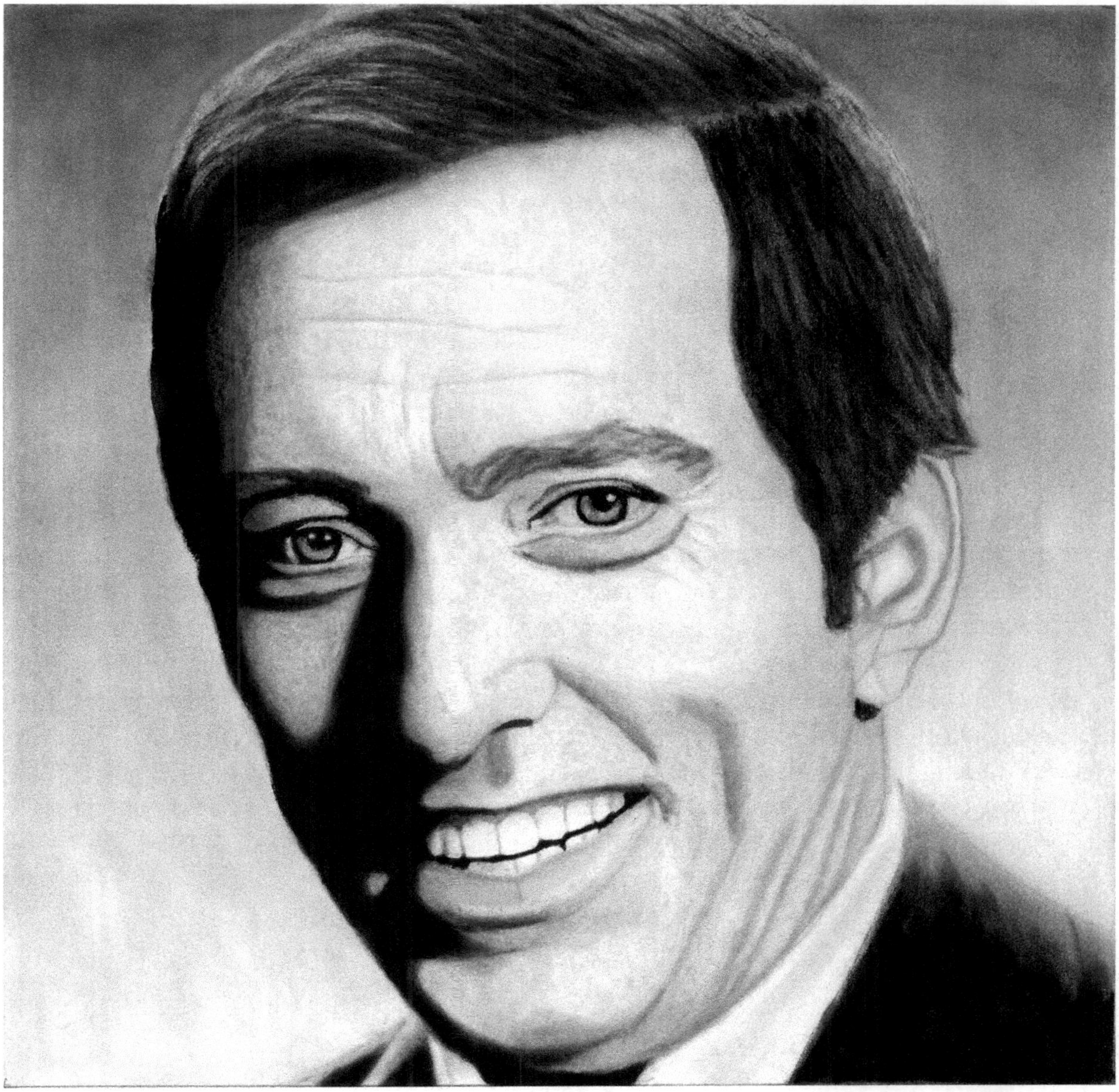

To view how this drawing was masterfully created or to purchase a Limited Edition Framed Artwork of Andy Williams type into your Internet Browser the URL shortcut ➡ **myportrait.art/andywilliams**

To listen to his Greatest Songs type into your Internet Browser the URL shortcut ➡ **radio.surf/andywilliams**

To view all channels on THE FACE OF MUSIC Internet Radio MEGA Station type into your Internet Browser the URL shortcut ➡ **radio.surf/music**

To inquire about purchasing a Limited Edtion NFT of this portrait type into your Internet Browser the URL shortcut ➡ **myartnft.shop/andywilliams**

To view all available NFTs type into your Internet Browser the URL shortcut ➡ **myartnft.shop/all**

# Animals, The

(Total Albums Sold: 5 Million) (Genre: Rock)

The Animals were an English rhythm and blues and rock band, formed in Newcastle upon Tyne in the early 1960s. The band moved to London upon finding fame in 1964. The Animals were known for their gritty, bluesy sound and deep-voiced frontman Eric Burdon, as exemplified by their signature song and transatlantic No. 1 hit single, "The House of the Rising Sun", as well as by hits such as "We Gotta Get Out of This Place", "It's My Life", "Inside Looking Out", "I'm Crying" and "Don't Let Me Be Misunderstood". The band balanced tough, rock-edged pop singles against rhythm and blues-oriented album material and were part of the British Invasion of the US.The Animals underwent numerous personnel changes in the mid-1960s and suffered from poor business management. Under the name Eric Burdon and the Animals, the much-changed act moved to California and achieved commercial success as a psychedelic and hard rock band with hits like "San Franciscan Nights", "When I Was Young" and "Sky Pilot", before disbanding at the end of the decade. Altogether, the group had ten Top Twenty hits in both the UK Singles Chart and the US Billboard Hot 100.The original lineup of Burdon, Alan Price, Chas Chandler, Hilton Valentine and John Steel reunited for a one-off benefit concert in Newcastle in 1968. They later had brief comebacks in 1975 and 1983. There have been several partial regroupings of the original era members since then under various names. The Animals were inducted into the Rock and Roll Hall of Fame in 1994.

# Eric Burdon

(Net Worth: $8 Million) (Height: 5'-7")

Eric Victor Burdon (born 11 May 1941) is an English singer-songwriter and actor. He was previously the vocalist of rock band The Animals and funk band War. He is regarded as one of the British Invasion's most distinctive singers with his deep, powerful blues-rock voice. He is also known for his aggressive stage performances.In 2008, he was ranked 57th in Rolling Stone's list The 100 Greatest Singers of All Time.Burdon was lead singer of the Animals, formed during 1962 in Newcastle upon Tyne. The original band was the Alan Price Rhythm and Blues Combo, which formed in 1958; they became the Animals shortly after Burdon joined the band. The Animals combined electric blues with rock; in the US they were considered one of the leading bands of the British Invasion. Along with the Beatles, the Rolling Stones, the Who, the Hollies, the Dave Clark Five, and the Kinks, the group introduced contemporary British music and fashion to American audiences. Burdon's powerful voice can be heard on the Animals' singles "The House of the Rising Sun", "Baby Let Me Take You Home", "I'm Crying", "Boom Boom", "Don't Let Me Be Misunderstood", "Bring It On Home to Me", "We Gotta Get Out of This Place", "It's My Life", "Don't Bring Me Down", "See See Rider", "Monterey", and "Sky Pilot".

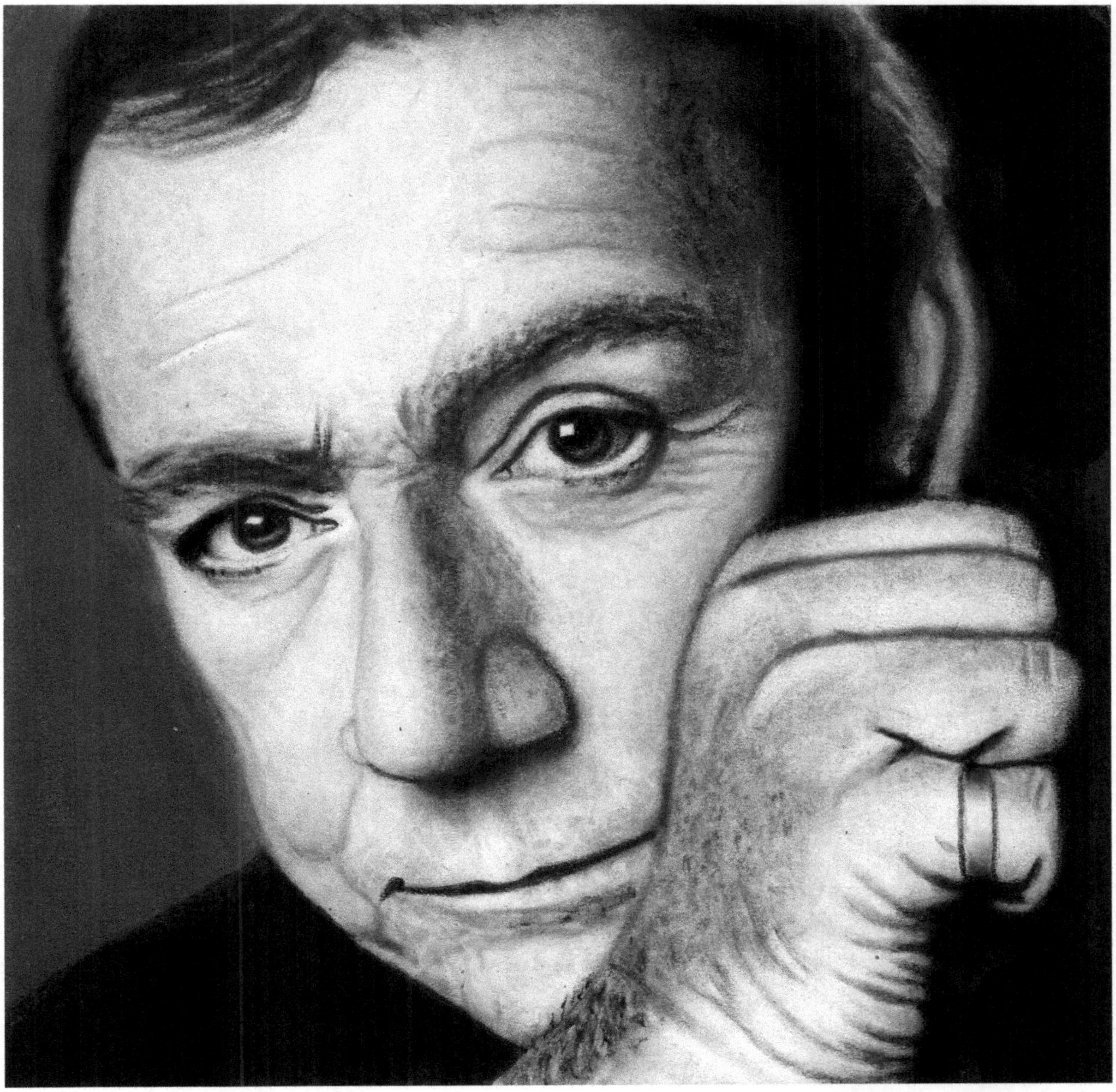

To view how this drawing was masterfully created or to purchase a Limited Edition Framed Artwork of Eric Burdon type into your Internet Browser the URL shortcut ➡ **myportrait.art/ericburdon**

To listen to their Greatest Songs type into your Internet Browser the URL shortcut ➡ **radio.surf/theanimals**

To view all channels on THE FACE OF MUSIC Internet Radio MEGA Station type into your Internet Browser the URL shortcut ➡ **radio.surf/music**

To inquire about purchasing a Limited Edtion NFT of this portrait type into your Internet Browser the URL shortcut ➡ **myartnft.shop/ericburdon**

To view all available NFTs type into your Internet Browser the URL shortcut ➡ **myartnft.shop/all**

# Anne Murray

(Net worth: $50 Million)(Total Albums Sold: 55 Million)
(Genre: Pop / Country)(Height: 5' - 7")

Morna Anne Murray CC ONS (born June 20, 1945) is a Canadian singer. Her albums consisting primarily of pop, country, and adult contemporary music have sold over 55 million copies worldwide during her 40-year career.Murray was the first Canadian female solo singer to reach No. 1 on the U.S. charts, and also the first to earn a Gold record for one of her signature songs, "Snowbird" (1970). She is often cited as one of the female Canadian artists who paved the way for other international Canadian success stories such as k.d. lang, Céline Dion, and Shania Twain. She is also the first woman and the first Canadian to win "Album of the Year" at the 1984 Country Music Association Awards for her Gold-plus 1983 album A Little Good News.Murray has received four Grammys, a record 24 Junos, three American Music Awards, three Country Music Association Awards, and three Canadian Country Music Association Awards. She has been inducted into the Canadian Country Music Hall of Fame, the Juno Hall of Fame, The Canadian Songwriters Hall of Fame, and Canadian Broadcast Hall of Fame. She is a member of the Country Music Hall of Fame Walkway of Stars in Nashville, and has her own star on the Hollywood Walk of Fame in Los Angeles and on Canada's Walk of Fame in Toronto.In 2011, Billboard ranked her 10th on their list of the 50 Biggest Adult Contemporary Artists Ever."What About Me," the lead single and title cut on her debut album, was written by Scott McKenzie and was a sizable Canadian radio hit. The project covered songs by Joni Mitchell, Ken Tobias, and John Denver. After a year-long stint on Arc, Murray switched to Capitol Records in 1969 to record her second album, This Way Is My Way, which was released in the fall of 1969. It featured the single that launched her career, "Snowbird", which became a No. 1 hit in Canada. "Snowbird" became a surprise hit on the U.S. charts as well, reaching No. 8 on the Billboard Hot 100 in 1970. It was also the first of her eight No. 1 Adult Contemporary hits. "Snowbird" was the first Gold record ever given to a Canadian artist in the United States (RIAA certified Gold on November 16, 1970). As one of the most successful female artists at that time, she became in demand for several television appearances in Canada and the United States, eventually becoming a regular on the hit U.S. television series The Glen Campbell Goodtime Hour. After the success of "Snowbird", she had a number of subsequent singles that charted both pop and country simultaneously. During the 1970s and 1980s, her hits included Kenny Loggins's "Danny's Song" (1972) (peaked at No. 7 on the Hot 100), "A Love Song" (1973), "He Thinks I Still Care", The Beatles' "You Won't See Me" (1974); her all-time biggest Hot 100 hit "You Needed Me" (1978), "I Just Fall in Love Again", "Shadows in the Moonlight", "Broken Hearted Me" (1979), "I'm Happy Just to Dance With You" (1980), which hit #64 on the Hot 100 and #23 on the Country chart, The Monkees' 1967 No. 1 hit "Daydream Believer", "Could I Have This Dance" from the Urban Cowboy motion picture soundtrack (1980), "Blessed Are the Believers" (1981), "Another Sleepless Night" (1982), "A Little Good News" (1983), "Just Another Woman in Love", "Nobody Loves Me Like You Do", and "Time, Don't Run Out on Me" (1985).

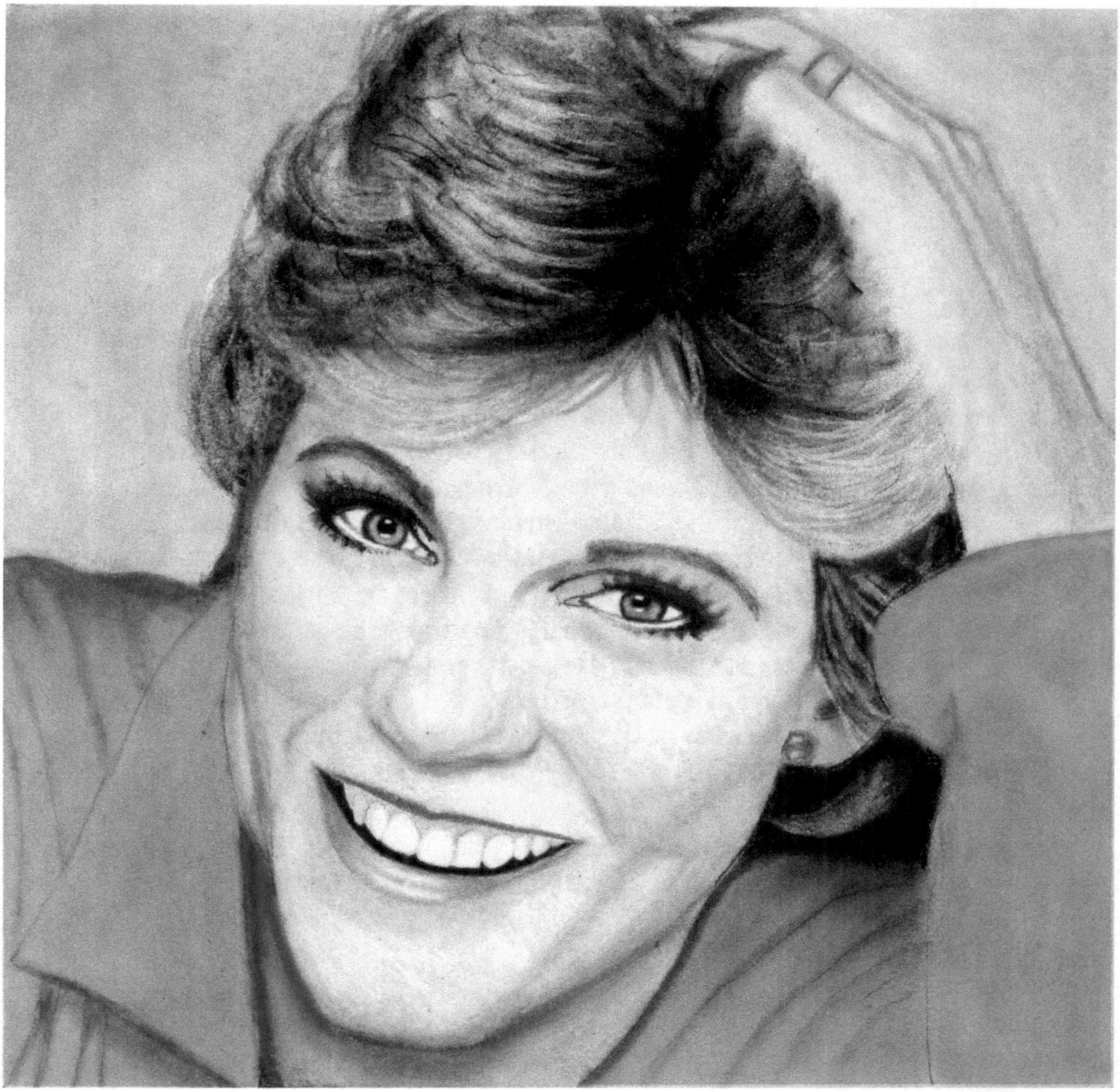

To view how this drawing was masterfully created or to purchase a Limited Edition Framed Artwork of Anne Murray type into your Internet Browser the URL shortcut ➡ **myportrait.art/annemurray**

To listen to herm Greatest Songs type into your Internet Browser the URL shortcut
➡ **radio.surf/annemurray**

To view all channels on THE FACE OF MUSIC Internet Radio MEGA Station type into your Internet Browser the URL shortcut ➡ **radio.surf/music**

To inquire about purchasing a Limited Edtion NFT of this portrait type into your Internet Browser the URL shortcut ➡ **myartnft.shop/annemurray**

To view all available NFTs type into your Internet Browser the URL shortcut ➡ **myartnft.shop/all**

# Anthrax

(Total Albums Sold: 10 Million) (Genre: Thrash Metal)

Anthrax is an American heavy metal band from New York City, formed in 1981 by rhythm guitarist Scott Ian and bassist Dan Lilker. The group is considered one of the leaders of the thrash metal scene from the 1980s and is part of the "Big Four" of the genre, along with Metallica, Megadeth and Slayer. They were also one of the first thrash metal bands (along with Overkill and Nuclear Assault) to emerge from the East Coast. The band has released 11 studio albums, several other albums, and 26 singles, including collaborating on a single with American hip hop group Public Enemy. According to Nielsen SoundScan, Anthrax sold 2.5 million records in the United States from 1991 to 2004, with worldwide sales of 10 million. Four of the band's studio albums have also achieved gold certifications by the RIAA, including their third full-length record Among the Living (1987), which cemented Anthrax's reputation as one of the most successful thrash metal bands. Anthrax's lineup has changed numerous times over their career, leaving Ian as the only constant member of the band. The band has had a revolving cast of singers and lead guitarists, including Neil Turbin, John Bush, Dan Spitz and Rob Caggiano. Since 2013, the band has consisted of Ian, drummer Charlie Benante, bassist Frank Bello, vocalist Joey Belladonna and lead guitarist Jonathan Donais. Ian and Benante (who replaced one-time drummer Greg D'Angelo in 1983) are the only two members to appear on every album, while Bello has been a member of Anthrax since 1984, replacing original bassist Dan Lilker. After two stints in Anthrax, from 1984 to 1992 and again from 2005 to 2007, Belladonna returned to the band in 2010.

# Joey Belladonna

(Net Worth: $85 Million) (Height: 5'-2")

Joey Belladonna (born Joseph Bellardini; October 13, 1960) is an American musician, best known as the vocalist for thrash metal band Anthrax. He is also the vocalist and drummer of the cover band Chief Big Way. Belladonna has six Grammy Award nominations and is known for his wild, energetic stage behavior, and tenor vocal range.

Belladonna was the lead singer of Anthrax from 1984 to 1992, and was considered part of the classic-lineup (also featuring Dan Spitz, Scott Ian, Frank Bello and Charlie Benante).

His voice has been featured on six studio albums and several EPs that have sold a total of eight million copies worldwide. During Belladonna's first tenure with Anthrax, the band was nominated for three Grammys, and he was voted the No. 1 metal singer two years in a row in Metal Forces magazine.

In early 2010, Belladonna officially rejoined Anthrax in time for the "Big Four" shows at the Sonisphere festival. Following these and other shows, Belladonna returned to the studio with the band to record new vocals for their long-awaited album Worship Music.

Since his return, Anthrax has been nominated for three additional Grammy awards.

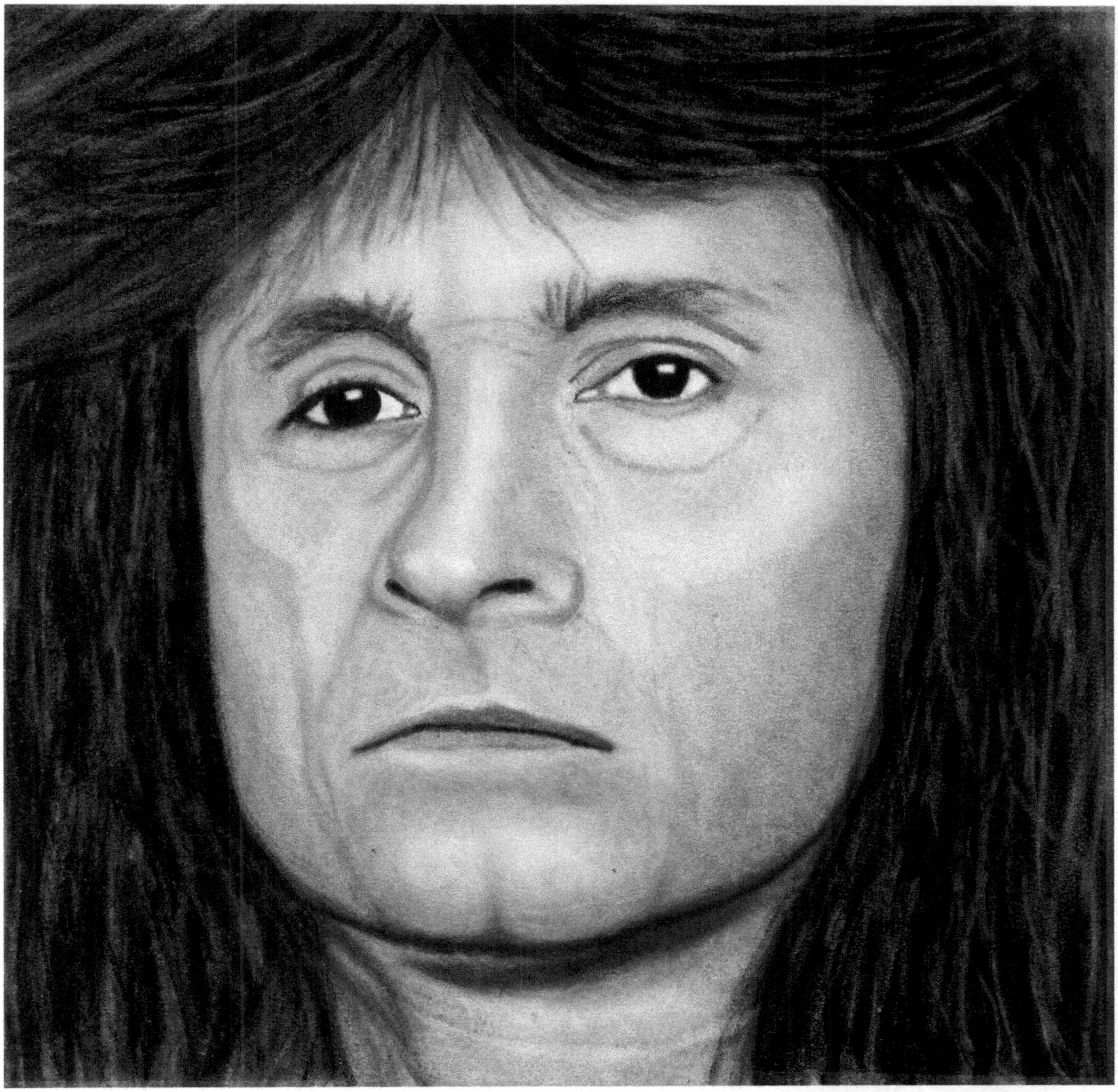

To view how this drawing was masterfully created or to purchase a Limited Edition Framed Artwork of Joey Belladonna type into your Internet Browser the URL shortcut ➡ **myportrait.art/joeybelladonna**

To listen to their Greatest Songs type into your Internet Browser the URL shortcut ➡ **radio.surf/anthrax**

To view all channels on THE FACE OF MUSIC Internet Radio MEGA Station type into your Internet Browser the URL shortcut ➡ **radio.surf/music**

To inquire about purchasing a Limited Edtion NFT of this portrait type into your Internet Browser the URL shortcut ➡ **myartnft.shop/joeybelladonna**

To view all available NFTs type into your Internet Browser the URL shortcut ➡ **myartnft.shop/all**

# Aretha Franklin

(Net worth: $ 17 Million)(Total Records Sold: 75 Million)
(Genre: Classic Soul)(Height: 5' - 5")

Aretha Louise Franklin (March 25, 1942 – August 16, 2018) was an American singer, songwriter, actress, pianist, and civil rights activist. Franklin began her career as a child singing gospel at New Bethel Baptist Church in Detroit, Michigan, where her father C. L. Franklin was a minister. At the age of 18, she embarked on a secular-music career as a recording artist for Columbia Records. While Franklin's career did not immediately flourish, she found acclaim and commercial success after signing with Atlantic Records in 1966. Hit songs such as "I Never Loved a Man (The Way I Love You)", "Respect", "(You Make Me Feel Like) A Natural Woman", "Chain of Fools", "Think", and "I Say a Little Prayer" propelled her past her musical peers. By the end of the 1960s, Aretha Franklin had come to be known as the "Queen of Soul".

Franklin continued to record acclaimed albums such as I Never Loved a Man the Way I Love You (1967), Lady Soul (1968), Spirit in the Dark (1970), Young, Gifted and Black (1972), Amazing Grace (1972), and Sparkle (1976) before experiencing problems with her record company. Franklin left Atlantic in 1979 and signed with Arista Records. She appeared in the 1980 film The Blues Brothers before releasing the successful albums Jump to It (1982), Who's Zoomin' Who? (1985), and Aretha (1986) on the Arista label. In 1998, Franklin returned to the Top 40 with the Lauryn Hill-produced song "A Rose Is Still a Rose"; later, she released an album of the same name which was certified gold. That same year, Franklin earned international acclaim for her performance of "Nessun dorma" at the Grammy Awards where she filled in at the last minute for Luciano Pavarotti, who canceled his appearance after the show had already begun. In a widely noted performance, she paid tribute to 2015 honoree Carole King by singing "(You Make Me Feel Like) A Natural Woman" at the Kennedy Center Honors.

Franklin recorded 112 charted singles on Billboard, including 77 Hot 100 entries, 17 top-ten pop singles, 100 R&B entries, and 20 number-one R&B singles. Besides the foregoing, Franklin's well-known hits also include "Ain't No Way", "Call Me", "Don't Play That Song (You Lied)", "Spanish Harlem", "Rock Steady", "Day Dreaming", "Until You Come Back to Me (That's What I'm Gonna Do)", "Something He Can Feel", "Jump to It", "Freeway of Love", "Who's Zoomin' Who", and "I Knew You Were Waiting (For Me)" (a duet with George Michael). She won 18 Grammy Awards, including the first eight awards given for Best Female R&B Vocal Performance (1968–1975). Franklin is one of the best-selling music artists of all time, having sold more than 75 million records worldwide.Franklin received numerous honors throughout her career. She was awarded the National Medal of Arts and the Presidential Medal of Freedom. In 1987, she became the first female performer to be inducted into the Rock and Roll Hall of Fame. She also was inducted into the UK Music Hall of Fame in 2005 and into the Gospel Music Hall of Fame in 2012. In 2010, Rolling Stone magazine ranked her number one on its list of the "100 Greatest Singers of All Time" and number nine on its list of "100 Greatest Artists of All Time". The Pulitzer Prize jury in 2019 awarded Franklin a posthumous special citation "for her indelible contribution to American music and culture for more than five decades". In 2020, she was inducted into the National Women's Hall of Fame.

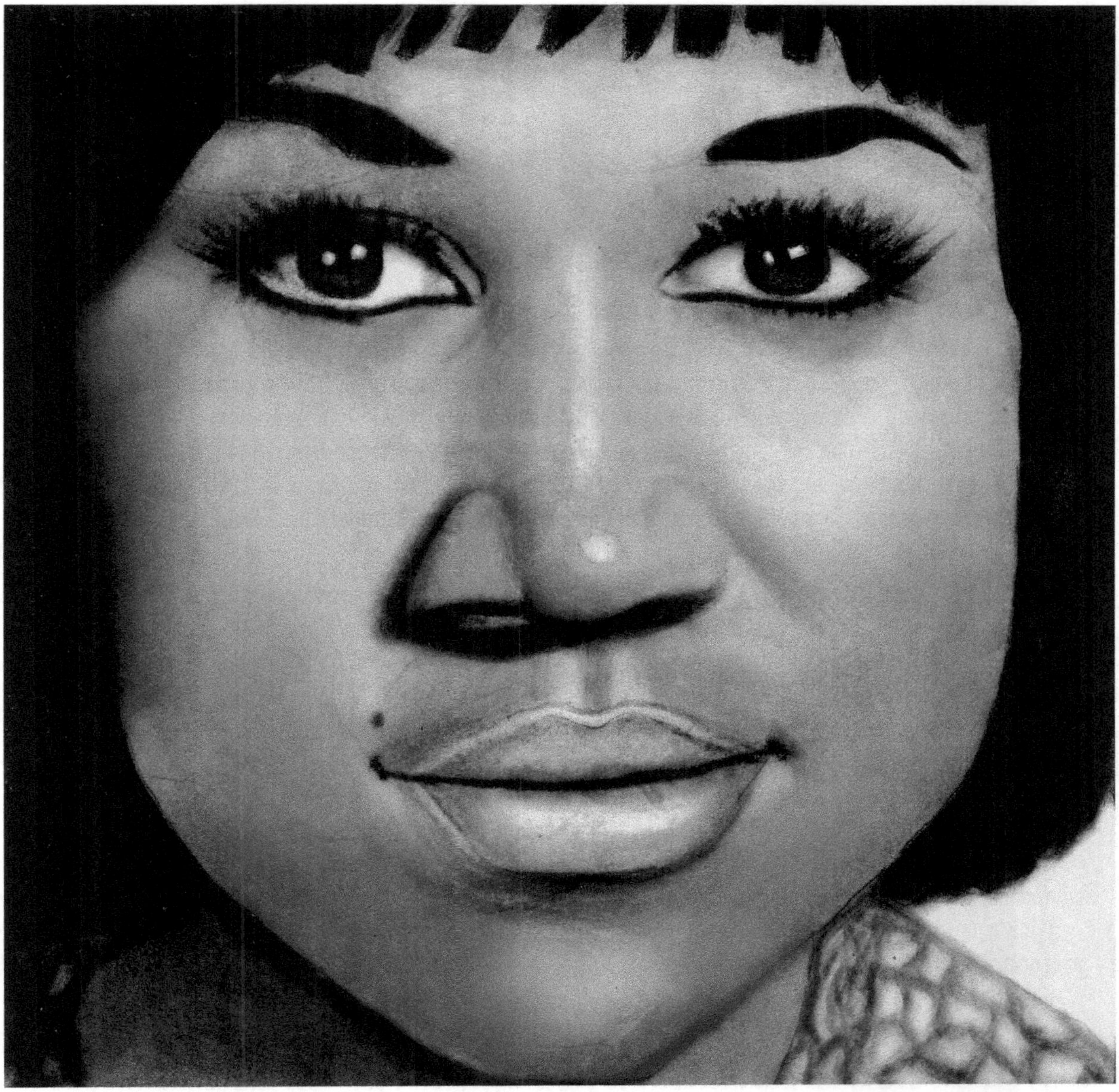

To view how this drawing was masterfully created or to purchase a Limited Edition Framed Artwork of Aretha Franklin type into your Internet Browser the URL shortcut ➡ **myportrait.art/arethafranklin**

To listen to her Greatest Songs type into your Internet Browser the URL shortcut
➡ **radio.surf/arethafranklin**

To view all channels on THE FACE OF MUSIC Internet Radio MEGA Station type into your Internet Browser the URL shortcut ➡ **radio.surf/music**

To inquire about purchasing a Limited Edtion NFT of this portrait type into your Internet Browser the URL shortcut ➡ **myartnft.shop/arethafranklin**

To view all available NFTs type into your Internet Browser the URL shortcut ➡ **myartnft.shop/all**

# B.B. King

(Net worth: $ 10 Million)(Total Records Sold: 1+ Million)
(Genre: Classic Blues)(Height: 5' - 10")

Riley B. King (September 16, 1925 – May 14, 2015), known professionally as B.B. King, was an American singer-songwriter, guitarist, and record producer. He introduced a sophisticated style of soloing based on fluid string bending, shimmering vibrato and staccato picking that influenced many later blues electric guitar players. AllMusic recognized King as "the single most important electric guitarist of the last half of the 20th century".King was inducted into the Rock and Roll Hall of Fame in 1987, and is one of the most influential blues musicians of all time, earning the nickname "The King of the Blues", and is considered one of the "Three Kings of the Blues Guitar" (along with Albert King and Freddie King, none of whom are blood related). King performed tirelessly throughout his musical career, appearing on average at more than 200 concerts per year into his 70s. In 1956 alone, he appeared at 342 shows.King was born on a cotton plantation in Itta Bena, Mississippi, and later worked at a cotton gin in Indianola, Mississippi. He was attracted to music and the guitar in church, and began his career in juke joints and local radio. He later lived in Memphis, Tennessee, and Chicago, and as his fame grew, toured the world extensively. King died at the age of 89 in Las Vegas, Nevada, on May 14, 2015.Riley B. King was born on September 16, 1925, on the Berclair cotton plantation near the town of Itta Bena, Mississippi, the son of sharecroppers Albert and Nora Ella King. He considered the nearby city of Indianola, Mississippi to be his home. When King was four years old, his mother left his father for another man, so he was raised by his maternal grandmother, Elnora Farr, in Kilmichael, Mississippi.While young, King sang in the gospel choir at Elkhorn Baptist Church in Kilmichael. King was attracted to the Pentecostal Church of God in Christ because of its music. The local minister performed with a Sears Roebuck Silvertone guitar during services. The minister taught King his first three chords. It seems that at the age of 12 he purchased his first guitar for $15.00, although another source indicates he was given his first guitar by Bukka White, his mother's first cousin (King's grandmother and White's mother were sisters).In November 1941, "King Biscuit Time" first aired, broadcasting on KFFA in Helena, Arkansas. It was a radio show featuring the Mississippi Delta blues. King listened to it while on break at a plantation. A self-taught guitarist, he then wanted to become a radio musician.In 1943, King left Kilmichael to work as a tractor driver and play guitar with the Famous St. John's Gospel Singers of Inverness, Mississippi, performing at area churches and on WGRM in Greenwood, Mississippi.Poster of B.B. King and Bill Harvey and Orchestra with photo of B.B. King holding his guitar and Evelyn Young playing saxophoneIn 1946, King followed Bukka White to Memphis, Tennessee. White took him in for the next ten months. However, King returned to Mississippi shortly afterward, where he decided to prepare himself better for the next visit, and returned to West Memphis, Arkansas, two years later in 1948. He performed on Sonny Boy Williamson's radio program on KWEM in West Memphis, where he began to develop an audience. King's appearances led to steady engagements at the Sixteenth Avenue Grill in West Memphis, and later to a ten-minute spot on the Memphis radio station WDIA. The radio spot became so popular that it was expanded and became the Sepia Swing Club.He worked at WDIA as a singer and disc jockey, where he was given the nickname "Beale Street Blues Boy", later shortened to "Blues Boy", and finally to B.B. It was there that he first met T-Bone Walker. King said, "Once I'd heard him for the first time, I knew I'd have to have [an electric guitar] myself. 'Had' to have one, short of stealing!"

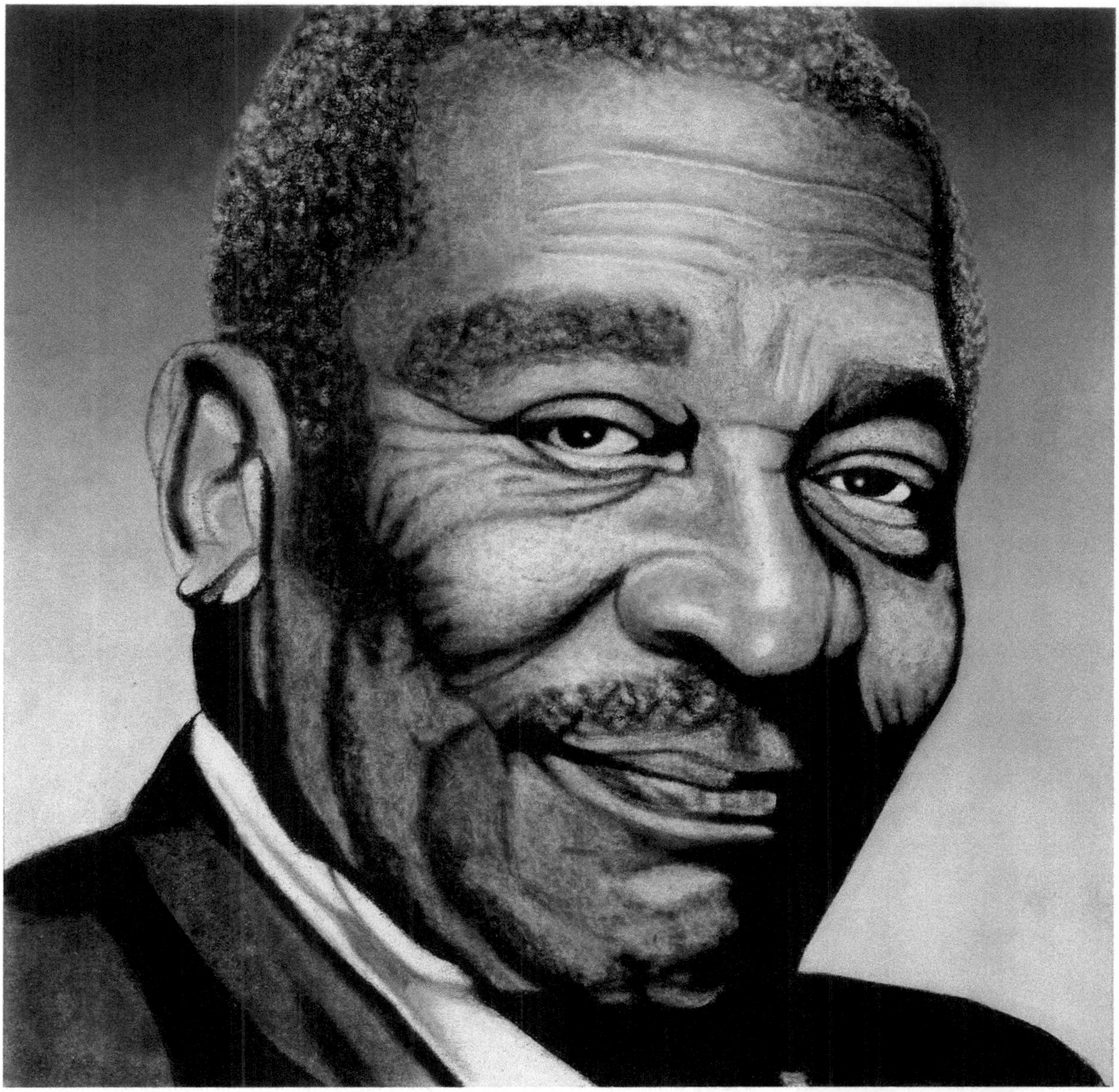

To view how this drawing was masterfully created or to purchase a Limited Edition Framed Artwork of B.B. King type into your Internet Browser the URL shortcut ➡ **myportrait.art/bbking**

To listen to his Greatest Songs type into your Internet Browser the URL shortcut ➡ **radio.surf/bbking**

To view all channels on THE FACE OF MUSIC Internet Radio MEGA Station type into your Internet Browser the URL shortcut ➡ **radio.surf/music**

To inquire about purchasing a Limited Edtion NFT of this portrait type into your Internet Browser the URL shortcut ➡ **myartnft.shop/bbking**

To view all available NFTs type into your Internet Browser the URL shortcut ➡ **myartnft.shop/all**

# Bachman Turner Overdrive

(Total Albums Sold: 30 Million) (Genre: Classic Rock)

Bachman–Turner Overdrive, often abbreviated as BTO, was a Canadian rock group from Winnipeg, Manitoba founded by Randy Bachman, Robbie Bachman and Fred Turner. Their 1970s catalogue included five Top 40 albums and six US Top 40 singles (eleven in Canada). BTO has five certified Gold albums and one certified Platinum album in the US; in Canada, they have six certified Platinum albums and one certified Gold album. The band has sold nearly 30 million albums worldwide, and has fans affectionately known as "gearheads" (derived from the band's gear-shaped logo). Many of their songs, including "Let It Ride", "You Ain't Seen Nothing Yet", "Takin' Care of Business", "Hey You", and "Roll on Down the Highway", still receive play on classic-rock stations.The original lineup consisted of Randy Bachman (lead guitar, lead vocals), Fred Turner (bass guitar, lead vocals), Tim Bachman (guitar, vocals) and Robbie Bachman (drums). This lineup released two albums in 1973. The second and most commercially successful lineup featured Blair Thornton (lead guitar), in place of Tim Bachman. This lineup released four albums between 1974 and 1977, including two that reached the Top 5 in the U.S. pop charts, as well as the band's only U.S. No. 1 single ("You Ain't Seen Nothing Yet"). Subsequent lineups enjoyed only moderate success.After the band went into a hiatus in 2005, Randy Bachman and Fred Turner reunited in 2009 to tour and collaborate on a new album. In 2010, they played the halftime show at the Grey Cup in Edmonton. The two stopped touring following Turner's amicable retirement in March 2018.On March 29, 2014, the classic Not Fragile line-up reunited for the first time since 1991 to mark Bachman–Turner Overdrive's induction into the Canadian Music Hall of Fame, and participated in performing in a tribute version of "Takin' Care of Business".

# Randy Bachman

(Net Worth: $15 Million) (Height: 5'-6")

Randolph Charles Bachman, OC OM (/ˈbækmən/; born September 27, 1943) is a Canadian musician, lead guitarist, songwriter and a founding member of classic rock band The Guess Who and hard rock band Bachman–Turner Overdrive. Bachman was also a member of Brave Belt, Union and Ironhorse, and has recorded as a solo artist. He is a national radio personality on CBC Radio, hosting the weekly music show, Vinyl Tap. Bachman was inducted into the Musicians Hall of Fame and Museum in 2016.In 1960, Bachman and Chad Allan co-founded Al and The Silvertones in Winnipeg. By 1962, the band changed their name to Chad Allan and the Expressions and later to The Guess Who. In 1965, the Guess Who had a #1 hit in Canada with their cover of Johnny Kidd's "Shakin' All Over", which also charted in the US at #22. In 1966, Chad Allan left the band and Burton Cummings became the primary vocalist. Between 1966 and 1968, The Guess Who laboured mostly in their home country, releasing a few singles that managed to crack the Top 40 in Canada. In early 1969, the group finally broke through internationally with the hit song "These Eyes", co-written by Bachman and Cummings. The Guess Who released three successful albums over the next two years: Wheatfield Soul (1969), Canned Wheat (1969), and American Woman (1970), which brought them mainstream attention. Bachman wrote or cowrote (primarily with Cummings) most of the group's songs during this period.

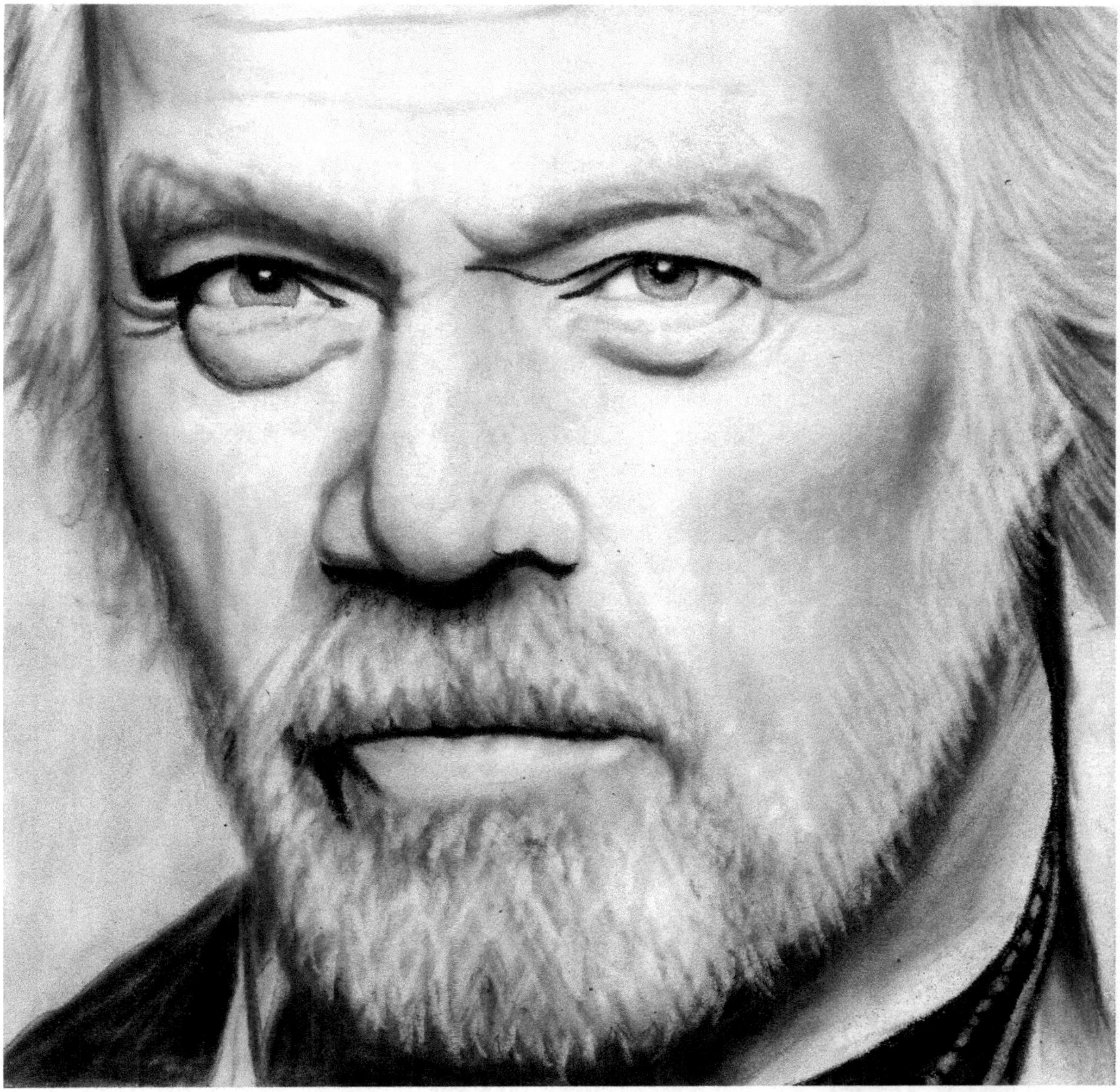

To view how this drawing was masterfully created or to purchase a Limited Edition Framed Artwork of Randy Bachman type into your Internet Browser the URL shortcut ➡ **myportrait.art/randybachman**

To listen to their Greatest Songs type into your Internet Browser the URL shortcut ➡ **radio.surf/bto**

To view all channels on THE FACE OF MUSIC Internet Radio MEGA Station type into your Internet Browser the URL shortcut ➡ **radio.surf/music**

To inquire about purchasing a Limited Edtion NFT of this portrait type into your Internet Browser the URL shortcut ➡ **myartnft.shop/randybachman**

To view all available NFTs type into your Internet Browser the URL shortcut ➡ **myartnft.shop/all**

# Bad Company

(Total Albums Sold: 40 Million) (Genre: Classic Rock)

Bad Company are an English rock supergroup formed in Albury, Surrey in 1973 by singer Paul Rodgers, guitarist Mick Ralphs, drummer Simon Kirke and later adding bassist Boz Burrell. Peter Grant, who managed the rock band Led Zeppelin, also managed Bad Company until 1982.

Bad Company enjoyed great success throughout the 1970s. Their first three albums, Bad Company (1974), Straight Shooter (1975), and Run with the Pack (1976), reached the top five in the album charts in both the UK and the US. Many of their singles and songs, such as "Bad Company", "Can't Get Enough", "Good Lovin' Gone Bad", "Feel Like Makin' Love", "Ready for Love", "Shooting Star", and "Rock 'n' Roll Fantasy", remain staples of classic rock radio. They have sold 20 million RIAA-certified albums in the US and 40 million worldwide.The band's 1974 debut album, Bad Company, was recorded at Headley Grange, Hampshire in Ronnie Lane's Mobile Studio. The album reached number one on the Billboard 200 in the US and number 3 in the UK Albums Chart, spending 25 weeks in the UK charts. The album has been certified five times platinum in the US and became the 46th–best-selling album of the 1970s. The singles "Can't Get Enough" and "Movin' On" reached No. 5 and No. 19 on the Billboard Hot 100.

# Paul Rodgers

(Net Worth: $14 Million) (Height: 5'-6")

Paul Rodgers (born 17 December 1949) is an English-Canadian singer, songwriter and multi-instrumentalist. In the 1960s and 1970s, he was vocalist of Free and Bad Company. After stints in two lesser-known bands in the 1980s and early 1990s, The Firm and The Law, he became a solo artist. He has more recently toured and recorded with Queen. A poll in Rolling Stone magazine ranked him number 55 on its list of the "100 Greatest Singers of All Time". In 2011 Rodgers received the British Academy's Ivor Novello Award for Outstanding Contribution to British Music.Rodgers has been cited as a significant influence on a number of notable rock singers. In 1991, John Mellencamp called Rodgers "the best rock singer ever". Freddie Mercury in particular liked Rodgers and his aggressive style.Rodgers joined in 1968 as singer/songwriter for bluesy rockers Free. In 1970, they shot up the international radio charts with "All Right Now", which Rodgers wrote with the group's bassist Andy Fraser. It was a number one hit in more than 20 territories and acknowledged by ASCAP in 1990 for having received over a million radio plays in the US.Rodgers formed his next band, Bad Company, with Mick Ralphs, former guitarist of Mott the Hoople. The lineup also included Rodgers' bandmate from Free, drummer Simon Kirke, and Boz Burrell, former vocalist and bassist of King Crimson. Rodgers said he and Ralphs were still trying to come up with a name for the band, "and I just said 'Bad Company', and there was this scuffling noise and he said, 'Shit, I dropped the phone—that's it!'Bad Company was the first act signed to Led Zeppelin's new record label, Swan Song. They toured from 1973 to 1982, and had several hits such as "Feel Like Makin' Love", "Can't Get Enough", "Shooting Star", "Bad Company", and "Run with the Pack". Rodgers played instruments on several tracks: "Bad Company" and "Run With The Pack" featured him on piano; "Rock and Roll Fantasy" on guitar; and on the ballad "Seagull" Rodgers played all of the instruments. Bad Company earned six platinum albums until Rodgers left in 1982, stating that he wanted to spend time with his young family.

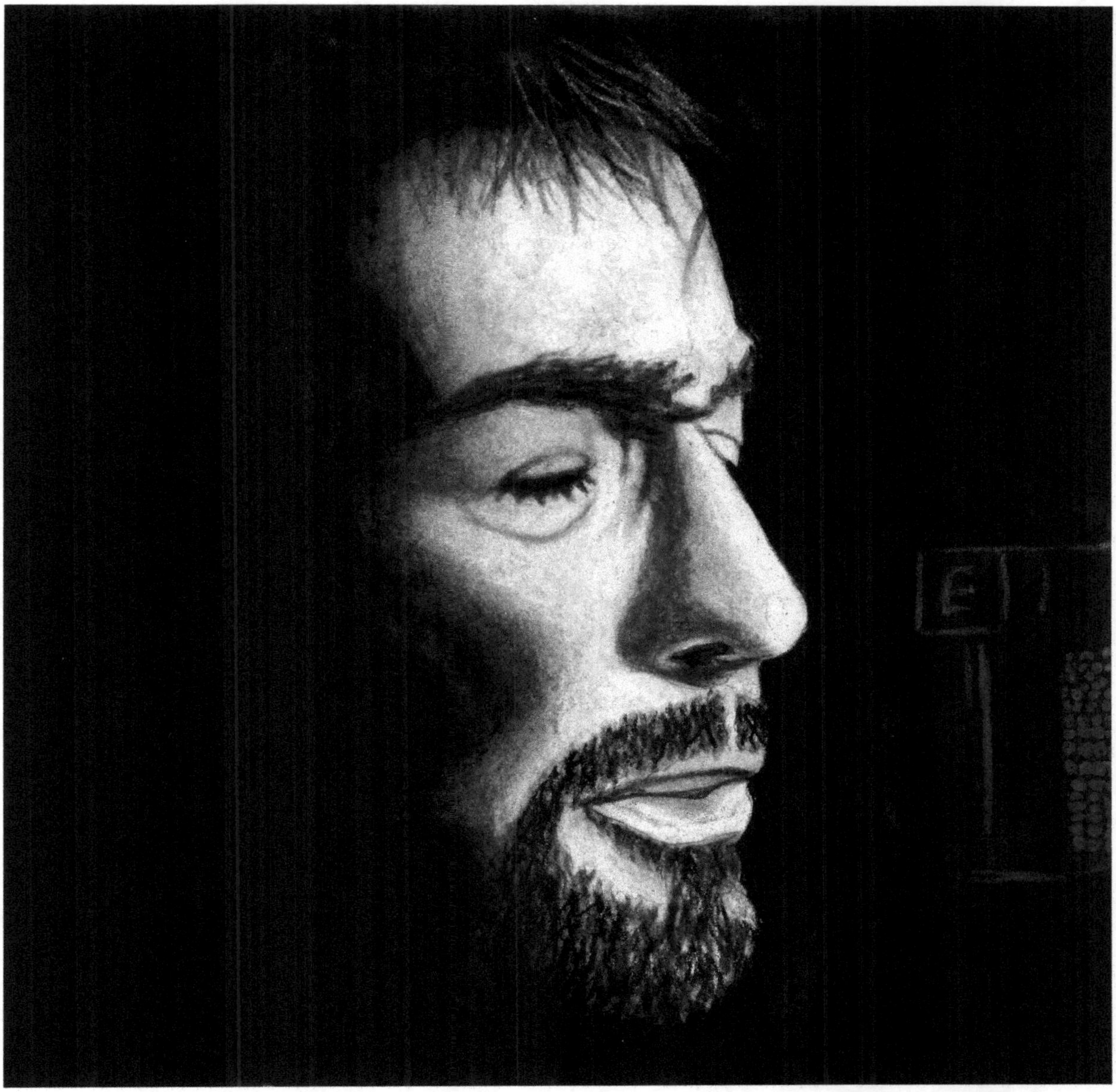


To view how this drawing was masterfully created or to purchase a Limited Edition Framed Artwork of Paul Rodgers type into your Internet Browser the URL shortcut ➡ **myportrait.art/paulrodgers**

To listen to their Greatest Songs type into your Internet Browser the URL shortcut
➡ **radio.surf/badcompany**

To view all channels on THE FACE OF MUSIC Internet Radio MEGA Station type into your Internet Browser the URL shortcut ➡ **radio.surf/music**

To inquire about purchasing a Limited Edtion NFT of this portrait type into your Internet Browser the URL shortcut ➡ **myartnft.shop/paulrodgers**

To view all available NFTs type into your Internet Browser the URL shortcut ➡ **myartnft.shop/all**

# Band, The

(Total Albums Sold: 5 Million) (Genre: Rock)

The Band was a Canadian-American rock group formed in Toronto, Ontario, in 1967. Originally the backing band for Ronnie Hawkins and later Bob Dylan, the group released its debut album, Music from Big Pink, in 1968 to critical acclaim. Described by music critic Bruce Eder as "one of the most popular and influential rock groups in the world, their music embraced by critics ... as seriously as the music of the Beatles and the Rolling Stones". The Band combined elements of Americana, folk, rock, jazz, country, and R&B influencing subsequent musicians such as the Eagles, Elton John, the Grateful Dead, the Flaming Lips, and Wilco.The band consisted of four Canadians and one American: Rick Danko (bass guitar, vocals, fiddle), Garth Hudson (keyboards, accordion, saxophone), Richard Manuel (keyboards, drums, vocals), Robbie Robertson (guitar, vocals), and Levon Helm (drums, vocals, mandolin, guitar). Between 1958 and 1963, the band was the Hawks, a backing band for rockabilly singer Ronnie Hawkins. In the mid-1960s it gained recognition backing Bob Dylan, and the 1966 tour was notable as Dylan's first with an electric band. After leaving Dylan and changing its name to "The Band", it released several albums to critical and popular acclaim, highlighted by the songs "The Weight" and "The Night They Drove Old Dixie Down". According to AllMusic, its influence on several generations of musicians has been substantial; Roger Waters called Music from Big Pink the second most influential record in the history of rock and roll, and music journalist Al Aronowitz called its "country soul ... a sound never heard before".The group was inducted into the Canadian Music Hall of Fame in 1989 and the Rock and Roll Hall of Fame in 1994. In 2004 Rolling Stone ranked it 50th on its list of the 100 greatest artists of all time, and in 2008 it received the Grammy Lifetime Achievement Award. In 2004, "The Weight" was ranked 41st on Rolling Stone's list of the 500 greatest songs of all time. In 2014, the Band was inducted into Canada's Walk of Fame.

# Richard Manuel

(Net Worth: $5 Million) (Height: 5'-7")

Richard George Manuel (April 3, 1943 – March 4, 1986) was a Canadian composer, singer, and multi-instrumentalist, best known as a pianist and lead singer of The Band. The five members existed from December 1961 as The Hawks, becoming The Band in 1967, effectively breaking up in 1976, then re-formed in 1983. Manuel was with them until his 1986 suicide, a few hours after The Band performed a show.

Manuel's singing alternated between a soul-influenced baritone that drew frequent comparisons to Ray Charles and a delicate falsetto. Though The Band had three vocalists sharing lead and harmony parts, Manuel was often seen as the group's primary vocalist.

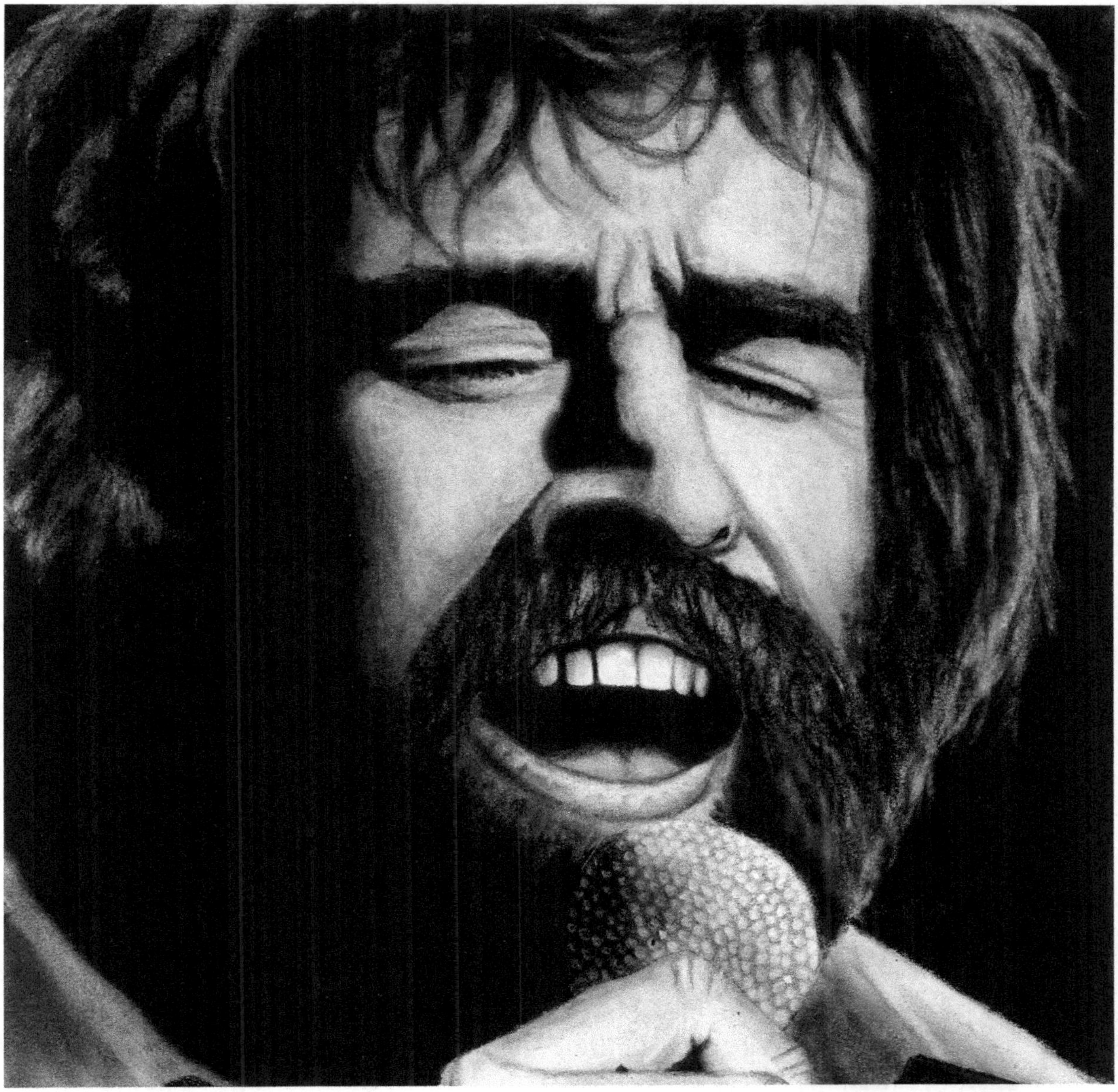

To view how this drawing was masterfully created or to purchase a Limited Edition Framed Artwork of Richard Manuel type into your Internet Browser the URL shortcut ➡ **myportrait.art/richardmanuel**

To listen to their Greatest Songs type into your Internet Browser the URL shortcut ➡ **radio.surf/theband**

To view all channels on THE FACE OF MUSIC Internet Radio MEGA Station type into your Internet Browser the URL shortcut ➡ **radio.surf/music**

To inquire about purchasing a Limited Edtion NFT of this portrait type into your Internet Browser the URL shortcut ➡ **myartnft.shop/richardmanuel**

To view all available NFTs type into your Internet Browser the URL shortcut ➡ **myartnft.shop/all**

# Barbra Streisand

(Net worth: $400 Million)(Total Records Sold: 150 Million)
(Genre: Broadway, Pop, Disco)(Height: 5' - 5")

Barbara Joan "Barbra" Streisand (/ˈstraɪsænd/; born April 24, 1942) is an American singer, actress, and filmmaker. With a career spanning seven decades, she has achieved success in multiple fields of entertainment and is one of the few entertainers who have been awarded an Emmy, Grammy, Oscar, and Tony Award (EGOT).

Streisand began her career by performing in nightclubs and Broadway theaters in the early 1960s. Following her guest appearances on various television shows, she signed to Columbia Records and released her debut album, The Barbra Streisand Album (1963). It won two Grammy Awards, including Album of the Year. Throughout her recording career, Streisand has topped the US Billboard 200 chart with 11 albums—a record for a woman—including People (1964), The Way We Were (1974), Guilty (1980), and Higher Ground (1997). She has attained five number-one singles on the US Billboard Hot 100 chart: "The Way We Were", "Evergreen", "You Don't Bring Me Flowers", "No More Tears (Enough Is Enough)", and "Woman in Love".

After becoming an established recording artist in the 1960s, Streisand ventured into film by the end of that decade. She starred in the critically acclaimed Funny Girl (1968), for which she won the Academy Award for Best Actress. Her other films include Hello, Dolly! (1969), What's Up, Doc? (1972), The Way We Were (1973), Funny Lady (1975), Yentl (1983), Nuts (1987), The Prince of Tides (1991), and The Mirror Has Two Faces (1996). For her film A Star Is Born (1976), she won her second Academy Award, composing music for the love theme "Evergreen", the first woman to be honored as a composer. With the release of Yentl (1983), Streisand became the first woman to write, produce, direct, and star in a major studio film. The film won an Oscar for Best Score and a Golden Globe for Best Motion Picture Musical. Streisand also received the Golden Globe Award for Best Director, becoming the first (and for thirty-seven years, the only) woman to win that award.

With sales of over 150 million records worldwide, Streisand is one of the best-selling recording artists of all time. According to the Recording Industry Association of America (RIAA), she is the highest-certified female artist in the United States, with 68.5 million certified album units tying with Mariah Carey. Billboard honored Streisand as the greatest Billboard 200 female artist of all time. Her accolades include two Academy Awards, ten Grammy Awards including the Grammy Lifetime Achievement Award and the Grammy Legend Award, five Emmy Awards, four Peabody Awards, the Presidential Medal of Freedom, and nine Golden Globes.

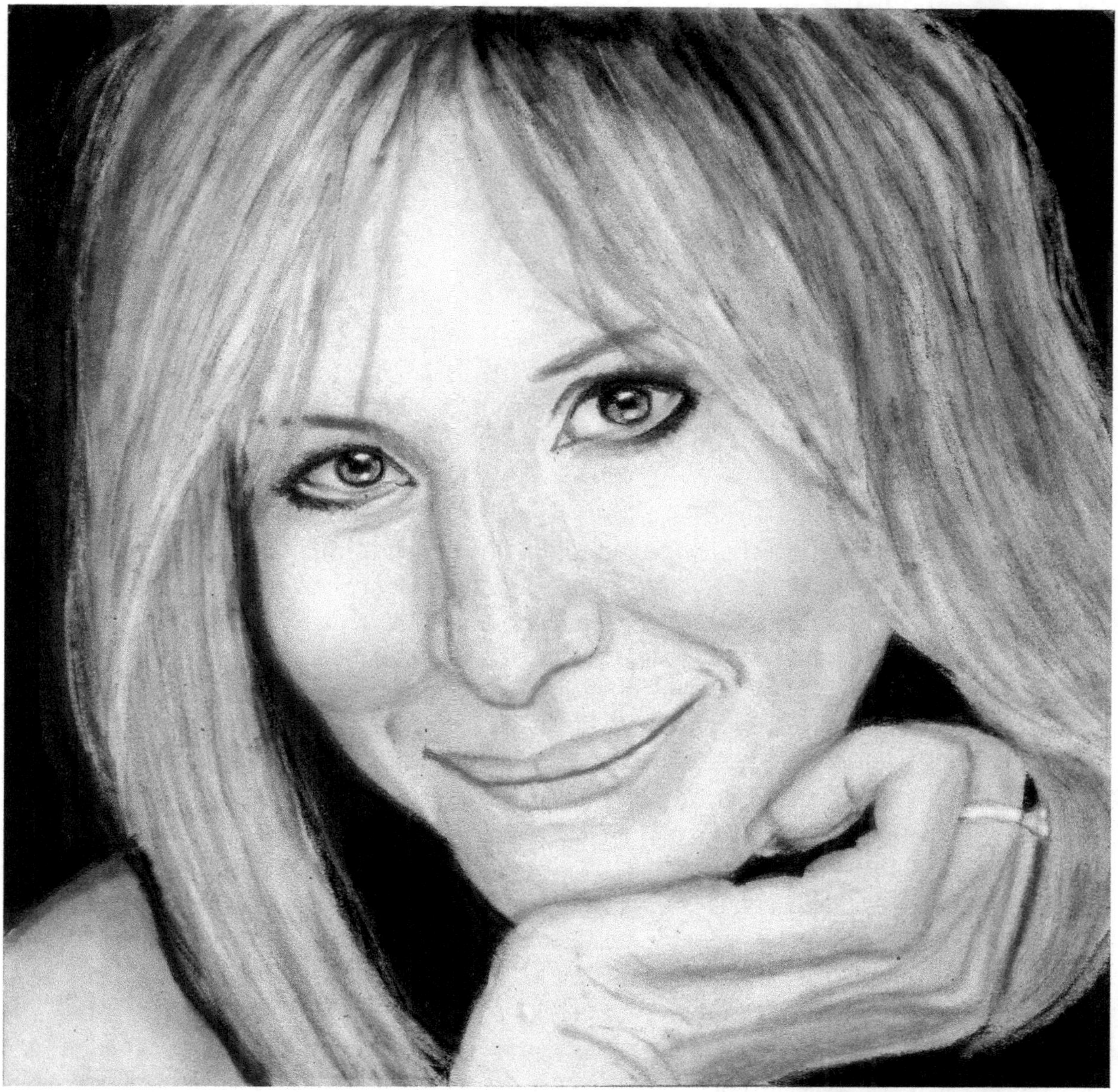

To view how this drawing was masterfully created or to purchase a Limited Edition Framed Artwork of Barbra Streisand type into your Internet Browser the URL shortcut ➡ **myportrait.art/barbrastreisand**

To listen to her Greatest Songs type into your Internet Browser the URL shortcut
➡ **radio.surf/barbrastreisand**

To view all channels on THE FACE OF MUSIC Internet Radio MEGA Station type into your Internet Browser the URL shortcut ➡ **radio.surf/music**

To inquire about purchasing a Limited Edtion NFT of this portrait type into your Internet Browser the URL shortcut ➡ **myartnft.shop/barbrastreisand**

To view all available NFTs type into your Internet Browser the URL shortcut ➡ **myartnft.shop/all**

# Barry Manilow

(Net worth: $100 Million)(Total Records Sold: 85 Million)
(Genre: Pop, Soft Rock)(Height: 6' - 0")

Barry Manilow (born Barry Alan Pincus, June 17, 1943) is an American singer-songwriter, arranger, musician, producer and actor, with a career that has spanned more than 50 years. His hit recordings include "Could It Be Magic", "Mandy", "I Write the Songs", "Can't Smile Without You" and "Copacabana (At the Copa)".

He recorded and released 51 Top 40 singles on the Adult Contemporary Chart, including 13 that hit number one, 28 appeared within the top ten, and 36 in the top twenty. Manilow has released 13 platinum and six multi-platinum albums. Although not a favorite artist of music critics, Manilow has been praised by entertainers including Frank Sinatra, who was quoted in the 1970s as saying, "He's next." In 1988, Bob Dylan stopped Manilow at a party, hugged him and said, "Don't stop what you're doing, man. We're all inspired by you."

As well as producing and arranging albums for himself and other artists, Manilow has written and performed songs for musicals, films, and commercials for corporations such as McDonald's, Pepsi-Cola, and Band-Aid, from the 1960s. He has been nominated for a Grammy Award (winning once) as a producer, arranger and performer a total of fifteen times (and in every decade) from 1973 to 2015. He has also produced Grammy-nominated albums for Bette Midler, Dionne Warwick, Nancy Wilson and Sarah Vaughan. Manilow has sold more than 85 million records as a solo artist worldwide, making him one of the world's best-selling artists.

Manilow was born Barry Alan Pincus on June 17, 1943, in Brooklyn, New York, the son of Edna Manilow and Harold Pincus (who went by his own stepfather's surname, Keliher). His father was born to a Jewish father, named Harry Pincus, and an Irish-American Catholic mother, while Manilow's maternal grandparents were of Russian Jewish background. His Irish roots trace back to Limerick, Ireland.

Manilow grew up in the Williamsburg neighborhood of Brooklyn, and graduated in 1961 from Eastern District High School, which closed in 1995. While in high school, he met Susan Deixler, who would later become his wife. He enrolled in the City College of New York, where he briefly studied before entering the New York College of Music. He also worked at CBS while he was a student in order to pay his expenses. He later studied Musical Theater at the Juilliard performing arts school.

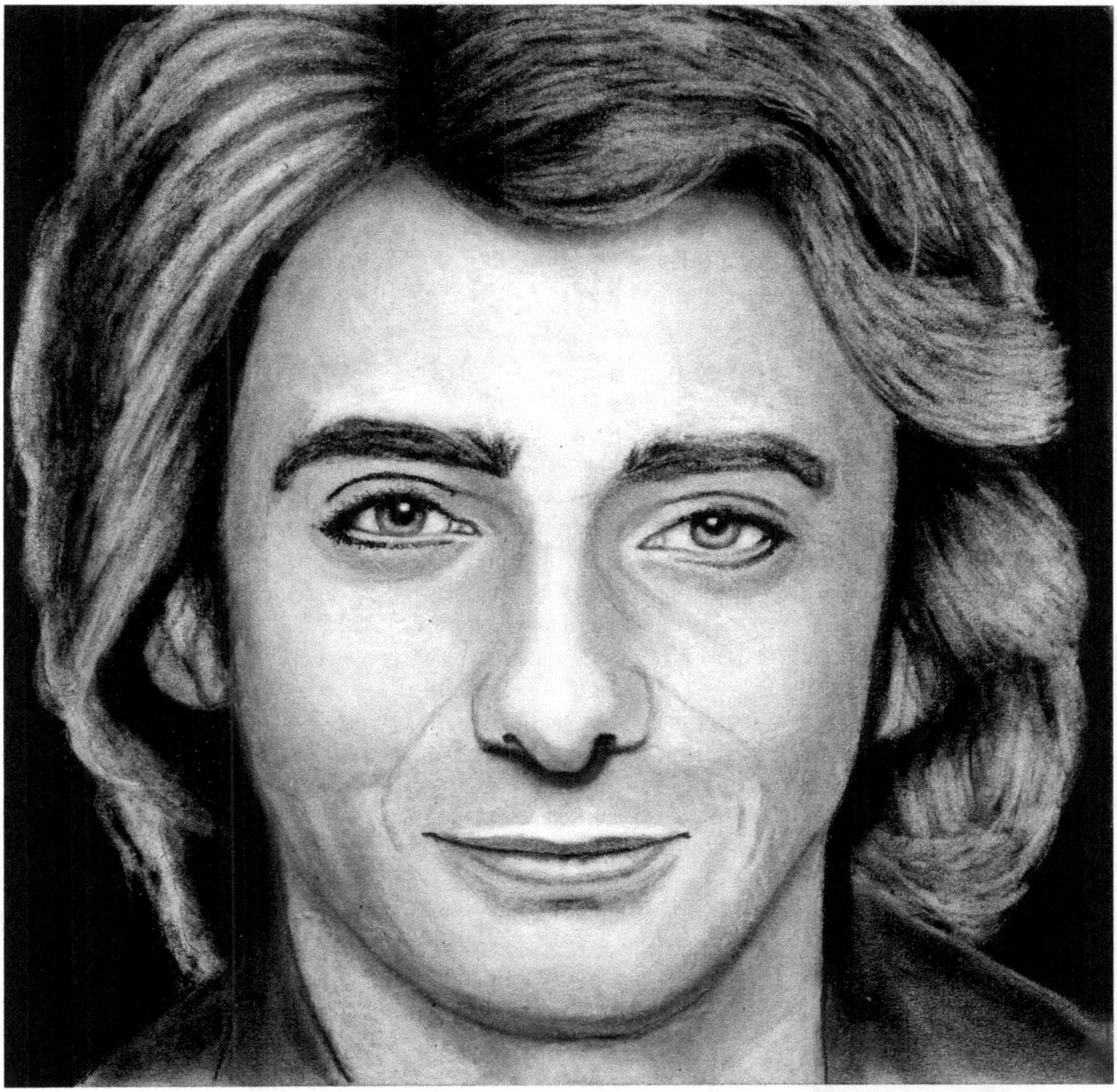

To view how this drawing was masterfully created or to purchase a Limited Edition Framed Artwork of Barry Manilow type into your Internet Browser the URL shortcut ➡ **myportrait.art/barrymanilow**

To listen to his Greatest Songs type into your Internet Browser the URL shortcut ➡ **radio.surf/barrymanilow**

To view all channels on THE FACE OF MUSIC Internet Radio MEGA Station type into your Internet Browser the URL shortcut ➡ **radio.surf/music**

To inquire about purchasing a Limited Edtion NFT of this portrait type into your Internet Browser the URL shortcut ➡ **myartnft.shop/barrymanilow**

To view all available NFTs type into your Internet Browser the URL shortcut ➡ **myartnft.shop/all**

# Beach Boys, The

(Total Albums Sold: 100 Million) (Genre: Rock)

The Beach Boys are an American rock band formed in Hawthorne, California in 1961. The group's original lineup consisted of brothers Brian (vocals, bass, keyboards), Dennis (drums, vocals), and Carl Wilson (lead guitar, vocals), their cousin Mike Love (vocals), and friend Al Jardine (rhythm guitar, vocals). Distinguished by their vocal harmonies, adolescent-oriented themes, and musical ingenuity, they are one of the most influential acts of the rock era. They drew on the music of older pop vocal groups, 1950s rock and roll, and black R&B to create their unique sound, and under Brian's direction, often incorporated classical or jazz elements and unconventional recording techniques in innovative ways.One of the first self-contained rock groups, the Beach Boys began as a garage band, managed by the Wilsons' father Murry, and with Brian as composer, arranger, producer, and de facto leader. In 1963, they had their first national hit with "Surfin' U.S.A.", beginning a string of top-ten singles that reflected a southern California youth culture of surfing, cars, and romance, dubbed the "California sound". They were one of the few American rock bands to sustain their commercial standing during the British Invasion. Starting with 1965's The Beach Boys Today!, they abandoned beachgoing themes for more personal lyrics and ambitious orchestrations. In 1966, the Pet Sounds album and "Good Vibrations" single raised the group's prestige as rock innovators; they also formed Brother Records, Inc., a corporation that continues to oversee affairs related to the band's legacy. After scrapping the Smile album in 1967, Brian's contributions diminished due to his mental health issues.The Beach Boys are one of the most critically acclaimed and commercially successful bands of all time, selling over 100 million records worldwide. They helped legitimize popular music as a recognized art form and influenced the development of music genres and movements such as psychedelia, power pop, progressive rock, punk, alternative, and lo-fi. Between the 1960s and 2010s, the group had 36 songs reach the US Top 40 (the most by an American band), with four topping the Billboard Hot 100. In 2004, Rolling Stone ranked the Beach Boys number 12 on its list of the greatest artists of all time. The founding members were inducted into the Rock and Roll Hall of Fame in 1988.

# Brian Wilson

(Net Worth: $100 Million) (Height: 6'-2")

Brian Douglas Wilson (born June 20, 1942) is an American musician, singer, songwriter, and record producer who co-founded the Beach Boys. After signing with Capitol Records in 1962, Wilson wrote or co-wrote more than two dozen Top 40 hits for the group. In addition to his unorthodox approaches to pop composition and mastery of recording techniques, Wilson is known for his lifelong struggles with mental illness. He is often referred to as a genius and is widely acknowledged as one of the most innovative and significant songwriters of the 20th century.Wilson was the first pop artist credited for writing, arranging, producing, and performing his own material. He is considered a major innovator in the field of music production, the principal originator of the California Sound, one of the first music producer auteurs, and among the first rock producers to use the studio as its own instrument. The unusual creative control Capitol gave him over his own records effectively set a precedent that allowed other bands and artists to act as their own producers or co-producers. Wilson's success also led to a proliferation of like-minded California producers who helped supplant New York as the center of popular records. The zeitgeist of the early 1960s is commonly associated with his early songs, and he was a major influence on the retrospectively-termed "sunshine pop" and Flower Power music that proceeded.

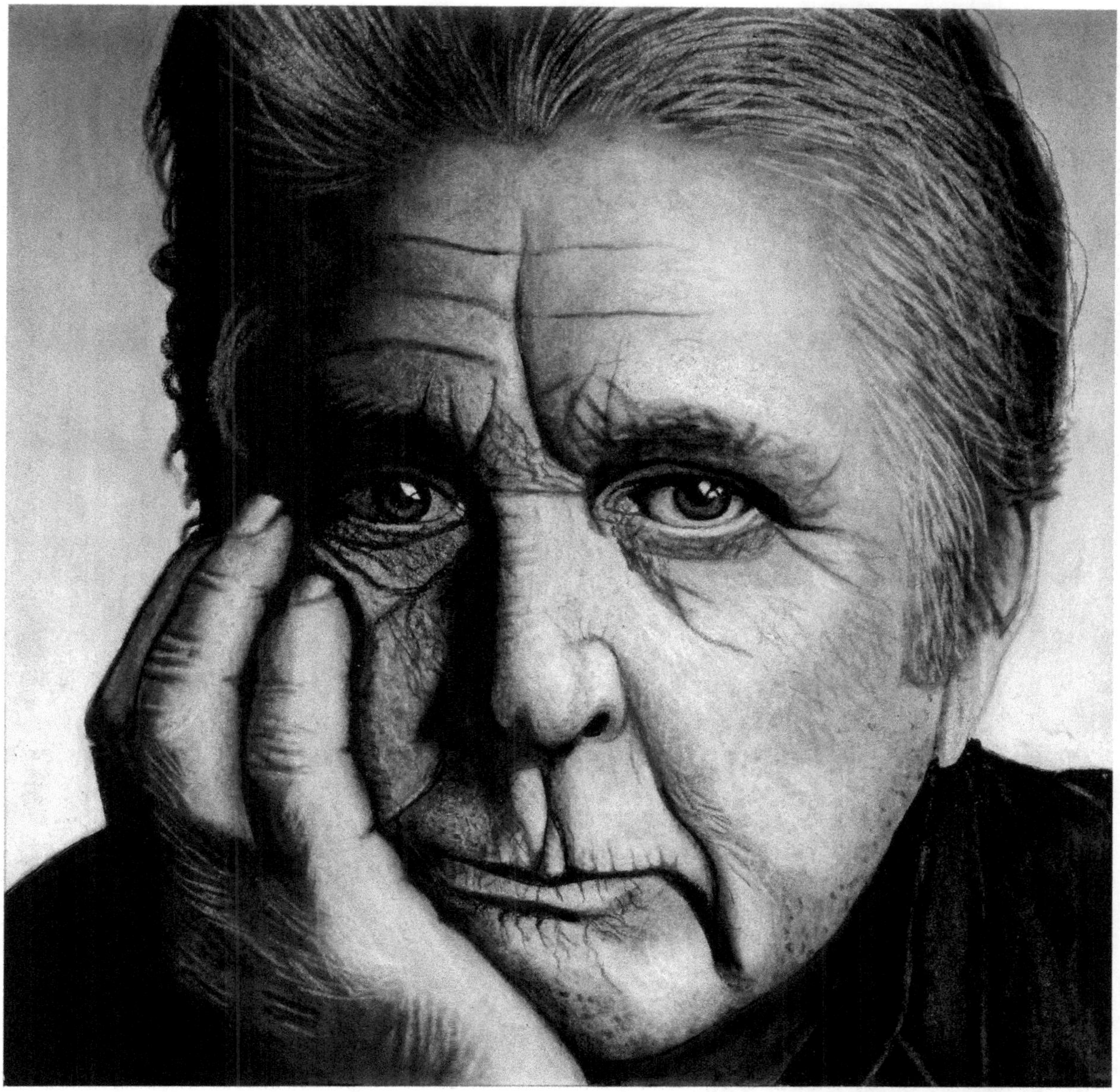

To view how this drawing was masterfully created or to purchase a Limited Edition Framed Artwork of Brian Wilson type into your Internet Browser the URL shortcut ➡ **myportrait.art/brianwilson**

To listen to their Greatest Songs type into your Internet Browser the URL shortcut
➡ **radio.surf/thebeachboys**

To view all channels on THE FACE OF MUSIC Internet Radio MEGA Station type into your Internet Browser the URL shortcut ➡ **radio.surf/music**

To inquire about purchasing a Limited Edtion NFT of this portrait type into your Internet Browser the URL shortcut ➡ **myartnft.shop/brianwilson**

To view all available NFTs type into your Internet Browser the URL shortcut ➡ **myartnft.shop/all**

# Beastie Boys

(Total Albums Sold: 10 Million) (Genre: Hip-Hop / Rap)

Beastie Boys were an American rap rock group from New York City, formed in 1978. The group was composed of Michael "Mike D" Diamond (vocals, drums), Adam "MCA" Yauch (vocals, bass) and Adam "Ad-Rock" Horovitz (vocals, guitar, programming).

Beastie Boys were formed out of members of experimental hardcore punk band the Young Aborigines in 1978, with Diamond as vocalist, Jeremy Shatan on bass guitar, guitarist John Berry and Kate Schellenbach on drums. When Shatan left in 1981, Yauch replaced him on bass and the band changed their name to Beastie Boys. Berry left shortly thereafter and was replaced by Horovitz. After achieving local success with the 1983 comedy hip hop single "Cooky Puss", Beastie Boys made a full transition to hip hop, and Schellenbach left. They toured with Madonna in 1985 and a year later released their debut album, Licensed to Ill, the first rap record to top the Billboard 200 chart. Their second album, Paul's Boutique (1989), composed almost entirely of samples, was a commercial failure, but later received critical acclaim. Check Your Head (1992) and Ill Communication (1994) found mainstream success, followed by Hello Nasty (1998), To the 5 Boroughs (2004), The Mix-Up (2007), and Hot Sauce Committee Part Two (2011). Beastie Boys have sold 20 million records in the United States, making them the biggest-selling rap group since Billboard began recording sales in 1991. With seven platinum-selling albums from 1986 to 2004, Beastie Boys were one of the longest-lived hip hop acts worldwide. In 2012, they became the third rap group to be inducted into the Rock and Roll Hall of Fame. In the same year, Yauch died of cancer and Beastie Boys disbanded.

# Adam MCA Yauch

(Net Worth: $75 Million) (Height: 5'-9")

Adam Nathaniel Yauch (August 5, 1964 – May 4, 2012), better known under the stage name MCA, was an American rapper, bass player, filmmaker and a founding member of the hip hop group Beastie Boys. Yauch founded Oscilloscope Laboratories, an independent film production and distribution company based in New York City. As a Buddhist, he was involved in the Tibetan independence movement and organized the Tibetan Freedom Concert. He died in 2012 from parotid cancer. Born in Brooklyn, New York City, Yauch was an only child. His father was an architect, and his mother was a social worker. Yauch's mother was Jewish, and his father Catholic but he had a non-religious upbringing in Brooklyn Heights, Brooklyn. Yauch attended Edward R. Murrow High School in Brooklyn's Midwood neighborhood. In high school, he taught himself to play the bass guitar and formed Beastie Boys with John Berry, Kate Schellenbach, and Michael Diamond. They played their first show—while still a hardcore punk band in the vein of Reagan Youth—on his 17th birthday. He attended Bard College for two years before dropping out. He directed the 2008 film Gunnin' For That #1 Spot about eight high school basketball prospects at the Boost Mobile Elite 24 Hoops Classic at Rucker Park in Harlem, New York City. Yauch produced Build a Nation, the comeback album from hardcore/punk band Bad Brains. In addition, Oscilloscope Laboratories also distributed Kelly Reichardt's Wendy and Lucy (2008) and Oren Moverman's The Messenger (2009).

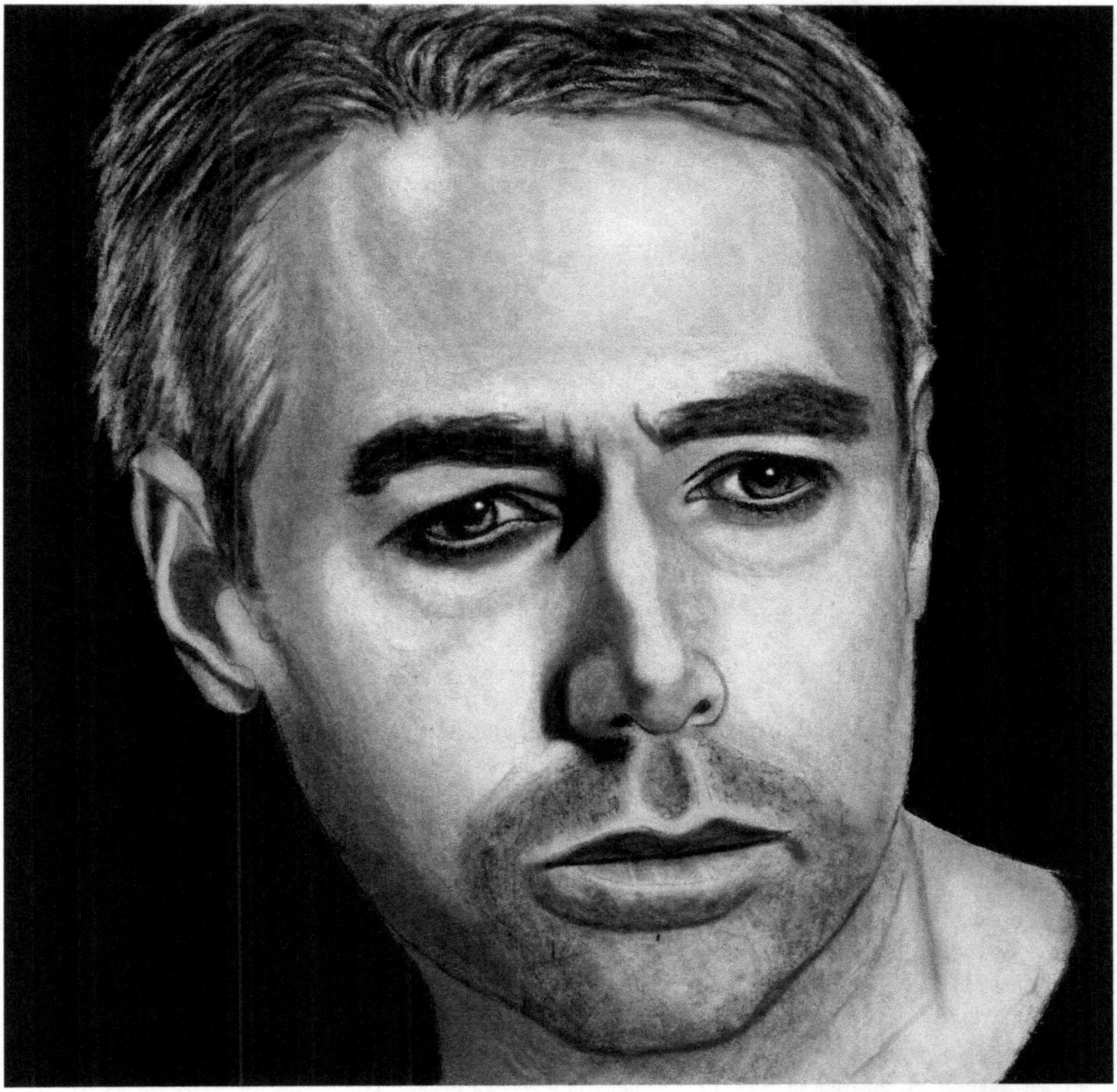

To view how this drawing was masterfully created or to purchase a Limited Edition Framed Artwork of Adam MCA Yauch type into your Internet Browser the URL shortcut ➡ **myportrait.art/adamyauch**

To listen to their Greatest Songs type into your Internet Browser the URL shortcut ➡ **radio.surf/beastieboys**

To view all channels on THE FACE OF MUSIC Internet Radio MEGA Station type into your Internet Browser the URL shortcut ➡ **radio.surf/music**

To inquire about purchasing a Limited Edtion NFT of this portrait type into your Internet Browser the URL shortcut ➡ **myartnft.shop/adamyauch**

To view all available NFTs type into your Internet Browser the URL shortcut ➡ **myartnft.shop/all**

# Beatles, The

(Total Records Sold: 600 Million) (Genre: Pop, Rock, Psychedelic Rock)

The Beatles were an English rock band formed in Liverpool in 1960. The group, whose best-known line-up comprised John Lennon, Paul McCartney, George Harrison and Ringo Starr, are regarded as the most influential band of all time. They were integral to the development of 1960s counterculture and popular music's recognition as an art form. Rooted in skiffle, beat and 1950s rock and roll, their sound incorporated elements of classical music and traditional pop in innovative ways; the band later explored music styles ranging from ballads and Indian music to psychedelia and hard rock. As pioneers in recording, songwriting and artistic presentation, the Beatles revolutionised many aspects of the music industry and were often publicised as leaders of the era's youth and sociocultural movements.

Continued on Page 51.....

# George Harrison

(Net Worth: $400 Million) (Height: 5'-10")

George Harrison MBE (25 February 1943 – 29 November 2001) was an English musician, singer, songwriter, and music and film producer who achieved international fame as the lead guitarist of the Beatles. Sometimes called "the quiet Beatle", Harrison embraced Indian culture and helped broaden the scope of popular music through his incorporation of Indian instrumentation and Hindu-aligned spirituality in the Beatles' work. Although the majority of the band's songs were written by John Lennon and Paul McCartney, most Beatles albums from 1965 onwards contained at least two Harrison compositions. His songs for the group include "Taxman", "Within You Without You", "While My Guitar Gently Weeps", "Here Comes the Sun" and "Something".Harrison's earliest musical influences included George Formby and Django Reinhardt; Carl Perkins, Chet Atkins and Chuck Berry were subsequent influences. By 1965, he had begun to lead the Beatles into folk rock through his interest in Bob Dylan and the Byrds, and towards Indian classical music through his use of the sitar on "Norwegian Wood (This Bird Has Flown)". Having initiated the band's embracing of Transcendental Meditation in 1967, he subsequently developed an association with the Hare Krishna movement. After the band's break-up in 1970, Harrison released the triple album All Things Must Pass, a critically acclaimed work that produced his most successful hit single, "My Sweet Lord", and introduced his signature sound as a solo artist, the slide guitar. He also organised the 1971 Concert for Bangladesh with Indian musician Ravi Shankar, a precursor to later benefit concerts such as Live Aid. In his role as a music and film producer, Harrison produced acts signed to the Beatles' Apple record label before founding Dark Horse Records in 1974 and co-founding HandMade Films in 1978.Harrison released several best-selling singles and albums as a solo performer. In 1988, he co-founded the platinum-selling supergroup the Traveling Wilburys. A prolific recording artist, he was featured as a guest guitarist on tracks by Badfinger, Ronnie Wood and Billy Preston, and collaborated on songs and music with Dylan, Eric Clapton, Ringo Starr and Tom Petty, among others. Rolling Stone magazine ranked him number 11 in their list of the "100 Greatest Guitarists of All Time". He is a two-time Rock and Roll Hall of Fame inductee – as a member of the Beatles in 1988, and posthumously for his solo career in 2004.Harrison's first marriage, to model Pattie Boyd in 1966, ended in divorce in 1977. The following year he married Olivia Arias, with whom he had a son, Dhani. Harrison died from lung cancer in 2001 at the age of 58, two years after surviving a knife attack by an intruder at his Friar Park home. His remains were cremated and the ashes were scattered according to Hindu tradition in a private ceremony in the Ganges and Yamuna rivers in India.

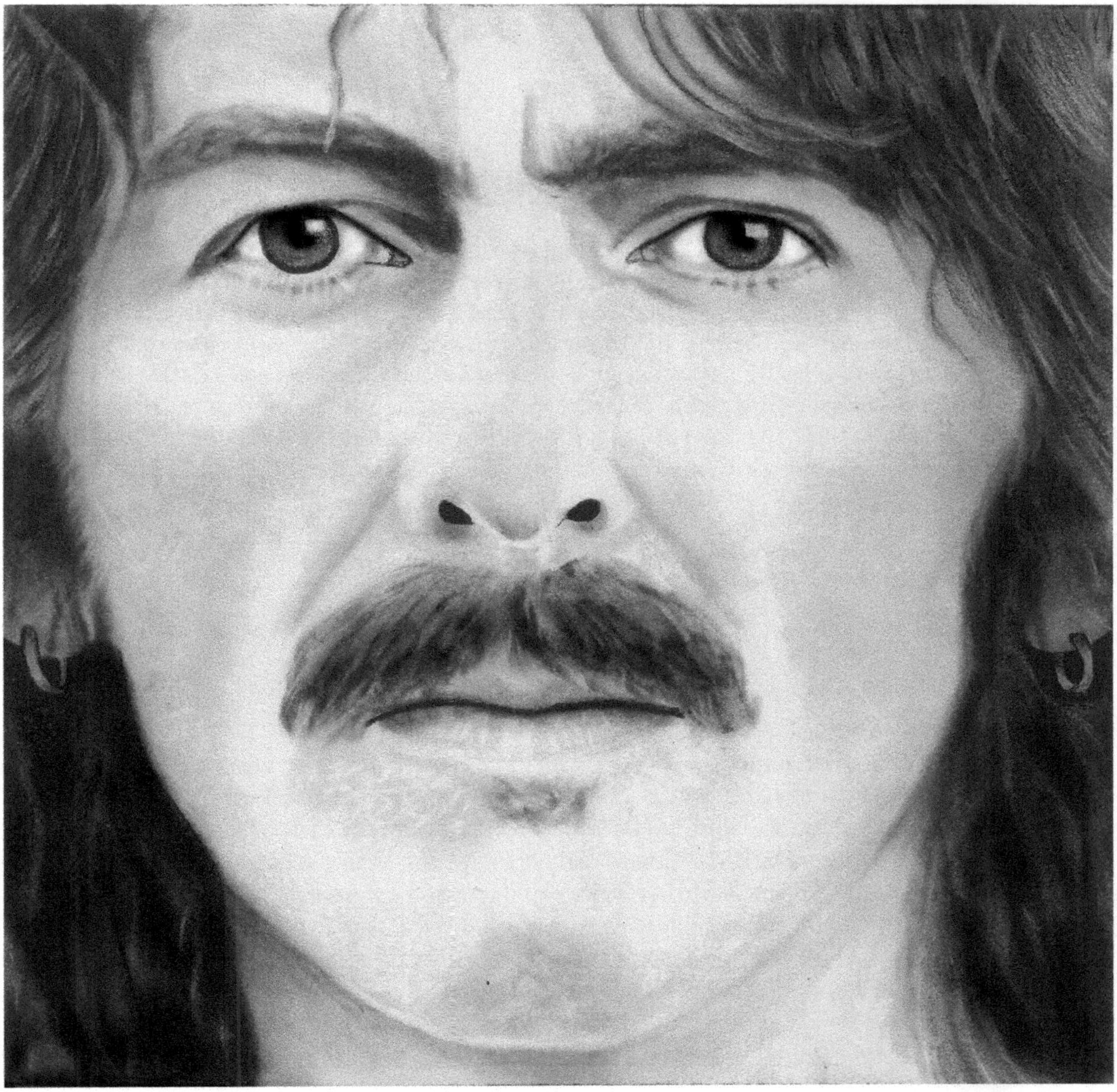

To view how this drawing was masterfully created or to purchase a Limited Edition Framed Artwork of George Harrison type into your Internet Browser the URL shortcut ➡ **myportrait.art/georgeharrison**

To listen to their Greatest Songs type into your Internet Browser the URL shortcut ➡ **radio.surf/thebeatles**

To view all channels on THE FACE OF MUSIC Internet Radio MEGA Station type into your Internet Browser the URL shortcut ➡ **radio.surf/music**

To inquire about purchasing a Limited Edtion NFT of this portrait type into your Internet Browser the URL shortcut ➡ **myartnft.shop/georgeharrison**

To view all available NFTs type into your Internet Browser the URL shortcut ➡ **myartnft.shop/all**

# Beatles, The

Contined....

Led by primary songwriters Lennon and McCartney, the Beatles built their reputation playing clubs in Liverpool and Hamburg over three years from 1960, initially with Stuart Sutcliffe playing bass. The core trio of Lennon, McCartney and Harrison, together since 1958, went through a succession of drummers, including Pete Best, before asking Starr to join them in 1962. Manager Brian Epstein moulded them into a professional act, and producer George Martin guided and developed their recordings, greatly expanding their domestic success after their first hit, "Love Me Do", in late 1962. As their popularity grew into the intense fan frenzy dubbed "Beatlemania", the band acquired the nickname "the Fab Four", with Epstein, Martin and other members of the band's entourage sometimes given the informal title of "fifth Beatle".

Continued on Page 53....

# John Lennon

(Net Worth: $800 Million) (Height: 5'-10")

John Winston Ono Lennon (born John Winston Lennon; 9 October 1940 – 8 December 1980) was an English singer, songwriter, musician and peace activist who achieved worldwide fame as the founder, co-lead vocalist, and rhythm guitarist of the Beatles. His songwriting partnership with Paul McCartney remains the most successful in history. In 1969, he started the Plastic Ono Band with his second wife, Yoko Ono. After the Beatles disbanded in 1970, Lennon continued a career as a solo artist and as Ono's collaborator. Born in Liverpool, Lennon became involved in the skiffle craze as a teenager. In 1956, he formed his first band, the Quarrymen, which evolved into the Beatles in 1960. He was initially the group's de facto leader, a role gradually ceded to McCartney. Lennon was characterised for the rebellious nature and acerbic wit in his music, writing, drawings, on film and in interviews. In the mid-1960s, he had two books published: In His Own Write and A Spaniard in the Works, both collections of nonsense writings and line drawings. Starting with 1967's "All You Need Is Love", his songs were adopted as anthems by the anti-war movement and the larger counterculture.

From 1968 to 1972, Lennon produced more than a dozen records with Ono, including a trilogy of avant-garde albums, his first solo LP John Lennon/Plastic Ono Band, and the international top 10 singles "Give Peace a Chance", "Instant Karma!", "Imagine" and "Happy Xmas (War Is Over)". In 1969, he held the two week-long anti-war demonstration Bed-Ins for Peace. After moving to New York City in 1971, his criticism of the Vietnam War resulted in a three-year attempt by the Nixon administration to deport him. In 1975, Lennon disengaged from the music business to raise his infant son Sean and, in 1980, returned with the Ono collaboration Double Fantasy. He was shot and killed in the archway of his Manhattan apartment building by a Beatles fan, Mark David Chapman, three weeks after the album's release.

As a performer, writer or co-writer, Lennon had 25 number one singles in the Billboard Hot 100 chart. Double Fantasy, his best-selling album, won the 1981 Grammy Award for Album of the Year. In 1982, Lennon was honoured with the Brit Award for Outstanding Contribution to Music. In 2002, Lennon was voted eighth in a BBC poll of the 100 Greatest Britons. Rolling Stone ranked him the fifth-greatest singer and thirty-eighth greatest artist of all time. He was inducted into the Songwriters Hall of Fame (in 1997) and the Rock and Roll Hall of Fame (twice, as a member of the Beatles in 1988 and as a solo artist in 1994).

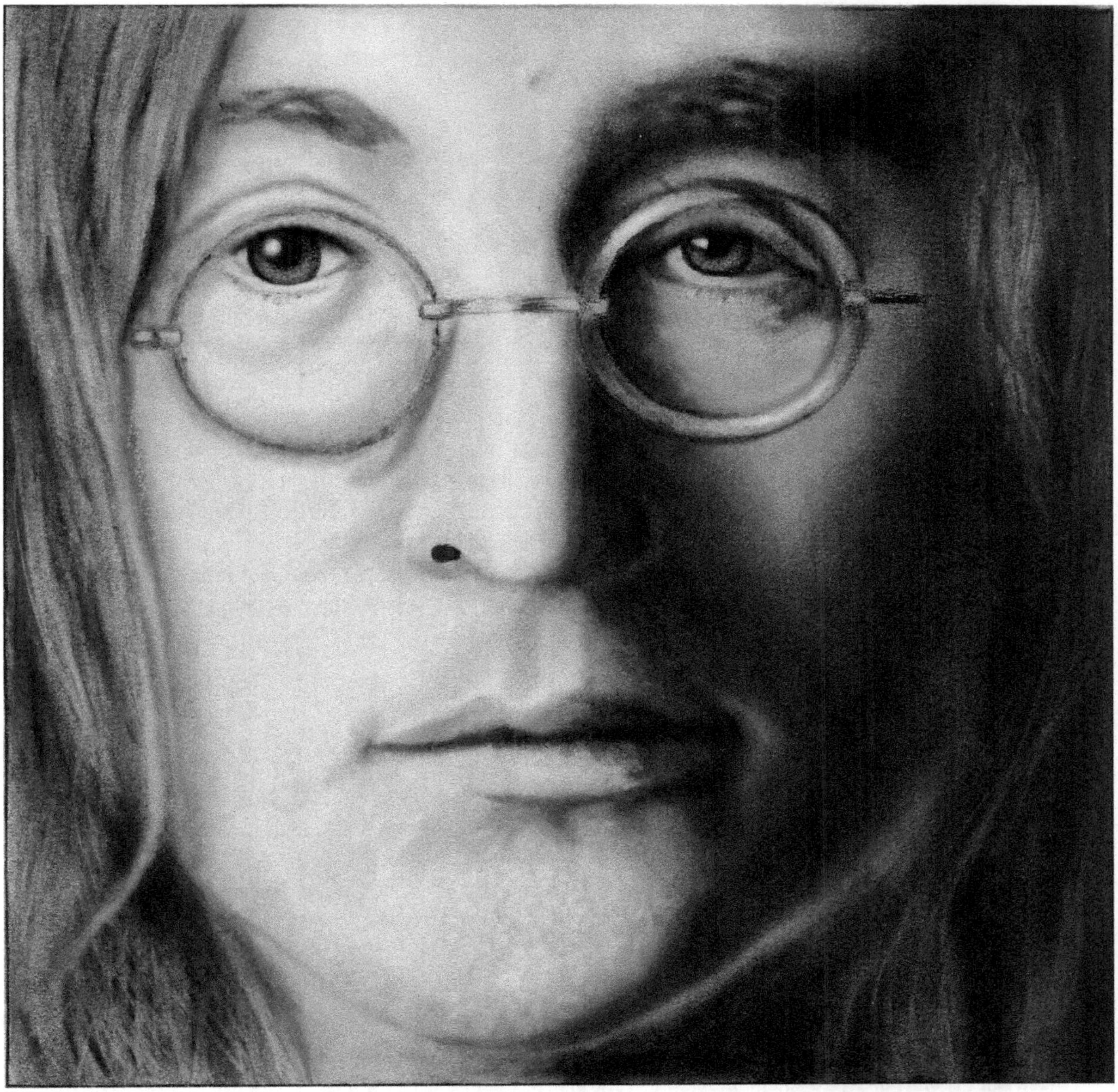

To view how this drawing was masterfully created or to purchase a Limited Edition Framed Artwork of John Lennon type into your Internet Browser the URL shortcut ➡ **myportrait.art/johnlennon**

To listen to their Greatest Songs type into your Internet Browser the URL shortcut ➡ **radio.surf/thebeatles**

To view all channels on THE FACE OF MUSIC Internet Radio MEGA Station type into your Internet Browser the URL shortcut ➡ **radio.surf/music**

To inquire about purchasing a Limited Edtion NFT of this portrait type into your Internet Browser the URL shortcut ➡ **myartnft.shop/johnlennon**

To view all available NFTs type into your Internet Browser the URL shortcut ➡ **myartnft.shop/all**

# Beatles, The

Continued....

By early 1964, the Beatles were international stars, leading the "British Invasion" of the United States pop market and breaking numerous sales records. They soon made their film debut with A Hard Day's Night (1964). From 1965 onwards, they produced records of greater complexity, including the albums Rubber Soul (1965), Revolver (1966) and Sgt. Pepper's Lonely Hearts Club Band (1967), and enjoyed further commercial success with The Beatles (also known as "the White Album", 1968) and Abbey Road (1969). Heralding the album era, their success led to the massive sales increase and popularity of the album format, which eventually replaced singles as the dominant form of recorded music. Their cultural impact extended to fashion, British identity, rock groups, interest in psychedelic drugs and Eastern spirituality, electronic music, album art and music videos. In 1968, they founded Apple Corps, a multi-armed multimedia corporation that continues to oversee projects related to the band's legacy. After the group's break-up in 1970, all four members enjoyed success as solo artists. Lennon was shot and killed in 1980, and Harrison died of lung cancer in 2001. McCartney and Starr remain musically active.

Continued on Page 55....

# Paul McCartney

(Net Worth: $1.2 Billion) (Height: 5'-10")

Sir James Paul McCartney CH MBE (born 18 June 1942) is an English singer, songwriter, musician, and record and film producer who gained worldwide fame as co-lead vocalist and bassist for the Beatles. His songwriting partnership with John Lennon remains the most successful in history. After the group disbanded in 1970, he pursued a solo career and formed the band Wings with his first wife, Linda, and Denny Laine. A self-taught musician, McCartney is proficient on bass, guitar, keyboards, and drums. He is known for his melodic approach to bass-playing (mainly playing with a plectrum), his versatile and wide tenor vocal range (spanning over four octaves), and his eclecticism (exploring styles ranging from pre-rock and roll pop to classical and electronica). McCartney began his career as a member of the Quarrymen in 1957, which evolved into the Beatles in 1960. Starting with the 1967 album Sgt. Pepper's Lonely Hearts Club Band, he gradually became the Beatles' de facto leader, providing the creative impetus for most of their music and film projects. His Beatles songs "And I Love Her" (1964), "Yesterday" (1965), "Eleanor Rigby" (1966) and "Blackbird" (1968) rank among the most covered songs in history.

In 1970, McCartney debuted as a solo artist with the album McCartney. Throughout the 1970s, he led Wings, one of the most successful bands of the decade, with more than a dozen international top 10 singles and albums. McCartney resumed his solo career in 1980. Since 1989, he has toured consistently as a solo artist. In 1993, he formed the music duo the Fireman with Youth of Killing Joke. Beyond music, he has taken part in projects to promote international charities related to such subjects as animal rights, seal hunting, land mines, vegetarianism, poverty, and music education.

McCartney is one of the most successful composers and performers of all time. He has written or co-written 32 songs that have reached No. 1 on the Billboard Hot 100, and as of 2009, had sales of 25.5 million RIAA-certified units in the United States. His honours include two inductions into the Rock and Roll Hall of Fame (as a member of the Beatles in 1988 and as a solo artist in 1999), 18 Grammy Awards, an appointment as a Member of the Order of the British Empire in 1965, and a knighthood in 1997 for services to music.

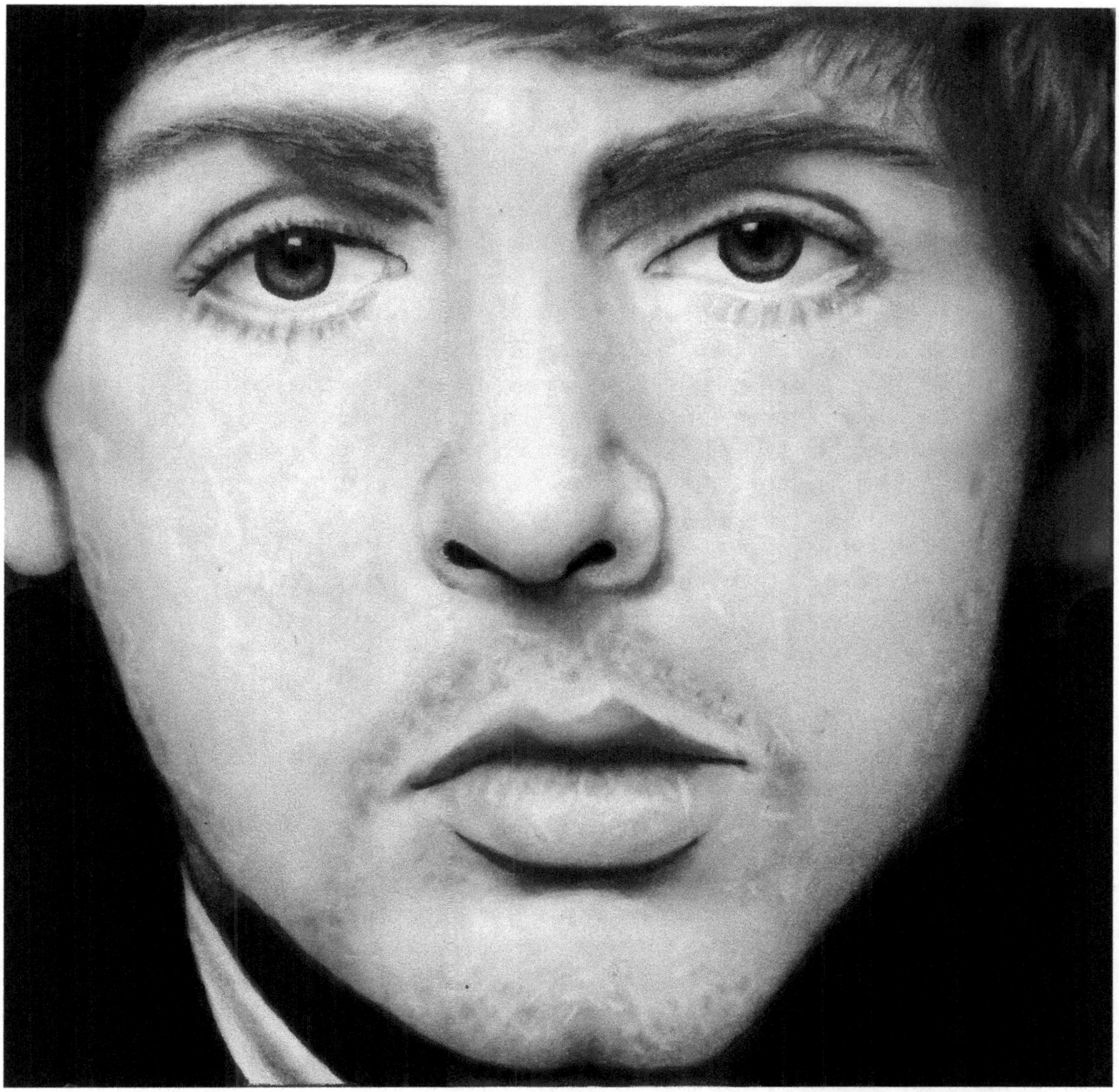

To view how this drawing was masterfully created or to purchase a Limited Edition Framed Artwork of Paul McCartney type into your Internet Browser the URL shortcut ➡ **myportrait.art/paulmccartney**

To listen to their Greatest Songs type into your Internet Browser the URL shortcut ➡ **radio.surf/thebeatles**

To view all channels on THE FACE OF MUSIC Internet Radio MEGA Station type into your Internet Browser the URL shortcut ➡ **radio.surf/music**

To inquire about purchasing a Limited Edtion NFT of this portrait type into your Internet Browser the URL shortcut ➡ **myartnft.shop/paulmccartney**

To view all available NFTs type into your Internet Browser the URL shortcut ➡ **myartnft.shop/all**

# Beatles, The

Contined....

The Beatles are the best-selling music act of all time, with estimated sales of 600 million units worldwide. They hold the record for most number-one albums on the UK Albums Chart (15), most number-one hits on the Billboard Hot 100 chart (20), and most singles sold in the UK (21.9 million). The band received seven Grammy Awards, four Brit Awards, an Academy Award (for Best Original Song Score for the 1970 film Let It Be) and fifteen Ivor Novello Awards. They were inducted into the Rock and Roll Hall of Fame in 1988, and all four main members were inducted individually between 1994 and 2015. In 2004 and 2011, the group topped Rolling Stone's lists of the greatest artists in history. Time magazine named them among the 20th century's 100 most important people.

# Ringo Starr

(Net Worth: $350 Million) (Height: 5'-6")

Sir Richard Starkey MBE (born 7 July 1940), better known by his stage name Ringo Starr, is an English musician, singer, songwriter and actor who achieved international fame during the 1960s as the drummer for the Beatles. He occasionally sang lead vocals with the group, usually for one song on each album, including "Yellow Submarine", "With a Little Help from My Friends" and their cover of "Act Naturally". He also wrote and sang the Beatles' songs "Don't Pass Me By" and "Octopus's Garden", and is credited as a co-writer of others.Starr was afflicted by life-threatening illnesses during childhood, with periods of prolonged hospitalisation. He briefly held a position with British Rail before securing an apprenticeship as a machinist at a Liverpool equipment manufacturer. Soon afterwards, he became interested in the UK skiffle craze and developed a fervent admiration for the genre. In 1957, he co-founded his first band, the Eddie Clayton Skiffle Group, which earned several prestigious local bookings before the fad succumbed to American rock and roll around early 1958. When the Beatles formed in 1960, Starr was a member of another Liverpool group, Rory Storm and the Hurricanes. After achieving moderate success in the UK and Hamburg, he quit the Hurricanes when he was asked to join the Beatles in August 1962, replacing Pete Best.In addition to the Beatles' films, Starr has acted in numerous others. After the band's break-up in 1970, he released several successful singles including the US top-ten hit "It Don't Come Easy", and number ones "Photograph" and "You're Sixteen". His most successful UK single was "Back Off Boogaloo", which peaked at number two. He achieved commercial and critical success with his 1973 album Ringo, which was a top-ten release in both the UK and the US. He has featured in numerous documentaries, hosted television shows, narrated the first two series of the children's television programme Thomas & Friends and portrayed "Mr. Conductor" during the first season of the PBS children's television series Shining Time Station. Since 1989, he has toured with thirteen variations of Ringo Starr & His All-Starr Band.r's playing style, which emphasised feel over technical virtuosity, influenced many drummers to reconsider their playing from a compositional perspective. He also influenced various modern drumming techniques, such as the matched grip, tuning the drums lower, and using muffling devices on tonal rings. In his opinion, his finest recorded performance was on the Beatles' "Rain". In 1999, he was inducted into the Modern Drummer Hall of Fame. In 2011, Rolling Stone readers named him the fifth-greatest drummer of all time. He was inducted twice into the Rock and Roll Hall of Fame, as a Beatle in 1988 and as a solo artist in 2015, and appointed a Knight Bachelor in the 2018 New Year Honours for services to music. In 2020, he was cited as the wealthiest drummer in the world, with a net worth of $350 million.

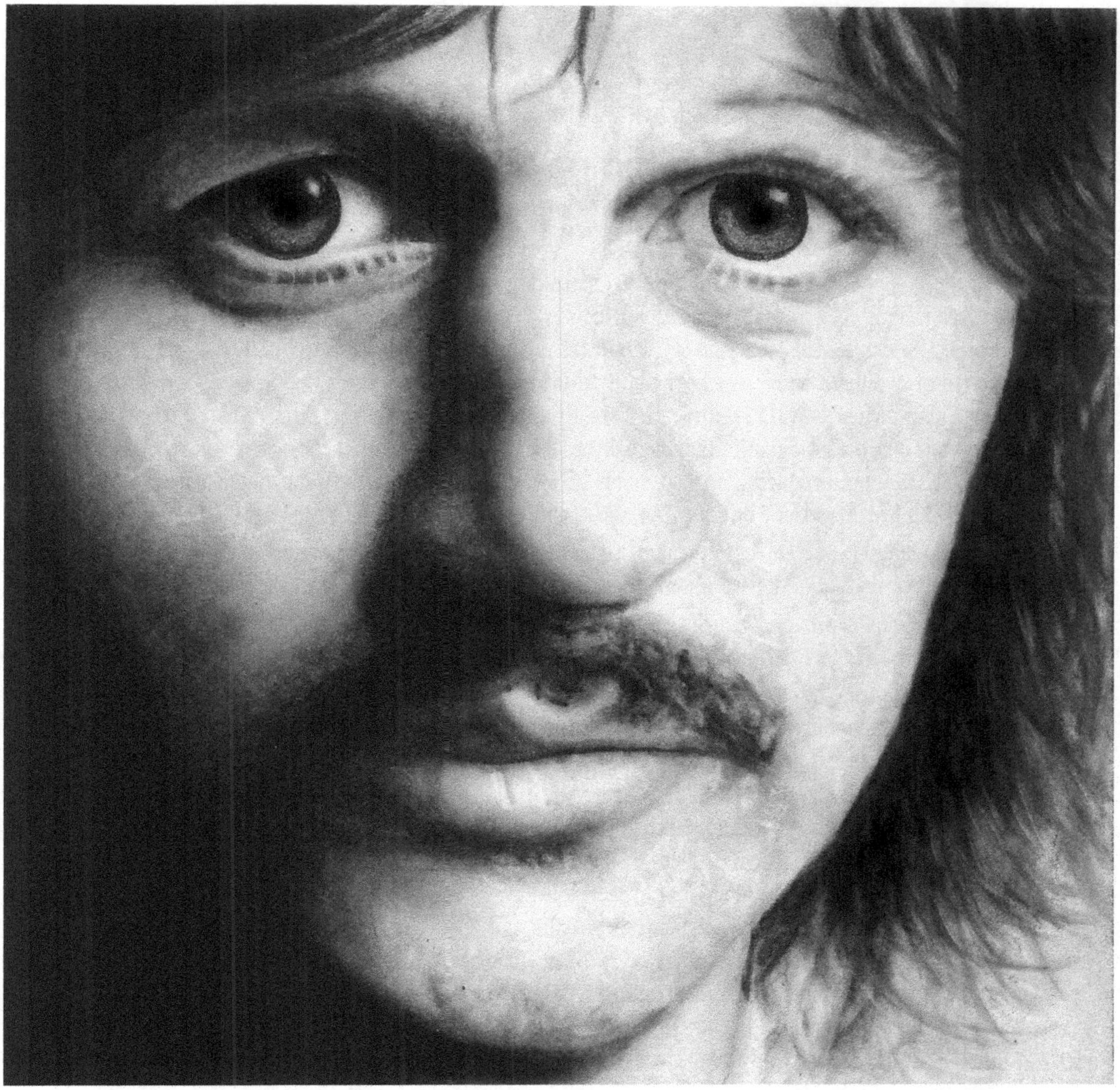

To view how this drawing was masterfully created or to purchase a Limited Edition Framed Artwork of Ringo Starr type into your Internet Browser the URL shortcut ➡ **myportrait.art/ringostarr**

To listen to their Greatest Songs type into your Internet Browser the URL shortcut ➡ **radio.surf/thebeatles**

To view all channels on THE FACE OF MUSIC Internet Radio MEGA Station type into your Internet Browser the URL shortcut ➡ **radio.surf/music**

To inquire about purchasing a Limited Edtion NFT of this portrait type into your Internet Browser the URL shortcut ➡ **myartnft.shop/ringostarr**

To view all available NFTs type into your Internet Browser the URL shortcut ➡ **myartnft.shop/all**

# Bee Gees

(Total Albums Sold: 120+ Million) (Genre: Pop , Disco , Soft Rock)

The Bee Gees were a music group formed in 1958, featuring brothers Barry, Robin, and Maurice Gibb. The trio were especially successful as a popular music act in the late 1960s and early 1970s, and later as prominent performers of the disco music era in the mid-to-late 1970s. The group sang recognisable three-part tight harmonies; Robin's clear vibrato lead vocals were a hallmark of their earlier hits, while Barry's R&B falsetto became their signature sound during the mid-to-late 1970s and 1980s. The Bee Gees wrote all of their own hits, as well as writing and producing several major hits for other artists.Born on the Isle of Man to English parents, the Gibb brothers lived in Chorlton, Manchester, England until the late 1950s. There, in 1955, they formed the skiffle/rock and roll group the Rattlesnakes. The family then moved to Redcliffe, in the Moreton Bay Region, Queensland, Australia, and then to Cribb Island. After achieving their first chart success in Australia as the Bee Gees with "Spicks and Specks" (their 12th single), they returned to the UK in January 1967, when producer Robert Stigwood began promoting them to a worldwide audience. The Bee Gees' Saturday Night Fever soundtrack (1977) was the turning point of their career, with both the film and soundtrack having a cultural impact throughout the world, enhancing the disco scene's mainstream appeal. They won five Grammy Awards for Saturday Night Fever, including Album of the Year.The Bee Gees have sold over 120 million records worldwide (with estimates as high as over 220 million), making them among the best-selling music artists of all time. They were inducted into the Rock and Roll Hall of Fame in 1997; the presenter of the award to "Britain's first family of harmony" was Brian Wilson, historical leader of the Beach Boys, another "family act" featuring three harmonising brothers. The Bee Gees' Hall of Fame citation says, "Only Elvis Presley, the Beatles, Michael Jackson, Garth Brooks and Paul McCartney have outsold the Bee Gees." The Bee Gees are the third most successful band in Billboard charts history after the Beatles and the Supremes. Following Maurice's sudden death in January 2003 at the age of 53, Barry and Robin retired the group's name after 45 years of activity. In 2009, Robin announced that he and Barry had agreed that the Bee Gees would re-form and perform again. Robin died in May 2012, aged 62, after a prolonged period of failing health, leaving Barry as the only surviving member of the group.

# Barry Gibb

(Net Worth: $90 Million) (Height: 5'-11")

Sir Barry Alan Crompton Gibb CBE (born 1 September 1946) is a British-American musician, singer-songwriter and record producer who rose to worldwide fame as a co-founder of the group the Bee Gees, one of the most commercially successful groups in the history of popular music. With his younger brothers, twins Robin and Maurice Gibb, he formed a songwriting partnership beginning in 1955. He has lived in Britain, Australia, and the United States, holding dual UK–US citizenship. Gibb's career has spanned over 60 years. In 1994, he was inducted into the Songwriters Hall of Fame with his brothers. In 1997, as a member of the Bee Gees, he was inducted into the Rock and Roll Hall of Fame and received the Brit Award for Outstanding Contribution to Music. He is a fellow of the British Academy of Songwriters, Composers and Authors. In 2007, Q magazine ranked him number 38 on its list of the "100 Greatest Singers"

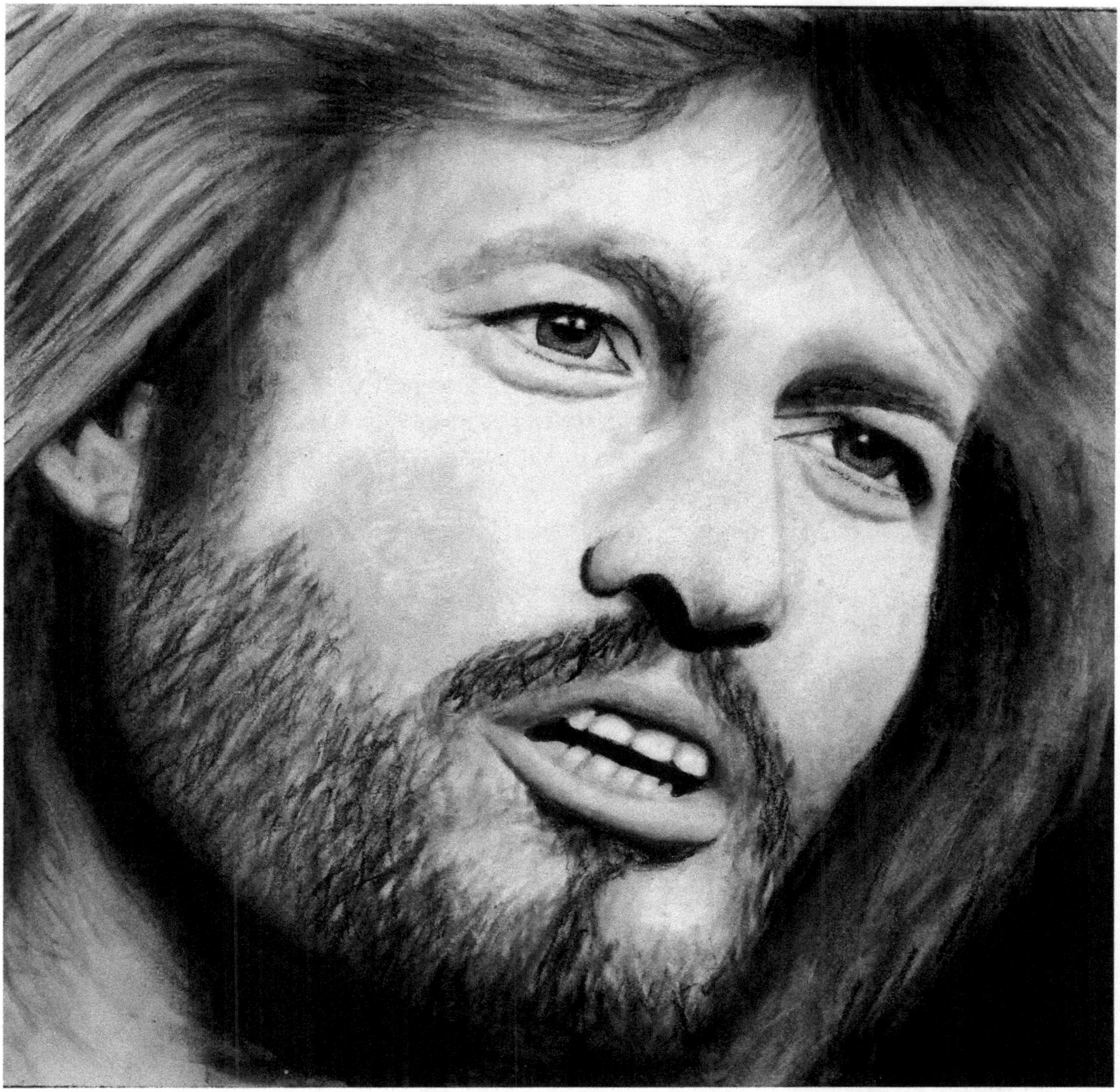

To view how this drawing was masterfully created or to purchase a Limited Edition Framed Artwork of Barry Gibb type into your Internet Browser the URL shortcut ➡ **myportrait.art/barrygibb**

To listen to their Greatest Songs type into your Internet Browser the URL shortcut ➡ **radio.surf/beegees**

To view all channels on THE FACE OF MUSIC Internet Radio MEGA Station type into your Internet Browser the URL shortcut ➡ **radio.surf/music**

To inquire about purchasing a Limited Edtion NFT of this portrait type into your Internet Browser the URL shortcut ➡ **myartnft.shop/barrygibb**

To view all available NFTs type into your Internet Browser the URL shortcut ➡ **myartnft.shop/all**

# Big Joe Turner

(Net worth: $3 Million)(Total Records Sold: 3+ Million)
(Genre: Jump Blues , Blues , R & B)(Height: 6' - 2")

B Joseph Vernon "Big Joe" Turner Jr. (May 18, 1911 – November 24, 1985) was an American blues shouter from Kansas City, Missouri. According to songwriter Doc Pomus, "Rock and roll would have never happened without him." His greatest fame was due to his rock-and-roll recordings in the 1950s, particularly "Shake, Rattle and Roll", but his career as a performer endured from the 1920s into the 1980s.

Turner was inducted into the Rock and Roll Hall of Fame in 1987, with the Hall lauding him as "the brawny voiced 'Boss of the Blues'"

Turner was born May 18, 1911 in Kansas City, Missouri, United States. His father was killed in a train accident when Turner was four years old. He sang in his church, and on street corners for money. He left school at age fourteen to work in Kansas City's nightclubs, first as a cook and later as a singing bartender. He became known as "The Singing Barman", and worked in such venues as the Kingfish Club and the Sunset, where he and his partner, the boogie-woogie pianist Pete Johnson, became resident performers. The Sunset was managed by Piney Brown. It featured "separate but equal" facilities for white patrons. Turner wrote "Piney Brown Blues" in his honor and sang it throughout his career.

At that time Kansas City nightclubs were subject to frequent raids by the police: Turner said, "The Boss man would have his bondsmen down at the police station before we got there. We'd walk in, sign our names and walk right out. Then we would cabaret until morning."

His partnership with Johnson proved fruitful. Together they went to New York City in 1936, where they appeared on a playbill with Benny Goodman, but as Turner recounted, "After our show with Goodman, we auditioned at several places, but New York wasn't ready for us yet, so we headed back to K.C." Eventually they were seen by the talent scout John Hammond in 1938, who invited them back to New York to appear in one of his From Spirituals to Swing concerts at Carnegie Hall, which were instrumental in introducing jazz and blues to a wider American audience.

In part because of their appearance at Carnegie Hall, Turner and Johnson had a major success with the song "Roll 'Em Pete". The track was basically a collection of traditional blues lyrics. It was a song that Turner recorded many times, with various musicians, over the ensuing years.

Turner died of heart failure in November 1985, at the age of 74, in Inglewood, California, having suffered from effects of arthritis, a stroke and diabetes. His funeral included musical tributes from Etta James and Barbara Morrison. He was buried at Roosevelt Memorial Park in Gardena, California.

He was posthumously inducted into the Rock and Roll Hall of Fame in 1987.

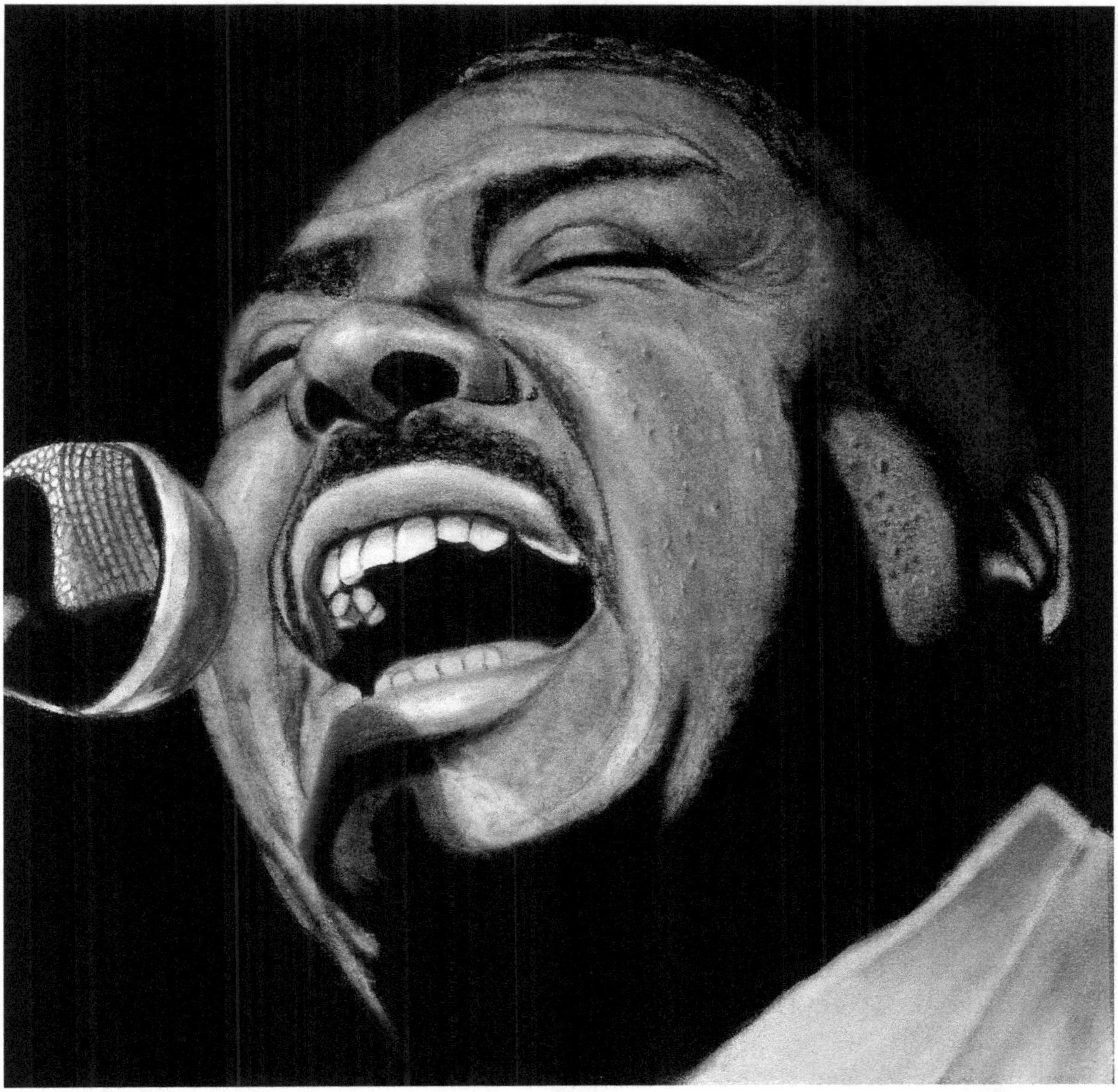

To view how this drawing was masterfully created or to purchase a Limited Edition Framed Artwork of Big Joe Turner type into your Internet Browser the URL shortcut ➡ **myportrait.art/bigjoeturner**

To listen to his Greatest Songs type into your Internet Browser the URL shortcut ➡ **radio.surf/bigjoeturner**

To view all channels on THE FACE OF MUSIC Internet Radio MEGA Station type into your Internet Browser the URL shortcut ➡ **radio.surf/music**

To inquire about purchasing a Limited Edtion NFT of this portrait type into your Internet Browser the URL shortcut ➡ **myartnft.shop/bigjoeturner**

To view all available NFTs type into your Internet Browser the URL shortcut ➡ **myartnft.shop/all**

# Big L

(Net worth: $3 Million)(Total Records Sold: 3+ Million)
(Genre: Hip-Hop)(Height: 5' - 8")

Lamont Coleman (May 30, 1974 – February 15, 1999), known professionally as Big L, was an American rapper and songwriter.

Emerging from Harlem in New York City in the early to mid-1990s, Coleman became well known amongst underground hip-hop fans for his freestyling ability. He was eventually signed to Columbia Records, where, in 1995, he released his debut album, Lifestylez ov da Poor & Dangerous. On February 15, 1999, Coleman was shot nine times by an unknown assailant, in East Harlem, New York, his hometown. He died from his injuries.

Noted for his use of wordplay, multiple writers at AllMusic, HipHopDX and The Source have praised Coleman for his lyrical ability, and he has also been described as "one of the most auspicious storytellers in hip-hop history." Regarding Coleman's legacy in an interview with Funkmaster Flex, Nas claimed "[Coleman] scared me to death. When I heard [his performance at the Apollo Theater] on tape, I was scared to death. I said, 'Yo, it's no way I can compete if this is what I gotta compete with.'"

Lamont Coleman was born in Harlem, New York City, on May 30, 1974, the third and youngest child of Gilda Terry (d. 2008) and Charles Davis. Davis left the family while Coleman was a child. His two older siblings, Donald Coleman and Leroy Phinazee (d. 2002), were the children of Gilda and a man named Mr. Phinazee. Coleman received the nicknames "Little L" and "'mont 'mont" as a child. At the age of 12, Coleman became a big hip hop fan and started freestyling with other people in his neighborhood. He founded a group known as Three the Hard Way in 1990, but it was quickly broken up due to a lack of enthusiasm amongst the members. It consisted of Coleman, Doc Reem, and Rodney. No projects were released, and after Rodney left, the group was renamed Two Hard Motherfuckers. Around this time, people started to refer to Coleman as "Big L". In the summer of 1990, Coleman met Lord Finesse at an autograph session in a record shop on 125th Street. After he did a freestyle, Finesse and Coleman exchanged numbers.

Coleman attended Julia Richman High School. While in high school, Coleman freestyle battled in his hometown; in his last interview, he stated, "in the beginning, all I ever saw me doing was battling everybody on the street corners, rhyming in the hallways, beating on the wall, rhyming to my friends. Every now and then, a house party, grab the mic, a block party, grab the mic." He graduated in 1992. Coleman began writing rhymes in 1990.

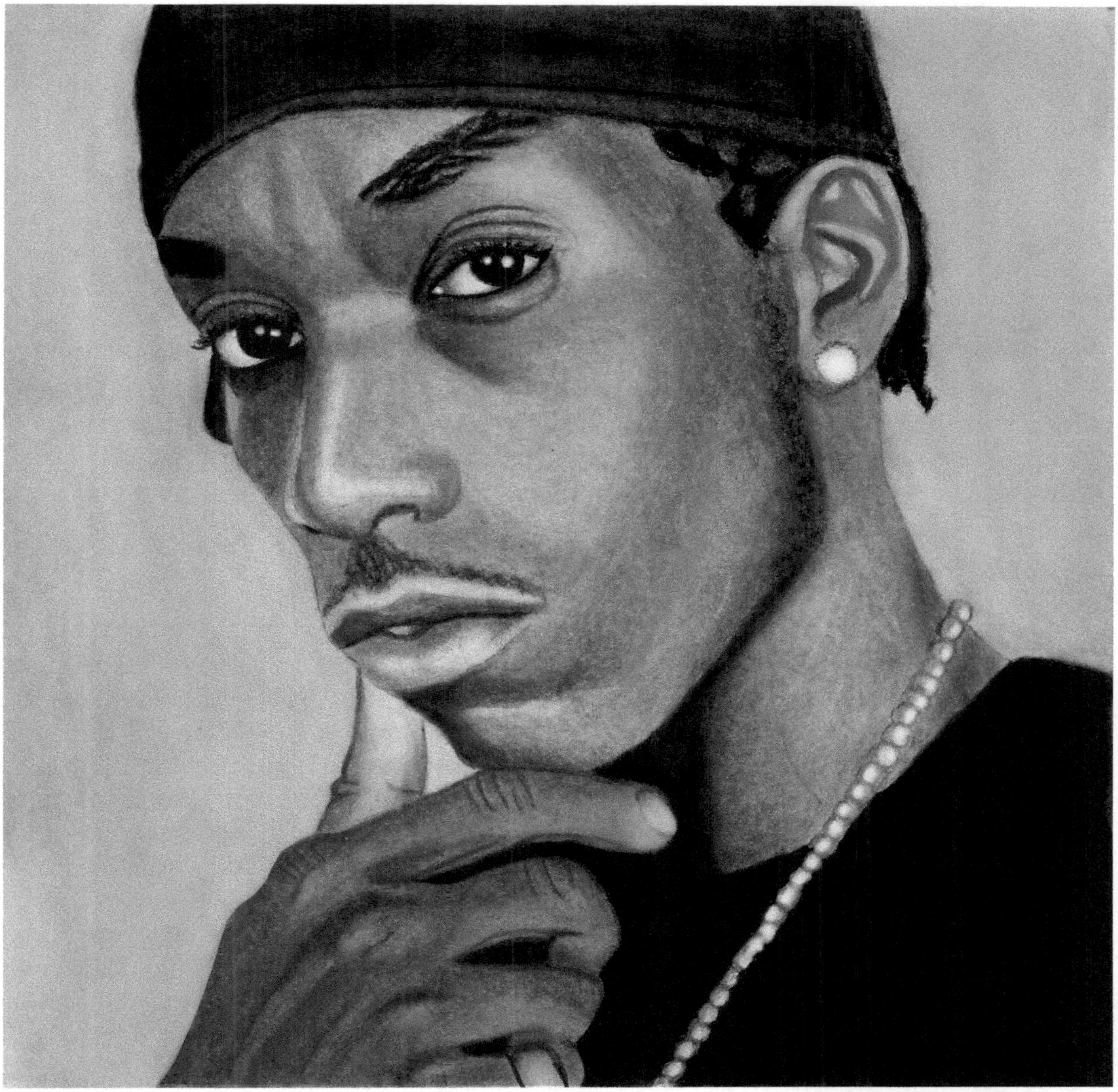

To view how this drawing was masterfully created or to purchase a Limited Edition Framed Artwork of Big L type into your Internet Browser the URL shortcut ➡ **myportrait.art/bigl**

To listen to his Greatest Songs type into your Internet Browser the URL shortcut ➡ **radio.surf/bigl**

To view all channels on THE FACE OF MUSIC Internet Radio MEGA Station type into your Internet Browser the URL shortcut ➡ **radio.surf/music**

To inquire about purchasing a Limited Edtion NFT of this portrait type into your Internet Browser the URL shortcut ➡ **myartnft.shop/bigl**

To view all available NFTs type into your Internet Browser the URL shortcut ➡ **myartnft.shop/all**

# Big Pun

(Net worth: $5 Million)(Total Records Sold: 5+ Million)
(Genre: Hip-Hop)(Height: 5' - 7")

Christopher Lee Rios (November 9, 1971 – February 7, 2000), better known by his stage name Big Pun (short for Big Punisher), was an American rapper and songwriter. Pun's lyrics are notable for their technical efficiency, having exceptional breath control, heavy use of alliteration, as well as internal and multi-syllabic rhyming schemes. He is frequently cited as one of the best MCs of all time. Emerging from the underground hip hop scene in the Bronx borough of New York City in the early 1990s, he came to prominence during the latter half of the decade for his work with Fat Joe and the Terror Squad.

Big Pun was initially discovered by Fat Joe, and made his earliest appearance on Fat Joe's 1995 album Jealous One's Envy. In 1997, he signed with Loud Records as a solo artist, and released his Grammy-nominated debut studio album Capital Punishment in April 1998 to critical acclaim and commercial success, peaking at #5 on the Billboard 200 and becoming the first solo hip hop record by a Latino artist to go Platinum.During the late 1980s, he began writing rap lyrics. He later formed the underground group Full-A-Clips with Lyrical Assassin, Joker Jamz and Toom. Rios made a number of recordings with the group in the early 1990s, which have not been released. At this point Rios was operating under the alias Big Moon Dawg. After changing his stage name to Big Punisher, Rios met fellow Puerto Rican and Bronx rapper Fat Joe in 1995 and made his commercial debut on Fat Joe's second album, Jealous One's Envy, in addition to appearing on the song, "Watch Out". He also appeared on The Beatnuts' song "Off the Books".In 1997, Big Pun began recording songs for his debut album Capital Punishment. In 1997, producer Knobody's production partner Sean C took advantage of his new role as A&R at Loud Records to play Knobody's tracks to Big Pun. Suitably impressed, the rapper hired Knobody to remix "I'm Not a Player". The remixed song, featuring Joe and titled "Still Not a Player", became Big Pun's first major mainstream hit and major breakthrough for Knobody. The full-length debut Capital Punishment followed in 1998, and became the first album by a solo Latino rapper to go platinum, peaking at No. 5 on the Billboard 200. Capital Punishment was also nominated for the Grammy Award for Best Rap Album.Big Pun became a member of Terror Squad, a New York-based group of rappers founded by Fat Joe, with most of the roster supplied by the now-defunct Full-A-Clips who released their debut album The Album in 1999. The album did not fare well commercially but it was well received critically and the album was meant to start the foundation for all other Terror Squad members to release their solo projects. Rios struggled with weight issues his entire adult life. He weighed 180 pounds (82 kg) at age 18, which increased to 300 pounds (140 kg) at 21. His weight fluctuated in the early 1990s between obese and morbidly obese. Rios enrolled in a weight-loss program at Duke University and shed 80 pounds (36 kg), but he prematurely quit the program and eventually regained the weight. His weight was a constant topic of argument among him and his friends to the point that Rios would not eat around them.

On February 5, 2000, Rios withdrew from a planned Saturday Night Live performance with Fat Joe and Jennifer Lopez due to illness. Two days later while staying at a hotel with his family in White Plains, New York, he suffered a heart attack and respiratory failure and was taken to a hospital, where he died at the age of 28 after paramedics were unable to revive him. His weight had reached a peak of 698 pounds (317 kg) at the time of his death. Rios was survived by his wife, Liza, and their three children, Star, Vanessa and Christopher Jr

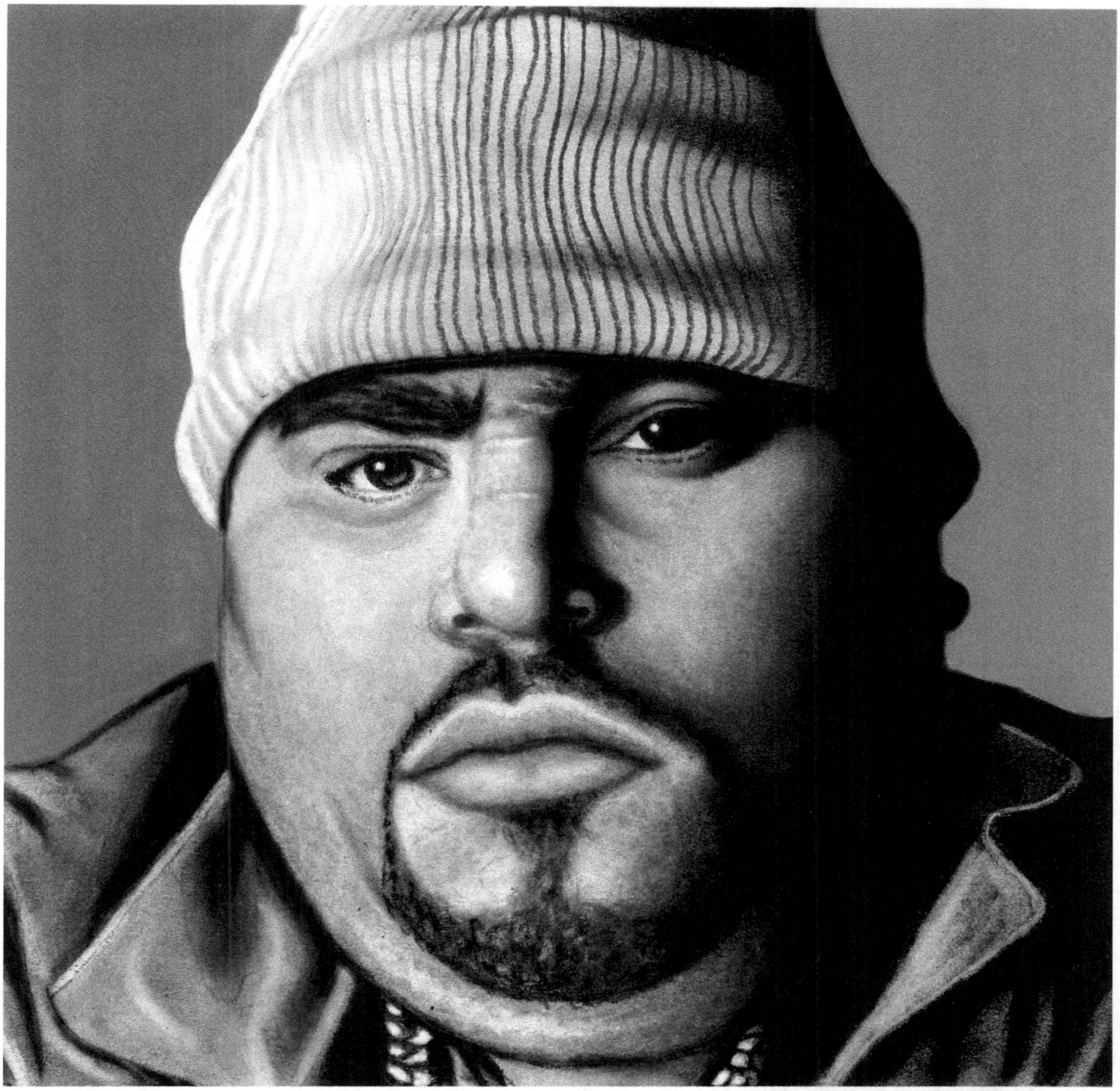

To view how this drawing was masterfully created or to purchase a Limited Edition Framed Artwork of Big Pun type into your Internet Browser the URL shortcut ➡ **myportrait.art/bigpun**

To listen to his Greatest Songs type into your Internet Browser the URL shortcut ➡ **radio.surf/bigpun**

To view all channels on THE FACE OF MUSIC Internet Radio MEGA Station type into your Internet Browser the URL shortcut ➡ **radio.surf/music**

To inquire about purchasing a Limited Edtion NFT of this portrait type into your Internet Browser the URL shortcut ➡ **myartnft.shop/bigpun**

To view all available NFTs type into your Internet Browser the URL shortcut ➡ **myartnft.shop/all**

# Bill Haley & his Comets

(Total Albums Sold: 60 Million) (Genre: Rock & Roll , Country , Rockabilly)
Bill Haley & His Comets were an American rock and roll band, founded in 1952 and continued until Haley's death in 1981. The band was also known as Bill Haley and the Comets and Bill Haley's Comets (and variations thereof). From late 1954 to late 1956, the group placed nine singles in the Top 20, one of those a number one and three more in the Top Ten. The single "Rock Around the Clock" became the biggest selling rock and roll single in the history of the genre and retained that position for some years.

Bandleader Bill Haley had previously been a country music performer; after recording a country and western-styled version of Jackie Brenston and his Delta Cats "Rocket 88", a rhythm and blues song, he changed musical direction to a new sound which came to be called rock and roll.

Although several members of the Comets became famous, Bill Haley remained the star. With his spit curl and the band's matching plaid dinner jackets and energetic stage behavior, many fans consider them to be as revolutionary in their time as the Beatles were a decade later.

Following Haley's death, no fewer than seven different groups have existed under the Comets name, all claiming (with varying degrees of authority) to be the continuation of Haley's group. As of the end of 2014, four such groups were still performing in the United States and internationally.

# Bill Haley

(Net Worth: $16 Million) (Height: 5'-5")
William John Clifton Haley (/ˈheɪli/; July 6, 1925 – February 9, 1981) was a pioneering American rock and roll musician. He is credited by many with first popularizing this form of music in the early 1950s with his group Bill Haley & His Comets and million-selling hits such as "Rock Around the Clock", "See You Later, Alligator", "Shake, Rattle and Roll", "Rocket 88", "Skinny Minnie", and "Razzle Dazzle".

Haley was born July 6, 1925 in Highland Park, Michigan. In 1929, the four-year-old Haley underwent an inner-ear mastoid operation which accidentally severed an optic nerve, leaving him blind in his left eye for the rest of his life. It is said that he adopted his trademark kiss curl over his right eye to draw attention from his left, but it also became his "gimmick", and added to his popularity. As a result of the effects of the Great Depression on the Detroit area, his father moved the family to Bethel, Pennsylvania, when Bill was seven years old. Haley's father William Albert Haley was from Kentucky and played the banjo and mandolin, and his mother, Maude Green, who was originally from Ulverston in Lancashire, England, was a technically accomplished keyboardist with classical training. Haley told the story that when he made a simulated guitar out of cardboard, his parents bought him a real one.

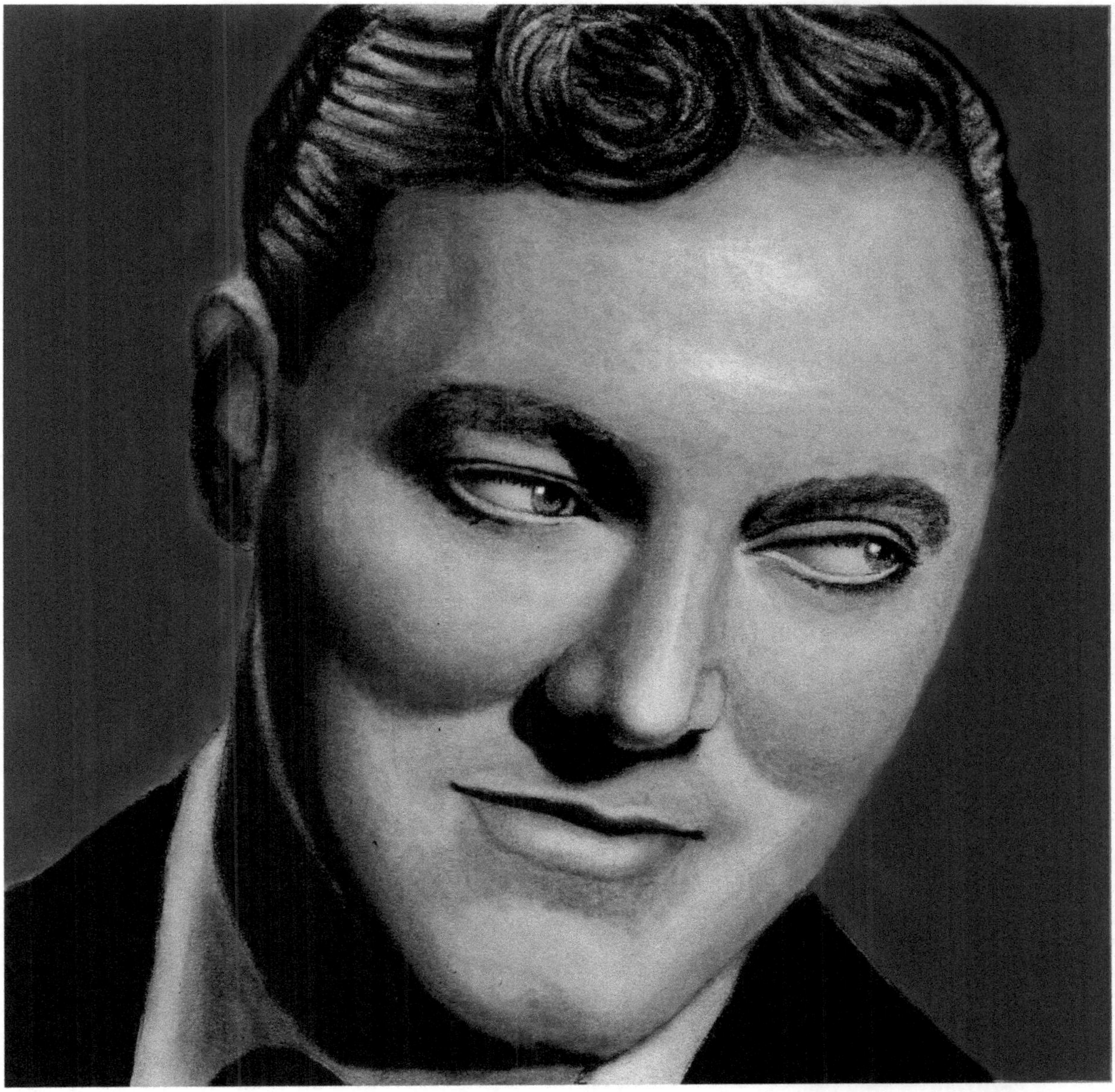

To view how this drawing was masterfully created or to purchase a Limited Edition Framed Artwork of Bill Haley type into your Internet Browser the URL shortcut ➡ **myportrait.art/billhaley**

To listen to their Greatest Songs type into your Internet Browser the URL shortcut ➡ **radio.surf/billhaleyandhiscomets**

To view all channels on THE FACE OF MUSIC Internet Radio MEGA Station type into your Internet Browser the URL shortcut ➡ **radio.surf/music**

To inquire about purchasing a Limited Edtion NFT of this portrait type into your Internet Browser the URL shortcut ➡ **myartnft.shop/billhaley**

To view all available NFTs type into your Internet Browser the URL shortcut ➡ **myartnft.shop/all**

# Billy Idol

(Net worth: $50 Million)(Total Albums Sold: 40 Million)
(Genre: Punk Rock , Hard Rock)(Height: 5' - 9")

William Michael Albert Broad (born 30 November 1955), known professionally as Billy Idol, is an English musician, singer, songwriter, and actor who holds dual British and American citizenship. He first achieved fame in the 1970s emerging from the London punk rock scene as the lead singer of the group Generation X. Subsequently, he embarked on a solo career which led to international recognition and made Idol a lead artist during the MTV-driven "Second British Invasion" in the United States. The name "Billy Idol" was inspired by a schoolteacher's description of him as "idle".

Idol began his music career in late 1976 as a guitarist in the punk rock band Chelsea. However, he soon left the group. With his former bandmate Tony James, Idol formed Generation X. With Idol as lead singer, the band achieved success in the United Kingdom and released three albums on Chrysalis Records, then disbanded. In 1981, Idol moved to New York City to pursue his solo career in collaboration with guitarist Steve Stevens. His debut studio album, Billy Idol (1982), was a commercial success. With music videos for singles "Dancing with Myself" and "White Wedding" Idol soon became a staple of then-newly established MTV.

Idol's second studio album, Rebel Yell (1983), was a major commercial success, featuring hit singles "Rebel Yell" and "Eyes Without a Face". The album was certified double platinum by the Recording Industry Association of America (RIAA) for shipment of two million copies in the US. In 1986, he released Whiplash Smile. Having accumulated three US top 10 singles ("Rebel Yell", "White Wedding" and "Mony Mony") Idol released a 1988 greatest hits album titled Idol Songs: 11 of the Best; the album went platinum in the United Kingdom. Idol then released Charmed Life (1990) and the concept album Cyberpunk (1993).

Idol spent the second half of the 1990s out of the public eye focusing on his personal life. He made a musical comeback with the release of Devil's Playground (2005) and again with Kings & Queens of the Underground (2014).

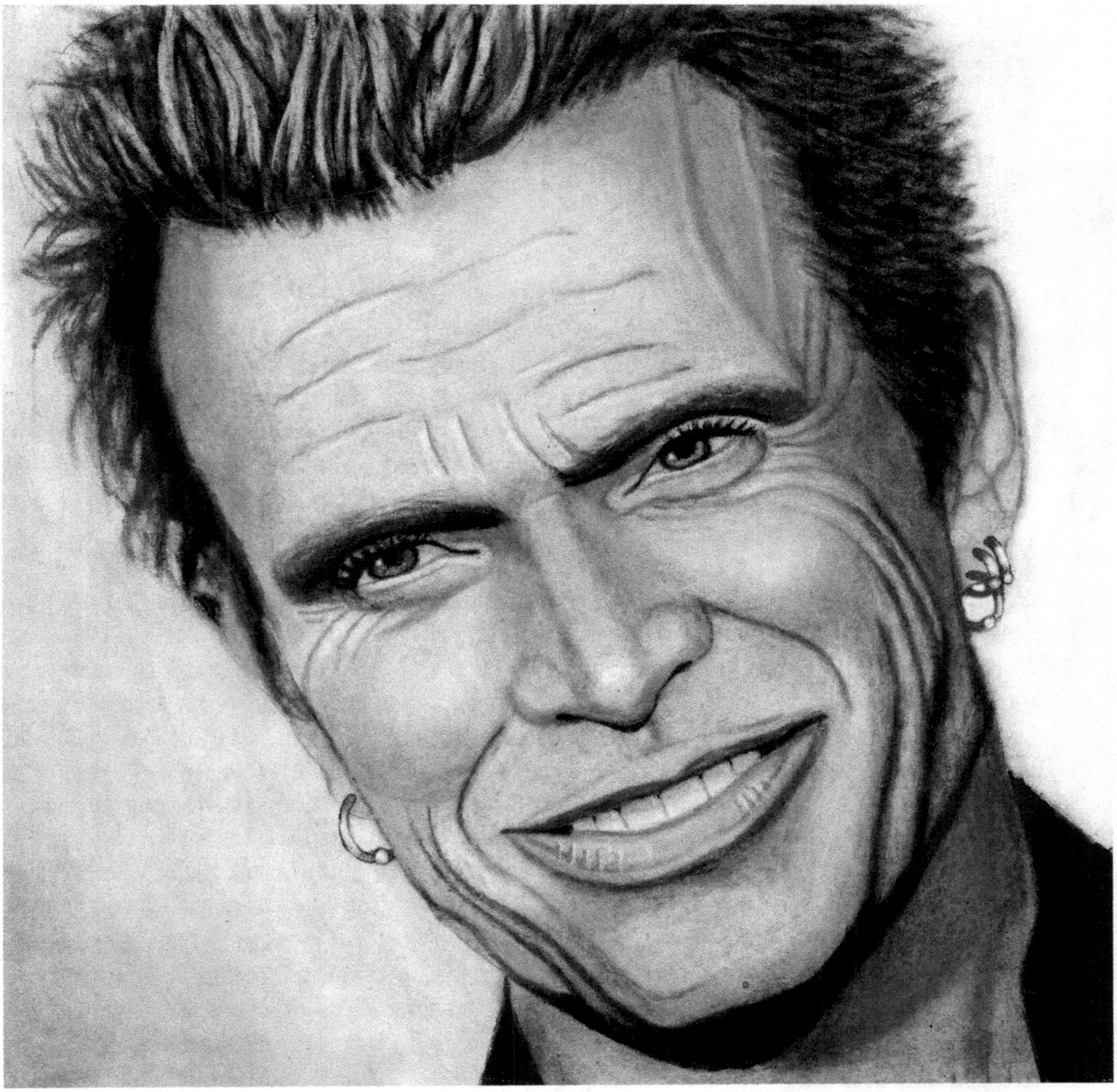

To view how this drawing was masterfully created or to purchase a Limited Edition Framed Artwork of Billy Idol type into your Internet Browser the URL shortcut ➡ **myportrait.art/billyidol**

To listen to his Greatest Songs type into your Internet Browser the URL shortcut ➡ **radio.surf/billyidol**

To view all channels on THE FACE OF MUSIC Internet Radio MEGA Station type into your Internet Browser the URL shortcut ➡ **radio.surf/music**

To inquire about purchasing a Limited Edtion NFT of this portrait type into your Internet Browser the URL shortcut ➡ **myartnft.shop/billyidol**

To view all available NFTs type into your Internet Browser the URL shortcut ➡ **myartnft.shop/all**

# Billy Joel

(Net worth: $225 Million)(Total: Records Sold: 150 Million)
(Genre: Rock)(Height: 5' - 5")

William Martin Joel (born May 9, 1949) is an American musician, singer-songwriter, and composer. Commonly nicknamed the "Piano Man" after his first major hit and signature song of the same name, he has led a commercially successful career as a solo artist since the 1970s, having released 12 studio albums from 1971 to 1993 as well as one studio album in 2001. He is one of the best-selling music artists of all time, as well as the seventh best-selling recording artist and the fourth best-selling solo artist in the United States, with over 150 million records sold worldwide. His 1985 compilation album, Greatest Hits Vol. 1 & 2, is one of the best-selling albums in the United States.

Joel was born in 1949 in the Bronx, New York, and grew up on Long Island, both places that influenced his music.

Growing up, he took piano lessons at the insistence of his mother. After dropping out of high school to pursue a musical career, Joel took part in two short-lived bands, The Hassles and Attila, before signing a record deal with Family Productions and kicking off a solo career in 1971 with his first release, Cold Spring Harbor. In 1972, Joel caught the attention of Columbia Records after a live radio performance of the song "Captain Jack" became popular in Philadelphia, prompting him to sign a new record deal with the company and release his second album, Piano Man, in 1973. After releasing the albums Streetlife Serenade and Turnstiles in 1974 and 1976 respectively, Joel released his critical and commercial breakthrough album, The Stranger, in 1977. This album became Columbia's best-selling release, selling over 10 million copies and spawning several hit singles, including "Just the Way You Are", "Movin' Out (Anthony's Song)", "Only the Good Die Young", and "She's Always a Woman"; another song on this album, "Scenes from an Italian Restaurant", is Joel's favorite of his own songs and has become a staple of his live shows.

Across the 20 years of his solo career, Joel produced 33 Top 40 hits in the U.S., all of which he wrote himself, and three of which ("It's Still Rock and Roll to Me", "Tell Her About It", and "We Didn't Start the Fire") peaked at the top of the Billboard Hot 100 charts. Joel has been nominated for 23 Grammy Awards, winning five of them, including Album of the Year for 52nd Street. Joel was inducted into the Songwriters Hall of Fame (1992), the Rock and Roll Hall of Fame (1999), and the Long Island Music Hall of Fame (2006). In 2001, Joel received the Johnny Mercer Award from the Songwriters Hall of Fame. In 2013, Joel received the Kennedy Center Honors, for influencing American culture through the arts. Since the advent of his solo career, Joel has held a successful touring career, holding live performances across the globe in which he sings several of his written songs. In 1987, he became one of the first artists to hold a rock and roll tour in the Soviet Union following the country's alleviation of the ban on rock and roll music. Despite largely retiring from writing and releasing pop music following the release of River of Dreams, he continues to tour; he frequently performs at Madison Square Garden. Joel has been in several relationships, including marriages to Elizabeth Weber Small, model Christie Brinkley, and chef Katie Lee; since 2015, he has been married to Alexis Roderick, his fourth spouse. He has three daughters: Alexa Ray Joel with Brinkley, and Della Rose and Remy Anne with Roderick.
oderick.

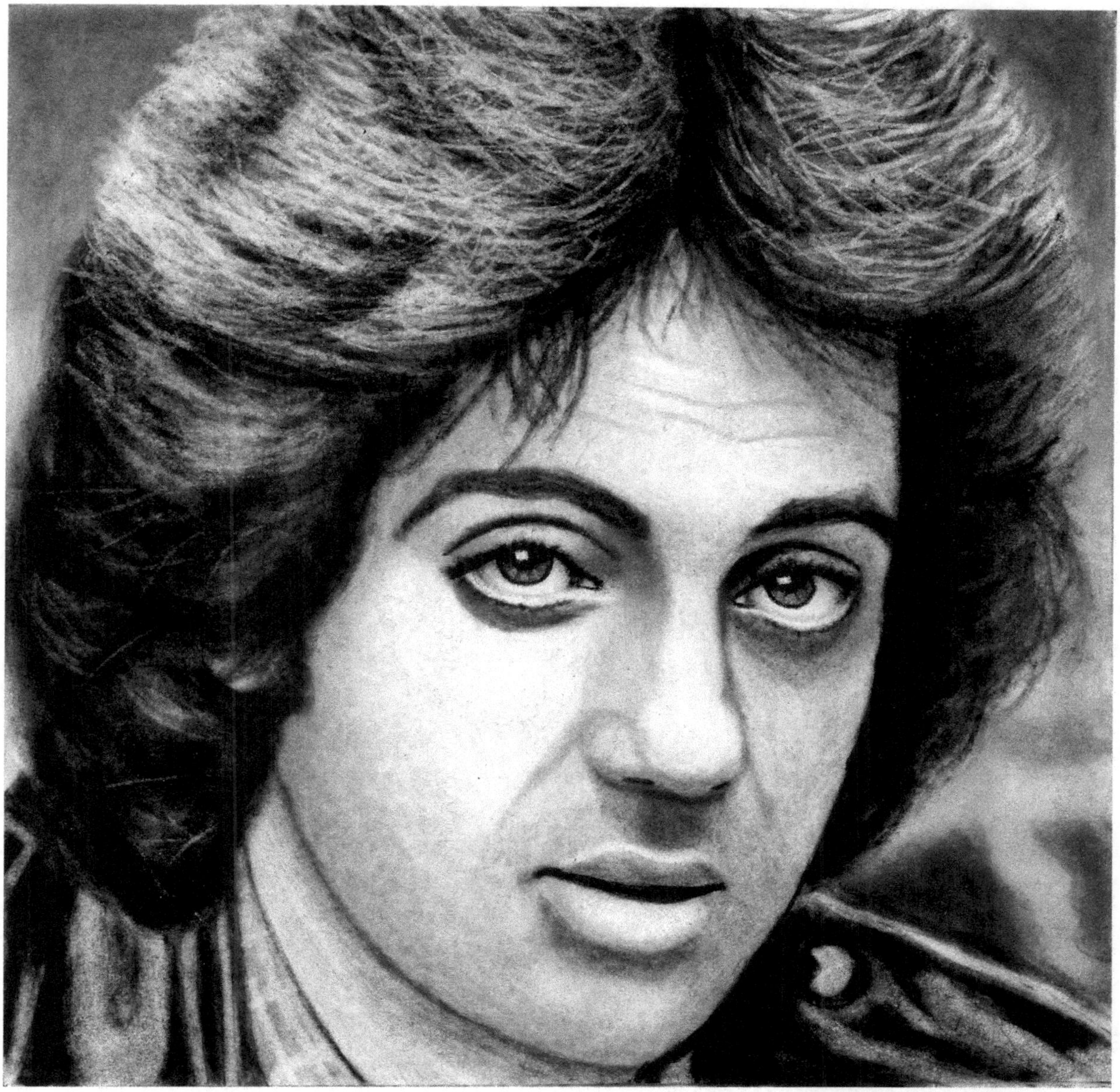

To view how this drawing was masterfully created or to purchase a Limited Edition Framed Artwork of Billy Joel type into your Internet Browser the URL shortcut ➡ **myportrait.art/billyjoel**

To listen to his Greatest Songs type into your Internet Browser the URL shortcut ➡ **radio.surf/billyjoel**

To view all channels on THE FACE OF MUSIC Internet Radio MEGA Station type into your Internet Browser the URL shortcut ➡ **radio.surf/music**

To inquire about purchasing a Limited Edtion NFT of this portrait type into your Internet Browser the URL shortcut ➡ **myartnft.shop/billyjoel**

To view all available NFTs type into your Internet Browser the URL shortcut ➡ **myartnft.shop/all**

# Bing Crosby

(Net worth: $50 Million)(Total Recordings Sold: 1 Billion)
(Genre: Crooner)(Height: 5' - 9")

Harry Lillis "Bing" Crosby Jr. (May 3, 1903 – October 14, 1977) was an American singer, comedian and actor. The first multimedia star, Crosby was one of the most popular and influential musical artists of the 20th century. He was a leader in record sales, radio ratings, and motion picture grosses from 1930 to 1954. He made over seventy feature films and recorded more than 1,600 different songs.

His early career coincided with recording innovations that allowed him to develop an intimate singing style that influenced many male singers who followed him, including Perry Como, Frank Sinatra, Dean Martin, Dick Haymes, Elvis Presley, and John Lennon.

Yank magazine said that he was "the person who had done the most for the morale of overseas servicemen" during World War II. In 1948, American polls declared him the "most admired man alive," ahead of Jackie Robinson and Pope Pius XII.:6 Also in 1948, Music Digest estimated that his recordings filled more than half of the 80,000 weekly hours allocated to recorded radio music.

Crosby won the Academy Award for Best Actor for his performance in Going My Way (1944), and was nominated for its sequel The Bells of St. Mary's (1945) opposite Ingrid Bergman, becoming the first of six actors to be nominated twice for playing the same character. In 1963, Crosby received the first Grammy Global Achievement Award. He is one of 33 people to have three stars on the Hollywood Walk of Fame, in the categories of motion pictures, radio, and audio recording. He was also known for his collaborations with longtime friend Bob Hope, starring in the Road to... films from 1940 to 1962.

Crosby influenced the development of the postwar recording industry. After seeing a demonstration of a German broadcast quality reel-to-reel tape recorder brought to America by John T. Mullin, he invested $50,000 in a California electronics company called Ampex to build copies. He then convinced ABC to allow him to tape his shows. He became the first performer to pre-record his radio shows and master his commercial recordings onto magnetic tape.

Through the medium of recording, he constructed his radio programs with the same directorial tools and craftsmanship (editing, retaking, rehearsal, time shifting) used in motion picture production, a practice that became an industry standard. In addition to his work with early audio tape recording, he helped to finance the development of videotape, bought television stations, bred racehorses, and co-owned the Pittsburgh Pirates baseball team.

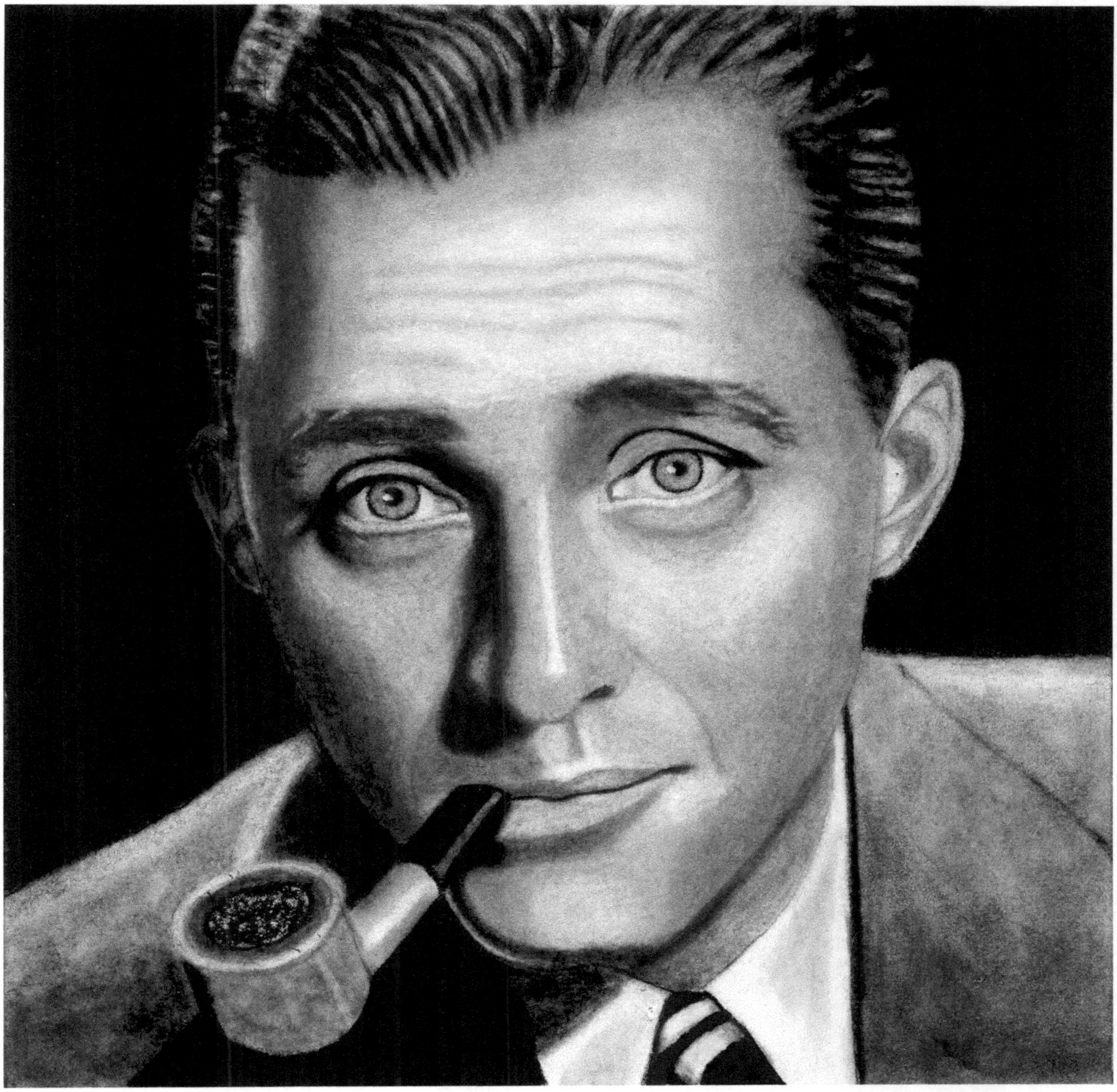

To view how this drawing was masterfully created or to purchase a Limited Edition Framed Artwork of Bing Crosby type into your Internet Browser the URL shortcut ➡ **myportrait.art/bingcrosby**

To listen to his Greatest Songs type into your Internet Browser the URL shortcut ➡ **radio.surf/bingcrosby**

To view all channels on THE FACE OF MUSIC Internet Radio MEGA Station type into your Internet Browser the URL shortcut ➡ **radio.surf/music**

To inquire about purchasing a Limited Edtion NFT of this portrait type into your Internet Browser the URL shortcut ➡ **myartnft.shop/bingcrosby**

To view all available NFTs type into your Internet Browser the URL shortcut ➡ **myartnft.shop/all**

# Black Eyed Peas

(Total Albums Sold: 80 Million) (Genre: Hip-Hop , Dance Pop)

Black Eyed Peas (also known as The Black Eyed Peas) is an American musical group, consisting of rappers will.i.am, apl.de.ap, Taboo and J. Rey Soul. Originally an alternative hip hop group, they subsequently refashioned themselves as a more marketable pop-rap act. Although the group was founded in Los Angeles in 1995, it was not until the release of their third album, Elephunk, in 2003, that they achieved high record sales. Black Eyed Peas and Shakira's music video ranked 4th in global charts.Black Eyed Peas' first major hit was the 2003 single "Where Is the Love?" from Elephunk, which topped the charts in 13 countries, including the United Kingdom, where it spent seven weeks at number one and went on to become Britain's biggest-selling single of 2003. Their fourth album, Monkey Business, was an even bigger worldwide success, and became certified 4× Platinum in the United States. In 2009, the group became one of only 11 artists to have simultaneously held the number-one and number-two spots on the Billboard Hot 100, with their singles "Boom Boom Pow" and "I Gotta Feeling", which topped the chart for an unprecedented 26 consecutive weeks.The album The E.N.D. produced a third Hot 100 number-one placement with "Imma Be", making the group one of few to ever place three number one singles on the chart from the same album, before being followed with "Rock That Body" and "Meet Me Halfway", which peaked in the top 10 of the Hot 100. "I Gotta Feeling" became the first single to sell more than one million downloads in the United Kingdom. At the 52nd Grammy Awards ceremony, held in January 2010, they won three awards out of six nominations. In November 2010, they released the album The Beginning. In February 2011, the group performed at the Super Bowl XLV halftime show.Black Eyed Peas have sold an estimated 80 million records, making them one of the best-selling groups of all time. According to Nielsen SoundScan, the group were the second-best-selling artist/group of all time for downloaded tracks, behind Rihanna, with over 42 million sales. They were ranked 12th on Billboard's 2000s Decade-End Artist of the Decade Chart, and 7th on the Hot 100 Artists of the Decade.

# Fergie

(Net Worth: $45 Million) (Height: 5'-4")

Fergie Duhamel : born Stacy Ann Ferguson; March 27, 1975), professionally known by her stage name Fergie, is an American singer, songwriter, and actress. She first achieved chart success as part of the hip hop group the Black Eyed Peas. Her debut solo album, The Dutchess (2006), saw commercial success and spawned three Billboard Hot 100 number one singles: "London Bridge", "Glamorous", and "Big Girls Don't Cry". Although she vocally incorporates rapping into her performances, she does not consider herself a rapper.Fergie was originally a member of the children's television series Kids Incorporated and the girl group Wild Orchid. In 2001, she left the group and in the subsequent year joined the Black Eyed Peas. She worked with the Black Eyed Peas on two albums before releasing her debut solo album, The Dutchess, in 2006. She continued her collaboration with the Black Eyed Peas and released a further two albums with them, The E.N.D. (2009) and The Beginning (2010). Fergie began touring with her own group in 2009. Her second solo album, Double Dutchess, was released in 2017.Fergie has additionally appeared in a number of films including Poseideon (2006), Grindhouse (2007), and Nine (2009). She launched her first fragrance, Outspoken, under Avon in May 2010 and has since released four more fragrances.

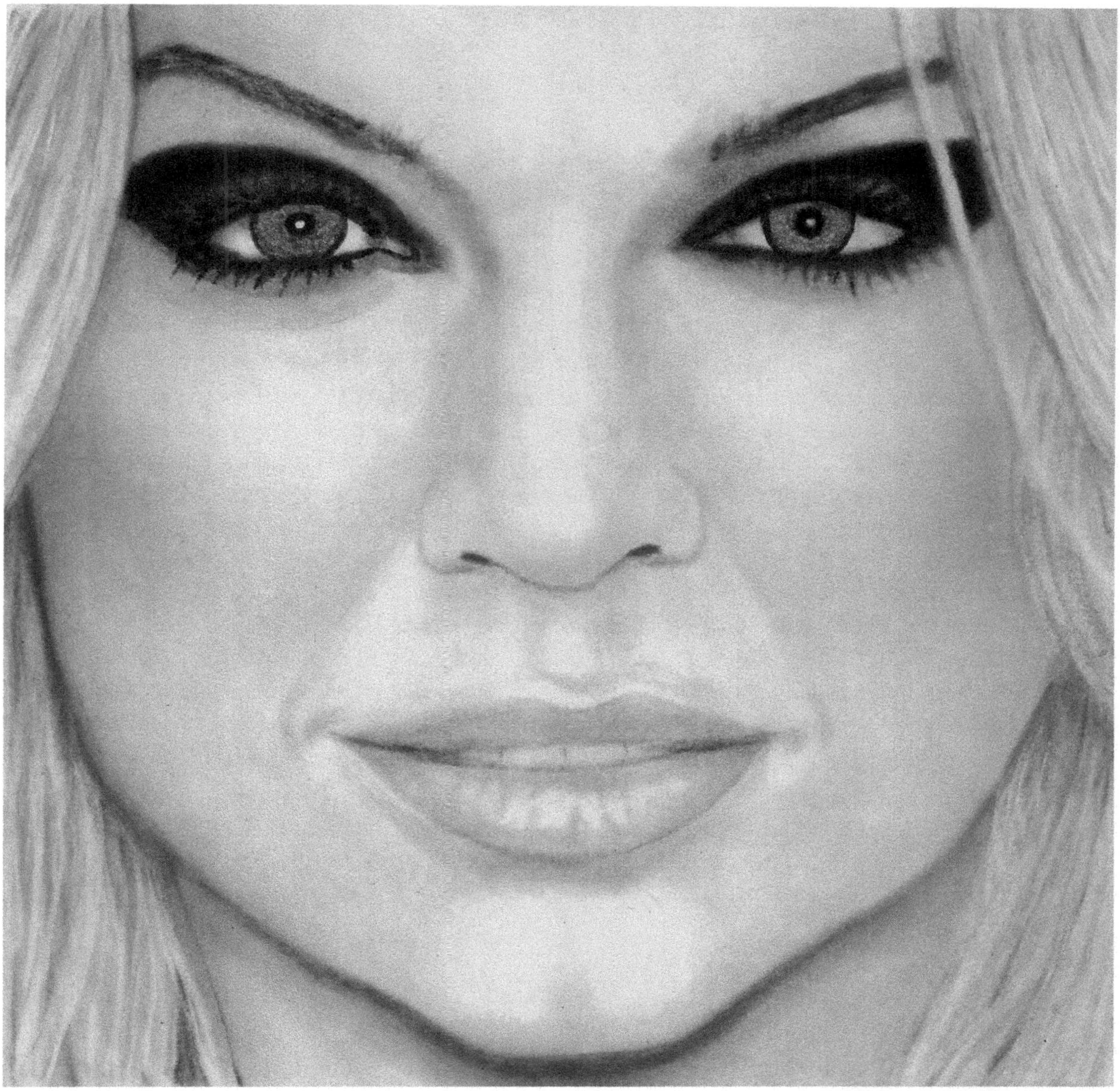

To view how this drawing was masterfully created or to purchase a Limited Edition Framed Artwork of Fergie type into your Internet Browser the URL shortcut ➡ **myportrait.art/fergie**

To listen to their Greatest Songs type into your Internet Browser the URL shortcut
➡ **radio.surf/blackeyedpeas**

To view all channels on THE FACE OF MUSIC Internet Radio MEGA Station type into your Internet Browser the URL shortcut ➡ **radio.surf/music**

To inquire about purchasing a Limited Edtion NFT of this portrait type into your Internet Browser the URL shortcut ➡ **myartnft.shop/fergie**

To view all available NFTs type into your Internet Browser the URL shortcut ➡ **myartnft.shop/all**

# Black Sabbath

[Total Albums Sold: 70+Million] Black Sabbath were an English rock band formed in Birmingham in 1968 by guitarist Tony Iommi, drummer Bill Ward, bassist Geezer Butler and vocalist Ozzy Osbourne. They are often cited as pioneers of heavy metal music. The band helped define the genre with releases such as Black Sabbath (1970), Paranoid (1970), and Master of Reality (1971). The band had multiple line-up changes following Osbourne's departure in 1979, with Iommi being the only constant member throughout its history. After previous iterations of the group called the Polka Tulk Blues Band and Earth, the band settled on the name Black Sabbath in 1969. They distinguished themselves through occult themes with horror-inspired lyrics and tuned-down guitars. Signing to Philips Records in November 1969, they released their first single, "Evil Woman" in January 1970. Their debut album, Black Sabbath, was released the following month. Though it received a negative critical response, the album was a commercial success, leading to a follow-up record, Paranoid, later in 1970. The band's popularity grew, and by 1973's Sabbath Bloody Sabbath, critics were starting to respond favourably. Osbourne's regular use of drugs and alcohol led to his firing in 1979. He was replaced by former Rainbow vocalist Ronnie James Dio. Following two albums with Dio, Black Sabbath endured many personnel changes in the 1980s and 1990s that included vocalists Ian Gillan, Glenn Hughes, Ray Gillen and Tony Martin, as well as several drummers and bassists. In 1991, Iommi and Butler rejoined Dio and drummer Vinny Appice to record Dehumanizer (1992). The original line-up reunited with Osbourne in 1997 and released a live album Reunion. Black Sabbath's final studio album and nineteenth overall, 13 (2013), features all of the original members except Ward. During their farewell tour, the band played their final concert in their home city of Birmingham on 4 February 2017.

# Ozzy Osbourne

[Net Worth: $220+Million][Total Albums Sold: 100+Million][Height: 5'-10"]John Michael "Ozzy" Osbourne (born 3 December 1948) is an English singer, songwriter, actor, and television personality. He rose to prominence during the 1970s as the lead vocalist of the heavy metal band Black Sabbath, during which he adopted the nickname the "Prince of Darkness". Osbourne was fired from the band in 1979 due to alcohol and drug problems, but he went on to have a successful solo career, releasing 12 studio albums, the first seven of which were awarded multi-platinum certifications in the US. Osbourne has since reunited with Black Sabbath on several occasions. He rejoined in 1997 and helped record the group's final studio album 13 (2013), before they embarked on a farewell tour which culminated in a final performance in their home city, Birmingham, England, in February 2017. His longevity and success have earned him the informal title of "Godfather of Heavy Metal".

Osbourne's total album sales from his years in Black Sabbath, combined with his solo work, is over 100 million. As a member of Black Sabbath, he was inducted into the Rock and Roll Hall of Fame, and he was inducted into the UK Music Hall of Fame as a solo artist and as a member of the band. Possessing a distinctive singing voice, Osbourne, as a native of Birmingham, is known for his strong Brummie accent – he has a star on the Birmingham Walk of Stars in his hometown as well as the Hollywood Walk of Fame. At 2014 MTV Europe Music Awards, he received the Global Icon Award. In 2015, Osbourne received the Ivor Novello Award for Lifetime Achievement from the British Academy of Songwriters, Composers and Authors.

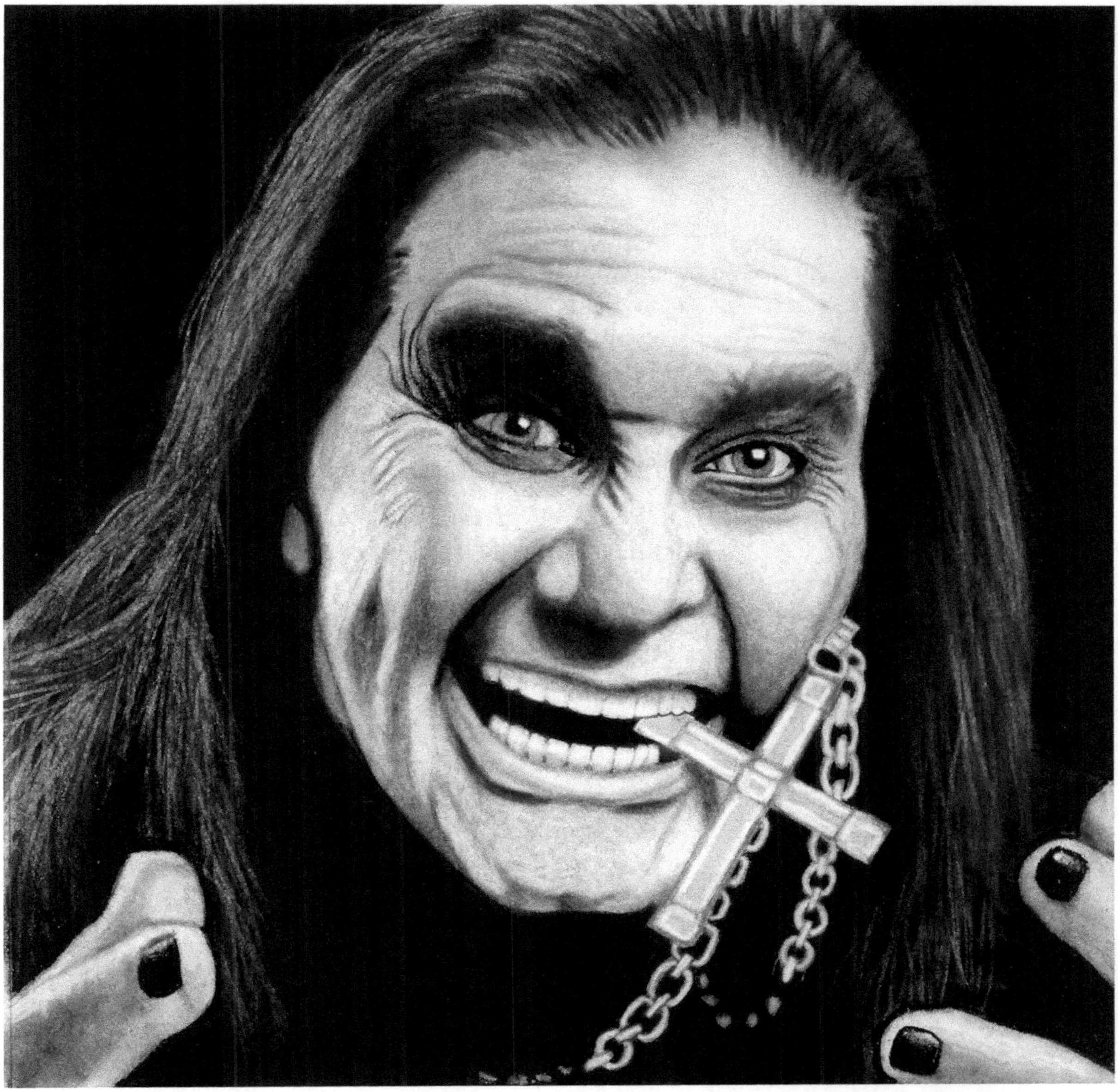

To view how this drawing was masterfully created or to purchase a Limited Edition Framed Artwork of Ozzy Osbourne type into your Internet Browser the URL shortcut ➡ **myportrait.art/ozzyosbourne**

To listen to Black Sabbath's Greatest Songs type into your Internet Browser the URL shortcut
➡ **radio.surf/blacksabbath**

To listen to Ozzy Osbournes's Greatest Songs type into your Internet Browser the URL shortcut
➡ **radio.surf/ozzyosbourne**

To view all channels on THE FACE OF MUSIC Internet Radio MEGA Station type into your Internet Browser the URL shortcut ➡ **radio.surf/music**

To inquire about purchasing a Limited Edtion NFT of this portrait type into your Internet Browser the URL shortcut ➡ **myartnft.shop/ozzyosbourne**

To view all available NFTs type into your Internet Browser the URL shortcut ➡ **myartnft.shop/all**

# Blondie

(Total Albums Sold: 40 Million) (Genre: New Wave / Post Punk)
Blondie is an American rock band co-founded by singer Debbie Harry and guitarist Chris Stein. The band were pioneers in the American punk and then the new wave scene of the mid-1970s in New York. Their first two albums contained strong elements of these genres, and although highly successful in the United Kingdom and Australia, Blondie was regarded as an underground band in the United States until the release of Parallel Lines in 1978. Over the next three years, the band achieved several hit singles including "Heart of Glass", "Call Me", "Rapture" and "The Tide Is High". The band became noted for its eclectic mix of musical styles, incorporating elements of disco, pop, reggae, and early rap music. Blondie disbanded after the release of its sixth studio album, The Hunter, in 1982. Debbie Harry continued to pursue a solo career with varied results after taking a few years off to care for partner Chris Stein, who was diagnosed with pemphigus, a rare autoimmune disease of the skin. The band re-formed in 1997, achieving renewed success and a number one single in the United Kingdom with "Maria" in 1999, exactly 20 years after their first UK No. 1 single ("Heart of Glass").The group toured and performed throughout the world during the following years, and was inducted into the Rock and Roll Hall of Fame in 2006. Blondie has sold around 40 million records worldwide and is still active. The band's eleventh studio album, Pollinator, was released on May 5, 2017.

# Debbie Harry

(Net Worth: $20 Million) (Height: 5'-3")
Deborah Ann Harry (born Angela Trimble; July 1, 1945) is an American singer, songwriter and actress, known as the lead vocalist of the band Blondie. Her recordings with the band reached No.1 in the US and UK charts on many occasions from 1979 to 2017.
Born in Miami, Florida, Harry was adopted as an infant and raised in Hawthorne, New Jersey. After attending college, she worked various jobs, including as a secretary (including at the BBC in New York), dancer, and Playboy Bunny, before breaking through in the music industry. Harry co-formed Blondie in 1974 in New York City. The band released their eponymous debut album in 1976, and released a further three albums between then and 1979, including Parallel Lines, which spawned six singles, including "Heart of Glass". Their fifth record, Autoamerican (1980), afforded Harry and the band further attention, spawning such hits as a cover of "The Tide Is High", and "Rapture", the latter of which is considered the first rap song to chart at number one in the United States.

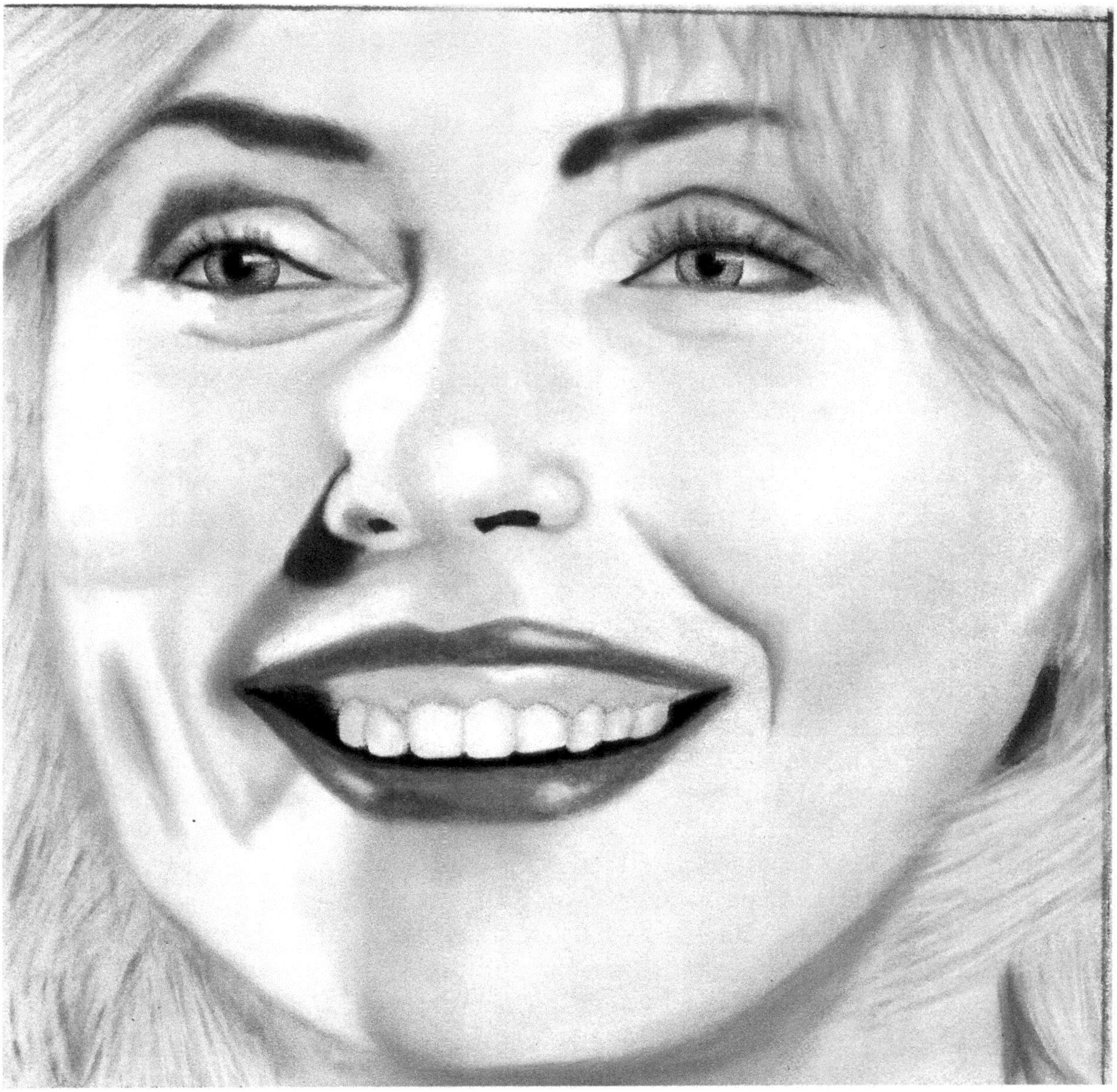

To view how this drawing was masterfully created or to purchase a Limited Edition Framed Artwork of Debbie Harry type into your Internet Browser the URL shortcut ➡ **myportrait.art/debbieharry**

To listen to their Greatest Songs type into your Internet Browser the URL shortcut ➡ **radio.surf/blondie**

To view all channels on THE FACE OF MUSIC Internet Radio MEGA Station type into your Internet Browser the URL shortcut ➡ **radio.surf/music**

To inquire about purchasing a Limited Edtion NFT of this portrait type into your Internet Browser the URL shortcut ➡ **myartnft.shop/debbieharry**

To view all available NFTs type into your Internet Browser the URL shortcut ➡ **myartnft.shop/all**

# Bo Diddley

(Net worth: $6 Million)(Total Records Sold: 5+ Million)
(Genre: R&B , Rock & Roll)(Height: 5' - 7")

Ellas McDaniel (born Ellas Otha Bates; December 30, 1928 – June 2, 2008), known as Bo Diddley, was an American singer, guitarist, songwriter and music producer who played a key role in the transition from the blues to rock and roll. He influenced many artists, including Buddy Holly, Elvis Presley, the Beatles, the Rolling Stones, the Animals, and the Clash.

His use of African rhythms and a signature beat, a simple five-accent hambone rhythm, is a cornerstone of hip hop, rock, and pop music. In recognition of his achievements, he was inducted into the Rock and Roll Hall of Fame in 1987, the Blues Hall of Fame in 2003, and the Rhythm and Blues Music Hall of Fame in 2017. He received a Lifetime Achievement Award from the Rhythm and Blues Foundation and the Grammy Lifetime Achievement Award. Diddley is also recognized for his technical innovations, including his distinctive rectangular guitar, with its unique booming, resonant, shimmering tones.

The origin of the stage name Bo Diddley is unclear. McDaniel claimed that his peers gave him the name, which he suspected was an insult. He also said that the name first belonged to a singer his adoptive mother knew. Harmonicist Billy Boy Arnold said that it was a local comedian's name, which Leonard Chess adopted as McDaniel's stage name and the title of his first single. McDaniel also stated that his school classmates in Chicago gave him the nickname, which he started using when sparring and boxing in the neighborhood with The Little Neighborhood Golden Gloves Bunch.

Bo Diddley died on June 2, 2008, of heart failure at his home in Archer, Florida at the age of 79. Garry Mitchell, his grandson and one of more than thirty-five family members at the musician's home when he died at 1:45 am. EDT, said his death was not unexpected. "There was a gospel song that was sang [at his bedside] and [when it was done] he said 'wow' with a thumbs up," Mitchell told Reuters, when asked to describe the scene at the deathbed. "The song was 'Walk Around Heaven' and in his last words he stated that he was going to heaven."

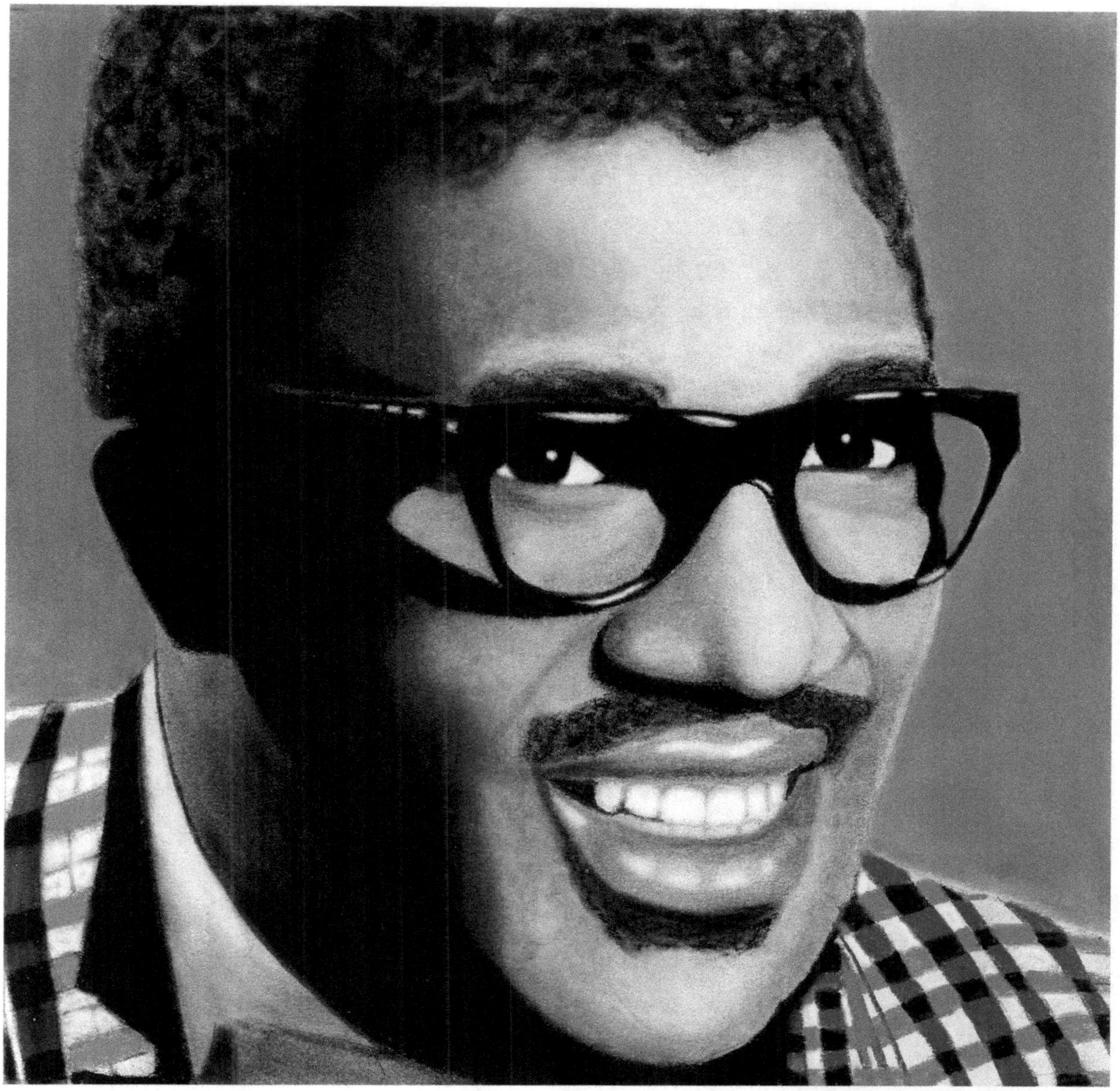

To view how this drawing was masterfully created or to purchase a Limited Edition Framed Artwork of Bo Diddley type into your Internet Browser the URL shortcut ➡ **myportrait.art/bodiddley**

To listen to his Greatest Songs type into your Internet Browser the URL shortcut ➡ **radio.surf/bodiddley**

To view all channels on THE FACE OF MUSIC Internet Radio MEGA Station type into your Internet Browser the URL shortcut ➡ **radio.surf/music**

To inquire about purchasing a Limited Edtion NFT of this portrait type into your Internet Browser the URL shortcut ➡ **myartnft.shop/bodiddley**

To view all available NFTs type into your Internet Browser the URL shortcut ➡ **myartnft.shop/all**

# Bob Dylan

(Net worth: $200 Million)(Total Records Sold: 100+ Million)
(Genre: Folk , Blues , Rock , Gospel )(Height: 5' - 7")

Bob Dylan (born Robert Allen Zimmerman; May 24, 1941) is an American singer-songwriter, author and visual artist. Often regarded as one of the greatest songwriters of all time, Dylan has been a major figure in popular culture for more than 50 years. Much of his most celebrated work dates from the 1960s, when songs such as "Blowin' in the Wind" (1963) and "The Times They Are a-Changin'" (1964) became anthems for the civil rights and anti-war movements. His lyrics during this period incorporated a range of political, social, philosophical, and literary influences, defying pop music conventions and appealing to the burgeoning counterculture.

Following his self-titled debut album in 1962, which mainly comprised traditional folk songs, Dylan made his breakthrough as a songwriter with the release of The Freewheelin' Bob Dylan the following year. The album features "Blowin' in the Wind" and the thematically complex "A Hard Rain's a-Gonna Fall". For many of these songs, he adapted the tunes and phraseology of older folk songs. He went on to release the politically charged The Times They Are a-Changin' and the more lyrically abstract and introspective Another Side of Bob Dylan in 1964. In 1965 and 1966, Dylan drew controversy when he adopted electrically amplified rock instrumentation, and in the space of 15 months recorded three of the most important and influential rock albums of the 1960s: Bringing It All Back Home (1965), Highway 61 Revisited (1965) and Blonde on Blonde (1966). Commenting on the six-minute single "Like a Rolling Stone" (1965), Rolling Stone wrote: "No other pop song has so thoroughly challenged and transformed the commercial laws and artistic conventions of its time, for all time." In July 1966, Dylan withdrew from touring after a motorcycle accident. During this period, he recorded a large body of songs with members of the Band, who had previously backed him on tour. These recordings were released as the collaborative album The Basement Tapes in 1975. In the late 1960s and early 1970s, Dylan explored country music and rural themes in John Wesley Harding (1967), Nashville Skyline (1969), and New Morning (1970). In 1975, he released Blood on the Tracks, which many saw as a return to form. In the late 1970s, he became a born-again Christian and released a series of albums of contemporary gospel music before returning to his more familiar rock-based idiom in the early 1980s. Dylan's 1997 album Time Out of Mind marked the beginning of a renaissance for his career. He has released five critically acclaimed albums of original material since then, the most recent being Rough and Rowdy Ways (2020). He also recorded a series of three albums in the 2010s comprising versions of traditional American standards, especially songs recorded by Frank Sinatra. Backed by a changing lineup of musicians, he has toured steadily since the late 1980s on what has been dubbed the Never Ending Tour. Since 1994, Dylan has published eight books of drawings and paintings, and his work has been exhibited in major art galleries. He has sold more than 100 million records, making him one of the best-selling music artists of all time. He has received numerous awards, including the Presidential Medal of Freedom, ten Grammy Awards, a Golden Globe Award and an Academy Award. Dylan has been inducted into the Rock and Roll Hall of Fame, Nashville Songwriters Hall of Fame and the Songwriters Hall of Fame. The Pulitzer Prize Board in 2008 awarded him a special citation for "his profound impact on popular music and American culture, marked by lyrical compositions of extraordinary poetic power". In 2016, Dylan was awarded the Nobel Prize in Literature "for having created new poetic expressions within the great American song tradition".

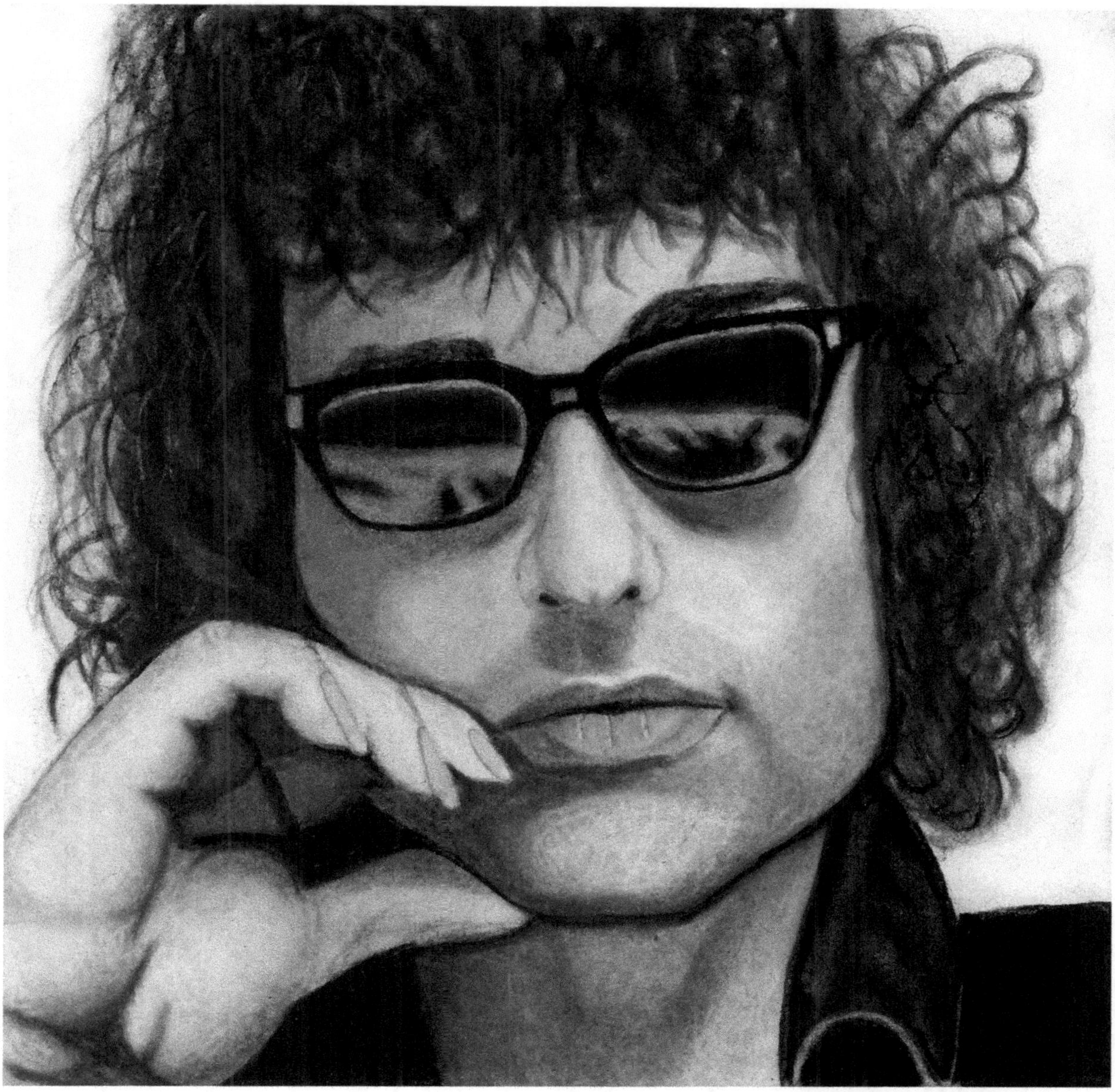

To view how this drawing was masterfully created or to purchase a Limited Edition Framed Artwork of Bob Dylan type into your Internet Browser the URL shortcut ➡ **myportrait.art/bobdylan**

To listen to his Greatest Songs type into your Internet Browser the URL shortcut ➡ **radio.surf/bobdylan**

To view all channels on THE FACE OF MUSIC Internet Radio MEGA Station type into your Internet Browser the URL shortcut ➡ **radio.surf/music**

To inquire about purchasing a Limited Edtion NFT of this portrait type into your Internet Browser the URL shortcut ➡ **myartnft.shop/bobdylan**

To view all available NFTs type into your Internet Browser the URL shortcut ➡ **myartnft.shop/all**

# Bob Marley

(Net worth: $32 Million)(Total Records Sold: 135 Million)
(Genre: Reggae )(Height: 5' - 7")

Robert Nesta "Bob" Marley, OM (6 February 1945 – 11 May 1981) was a Jamaican singer, songwriter, and musician. Considered one of the pioneers of reggae, his musical career was marked by fusing elements of reggae, ska, and rocksteady, as well as his distinctive vocal and songwriting style. Marley's contributions to music increased the visibility of Jamaican music worldwide, and made him a global figure in popular culture for over a decade. Over the course of his career Marley became known as a Rastafari icon, and he infused his music with a sense of spirituality. He is also considered a global symbol of Jamaican music and culture and identity, and was controversial in his outspoken support for the legalization of marijuana, while he also advocated for Pan-Africanism.

Born in Nine Mile, British Jamaica, Marley began his professional musical career in 1963, after forming Bob Marley and the Wailers. The group released its debut studio album The Wailing Wailers in 1965, which contained the single "One Love/People Get Ready"; the song was popular worldwide, and established the group as a rising figure in reggae. The Wailers subsequently released eleven further studio albums; while initially employing louder instrumentation and singing, the group began engaging in rhythmic-based song construction in the late 1960s and early 1970s, which coincided with the singer's conversion to Rastafari. During this period Marley relocated to London, and the group embodied their musical shift with the release of the album The Best of The Wailers (1971).

The group attained international success after the release of the albums Catch a Fire and Burnin' (both 1973), and forged a reputation as touring artists. Following the disbandment of the Wailers a year later, Marley went on to release his solo material under the band's name. His debut studio album Natty Dread (1974) received positive reception, as did its follow-up Rastaman Vibration (1976). A few months after the album's release Marley survived an assassination attempt at his home in Jamaica, which prompted him to permanently relocate to London. During his time in London he recorded the album Exodus (1977); it incorporated elements of blues, soul, and British rock and enjoyed widespread commercial and critical success.

In 1977, Marley was diagnosed with acral lentiginous melanoma; he died as a result of the illness in 1981. His fans around the world expressed their grief, and he received a state funeral in Jamaica. The greatest hits album Legend was released in 1984, and became the best-selling reggae album of all time. Marley also ranks as one of the best-selling music artists of all time, with estimated sales of more than 75 million records worldwide. He was posthumously honored by Jamaica soon after his death with a designated Order of Merit by his nation. In 1994, he was inducted into the Rock and Roll Hall of Fame. Rolling Stone ranked him No. 11 on its list of the 100 Greatest Artists of All Time.

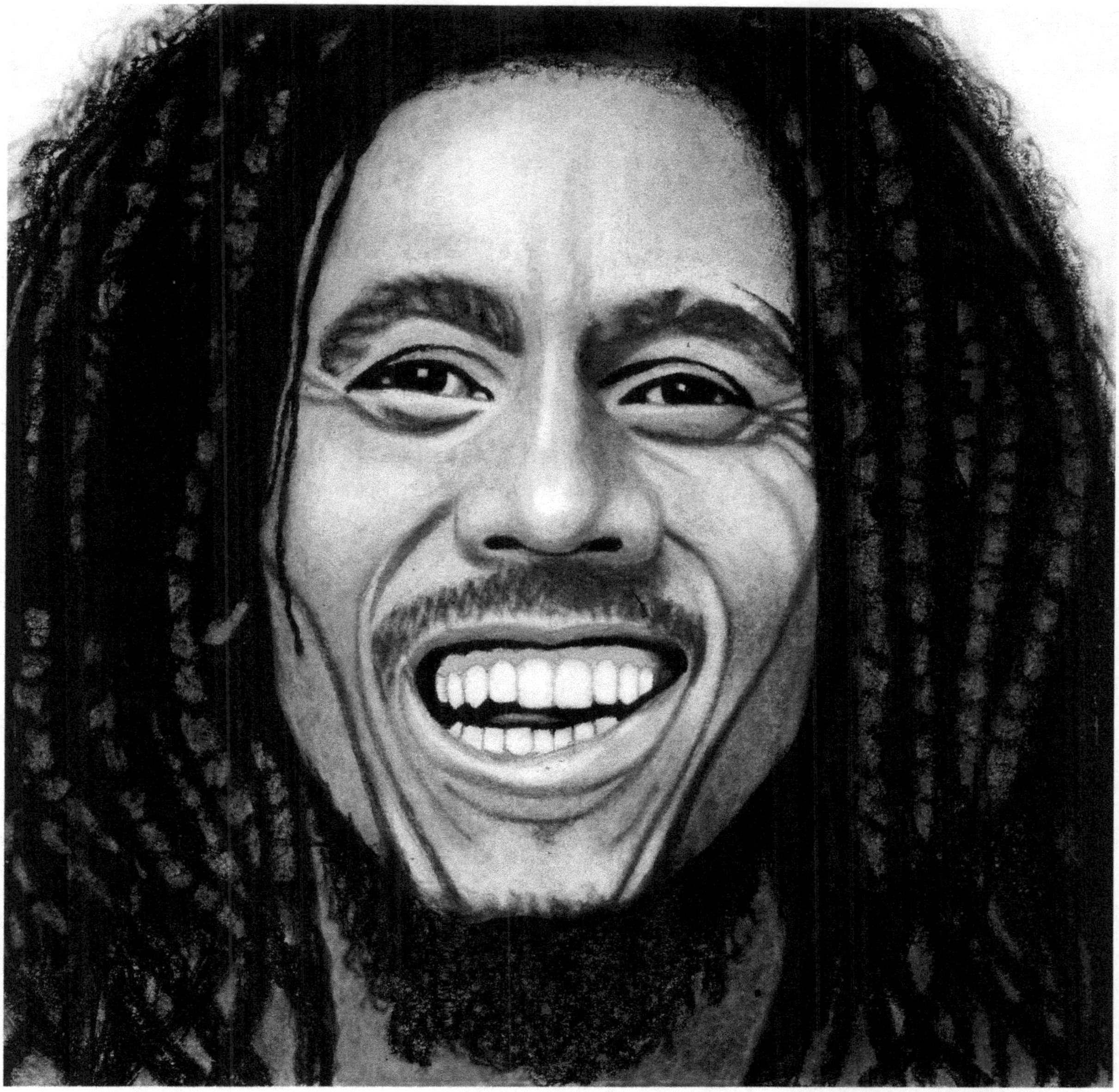

To view how this drawing was masterfully created or to purchase a Limited Edition Framed Artwork of Bob Marley type into your Internet Browser the URL shortcut ➡ **myportrait.art/bobmarley**

To listen to his Greatest Songs type into your Internet Browser the URL shortcut ➡ **radio.surf/bobmarley**

To view all channels on THE FACE OF MUSIC Internet Radio MEGA Station type into your Internet Browser the URL shortcut ➡ **radio.surf/music**

To inquire about purchasing a Limited Edtion NFT of this portrait type into your Internet Browser the URL shortcut ➡ **myartnft.shop/bobmarley**

To view all available NFTs type into your Internet Browser the URL shortcut ➡ **myartnft.shop/all**

# Bob Seger

(Net worth: $60 Million)(Total Records Sold: 75 Million)
(Genre: Classic Rock )(Height: 5' - 10")

Robert Clark Seger (born May 6, 1945) is an American singer, songwriter, and musician. As a locally successful Detroit-area artist, he performed and recorded as Bob Seger and the Last Heard and Bob Seger System throughout the 1960s, breaking through with his first album, Ramblin' Gamblin' Man (which contained his first national hit of the same name) in 1968. By the early 1970s, he had dropped the 'System' from his recordings and continued to strive for broader success with various other bands. In 1973, he put together the Silver Bullet Band, with a group of Detroit-area musicians, with whom he became most successful on the national level with the album Live Bullet (1976), recorded live with the Silver Bullet Band in 1975 at Cobo Hall in Detroit, Michigan. In 1976, he achieved a national breakout with the studio album Night Moves. On his studio albums, he also worked extensively with the Alabama-based Muscle Shoals Rhythm Section, which appeared on several of Seger's best-selling singles and albums.

A roots rocker with a classic raspy, powerful voice, Seger wrote and recorded songs that dealt with love, women, and blue-collar themes, and is an example of a heartland rock artist. He has recorded many hits, including "Night Moves", "Turn the Page", "Still the Same", "We've Got Tonite", "Against the Wind", "You'll Accomp'ny Me", "Hollywood Nights", "Shame on the Moon", "Like a Rock", and "Shakedown", the last of which was written for the 1987 film Beverly Hills Cop II and topped the Billboard Hot 100 chart. He also co-wrote the Eagles' number-one hit "Heartache Tonight", and his recording of "Old Time Rock and Roll" was named one of the Songs of the Century in 2001.

With a career spanning six decades, Seger has sold more than 75 million records worldwide, making him one of the world's best-selling artists of all time. Seger was inducted into the Rock and Roll Hall of Fame in 2004 and the Songwriters Hall of Fame in 2012. Seger was named Billboard's 2015 Legend of Live honoree at the 12th annual Billboard Touring Conference & Awards, held November 18–19 at the Roosevelt Hotel in New York. He announced his farewell tour in September 2018.

Seger was born at Henry Ford Hospital in Detroit, Michigan, the son of Charlotte and Stewart Seger. At age five, he moved with his family to Ann Arbor. He has an older brother, George.

Seger's father, a medical technician for the Ford Motor Company, played several instruments and Seger was exposed to music from an early age. Seger was also exposed to frequent arguments between his parents that disturbed the neighborhood at night. In 1956, when Seger was 10 years old, his father abandoned the family and moved to California. The remaining family soon lost their comfortable middle-class status and struggled financially.

Seger attended Tappan Junior High School (now Tappan Middle School) in Ann Arbor, Michigan, and graduated in 1963 from Pioneer High School, known at the time as Ann Arbor High School. He ran track and field in high school. Seger also went to Lincoln Park High School for a time.

Regarding his early musical inspirations, Seger has stated, "Little Richard – he was the first one that really got to me. Little Richard and, of course, Elvis Presley." "Come Go with Me" by The Del-Vikings, a hit in 1957, was the first record he bought.

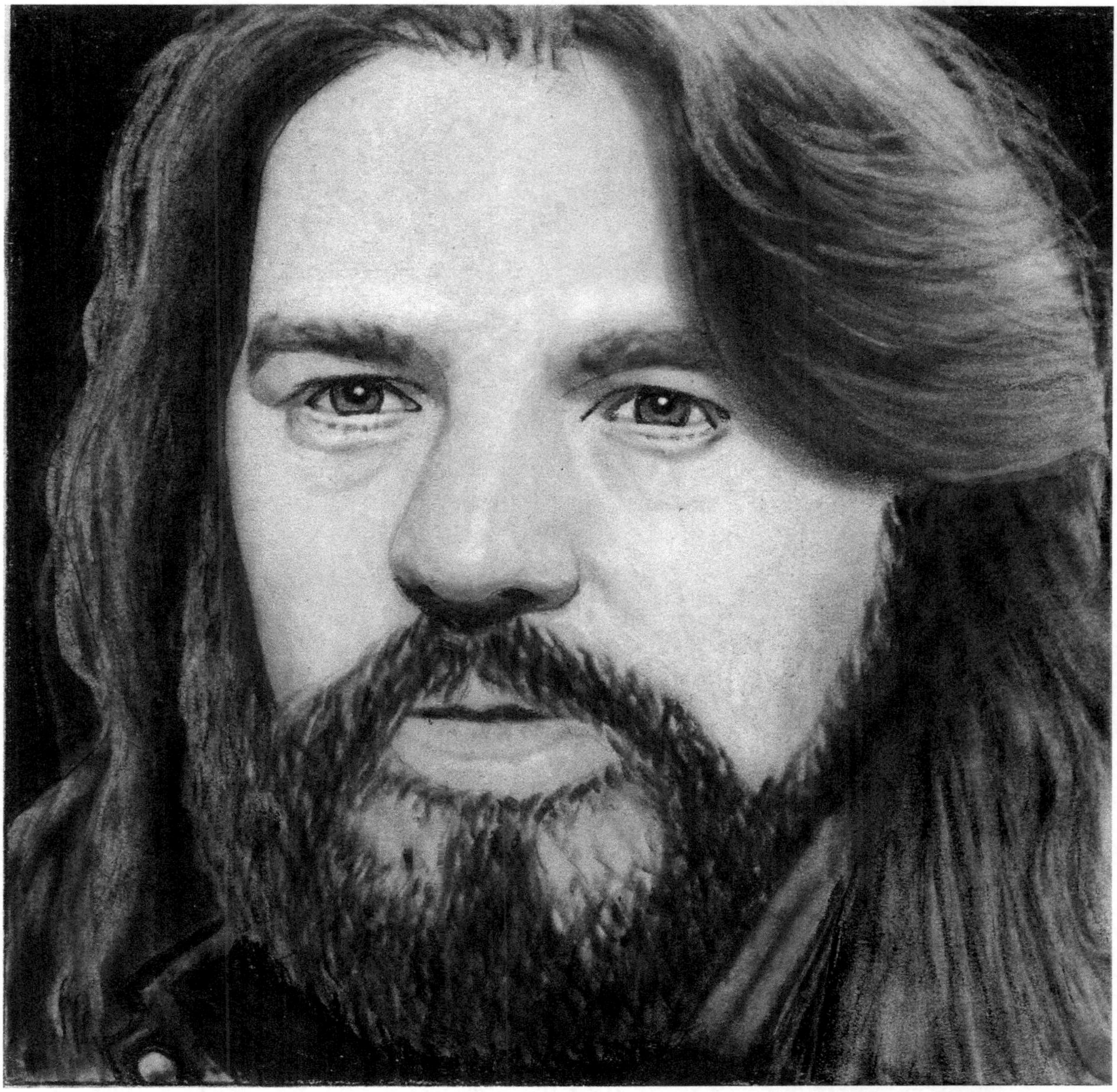

To view how this drawing was masterfully created or to purchase a Limited Edition Framed Artwork of Bob Seger type into your Internet Browser the URL shortcut ➡ **myportrait.art/bobseger**

To listen to his Greatest Songs type into your Internet Browser the URL shortcut ➡ **radio.surf/bobseger**

To view all channels on THE FACE OF MUSIC Internet Radio MEGA Station type into your Internet Browser the URL shortcut ➡ **radio.surf/music**

To inquire about purchasing a Limited Edtion NFT of this portrait type into your Internet Browser the URL shortcut ➡ **myartnft.shop/bobseger**

To view all available NFTs type into your Internet Browser the URL shortcut ➡ **myartnft.shop/all**

# Bobby Bland

(Net worth: $5 Million)(Total Records Sold: 5+ Million)
(Genre: Blues , R&B , Soul )(Height: 5' - 11")

Robert Calvin Bland (born Robert Calvin Brooks; January 27, 1930 – June 23, 2013), known professionally as Bobby "Blue" Bland, was an American blues singer.

Bland developed a sound that mixed gospel with the blues and R&B. He was described as "among the great storytellers of blues and soul music... [who] created tempestuous arias of love, betrayal and resignation, set against roiling, dramatic orchestrations, and left the listener drained but awed." He was sometimes referred to as the "Lion of the Blues" and as the "Sinatra of the Blues". His music was also influenced by Nat King Cole.

Bland was inducted into the Blues Hall of Fame in 1981, the Rock and Roll Hall of Fame in 1992, and the Memphis Music Hall of Fame in 2012. He received the Grammy Lifetime Achievement Award in 1997. The Rock and Roll Hall of Fame described him as "second in stature only to B.B. King as a product of Memphis's Beale Street blues scene".

Bland's first chart success came in 1957 with "Farther Up the Road", which reached number 1 on the R&B chart and number 43 on the Billboard Hot 100. It was followed by a series of hits on the R&B chart, including "Little Boy Blue" (1958). He also recorded an album with Parker, Blues Consolidated, in 1958. Bland's craft was most clearly heard on a series of early-1960s releases, including "Cry Cry Cry", "I Pity the Fool" (number 1 on the R&B chart in 1961) and "Turn On Your Love Light", which became a much-covered standard by many bands. Despite credits to the contrary—often claimed by Robey—many of these classic works were written by Joe Scott. Bland also recorded a hit version of T-Bone Walker's "Call It Stormy Monday (But Tuesday Is Just as Bad)", which was erroneously given the title of a different song, "Stormy Monday Blues".

His last record to reach number 1 on the R&B chart was "That's the Way Love Is", in 1963, but he continued to produce a consistent run of R&B chart entries through the mid-1960s. He barely broke into the mainstream market; his highest-charting song on the pop chart, "Ain't Nothing You Can Do", peaked at number 20 in 1964, in the same week in which the Beatles held down the top five spots. Bland's records mostly sold on the R&B market rather than achieving crossover success. He had 23 Top Ten hits on the Billboard R&B chart. In the book Top R&B/Hip-Hop Singles: 1942–1995, by Joel Whitburn, Bland was ranked number 13 of the all-time top-charting artists.

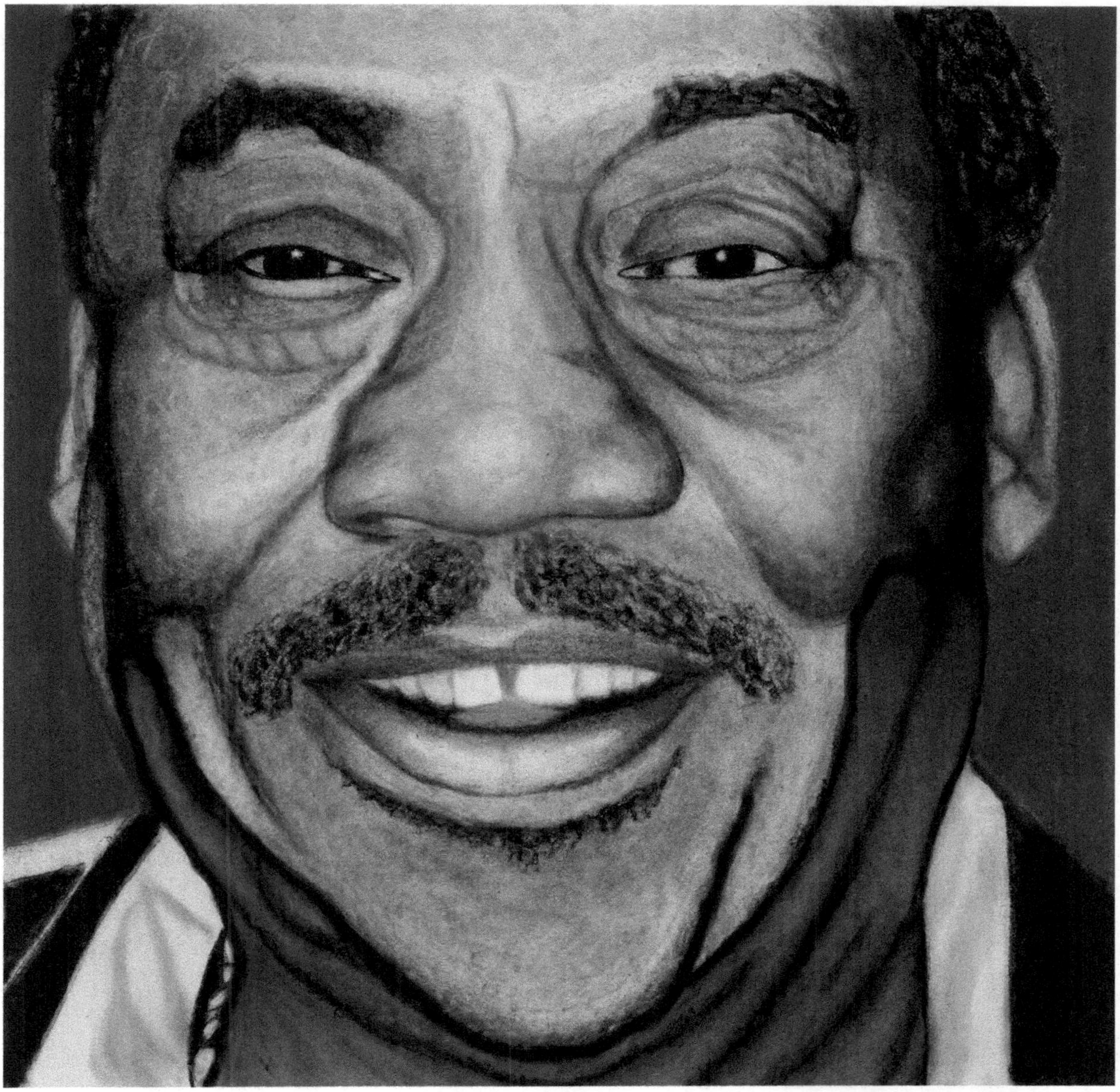

To view how this drawing was masterfully created or to purchase a Limited Edition Framed Artwork of Bobby Bland type into your Internet Browser the URL shortcut ➡ **myportrait.art/bobbybland**

To listen to his Greatest Songs type into your Internet Browser the URL shortcut ➡ **radio.surf/bobbybland**

To view all channels on THE FACE OF MUSIC Internet Radio MEGA Station type into your Internet Browser the URL shortcut ➡ **radio.surf/music**

To inquire about purchasing a Limited Edtion NFT of this portrait type into your Internet Browser the URL shortcut ➡ **myartnft.shop/bobbybland**

To view all available NFTs type into your Internet Browser the URL shortcut ➡ **myartnft.shop/all**

# Bobby Darin

(Net worth: $5 Million)(Total Records Sold: 5+ Million)
(Genre: Vocal / Easy Listening , Rock & Roll )(Height: 5' - 8")

Bobby Darin (born Walden Robert Cassotto; May 14, 1936 – December 20, 1973) was an American singer, songwriter, multi-instrumentalist, impressionist, and actor in film and television. He performed jazz, pop, rock and roll, folk, swing, and country music.

He started his career as a songwriter for Connie Francis. He recorded his first million-selling single, "Splish Splash", in 1958. That was followed by "Dream Lover", "Mack the Knife", and "Beyond the Sea", which brought him worldwide fame. In 1962 he won a Golden Globe Award for his first film, Come September, co-starring his first wife, actress Sandra Dee.

During the 1960s, he became more politically active and worked on Robert F. Kennedy's Democratic presidential campaign. He was present on the night of June 4/5, 1968, at the Ambassador Hotel in Los Angeles at the time of Kennedy's assassination. During the same year, he discovered the woman who had raised him was his grandmother, not his mother as he thought, and learned that the woman he thought was his sister was actually his mother. Those events deeply affected Darin and sent him into a long period of seclusion.

Although he made a successful comeback (in television) in the early 1970s, his health was beginning to fail, as he had always expected, following bouts of rheumatic fever in childhood. The knowledge of his vulnerability had always spurred him on to use his musical talent while still young. He died at the age of 37 after a heart operation in Los Angeles.

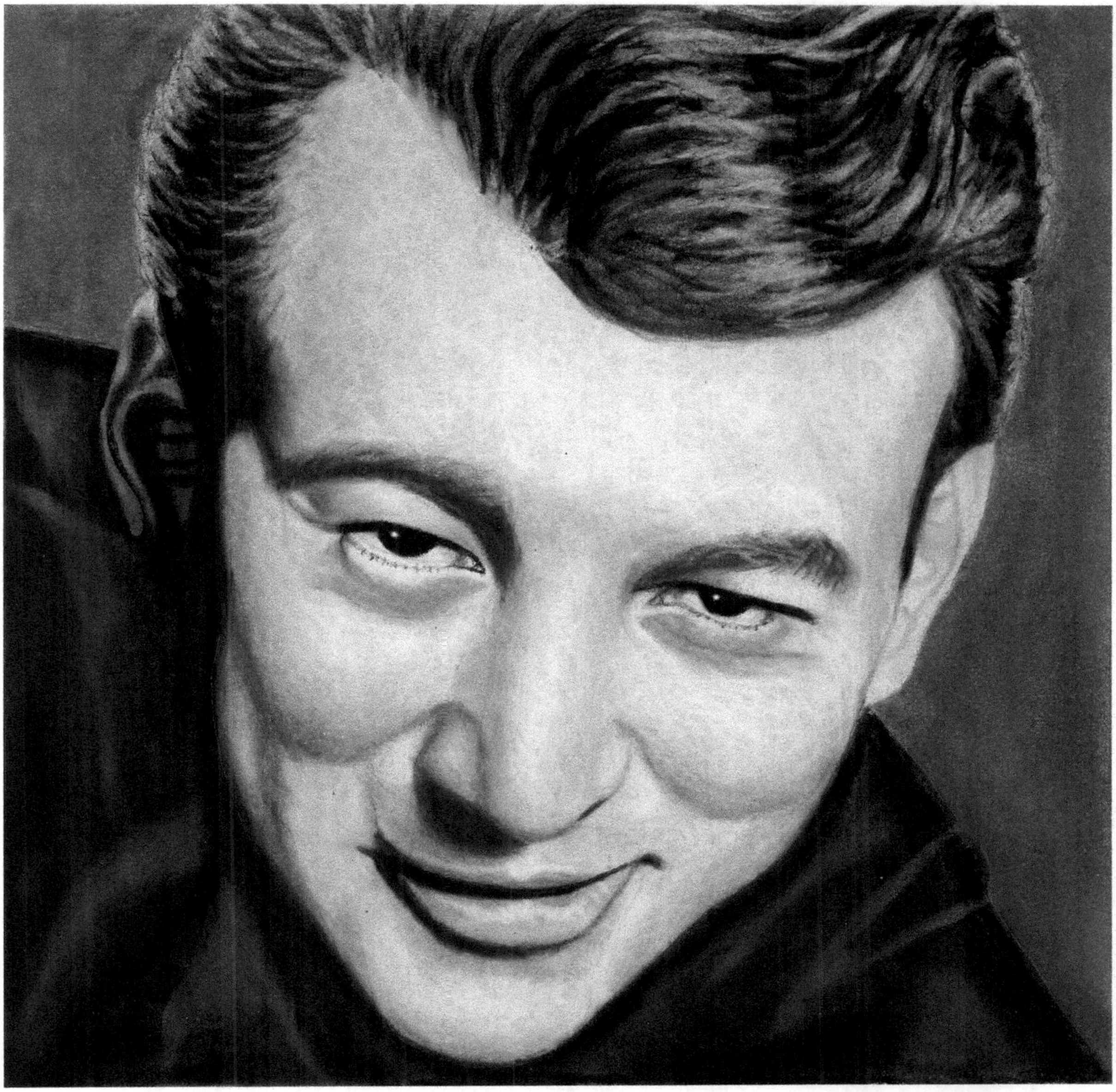

To view how this drawing was masterfully created or to purchase a Limited Edition Framed Artwork of Bobby Darin type into your Internet Browser the URL shortcut ➡ **myportrait.art/bobbydarin**

To listen to his Greatest Songs type into your Internet Browser the URL shortcut ➡ **radio.surf/bobbydarin**

To view all channels on THE FACE OF MUSIC Internet Radio MEGA Station type into your Internet Browser the URL shortcut ➡ **radio.surf/music**

To inquire about purchasing a Limited Edtion NFT of this portrait type into your Internet Browser the URL shortcut ➡ **myartnft.shop/bobbydarin**

To view all available NFTs type into your Internet Browser the URL shortcut ➡ **myartnft.shop/all**

# Bon Jovi

(Total Albums Sold: 100 Million) (Genre: Hard Rock)
Bon Jovi is an American rock band formed in 1983 in Sayreville, New Jersey. It consists of singer Jon Bon Jovi, keyboardist David Bryan, drummer Tico Torres, guitarist Phil X, and bassist Hugh McDonald. Original bassist Alec John Such quit the band in 1994, and longtime guitarist and co-songwriter Richie Sambora left in 2013.
Bon Jovi has released 15 studio albums, five compilations and three live albums. They have sold more than 100 million records worldwide, making them one of the best-selling American rock bands, and performed more than 2,700 concerts in over 50 countries for more than 34 million fans. Bon Jovi was inducted into the UK Music Hall of Fame in 2006, and into the US Rock and Roll Hall of Fame in 2018. The band received the Award of Merit at the American Music Awards in 2004, and Jon Bon Jovi and Richie Sambora were inducted into Songwriters Hall of Fame in 2009.

# Jon Bon Jovi

(Net Worth: $410 Million) (Height: 5'-9")
John Francis Bongiovi Jr. (born March 2, 1962), known professionally as Jon Bon Jovi, is an American singer-songwriter, record producer, philanthropist, and actor. He is best known as the founder and frontman of the Grammy Award-winning rock band Bon Jovi, which was formed in 1983. He has released 15 studio albums with his band as well as two solo albums.
In the 1990s, Bon Jovi started an acting career, starring in the films Moonlight and Valentino and U-571 and appearing on television in Sex and the City, Ally McBeal and The West Wing.
As a songwriter, Bon Jovi was inducted into the Songwriters Hall of Fame in 2009. In 2012, he ranked number 50 on the list of Billboard Magazine's "Power 100", a ranking of "The Most Powerful and Influential People in the Music Business". In 1996, People magazine named him one of the "50 Most Beautiful People in the World". In 2000, People awarded him the title "Sexiest Rock Star".
Bon Jovi was a founder and former majority owner of the Arena Football League team, the Philadelphia Soul. He is the founder of The Jon Bon Jovi Soul Foundation, founded in 2006.

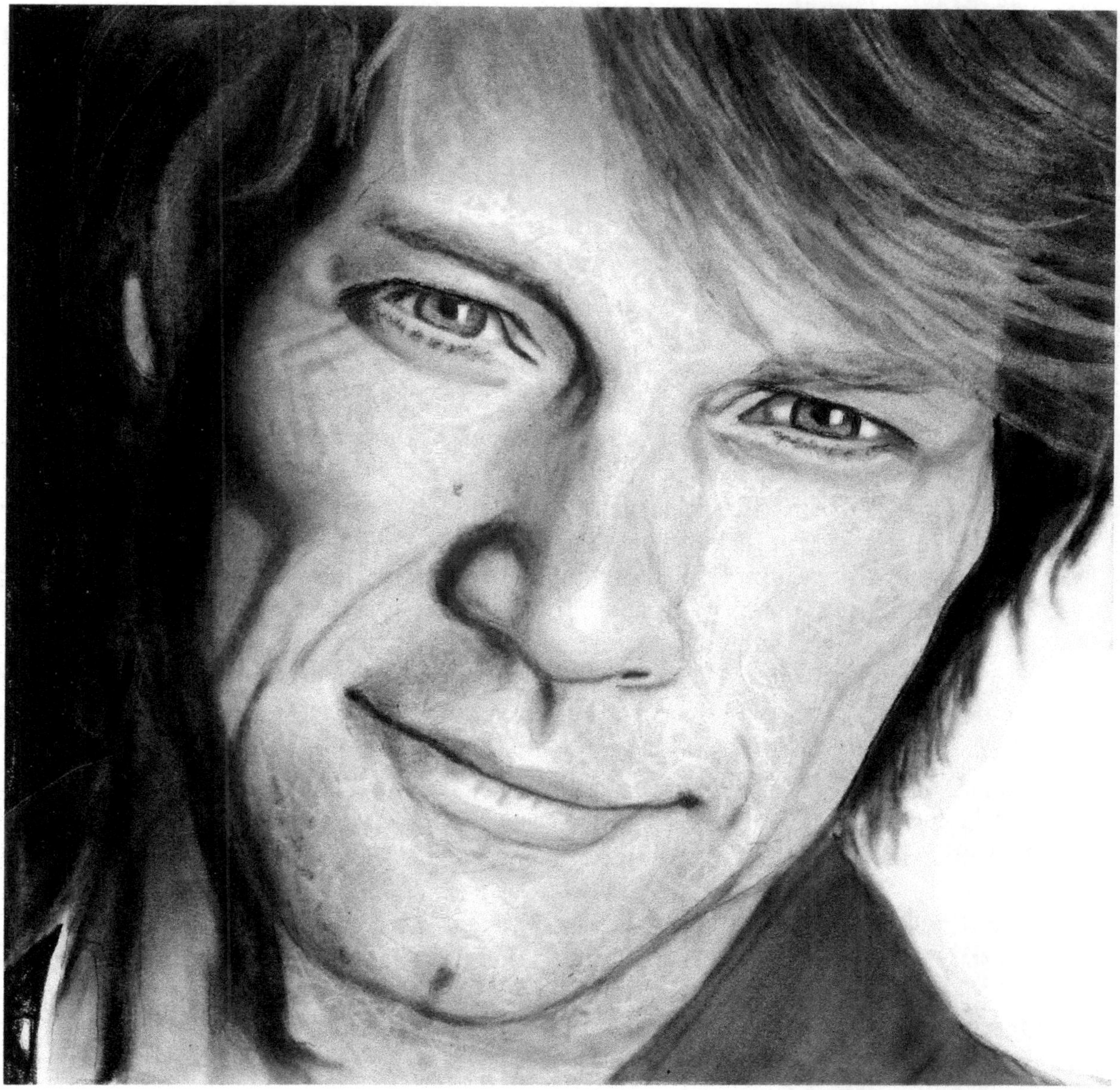

To view how this drawing was masterfully created or to purchase a Limited Edition Framed Artwork of Jon Bon Jovin type into your Internet Browser the URL shortcut ➡ **myportrait.art/jonbonjovi**

To listen to their Greatest Songs type into your Internet Browser the URL shortcut ➡ **radio.surf/bonjovi**

To view all channels on THE FACE OF MUSIC Internet Radio MEGA Station type into your Internet Browser the URL shortcut ➡ **radio.surf/music**

To inquire about purchasing a Limited Edtion NFT of this portrait type into your Internet Browser the URL shortcut ➡ **myartnft.shop/jonbonjovi**

To view all available NFTs type into your Internet Browser the URL shortcut ➡ **myartnft.shop/all**

# Boston

(Total Albums Sold: 75 Million) (Genre: Classic Rock)

Boston is an American rock band from Boston, Massachusetts, which had its most notable successes during the 1970s and 1980s. The band is centered on multi-instrumentalist founder and leader Tom Scholz, who played the majority of instruments on the debut album, and lead vocalist Brad Delp. Boston's best-known songs include "More Than a Feeling", "Peace of Mind", "Foreplay/Long Time", "Rock and Roll Band", "Smokin'", "Don't Look Back", "A Man I'll Never Be", and "Amanda". The band has sold more than 75 million records worldwide, including 31 million albums in the United States, of which 17 million were from its self-titled debut album and seven million were for its second album, Don't Look Back, making the group one of the world's best-selling artists. Altogether, the band has released six studio albums over a career spanning over 46 years. Boston was ranked the 63rd best hard rock artist by VH1. The debut album, Boston, released on August 25, 1976, ranks as one of the best-selling debut albums in U.S. history with over 17 million copies sold.

During the late summer and early autumn of 1976, Boston attracted publicity due to the record sales. However, there was "a conscious effort to de-emphasize Scholz as the total mastermind behind Boston".

After opening for Black Sabbath, Blue Öyster Cult, Foghat and others in the autumn, the band embarked on a headlining tour in the winter and spring of 1976–1977 to support the album. This helped establish Boston as one of rock's top acts within a short time, being nominated for a Grammy award as a "Best New Artist". Boston was the first band in history to make their New York City debut at Madison Square Garden.

The album spawned three singles, "More Than a Feeling", "Long Time", and "Peace of Mind", all of which made the national charts. Additionally, the album peaked at No. 3 on the Billboard 200 and remained on the charts for 132 weeks.

Despite having problems with manager Paul Ahern, being caught in the middle of a fight between Ahern and his business partner Charles McKenzie, and doing most of the recording work alone, Scholz completed the second Boston album two years after the debut album's release. The second album, Don't Look Back, was released by Epic in August 1978.

At the time this was considered a long gap between albums, but Scholz still considered Don't Look Back to be a rush job and was unhappy with the album's second side in particular. Overall, Don't Look Back sold about half as well as the debut album, eventually selling over 7 million records.

# Brad Delp

(Net Worth: $0.5 Million) (Height: 5'-9")

Bradley Edward Delp (June 12, 1951 – March 9, 2007) was an American singer and songwriter, widely known as the lead vocalist of the rock bands Boston and RTZ.

Delp died by suicide by carbon monoxide poisoning at his home on Academy Avenue, in Atkinson, New Hampshire.

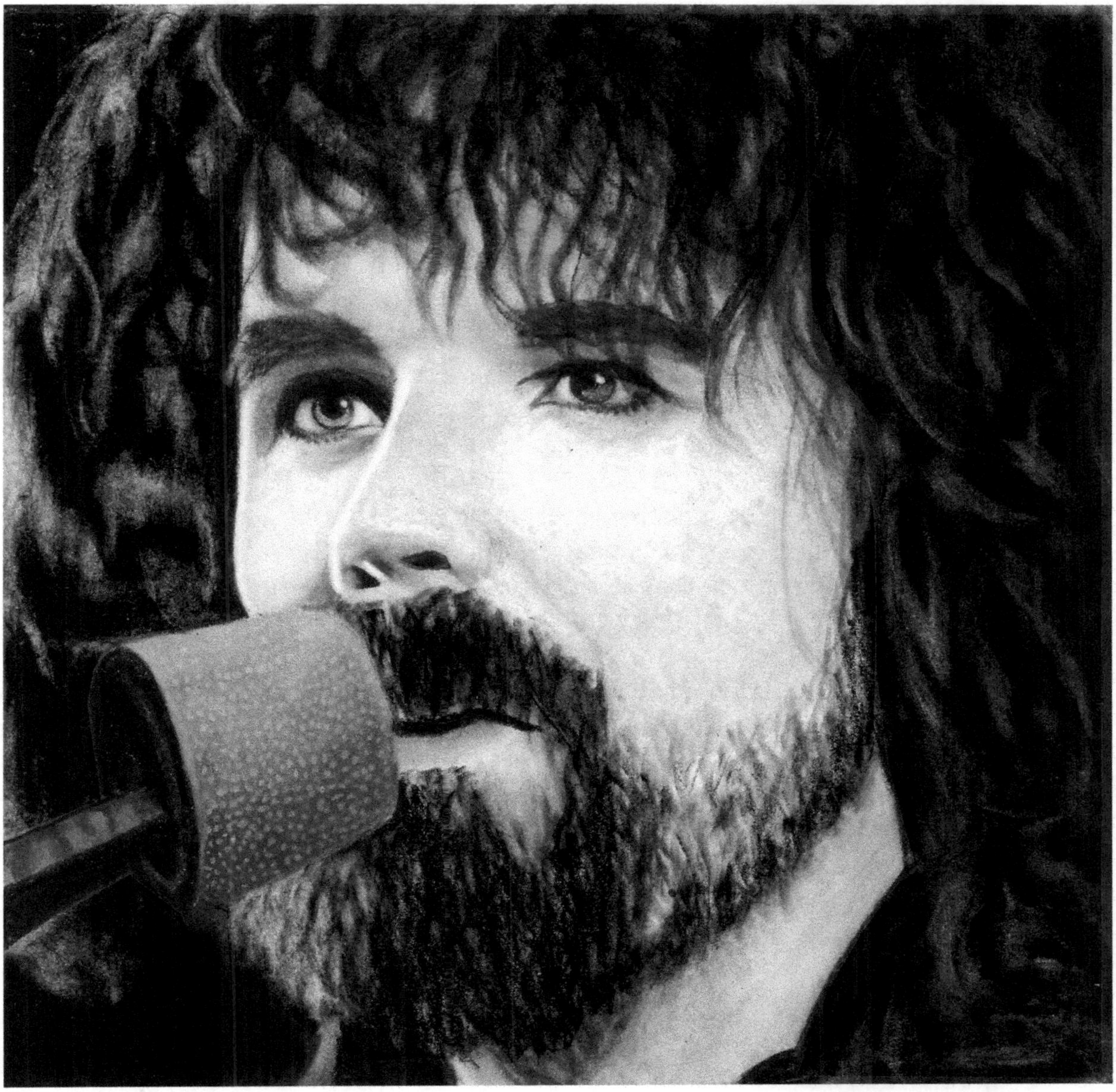

To view how this drawing was masterfully created or to purchase a Limited Edition Framed Artwork of Brad Delp type into your Internet Browser the URL shortcut ➡ **myportrait.art/braddelp**

To listen to their Greatest Songs type into your Internet Browser the URL shortcut ➡ **radio.surf/boston**

To view all channels on THE FACE OF MUSIC Internet Radio MEGA Station type into your Internet Browser the URL shortcut ➡ **radio.surf/music**

To inquire about purchasing a Limited Edtion NFT of this portrait type into your Internet Browser the URL shortcut ➡ **myartnft.shop/braddelp**

To view all available NFTs type into your Internet Browser the URL shortcut ➡ **myartnft.shop/all**

# Britney Spears

(Net worth: $70 Million)(Total Records Sold: 100+Million)
(Genre: Pop)(Height: 5' - 4")

Britney Jean Spears (born December 2, 1981) is an American singer, songwriter, dancer, and actress. She is credited with influencing the revival of teen pop during the late 1990s and early 2000s, for which she is referred to as the "Princess of Pop". After appearing in stage productions and television series, Spears signed with Jive Records in 1997 at age 15. Her first two studio albums, certified diamond in the US ...Baby One More Time (1999) and Oops!... I Did It Again (2000), were global successes and became two of the best-selling albums of all time, along with making her the best-selling teenage artist of all time. The former's title track was named the greatest debut single of all time by Rolling Stone in 2020 and the latter held a 15-year record for fastest-selling album by a female artist in the United States with first-week sales of over 1.3 million copies.

Spears adopted more mature and provocative themes and aesthetics for her next two studio albums, Britney (2001) and In the Zone (2003), and made her feature film debut in a starring role in Crossroads (2002). She became the executive producer of her fifth studio album Blackout (2007), which is often critically referred to as her best work. Due to a series of highly publicized personal struggles, promotion for the album was limited and she was later involuntarily placed in a conservatorship. Since then, she released the chart-topping albums, Circus (2008) and Femme Fatale (2011), the latter of which became her most successful era of singles in the US charts. She embarked on a four-year concert residency, Britney: Piece of Me, at Planet Hollywood Resort & Casino in Las Vegas to promote her next two albums Britney Jean (2013) and Glory (2016). Since 2019, Spears has been involved in a legal dispute over her conservatorship.

Spears has scored six number-one albums on the Billboard 200. She also has four solo number-one singles on the US Billboard Hot 100: "...Baby One More Time", "Womanizer", "3", and "Hold It Against Me". As a featured artist, the "S&M" remix also topped the Billboard chart. Other singles, "Oops!... I Did It Again", "Toxic", and "Scream & Shout", topped the charts in most countries. With "3" in 2009 and "Hold It Against Me" in 2011, she became the second artist after Mariah Carey in the Hot 100's history to debut at number one with two or more songs. Spears's heavily choreographed videography is considered a focal point to the success of her career, for which she has been awarded the Michael Jackson Video Vanguard Award. She has earned numerous awards and accolades, including a Grammy Award; thirteen Guinness World Records; six MTV Video Music Awards; seven Billboard Music Awards, including the Millennium Award; the inaugural Radio Disney Icon Award; and a star on the Hollywood Walk of Fame.Regarded as a pop icon, Spears has sold over 100 million records worldwide, including over 70 million solely in the United States, making her one of the world's best-selling music artists. She was ranked by Billboard as the eighth-biggest artist of the 2000s decade. In the United States, she is the fourth best-selling female album artist of the Nielsen SoundScan era as well as the best-selling female album artist of the 2000s. In 2004, Spears launched a perfume brand with Elizabeth Arden, Inc.; sales exceeded US$1.5 billion as of 2012. Forbes has reported Spears as the highest-paid female musician of 2002 and 2012. She has also topped the list of most searched celebrities seven times in 12 years, a record since the inception of the internet

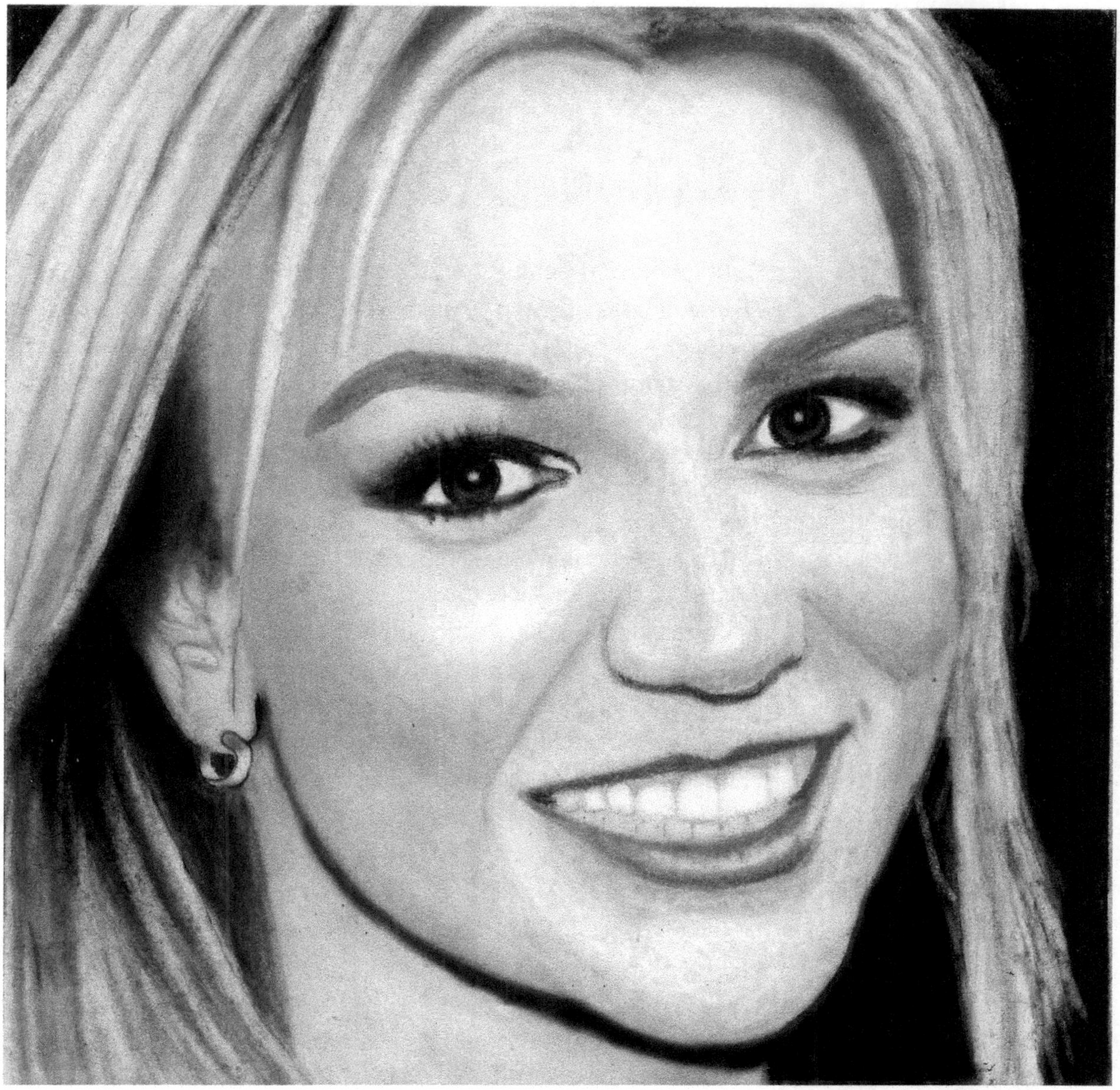

To view how this drawing was masterfully created or to purchase a Limited Edition Framed Artwork of Britney Spears type into your Internet Browser the URL shortcut ➡ **myportrait.art/britneyspears**

To listen to her Greatest Songs type into your Internet Browser the URL shortcut➡ **radio.surf/britneyspears**

To view all channels on THE FACE OF MUSIC Internet Radio MEGA Station type into your Internet Browser the URL shortcut ➡ **radio.surf/music**

To inquire about purchasing a Limited Edtion NFT of this portrait type into your Internet Browser the URL shortcut ➡ **myartnft.shop/britneyspears**

To view all available NFTs type into your Internet Browser the URL shortcut ➡ **myartnft.shop/all**

# Bruce Springsteen

(Net worth: $500 Million)(Total Records Sold: 150+Million)
(Genre: Classic Rock )(Height: 5' - 9")

Bruce Frederick Joseph Springsteen (born September 23, 1949) is an American singer, songwriter, and musician who is both a solo artist and the leader of the E Street Band. Originally from the Jersey Shore, he received critical acclaim for his early 1970s albums and attained worldwide fame upon the release of Born to Run in 1975. During a career that has spanned five decades, Springsteen has become known for his poetic, socially conscious lyrics and energetic stage performances, sometimes lasting up to four hours in length. He has been given the nickname "The Boss". He has recorded both rock albums and folk-oriented works, and his lyrics often address the experiences and struggles of working-class Americans.

Born in the U.S.A. (1984) is Springsteen's most commercially successful album, making him one of the most successful rock figures of the 1980s. It was certified 15× platinum in the US and has sold 30 million copies worldwide, making it one of the best-selling albums of all time. Seven of its singles reached the top 10 of the Billboard Hot 100 including the title track, which was a bitter commentary on the treatment of Vietnam veterans — some of whom were Springsteen's friends. Advocating for the rights of the common working-class man, the song made a huge political impact. Springsteen's other best-known songs include "Born to Run" (1975), "Thunder Road" (1975), "Badlands" (1978), "Hungry Heart" (1980), "The River" (1980), "Atlantic City" (1982), "Dancing in the Dark" (1984), "I'm on Fire" (1984), "Glory Days" (1985), "Brilliant Disguise" (1987), "Human Touch" (1992), "Streets of Philadelphia" (1994), and "The Rising" (2002).

Among the album era's prominent acts, Springsteen has sold more than 150 million records worldwide and more than 64 million albums in the United States, making him one of the world's best-selling music artists. He has earned numerous awards for his work, including 20 Grammy Awards, two Golden Globes, an Academy Award, and a Tony Award (for Springsteen on Broadway). Springsteen was inducted into both the Songwriters Hall of Fame and the Rock and Roll Hall of Fame in 1999, received the Kennedy Center Honors in 2009, was named MusiCares person of the year in 2013, and was awarded the Presidential Medal of Freedom by President Barack Obama in 2016. He is ranked 23rd on Rolling Stone's list of the Greatest Artists of All Time.

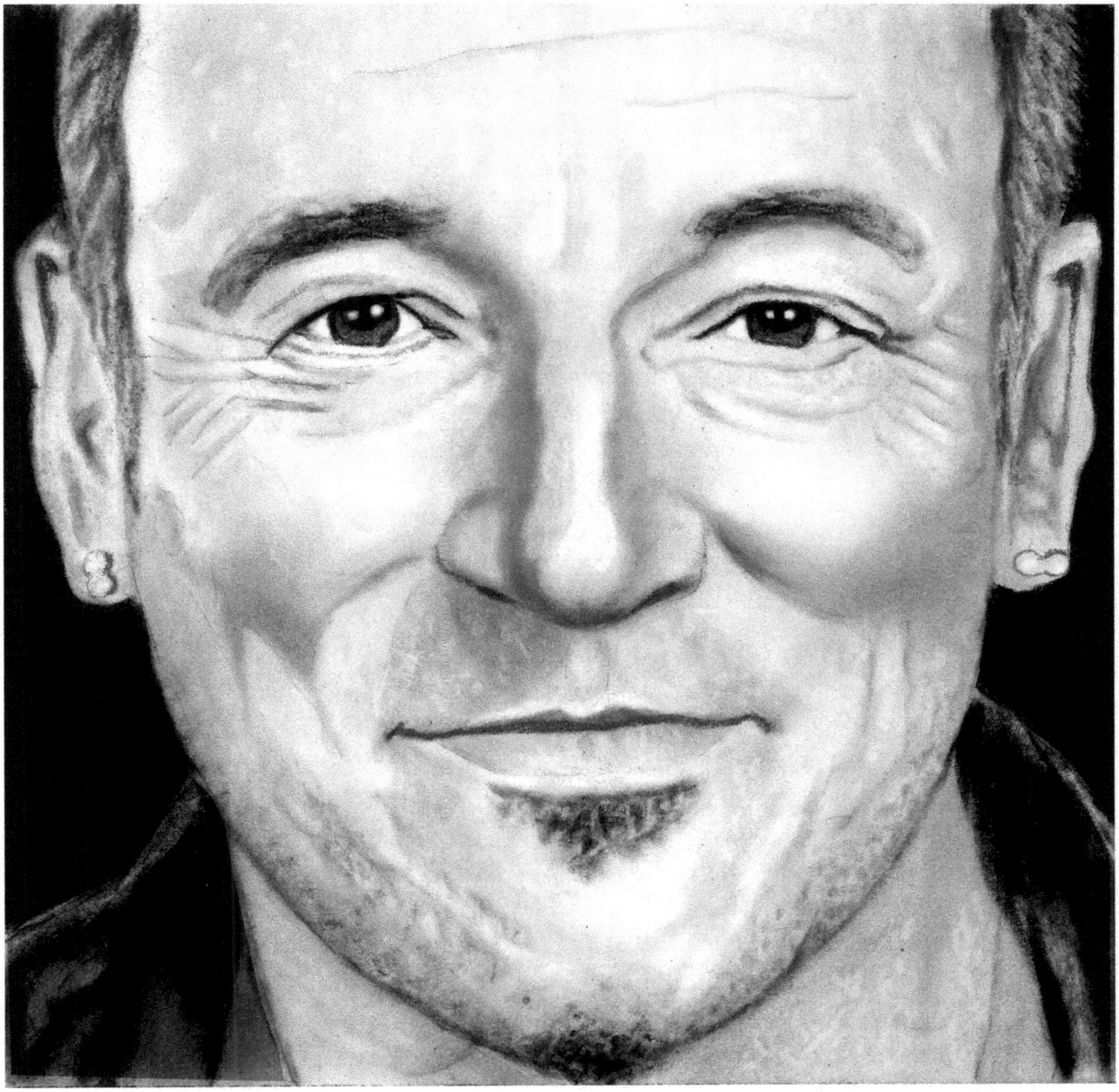

To view how this drawing was masterfully created or to purchase a Limited Edition Framed Artwork of Bruce Springsteen type into your Internet Browser the URL shortcut ➡ **myportrait.art/brucespringsteen**

To listen to his Greatest Songs type into your Internet Browser the URL shortcut ➡ **radio.surf/brucespringsteen**

To view all channels on THE FACE OF MUSIC Internet Radio MEGA Station type into your Internet Browser the URL shortcut ➡ **radio.surf/music**

To inquire about purchasing a Limited Edtion NFT of this portrait type into your Internet Browser the URL shortcut ➡ **myartnft.shop/brucespringsteen**

To view all available NFTs type into your Internet Browser the URL shortcut ➡ **myartnft.shop/all**

# Bryan Adams

(Net worth: $65 Million)(Total Records Sold: 100+ Million)
(Genre: Rock )(Height: 5' - 8")

Bryan Guy Adams OC OBC (born 5 November 1959) is a Canadian guitarist, singer, composer, record producer, photographer, and philanthropist. With several number 1 singles and albums in various countries, Adams has sold over 100 million records worldwide. Adams was the most played artist on Canadian radio in the 2010s and he has had 25 Top 15 singles in Canada, and a dozen or more in the US, UK and Australia.

Adams joined his first band at age 15 and at age 20 his eponymous debut album was released. He rose to fame in North America with 1983 Top 10 album Cuts Like a Knife, featuring its title track and the ballad "Straight From the Heart", his first US Top 10 hit. His 1984 album, Reckless, made him a global star with tracks like "Run to You" and "Summer of '69", both Top 10 hits in the US and Canada, and the power ballad "Heaven", a US number 1 hit. His 1987 album Into the Fire went to number 2 in Canada and the Top 10 in several other countries.

In 1991, Adams's released "(Everything I Do) I Do It for You", which went to number 1 in at least 19 countries, including for 16 and 18 straight weeks in the UK, and Europe overall, both records. It is one of the best-selling singles of all time, having sold more than 15 million copies worldwide. The song was included on Adams' Waking Up the Neighbours (1991), a worldwide number 1 album that sold 16 million copies, including being certified diamond in Canada. Other international Top 10 hits off the album were the Canadian number 1 songs "Can't Stop This Thing We Started" and "Thought I'd Died and Gone to Heaven". Beginning in 1993, Adams' hits were mostly ballads, including the worldwide number 1 or 2 hits: "Please Forgive Me"; "All for Love" (1993); and "Have You Ever Really Loved a Woman?" (1995), the latter two topping the U.S. Billboard Hot 100.

In 1996, Adams' 18 til I Die was a Top 5 album in many countries, but only reached number 31 in the US. He did duets with Barbra Streisand ("I Finally Found Someone" (1996), his last US Top 10 hit) and Melanie C ("When You're Gone" (1998), an international Top 5 hit). In the 1990s, Adams had six European Radio Airplay number 1 songs for 32 weeks, the fourth and third most, respectively; and three number 1 songs on the European Sales Chart for 29 weeks total, the most weeks of any artist. Since 1999, Adams released seven albums, three reaching number 1 in Canada, and most reaching the Top 10 in the UK, Germany and elsewhere.

In 2008, Adams was ranked 38th on the list of all-time top artists on the Billboard Hot 100. Adams has won 20 Juno Awards and a Grammy Award for Best Song Written for a Motion Picture or Television amongst 15 Grammy nominations, and has been nominated for five Golden Globe Awards and three Academy Awards for his songwriting for films. Adams has been inducted into the Hollywood Walk of Fame, Canada's Walk of Fame, the Canadian Broadcast Hall of Fame, and the Canadian Music Hall of Fame. On 1 May 2010, Adams received the Governor General's Performing Arts Award for his 30 years of contributions to the arts.

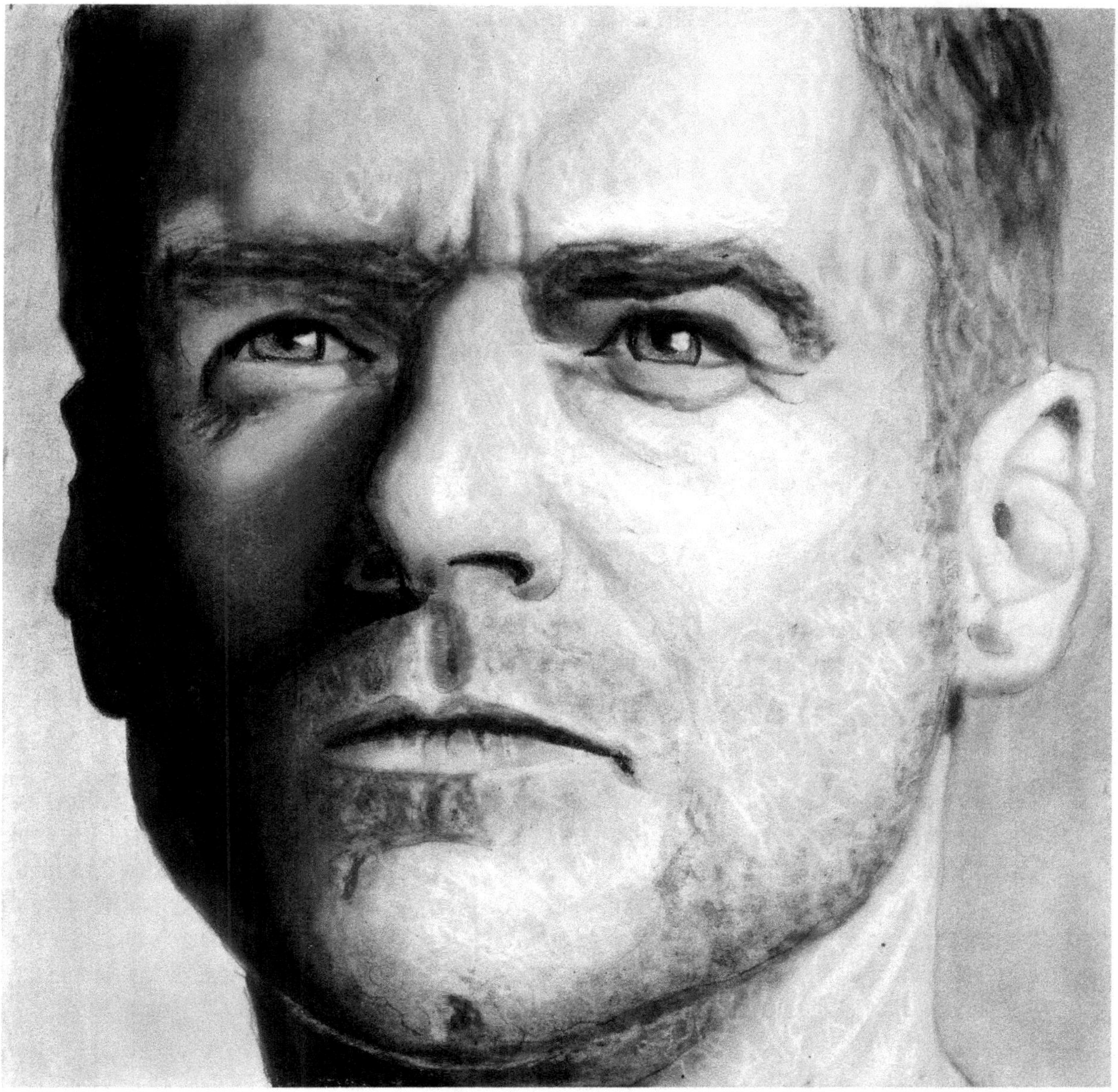

To view how this drawing was masterfully created or to purchase a Limited Edition Framed Artwork of Bryan Adams type into your Internet Browser the URL shortcut ➡ **myportrait.art/bryanadams**

To listen to his Greatest Songs type into your Internet Browser the URL shortcut ➡ **radio.surf/bryanadams**

To view all channels on THE FACE OF MUSIC Internet Radio MEGA Station type into your Internet Browser the URL shortcut ➡ **radio.surf/music**

To inquire about purchasing a Limited Edtion NFT of this portrait type into your Internet Browser the URL shortcut ➡ **myartnft.shop/bryanadams**

To view all available NFTs type into your Internet Browser the URL shortcut ➡ **myartnft.shop/all**

# Buddy Holly

(Net worth: $1 Million)(Total Records Sold: 5 Million)
(Genre: Rock & Roll , Rockabilly , Pop , Country )(Height: 6' - 0")

Charles Hardin Holley (September 7, 1936 – February 3, 1959), known professionally as Buddy Holly, was an American singer-songwriter who was a central and pioneering figure of mid-1950s rock and roll. He was born in Lubbock, Texas, to a musical family during the Great Depression, and learned to play guitar and sing alongside his siblings. His style was influenced by gospel music, country music, and rhythm and blues acts, which he performed in Lubbock with his friends from high school.

He made his first appearance on local television in 1952, and the following year he formed the group "Buddy and Bob" with his friend Bob Montgomery. In 1955, after opening for Elvis Presley, he decided to pursue a career in music. He opened for Presley three times that year; his band's style shifted from country and western to entirely rock and roll. In October that year, when he opened for Bill Haley & His Comets, he was spotted by Nashville scout Eddie Crandall, who helped him get a contract with Decca Records.

Holly's recording sessions at Decca were produced by Owen Bradley, who had become famous for producing orchestrated country hits for stars like Patsy Cline. Unhappy with Bradley's musical style and control in the studio, Holly went to producer Norman Petty in Clovis, New Mexico, and recorded a demo of "That'll Be the Day", among other songs. Petty became the band's manager and sent the demo to Brunswick Records, which released it as a single credited to "The Crickets", which became the name of Holly's band. In September 1957, as the band toured, "That'll Be the Day" topped the US and UK singles charts. Its success was followed in October by another major hit, "Peggy Sue".

The album The "Chirping" Crickets, released in November 1957, reached number five on the UK Albums Chart. Holly made his second appearance on The Ed Sullivan Show in January 1958 and soon after toured Australia and then the UK. In early 1959, he assembled a new band, consisting of future country music star Waylon Jennings (bass), famed session musician Tommy Allsup (guitar), and Carl Bunch (drums), and embarked on a tour of the midwestern U.S. After a show in Clear Lake, Iowa, he chartered an airplane to travel to his next show, in Moorhead, Minnesota. Soon after takeoff, the plane crashed, killing Holly, Ritchie Valens, The Big Bopper, and pilot Roger Peterson in a tragedy later referred to by Don McLean as "The Day the Music Died" in his song "American Pie".

During his short career, Holly wrote and recorded many songs. He is often regarded as the artist who defined the traditional rock-and-roll lineup of two guitars, bass, and drums. He was a major influence on later popular music artists, including Elvis Presley, Bob Dylan, The Beatles, The Rolling Stones, Eric Clapton, The Hollies (who named themselves in his honor), Elvis Costello, Marshall Crenshaw (who later played Holly), and Elton John. He was among the first artists inducted into the Rock and Roll Hall of Fame, in 1986. Rolling Stone magazine ranked him number 13 in its list of "100 Greatest Artists".

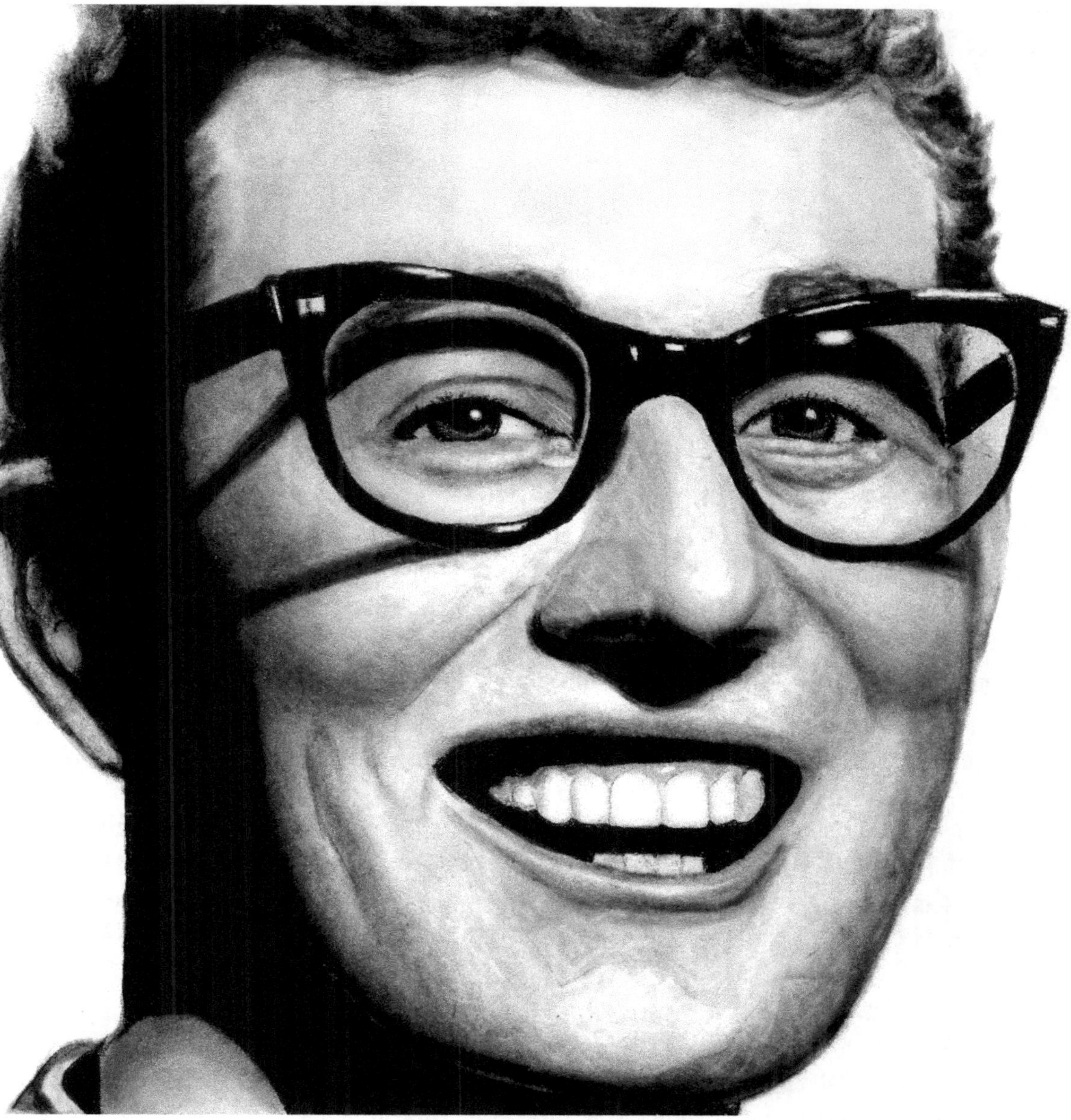

To view how this drawing was masterfully created or to purchase a Limited Edition Framed Artwork of Buddy Holly type into your Internet Browser the URL shortcut ➡ **myportrait.art/buddyholly**

To listen to his Greatest Songs type into your Internet Browser the URL shortcut ➡ **radio.surf/buddyholly**

To view all channels on THE FACE OF MUSIC Internet Radio MEGA Station type into your Internet Browser the URL shortcut ➡ **radio.surf/music**

To inquire about purchasing a Limited Edtion NFT of this portrait type into your Internet Browser the URL shortcut ➡ **myartnft.shop/buddyholly**

To view all available NFTs type into your Internet Browser the URL shortcut ➡ **myartnft.shop/all**

# Busta Rhymes

(Net worth: $20 Million)(Total Records Sold: 9 Million)
(Genre: Hip-Hop)(Height: 6′ - 2″)

Trevor George Smith Jr. (born May 20, 1972), known professionally as Busta Rhymes, is a Jamaican-American rapper, singer, record producer, actor, and record executive. Chuck D of Public Enemy gave him the moniker Busta Rhymes, after NFL and CFL wide receiver George "Buster" Rhymes. He has received 11 Grammy Award nominations for his work.

About.com included him on its list of the 50 Greatest MCs of Our Time (1987–2007), while Steve Huey of AllMusic called him one of the best and most prolific rappers of the 1990s. In 2012, The Source placed him on their list of the Top 50 Lyricists of All Time. MTV has called him "one of hip-hop's greatest visual artists".

Busta Rhymes was an original member of Leaders of the New School. He later went on and founded the record label Conglomerate (initially Flipmode Entertainment) and production crew The Conglomerate (formerly Flipmode Squad). In November 2011, Busta Rhymes signed a deal with Cash Money Records. On July 23, 2014, Busta Rhymes announced that he left Cash Money Records due to creative differences and was no longer on Republic.

He has released ten studio albums, with the first being the 1996 platinum-selling album The Coming. His list of hit singles include "Woo Hah!! Got You All in Check", "Put Your Hands Where My Eyes Could See", "Dangerous", "Turn It Up" (Remix)/"Fire It Up", "Gimme Some More", "What's It Gonna Be?", "Pass the Courvoisier, Part II", "I Know What You Want" and "Touch It".

Busta Rhymes was born Trevor George Smith Jr. in Brooklyn, New York City on May 20, 1972, to Geraldine Green and Trevor Smith Sr., both from Jamaica. At age 12, Smith's family moved to Uniondale, Long Island,. For a short while, Smith attended George Westinghouse Career and Technical Education High School in Brooklyn with future rappers Christopher "The Notorious B.I.G" Wallace and Shawn "Jay Z" Carter. Smith eventually graduated from Long Island's Uniondale High School in 1991.

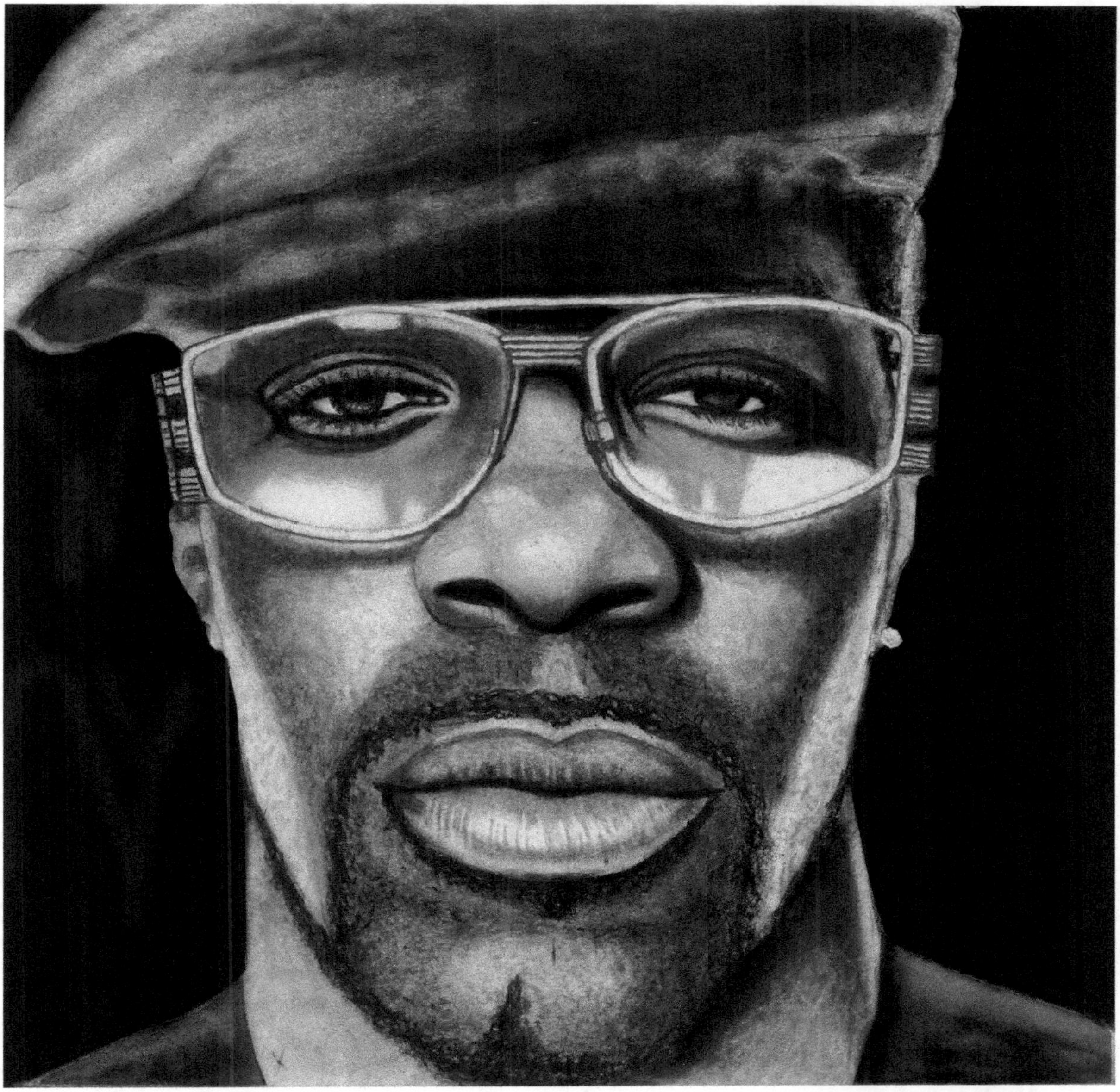

To view how this drawing was masterfully created or to purchase a Limited Edition Framed Artwork of Busta Rhymes type into your Internet Browser the URL shortcut ➡ **myportrait.art/bustarhymes**

To listen to his Greatest Songs type into your Internet Browser the URL shortcut ➡ **radio.surf/bustarhymes**

To view all channels on THE FACE OF MUSIC Internet Radio MEGA Station type into your Internet Browser the URL shortcut ➡ **radio.surf/music**

To inquire about purchasing a Limited Edition NFT of this portrait type into your Internet Browser the URL shortcut ➡ **myartnft.shop/bustarhymes**

To view all available NFTs type into your Internet Browser the URL shortcut ➡ **myartnft.shop/all**

# Byrds, The

(Genre: Rock , Pop , Psychedelic , Folk Rock)

The Byrds were an American rock band formed in Los Angeles, California in 1964 The band underwent multiple lineup changes throughout its existence, with frontman Roger McGuinn (known as Jim McGuinn until mid-1967) remaining the sole consistent member. Although their time as one of the most popular groups in the world only lasted for a short period in the mid-1960s, the Byrds are today considered by critics to be among the most influential rock acts of their era. Their signature blend of clear harmony singing and McGuinn's jangly twelve-string Rickenbacker guitar was "absorbed into the vocabulary of rock" and has continued to be influential.

Initially, the Byrds pioneered the musical genre of folk rock as a popular format in 1965, by melding the influence of the Beatles and other British Invasion bands with contemporary and traditional folk music on their first and second albums, and the hit singles "Mr. Tambourine Man" and "Turn! Turn! Turn!". As the 1960s progressed, the band was influential in originating psychedelic rock and raga rock, with their song "Eight Miles High" and the albums Fifth Dimension (1966), Younger Than Yesterday (1967) and The Notorious Byrd Brothers (1968). The band also played a pioneering role in the development of country rock, with the 1968 album Sweetheart of the Rodeo representing their fullest immersion into the genre.

The original five-piece lineup of the band consisted of Jim McGuinn (lead guitar, vocals), Gene Clark (tambourine, vocals), David Crosby (rhythm guitar, vocals), Chris Hillman (bass guitar, vocals), and Michael Clarke (drums). This version of the band was relatively short-lived and by early 1966 Clark had left due to problems associated with anxiety and his increasing isolation within the group. The Byrds continued as a quartet until late 1967, when Crosby and Clarke also departed. McGuinn and Hillman decided to recruit new members, including country rock pioneer Gram Parsons, but by late 1968, Hillman and Parsons had also exited the band. McGuinn elected to rebuild the band's membership; between 1968 and 1973, he helmed a new incarnation of the Byrds that featured guitarist Clarence White, among others. McGuinn disbanded the then-current lineup in early 1973 to make way for a reunion of the original quintet. The Byrds' final album was released in March 1973, with the reunited group disbanding later that year.Several former members of the Byrds went on to successful careers of their own, either as solo artists or as members of such groups as Crosby, Stills, Nash & Young, the Flying Burrito Brothers, McGuinn, Clark & Hillman, and the Desert Rose Band. In 1991, the Byrds were inducted into the Rock and Roll Hall of Fame, an occasion that saw the five original members performing together for the last time. Gene Clark died of a heart attack later that year, while Michael Clarke died of liver failure in 1993. McGuinn, Crosby, and Hillman remain active.

# Roger McGuinn

(Net Worth: $30 Million) (Height: 6'-1")

James Roger McGuinn (born James Joseph McGuinn III; July 13, 1942) is an American musician. He is best known for being the frontman and leader of the Byrds. He was inducted into the Rock and Roll Hall of Fame for his work with the Byrds.

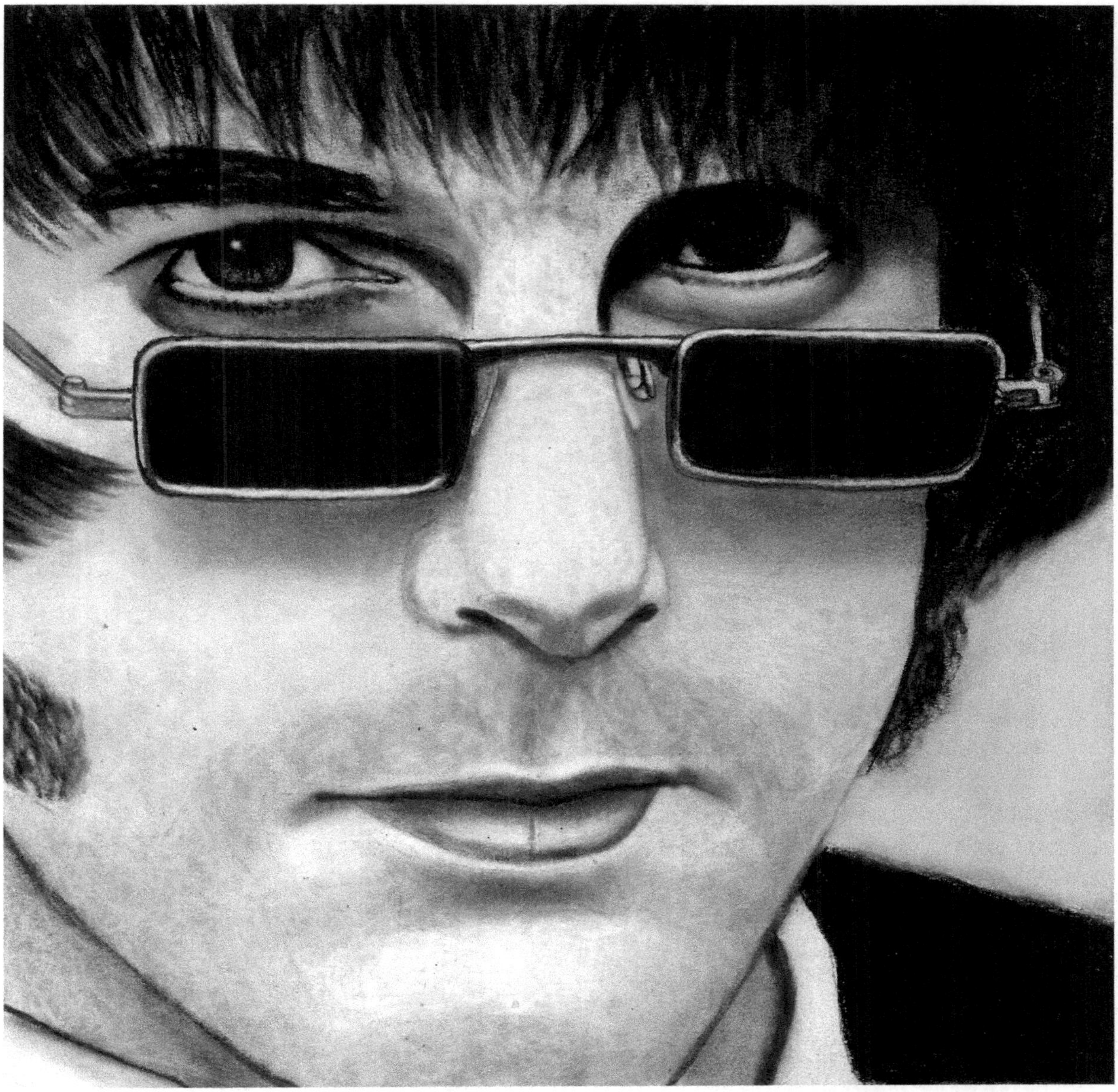

To view how this drawing was masterfully created or to purchase a Limited Edition Framed Artwork of Roger McGuinn type into your Internet Browser the URL shortcut ➡ **myportrait.art/rogermcguinn**

To listen to their Greatest Songs type into your Internet Browser the URL shortcut ➡ **radio.surf/thebyrds**

To view all channels on THE FACE OF MUSIC Internet Radio MEGA Station type into your Internet Browser the URL shortcut ➡ **radio.surf/music**

To inquire about purchasing a Limited Edtion NFT of this portrait type into your Internet Browser the URL shortcut ➡ **myartnft.shop/rogermcguinn**

To view all available NFTs type into your Internet Browser the URL shortcut ➡ **myartnft.shop/all**

# Captain and Tennille

(Total Records Sold: Millions) (Genre: Soft Rock, Pop)

Captain & Tennille were American recording artists whose primary success occurred in the 1970s. The husband-and-wife team were "Captain" Daryl Dragon (August 27, 1942 – January 2, 2019) and Toni Tennille (born May 8, 1940). They have five albums certified gold or platinum and scored numerous hits on the US singles charts, the most enduring of which included "Love Will Keep Us Together", "Do That to Me One More Time", and "Muskrat Love". They hosted their own television variety series on ABC in 1976–77.

In 1972, Toni Tennille was the co-writer of an ecology-themed musical, Mother Earth. At that time, Daryl Dragon (son of composer Carmen Dragon) was working as a keyboardist for the Beach Boys, where thanks to his habit of wearing a ship captain's hat while performing he got his stage name "Captain". When Tennille's show was preparing to move from San Francisco's Marines Memorial Theatre to Southern California's South Coast Repertory, a call was put out for a replacement keyboardist. Dragon was between tours when he heard about the opening, met Tennille in San Francisco to audition, and landed the gig. Dragon later reciprocated by recommending Tennille to the Beach Boys when the band needed an additional keyboardist, and they hired her. She toured with them for a year, and has since been known as the Beach Boys' one and only "Beach Girl." Realizing their collaborative potential when the tour was over, Tennille and Dragon began performing as a duo at the Smokehouse Restaurant in Encino, California. They started to become popular in the Los Angeles area, and their early version of the Tennille-penned "The Way I Want to Touch You" became popular on a local radio station. This led to a recording contract with A&M Records.

Their first hit single, a rendition of Neil Sedaka's and Howard Greenfield's "Love Will Keep Us Together", reached #1 on the Billboard Hot 100 singles chart nine weeks after its 1975 debut, and went on to win the Grammy Award for Record of the Year. It sold over 1 million copies and was awarded a Gold disc by the RIAA on July 1, 1975. Tennille paid tribute to Sedaka in the recording when she sang the overdub "Sedaka's back" at the outro. The duo successfully mined the Sedaka songbook a number of times over their chartmaking career. Two of their other hit singles were the Sedaka co-writes "Lonely Night (Angel Face)" and "You Never Done It Like That". Their Spanish recording of "Love Will Keep Us Together", "Por Amor Viviremos", also charted in 1975; it was the first time two versions of the same single charted simultaneously. Tennille and Dragon included renditions of several other Sedaka songs on their albums.

Tennille and Dragon married on November 11, 1975. A wedding date of Valentine's Day 1974 had long been erroneously reported (on their show, Tennille claimed they were married on Valentine's Day), such as on the February 14, 1976 edition of Casey Kasem's American Top 40.

# Toni Tennille

(Net Worth: $4.5 Million) (Height: 5'-10")

Cathryn Antoinette "Toni" Tennille (born May 8, 1940) is an American singer-songwriter and keyboardist, best known as one-half of the 1970s duo Captain & Tennille with her former husband Daryl Dragon; their signature song is "Love Will Keep Us Together". Tennille also did musical work independently of Dragon, including solo albums and session work.

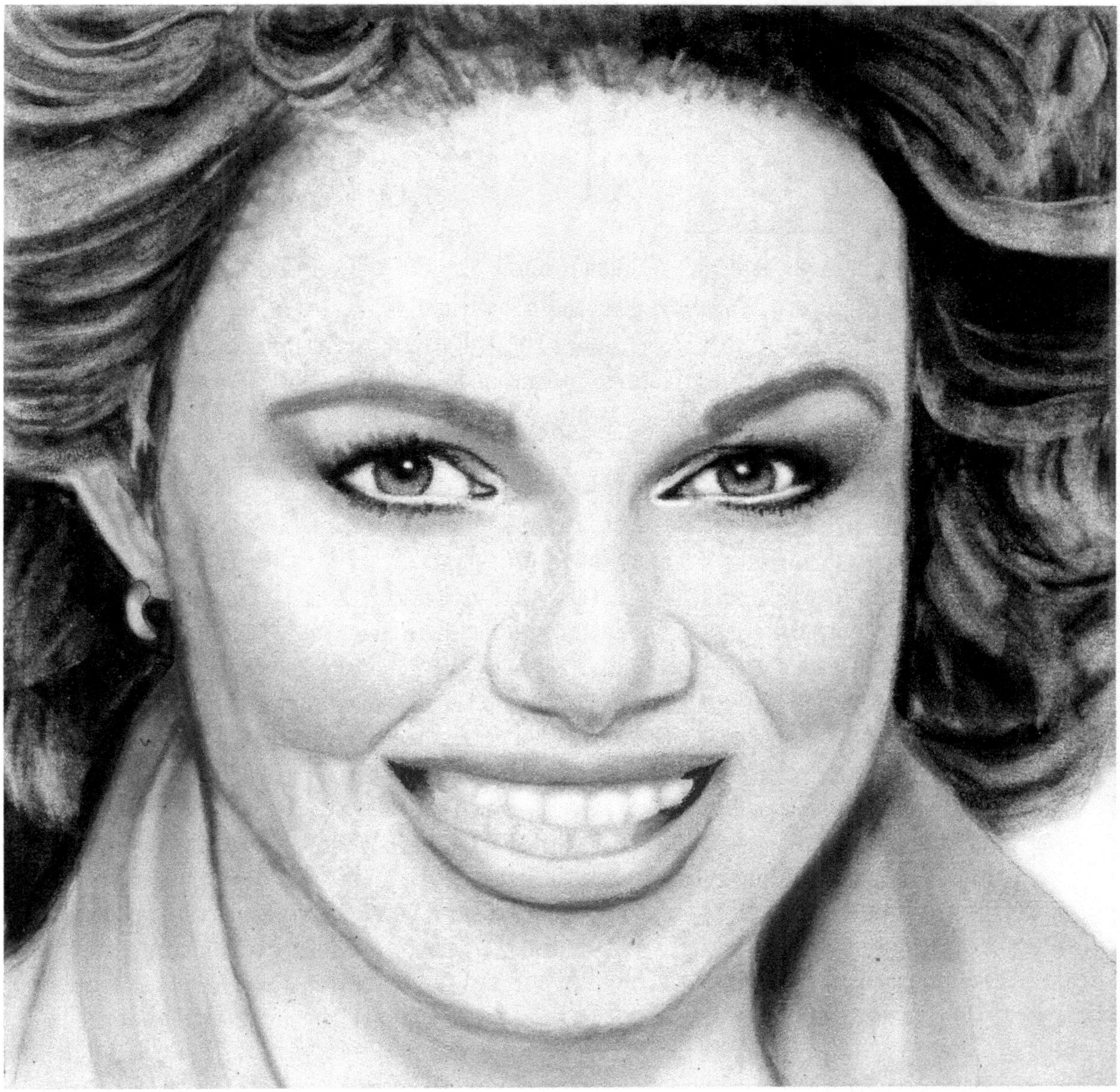

To view how this drawing was masterfully created or to purchase a Limited Edition Framed Artwork of Toni Tennille type into your Internet Browser the URL shortcut ➡ **myportrait.art/tonitennille**

To listen to their Greatest Songs type into your Internet Browser the URL shortcut
➡ **radio.surf/captainandtennille**

To view all channels on THE FACE OF MUSIC Internet Radio MEGA Station type into your Internet Browser the URL shortcut ➡ **radio.surf/music**

To inquire about purchasing a Limited Edition NFT of this portrait type into your Internet Browser the URL shortcut ➡ **myartnft.shop/tonitennille**

To view all available NFTs type into your Internet Browser the URL shortcut ➡ **myartnft.shop/all**

# Carl Perkins

(Net worth: $7 Million)(Total Records Sold: Millions)
(Genre: Rockabilly)(Height: 6' - 1")

Carl Lee Perkins (April 9, 1932 – January 19, 1998) was an American singer-songwriter who recorded most notably at the Sun Studio, in Memphis, beginning in 1954. Amongst his best-known songs are "Blue Suede Shoes", "Matchbox" and "Everybody's Trying to Be My Baby".

According to Charlie Daniels, "Carl Perkins' songs personified the rockabilly era, and Carl Perkins' sound personifies the rockabilly sound more so than anybody involved in it, because he never changed."

Perkins's songs were recorded by artists (and friends) as influential as Elvis Presley, the Beatles, Jimi Hendrix, Johnny Cash and Eric Clapton which further established his place in the history of popular music. Paul McCartney claimed that "if there were no Carl Perkins, there would be no Beatles."

Called "the King of Rockabilly", he was inducted into the Rock and Roll Hall of Fame, the Rockabilly Hall of Fame, the Memphis Music Hall of Fame, and the Nashville Songwriters Hall of Fame. He also received a Grammy Hall of Fame Award.

Perkins was born in Tiptonville, Tennessee, the son of poor sharecroppers Buck and Louise Perkins (misspelled on his birth certificate as "Perkings"). Beginning at the age of six, he worked long hours in the cotton fields with his family, whether school was in session or not. He grew up hearing southern gospel music sung by white friends in church and by African-American field workers working in the cotton fields. On Saturday nights Perkins would listen to the Grand Ole Opry on his father's radio. Roy Acuff's broadcasts inspired him to ask his parents for a guitar. Since they could not afford one, his father made one from a cigar box and a broomstick. Eventually, a neighbor sold his father a worn-out Gene Autry guitar. Perkins could not afford new strings, and when they broke he had to retie them. The knots cut his fingers when he would slide to another note, so he began bending the notes, stumbling onto a type of blue note.

Perkins taught himself parts of Acuff's "Great Speckled Bird" and "The Wabash Cannonball", having heard them played on the Opry. He also cited Bill Monroe's fast playing and vocals as an early influence. Perkins also learned from John Westbrook, an African-American field worker in his sixties who played blues and gospel music on an old acoustic guitar. Westbrook advised Perkins to "Get down close to it. You can feel it travel down the strangs, come through your head and down to your soul where you live. You can feel it. Let it rib-a-rate."

In January 1947, the Perkins family moved from Lake County, Tennessee, to Madison County. Now in closer proximity to Memphis, Perkins was exposed to a greater variety of music. At age fourteen, he wrote a country song called "Let Me Take You to the Movie, Magg". It was that song that eventually persuaded Sam Phillips to sign Perkins to his Sun Records label..

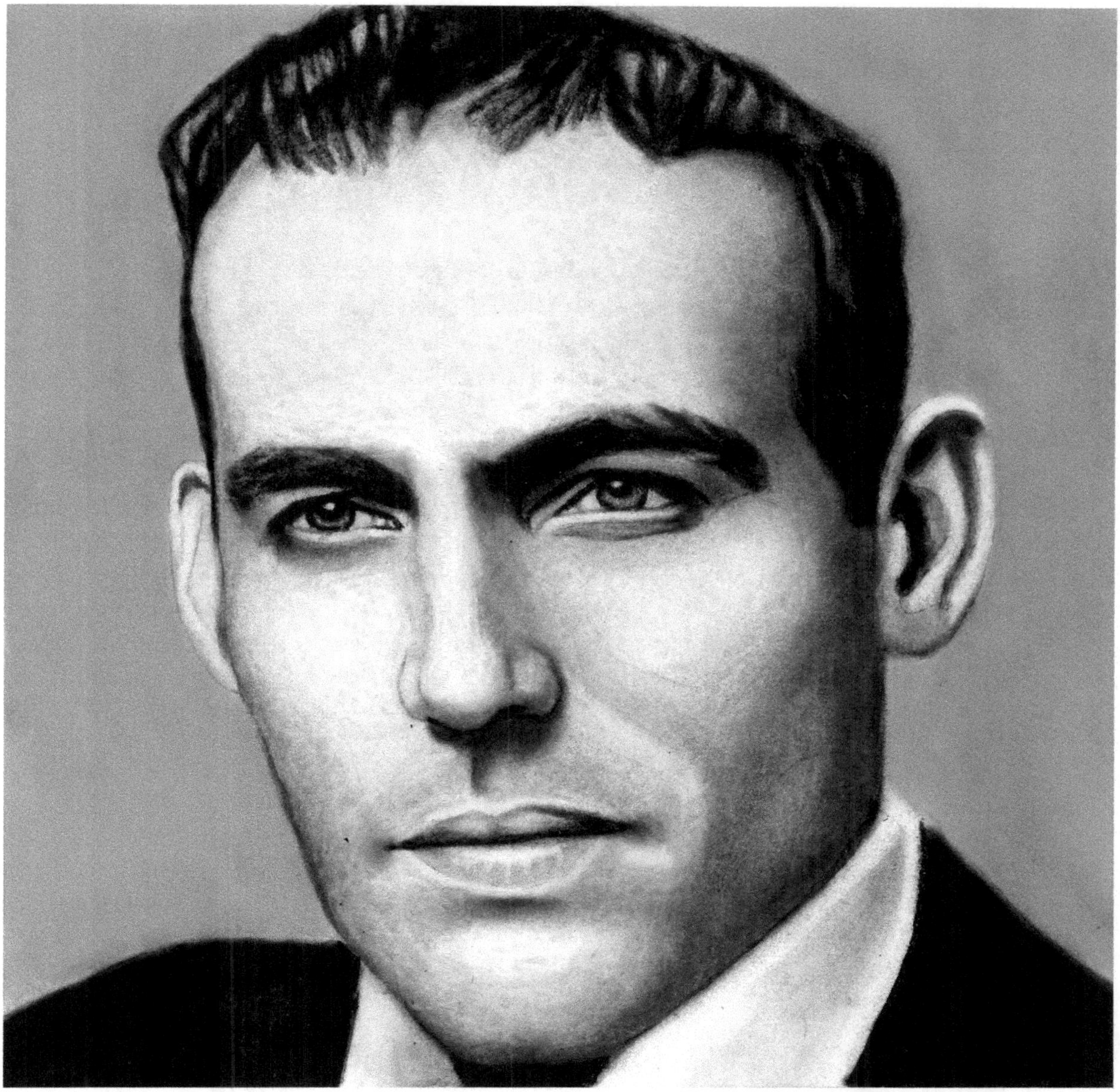

To view how this drawing was masterfully created or to purchase a Limited Edition Framed Artwork of Carl Perkins type into your Internet Browser the URL shortcut ➡ **myportrait.art/carlperkins**

To listen to his Greatest Songs type into your Internet Browser the URL shortcut ➡ **radio.surf/carlperkins**

To view all channels on THE FACE OF MUSIC Internet Radio MEGA Station type into your Internet Browser the URL shortcut ➡ **radio.surf/music**

To inquire about purchasing a Limited Edtion NFT of this portrait type into your Internet Browser the URL shortcut ➡ **myartnft.shop/carlperkins**

To view all available NFTs type into your Internet Browser the URL shortcut ➡ **myartnft.shop/all**

# Carpenters, The

(Total Records Sold: 90+ Million)(Genre: Pop)

The Carpenters were an American vocal and instrumental duo consisting of siblings Karen (1950–1983) and Richard Carpenter (born 1946). They produced a distinct soft musical style, combining Karen's contralto vocals with Richard's harmonizing, arranging and composition skills. During their 14-year career, the Carpenters recorded ten albums, along with numerous singles and several television specials.

The siblings were born in New Haven, Connecticut, and moved to Downey, California, in 1963. Richard took piano lessons as a child, progressing to California State University, Long Beach, while Karen learned the drums. They first performed together as a duo in 1965 and formed the jazz-oriented Richard Carpenter Trio followed by the middle-of-the-road group Spectrum. Signing as Carpenters to A&M Records in 1969, they achieved major success the following year with the hit singles "(They Long to Be) Close to You" and "We've Only Just Begun". Subsequently, the duo's brand of melodic pop produced a record-breaking run of hit recordings on the American Top 40 and Adult Contemporary charts, and they became leading sellers in the soft rock, easy listening and adult contemporary music genres. The Carpenters had three number-one singles and five number-two singles on the Billboard Hot 100 and fifteen number-one hits on the Adult Contemporary chart, in addition to twelve top-10 singles.

They have sold more than 90 million records worldwide, making them one of the best-selling music artists of all time. The duo toured continually during the 1970s, which put them under increased strain; Richard took a year off in 1979 after he had become addicted to Quaalude, while Karen suffered from anorexia nervosa.Their career together ended in 1983 when Karen died from heart failure brought on by complications of anorexia. Extensive news coverage surrounding these circumstances increased public awareness of eating disorders. Though the Carpenters were criticized for their clean-cut and wholesome conservative image in the 1970s, their music has since been re-evaluated, attracting critical acclaim and continued commercial success.

# Karen Carpenter

(Net Worth: $6 Million) (Height: 5'-4")

Karen Anne Carpenter (March 2, 1950 – February 4, 1983) was an American singer and drummer who, along with her elder brother Richard, was part of the duo the Carpenters. She was praised for her three-octave contralto vocal range and drumming abilities. Her struggles with eating disorders would later raise awareness of anorexia and body dysmorphia.

Carpenter was born in New Haven, Connecticut, and moved to Downey, California, in 1963 with her family. She began to study the drums in high school and joined the Long Beach State choir after graduating. After several years of touring and recording, Carpenters were signed to A&M Records in 1969, achieving commercial and critical success throughout the 1970s. Initially, Carpenter was the band's full-time drummer, but gradually took the role of frontwoman as drumming was reduced to a handful of live showcases or tracks on albums. While Carpenters were on hiatus in the late 1970s, she recorded a solo album, which was released years after her death. Briefly married in the early 1980s, Carpenter suffered from anorexia nervosa, which was little-known at the time. Her death from heart failure at age 32, related to complications of her illness, led to increased visibility and awareness of eating disorders. Her work continues to attract praise, including appearing on Rolling Stone's 2010 list of the 100 greatest singers of all time.

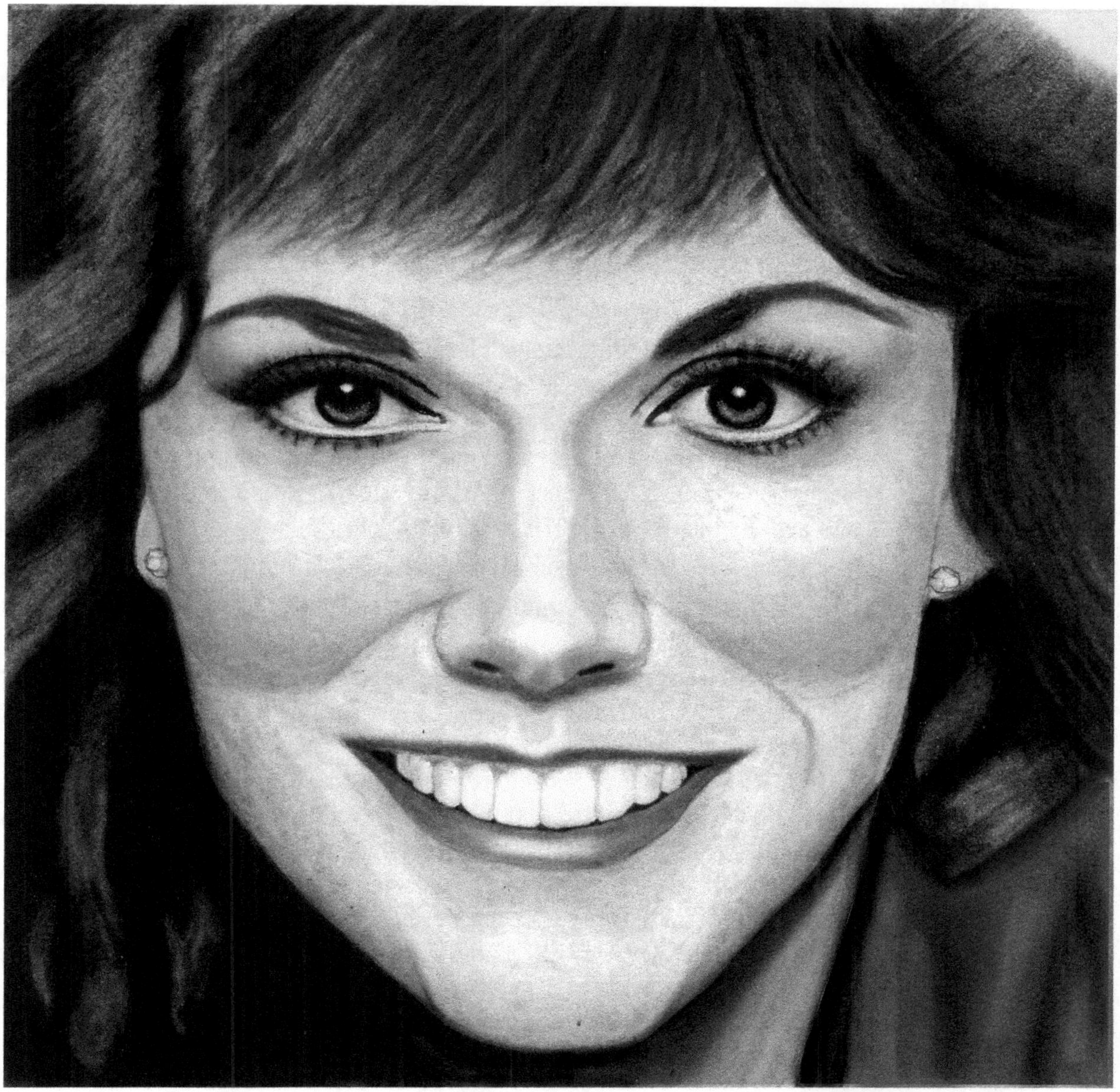

To view how this drawing was masterfully created or to purchase a Limited Edition Framed Artwork of Karen Carpenter type into your Internet Browser the URL shortcut ➡ **myportrait.art/karencarptener**

To listen to their Greatest Songs type into your Internet Browser the URL shortcut ➡ **radio.surf/thecarpenters**

To view all channels on THE FACE OF MUSIC Internet Radio MEGA Station type into your Internet Browser the URL shortcut ➡ **radio.surf/music**

To inquire about purchasing a Limited Edition NFT of this portrait type into your Internet Browser the URL shortcut ➡ **myartnft.shop/karencarptener**

To view all available NFTs type into your Internet Browser the URL shortcut ➡ **myartnft.shop/all**

# Cars, The

(Total Records Sold: 23+ Million)(Genre: New Wave , Pop)
The Cars were an American rock band formed in Boston in 1976. Emerging from the new wave scene in the late 1970s, the line-up consisted of Elliot Easton (lead guitar), Greg Hawkes (keyboards), Ric Ocasek (rhythm guitar), Benjamin Orr (bass guitar), and David Robinson (drums). Ocasek and Orr split lead vocal duties, and Ocasek served as the band's principal songwriter.
The Cars were at the forefront of merging 1970s guitar-oriented rock with the new synthesizer-oriented pop that was then becoming popular and flourishing in the early 1980s. Robert Palmer, music critic for The New York Times and Rolling Stone, described the Cars' musical style: "they have taken some important but disparate contemporary trends—punk minimalism, the labyrinthine synthesizer and guitar textures of art rock, the '50s rockabilly revival and the melodious terseness of power pop—and mixed them into a personal and appealing blend."
The Cars were named Best New Artist in the 1978 Rolling Stone Readers' Poll and won Video of the Year for "You Might Think" at the first MTV Video Music Awards in 1984. Their debut album The Cars sold six million copies and appeared on the Billboard 200 album chart for 139 weeks. As of 2001, the Cars had sold over 23 million albums in the United States.
The band disbanded in 1988 and Ocasek stated that a reunion would never happen. Orr died in 2000 from pancreatic cancer. In 2005, Easton and Hawkes joined with Todd Rundgren to form the spin-off band the New Cars, which performed classic Cars and Rundgren songs along with new material. The surviving original members reunited in 2010 to record the album Move Like This, which was released in May 2011, followed by a short tour.In April 2018, the Cars were inducted into the Rock and Roll Hall of Fame and reunited to perform at the induction ceremony. The reunion was their final performance with Ocasek, who died on September 15, 2019 of cardiovascular disease

# Ric Ocasek

(Net Worth: $80 Million) (Height: 6'- 4")
Richard Theodore Otcasek (March 23, 1944 – September 15, 2019), known as Ric Ocasek, was an American singer, songwriter, musician and record producer. He was co-lead vocalist, rhythm guitarist and songwriter for the rock band the Cars. In addition to his work with the Cars, Ocasek recorded seven solo albums, and his song "Emotion in Motion" was a top 20 hit in the United States in 1986. Ocasek also worked as a record producer for artists such as Suicide, Bad Brains, Weezer, Nada Surf, Guided by Voices, and No Doubt. In 2018, Ocasek was inducted into the Rock and Roll Hall of Fame as a member of the Cars.

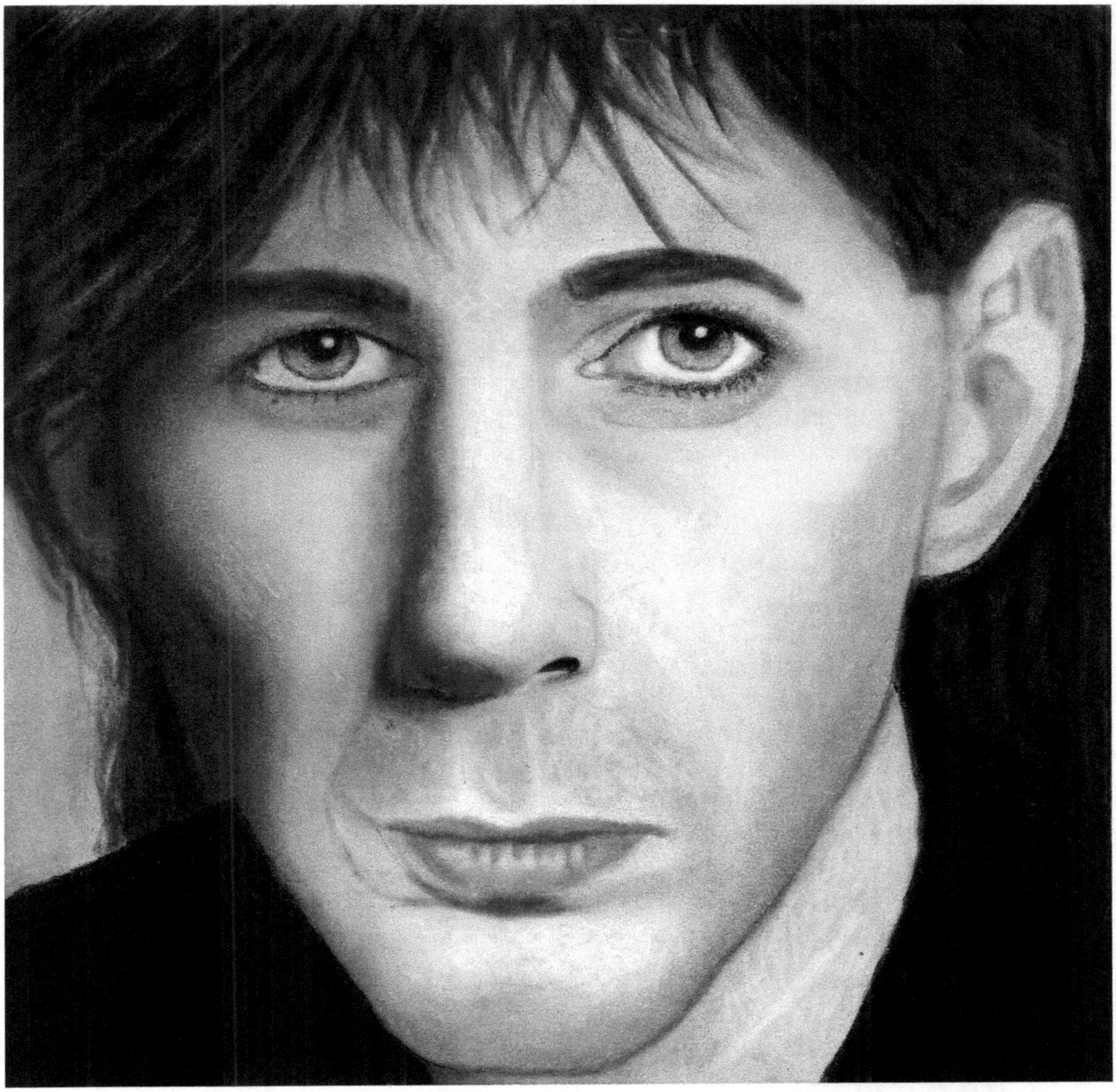

To view how this drawing was masterfully created or to purchase a Limited Edition Framed Artwork of Ric Ocasek type into your Internet Browser the URL shortcut ➡ **myportrait.art/ricocasek**

To listen to their Greatest Songs type into your Internet Browser the URL shortcut ➡ **radio.surf/thecars**

To view all channels on THE FACE OF MUSIC Internet Radio MEGA Station type into your Internet Browser the URL shortcut ➡ **radio.surf/music**

To inquire about purchasing a Limited Edtion NFT of this portrait type into your Internet Browser the URL shortcut ➡ **myartnft.shop/ricocasek**

To view all available NFTs type into your Internet Browser the URL shortcut ➡ **myartnft.shop/all**

# Cat Stevens

(Net worth: $10 Million)(Total Records Sold: 40 Million)
(Genre: Folk , Pop , Rock , Islamic)(Height: 5' - 10")

Yusuf Islam (born Steven Demetre Georgiou; 21 July 1948), commonly known by his stage names Cat Stevens, Yusuf, and Yusuf / Cat Stevens, is a British singer-songwriter and multi-instrumentalist. His musical style consists of folk, pop, rock, and, in his later career, Islamic music, before returning to secular music in 2006. He was inducted into the Rock and Roll Hall of Fame in 2014.

His 1967 debut album and its title song "Matthew and Son" both reached top ten in the UK charts. Stevens' albums Tea for the Tillerman (1970) and Teaser and the Firecat (1971) were certified triple platinum in the US. His 1972 album Catch Bull at Four spent weeks at the top of several major charts. He earned ASCAP songwriting awards in 2005 and 2006 for "The First Cut Is the Deepest", and the song has been a hit for four artists. His other hit songs include "Father and Son", "Wild World", "Moonshadow", "Peace Train", and "Morning Has Broken".

In December 1977, Stevens converted to Islam and adopted the name Yusuf Islam the following year. In 1979, he auctioned all of his guitars for charity. He has since bought back at least one of these guitars as a result of the efforts of his son Yoriyos, and left his musical career to devote himself to educational and philanthropic causes in the Muslim community. He was embroiled in a long-running controversy regarding comments he made in 1989 about the death fatwa on author Salman Rushdie. His current stance is that he never supported the fatwa: "I was cleverly framed by certain questions. I never supported the fatwa." He has received two honorary doctorates and awards for promoting peace as well as other humanitarian awards.

In 2006, he returned to pop music – releasing his first new studio album of new pop songs in 28 years, entitled An Other Cup. With that release and subsequent ones, he dropped the surname "Islam" from the album cover art – using the stage name Yusuf as a mononym. In 2009, he released the album Roadsinger and, in 2014, he released the album Tell 'Em I'm Gone and began his first US tour since 1978. His second North American tour since his resurgence, featuring 12 shows in intimate venues, ran from 12 September to 7 October 2016. In 2017, he released the album The Laughing Apple, now using the stage name Yusuf / Cat Stevens, using the Cat Stevens name for the first time in 39 years. In September 2020, he released Tea for the Tillerman 2, a reimagining of his classic album Tea for the Tillerman to celebrate its 50th anniversary.

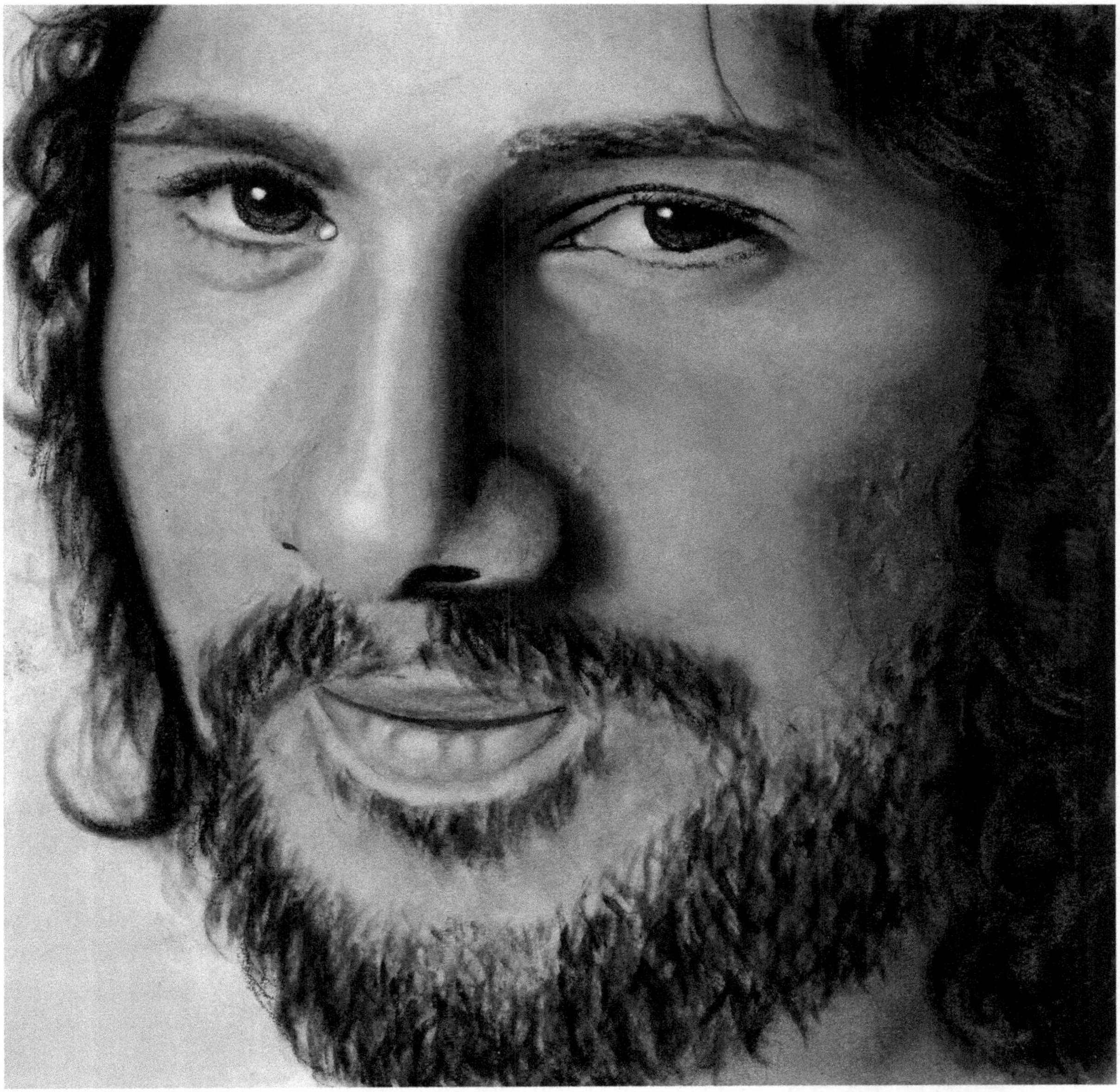

To view how this drawing was masterfully created or to purchase a Limited Edition Framed Artwork of Cat Stevens type into your Internet Browser the URL shortcut ➡ **myportrait.art/catstevens**

To listen to his Greatest Songs type into your Internet Browser the URL shortcut ➡ **radio.surf/catstevens**

To view all channels on THE FACE OF MUSIC Internet Radio MEGA Station type into your Internet Browser the URL shortcut ➡ **radio.surf/music**

To inquire about purchasing a Limited Edtion NFT of this portrait type into your Internet Browser the URL shortcut ➡ **myartnft.shop/catstevens**

To view all available NFTs type into your Internet Browser the URL shortcut ➡ **myartnft.shop/all**

# Céline Dion

(Net worth: $455 Million)(Total Records Sold: 200+ Million)
(Genre: Pop , Soft Rock , Chanson)(Height: 5' - 7")

Céline Marie Claudette Dion : French: , Quebec French: ; born 30 March 1968) is a Quebecois Canadian singer. She is renowned for her powerful, technically skilled vocals, and remains the best-selling Canadian recording artist and one of the best-selling artists of all time with record sales of over 200 million worldwide. Born into a large family from Charlemagne, Quebec, she emerged as a teen star in her home country with a series of French-language albums during the 1980s. She first gained international recognition by winning both the 1982 Yamaha World Popular Song Festival and the 1988 Eurovision Song Contest, where she represented Switzerland. After learning to speak English, she signed on to Epic Records in the United States. In 1990, Dion released her debut English-language album, Unison, establishing herself as a viable pop artist in North America and other English-speaking areas of the world.

During the 1990s, she achieved worldwide fame after releasing several best-selling English-language albums, such as Falling into You (1996) and Let's Talk About Love (1997), which were both certified diamond in the US. She also scored a series of international number-one hits, including "The Power of Love", "Think Twice", "Because You Loved Me", "It's All Coming Back to Me Now", "My Heart Will Go On", and "I'm Your Angel". Dion continued releasing French albums between each English record: D'eux (1995) became the best-selling French-language album of all time, while S'il suffisait d'aimer (1998), Sans attendre (2012), and Encore un soir (2016), were all certified diamond in France. During the 2000s, she built her reputation as a highly successful live performer with A New Day... on the Las Vegas Strip (2003–07), which remains the highest-grossing concert residency of all time, as well as the Taking Chances World Tour (2008–09), one of the highest-grossing concert tours of all time.

Dion's music has been influenced by genres ranging from rock and R&B to gospel and classical. Her recordings are mainly in French and English, although she also sings in Spanish, Italian, German, Latin, Japanese, and Mandarin Chinese. While her releases have often received mixed critical reception, she is regarded as one of pop music's most influential vocalists. She has won five Grammy Awards, including Album of the Year and Record of the Year. Billboard named her the "Queen of Adult Contemporary" for having the most number-one songs on the radio format for a female artist. She is the second best-selling female artist in the US during the Nielsen SoundScan era. In 2003, she was honoured by the International Federation of the Phonographic Industry (IFPI) for selling over 50 million albums in Europe.

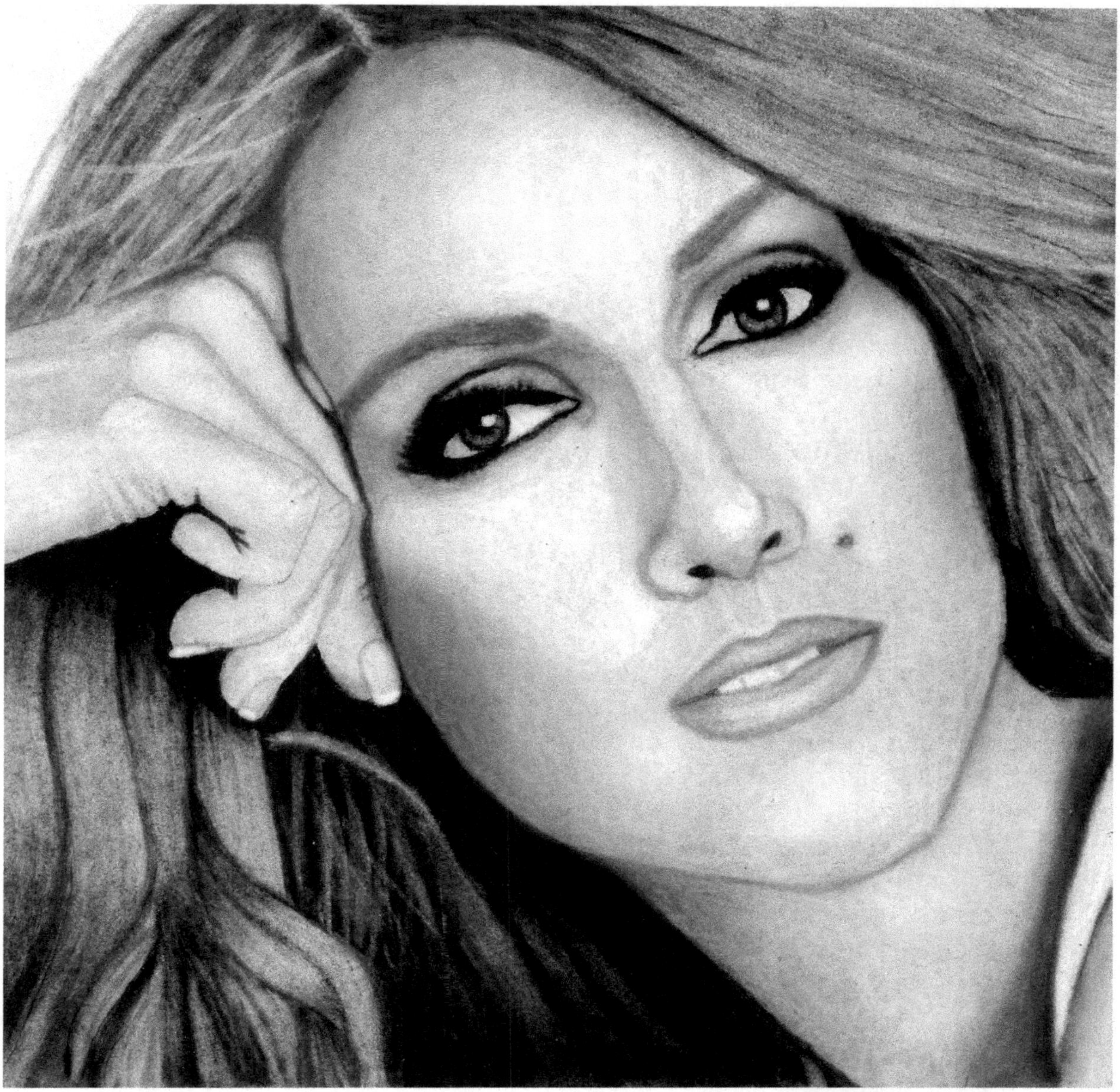

To view how this drawing was masterfully created or to purchase a Limited Edition Framed Artwork of Celine Dion type into your Internet Browser the URL shortcut ➡ **myportrait.art/celinedion**

To listen to her Greatest Songs type into your Internet Browser the URL shortcut ➡ **radio.surf/celinedion**

To view all channels on THE FACE OF MUSIC Internet Radio MEGA Station type into your Internet Browser the URL shortcut ➡ **radio.surf/music**

To inquire about purchasing a Limited Edtion NFT of this portrait type into your Internet Browser the URL shortcut ➡ **myartnft.shop/celinedion**

To view all available NFTs type into your Internet Browser the URL shortcut ➡ **myartnft.shop/all**

# Charley Pride

(Net worth: $40 Million)(Total Records Sold: 70+ Million)
(Genre:Country)(Height: 6' - 0")

Charley Frank Pride (March 18, 1934 – December 12, 2020) was an American singer, guitarist, and professional baseball player. His greatest musical success came in the early to mid 1970s, when he was the best-selling performer for RCA Records since Elvis Presley. During the peak years of his recording career (1966–1987), he had 52 top-10 hits on the Billboard Hot Country Songs chart, 30 of which made it to number one. He won the Entertainer of the Year award at the Country Music Association Awards in 1971.

Pride is one of three African-American members of the Grand Ole Opry (the others being DeFord Bailey and Darius Rucker). He was inducted into the Country Music Hall of Fame in 2000.

While he was active in baseball, Pride had been encouraged to join the music business by country stars such as Red Sovine and Red Foley, and was working towards this career. In 1958, in Memphis, Pride visited Sun Studio and recorded some songs.

He performed his music solo at clubs and with a four-piece combo called the Night Hawks during the time he lived in Montana. His break came when Chet Atkins at RCA Victor heard a demonstration tape and got Pride a contract. In 1966, he released his first RCA Victor single, "The Snakes Crawl at Night". Nashville manager and agent Jack D. Johnson signed Pride. Atkins was the longtime producer at RCA Victor who had made stars out of country singers such as Jim Reeves, Skeeter Davis, and others. Pride was signed to RCA Victor in 1965. "The Snakes Crawl at Night" did not chart. On the records of this song submitted to radio stations for airplay, the singer was listed as "Country Charley Pride". Pride disputes that the omission of a photo was deliberate; he stated that getting promoters to bring in a black country singer was a bigger problem: "People didn't care if I was pink. RCA signed me ... they knew I was colored ... They decided to put the record out and let it speak for itself."

While living in Montana, he continued to sing at local clubs, and in Great Falls had an additional boost to his career when he befriended local businessman Louis Allen "Al" Donohue, who owned radio stations, including KMON, the first stations to play Pride's records in Montana.

Soon after the release of "The Snakes Crawl at Night", Pride released another single called "Before I Met You", which also did not chart. Not long afterwards, his third single, "Just Between You and Me", was released. This song finally brought Pride success on the country charts. The song reached number nine on Hot Country Songs on February 25, 1967.

According to a news item by the Associated Press, Pride made this comment in a 1992 interview: "They used to ask me how it feels to be the 'first colored country singer' ... Then it was 'first Negro country singer;' then 'first black country singer.' Now I'm the 'first African-American country singer.' That's about the only thing that's changed".

Pride died in Dallas on December 12, 2020, of complications related to COVID-19. He was 86 years old.

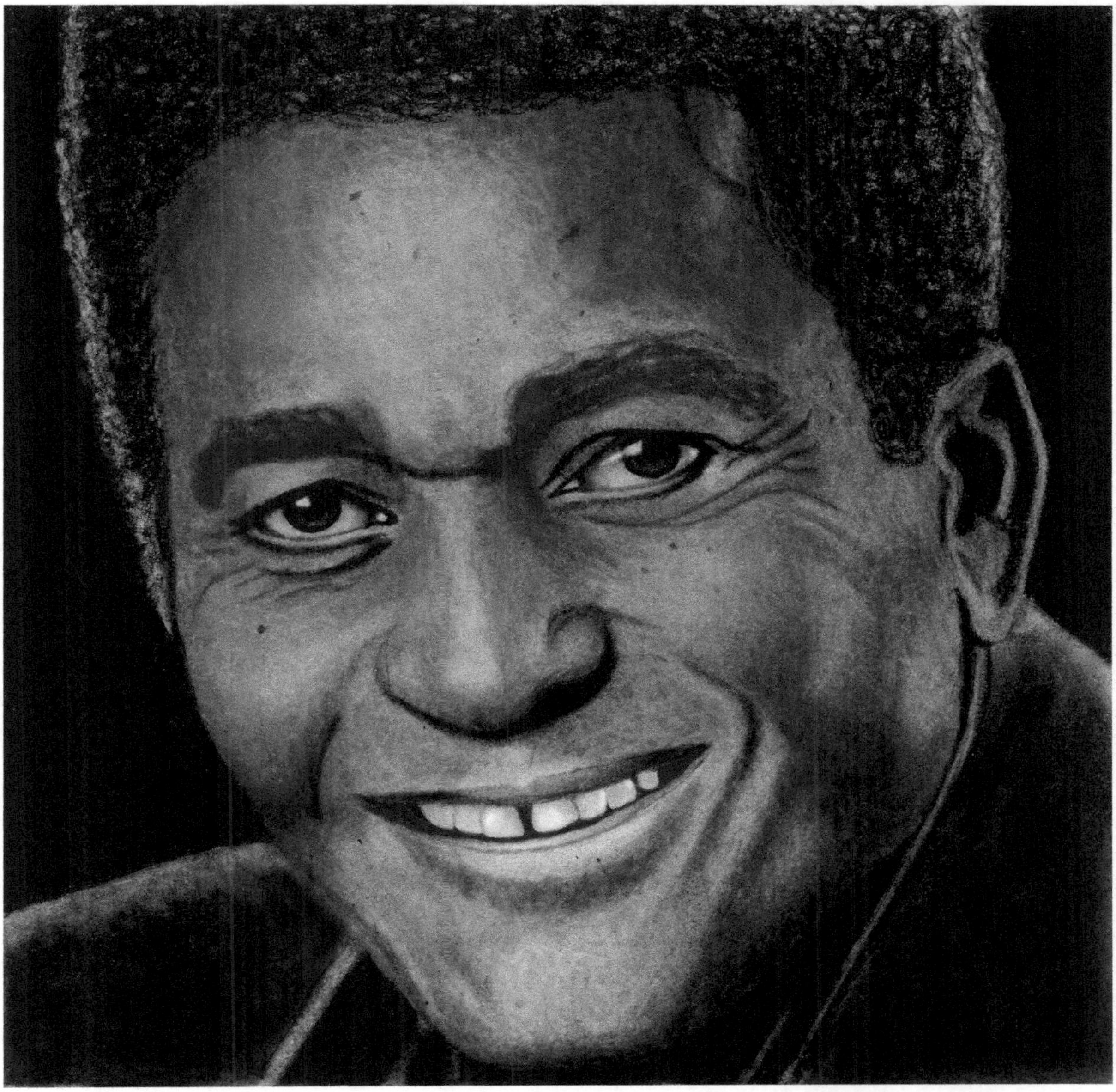

To view how this drawing was masterfully created or to purchase a Limited Edition Framed Artwork of Charley Pride type into your Internet Browser the URL shortcut ➡ **myportrait.art/charleypride**

To listen to his Greatest Songs type into your Internet Browser the URL shortcut ➡ **radio.surf/charleypride**

To view all channels on THE FACE OF MUSIC Internet Radio MEGA Station type into your Internet Browser the URL shortcut ➡ **radio.surf/music**

To inquire about purchasing a Limited Edtion NFT of this portrait type into your Internet Browser the URL shortcut ➡ **myartnft.shop/charleypride**

To view all available NFTs type into your Internet Browser the URL shortcut ➡ **myartnft.shop/all**

# Charlie Daniels

(Net worth: $20 Million)(Total Records Sold: 13.5+ Million)
(Genre:Country , Rock)(Height: 6' - 2")

Charles Edward Daniels (October 28, 1936 – July 6, 2020) was an American singer, songwriter and multi-instrumentalist known for his contributions to Southern rock, country, and bluegrass music. He was best known for his number-one country hit "The Devil Went Down to Georgia". Much of his output, including all but one of his eight Billboard Hot 100 charting singles, was credited to the Charlie Daniels Band.

Daniels was active as a singer and musician from the 1950s until his death. He was inducted into the Cheyenne Frontier Days Hall of Fame in 2002, the Grand Ole Opry in 2008, the Musicians Hall of Fame and Museum in 2009, and the Country Music Hall of Fame in 2016.

Daniels was born October 28, 1936, in Wilmington, North Carolina, and raised on a musical diet that included Pentecostal gospel, local bluegrass bands, and the rhythm & blues and country music from Nashville's 50,000-watt AM radio stations WLAC and WSM. In 2016, he shared memories of his youth and baseball in Wilmington when he wrote the foreword for a book on the Tobacco State League. As a teenager, Daniels moved to the small town of Gulf, Chatham County, North Carolina. He graduated from high school in 1955. Already skilled on guitar, fiddle, banjo, and mandolin, he formed a rock 'n' roll band and hit the road.

Daniels died on July 6, 2020, at the age of 83 of a hemorrhagic stroke at Summit Medical Center in Hermitage, TN.

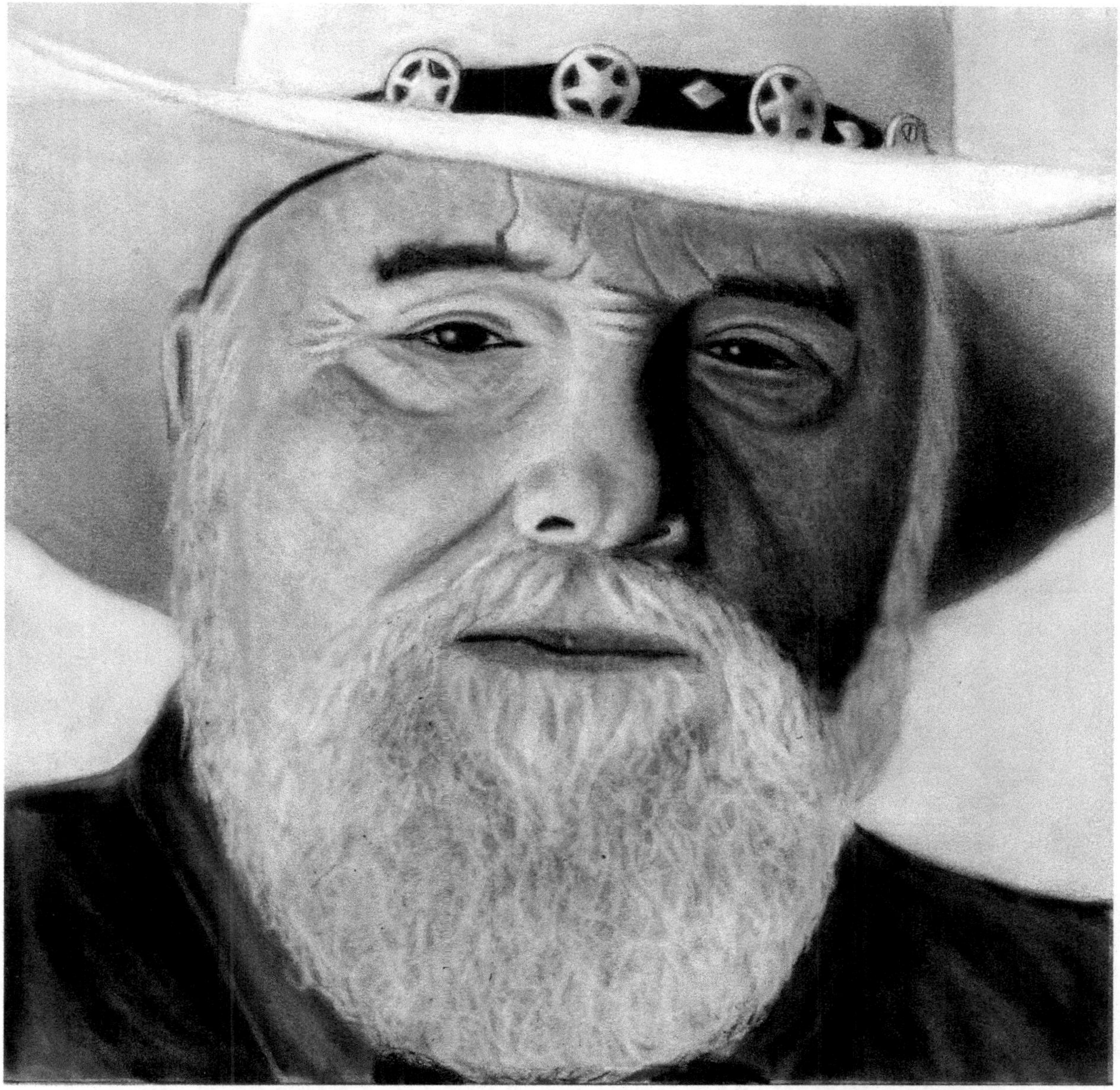

To view how this drawing was masterfully created or to purchase a Limited Edition Framed Artwork of Charlie Daniels type into your Internet Browser the URL shortcut ➡ **myportrait.art/charliedaniels**

To listen to his Greatest Songs type into your Internet Browser the URL shortcut ➡ **radio.surf/charliedaniels**

To view all channels on THE FACE OF MUSIC Internet Radio MEGA Station type into your Internet Browser the URL shortcut ➡ **radio.surf/music**

To inquire about purchasing a Limited Edtion NFT of this portrait type into your Internet Browser the URL shortcut ➡ **myartnft.shop/charliedaniels**

To view all available NFTs type into your Internet Browser the URL shortcut ➡ **myartnft.shop/all**

# Cheap Trick

(Total Albums Sold: 20+ Million)(Genre: Hard Rock)

Cheap Trick are an American rock band from Rockford, Illinois, formed in 1973. The band's classic line-up consisted of frontman Robin Zander, guitarist Rick Nielsen, bassist Tom Petersson, and drummer Bun E. Carlos.

Cheap Trick released their self-titled debut album in 1977 and found success in Japan with the release of their second album, In Color, later that year. The band would achieve mainstream popularity in the United States in 1979 with their breakthrough album Cheap Trick at Budokan. Cheap Trick reached the Top 10 in the US charts in 1979 with the Budokan live version of "I Want You to Want Me" and topped the charts in 1988 with "The Flame".

Cheap Trick have performed live more than 3,700 times and sold more than 20 million albums. Over the course of its career, Cheap Trick has experienced several resurgences of popularity.

Cheap Trick were inducted into the Rock and Roll Hall of Fame in 2016.

# Robin Zander

(Net Worth: $25 Million) (Height: 5'- 8")

Robin Wayne Zander (born January 23, 1953) is an American singer, songwriter and rhythm guitarist. He is best known as the lead singer and rhythm guitarist for the rock band Cheap Trick, but is also a solo artist. Zander was inducted into the Rock and Roll Hall of Fame in 2016 as a member of Cheap Trick.

In 1974, Zander accepted an invitation to join Cheap Trick. Along with Zander, the band consisted of guitarist Rick Nielsen, bassist Tom Petersson, and drummer Bun E. Carlos. Cheap Trick's 1979 album, Cheap Trick at Budokan, catapulted the band to stardom. The band reached the Top 10 in the U.S. charts in 1979 with "I Want You to Want Me" and topped the charts in 1988 with "The Flame". As of 2018, Cheap Trick had been a band for over 40 years. Cheap Trick has performed more than 5,000 shows and has sold more than 20 million albums. Zander was inducted into the Rock and Roll Hall of Fame as a member of Cheap Trick in 2016.

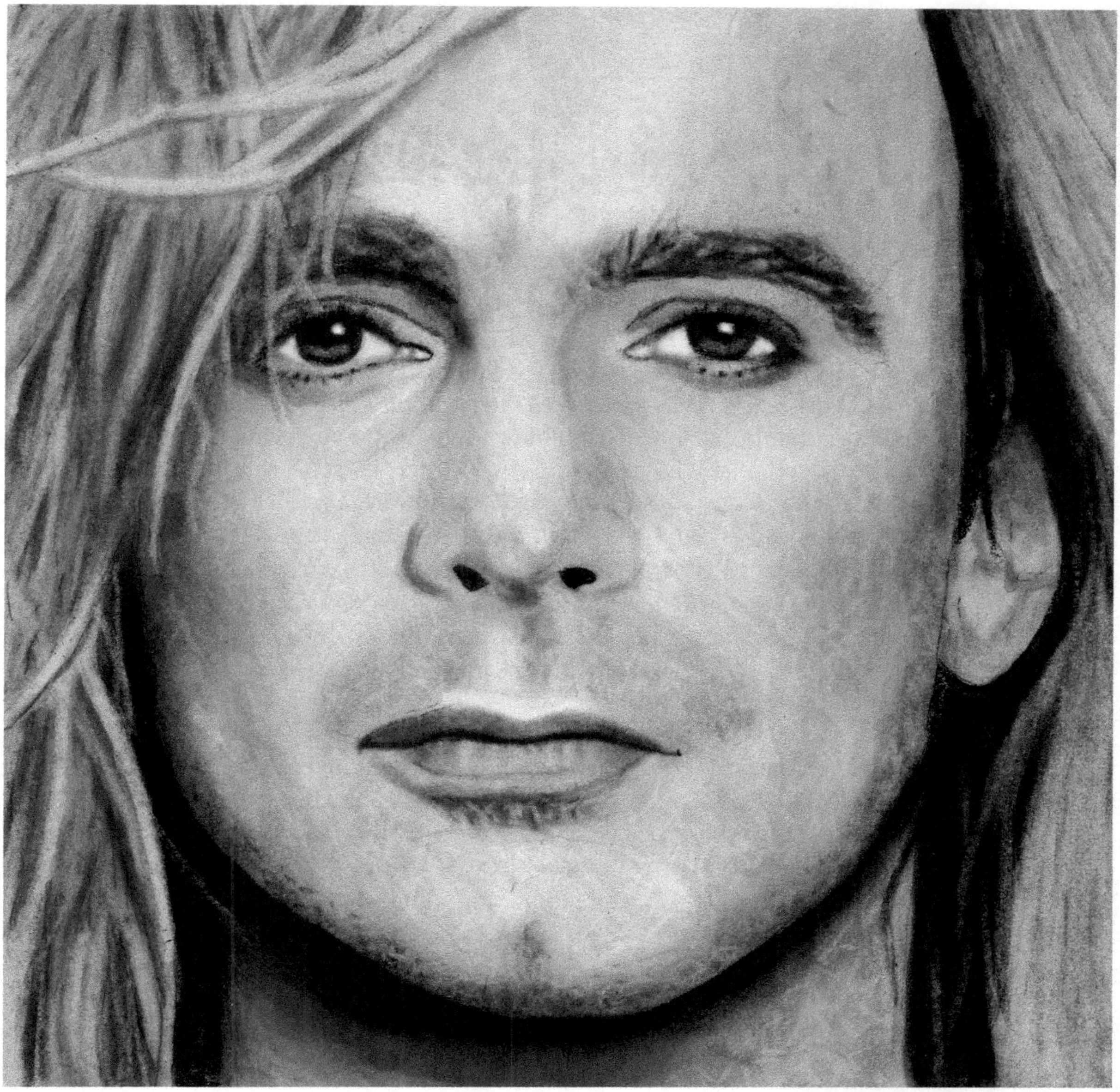

To view how this drawing was masterfully created or to purchase a Limited Edition Framed Artwork of Robin Zander type into your Internet Browser the URL shortcut ➡ **myportrait.art/robinzander**

To listen to their Greatest Songs type into your Internet Browser the URL shortcut ➡ **radio.surf/cheaptrick**

To view all channels on THE FACE OF MUSIC Internet Radio MEGA Station type into your Internet Browser the URL shortcut ➡ **radio.surf/music**

To inquire about purchasing a Limited Edtion NFT of this portrait type into your Internet Browser the URL shortcut ➡ **myartnft.shop/robinzander**

To view all available NFTs type into your Internet Browser the URL shortcut ➡ **myartnft.shop/all**

# Cher

(Net worth: $360 Million)(Total Records Sold: 100 Million)
(Genre: Dance , Dico , Folk , Rock)(Height: 5' - 6")

Cher (born Cherilyn Sarkisian; May 20, 1946) is an American singer, actress and television personality. Commonly referred to by the media as the "Goddess of Pop", she has been described as embodying female autonomy in a male-dominated industry. Cher is known for her distinctive contralto singing voice and for having worked in numerous areas of entertainment, as well as adopting a variety of styles and appearances throughout her six-decade-long career.Cher gained popularity in 1965 as one-half of the folk rock husband-wife duo Sonny & Cher after their song "I Got You Babe" peaked at number one on the US and UK charts. By the end of 1967, they had sold 40 million records worldwide and had become, according to Time magazine, rock's "it" couple. She began her solo career simultaneously, releasing in 1966 the transatlantic top three single "Bang Bang (My Baby Shot Me Down)". She became a television personality in the 1970s with her CBS shows The Sonny & Cher Comedy Hour, watched by over 30 million viewers weekly during its three-year run, and Cher. She emerged as a fashion trendsetter by wearing elaborate outfits on her television shows.While working on television, Cher established herself as a solo artist with the US Billboard Hot 100 number-one singles "Gypsys, Tramps & Thieves", "Half-Breed", and "Dark Lady", becoming the female artist with the most number-one singles in United States history at the time. After her divorce from Sonny Bono in 1975, she launched a comeback with the disco album Take Me Home (1979) and earned $300,000 a week for her 1979–1982 concert residency in Las Vegas.In 1982, Cher made her Broadway debut in the play Come Back to the Five and Dime, Jimmy Dean, Jimmy Dean and starred in its film adaptation. She subsequently garnered critical acclaim for her performances in films such as Silkwood (1983), Mask (1985), The Witches of Eastwick (1987), and Moonstruck (1987), the latter of which won her the Academy Award for Best Actress. She then revived her music career by recording the rock-inflected albums Cher (1987), Heart of Stone (1989), and Love Hurts (1991), all of which yielded successful singles such as "I Found Someone", "If I Could Turn Back Time", and "Love and Understanding". Cher contributed to the soundtrack for her next film, Mermaids (1990), which spawned the UK number-one single "The Shoop Shoop Song (It's in His Kiss)". She made her directorial debut with a segment in the abortion-themed anthology If These Walls Could Talk (1996), which received widespread critical acclaim after premiering on HBO.Cher reached a new commercial peak in 1998 with the dance-pop album Believe, whose title track won her the Billboard Music Award for Hot 100 Single of the Year and became the biggest-selling single of all time by a female artist in the UK. It features pioneering use of Auto-Tune to distort her vocals, known as the "Cher effect". Her 2002–2005 Living Proof: The Farewell Tour became one of the highest-grossing concert tours of all time, earning $250 million. In 2008, she signed a $60 million deal to headline the Colosseum at Caesars Palace in Las Vegas for three years. In 2018, Cher returned to film for her first on-screen role since 2010's Burlesque, starring in the musical romantic comedy film Mamma Mia! Here We Go Again. Inspired by the film, the album Dancing Queen (2018) debuted at number three on the Billboard 200, tying with 2013's Closer to the Truth for Cher's highest-charting solo album in the US.Having sold 100 million records to date, Cher is one of the world's best-selling music artists. Her achievements include a Grammy Award, an Emmy Award, an Academy Award, three Golden Globe Awards, a Cannes Film Festival Award, the Billboard Icon Award, and awards from the Kennedy Center Honors and the Council of Fashion Designers of America. She is the only artist to date to have a number-one single on a Billboard chart in six consecutive decades, from the 1960s to the 2010s. Outside of her music and acting, she is noted for her political views, social media presence, philanthropic endeavors, and social activism, including LGBT rights and HIV/AIDS prevention.

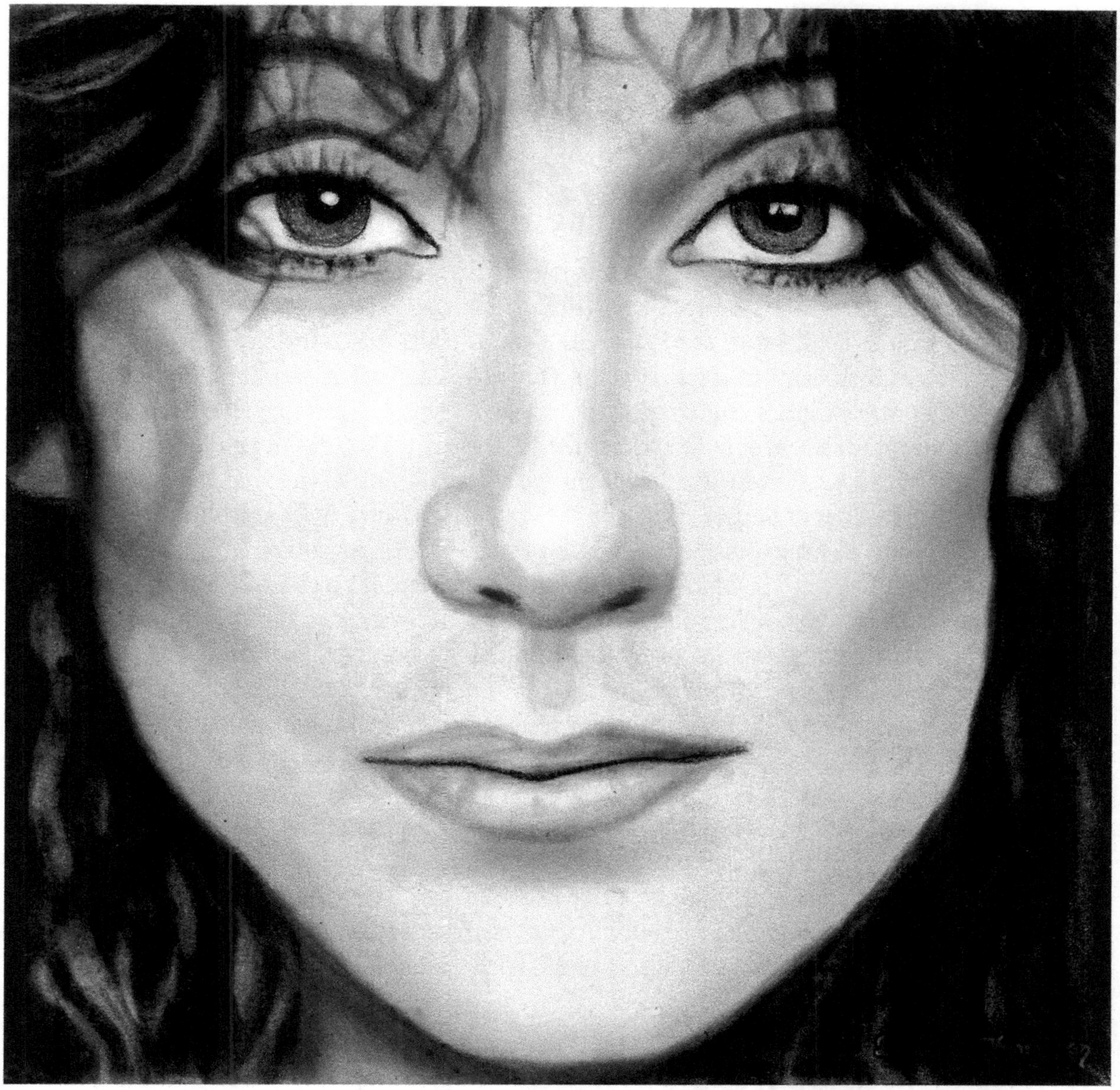

To view how this drawing was masterfully created or to purchase a Limited Edition Framed Artwork of Cher type into your Internet Browser the URL shortcut ➡ **myportrait.art/cher**

To listen to her Greatest Songs type into your Internet Browser the URL shortcut ➡ **radio.surf/cher**

To view all channels on THE FACE OF MUSIC Internet Radio MEGA Station type into your Internet Browser the URL shortcut ➡ **radio.surf/music**

To inquire about purchasing a Limited Edtion NFT of this portrait type into your Internet Browser the URL shortcut ➡ **myartnft.shop/cher**

To view all available NFTs type into your Internet Browser the URL shortcut ➡ **myartnft.shop/all**

# Chicago

(Total Albums Sold: 100+ Million)(Genre: Soft Pop, Pop Rock, Jazz Rock)
Chicago is an American rock band formed in 1967 in Chicago, Illinois, calling themselves the Chicago Transit Authority in 1968 before shortening the name in 1969. The self-described "rock and roll band with horns" blended elements of classical music, jazz, R&B and pop music. They began writing songs with politically charged lyrics, and later moved to a softer sound, generating several hit ballads. The group had a steady stream of hits throughout the 1970s and 1980s. In September 2008, Billboard ranked Chicago at number thirteen in a list of the top 100 artists of all time for Hot 100 singles chart success, and ranked them at number fifteen on the same list produced in October 2015. Billboard also ranked Chicago ninth on the list of the 100 greatest artists of all time in terms of Billboard 200 album chart success in October 2015. Chicago is one of the longest-running and most successful rock groups, and one of the world's best-selling groups of all time, having sold more than 100 million records. In 1971, Chicago was the first rock act to sell out Carnegie Hall for a week.

To date, Chicago has sold over 40 million units in the U.S., with 23 gold, 18 platinum, and eight multi-platinum albums. They have had five consecutive number-one albums on the Billboard 200 and 20 top-ten singles on the Billboard Hot 100. In 1974 the group had seven albums, its entire catalog at the time, on the Billboard 200 simultaneously. The group has received ten Grammy Award nominations, winning one for the song, "If You Leave Me Now". The group's first album, Chicago Transit Authority, released in 1969, was inducted into the Grammy Hall of Fame in 2014. Chicago was inducted into the Rock and Roll Hall of Fame in 2016. In 2017, Peter Cetera, Robert Lamm, and James Pankow were elected to the Songwriters Hall of Fame for their songwriting efforts as members of the music group. Chicago received a Grammy Lifetime Achievement Award on October 16, 2020.

# Peter Cetera

(Net Worth: $40 Million) (Height: 5'-11")
Peter Paul Cetera (born September 13, 1944) is an American retired singer, songwriter, and bassist best known for being an original member of the rock band Chicago (1967–1985), before launching a successful solo career. His career as a recording artist encompasses 17 albums with Chicago and eight solo albums.

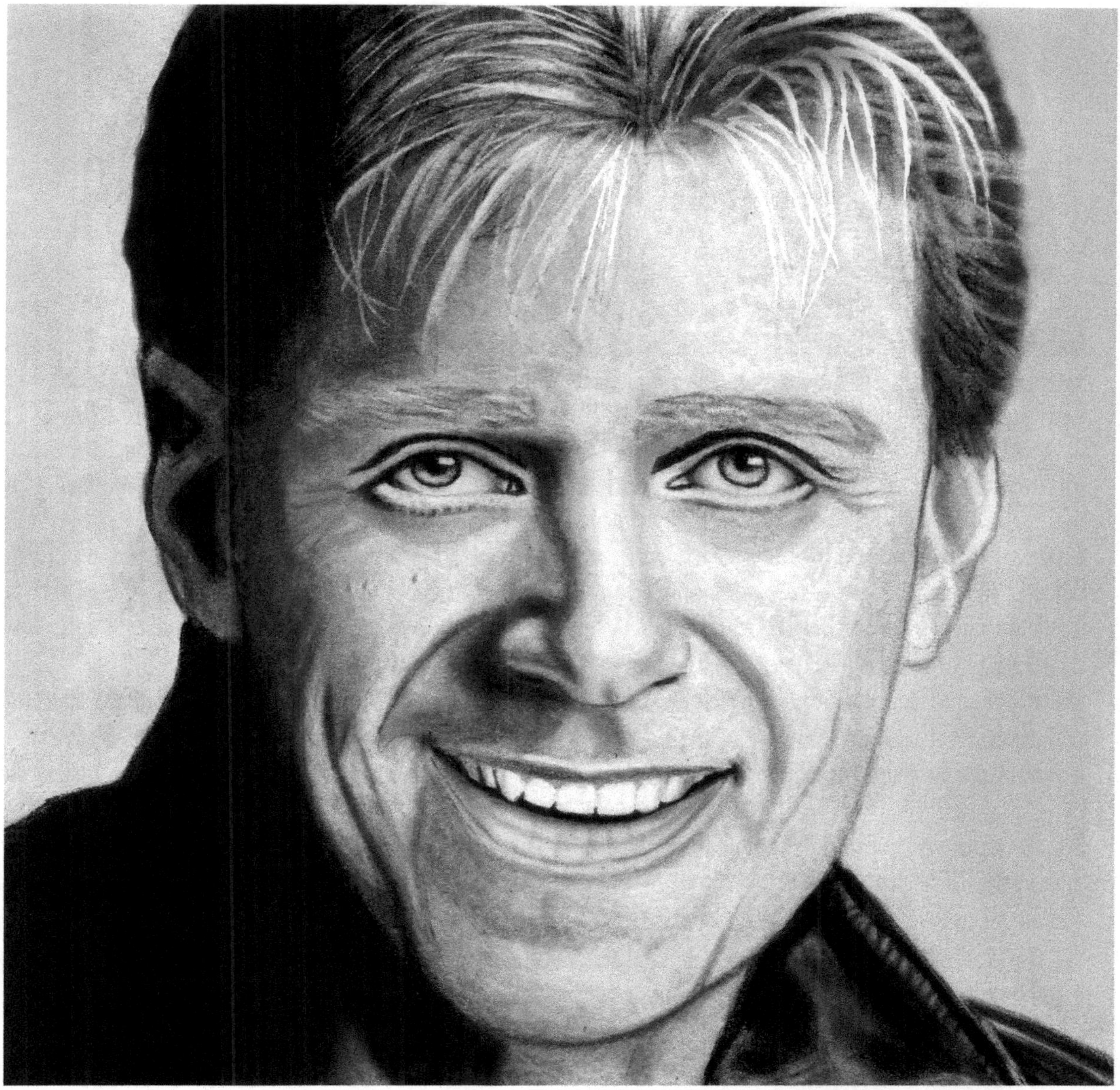

To view how this drawing was masterfully created or to purchase a Limited Edition Framed Artwork of Peter Cetera type into your Internet Browser the URL shortcut ➡ **myportrait.art/petercetera**

To listen to their Greatest Songs type into your Internet Browser the URL shortcut ➡ **radio.surf/chicago**

To view all channels on THE FACE OF MUSIC Internet Radio MEGA Station type into your Internet Browser the URL shortcut ➡ **radio.surf/music**

To inquire about purchasing a Limited Edtion NFT of this portrait type into your Internet Browser the URL shortcut ➡ **myartnft.shop/petercetera**

To view all available NFTs type into your Internet Browser the URL shortcut ➡ **myartnft.shop/all**

# Christina Aguilera

(Net worth: $160 Million)(Total Records Sold: 100 Million)
(Genre: Pop , R&B , Dance , Soul)(Height: 5' - 1 1/2")

Christina María Aguilera ( born December 18, 1980) is an American singer, songwriter, actress, and television personality. Her accolades include five Grammy Awards, one Latin Grammy Award, and a star on the Hollywood Walk of Fame. Aguilera ranked at number 58 on Rolling Stone's list of 100 Greatest Singers of All Time in 2008, and was included on Time's annual list of the 100 most influential people in the world in 2013. With estimated sales of 100 million records, she is one of the world's best-selling music artists.

Born in Staten Island of New York City and raised in Pennsylvania, Aguilera appeared on television shows in her early years before signing a recording contract with RCA Records in 1998. Her self-titled debut album, released in 1999, reached number one in the US and spawned three US number-one singles: "Genie in a Bottle", "What a Girl Wants", and "Come On Over Baby ( All I Want Is You)". While recognized as a prominent figure in the contemporary teen pop scene, Aguilera sought to assume artistic control with Stripped (2002) and its lead single "Dirrty", which displayed her sexuality. The second single from the album, "Beautiful", received favorable response for its empowering lyrics and became an anthem for the LGBT community.

Aguilera scored her second US number-one album with Back to Basics (2006), which drew inspiration from early 20th-century jazz, soul, and blues, and spawned the top-ten singles "Ain't No Other Man", "Hurt", and "Candyman". Her next three albums, Bionic (2010), Lotus (2012), and Liberation (2018), all experimented with various musical styles and reached the top ten in the US. Besides solo materials, Aguilera earned chart-topping entries with collaborations including "Lady Marmalade", "Moves like Jagger", "Feel This Moment", "Say Something" and "Hoy Tengo Ganas de Ti". Alongside her music career, Aguilera starred in the film Burlesque (2010) and was a coach on six seasons of the singing competition television series The Voice from 2011 to 2016.

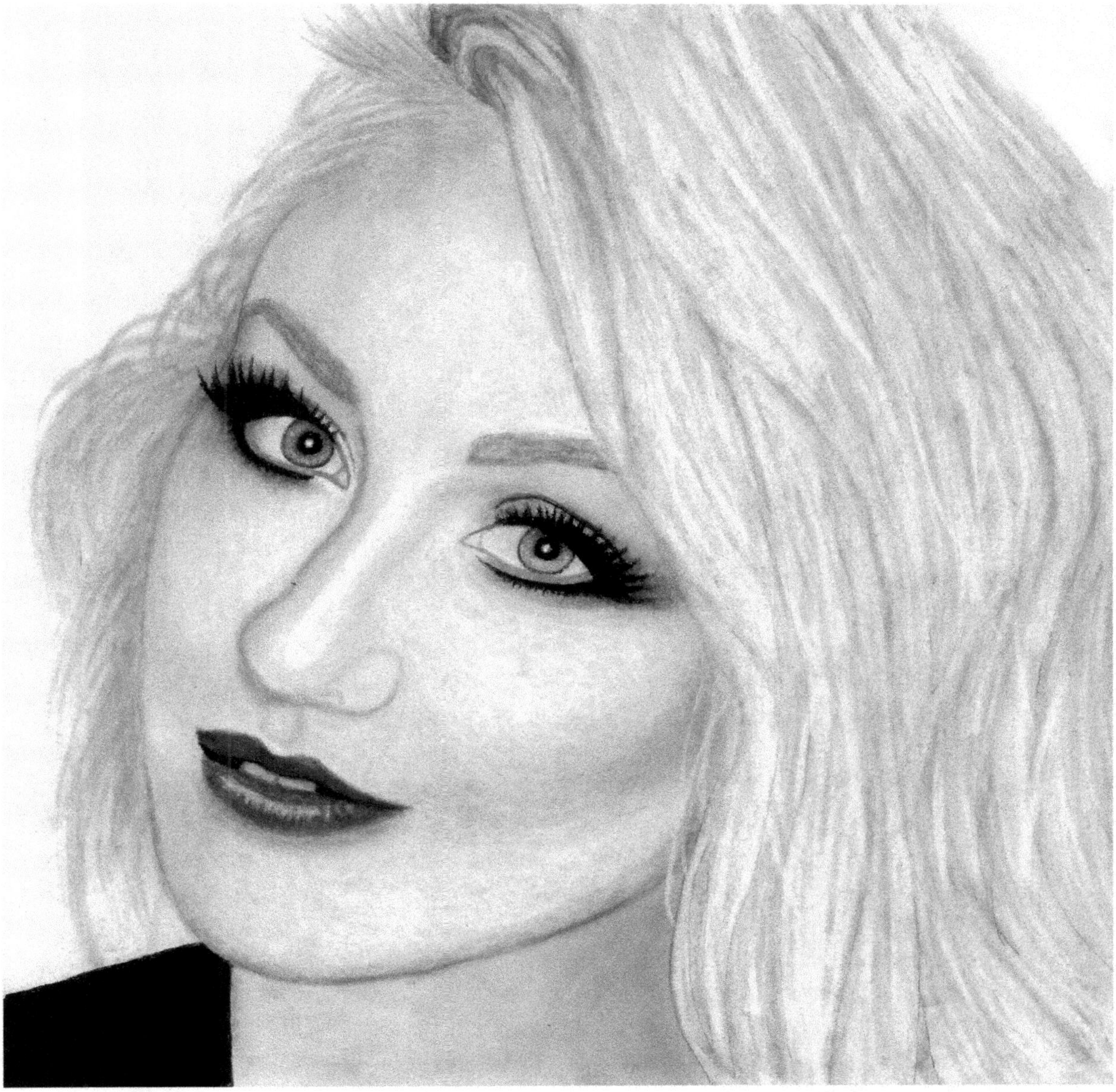

To view how this drawing was masterfully created or to purchase a Limited Edition Framed Artwork of Christina Aguilera type into your Internet Browser the URL shortcut ➡ **myportrait.art/christinaaguilera**

To listen to her Greatest Songs type into your Internet Browser the URL shortcut
➡ **radio.surf/christinaaguilera**

To view all channels on THE FACE OF MUSIC Internet Radio MEGA Station type into your Internet Browser the URL shortcut ➡ **radio.surf/music**

To inquire about purchasing a Limited Edition NFT of this portrait type into your Internet Browser the URL shortcut ➡ **myartnft.shop/christinaaguilera**

To view all available NFTs type into your Internet Browser the URL shortcut ➡ **myartnft.shop/all**

# Chubby Checker

(Net worth: $4 Million)(Total Records Sold: 15+ Million)
(Genre:Rock & Roll , R&B)(Height: 5' - 9")

Chubby Checker (born Ernest Evans; October 3, 1941) is an American rock 'n roll singer and dancer. He is widely known for popularizing many dance styles including the twist dance style, with his 1960 hit cover of Hank Ballard & The Midnighters' R&B hit "The Twist" and the Pony with hit "Pony Time". In September 2008, "The Twist" topped Billboard's list of the most popular singles to have appeared in the Hot 100 since its debut in 1958, an honor it maintained for an August 2013 update of the list. He also popularized the "Limbo Rock" and its trademark limbo dance, as well as various dance styles such as The Fly. Checker privately recorded a novelty single for Clark in which the singer portrayed a school teacher with an unruly classroom of musical performers. The premise allowed Checker to imitate such acts as Fats Domino, The Coasters, Elvis Presley, Cozy Cole, and Ricky Nelson, Frankie Avalon, and Fabian Forte as The Chipmunks, each singing "Mary Had a Little Lamb". Clark sent the song out as his Christmas greeting, and it received such good response that Cameo-Parkway signed Checker to a recording contract. Titled "The Class", the single became Checker's first release, charting at #38 in the spring of 1959.

Checker introduced his version of "The Twist" at the age of 18 in July 1960 in Wildwood, New Jersey at the Rainbow Club. "The Twist" went on to become the only single to top the Billboard Hot 100 twice, in two separate chart runs. (Bing Crosby's "White Christmas" had done so on Billboard's earlier chart.)

"The Twist" had previously peaked at #16 on the Billboard rhythm and blues chart, in the 1959 version recorded by its author, Hank Ballard, whose band The Midnighters first performed the dance on stage. Checker's "Twist", however, was a nationwide smash, aided by his many appearances on Dick Clark's American Bandstand, the Top 10 American Bandstand ranking of the song, and the teenagers on the show who enjoyed dancing the Twist. The song was so ubiquitous that Checker felt that his critics thought that he could only succeed with dance records typecasting him as a dance artist. Checker later lamented: "... in a way, "The Twist" really ruined my life. I was on my way to becoming a big nightclub performer, and "The Twist" just wiped it out ... It got so out of proportion. No one ever believes I have talent." By 1965 alone, "The Twist" had sold over 15 million copies, and was awarded multiple gold discs by the RIAA.

Despite Checker's initial disapproval, he found follow-up success with a succession of up-tempo dance tracks, including "The Hucklebuck" (#14), "The Fly" (#7), "Dance the Mess Around" (#24), and "Pony Time", which became his second #1 single. Checker's follow-up "twist" single, "Let's Twist Again", won the 1961 Grammy Award for Best Rock and Roll Solo Vocal Performance. A 1962 duet with Dee Dee Sharp, "Slow Twistin'", reached #3 on the national charts. Other substantial hits included "Dancin' Party", "Popeye the Hitchhiker", "Twenty Miles", "Birdland", "Loddy Lo", and a Christmas duet with Bobby Rydell, "Jingle Bell Rock". "Limbo Rock" reached #2 on 22–29 December 1962, becoming Checker's last Top Ten hit. Chubby Checker continued to have Top 40 singles until 1965, his last being "Let's Do the Freddie" (#40), a variation on Freddie and the Dreamers' dance tune "Do the Freddie", with new melody and lyrics. Changes in public tastes, owing mostly to the British Invasion and counterculture era, ended his hit-making career. He spent much of the rest of the 1960s touring and recording in Europe.

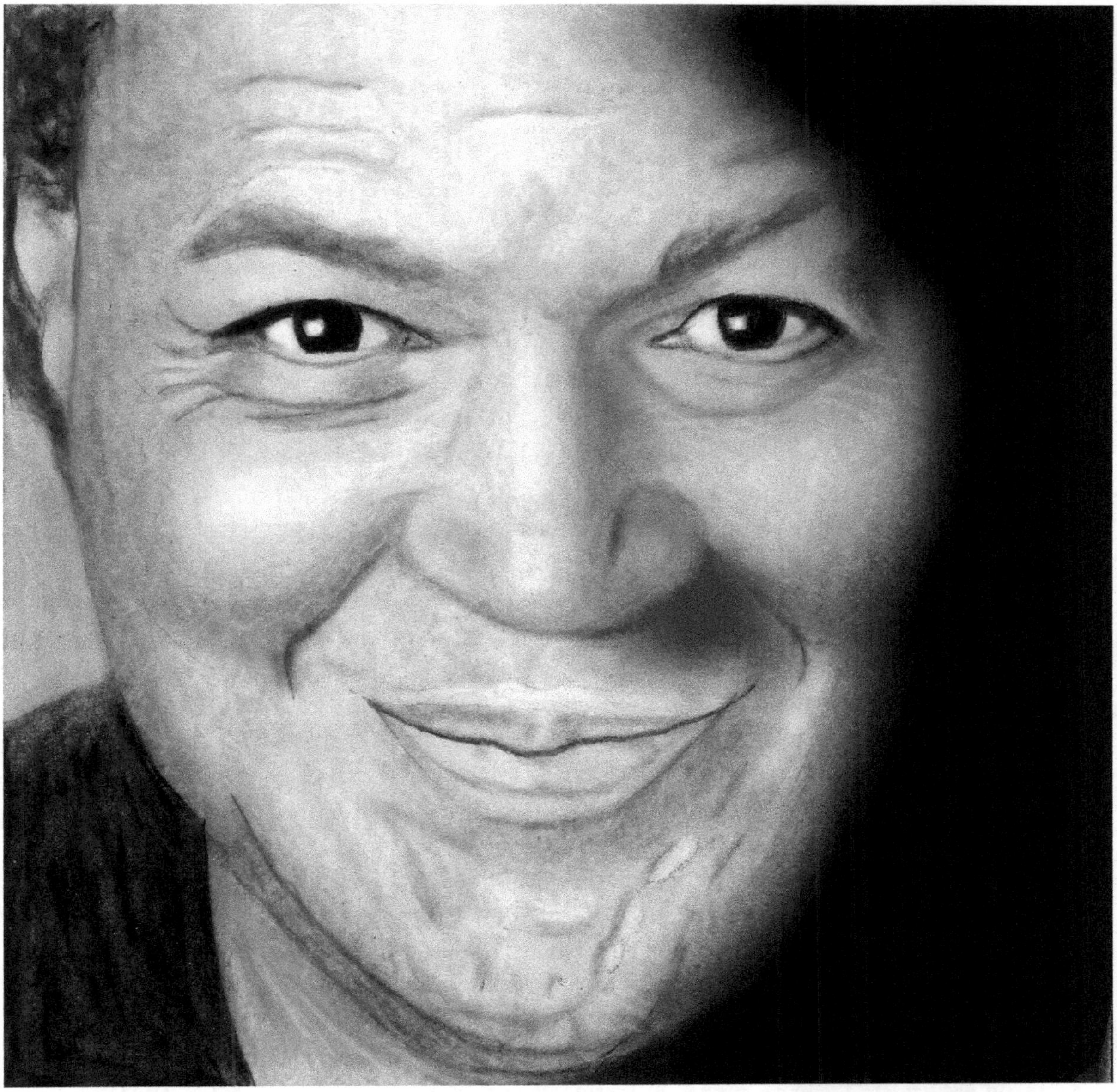

To view how this drawing was masterfully created or to purchase a Limited Edition Framed Artwork of Chubby Checker type into your Internet Browser the URL shortcut ➡ **myportrait.art/chubbychecker**

To listen to his Greatest Songs type into your Internet Browser the URL shortcut ➡ **radio.surf/chubbychecker**

To view all channels on THE FACE OF MUSIC Internet Radio MEGA Station type into your Internet Browser the URL shortcut ➡ **radio.surf/music**

To inquire about purchasing a Limited Edtion NFT of this portrait type into your Internet Browser the URL shortcut ➡ **myartnft.shop/chubbychecker**

To view all available NFTs type into your Internet Browser the URL shortcut ➡ **myartnft.shop/all**

# Chuck Berry

(Net worth: $10 Million)(Total Records Sold: Multi-Millions)
(Genre:Rock & Roll)(Height: 6' - 2")

Charles Edward Anderson Berry (October 18, 1926 – March 18, 2017) was an American singer, songwriter and guitarist, and one of the pioneers of rock and roll music. Nicknamed the "Father of Rock and Roll", Berry refined and developed rhythm and blues into the major elements that made rock and roll distinctive with songs such as "Maybellene" (1955), "Roll Over Beethoven" (1956), "Rock and Roll Music" (1957) and "Johnny B. Goode" (1958). Writing lyrics that focused on teen life and consumerism, and developing a music style that included guitar solos and showmanship, Berry was a major influence on subsequent rock music.

Born into a middle-class African-American family in St. Louis, Berry had an interest in music from an early age and gave his first public performance at Sumner High School. While still a high school student he was convicted of armed robbery and was sent to a reformatory, where he was held from 1944 to 1947. After his release, Berry settled into married life and worked at an automobile assembly plant. By early 1953, influenced by the guitar riffs and showmanship techniques of the blues musician T-Bone Walker, Berry began performing with the Johnnie Johnson Trio. His break came when he traveled to Chicago in May 1955 and met Muddy Waters, who suggested he contact Leonard Chess, of Chess Records. With Chess, he recorded "Maybellene"—Berry's adaptation of the country song "Ida Red"—which sold over a million copies, reaching number one on Billboard magazine's rhythm and blues chart. By the end of the 1950s, Berry was an established star, with several hit records and film appearances and a lucrative touring career. He had also established his own St. Louis nightclub, Berry's Club Bandstand. He was sentenced to three years in prison in January 1962 for offenses under the Mann Act—he had transported a 14-year-old girl across state lines. After his release in 1963, Berry had several more hits, including "No Particular Place to Go", "You Never Can Tell", and "Nadine". But these did not achieve the same success, or lasting impact, of his 1950s songs, and by the 1970s he was more in demand as a nostalgic performer, playing his past hits with local backup bands of variable quality. In 1972 he reached a new level of achievement when a rendition of "My Ding-a-Ling" became his only record to top the charts. His insistence on being paid in cash led in 1979 to a four-month jail sentence and community service, for tax evasion.

Berry was among the first musicians to be inducted into the Rock and Roll Hall of Fame on its opening in 1986; he was cited for having "laid the groundwork for not only a rock and roll sound but a rock and roll stance." Berry is included in several of Rolling Stone magazine's "greatest of all time" lists; he was ranked fifth on its 2004 and 2011 lists of the 100 Greatest Artists of All Time. The Rock and Roll Hall of Fame's 500 Songs That Shaped Rock and Roll includes three of Berry's: "Johnny B. Goode", "Maybellene", and "Rock and Roll Music". Berry's "Johnny B. Goode" is the only rock-and-roll song included on the Voyager Golden Record.

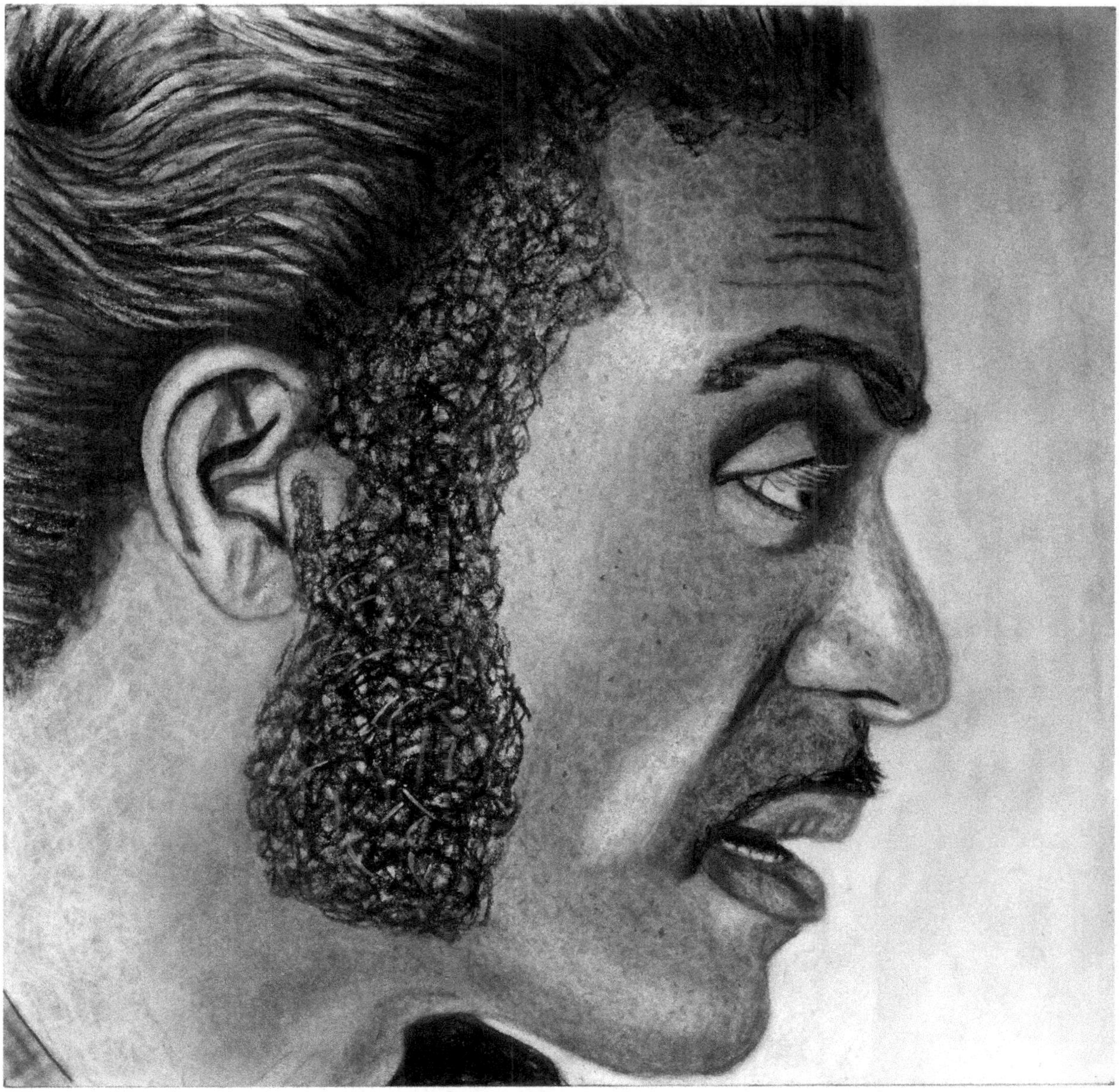

To view how this drawing was masterfully created or to purchase a Limited Edition Framed Artwork of Chuck Berry type into your Internet Browser the URL shortcut ➡ **myportrait.art/chuckberry**

To listen to his Greatest Songs type into your Internet Browser the URL shortcut ➡ **radio.surf/chuckberry**

To view all channels on THE FACE OF MUSIC Internet Radio MEGA Station type into your Internet Browser the URL shortcut ➡ **radio.surf/music**

To inquire about purchasing a Limited Edtion NFT of this portrait type into your Internet Browser the URL shortcut ➡ **myartnft.shop/chuckberry**

To view all available NFTs type into your Internet Browser the URL shortcut ➡ **myartnft.shop/all**

# Clash, The

(Total Albums Sold: Millions)(Genre: Punk Rock , New Wave)

The Clash were an English rock band formed in London in 1976 as a key player in the original wave of British punk rock. They also contributed to the post-punk and new wave movements that emerged in the wake of punk and employed elements of a variety of genres including reggae, dub, funk, ska, and rockabilly. For most of their recording career, the Clash consisted of lead vocalist and rhythm guitarist Joe Strummer, lead guitarist and vocalist Mick Jones, bassist Paul Simonon, and drummer Nicky "Topper" Headon. Headon left the group in 1982 and internal friction led to Jones' departure the following year. The group continued with new members, but finally disbanded in early 1986.

The Clash achieved commercial success in the United Kingdom with the release of their self-titled debut album, The Clash, in 1977. Their third album, London Calling, released in the UK in December 1979, earned them popularity in the United States when it was released there the following month. It was declared the best album of the 1980s a decade later by Rolling Stone. In 1982, they reached new heights of success with the release of Combat Rock, which spawned the US top 10 hit "Rock the Casbah", helping the album to achieve a 2× Platinum certification there. A final album, Cut the Crap, was released in 1985.

In January 2003, shortly after the death of Joe Strummer, the band—including original drummer Terry Chimes—were inducted into the Rock and Roll Hall of Fame. In 2004, Rolling Stone ranked the Clash number 28 on its list of the "100 Greatest Artists of All Time".

# Joe Strummer

(Net Worth: $4 Million) (Height: 5'- 8")

John Graham Mellor (21 August 1952 – 22 December 2002), better known as Joe Strummer, was a British musician, singer, songwriter, composer, actor, and radio host who was best known as the co-founder, lyricist, rhythm guitarist, and co-lead vocalist of punk rock band The Clash. Formed in 1976, the Clash's second album Give 'Em Enough Rope (1978) reached No. 2 on the UK charts. Soon after, they achieved success in the US starting with London Calling (1979) and peaking with Combat Rock (1982), which reached No. 7 on the US charts and was certified 2× platinum there. The Clash's explosive political lyrics, musical experimentation, and rebellious attitude had a far-reaching influence on rock music in general, especially alternative rock. Their music incorporated reggae, ska, dub, funk, rap and rockabilly.Strummer's other career highlights included stints with the 101ers, Latino Rockabilly War, the Mescaleros, and the Pogues, as well as solo music. His work as a musician allowed him to explore other interests such as acting, scoring television shows and films, hosting radio shows, and as a radio host on the BBC Radio show London Calling. Strummer and the Clash were inducted into the Rock and Roll Hall of Fame in January 2003. In his remembrance, Strummer's friends and family established the Joe Strummer Foundation (initially known as Strummerville), a non-profit organisation which gives opportunities to musicians and support to projects around the world that create empowerment through music.

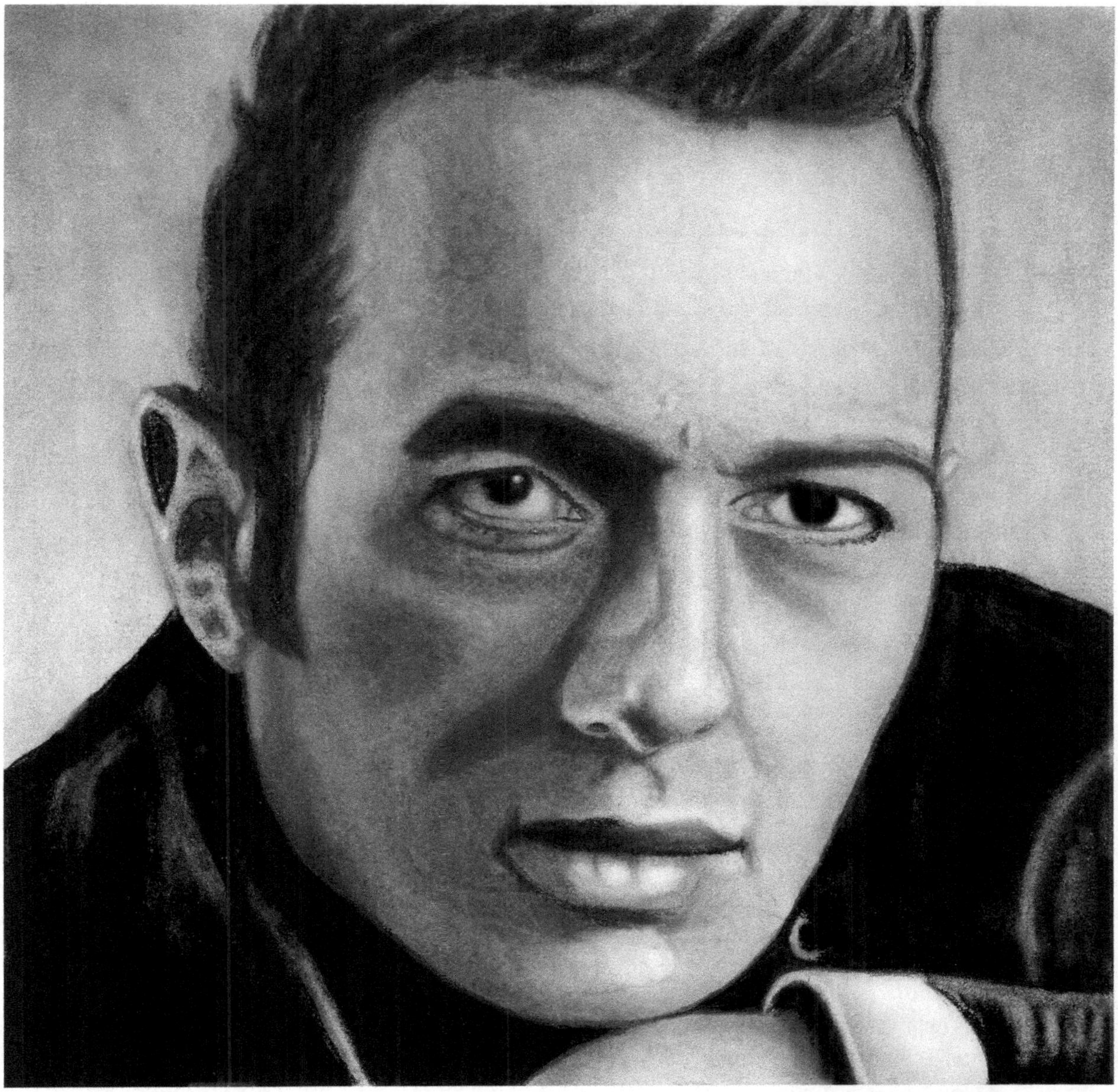

To view how this drawing was masterfully created or to purchase a Limited Edition Framed Artwork of Joe Strummer type into your Internet Browser the URL shortcut ➡ **myportrait.art/joestrummer**

To listen to their Greatest Songs type into your Internet Browser the URL shortcut ➡ **radio.surf/theclash**

To view all channels on THE FACE OF MUSIC Internet Radio MEGA Station type into your Internet Browser the URL shortcut ➡ **radio.surf/music**

To inquire about purchasing a Limited Edtion NFT of this portrait type into your Internet Browser the URL shortcut ➡ **myartnft.shop/joestrummer**

To view all available NFTs type into your Internet Browser the URL shortcut ➡ **myartnft.shop/all**

# Commodores

(Total Albums Sold: 70 Million)(Genre: Funk , Soul , R&B , Pop)

Commodores are an American funk and soul band, which were at their peak in the late 1970s through the mid 1980s. The members of the group met as mostly freshmen at Tuskegee Institute (now Tuskegee University) in 1968, and signed with Motown in November 1972, having first caught the public eye opening for the Jackson 5 while on tour.

The group's most successful period was in the late 1970s and early 1980s when Lionel Richie was the co-lead singer. The band's biggest hit singles are ballads such as "Easy", "Three Times a Lady", and "Nightshift"; and funky dance hits which include "Brick House", "Fancy Dancer", "Lady (You Bring Me Up)", and "Too Hot ta Trot".

Commodores were inducted into the Alabama Music Hall of Fame and Vocal Group Hall of Fame. The band has also won one Grammy Award out of nine nominations. As well the Commodores have sold over 70 million albums worldwide.

# Lionel Richie

(Net Worth: $200 Million) (Height: 5'- 11")

Lionel Brockman Richie Jr. (born June 20, 1949) is an American singer, songwriter, composer, record producer, actor, and television judge. During the 1970s, he recorded with the funk band the Commodores, and his solo career made him one of the most successful balladeers of the 1980s.

Beginning in 1968, Richie was a member of the Commodores. The Commodores became established as a popular soul group; their first several albums had a danceable, funky sound, as in such tracks as "Machine Gun" and "Brick House". Over time, Richie wrote and sang more romantic, easy-listening ballads such as "Easy", "Three Times a Lady", "Still", and the breakup ballad "Sail On". Richie launched a solo career in 1982 and his 1982 debut solo album, Lionel Richie, contained three hit singles: the U.S. number-one song "Truly", and the top five hits "You Are" and "My Love". The album hit No. 3 on the music charts and sold over four million copies. His 1983 follow-up album, Can't Slow Down, sold over twice as many copies, propelling him into the first rank of international superstars. He also co-wrote the 1985 charity single "We Are the World" with Michael Jackson, which sold over 20 million copies.

Over the course of his career, Richie has sold over 90 million records worldwide, making him one of the world's best-selling artists of all time. He won the Grammy Award for Album of the Year for Can't Slow Down, and his other Grammy Awards include Producer of the Year (Non-Classical) in 1985 and Best Male Pop Vocal Performance for "Truly" in 1983. Richie has also been nominated for two Golden Globe awards and won one. In 1982, he was nominated for Best Original Song for the film Endless Love. In 1986, he won the Golden Globe award for Best Original Song for "Say You, Say Me", featured in the film White Nights. The song also won the Academy Award for Best Original Song. In 2016, Richie received the Songwriters Hall of Fame's highest honor, the Johnny Mercer Award. He has served with Luke Bryan and Katy Perry as a judge for the singing competition American Idol since its move to ABC from the Fox network, since 2018.

To view how this drawing was masterfully created or to purchase a Limited Edition Framed Artwork of Lionel Richie type into your Internet Browser the URL shortcut ➡ **myportrait.art/lionelrichie**

To listen to the Commodore's Greatest Songs type into your Internet Browser the URL shortcut
➡ **radio.surf/commodores**

To listen to Lion Richie's Greatest Songs type into your Internet Browser the URL shortcut
➡ **radio.surf/lionelrichie**

To view all channels on THE FACE OF MUSIC Internet Radio MEGA Station type into your Internet Browser the URL shortcut ➡ **radio.surf/music**

To inquire about purchasing a Limited Edtion NFT of this portrait type into your Internet Browser the URL shortcut ➡ **myartnft.shop/lionelrichie**

To view all available NFTs type into your Internet Browser the URL shortcut ➡ **myartnft.shop/all**

# Common

(Net worth: $45 Million)(Total Albums Sold: 2.8 Million)
(Genre:Hip-Hop)(Height: 6' - 0")

Lonnie Rashid Lynn (born March 13, 1972), known by his stage name Common (formerly Common Sense), is an American rapper, actor, and writer. He debuted in 1992, with the album Can I Borrow a Dollar?, and gained critical acclaim with his 1994 album Resurrection. He maintained an underground following into the late 1990s. He achieved mainstream success through his work with the Soulquarians. Common's first major-label album Like Water for Chocolate (2000), received commercial success. In 2003, he won the Grammy Award for Best R&B Song for the Erykah Badu single "Love of My Life". His 2005 album Be was also a commercial success and was nominated for Best Rap Album at the 2006 Grammy Awards. Common received his second Grammy Award for Best Rap Performance by a Duo or Group for "Southside" (featuring Kanye West), from his 2007 album Finding Forever. His best-of album, Thisisme Then: The Best of Common, was released in late 2007. In 2011, Common launched Think Common Entertainment, his own record label imprint, having previously released music under various other labels including Relativity, Geffen, and GOOD Music.

Common won the 2015 Golden Globe Award for Best Original Song and the Academy Award for Best Original Song, for his song "Glory" from the 2014 film Selma, in which he co-starred as Civil Rights Movement leader James Bevel. Common's acting career also includes roles in the films Smokin' Aces, Street Kings, American Gangster, Wanted, Terminator Salvation, Date Night, Just Wright, Happy Feet Two, New Year's Eve, Run All Night, Being Charlie, Rex, John Wick: Chapter 2, Smallfoot and Hunter Killer. He also narrated the documentary Bouncing Cats, about one man's efforts to improve the lives of children in Uganda through hip-hop/b-boy culture. He starred as Elam Ferguson on the AMC western television series Hell on Wheels.

Common was born on March 13, 1972 at the Chicago Osteopathic Hospital in Chicago's Hyde Park neighborhood, the son of educator and former principal of John Hope College Preparatory High School, Mahalia Ann Hines and former ABA basketball player turned youth counselor Lonnie Lynn. He was raised in the Calumet Heights neighborhood. Lynn's parents divorced when he was six years old, resulting in his father moving to Denver, Colorado. This left Lynn to be raised by his mother; however, his father remained active in his life, and was able to get Lynn a job with the Chicago Bulls as a teenager. Lynn attended Florida A&M University for two years under a scholarship and majored in business administration.

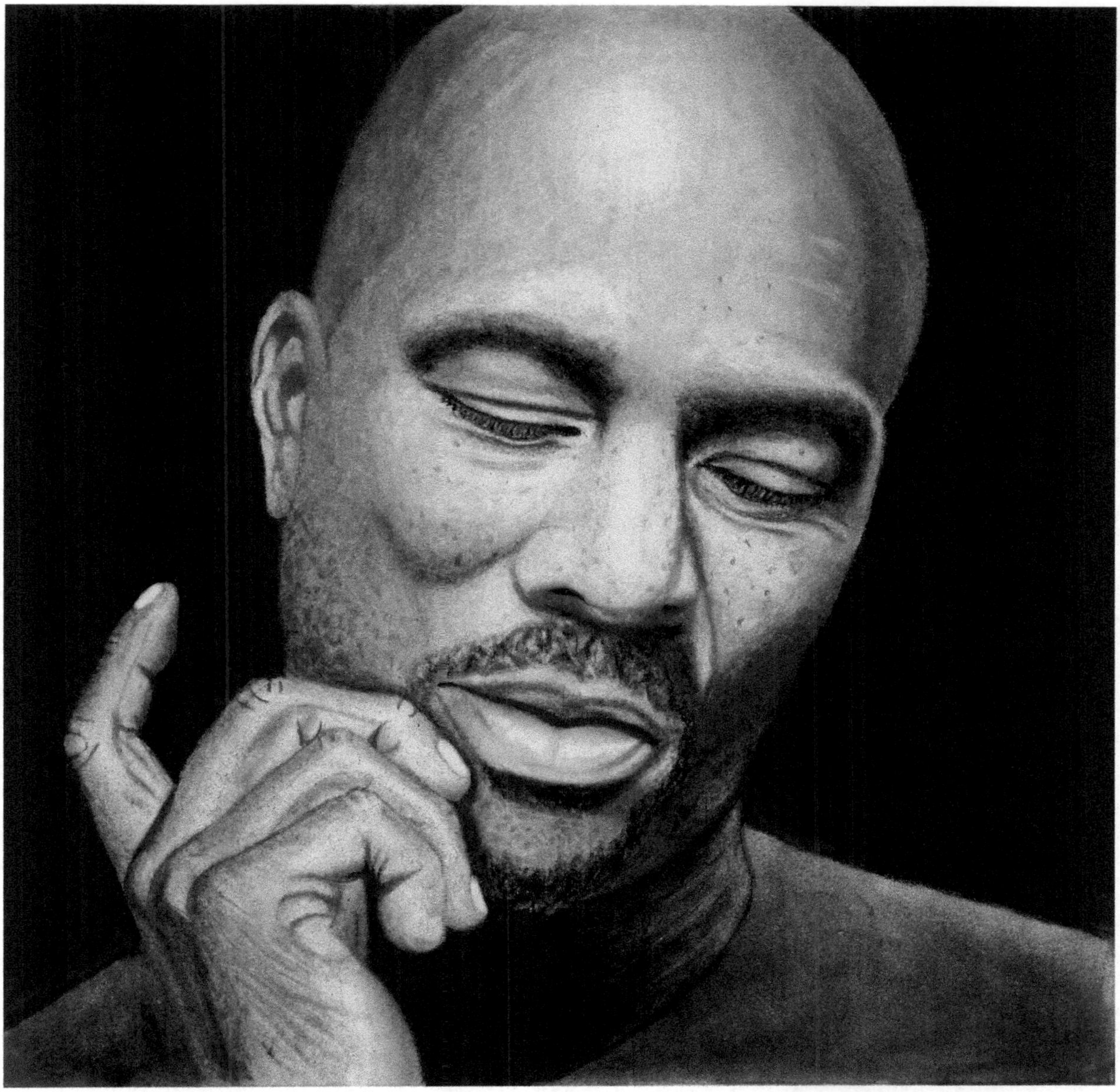

To view how this drawing was masterfully created or to purchase a Limited Edition Framed Artwork of Common type into your Internet Browser the URL shortcut ➡ **myportrait.art/common**

To listen to his Greatest Songs type into your Internet Browser the URL shortcut ➡ **radio.surf/common**

To view all channels on THE FACE OF MUSIC Internet Radio MEGA Station type into your Internet Browser the URL shortcut ➡ **radio.surf/music**

To inquire about purchasing a Limited Edtion NFT of this portrait type into your Internet Browser the URL shortcut ➡ **myartnft.shop/common**

To view all available NFTs type into your Internet Browser the URL shortcut ➡ **myartnft.shop/all**

# Conway Twitty

(Net worth: $14 Million)(Total Records Sold: 50 Million)
(Genre: Country , Rock & Roll , Rockabilly)(Height: 6' - 0")

Harold Lloyd Jenkins (September 1, 1933 – June 5, 1993), better known by his stage name Conway Twitty, was an American country music singer. He also had success in the rock and roll, R&B, and pop genres. From 1971 to 1976, Twitty received a string of Country Music Association awards for duets with Loretta Lynn. He was inducted into the Country Music Hall of Fame and the Rockabilly Hall of Fame.

Twitty was born Harold Lloyd Jenkins on September 1, 1933, in Friars Point, in Coahoma County, in northwestern Mississippi. The Jenkins family were of Welsh descent. He was named by his great-uncle, after his favorite silent movie actor, Harold Lloyd. The Jenkins family moved to Helena, Arkansas, when Jenkins was 10 years old. In Helena, Jenkins formed his first singing group, the Phillips County Ramblers.

Jenkins had his own local radio show every Saturday morning. He also played baseball, his second passion. He received an offer to play with the Philadelphia Phillies after high school, but he was drafted into the United States Army. He served in the Far East and organized a group called the Cimmerons to entertain his fellow soldiers.

Wayne Hause, a neighbor, suggested that Jenkins could make it in the music industry. Soon after hearing Elvis Presley's song "Mystery Train", Jenkins began writing rock and roll material. He went to the Sun Studios in Memphis, Tennessee, and worked with Sam Phillips, the owner and founder, to get the "right" sound.

None of Jenkins' Sun recordings were released at the time, but Roy Orbison did record his composition "Rockhouse" which was issued on SUN 251 (flipside "You're My Baby") in 1956.

Allegedly, in 1957, Jenkins decided that his real name was not memorable enough and sought a better show business name. In The Billboard Book of Number One Hits, Fred Bronson states that the singer was looking at a road map when he spotted Conway, Arkansas, and Twitty, Texas, and chose the name Conway Twitty Also, in 1957, under his new name, He recorded briefly for Mercury Records, releasing two unsuccessful singles.

On June 4, 1993, Twitty became ill while performing at the Jim Stafford Theatre in Branson, Missouri. He collapsed on his tour bus after the show and was rushed to a hospital. He was rushed into surgery, but died of an abdominal aortic aneurysm, in the early hours of the following morning at Cox South Hospital in Springfield, Missouri, at the age of 59. .

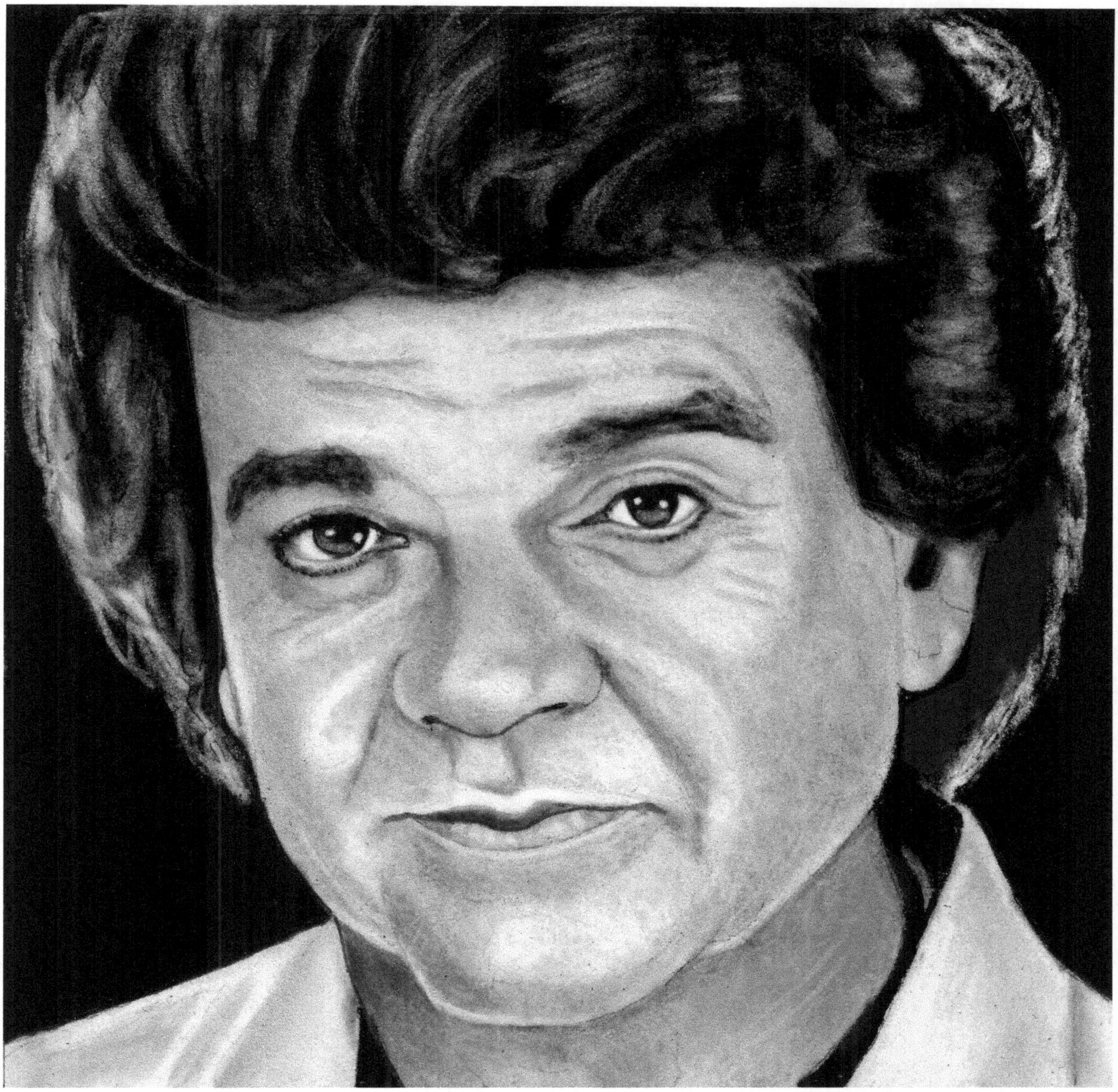

To view how this drawing was masterfully created or to purchase a Limited Edition Framed Artwork of Conway Twitty type into your Internet Browser the URL shortcut ➡ **myportrait.art/conwaytwitty**

To listen to his Greatest Songs type into your Internet Browser the URL shortcut ➡ **radio.surf/conwaytwitty**

To view all channels on THE FACE OF MUSIC Internet Radio MEGA Station type into your Internet Browser the URL shortcut ➡ **radio.surf/music**

To inquire about purchasing a Limited Edtion NFT of this portrait type into your Internet Browser the URL shortcut ➡ **myartnft.shop/conwaytwitty**

To view all available NFTs type into your Internet Browser the URL shortcut ➡ **myartnft.shop/all**

# Cream

(Total Albums Sold: 15+ Million)(Genre: Psychedelic Rock , Hard Rock , Blues Rock)
Cream were a British rock band formed in London in 1966. The group consisted of bassist Jack Bruce, guitarist Eric Clapton, and drummer Ginger Baker. Bruce was the primary songwriter and vocalist, although Clapton and Baker also sang and contributed songs. Formed from members of previously successful bands, they are widely regarded as the world's first supergroup. Cream were highly regarded for the instrumental proficiency of each of their members. Tensions between Bruce and Baker led to their decision in May 1968 to break up, though the band were persuaded to make a final album, Goodbye, and to tour, culminating in two final farewell concerts at the Royal Albert Hall on 25 and 26 November 1968 which were filmed and shown in theatres, then in 1977 released as a home video, Farewell Concert.
In 1993, Cream were inducted into the Rock and Roll Hall of Fame. They were included in both Rolling Stone and VH1's lists of the "100 Greatest Artists of All Time", at number 67 and 61 respectively. They were also ranked number 16 on VH1's "100 Greatest Artists of Hard Rock".

# Eric Clapton

(Net Worth: $250 Million) (Height: 5'- 10")
Eric Patrick Clapton, CBE (born 30 March 1945) is an English rock and blues guitarist, singer, and songwriter. He is the only three-time inductee to the Rock and Roll Hall of Fame: once as a solo artist and separately as a member of the Yardbirds and of Cream. Clapton has been referred to as one of the most important and influential guitarists of all time. Clapton ranked second in Rolling Stone's list of the "100 Greatest Guitarists of All Time" and fourth in Gibson's "Top 50 Guitarists of All Time". He was also named number five in Time magazine's list of "The 10 Best Electric Guitar Players" in 2009.
Alongside his solo career, he also performed with Delaney & Bonnie and Derek and the Dominos, with whom he recorded "Layla", one of his signature songs.
Clapton has received 18 Grammy Awards as well as the Brit Award for Outstanding Contribution to Music. In 2004 he was awarded a CBE at Buckingham Palace for services to music. He has received four Ivor Novello Awards from the British Academy of Songwriters, Composers and Authors, including the Lifetime Achievement Award. In his solo career, Clapton has sold more than 100 million records worldwide, making him one of the best-selling musicians of all time. In 1998, Clapton, a recovering alcoholic and drug addict, founded the Crossroads Centre on Antigua, a medical facility for recovering substance abusers.

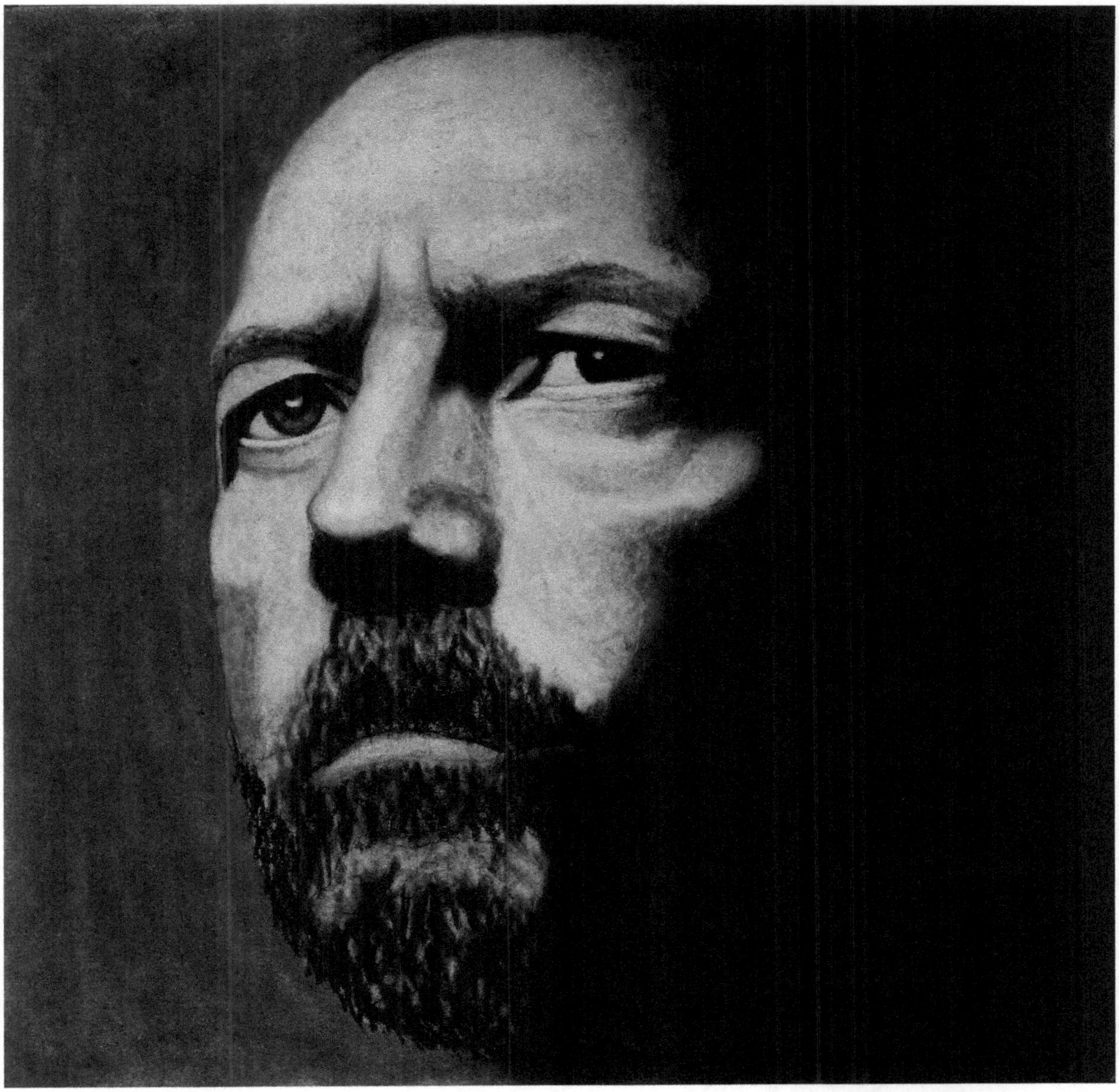

To view how this drawing was masterfully created or to purchase a Limited Edition Framed Artwork of Eric Clapton type into your Internet Browser the URL shortcut ➡ **myportrait.art/ericclapton**

To listen to their Greatest Songs type into your Internet Browser the URL shortcut ➡ **radio.surf/ericclapton**

To view all channels on THE FACE OF MUSIC Internet Radio MEGA Station type into your Internet Browser the URL shortcut ➡ **radio.surf/music**

To inquire about purchasing a Limited Edtion NFT of this portrait type into your Internet Browser the URL shortcut ➡ **myartnft.shop/ericclapton**

To view all available NFTs type into your Internet Browser the URL shortcut ➡ **myartnft.shop/all**

# Creedence Clearwater Revival

(Total Albums Sold: 26+ Million)(Genre: Classic Rock)

Creedence Clearwater Revival, also referred to as Creedence and CCR, was an American rock band which recorded and performed from 1967 to 1972. The band initially consisted of lead vocalist, lead guitarist, and primary songwriter John Fogerty; his brother, rhythm guitarist Tom Fogerty; bassist Stu Cook; and drummer Doug Clifford. These members had played together since 1959, first as the Blue Velvets and later as the Golliwogs.

CCR's musical style encompassed roots rock, swamp rock, blues rock, Southern rock, and country rock. Despite their San Francisco Bay Area origin, the band played in a Southern rock style, with lyrics about bayous, catfish, the Mississippi River and other popular elements of Southern United States iconography. The band's songs rarely dealt with romantic love, concentrating instead on political and socially conscious lyrics about topics such as the Vietnam War. The band performed at the 1969 Woodstock festival in Upstate New York, and was the first major act signed to appear there.

CCR disbanded acrimoniously in late 1972 after four years of chart-topping success. Tom Fogerty had officially left the previous year, and John was at odds with the remaining members over matters of business and artistic control, all of which resulted in subsequent lawsuits among the former bandmates. Fogerty's ongoing disagreements with Fantasy Records owner Saul Zaentz created further protracted court battles, and John Fogerty refused to perform with the two other surviving members at Creedence's 1993 induction into the Rock and Roll Hall of Fame.

CCR's music is still a staple of U.S. classic rock radio airplay; 28 million CCR records have been sold in the U.S alone. The compilation album Chronicle The 20 Greatest Hits, originally released in 1976, is still on the Billboard 200 album chart and reached the 500-weeks mark in December, 2020. It has been awarded 10x platinum, indicating it has sold over 10 million copies. Rolling Stone ranked them 82nd on its 100 Greatest Artists of All Time.

# John Fogerty

(Net Worth: $90 Million) (Height: 5'- 10")

John Cameron Fogerty (born May 28, 1945) is an American musician, singer, and songwriter. Together with Doug Clifford, Stu Cook, and his brother Tom Fogerty, he founded the band Creedence Clearwater Revival (CCR), for which he was the lead singer, lead guitarist, and principal songwriter. The group had nine top-10 singles and eight gold albums between 1968 and 1972, and was inducted into the Rock and Roll Hall of Fame in 1993.

Since CCR parted ways in 1972, Fogerty has had a successful solo career, which continues. He was listed on Rolling Stone magazine's list of 100 Greatest Songwriters (at number 40) and the list of 100 Greatest Singers (at number 72). His songs include "Proud Mary", "Bad Moon Rising", "Fortunate Son", "Green River", "Down on the Corner", "Who'll Stop the Rain", and "Centerfield".

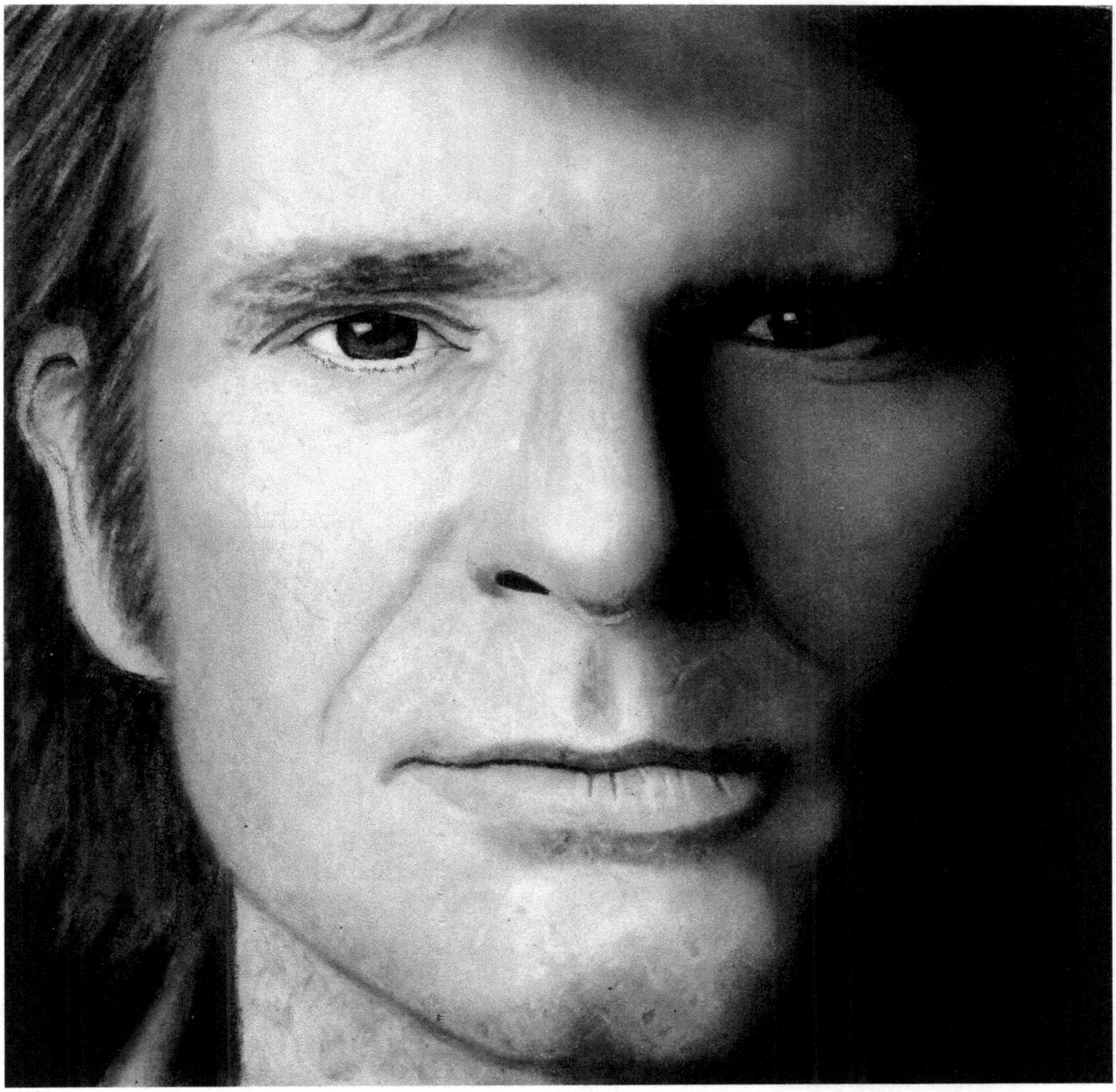

To view how this drawing was masterfully created or to purchase a Limited Edition Framed Artwork of John Fogerty type into your Internet Browser the URL shortcut ➡ **myportrait.art/johnfogerty**

To listen to their Greatest Songs type into your Internet Browser the URL shortcut ➡ **radio.surf/ccr**

To view all channels on THE FACE OF MUSIC Internet Radio MEGA Station type into your Internet Browser the URL shortcut ➡ **radio.surf/music**

To inquire about purchasing a Limited Edtion NFT of this portrait type into your Internet Browser the URL shortcut ➡ **myartnft.shop/johnfogerty**

To view all available NFTs type into your Internet Browser the URL shortcut ➡ **myartnft.shop/all**

# Crosby, Stills & Nash

(Total Albums Sold: 13 Million)(Genre: Folk Rock, Country Rock, Soft Rock)

Crosby, Stills & Nash (CSN) is a folk rock supergroup made up of American singer-songwriters David Crosby and Stephen Stills, and English singer-songwriter Graham Nash. When joined by Canadian singer-songwriter Neil Young as a fourth member, they are called Crosby, Stills, Nash & Young (CSNY). They are noted for their intricate vocal harmonies, often tumultuous interpersonal relationships, political activism, and lasting influence on American music and culture.

CSN formed in 1968 shortly after Crosby, Stills and Nash performed together informally in July of that year, discovering they harmonized well. Crosby had been asked to leave The Byrds in late 1967, and Stills' band Buffalo Springfield had broken up in early 1968; Nash left his band The Hollies in December, and by early 1969 the trio had signed a recording contract with Atlantic Records. Their first album, Crosby, Stills & Nash, was released in May 1969, from which came two Top 40 hits, "Suite: Judy Blue Eyes" [#21] and "Marrakesh Express" [#28]. In order to tour the album, the trio hired drummer Dallas Taylor and session bassist Greg Reeves, though they still needed a keyboardist; Ahmet Ertegun suggested Neil Young, who had played with Stills in Buffalo Springfield, and after some initial reluctance, the trio agreed, signing him on as a full member. The band, now named Crosby, Stills, Nash & Young, started their tour, and played their second gig at Woodstock Festival in the early morning hours of August 18, 1969. The first album with Young, Déjà Vu, reached number one in several international charts in 1970, and remains their best selling album, going on to sell over 8 million copies with three hit singles. Four singles were released from the album including "Woodstock", "Teach Your Children", and "Our House". The group's second tour, which produced the live double album 4 Way Street (1971), was fraught with arguments between Young and Taylor, which resulted in Taylor being replaced by John Barbata, and tensions with Stills, which resulted in his being temporarily dismissed from the band. At the end of the tour the band split up. The group have since reunited several times, sometimes with and sometimes without Young, and have released eight studio and four live albums.Crosby, Stills & Nash were inducted into the Rock and Roll Hall of Fame and all three members were also inducted for their work in other groups (Crosby for the Byrds, Stills for Buffalo Springfield and Nash for the Hollies). Neil Young has also been inducted as a solo artist and as a member of Buffalo Springfield but not as a member of CSN. They have not made a group studio album since 1999's Looking Forward, and have been inactive as a performing unit since the end of 2015. Whether or not this break is permanent remains to be seen, as the group has often been inactive for years at a time.

# David Crosby

(Net Worth: $10 Million) (Height: 5'- 8")

David Van Cortlandt Crosby (born August 14, 1941) is an American singer-songwriter and musician. In addition to his solo career, he was a founding member of both the Byrds and Crosby, Stills & Nash.

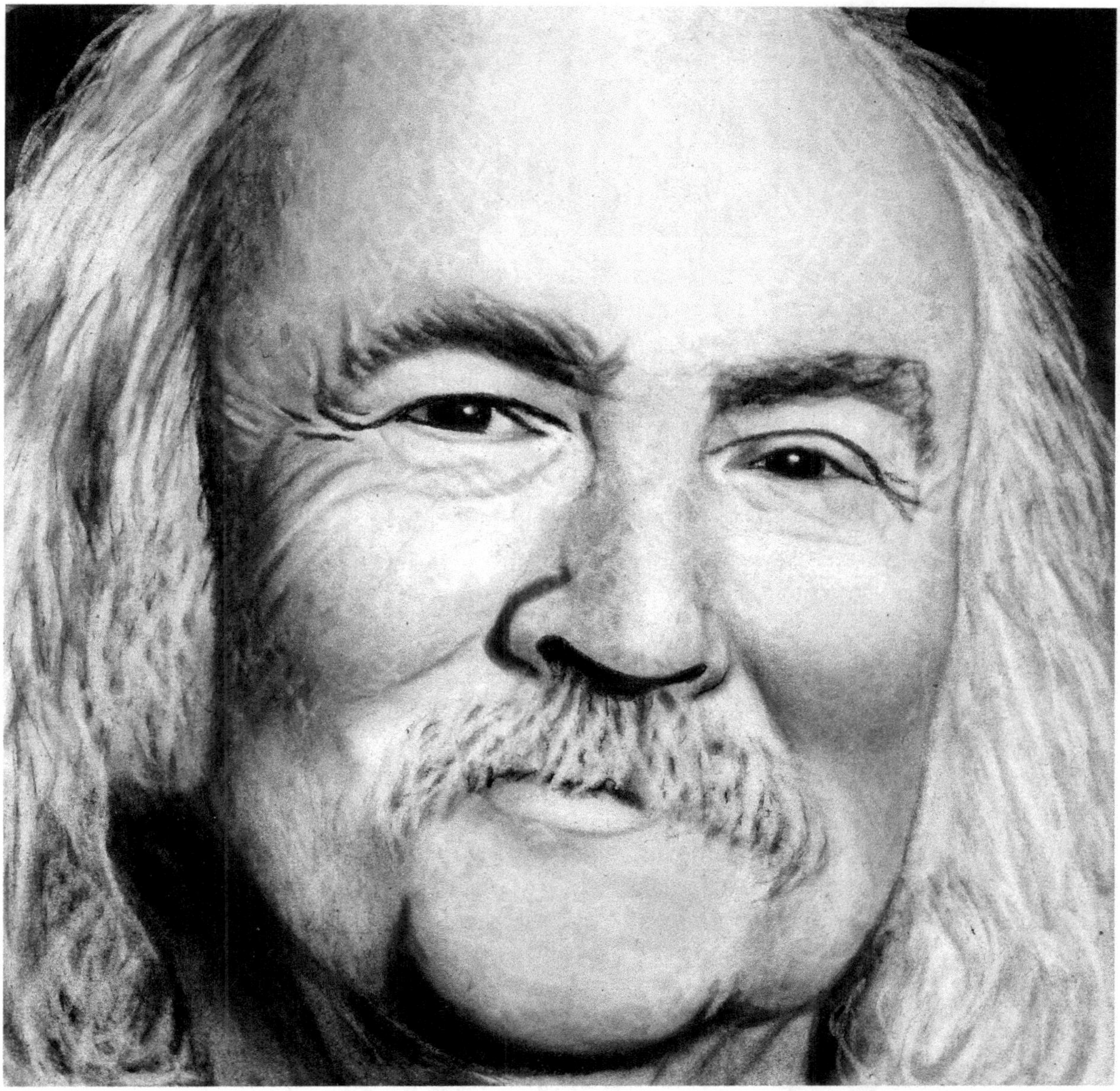

To view how this drawing was masterfully created or to purchase a Limited Edition Framed Artwork of David Crosby type into your Internet Browser the URL shortcut ➡ **myportrait.art/davidcrosby**

To listen to their Greatest Songs type into your Internet Browser the URL shortcut
➡ **radio.surf/crosbystillsandnash**

To view all channels on THE FACE OF MUSIC Internet Radio MEGA Station type into your Internet Browser the URL shortcut ➡ **radio.surf/music**

To inquire about purchasing a Limited Edtion NFT of this portrait type into your Internet Browser the URL shortcut ➡ **myartnft.shop/davidcrosby**

To view all available NFTs type into your Internet Browser the URL shortcut ➡ **myartnft.shop/all**

# Cult, The

(Total Albums Sold: 2.5 Million)(Genre: Gothic Rock , Post Punk)

The Cult are a British rock band formed in 1983. Before settling on their current name in January 1984, the band performed under the name Death Cult, which was an evolution of the name of lead singer Ian Astbury's previous band Southern Death Cult. They gained a dedicated following in the United Kingdom in the mid-1980s as a post-punk/gothic rock band, with singles such as "She Sells Sanctuary", before breaking into the mainstream in the United States in the late 1980s establishing themselves as a hard rock band with singles such as "Love Removal Machine" and "Fire Woman". Since the initial formation of Southern Death Cult in Bradford in 1981, the band have had various line-ups; the longest-serving members are Astbury and guitarist Billy Duffy, who are the band's two songwriters. After moving to London, the band released their second album Love in 1985, which charted at No. 4 in the UK and included singles such as "She Sells Sanctuary" and "Rain". On their third album, Electric (1987), the band supplemented their post-punk sound with hard rock; the polish on this new sound was facilitated by producer Rick Rubin. Their fourth album, Sonic Temple (1989), proceeded in a similar vein, and these two albums enabled them to break into the North American market. It was also during this period that The Cult relocated to Los Angeles, California, where they are currently based in.The Cult released two more studio albums – Ceremony (1991) and The Cult (1994) – before breaking up in 1995, due to internal conflicts. The band reunited in 1999 and released their seventh album Beyond Good and Evil two years later. After going on hiatus in 2002, they returned in 2006 to perform a series of worldwide tours, and have since released three more studio albums: Born into This (2007), Choice of Weapon (2012) and Hidden City (2016).

## Ian Astbury

(Net Worth: $15 Million) (Height: 5'- 10")

Ian Robert Astbury (born 14 May 1962) is a British singer and songwriter. He is best known as a founding member and lead vocalist for the rock band the Cult.

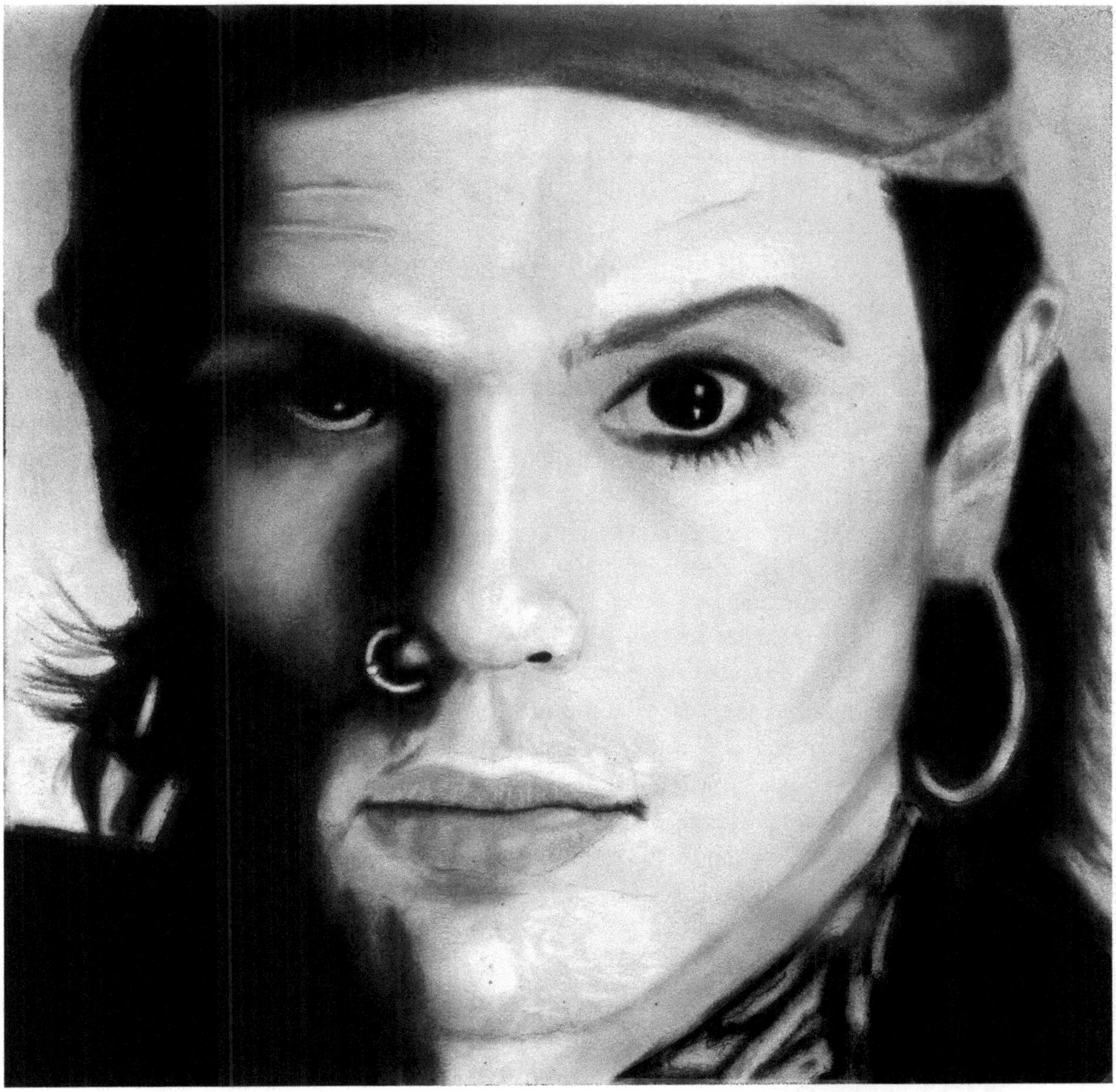

To view how this drawing was masterfully created or to purchase a Limited Edition Framed Artwork of Ian Astbury type into your Internet Browser the URL shortcut ➡ **myportrait.art/ianastbury**

To listen to their Greatest Songs type into your Internet Browser the URL shortcut ➡ **radio.surf/thecult**

To view all channels on THE FACE OF MUSIC Internet Radio MEGA Station type into your Internet Browser the URL shortcut ➡ **radio.surf/music**

To inquire about purchasing a Limited Edtion NFT of this portrait type into your Internet Browser the URL shortcut ➡ **myartnft.shop/ianastbury**

To view all available NFTs type into your Internet Browser the URL shortcut ➡ **myartnft.shop/all**

# Culture Club

(Total Albums Sold: 50+ Million)(Genre: New Wave, Pop, Dance-Rock)

Culture Club is an English band that formed in London in 1981. The band comprises Boy George (lead vocals), Roy Hay (guitar and keyboards), Mikey Craig (bass guitar) and Jon Moss (drums and percussion). They are considered one of the most representative and influential groups of the 1980s. Led by singer and frontman Boy George, whose androgynous style of dressing caught the attention of the public and the media in the early 1980s, the band have sold more than 50 million records including over 6 million BPI certified records sold in the UK and over 7 million RIAA certified records sold in the US. Their hits include "Do You Really Want to Hurt Me", "Time (Clock of the Heart)", "I'll Tumble 4 Ya", "Church of the Poison Mind", "Karma Chameleon", "Victims", "Miss Me Blind", "It's a Miracle", "The War Song", "Move Away", and "I Just Wanna Be Loved". In the UK they amassed twelve Top 40 hit singles between 1982 and 1999, including the number ones "Do You Really Want To Hurt Me" and "Karma Chameleon", the latter being the biggest selling single of 1983 in the UK, and hit number one on the US Hot 100 in 1984. The song "Time (Clock of the Heart)" is included on the Rock and Roll Hall of Fame's list of 500 songs that shaped rock and roll.

In 1984, Culture Club won Brit Awards for Best British Group, Best British Single ("Karma Chameleon"), and the Grammy Award for Best New Artist. They were nominated the same year for the Grammy Award for Pop Vocal by Group or Duo. The band were also nominated for a Canadian Juno Award for International Album of the Year. In January 1985, Culture Club were nominated for an American Music Award for Favorite Pop/Rock Band/Duo/Group Video Artist, and in September 1985, they were nominated for two MTV Video Music Awards for Best Special Effects and Best Art Direction for their video "It's a Miracle". In 1987, they received another nomination for an American Music Award for Favorite Pop/Rock Band/Duo/Group Video Artist.

# Boy George

(Net Worth: $35 Million) (Height: 6'-0")

George Alan O'Dowd (born 14 June 1961), known professionally as Boy George, is an English singer, songwriter, DJ, fashion designer, photographer and record producer. He is the lead singer of the pop band Culture Club. At the height of the band's fame, during the 1980s, they recorded global hit songs such as "Karma Chameleon", "Do You Really Want to Hurt Me" and "Time (Clock of the Heart)". George is known for his soulful voice and his androgynous appearance. He was part of the English New Romantic movement which emerged in the late 1970s to the early 1980s.

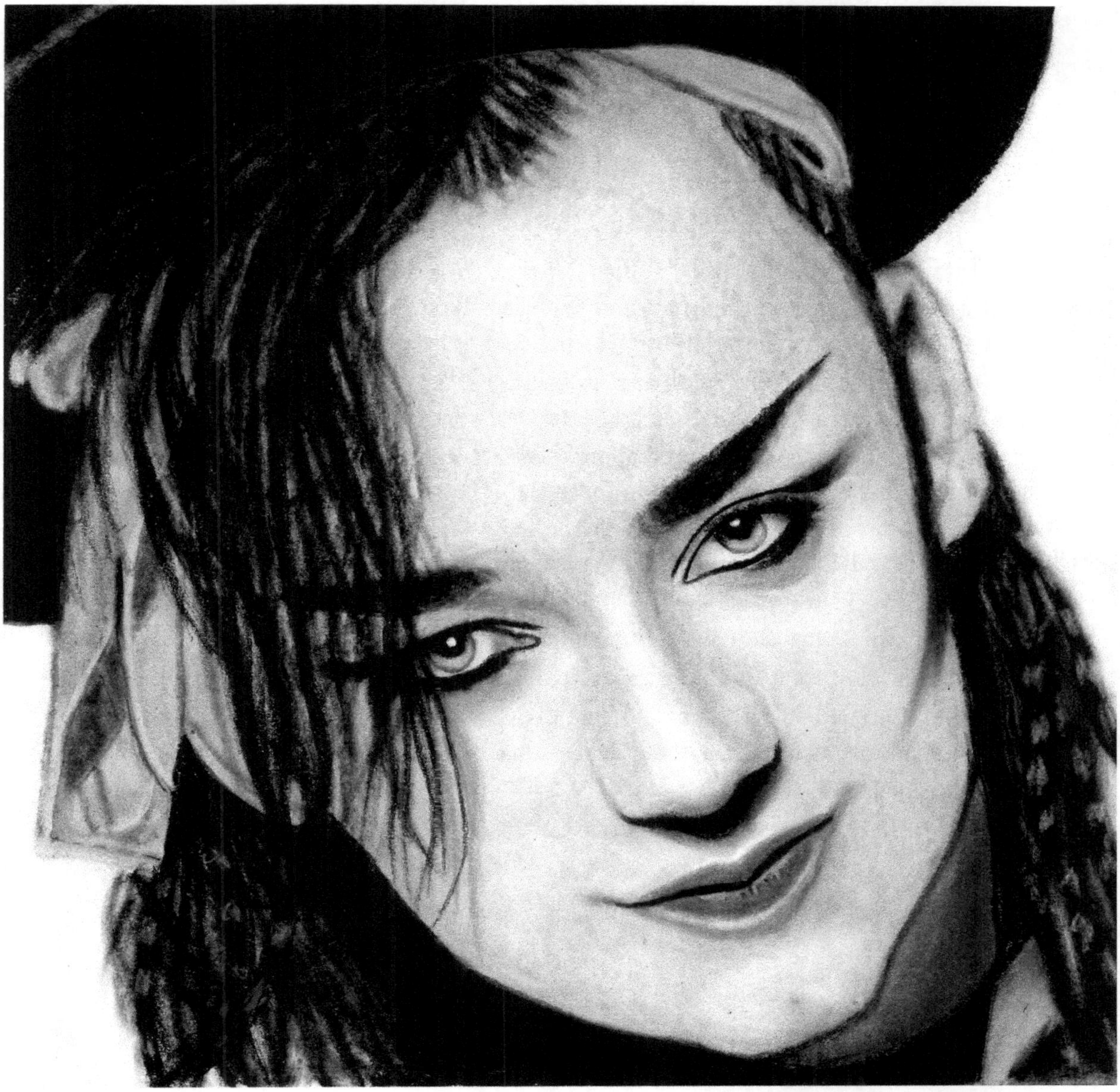

To view how this drawing was masterfully created or to purchase a Limited Edition Framed Artwork of Boy George type into your Internet Browser the URL shortcut ➡ **myportrait.art/boygeorge**

To listen to their Greatest Songs type into your Internet Browser the URL shortcut ➡ **radio.surf/cultureclub**

To view all channels on THE FACE OF MUSIC Internet Radio MEGA Station type into your Internet Browser the URL shortcut ➡ **radio.surf/music**

To inquire about purchasing a Limited Edtion NFT of this portrait type into your Internet Browser the URL shortcut ➡ **myartnft.shop/boygeorge**

To view all available NFTs type into your Internet Browser the URL shortcut ➡ **myartnft.shop/all**

# Cure, The

(Total Albums Sold: 30+ Million)(Genre: New Wave , Post Punk , Gothic Rock)
The Cure are an English rock band formed in Crawley, West Sussex, in 1978. The band members have changed several times, and guitarist, lead vocalist, and songwriter Robert Smith is the only constant member. The band's debut album was Three Imaginary Boys (1979) and this, along with several early singles, placed the band in the post-punk and new wave movements that had sprung up in the United Kingdom. Beginning with their second album, Seventeen Seconds (1980), the band adopted a new, increasingly dark and tormented style, which, together with Smith's stage look, had a strong influence on the emerging genre of gothic rock as well as the subculture that eventually formed around the genre. Following the release of their fourth album Pornography in 1982, the band's future was uncertain. Smith was keen to move past the gloomy reputation his band had acquired, introducing a greater pop sensibility into the band's music. Songs such as "Let's Go to Bed" (1982), "The Love Cats" (1983), "Inbetween Days" (1985), "Close To Me" (1985), "Just Like Heaven" (1987), "Lovesong" (1989), and "Friday I'm in Love" (1992) aided the band in receiving commercial popularity. The band have released 13 studio albums, two EPs, over 30 singles, and have sold over 30 million albums worldwide. The Cure were inducted into the Rock and Roll Hall of Fame in 2019.

# Robert Smith

(Net Worth: $25 Million) (Height: 5'- 10")
Robert James Smith (born 21 April 1959) is an English singer, songwriter, musician, and record producer. He is best known as the lead singer, guitarist, primary songwriter, and only continuous member of the rock band The Cure, which he co-founded in 1976. He was also the lead guitarist for the band Siouxsie and the Banshees from 1982 to 1984, and was part of the short-lived group The Glove in 1983. Considered to be one of the most influential and underrated guitarists of the 20th century, Smith is known for his guitar-playing style, distinctive voice, and unique fashion sense, with the latter—a pale complexion, smeared red lipstick, black eye-liner, a dishevelled nest of wiry black hair, and all-black clothes—being highly influential on the goth subculture that rose to prominence in the 1980s. He was inducted into the Rock and Roll Hall of Fame as a member of The Cure in 2019.

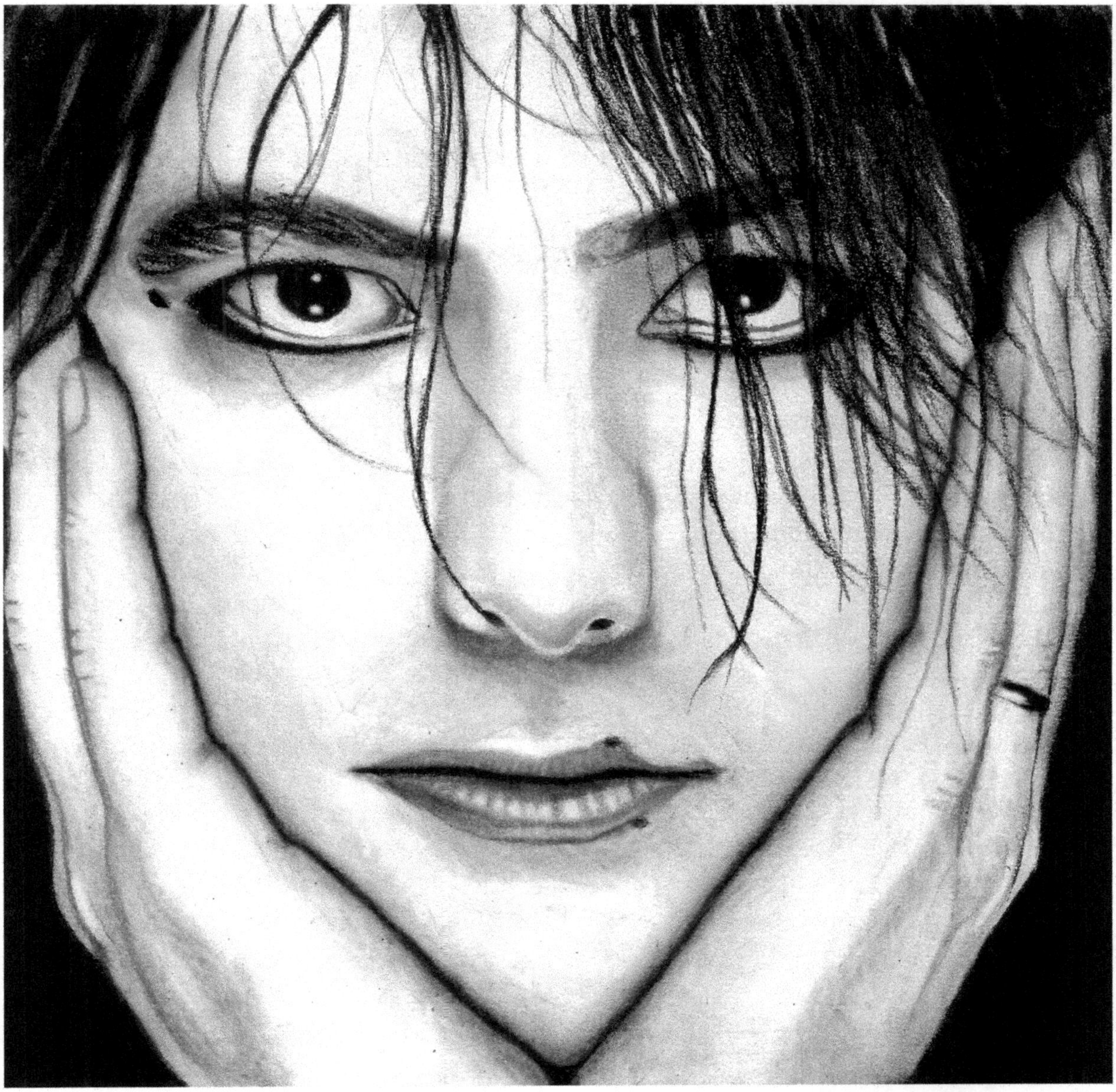

To view how this drawing was masterfully created or to purchase a Limited Edition Framed Artwork of Robert Smith type into your Internet Browser the URL shortcut ➡ **myportrait.art/robertsmith**

To listen to their Greatest Songs type into your Internet Browser the URL shortcut ➡ **radio.surf/thecure**

To view all channels on THE FACE OF MUSIC Internet Radio MEGA Station type into your Internet Browser the URL shortcut ➡ **radio.surf/music**

To inquire about purchasing a Limited Edtion NFT of this portrait type into your Internet Browser the URL shortcut ➡ **myartnft.shop/robertsmith**

To view all available NFTs type into your Internet Browser the URL shortcut ➡ **myartnft.shop/all**

# Cyndi Lauper

(Net worth: $50 Million)(Total Albums Sold: 50+ Million)
(Genre: New Wave, Pop, Rock, Soul)(Height: 5' - 2")

Cynthia Ann Stephanie Lauper (born June 22, 1953) is an American singer, songwriter, actress and activist. Her career has spanned over 40 years. Her album She's So Unusual (1983) was the first debut album by a female artist to achieve four top-five hits on the Billboard Hot 100—"Girls Just Want to Have Fun", "Time After Time", "She Bop", and "All Through the Night"—and earned Lauper the Best New Artist award at the 27th Grammy Awards in 1985. Her success continued with the soundtrack for the motion picture The Goonies and her second record True Colors (1986). This album included the number one single "True Colors" and "Change of Heart", which peaked at number three. In 1989, she had a hit with a cover of Roy Orbison's "I Drove All Night".

Since 1983, Lauper has released eleven studio albums and participated in many other projects. In 2010, Memphis Blues became Billboard's most successful blues album of the year, remaining at number one on the Billboard Blues Albums chart for 13 consecutive weeks. In 2013, Lauper won the Tony Award for best original score for composing the Broadway musical Kinky Boots, making her the first woman to win the category by herself. The musical was awarded five other Tonys including Tony Award for Best New Musical. In 2014, Lauper was awarded the Grammy Award for Best Musical Theater Album for the cast recording. In 2016, the West End production won Best New Musical at the Olivier Awards. Lauper has sold over 50 million records worldwide. She has won awards at the Grammys, Emmys, Tonys, the New York's Outer Critics Circle, MTV Video Music Awards (VMAs), Billboard Awards, and American Music Awards (AMAs). An inductee into both the Songwriters Hall of Fame and the Hollywood Walk of Fame, Lauper is one of the few singers to win three of the four major American entertainment awards (EGOT). Lauper won the inaugural Best Female Video prize at the 1984 VMAs for "Girls Just Want to Have Fun". This music video is recognized by MTV, VH1 and Rolling Stone as one of the greatest music videos of the era. She is featured in the Rock and Roll Hall of Fame Museum's Women Who Rock exhibit. Her debut album is included in Rolling Stone's list of the 500 Greatest Albums of All Time, while "Time After Time" is included in VH1's list of the 100 Best Songs of the Past 25 years. VH1 has ranked Lauper No. 58 of the 100 Greatest Women of Rock & Roll.

Lauper is known for her distinctive image, featuring a variety of hair colors and eccentric clothing, and for her powerful and distinctive four-octave singing range. She has been celebrated for her humanitarian work, particularly as an advocate for LGBT rights in the United States. Her charitable efforts were acknowledged in 2013 when she was invited as a special guest to attend U.S. President Barack Obama's second-term inauguration.

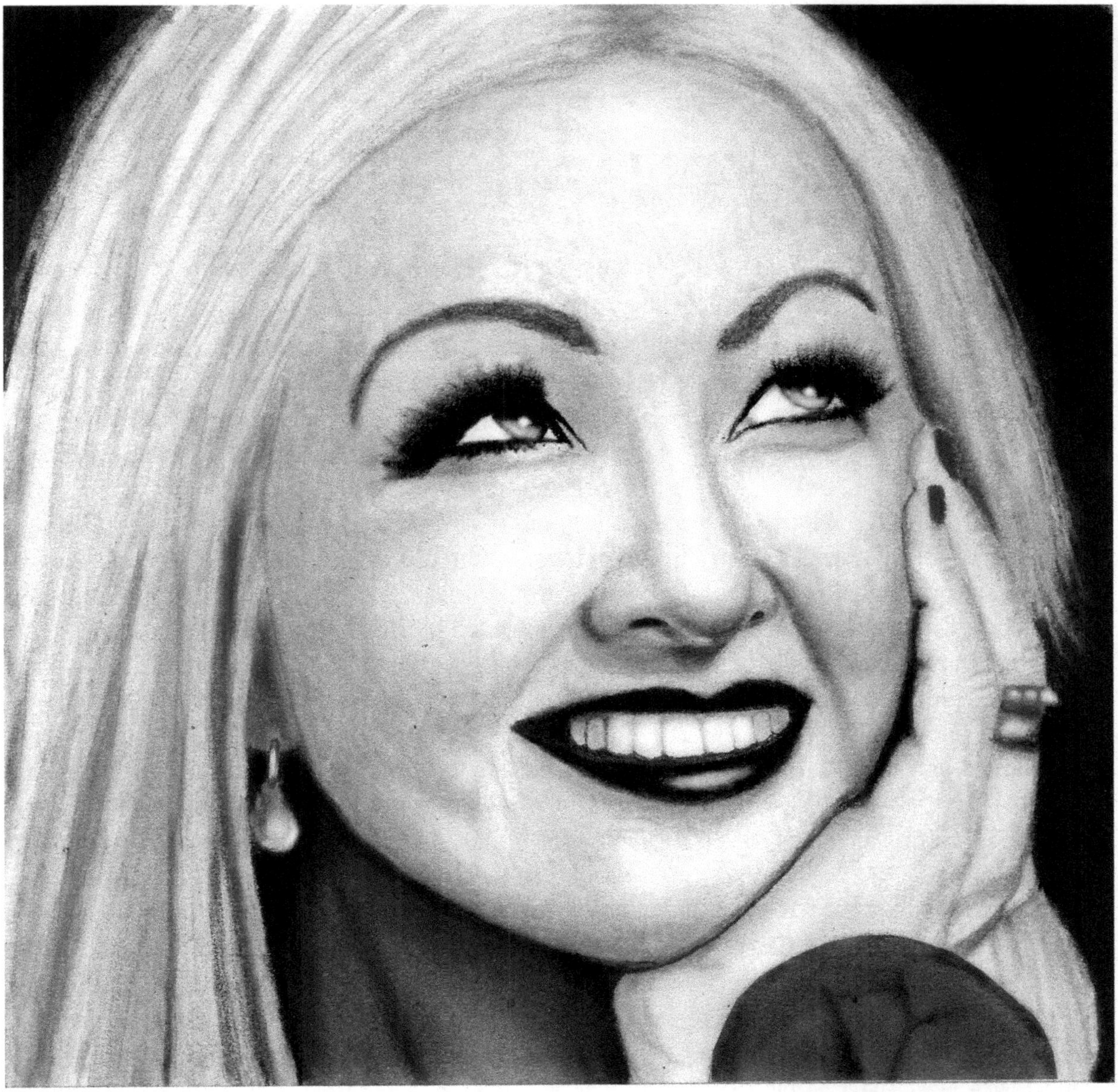

To view how this drawing was masterfully created or to purchase a Limited Edition Framed Artwork of Cyndi Lauper type into your Internet Browser the URL shortcut ➡ **myportrait.art/cyndilauper**

To listen to her Greatest Songs type into your Internet Browser the URL shortcut ➡ **radio.surf/cyndilauper**

To view all channels on THE FACE OF MUSIC Internet Radio MEGA Station type into your Internet Browser the URL shortcut ➡ **radio.surf/music**

To inquire about purchasing a Limited Edtion NFT of this portrait type into your Internet Browser the URL shortcut ➡ **myartnft.shop/cyndilauper**

To view all available NFTs type into your Internet Browser the URL shortcut ➡ **myartnft.shop/all**

# Dave Matthews

(Net worth: $300 Million)(Total Albums Sold: 33+ Million)
(Genre: Blues Rock)(Height: 6' - 1 1/2")

David John Matthews (born January 9, 1967) is an American singer, songwriter, musician, actor and record label owner, best known as the lead vocalist, songwriter and guitarist for the Dave Matthews Band (DMB). Matthews was born in Johannesburg, and moved frequently between South Africa, the United Kingdom and the United States while growing up. Matthews started playing acoustic guitar at the age of nine.

From 1991 to 2003, Matthews predominantly focused on songwriting and performing with the Dave Matthews Band, which he started in Charlottesville, Virginia in 1991. Since then, he has also done various solo performances and produced other records. During the period from 2000 to 2010, his band sold more tickets and earned more money than any other act in North America. The band's 2012 album Away from the World made them the only group to have six consecutive studio albums debut at number one on the Billboard charts. This record was extended to seven consecutive number one albums with the 2018 release, Come Tomorrow.

In addition to music, Matthews has had multiple acting roles. He has also won two Grammy Awards: one with the Dave Matthews Band in 1997 for Best Rock Vocal Performance by a Duo or Group ("So Much to Say") and one in 2004 for Best Male Rock Vocal Performance ("Gravedigger") from his solo album.

After writing his first few songs, including "I'll Back You Up", "The Song that Jane Likes" and "Recently", Matthews formed Dave Matthews Band in early 1991 with LeRoi Moore, Carter Beauford, Stefan Lessard, Peter Griesar (who left the band in 1993), and Boyd Tinsley while working at Miller's. The band's first show was on March 14, 1991, as part of a benefit for the Middle East Children's Alliance at Trax Nightclub in Charlottesville.

Matthews' older sister Anne, who lived in South Africa, was murdered by her husband in early 1994. Her husband subsequently died by suicide, on or around January 27 of that year. The event had a profound effect on Matthews' outlook on life and was referenced in a few of his songs. On January 29, 1994, he performed with Tim Reynolds at the Wetlands in New York, where he dedicated that performance "to her [Anne's] memory". Dave Matthews Band's Under the Table and Dreaming, released later that year, was dedicated to her. Anne Matthews was survived by her two children and they traveled to the United States following her death. Dave and his younger sister Jane (after whom the Dave Matthews Band song "The Song That Jane Likes" is named) took responsibility for the children's upbringing.

Dave Matthews married longtime girlfriend Jennifer Ashley Harper in 2000. They have twin daughters, Stella Busina and Grace Anne, born August 15, 2001, and a son, August Oliver, born June 19, 2007. They reside in Seattle. In a 2001 interview, Matthews stated that he was agnostic. Matthews is also on the Farm Aid board of directors along with fellow musicians Willie Nelson, John Mellencamp and Neil Young, who raise money for family farmers in the United States.

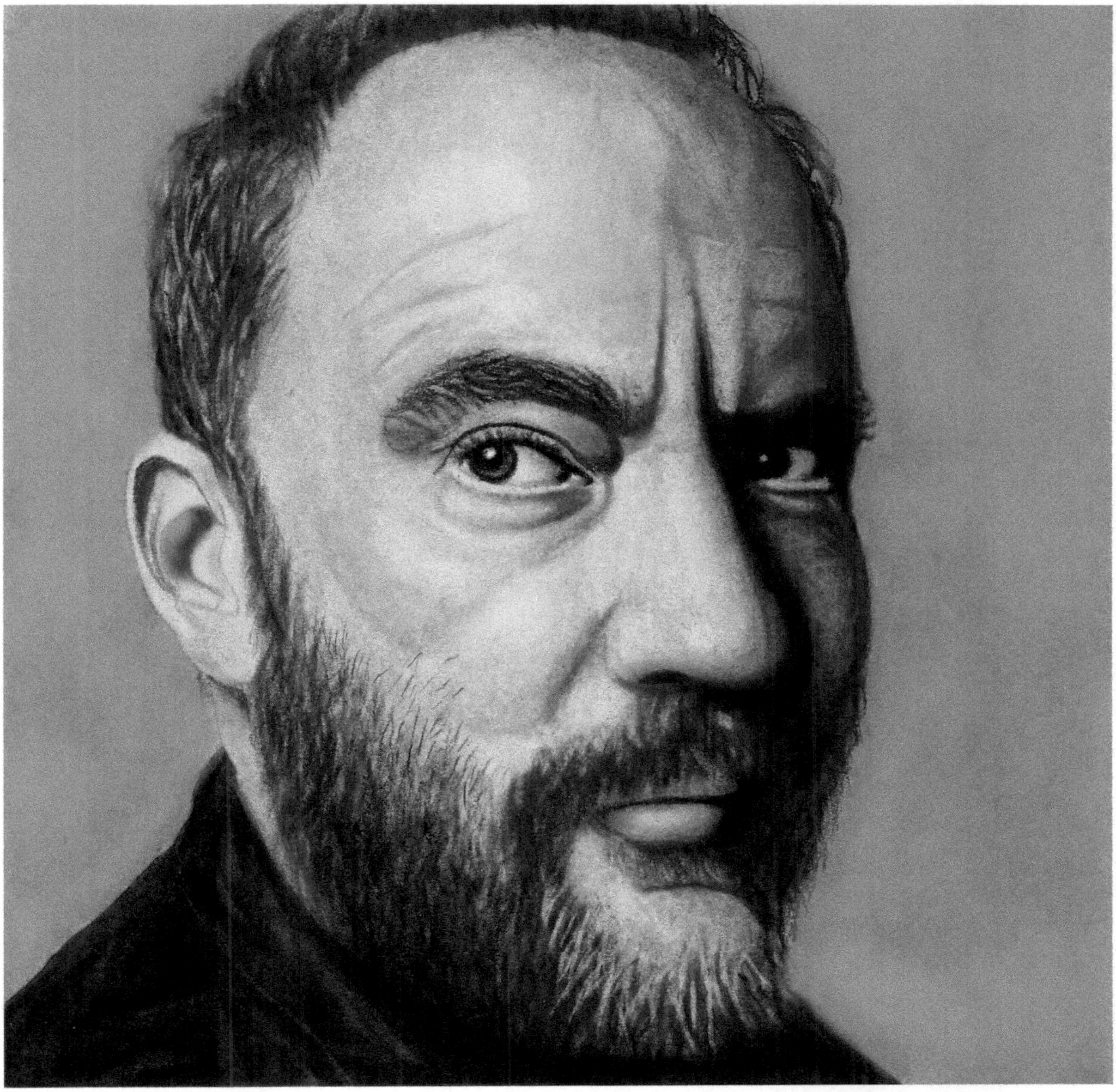

To view how this drawing was masterfully created or to purchase a Limited Edition Framed Artwork of Dave Matthews type into your Internet Browser the URL shortcut ➡ **myportrait.art/davematthews**

To listen to their Greatest Songs type into your Internet Browser the URL shortcut ➡ **radio.surf/davematthewsband**

To view all channels on THE FACE OF MUSIC Internet Radio MEGA Station type into your Internet Browser the URL shortcut ➡ **radio.surf/music**

To inquire about purchasing a Limited Edtion NFT of this portrait type into your Internet Browser the URL shortcut ➡ **myartnft.shop/davematthews**

To view all available NFTs type into your Internet Browser the URL shortcut ➡ **myartnft.shop/all**

# David Bowie

(Net worth: $230 Million)(Total Recordss Sold: 140 Million)
(Genre: Rock , Pop)(Height: 5' - 10")

David Robert Jones (8 January 1947 – 10 January 2016), known professionally as David Bowie , was an English singer-songwriter and actor. He was a leading figure in the music industry and is regarded as one of the most influential musicians of the 20th century. He was acclaimed by critics and musicians, particularly for his innovative work during the 1970s. His career was marked by reinvention and visual presentation, with his music and stagecraft having a significant impact on popular music. During his lifetime, his record sales, estimated at over 100 million records worldwide, made him one of the best-selling music artists of all time. In the UK, he was awarded ten platinum album certifications, eleven gold and eight silver, and released eleven number-one albums. In the US he received five platinum and nine gold certifications. He was inducted into the Rock and Roll Hall of Fame in 1996. Rolling Stone placed him among its list of the 100 Greatest Artists of All Time and named him the "Greatest Rock Star Ever" following his death in 2016.

Born in Brixton, South London, Bowie developed an interest in music as a child. He studied art, music and design before embarking on a professional career as a musician in 1963. "Space Oddity", released in 1969, was his first top-five entry on the UK Singles Chart. After a period of experimentation, he re-emerged in 1972 during the glam rock era with his flamboyant and androgynous alter ego Ziggy Stardust. The character was spearheaded by the success of Bowie's single "Starman" and album The Rise and Fall of Ziggy Stardust and the Spiders from Mars, which won him widespread popularity. In 1975, Bowie's style shifted towards a sound he characterised as "plastic soul", initially alienating many of his UK fans but garnering him his first major US crossover success with the number-one single "Fame" and the album Young Americans. In 1976, Bowie starred in the cult film The Man Who Fell to Earth, directed by Nicolas Roeg, and released Station to Station. In 1977, he further confounded expectations with the electronic-inflected album Low, the first of three collaborations with Brian Eno that came to be known as the "Berlin Trilogy". "Heroes" (1977) and Lodger (1979) followed; each album reached the UK top five and received lasting critical praise. After uneven commercial success in the late 1970s, Bowie had UK number ones with the 1980 single "Ashes to Ashes", its album Scary Monsters (and Super Creeps), and "Under Pressure", a 1981 collaboration with Queen. He reached his commercial peak in 1983 with Let's Dance; its title track topped both UK and US charts. Throughout the 1990s and 2000s, Bowie continued to experiment with musical styles, including industrial and jungle. He also continued acting; his roles included Major Jack Celliers in Merry Christmas, Mr. Lawrence (1983), Jareth the Goblin King in Labyrinth (1986), Pontius Pilate in The Last Temptation of Christ (1988), and Nikola Tesla in The Prestige (2006), among other film and television appearances and cameos. He stopped touring after 2004 and his last live performance was at a charity event in 2006. In 2013, Bowie returned from a decade-long recording hiatus with The Next Day. He remained musically active until his death of liver cancer at his home in New York City, two days after his 69th birthday and the release of his final album, Blackstar (2016). Blackstar won British Album of the Year at the 2017 Brit Awards and five Grammy Awards at the 2017 Grammy Awards.

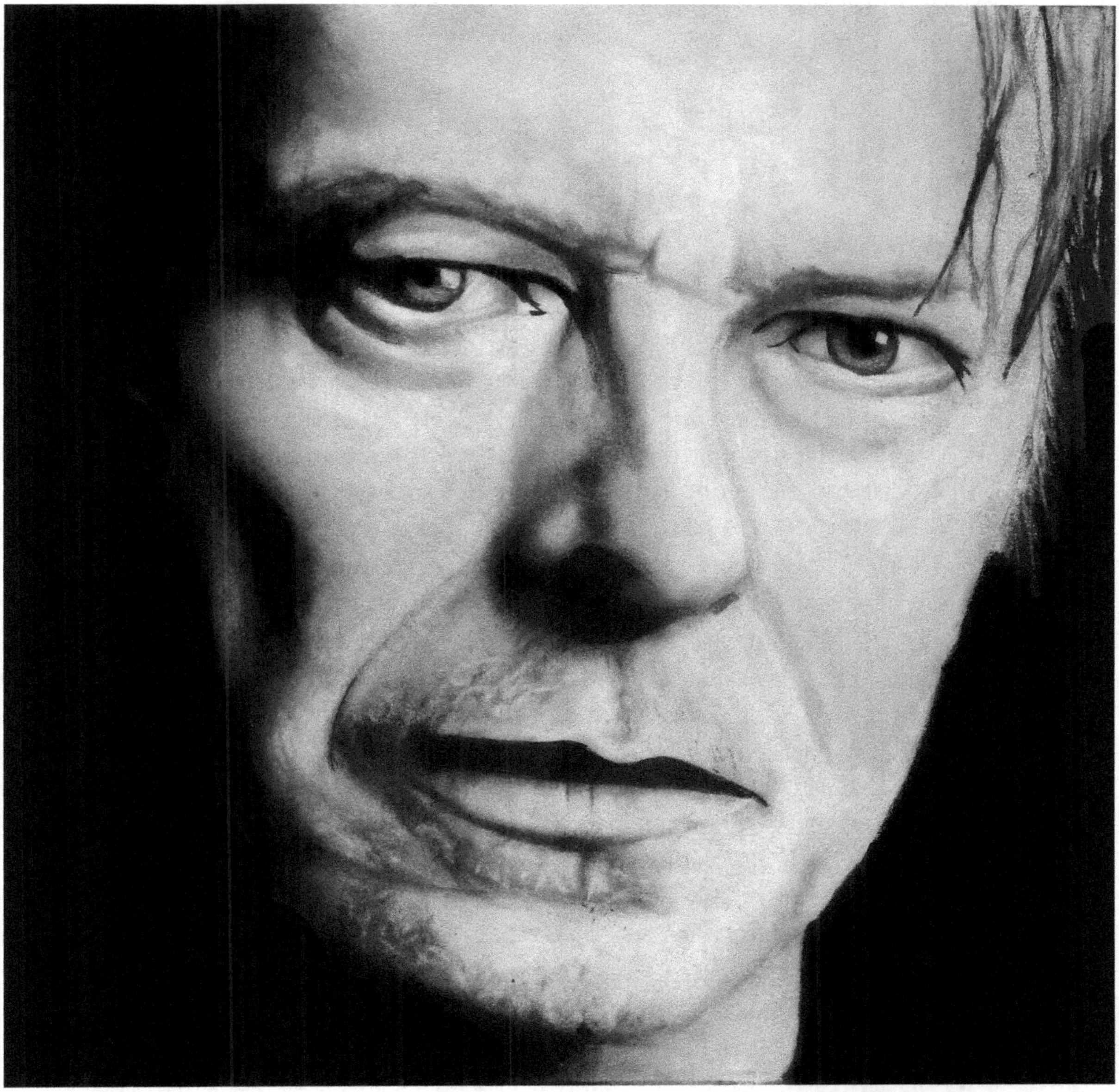

To view how this drawing was masterfully created or to purchase a Limited Edition Framed Artwork of David Bowie type into your Internet Browser the URL shortcut ➡ **myportrait.art/davidbowie**

To listen to his Greatest Songs type into your Internet Browser the URL shortcut ➡ **radio.surf/davidbowie**

To view all channels on THE FACE OF MUSIC Internet Radio MEGA Station type into your Internet Browser the URL shortcut ➡ **radio.surf/music**

To inquire about purchasing a Limited Edtion NFT of this portrait type into your Internet Browser the URL shortcut ➡ **myartnft.shop/davidbowie**

To view all available NFTs type into your Internet Browser the URL shortcut ➡ **myartnft.shop/all**

# David Cassidy

(Net worth: $0.5 Million)(Total Records Sold: 30 Million)
(Genre: Pop , Rock)(Height: 5' - 8")

David Bruce Cassidy ( April 12, 1950 – November 21, 2017) was an American actor, singer, songwriter, and guitarist. He was best known for his role as Keith Partridge, the son of Shirley Partridge (played by his stepmother, Shirley Jones), in the 1970s musical-sitcom The Partridge Family. This role catapulted Cassidy to teen idol status as a superstar pop singer of the 1970s.

In 1970, Cassidy took the role of Keith Partridge on the musical television show The Partridge Family. After demonstrating his singing talent, Cassidy was allowed to join the studio ensemble as the lead singer. (He and Shirley Jones were the only TV cast members to appear on any Partridge Family recordings.) The show proved popular, but the fame took its toll on Cassidy. In the midst of his rise to fame, Cassidy felt stifled by the show and trapped by the mass hysteria surrounding his every move.:92–95 In May 1972, to alter his public image, he appeared nude on the cover of Rolling Stone in a cropped Annie Leibovitz photo.

Once "I Think I Love You"—the first single released by The Partridge Family pop group—became a hit, Cassidy began work on solo albums. Within the first year, he had produced his own single, a cover of The Association's "Cherish" (from the album of the same title); the song reached number nine in the United States, number two in the United Kingdom (a double A-side with "Could It Be Forever"), and number one in Australia and New Zealand. He began tours that featured Partridge tunes and his own hits. Cassidy achieved far greater solo chart success in the UK than in his native America, including a cover of The Young Rascals' "How Can I Be Sure" and the double A-side single "Daydreamer" / "The Puppy Song" – a UK number one which failed to chart in the States. In Britain, Cassidy the solo star remains best known for "Daydreamer", "How Can I Be Sure" and "Could It Be Forever" (UK number 2/US number 37), all released during his 1972–73 solo chart peak. Though he wanted to become a respected rock musician along the lines of Mick Jagger, his channel to stardom launched him into the ranks of teen idol, a brand he loathed until much later in life, when he managed to come to terms with his pop idol beginnings. Ten albums by The Partridge Family and five solo albums by Cassidy were produced during the series, with most selling more than a million copies each.

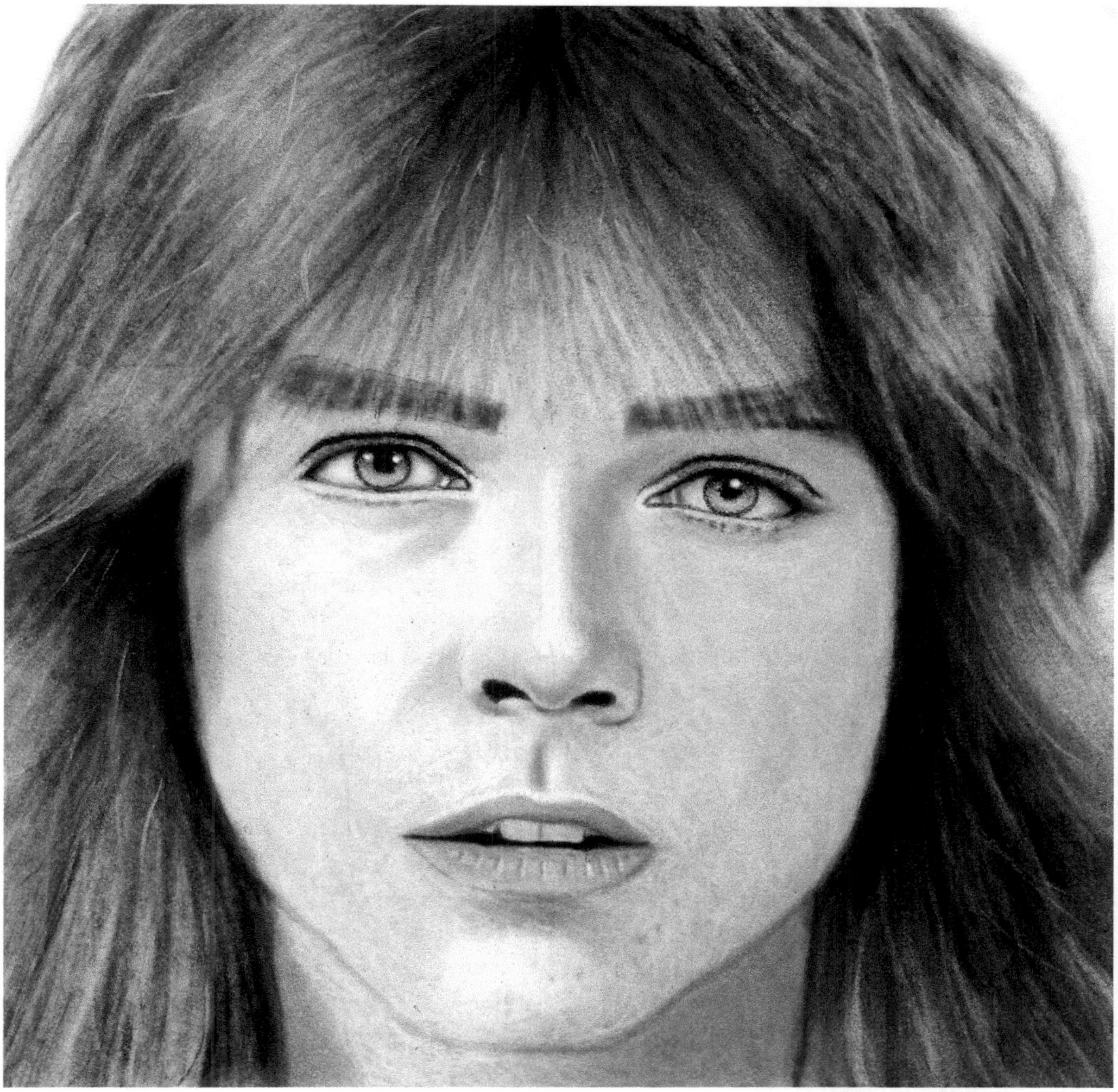

To view how this drawing was masterfully created or to purchase a Limited Edition Framed Artwork of David Cassidy type into your Internet Browser the URL shortcut ➡ **myportrait.art/davidcassidy**

To listen to his Greatest Songs type into your Internet Browser the URL shortcut ➡ **radio.surf/davidcassidy**

To view all channels on THE FACE OF MUSIC Internet Radio MEGA Station type into your Internet Browser the URL shortcut ➡ **radio.surf/music**

To inquire about purchasing a Limited Edtion NFT of this portrait type into your Internet Browser the URL shortcut ➡ **myartnft.shop/davidcassidy**

To view all available NFTs type into your Internet Browser the URL shortcut ➡ **myartnft.shop/all**

# Dean Martin

(Net worth: $30 Million)(Total Records Sold: Millions)
(Genre: Crooner)(Height: 5' - 10")

Dean Martin (born Dino Paul Crocetti; June 7, 1917 – December 25, 1995) was an American singer, actor, and comedian. One of the most popular and enduring American entertainers of the mid-20th century, Martin was nicknamed "The King of Cool".

Martin gained his career breakthrough together with comedian Jerry Lewis, billed as Martin & Lewis, in 1946. They performed in nightclubs and later had numerous appearances on radio, television and in films. Following an acrimonious ending of the partnership in 1956, Martin pursued a solo career as a performer and actor.

Martin established himself as a singer, recording numerous contemporary songs as well as standards from the Great American Songbook. He became one of the most popular acts in Las Vegas and was known for his friendship with fellow artists Frank Sinatra and Sammy Davis Jr., who together formed the Rat Pack.

Starting in 1965, Martin was the host of the television variety program The Dean Martin Show, which centered on Martin's singing and comedic talents and was characterized by his relaxed, easy-going demeanor. From 1974 to 1984, he was roastmaster on the popular Dean Martin Celebrity Roast, which drew celebrities, comedians and politicians.

Throughout his career, Martin performed in concert stages, nightclubs, audio recordings and appeared in 85 film and television productions. His most iconic songs include "Ain't That a Kick in the Head?", "Memories Are Made of This", "That's Amore", "Everybody Loves Somebody", "You're Nobody till Somebody Loves You", "Sway", and "Volare".

In October 1941, Martin married Elizabeth "Betty" Anne McDonald in Cleveland, Ohio, and the couple had an apartment in Cleveland Heights for a while. They eventually had four children before the marriage ended in 1949.

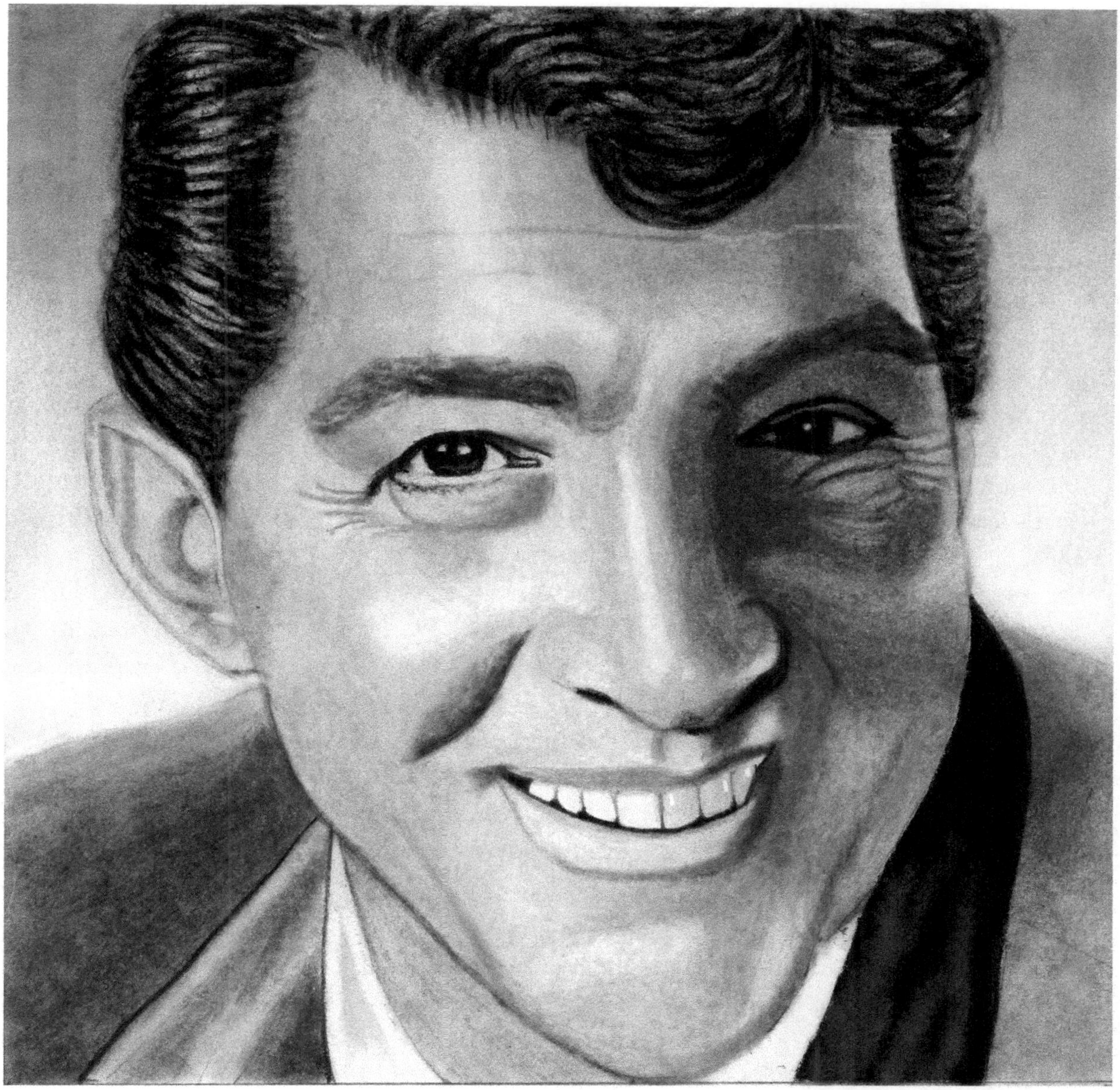

To view how this drawing was masterfully created or to purchase a Limited Edition Framed Artwork of Dean Martin type into your Internet Browser the URL shortcut ➡ **myportrait.art/deanmartin**

To listen to his Greatest Songs type into your Internet Browser the URL shortcut ➡ **radio.surf/deanmartin**

To view all channels on THE FACE OF MUSIC Internet Radio MEGA Station type into your Internet Browser the URL shortcut ➡ **radio.surf/music**

To inquire about purchasing a Limited Edition NFT of this portrait type into your Internet Browser the URL shortcut ➡ **myartnft.shop/deanmartin**

To view all available NFTs type into your Internet Browser the URL shortcut ➡ **myartnft.shop/all**

# Deep Purple

(Total Albums Sold: 100+ Million)(Genre: Hard Rock)

Deep Purple are an English rock band formed in Hertford, Hertfordshire, in 1968. They are considered to be among the pioneers of heavy metal and modern hard rock, although their musical approach has changed over the years. Originally formed as a psychedelic rock and progressive rock band, they shifted to a heavier sound with their 1970 album Deep Purple in Rock. Deep Purple, together with Led Zeppelin and Black Sabbath, have been referred to as the "unholy trinity of British hard rock and heavy metal in the early to mid-seventies". They were listed in the 1975 Guinness Book of World Records as "the globe's loudest band" for a 1972 concert at London's Rainbow Theatre and have sold over 100 million albums worldwide.

Deep Purple have had several line-up changes and an eight-year hiatus (1976–1984). The 1968–1976 line-ups are commonly labelled Mark I, II, III and IV. Their second and most commercially successful line-up consisted of Ian Gillan (vocals) and Roger Glover (bass), who joined founding members Jon Lord (keyboards), Ian Paice (drums) and Ritchie Blackmore (guitar). This line-up was active from 1969 to 1973 and was revived from 1984 to 1989 and again from 1992 to 1993. The band achieved more modest success in the intervening periods between 1968 and 1969 with the line-up including Rod Evans (lead vocals) and Nick Simper (bass, backing vocals), between 1974 and 1976 with the line-up including David Coverdale (lead vocals) and Glenn Hughes (bass, vocals) (and Tommy Bolin replacing Blackmore in 1975), and between 1989 and 1992 with the line-up including Joe Lynn Turner (vocals). The band's line-up (currently including Ian Gillan, and guitarist Steve Morse from 1994) has been much more stable in recent years, although keyboardist Jon Lord's retirement from the band in 2002 (being succeeded by Don Airey) left Ian Paice as the only original Deep Purple member still in the band.

Deep Purple were ranked number 22 on VH1's Greatest Artists of Hard Rock programme, and a poll on radio station Planet Rock ranked them 5th among the "most influential bands ever". The band received the Legend Award at the 2008 World Music Awards. Deep Purple (specifically Blackmore, Lord, Paice, Gillan, Glover, Coverdale, Evans, and Hughes) were inducted into the Rock and Roll Hall of Fame in 2016.

# Ian Gillan

(Net Worth: $40 Million) (Height: 6'- 0")

Ian Gillan (born 19 August 1945) is an English singer and songwriter. He is the lead singer and lyricist for the rock band Deep Purple and is known for his powerful and wide-ranging singing voice, in particular his high pitched banshee screams.

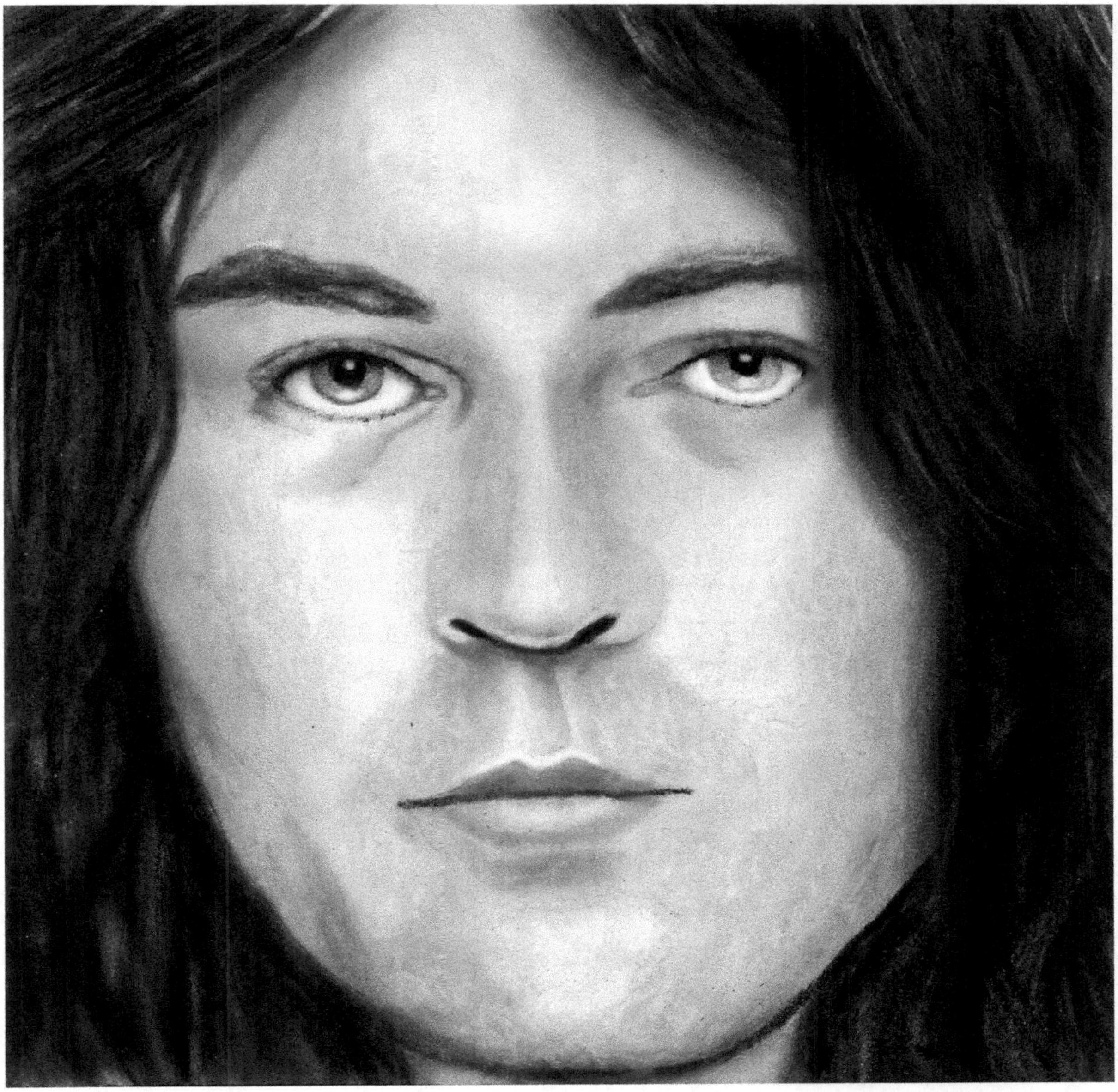

To view how this drawing was masterfully created or to purchase a Limited Edition Framed Artwork of Ian Gillan type into your Internet Browser the URL shortcut ➡ **myportrait.art/iangillan**

To listen to their Greatest Songs type into your Internet Browser the URL shortcut ➡ **radio.surf/deeppurple**

To view all channels on THE FACE OF MUSIC Internet Radio MEGA Station type into your Internet Browser the URL shortcut ➡ **radio.surf/music**

To inquire about purchasing a Limited Edition NFT of this portrait type into your Internet Browser the URL shortcut ➡ **myartnft.shop/iangillan**

To view all available NFTs type into your Internet Browser the URL shortcut ➡ **myartnft.shop/all**

# Def Leppard

(Total Albums Sold: 100+ Million)(Genre: Hard Rock)

Def Leppard are an English rock band formed in 1977 in Sheffield. Since 1992, the band has consisted of Joe Elliott (lead vocals), Rick Savage (bass, backing vocals), Rick Allen (drums, backing vocals), Phil Collen (guitars, backing vocals), and Vivian Campbell (guitars, backing vocals). They established themselves as part of the new wave of British heavy metal movement of the early 1980s. The band's greatest commercial success came between the early 1980s and the early 1990s. Their first album, 1980's On Through the Night, reached the Top 15 in the UK but received little notice elsewhere. Their second album, 1981's High 'n' Dry, was produced by Mutt Lange, who helped them begin to define their melodic, hard rock style, and the album's most popular track "Bringin' On the Heartbreak" became one of the first rock videos played on MTV in 1982, but the album only reached the Top 30 and 40 in the UK and US. Def Leppard's next studio album, Pyromania, was released in January 1983, with "Photograph" and "Rock of Ages" both topping the US Rock Tracks chart and reaching the Top 20 of the Hot 100. Reaching No. 2 on the US album chart, Pyromania was certified Diamond in the US and 7x platinum in Canada and reached the Top 20 in the UK but did not sell much elsewhere.

Def Leppard's fourth album, the more pop-orientated Hysteria (1987), topped the UK, US, New Zealand, Canadian, Australian and Norway charts. It also went to No. 2 in Sweden and No. 10 in Germany without any Top 50 singles in those countries. It has been certified 12× platinum for sales in the US and 13x platinum in Canada, selling over 25 million copies worldwide, making it one of the best-selling albums of all time. The album spawned six Top 20 US singles, including the US Billboard Hot 100 No. 1 "Love Bites" (went Top 10 in several other countries including No. 2 in NZ), alongside "Pour Some Sugar on Me" (US No. 2), "Hysteria", "Armageddon It" (No. 2 in NZ), "Animal" (at No. 6, the biggest UK hit), and "Rocket" (a Top 15 hit in many countries). Hysteria had four Top 10 hits in NZ.

As one of the world's best-selling music artists, Def Leppard have sold more than 100 million records worldwide, and have two albums with RIAA diamond certification: Pyromania and Hysteria, making them one of only five rock bands with two original studio albums selling more than 10 million copies in the US. The band were ranked No. 31 in VH1's "100 Greatest Artists of Hard Rock" and ranked No. 70 in "100 Greatest Artists of All Time". Def Leppard were inducted into the Rock and Roll Hall of Fame in 2019.

# Joe Elliott

(Net Worth: $70 Million) (Height: 6'-1 1/2")

Joseph Thomas Elliott Jr. (born 1 August 1959) is an English singer-songwriter, musician, record producer and radio presenter, best known as the lead singer and one of the founding members of the English hard rock band Def Leppard.

Elliott is known for his distinctive and wide ranging raspy singing voice.

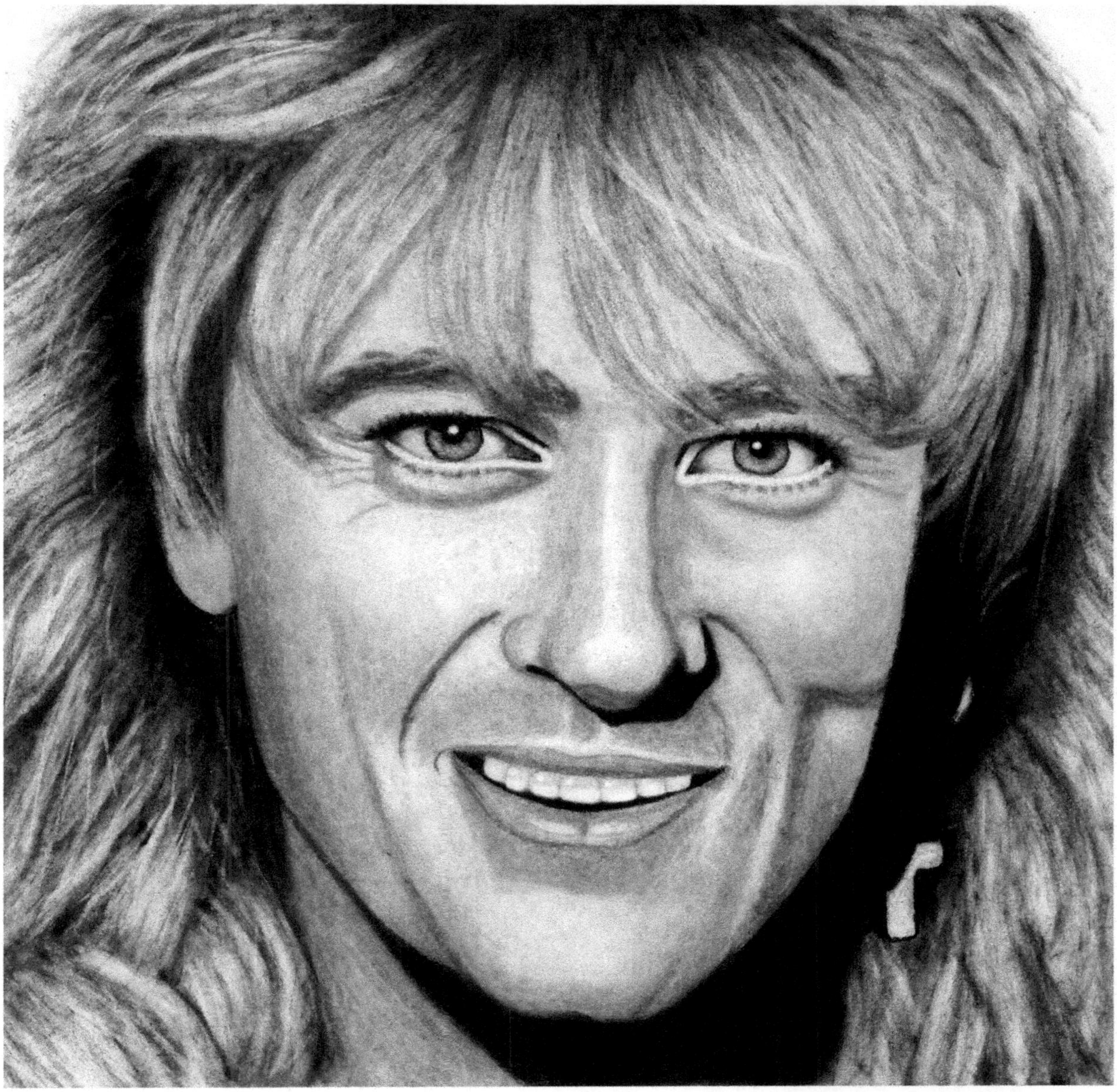

To view how this drawing was masterfully created or to purchase a Limited Edition Framed Artwork of Joe Elliott type into your Internet Browser the URL shortcut ➡ **myportrait.art/joeelliott**

To listen to their Greatest Songs type into your Internet Browser the URL shortcut ➡ **radio.surf/defleppard**

To view all channels on THE FACE OF MUSIC Internet Radio MEGA Station type into your Internet Browser the URL shortcut ➡ **radio.surf/music**

To inquire about purchasing a Limited Edtion NFT of this portrait type into your Internet Browser the URL shortcut ➡ **myartnft.shop/joeelliott**

To view all available NFTs type into your Internet Browser the URL shortcut ➡ **myartnft.shop/all**

# Destiny's Child

(Total Albums Sold: 60 Million) (Genre: Contemporary R&B)

Destiny's Child was an American girl group whose final and best-known lineup comprised Beyoncé Knowles, Kelly Rowland, and Michelle Williams. The group began their musical career as Girl's Tyme, formed in 1990 in Houston, Texas. After years of limited success, the quartet comprising Knowles, Rowland, LaTavia Roberson, and LeToya Luckett were signed in 1997 to Columbia Records as Destiny's Child. The group was launched into mainstream recognition following the release of their best-selling second album, The Writing's on the Wall (1999), which contained the number-one singles "Bills, Bills, Bills" and "Say My Name". Despite critical and commercial success, the group was plagued by internal conflict and legal turmoil, as Roberson and Luckett attempted to split from the group's manager Mathew Knowles, citing favoritism of Knowles and Rowland.In early 2000, both Roberson and Luckett were replaced with Williams and Farrah Franklin; however, Franklin quit after five months, leaving the group as a trio. Their third album, Survivor (2001), whose themes the public interpreted as a channel to the group's experience, produced the worldwide hits "Independent Women", "Survivor" and "Bootylicious". In 2001, they announced a hiatus to pursue solo careers. The trio reunited two years later for the release of their fifth and final studio album, Destiny Fulfilled (2004), which spawned the international hits "Lose My Breath" and "Soldier". Since the group's official disbandment in 2006, Knowles, Rowland, and Williams have reunited a couple of times, including at the 2013 Super Bowl halftime show and 2018 Coachella festival.Destiny's Child has sold more than sixty million records worldwide to date. Billboard ranks the group as one of the greatest musical trios of all time, the ninth most successful artist/band of the 2000s, placed the group 68th in its All-Time Hot 100 Artists list in 2008 and in December 2016, the magazine ranked them as the 90th most successful dance club artist of all time. The group was nominated for 14 Grammy Awards, winning twice for Best R&B Performance by a Duo or Group with Vocals and once for Best R&B Song.

# Beyonce'

(Total Albums Sold: 110 Million)(Net Worth: $400 Million) (Height: 5'-9")

Beyoncé Giselle Knowles-Carter (/biːˈjɒnseɪ/ bee-YON-say; née Knowles; born September 4, 1981) is an American singer, songwriter, actress, director, humanitarian, and record producer. Born and raised in Houston, Texas, Beyoncé performed in various singing and dancing competitions as a child. She rose to fame in the late 1990s as the lead singer of Destiny's Child, one of the best-selling girl groups of all time. Their hiatus saw the release of her first solo album, Dangerously in Love (2003), which featured the US Billboard Hot 100 number-one singles "Crazy in Love" and "Baby Boy".

Beyoncé is one of the world's best-selling recording artists, having sold 118 million records worldwide. She is the first artist to debut at number one on the Billboard 200 with their first six solo studio albums. Her success during the 2000s was recognized with the RIAA's Top Certified Artist of the Decade as well as Billboard's Top Female Artist of the Decade. Beyoncé's accolades include 28 Grammy Awards, 24 MTV Video Music Awards (including the Video Vanguard Award in 2014), 31 BET Awards, and 17 Soul Train Music Awards; all of which are more than any other singer. In 2014, Billboard named her the highest-earning black musician of all time, while in 2020, she was included on Time's list of 100 women who defined the last century.

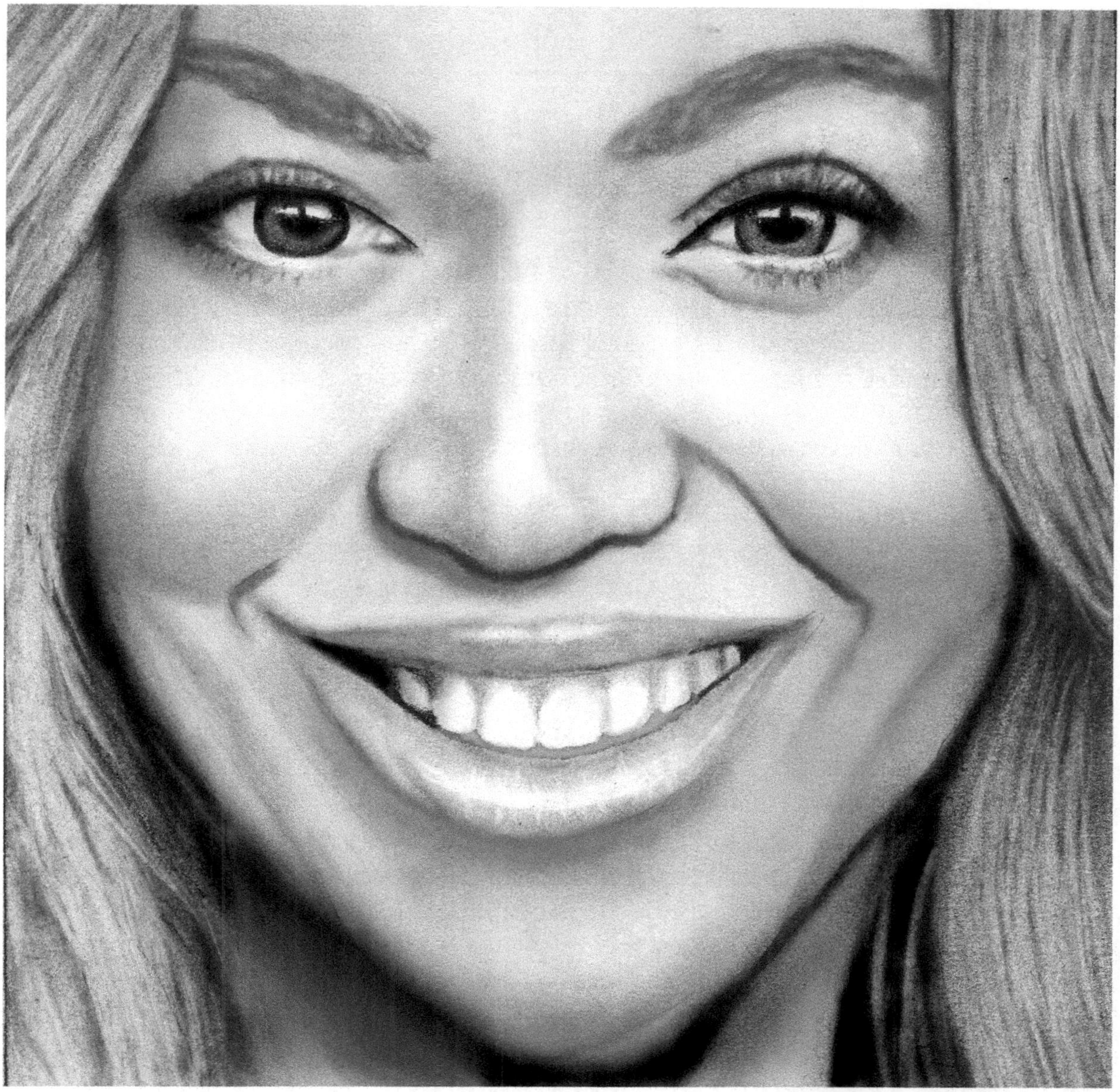

To view how this drawing was masterfully created or to purchase a Limited Edition Framed Artwork of Beyonce type into your Internet Browser the URL shortcut ➡ **myportrait.art/beyonce**

To listen to their Greatest Songs type into your Internet Browser the URL shortcut ➡ **radio.surf/beyonce**

To view all channels on THE FACE OF MUSIC Internet Radio MEGA Station type into your Internet Browser the URL shortcut ➡ **radio.surf/music**

To inquire about purchasing a Limited Edtion NFT of this portrait type into your Internet Browser the URL shortcut ➡ **myartnft.shop/beyonce**

To view all available NFTs type into your Internet Browser the URL shortcut ➡ **myartnft.shop/all**

# Dio

(Total Albums Sold: 20+ Million)(Genre: Heavy Metal)

Dio was an American heavy metal band formed in 1982 and led by vocalist Ronnie James Dio. Dio left Black Sabbath with intentions to form a new band with fellow former Black Sabbath member Vinny Appice, the band's drummer. The name Dio was chosen because it made sense from a commercial standpoint, as the name was already well known at that time.

The band released ten studio albums and had numerous line-up changes over the years with Dio himself being the only constant member. Guitarists included Vivian Campbell, Craig Goldy, Doug Aldrich, Warren DeMartini, Tracy G, Jake E. Lee and Rowan Robertson.

The band dissolved in 2010 when Ronnie James Dio died of stomach cancer at the age of 67. Dio has sold more than 20 million albums worldwide.

# Ronnie James Dio

(Net Worth: $10 Million) (Height: 5'-4")

Ronald James Padavona (July 10, 1942 – May 16, 2010), known professionally as Ronnie James Dio, was an American heavy metal singer-songwriter and composer. He fronted or founded numerous groups throughout his career, including Elf, Rainbow, Black Sabbath, Dio, and Heaven & Hell. Though his parents were from Cortland, New York, Dio was born in Portsmouth, New Hampshire, where his family resided for his father's service in the U.S. Army during World War II; they soon returned to Cortland. Dio's music career began there in 1957 as part of the Vegas Kings (later Ronnie and the Rumblers). In 1967, he formed the rock band Elf, which became a regular opening act for Deep Purple. In 1975, Deep Purple guitarist Ritchie Blackmore founded the band Rainbow and hired Dio to be his lead singer; during his tenure, the band released three studio albums. Dio quickly emerged as one of heavy rock's pre-eminent vocalists. In 1979, Dio replaced Ozzy Osbourne as Black Sabbath's lead singer and appeared on three studio albums with the band, all three of which met with success: Heaven & Hell (1980), Mob Rules (1981) and Dehumanizer (1992). In 1982, he left to form the band Dio, which itself had two albums certified platinum by the RIAA. In 2006, he founded the band Heaven & Hell with ex-bandmate Tony Iommi. In November 2009, Dio was diagnosed with stomach cancer, and he died of the disease in May 2010.

Dio is regarded as one of the greatest and most influential heavy metal artists of all time. He is known for popularizing the "Metal Horns" hand gesture in metal culture and his medieval-themed song lyrics. According to a version provided by the singer himself, the act derives directly from the classic Italian apotropaic gesture, which his grandmother usually did. Dio had a powerful, versatile vocal range and was capable of singing both hard rock and lighter ballads. He was awarded the "Metal Guru Award" by Classic Rock Magazine in 2006. He was also named the "Best Metal singer" at the Revolver Golden Gods Awards in 2010 and ranked as the genre's best vocalist in 2013 by music journalist Sacha Jenkins.

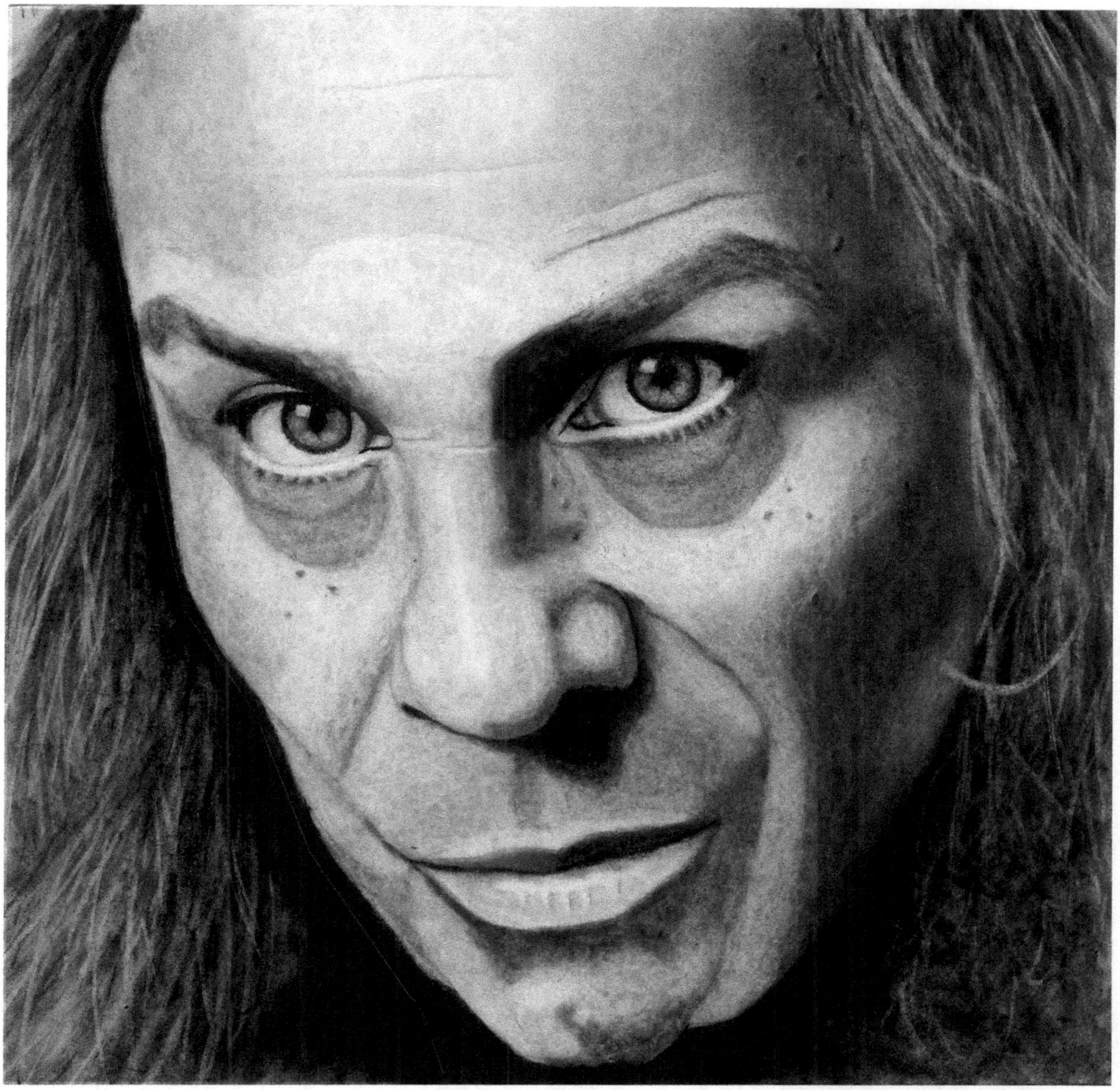

To view how this drawing was masterfully created or to purchase a Limited Edition Framed Artwork of Ronnie James Dio type into your Internet Browser the URL shortcut ➡ **myportrait.art/ronniejamesdio**

To listen to his Greatest Songs type into your Internet Browser the URL shortcut ➡ **radio.surf/dio**

To view all channels on THE FACE OF MUSIC Internet Radio MEGA Station type into your Internet Browser the URL shortcut ➡ **radio.surf/music**

To inquire about purchasing a Limited Edtion NFT of this portrait type into your Internet Browser the URL shortcut ➡ **myartnft.shop/ronniejamesdio**

To view all available NFTs type into your Internet Browser the URL shortcut ➡ **myartnft.shop/all**

# Dion

(Net worth: $5 Million)(Total Records Sold: Millions)
(Genre: Rock , Pop , R&B , Blues)(Height: 5' - 10")

Dion Francis DiMucci (born July 18, 1939), better known mononymously as Dion, is an American singer and songwriter whose work has incorporated elements of doo-wop, rock and R&B styles, and, most recently, straight blues. Initially as lead singer of Dion and the Belmonts and then in his solo career, he was one of the most popular American rock and roll performers of the pre-British Invasion era. He had 39 Top 40 hits in the late 1950s and early 1960s as a solo performer, with the Belmonts or with the Del Satins. He is best remembered for the singles "Runaround Sue", "The Wanderer", "Ruby Baby" and "Lovers Who Wander", among his other hits.

Dion's popularity waned in the mid-1960s. Toward the end of the decade, he shifted his style and produced songs with a more mature, contemplative feeling, such as "Abraham, Martin and John." He became popular again in the late 1960s and into the mid-1970s, and he has continued making music ever since. Critics who had dismissed his early work, pegging him as merely a teen idol, praised his later work, and noted the influence he has had on other musicians

Dion was inducted into the Rock & Roll Hall of Fame in 1989.

Dion was born to an Italian-American family in the Bronx, New York As a child, he accompanied his father, Pasquale DiMucci, a vaudeville entertainer, on tour, and developed a love of country music – particularly the work of Hank Williams. He also developed a fondness for the blues and doo-wop musicians he heard performing in local bars and on the radio. His singing was honed on the street corners and local clubs of the Bronx, where he and other neighborhood singers created a cappella riffs.

In early 1957, he auditioned for Bob and Gene Schwartz for their short-lived Mohawk Records label. They asked Dion to sing a song which had been arranged by Hugo Montenegro and recorded featuring Vic Damone doing vocals. At first Dion refused, stating the song would sound like something his old fashioned parents would listen to, but the Schwartzes convinced him to give it a try. The backing vocals were by a group called "The Timberlanes", whom Dion had never met. The resulting single, "The Chosen Few", was released under the name'Dion and the Timberlanes, and became a minor regional hit. Dion himself stated in 2019 during an interview at "Crashing the Party" (a Radio Show related to Norton Records, Brooklyn, New York) that "The Chosen Few" hit the Top Ten locally in Boston and enabled him to perform this song on American Bandstand where the kids at the show started screaming during his performance, which gave him his first impression of being a record star. Writing about this experience later, in his autobiography, The Wanderer, Dion said that he had never met the Timberlanes and did not even know who they were. "The vocal group was so white bread, I went back to my neighborhood and I recruited a bunch of guys – three guys – and we called ourselves Dion and the Belmonts.".

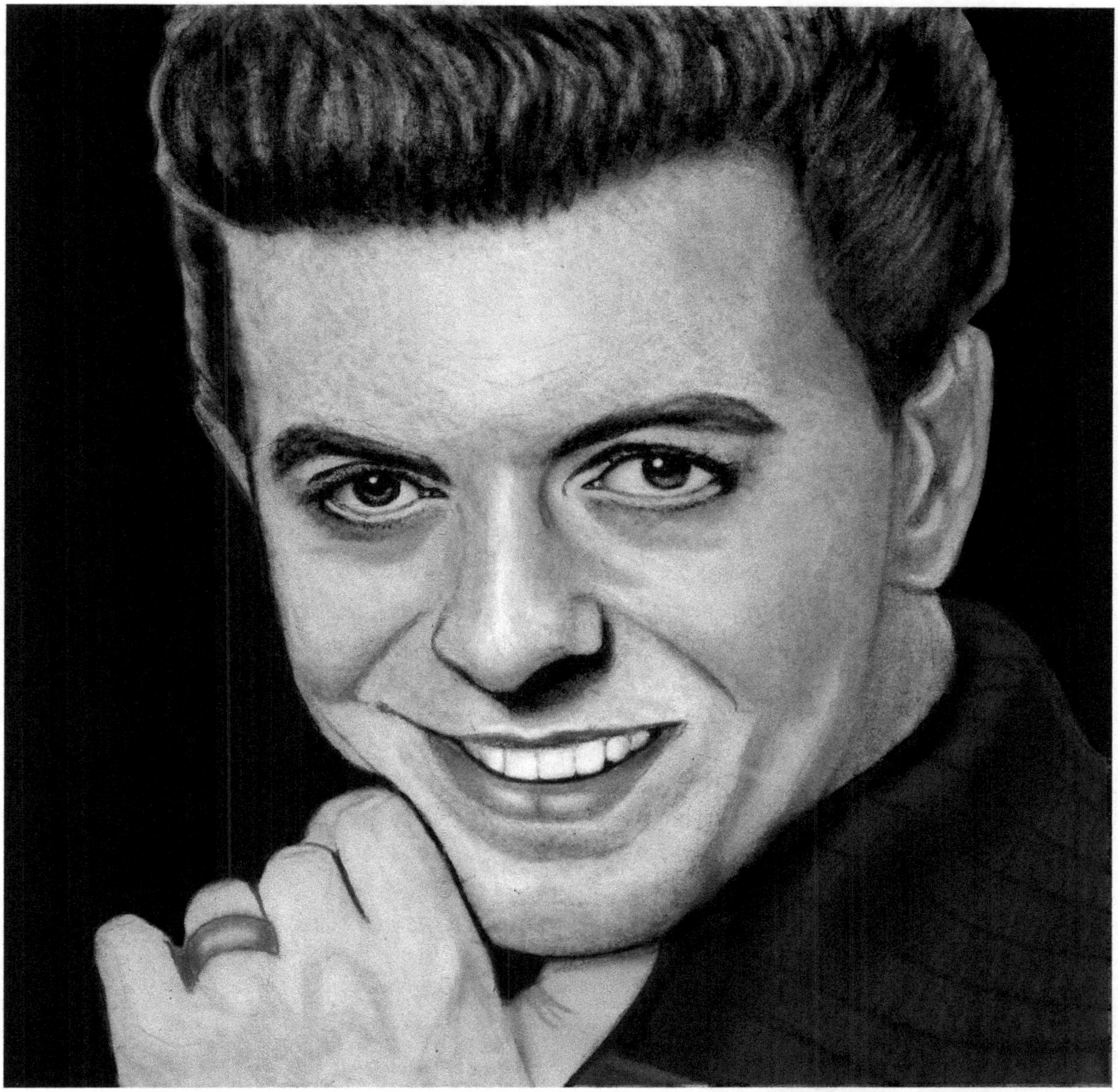

To view how this drawing was masterfully created or to purchase a Limited Edition Framed Artwork of Dion type into your Internet Browser the URL shortcut ➡ **myportrait.art/dion**

To listen to his Greatest Songs type into your Internet Browser the URL shortcut ➡ **radio.surf/dion**

To view all channels on THE FACE OF MUSIC Internet Radio MEGA Station type into your Internet Browser the URL shortcut ➡ **radio.surf/music**

To inquire about purchasing a Limited Edtion NFT of this portrait type into your Internet Browser the URL shortcut ➡ **myartnft.shop/dion**

To view all available NFTs type into your Internet Browser the URL shortcut ➡ **myartnft.shop/all**

# Dire Straits

(Total Albums Sold: 100+ Million) (Genre: Classic Rock)

Dire Straits were a British rock band formed in London in 1977 by Mark Knopfler (lead vocals and lead guitar), David Knopfler (rhythm guitar and backing vocals), John Illsley (bass guitar and backing vocals), and Pick Withers (drums and percussion). They were active from 1977 to 1988 and again from 1991 to 1995. Dire Straits are one of the world's best-selling music artists, with album sales of over 100 million.

Their first single, "Sultans of Swing", from their 1978 self-titled debut album, reached the top ten in the UK and US charts. It was followed by hit singles including "Romeo and Juliet" (1981), "Private Investigations" (1982), "Twisting by the Pool" (1983), "Money for Nothing" (1985), and "Walk of Life" (1985). Their most commercially successful album, Brothers in Arms (1985), has sold more than 30 million copies; it was the first album to sell a million copies on compact disc, and is the eighth-bestselling album in UK history. According to the Guinness Book of British Hit Albums, Dire Straits have spent over 1,100 weeks on the UK albums chart, the fifth most of all time.Dire Straits' sound draws from various influences including country, folk, the blues rock of J. J. Cale, and jazz. Their stripped-down sound contrasted with punk rock and demonstrated a roots rock influence that emerged from pub rock. There were several changes in personnel, with Mark Knopfler and Illsley being the only members who lasted from the beginning of the band's existence, to the end. After their first breakup in 1988, Knopfler told Rolling Stone: "A lot of press reports were saying we were the biggest band in the world. There's not an accent then on the music, there's an accent on popularity. I needed a rest." They disbanded for good in 1995, after which Knopfler launched a solo career full-time. He has since declined reunion offers.Called "the biggest British rock band of the 80s" by Classic Rock magazine, their 1985–1986 world tour, which included a performance at Live Aid in July 1985, set a record in Australasia. Their final world tour from 1991 to 1992 sold 7.1 million tickets. Dire Straits won four Grammy Awards, three Brit Awards (Best British Group twice), two MTV Video Music Awards, and various other awards. They were inducted into the Rock and Roll Hall of Fame in 2018.

# Mark Knopfler

(Net Worth: $95 Million) (Height: 6' - 0")

Mark Freuder Knopfler ( born 12 August 1949) is a British singer-songwriter, guitarist, and record producer. He became known as the lead guitarist, singer and songwriter of the rock band Dire Straits. He pursued a solo career after leaving the band in 1987. Dire Straits reunited in early 1991, but dissolved again in 1995. He is now an independent solo artist.

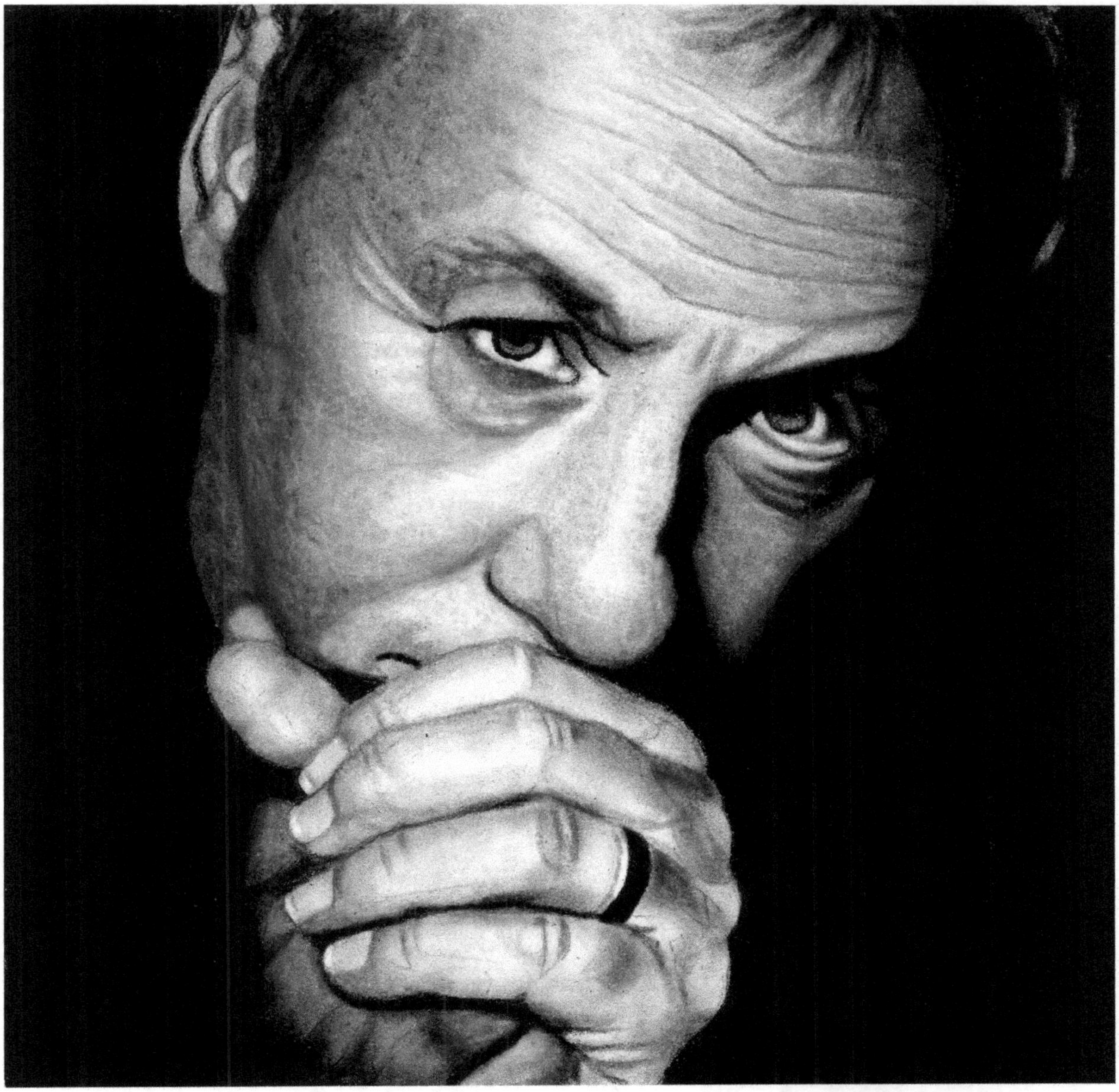

To view how this drawing was masterfully created or to purchase a Limited Edition Framed Artwork of Mark Knopfler type into your Internet Browser the URL shortcut ➡ **myportrait.art/markknopfler**

To listen to their Greatest Songs type into your Internet Browser the URL shortcut ➡ **radio.surf/direstraits**

To view all channels on THE FACE OF MUSIC Internet Radio MEGA Station type into your Internet Browser the URL shortcut ➡ **radio.surf/music**

To inquire about purchasing a Limited Edtion NFT of this portrait type into your Internet Browser the URL shortcut ➡ **myartnft.shop/markknopfler**

To view all available NFTs type into your Internet Browser the URL shortcut ➡ **myartnft.shop/all**

# Dixie Chicks

(Total Albums Sold: 33 Million) (Genre: Country)

Dixie Chicks (now they go by The Chicks) are an American country music band composed of lead singer Natalie Maines and multi-instrumentalist sisters Martie Maguire and Emily Strayer (both née Erwin). The Erwin sisters founded the band in 1989 in Dallas, Texas with bassist Laura Lynch and vocalist/guitarist Robin Lynn Macy, and performed bluegrass and country music, busking and touring the bluegrass festival circuits and small venues for six years without attracting a major label. Macy left in 1992 and Lynch became the lead vocalist soon afterward. Following the replacement of Lynch with Maines and a change in repertoire, the Chicks achieved commercial success, beginning in 1998 with hit songs "There's Your Trouble" and "Wide Open Spaces".

Days before the 2003 invasion of Iraq, Maines told a London audience the band did not endorse the war and were "ashamed" of US President George W. Bush being from Texas. The remarks triggered boycotts in the US and backlash from fans. After a hiatus, they toured again in 2010, 2013 and 2016. In 2020, they dropped "Dixie" from their name, citing negative connotations, and released their first album in 14 years, Gaslighter.

The Chicks have won 13 Grammy Awards, including five in 2007 for Taking the Long Way—which received the Grammy Award for Album of the Year—and its single "Not Ready to Make Nice"—which received the Grammy Award for Record of the Year and the Grammy Award for Song of the Year. By July 2020, with 33 million certified albums sold, and sales of 27.9 million albums in the U.S alone, they had become the best-selling female band and best-selling country group in the U.S during the Nielsen SoundScan era (1991–present).

# Natalie Maines

(Net Worth: $40 Million) (Height: 5' - 2")

Natalie Louise Maines (born October 14, 1974) is the lead vocalist for the all-female country band The Chicks.

In 1995, after leaving Berklee College of Music, Maines was recruited by the Dixie Chicks to replace their lead singer, Laura Lynch. With Maines as lead vocalist, the band earned 10 Country Music Association Awards and 13 Grammy Awards for their work between 1998 and 2007.

In 2006, with Maines still acting as lead singer, the Dixie Chicks released Taking the Long Way. The album subsequently won five Grammy Awards (including Album of the Year). The Chicks album Gaslighter was released on July 17, 2020. Maines released a solo album, Mother, on May 7, 2013.

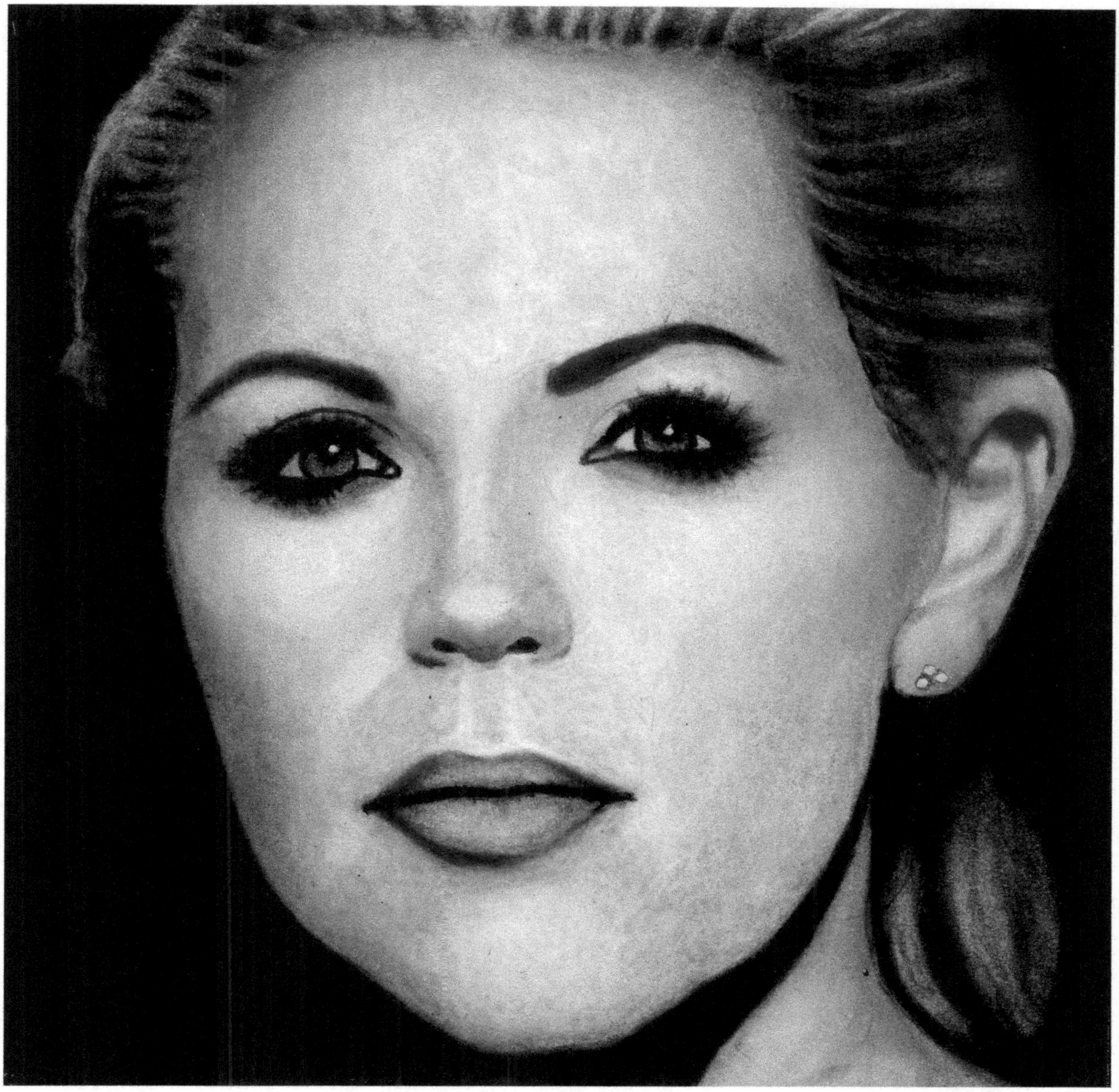

To view how this drawing was masterfully created or to purchase a Limited Edition Framed Artwork of Natalie Maines type into your Internet Browser the URL shortcut ➡ **myportrait.art/nataliemaines**

To listen to their Greatest Songs type into your Internet Browser the URL shortcut ➡ **radio.surf/dixiechicks**

To view all channels on THE FACE OF MUSIC Internet Radio MEGA Station type into your Internet Browser the URL shortcut ➡ **radio.surf/music**

To inquire about purchasing a Limited Edtion NFT of this portrait type into your Internet Browser the URL shortcut ➡ **myartnft.shop/nataliemaines**

To view all available NFTs type into your Internet Browser the URL shortcut ➡ **myartnft.shop/all**

# DMX

(Net worth: Negative $1 Million in Debt)(Total Records Sold: 70 Million)
(Genre: Hip-Hop)(Height: 5' - 10")

Earl Simmons (December 18, 1970 – April 9, 2021), better known by his stage name DMX (Dark Man X), is an American rapper and songwriter. He began rapping in the early 1990s, and released his debut album It's Dark and Hell Is Hot in 1998, to both critical acclaim and commercial success, selling 251,000 copies within its first week of release. He released his best-selling album, ... And Then There Was X, in 1999, which included the hit single "Party Up (Up in Here)". Since his debut, DMX has released seven studio albums.

He has been featured in films such as Belly, Romeo Must Die, Exit Wounds, Cradle 2 the Grave and Last Hour. In 2006, he starred in the reality television series DMX: Soul of a Man, which was primarily aired on the BET cable television network. In 2003, DMX published a book of his memoirs entitled, E.A.R.L.: The Autobiography of DMX.

DMX got his start in the music industry in 1984, when he would beatbox for a local rapper named Ready Ron. After serving time in prison, he began writing his own lyrics and would perform at the local rec center for younger children. After going to prison again in 1988, he began taking rapping more seriously, dedicating almost all of his free time to writing lyrics and also meeting and rapping with K-Solo while incarcerated. When he was released that summer, he began producing and selling his own mixtapes where he would rap over instrumentals from other songs and sell them on street corners, which helped him build a local fan base all over New York. In 1991, Gabriel Grevenstuk from The Source magazine praised DMX in his Unsigned Hype column that highlighted unsigned hip-hop artists. The same year, he recorded his first demos, Unstoppable Force and Three Little Pigs.

In 1992, Columbia Records signed DMX to their subsidiary label Ruffhouse, which released his debut single "Born Loser". The single did not receive much airplay, and the label eventually agreed to release DMX from their contract.

He released his second single, "Make a Move" in 1994, and made a guest appearance alongside Jay Z, Ja Rule, and Mic Geronimo on the classic underground track "Time To Build" on Mic Geronimo's debut album in 1995. He also appeared on LL Cool J's single "4, 3, 2, 1" in 1997. Additional guest spots on Mase singles "24 Hrs. to Live" and "Take What's Yours", and The LOX's single "Money, Power & Respect" created a strong buzz for the then-unsigned rapper. DMX also made a cameo appearance in the Sum 41 music video for "Makes No Difference".

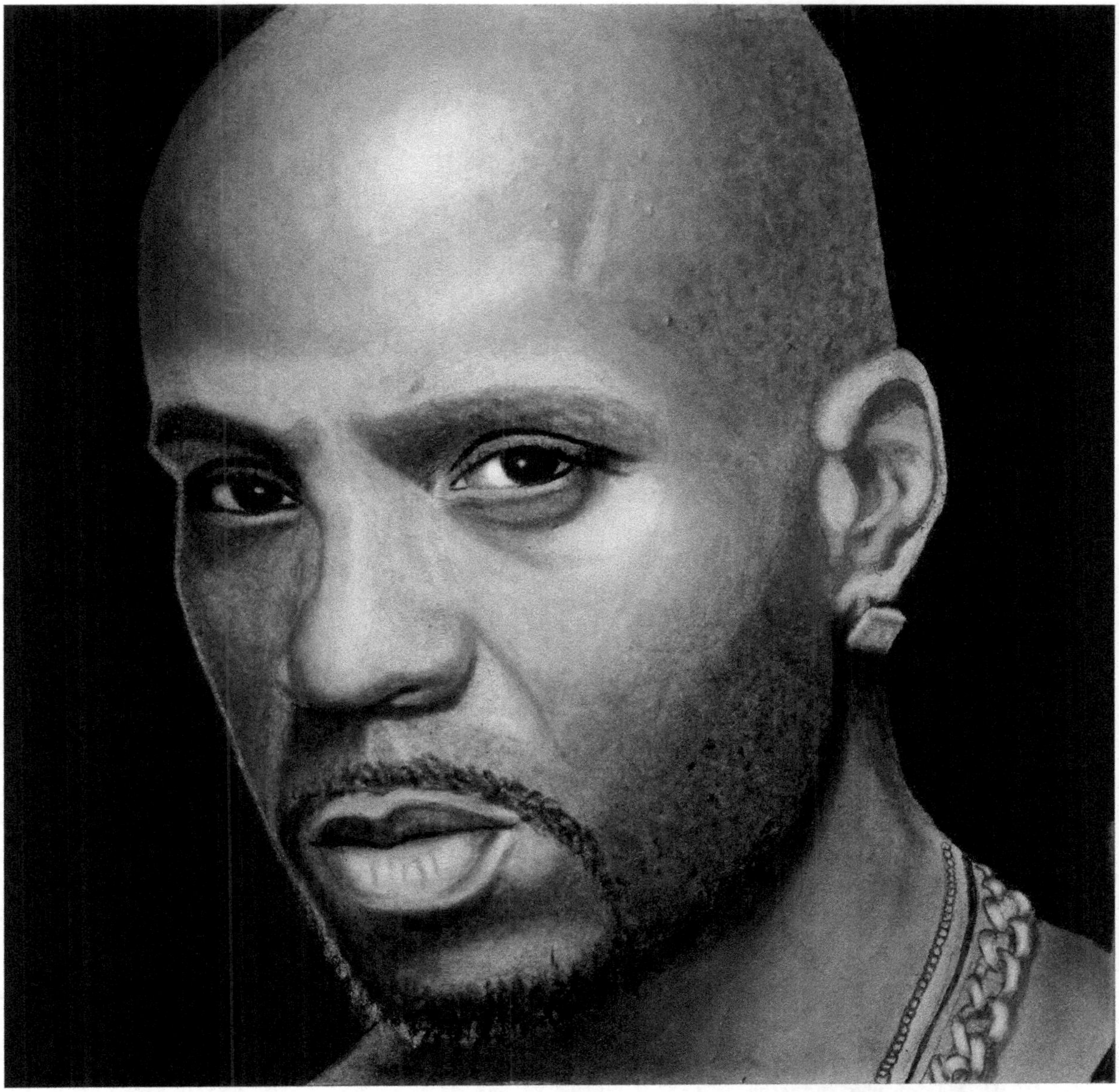

To view how this drawing was masterfully created or to purchase a Limited Edition Framed Artwork of DMX type into your Internet Browser the URL shortcut ➡ **myportrait.art/dmx**

To listen to their Greatest Songs type into your Internet Browser the URL shortcut ➡ **radio.surf/dmx**

To view all channels on THE FACE OF MUSIC Internet Radio MEGA Station type into your Internet Browser the URL shortcut ➡ **radio.surf/music**

To inquire about purchasing a Limited Edition NFT of this portrait type into your Internet Browser the URL shortcut ➡ **myartnft.shop/dmx**

To view all available NFTs type into your Internet Browser the URL shortcut ➡ **myartnft.shop/all**

# Dolly Parton

(Net worth: $600 Million)(Total Records Sold: 100 Million)
(Genre: Country)(Height: 5' - 0")

Dolly Rebecca Parton (born January 19, 1946) is an American singer, songwriter, multi-instrumentalist, actress, author, businesswoman, and humanitarian, known primarily for her work in country music. After achieving success as a songwriter for others, Parton made her album debut in 1967 with Hello, I'm Dolly, which led to success during the remainder of the 1960s (both as a solo artist and with a series of duet albums with Porter Wagoner), before her sales and chart peak came during the 1970s and continued into the 1980s. Parton's albums in the 1990s did not sell as well, but she achieved commercial success again in the new millennium and has released albums on various independent labels since 2000, including her own label, Dolly Records. She has sold more than a hundred million records worldwide.

Parton's music includes Recording Industry Association of America (RIAA)-certified gold, platinum and multi-platinum awards. She has had 25 songs reach no. 1 on the Billboard country music charts, a record for a female artist (tied with Reba McEntire). She has 44 career Top 10 country albums, a record for any artist, and she has 110 career-charted singles over the past forty years. She has garnered ten Grammy Awards and fifty nominations, including the Lifetime Achievement Award and a 2020 Grammy Award with for KING & COUNTRY for their collaboration on "God Only Knows"; ten Country Music Association Awards, including Entertainer of the Year and is one of only seven female artists to win the Country Music Association's Entertainer of the Year Award; five Academy of Country Music Awards, also including a nod for Entertainer of the Year; four People's Choice Awards; and three American Music Awards.

In 1999, Parton was inducted into the Country Music Hall of Fame. She has composed over 3,000 songs, including "I Will Always Love You" (a two-time U.S. country chart-topper, as well as an international pop hit for Whitney Houston), "Jolene", "Coat of Many Colors", and "9 to 5". She is also in a select group to have received at least one nomination from the Academy Awards, Grammy Awards, Tony Awards, and Emmy Awards. As an actress, she has starred in films such as 9 to 5 (1980) and The Best Little Whorehouse in Texas (1982), for which she earned Golden Globe nominations for Best Actress, as well as Rhinestone (1984), Steel Magnolias (1989), Straight Talk (1992) and Joyful Noise (2012).

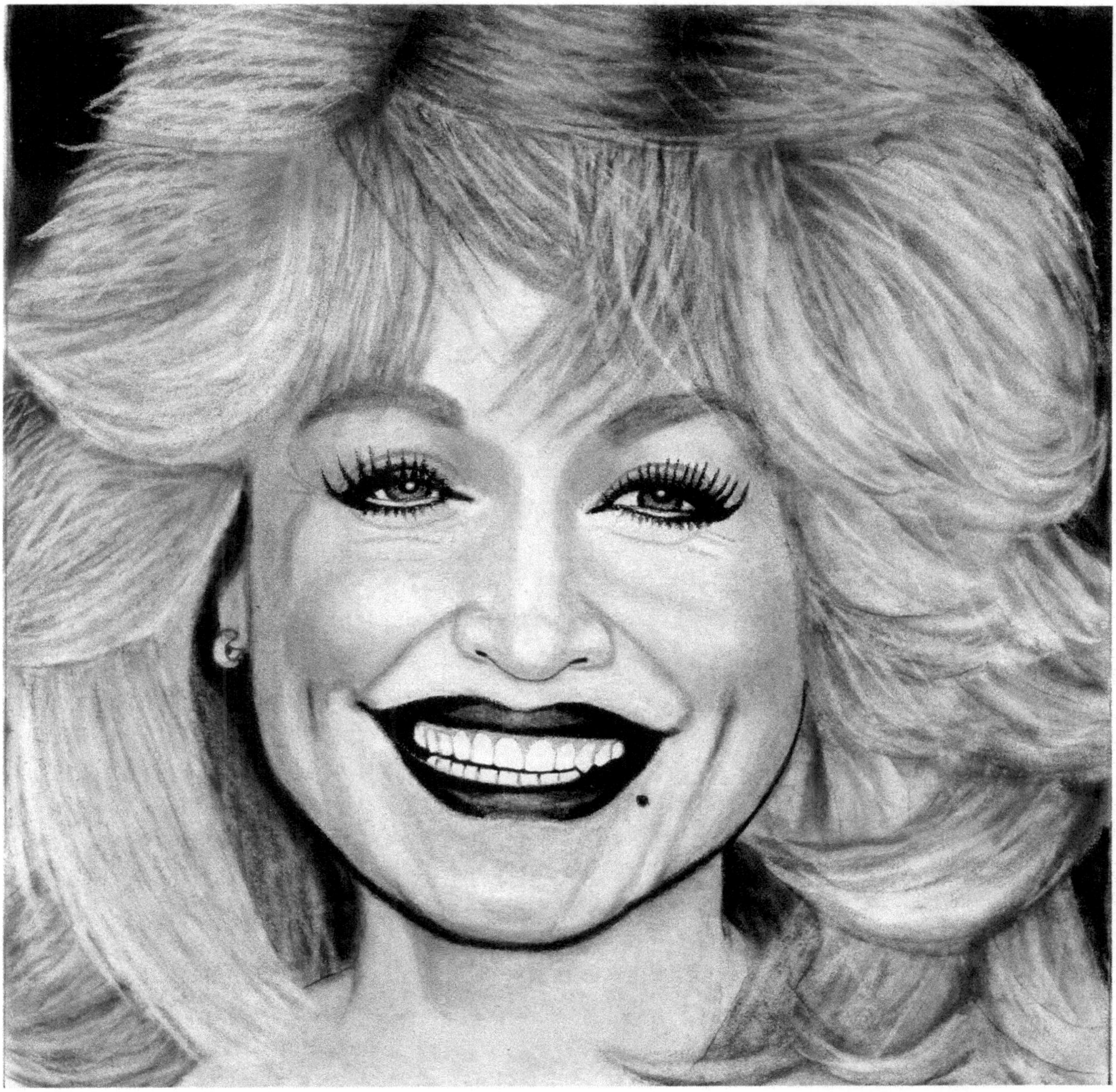

To view how this drawing was masterfully created or to purchase a Limited Edition Framed Artwork of Dolly Parton type into your Internet Browser the URL shortcut ➡ **myportrait.art/dollyparton**

To listen to her Greatest Songs type into your Internet Browser the URL shortcut ➡ **radio.surf/dollyparton**

To view all channels on THE FACE OF MUSIC Internet Radio MEGA Station type into your Internet Browser the URL shortcut ➡ **radio.surf/music**

To inquire about purchasing a Limited Edtion NFT of this portrait type into your Internet Browser the URL shortcut ➡ **myartnft.shop/dollyparton**

To view all available NFTs type into your Internet Browser the URL shortcut ➡ **myartnft.shop/all**

# Don McLean

(Net worth: $50 Million)(Total Records Sold: Millions)
(Genre: Folk Rock)(Height: 5' - 10")

Donald McLean III (born October 2, 1945) is an American singer-songwriter, best known for his 1971 hit song "American Pie", an 8.5-minute folk rock "cultural touchstone" about the loss of innocence of the early rock and roll generation.

His other hit singles include "Vincent", "Dreidel", a rendition of Roy Orbison's "Crying", a rendition of the Skyliners' "Since I Don't Have You", and "Wonderful Baby".

His composition "And I Love You So" has been sung by Elvis Presley, Perry Como, Helen Reddy, Glen Campbell, and others, and in 2000, Madonna had a hit with a rendition of "American Pie".

In 2004, he was inducted into the Songwriters Hall of Fame. In January 2018, BMI certified that "American Pie" and "Vincent" had reached five million and three million airplays respectively.

McLean's magnum opus "American Pie" is a sprawling, impressionistic ballad inspired partly by the deaths of Buddy Holly, Ritchie Valens, and J.P. Richardson (The Big Bopper) in a plane crash in 1959, and developments in American youth culture in the subsequent decade. The song popularized the expression "The Day the Music Died" in reference to the crash.

The song was recorded on May 26, 1971, and a month later received its first radio airplay on New York's WNEW-FM and WPLJ-FM to mark the closing of Fillmore East, the famous New York concert hall. "American Pie" reached number one on the Billboard Hot 100 from January 15 to February 5, 1972, and remains McLean's most successful single release. The single also topped the Billboard Easy Listening chart. With a total running time of 8:36 encompassing both sides of the single, it is also the longest song to reach number 1. Some stations played only part one of the original split-sided single release.

WCFL DJ Bob Dearborn unraveled the lyrics and first published his interpretation on January 7, 1972, four days after the song reached number 1 on rival station WLS six days before it reached number 1 on WCFL, and eight days before it reached number 1 nationally (see "Further reading" under "American Pie"). Numerous other interpretations, which together largely converged on Dearborn's interpretation, quickly followed. McLean declined to say anything definitive about the lyrics until 1978. Since then McLean has stated that the lyrics are also somewhat autobiographical and present an abstract story of his life from the mid-1950s until the time he wrote the song in the late 1960s.

In 2001, "American Pie" was voted number 5 in a poll of the 365 Songs of the Century compiled by the Recording Industry Association of America and the National Endowment for the Arts.

On April 7, 2015, McLean's original working manuscript for "American Pie" sold for $1,205,000 (£809,524/€1,109,182) at Christie's auction rooms, New York, making it the third highest auction price achieved for an American literary manuscript.

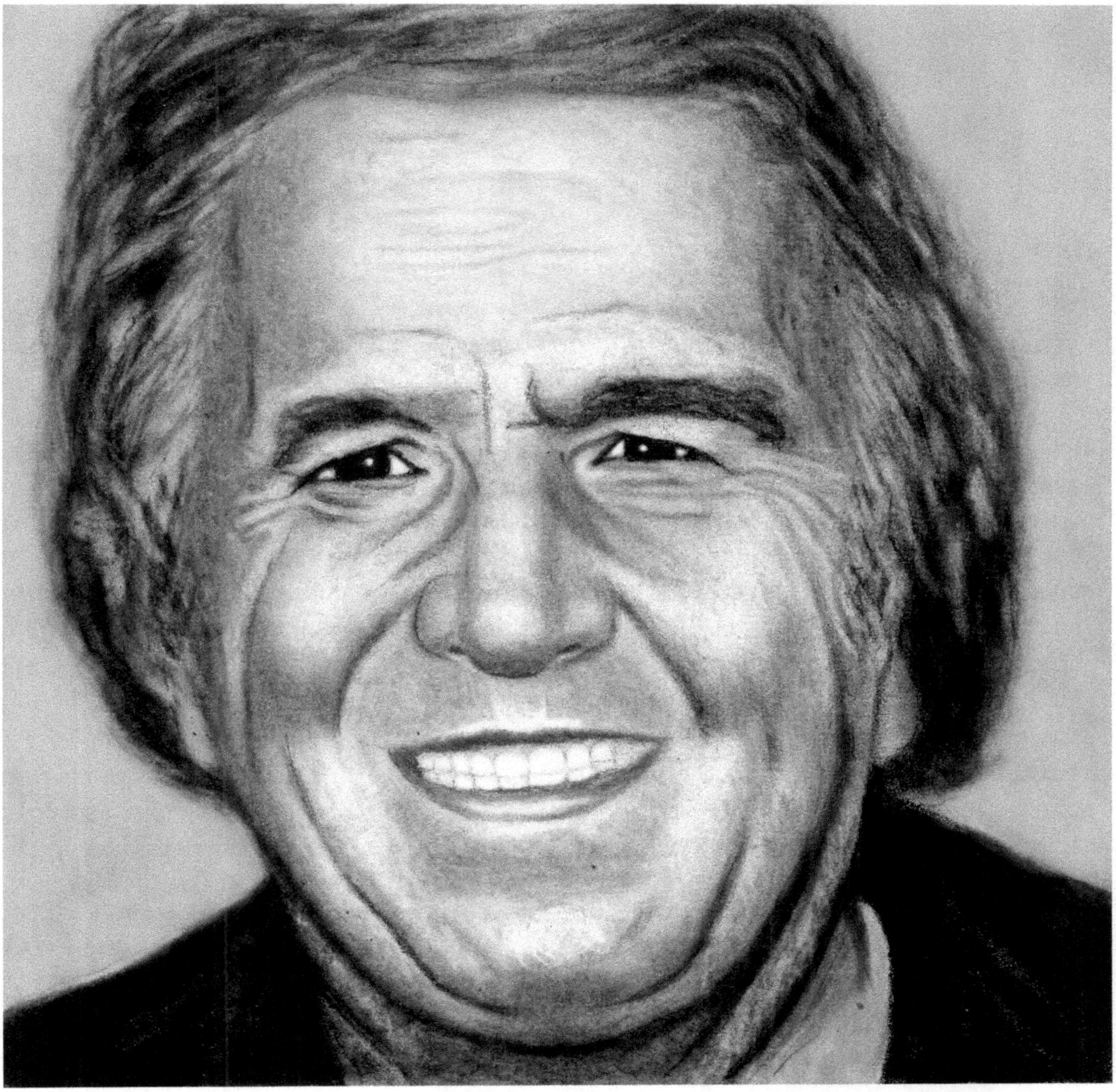

To view how this drawing was masterfully created or to purchase a Limited Edition Framed Artwork of Don McLean type into your Internet Browser the URL shortcut ➡ **myportrait.art/donmclean**

To listen to his Greatest Songs type into your Internet Browser the URL shortcut ➡ **radio.surf/donmclean**

To view all channels on THE FACE OF MUSIC Internet Radio MEGA Station type into your Internet Browser the URL shortcut ➡ **radio.surf/music**

To inquire about purchasing a Limited Edtion NFT of this portrait type into your Internet Browser the URL shortcut ➡ **myartnft.shop/donmclean**

To view all available NFTs type into your Internet Browser the URL shortcut ➡ **myartnft.shop/all**

# Donna Summer

(Net worth: $75 Million)(Total Records Sold: 100+ Million)
(Genre: Disco)(Height: 5' - 7")

LaDonna Adrian Gaines (December 31, 1948 – May 17, 2012), known professionally as Donna Summer, was an American singer, songwriter and actress. She gained prominence during the disco era of the 1970s and became known as the "Queen of Disco", while her music gained a global following.
While influenced by the counterculture of the 1960s, Summer became the lead singer of a psychedelic rock band named Crow and moved to New York City. Joining a touring version of the musical Hair, she left New York and spent several years living, acting and singing in Europe, where she met music producers Giorgio Moroder and Pete Bellotte in Munich, where they recorded influential disco hits such as "Love to Love You Baby" and "I Feel Love", marking her breakthrough into an international career. Summer returned to the United States in 1975, and other hits such as "Last Dance", "MacArthur Park", "Heaven Knows", "Hot Stuff", "Bad Girls", "Dim All the Lights", "No More Tears (Enough Is Enough)" (duet with Barbra Streisand) and "On the Radio" followed.
Summer earned a total of 42 hit singles on the US Billboard Hot 100 in her lifetime, with 14 of those reaching the top-ten. She claimed a top 40 hit every year between 1975 and 1984, and from her first top-ten hit in 1976, to the end of 1982, she had 12 top-ten hits (10 were top-five hits), more than any other act during that time period. She returned to the Hot 100's top-five in 1983, and claimed her final top-ten hit in 1989 with "This Time I Know It's for Real". She was the first artist to have three consecutive double albums reach number one on the US Billboard 200 chart and charted four number-one singles in the US within a 12-month period. She also charted two number-one singles on the R&B Singles chart in the US and a number-one single in the United Kingdom. Her most recent Hot 100 hit came in 1999 with "I Will Go with You (Con Te Partiro)". While her fortunes on the Hot 100 waned through those decades, Summer remained a force on the Billboard Dance Club Songs chart over her entire career.
Summer died on May 17, 2012, from lung cancer, at her home in Naples, Florida. She sold over 100 million records worldwide, making her one of the best-selling music artists of all time. She won five Grammy Awards. In her obituary in The Times, she was described as the "undisputed queen of the Seventies disco boom" who reached the status of "one of the world's leading female singers." Giorgio Moroder described Summer's work with them on the song "I Feel Love" as "really the start of electronic dance" music. In 2013, Summer was inducted into the Rock and Roll Hall of Fame. In December 2016, Billboard ranked her at No. 6 on its list of the Greatest of All Time Top Dance Club Artists.

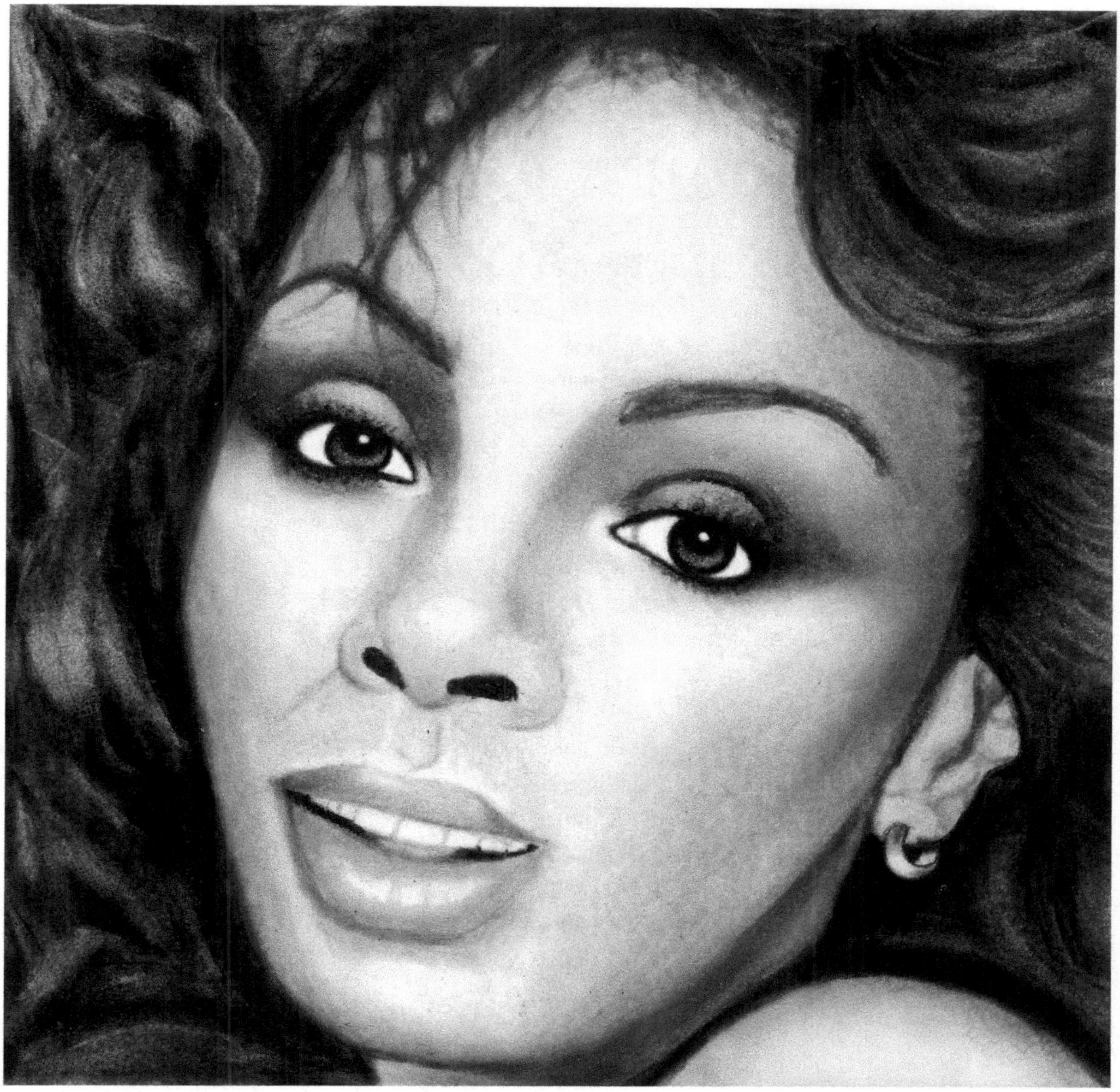

To view how this drawing was masterfully created or to purchase a Limited Edition Framed Artwork of Donna Summer type into your Internet Browser the URL shortcut ➡ **myportrait.art/donnasummer**

To listen to her Greatest Songs type into your Internet Browser the URL shortcut
➡ **radio.surf/donnasummer**

To view all channels on THE FACE OF MUSIC Internet Radio MEGA Station type into your Internet Browser the URL shortcut ➡ **radio.surf/music**

To inquire about purchasing a Limited Edtion NFT of this portrait type into your Internet Browser the URL shortcut ➡ **myartnft.shop/donnasummer**

To view all available NFTs type into your Internet Browser the URL shortcut ➡ **myartnft.shop/all**

# Donny Osmond

(Net worth: $18 Million)(Total Records Sold: 80 Million)
(Genre: Pop)(Height: 5' - 9")

Donald Clark Osmond (born December 9, 1957) is an American singer, dancer, actor, television host and former teen idol. Osmond first gained fame performing with four of his elder brothers as the Osmonds, earning several top ten hits and gold albums. Then, in the early 1970s, Osmond began a solo career, earning several additional top ten songs.

Osmond further gained fame due to the success of the 1976–1979 variety series Donny & Marie. The Donny & Marie duo also released a series of top ten hits and gold albums and hosted a syndicated and Daytime Emmy Award-nominated 1998–2000 talk show. Most recently, Donny & Marie headlined an 11-year Las Vegas residency at the Flamingo Las Vegas (2008–2019).

Osmond also successfully competed on two reality TV shows, winning season 9 of Dancing with the Stars and being named runner-up for season 1 of The Masked Singer. He also hosted the game show Pyramid from 2002 to 2004.

Andy Williams' father, Jay Emerson Williams, saw the Osmond Brothers ( Alan, Wayne, Merrill and Jay) perform on a Disneyland televised special as a barbershop quartet. In short order, the group was invited to audition for The Andy Williams Show. Williams initially had reservations about featuring children on the program, however, encouraged by his father to try them out, they proved in a short period of time to become an asset to the program, and soon became regulars on the show and gained popularity quickly. In 1963, Donny Osmond made his debut on the show at the age of five singing "You Are My Sunshine". The brothers continued to perform on the show throughout the 1960s along with a visit from their sister Marie.

Osmond became a teen idol in the early 1970s as a solo singer, while continuing to sing with his older brothers. Osmond was one of the biggest "Cover Boy" pop stars for Tiger Beat magazine in the early 1970s. His first solo hit was a cover of Roy Orbison's 1958 recording of "Sweet and Innocent", which peaked at No. 7 in the U.S. in 1971. Osmond's follow-ups "Go Away Little Girl" (1971) (U.S. No. 1), "Puppy Love" (U.S. No. 3), and "Hey Girl/I Knew You When" (U.S. No. 9) (1972) vaulted him into international fame, further advanced by his November 20, 1972 appearance on the Here's Lucy show, where he sang "Too Young" to Lucy's niece, played by Eve Plumb, and sang with Lucie Arnaz ("I'll Never Fall in Love Again").

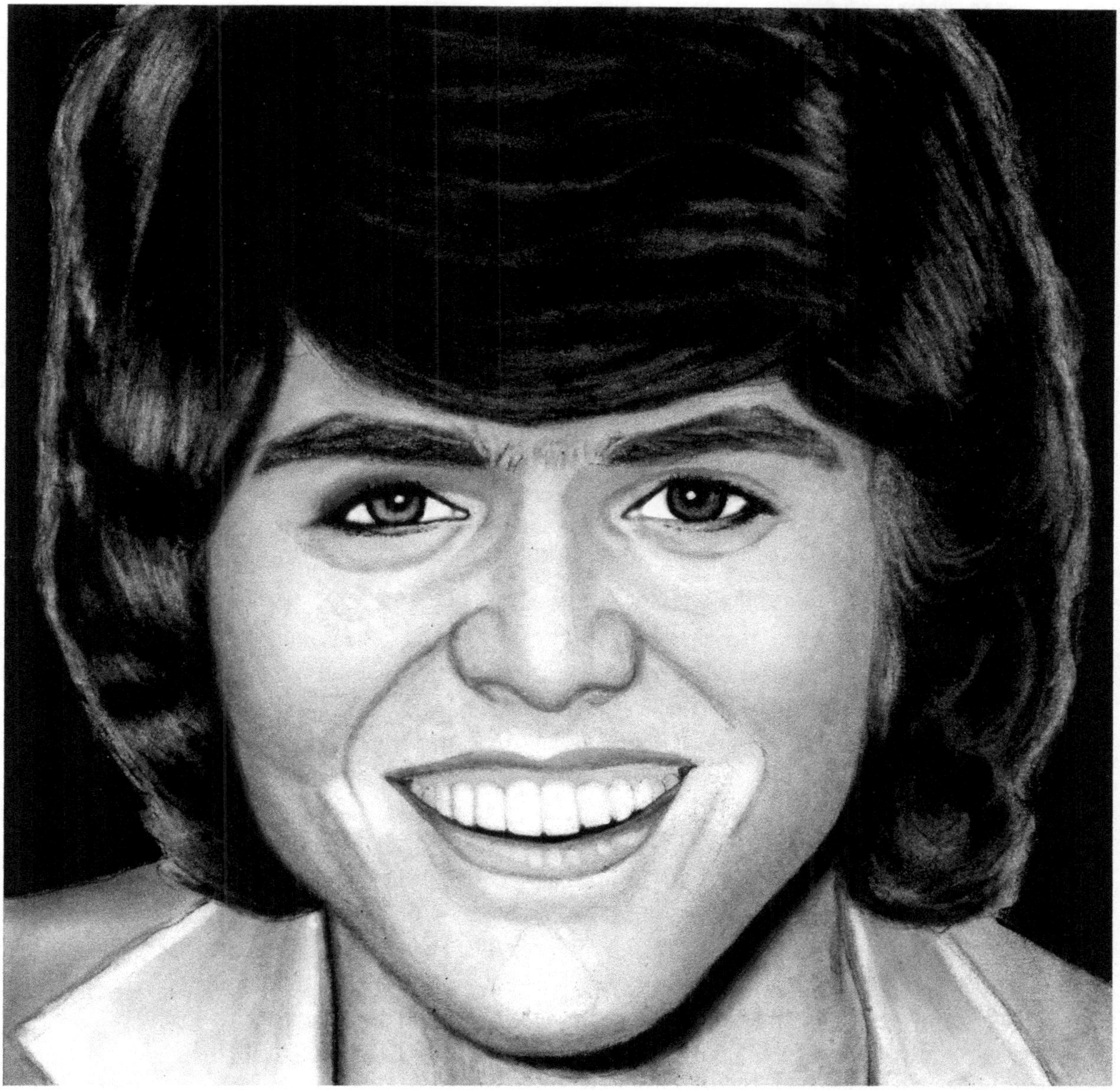

To view how this drawing was masterfully created or to purchase a Limited Edition Framed Artwork of Donny Osmond type into your Internet Browser the URL shortcut ➡ **myportrait.art/donnyosmond**

To listen to his Greatest Songs type into your Internet Browser the URL shortcut
➡ **radio.surf/donnyosmond**

To view all channels on THE FACE OF MUSIC Internet Radio MEGA Station type into your Internet Browser the URL shortcut ➡ **radio.surf/music**

To inquire about purchasing a Limited Edtion NFT of this portrait type into your Internet Browser the URL shortcut ➡ **myartnft.shop/donnyosmond**

To view all available NFTs type into your Internet Browser the URL shortcut ➡ **myartnft.shop/all**

# Donovan

(Net worth: $10 Million)(Total Records Sold: Millions)
(Genre: Folk , Rock , Psychedelic Rock)(Height: 5' - 9 1/2")

Donovan Phillips Leitch (born 10 May 1946) is a Scottish singer, songwriter and guitarist. He developed an eclectic and distinctive style that blended folk, jazz, pop, psychedelic rock, and world music (notably calypso). He has lived in Scotland, Hertfordshire (England), London, California, and since at least 2008 in County Cork, Ireland, with his family. Emerging from the British folk scene, Donovan reached fame in the United Kingdom in early 1965 with live performances on the pop TV series Ready Steady Go!.

Having signed with Pye Records in 1965, he recorded singles and two albums in the folk vein for Hickory Records (US company), after which he signed to CBS/Epic Records in the US – the first signing by the company's new vice-president Clive Davis – and became more successful internationally. He began a long and successful collaboration with leading British independent record producer Mickie Most, scoring multiple hit singles and albums in the UK, US and other countries.

His most successful singles were the early UK hits "Catch the Wind", "Colours" and "Universal Soldier" in 1965, the last written by Buffy Sainte-Marie. In September 1966 "Sunshine Superman" topped America's Billboard Hot 100 chart for one week and went to number two in Britain, followed by "Mellow Yellow" at US No. 2 in December 1966, then 1968's "Hurdy Gurdy Man" in the Top 5 in both countries, then "Atlantis", which reached US No. 7 in May 1969.

He became a friend of pop musicians including Joan Baez, Brian Jones and the Beatles. He taught John Lennon a finger-picking guitar style in 1968 that Lennon employed in "Dear Prudence", "Julia", "Happiness Is a Warm Gun" and other songs. Donovan's commercial fortunes waned after parting with Most in 1969, and he left the industry for a time.

Donovan continued to perform and record sporadically in the 1970s and 1980s. His musical style and hippie image were scorned by critics, especially after punk rock. His performing and recording became sporadic until a revival in the 1990s with the emergence of Britain's rave scene. He recorded the 1996 album Sutras with producer Rick Rubin and in 2004 made a new album, Beat Cafe. Donovan was inducted into the Rock and Roll Hall of Fame in 2012 and the Songwriters Hall of Fame in 2014.

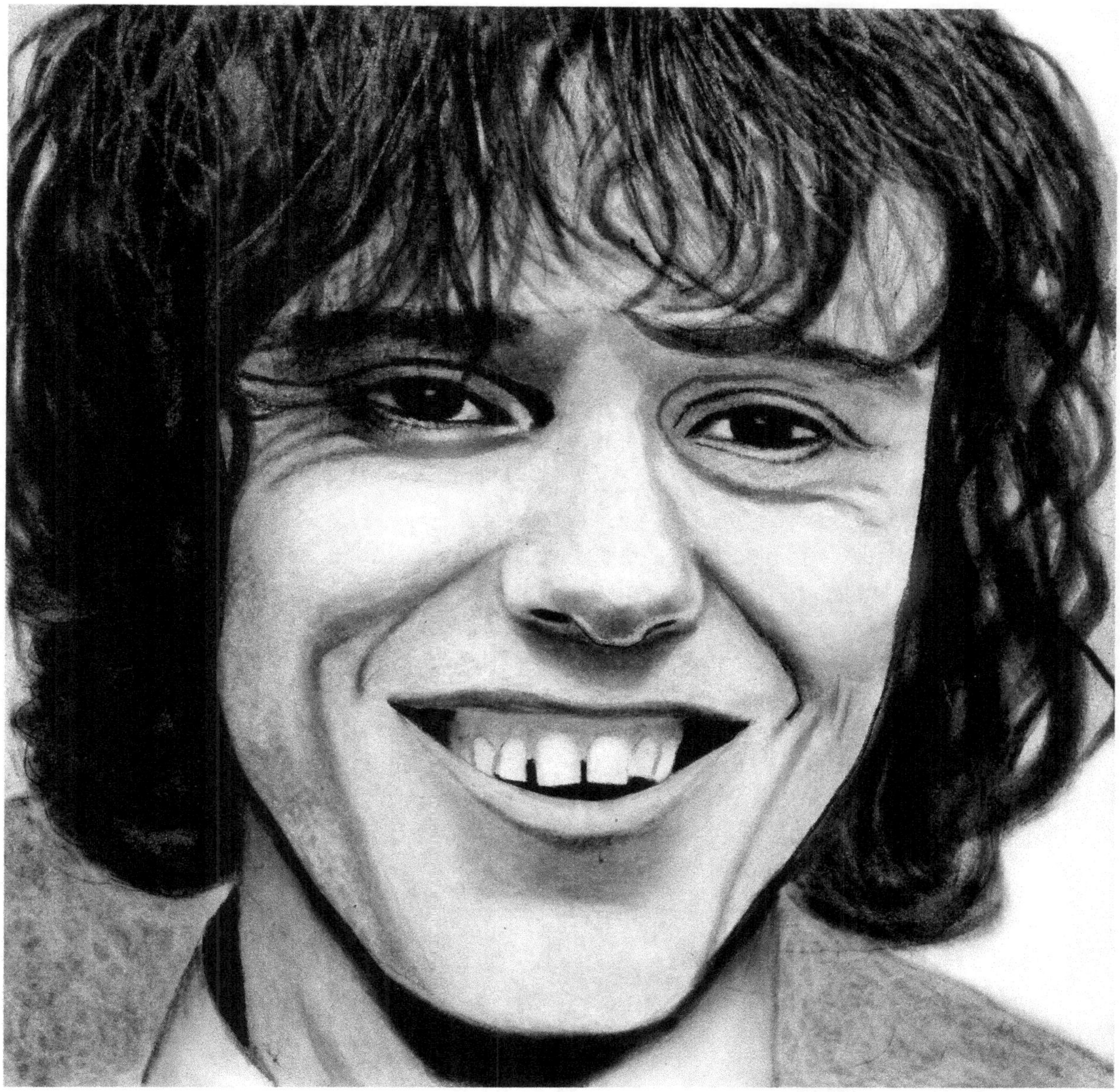

To view how this drawing was masterfully created or to purchase a Limited Edition Framed Artwork of Donovan type into your Internet Browser the URL shortcut ➡ **myportrait.art/donovan**

To listen to his Greatest Songs type into your Internet Browser the URL shortcut ➡ **radio.surf/donovan**

To view all channels on THE FACE OF MUSIC Internet Radio MEGA Station type into your Internet Browser the URL shortcut ➡ **radio.surf/music**

To inquire about purchasing a Limited Edtion NFT of this portrait type into your Internet Browser the URL shortcut ➡ **myartnft.shop/donovan**

To view all available NFTs type into your Internet Browser the URL shortcut ➡ **myartnft.shop/all**

# Doobie Brothers, The

(Total Albums Sold: 48+ Million) (Genre: Classic Rock)

The Doobie Brothers are an American rock band from San Jose, California. Active for five decades, with their greatest success in the 1970s, the group's current lineup consists of founding members Tom Johnston (guitars, vocals) and Patrick Simmons (guitars, vocals), veteran member Michael McDonald (keyboards, vocals), longtime member John McFee (guitars, pedal steel, violin, backing vocals), and touring musicians including John Cowan (bass, vocals), Bill Payne (keyboards), Marc Russo (saxophones), Ed Toth (drums), and Marc Quiñones (percussion).

The band's history can be roughly divided into three eras. From 1970 to 1975 it featured lead vocalist Johnston and a mainstream rock and roll sound with elements of folk, country and R&B. Johnston left the group in 1977 due to health reasons, and was replaced by Michael McDonald, whose interest in soul music changed the band's sound until it broke up in 1982 with Simmons being the only constant member having appeared on all of their albums. In 1987, the Doobie Brothers reformed with Johnston back in the fold; McDonald, who had previously made several guest appearances since their reformation, returned to the band full-time in 2019 for their upcoming 50th anniversary tour. Every incarnation of the group has emphasized vocal harmonies. The Doobie Brothers were inducted into the Vocal Group Hall of Fame in 2004, and the Rock and Roll Hall of Fame on November 7, 2020. The group has sold more than 48 million albums worldwide. Founding members John Hartman and Dave Shogren, Tiran Porter, Michael Hossack,

Keith Knudsen and Jeff "Skunk" Baxter are former members of the band.

# Tom Johnston

(Net Worth: $13 Million)

Charles Thomas Johnston (born August 15, 1948) is an American musician. He is a guitarist and vocalist, known principally as a founder, guitarist, lead vocalist and songwriter for the rock group The Doobie Brothers, as well as for his own solo career. He has played off and on with The Doobie Brothers for 50 years, in several styles. He was inducted into the Rock and Roll Hall of Fame as a member of The Doobie Brothers in 2020.

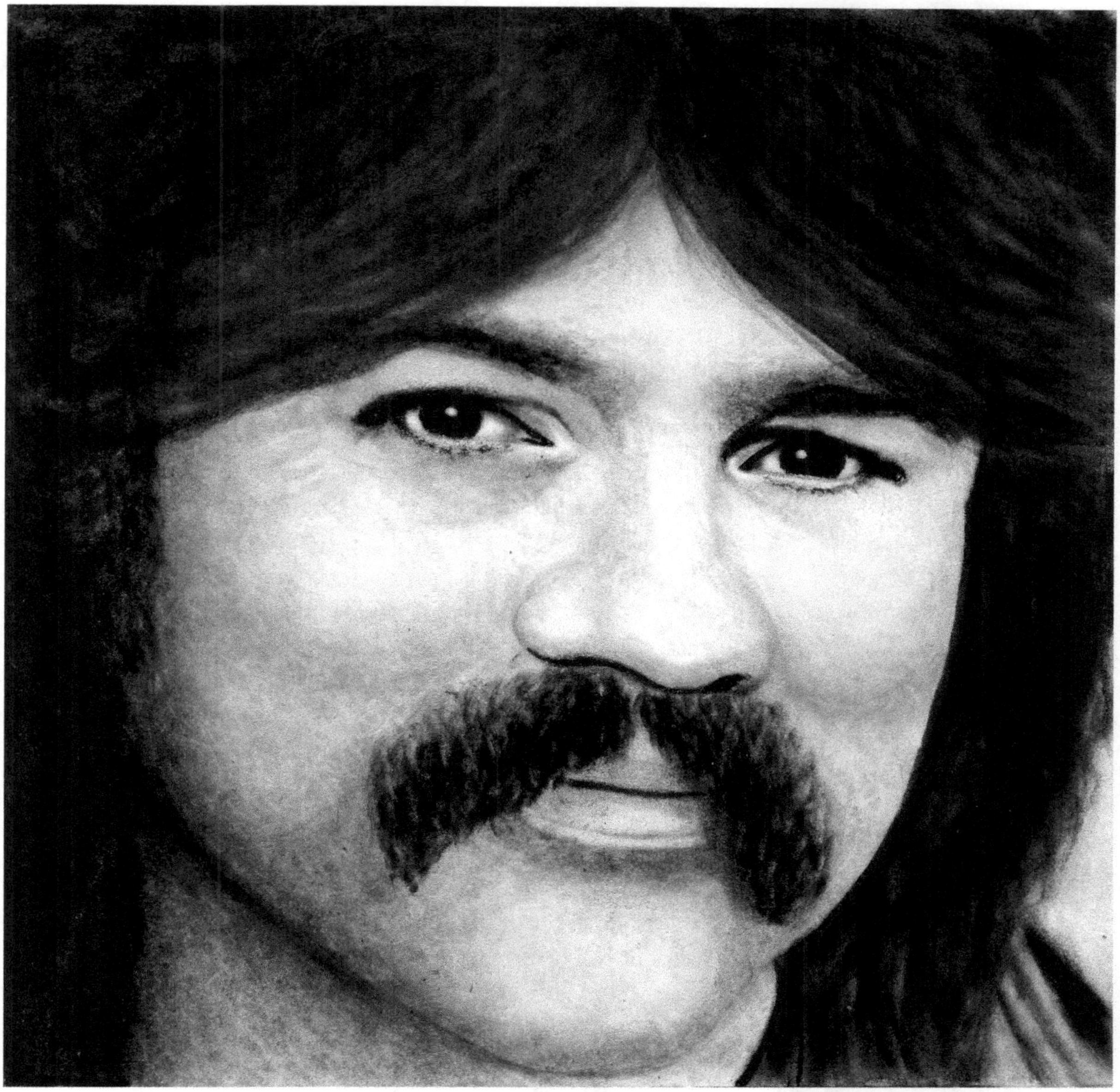

To view how this drawing was masterfully created or to purchase a Limited Edition Framed Artwork of Tom Johnston type into your Internet Browser the URL shortcut ➡ **myportrait.art/tomjohnston**

To listen to their Greatest Songs type into your Internet Browser the URL shortcut
➡ **radio.surf/thedoobiebrothers**

To view all channels on THE FACE OF MUSIC Internet Radio MEGA Station type into your Internet Browser the URL shortcut ➡ **radio.surf/music**

To inquire about purchasing a Limited Edtion NFT of this portrait type into your Internet Browser the URL shortcut ➡ **myartnft.shop/tomjohnston**

To view all available NFTs type into your Internet Browser the URL shortcut ➡ **myartnft.shop/all**

# Doors, The

(Total Albums Sold: 100+ Million) (Genre: Classic Rock)

The Doors were an American rock band formed in Los Angeles in 1965, with vocalist Jim Morrison, keyboardist Ray Manzarek, guitarist Robby Krieger, and drummer John Densmore. They were among the most controversial and influential rock acts of the 1960s, also because of Morrison's lyrics and voice, along with his erratic stage persona, and the group was widely regarded as an important part of the era's counterculture.

The band took its name from the title of Aldous Huxley's book The Doors of Perception, itself a reference to a quote by William Blake. After signing with Elektra Records, the Doors with Morrison released six albums in five years, some of which are considered among the greatest of all time, including The Doors (1967), Strange Days (1967), and L.A. Woman (1971). They were one of the most successful bands during that time and by 1972 the Doors had sold over 4 million albums domestically and nearly 8 million singles.Morrison died in uncertain circumstances in 1971. The band continued as a trio until disbanding in 1973. They released three more albums in the 1970s, two of which featured earlier recordings by Morrison, and over the decades reunited on stage in various configurations. In 2002, Manzarek, Krieger and Ian Astbury of the Cult on vocals started performing as "The Doors of the 21st Century". Densmore and the Morrison estate successfully sued them over the use of the band's name. After a short time as Riders on the Storm, they settled on the name Manzarek–Krieger and toured until Manzarek's death in 2013.The Doors were the first American band to accumulate eight consecutive gold LPs. According to the RIAA, they have sold 33 million records in the US and over 100 million records worldwide, making them one of the best-selling bands of all time. The Doors have been listed as one of the greatest artists of all time by magazines including Rolling Stone, which ranked them 41st on its list of the "100 Greatest Artists of All Time". In 1993, they were inducted into the Rock and Roll Hall of Fame.

# Jim Morrison

(Net Worth: $20 Million) (Height: 5' - 10")

James "Jim" Douglas Morrison (December 8, 1943 – July 3, 1971) was an American singer, songwriter and poet, who was the lead vocalist of the rock band the Doors. Due to his wild personality, poetic lyrics, distinctive voice, unpredictable and erratic performances, and the dramatic circumstances surrounding his life and early death, Morrison is regarded by music critics and fans as one of the most iconic and influential frontmen in rock history. Since his death, his fame has endured as one of popular culture's most rebellious and oft-displayed icons, representing the generation gap and youth counterculture.Morrison developed an alcohol dependency in the 1960s, which at times affected his performances on stage. He died unexpectedly in Paris at the age of 27, amid conflicting witness reports. Since no autopsy was performed, the cause of Morrison's death remains disputed. Though the Doors recorded two more albums after Morrison died, his death severely affected the band's fortunes, and they split up in 1973. In 1993, Morrison was inducted into the Rock and Roll Hall of Fame as a member of the Doors.

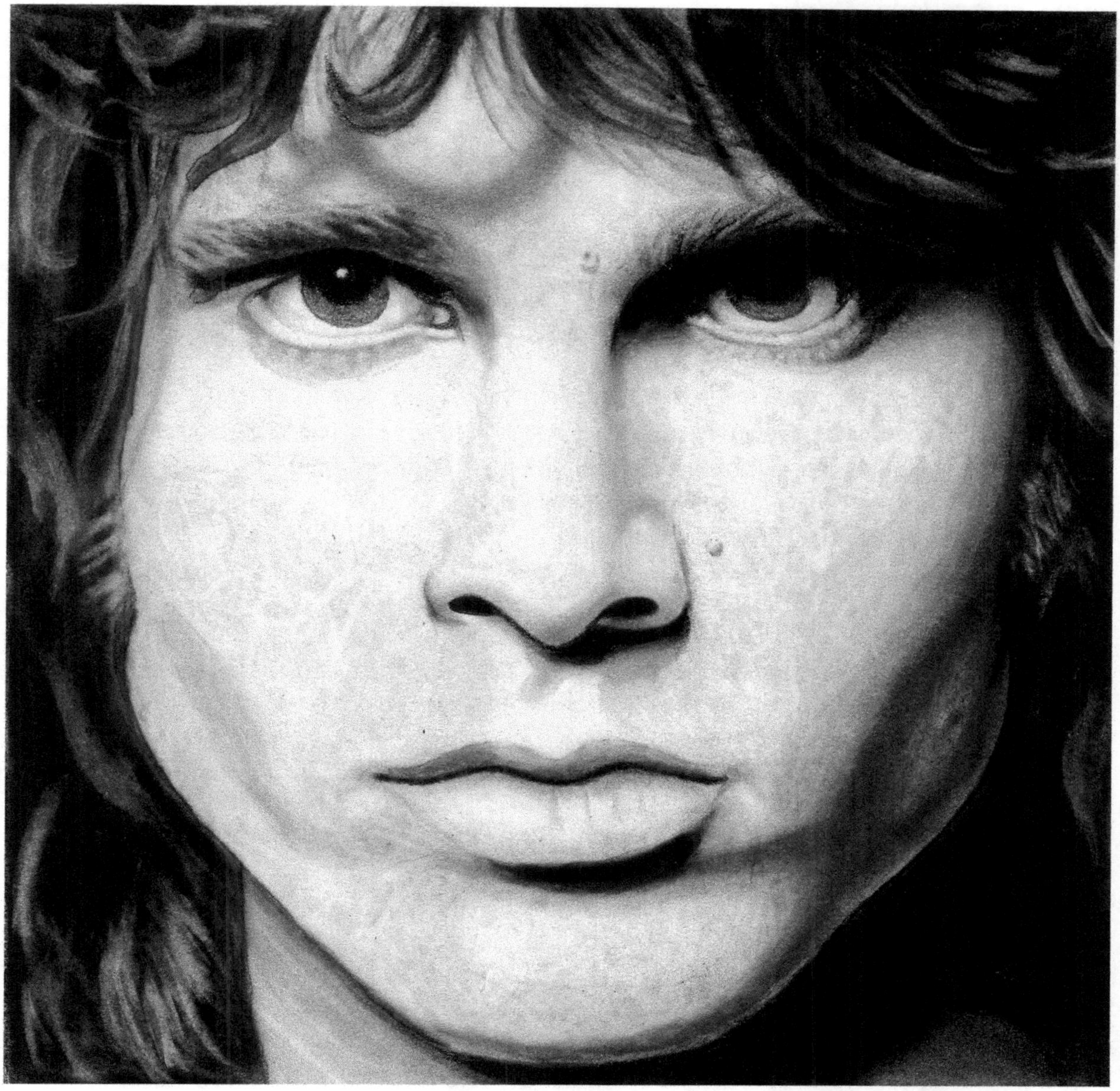

To view how this drawing was masterfully created or to purchase a Limited Edition Framed Artwork of Jim Morrison type into your Internet Browser the URL shortcut ➡ **myportrait.art/jimmorrison**

To listen to their Greatest Songs type into your Internet Browser the URL shortcut ➡ **radio.surf/thedoors**

To view all channels on THE FACE OF MUSIC Internet Radio MEGA Station type into your Internet Browser the URL shortcut ➡ **radio.surf/music**

To inquire about purchasing a Limited Edtion NFT of this portrait type into your Internet Browser the URL shortcut ➡ **myartnft.shop/jimmorrison**

To view all available NFTs type into your Internet Browser the URL shortcut ➡ **myartnft.shop/all**

# Drifters, The

(Total Records Sold: Millions) (Genre: R&B , Soul , Pop)

The Drifters are an American doo-wop and R&B/soul vocal group. They were originally formed as a backing group for Clyde McPhatter, formerly the lead tenor of Billy Ward and his Dominoes in 1953. According to Rolling Stone, the Drifters were the least stable of the great vocal groups, as they were low-paid musicians hired by George Treadwell, who owned the Drifters' name from 1955, after McPhatter left. The Treadwell Drifters line has had 60 musicians, including several splinter groups by former Drifters members (not under Treadwell's management). These groups are usually identified with a possessive credit such as "Bill Pinkney's Original Drifters", "Charlie Thomas' Drifters".

The three golden eras of the Drifters were the early 1950s, the 1960s, and the early 1970s (post-Atlantic period). From these, the first Drifters, formed by Clyde McPhatter, were inducted into the Vocal Group Hall of Fame as "The Drifters". The second Drifters, featuring Ben E. King, were separately inducted into the Vocal Group Hall of Fame as "Ben E. King and the Drifters". In their induction, the Rock and Roll Hall of Fame selected four members from the first Drifters, two from the second Drifters, and one from the post-Atlantic Drifters. There were other lead singers too, but the group was less successful during those times. According to the Vocal Group Hall of Fame: "Through turmoil and changes, the (original) Drifters managed to set musical trends and give the public 13 chart hits, most of which are legendary recordings today." Matching that feat, subsequent formations of the Drifters recorded 13 Billboard Hot 100 top-30 chart hits. The 1950s and '60s incarnations of the group were also a force on the US R&B charts, notching six number-one R&B hits: "Money Honey" (1953), "Honey Love" (1954), "Adorable" (1955), "There Goes My Baby" (1959), "Save The Last Dance For Me" (1960), and "Under The Boardwalk" (1964). A 1970s revival in Britain, with both old and new material, was not matched in the United States, although they had their biggest successes on the UK pop charts, peaking with the number-two hit "Kissin' in the Back Row of the Movies".

# Clyde McPhatter

(Net Worth: $5 Million)

Clyde Lensley McPhatter (November 15, 1932 – June 13, 1972) was an American rhythm and blues, soul, and rock and roll singer. He was one of the most widely imitated R&B singers of the 1950s and early 1960s and was a key figure in the shaping of doo-wop and R&B.

McPhatter's high-pitched tenor voice was steeped in the gospel music he sang in much of his early life. He was the lead tenor of the Mount Lebanon Singers, a gospel group he formed as a teenager. He was later the lead tenor of Billy Ward and his Dominoes and was largely responsible for the initial success of the group. After his tenure with the Dominoes, McPhatter formed his own group, the Drifters, and later worked as a solo performer. Only 39 at the time of his death, he had struggled for years with alcoholism and depression, and was, according to Jay Warner's On This Day in Music History, "broke and despondent over a mismanaged career that made him a legend but hardly a success." McPhatter left a legacy of over 22 years of recording history. He was the first artist to be inducted twice into the Rock and Roll Hall of Fame, first as a solo artist and later as a member of the Drifters.

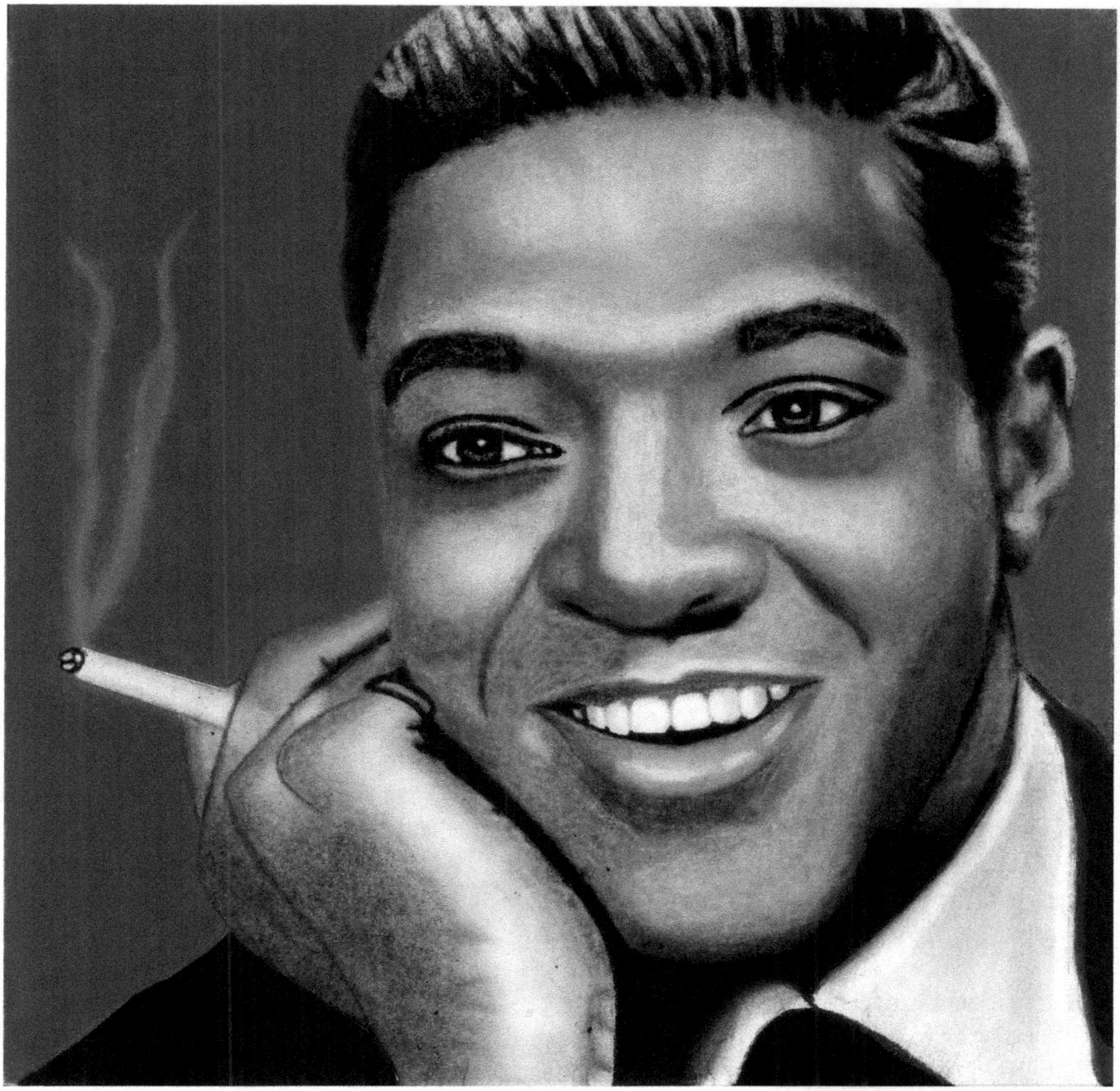

To view how this drawing was masterfully created or to purchase a Limited Edition Framed Artwork of Clyde McPhatter type into your Internet Browser the URL shortcut ➡ **myportrait.art/clydemcphatter**

To listen to their Greatest Songs type into your Internet Browser the URL shortcut ➡ **radio.surf/thedrifters**

To view all channels on THE FACE OF MUSIC Internet Radio MEGA Station type into your Internet Browser the URL shortcut ➡ **radio.surf/music**

To inquire about purchasing a Limited Edtion NFT of this portrait type into your Internet Browser the URL shortcut ➡ **myartnft.shop/clydemcphatter**

To view all available NFTs type into your Internet Browser the URL shortcut ➡ **myartnft.shop/all**

# Duran Duran

(Total Albums Sold: 100+ Million) (Genre: New Wave, Pop)

Duran Duran are an English new wave band formed in Birmingham in 1978. The group were a leading band in the MTV-driven Second British Invasion of the US in the 1980s. The group was formed by keyboardist Nick Rhodes and bassist John Taylor, with the later addition of drummer Roger Taylor, and after numerous personnel changes, guitarist Andy Taylor (none of the Taylors are related) and lead singer Simon Le Bon. These five members featured the most commercially successful line-up.

When Duran Duran emerged they were generally considered part of the New Romantic scene, along with bands such as Spandau Ballet and Visage. The video age catapulted Duran Duran into the mainstream with the introduction of the 24-hour music channel MTV. Many of their videos were shot on 35 mm film, which gave a much more polished look than was standard at the time. They also collaborated with professional film directors to take the quality a step further, often teaming up with Australian director Russell Mulcahy for some of their most memorable video offerings. In 1984, the band were early innovators with video technology in their live stadium shows. The band were one of the most successful acts of the 1980s, though by the end of the decade, membership and music style changes challenged the band before a resurgence in the early 1990s.

The group have never disbanded, but after the departures of Andy and Roger Taylor in 1986, the line-up has changed to include former Missing Persons American guitarist Warren Cuccurullo from 1989 to 2001 and American drummer Sterling Campbell from 1989 to 1991. The reunion of the original five members in the early 2000s created a stir among the band's fans and music media. Andy Taylor left the band once again in mid-2006, and guitarist Dominic Brown has since been working with the band as a session player and touring member.

Duran Duran have sold over 100 million records worldwide, making them one of the world's best-selling music artists. They achieved 14 singles in the top 10 of the UK Singles Chart and 21 in the US Billboard Hot 100. The band have won numerous awards throughout their career: two Brit Awards including the 2004 award for Outstanding Contribution to Music, two Grammy Awards, an MTV Video Music Award for Lifetime Achievement, and a Video Visionary Award from the MTV Europe Music Awards. They were also awarded a star on the Hollywood Walk of Fame.

# Simon Le Bon

(Net Worth: $80 Million) (Height: 6' - 1 1/2")

Simon John Charles Le Bon (born 27 October 1958) is an English musician, singer, songwriter and lyricist, best known as the lead singer and lyricist of the band Duran Duran and its offshoot, Arcadia. Le Bon has received three Ivor Novello Awards from the British Academy of Songwriters, Composers and Authors, including the award for Outstanding Contribution to British Music.

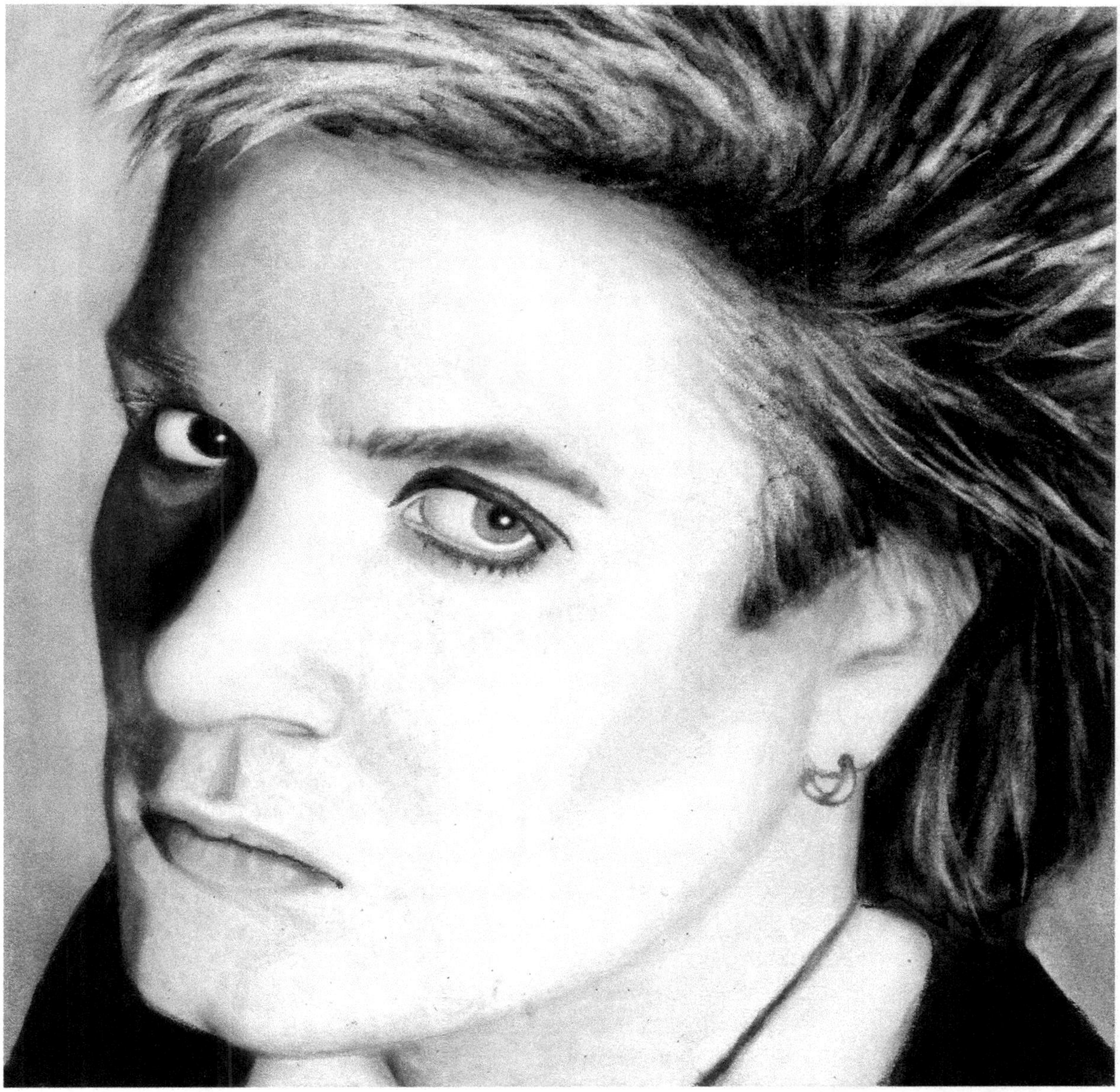

To view how this drawing was masterfully created or to purchase a Limited Edition Framed Artwork of Simon Le Bon type into your Internet Browser the URL shortcut ➡ **myportrait.art/simonlebon**

To listen to their Greatest Songs type into your Internet Browser the URL shortcut ➡ **radio.surf/duranduran**

To view all channels on THE FACE OF MUSIC Internet Radio MEGA Station type into your Internet Browser the URL shortcut ➡ **radio.surf/music**

To inquire about purchasing a Limited Edition NFT of this portrait type into your Internet Browser the URL shortcut ➡ **myartnft.shop/simonlebon**

To view all available NFTs type into your Internet Browser the URL shortcut ➡ **myartnft.shop/all**

# Eagles

(Total Albums Sold: 200+ Million) (Genre: Classic Rock)

The Eagles are an American rock band formed in Los Angeles in 1971. With five number one singles and six number one albums, six Grammy Awards, and five American Music Awards, the Eagles were one of the most successful musical acts of the 1970s in North America. Founding members Glenn Frey (guitars, vocals), Don Henley (drums, vocals), Bernie Leadon (guitars, vocals) and Randy Meisner (bass guitar, vocals), were recruited by Linda Ronstadt as band members, some touring with her, and all playing on her third solo album, before venturing out on their own on David Geffen's new Asylum Records label.Their debut, Eagles (1972), spawned two top 20 singles in the US and Canada: "Take It Easy" and "Witchy Woman". The next year's follow up, Desperado, only peaked at number 41 in the US although "Desperado" became a popular track. In 1974, guitarist Don Felder joined, and On the Border produced the top 40 hit "Already Gone" and the Eagles' first number one song in the US and Canada, "Best of My Love", which made the top 15 in Australia, their first hit overseas. In 1975, guitarist and vocalist Joe Walsh replaced Leadon, and the album One of These Nights became their first number one album in the US and top 10 album in many countries. It included the US number one hit "One of These Nights", which was their first top 10 hit outside of North America, and US top five songs "Lyin' Eyes" and "Take It to the Limit". Their Greatest Hits (1971–1975) (1976) is the best-selling album in the United States, with 38 million sold, and primed the public for late 1976 release of Hotel California, which would sell more than 26 million copies in the U.S., (ranking 3rd all time for US sales), and more than 42 million copies worldwide. The album yielded two number one singles in the US and Canada, "New Kid in Town" and "Hotel California", the latter of which became their only top 10 hit in the United Kingdom, while also reaching the top 10 in New Zealand and many European countries, including number two in France.

- Continued on Page 201 -.

# Don Henley

(Net Worth: $200 Million) (Height: 5' - 10")

Donald Hugh Henley (born July 22, 1947) is an American musician, singer, songwriter, record producer, and a founding member of the Eagles. He was the drummer and co-lead vocalist for the Eagles from 1971 until the band broke up in 1980, and has reprised those duties for the group's reunions since 1994. Henley sang the lead vocals on Eagles hits such as "Witchy Woman", "Desperado", "Best of My Love", "One of These Nights", "Hotel California", "Life in the Fast Lane", "The Long Run" and "Get Over It". After the Eagles broke up in 1980, Henley pursued a solo career and released his debut album I Can't Stand Still, in 1982. He has released five studio albums, two compilation albums, and one live DVD. His solo hits include "Dirty Laundry", "The Boys of Summer", "All She Wants to Do Is Dance", "The Heart of the Matter", "The Last Worthless Evening", "Sunset Grill", "Not Enough Love in the World", and "The End of the Innocence".

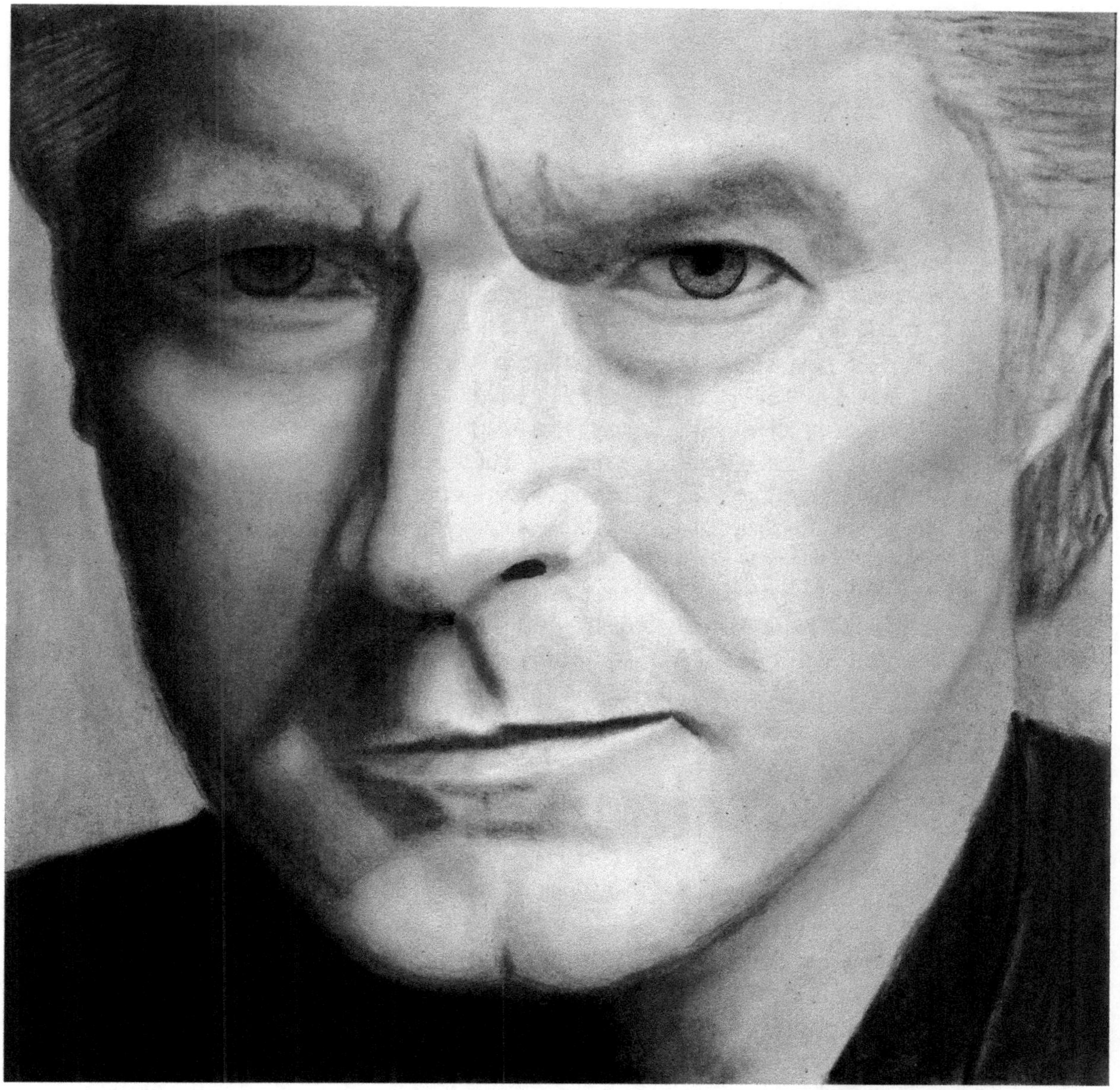

To view how this drawing was masterfully created or to purchase a Limited Edition Framed Artwork of Don Henley type into your Internet Browser the URL shortcut ➡ **myportrait.art/donhenley**

To listen to Eagles Greatest Songs type into your Internet Browser the URL shortcut ➡ **radio.surf/eagles**

To listen to Don Henley's Greatest Songs type into your Internet Browser the URL shortcut
➡ **radio.surf/donhenley**

To view all channels on THE FACE OF MUSIC Internet Radio MEGA Station type into your Internet Browser the URL shortcut ➡ **radio.surf/music**

To inquire about purchasing a Limited Edtion NFT of this portrait type into your Internet Browser the URL shortcut ➡ **myartnft.shop/donhenley**

To view all available NFTs type into your Internet Browser the URL shortcut ➡ **myartnft.shop/all**

# Eagles

- Continued -

Meisner was replaced by Timothy B. Schmit in 1977, and the Eagles released their last studio album for nearly 28 years in 1979 with The Long Run, which spawned the North American number one song "Heartache Tonight", which became their biggest hit in Australia (number 13), and the North American top 10 hits "The Long Run" and "I Can't Tell You Why". The Eagles broke up in 1980 but reunited in 1994 for the album Hell Freezes Over, a mix of live and new studio tracks, and toured consistently. In 2007, the Eagles released Long Road Out of Eden, their sixth number one album in the US, and in 2008 launched the Long Road Out of Eden Tour. In 2013, they began the extended History of the Eagles Tour in conjunction with the documentary release, History of the Eagles. Following Frey's death in January 2016, the Eagles re-formed in 2017, with Glenn's son Deacon Frey and Vince Gill sharing lead vocals for Frey's songs.The Eagles are one of the world's best-selling bands, having sold more than 200 million records, including 100 million sold in U.S alone. They were inducted into the Rock and Roll Hall of Fame in 1998 and were ranked number 75 on Rolling Stone's 2004 list of the 100 Greatest Artists of All Time.

# Glenn Frey

(Net Worth: $120 Million) (Height: 5' - 8")

Glenn Lewis Frey (November 6, 1948 – January 18, 2016) was an American singer, songwriter, actor and founding member of the rock band the Eagles. Frey was the co-lead singer and frontman for the Eagles, roles he came to share with fellow member Don Henley, with whom he wrote most of the Eagles' material. Frey played guitar and keyboards as well as singing lead vocals on songs such as "Take It Easy", "Peaceful Easy Feeling", "Tequila Sunrise", "Already Gone", "James Dean", "Lyin' Eyes", "New Kid in Town", and "Heartache Tonight".After the breakup of the Eagles in 1980, Frey embarked on a successful solo career. He released his debut album, No Fun Aloud, in 1982 and went on to record Top 40 hits "The One You Love", "Smuggler's Blues", "Sexy Girl", "The Heat Is On", "You Belong to the City", "True Love", "Soul Searchin'" and "Livin' Right". As a member of the Eagles, Frey won six Grammy Awards, and five American Music Awards. The Eagles were inducted into the Rock and Roll Hall of Fame in 1998, the first year they were nominated. Consolidating his solo recordings and those with the Eagles, Frey had 24 Top 40 singles on the Billboard Hot 100.

From about 2000, Frey had suffered from rheumatoid arthritis, which affected various joints of his body. The medication that he was prescribed to control the disease eventually led to colitis and pneumonia, and in November 2015, the Eagles announced that they were postponing their appearance at the Kennedy Center Honors because Frey required surgery for intestinal problems and needed a lengthy recovery period. He never had the surgery due to complications from pneumonia and was placed in a medically induced coma at Columbia University Medical Center. Frey died there on January 18, 2016, at the age of 67 from complications of rheumatoid arthritis, acute ulcerative colitis, and pneumonia. Medications for rheumatoid arthritis or ulcerative colitis can compromise the immune system's ability to fight off pneumonia.

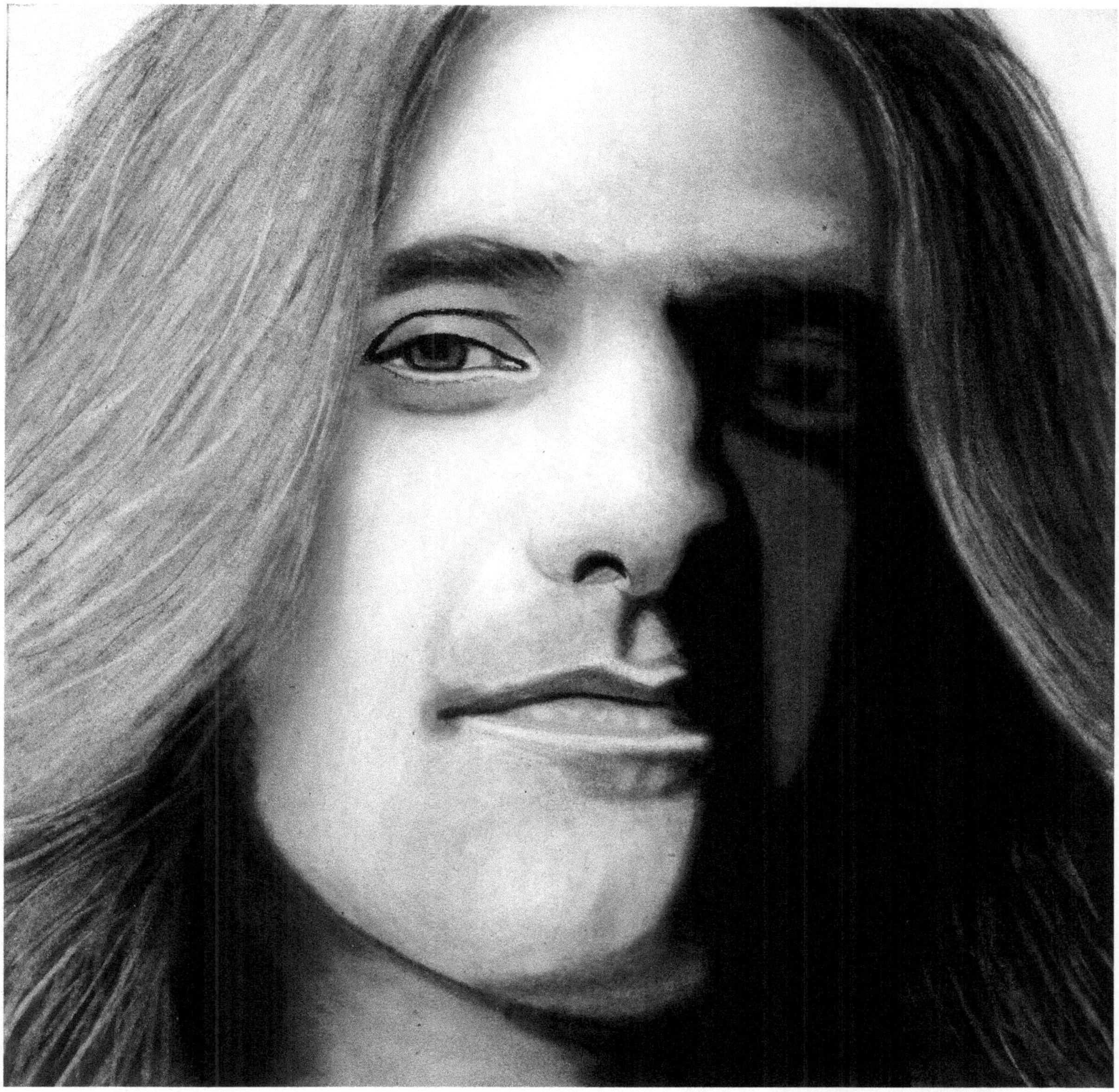

To view how this drawing was masterfully created or to purchase a Limited Edition Framed Artwork of Glenn Frey type into your Internet Browser the URL shortcut ➡ **myportrait.art/glennfrey**

To listen to Eagles Greatest Songs type into your Internet Browser the URL shortcut ➡ **radio.surf/eagles**

To listen to Glenn Frey's Greatest Songs type into your Internet Browser the URL shortcut ➡ **radio.surf/glennfrey**

To view all channels on THE FACE OF MUSIC Internet Radio MEGA Station type into your Internet Browser the URL shortcut ➡ **radio.surf/music**

To inquire about purchasing a Limited Edtion NFT of this portrait type into your Internet Browser the URL shortcut ➡ **myartnft.shop/glennfrey**

To view all available NFTs type into your Internet Browser the URL shortcut ➡ **myartnft.shop/all**

# Earth, Wind & Fire

(Total Records Sold: 80+ Million)

(Genre: R&B, Soul, Funk, Jazz, Disco, Pop, Dance, Latin, Afro Pop)

Earth, Wind & Fire (EW&F or EWF) is an American band that has spanned the musical genres of R&B, soul, funk, jazz, disco, pop, dance, Latin, and Afro pop. They have been described as one of the most innovative and commercially successful acts of all time. Rolling Stone called them "innovative, precise yet sensual, calculated yet galvanizing" and declared that the band "changed the sound of black pop". VH1 has also described EWF as "one of the greatest bands" ever.The band was founded in Chicago by Maurice White in 1969, having grown out of a previous band known as the Salty Peppers. As well other prominent members of EWF have included Philip Bailey, Verdine White, Ralph Johnson, Larry Dunn, Al McKay, Roland Bautista, Robert Brookins, Sonny Emory, Fred Ravel, Ronnie Laws, Sheldon Reynolds and Andrew Woolfolk. The band is known for its kalimba sound, dynamic horn section, energetic and elaborate stage shows, and the contrast between Philip Bailey's falsetto vocals and Maurice White's baritone.

The band has won six Grammys from their 17 nominations and four American Music Awards out of 12 nominations. They have been inducted into the Rock and Roll Hall of Fame, the Vocal Group Hall of Fame, the NAACP Image Award Hall of Fame, and Hollywood's Rockwalk, in addition to receiving a star on the Hollywood Walk of Fame. With sales of over 90 million records, they are one of the world's best-selling bands of all time. The band has also received an ASCAP Rhythm & Soul Heritage Award, BET Lifetime Achievement Award, and the Soul Train Legend Award, as well as a NARAS Signature Governor's Award, a Grammy Lifetime Achievement Award, the 2012 Congressional Horizon Award, and the Kennedy Center Honors in 2019, along with Sally Field, Linda Roustadt, Sesame Street and Michael Tilson Thomas.

# Maurice White

(Net Worth: $5 Million) (Height: 5' - 10")

Maurice White (December 19, 1941 – February 4, 2016) was an American singer, musician, songwriter, and record producer. He was the founder, leader, main songwriter, and producer of the band Earth, Wind & Fire, and served as the band's co-lead singer with Philip Bailey. Described as a "visionary" by Vibe and a "mastermind" by Variety, White was nominated for a total of 22 Grammys, of which he won seven. He was inducted into the Rock and Roll Hall of Fame and the Vocal Group Hall of Fame as a member of Earth, Wind & Fire, and was also inducted individually into the Songwriters Hall of Fame. He additionally worked with artists such as Deniece Williams, Cher, the Emotions, Barbra Streisand, Ramsey Lewis, and Neil Diamond.

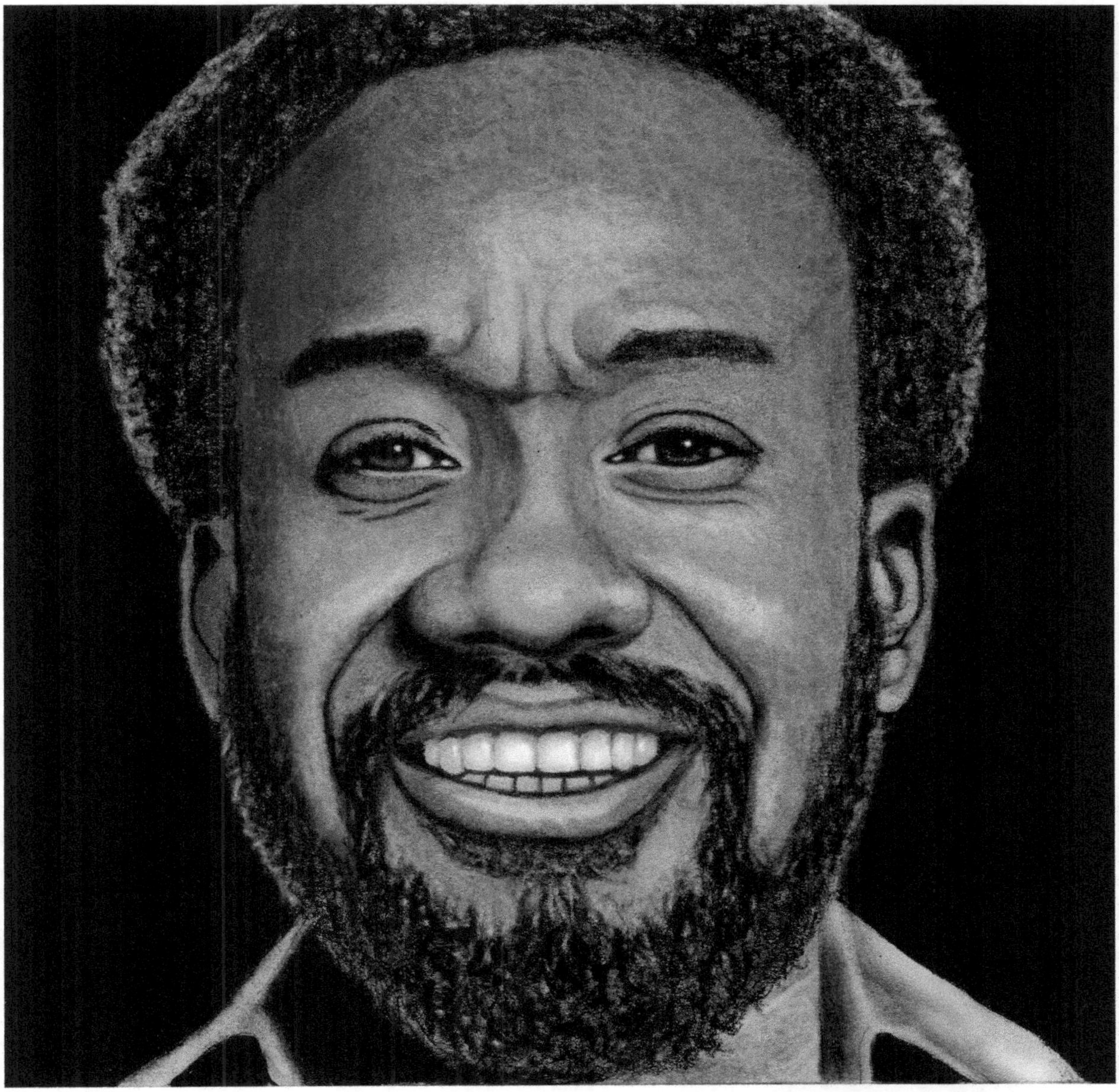

To view how this drawing was masterfully created or to purchase a Limited Edition Framed Artwork of Maurice White type into your Internet Browser the URL shortcut ➡ **myportrait.art/mauricewhite**

To listen to their Greatest Songs type into your Internet Browser the URL shortcut ➡ **radio.surf/earthwindandfire**

To view all channels on THE FACE OF MUSIC Internet Radio MEGA Station type into your Internet Browser the URL shortcut ➡ **radio.surf/music**

To inquire about purchasing a Limited Edition NFT of this portrait type into your Internet Browser the URL shortcut ➡ **myartnft.shop/mauricewhite**

To view all available NFTs type into your Internet Browser the URL shortcut ➡ **myartnft.shop/all**

# Eddie Cochran

(Net worth: $15 Million)(Total Records Sold: Millions)
(Genre: Folk , Rock & Roll , Pop , Country , Rockabilly , R&B)(Height: 5' - 9")

Ray Edward Cochran (October 3, 1938 – April 17, 1960) was an American rock and roll musician. Cochran's songs, such as "Twenty Flight Rock", "Summertime Blues", "C'mon Everybody", and "Somethin' Else", captured teenage frustration and desire in the mid-1950s and early 1960s. He experimented with multitrack recording, distortion techniques, and overdubbing even on his earliest singles. He played the guitar, piano, bass, and drums. His image as a sharply dressed and attractive young man with a rebellious attitude epitomized the stance of the 1950s rocker, and in death he achieved iconic status. Cochran was involved with music from an early age, playing in the school band and teaching himself to play blues guitar. In 1954, he formed a duet with the guitarist Hank Cochran (no relation). When they split the following year, Eddie began a songwriting career with Jerry Capehart. His first success came when he performed the song "Twenty Flight Rock" in the film The Girl Can't Help It, starring Jayne Mansfield. Soon afterward, he signed a recording contract with Liberty Records and his first record for the label, Sittin' in the Balcony, rose to number 18 on the Billboard charts.

Cochran died at age 21 in Chippenham, Wiltshire, after a road accident in Bath during his British tour in April 1960. He had just performed at the Bristol Hippodrome. Though his best-known songs were released during his lifetime, more of his songs were released posthumously. In 1987, Cochran was inducted into the Rock and Roll Hall of Fame. His songs have been recorded by a wide variety of recording artists.

Cochran was born October 3, 1938, in Albert Lea, Minnesota, to Alice and Frank R. Cochran. His parents were from Oklahoma, and he always said in interviews that his parents had some roots in Oklahoma. He took music lessons in school but quit the band to play drums. Also, rather than taking piano lessons, he began learning guitar, playing country and other music he heard on the radio.

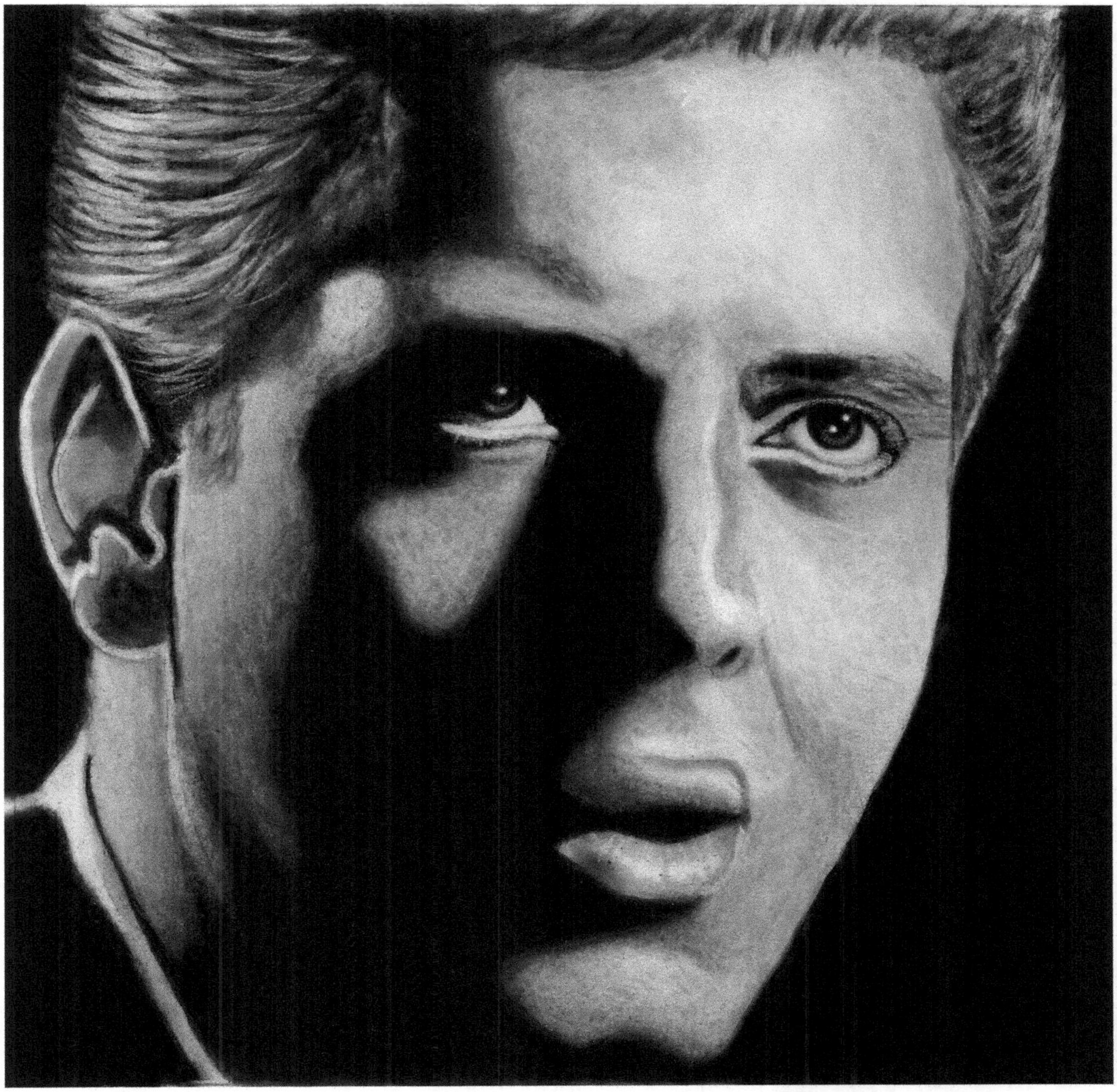

To view how this drawing was masterfully created or to purchase a Limited Edition Framed Artwork of Eddie Cochran type into your Internet Browser the URL shortcut ➡ **myportrait.art/eddiecochran**

To listen to his Greatest Songs type into your Internet Browser the URL shortcut ➡ **radio.surf/eddiecochran**

To view all channels on THE FACE OF MUSIC Internet Radio MEGA Station type into your Internet Browser the URL shortcut ➡ **radio.surf/music**

To inquire about purchasing a Limited Edtion NFT of this portrait type into your Internet Browser the URL shortcut ➡ **myartnft.shop/eddiecochran**

To view all available NFTs type into your Internet Browser the URL shortcut ➡ **myartnft.shop/all**

# Electric Light Orchestra

(Total Records Sold: 50+ Million) (Genre: Progressive / Art Rock)

The Electric Light Orchestra (ELO) are an English rock band formed in Birmingham in 1970 by songwriters-multi-instrumentalists Jeff Lynne and Roy Wood with drummer Bev Bevan. Their music is characterised by a fusion of Beatlesque pop, classical arrangements and futuristic iconography. After Wood's departure in 1972, Lynne became the band's sole leader, arranging and producing every album while writing nearly all of their original material. For their initial tenure, Lynne, Bevan and keyboardist Richard Tandy were the group's only consistent members. ELO was formed out of Lynne's and Wood's desire to create modern rock and pop songs with classical overtones. It derived as an offshoot of Wood's previous band, the Move, of which Lynne and Bevan were also members. During the 1970s and 1980s, ELO released a string of top 10 albums and singles, including two LPs that reached the top of British charts: the disco-inspired Discovery (1979) and the science-fiction-themed concept album Time (1981). In 1986 Lynne lost interest in the band and disbanded the group. Bevan responded by forming his own band, ELO Part II, which later became the Orchestra. After a brief reunion from 2000–01, ELO remained largely inactive until 2014, when Lynne re-formed the band again with Tandy as Jeff Lynne's ELO.

During ELO's original 13-year period of active recording and touring, they sold over 50 million records worldwide, and collected 19 CRIA, 21 RIAA, and 38 BPI awards. From 1972 to 1986, ELO accumulated 27 top 40 songs on the UK Singles Chart, and fifteen top 20 songs on the US Billboard Hot 100. The band also holds the record for having the most Billboard Hot 100 top 40 hits (20) without a number one single of any band in US chart history. In 2017, the key members of ELO (Wood, Lynne, Bevan and Tandy) were inducted into the Rock and Roll Hall of Fame.

# Jeff Lynne

(Net Worth: $100 Million) (Height: 5' - 9 1/2")

Jeffrey Lynne OBE (born 30 December 1947) is an English singer, songwriter, record producer, and multi-instrumentalist who co-founded the rock band Electric Light Orchestra (ELO). The group formed in 1970 as an offshoot of the Move, of which Lynne was also a member. Following the departure of Roy Wood in 1972, Lynne assumed sole leadership of the band and wrote, arranged and produced virtually all of its subsequent records. Previously, Lynne had been involved with the Idle Race as a founding member and principal songwriter.

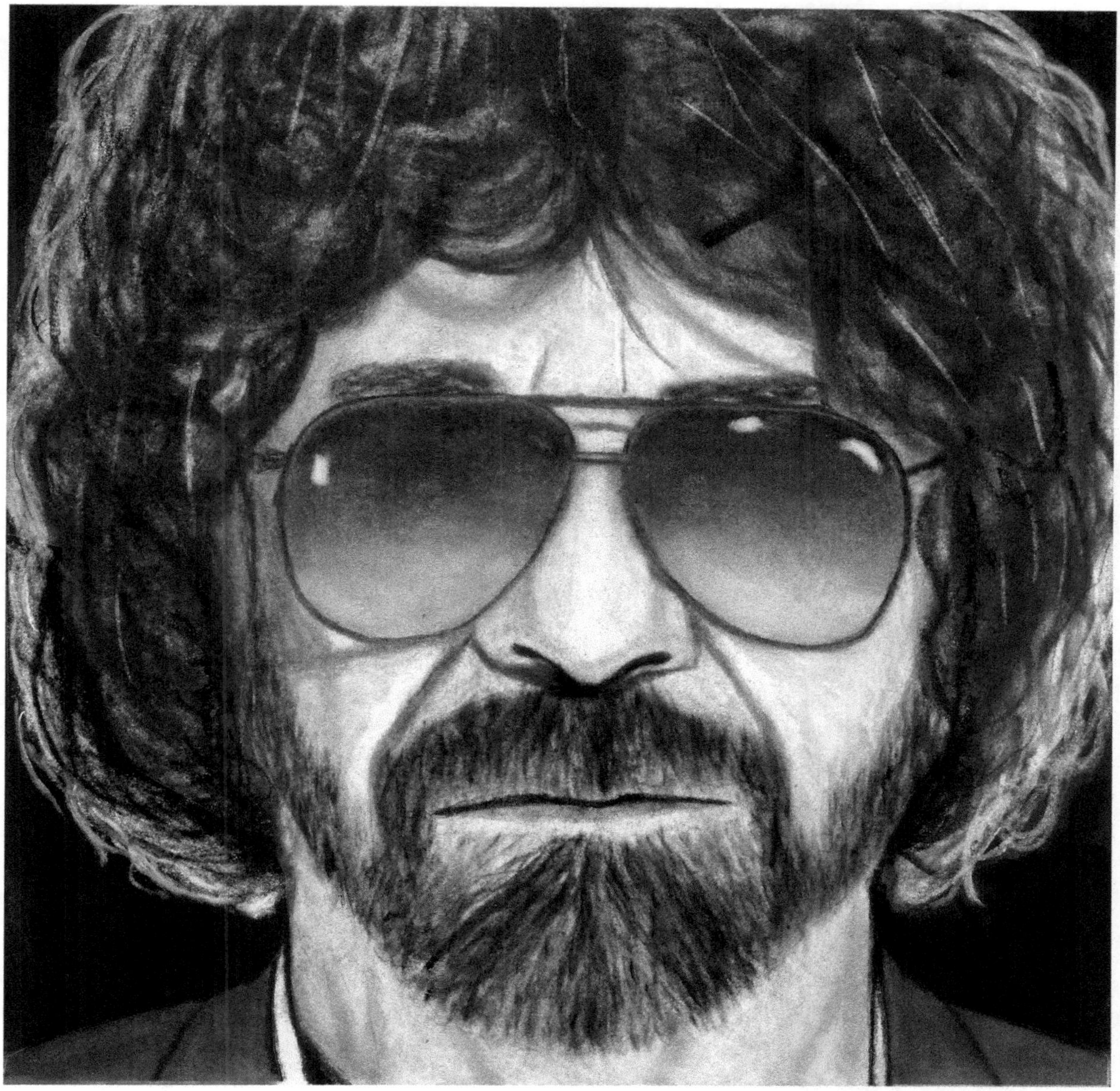

To view how this drawing was masterfully created or to purchase a Limited Edition Framed Artwork of Jeff Lynne type into your Internet Browser the URL shortcut ➡ **myportrait.art/jefflynne**

To listen to their Greatest Songs type into your Internet Browser the URL shortcut ➡ **radio.surf/elo**

To view all channels on THE FACE OF MUSIC Internet Radio MEGA Station type into your Internet Browser the URL shortcut ➡ **radio.surf/music**

To inquire about purchasing a Limited Edtion NFT of this portrait type into your Internet Browser the URL shortcut ➡ **myartnft.shop/jefflynne**

To view all available NFTs type into your Internet Browser the URL shortcut ➡ **myartnft.shop/all**

# Ella Fitzgerald

(Net worth: $10 Million)(Total Albums Sold: 40 Million)
(Genre: Swing , Bebop , Pop , Jazz , Blues)(Height: 5' - 4 1/2")

Ella Jane Fitzgerald ( April 25, 1917 – June 15, 1996) was an American jazz singer, sometimes referred to as the First Lady of Song, Queen of Jazz, and Lady Ella. She was noted for her purity of tone, impeccable diction, phrasing, timing, intonation, and a "horn-like" improvisational ability, particularly in her scat singing.

After a tumultuous adolescence, Fitzgerald found stability in musical success with the Chick Webb Orchestra, performing across the country but most often associated with the Savoy Ballroom in Harlem. Her rendition of the nursery rhyme "A-Tisket, A-Tasket" helped boost both her and Webb to national fame. After taking over the band when Webb died, Fitzgerald left it behind in 1942 to start her solo career.

Her manager was Moe Gale, co-founder of the Savoy, until she turned the rest of her career over to Norman Granz, who founded Verve Records to produce new records by Fitzgerald. With Verve she recorded some of her more widely noted works, particularly her interpretations of the Great American Songbook.

While Fitzgerald appeared in movies and as a guest on popular television shows in the second half of the twentieth century, her musical collaborations with Louis Armstrong, Duke Ellington, and The Ink Spots were some of her most notable acts outside of her solo career. These partnerships produced some of her best-known songs such as "Dream a Little Dream of Me", "Cheek to Cheek", "Into Each Life Some Rain Must Fall", and "It Don't Mean a Thing (If It Ain't Got That Swing)".

In 1993, after a career of nearly 60 years, she gave her last public performance. Three years later, she died at the age of 79 after years of declining health. Her accolades included fourteen Grammy Awards, the National Medal of Arts, and the Presidential Medal of Freedom.

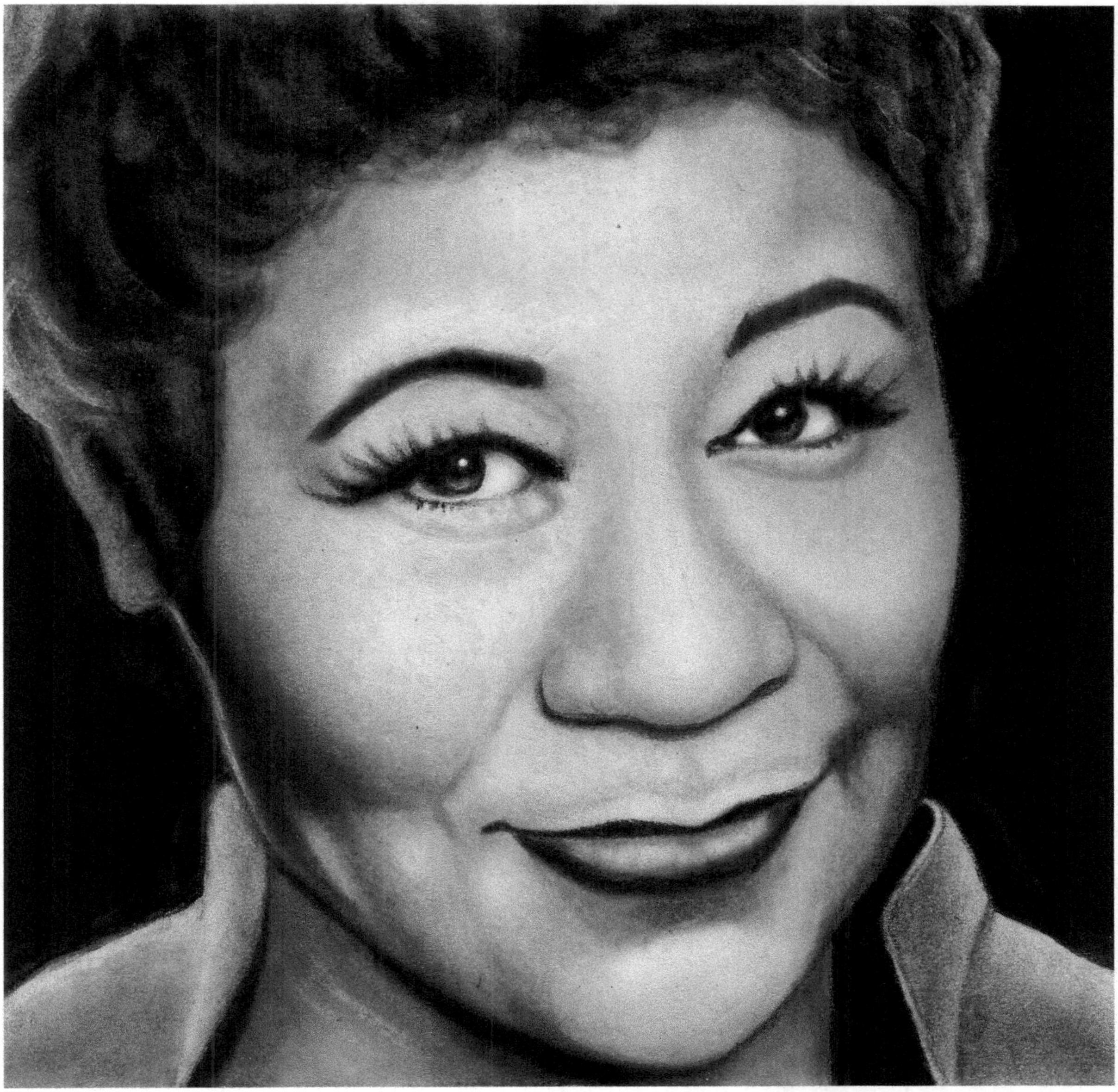

To view how this drawing was masterfully created or to purchase a Limited Edition Framed Artwork of Ella Fitzgerald type into your Internet Browser the URL shortcut ➡ **myportrait.art/ellafitzgerald**

To listen to her Greatest Songs type into your Internet Browser the URL shortcut ➡ **radio.surf/ellafitzgerald**

To view all channels on THE FACE OF MUSIC Internet Radio MEGA Station type into your Internet Browser the URL shortcut ➡ **radio.surf/music**

To inquire about purchasing a Limited Edtion NFT of this portrait type into your Internet Browser the URL shortcut ➡ **myartnft.shop/ellafitzgerald**

To view all available NFTs type into your Internet Browser the URL shortcut ➡ **myartnft.shop/all**

# Elton John

(Net worth: $500 Million)(Total Albums Sold: 300+ Million)
(Genre: Rock, Pop, Soft Rock)(Height: 5' - 6 1/2")

Sir Elton Hercules John CH Kt CBE (born Reginald Kenneth Dwight; 25 March 1947) is an English singer, songwriter, pianist, and composer. Collaborating with lyricist Bernie Taupin since 1967 on more than 30 albums, John has sold over 300 million records, making him one of the best-selling music artists of all time. He has more than fifty Top 40 hits in the UK Singles Chart and US Billboard Hot 100, including seven number ones in the UK and nine in the US, as well as seven consecutive number-one albums in the US. His tribute single "Candle in the Wind 1997", rewritten in dedication to Diana, Princess of Wales, sold over 33 million copies worldwide and is the best-selling single in the history of the UK and US singles charts. He has also produced records and occasionally acted in films. John owned Watford F.C. from 1976 to 1987 and from 1997 to 2002. He is an honorary life president of the club.

Raised in the Pinner area of Greater London, John learned to play piano at an early age, and by 1962 had formed Bluesology, an R&B band with whom he played until 1967. He met his longtime musical partner Taupin in 1967, after they both answered an advert for songwriters. For two years, they wrote songs for artists including Lulu, and John worked as a session musician for artists including the Hollies and the Scaffold. In 1969, John's debut album, Empty Sky, was released. In 1970, his first hit single, "Your Song", from his second album, Elton John, became his first top ten in both the UK and the US. His most commercially successful period, 1970–1976, included Honky Château (1972), Don't Shoot Me I'm Only the Piano Player (1973), Goodbye Yellow Brick Road (1973) and his first Greatest Hits compilation — the latter two listed among the best-selling albums worldwide. John has also had success in musical films and theatre, composing for The Lion King and its stage adaptation, Aida and Billy Elliot the Musical. John has received five Grammy Awards, five Brit Awards; including for Outstanding Contribution to Music; two Academy Awards, two Golden Globes, a Tony Award, a Disney Legends Award, and the Kennedy Center Honor. In 2004, Rolling Stone ranked him 49th on its list of 100 influential musicians of the rock and roll era. In 2013, Billboard ranked him the most successful male solo artist on the Billboard Hot 100 Top All-Time Artists, and third overall, behind the Beatles and Madonna. He was inducted into the Songwriters Hall of Fame in 1992 and the Rock and Roll Hall of Fame in 1994, and is a fellow of the British Academy of Songwriters, Composers and Authors. He was knighted by Queen Elizabeth II for "services to music and charitable services" in 1998.

John has been involved in the fight against AIDS since the late 1980s. In 1992, he established the Elton John AIDS Foundation, and a year later he began hosting his annual Academy Awards Party, which has since become one of the biggest high-profile Oscar parties in the Hollywood film industry. Since its inception, the foundation has raised over £300 million. John has performed at a number of royal events, such as the funeral of Princess Diana at Westminster Abbey in 1997, the Party at the Palace in 2002 and the Queen's Diamond Jubilee Concert outside Buckingham Palace in 2012. John, who announced he was bisexual in 1976 and has been openly gay since 1988, entered into a civil partnership with David Furnish on 21 December 2005; they married after same-sex marriage became legal in England and Wales in 2014. Presenting John with France's highest civilian award, the Legion d'honneur, in 2019, French President Emmanuel Macron called him a "melodic genius" and praised his work on behalf of the LGBT community. In 2018, John embarked on a three-year farewell tour.

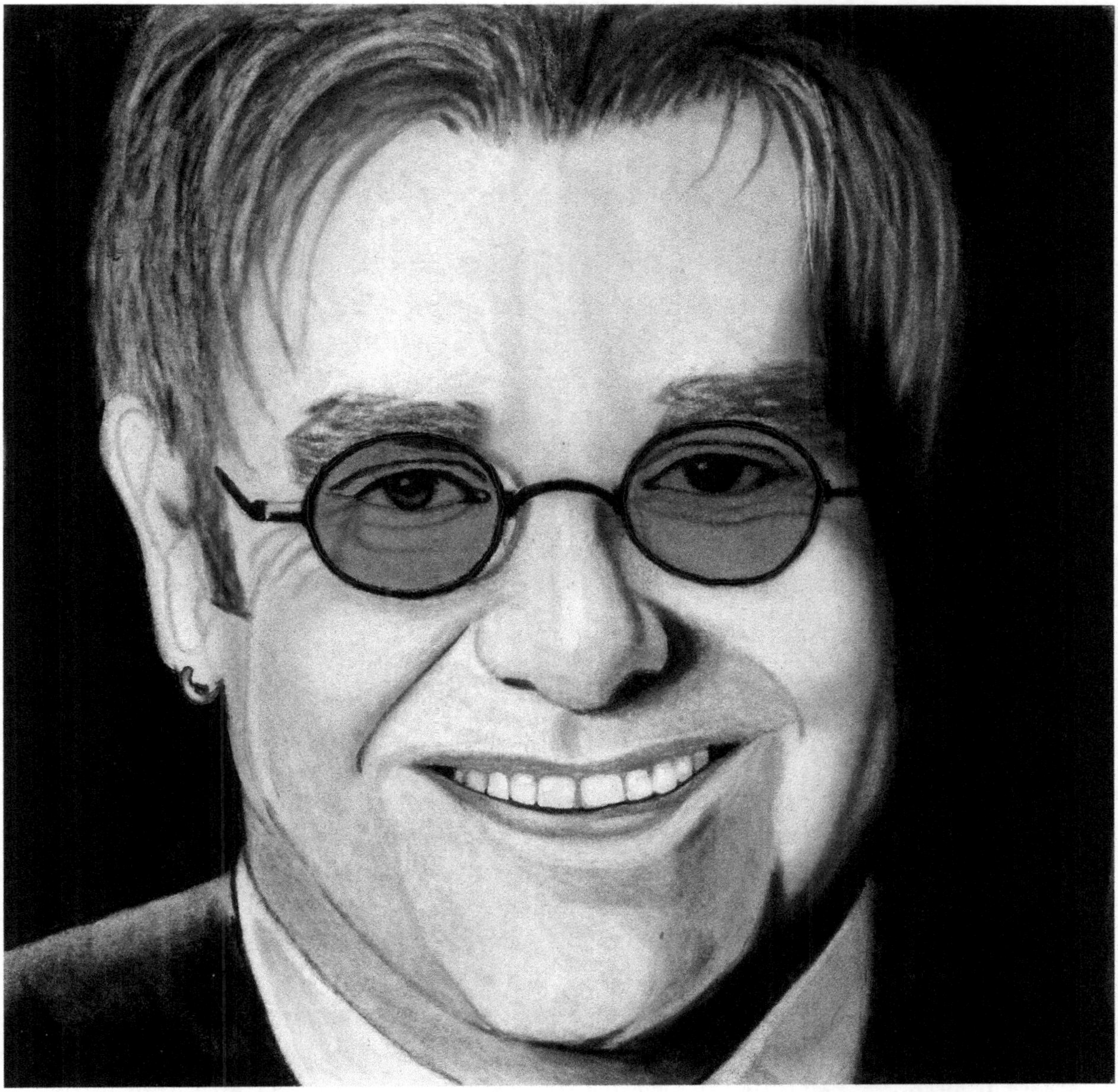

To view how this drawing was masterfully created or to purchase a Limited Edition Framed Artwork of Elton John type into your Internet Browser the URL shortcut ➡ **myportrait.art/eltonjohn**

To listen to his Greatest Songs type into your Internet Browser the URL shortcut ➡ **radio.surf/eltonjohn**

To view all channels on THE FACE OF MUSIC Internet Radio MEGA Station type into your Internet Browser the URL shortcut ➡ **radio.surf/music**

To inquire about purchasing a Limited Edition NFT of this portrait type into your Internet Browser the URL shortcut ➡ **myartnft.shop/eltonjohn**

To view all available NFTs type into your Internet Browser the URL shortcut ➡ **myartnft.shop/all**

# Elvis Costello

(Net worth: $70 Million)(Total Albums Sold: Millions)
(Genre: New Wave , Power Pop , Punk Rock)(Height: 5' - 9 1/4")

Declan Patrick Aloysius McManus, OBE (born 25 August 1954), known professionally as Elvis Costello, is an English singer-songwriter. He has won multiple awards in his career, including Grammy Awards in 1999 and 2020, and has twice been nominated for the Brit Award for Best British Male Artist. In 2003, he was inducted into the Rock and Roll Hall of Fame. In 2004, Rolling Stone ranked Costello number 80 on its list of the 100 Greatest Artists of All Time.

Costello began his career as part of London's pub rock scene in the early 1970s and later became associated with the first wave of the British punk and new wave movement that emerged in the mid-to-late 1970s. His critically acclaimed debut album My Aim Is True was released in 1977. Shortly after recording it, he formed the Attractions as his backing band. His second album This Year's Model was released in 1978, and was ranked number 11 by Rolling Stone on its list of the best albums from 1967 to 1987. His third album Armed Forces was released in 1979, and features his highest-charting single, "Oliver's Army" (number 2 in the UK). His first three albums all appeared on Rolling Stone's list of the 500 Greatest Albums of All Time.

Costello and the Attractions toured and recorded together for the better part of a decade, though differences between them caused a split by 1986. Much of Costello's work since has been as a solo artist, though reunions with members of the Attractions have been credited to the group over the years. Costello's lyrics employ a wide vocabulary and frequent wordplay. His music has drawn on many diverse genres; one critic described him as a "pop encyclopaedia", able to "reinvent the past in his own image".

Costello has co-written several original songs for motion pictures, including "God Give Me Strength" from Grace of My Heart (1996, with Burt Bacharach) and "The Scarlet Tide" from Cold Mountain (2003, with T-Bone Burnett). For the latter, Elvis was nominated (along with Burnett) for the Academy Award for Best Original Song and the Grammy Award for Best Song Written for Visual Media.

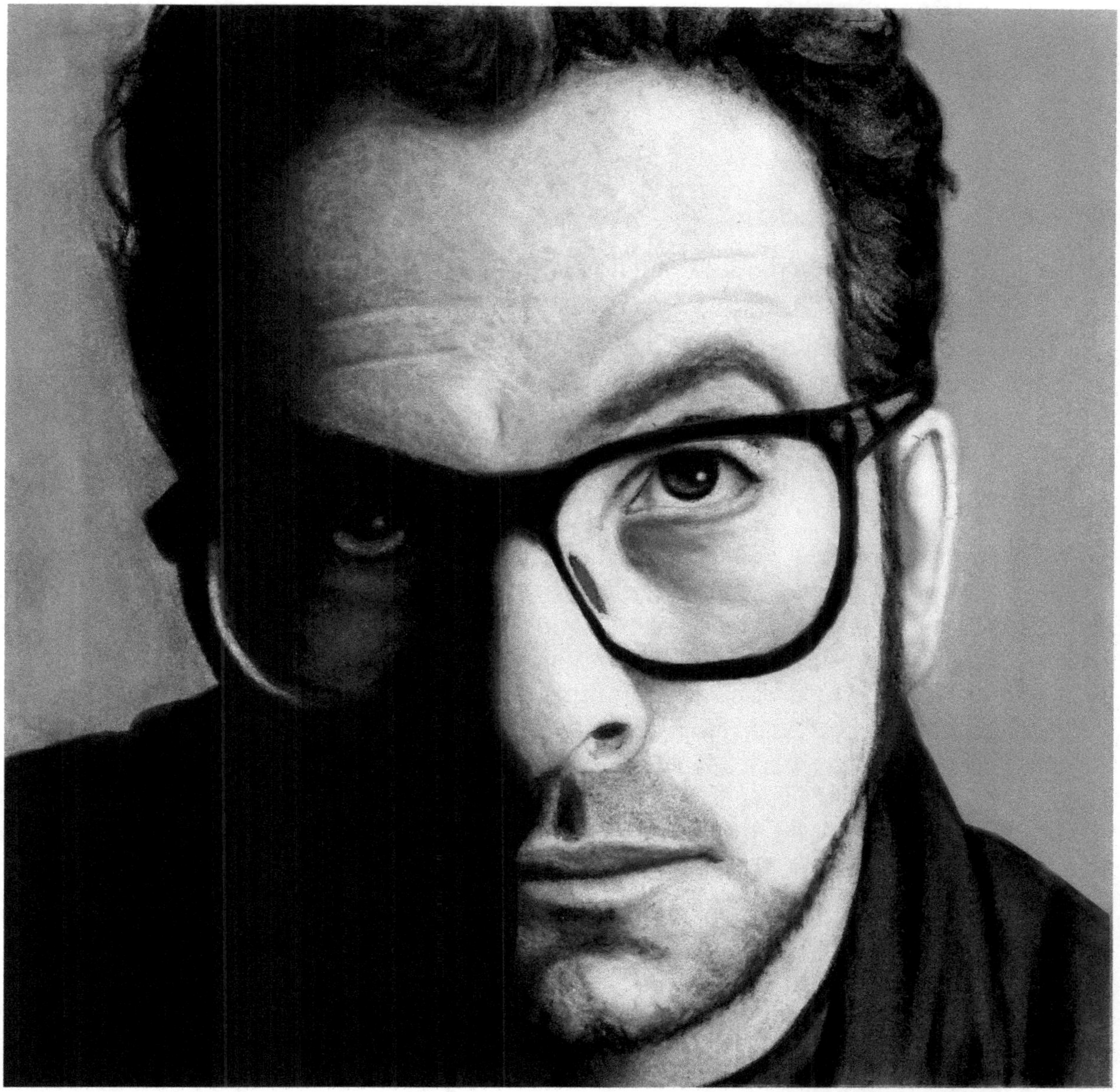

To view how this drawing was masterfully created or to purchase a Limited Edition Framed Artwork of Elvis Costello type into your Internet Browser the URL shortcut ➡ **myportrait.art/elviscostello**

To listen to his Greatest Songs type into your Internet Browser the URL shortcut ➡ **radio.surf/elviscostello**

To view all channels on THE FACE OF MUSIC Internet Radio MEGA Station type into your Internet Browser the URL shortcut ➡ **radio.surf/music**

To inquire about purchasing a Limited Edtion NFT of this portrait type into your Internet Browser the URL shortcut ➡ **myartnft.shop/elviscostello**

To view all available NFTs type into your Internet Browser the URL shortcut ➡ **myartnft.shop/all**

# Elvis Presley

(Net worth: $20 Million)(Total Albums Sold: 1+ Billion)
(Genre: Rock N Roll , Pop , Rockabilly , Country , Gospel , R&B)(Height: 6' - 0")

Elvis Aaron Presley (January 8, 1935 – August 16, 1977), also known simply as Elvis, was an American singer, musician and actor. He is regarded as one of the most significant cultural icons of the 20th century and is often referred to as the "King of Rock and Roll". His energized interpretations of songs and sexually provocative performance style, combined with a singularly potent mix of influences across color lines during a transformative era in race relations, led him to both great success and initial controversy.

Presley was born in Tupelo, Mississippi, and relocated to Memphis, Tennessee with his family when he was 13 years old. His music career began there in 1954, recording at Sun Records with producer Sam Phillips, who wanted to bring the sound of African-American music to a wider audience. Presley, on rhythm acoustic guitar, and accompanied by lead guitarist Scotty Moore and bassist Bill Black, was a pioneer of rockabilly, an uptempo, backbeat-driven fusion of country music and rhythm and blues. In 1955, drummer D. J. Fontana joined to complete the lineup of Presley's classic quartet and RCA Victor acquired his contract in a deal arranged by Colonel Tom Parker, who would manage him for more than two decades. Presley's first RCA single, "Heartbreak Hotel", was released in January 1956 and became a number-one hit in the United States. With a series of successful network television appearances and chart-topping records, he became the leading figure of the newly popular sound of rock and roll.

In November 1956, Presley made his film debut in Love Me Tender. Drafted into military service in 1958, Presley relaunched his recording career two years later with some of his most commercially successful work. He held few concerts, however, and guided by Parker, proceeded to devote much of the 1960s to making Hollywood films and soundtrack albums, most of them critically derided. In 1968, following a seven-year break from live performances, he returned to the stage in the acclaimed television comeback special Elvis, which led to an extended Las Vegas concert residency and a string of highly profitable tours. In 1973, Presley gave the first concert by a solo artist to be broadcast around the world, Aloha from Hawaii. Years of prescription drug abuse severely compromised his health, and he died suddenly in 1977 at his Graceland estate at the age of 42.

With his rise from poverty to significant fame, Presley's success seemed to epitomize the American Dream. He is the best-selling solo music artist of all time, and was commercially successful in many genres, including pop, country, R&B, adult contemporary, and gospel. He won three Grammy Awards, received the Grammy Lifetime Achievement Award at age 36, and has been inducted into multiple music halls of fame. Presley holds several records; the most RIAA certified gold and platinum albums, the most albums charted on the Billboard 200, and the most number-one albums by a solo artist on the UK Albums Chart and the most number-one singles by any act on the UK Singles Chart. In 2018, Presley was posthumously awarded the Presidential Medal of Freedom by Donald Trump.

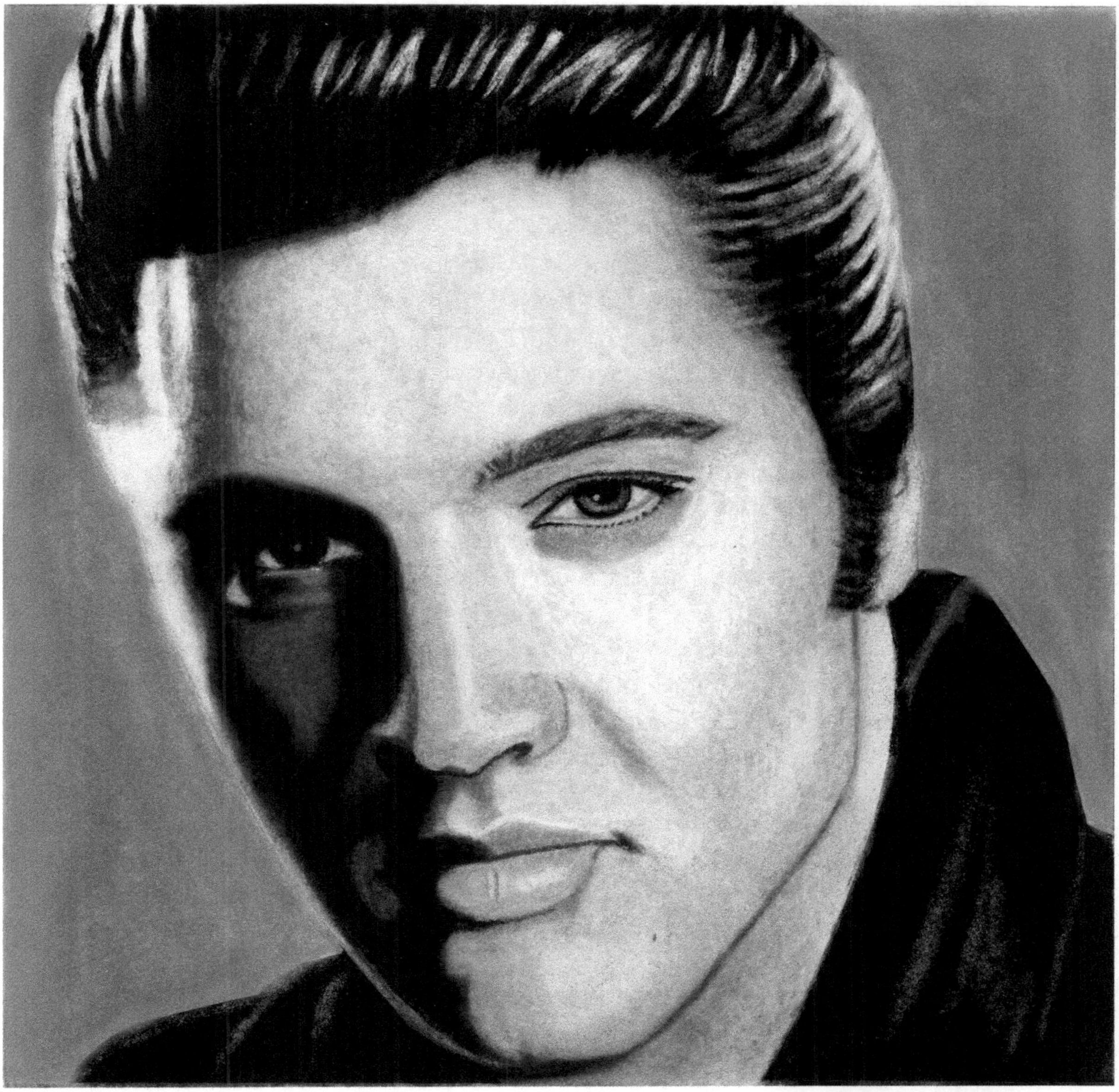

To view how this drawing was masterfully created or to purchase a Limited Edition Framed Artwork of Elvis Presley type into your Internet Browser the URL shortcut ➡ **myportrait.art/elvispresley**

To listen to his Greatest Songs type into your Internet Browser the URL shortcut ➡ **radio.surf/elvispresley**

To view all channels on THE FACE OF MUSIC Internet Radio MEGA Station type into your Internet Browser the URL shortcut ➡ **radio.surf/music**

To inquire about purchasing a Limited Edtion NFT of this portrait type into your Internet Browser the URL shortcut ➡ **myartnft.shop/elvispresley**

To view all available NFTs type into your Internet Browser the URL shortcut ➡ **myartnft.shop/all**

# Eminem

(Net worth: $230 Million)(Total Albums Sold: 220+ Million)
(Genre: Hip-Hop)(Height: 5' - 8")

Marshall Bruce Mathers III (born October 17, 1972), known professionally as Eminem is an American rapper, songwriter, and record producer. Eminem is among the best-selling music artists of all time, with estimated worldwide sales of more than 220 million records. He is credited with popularizing hip hop in Middle America and is critically acclaimed as one of the greatest rappers of all time.

Eminem's global success and acclaimed works are widely regarded as having broken racial barriers for the acceptance of white rappers in popular music. While much of his transgressive work during the early 2000s made him hugely controversial, he came to be a representation of popular angst of the American underclass. He has been influential for many artists of various genres. After his debut album Infinite (1996) and the extended play Slim Shady EP (1997), Eminem signed with Dr. Dre's Aftermath Entertainment and subsequently achieved mainstream popularity in 1999 with The Slim Shady LP. His next two releases The Marshall Mathers LP (2000) and The Eminem Show (2002) were worldwide successes and were both nominated for the Grammy Award for Album of the Year. After the release of his next album, Encore (2004), Eminem went on hiatus in 2005 partly due to a prescription drug addiction. He returned to the music industry four years later with the release of Relapse (2009), and Recovery was released the following year. Recovery was the best-selling album worldwide of 2010, making it Eminem's second album, after The Eminem Show in 2002, to be the best-selling album of the year worldwide. In the following years, he released the US number one albums The Marshall Mathers LP 2 (2013), Revival (2017), Kamikaze (2018) and Music to Be Murdered By (2020).

Eminem made his debut in the film industry with the musical drama film 8 Mile (2002), playing a fictionalized version of himself, and his track "Lose Yourself" from its soundtrack won the Academy Award for Best Original Song, making him the first hip hop artist ever to win the award. Eminem has made cameo appearances in the films The Wash (2001), Funny People (2009), and The Interview (2014), and the television series Entourage (2010). He has also developed other ventures, including Shady Records, a joint venture with manager Paul Rosenberg, which helped launch the careers of artists such as 50 Cent, Yelawolf and Obie Trice, among others. He has also established his own channel, Shade 45, on Sirius XM Radio. In addition to his solo career, Eminem was a member of the hip hop group D12. He is also known for collaborations with fellow Detroit-based rapper Royce Da 5'9"; the two are collectively known as Bad Meets Evil.

He was the best-selling music artist in the United States of the 2000s and the best-selling male music artist in the United States of the 2010s, third overall. Billboard named him the "Artist of the Decade (2000–2009)". The Marshall Mathers LP, The Eminem Show, "Lose Yourself", "Love the Way You Lie" and "Not Afraid" have all been certified Diamond or higher by the Recording Industry Association of America (RIAA). Rolling Stone has included him in its lists of the 100 Greatest Artists of All Time and the 100 Greatest Songwriters of All Time. He has won numerous awards, including 15 Grammy Awards, eight American Music Awards, 17 Billboard Music Awards, an Academy Award and an MTV Europe Music Global Icon Award. He has had ten number-one albums on the Billboard 200—which all consecutively debuted at number one on the chart, making him the only artist to achieve this—and five number-one singles on the Billboard Hot 100.

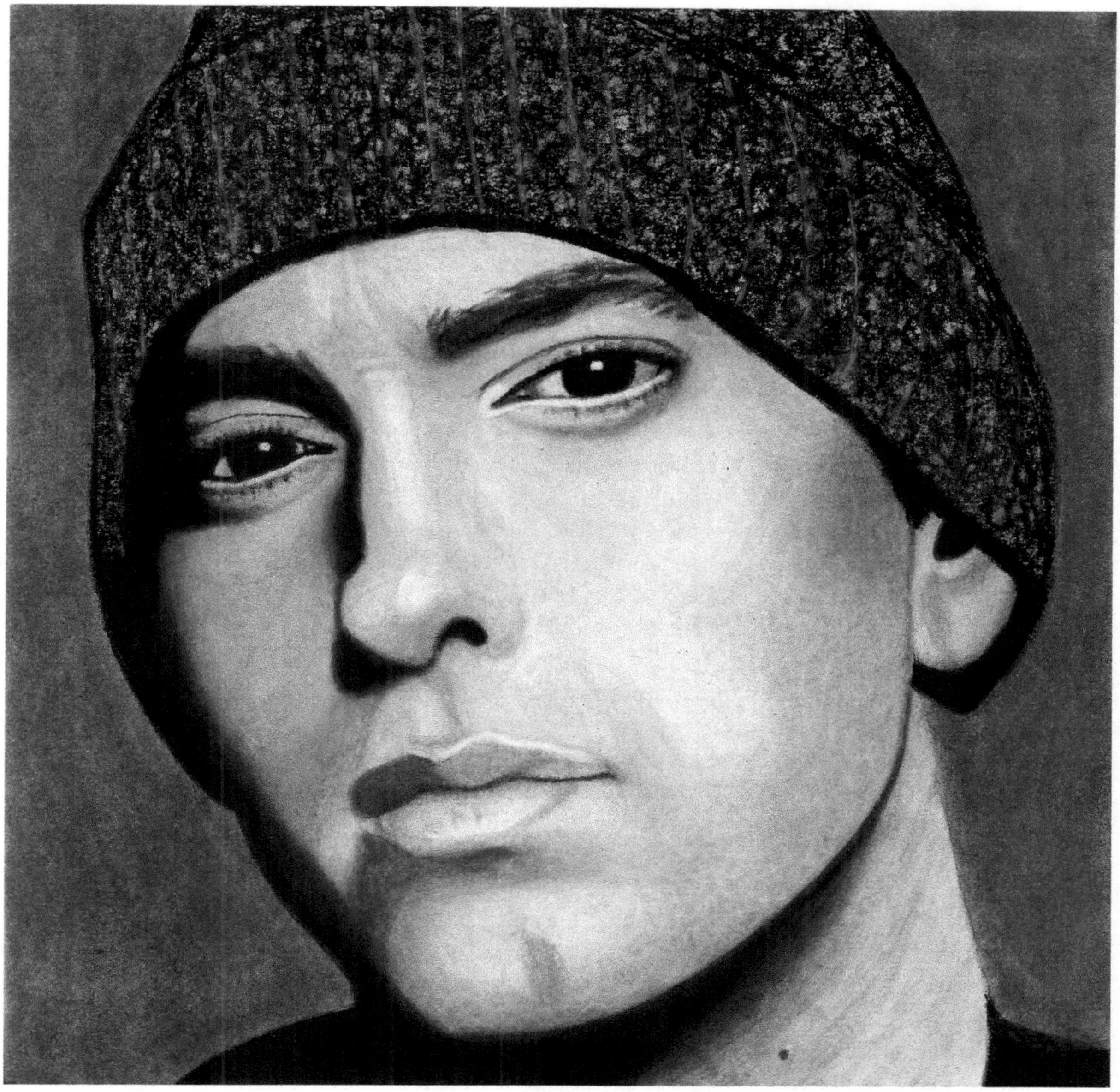

To view how this drawing was masterfully created or to purchase a Limited Edition Framed Artwork of Eminem type into your Internet Browser the URL shortcut ➡ **myportrait.art/eminem**

To listen to his Greatest Songs type into your Internet Browser the URL shortcut ➡ **radio.surf/eminem**

To view all channels on THE FACE OF MUSIC Internet Radio MEGA Station type into your Internet Browser the URL shortcut ➡ **radio.surf/music**

To inquire about purchasing a Limited Edition NFT of this portrait type into your Internet Browser the URL shortcut ➡ **myartnft.shop/eminem**

To view all available NFTs type into your Internet Browser the URL shortcut ➡ **myartnft.shop/all**

# Engelbert Humperdinck

(Net worth: $180 Million)(Total Records Sold: 140+ Million)
(Genre: Crooner)(Height: 6' - 1 1/2")

Engelbert Humperdinck (born Arnold George Dorsey; 2 May 1936) is an English pop singer. Humperdinck has been described as "one of the finest middle-of-the-road balladeers around". His singles "Release Me" and "The Last Waltz" both topped the UK music charts in 1967, and sold more than a million copies each. In North America, he also had chart successes with "After the Lovin'" (1976) and "This Moment in Time" (1979). Overall he has sold more than 140 million records worldwide.

Arnold George Dorsey was born in Madras, British India, in 1936, one of ten children to British Army NCO Mervyn Dorsey, who was of Welsh descent, and his wife Olive, who, according to the singer, was of German descent. Various sources also say that he has Anglo-Indian heritage. His family moved to Leicester, England, when he was ten years old. He later showed an interest in music and began learning the saxophone. By the early 1950s, he was playing saxophone in nightclubs, but he is believed not to have begun singing until he was in his late teens. His impression of Jerry Lewis prompted friends to begin calling him "Gerry Dorsey", a name that he worked under for almost a decade.

Dorsey's attempt to get his music career off the ground was interrupted by conscription into the British Army Royal Corps of Signals during the mid-1950s. Later, he got his first chance to record in 1958 with Decca Records after his discharge. His first single "I'll Never Fall in Love Again" was not a hit, but Dorsey recorded for the same company almost a decade later with very different results. He continued working the nightclubs but in 1961, he was stricken with tuberculosis. He eventually regained his health and returned to nightclub work, but with little success.

In 1965, Dorsey teamed up with Gordon Mills, his former roommate whilst in Bayswater, London, who had become a music impresario and the manager of Tom Jones. Mills, aware that Dorsey had been struggling for several years to become successful in the music industry, suggested a name-change to the more arresting Engelbert Humperdinck, borrowed from the 19th-century German composer of operas such as Hansel and Gretel. Dorsey adopted the name professionally but not legally. Mills arranged a new deal for him with Decca Records, and Dorsey has been performing under this name ever since.

Humperdinck enjoyed his first real success during July 1966 in Belgium, where he and four others represented Britain in the annual Knokke song contest. Three months later in October 1966, he was on stage in Mechelen. He made a mark on the Belgian charts with "Dommage, Dommage", and an early music video was filmed with him in the harbour of Zeebrugge.

In the mid-1960s, Humperdinck visited German songwriter Bert Kaempfert at his house in Spain and was offered arrangements of three songs: "Spanish Eyes"; "Strangers in the Night" and "Wonderland by Night". He returned to Britain where he recorded all three songs. He recognised the potential of "Strangers in the Night" and asked manager Gordon Mills whether it could be released as a single—but his request was refused, since the song had already been requested by Frank Sinatra.

In early 1967, the changes paid off when Humperdinck's version of "Release Me" made the top ten on both sides of the Atlantic and number one in Britain, recorded in a smooth ballad style with a full chorus joining him on the third refrain, and keeping The Beatles' "Strawberry Fields Forever"/"Penny Lane" from the top slot in the United Kingdom. His song "Ten Guitars", a B-side on the single "Release Me" became a huge hit in New Zealand. Another groundbreaking video showed Engelbert tied up with a lasso. "Release Me" spent 56 weeks in the Top 50 in a single chart run. "Release Me" was believed to have sold 85,000 copies a day at the height of its popularity, and it was the best known of his songs for years.

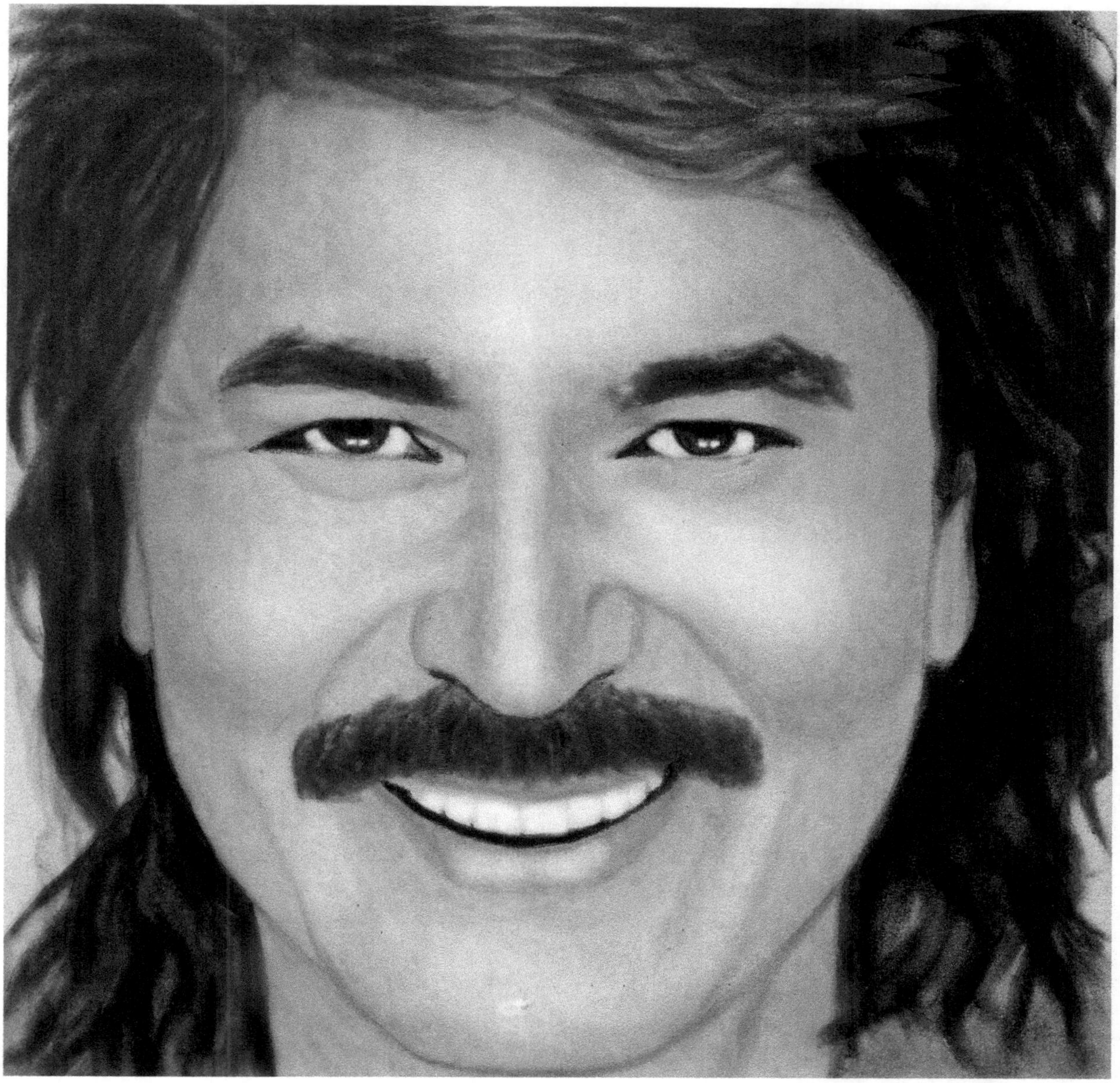

To view how this drawing was masterfully created or to purchase a Limited Edition Framed Artwork of Engelbert Humperdinck type into your Internet Browser the URL shortcut
➡ **myportrait.art/engelberthumperdinck**

To listen to his Greatest Songs type into your Internet Browser the URL shortcut
➡ **radio.surf/engelberthumperdinck**

To view all channels on THE FACE OF MUSIC Internet Radio MEGA Station type into your Internet Browser the URL shortcut ➡ **radio.surf/music**

To inquire about purchasing a Limited Edtion NFT of this portrait type into your Internet Browser the URL shortcut ➡ **myartnft.shop/engelberthumperdinck**

To view all available NFTs type into your Internet Browser the URL shortcut ➡ **myartnft.shop/all**

# Eric B. & Rakim

(Total Records Sold: Millions) (Genre: Hip-Hop)

Eric B. & Rakim are an American hip hop duo formed in Long Island, New York, in 1986, composed of DJ Eric B. (born Eric Barrier) and MC Rakim (born William Michael Griffin Jr.).

AllMusic wrote that "during rap's so-called golden age in the late '80s, Eric B. & Rakim were almost universally recognized as the premier DJ/MC team in all of hip-hop." Tom Terrell of NPR called them "the most influential DJ/MC combo in contemporary pop music period." The editors of About.com ranked them as No. 5 on their list of the 10 Greatest Hip-Hop Duos of All-Time, and Rolling Stone ranked them No. 5 on its list of the 20 Greatest Duos of All Time.

# Rakim

(Net Worth: $2 Million) (Height: 6' - 0")

William Michael Griffin Jr. (born January 28, 1968), better known by his stage name Rakim, is an American rapper and record producer. One half of golden age hip hop duo Eric B. & Rakim, he is widely regarded as one of the most influential and most skilled MCs of all time.

Rakim is considered a transformational figure in hip hop by raising the bar for MC technique higher than it had ever been. Rakim helped to pioneer the use of internal rhymes and multisyllabic rhymes, and he was among the first to demonstrate the possibilities of sitting down to write intricately crafted lyrics packed with clever word choices and metaphors rather than the more improvisational styles and simpler rhyme patterns that predominated before him. Rakim is also credited with creating the overall shift from the more simplistic old school flows to more complex flows. Rapper Kool Moe Dee explained that before Rakim, the term 'flow' wasn't widely used – "Rakim is basically the inventor of flow. We were not even using the word flow until Rakim came along. It was called rhyming, it was called cadence, but it wasn't called flow. Rakim created flow!" Rakim released four albums with DJ Eric B.: Paid in Full, Follow the Leader, Let the Rhythm Hit 'Em and Don't Sweat the Technique. He has released three solo albums: The 18th Letter, The Master and The Seventh Seal.

Paid in Full was named the greatest hip hop album of all time by MTV in 2006, while Rakim himself was ranked No. 4 on MTV's list of the Greatest MCs of All Time. Steve Huey of AllMusic stated that "Rakim is near-universally acknowledged as one of the greatest MCs – perhaps the greatest – of all time within the hip-hop community". The editors of About.com ranked him No. 2 on their list of the 'Top 50 MCs of Our Time (1987–2007)'. In 2012, The Source ranked him No. 1 on their list of the "Top 50 Lyricists of All Time".

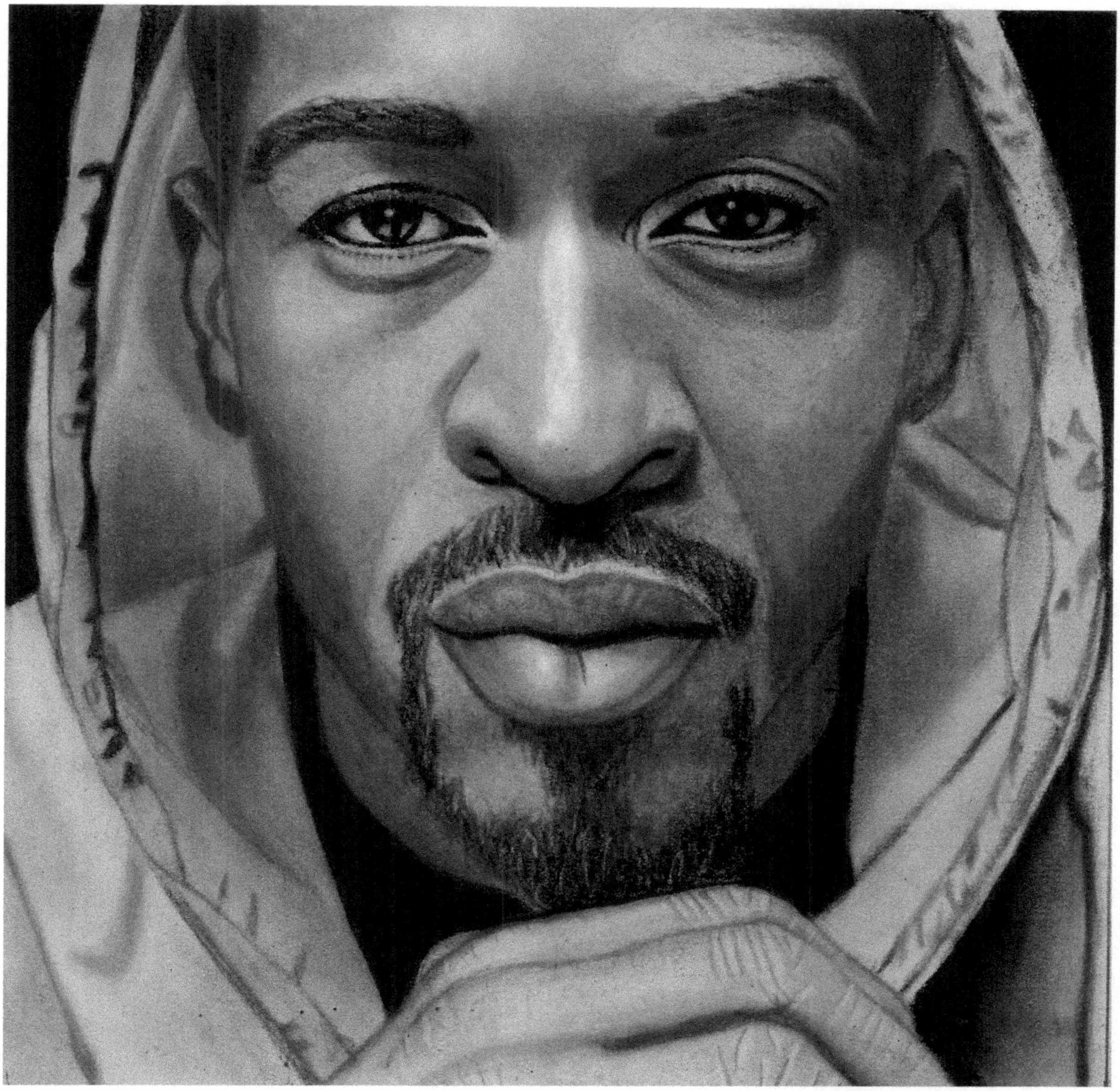

To view how this drawing was masterfully created or to purchase a Limited Edition Framed Artwork of Rakim type into your Internet Browser the URL shortcut ➡ **myportrait.art/rakim**

To listen to their Greatest Songs type into your Internet Browser the URL shortcut ➡ **radio.surf/ericbandrakim**

To view all channels on THE FACE OF MUSIC Internet Radio MEGA Station type into your Internet Browser the URL shortcut ➡ **radio.surf/music**

To inquire about purchasing a Limited Edtion NFT of this portrait type into your Internet Browser the URL shortcut ➡ **myartnft.shop/rakim**

To view all available NFTs type into your Internet Browser the URL shortcut ➡ **myartnft.shop/all**

# Eurythmics

(Total Records Sold: 75 Million) (Genre: New Wave , Pop)

Eurythmics were a British pop duo consisting of members Annie Lennox and Dave Stewart. Stewart and Lennox were both previously in The Tourists, a band which broke up in 1980; Eurythmics were formed later that year in Wagga Wagga, Australia. The duo released their first studio album, In the Garden, in 1981 to little success, but went on to achieve global success when their second album Sweet Dreams ( Are Made of This), was released in 1983. The title track became a worldwide hit which topped the charts in various countries including the US. The duo went on to release a string of hit singles and albums before they split up in 1990. By this time, Stewart was a sought-after record producer, while Lennox began a solo recording career in 1992 with her debut album Diva. After almost a decade apart, Eurythmics reunited to record their ninth album, Peace, released in late 1999. They reunited again in 2005 to release the single "I've Got a Life", as part of a new Eurythmics compilation album, Ultimate Collection.

The duo have won an MTV Video Music Award for Best New Artist in 1984, the Grammy Award for Best Rock Performance by a Duo or Group with Vocal in 1987, the Brit Award for Outstanding Contribution to Music in 1999, and in 2005 were inducted into the UK Music Hall of Fame. The Eurythmics have sold an estimated 75 million records worldwide. In 2017, the group was nominated for induction into the Rock & Roll Hall of Fame, and were nominated again in 2018.

# Annie Lennox

(Net Worth: $60 Million) (Height: 5' - 8")

Ann Lennox (born 25 December 1954) is a Scottish singer-songwriter, political activist and philanthropist. After achieving moderate success in the late 1970s as part of the new wave band The Tourists, she and fellow musician Dave Stewart went on to achieve international success in the 1980s as Eurythmics. Appearing in the 1983 music video for "Sweet Dreams ( Are Made of This)" with orange cropped hair and wearing a man's business suit, the BBC states, "all eyes were on Annie Lennox, the singer whose powerful androgynous look defied the male gaze". Subsequent hits with Eurythmics include "There Must Be an Angel (Playing with My Heart)" and "Here Comes the Rain Again".Lennox embarked on a solo career in 1992 with her debut album, Diva, which produced several hit singles including "Why" and "Walking on Broken Glass". The same year, she performed "Love Song for a Vampire" for Bram Stoker's Dracula. Her 1995 studio album, Medusa, includes "No More I Love You's" and "A Whiter Shade of Pale". To date, she has released six solo studio albums and a compilation album, The Annie Lennox Collection (2009). With eight Brit Awards, which includes being named Best British Female Artist a record six times, Lennox has been named the "Brits Champion of Champions". She has also collected four Grammy Awards and an MTV Video Music Award. In 2002, Lennox received a Billboard Century Award; the highest accolade from Billboard magazine. In 2004, she received both the Golden Globe and the Academy Award for Best Original Song for "Into the West", written for the soundtrack to the feature film The Lord of the Rings: The Return of the King.

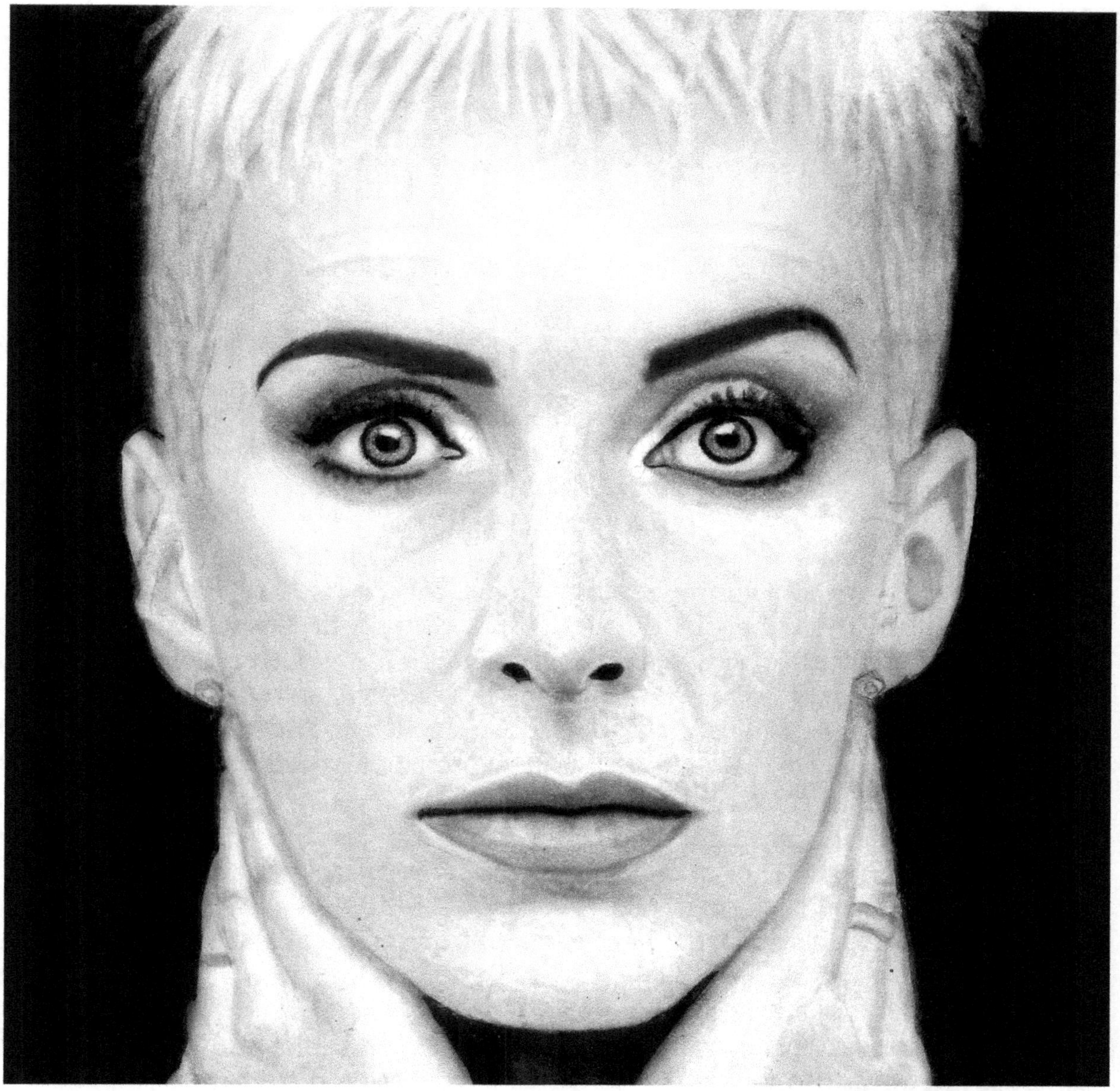

To view how this drawing was masterfully created or to purchase a Limited Edition Framed Artwork of Annie Lennox type into your Internet Browser the URL shortcut ➡ **myportrait.art/annielennox**

To listen to their Greatest Songs type into your Internet Browser the URL shortcut ➡ **radio.surf/eurythmics**

To view all channels on THE FACE OF MUSIC Internet Radio MEGA Station type into your Internet Browser the URL shortcut ➡ **radio.surf/music**

To inquire about purchasing a Limited Edtion NFT of this portrait type into your Internet Browser the URL shortcut ➡ **myartnft.shop/annielennox**

To view all available NFTs type into your Internet Browser the URL shortcut ➡ **myartnft.shop/all**

# Everly Brothers, The

(Total Records Sold: Millions) (Genre: Rock N Roll , Rockabilly , Country)
The Everly Brothers were an American country-influenced rock and roll duo, known for steel-string acoustic guitar playing and close harmony singing. Consisting of Isaac Donald "Don" Everly (born February 1, 1937) and Phillip "Phil" Jason Everly (January 19, 1939 – January 3, 2014), the duo was raised in a musical family, first appearing on radio singing along with their father Ike Everly and mother Margaret Everly as "The Everly Family" in the 1940s. When the brothers were still in high school, they gained the attention of prominent Nashville musicians like Chet Atkins, who began to groom them for national attention.

They began writing and recording their own music in 1956, and their first hit song came in 1957, with "Bye Bye Love", written by Felice and Boudleaux Bryant. The song hit No. 1 in the spring of 1957, and additional hits would follow through 1958, many of them written by the Bryants, including "Wake Up Little Susie", "All I Have to Do Is Dream", and "Problems". In 1960, they signed with the major label Warner Bros. Records and recorded "Cathy's Clown", written by the brothers themselves, which was their biggest selling single. The brothers enlisted in the United States Marine Corps Reserve in 1961, and their output dropped off, though additional hit singles continued through 1962, with "That's Old Fashioned (That's the Way Love Should Be)" being their last top-10 hit.

Long-simmering disputes with Wesley Rose, the CEO of Acuff-Rose Music, which managed the group, a growing drug usage in the 1960s, as well as changing tastes in popular music, led to the group's decline in popularity in its native U.S., though the brothers continued to release hit singles in the U.K. and Canada, and had many highly successful tours throughout the 1960s. In the early 1970s, the brothers began releasing solo recordings, and in 1973 they officially broke up. Starting in 1983, the brothers got back together, and would continue to perform periodically until Phil's death in 2014.

The group was highly influential on the music of the generation that followed it. Many of the top acts of the 1960s were heavily influenced by the close-harmony singing and acoustic guitar playing of the Everly Brothers, including the Beatles, the Beach Boys, the Bee Gees, and Simon & Garfunkel. Rolling Stone ranked the Everly Brothers No. 1 on its list of the 20 Greatest Duos of All Time. They were inducted into the Rock and Roll Hall of Fame as part of the inaugural class of 1986, and into the Country Music Hall of Fame in 2001. Don was inducted into the Musicians Hall of Fame and Museum in 2019, earning the organization's first Iconic Riff Award for his distinctive rhythm guitar intro to the Everlys' massive 1957 hit "Wake Up Little Susie".

# Phil Everly

(Net Worth: $20 Million) (Height: 6' - 1")
Phil Everly was born on January 19, 1939 in Chicago, Illinois, USA as Phillip Jason Everly. He was married to Patrice Yvonne Arnold, Patricia Mickey and Jacqueline Alice Ertel. He died on January 3, 2014 in Burbank, California, USA.

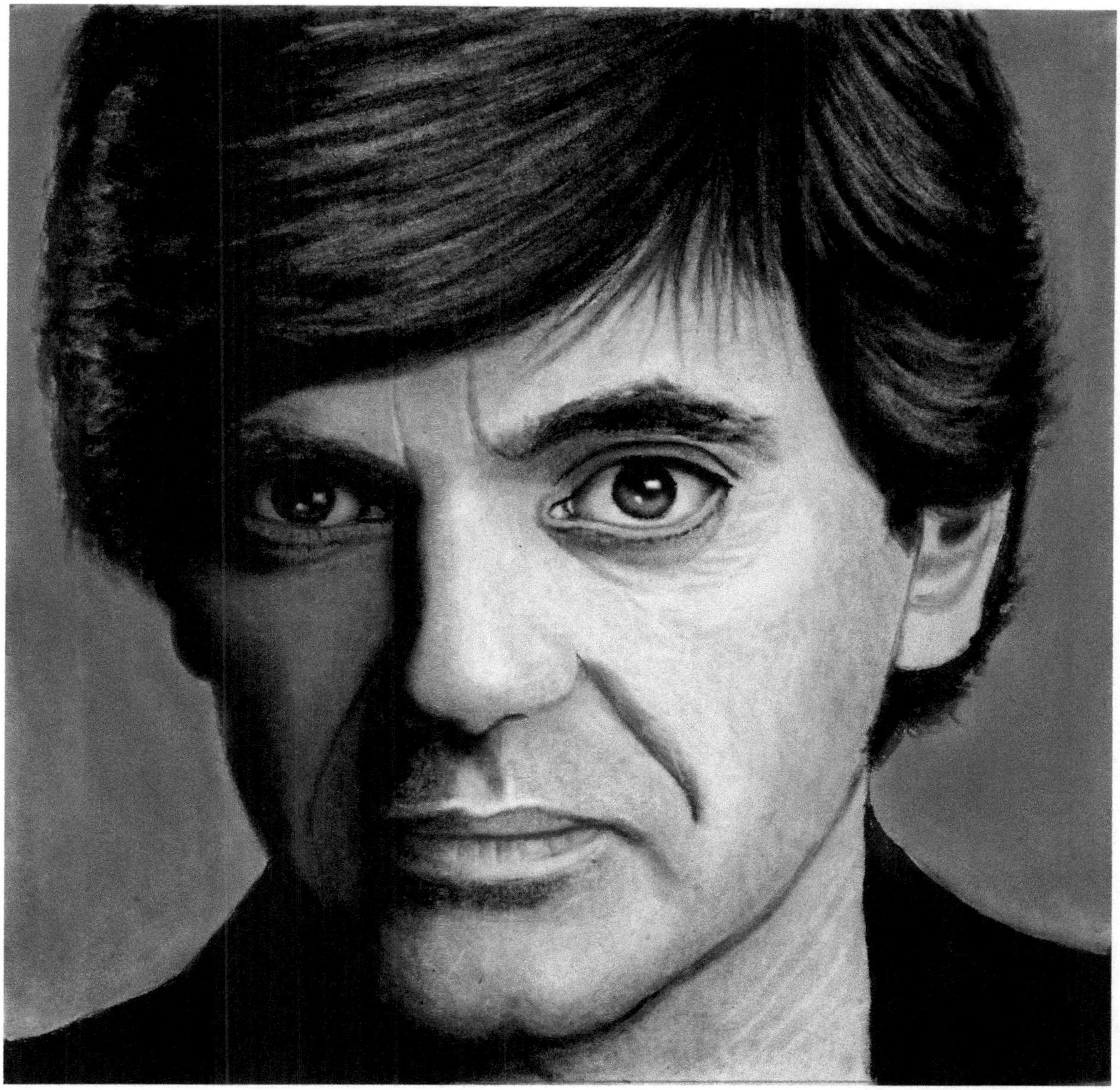

To view how this drawing was masterfully created or to purchase a Limited Edition Framed Artwork of Phil Everly type into your Internet Browser the URL shortcut ➡ **myportrait.art/phileverly**

To listen to their Greatest Songs type into your Internet Browser the URL shortcut
➡ **radio.surf/theeverlybrothers**

To view all channels on THE FACE OF MUSIC Internet Radio MEGA Station type into your Internet Browser the URL shortcut ➡ **radio.surf/music**

To inquire about purchasing a Limited Edtion NFT of this portrait type into your Internet Browser the URL shortcut ➡ **myartnft.shop/phileverly**

To view all available NFTs type into your Internet Browser the URL shortcut ➡ **myartnft.shop/all**

# Faith Hill

(Net worth: $165 Million)(Total Albums Sold: 40+ Million)
(Genre: Pop , Country)(Height: 5' - 10")

Audrey Faith McGraw (born September 21, 1967), known professionally as Faith Hill, is an American singer and record producer. She is one of the most successful country music artists of all time, having sold more than 40 million albums worldwide.

Hill's first two albums, Take Me as I Am (1993) and It Matters to Me (1995), were major successes and placed a combined three number ones on Billboard's country charts. She then achieved mainstream and crossover success with her next two albums, Faith (1998) and Breathe (1999). Faith spawned her first international success in early 1998, "This Kiss", while Breathe became one of the best-selling country albums of all time, led by the huge crossover success of the songs "Breathe" and "The Way You Love Me". It had massive sales worldwide and earned Hill three Grammy Awards.

In 2001, she recorded "There You'll Be" for the Pearl Harbor soundtrack and it became an international success and her best-selling single in Europe. Hill's next two albums, Cry (2002) and Fireflies (2005), were both commercial successes: the former spawned another crossover single, "Cry", which won Hill a Grammy Award, and the latter produced the singles "Mississippi Girl" and "Like We Never Loved at All", which earned her another Grammy Award.

Hill has won five Grammy Awards, 15 Academy of Country Music Awards, six American Music Awards, and several other awards. Her Soul2Soul II Tour 2006 with McGraw became the highest-grossing country tour of all time. In 2001, she was named one of the "30 Most Powerful Women in America" by Ladies Home Journal. In 2009, Billboard named her as the No. 1 Adult Contemporary artist of the 2000s decade and also as the 39th best artist. From 2007 to 2012, Hill was the voice of NBC Sunday Night Football's intro song. Hill received a star on the Hollywood Walk of Fame in 2019. Hill is married to American singer Tim McGraw, with whom she has recorded several duets.

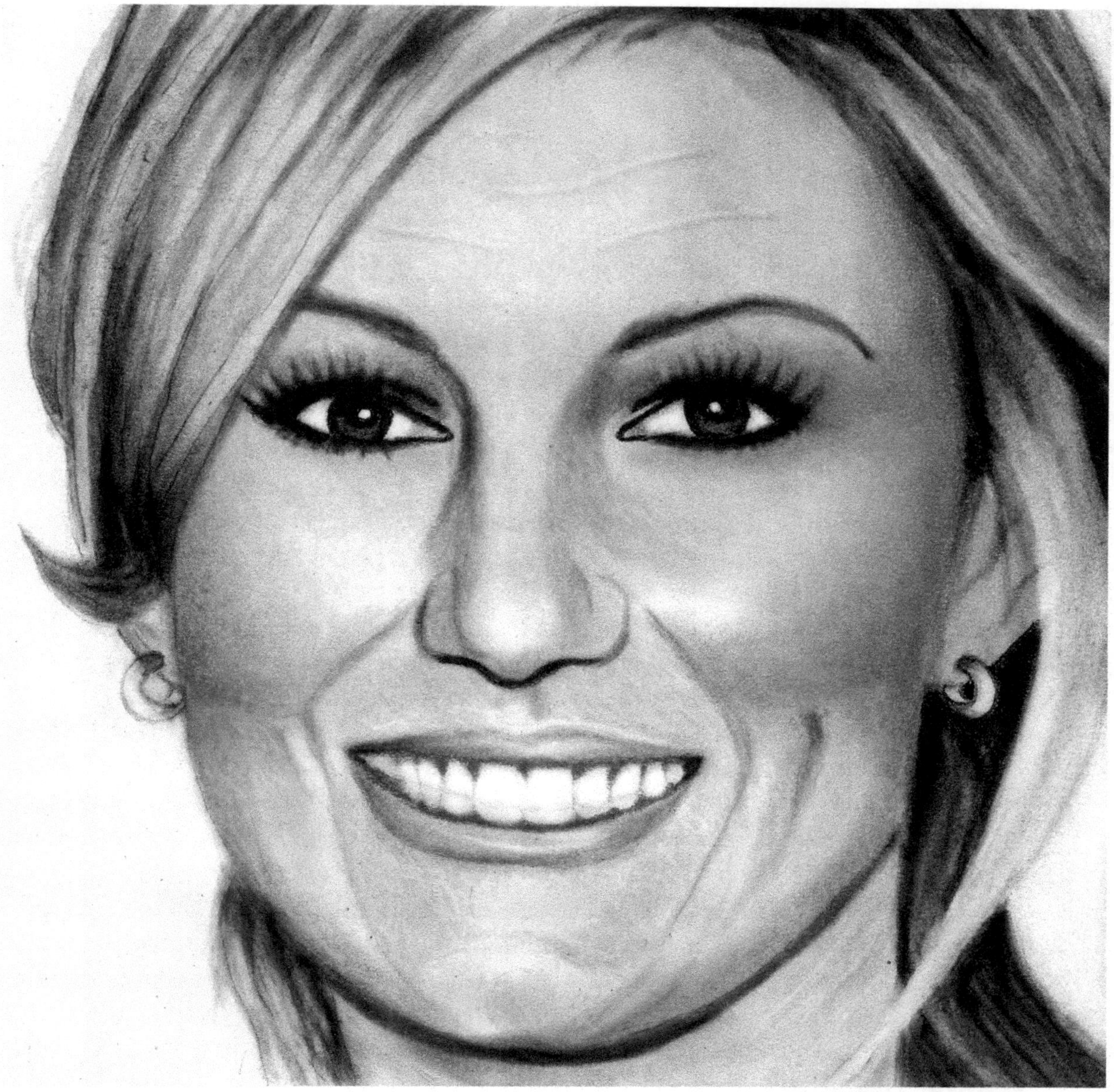

To view how this drawing was masterfully created or to purchase a Limited Edition Framed Artwork of Faith Hill type into your Internet Browser the URL shortcut ➡ **myportrait.art/faithhill**

To listen to her Greatest Songs type into your Internet Browser the URL shortcut ➡ **radio.surf/faithhill**

To view all channels on THE FACE OF MUSIC Internet Radio MEGA Station type into your Internet Browser the URL shortcut ➡ **radio.surf/music**

To inquire about purchasing a Limited Edtion NFT of this portrait type into your Internet Browser the URL shortcut ➡ **myartnft.shop/faithhill**

To view all available NFTs type into your Internet Browser the URL shortcut ➡ **myartnft.shop/all**

# Fats Domino

(Net worth: $5 Million)(Total Albums Sold: 110+ Million)
(Genre: Rock N Roll , R&B)(Height: 5' - 4")

Antoine Dominique Domino Jr. (February 26, 1928 – October 24, 2017), known as Fats Domino, was an American pianist and singer-songwriter. One of the pioneers of rock and roll music, Domino sold more than 65 million records.

Between 1955 and 1960, he had eleven Top 10 US pop hits. By 1955 five of his records had sold more than a million copies, being certified gold. The Associated Press estimates that during his career, the artist "sold more than 110 million records and the Grammy organization states that Domino landed 37 songs in the Top 40 on the Billboard Hot 100 throughout his career, including 11 that peaked inside the Top 10".

His humility and shyness may be one reason his contribution to the genre has been overlooked. The significance of his work was great however; Elvis Presley declared Domino to be "the real king of Rock 'N' Roll" and once announced that Domino "was a huge influence on me when I started out".

Four of Domino's records were named to the Grammy Hall of Fame for their significance: "Blueberry Hill", "Ain't It A Shame", "Walking to New Orleans" and "The Fat Man". "The Fat Man" "is cited by some historians as the first rock and roll single and the first to sell more than 1 million copies"

Antoine Domino Jr. was born and raised in New Orleans, Louisiana, the youngest of eight children born to Antoine Caliste Domino (1879–1964) and Marie-Donatille Gros (1886–1971). The Domino family was of French Creole background, and Louisiana Creole was his first language. Antoine was born at home with the assistance of his grandmother, a midwife. His name was initially misspelled as Anthony on his birth certificate. His family had recently arrived in the Lower Ninth Ward from Vacherie, Louisiana. His father was a part-time violin player who worked at a racetrack. He attended Howard University, leaving to start work as a helper to an ice delivery man. Domino learned to play the piano in about 1938 from his brother-in-law, the jazz guitarist Harrison Verrett.

The musician was married to Rosemary Domino (née Hall) from 1947 until her death in 2008; the couple had eight children: Antoine III (1950-2015), Anatole, Andre (1952-1997), Antonio, Antoinette, Andrea, Anola, and Adonica. Even after his success he continued to live in his old neighborhood, the Lower Ninth Ward, until after Hurricane Katrina, when he moved to a suburb of New Orleans.

By age 14, Domino was performing in New Orleans bars. In 1947, Billy Diamond, a New Orleans bandleader, accepted an invitation to hear the young pianist perform at a backyard barbecue. Domino played well enough that Diamond asked him to join his band, the Solid Senders, at the Hideaway Club in New Orleans, where he would earn $3 a week playing the piano. Diamond nicknamed him "Fats", because Domino reminded him of the renowned pianists Fats Waller and Fats Pichon, but also because of his large appetite.

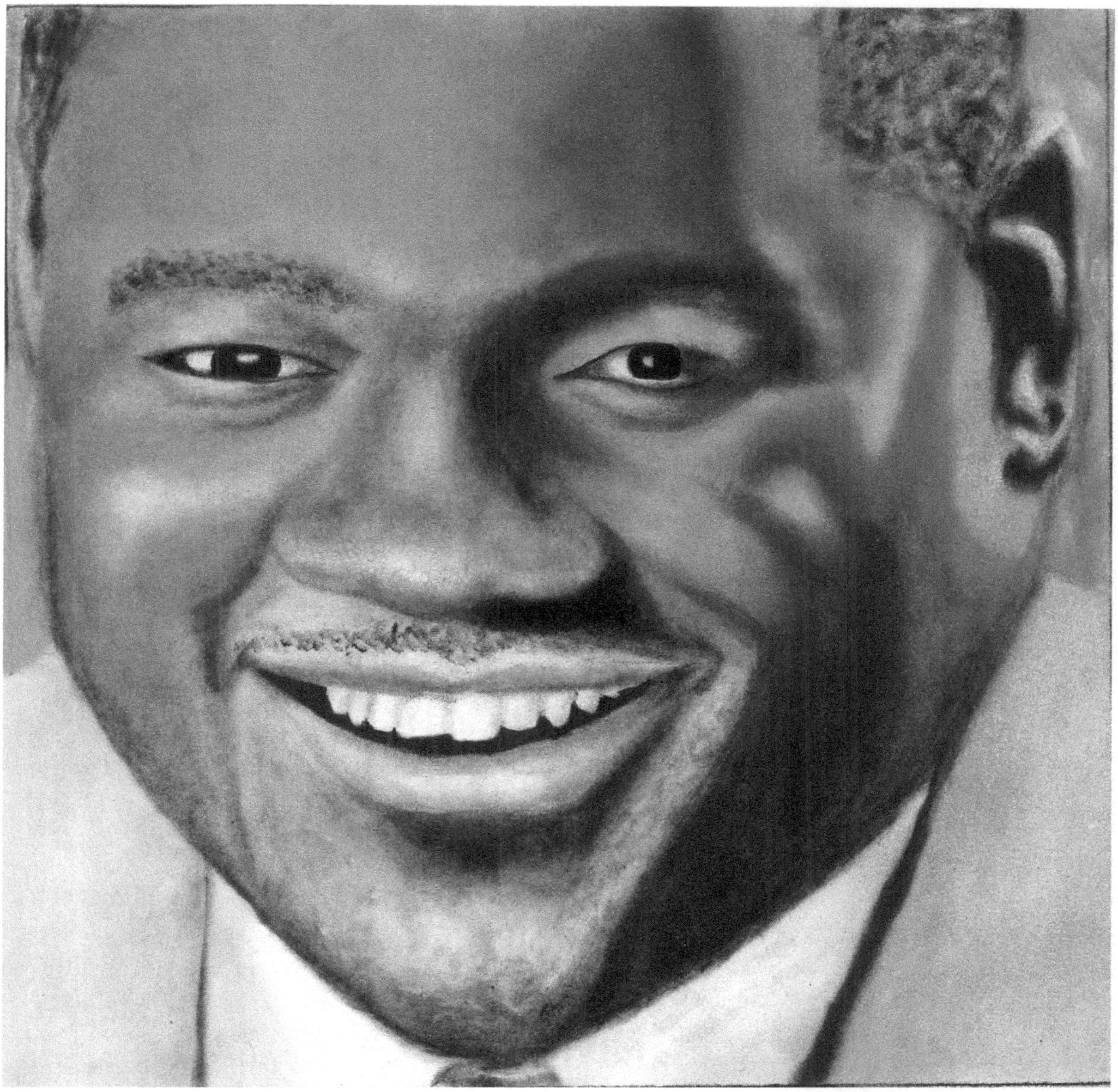

To view how this drawing was masterfully created or to purchase a Limited Edition Framed Artwork of Fats Domino type into your Internet Browser the URL shortcut ➡ **myportrait.art/fatsdomino**

To listen to his Greatest Songs type into your Internet Browser the URL shortcut ➡ **radio.surf/fatsdomino**

To view all channels on THE FACE OF MUSIC Internet Radio MEGA Station type into your Internet Browser the URL shortcut ➡ **radio.surf/music**

To inquire about purchasing a Limited Edtion NFT of this portrait type into your Internet Browser the URL shortcut ➡ **myartnft.shop/fatsdomino**

To view all available NFTs type into your Internet Browser the URL shortcut ➡ **myartnft.shop/all**

# Fifty Cent

(Net worth: $30 Million)(Total Albums Sold: 30+ Million)
(Genre: Hip-Hop)(Height: 6' - 0")

Curtis James Jackson III (born July 6, 1975), known professionally as 50 Cent, is an American rapper, songwriter, television producer, actor, and entrepreneur. Known for his impact in the hip hop industry, he has been described as a "master of the nuanced art of lyrical brevity".

Born in the South Jamaica neighborhood of Queens, Jackson began selling drugs at age 12 during the 1980s crack epidemic. He later began pursuing a musical career and in 2000 he produced Power of the Dollar for Columbia Records, but days before the planned release he was shot and the album was never released. In 2002, after 50 Cent released the compilation album Guess Who's Back?, he was discovered by Eminem and signed to Shady Records, under the aegis of Dr. Dre's Aftermath Entertainment and Interscope Records.

With the aid of Eminem and Dr. Dre (who produced his first major-label album Get Rich or Die Tryin'), 50 Cent became one of the world's best selling rappers and rose to prominence as de facto leader of East Coast hip hop group G-Unit. In 2003, he founded G-Unit Records, signing his G-Unit associates Young Buck, Lloyd Banks and Tony Yayo. 50 Cent had similar commercial and critical success with his second album, The Massacre, which was released in 2005. He underwent musical changes by his fifth album, Animal Ambition (2014), and as of 2021, is working on his sixth album, Street King Immortal. He executive-produced and starred in the television series Power (2014–2020) and is slated to produce its spin-offs.

50 Cent has sold over 30 million albums worldwide and won several awards, including a Grammy Award, thirteen Billboard Music Awards, six World Music Awards, three American Music Awards and four BET Awards. As an actor, Jackson appeared in the semi-autobiographical film Get Rich or Die Tryin' (2005), the war film Home of the Brave (2006), and the crime thriller film Righteous Kill (2008). 50 Cent was ranked the sixth-best artist of the 2000s and the third-best rapper (behind Eminem and Nelly) by Billboard. Rolling Stone ranked Get Rich or Die Tryin' and "In da Club" in its lists of the "100 Best Albums of the 2000s" and "100 Best Songs of the 2000s" at numbers 37 and 13, respectively.

Jackson was born in the borough of Queens, New York City, and raised in its South Jamaica neighborhood by his mother Sabrina. A drug dealer, Sabrina raised Jackson until she died in a fire when Jackson was 8. After his mother's death and his father's departure, Jackson was raised by his grandmother.

He began boxing at about age 11, and when he was 14, a neighbor opened a boxing gym for local youth. "When I wasn't killing time in school, I was sparring in the gym or selling crack on the strip," Jackson remembered. He sold crack during primary school. "I was competitive in the ring and hip-hop is competitive too ... I think rappers condition themselves like boxers, so they all kind of feel like they're the champ." At age 12, Jackson began dealing narcotics when his grandparents thought he was in after-school programs and brought guns and drug money to school. In the tenth grade, he was caught by metal detectors at Andrew Jackson High School: "I was embarrassed that I got arrested like that ... After I got arrested I stopped hiding it. I was telling my grandmother [openly], 'I sell drugs.'"

On June 29, 1994, Jackson was arrested for selling four vials of cocaine to an undercover police officer. He was arrested again three weeks later, when police searched his home and found heroin, ten ounces of crack cocaine, and a starting pistol. Although Jackson was sentenced to three to nine years in prison, he served six months in a boot camp and earned his GED. He has said that he did not use cocaine himself. Jackson adopted the nickname "50 Cent" as a metaphor for change. The name was inspired by Kelvin Martin, a 1980s Brooklyn robber known as "50 Cent"; Jackson chose it "because it says everything I want it to say. I'm the same kind of person 50 Cent was. I provide for myself by any means."

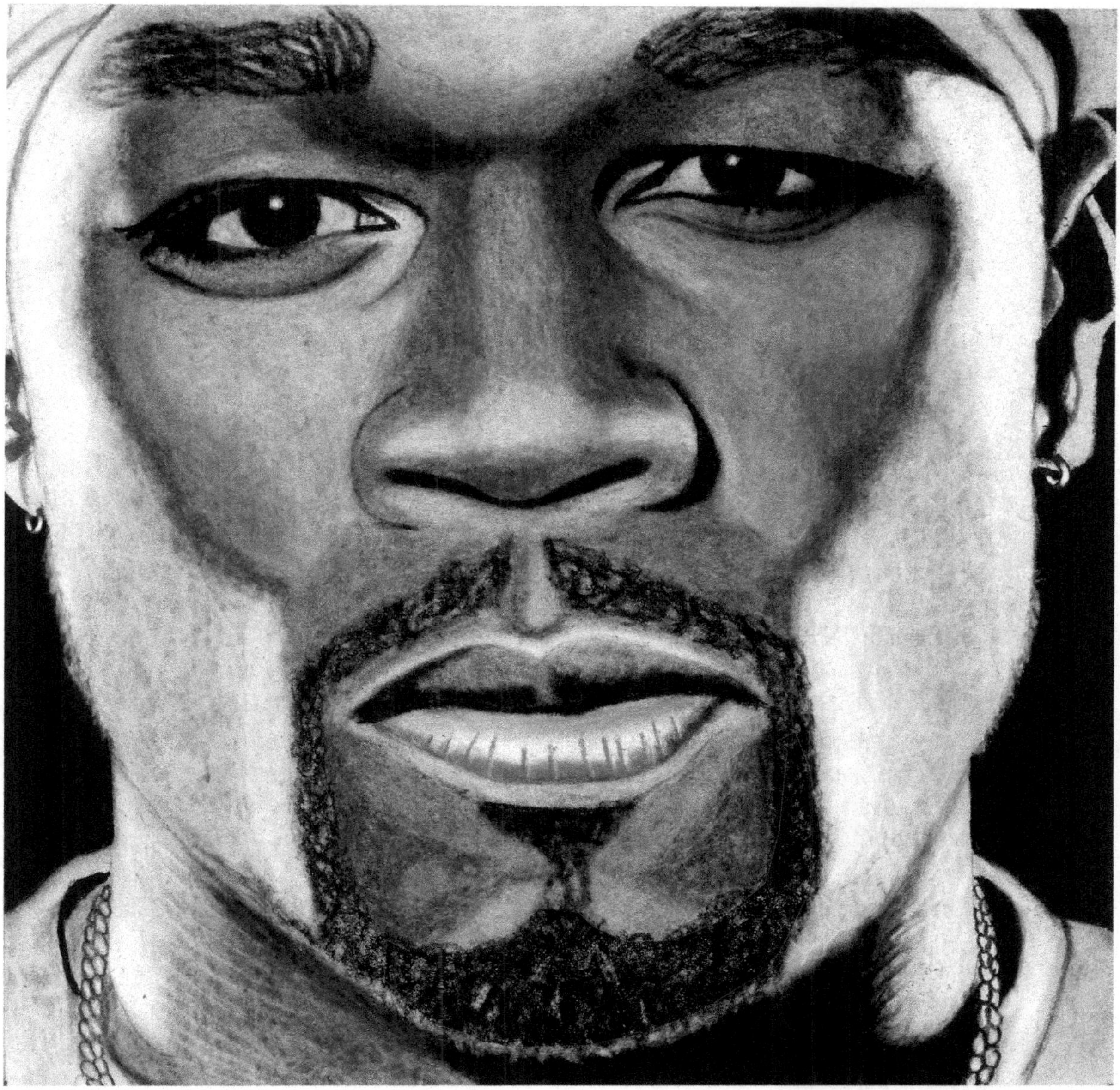

To view how this drawing was masterfully created or to purchase a Limited Edition Framed Artwork of 50 Cent type into your Internet Browser the URL shortcut ➡ **myportrait.art/50cent**

To listen to his Greatest Songs type into your Internet Browser the URL shortcut ➡ **radio.surf/50cent**

To view all channels on THE FACE OF MUSIC Internet Radio MEGA Station type into your Internet Browser the URL shortcut ➡ **radio.surf/music**

To inquire about purchasing a Limited Edition NFT of this portrait type into your Internet Browser the URL shortcut ➡ **myartnft.shop/50cent**

To view all available NFTs type into your Internet Browser the URL shortcut ➡ **myartnft.shop/all**

# Fleetwood Mac

(Total Records Sold: 120 Million) (Genre: Classic Rock)

Fleetwood Mac are a British-American rock band, formed in London in 1967. Fleetwood Mac were founded by guitarist Peter Green, drummer Mick Fleetwood and guitarist Jeremy Spencer, before bassist John McVie joined the lineup for their self-titled debut album. Danny Kirwan joined as a third guitarist in 1968. Keyboardist Christine Perfect, who contributed as a session musician from the second album, married McVie and joined in 1970.

Originally primarily a British blues band, Fleetwood Mac scored a UK number one with "Albatross", and had other hits such as the singles "Oh Well" and "Man of the World". All three guitarists left in succession during the early 1970s, to be replaced by guitarists Bob Welch and Bob Weston and vocalist Dave Walker. By 1974, all three of them had either departed or been dismissed, leaving the band without a male lead vocalist or guitarist. In late 1974, while Fleetwood was scouting studios in Los Angeles, he was introduced to American folk-rock duo Lindsey Buckingham and Stevie Nicks. The band soon asked Buckingham to be their new lead guitarist, and Buckingham agreed on condition that Nicks could also join the band.

The addition of Buckingham and Nicks gave the band a more pop rock sound, and their 1975 self-titled album, Fleetwood Mac, reached No. 1 in the United States. Rumours (1977), Fleetwood Mac's second album after the arrival of Buckingham and Nicks, produced four U.S. Top 10 singles and remained at number one on the American albums chart for 31 weeks. It also reached the top spot in various countries around the world and won a Grammy Award for Album of the Year in 1978. Rumours has sold over 40 million copies worldwide, making it one of the best-selling albums in history. The band went through personal turmoil while recording the album, as all of the romantic partnerships in the band (John and Christine McVie, Buckingham and Nicks, and Fleetwood and his wife Jenny) separated while continuing to write and record music together.

Fleetwood Mac have sold more than 120 million records worldwide, making them one of the world's best-selling bands. In 1979, the group were honoured with a star on the Hollywood Walk of Fame. In 1998 the band were inducted into the Rock and Roll Hall of Fame and received the Brit Award for Outstanding Contribution to Music. In 2018, the band received the MusiCares Person of the Year award by The Recording Academy in recognition of their artistic achievement in the music industry and dedication to philanthropy's best-selling bands. In 1979, the group were honoured with a star on the Hollywood Walk of Fame. In 1998 the band were inducted into the Rock and Roll Hall of Fame and received the Brit Award for Outstanding Contribution to Music. In 2018, the band received the MusiCares Person of the Year award by The Recording Academy in recognition of their artistic achievement in the music industry and dedication to philanthropy.

# Stevie Nicks

(Net Worth: $75 Million) (Height: 5' - 1")

Stephanie Lynn Nicks (born May 26, 1948) is an American singer and songwriter known for her work with the band Fleetwood Mac and as a solo artist. She is known for her distinctive voice, mystical stage persona and poetic, symbolic lyrics.

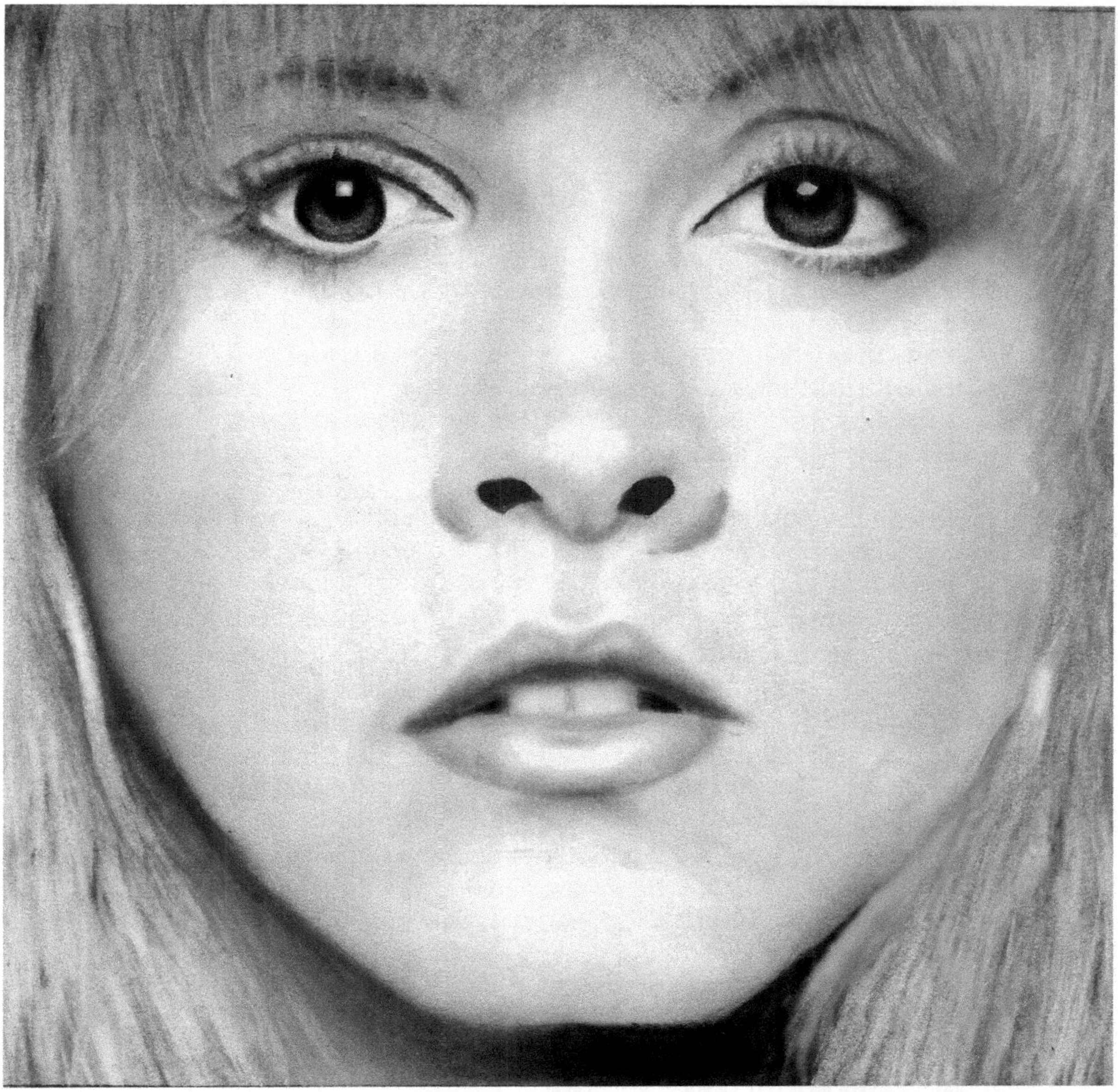

To view how this drawing was masterfully created or to purchase a Limited Edition Framed Artwork of Stevie Nicks type into your Internet Browser the URL shortcut ➡ **myportrait.art/stevienicks**

To listen to their Greatest Songs type into your Internet Browser the URL shortcut
➡ **radio.surf/fleetwoodmac**

To view all channels on THE FACE OF MUSIC Internet Radio MEGA Station type into your Internet Browser the URL shortcut ➡ **radio.surf/music**

To inquire about purchasing a Limited Edtion NFT of this portrait type into your Internet Browser the URL shortcut ➡ **myartnft.shop/stevienicks**

To view all available NFTs type into your Internet Browser the URL shortcut ➡ **myartnft.shop/all**

# Foo Fighters

(Total Albums Sold: 12+ Million) (Genre: Rock)

Foo Fighters is an American rock band formed in Seattle, Washington in 1994. It was founded by former Nirvana drummer Dave Grohl as a one-man project following the dissolution of Nirvana after the suicide of Kurt Cobain. The group took its name from "Foo fighter", a nickname coined by Allied aircraft pilots for UFOs and other aerial phenomena. Over the course of their career, Foo Fighters have won 12 Grammy Awards, including Best Rock Album four times. The band has also won an American Music Award, four Brit Awards, and two MTV Video Music Awards. As of 2015, Foo Fighters have sold over 12 million albums in the U.S.

Prior to the release of Foo Fighters' 1995 debut album Foo Fighters, which featured Grohl as the only official member, Grohl recruited bassist Nate Mendel and drummer William Goldsmith, both formerly of Sunny Day Real Estate, as well as Nirvana touring guitarist Pat Smear. The band began with performances in Portland, Oregon. Goldsmith quit during the recording of their second album, The Colour and the Shape (1997); most of the drum parts were re-recorded by Grohl. Smear departed soon afterward but appeared as a guest with the band frequently from 2005; he rejoined the band in 2010.

Smear and Goldsmith were replaced by Franz Stahl and Taylor Hawkins, respectively, although Stahl was fired before the recording of the group's third album, There Is Nothing Left to Lose (1999). The band briefly continued as a trio until Chris Shiflett joined on guitar after the completion of There Is Nothing Left to Lose. The band released its fourth album, One by One, in 2002. The group followed that release with the two-disc In Your Honor (2005), which was split between acoustic songs and heavier material. Foo Fighters released their sixth album, Echoes, Silence, Patience & Grace, in 2007.

The band's seventh studio album, Wasting Light, produced by Butch Vig, was released in 2011, in which Smear returned as a full member. In November 2014, the band's eighth studio album, Sonic Highways, was released as an accompanying soundtrack to the Grohl-directed 2014 miniseries of the same name. On September 15, 2017, the band released their ninth studio album, Concrete and Gold, which became their second to reach number one in the United States and was the band's first studio album to feature longtime session and touring keyboardist Rami Jaffee as a full member. In February 2021, the band released its tenth album, Medicine at Midnight, and was nominated for induction into the Rock and Roll Hall of Fame.

# Dave Grohl

(Net Worth: $320 Million) (Height: 6' - 0")

David Eric Grohl (born January 14, 1969) is an American musician, singer, and songwriter. He was the drummer for rock band Nirvana and founded the band Foo Fighters, for whom he is the singer, guitarist, and primary songwriter. Grohl is also the drummer and co-founder of the rock supergroup Them Crooked Vultures, and wrote the music for his short-lived side projects Late! and Probot. He has also recorded and toured with Queens of the Stone Age.

Grohl established himself as a respected drummer with Nirvana and in 2014 was inducted into the Rock and Roll Hall of Fame, along with former bandmates Kurt Cobain and Krist Novoselic, in the group's first year of eligibility. In 2010, Grohl was described by Ken Micallef, co-author of the book Classic Rock Drummers, as one of the most influential rock musicians of the last 20 years.

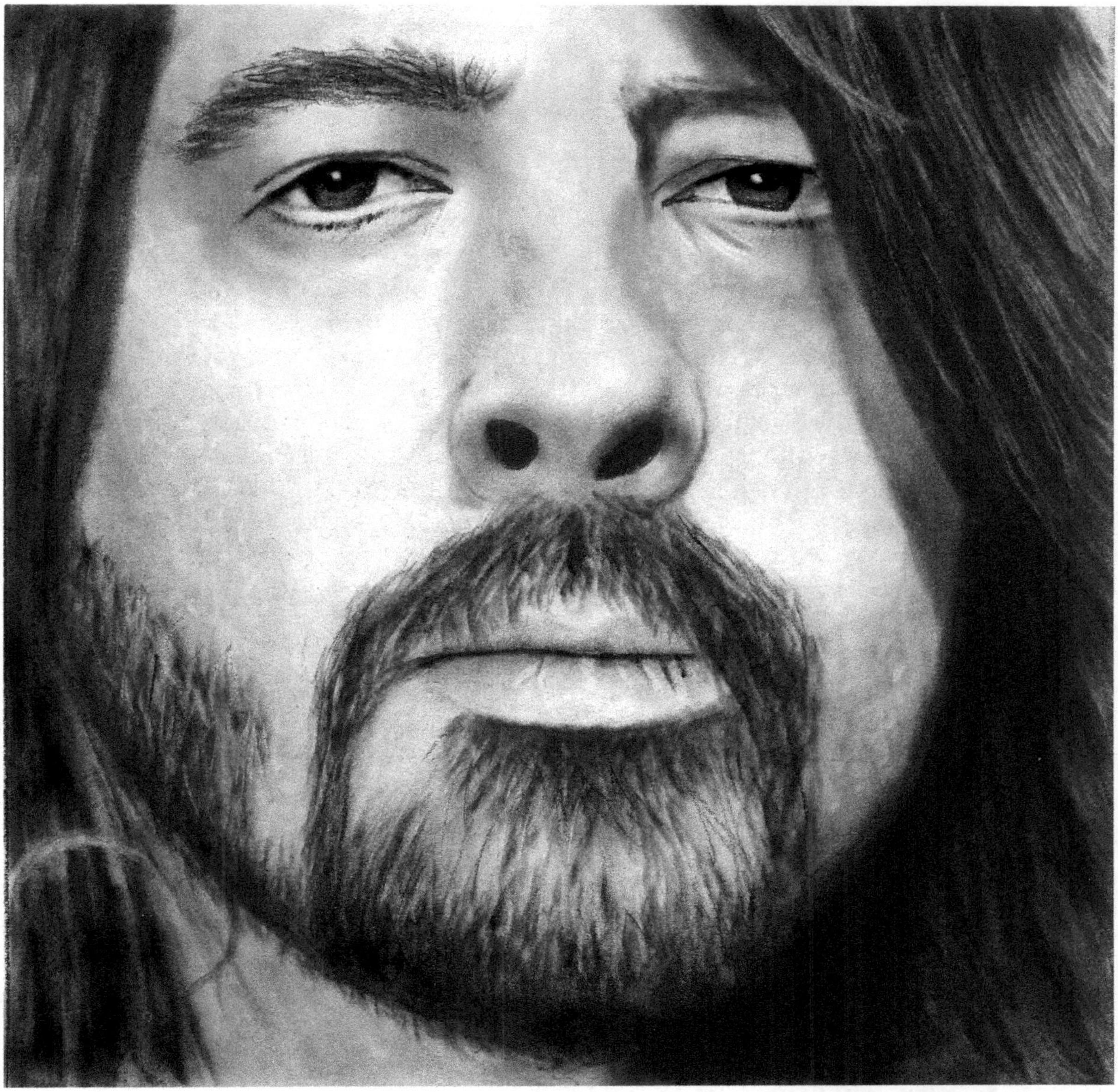

To view how this drawing was masterfully created or to purchase a Limited Edition Framed Artwork of Dave Grohl type into your Internet Browser the URL shortcut ➡ **myportrait.art/davegrohl**

To listen to their Greatest Songs type into your Internet Browser the URL shortcut ➡ **radio.surf/foofighters**

To view all channels on THE FACE OF MUSIC Internet Radio MEGA Station type into your Internet Browser the URL shortcut ➡ **radio.surf/music**

To inquire about purchasing a Limited Edtion NFT of this portrait type into your Internet Browser the URL shortcut ➡ **myartnft.shop/davegrohl**

To view all available NFTs type into your Internet Browser the URL shortcut ➡ **myartnft.shop/all**

# Foreigner

(Total Records Sold: 80+ Million) (Genre: Classic Rock)

Foreigner is a British-American rock band, originally formed in New York City in 1976 by veteran British guitarist and songwriter Mick Jones, and fellow Briton and ex-King Crimson member Ian McDonald, along with American vocalist Lou Gramm. Jones came up with the band's name as he, McDonald and Dennis Elliott were British, whereas Gramm, Al Greenwood and Ed Gagliardi were American.

In 1977, Foreigner released its self-titled debut album, the first of four straight albums to be certified at least 5x platinum in the US. Foreigner peaked at No. 4 on the US album chart and in the Top 10 in Canada and Australia, while yielding two Top 10 hits in North America, "Feels Like the First Time" and "Cold as Ice". Their 1978 follow-up, Double Vision, was even more successful peaking at No. 3 in North America with two hit singles, "Hot Blooded" a No. 3 hit in both countries, and the title track, a US No. 2 and a Canadian No. 7. Foreigner's third album, Head Games (1979) went to No. 5 in North America producing two Top 20 singles including its titletrack.

Reduced to a quartet, 4 (1981) hit No. 1 (for 10 weeks) in the US and No. 2 in Canada, while becoming Foreigner's break-through album outside of North America, going Top 5 in the UK, Germany and Australia. Two of 4's singles were smashes: "Urgent" reached No. 1 in Canada and on the new US Rock Tracks chart, No. 4 on the US Hot 100 and, became their first Top 15 hit in Germany; and, the ballad "Waiting for a Girl Like You" peaked at No. 2 in both the US (for a record 10 weeks) and Canada, topped the US Rock Tracks chart, and became their first Top 10 hit in the UK and Australia. In 1982, Foreigner released its first greatest hits album, Records, which has gone on to sell 7 million copies in the US. In 1984, Foreigner had its biggest hit single, the anthemic ballad "I Want to Know What Love Is", which topped the US, UK, Canadian and Australian charts, while hitting No. 3 in Germany and the Top 10 in numerous other countries. Its source album, Agent Provocateur, was the band's most successful in the UK, Germany and some other countries in Europe, where it peaked at No. 1, and in Australia (No. 3), while performing well in the US (No. 4) and Canada (No. 3).

After a break, Foreigner released Inside Information (1987), which despite the No. 6 US and Australian hit, "Say You Will" (which also rose to No. 1 on the US Rock Tracks chart), had a large sales drop-off, only hitting the Top 10 in a few European countries with a No. 15 peak in the US. The band's most recent albums, Unusual Heat (1991), without Gramm, who departed due to the band's shift towards the use of synthesizers, Mr. Moonlight (1994), with Gramm back on vocals, and Can't Slow Down (2009), once again without Gramm, were not major sellers; the highest chart positions were obtained in Germany, where the last album peaked at No. 16. Foreigner is one of the world's best-selling bands of all time with worldwide sales of more than 80 million records, including 37.5 million in the US. Leader Mick Jones has been for many years the only founding member still involved.

# Lou Gramm

(Net Worth: $25 Million) (Height: 5' - 5")

Lou Gramm (born Louis Andrew Grammatico; May 2, 1950) is an American rock singer-songwriter, best known for being the lead singer of the rock band Foreigner.

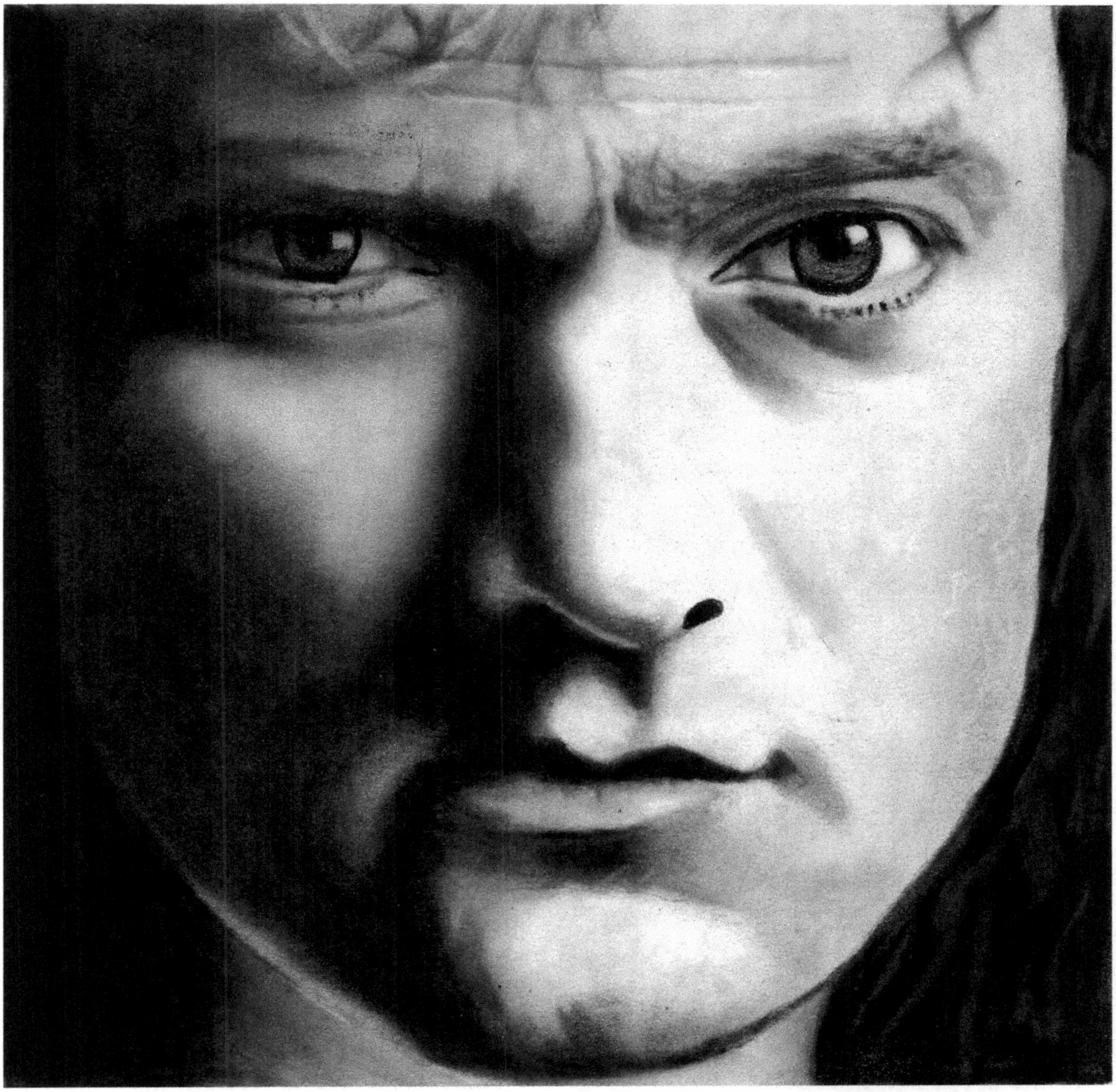

To view how this drawing was masterfully created or to purchase a Limited Edition Framed Artwork of Lou Gramm type into your Internet Browser the URL shortcut ➡ **myportrait.art/lougramm**

To listen to their Greatest Songs type into your Internet Browser the URL shortcut ➡ **radio.surf/foreigner**

To view all channels on THE FACE OF MUSIC Internet Radio MEGA Station type into your Internet Browser the URL shortcut ➡ **radio.surf/music**

To inquire about purchasing a Limited Edtion NFT of this portrait type into your Internet Browser the URL shortcut ➡ **myartnft.shop/lougramm**

To view all available NFTs type into your Internet Browser the URL shortcut ➡ **myartnft.shop/all**

# Four Seasons, The

(Total Records Sold: 175 Million) (Genre: Rock , Pop)

The Four Seasons are an American rock band that became internationally successful in the 1960s and 1970s. Since 1970, they have also been known at times as Frankie Valli and the Four Seasons. In 1960, the band known as the Four Lovers evolved into the Four Seasons, with Frankie Valli as the lead singer, Bob Gaudio (formerly of the Royal Teens) on keyboards and tenor vocals, Tommy DeVito on lead guitar and baritone vocals, and Nick Massi on electric bass and bass vocals. On nearly all of their 1960s hits they were credited as the 4 Seasons.

The legal name of the organization is the Four Seasons Partnership, formed by Gaudio and Valli, and was taken after a failed audition in 1960. While singers, producers, and musicians have come and gone, Gaudio and Valli remain the band's constant (with each owning fifty percent of the act and its assets, including virtually all of its recording catalog). Gaudio no longer plays live, leaving Valli as the only member of the band from its inception who is touring as of 2019.

The Four Seasons were one of only two American bands (the other being the Beach Boys) to enjoy substantial chart success before, during, and after the British Invasion. The band's original line-up was inducted into the Rock and Roll Hall of Fame in 1990, and joined the Vocal Group Hall of Fame in 1999. They are one of the best-selling musical groups of all time, having sold an estimated 175 million records worldwide.

# Frankie Valli

(Net Worth: $80 Million) (Height: 5' - 5")

Francesco Stephen Castelluccio (born May 3, 1934), known professionally as Frankie Valli, is an American singer, known as the frontman of the Four Seasons beginning in 1960. He is known for his unusually powerful lead falsetto voice. Valli scored 29 top 40 hits with the Four Seasons, one top 40 hit under the Four Seasons alias the Wonder Who?, and nine top 40 hits as a solo artist. As a member of the Four Seasons, Valli's number-one hits include "Sherry" (1962), "Big Girls Don't Cry" (1962), "Walk Like a Man" (1963), "Rag Doll" (1964) and "December, 1963 (Oh, What a Night)" (1975). Valli's recording of the song "Can't Take My Eyes Off You" reached number two in 1967. As a solo artist, Valli scored number-one hits with the songs "My Eyes Adored You" (1974) and "Grease" (1978).

Valli, Tommy DeVito, Nick Massi and Bob Gaudio – the original members of the Four Seasons – were inducted into the Rock and Roll Hall of Fame in 1990 and the Vocal Group Hall of Fame in 1999.

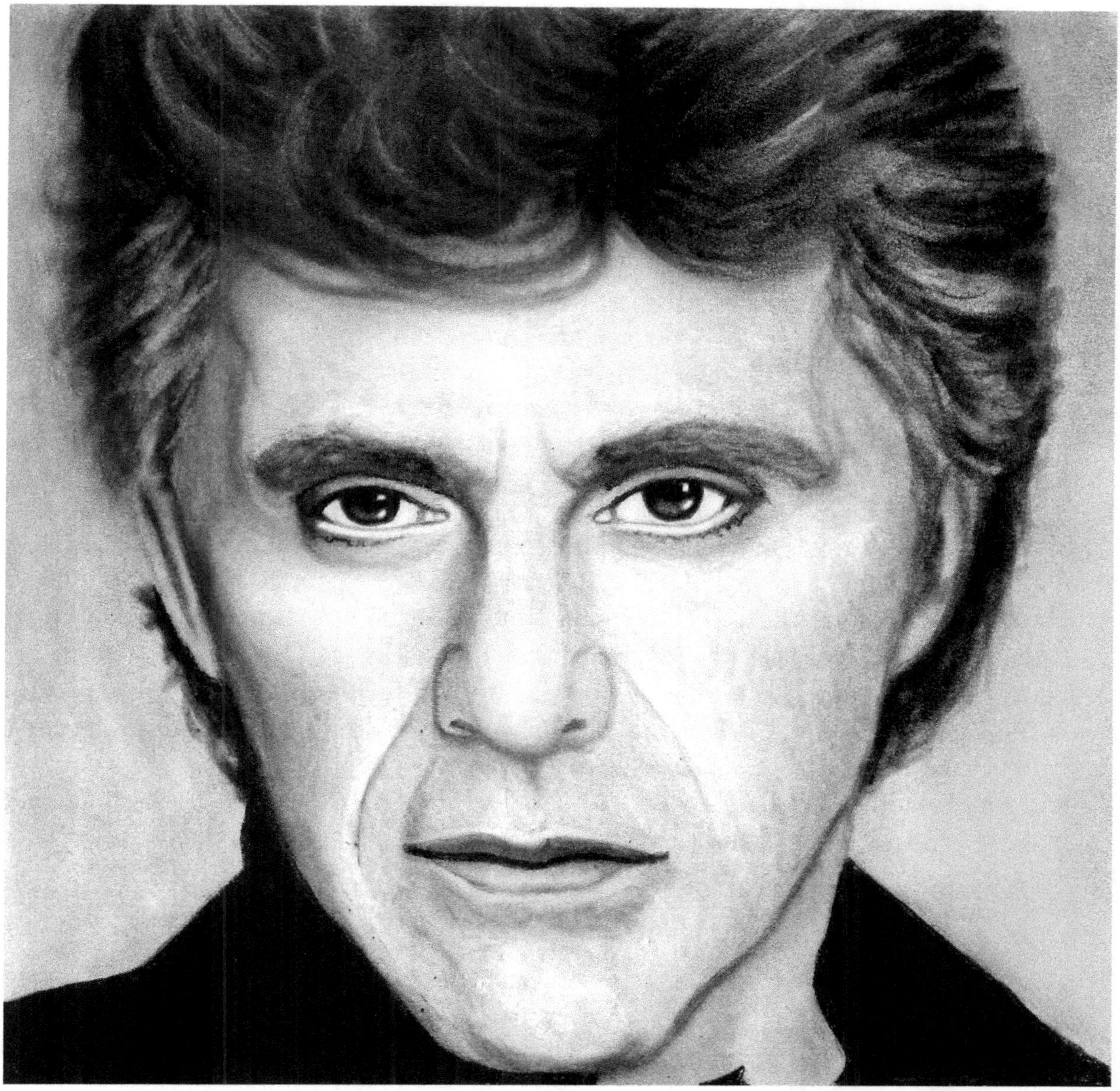

To view how this drawing was masterfully created or to purchase a Limited Edition Framed Artwork of Frankie Valli type into your Internet Browser the URL shortcut ➡ **myportrait.art/frankievalli**

To listen to their Greatest Songs type into your Internet Browser the URL shortcut
➡ **radio.surf/thefourseasons**

To view all channels on THE FACE OF MUSIC Internet Radio MEGA Station type into your Internet Browser the URL shortcut ➡ **radio.surf/music**

To inquire about purchasing a Limited Edtion NFT of this portrait type into your Internet Browser the URL shortcut ➡ **myartnft.shop/frankievalli**

To view all available NFTs type into your Internet Browser the URL shortcut ➡ **myartnft.shop/all**

# Four Tops

(Total Records Sold: 50 Million) (Genre: Soul , R&B , Pop)

The Four Tops are an American vocal quartet from Detroit, Michigan who helped to define the city's Motown sound of the 1960s.

Founded as the Four Aims, lead singer Levi Stubbs, Abdul "Duke" Fakir, Renaldo "Obie" Benson and Lawrence Payton remained together for over four decades, performing from 1953 until 1997 without a change in personnel. The Four Tops were among a number of groups, including the Miracles, the Marvelettes, Martha and the Vandellas, the Temptations, and the Supremes, who established the Motown Sound heard around the world during the 1960s. They were notable for having Stubbs, a baritone, as their lead singer, whereas most other male and mixed vocal groups of the time were fronted by tenors.

The group was the main male vocal group for the highly successful songwriting and production team of Holland–Dozier–Holland, who crafted a stream of hit singles for Motown. These included two Billboard Hot 100 number-one hits for the Tops: "I Can't Help Myself (Sugar Pie Honey Bunch)" in 1965 and "Reach Out I'll Be There" in 1966. The group continued to have chart singles into the 1970s, including the million-seller "Ain't No Woman" (1973).

The group was inducted into the Rock and Roll Hall of Fame in 1990 and into the Vocal Group Hall of Fame in 1999. In 2004, Rolling Stone ranked them #79 on its list of the 100 Greatest Artists of All Time.

The Four Tops continue to perform with Fakir as the last surviving original member.

# Levi Stubbs

(Net Worth: $7 Million) (Height: 5' - 11")

Levi Stubbs (born Levi Stubbles, June 6, 1936 – October 17, 2008) was an American baritone singer, best known as the lead vocalist of the R&B group the Four Tops, who released a variety of Motown hit records during the 1960s and 1970s. He has been noted for his powerful, emotional, dramatic style of singing.

Stubbs was also a voice artist in film and television, and provided the voice of "Audrey II", the alien plant in the 1986 musical horror comedy film Little Shop of Horrors (an adaption of the stage musical of the same name), as well as Mother Brain in the 1989 TV series Captain N: The Game Master.

Stubbs was admired by his peers for his impressive vocal range, and influenced many later pop and soul artists, such as Daryl Hall of Hall and Oates.

Stubbs was born and spent much of his life in Detroit, Michigan. He had five children with his wife Clineice Stubbs, to whom he was married for almost 50 years. His last performance was at the Four Tops' "50th Anniversary Concert" on July 28, 2004, at the Detroit Opera House.

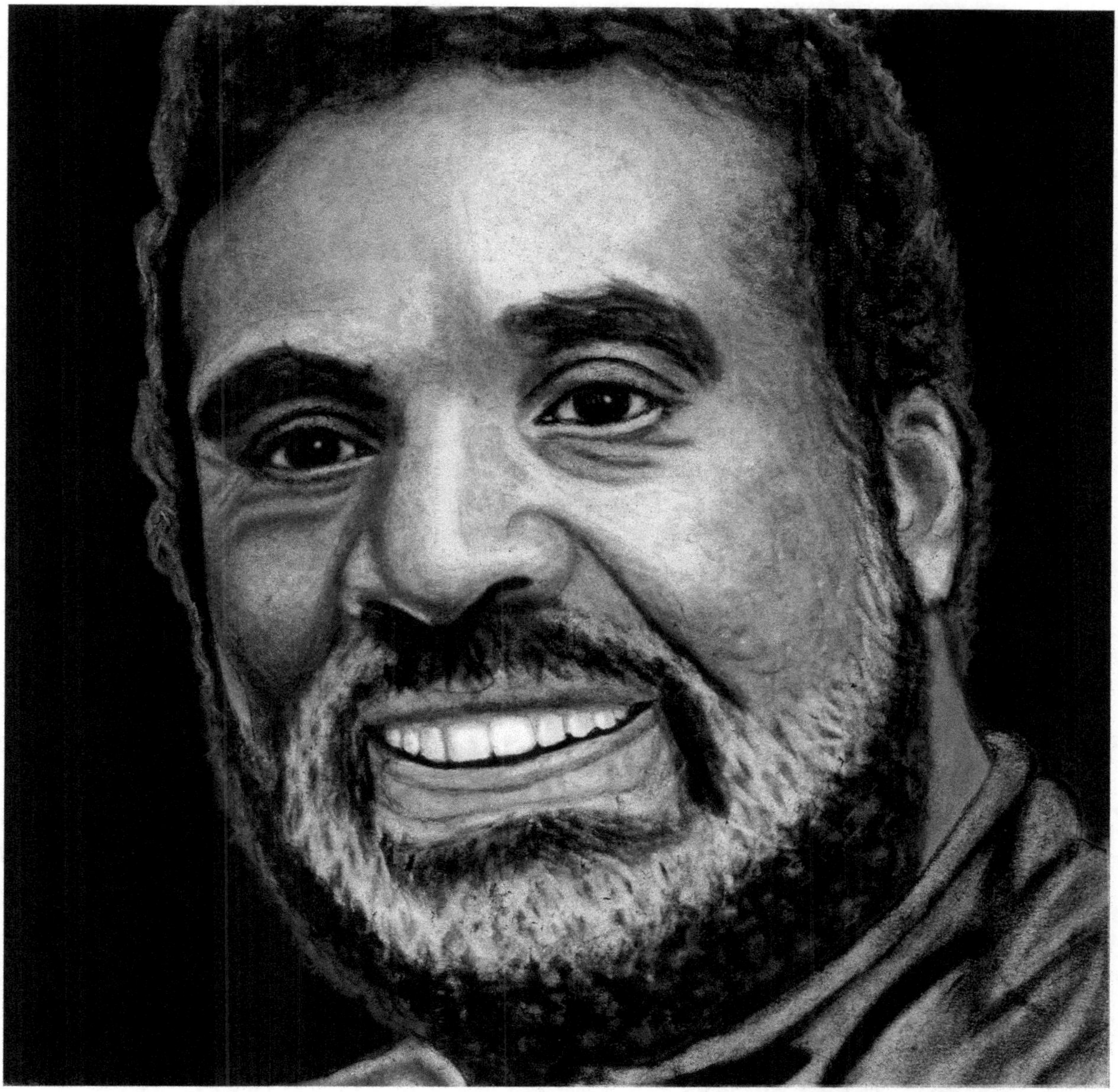

To view how this drawing was masterfully created or to purchase a Limited Edition Framed Artwork of Levi Stubbs type into your Internet Browser the URL shortcut ➡ **myportrait.art/levistubbs**

To listen to their Greatest Songs type into your Internet Browser the URL shortcut ➡ **radio.surf/fourtops**

To view all channels on THE FACE OF MUSIC Internet Radio MEGA Station type into your Internet Browser the URL shortcut ➡ **radio.surf/music**

To inquire about purchasing a Limited Edtion NFT of this portrait type into your Internet Browser the URL shortcut ➡ **myartnft.shop/levistubbs**

To view all available NFTs type into your Internet Browser the URL shortcut ➡ **myartnft.shop/all**

# Frank Sinatra

(Net worth: $200 Million)(Total Albums Sold: 150+ Million)
(Genre: Crooner , Jazz , Swing)(Height: 5' - 7")

Francis Albert Sinatra ( December 12, 1915 – May 14, 1998) was an American singer, actor, and producer who was one of the most popular and influential musical artists of the 20th century. He is one of the best-selling music artists of all time, having sold more than 150 million records worldwide.

Born to Italian immigrants in Hoboken, New Jersey, Sinatra was greatly influenced by the intimate easy listening vocal style of Bing Crosby and began his musical career in the swing era with bandleaders Harry James and Tommy Dorsey. Sinatra found success as a solo artist after he signed with Columbia Records in 1943, becoming the idol of the "bobby soxers". He released his debut album, The Voice of Frank Sinatra, in 1946. But by the early 1950s, his professional career had stalled and he turned to Las Vegas, where he became one of its best known residency performers as part of the Rat Pack. His career was reborn in 1953 with the success of From Here to Eternity, with his performance subsequently earning him an Academy Award and Golden Globe Award for Best Supporting Actor. Sinatra subsequently released several critically lauded albums, some of which are retrospectively noted as being among the first "concept albums", including In the Wee Small Hours (1955), Songs for Swingin' Lovers! (1956), Come Fly with Me (1958), Only the Lonely (1958), No One Cares (1959), and Nice 'n' Easy (1960).

Sinatra left Capitol in 1960 to start his own record label, Reprise Records, and released a string of successful albums. In 1965, he recorded the retrospective album September of My Years and starred in the Emmy-winning television special Frank Sinatra: A Man and His Music. After releasing Sinatra at the Sands, recorded at the Sands Hotel and Casino in Vegas with frequent collaborator Count Basie in early 1966, the following year he recorded one of his most famous collaborations with Tom Jobim, the album Francis Albert Sinatra & Antonio Carlos Jobim. It was followed by 1968's Francis A. & Edward K. with Duke Ellington. Sinatra retired for the first time in 1971, but came out of retirement two years later. He recorded several albums and resumed performing at Caesars Palace, and released "New York, New York" in 1980. Using his Las Vegas shows as a home base, he toured both within the United States and internationally until shortly before his death in 1998.

While Sinatra never learned how to read music, he worked very hard from a young age to improve his abilities in all aspects of music. A perfectionist, renowned for his dress sense and performing presence, he always insisted on recording live with his band. His bright blue eyes earned him the popular nickname "Ol' Blue Eyes".

Sinatra led a colorful personal life, and was often involved in turbulent affairs with women, such as with his second wife Ava Gardner. He later married Mia Farrow in 1966 and Barbara Marx in 1976. Sinatra had several violent confrontations, usually with journalists he felt had crossed him, or work bosses with whom he had disagreements. He was honored at the Kennedy Center Honors in 1983, was awarded the Presidential Medal of Freedom by Ronald Reagan in 1985, and the Congressional Gold Medal in 1997. Sinatra was also the recipient of eleven Grammy Awards, including the Grammy Trustees Award, Grammy Legend Award and the Grammy Lifetime Achievement Award. He was collectively included in Time magazine's compilation of the 20th century's 100 most influential people. After Sinatra's death, American music critic Robert Christgau called him "the greatest singer of the 20th century", and he continues to be seen as an iconic figure.

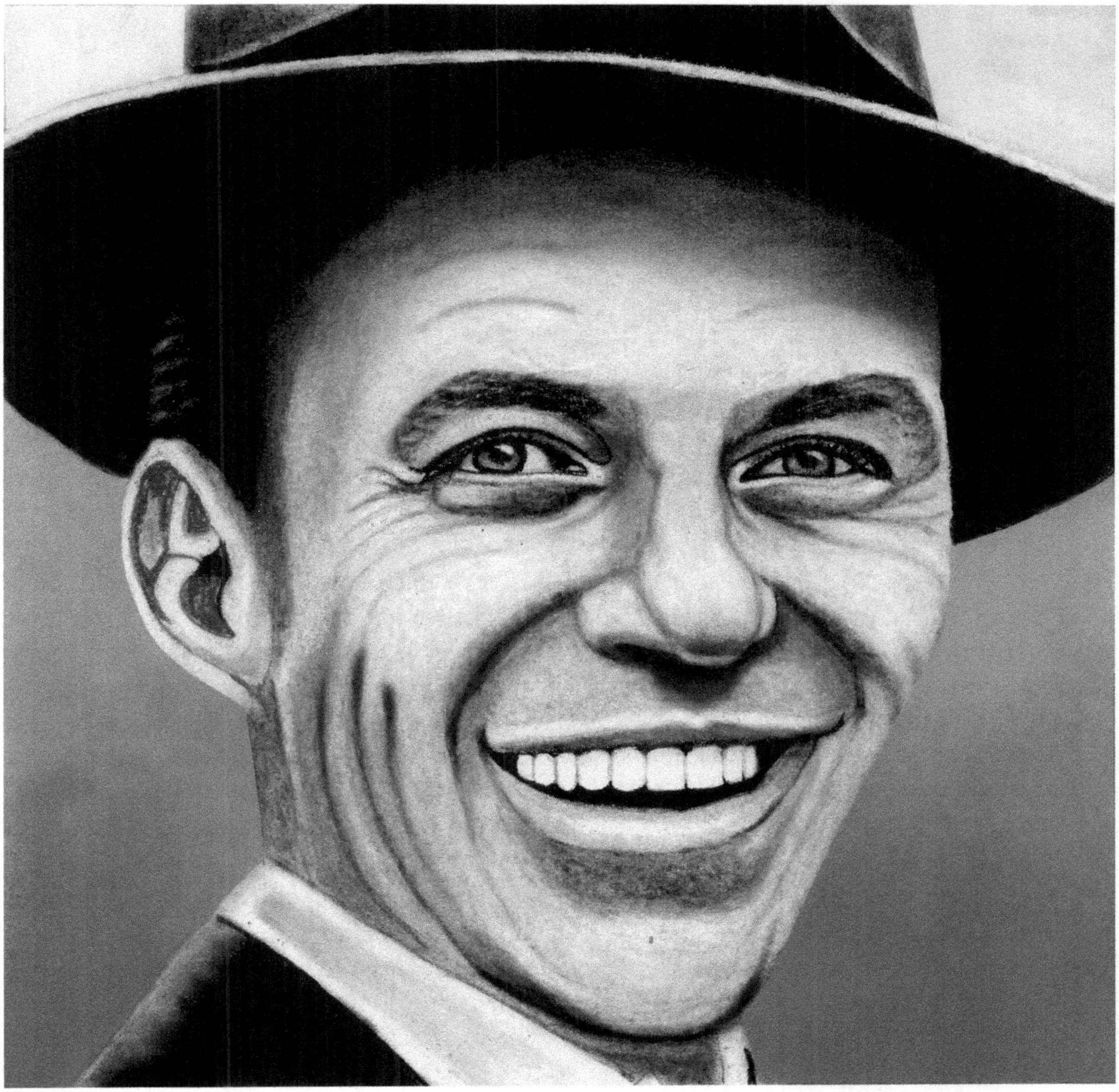

To view how this drawing was masterfully created or to purchase a Limited Edition Framed Artwork of Frank Sinatra type into your Internet Browser the URL shortcut ➡ **myportrait.art/franksinatra**

To listen to his Greatest Songs type into your Internet Browser the URL shortcut ➡ **radio.surf/franksinatra**

To view all channels on THE FACE OF MUSIC Internet Radio MEGA Station type into your Internet Browser the URL shortcut ➡ **radio.surf/music**

To inquire about purchasing a Limited Edtion NFT of this portrait type into your Internet Browser the URL shortcut ➡ **myartnft.shop/franksinatra**

To view all available NFTs type into your Internet Browser the URL shortcut ➡ **myartnft.shop/all**

# Frank Zappa

(Net worth: $40 Million)(Total Albums Sold: 11 Million)
(Genre: Progressive / Art Rock)(Height: 5' - 11 1/2")

Frank Vincent Zappa (December 21, 1940 – December 4, 1993) was an American singer-songwriter, innovative rock guitarist, modernist composer, multi-instrumentalist, satirist, film-maker, and bandleader. His work is characterized by nonconformity, free-form improvisation, sound experiments, musical virtuosity, and satire of American culture. In a career spanning more than 30 years, Zappa composed rock, pop, jazz, jazz fusion, orchestral and musique concrète works, and produced almost all of the 60-plus albums that he released with his band the Mothers of Invention and as a solo artist. Zappa also directed feature-length films and music videos, and designed album covers. He is considered one of the most innovative and stylistically diverse rock musicians of his era.

As a self-taught composer and performer, Zappa had diverse musical influences that led him to create music that was sometimes difficult to categorize. While in his teens, he acquired a taste for 20th-century classical modernism, African-American rhythm and blues, and doo-wop music. He began writing classical music in high school, while at the same time playing drums in rhythm and blues bands, later switching to electric guitar. His 1966 debut album with the Mothers of Invention, Freak Out!, combined songs in conventional rock and roll format with collective improvisations and studio-generated sound collages. He continued this eclectic and experimental approach whether the fundamental format was rock, jazz, or classical.

Zappa's output is unified by a conceptual continuity he termed "Project/Object", with numerous musical phrases, ideas, and characters reappearing across his albums. His lyrics reflected his iconoclastic views of established social and political processes, structures and movements, often humorously so, and he has been described as the "godfather" of comedy rock. He was a strident critic of mainstream education and organized religion, and a forthright and passionate advocate for freedom of speech, self-education, political participation and the abolition of censorship. Unlike many other rock musicians of his generation, he disapproved of drugs but supported their decriminalization and regulation.

Zappa was a highly productive and prolific artist with a controversial critical standing: supporters of his music admired its compositional complexity, while critics found it lacking emotional depth. He had some commercial success, particularly in Europe, and worked as an independent artist for most of his career. He remains a major influence on musicians and composers. His honors include his 1995 induction into the Rock and Roll Hall of Fame and the 1997 Grammy Lifetime Achievement Award. In 2000, he was ranked number 36 on VH1's 100 Greatest Artists of Hard Rock. In 2004, Rolling Stone magazine ranked him at number 71 on its list of the "100 Greatest Artists of All Time", and in 2011 at number 22 on its list of the "100 Greatest Guitarists of All Time".

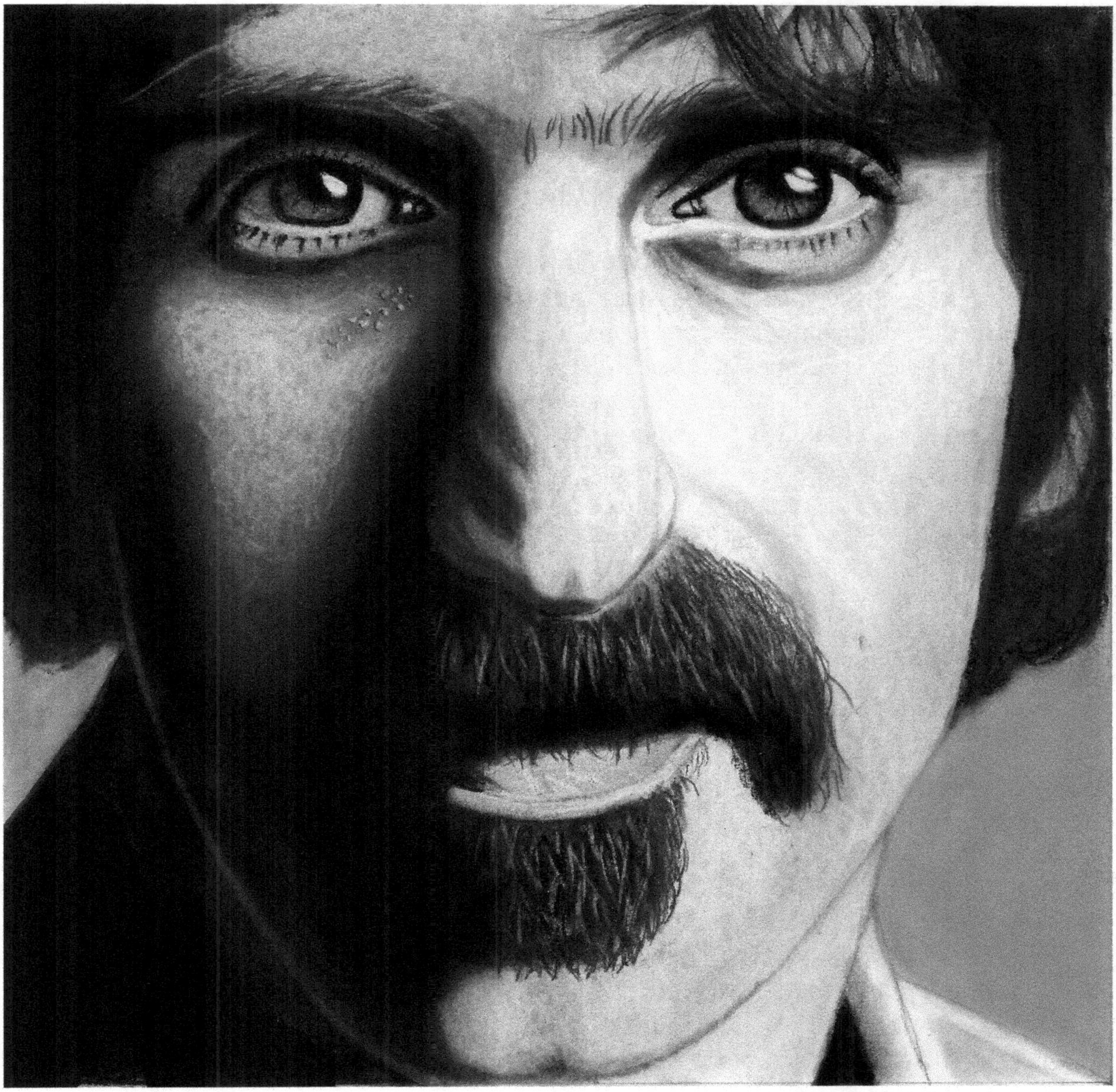

To view how this drawing was masterfully created or to purchase a Limited Edition Framed Artwork of Frank Zappa type into your Internet Browser the URL shortcut ➡ **myportrait.art/frankzappa**

To listen to his Greatest Songs type into your Internet Browser the URL shortcut ➡ **radio.surf/frankzappa**

To view all channels on THE FACE OF MUSIC Internet Radio MEGA Station type into your Internet Browser the URL shortcut ➡ **radio.surf/music**

To inquire about purchasing a Limited Edtion NFT of this portrait type into your Internet Browser the URL shortcut ➡ **myartnft.shop/frankzappa**

To view all available NFTs type into your Internet Browser the URL shortcut ➡ **myartnft.shop/all**

# Fugees

(Total Records Sold: 50 Million) (Genre: Hip-Hop)

Fugees (sometimes The Fugees) was an American hip hop group who rose to fame in the mid-1990s. Their repertoire included elements of hip hop, soul and Caribbean music, particularly reggae. The members of the group were Wyclef Jean, Lauryn Hill, and Pras Michel. Deriving their name from a shortening of the word "refugees", Jean and Michel are Haitian while Hill is American.Before disbanding in 1997, the group recorded two albums, one of which, The Score (1996), was a multi-Platinum and Grammy-winning success and contains their hit single "Killing Me Softly". Hill and Jean each went on to successful solo recording careers; Michel focused on soundtrack recordings and acting, though he found commercial success with his song "Ghetto Supastar". In 2007, MTV ranked them the ninth greatest hip-hop group of all time.

# Lauryn Hill

(Net Worth: $9 Million) (Height: 5' - 4")

Lauryn Noelle Hill (born May 26, 1975) is an American singer, rapper, songwriter, and record producer. She is often regarded as one of the greatest rappers of all time, as well as being one of the most influential singers of her generation. Hill is credited for breaking barriers for female rappers, popularizing melodic rapping and for bringing hip hop and neo soul to popular music. She is known for being a member of Fugees and her solo album The Miseducation of Lauryn Hill, which became one of the best-selling albums of all-time. Hill has won many awards, including eight Grammy Awards, the most for a female rapper.

Raised mostly in South Orange, New Jersey, Hill began singing with her music-oriented family during her childhood. She appeared in the 1993 film Sister Act 2: Back in the Habit alongside Whoopi Goldberg. In high school, Hill was approached by Pras Michel for a band he started, which his cousin Wyclef Jean soon joined. They renamed themselves the Fugees and released the albums Blunted on Reality (1994) and the Grammy Award-winning The Score (1996), which sold seven million copies in the U.S. Hill rose to prominence for her African-American and Caribbean music influences on her rapping and singing as well as her performance on the Fugees version of "Killing Me Softly". She began to focus on solo projects, writing and producing "A Rose Is Still a Rose" by Aretha Franklin, then featuring on the Grammy Award-nominated songs "If I Ruled the World (Imagine That)" by Nas and Guantanamera by Wyclef Jean. Her tumultuous romantic relationship with Jean led to the split of the band in 1997, after which she began work on her solo album.

The Miseducation of Lauryn Hill (1998) remains Hill's sole solo studio album. It received widespread critical acclaim for showcasing a representation of life and relationships and locating a contemporary voice within the neo soul genre. The album debuted at number one on the U.S. Billboard 200 and has sold approximately ten million copies there, being certified Diamond by the Recording Industry Association of America. This included the singles "Doo Wop (That Thing)", "Ex-Factor", and "Everything Is Everything". At the 41st Grammy Awards, the record earned her five awards, including Album of the Year and Best New Artist. During this time, she won several other awards and became a common sight on the cover of magazines.

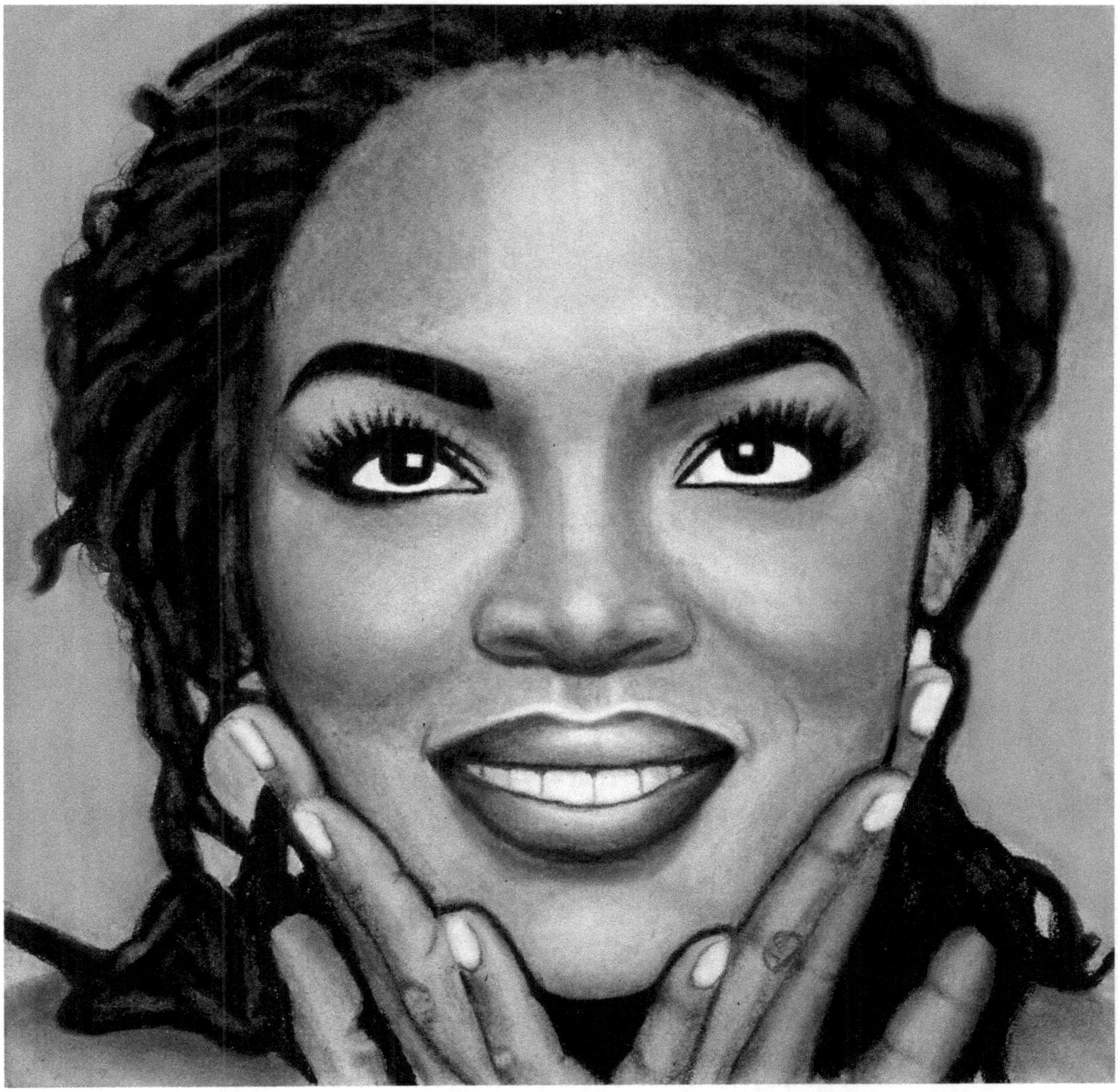

To view how this drawing was masterfully created or to purchase a Limited Edition Framed Artwork of Lauryn Hill type into your Internet Browser the URL shortcut ➡ **myportrait.art/laurynhill**

To listen to their Greatest Songs type into your Internet Browser the URL shortcut ➡ **radio.surf/fugees**

To view all channels on THE FACE OF MUSIC Internet Radio MEGA Station type into your Internet Browser the URL shortcut ➡ **radio.surf/music**

To inquire about purchasing a Limited Edition NFT of this portrait type into your Internet Browser the URL shortcut ➡ **myartnft.shop/laurynhill**

To view all available NFTs type into your Internet Browser the URL shortcut ➡ **myartnft.shop/all**

# Garth Brooks

(Net worth: $400 Million)(Total Records Sold: 170+Million)
(Genre: Country)(Height: 6' - 0")

Troyal Garth Brooks (born February 7, 1962) is an American singer and songwriter. His integration of rock and pop elements into the country genre has earned him popularity, particularly in the United States with success on the country music single and album charts, multi-platinum recordings and record-breaking live performances, while also crossing over into the mainstream pop arena.

As of 2020, Brooks is now the only artist in music history to have released nine albums that achieved diamond status in the United States (surpassing the Beatles' former record of six); those albums are Garth Brooks (diamond), No Fences (17× platinum), Ropin' the Wind (14× platinum), The Chase (diamond), In Pieces (diamond), The Hits (diamond), Sevens (diamond), Double Live (21× platinum), and The Ultimate Hits (diamond). Since 1989, Brooks has released 23 records in all, which include 13 studio albums, two live albums, three compilation albums, three Christmas albums and four box sets, along with 77 singles. He has won several awards in his career, including two Grammy Awards, 17 American Music Awards (including "Artist of the '90s") and the RIAA Award for best-selling solo albums artist of the century in the U.S.

Troubled by conflicts between career and family, Brooks retired from recording and performing from 2001 until 2005. During this time, he sold millions of albums through an exclusive distribution deal with Walmart and sporadically released new singles. In 2005, Brooks started a partial comeback, giving select performances and releasing two compilation albums. In 2009, he began Garth at Wynn, a periodic weekend concert residency at Las Vegas' Encore Theatre from December 2009 to January 2014. Following the conclusion of the residency, Brooks announced his signing with Sony Music Nashville in July 2014. In September 2014, he began his comeback world tour, with wife and musician Trisha Yearwood, which culminated in 2017. This was followed by his Stadium Tour, which began in 2019. His most recent album, Fun, was released in November 2020.

Brooks is one of the world's best-selling music artists, having sold more than 170 million records. As of 2020, according to the RIAA, he is the best-selling solo albums artist in the United States with 156 million domestic units sold, ahead of Elvis Presley, and is second only to the Beatles in total album sales overall. Brooks was inducted into the Country Music Hall of Fame on October 21, 2012, having been inducted into the Songwriters Hall of Fame the year before. He was also inducted into the Musicians Hall of Fame and Museum in 2016 with his studio musicians, The G-Men. On March 4, 2020, Brooks received the Library of Congress Gershwin Prize for Popular Song. At age 58, he is the youngest recipient of the award.

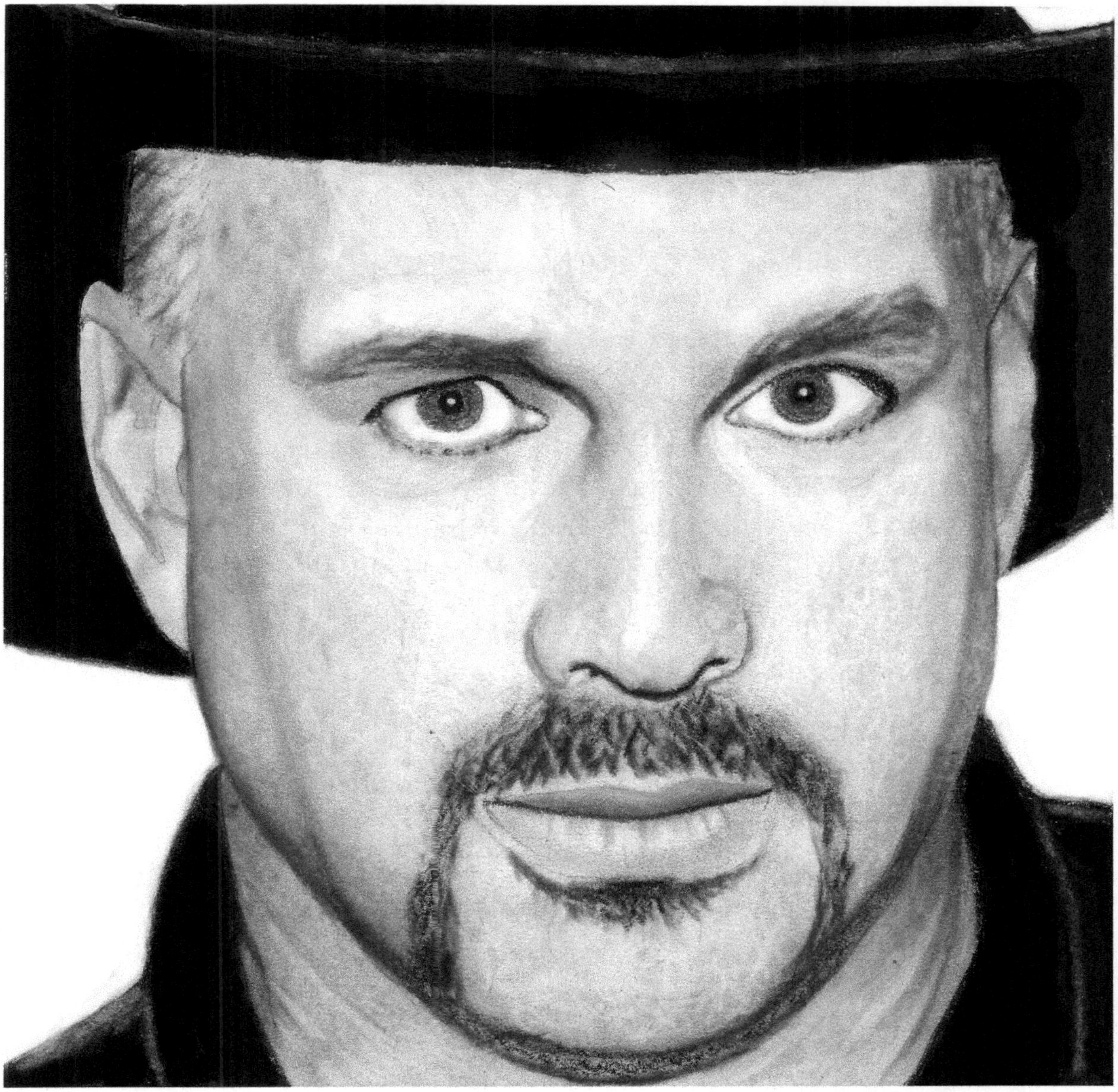

To view how this drawing was masterfully created or to purchase a Limited Edition Framed Artwork of Garth Brooks type into your Internet Browser the URL shortcut ➡ **myportrait.art/garthbrooks**

To listen to his Greatest Songs type into your Internet Browser the URL shortcut ➡ **radio.surf/garthbrooks**

To view all channels on THE FACE OF MUSIC Internet Radio MEGA Station type into your Internet Browser the URL shortcut ➡ **radio.surf/music**

To inquire about purchasing a Limited Edition NFT of this portrait type into your Internet Browser the URL shortcut ➡ **myartnft.shop/garthbrooks**

To view all available NFTs type into your Internet Browser the URL shortcut ➡ **myartnft.shop/all**

# Genesis

(Total Records Sold: 150 Million) (Genre: Progressive / Art Rock)
Genesis are an English rock band formed at Charterhouse School, Godalming, Surrey, in 1967. The band's most commercially successful line-up consists of keyboardist Tony Banks, bassist/guitarist Mike Rutherford and drummer/singer Phil Collins. The 1970s line-up featuring singer Peter Gabriel and guitarist Steve Hackett was among the pioneers of progressive rock.

With 150 million albums sold worldwide, Genesis are one of the world's best-selling music artists. Their discography includes 15 studio and six live albums. They have won numerous awards (including a Grammy Award for Best Concept Music Video with "Land of Confusion") and have inspired a number of tribute bands recreating Genesis shows from various stages of the band's career. In 2010, Genesis were inducted into the Rock and Roll Hall of Fame.

# Phil Collins

(Net Worth: $260 Million) (Height: 5' - 6")
Philip David Charles Collins (born 30 January 1951) is an English drummer, singer, songwriter, and record producer, best known as the drummer/singer of the rock band Genesis and for his solo career. Between 1982 and 1990, Collins achieved three UK and seven US number-one singles in his solo career. When his work with Genesis, his work with other artists, as well as his solo career is totalled, he had more US top 40 singles than any other artist during the 1980s. His most successful singles from the period include "In the Air Tonight", "I Don't Care Anymore", "Against All Odds (Take a Look at Me Now)", "One More Night", "Sussudio", "Take Me Home", "Two Hearts", "A Groovy Kind of Love", "I Wish It Would Rain Down", and "Another Day in Paradise".

Collins's discography includes eight studio albums that have sold 33.5 million certified units in the US and an estimated 150 million records sold worldwide, making him one of the world's best-selling artists. He is one of only three recording artists, along with Paul McCartney and Michael Jackson, who have sold over 100 million records both as solo artists and separately as principal members of a band. He has won eight Grammy Awards, six Brit Awards (winning Best British Male Artist three times), two Golden Globe Awards, one Academy Award, and a Disney Legend Award. He was awarded six Ivor Novello Awards from the British Academy of Songwriters, Composers and Authors, including the International Achievement Award. He received a star on the Hollywood Walk of Fame in 1999, and was inducted into the Songwriters Hall of Fame in 2003 and the Rock and Roll Hall of Fame as a member of Genesis in 2010. He has also been recognised by music publications with induction into the Modern Drummer
Hall of Fame in 2012, and the Classic Drummer Hall of Fame in 2013.

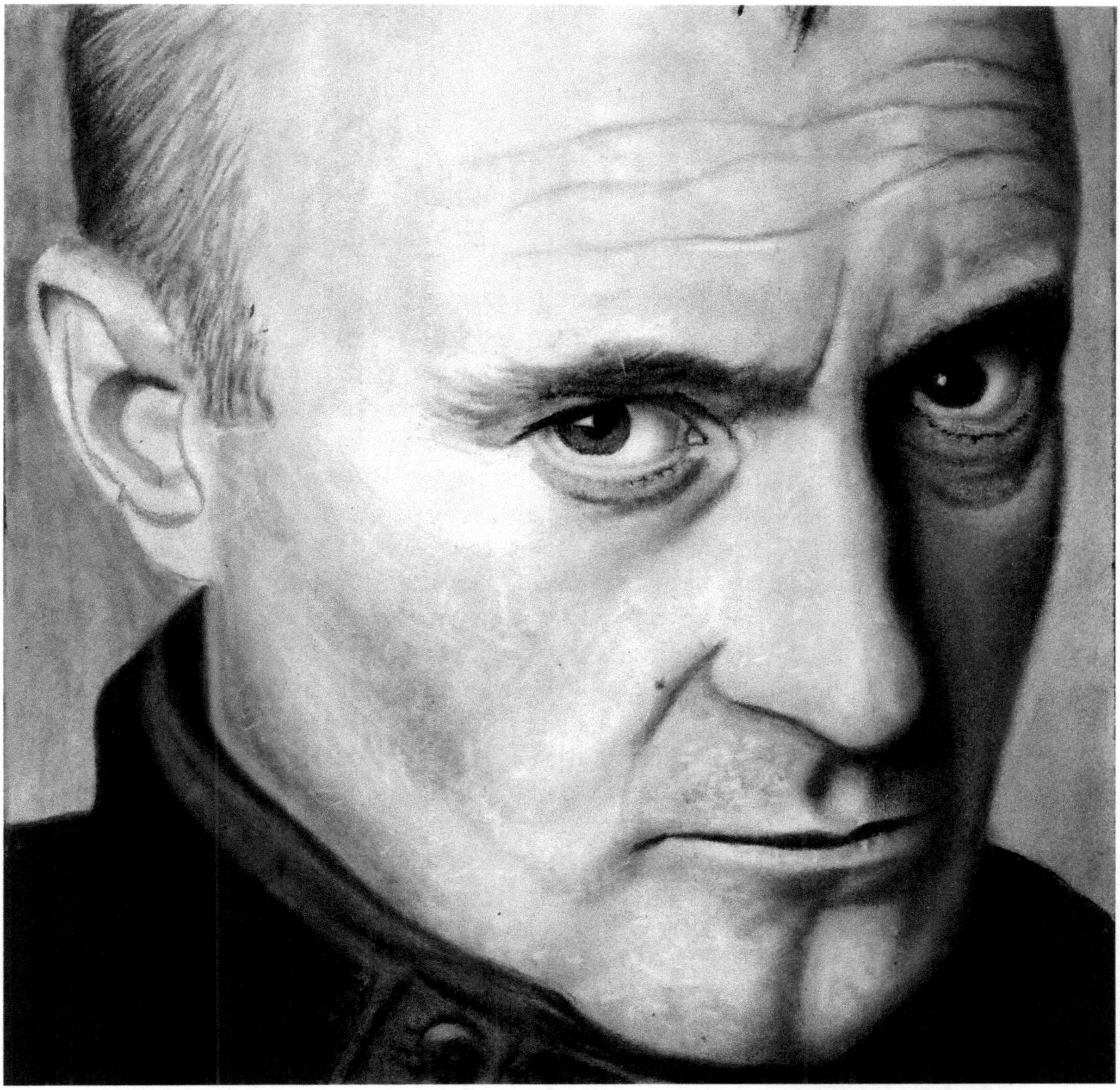

To view how this drawing was masterfully created or to purchase a Limited Edition Framed Artwork of Phil Collins type into your Internet Browser the URL shortcut ➡ **myportrait.art/philcollins**

To listen to Genesis's Greatest Songs type into your Internet Browser the URL shortcut ➡ **radio.surf/genesis**

To listen to Phil Collins Greatest Songs type into your Internet Browser the URL shortcut
➡ **radio.surf/philcollins**

To view all channels on THE FACE OF MUSIC Internet Radio MEGA Station type into your Internet Browser the URL shortcut ➡ **radio.surf/music**

To inquire about purchasing a Limited Edition NFT of this portrait type into your Internet Browser the URL shortcut ➡ **myartnft.shop/philcollins**

To view all available NFTs type into your Internet Browser the URL shortcut ➡ **myartnft.shop/all**

# George Jones

(Net worth: $35 Million)(Total Records Sold: Millions)
(Genre: Country)(Height: 5' - 7")

George Glenn Jones (September 12, 1931 – April 26, 2013) was an American musician, singer, and songwriter. He achieved international fame for his long list of hit records, including his best-known song "He Stopped Loving Her Today", as well as his distinctive voice and phrasing. For the last two decades of his life, Jones was frequently referred to as the greatest living country singer. Country music scholar Bill Malone writes, "For the two or three minutes consumed by a song, Jones immerses himself so completely in its lyrics, and in the mood it conveys, that the listener can scarcely avoid becoming similarly involved." Waylon Jennings expressed a similar opinion in his song "It's Alright": "If we all could sound like we wanted to, we'd all sound like George Jones." The shape of his nose and facial features earned Jones the nickname "The Possum".

Born in Texas, Jones first heard country music when he was seven, and was given a guitar at the age of nine. He married his first wife, Dorothy Bonvillion, in 1950, and was divorced in 1951. He served in the United States Marine Corps and was discharged in 1953. He married Shirley Ann Corley in 1954. In 1959, Jones recorded "White Lightning", written by J. P. Richardson, which launched his career as a singer. His second marriage ended in divorce in 1968; he married fellow country music singer Tammy Wynette a year later. Years of alcoholism compromised his health and led to his missing many performances, earning him the nickname "No Show Jones". After his divorce from Wynette in 1975, Jones married his fourth wife, Nancy Sepulvado, in 1983 and became sober for good in 1999. Jones died in 2013, aged 81, from hypoxic respiratory failure.

George Jones has been called "The Rolls Royce Of Country Music" and had more than 160 chart singles to his name from 1955 until his death in 2013. Johnny Cash once said, "When people ask me who my favorite country singer is, I say, 'You mean besides George Jones?'"

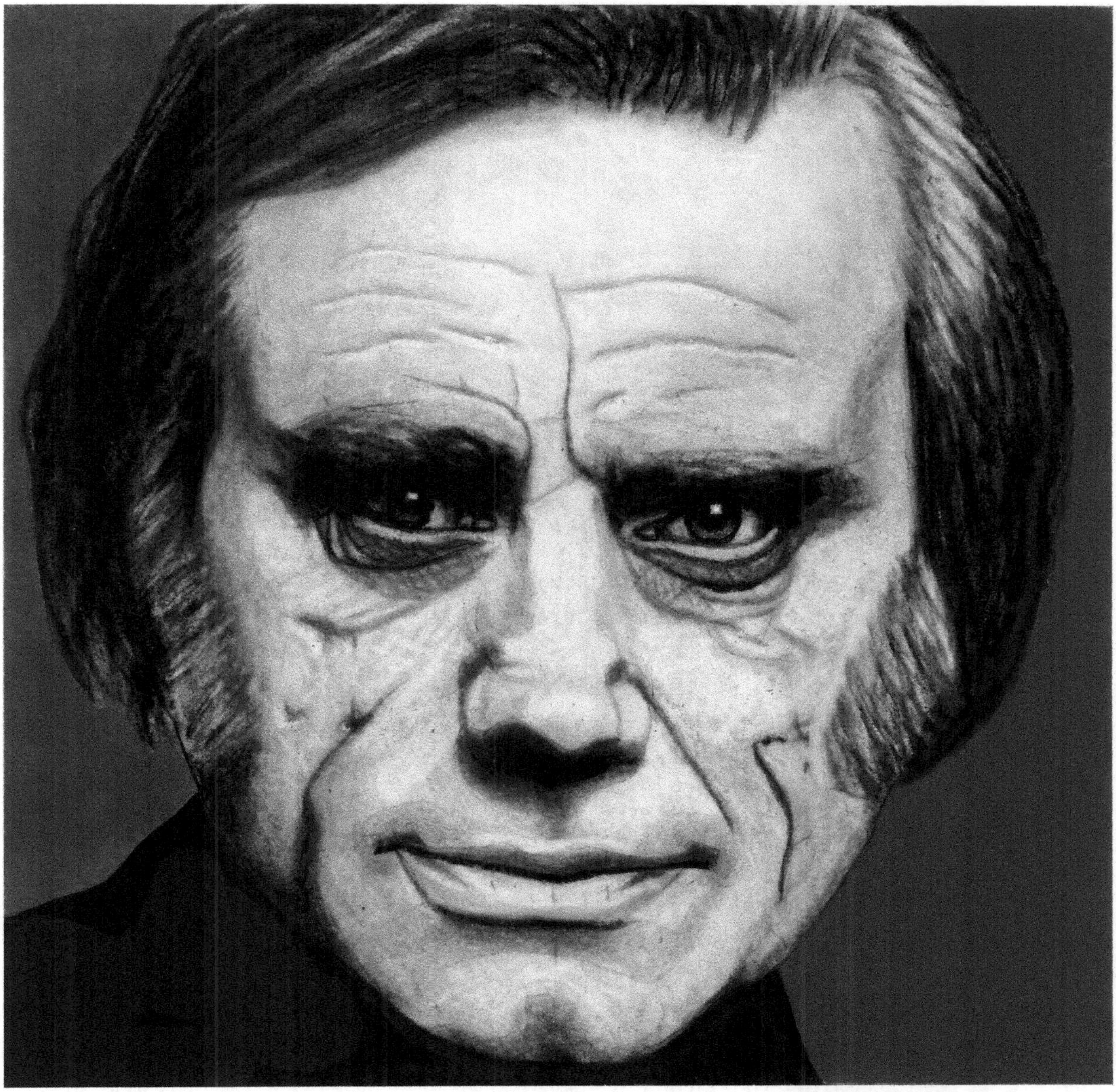

To view how this drawing was masterfully created or to purchase a Limited Edition Framed Artwork of George Jones type into your Internet Browser the URL shortcut ➡ **myportrait.art/georgejones**

To listen to his Greatest Songs type into your Internet Browser the URL shortcut ➡ **radio.surf/georgejones**

To view all channels on THE FACE OF MUSIC Internet Radio MEGA Station type into your Internet Browser the URL shortcut ➡ **radio.surf/music**

To inquire about purchasing a Limited Edtion NFT of this portrait type into your Internet Browser the URL shortcut ➡ **myartnft.shop/georgejones**

To view all available NFTs type into your Internet Browser the URL shortcut ➡ **myartnft.shop/all**

# George Michael

(Net worth: $200 Million)(Total Records Sold: 115 Million)
(Genre: Pop , R&B)(Height: 6' - 0")

George Michael (born Georgios Kyriacos Panayiotou; 25 June 1963 – 25 December 2016) was an English singer, songwriter, record producer, and philanthropist who rose to fame as a member of the music duo Wham! and later embarked on a solo career. At the time of his death, Michael had sold over 115 million records worldwide, making him one of the best-selling music artists of all time. He achieved seven number-one songs on the UK Singles Chart and eight number-one songs on the US Billboard Hot 100. Michael won various music awards, including two Grammy Awards, three Brit Awards, three American Music Awards, 12 Billboard Music Awards, four MTV Video Music Awards, and six Ivor Novello Awards. In 2008, he was ranked 40th on Billboard's list of the Greatest Hot 100 Artists of All Time.

Born in East Finchley, Michael formed the duo Wham! with Andrew Ridgeley in 1981. The band's first two albums, Fantastic (1983) and Make It Big (1984), reached number one on the UK Albums Chart and the US Billboard 200. Their hit singles included "Wake Me Up Before You Go-Go" and "Last Christmas". Certifying themselves as a global act, Wham!'s tour of China in April 1985 was the first visit to China by a Western popular music act, and generated worldwide media coverage. Michael's first solo single, "Careless Whisper", reached number one in over 20 countries, including the UK and US. His debut solo album, Faith, was released in 1987, topping the UK Albums Chart and staying at number one on the Billboard 200 for 12 weeks. Four singles from the album—"Faith", "Father Figure", "One More Try", and "Monkey"—reached number one on the Billboard Hot 100. Faith was awarded Album of the Year at the 1989 Grammy Awards. Listen Without Prejudice Vol. 1 (1990) was a UK number-one and included the Billboard Hot 100 number-one "Praying for Time". "Don't Let the Sun Go Down on Me", a 1991 duet with Elton John, was also a transatlantic number one. Michael went on to release the albums Older (1996), Songs from the Last Century (1999) and Patience (2004). In 2004, the Radio Academy named him the most played artist on British radio during the period 1984–2004.

Michael, who came out as gay in 1998, was an active LGBT rights campaigner and HIV/AIDS charity fundraiser. Michael's personal life and legal troubles made headlines during the late 1990s and 2000s, as he was arrested for public lewdness in 1998 and was arrested for multiple drug-related offences after that time. The 2005 documentary A Different Story covered his career and personal life. Michael's first tour since 1991, the 25 Live tour, spanned three tours over the course of three years: 2006, 2007, and 2008. Four years later, he performed his final concert at London's Earls Court in 2012. In the early hours of 25 December 2016, Michael was found dead at his home in Goring-on-Thames, Oxfordshire, aged 53. A coroner's report attributed his death to natural causes.

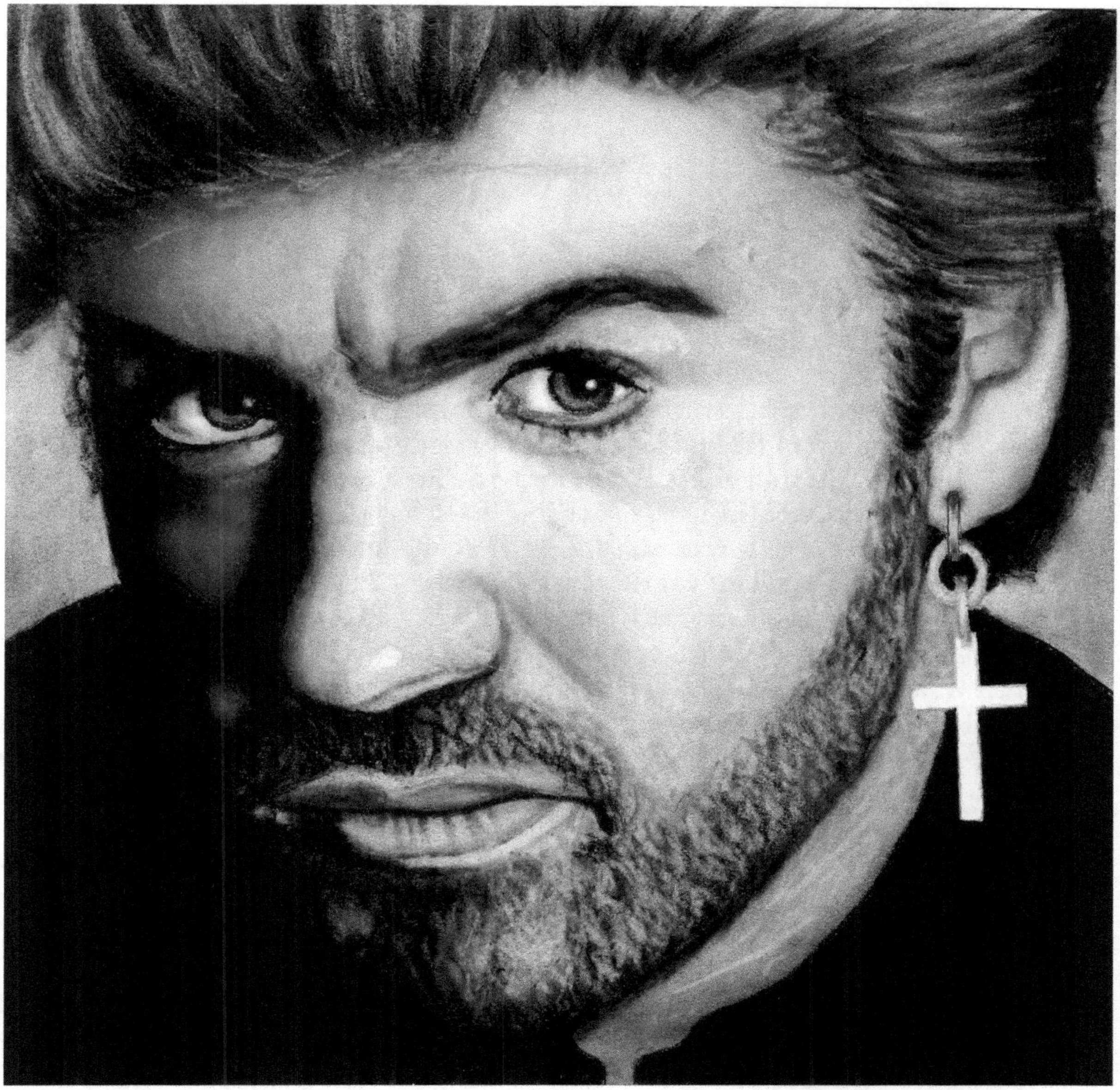

To view how this drawing was masterfully created or to purchase a Limited Edition Framed Artwork of George Michael type into your Internet Browser the URL shortcut ➡ **myportrait.art/georgemichael**

To listen to his Greatest Songs type into your Internet Browser the URL shortcut
➡ **radio.surf/georgemichael**

To view all channels on THE FACE OF MUSIC Internet Radio MEGA Station type into your Internet Browser the URL shortcut ➡ **radio.surf/music**

To inquire about purchasing a Limited Edtion NFT of this portrait type into your Internet Browser the URL shortcut ➡ **myartnft.shop/georgemichael**

To view all available NFTs type into your Internet Browser the URL shortcut ➡ **myartnft.shop/all**

# George Strait

(Net worth: $300 Million)(Total Records Sold: 100+ Million)
(Genre: Country)(Height: 5' - 10")

George Harvey Strait Sr. (born May 18, 1952) is an American country music singer, songwriter, actor, and music producer. George Strait is known as the "King of Country" and is considered one of the most influential and popular recording artists of all time. He is known for his neotraditionalist country style, cowboy look, and being one of the first and most prominent country artists to bring country music back to its roots and away from the pop country era in the 1980s.

Strait's success began when his first single "Unwound" was a hit in 1980. During the 1980s, seven of his albums reached number one on the country charts. In the 2000s, Strait was named Artist of the Decade by the Academy of Country Music, was elected into the Country Music Hall of Fame, and won his first Grammy award for the album Troubadour. Strait was named CMA Entertainer of the Year in 1989, 1990 and 2013, and ACM Entertainer of the Year in 1990 and 2014. He has been nominated for more CMA and ACM awards and has more wins in both categories than any other artist.

By 2009, he broke Conway Twitty's previous record for the most number-one hits on Billboard's Hot Country Songs chart when his 44 number one singles surpassed Twitty's 40. Counting all music charts, Strait has amassed a total of 60 number-one hits, breaking a record also previously set by Twitty, giving him more number one songs than any other artist in any genre of music.

Strait is also known for his touring career when he designed a 360-degree configuration and introduced festival style tours. For example, the Strait Tours earned $99 million in three years. His concert at AT&T Stadium in Arlington, Texas, in June 2014 drew 104,793 people, marking a new record for largest indoor concert in North America.

Strait has sold more than 100 million records worldwide, making him one of the best-selling music artists of all time. His certifications from the RIAA include 13 multi-platinum, 33 platinum, and 38 gold albums. His best-selling album is Pure Country (1992), which sold 6 million (6× platinum). His highest certified album is Strait Out of the Box (1995), which sold 2 million copies (8× Platinum due to being a box set with four CDs). According to the RIAA, Strait is the 12th best-selling album recording artist in the United States overall.

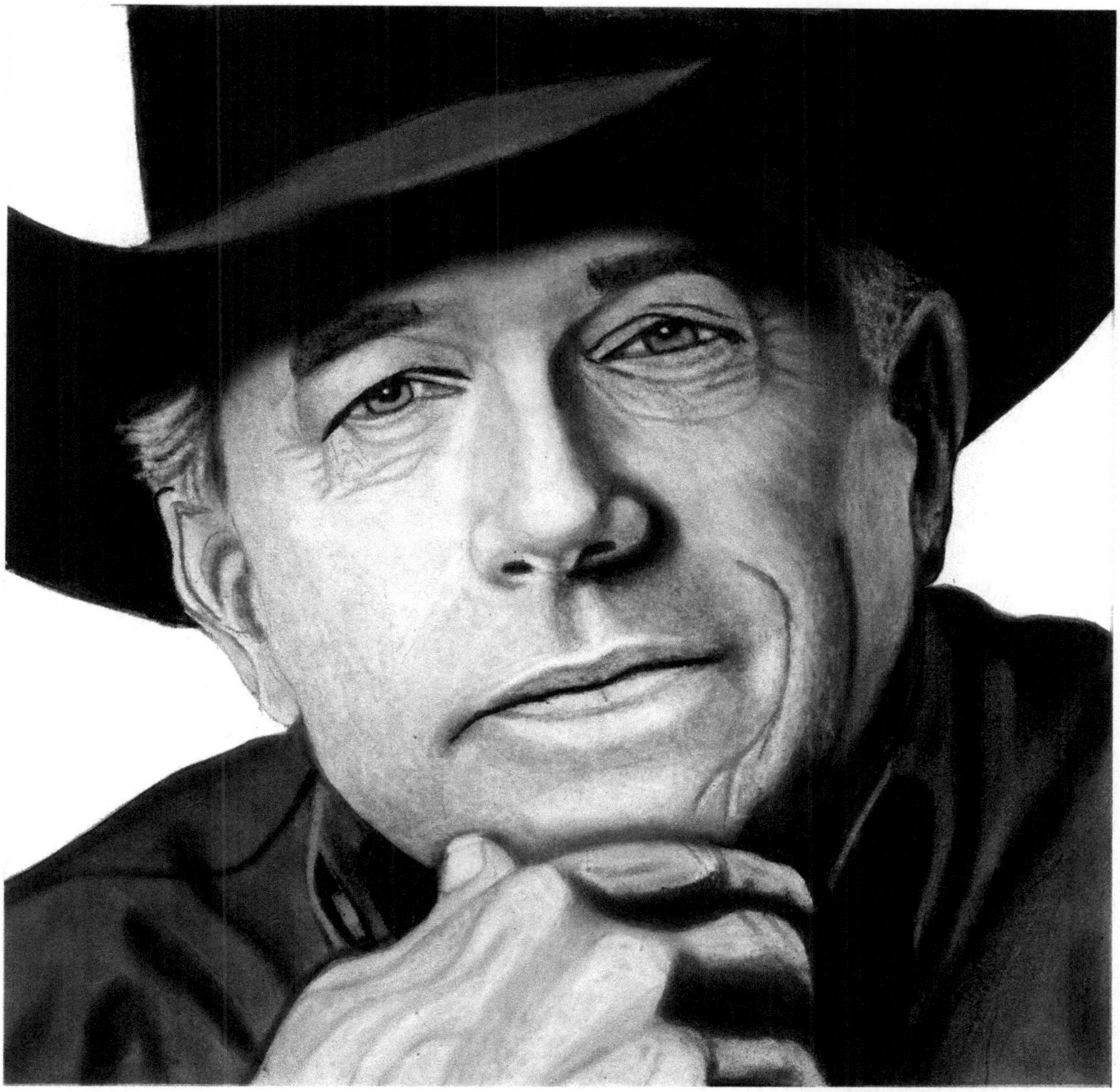

To view how this drawing was masterfully created or to purchase a Limited Edition Framed Artwork of George Strait type into your Internet Browser the URL shortcut ➡ **myportrait.art/georgestrait**

To listen to his Greatest Songs type into your Internet Browser the URL shortcut ➡ **radio.surf/georgestrait**

To view all channels on THE FACE OF MUSIC Internet Radio MEGA Station type into your Internet Browser the URL shortcut ➡ **radio.surf/music**

To inquire about purchasing a Limited Edtion NFT of this portrait type into your Internet Browser the URL shortcut ➡ **myartnft.shop/georgestrait**

To view all available NFTs type into your Internet Browser the URL shortcut ➡ **myartnft.shop/all**

# George Thorogood

(Net worth: $60 Million)(Total Albums Sold: 15 Million)
(Genre: Blues Rock , Rock & Roll)(Height: 6' - 1")

George Lawrence Thorogood (born February 24, 1950) is an American musician, singer and songwriter from Wilmington, Delaware. His "high-energy boogie-blues" sound became a staple of 1980s rock radio, with hits like his original songs "Bad to the Bone" and "I Drink Alone". He has also helped to popularize older songs by American icons, such as "Move It on Over", "Who Do You Love?", and "House Rent Blues/One Bourbon, One Scotch, One Beer".

With his band, the Destroyers, Thorogood has released over 20 albums, of which two have been certified Platinum and six have been certified Gold. He has sold 15 million albums worldwide. Thorogood and band continue to tour extensively, and in 2014 the band celebrated their 40th anniversary of performing.

Thorogood began his career as a solo acoustic performer in the style of Robert Johnson and Elmore James after being inspired in 1970 by a John P. Hammond concert. In 1973, he formed a band, the Delaware Destroyers, with high school friend and drummer Jeff Simon. With additional players, the Delaware Destroyers developed its sound, a mixture of Chicago blues and rock and roll. The band's first shows were in the Rathskeller bar at the University of Delaware and at Deer Park Tavern, both in Newark, Delaware. Eventually, the band's name was shortened to the Destroyers. During this time, Thorogood supplemented his income by working as a roadie for Hound Dog Taylor.

Thorogood gained his first mainstream exposure as a support act for the Rolling Stones during their 1981 U.S. tour. He was also the featured musical guest on Saturday Night Live (Season 8, Episode 2) on the October 2, 1982, broadcast. During this time, Thorogood and the Destroyers became known for their rigorous touring schedule, including the "50/50" tour in 1981, on which the band toured all 50 US states in 50 days. After two shows in Boulder, Colorado, Thorogood and his band flew to Hawaii for one show and then performed a show in Alaska the following night. The next day, Thorogood and his band met his roadies in Washington and continued the one-show-per-state tour. In addition, he played Washington, D.C. on the same day that he performed a show in Maryland, thereby playing 51 shows in 50 days.

Thorogood's popularity waned in the 1990s, although he had a No. 2 hit on the Billboard Album Rock Tracks chart in 1992 with "Get a Haircut".

In 2012, Thorogood was named one of the "50 Most Influential Delawareans of the Past 50 Years". He released his first proper solo album in 2017 titled Party of One..

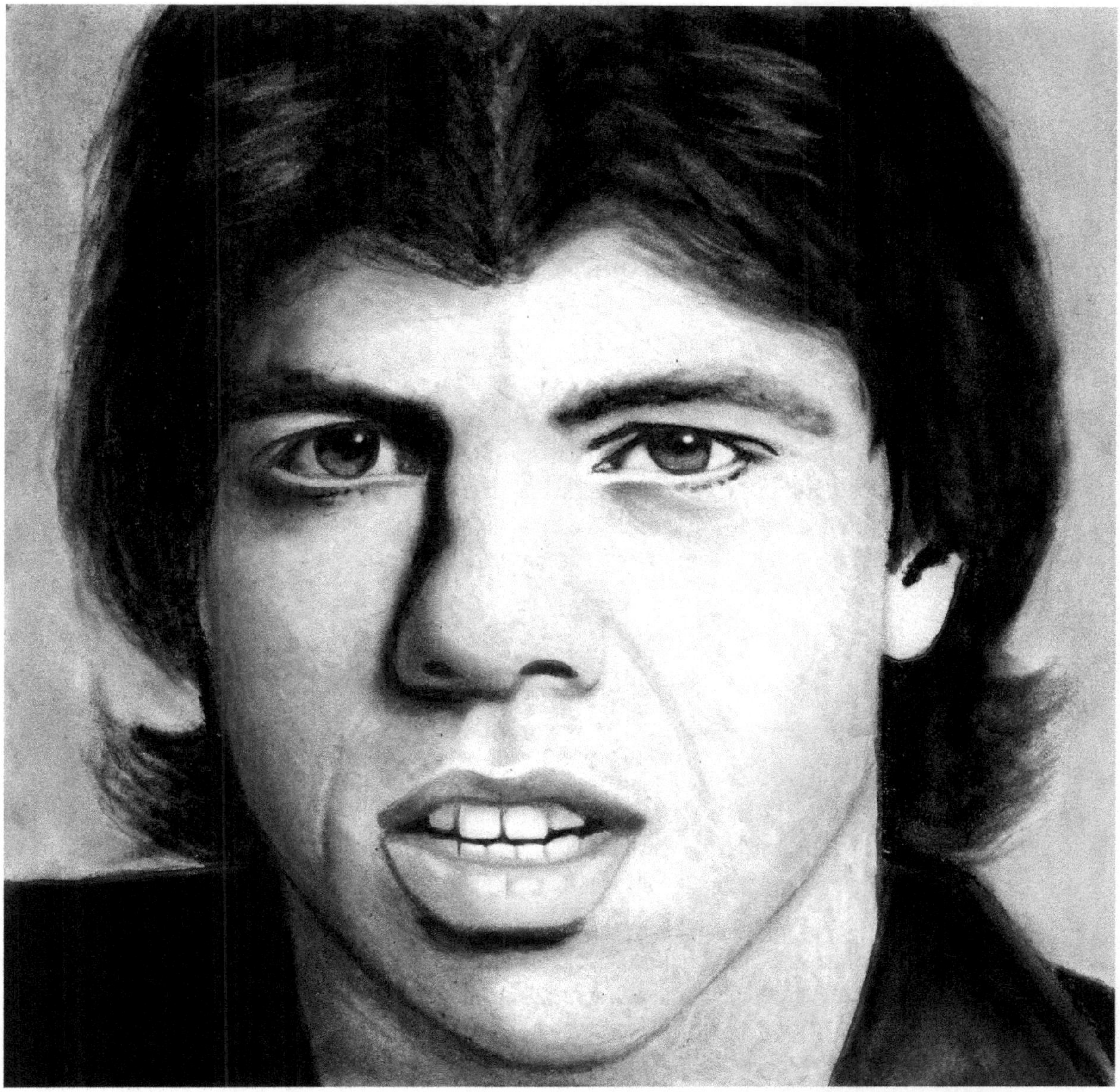

To view how this drawing was masterfully created or to purchase a Limited Edition Framed Artwork of George Thorogood type into your Internet Browser the URL shortcut ➡ **myportrait.art/georgethorogood**

To listen to his Greatest Songs type into your Internet Browser the URL shortcut
➡ **radio.surf/georgethorogood**

To view all channels on THE FACE OF MUSIC Internet Radio MEGA Station type into your Internet Browser the URL shortcut ➡ **radio.surf/music**

To inquire about purchasing a Limited Edtion NFT of this portrait type into your Internet Browser the URL shortcut ➡ **myartnft.shop/georgethorogood**

To view all available NFTs type into your Internet Browser the URL shortcut ➡ **myartnft.shop/all**

# Geto Boys

(Total Records Sold: Millions) (Genre: Southern Hip-Hop)

The Geto Boys (originally spelled Ghetto Boys) were an American hip hop group originally formed in Houston, Texas. The group was formed in 1987. The Geto Boys enjoyed success in the 1990s with the group's classic lineup consisting of Bushwick Bill, Scarface and Willie D, earning several certified albums and hit singles, including "Mind Playing Tricks on Me" which reached No. 1 on the Hot Rap Songs and #23 on the Billboard Hot 100.

The Geto Boys earned notoriety for lyrics covering controversial topics such as misogyny, gore, psychotic experiences, and necrophilia. About.com ranked the Geto Boys No. 10 on its list of the 25 Best Rap Groups of All-Time, describing them as "southern rap pioneers who paved the way for future southern hip-hop acts."

# Scarface

(Net Worth: $100 Thousand) (Height: 5' - 9")

Brad Terrence Jordan (born November 9, 1970), better known by his stage name Scarface, is an American rapper, record producer, and politician, best known as a member of the Geto Boys, a hip hop group from Houston, Texas. He grew up in Houston and is originally from the city's South Acres (Crestmont Park) neighborhood. In 2012, The Source ranked him #16 on their list of the Top 50 Lyricists of All Time, while About.com ranked him #6 on its list of the 50 Greatest MCs of Our Time (1987–2007) Scarface attended Woodson Middle School in Houston, Texas. He dropped out of high school and worked as a drug dealer. As a teenager, he attempted suicide, and subsequently spent time in a hospital psychiatric ward. He was brought up as a Christian, and converted to Islam in 2006.

He began his career as DJ Akshen (pronounced Action) recording and deejaying for Lil' Troy's Short Stop, a local record label in Houston. After releasing the 12" single "Scarface/ Another Head Put To Rest" (1989), written by Chris "Mr. 3-2" Barriere and produced by Def Jam Blaster, Bruce "Grim" Rhodes, he would go on to sign with Rap-A-Lot and join a group who were collectively known as Geto Boys replacing a member who left, and released the group's second album Grip It! On That Other Level (1989), a highly successful album that garnered the group a large fanbase, in spite of their violent lyrics keeping them from radio and MTV. He took his stage name from the 1983 film Scarface.

In 1992, Scarface appeared (along with Bushwick Bill) on the Kool G Rap & DJ Polo album Live and Let Die.The album Mr. Scarface Is Back was a success, and Scarface's popularity soon overshadowed the other Geto Boys. Scarface remained in the group while releasing a series of solo albums that kept him in the public view with increasing sales, making him the only Geto Boys member that has always remained with the group since the group personnel was revamped in 1989. This peaked with The Diary and The Last of a Dying Breed, the latter of which received positive reviews and sales, and earned him Lyricist of the Year at the 2001 Source Awards.

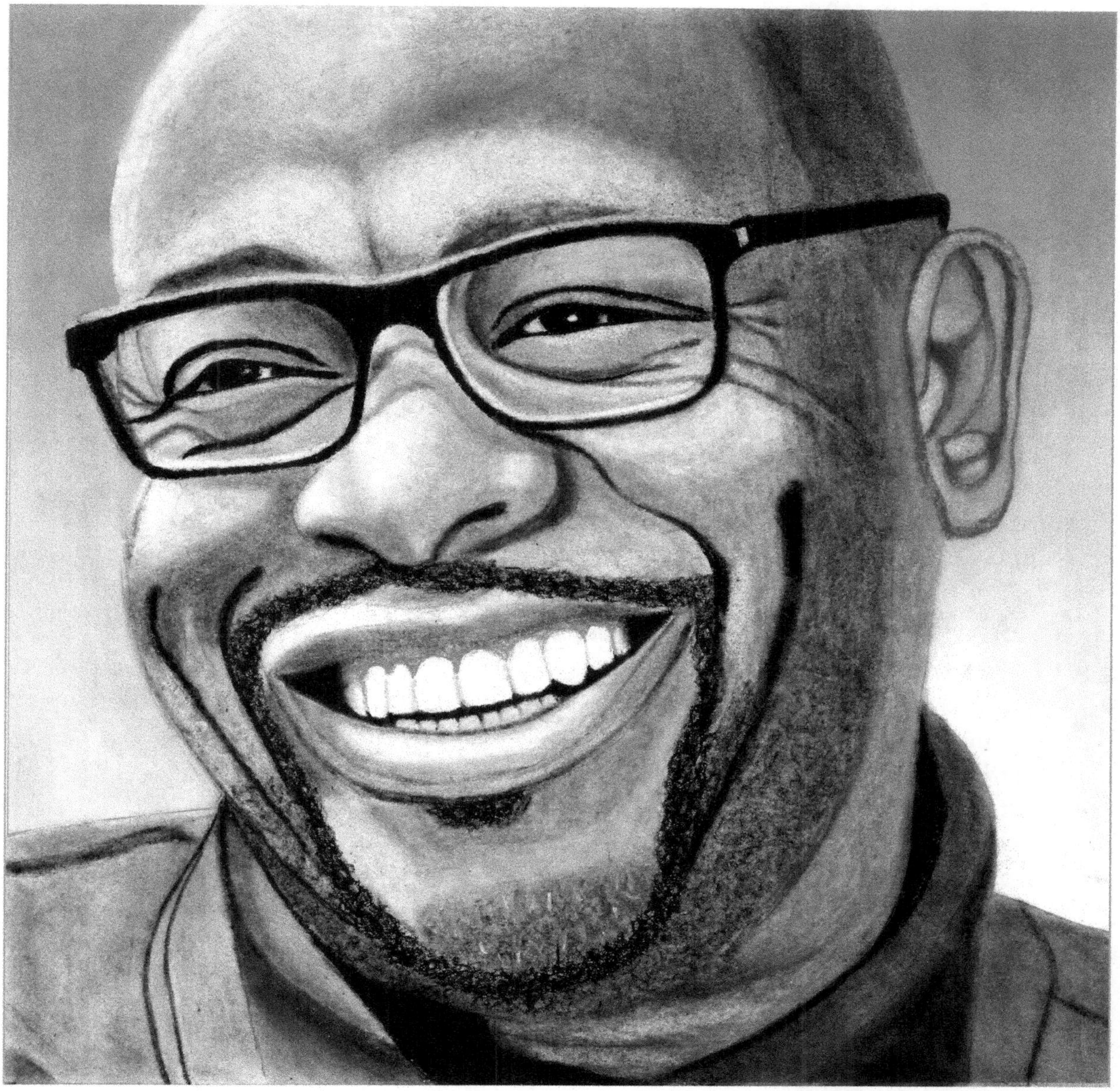

To view how this drawing was masterfully created or to purchase a Limited Edition Framed Artwork of Scareface type into your Internet Browser the URL shortcut ➡ **myportrait.art/scareface**

To listen to their Greatest Songs type into your Internet Browser the URL shortcut ➡ **radio.surf/getoboys**

To view all channels on THE FACE OF MUSIC Internet Radio MEGA Station type into your Internet Browser the URL shortcut ➡ **radio.surf/music**

To inquire about purchasing a Limited Edition NFT of this portrait type into your Internet Browser the URL shortcut ➡ **myartnft.shop/scareface**

To view all available NFTs type into your Internet Browser the URL shortcut ➡ **myartnft.shop/all**

# Ghostface Killah

(Net worth: $17 Million)(Total Albums Sold: 7 Million)
(Genre: Hip-Hop)(Height: 6' - 2 1/2")

Dennis Coles (born May 9, 1970), better known by his stage name Ghostface Killah, is an American rapper, songwriter and actor and lead member of the hip hop group Wu-Tang Clan. After the group achieved breakthrough success in the aftermath of Enter the Wu-Tang (36 Chambers), the members went on to pursue solo careers to varying levels of success. Ghostface Killah debuted his solo career with Ironman, which was well received by music critics, in 1996. He has enjoyed continued success in the years that have followed, releasing critically acclaimed albums such as Supreme Clientele (2000) and Fishscale (2006). His stage name was taken from one of the characters in the 1979 kung fu film Mystery of Chessboxing. He is the founder of his own record label, Starks Enterprises.

Ghostface Killah is critically acclaimed for his loud, fast-paced flow, and his emotional stream-of-consciousness narratives containing cryptic slang and non-sequiturs. In 2006, MTV included him as an "honourable mention" on their list of the "Greatest MCs of All Time", while the editors of About.com placed him on their list of the "Top 50 MCs of Our Time (1987–2007)", calling him "one of the most imaginative storytellers of our time." Q magazine called him "rap's finest storyteller." Pitchfork Media has stated that "Ghostface has unparalleled storytelling instincts; he might be the best, most colorful storyteller rap has ever seen." NPR has called him "a compulsive storyteller", and asserts that "his fiction is painterly."

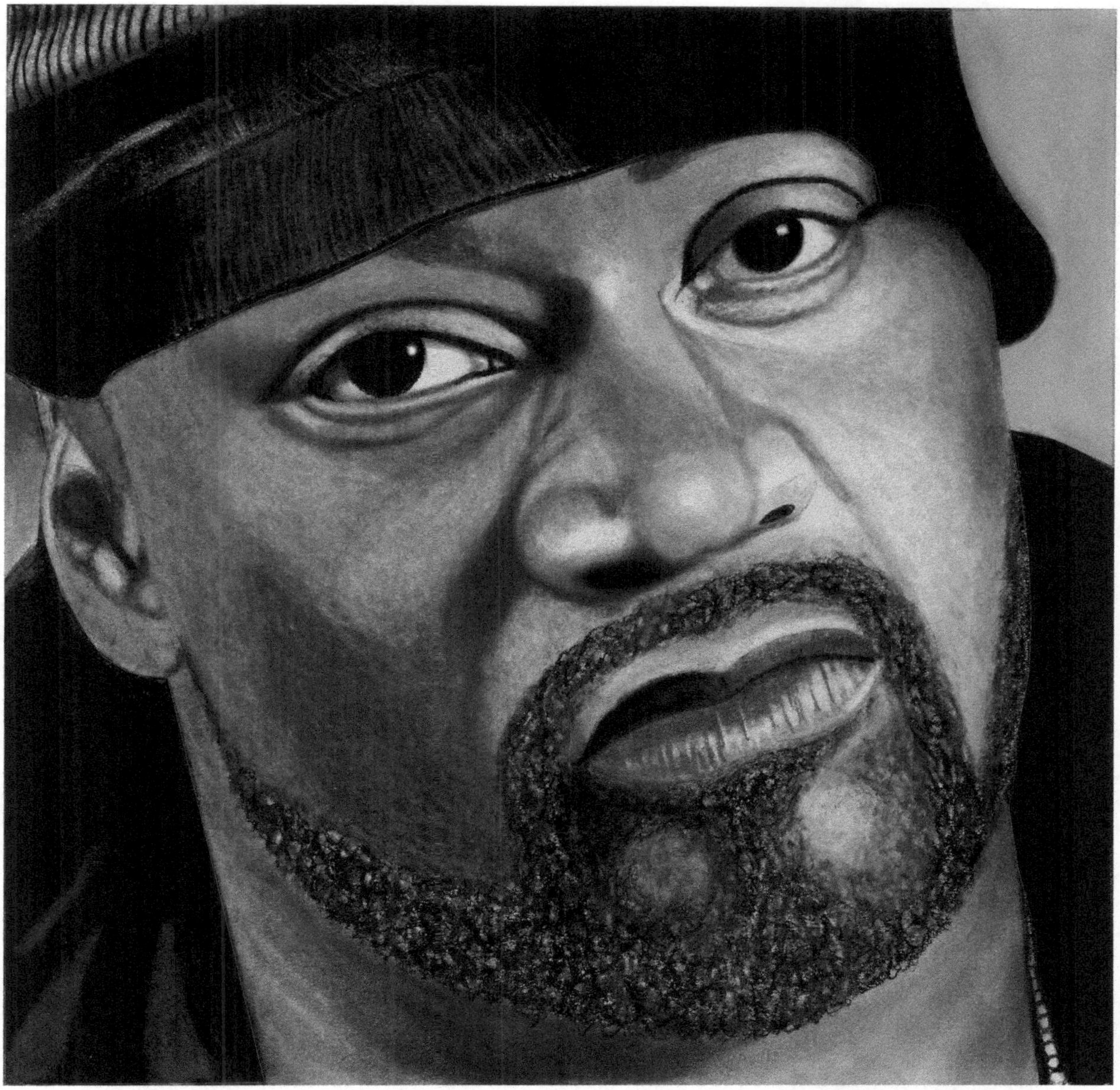

To view how this drawing was masterfully created or to purchase a Limited Edition Framed Artwork of Ghostface Killah type into your Internet Browser the URL shortcut ➡ **myportrait.art/ghostfacekillah**

To listen to his Greatest Songs type into your Internet Browser the URL shortcut
➡ **radio.surf/ghostfacekillah**

To view all channels on THE FACE OF MUSIC Internet Radio MEGA Station type into your Internet Browser the URL shortcut ➡ **radio.surf/music**

To inquire about purchasing a Limited Edition NFT of this portrait type into your Internet Browser the URL shortcut ➡ **myartnft.shop/ghostfacekillah**

To view all available NFTs type into your Internet Browser the URL shortcut ➡ **myartnft.shop/all**

# Gladys Knight & the Pips

(Total Records Sold: Millions) (Genre: R&B, Soul)

Gladys Knight & the Pips were an American R&B/soul/funk family music group from Atlanta, Georgia, that remained active on the music charts and performing circuit for over three decades.Starting out as simply The Pips in 1952, derived from a cousin's nickname, the founding members were Gladys Knight, brother Merald "Bubba" Knight, sister Brenda Knight and cousins Eleanor and William Guest. After a couple of years performing in talent shows, the group signed with Brunswick Records in 1957, recording a couple of singles that failed to chart. Brenda Knight and Eleanor Guest eventually left the group and were replaced by another cousin, Edward Patten and a non-relative, Langston George in 1959. This lineup produced the group's first hit single, "Every Beat of My Heart". After the single was released on three different labels, they changed their name to Gladys Knight & the Pips in 1961. Langston George left the same year and Gladys Knight left in 1962 to start a family with musician Jimmy Newman. Knight rejoined in 1964 and this lineup continued until the group's disbandment in 1989.The group reached commercial success after signing with Motown Records in 1966. After a year and a half, the group recorded the first hit single version of "I Heard It Through the Grapevine" in 1967, which led to several hit singles for Motown's Soul Records label, including "Nitty Gritty", "Friendship Train", "If I Were Your Woman", "I Don't Want to Do Wrong" and the Grammy-winning "Neither One of Us (Wants to Be the First to Say Goodbye)", before leaving the label for Buddah Records in 1973. At Buddah, they recorded the hits "Best Thing That Ever Happened to Me", "I've Got to Use My Imagination", "I Feel a Song (In My Heart)" and their Grammy-winning and number-one hit single, "Midnight Train to Georgia". In 1974, they recorded the soundtrack to the successful film Claudine with producer Curtis Mayfield, which included the songs "On and On", "The Makings of You" and "Make Yours a Happy Home". Contractual difficulties with their labels forced the group to record side projects from 1977 until 1980 when they signed with Columbia Records. Later hits included "Landlord", "Save the Overtime (For Me)" and the Grammy-winning single "Love Overboard". In 1989, the group disbanded with the Pips retiring and Knight embarking on a successful solo career.Gladys Knight & the Pips are multiple Grammy and American Music Award winners and are inductees into the Rock and Roll Hall of Fame and the Vocal Group Hall of Fame in 1996 and 2001 respectively.

# Gladys Knight

(Net Worth: $28 Million) (Height: 5' - 3 1/2")

Gladys Maria Knight (born May 28, 1944), known as the "Empress of Soul", is an American singer, songwriter, actress, businesswoman, and author. A seven-time Grammy Award-winner, Knight is known for the hits she recorded during the 1960s, 1970s, and 1980s with her group Gladys Knight & the Pips, which also included her brother Merald "Bubba" Knight and cousins William Guest and Edward Patten.

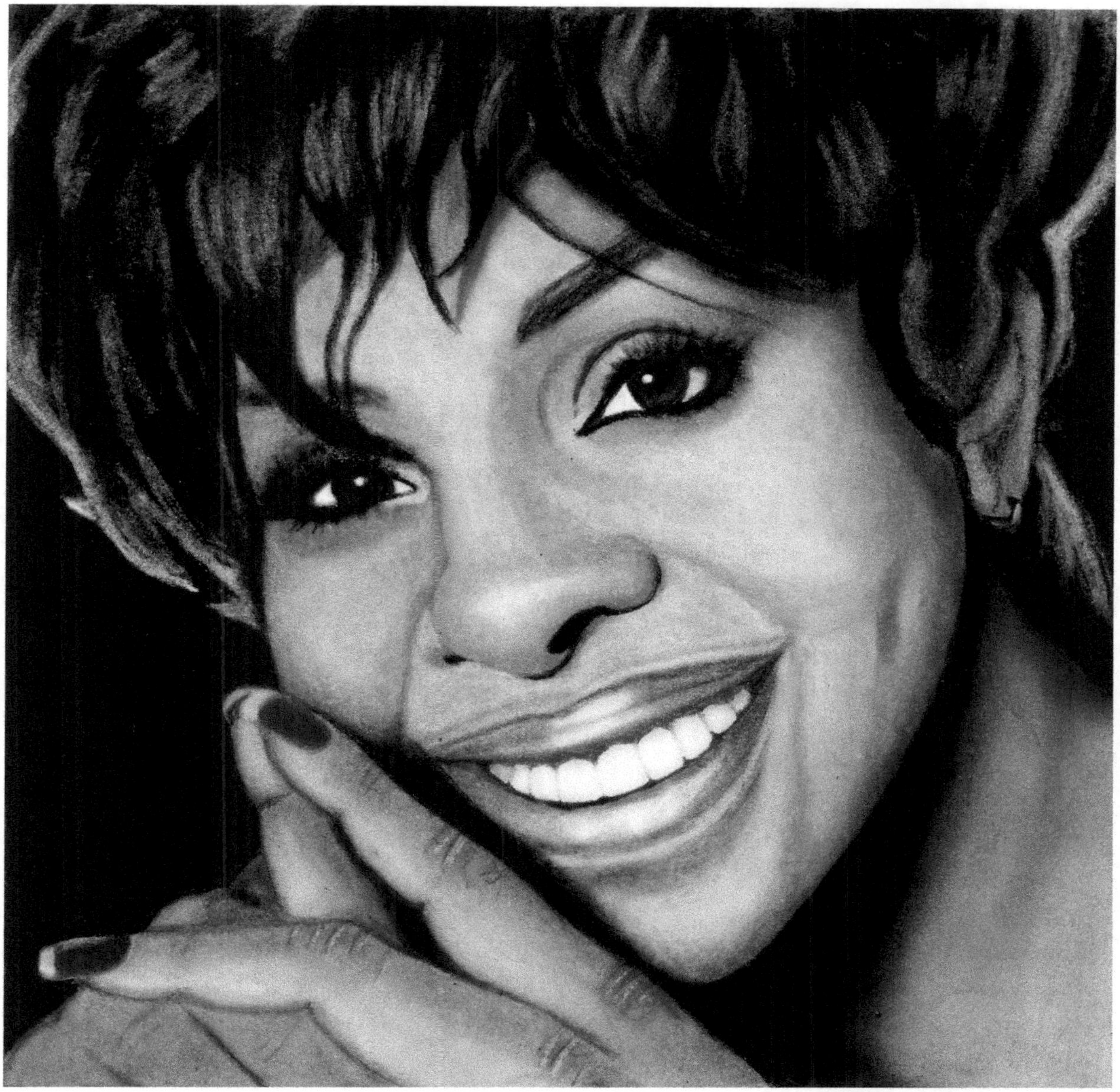

To view how this drawing was masterfully created or to purchase a Limited Edition Framed Artwork of Gladys Knight type into your Internet Browser the URL shortcut ➡ **myportrait.art/gladysknight**

To listen to their Greatest Songs type into your Internet Browser the URL shortcut
➡ **radio.surf/gladysknightandthepips**

To view all channels on THE FACE OF MUSIC Internet Radio MEGA Station type into your Internet Browser the URL shortcut ➡ **radio.surf/music**

To inquire about purchasing a Limited Edtion NFT of this portrait type into your Internet Browser the URL shortcut ➡ **myartnft.shop/gladysknight**

To view all available NFTs type into your Internet Browser the URL shortcut ➡ **myartnft.shop/all**

# Glen Campbell

(Net worth: $50 Million)(Total Albums Sold: 50 Million)
(Genre: Country)(Height: 6' - 0")

Glen Travis Campbell (April 22, 1936 – August 8, 2017) was an American singer, guitarist, songwriter, television host, and actor. He was best known for a series of hit songs in the 1960s and 1970s, and for hosting The Glen Campbell Goodtime Hour on CBS television from 1969 until 1972. He released 64 albums in a career that spanned five decades, selling over 45 million records worldwide, including twelve gold albums, four platinum albums, and one double-platinum album.

Born in Billstown, Arkansas, Campbell began his professional career as a studio musician in Los Angeles, spending several years playing with the group of instrumentalists later known as "The Wrecking Crew". After becoming a solo artist, he placed a total of 80 different songs on either the Billboard Country Chart, Billboard Hot 100, or Adult Contemporary Chart, of which 29 made the top 10 and of which nine reached number one on at least one of those charts. Among Campbell's hits are "Universal Soldier", his first hit from 1965, along with "Gentle on My Mind" (1967), "By the Time I Get to Phoenix" (1967), "Dreams of the Everyday Housewife" (1968), "Wichita Lineman" (1968), "Galveston" (1969), "Rhinestone Cowboy" (1975) and "Southern Nights" (1977).

In 1967, Campbell won four Grammys in the country and pop categories. For "Gentle on My Mind", he received two awards in country and western; "By the Time I Get to Phoenix" did the same in pop. Three of his early hits later won Grammy Hall of Fame Awards (2000, 2004, 2008), while Campbell himself won the Grammy Lifetime Achievement Award in 2012. He owned trophies for Male Vocalist of the Year from both the Country Music Association (CMA) and the Academy of Country Music (ACM), and took the CMA's top award as 1968 Entertainer of the Year. Campbell played a supporting role in the film True Grit (1969), which earned him a Golden Globe nomination for Most Promising Newcomer. He also sang the title song, which was nominated for an Academy Award.

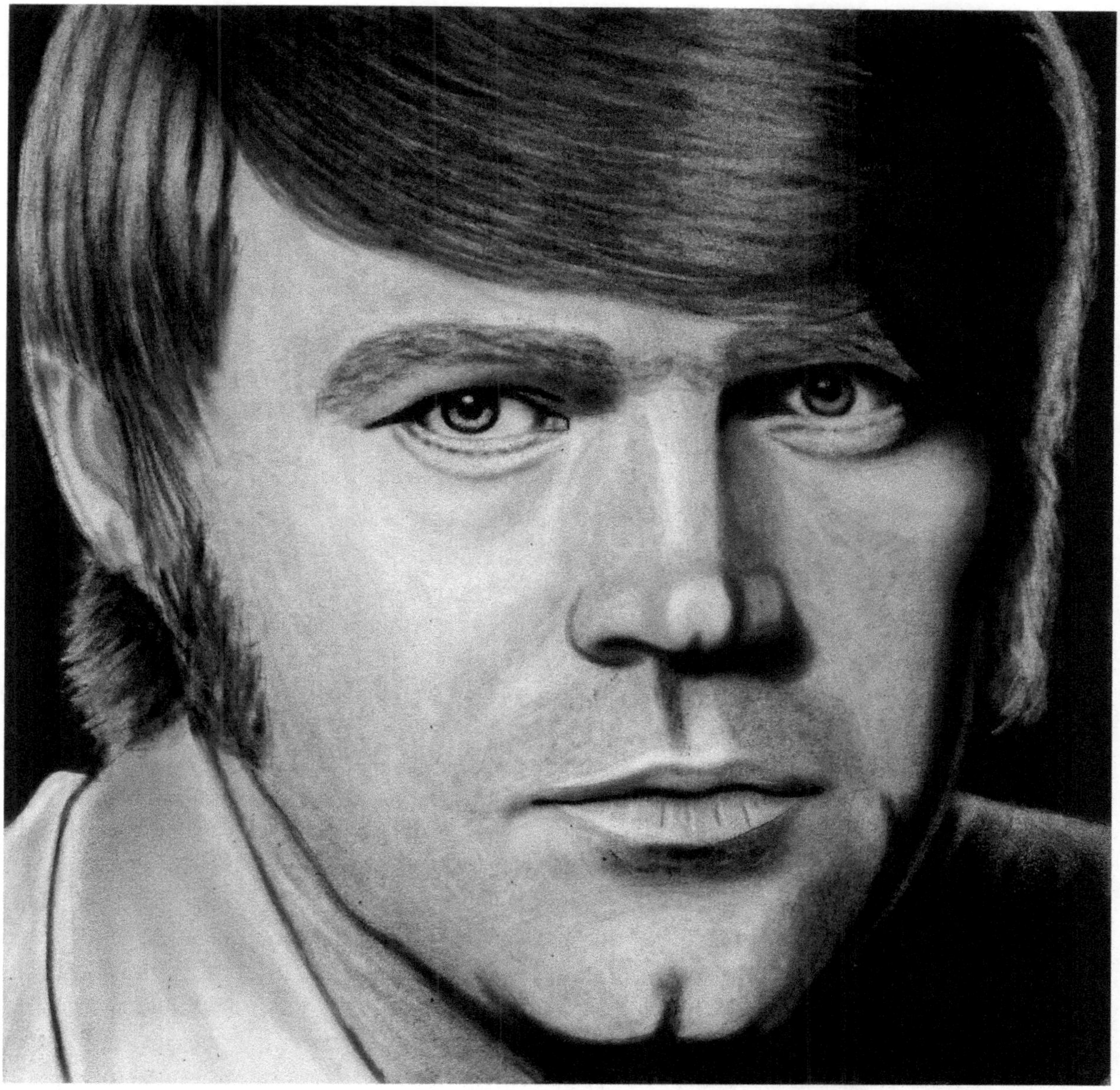

To view how this drawing was masterfully created or to purchase a Limited Edition Framed Artwork of Glen Campbell type into your Internet Browser the URL shortcut ➡ **myportrait.art/glencampbell**

To listen to his Greatest Songs type into your Internet Browser the URL shortcut ➡ **radio.surf/glencampbell**

To view all channels on THE FACE OF MUSIC Internet Radio MEGA Station type into your Internet Browser the URL shortcut ➡ **radio.surf/music**

To inquire about purchasing a Limited Edtion NFT of this portrait type into your Internet Browser the URL shortcut ➡ **myartnft.shop/glencampbell**

To view all available NFTs type into your Internet Browser the URL shortcut ➡ **myartnft.shop/all**

# Glenn Miller

(Net worth: $29 Million)(Total Records Sold: Multi-Millions)
(Genre: Big Band , Swing)

Alton Glenn Miller (March 1, 1904 – disappeared December 15, 1944) was an American big-band trombonist, arranger, composer, and bandleader in the swing era. He was the best-selling recording artist from 1939 to 1942, leading one of the best-known big bands. Miller's recordings include "In the Mood", "Moonlight Serenade", "Pennsylvania 6-5000", "Chattanooga Choo Choo", " A String of Pearls", "At Last", "(I've Got a Gal In) Kalamazoo", "American Patrol", "Tuxedo Junction", "Elmer's Tune", "Little Brown Jug" and "Anvil Chorus". In just four years Glenn Miller scored 16 number-one records and 69 top ten hits—more than Elvis Presley (38 top 10s) and the Beatles (33 top 10s) did in their careers.

In 1942, Miller volunteered to join the U.S. military to entertain troops during World War II, ending up with the U.S. Army Air Forces. On December 15, 1944, while flying to Paris, Miller's aircraft disappeared in bad weather over the English Channel. He was posthumously awarded the Bronze Star Medal.

Miller realized that he needed to develop a unique sound, and decided to make the clarinet play a melodic line with a tenor saxophone holding the same note, while three other saxophones harmonized within a single octave. George T. Simon discovered a saxophonist named Wilbur Schwartz for Glenn Miller. Miller hired Schwartz, but instead had him play lead clarinet. According to Simon, "Willie's tone and way of playing provided a fullness and richness so distinctive that none of the later Miller imitators could ever accurately reproduce the Miller sound." With this new sound-combination, Glenn Miller found a way to differentiate his band's style from that of many bands that existed in the late thirties. Miller talked about his style in the May 1939 issue of Metronome magazine. "You'll notice today some bands use the same trick on every introduction; others repeat the same musical phrase as a modulation into a vocal ... We're fortunate in that our style doesn't limit us to stereotyped intros, modulations , first choruses, endings or even trick rhythms. The fifth sax, playing clarinet most of the time, lets you know whose band you're listening to. And that's about all there is to it."

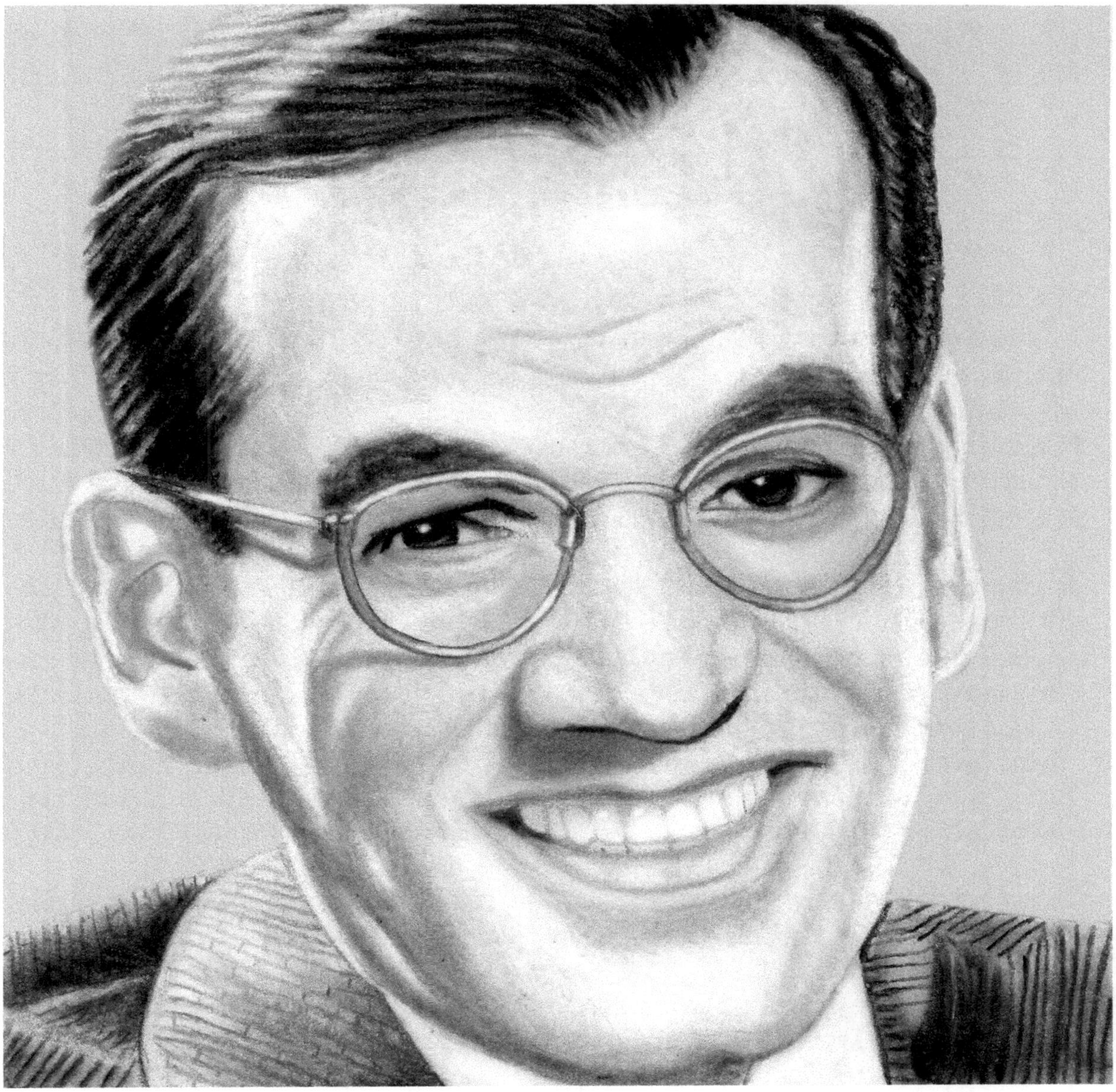

To view how this drawing was masterfully created or to purchase a Limited Edition Framed Artwork of Glenn Miller type into your Internet Browser the URL shortcut ➡ **myportrait.art/glennmiller**

To listen to his Greatest Songs type into your Internet Browser the URL shortcut ➡ **radio.surf/glennmiller**

To view all channels on THE FACE OF MUSIC Internet Radio MEGA Station type into your Internet Browser the URL shortcut ➡ **radio.surf/music**

To inquire about purchasing a Limited Edtion NFT of this portrait type into your Internet Browser the URL shortcut ➡ **myartnft.shop/glennmiller**

To view all available NFTs type into your Internet Browser the URL shortcut ➡ **myartnft.shop/all**

# Gloria Estefan

(Net worth: $500 Million)(Total Records Sold: 75+ Million)
(Genre: Latin Pop , Dance Pop) (Height: 5' - 0")

Gloria Estefan (Spanish: [ˈɡloɾja esˈtefan]; born Gloria María Milagrosa Fajardo García; September 1, 1957) is a Cuban-American singer, songwriter, actress and businesswoman. A contralto, she started her career as the lead singer in the group Miami Latin Boys, which later became known as Miami Sound Machine. She experienced worldwide success with "Conga" in 1985; this became Estefan's signature song and led to the Miami Sound Machine winning the grand prix in the 15th annual Tokyo Music Festival in 1986. In the middle of 1988, she and the band got their first number-one hit with the song "Anything for You".

In March 1990, Estefan had a severe accident in her tour bus. She made her comeback in March 1991 with a new world tour and album called Into the Light. Her 1993 Spanish-language album, Mi Tierra, won the first of her three Grammy Awards for Best Tropical Latin Album. It was the first number-one album on the Billboard Top Latin Albums chart, established when it was released. It was also the first Diamond album in Spain. Many of her songs, such as "Rhythm Is Gonna Get You", "1-2-3", "Don't Wanna Lose You", "Get On Your Feet", "Here We Are", "Coming Out of the Dark", "Bad Boy", "Oye!", "Party Time" and a remake of "Turn the Beat Around" became international chart-topping hits. Estefan's record sales surpass more than 75 million worldwide, making her one of the best-selling female singers of all-time.

She has won three Grammy Awards and received a star on the Hollywood Walk of Fame and Las Vegas Walk of Fame. In 2015, she received the Presidential Medal of Freedom for her contributions to American music and received the Kennedy Center Honors in December 2017 for her contributions to American Culture Life. Estefan also won an MTV Video Music Award, was honored with the American Music Award for Lifetime Achievement, as well as being named BMI Songwriter of the Year. She was inducted into the Songwriters Hall of Fame and has received multiple Billboard Awards. She is also on the Top 100 Greatest Artists of All Time lists of VH1 and Billboard. Richard Blanco, the 2013 Presidential Inaugural Poet, author of "How to Love a Country", told the Boston Globe that Gloria Estefan is among the Latin singers who helped him to ground " in the musical poetry of my culture and rejuvenate my spirits".

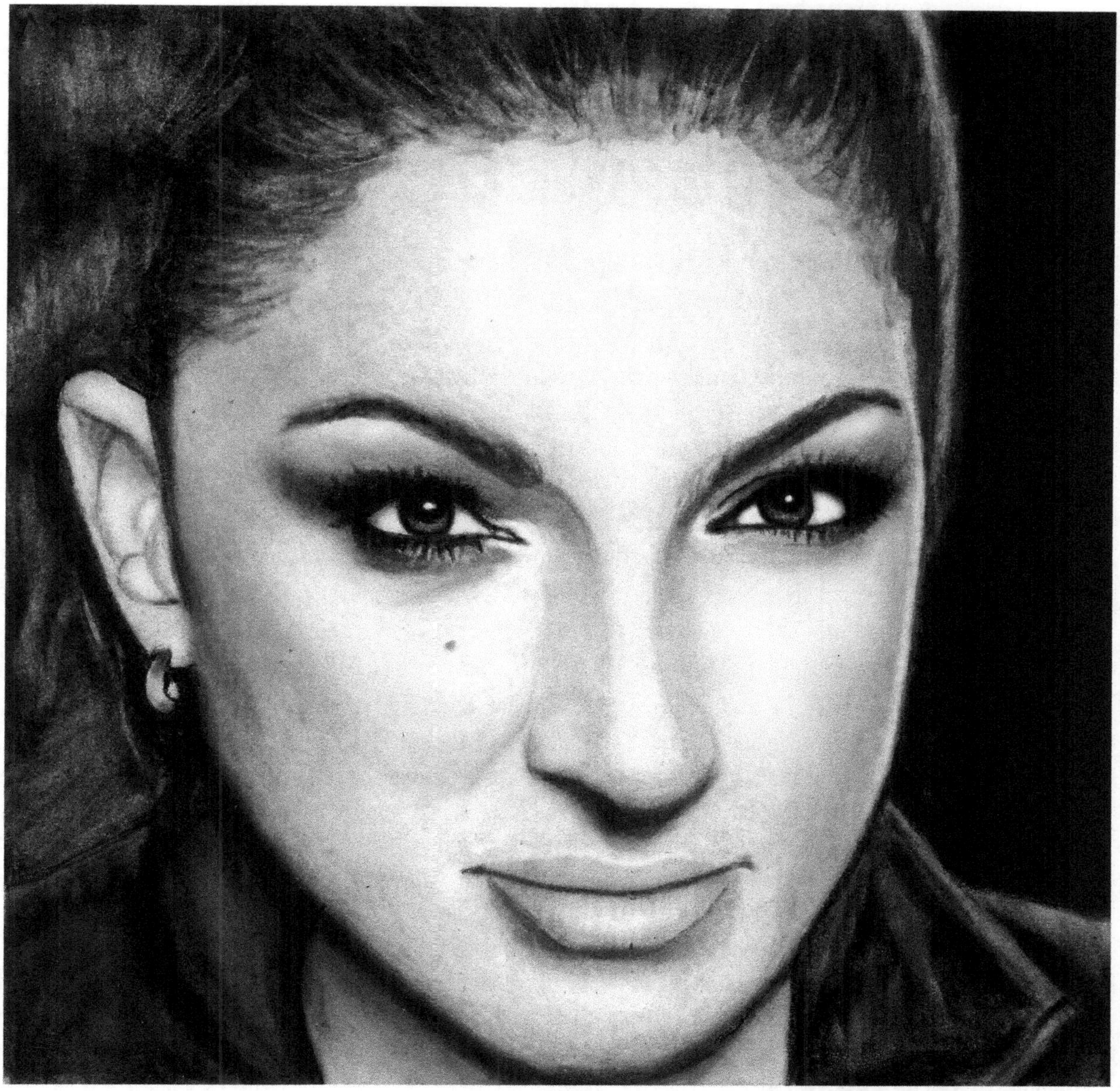

To view how this drawing was masterfully created or to purchase a Limited Edition Framed Artwork of Gloria Estefan type into your Internet Browser the URL shortcut ➡ **myportrait.art/gloriaestefan**

To listen to her Greatest Songs type into your Internet Browser the URL shortcut ➡ **radio.surf/gloriaestefan**

To view all channels on THE FACE OF MUSIC Internet Radio MEGA Station type into your Internet Browser the URL shortcut ➡ **radio.surf/music**

To inquire about purchasing a Limited Edtion NFT of this portrait type into your Internet Browser the URL shortcut ➡ **myartnft.shop/gloriaestefan**

To view all available NFTs type into your Internet Browser the URL shortcut ➡ **myartnft.shop/all**

# Gordon Lightfoot

(Net worth: $30 Million)(Total Records Sold: Multi-Millions)
(Genre: Folk , Country) (Height: 6' - 0")

Gordon Meredith Lightfoot Jr. (born November 17, 1938) is a Canadian singer-songwriter and guitarist who achieved international success in folk, folk-rock, and country music. He is credited with helping to define the folk-pop sound of the 1960s and 1970s. He is often referred to as Canada's greatest songwriter and is known internationally as a folk-rock legend.

Lightfoot's songs, including "For Lovin' Me", "Early Morning Rain", "Steel Rail Blues", "Ribbon of Darkness"—a number one hit on the U.S country chart with Marty Robbins's cover in 1965—and "Black Day in July," about the 1967 Detroit riot, brought him wide recognition in the 1960s. Canadian chart success with his own recordings began in 1962 with the No. 3 hit "(Remember Me) I'm the One", followed by recognition and charting abroad in the 1970s. He topped the US Hot 100 or AC chart with the hits "If You Could Read My Mind" (1970), "Sundown" (1974); "Carefree Highway" (1974), "Rainy Day People" (1975), and "The Wreck of the Edmund Fitzgerald" (1976), and had many other hits that appeared in the top 40.

Several of Lightfoot's albums achieved gold and multi-platinum status internationally. His songs have been recorded by renowned artists such as Elvis Presley, Johnny Cash, Hank Williams Jr., The Kingston Trio, Jerry Lee Lewis, Neil Young, Bob Dylan, Judy Collins, Barbra Streisand, Johnny Mathis, Herb Alpert, Harry Belafonte, Sarah McLachlan, Eric Clapton, John Mellencamp, Peter, Paul and Mary, Glen Campbell, The Grateful Dead, Nico, and Olivia Newton-John.

Robbie Robertson of the Band described Lightfoot as "a national treasure". Bob Dylan, also a Lightfoot fan, called him one of his favorite songwriters and, in an often-quoted tribute, Dylan observed that when he heard a Lightfoot song he wished "it would last forever". Lightfoot was a featured musical performer at the opening ceremonies of the 1988 Winter Olympic Games in Calgary, Alberta. He received an honorary Doctor of Laws degree from Trent University in Spring 1979 and was made a Companion of the Order of Canada in May 2003. In November 1997, the Governor General's Performing Arts Award, Canada's highest honour in the performing arts, was bestowed on Lightfoot. On February 6, 2012, Lightfoot was presented with the Queen Elizabeth II Diamond Jubilee Medal by the Lieutenant Governor of Ontario. June of that year saw his induction into the Songwriters Hall of Fame. On June 6, 2015, Lightfoot received an honorary doctorate of music in his hometown of Orillia from Lakehead Universit

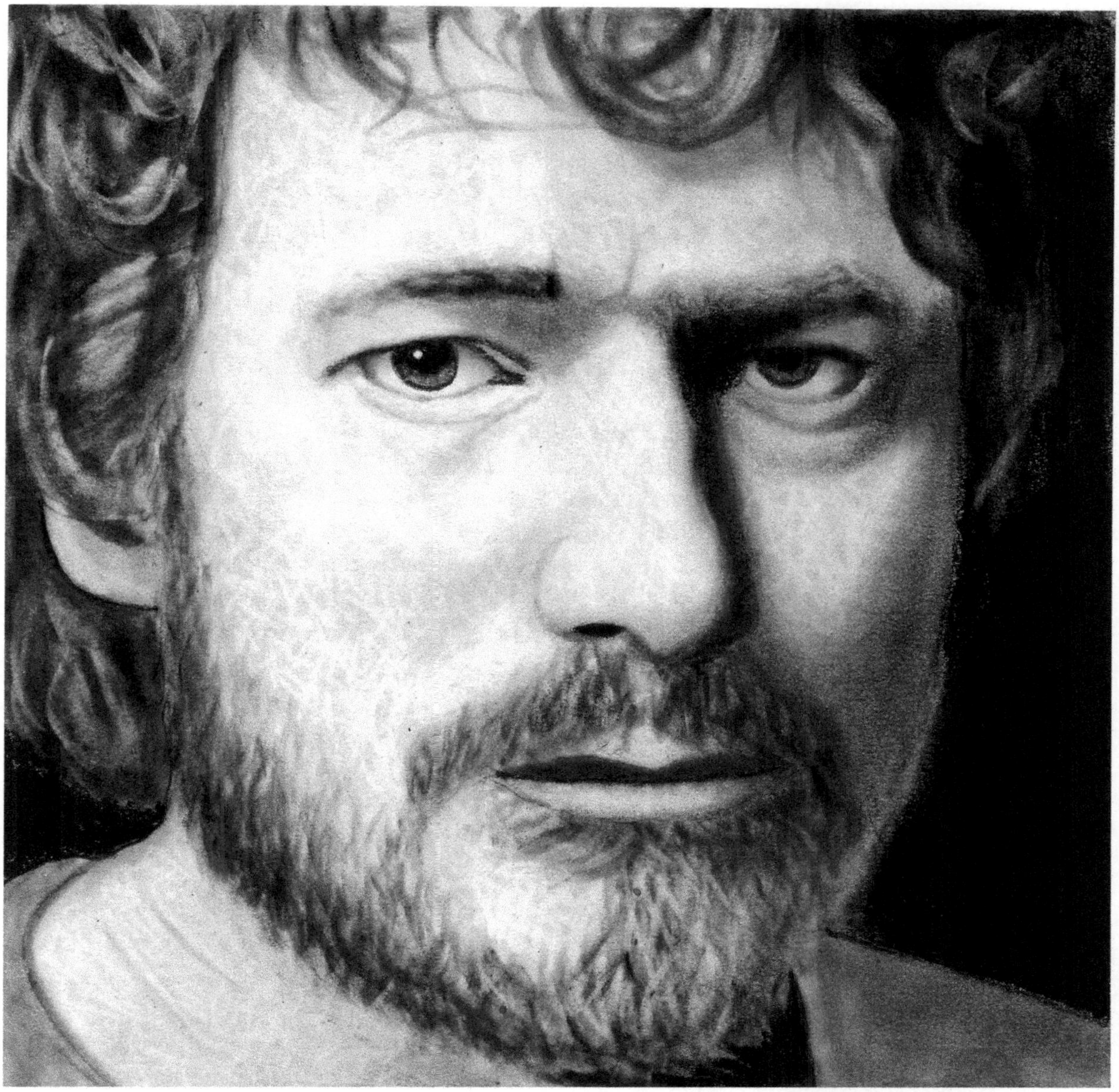

To view how this drawing was masterfully created or to purchase a Limited Edition Framed Artwork of Gordon Lightfoot type into your Internet Browser the URL shortcut ➡ **myportrait.art/gordonlightfoot**

To listen to his Greatest Songs type into your Internet Browser the URL shortcut ➡ **radio.surf/gordonlightfoot**

To view all channels on THE FACE OF MUSIC Internet Radio MEGA Station type into your Internet Browser the URL shortcut ➡ **radio.surf/music**

To inquire about purchasing a Limited Edtion NFT of this portrait type into your Internet Browser the URL shortcut ➡ **myartnft.shop/gordonlightfoot**

To view all available NFTs type into your Internet Browser the URL shortcut ➡ **myartnft.shop/all**

# Grateful Dead

(Total Albums Sold: 35+ Million) (Genre: Blues Rock , Rock)

The Grateful Dead was an American rock band formed in 1965 in Palo Alto, California. The band is known for its eclectic style, which fused elements of rock, folk, country, jazz, bluegrass, blues, gospel, and psychedelic rock; for live performances of lengthy instrumental jams; and for its devoted fan base, known as "Deadheads". "Their music", writes Lenny Kaye, "touches on ground that most other groups don't even know exists." These various influences were distilled into a diverse and psychedelic whole that made the Grateful Dead "the pioneering Godfathers of the jam band world". The band was ranked 57th by Rolling Stone magazine in its The Greatest Artists of All Time issue. The band was inducted into the Rock and Roll Hall of Fame in 1994 and a recording of their May 8, 1977 performance at Cornell University's Barton Hall was added to the National Recording Registry of the Library of Congress in 2012. The Grateful Dead has sold more than 35 million albums worldwide.The Grateful Dead was founded in the San Francisco Bay Area amid the rise of the counterculture of the 1960s. The founding members were Jerry Garcia (lead guitar, vocals), Bob Weir (rhythm guitar, vocals), Ron "Pigpen" McKernan (keyboards, harmonica, vocals), Phil Lesh (bass, vocals), and Bill Kreutzmann (drums). Members of the Grateful Dead had played together in various San Francisco bands, including Mother McCree's Uptown Jug Champions and the Warlocks. Lesh was the last member to join the Warlocks before they became the Grateful Dead; he replaced Dana Morgan Jr., who had played bass for a few gigs. Drummer Mickey Hart and non-performing lyricist Robert Hunter joined in 1967. With the exception of McKernan, who died in 1973, and Hart, who took time off from 1971 to 1974, the core of the band stayed together for its entire 30-year history. The other official members of the band are Tom Constanten (keyboards; 1968–1970), John Perry Barlow (nonperforming lyricist; 1971–1995), Keith Godchaux (keyboards; 1971–1979), Donna Godchaux (vocals; 1972–1979), Brent Mydland (keyboards, vocals; 1979–1990), and Vince Welnick (keyboards, vocals; 1990–1995). Bruce Hornsby (accordion, piano, vocals) was a touring member from 1990 to 1992, as well as a guest with the band on occasion before and after the tours. After the death of Garcia in 1995, former members of the band, along with other musicians, toured as the Other Ones in 1998, 2000, and 2002, and the Dead in 2003, 2004, and 2009. In 2015, the four surviving core members marked the band's 50th anniversary in a series of concerts that were billed as their last performances together. There have also been several spin-offs featuring one or more core members, such as Dead & Company, Furthur, the Rhythm Devils, Phil Lesh and Friends, RatDog, and Billy & the Kids.

# Jerry Garcia

(Net Worth: $15 Million) (Height: 5' - 11")

Jerome John Garcia ( August 1, 1942 – August 9, 1995) was an American singer-songwriter and guitarist, best known for being a principal songwriter, the lead guitarist and a vocalist with the rock band the Grateful Dead, of which he was a founding member and which came to prominence during the counterculture of the 1960s. Although he disavowed the role, Garcia was viewed by many as the leader or "spokesman" of the group.

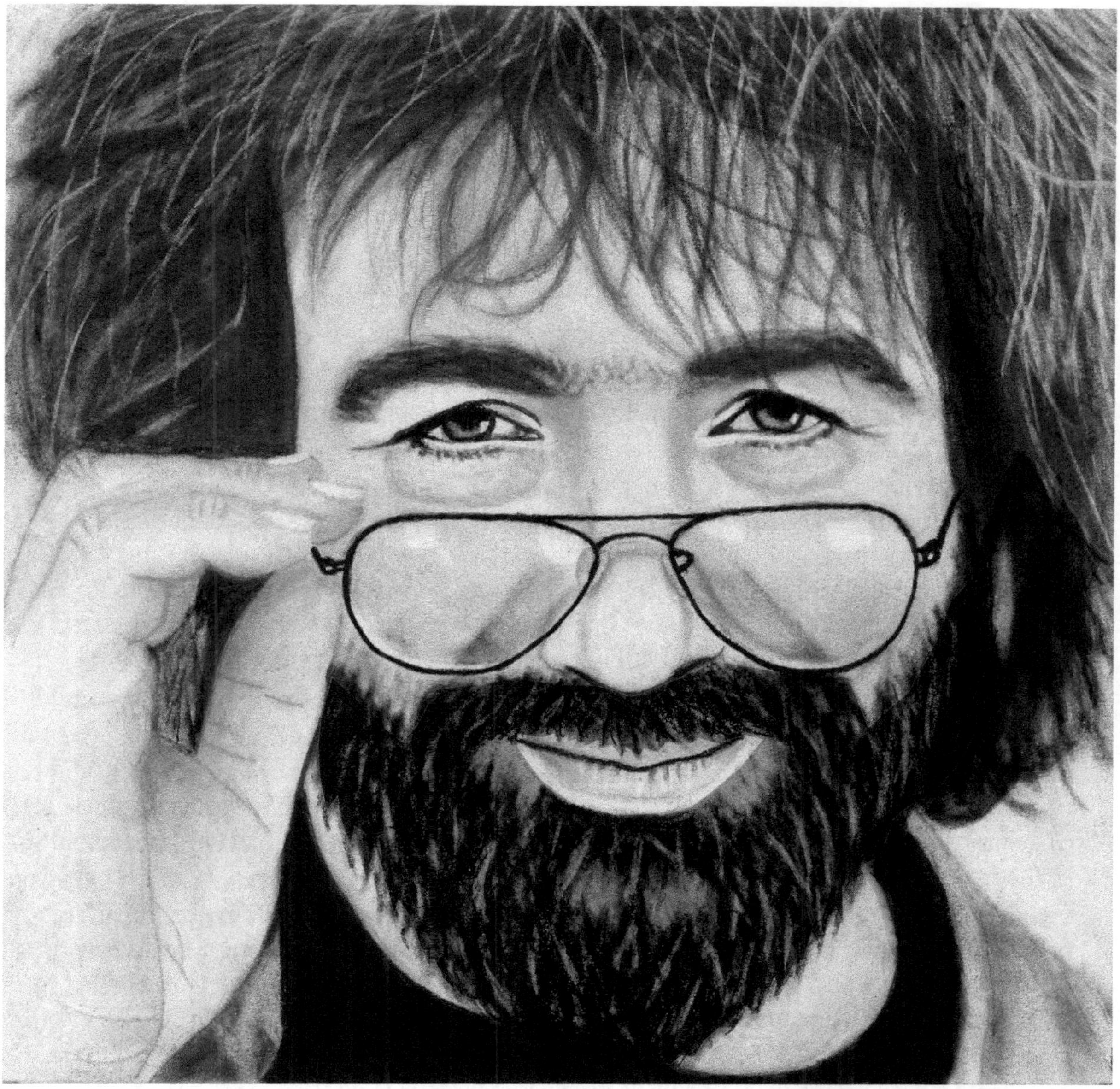

To view how this drawing was masterfully created or to purchase a Limited Edition Framed Artwork of Jerry Garcia type into your Internet Browser the URL shortcut ➡ **myportrait.art/jerrygarcia**

To listen to their Greatest Songs type into your Internet Browser the URL shortcut
➡ **radio.surf/gratefuldead**

To view all channels on THE FACE OF MUSIC Internet Radio MEGA Station type into your Internet Browser the URL shortcut ➡ **radio.surf/music**

To inquire about purchasing a Limited Edtion NFT of this portrait type into your Internet Browser the URL shortcut ➡ **myartnft.shop/jerrygarcia**

To view all available NFTs type into your Internet Browser the URL shortcut ➡ **myartnft.shop/all**

# Green Day

(Total Albums Sold: 75+ Million) (Genre: Punk)

Green Day is an American rock band formed in the East Bay of California in 1987 by lead vocalist and guitarist Billie Joe Armstrong and bassist and backing vocalist Mike Dirnt. For much of the band's career, they have been a trio with drummer Tré Cool, who replaced John Kiffmeyer in 1990 before the recording of the band's second studio album, Kerplunk (1991). Touring guitarist Jason White became a full-time member in 2012, but returned to his role as a touring member in 2016. Green Day was originally part of the late-'80s/early-'90s punk scene at the DIY 924 Gilman Street club in Berkeley, California. The band's early releases were with the independent record label Lookout! Records. In 1994, their major-label debut Dookie, released through Reprise Records, became a breakout success and eventually shipped over 10 million copies in the U.S. Green Day is credited alongside fellow California punk bands NOFX, Sublime, Bad Religion, the Offspring, Rancid, and Jawbreaker with popularizing mainstream interest in punk rock in the U.S.

Though the albums Insomniac (1995), Nimrod (1997), and Warning (2000) did not match the success of Dookie, they were still successful with the former two reaching double platinum status while the latter achieved gold. Green Day's seventh album, a rock opera called American Idiot (2004), found popularity with a younger generation, selling six million copies in the U.S. Their next album, 21st Century Breakdown, was released in 2009 and achieved the band's best chart performance. It was followed by a trilogy of albums, ¡Uno!, ¡Dos!, and ¡Tré!, released in September, November, and December 2012, respectively. The trilogy did not perform as well as expected commercially in comparison to their previous albums largely due to lack of promotion and Armstrong entering rehab. Their twelfth studio album, Revolution Radio, was released in October 2016 and became their third to debut at No. 1 on the Billboard 200. The band's thirteenth studio album, Father of All Motherfuckers, was released on February 7, 2020.

Green Day has sold more than 75 million records worldwide, making them one of the best-selling music artists of all time. The group has been nominated for 20 Grammy awards and has won five of them with Best Alternative Album for Dookie, Best Rock Album for American Idiot and 21st Century Breakdown, Record of the Year for "Boulevard of Broken Dreams", and Best Musical Show Album

# Billy Joe Armstrong

(Net Worth: $75 Million) (Height: 5' - 7")

Billie Joe Armstrong (born February 17, 1972) is an American singer, songwriter, musician, actor, and record producer. He is best known as the lead vocalist, primary songwriter, and lead guitarist of the rock band Green Day, which he co-founded with Mike Dirnt in 1985. He is also a guitarist and vocalist for the punk rock band Pinhead Gunpowder, and provides lead vocals for Green Day's side projects Foxboro Hot Tubs, The Network, The Longshot, and The Coverups.

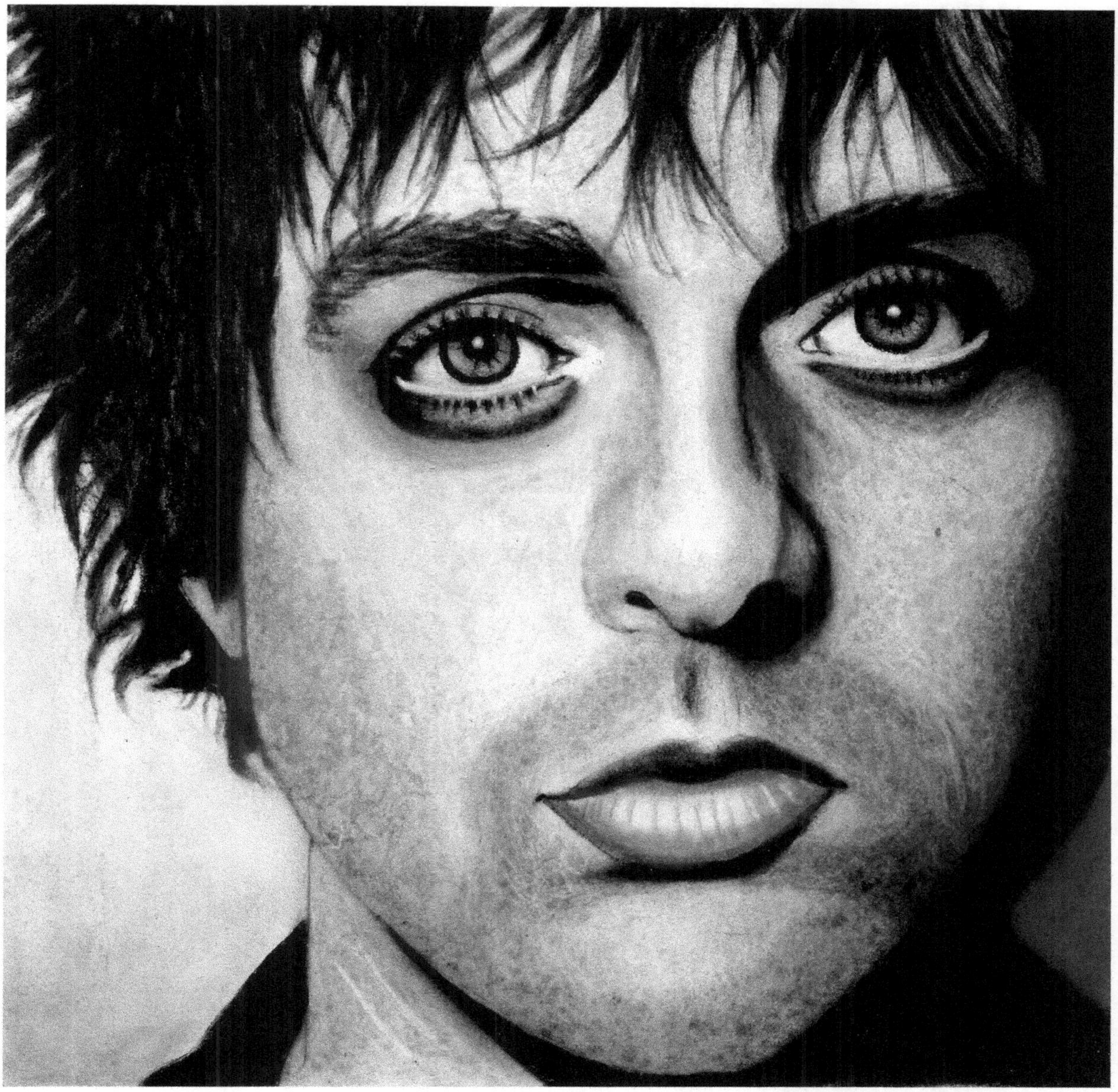

To view how this drawing was matersfully created or to purchase a Limited Edition Framed Artwork of Billy Joe Armstrong type into your Internet Browser the URL shortcut ➡ **myportrait.art/billyjoearmstrong**

To listen to their Greatest Songs type into your Internet Browser the URL shortcut ➡ **radio.surf/greenday**

To view all channels on THE FACE OF MUSIC Internet Radio MEGA Station type into your Internet Browser the URL shortcut ➡ **radio.surf/music**

To inquire about purchasing a Limited Edtion NFT of this portrait type into your Internet Browser the URL shortcut ➡ **myartnft.shop/billyjoearmstrong**

To view all available NFTs type into your Internet Browser the URL shortcut ➡ **myartnft.shop/all**

# Guess Who, The

(Total Albums Sold: 75+ Million) (Genre: Classic Rock , Psychedelic Rock)

The Guess Who are a Canadian rock band from Winnipeg, Manitoba, best-known for their Classic Rock and Psychedelic Rock hits from 1968 to 1975.

The band originated in 1962 and achieved an international hit single with a cover of "Shakin' All Over" in 1965. They found their greatest success, however, in the late 60s and early 70s, under the leadership of singer/keyboardist Burton Cummings and guitarist Randy Bachman, with hit songs including "American Woman", "These Eyes", "No Time" and many others.

During their most successful period, the Guess Who released eleven studio albums, all of which reached the charts in Canada and the United States. They may be best known for their 1970 album American Woman, which reached no. 1 in Canada and no. 9 in the United States, while five other albums reached the top ten in Canada. The Guess Who charted fourteen Top 40 singles in the United States and more than thirty in Canada.

The Guess Who was disbanded by Cummings in 1975, though bassist Jim Kale and/or drummer Garry Peterson have toured and recorded under the Guess Who name since 1977, frequently with no other original band members involved.

# Burton Cummings

(Net Worth: $14 Million) (Height: 5' - 6")

Burton Lorne Cummings, (born December 31, 1947) is a Canadian musician, singer and songwriter.Cummings is the former lead singer and keyboardist for the Canadian rock band The Guess Who. During his decade in the band, from 1965 to 1975, he sang, wrote or co-wrote many hit songs, including "American Woman," "No Time", "Share the Land", "Hand Me Down World", "Laughing", "Star Baby", "New Mother Nature", "These Eyes", and "Clap for the Wolfman".

In October 1975 Cummings left The Guess Who after 10 years to become a solo artist, and the group disbanded. One of his first projects was providing back-up vocals on Eric Carmen's second solo LP, Boats Against the Current, including "She Did It". In 1977 he was presented with a Juno Award as best male vocalist.

Cummings' subsequent hits in Canada included "Stand Tall," which was his greatest American solo hit, peaking at #10 on the Billboard Hot 100 and number two on the Adult Contemporary chart. Other hits included "I'm Scared," "Break It to Them Gently," and "Fine State of Affairs." Cummings charted outside Canada with "Stand Tall" and "You Saved My Soul," as well as "I Will Play a Rhapsody," which spent a few weeks on the Billboard Adult Contemporary Chart, peaking at #38. His Dream of a Child album, released in 1978, was the biggest Canadian album in history at that time going triple platinum. Cummings released a total of eight solo albums and collections from 1976 to 1994.

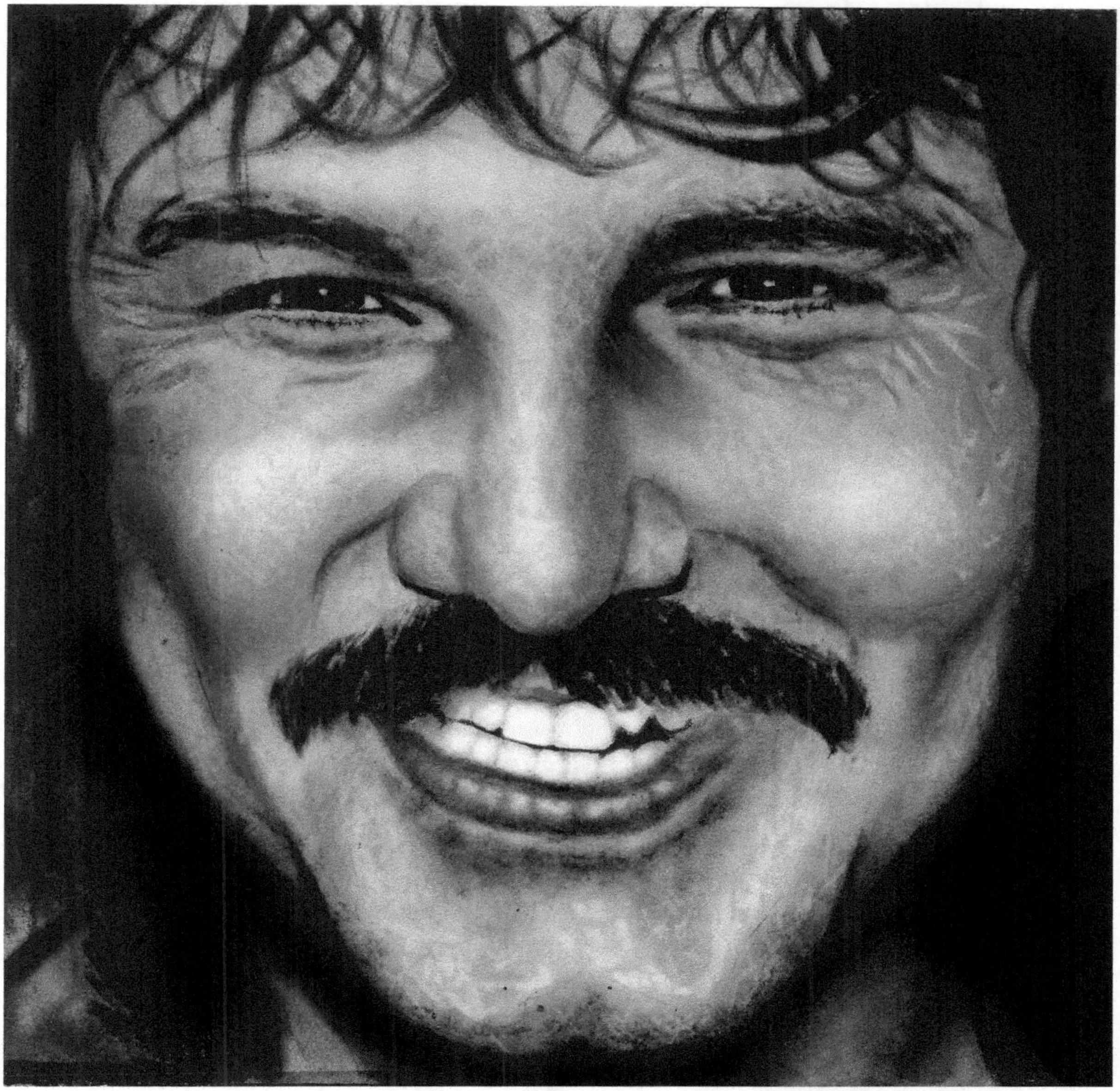

To view how this drawing was masterfully created or to purchase a Limited Edition Framed Artwork of Burton Cummings type into your Internet Browser the URL shortcut ➡ **myportrait.art/burtoncummings**

To listen to their Greatest Songs type into your Internet Browser the URL shortcut ➡ **radio.surf/theguesswho**

To view all channels on THE FACE OF MUSIC Internet Radio MEGA Station type into your Internet Browser the URL shortcut ➡ **radio.surf/music**

To inquire about purchasing a Limited Edtion NFT of this portrait type into your Internet Browser the URL shortcut ➡ **myartnft.shop/burtoncummings**

To view all available NFTs type into your Internet Browser the URL shortcut ➡ **myartnft.shop/all**

# Guns N' Roses

(Total Albums Sold: 100+ Million) (Genre: Hard Rock)

Guns N' Roses, often abbreviated as GNR, is an American hard rock band from Los Angeles, California, formed in 1985. When they signed to Geffen Records in 1986, the band comprised vocalist Axl Rose, lead guitarist Slash, rhythm guitarist Izzy Stradlin, bassist Duff McKagan, and drummer Steven Adler. The current lineup consists of Rose, Slash, McKagan, guitarist Richard Fortus, drummer Frank Ferrer and keyboardists Dizzy Reed and Melissa Reese.

Guns N' Roses' debut album, Appetite for Destruction (1987), reached number one on the Billboard 200 a year after its release, on the strength of the top 10 singles "Welcome to the Jungle", "Paradise City", and "Sweet Child o' Mine", the band's only single to reach number one on the Billboard Hot 100. The album has sold approximately 30 million copies worldwide, including 18 million units in the United States, making it the country's bestselling debut album and eleventh-bestselling album. Their next studio album, G N' R Lies (1988), reached number two on the Billboard 200, sold ten million copies worldwide (including five million in the U.S), and included the top 5 hit "Patience". Use Your Illusion I and Use Your Illusion II, recorded simultaneously and released in 1991, debuted at number two and number one on the Billboard 200 respectively and have sold a combined 35 million copies worldwide, including 14 million units in the United States. The Illusion albums included the lead single "You Could Be Mine" (also featured in the film soundtrack for Terminator 2), covers of "Live and Let Die" and "Knockin' on Heaven's Door", and a trilogy of ballads ("Don't Cry", "November Rain", and "Estranged"), which featured notably high-budget music videos. The Illusion records were also supported by the extensive Use Your Illusion Tour, a world tour that lasted from 1991–1993. "The Spaghetti Incident?" (1993), an album of covers, was the band's last studio album to feature Slash and McKagan before their initial departure.

Work on a follow-up album stalled due to creative differences between band members; by 1998 only Rose and Reed remained from the Illusion-era lineup. After a decade of work and several lineup changes, Guns N' Roses's long-awaited sixth studio album, Chinese Democracy (2008), was released. At an estimated $14 million in production costs, it is the most expensive rock album in history. It debuted at number three on the Billboard 200, but undersold industry expectations despite mostly positive critical reception. Slash and McKagan rejoined the band in 2016 for the Not in This Lifetime... Tour, which became the third-highest-grossing concert tour on record, grossing over $584 million by its conclusion in 2019.

# Axl Rose

(Net Worth: $200 Million) (Height: 5' - 9")

W. Axl Rose (born William Bruce Rose Jr.; raised as William Bruce Bailey; born February 6, 1962) is an American singer, songwriter and record producer. He is best known for being the lead vocalist and lyricist of the hard rock band Guns N' Roses, and has also been the band's sole constant member since their inception in 1985.

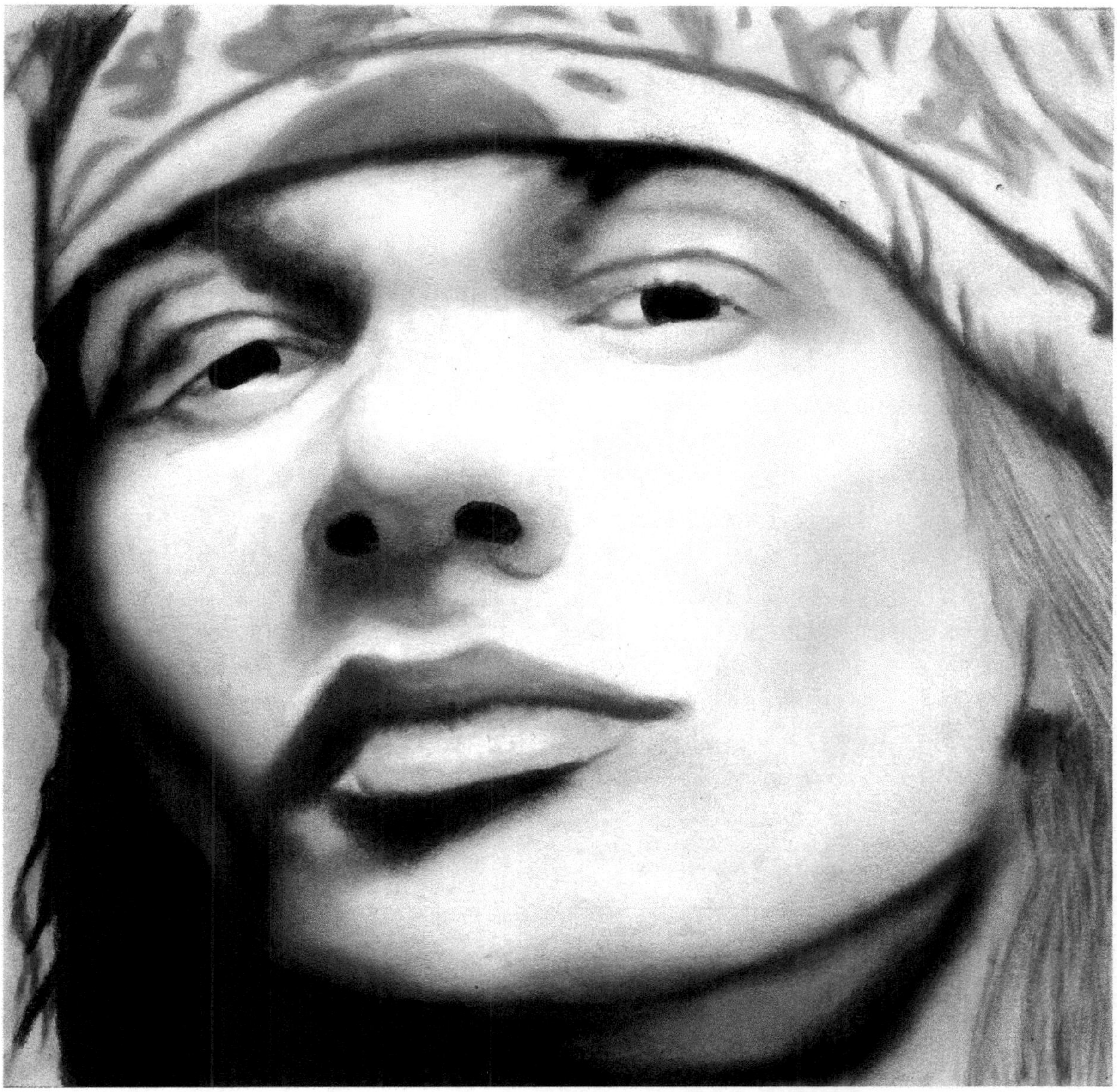

To view how this drawing was masterfully created or to purchase a Limited Edition Framed Artwork of Axl Rose type into your Internet Browser the URL shortcut ➡ **myportrait.art/axlrose**

To listen to their Greatest Songs type into your Internet Browser the URL shortcut ➡ **radio.surf/gunsnroses**

To view all channels on THE FACE OF MUSIC Internet Radio MEGA Station type into your Internet Browser the URL shortcut ➡ **radio.surf/music**

To inquire about purchasing a Limited Edtion NFT of this portrait type into your Internet Browser the URL shortcut ➡ **myartnft.shop/axlrose**

To view all available NFTs type into your Internet Browser the URL shortcut ➡ **myartnft.shop/all**

# Hall & Oates

(Total Albums Sold: 13 Million) (Genre: Pop , R&B)

Hall & Oates are an American pop rock duo formed in 1970 in Philadelphia. Daryl Hall is generally the lead vocalist; John Oates primarily plays electric guitar and provides backing vocals. The two write most of the songs they perform, separately or in collaboration. They achieved their greatest fame from the mid-1970s to the mid-1980s with a fusion of rock and roll and rhythm and blues.

Credited as Daryl Hall & John Oates (or Daryl Hall John Oates) on all of their US releases, the duo reached the US Top 40 with 29 of their 33 singles charting on Billboard's Hot 100 between 1974 and 1991. Six of these peaked at number one: "Rich Girl" (1977), the three 1981 releases "Kiss on My List", "Private Eyes" and "I Can't Go for That (No Can Do)" (also a Hot Soul no. 1), "Maneater" (1982) and "Out of Touch" (1984). Their overall 16 US Top Tens also include "She's Gone", "Sara Smile", "You Make My Dreams", "Family Man", "Say It Isn't So" and "Method of Modern Love". Seven of their albums have been RIAA-certified platinum and six of them gold. In the United Kingdom they have achieved success with two Top Ten albums and six Top 40 singles, two of which – "I Can't Go for That (No Can Do)" and "Maneater" – reached the Top Ten. The duo have spent 120 weeks in the UK Top 75 albums chart and 84 weeks in the UK Top 75 singles chart.

In 2003 Hall & Oates were inducted into the Songwriters Hall of Fame. In August 2018, in a 60th-anniversary celebration of Billboard's Hot 100, the duo ranked 18 in a list of the top Hot 100 artists of all time and six in a list of the Hot 100's top duos/groups. They remain the most successful duo, ahead of the Carpenters, the Everly Brothers and Simon & Garfunkel. In September 2010 VH1 placed the duo at no. 99 in their list of the 100 greatest artists of all time. In April 2014 they were inducted into the Rock and Roll Hall of Fame, and on September 2, 2016 they received a star on the Hollywood Walk of Fame.

# Daryl Hall

(Net Worth: $45 Million) (Height: 6' - 1")

Daryl Franklin Hohl (born October 11, 1946), known professionally as Daryl Hall, is an American rock, R&B and soul singer and musician, best known as the co-founder and principal lead vocalist of Hall & Oates (with guitarist and songwriter John Oates).

In the 1970s and early 1980s, Hall scored numerous Billboard chart hits and is regarded as one of the best soul singers of his generation. Guitarist Robert Fripp, who collaborated with him in the late 1970s and early 1980s, has written, "Daryl's pipes were a wonder. I have never worked with a more able singer."

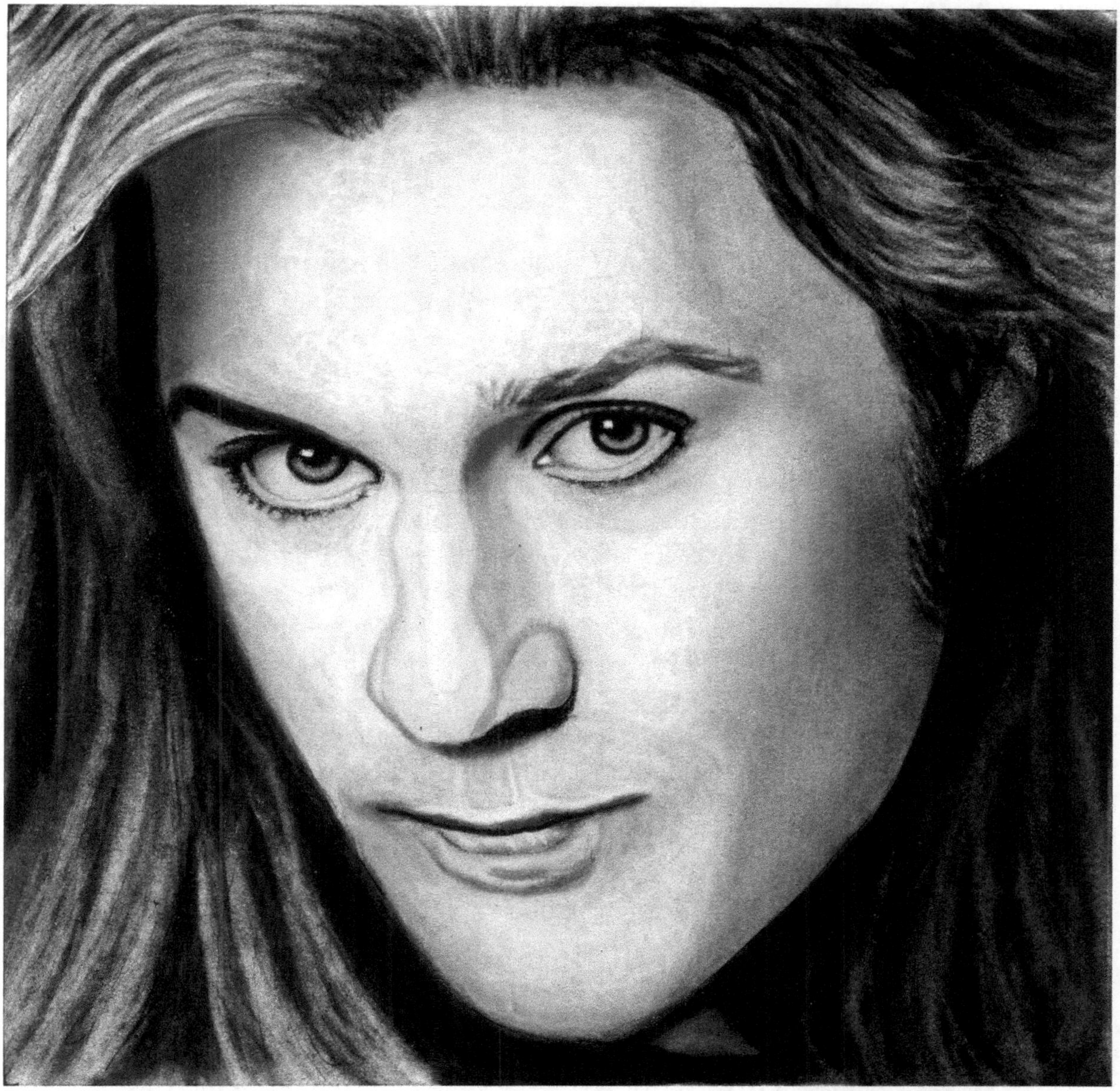

To view how this drawing was masterfully created or to purchase a Limited Edition Framed Artwork of Daryl Hall type into your Internet Browser the URL shortcut ➡ **myportrait.art/darlyhall**

To listen to their Greatest Songs type into your Internet Browser the URL shortcut
➡ **radio.surf/hallandoates**

To view all channels on THE FACE OF MUSIC Internet Radio MEGA Station type into your Internet Browser the URL shortcut ➡ **radio.surf/music**

To inquire about purchasing a Limited Edition NFT of this portrait type into your Internet Browser the URL shortcut ➡ **myartnft.shop/darlyhall**

To view all available NFTs type into your Internet Browser the URL shortcut ➡ **myartnft.shop/all**

# Hank Ballard

(Net worth: $15 Million)(Total Records Sold: Multi-Millions)
(Genre: Rock & Roll , R&B , Funk)

Hank Ballard (born John Henry Kendricks; November 18, 1927 – March 2, 2003) was an American R&B singer and songwriter, the lead vocalist of The Midnighters and one of the first rock and roll artists to emerge in the early 1950s. He played an integral part in the development of the genre, releasing the hit singles "Work With Me, Annie" and answer songs "Annie Had a Baby" and "Annie's Aunt Fannie" with his Midnighters. He later wrote and originally recorded (in 1959) "The Twist" which was notably covered a year later by Chubby Checker, this second version spreading the popularity of the dance. He was inducted into the Rock and Roll Hall of Fame in 1990.

In 1953, Ballard joined doo-wop group the Royals, which had previously been discovered by Johnny Otis and signed to Federal Records (a division of King Records), in Cincinnati. Ballard joined Henry Booth, Charles Sutton, Sonny Woods and Alonzo Tucker in the group, replacing previous singer Lawson Smith. The Royals released "Get It" (1953), an R&B song with possibly sexually oriented lyrics, which some radio stations refused to play, although it still made it to number 6 on the Billboard R&B chart.

The group then changed its name to the Midnighters to avoid confusion with the "5" Royales. In 1954, Ballard wrote a song called "Work with Me, Annie" that was drawn from "Get It". It became the Midnighters' first major R&B hit, spending seven weeks at number 1 on the R&B charts and also selling well in mainstream markets, along with the answer songs "Annie Had a Baby" and "Annie's Aunt Fannie"; all were banned by the FCC from radio air play. Their third major hit was "Sexy Ways", a song that cemented the band's reputation as one of the most risqué groups of the time.

They had four other R&B chart hits in 1954–55, but no others until 1959, by which time the group was billed as "Hank Ballard and The Midnighters" with their label changed from Federal to King, the parent label. Between 1959 and 1961 they had several more both on the R&B and Pop charts, starting with "Teardrops on Your Letter", a number 4 R&B hit in 1959 that had as its B-side the Ballard-written song "The Twist". A few months later, Chubby Checker's cover version of the song went to number 1 on the pop charts. It would return to the top of the charts again in 1962 – the only song in the rock and roll era to reach number 1 in two different non-consecutive years.

Ballard and the Midnighters had several other hit singles in 1962, including the Grammy-nominated "Finger Poppin' Time" (1960) and "Let's Go, Let's Go, Let's Go" (1960) which hit number 7 and number 6, respectively, on the Billboard pop charts. They did not reach the charts again after 1962 and dissolved in 1965.

After the Midnighters disbanded, Ballard launched a solo career. His 1968 single, "How You Gonna Get Respect (When You Haven't Cut Your Process Yet)", was his biggest post-Midnighters hit, peaking at number 15 on the R&B chart. James Brown produced Ballard's 1969 album You Can't Keep a Good Man Down. A 1972 single, "From the Love Side", credited to Hank Ballard and the Midnight Lighters, went to number 43 on the R&B chart. Ballard also appeared on Brown's 1972 album Get on the Good Foot, on two tracks, "Recitation By Hank Ballard", that features Ballard describing Brown and the album, and "Funky Side of Town", in duet, with James Brown..

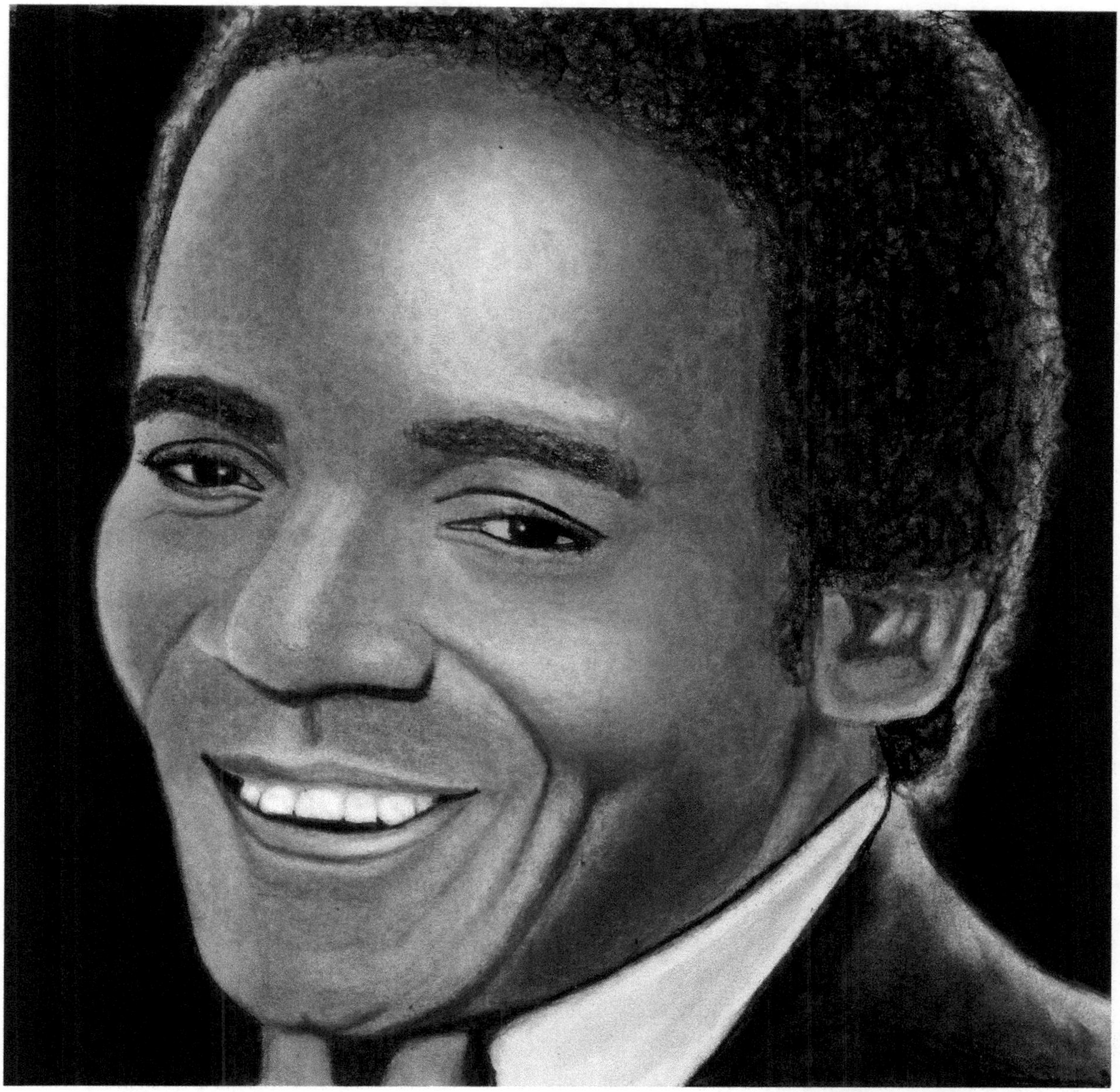

To view how this drawing was masterfully created or to purchase a Limited Edition Framed Artwork of Hank Ballard type into your Internet Browser the URL shortcut ➡ **myportrait.art/hankballard**

To listen to his Greatest Songs type into your Internet Browser the URL shortcut ➡ **radio.surf/hankballard**

To view all channels on THE FACE OF MUSIC Internet Radio MEGA Station type into your Internet Browser the URL shortcut ➡ **radio.surf/music**

To inquire about purchasing a Limited Edtion NFT of this portrait type into your Internet Browser the URL shortcut ➡ **myartnft.shop/hankballard**

To view all available NFTs type into your Internet Browser the URL shortcut ➡ **myartnft.shop/all**

# Hank Williams

(Net worth: $100 Thousand)(Total Records Sold: Millions)
(Genre: Country, Honk-Tonk, Folk, Rockabilly)(Height: 6' - 0")

Hiram "Hank" Williams (September 17, 1923 – January 1, 1953) was an American singer, songwriter, and musician. Regarded as one of the most significant and influential American singers and songwriters of the 20th century, he recorded 35 singles (five released posthumously) that reached the top 10 of the Billboard Country & Western Best Sellers chart, including 11 that reached No. 1 (three posthumously).

Born and raised in Alabama, Williams was given guitar lessons by African-American blues musician Rufus Payne in exchange for meals or money. Payne, along with Roy Acuff and Ernest Tubb, had a major influence on Williams's later musical style. Williams began his music career in Montgomery in 1937, when producers at local radio station WSFA hired him to perform and host a 15-minute program. He formed the Drifting Cowboys backup band, which was managed by his mother, and dropped out of school to devote his time to his career. When several of his band members were drafted during World War II, he had trouble with their replacements, and WSFA terminated his contract because of his alcoholism. Williams married singer Audrey Sheppard, who was his manager for nearly a decade. After recording "Never Again" and "Honky Tonkin'" with Sterling Records, he signed a contract with MGM Records. In 1947, he released "Move It on Over", which became a hit, and also joined the Louisiana Hayride radio program. One year later, he released a cover of "Lovesick Blues", which carried him into the mainstream. After an initial rejection, Williams joined the Grand Ole Opry. He was unable to read or notate music to any significant degree. Among the hits he wrote were "Your Cheatin' Heart", "Hey, Good Lookin'", and "I'm So Lonesome I Could Cry".

Years of back pain, alcoholism, and prescription drug abuse severely compromised Williams's health. In 1952, he divorced Sheppard and married singer Billie Jean Horton. He was dismissed by the Grand Ole Opry because of his unreliability and alcoholism. On New Year's Day 1953, he suffered from heart failure and died suddenly at the age of 29 in Oak Hill, West Virginia. Despite his relatively brief career, he is one of the most celebrated and influential musicians of the 20th century, especially in country music. Many artists have covered his songs and he has influenced Elvis Presley, Johnny Cash, Chuck Berry, Jerry Lee Lewis, George Jones, George Strait, Charley Pride, and The Rolling Stones, among others. Williams was inducted into the Country Music Hall of Fame in 1961, the Songwriters Hall of Fame in 1970, and the Rock and Roll Hall of Fame in 1987. The Pulitzer Prize jury awarded him a posthumous special citation in 2010 for his "craftsmanship as a songwriter who expressed universal feelings with poignant simplicity and played a pivotal role in transforming country music into a major musical and cultural force in American life".

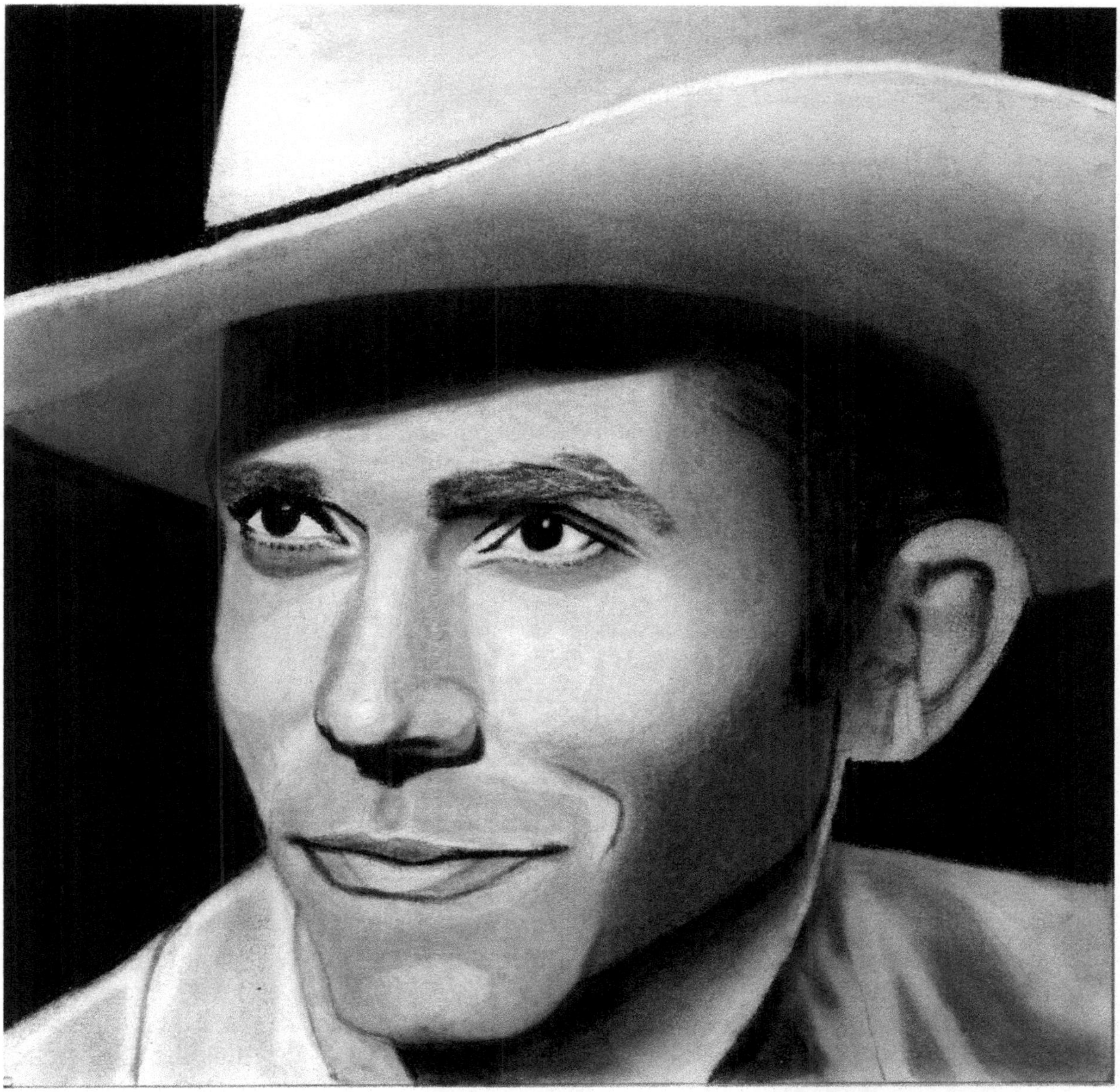

To view how this drawing was masterfully created or to purchase a Limited Edition Framed Artwork of Hank Williams type into your Internet Browser the URL shortcut ➡ **myportrait.art/hankwilliams**

To listen to his Greatest Songs type into your Internet Browser the URL shortcut ➡ **radio.surf/hankwilliams**

To view all channels on THE FACE OF MUSIC Internet Radio MEGA Station type into your Internet Browser the URL shortcut ➡ **radio.surf/music**

To inquire about purchasing a Limited Edition NFT of this portrait type into your Internet Browser the URL shortcut ➡ **myartnft.shop/hankwilliams**

To view all available NFTs type into your Internet Browser the URL shortcut ➡ **myartnft.shop/all**

# Harry Chapin

(Net worth: $5 Million)(Total Records Sold: Multi-Millions)
(Genre: Folk , Pop)

Harold Forster Chapin (December 7, 1942 – July 16, 1981) was an American singer-songwriter and philanthropist best known for his folk rock and pop rock songs. He achieved worldwide success in the 1970s and became one of the most popular artists and highest-paid performers. Chapin is also one of the best charting musical artists in the United States. Chapin, a Grammy Award-winning artist and Grammy Hall of Fame inductee, has sold over 16 million records worldwide. He has been described as one of the most beloved performers in music history.

As a dedicated humanitarian, Chapin fought to end world hunger. He was a key participant in the creation of the Presidential Commission on World Hunger in 1977. Chapin is credited with being the most politically and socially active American performer of the 1970s. In 1987, Chapin was posthumously awarded the Congressional Gold Medal for his humanitarian work.

In 1972 he released his debut album, Heads & Tales. The album was an international success, selling over 1 million units. Its success was due to the top 25 Billboard Hot 100 hit single, "Taxi". The song also became a top 5 hit in Canada.

The follow up album, Sniper and Other Love Songs, was also released in 1972. The album's title song, "Sniper", is a semi-fictional account of the University of Texas tower shooting. The single release from the album, "Sunday Morning Sunshine", charted on the Billboard Hot 100 and became a top 40 on Billboard Adult Contemporary.

In 1973, Chapin released his third album, Short Stories. The album produced another international hit, "W·O·L·D". Short Stories sold over 1 million units. The song is about an aging disc jockey who has given up his entire life and family for his career. The song is sung from the point of view of the disc jockey, who is singing to his ex-wife. It was inspired by American radio personality Jim Connors. Chapin wrote the song when he listened to Connors calling his ex-wife in the WMEX studio. The song became a top 40 hit on the Billboard Hot 100, a top 10 in Canada, and top 10 and 20 in various other countries. Other notable songs from the album, but not released as singles, are "Mr. Tanner", "Mail Order Annie", and "They Call Her Easy". The song, "Mr. Tanner", was loosely based on a pair of New York Times concert reviews of baritone Martin Tubridy – once in 1971 and once in 1972.

In 1974, Chapin released his most successful album, Verities and Balderdash. The album sold 2.5 million units due to the number 1 hit, "Cat's in the Cradle". The song is about a father who doesn't find time for his son during his childhood; and ultimately his son grows up to be just like his father, not making any time for his dad. The song earned Chapin another Grammy nomination for Best Male Pop Vocal Performance, and he was inducted into the Grammy Hall of Fame. Verities and Balderdash peaked at number 4 on the Billboard 200. The album's follow-up single, "I Wanna Learn a Love Song", charted at number 7 on Billboard Adult Contemporary. The song is a true story about how he met his wife, Sandra Chapin. "30,000 Pounds of Bananas" is a song that was included on the album but not released as a single. The song also became the number one requested song for a few weeks. It is a semi-fictional account of a truck crash that occurred in Scranton, Pennsylvania, transporting bananas - based loosely on a March 18, 1965 accident involving truck driver Gene Sesky. Other notable songs from the album include "Shooting Star", "Halfway to Heaven", and "Six String Orchestra".

In 1975, Chapin released his fifth album, Portrait Gallery. The album produced a top 40 Billboard Adult Contemporary hit, "Dreams Go By".

On the afternoon of July 16, 1981, Chapin was killed in a car accident.

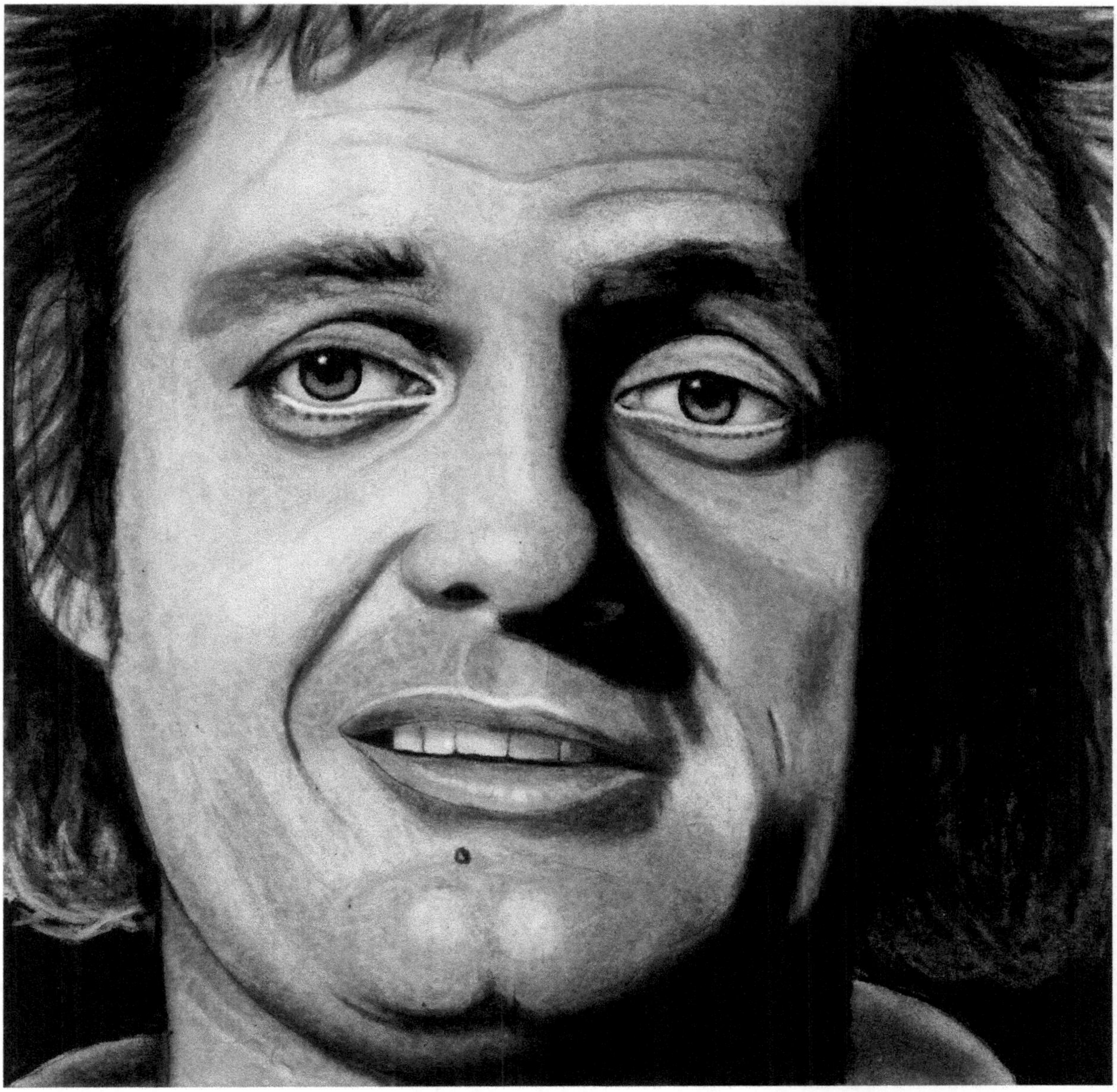

To view how this drawing was masterfully created or to purchase a Limited Edition Framed Artwork of Harry Chapin type into your Internet Browser the URL shortcut ➡ **myportrait.art/harrychapin**

To listen to his Greatest Songs type into your Internet Browser the URL shortcut ➡ **radio.surf/harrychapin**

To view all channels on THE FACE OF MUSIC Internet Radio MEGA Station type into your Internet Browser the URL shortcut ➡ **radio.surf/music**

To inquire about purchasing a Limited Edtion NFT of this portrait type into your Internet Browser the URL shortcut ➡ **myartnft.shop/harrychapin**

To view all available NFTs type into your Internet Browser the URL shortcut ➡ **myartnft.shop/all**

# Heart

(Total Records Sold: 35+ Million) (Genre: Classic Rock)
Heart is an American rock band formed in 1967 in Seattle, Washington, which evolved from an existing band, White Heart. By the mid-1970s, original members Roger Fisher (guitar) and Steve Fossen (bass guitar) had been joined by sisters Ann Wilson (lead vocals and flute) and Nancy Wilson (rhythm guitar, backing and occasional lead vocals), Michael Derosier (drums), and Howard Leese (guitar and keyboards) to form the lineup for the band's initial mid- to late-1970s success period. These core members were included in the band's 2013 induction into the Rock and Roll Hall of Fame.
Heart rose to fame with music influenced by hard rock and heavy metal, as well as folk music. The band's popularity declined in the early 1980s, but the band began a successful comeback in 1985 which continued into the mid-1990s. Heart disbanded in 1998, resumed performing in 2002, went on hiatus in 2016, and resumed performing in the summer of 2019. Heart's US Top 40 singles include "Magic Man" (1975), "Crazy on You" (1976), "Barracuda" (1977), "What About Love" (1985), "Never" (1985), and "All I Wanna Do Is Make Love to You" (1990), along with no. 1 hits "These Dreams" (1986) and "Alone" (1987).
Heart has sold over 35 million records worldwide, including approximately 22.5 million albums in the United States. It has placed top 10 albums on the Billboard 200 in the 1970s, 1980s, 1990 and 2010s. Heart was ranked number 57 on VH1's "100 Greatest Artists of Hard Rock".

# Ann Wilson

(Net Worth: $18 Million) (Height: 5' - 7")
Ann Dustin Wilson (born June 19, 1950) is an American musician best known as the lead singer and songwriter of the rock band Heart.
Wilson has been a member of Heart since the early 1970s; her younger sister, Nancy Wilson, is also a member of the band. The first hard rock band fronted by women, Heart released numerous albums throughout the late 1970s and 1980s; the albums Dreamboat Annie (1975), and Little Queen (1977) generated chart singles such as "Magic Man", "Crazy on You", and "Barracuda". Heart has sold over 35 million records worldwide and has placed top 10 albums on the Billboard 200 in the 1970s, 1980s, 1990 and 2010s.
Wilson was ranked no. 78 in Hit Parader's 2006 list of "Greatest Heavy Metal Vocalists of All Time". In 2013, she was inducted into the Rock and Roll Hall of Fame as a member of Heart.

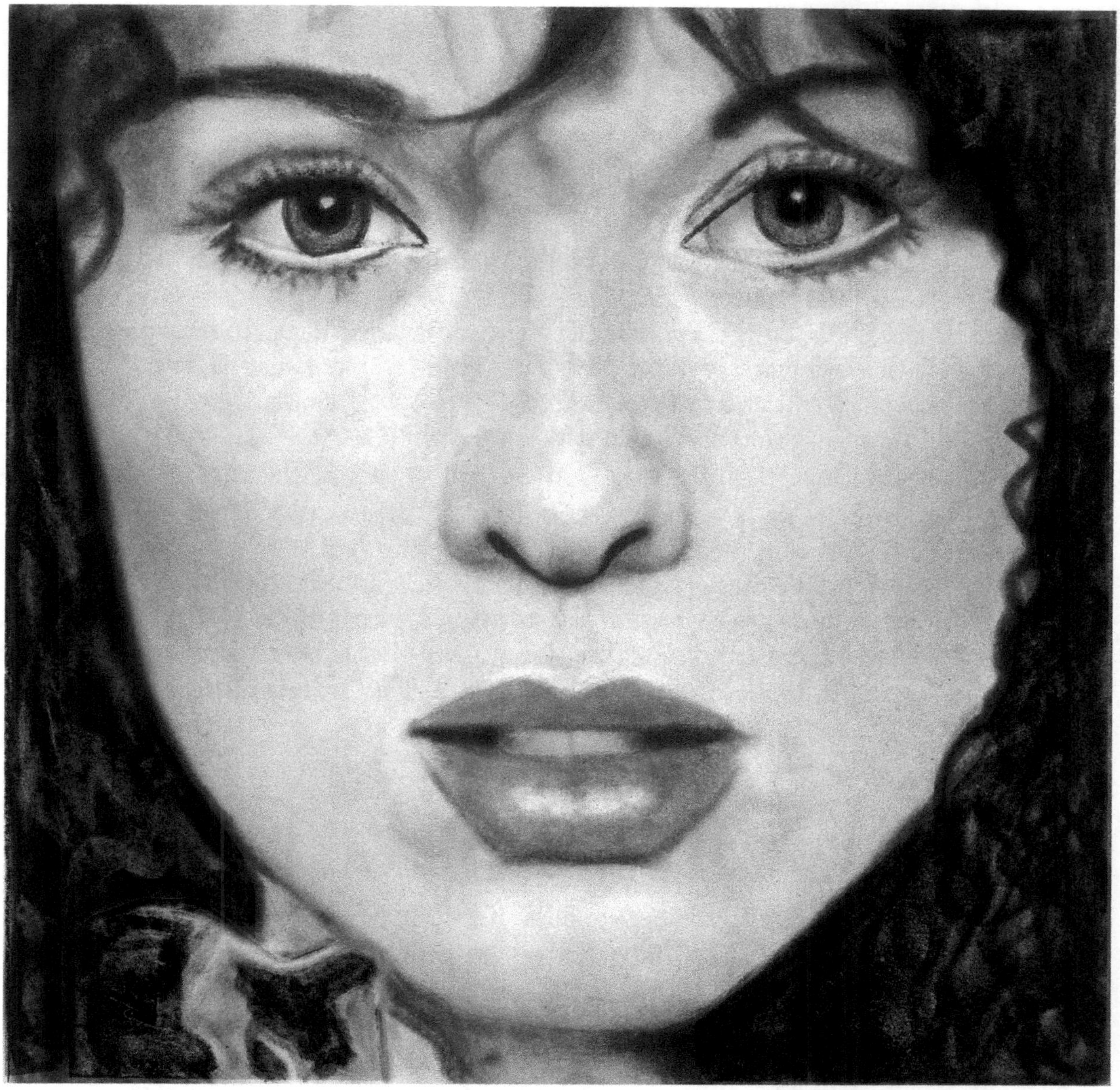

To view how this drawing was masterfully created or to purchase a Limited Edition Framed Artwork of Ann Wilson type into your Internet Browser the URL shortcut ➡ **myportrait.art/annwilson**

To listen to their Greatest Songs type into your Internet Browser the URL shortcut ➡ **radio.surf/heart**

To view all channels on THE FACE OF MUSIC Internet Radio MEGA Station type into your Internet Browser the URL shortcut ➡ **radio.surf/music**

To inquire about purchasing a Limited Edtion NFT of this portrait type into your Internet Browser the URL shortcut ➡ **myartnft.shop/annwilson**

To view all available NFTs type into your Internet Browser the URL shortcut ➡ **myartnft.shop/all**

# Hollies, The

(Total Records Sold: 30 Million) (Genre: Rock & Roll , Pop)
The Hollies are a British rock group formed in 1962. One of the leading British groups of the 1960s and into the mid 1970s, they are known for their distinctive three-part vocal harmony style. Allan Clarke and Graham Nash founded the band as a Merseybeat-type music group in Manchester, although some of the band members came from towns further north in East Lancashire. Graham Nash left the group in 1968 to form Crosby, Stills & Nash.

They enjoyed considerable popularity in many countries (with at least 60 singles or EPs and 26 albums charting somewhere in the world, spanning over five decades), although they did not achieve major US chart success until "Bus Stop" was released in 1966. The Hollies had over 30 charting singles on the UK Singles Chart and 22 on the Billboard Hot 100.

The Hollies are one of the few UK groups of the early 1960s, along with the Rolling Stones, that have never disbanded and continue to record and perform. In recognition of their achievements, the Hollies were inducted into the Rock and Roll Hall of Fame in 2010.

# Allan Clarke

(Net Worth: $20 Million) (Height: 5' - 10")
Harold Allan Clarke (born 5 April 1942, Salford, Lancashire, England) is an English pop rock singer, who was one of the founding members and the original lead singer of the Hollies. He achieved international hit singles with the group and is credited as co-writer on several of their best-known songs, including "On a Carousel", "Carrie Anne", "Jennifer Eccles" and "Long Cool Woman in a Black Dress". He retired from performing in 1999, but returned to the music industry in 2019. Clarke was inducted into the Rock and Roll Hall of Fame in 2010.

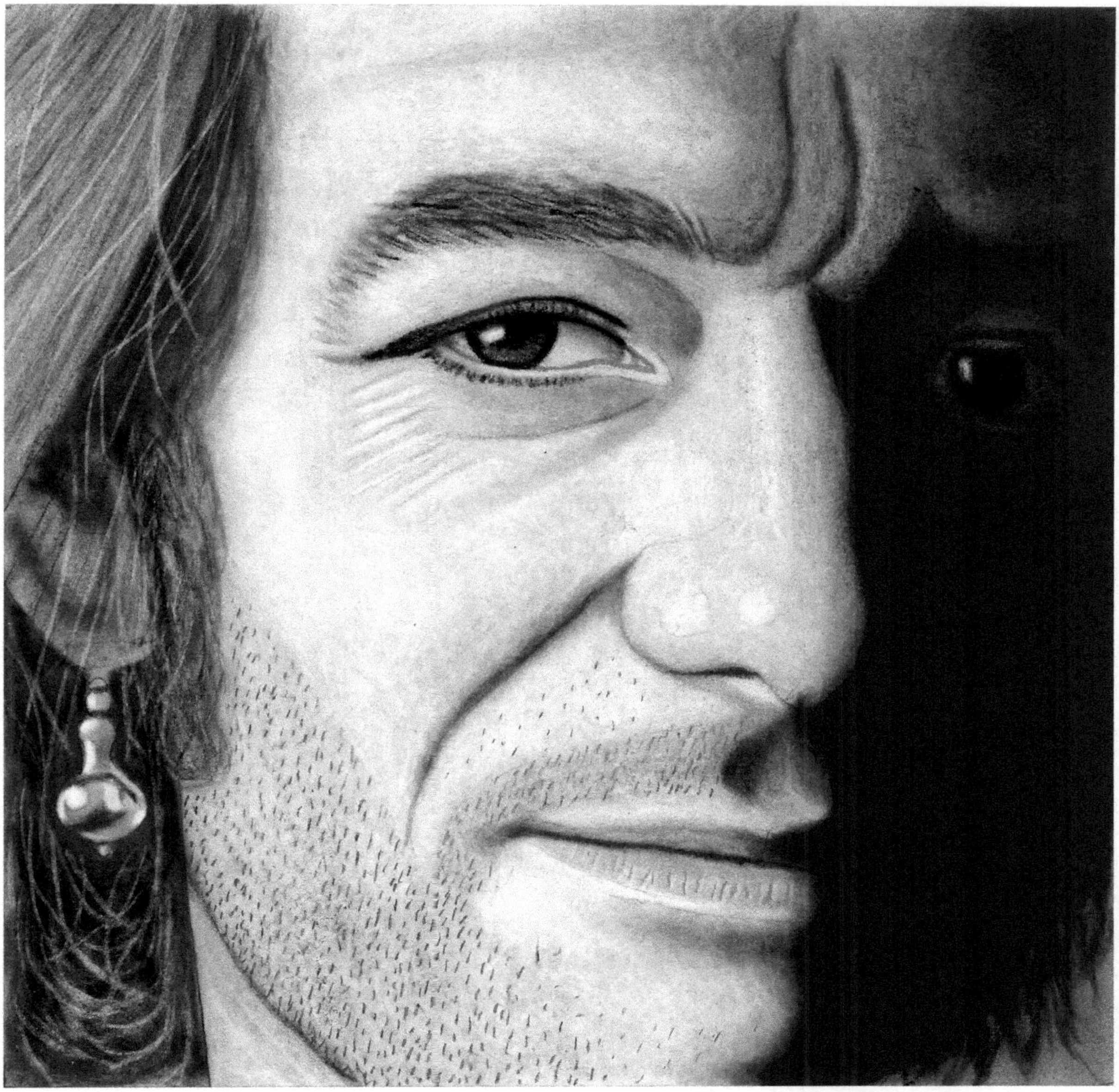

To view how this drawing was masterfully created or to purchase a Limited Edition Framed Artwork of Allan Clarke type into your Internet Browser the URL shortcut ➡ **myportrait.art/allanckarke**

To listen to their Greatest Songs type into your Internet Browser the URL shortcut ➡ **radio.surf/thehollies**

To view all channels on THE FACE OF MUSIC Internet Radio MEGA Station type into your Internet Browser the URL shortcut ➡ **radio.surf/music**

To inquire about purchasing a Limited Edition NFT of this portrait type into your Internet Browser the URL shortcut ➡ **myartnft.shop/allanckarke**

To view all available NFTs type into your Internet Browser the URL shortcut ➡ **myartnft.shop/all**

# Hootie & the Blowfish

(Total Records Sold: 21+ Million) (Genre: Soft Rock , Country Rock)

Hootie & the Blowfish is an American rock band that was formed in Columbia, South Carolina, in 1986. The band's lineup for most of its existence has been the quartet of Darius Rucker, Mark Bryan, Dean Felber, and Jim Sonefeld. The band went on hiatus in 2008 until they announced plans for a full reunion tour in 2019 and released their first new studio album in fourteen years, Imperfect Circle.

As of 2019, the band had charted sixteen singles on various Billboard singles charts and recorded six studio albums. Their debut album, Cracked Rear View (1994), is the 19th-best-selling album of all time in the United States, and was certified platinum 21 times. They have sold over 21 million copies of their albums in the United States. The group was also popular in Canada, having three number-one singles in the country.

# Darius Rucker

(Net Worth: $12 Million) (Height: 5' - 10")

Darius Carlos Rucker (born May 13, 1966) is an American singer and songwriter. He first gained fame as the lead vocalist and rhythm guitarist of rock band Hootie & the Blowfish, which he founded in 1986 at the University of South Carolina along with Mark Bryan, Jim "Soni" Sonefeld, and Dean Felber. The band released five studio albums with him as a member and charted six top 40 hits on the Billboard Hot 100. Rucker co-wrote most of the songs with the other members.

He released a solo R&B album, Back to Then in 2002 on Hidden Beach Recordings but no singles from it charted. Six years later, Rucker signed to Capitol Nashville as a country music singer, releasing the album, Learn to Live that year. Its first single, "Don't Think I Don't Think About It", made him the first black artist to reach number one on the Hot Country Songs charts since Charley Pride in 1983. (Ray Charles hit number one in March 1985 in a duet with Willie Nelson with "Seven Spanish Angels".) It was followed by two more number one singles, "It Won't Be Like This for Long" and "Alright" and the number three hit "History in the Making". In 2009, he became the first black American to win the New Artist Award from the Country Music Association, and the second black person to win any award from the association. A second album, Charleston, SC 1966, was released on October 12, 2010. The album includes the number one singles, "Come Back Song" and "This". His third country album True Believers (2013) reach No. 2 on the US Billboard 200 and No. 1 on the US Top Country Albums Billboard chart with singles "True Believers" (#24), "Wagon Wheel" (#1), and "Radio" (#14), all charting on the Billboard U.S. Country charts. His first country Christmas album, Home for the Holidays (2014) reached No. 31 on the US Billboard 200 chart and No. 7 on the US Country Chart. His fourth country album, Southern Style (2014) reached No. 6 (US Billboard 200) and No. 7 (Billboard US Top Country Albums), respectively with singles "Homegrown Honey" (#6) and "Southern Style" (#8) both charting on the U.S. Country charts in 2014 and 2015. His most recent country album When Was the Last Time (2017) charted #8 on the US Billboard 200 and #2 on the US Top Country Albums (Billboard).

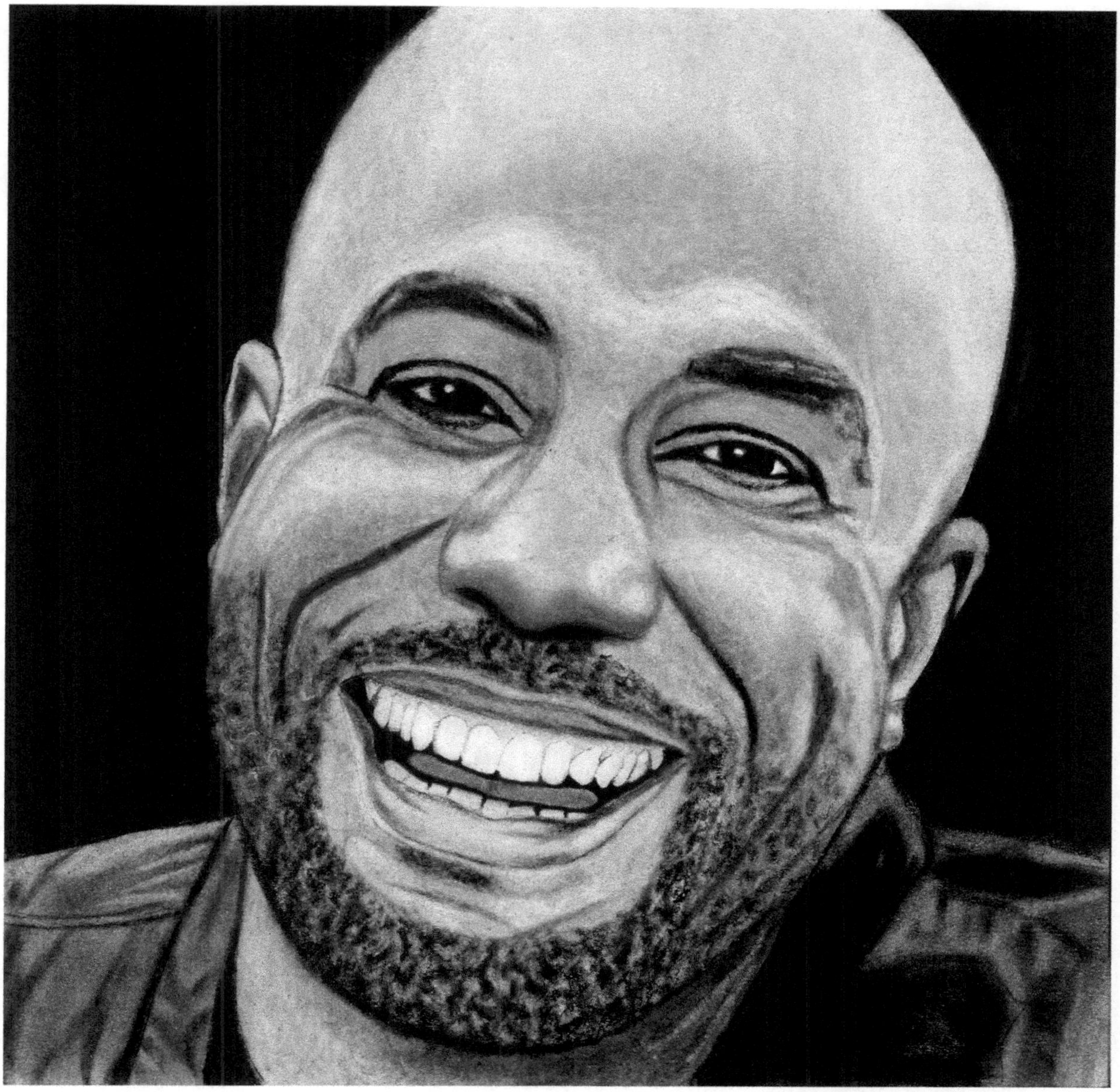

To view how this drawing was masterfully created or to purchase a Limited Edition Framed Artwork of Darius Rucker type into your Internet Browser the URL shortcut ➡ **myportrait.art/dariusrucker**

To listen to their Greatest Songs type into your Internet Browser the URL shortcut
➡ **radio.surf/hootieandtheblowfish**

To view all channels on THE FACE OF MUSIC Internet Radio MEGA Station type into your Internet Browser the URL shortcut ➡ **radio.surf/music**

To inquire about purchasing a Limited Edtion NFT of this portrait type into your Internet Browser the URL shortcut ➡ **myartnft.shop/dariusrucker**

To view all available NFTs type into your Internet Browser the URL shortcut ➡ **myartnft.shop/all**

# Huey Lewis & the News

(Total Records Sold: 30+ Million) (Genre: Pop)

Huey Lewis and the News is an American rock band based in San Francisco, California. They had a run of hit singles during the 1980s and early 1990s, eventually achieving 19 top ten singles across the Billboard Hot 100, Adult Contemporary, and Mainstream Rock charts.

Their most successful album, Sports, was released in 1983. The album, along with its videos being featured on MTV, catapulted the group to worldwide fame. Their popularity expanded when the song "The Power of Love" was featured in the 1985 film Back to the Future. "The Power of Love" reached number one on the Billboard Hot 100 singles chart and was nominated for the Academy Award for Best Original Song.

# Huey Lewis

(Net Worth: $25 Million) (Height: 5' - 11")

Hugh Anthony Cregg III (born July 5, 1950), known professionally as Huey Lewis, is an American singer, songwriter, and actor.

Lewis sings lead and plays harmonica for his band, Huey Lewis and the News, in addition to writing or co-writing many of the band's songs. The band is known for their third, and best-selling, album Sports, and their contribution to the soundtrack of the 1985 feature film Back to the Future. Lewis previously played with the band Clover from 1972 to 1979.

Huey Lewis was born in New York City. His father, Hugh Anthony Cregg Jr., was an Irish-American from Boston, and his mother, Maria Magdalena Barcinski, was Polish, from Warsaw. His grandfather, Hugh Cregg, was district attorney of Essex County, Massachusetts from 1931 to 1959..

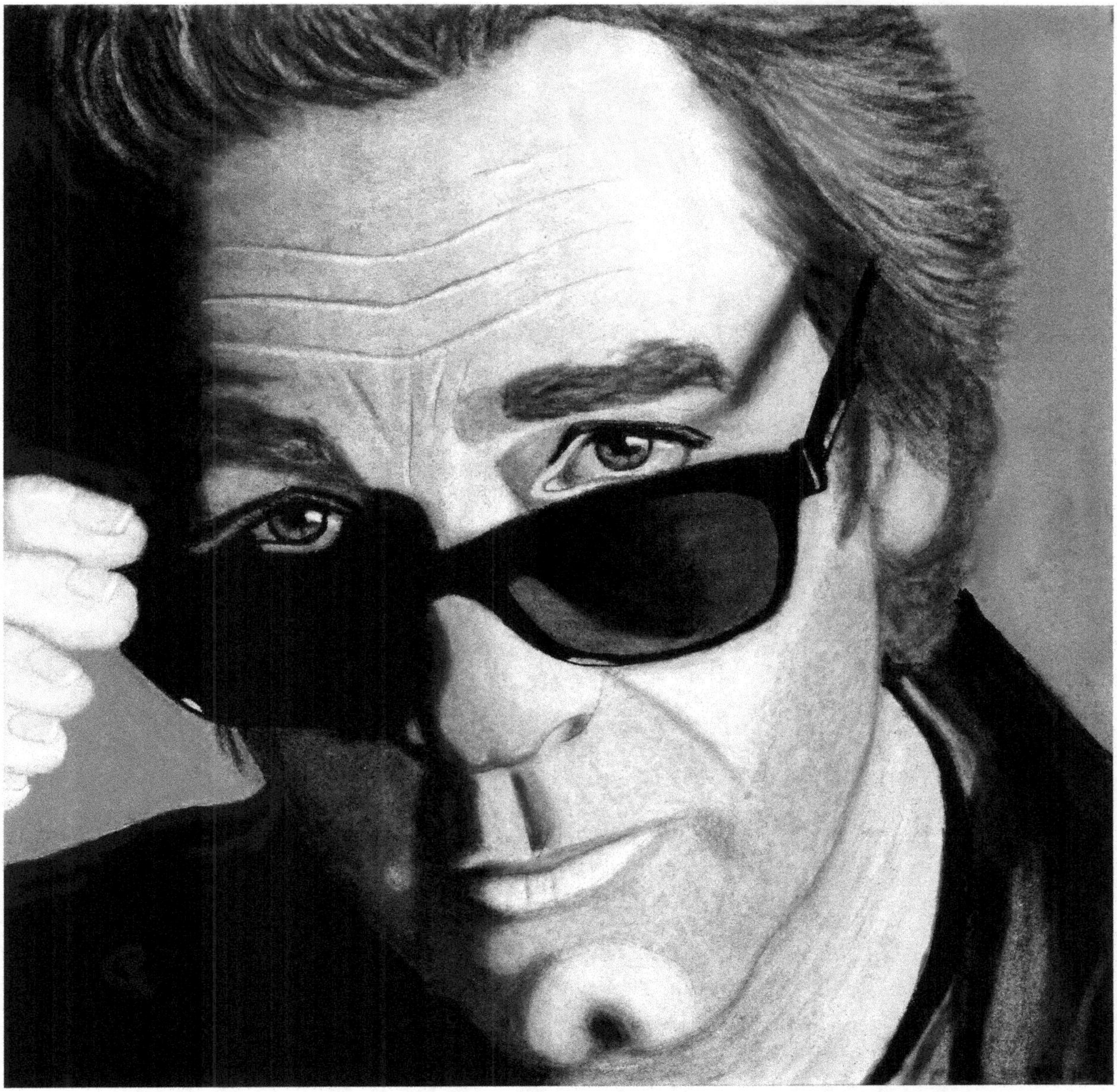

To view how this drawing was masterfully created or to purchase a Limited Edition Framed Artwork of Huey Lewis type into your Internet Browser the URL shortcut ➡ **myportrait.art/hueylewis**

To listen to their Greatest Songs type into your Internet Browser the URL shortcut
➡ **radio.surf/hueylewisandthenews**

To view all channels on THE FACE OF MUSIC Internet Radio MEGA Station type into your Internet Browser the URL shortcut ➡ **radio.surf/music**

To inquire about purchasing a Limited Edition NFT of this portrait type into your Internet Browser the URL shortcut ➡ **myartnft.shop/hueylewis**

To view all available NFTs type into your Internet Browser the URL shortcut ➡ **myartnft.shop/all**

# INXS

(Total Records Sold: 70+ Million) (Genre: New Wave, Rock)

INXS (pronounced "in excess") were an Australian rock band, formed as The Farriss Brothers in 1977 in Sydney, New South Wales. The band's founding members were bassist Garry Gary Beers, main composer and keyboardist Andrew Farriss, drummer Jon Farriss, guitarist Tim Farriss, lead singer and main lyricist Michael Hutchence, and guitarist and saxophonist Kirk Pengilly. For 20 years, INXS was fronted by Hutchence, whose magnetic stage presence made him the focal point of the band. Initially known for their new wave/pop style, the band later developed a harder pub rock style that included funk and dance elements.

In 1984, INXS had their first number-one hit in Australia with "Original Sin". The band would later achieve international success in the mid-to-late 1980s and early 1990s with the hit albums Listen Like Thieves, Kick, and X, as well as the singles "What You Need", "Need You Tonight" (the band's number-one single in the United States), "Devil Inside", "Never Tear Us Apart", "Suicide Blonde" and "New Sensation".

After Hutchence's death on 22 November 1997, INXS made appearances with several guest singers, and toured and recorded with Jon Stevens as lead singer, beginning in 2000. In 2005, members of INXS participated in Rock Star: INXS a reality television series that culminated in the selection of Canadian J.D. Fortune as their new lead singer. Irish singer-songwriter Ciaran Gribbin replaced Fortune as lead singer in 2011. During a concert on 11 November 2012, INXS stated that the performance would be their last, although they did not announce the band's permanent retirement.

INXS won six Australian Recording Industry Association (ARIA) awards, including three for "Best Group" in 1987, 1989 and 1992; the band was inducted into the ARIA Hall of Fame in 2001. INXS has sold over 70 million albums worldwide, making them one of Australia's highest selling music acts of all time.

# Michael Hutchence

(Net Worth: $1 Million) (Height: 5' - 10 1/2")

Michael Kelland John Hutchence (22 January 1960 – 22 November 1997) was an Australian musician, singer-songwriter and actor. Hutchence co-founded the rock band INXS which sold over 70 million records worldwide and was inducted into the ARIA Hall of Fame in 2001. He was the lead singer and lyricist of INXS from 1977 until his death.

Hutchence was a member of the short-lived pop rock group Max Q. He also recorded some solo material and acted in feature films, including Dogs in Space (1986), Frankenstein Unbound (1990), and Limp (1999).

Hutchence had a string of love affairs with prominent actresses, models and singers, and his private life was often reported in the Australian and international press. In July 1996, Hutchence and English television presenter Paula Yates had a daughter, Heavenly Hiraani Tiger Lily.

On the morning of 22 November 1997, Hutchence was found dead in his hotel room in Sydney. His death was reported by the New South Wales Coroner to be the result of suicide by hanging.

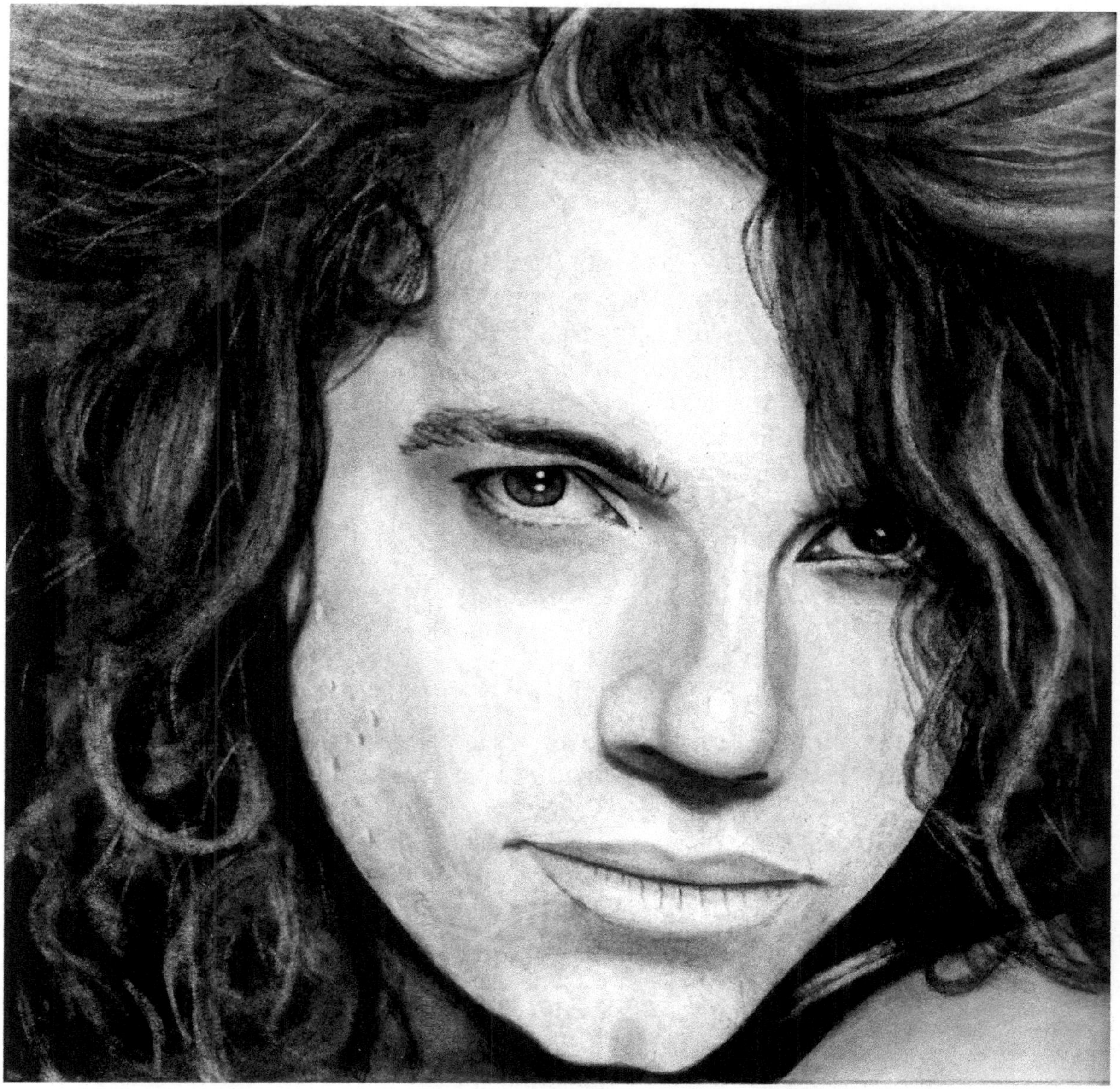

To view how this drawing was masterfully created or to purchase a Limited Edition Framed Artwork of Michael Hutchence type into your Internet Browser the URL shortcut ➡ **myportrait.art/michaelhutchence**

To listen to their Greatest Songs type into your Internet Browser the URL shortcut ➡ **radio.surf/inxs**

To view all channels on THE FACE OF MUSIC Internet Radio MEGA Station type into your Internet Browser the URL shortcut ➡ **radio.surf/music**

To inquire about purchasing a Limited Edtion NFT of this portrait type into your Internet Browser the URL shortcut ➡ **myartnft.shop/michaelhutchence**

To view all available NFTs type into your Internet Browser the URL shortcut ➡ **myartnft.shop/all**

# Iron Butterfly

(Total Records Sold: 30+ Million) (Genre: Heavy Metal , Psychedelic Rock)
Iron Butterfly is an American rock band best known for the 1968 hit "In-A-Gadda-Da-Vida", providing a dramatic sound that led the way towards the development of hard rock and heavy metal music. Formed in San Diego, California, among band members who used to be "arch enemies", their heyday was the late 1960s, but the band has been reincarnated with various members with varying levels of success, with no new recordings since 1975. The band's seminal 1968 album In- A-Gadda-Da-Vida was a best-seller. Iron Butterfly was the first group to receive an In-House platinum album award from Atlantic Records.

# Martin Gerschwitz

(Net Worth: $8 Million)
Martin Gerschwitz (born 25 June 1952) is a German violinist, keyboardist, singer and composer. Since 2005 he has played with the psychedelic rock band Iron Butterfly, both as a singer and keyboardist.
In the 2000s, he formed "Martin Gerschwitz & Friends", including Dieter Rubach on bass, Jan Mengeling on lead guitar and his childhood friend Martin Schwebel on drums. They also recorded a live DVD at the SAE, Frankfurt, in 2004. He continues to play worldwide tours with Iron Butterfly and solo.
Martin has worked and shared the stage with Scorpions, Cinderella, Eddie Van Halen, Loverboy, Tim Bogert, Robert Plant (Led Zeppelin), John Entwistle (The Who), Steve Stevens, Brituy Fox, U.D.O., Melanie Safka, Robben Ford, Andy Susemihl, Artimus Pyle (Lynyrd Skynyrd) and many more.

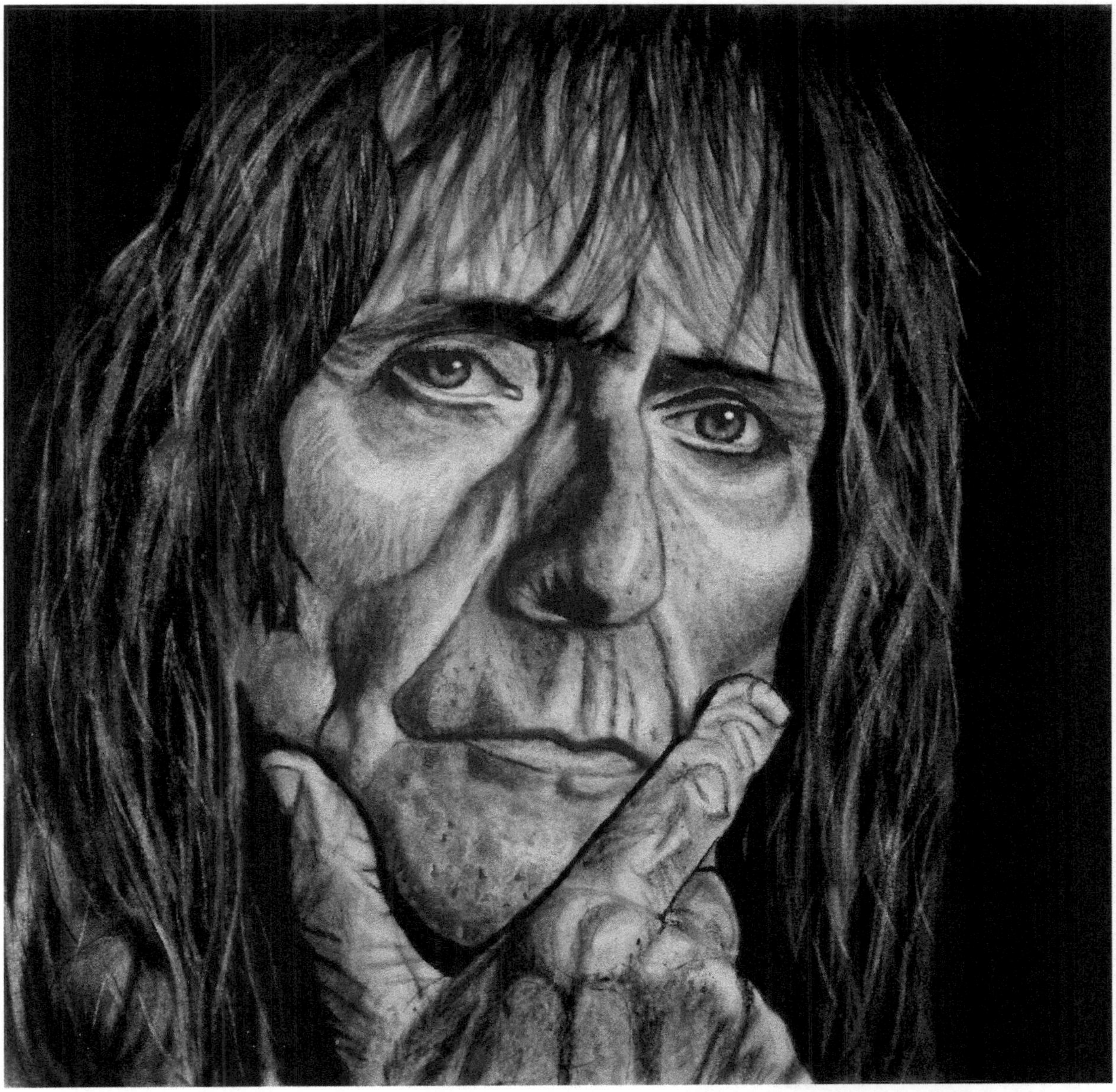

To view how this drawing was masterfully created or to purchase a Limited Edition Framed Artwork of Martin Gerschwitz type into your Internet Browser the URL shortcut ➡ **myportrait.art/martingerschwitz**

To listen to their Greatest Songs type into your Internet Browser the URL shortcut ➡ **radio.surf/ironbutterfly**

To view all channels on THE FACE OF MUSIC Internet Radio MEGA Station type into your Internet Browser the URL shortcut ➡ **radio.surf/music**

To inquire about purchasing a Limited Edition NFT of this portrait type into your Internet Browser the URL shortcut ➡ **myartnft.shop/martingerschwitz**

To view all available NFTs type into your Internet Browser the URL shortcut ➡ **myartnft.shop/all**

# Iron Maiden

(Total Records Sold: 100+ Million) (Genre: Heavy Metal)

Iron Maiden are an English heavy metal band formed in Leyton, East London, in 1975 by bassist and primary songwriter Steve Harris. The band's discography has grown to 40 albums, including 16 studio albums, 13 live albums, four EPs, and seven compilations.

Pioneers of the new wave of British heavy metal, Iron Maiden achieved initial success during the early 1980s. After several line-up changes, the band went on to release a series of UK and US platinum and gold albums, including 1982's The Number of the Beast, 1983's Piece of Mind, 1984's Powerslave, 1985's live release Live After Death, 1986's Somewhere in Time, 1988's Seventh Son of a Seventh Son, 1990's No Prayer for the Dying, and 1992's Fear of the Dark. Since the return of lead vocalist Bruce Dickinson and guitarist Adrian Smith in 1999, the band has undergone a resurgence in popularity, with a series of new albums and tours. Their 2010 studio offering, The Final Frontier, peaked at No. 1 in 28 countries and received widespread critical acclaim. The sixteenth studio album, The Book of Souls, was released on 4 September 2015 to similar success, topping the charts in 24 countries. Iron Maiden are considered one of the most influential and successful heavy metal bands in history, with The Sunday Times reporting in 2017 that the band have sold over 100 million copies of their albums worldwide, despite little radio or television support. The band won the Ivor Novello Award for international achievement in 2002. As of October 2013, the band have played over 2000 live shows throughout their career. For 40 years, the band have been supported by their famous mascot, "Eddie", who has appeared on almost all of their album and single covers, as well as in their live shows.

# Bruce Dickinson

(Net Worth: $130 Million)(Height: 5' - 6"|

Paul Bruce Dickinson (born 7 August 1958) is an English singer and songwriter. He is known for his work as the lead singer of the heavy metal band Iron Maiden since 1981, and is renowned for his wide-ranging operatic vocal style and energetic stage presence.

Dickinson began his career in music fronting small pub bands in the 1970s while attending school in Sheffield and university in London. In 1979, he joined British new wave heavy metal band Samson, with whom he gained some popularity under the stage name "Bruce Bruce" and performed on two studio records. He left Samson in 1981 to join Iron Maiden, replacing Paul Di'Anno, and debuted on their 1982 album The Number of the Beast. During his first tenure in the band, they issued a series of US and UK platinum and gold albums in the 1980s and early 1990s.

Dickinson quit Iron Maiden in 1993 (being replaced by Blaze Bayley) to pursue his solo career, which saw him experiment with a wide variety of heavy metal and rock styles. He re-joined the band in 1999, along with guitarist Adrian Smith, with whom he has released five subsequent studio albums. Since his return to Iron Maiden, he issued one further solo record in 2005, Tyranny of Souls. His younger cousin, Rob Dickinson, is the former lead singer of British alternative rock band Catherine Wheel, while his son, Austin, fronted the metalcore band Rise to Remain.

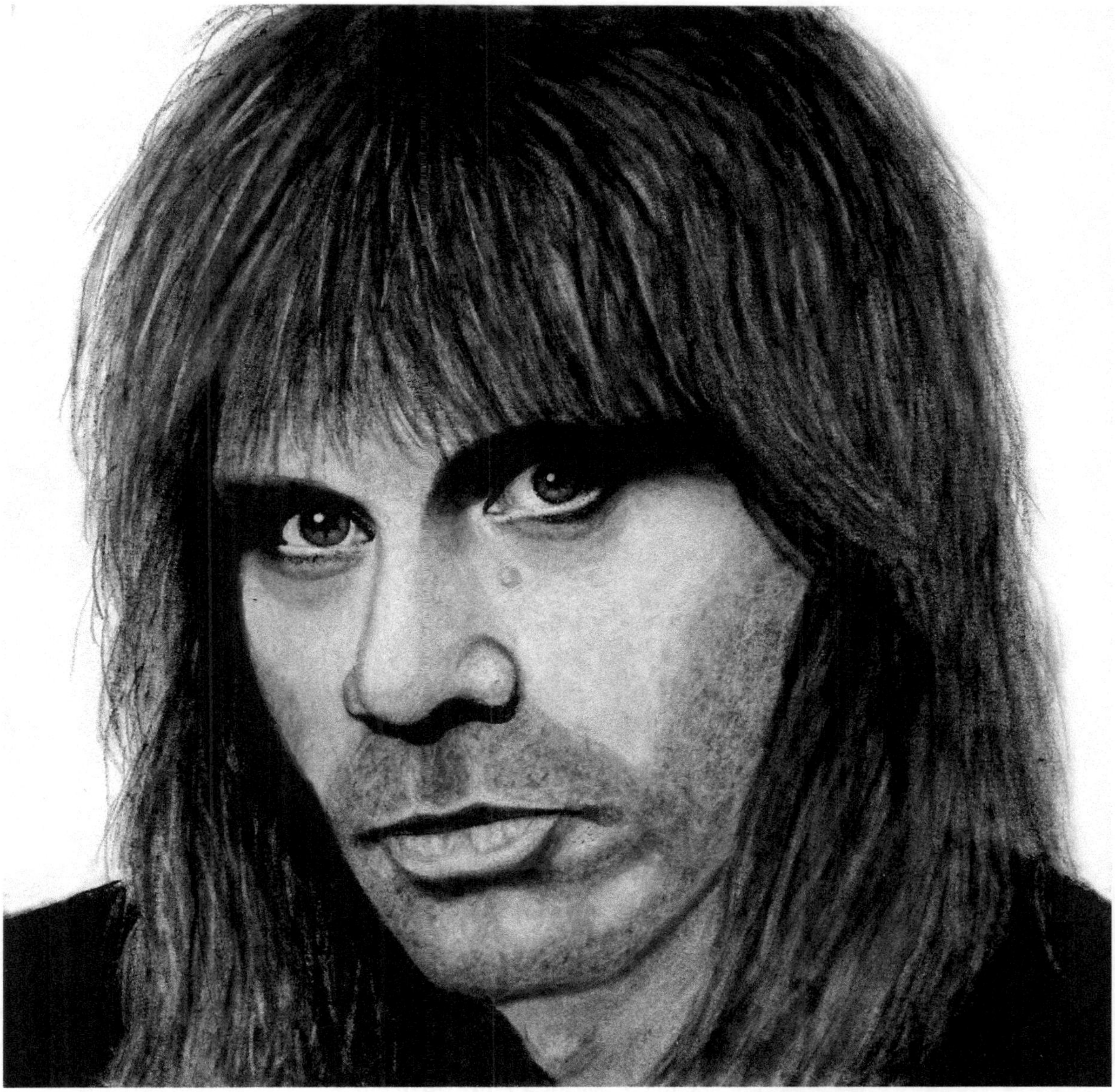

To view how this drawing was masterfully created or to purchase a Limited Edition Framed Artwork of Bruce Dickinson type into your Internet Browser the URL shortcut ➡ **myportrait.art/brucedickinson**

To listen to their Greatest Songs type into your Internet Browser the URL shortcut ➡ **radio.surf/ironmaiden**

To view all channels on THE FACE OF MUSIC Internet Radio MEGA Station type into your Internet Browser the URL shortcut ➡ **radio.surf/music**

To inquire about purchasing a Limited Edition NFT of this portrait type into your Internet Browser the URL shortcut ➡ **myartnft.shop/brucedickinson**

To view all available NFTs type into your Internet Browser the URL shortcut ➡ **myartnft.shop/all**

# Jackie Wilson

(Net worth: $10 Thousand)(Total Records Sold: Millions)
(Genre: R&B , Soul , Pop , Rock & Roll , Dop-Wop)

Jack Leroy Wilson Jr. (June 9, 1934 – January 21, 1984) was an American soul singer and performer. A tenor with a four-octave range, Wilson was a prominent figure in the transition of rhythm and blues into soul. Wilson was considered a master showman and one of the most dynamic singers and performers in pop, R&B and rock & roll history, earning the nickname "Mr. Excitement".

Wilson gained initial fame as a member of the R&B vocal group Billy Ward and His Dominoes. He went solo in 1957 and scored over 50 chart singles spanning the genres of R&B, pop, soul, doo-wop and easy listening, including 16 R&B Top 10 hits, in which six R&B of the repertoire ranked as number ones. On the Billboard Hot 100, Wilson scored 14 top 20 pop hits, six of which reached the top 10. Jackie Wilson was one of the most important and influential musical artists of his generation.

Wilson was posthumously inducted to the Rock and Roll Hall of Fame in 1987. He is also inducted into the National Rhythm & Blues Hall of Fame. Two of Wilson's recordings were inducted into the Grammy Hall of Fame in 1999. He was honored with the Rhythm and Blues Foundation's Legacy Tribute Award in 2003. In 2004, Rolling Stone magazine ranked Jackie Wilson No. 69 on its list of the 100 Greatest Artists of All Time.

Jack Leroy Wilson Jr. was born on June 9, 1934, in Highland Park, Michigan, as the third and only surviving child of singer-songwriter Jack Leroy Wilson, Sr. (1903–1983) and Eliza Mae Wilson (1900–1975). Eliza Mae was born on the Billups-Whitfield Place in Lowndes County, Mississippi. Eliza Mae's parents were Tom and Virginia Ransom. Wilson often visited his family in Columbus and was greatly influenced by the choir at Billups Chapel. Growing up in the suburban Detroit enclave of Highland Park, Wilson joined a gang called the Shakers and often got himself in trouble. Wilson's alcoholic father was frequently absent and usually unemployed. In 1943, his parents separated shortly after Jackie's ninth birthday.

Jackie Wilson began singing as a youth, accompanying his mother, an excellent church choir singer. In his early teens he joined a quartet, the Ever Ready Gospel Singers, who gained popularity in local churches. Wilson was not very religious, but he enjoyed singing in public. The money the quartet earned from performing was often spent on alcohol, and Wilson began drinking at an early age.

Wilson dropped out of high school at age 15, having been sentenced to detention in the Lansing Corrections system for juveniles twice. During his second stint in detention, Wilson learned to box and began competing in the Detroit amateur circuit at age 16. Wilson's record in the Golden Gloves was 2 and 8. After his mother forced Jackie to quit boxing, Wilson was forced by his father to marry Freda Hood, and he became a father at age 17.

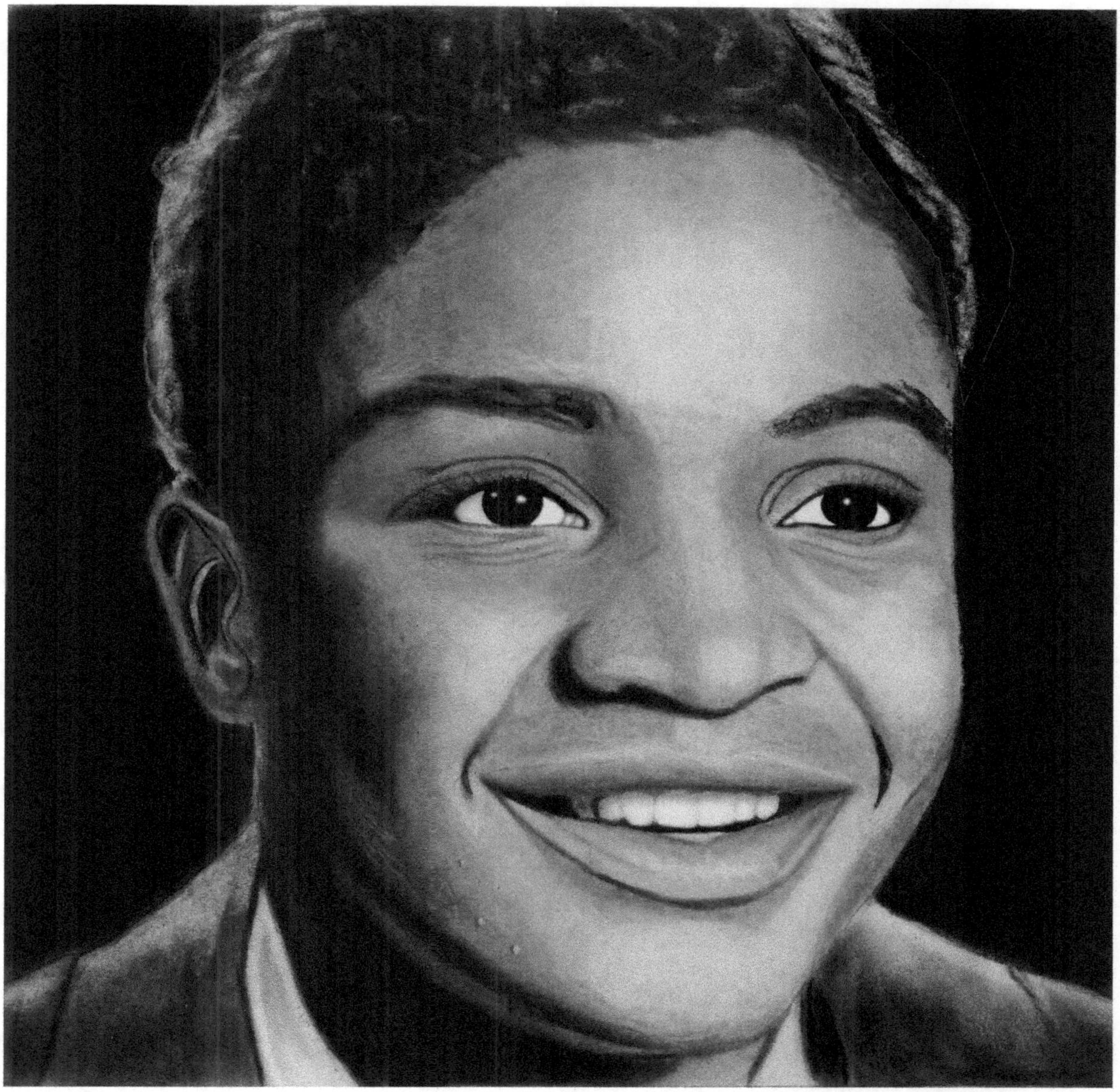

To view how this drawing was masterfully created or to purchase a Limited Edition Framed Artwork of Jackie Wilson type into your Internet Browser the URL shortcut ➡ **myportrait.art/jackiewilson**

To listen to his Greatest Songs type into your Internet Browser the URL shortcut ➡ **radio.surf/jackiewilson**

To view all channels on THE FACE OF MUSIC Internet Radio MEGA Station type into your Internet Browser the URL shortcut ➡ **radio.surf/music**

To inquire about purchasing a Limited Edtion NFT of this portrait type into your Internet Browser the URL shortcut ➡ **myartnft.shop/jackiewilson**

To view all available NFTs type into your Internet Browser the URL shortcut ➡ **myartnft.shop/all**

# James Brown

(Net worth: $100 Million)(Total Records Sold: 50+ Million)
(Genre: Funk , Soul , R&B)(Height: 5" - 6")

James Joseph Brown (May 3, 1933 – December 25, 2006) was an American singer, songwriter, dancer, musician, record producer and bandleader. The central progenitor of funk music and a major figure of 20th-century music, he is often referred to by the honorific nicknames "Godfather of Soul", "Mr. Dynamite", and "Soul Brother No. 1". In a career that lasted over 50 years, he influenced the development of several music genres. Brown was one of the first ten inductees into the Rock and Roll Hall of Fame at its inaugural induction in New York on January 23, 1986.

Brown began his career as a gospel singer in Toccoa, Georgia. He came to national public attention in the mid-1950s as the lead singer of the Famous Flames, a rhythm and blues vocal group founded by Bobby Byrd. With the hit ballads "Please, Please, Please" and "Try Me", Brown built a reputation as a tireless live performer with the Famous Flames and his backing band, sometimes known as the James Brown Band or the James Brown Orchestra. His success peaked in the 1960s with the live album Live at the Apollo and hit singles such as "Papa's Got a Brand New Bag", "I Got You (I Feel Good)" and "It's a Man's Man's Man's World".

During the late 1960s, Brown moved from a continuum of blues and gospel-based forms and styles to a profoundly "Africanized" approach to music-making, emphasizing stripped-down interlocking rhythms that influenced the development of funk music. By the early 1970s, Brown had fully established the funk sound after the formation of the J.B.s with records such as "Get Up (I Feel Like Being a) Sex Machine" and "The Payback". He also became noted for songs of social commentary, including the 1968 hit "Say It Loud – I'm Black and I'm Proud". Brown continued to perform and record until his death from pneumonia in 2006.

Brown recorded 17 singles that reached No. 1 on the Billboard R&B charts. He also holds the record for the most singles listed on the Billboard Hot 100 chart which did not reach No. 1. Brown was inducted into the first class of the Rhythm & Blues Music Hall of Fame in 2013 as an artist and then in 2017 as a songwriter. He also received honors from several other institutions, including inductions into the Songwriters Hall of Fame. In Joel Whitburn's analysis of the Billboard R&B charts from 1942 to 2010, Brown is ranked No. 1 in The Top 500 Artists. He is ranked seventh on Rolling Stone's list of the 100 Greatest Artists of All Time.

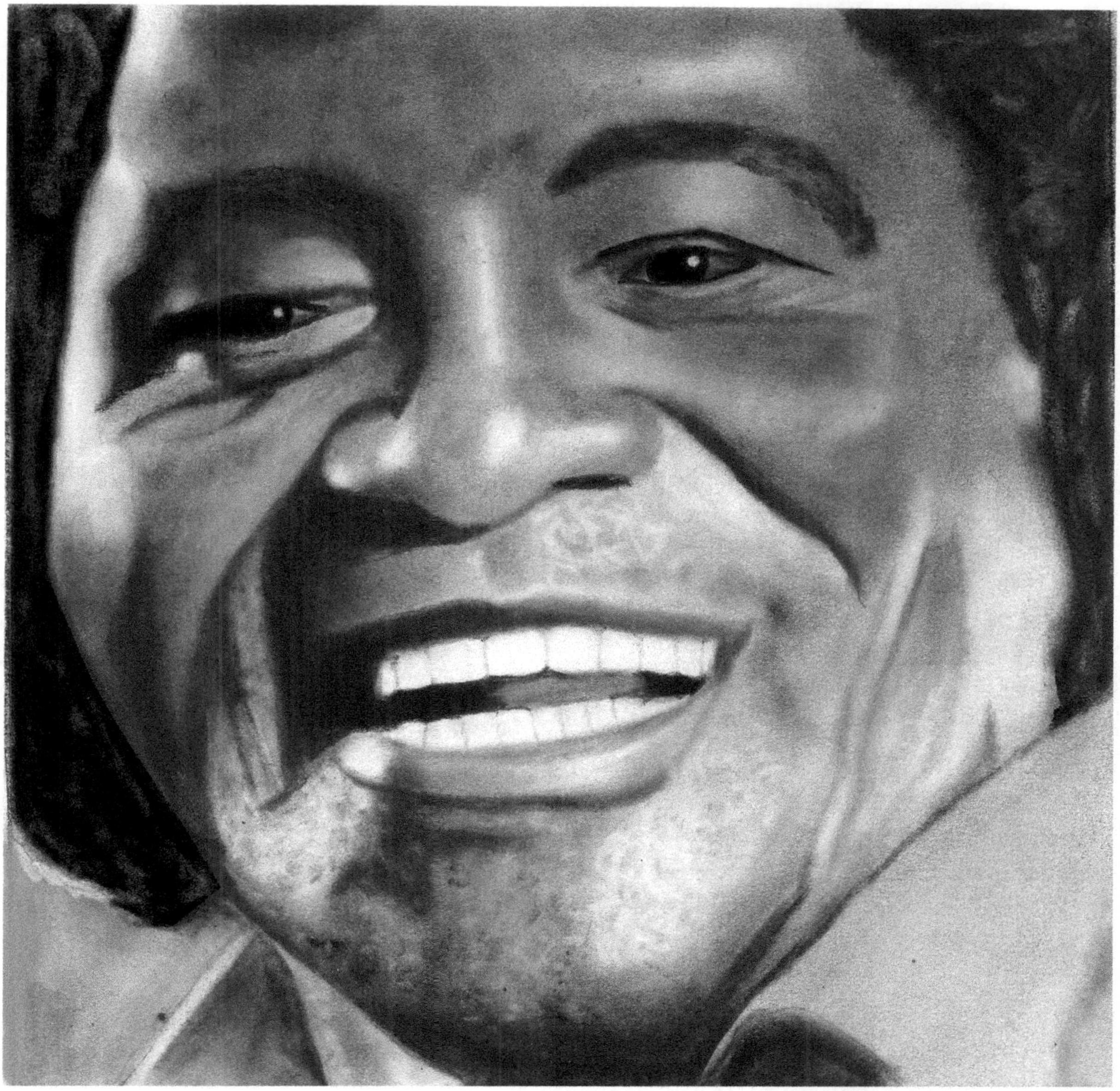

To view how this drawing was masterfully created or to purchase a Limited Edition Framed Artwork of James Brown type into your Internet Browser the URL shortcut ➡ **myportrait.art/jamesbrown**

To listen to his Greatest Songs type into your Internet Browser the URL shortcut ➡ **radio.surf/jamesbrown**

To view all channels on THE FACE OF MUSIC Internet Radio MEGA Station type into your Internet Browser the URL shortcut ➡ **radio.surf/music**

To inquire about purchasing a Limited Edtion NFT of this portrait type into your Internet Browser the URL shortcut ➡ **myartnft.shop/jamesbrown**

To view all available NFTs type into your Internet Browser the URL shortcut ➡ **myartnft.shop/all**

# Janis Joplin

(Net worth: $2 Million)(Total Albums Sold: 18.5+ Million)
(Genre: Psychedelic Rock , Soul , Blues)(Height: 5" - 6")

Janis Lyn Joplin (January 19, 1943 – October 4, 1970) was an American singer-songwriter who sang rock, soul and blues music. One of the most successful and widely known rock stars of her era, she was noted for her powerful mezzo-soprano vocals and "electric" stage presence.

In 1967, Joplin rose to fame following an appearance at Monterey Pop Festival, where she was the lead singer of the then little-known San Francisco psychedelic rock band Big Brother and the Holding Company. After releasing two albums with the band, she left Big Brother to continue as a solo artist with her own backing groups, first the Kozmic Blues Band and then the Full Tilt Boogie Band. She appeared at the Woodstock festival and the Festival Express train tour. Five singles by Joplin reached the Billboard Hot 100, including a cover of the Kris Kristofferson song "Me and Bobby McGee", which reached number one in March 1971. Her most popular songs include her cover versions of "Piece of My Heart", "Cry Baby", "Down on Me", "Ball and Chain", and "Summertime"; and her original song "Mercedes Benz", her final recording.

Joplin died of an accidental heroin overdose in 1970 aged 27, after releasing three albums (two with Big Brother, and one solo album). A second solo album, Pearl, was released in January 1971, just over three months after her death. It reached number one on the Billboard charts. She was posthumously inducted into the Rock and Roll Hall of Fame in 1995. Rolling Stone ranked Joplin number 46 on its 2004 list of the 100 Greatest Artists of All Time and number 28 on its 2008 list of 100 Greatest Singers of All Time. She remains one of the top-selling musicians in the United States, with Recording Industry Association of America certifications of 18.5 million albums sold.

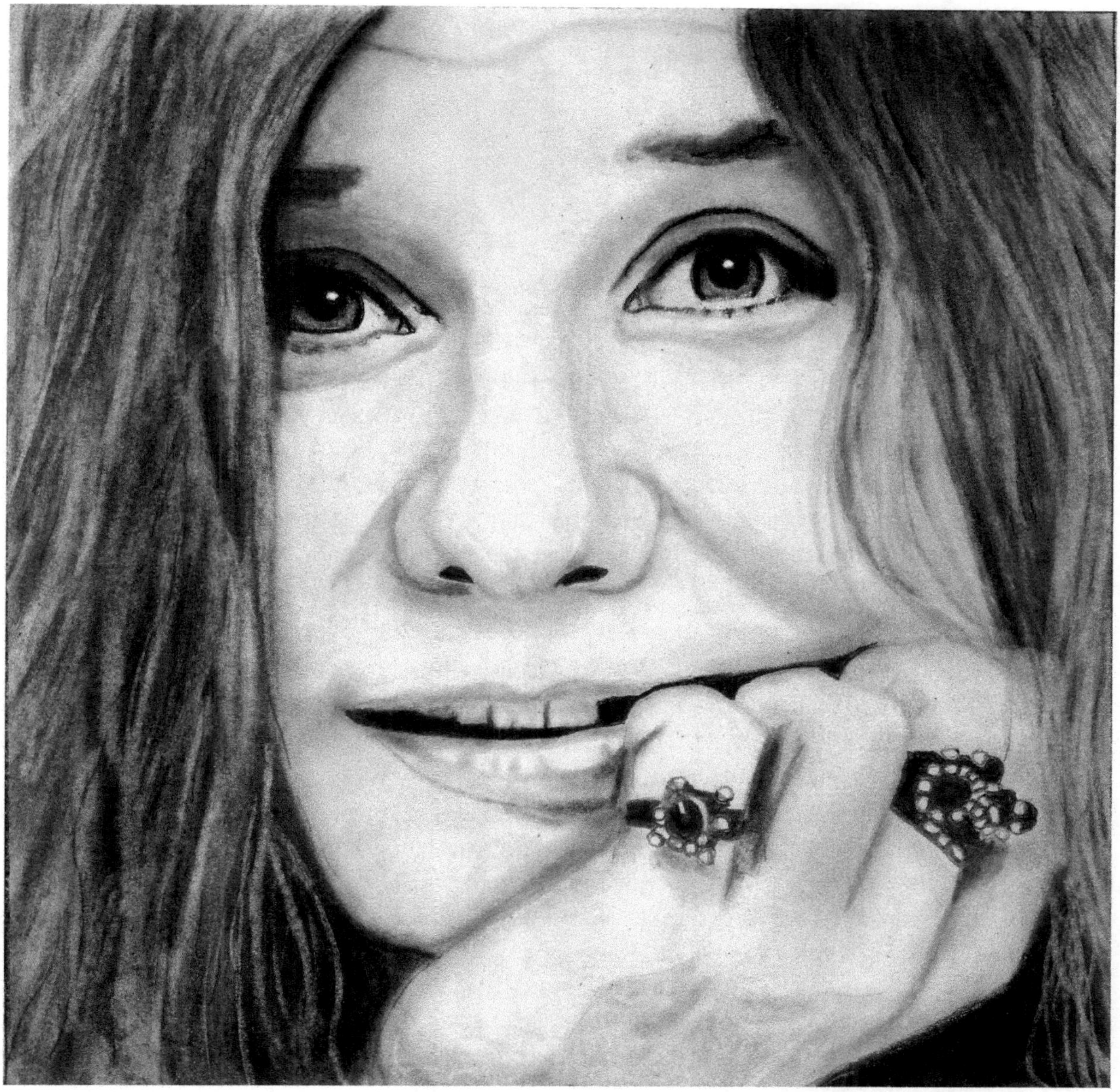

To view how this drawing was masterfully created or to purchase a Limited Edition Framed Artwork of Janis Joplin type into your Internet Browser the URL shortcut ➡ **myportrait.art/janisjoplin**

To listen to her Greatest Songs type into your Internet Browser the URL shortcut ➡ **radio.surf/janisjoplin**

To view all channels on THE FACE OF MUSIC Internet Radio MEGA Station type into your Internet Browser the URL shortcut ➡ **radio.surf/music**

To inquire about purchasing a Limited Edition NFT of this portrait type into your Internet Browser the URL shortcut ➡ **myartnft.shop/janisjoplin**

To view all available NFTs type into your Internet Browser the URL shortcut ➡ **myartnft.shop/all**

# Jay-Z

(Net worth: $ 1 . 4 Billion)(Total Albums Sold: 50+ Million)
(Genre: Hip-Hop)(Height: 6" - 1 1/2")

Shawn Corey Carter (born December 4, 1969), known professionally as Jay-Z is an American rapper, songwriter, record executive, businessman, and record producer. He is widely regarded as one of the most influential hip-hop artists in history and often cited as one of the greatest rappers of all time.[6][7] Born and raised in New York City, Jay-Z first began his musical career after founding the record label Roc-A-Fella Records in 1995, and subsequently released his debut studio album Reasonable Doubt in 1996. The album was released to widespread critical success, and solidified his standing in the music industry. He has gone on to release twelve additional albums, including the acclaimed albums The Blueprint (2001), The Black Album (2003), American Gangster (2007), and 4:44 (2017). Jay-Z has also released the full-length collaborative albums Watch the Throne (2011) with Kanye West and Everything Is Love (2018) with his wife Beyoncé, respectively.

Outside of his musical career, Jay-Z has also attained significant success and media attention for his career as a businessman. In 1999, he founded the clothing retailer Rocawear, and in 2003, he founded the luxury sports bar chain 40/40 Club. Both businesses have grown to become multi-million-dollar corporations, and allowed Jay-Z to fund the start-up for the entertainment company Roc Nation, which was founded in 2008. In 2015, he acquired the tech company Aspiro and took charge of their media streaming service Tidal.

Jay-Z is one of the world's best-selling music artists, with over 50 million albums and 75 million singles sold worldwide. He has won a total of 23 Grammy Awards, the most by a rapper, and holds the record for the most number-one albums by a solo artist on the Billboard 200, with 14. He has been ranked by Billboard and fellow music publication Rolling Stone as one of the 100 Greatest Artists of All Time.In 2017, he became the first rapper to be honored into the Songwriters Hall of Fame, and in 2018, received the commemorative "Salute to Industry Icons" award at the 60th Grammy Awards. In June 2019, Jay-Z officially became the first hip hop billionaire, making him the among the top wealthiest black Americans and the 2nd wealthiest American musician to date. In December 2020, Jay-Z launched a line of cannabis products called "Monogram".

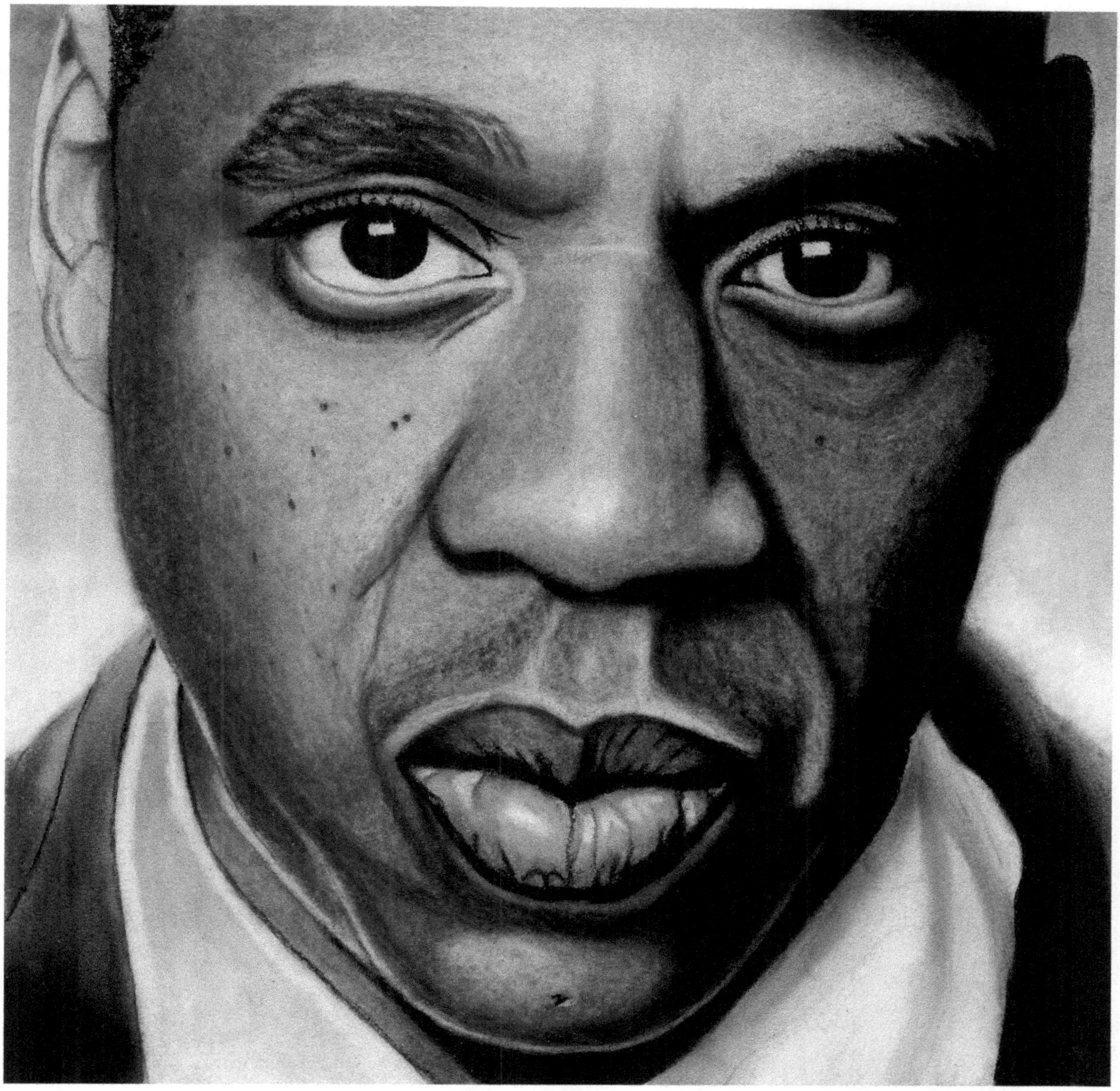

To view how this drawing was masterfully created or to purchase a Limited Edition Framed Artwork of Jay-Z type into your Internet Browser the URL shortcut ➡ **myportrait.art/jayz**

To listen to his Greatest Songs type into your Internet Browser the URL shortcut ➡ **radio.surf/jayz**

To view all channels on THE FACE OF MUSIC Internet Radio MEGA Station type into your Internet Browser the URL shortcut ➡ **radio.surf/music**

To inquire about purchasing a Limited Edition NFT of this portrait type into your Internet Browser the URL shortcut ➡ **myartnft.shop/jayz**

To view all available NFTs type into your Internet Browser the URL shortcut ➡ **myartnft.shop/all**

# Jefferson Airplane

(Total Records Sold: Millions) (Genre: Psychedelic Rock)

Jefferson Airplane was an American rock band based in San Francisco, California, that became one of the pioneering bands of psychedelic rock. Formed in 1965, the group defined the San Francisco Sound and was the first from the Bay Area to achieve international commercial success. They were headliners at the Monterey Pop Festival (1967), Woodstock (1969), Altamont Free Concert (1969), and the first Isle of Wight Festival (1968) in England. Their 1967 break-out album Surrealistic Pillow ranks on the short list of the most significant recordings of the Summer of Love. Two songs from that album, "Somebody to Love" and "White Rabbit", are among Rolling Stone's "500 Greatest Songs of All Time".

The October 1966 to February 1970 lineup of Jefferson Airplane, consisting of Marty Balin (vocals), Paul Kantner (guitar, vocals), Grace Slick (vocals), Jorma Kaukonen (lead guitar, vocals), Jack Casady (bass), and Spencer Dryden (drums), was inducted into the Rock and Roll Hall of Fame in 1996. Marty Balin left the band in 1971. After 1972, Jefferson Airplane effectively split into two groups. Kaukonen and Casady moved on full-time to their own band, Hot Tuna. Slick, Kantner, and the remaining members of Jefferson Airplane recruited new members and regrouped as Jefferson Starship in 1974, with Marty Balin eventually joining them. Jefferson Airplane was presented with the Grammy Lifetime Achievement Award in 2016.

# Grace Slick

(Net Worth: $20 Million)(Height: 5' - 7")

Grace Slick (born Grace Barnett Wing, October 30, 1939) is a retired American singer-songwriter and current artist who was a key figure in San Francisco's burgeoning psychedelic music scene in the mid-1960s. Her music career spanned four decades. She performed with The Great Society, Jefferson Airplane with whom she first found fame with the Surrealistic Pillow album, Jefferson Starship and Starship. She also had a sporadic solo career. Slick provided vocals on a number of well-known songs, including "Somebody to Love", "White Rabbit", "We Built This City", and "Nothing's Gonna Stop Us Now".

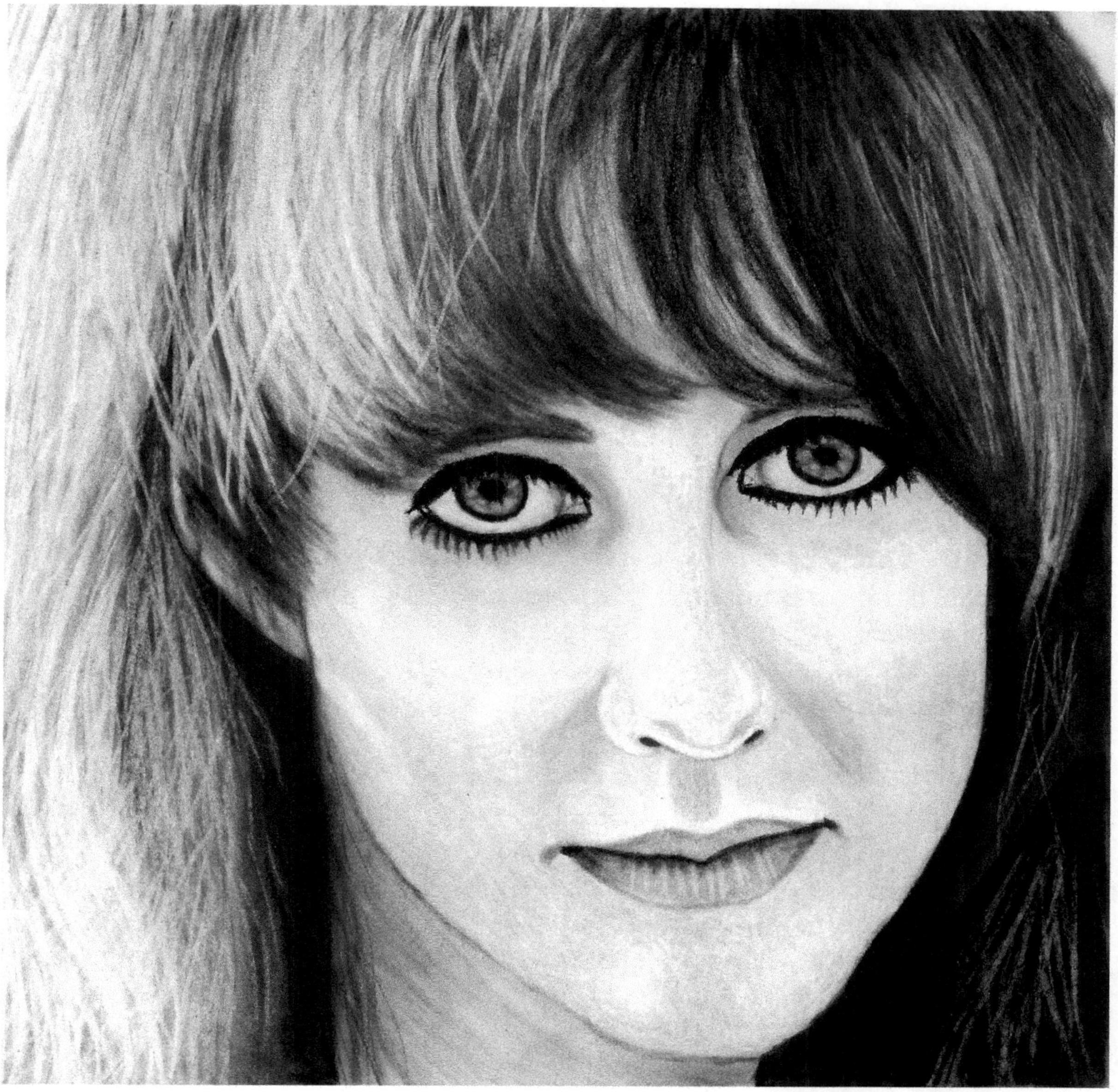

To view how this drawing was masterfully created or to purchase a Limited Edition Framed Artwork of Grace Slick type into your Internet Browser the URL shortcut ➡ **myportrait.art/graceslick**

To listen to their Greatest Songs type into your Internet Browser the URL shortcut
➡ **radio.surf/jeffersonairplane**

To view all channels on THE FACE OF MUSIC Internet Radio MEGA Station type into your Internet Browser the URL shortcut ➡ **radio.surf/music**

To inquire about purchasing a Limited Edtion NFT of this portrait type into your Internet Browser the URL shortcut ➡ **myartnft.shop/graceslick**

To view all available NFTs type into your Internet Browser the URL shortcut ➡ **myartnft.shop/all**

# Jennifer Lopez

(Net worth: $400 Million)(Total Records Sold: 70 Million)
(Genre: R&B , Hip-Hop , Dance , Latin , Pop)(Height: 5" - 2")

Jennifer Lynn Lopez (born July 24, 1969), also known by her nickname J.Lo, is an American actress, singer, songwriter and dancer. In 1991, Lopez began appearing as a Fly Girl dancer on In Living Color, where she remained a regular until she decided to pursue an acting career in 1993. For her first leading role in the 1997 Selena biopic of the same name, Lopez became the first Latin actress to earn over US$1 million for a film. She went on to star in Anaconda (1997) and Out of Sight (1998), and has subsequently established herself as one of the highest-paid Latin actresses worldwide as of 2017. Lopez is considered a pop culture icon, and is often described as a triple threat entertainer.

Lopez ventured into the music industry with her debut studio album On the 6 (1999), which helped propel the Latin pop movement in American music. With the simultaneous release of her second studio album J.Lo and her romantic comedy The Wedding Planner in 2001, Lopez became the first woman to have a number-one album and film in the same week. Her 2002 release, J to tha L–O! The Remixes, became the first remix album in history to debut atop the US Billboard 200. Later that year, she released her third studio album This Is Me... Then and starred in the film Maid in Manhattan.

After starring in Gigli (2003), a critical and commercial failure, Lopez subsequently starred in the successful romantic comedies Shall We Dance? (2004) and Monster-in-Law (2005). Her fifth studio album, Como Ama una Mujer (2007), received the highest first week sales for a debut Spanish album in the United States. Following a relatively unsuccessful period, she returned to prominence in 2011 with her appearance as a judge on American Idol and released her seventh studio album Love?. From 2016 to 2018, she starred in the police drama series Shades of Blue and performed a residency show, Jennifer Lopez: All I Have, at Planet Hollywood Las Vegas. Since 2017, Lopez has produced and served as a judge on World of Dance. In 2019, she garnered critical acclaim for her performance as a stripper in the crime drama Hustlers.

With a cumulative film gross of US$3.1 billion and estimated global sales of 70 million records, Lopez is regarded as the most influential Latin entertainer in North America. In 2012, Forbes ranked her as the most powerful celebrity in the world, as well as the 38th most powerful woman in the world. Time listed her among the 100 most influential people in the world in 2018. Her most successful singles on the US Billboard Hot 100 include: "If You Had My Love", "I'm Real", "Ain't It Funny", "All I Have", and "On the Floor". For her contributions to the recording industry, Lopez has received a landmark star on the Hollywood Walk of Fame, the Billboard Icon Award, and the Michael Jackson Video Vanguard Award among other honors. Her other ventures include beauty and clothing lines, fragrances, a production company, and a charitable foundation.

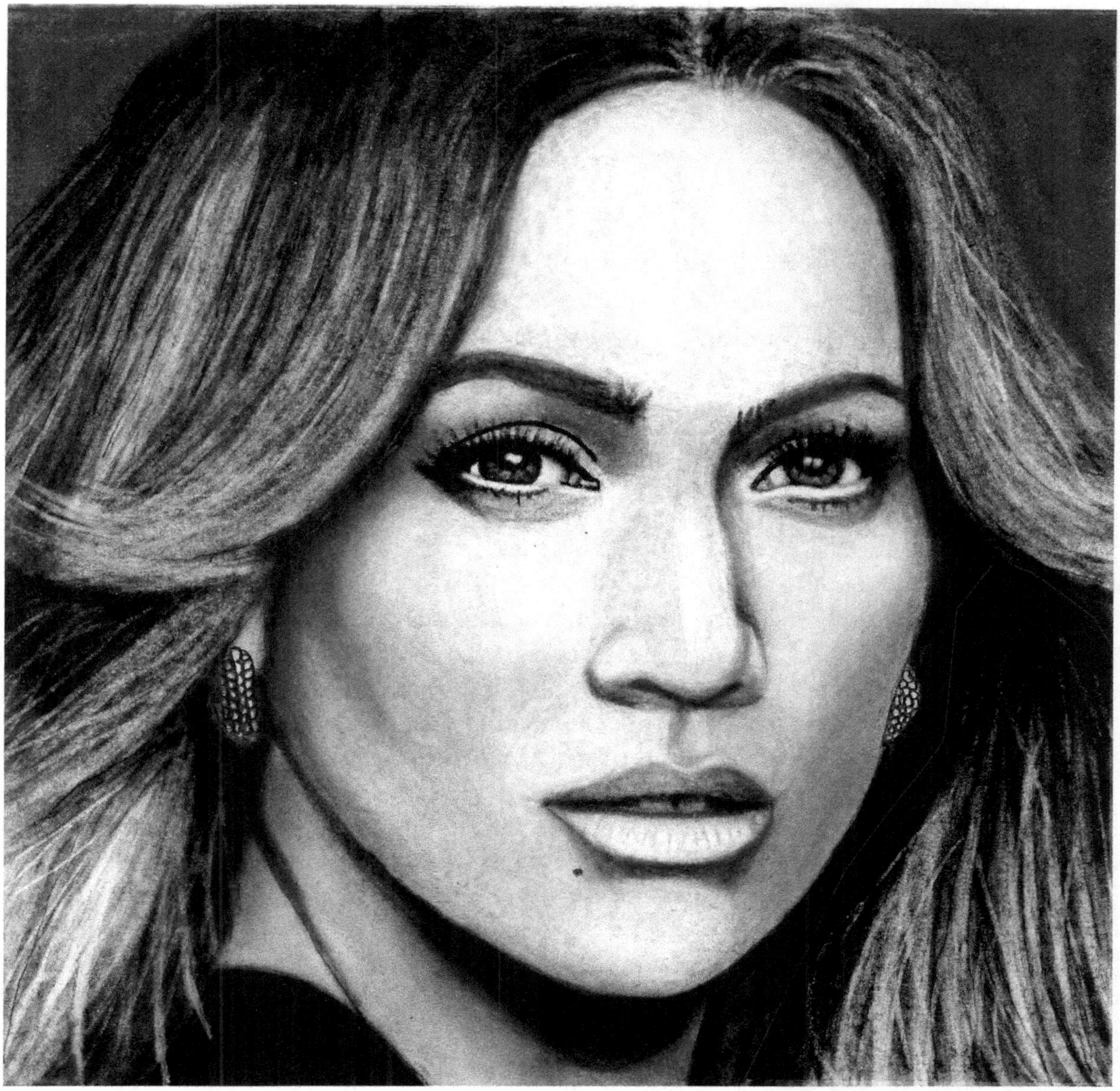

To view how this drawing was masterfully created or to purchase a Limited Edition Framed Artwork of Jennifer Lopez type into your Internet Browser the URL shortcut ➡ **myportrait.art/jenniferlopez**

To listen to he`r Greatest Songs type into your Internet Browser the URL shortcut➡ **radio.surf/jenniferlopez**

To view all channels on THE FACE OF MUSIC Internet Radio MEGA Station type into your Internet Browser the URL shortcut ➡ **radio.surf/music**

To inquire about purchasing a Limited Edtion NFT of this portrait type into your Internet Browser the URL shortcut ➡ **myartnft.shop/jenniferlopez**

To view all available NFTs type into your Internet Browser the URL shortcut ➡ **myartnft.shop/all**

# Jerry Lee Lewis

(Net worth: $10 Million)(Total Records Sold: Millions)
(Genre: Rock & Roll , Rockabilly)(Height: 5" - 11")

Jerry Lee Lewis (born September 29, 1935) is an American singer and pianist, often known by his nickname, The Killer. He has been described as "rock n' roll's first great wild man and one of the most influential pianists of the twentieth century."

A pioneer of rock and roll and rockabilly music, Lewis made his first recordings in 1956 at Sun Records in Memphis. "Crazy Arms" sold 300,000 copies in the South, but it was his 1957 hit "Whole Lotta Shakin' Goin' On" that shot Lewis to fame worldwide. He followed this with "Great Balls of Fire", "Breathless" and "High School Confidential". However, Lewis's rock and roll career faltered in the wake of his marriage to Myra Gale Brown, his 13-year-old cousin.

His popularity quickly eroded following the scandal and with few exceptions such as a cover of Ray Charles's "What'd I Say", he did not have much chart success in the early 1960s. His live performances at this time were increasingly wild and energetic. His 1964 live album Live at the Star Club, Hamburg is regarded by music journalists and fans as one of the wildest and greatest live rock albums ever. In 1968, Lewis made a transition into country music and had hits with songs such as "Another Place, Another Time". This reignited his career, and throughout the late 1960s and 1970s he regularly topped the country-western charts; throughout his seven-decade career, Lewis has had 30 songs reach the Top 10 on the Billboard Country and Western Chart. His No. 1 country hits included "To Make Love Sweeter for You", "There Must Be More to Love Than This", "Would You Take Another Chance on Me" and "Me and Bobby McGee".

Lewis's successes continued throughout the decades and he embraced his rock and roll past with songs such as a cover of the Big Bopper's "Chantilly Lace" and Mack Vickery's "Rockin' My Life Away". In the 21st century, Lewis continues to tour around the world and still releases new albums. His 2006 album Last Man Standing is his best-selling release to date, with over a million copies sold worldwide. This was followed by Mean Old Man in 2010, which has received some of the best sales of Lewis's career.

Lewis has a dozen gold records in both rock and country. He received four Grammy awards, including a Grammy Lifetime Achievement Award and two Grammy Hall of Fame Awards. Lewis was inducted into the Rock and Roll Hall of Fame in 1986, and his pioneering contribution to the genre has been recognized by the Rockabilly Hall of Fame. He was also a member of the inaugural class inducted into the Memphis Music Hall of Fame. In 1989, his life was chronicled in the movie Great Balls of Fire, starring Dennis Quaid. In 2003, Rolling Stone listed his box set All Killer, No Filler: The Anthology number 242 on their list of "500 Greatest Albums of All Time". In 2004, they ranked him No. 24 on their list of the 100 Greatest Artists of All Time. Lewis is the last surviving member of Sun Records' Million Dollar Quartet and the album Class of '55, which also included Johnny Cash, Carl Perkins, Roy Orbison and Elvis Presley.

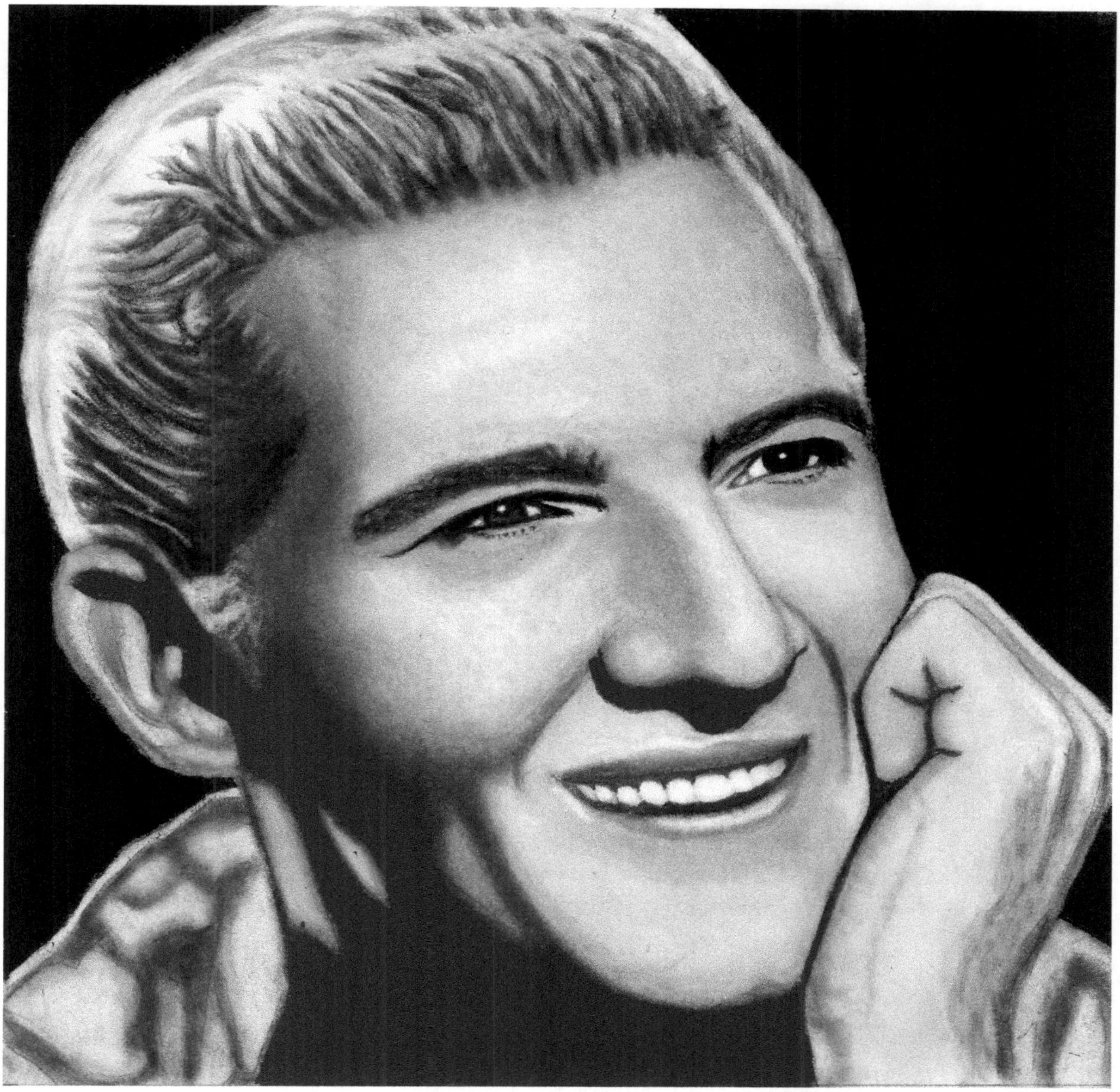

To view how this drawing was masterfully created or to purchase a Limited Edition Framed Artwork of Jerry Lee Lewis type into your Internet Browser the URL shortcut ➡ **myportrait.art/jerryleelewis**

To listen to his Greatest Songs type into your Internet Browser the URL shortcut ➡ **radio.surf/jerryleelewis**

To view all channels on THE FACE OF MUSIC Internet Radio MEGA Station type into your Internet Browser the URL shortcut ➡ **radio.surf/music**

To inquire about purchasing a Limited Edition NFT of this portrait type into your Internet Browser the URL shortcut ➡ **myartnft.shop/jerryleelewis**

To view all available NFTs type into your Internet Browser the URL shortcut ➡ **myartnft.shop/all**

# Jethro Tull

(Total Albums Sold: 60 Million) (Genre: Progressive Rock , Folk Rock , Jazz Fusion)

Jethro Tull are a British rock band formed in Blackpool, England in 1967. Initially playing blues rock and jazz fusion, the band later developed their sound to incorporate elements of hard rock and folk to forge a progressive rock signature. The band is led by vocalist/flautist/guitarist Ian Anderson, and has featured a revolving door of lineups through the years among of which include significant members such as longtime guitarist Martin Barre, keyboardists John Evan, Dee Palmer and Peter-John Vettese, drummers Clive Bunker, Barrie "Barriemore" Barlow and Doane Perry, and bassists Glenn Cornick, Jeffrey Hammond, John Glascock and Dave Pegg.

After achieving moderate recognition performing in the London club scene, the band released their debut album This Was in 1968. After a lineup change which saw original guitarist Mick Abrahams replaced by Martin Barre, the band released the folk-tinged blues album Stand Up (1969). Stand Up saw the band achieve their first commercial success, with the album reaching No. 1 in the UK, followed by regular tours of the UK and the US. Their musical style shifted in the direction of progressive rock with the albums Aqualung (1971), Thick as a Brick (1972) and A Passion Play (1973), and shifted again to folk rock with Songs from the Wood (1977), Heavy Horses (1978) and Stormwatch (1979). In the early 1980s the band underwent a major lineup change and shifted towards electronic rock, with the albums A (1980), The Broadsword and the Beast (1982) and Under Wraps (1984). The band won their sole Grammy Award for the 1987 album Crest of a Knave, which saw the band return to a hard rock style.

Jethro Tull have sold an estimated 60 million albums worldwide, with 11 gold and five platinum albums among them. They have been described by Rolling Stone as "one of the most commercially successful and eccentric progressive rock bands."

The last works as a group to contain new material were released in 2003, though the band continued to tour until 2011. Both Anderson and Barre have continued to record and tour as solo artists, with Anderson saying in 2014 that Jethro Tull "came more or less to an end." However in 2017 Anderson announced plans for a tour to commemorate the fiftieth anniversary of This Was. The current group—now billed as "Ian Anderson and the Jethro Tull band"—includes musicians who have been members of Anderson's solo band since 2012. In March 2021, Anderson announced plans for a new album by the group, The Zealot Gene.

# Ian Anderson

(Net Worth: $100 Million)(Height: 5' - 10")

Ian Scott Anderson (born 10 August 1947) is a Scottish musician, singer and songwriter best known for his work as lead vocalist, flautist and acoustic guitarist of British rock band Jethro Tull. He is a multi-instrumentalist who, in addition to flute, plays keyboards, acoustic and bass guitar, bouzouki, balalaika, saxophone, harmonica, and a variety of whistles. His solo work began with the 1983 album Walk into Light; since then he has released another five works, including the sequel to the Jethro Tull album Thick as a Brick (1972) in 2012, entitled Thick as a Brick 2.

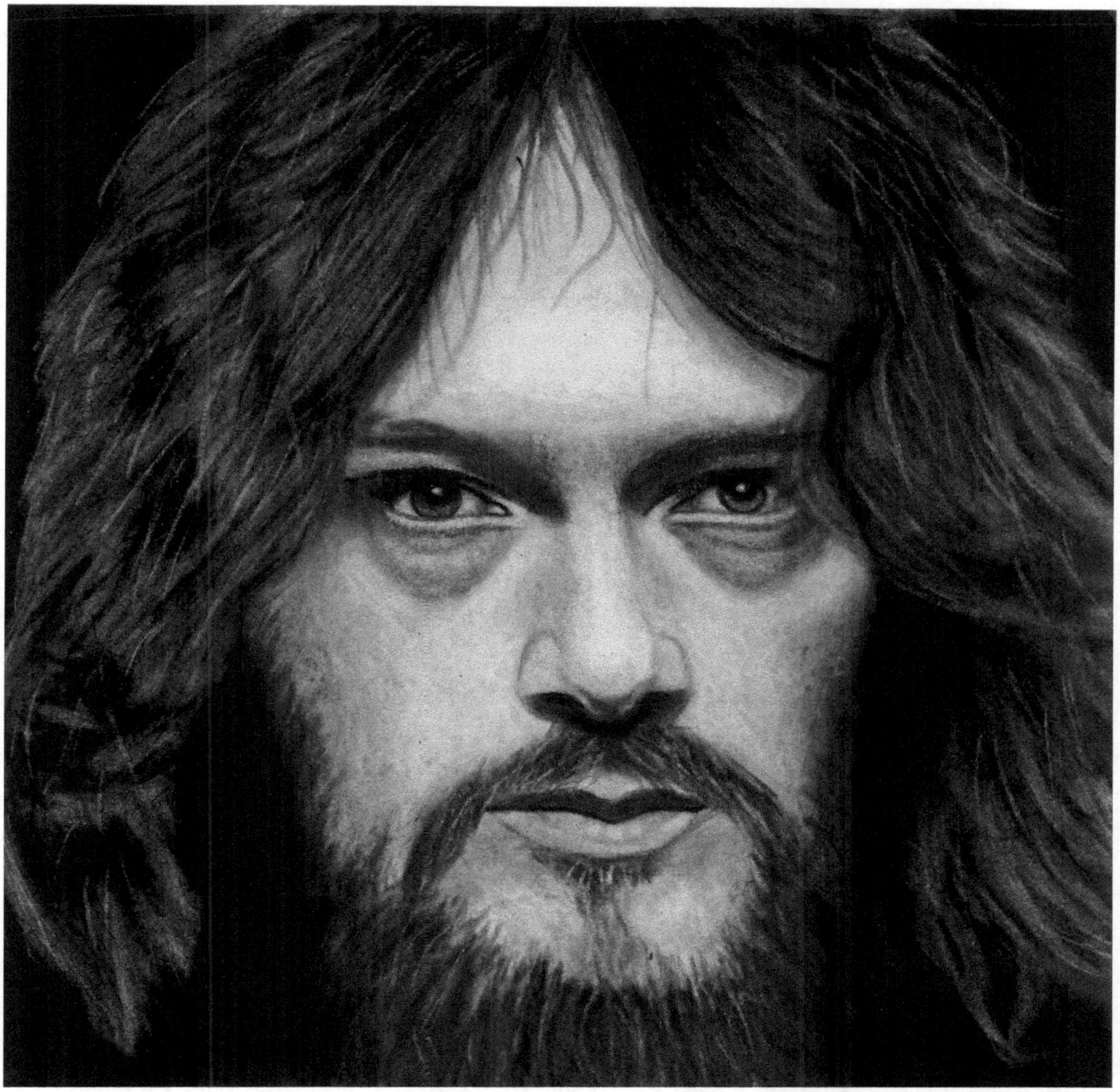

To view how this drawing was masterfully created or to purchase a Limited Edition Framed Artwork of Ian Anderson type into your Internet Browser the URL shortcut ➡ **myportrait.art/iananderson**

To listen to their Greatest Songs type into your Internet Browser the URL shortcut ➡ **radio.surf/jethrotull**

To view all channels on THE FACE OF MUSIC Internet Radio MEGA Station type into your Internet Browser the URL shortcut ➡ **radio.surf/music**

To inquire about purchasing a Limited Edition NFT of this portrait type into your Internet Browser the URL shortcut ➡ **myartnft.shop/iananderson**

To view all available NFTs type into your Internet Browser the URL shortcut ➡ **myartnft.shop/all**

# Jim Croce

(Net worth: $5 Million)(Total Records Sold: Millions)
(Genre: Folk , Soft Rock)(Height: 5" - 8")

James Joseph Croce (January 10, 1943 – September 20, 1973) was an American folk and rock singer-songwriter. Between 1966 and 1973, Croce released five studio albums and numerous singles. During this period, Croce took a series of odd jobs to pay bills while he continued to write, record, and perform concerts. After forming a partnership with songwriter and guitarist Maury Muehleisen his fortunes turned in the early 1970s. His breakthrough came in 1972; his third album You Don't Mess Around with Jim produced three charting singles, including "Time in a Bottle", which reached No. 1 after his death. The follow-up album, Life and Times, contained the song "Bad, Bad Leroy Brown", which was the only No. 1 hit he had during his lifetime.

On September 20, 1973, the day before the lead single to his fifth album, I Got a Name, was released, Croce, (along with five others), was killed in a plane crash, at the height of his popularity. Croce's music continued to chart throughout the 1970s following his death. His wife, Ingrid Croce, was his early songwriting partner and she continued to write and record after his death, and his son A. J. Croce himself became a singer-songwriter in the 1990s.

Croce did not take music seriously until he studied at Villanova, where he formed bands and performed at fraternity parties, coffee houses, and universities around Philadelphia, playing "anything that the people wanted to hear: blues, rock, a cappella, railroad music ... anything." Croce's band was chosen for a foreign exchange tour of Africa, the Middle East, and Yugoslavia. He later said, "We just ate what the people ate, lived in the woods, and played our songs. Of course they didn't speak English over there but if you mean what you're singing, people understand." On November 29, 1963, Croce met his future wife Ingrid Jacobson at the Philadelphia Convention Hall during a hootenanny, where he was judging a contest. Croce released his first album, Facets, in 1966, with 500 copies pressed. The album had been financed with a $500 ($3,940 in 2019 dollars) wedding gift from Croce's parents, who set a condition that the money must be spent to make an album. They hoped that he would give up music after the album failed, and use his college education to pursue a "respectable" profession. However, the album proved a success, with every copy sold.

On Thursday night, September 20, 1973, during Croce's Life and Times tour and the day before his ABC single "I Got a Name" was released, Croce and all five others on board were killed when their chartered Beechcraft E18S crashed into a tree during takeoff from the Natchitoches Regional Airport in Natchitoches, Louisiana. Croce was 30 years old..

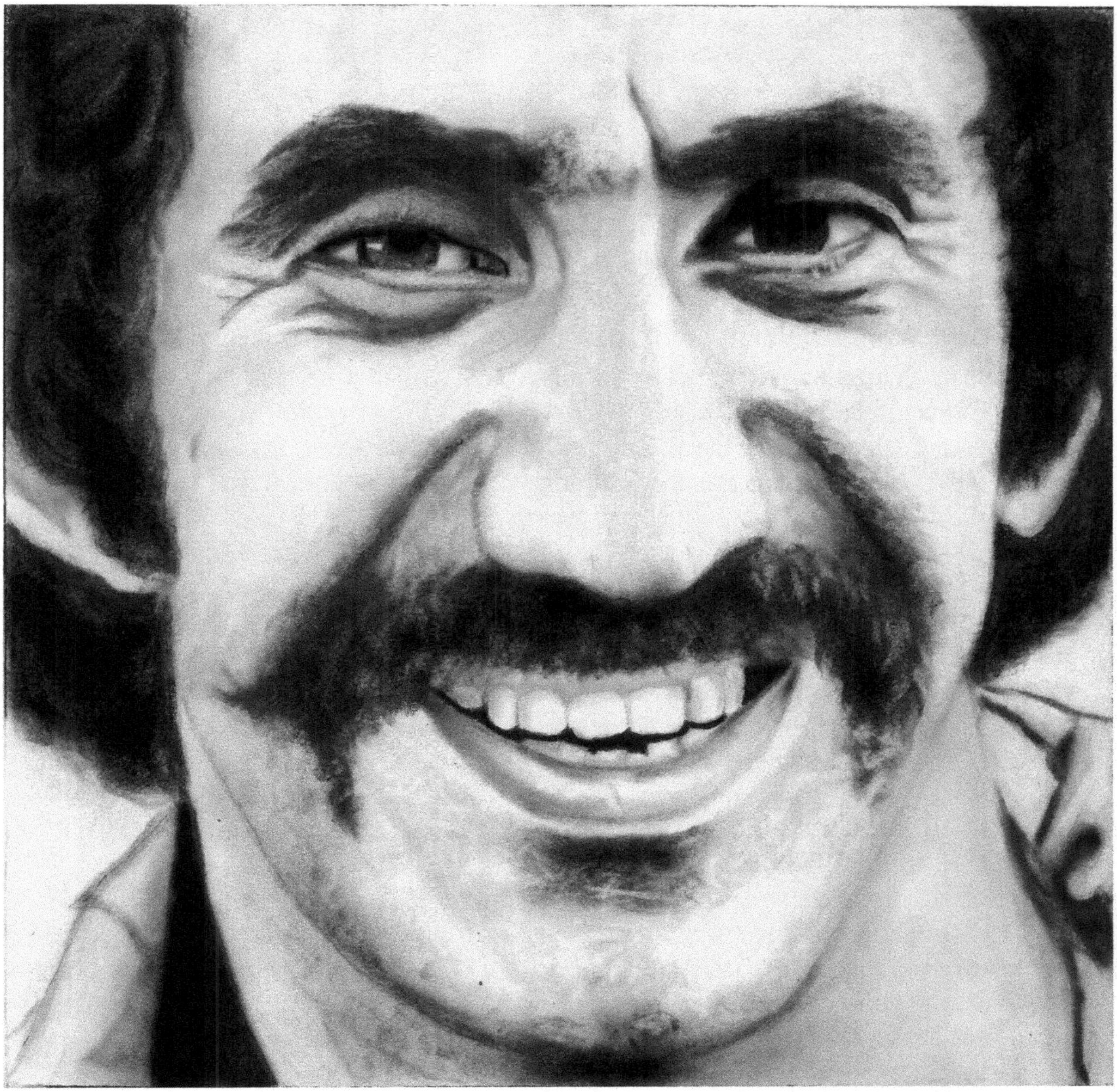

To view how this drawing was masterfully created or to purchase a Limited Edition Framed Artwork of Jim Croce type into your Internet Browser the URL shortcut ➡ **myportrait.art/jimcroce**

To listen to his Greatest Songs type into your Internet Browser the URL shortcut ➡ **radio.surf/jimcroce**

To view all channels on THE FACE OF MUSIC Internet Radio MEGA Station type into your Internet Browser the URL shortcut ➡ **radio.surf/music**

To inquire about purchasing a Limited Edtion NFT of this portrait type into your Internet Browser the URL shortcut ➡ **myartnft.shop/jimcroce**

To view all available NFTs type into your Internet Browser the URL shortcut ➡ **myartnft.shop/all**

# Jimi Hendrix

(Net worth: $150 Thousand)(Total Albums Sold: 30+ Million)
(Genre: Psychedelic Rock, Blues, R&B)(Height: 5" - 10")

James Marshall "Jimi" Hendrix (born Johnny Allen Hendrix; November 27, 1942 – September 18, 1970) was an American musician, singer, and songwriter. Although his mainstream career spanned only four years, he is widely regarded as one of the most influential electric guitarists in the history of popular music, and one of the most celebrated musicians of the 20th century. The Rock and Roll Hall of Fame describes him as "arguably the greatest instrumentalist in the history of rock music".

Born in Seattle, Washington, Hendrix began playing guitar at the age of 15. In 1961, he enlisted in the US Army, but was discharged the following year. Soon afterward, he moved to Clarksville, Tennessee, and began playing gigs on the chitlin' circuit, earning a place in the Isley Brothers' backing band and later with Little Richard, with whom he continued to work through mid-1965. He then played with Curtis Knight and the Squires before moving to England in late 1966 after bassist Chas Chandler of the Animals became his manager. Within months, Hendrix had earned three UK top ten hits with the Jimi Hendrix Experience: "Hey Joe", "Purple Haze", and "The Wind Cries Mary". He achieved fame in the US after his performance at the Monterey Pop Festival in 1967, and in 1968 his third and final studio album, Electric Ladyland, reached number one in the US. The double LP was Hendrix's most commercially successful release and his first and only number one album. The world's highest-paid performer, he headlined the Woodstock Festival in 1969 and the Isle of Wight Festival in 1970 before his accidental death in London from barbiturate-related asphyxia on September 18, 1970.

Hendrix was inspired by American rock and roll and electric blues. He favored overdriven amplifiers with high volume and gain, and was instrumental in popularizing the previously undesirable sounds caused by guitar amplifier feedback. He was also one of the first guitarists to make extensive use of tone-altering effects units in mainstream rock, such as fuzz distortion, Octavia, wah-wah, and Uni-Vibe. He was the first musician to use stereophonic phasing effects in recordings. Holly George-Warren of Rolling Stone commented: "Hendrix pioneered the use of the instrument as an electronic sound source. Players before him had experimented with feedback and distortion, but Hendrix turned those effects and others into a controlled, fluid vocabulary every bit as personal as the blues with which he began."

Hendrix was the recipient of several music awards during his lifetime and posthumously. In 1967, readers of Melody Maker voted him the Pop Musician of the Year and in 1968, Billboard named him the Artist of the Year and Rolling Stone declared him the Performer of the Year. Disc and Music Echo honored him with the World Top Musician of 1969 and in 1970, Guitar Player named him the Rock Guitarist of the Year. The Jimi Hendrix Experience was inducted into the Rock and Roll Hall of Fame in 1992 and the UK Music Hall of Fame in 2005. Rolling Stone ranked the band's three studio albums, Are You Experienced, Axis: Bold as Love, and Electric Ladyland, among the 100 greatest albums of all time, and they ranked Hendrix as the greatest guitarist and the sixth greatest artist of all time.

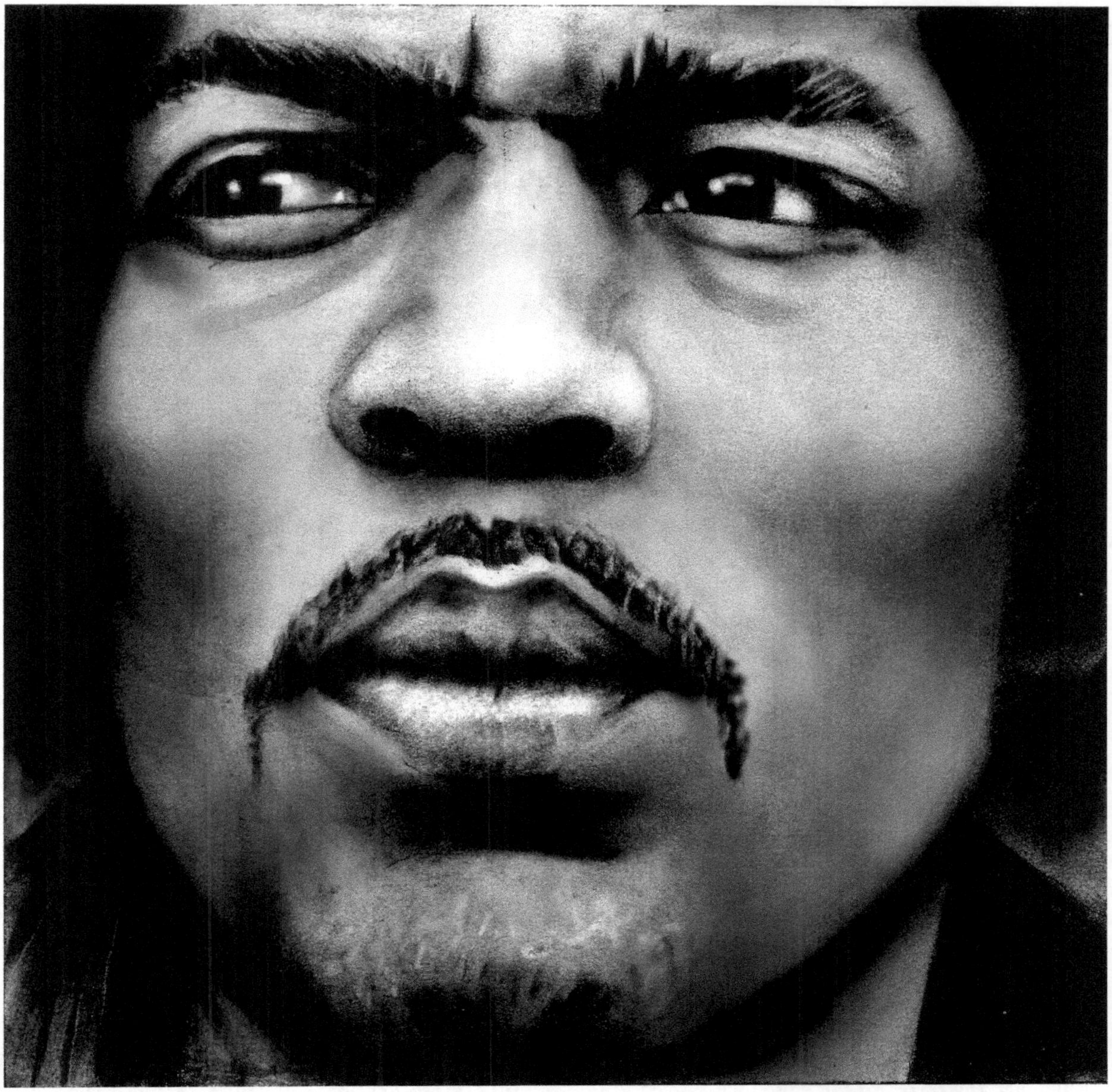

To view how this drawing was masterfully created or to purchase a Limited Edition Framed Artwork of Jimi Hendrix type into your Internet Browser the URL shortcut ➡ **myportrait.art/jimihendrix**

To listen to his Greatest Songs type into your Internet Browser the URL shortcut ➡ **radio.surf/jimihendrix**

To view all channels on THE FACE OF MUSIC Internet Radio MEGA Station type into your Internet Browser the URL shortcut ➡ **radio.surf/music**

To inquire about purchasing a Limited Edition NFT of this portrait type into your Internet Browser the URL shortcut ➡ **myartnft.shop/jimihendrix**

To view all available NFTs type into your Internet Browser the URL shortcut ➡ **myartnft.shop/all**

# Jimmy Reed

(Net worth: $5 Million)(Total Records Sold: Millions)
(Genre: Blues)

Mathis James Reed (September 6, 1925 – August 29, 1976) was an American blues musician and songwriter. His particular style of electric blues was popular with blues as well as non-blues audiences. Reed's songs such as "Honest I Do" (1957), "Baby What You Want Me to Do" (1960), "Big Boss Man" (1961), and "Bright Lights, Big City" (1961) appeared on both Billboard magazine's rhythm and blues and Hot 100 singles charts.

Reed influenced other musicians, such as Elvis Presley, Hank Williams Jr., and the Rolling Stones, who recorded his songs. Music critic Cub Koda describes him as "perhaps the most influential bluesman of all," due to his easily accessible style.

Reed was born in Dunleith, Mississippi, on September 6, 1925. He learned the harmonica and guitar from his friend Eddie Taylor. After several years of busking and performing there, he moved to Chicago, Illinois, in 1943. He was then drafted into the U.S. Navy and served in World War II. He was discharged in 1945 and returned briefly to Mississippi, marrying his girlfriend, Mary (henceforth known as Mama Reed). He then moved to Gary, Indiana, to work at an Armour meat-packing plant. Mama Reed was an uncredited background singer on many of his recordings, notably the hits "Baby What You Want Me to Do", "Big Boss Man" and "Bright Lights, Big City".

By the 1950s, Reed had established himself as a popular musician. He joined the Gary Kings with John Brim and played on the street with Willie Joe Duncan. Reed failed to gain a recording contract with Chess Records, but signed with Vee-Jay Records through Brim's drummer, Albert King. At Vee-Jay, Reed began playing again with Eddie Taylor and soon released "You Don't Have to Go", his first hit record. It was followed by a long string of hit songs.

Reed maintained his reputation despite his rampant alcoholism; his wife sometimes had to help him remember the lyrics to his songs while recording. In 1957, Reed developed epilepsy, though the condition was not correctly diagnosed for a long time, as Reed and doctors assumed it was delirium tremens. When Vee-Jay Records closed, his manager signed a contract with the fledgling ABC-Bluesway label, but Reed never produced another hit. In 1968, he toured Europe with the American Folk Blues Festival.

Reed died of respiratory failure in 1976, in Oakland, California, eight days short of his 51st birthday. He is interred in the Lincoln Cemetery, in Worth, Illinois. Reed was posthumously inducted into the Blues Hall of Fame in 1980, and the Rock and Roll Hall of Fame in 1991.

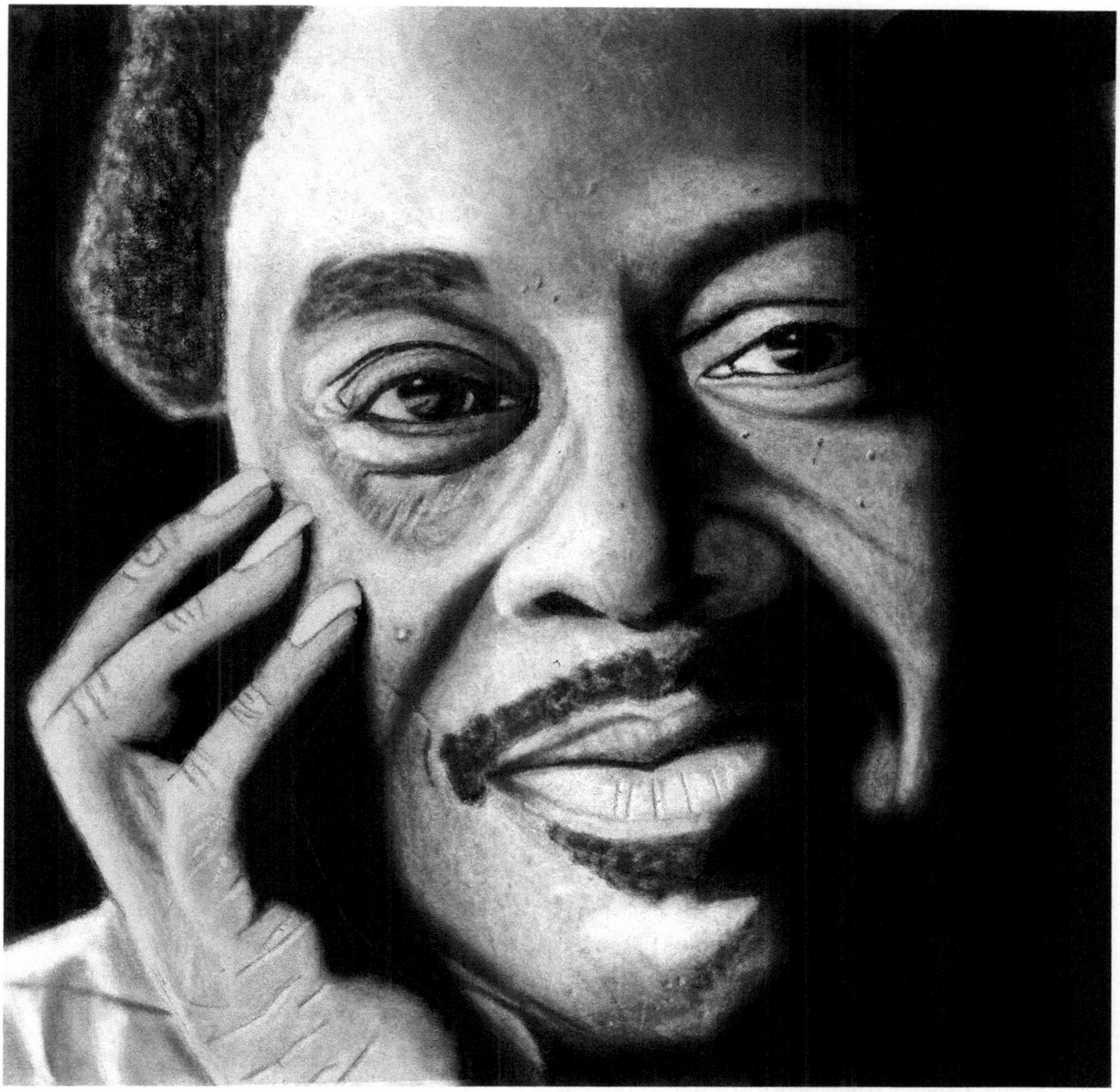

To view how this drawing was masterfully created or to purchase a Limited Edition Framed Artwork of Jimi Reed type into your Internet Browser the URL shortcut ➡ **myportrait.art/jimmyreed**

To listen to his Greatest Songs type into your Internet Browser the URL shortcut ➡ **radio.surf/jimmyreed**

To view all channels on THE FACE OF MUSIC Internet Radio MEGA Station type into your Internet Browser the URL shortcut ➡ **radio.surf/music**

To inquire about purchasing a Limited Edition NFT of this portrait type into your Internet Browser the URL shortcut ➡ **myartnft.shop/jimmyreed**

To view all available NFTs type into your Internet Browser the URL shortcut ➡ **myartnft.shop/all**

# Joan Jett

(Net worth: $10 Million)(Total Records Sold: 10+ Million)
(Genre: Hard Rock)(5' - 5")

Joan Jett (born Joan Marie Larkin, September 22, 1958) is an American rock singer, songwriter, composer, musician, record producer, and actress. Jett is best known for her work as the frontwoman of her band Joan Jett & the Blackhearts, and for earlier founding and performing with the Runaways, which recorded and released the hit song "Cherry Bomb". With The Blackhearts, Jett is known for her rendition of the song "I Love Rock 'n Roll" which was number-one on the Billboard Hot 100 for seven weeks in 1982. Jett's other notable songs include "Bad Reputation", "Crimson and Clover", "Do You Wanna Touch Me (Oh Yeah)", "Light of Day", "I Hate Myself for Loving You" and "Dirty Deeds". Jett has a mezzo-soprano vocal range. She has three albums that have been certified platinum or gold. She has been described as the Queen of Rock 'n' Roll. In 2015, Joan Jett & the Blackhearts were inducted into the Rock and Roll Hall of Fame.

Jett lives in Long Beach, New York, and has been a New York resident since the late 1970s.

Joan Marie Larkin was born on September 22, 1958, to James and Dorothy Larkin, at Lankenau Hospital in Wynnewood, Pennsylvania, a suburb of Philadelphia (although some sources list her birth date as September 22, 1960, which is incorrect). She is the oldest of three children. Her father was an insurance salesman and her mother was a secretary. Her family was Protestant, attended church, and went to Sunday school, but were not strict in their religious beliefs. In 1967, her family moved to Rockville, Maryland, where she attended Randolph Junior High and Wheaton High School. Jett got her first guitar at the age of 13. She took some guitar lessons, but soon quit because the instructor kept trying to teach her folk songs. Her family then moved to West Covina, California, in Los Angeles County, providing Jett the opportunity to pursue her musical interests. Shortly after the move, her parents divorced and she changed her name to Joan Jett,

because she thought it had more of a rock-star sound than her birth name (she has admitted in recent years that "Jett" was not actually her mother's maiden name, even though that is what she used to tell people).

In Los Angeles, Jett's favorite night spot was Rodney Bingenheimer's English Disco, a venue that provided the glam rock style she loved.

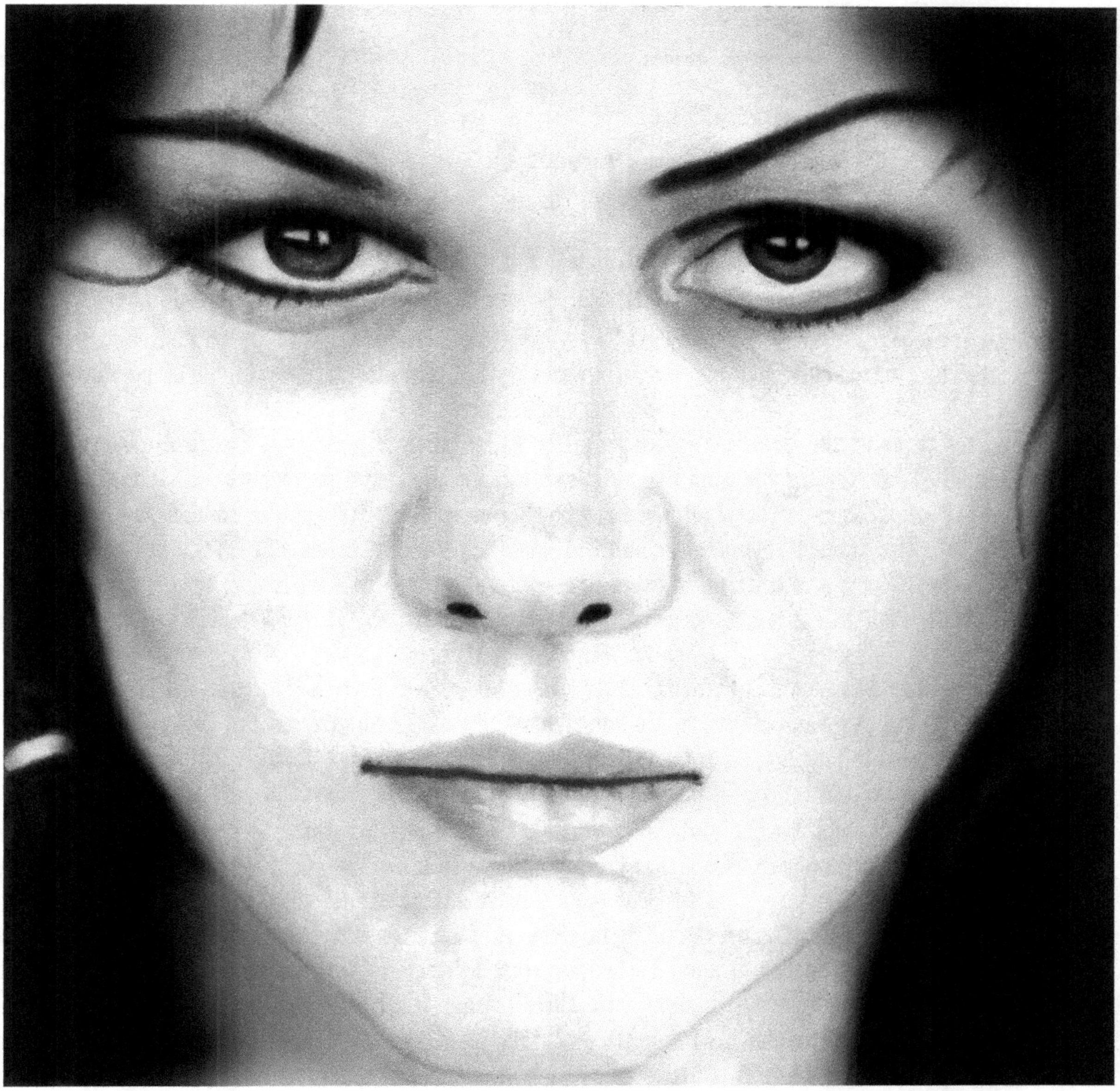

To view how this drawing was masterfully created or to purchase a Limited Edition Framed Artwork of Joan Jett type into your Internet Browser the URL shortcut ➡ **myportrait.art/joanjett**

To listen to her Greatest Songs type into your Internet Browser the URL shortcut ➡ **radio.surf/joanjett**

To view all channels on THE FACE OF MUSIC Internet Radio MEGA Station type into your Internet Browser the URL shortcut ➡ **radio.surf/music**

To inquire about purchasing a Limited Edtion NFT of this portrait type into your Internet Browser the URL shortcut ➡ **myartnft.shop/joanjett**

To view all available NFTs type into your Internet Browser the URL shortcut ➡ **myartnft.shop/all**

# Joe Cocker

(Net worth: $60 Million)(Total Records Sold: Millions)
(Genre: Rock , Blues , Soul , Pop)(5' - 9")

John Robert "Joe" Cocker (20 May 1944 – 22 December 2014) was an English singer known for his gritty voice, spasmodic body movement in performance, and distinctive versions of popular songs of varying genres.

Cocker's recording of the Beatles' "With a Little Help from My Friends" reached number one in the UK in 1968. He performed the song live at Woodstock in 1969 and performed the same year at the Isle of Wight Festival, and at the Party at the Palace concert in 2002 for the Golden Jubilee of Queen Elizabeth II. His version also became the theme song for the TV series The Wonder Years. His 1974 cover of "You Are So Beautiful" reached number five in the US. Cocker was the recipient of several awards, including a 1983 Grammy Award for his US number one "Up Where We Belong", a duet with Jennifer Warnes.

In 1993, Cocker was nominated for the Brit Award for Best British Male, in 2007 was awarded a bronze Sheffield Legends plaque in his hometown and in 2008 he received an OBE at Buckingham Palace for services to music. Cocker was ranked number 97 on Rolling Stone's 100 greatest singers list. Cocker was born on 20 May 1944 at 38 Tasker Road, Crookes, Sheffield. He was the youngest son of a civil servant, Harold Cocker, and Madge Cocker, née Lee. According to differing family stories, Cocker received his nickname of Joe either from playing a childhood game called "Cowboy Joe", or from a local window cleaner named Joe.

Cocker's main musical influences growing up were Ray Charles and Lonnie Donegan. Cocker's first experience singing in public was at age 12 when his elder brother Victor invited him on stage to sing during a gig of his skiffle group. In 1960, along with three friends, Cocker formed his first group, the Cavaliers. For the group's first performance at a youth club, they were required to pay the price of admission before entering. The Cavaliers eventually broke up after a year and Cocker left school to become an apprentice gasfitter working for the East Midlands Gas Board, later British Gas, while simultaneously pursuing a career in music.

Cocker is not related to fellow Sheffield-born musician Jarvis Cocker, despite a rumour to this effect (particularly in Australia, where Jarvis Cocker's father, radio presenter Mac Cocker, allowed listeners to believe that he was Joe's brother), although Joe was a friend of the family and even did some babysitting for Jarvis when he was an infant.

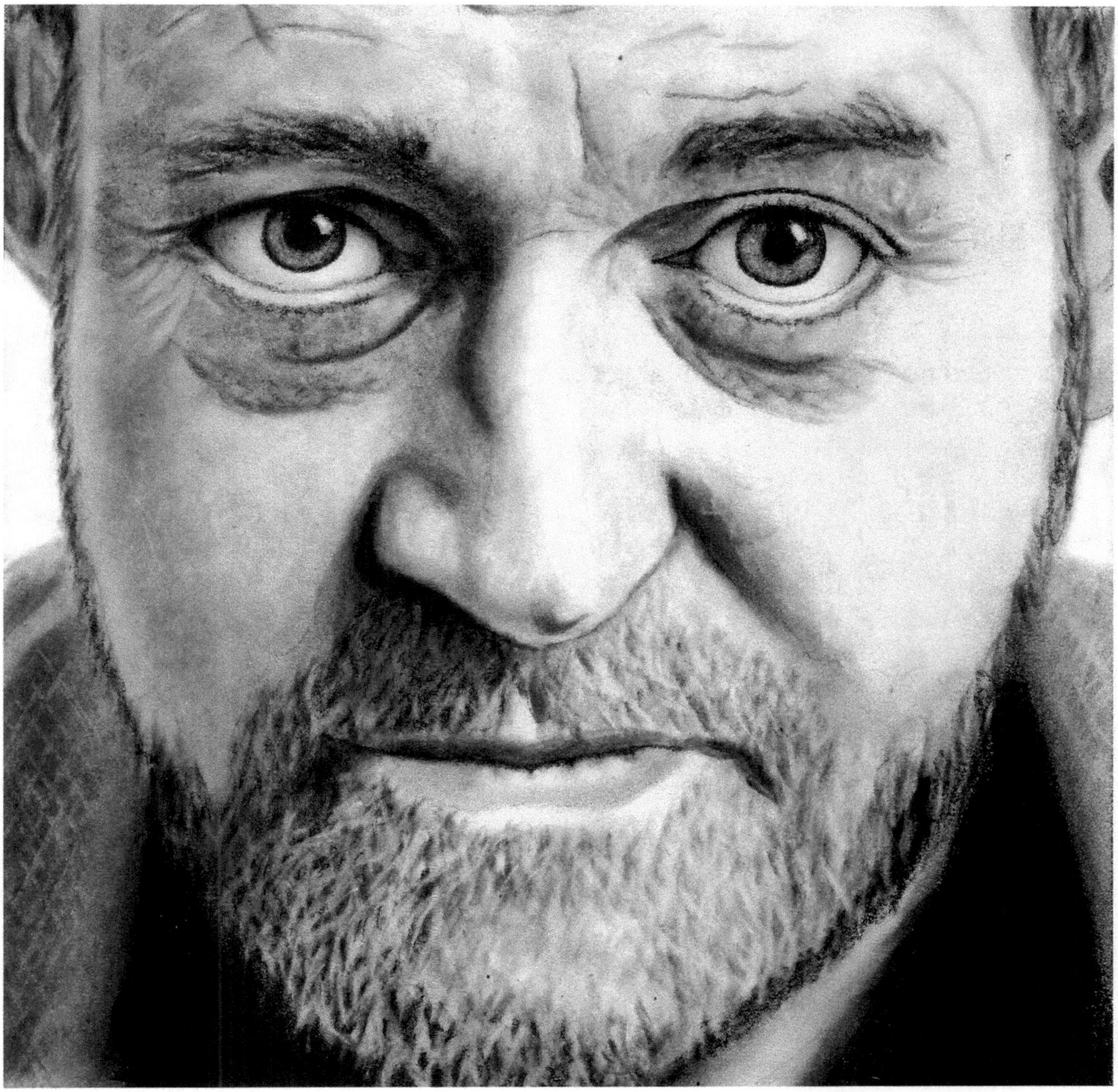

To view how this drawing was masterfully created or to purchase a Limited Edition Framed Artwork of Joe Cocker type into your Internet Browser the URL shortcut ➡ **myportrait.art/joecocker**

To listen to his Greatest Songs type into your Internet Browser the URL shortcut ➡ **radio.surf/joecocker**

To view all channels on THE FACE OF MUSIC Internet Radio MEGA Station type into your Internet Browser the URL shortcut ➡ **radio.surf/music**

To inquire about purchasing a Limited Edition NFT of this portrait type into your Internet Browser the URL shortcut ➡ **myartnft.shop/joecocker**

To view all available NFTs type into your Internet Browser the URL shortcut ➡ **myartnft.shop/all**

# John Denver

(Net worth: $60 Million)(Total Records Sold: 33 Million)
(Genre: Folk , Pop , Country)(5' - 9")

Henry John Deutschendorf Jr. (December 31, 1943 – October 12, 1997), known professionally as John Denver, was an American singer-songwriter, record producer, actor, activist, and humanitarian, whose greatest commercial success was as a solo singer. After traveling and living in numerous locations while growing up in his military family, Denver began his music career with folk music groups during the late 1960s. Starting in the 1970s, he was one of the most popular acoustic artists of the decade and one of its best-selling artists. By 1974, he was one of America's best-selling performers; AllMusic has called Denver "among the most beloved entertainers of his era".

Denver recorded and released approximately 300 songs, about 200 of which he composed. He had 33 albums and singles that were certified Gold and Platinum in the U.S by the RIAA, with estimated sales of more than 33 million units. He recorded and performed primarily with an acoustic guitar and sang about his joy in nature, disdain for city life, enthusiasm for music, and relationship trials. Denver's music appeared on a variety of charts, including country music, the Billboard Hot 100, and adult contemporary, earning 12 gold and four platinum albums with his signature songs "Take Me Home, Country Roads", "Annie's Song", "Rocky Mountain High", "Calypso", "Thank God I'm a Country Boy", and "Sunshine on My Shoulders".

Denver appeared in several films and television specials during the 1970s and 1980s, including the 1977 hit Oh, God!, in which he starred alongside George Burns. He continued to record into the 1990s, also focusing on environmental issues as well as lending vocal support to space exploration and testifying in front of Congress to protest censorship in music. He lived in Aspen for much of his life, where he was known for his love of Colorado. In 1974, Denver was named poet laureate of the state. The Colorado state legislature also adopted "Rocky Mountain High" as one of its two state songs in 2007.

An avid pilot, Denver died at age 53 in a single-fatality crash while piloting a recently purchased light plane.

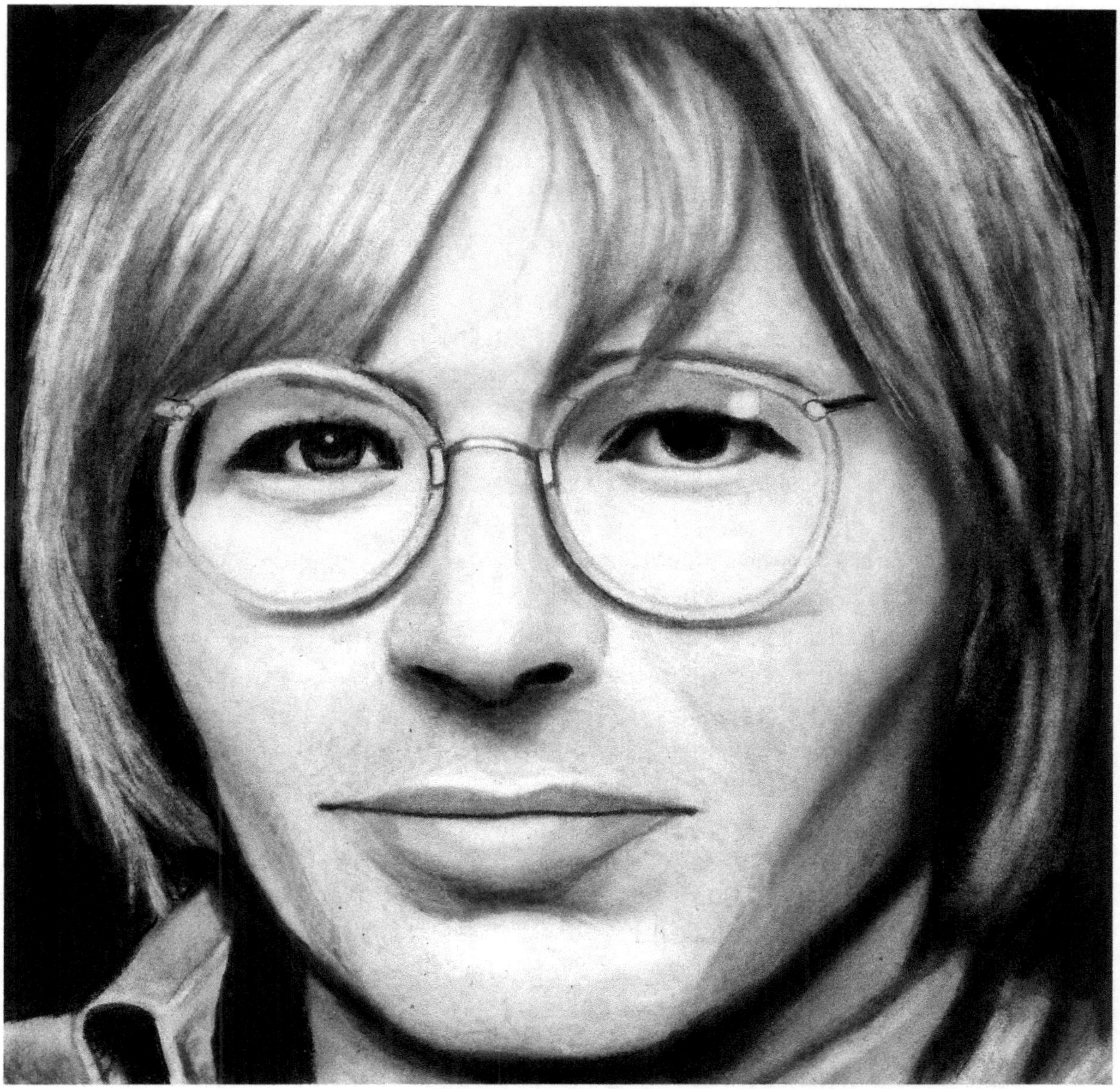

To view how this drawing was masterfully created or to purchase a Limited Edition Framed Artwork of John Denver type into your Internet Browser the URL shortcut ➡ **myportrait.art/johndenver**

To listen to his Greatest Songs type into your Internet Browser the URL shortcut ➡ **radio.surf/johndenver**

To view all channels on THE FACE OF MUSIC Internet Radio MEGA Station type into your Internet Browser the URL shortcut ➡ **radio.surf/music**

To inquire about purchasing a Limited Edtion NFT of this portrait type into your Internet Browser the URL shortcut ➡ **myartnft.shop/johndenver**

To view all available NFTs type into your Internet Browser the URL shortcut ➡ **myartnft.shop/all**

# John Lee Hooker

(Net worth: $10 Million)(Total Records Sold: Millions)
(Genre: Blues)(5' - 10")

John Lee Hooker (August 22, 1917 – June 21, 2001) was an American blues singer, songwriter, and guitarist. The son of a sharecropper, he rose to prominence performing an electric guitar-style adaptation of Delta blues. Hooker often incorporated other elements, including talking blues and early North Mississippi Hill country blues. He developed his own driving-rhythm boogie style, distinct from the 1930s–1940s piano-derived boogie-woogie. Hooker was ranked 35 in Rolling Stone's 2015 list of 100 greatest guitarists.

Some of his best known songs include "Boogie Chillen'" (1948), "Crawling King Snake" (1949), "Dimples" (1956), "Boom Boom" (1962), and "One Bourbon, One Scotch, One Beer" (1966). Several of his later albums, including The Healer (1989), Mr. Lucky (1991), Chill Out (1995), and Don't Look Back (1997), were album chart successes in the U.S and UK. The Healer (for the song "I'm In The Mood") and Chill Out (for the album) both earned him Grammy wins as well as Don't Look Back, which went on to earn him a double-Grammy win for Best Traditional Blues Recording and Best Pop Collaboration with Vocals (with Van Morrison).

It is believed that he was born in Tutwiler, in Tallahatchie County, although some sources say his birthplace was near Clarksdale, in Coahoma County. He was the youngest of the 11 children of William Hooker (born 1871, died after 1923), a sharecropper and Baptist preacher, and Minnie Ramsey (born c. 1880, date of death unknown). In the 1920 federal census, William and Minnie were recorded as being 48 and 39 years old, respectively, which implies that Minnie was born about 1880, not 1875. She was said to have been a "decade or so younger" than her husband (Boogie Man, p. 23), which gives additional credibility to this census record as evidence of Hooker's origins.

The Hooker children were homeschooled. They were permitted to listen only to religious songs; the spirituals sung in church were their earliest exposure to music. In 1921, their parents separated. The next year, their mother married William Moore, a blues singer, who provided John Lee with an introduction to the guitar (and whom he would later credit for his distinctive playing style).

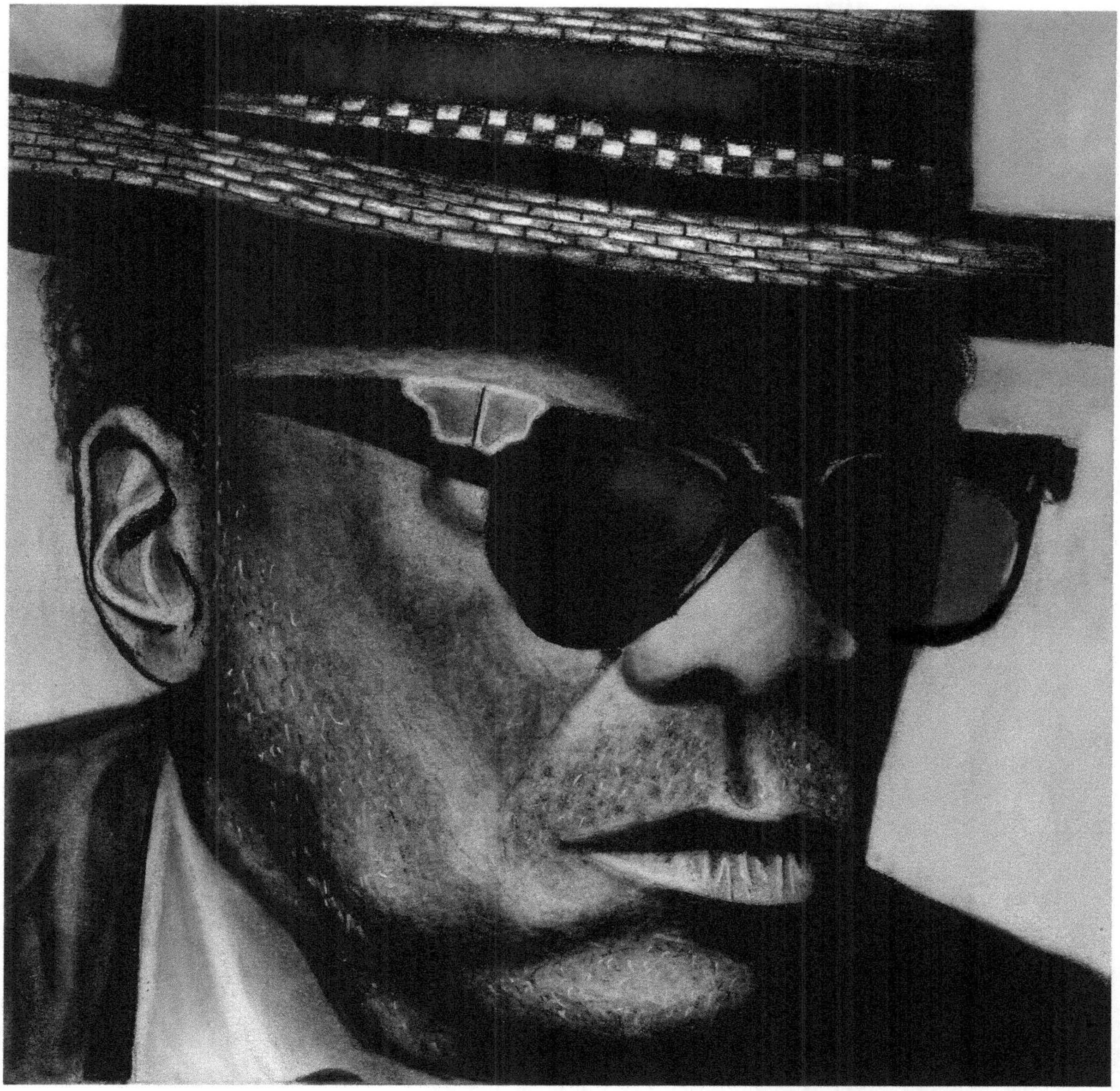

To view how this drawing was masterfully created or to purchase a Limited Edition Framed Artwork of John Lee Hooker type into your Internet Browser the URL shortcut ➡ **myportrait.art/johnleehooker**

To listen to his Greatest Songs type into your Internet Browser the URL shortcut ➡ **radio.surf/johnleehooker**

To view all channels on THE FACE OF MUSIC Internet Radio MEGA Station type into your Internet Browser the URL shortcut ➡ **radio.surf/music**

To inquire about purchasing a Limited Edtion NFT of this portrait type into your Internet Browser the URL shortcut ➡ **myartnft.shop/johnleehooker**

To view all available NFTs type into your Internet Browser the URL shortcut ➡ **myartnft.shop/all**

# John Mellencamp

(Net worth: $25 Million)(Total Records Sold: 60+ Million)
(Genre: Classic Rock)(5' - 8")

John J Mellencamp (born October 7, 1951), previously known as Johnny Cougar, John Cougar, and John Cougar Mellencamp, is an American musician, singer-songwriter, painter, actor, and film director. He is known for his catchy, populist brand of heartland rock, which emphasizes traditional instrumentation. Mellencamp rose to fame in the 1980s while "honing an almost startlingly plainspoken writing style" that, starting in 1982, yielded a string of Top 10 singles, including "Hurts So Good", "Jack & Diane", "Crumblin' Down", "Pink Houses", "Lonely Ol' Night", "Small Town", "R.O.C.K. in the U.S.A.", "Paper in Fire", and "Cherry Bomb". He has amassed 22 Top 40 hits in the United States. In addition, he holds the record for the most tracks by a solo artist to hit number one on the Hot Mainstream Rock Tracks chart, with seven. Mellencamp has been nominated for 13 Grammy Awards, winning one. His latest album of original songs, Sad Clowns & Hillbillies, was released on April 28, 2017 to widespread critical acclaim. Mellencamp has sold over 30 million albums in the US and over 60 million worldwide.

Mellencamp is also one of the founding members of Farm Aid, an organization that began in 1985 with a concert in Champaign, Illinois, to raise awareness about the loss of family farms and to raise funds to keep farm families on their land. Farm Aid concerts have remained an annual event over the past 36 years, and as of 2021 the organization has raised over $60 million.

Mellencamp was inducted into the Rock and Roll Hall of Fame on March 10, 2008. On June 14, 2018, Mellencamp was inducted into the Songwriters Hall of Fame. His biggest musical influences are Bob Dylan, Woody Guthrie, James Brown, and the Rolling Stones.

Rolling Stone contributor Anthony DeCurtis said: "Mellencamp has created an important body of work that has earned him both critical regard and an enormous audience. His songs document the joys and struggles of ordinary people seeking to make their way, and he has consistently brought the fresh air of common experience to the typically glamour-addled world of popular music."

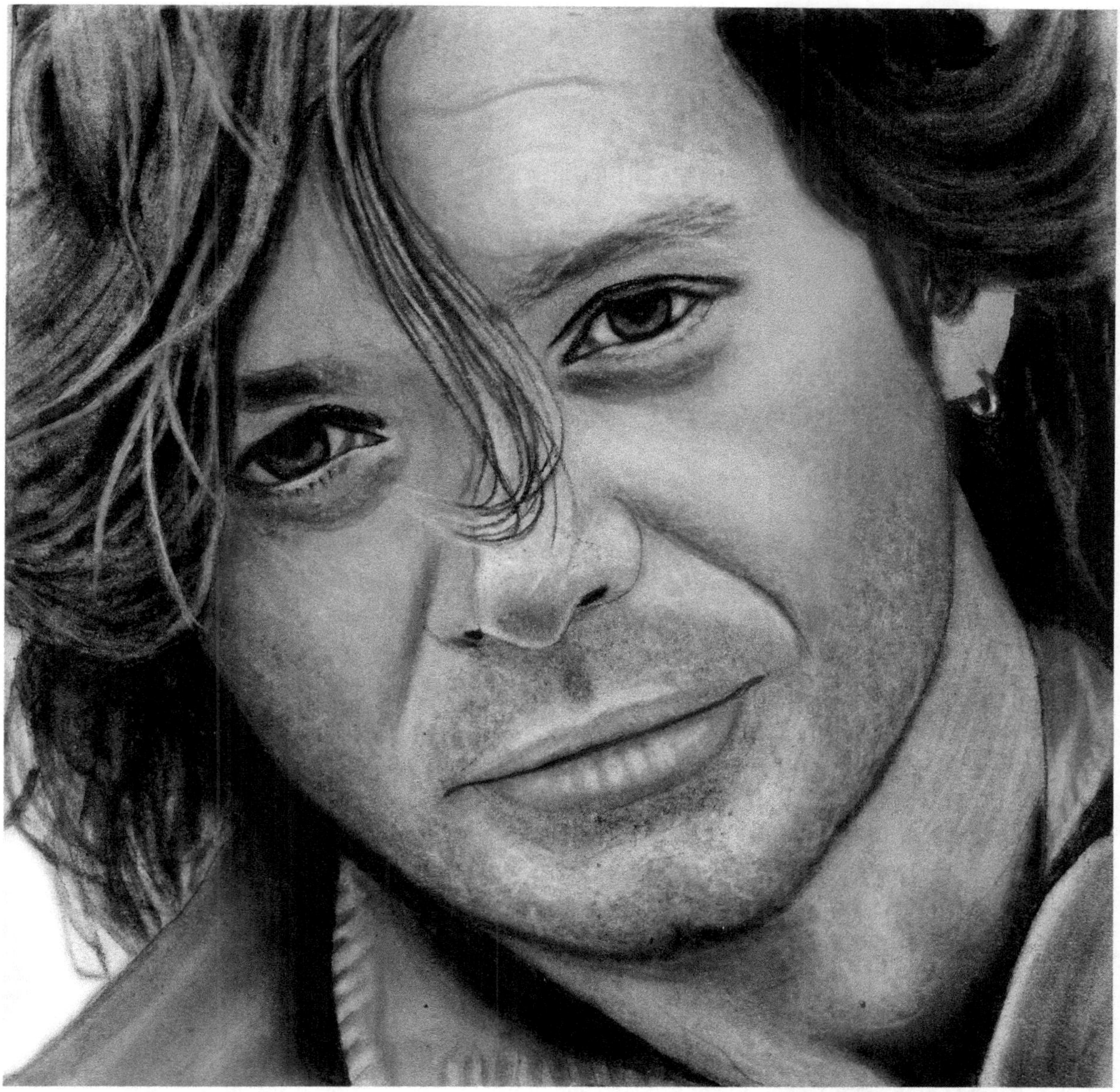

To view how this drawing was masterfully created or to purchase a Limited Edition Framed Artwork of John Mellencamp type into your Internet Browser the URL shortcut ➡ **myportrait.art/johnmellencamp**

To listen to his Greatest Songs type into your Internet Browser the URL shortcut
➡ **radio.surf/johnmellencamp**

To view all channels on THE FACE OF MUSIC Internet Radio MEGA Station type into your Internet Browser the URL shortcut ➡ **radio.surf/music**

To inquire about purchasing a Limited Edition NFT of this portrait type into your Internet Browser the URL shortcut ➡ **myartnft.shop/johnmellencamp**

To view all available NFTs type into your Internet Browser the URL shortcut ➡ **myartnft.shop/all**

# Johnny Cash

(Net worth: $60 Million)(Total Records Sold: 90+ Million)
(Genre: Country , Rockabilly , Gospel , Folk)(Height: 6' - 1")

John R. Cash (born J. R. Cash; February 26, 1932 – September 12, 2003) was an American singer, songwriter, musician, and actor. Much of Cash's music contained themes of sorrow, moral tribulation, and redemption, especially in the later stages of his career. He was known for his deep, calm bass-baritone voice, the distinctive sound of his Tennessee Three backing band characterized by train-like chugging guitar rhythms, a rebelliousness coupled with an increasingly somber and humble demeanor, free prison concerts, and a trademark all-black stage wardrobe which earned him the nickname "The Man in Black".

Born to poor cotton farmers in Kingsland, Arkansas, Cash rose to fame in the burgeoning rockabilly scene in Memphis, Tennessee, after four years in the Air Force. He traditionally began his concerts by simply introducing himself, "Hello, I'm Johnny Cash", followed by "Folsom Prison Blues", one of his signature songs. Alongside "Folsom Prison Blues", his other signature songs include "I Walk the Line", "Ring of Fire", "Get Rhythm", and "Man in Black". He also recorded humorous numbers like "One Piece at a Time" and "A Boy Named Sue", a duet with his future wife June called "Jackson" (followed by many further duets after their wedding), and railroad songs such as "Hey, Porter", "Orange Blossom Special", and "Rock Island Line". During the last stage of his career, he covered songs by contemporary rock artists of the time; his most notable covers were "Hurt" by Nine Inch Nails, "Rusty Cage" by Soundgarden and, "Personal Jesus" by Depeche Mode.

Cash is one of the best-selling music artists of all time, having sold more than 90 million records worldwide. His genre-spanning music embraced country, rock and roll, rockabilly, blues, folk, and gospel sounds. This crossover appeal earned him the rare honor of being inducted into the Country Music, Rock and Roll, and Gospel Music Halls of Fame.

Cash was born J. R. Cash in Kingsland, Arkansas, on February 26, 1932, the son of Carrie Cloveree (née Rivers) and Ray Cash. He had three older siblings, named Roy, Margaret Louise, and Jack, and three younger siblings, named Reba, Joanne, and Tommy (who also became a successful country artist). He was primarily of English and Scottish descent. His paternal grandmother also claimed Cherokee ancestry, though a DNA test of Cash's daughter Rosanne found she has no known Native American markers. He traced his Scottish surname to 11th-century Fife after meeting with the then-laird of Falkland, Major Michael Crichton-Stuart. Cash Loch and other locations in Fife bear the name of his family. He is a distant cousin of British Conservative politician Sir William Cash. His mother wanted to name him John and his father preferred to name him Ray, so J. R. ended up being the only compromise they could agree on. When Cash enlisted in the Air Force,
he was not permitted to use initials as a first name, so he changed it to John R. Cash. In 1955, when signing with Sun Records, he started using the name Johnny Cash.

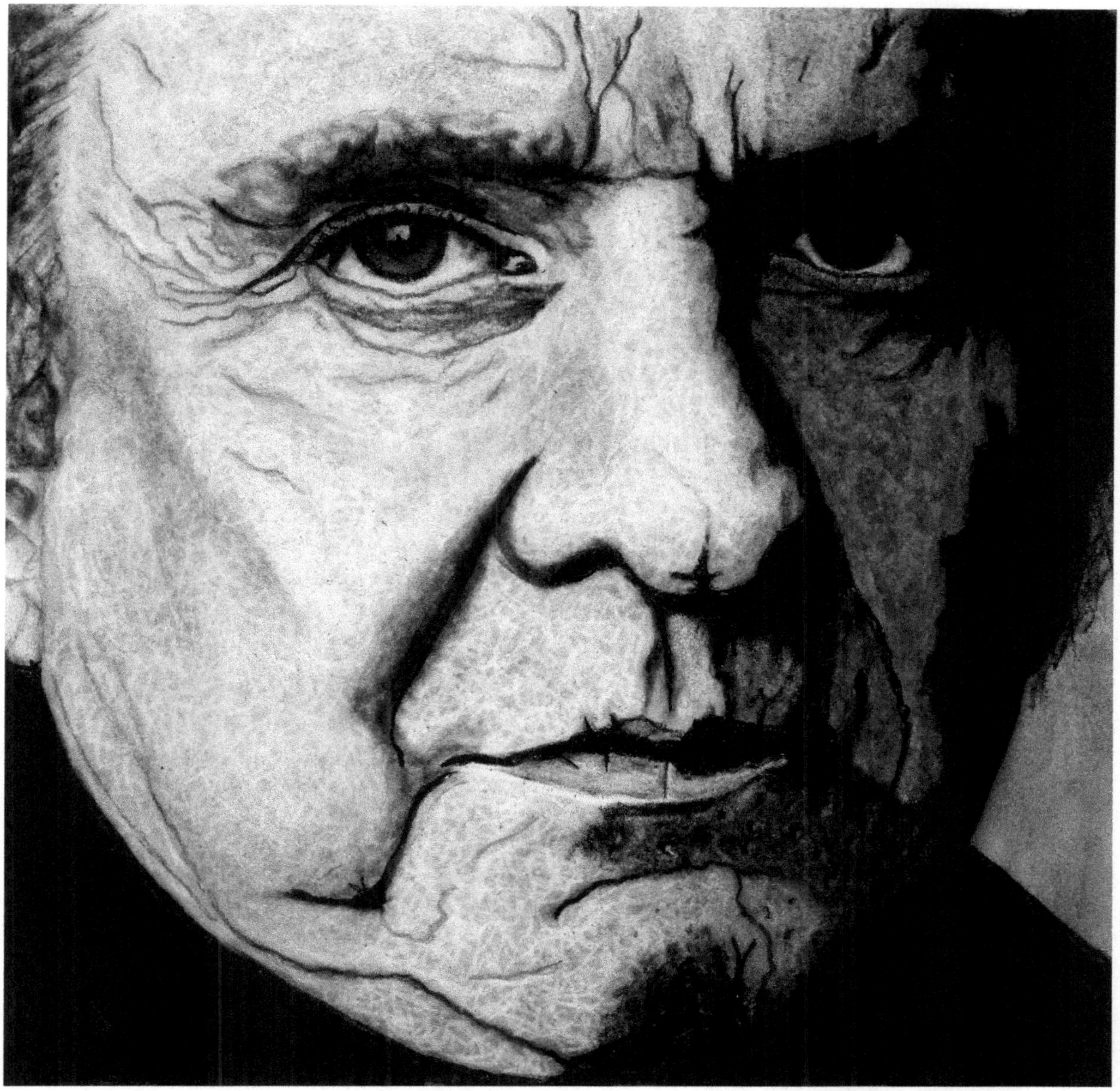

To view how this drawing was masterfully created or to purchase a Limited Edition Framed Artwork of Johnny Cash type into your Internet Browser the URL shortcut ➡ **myportrait.art/johnnycash**

To listen to his Greatest Songs type into your Internet Browser the URL shortcut ➡ **radio.surf/johnnycash**

To view all channels on THE FACE OF MUSIC Internet Radio MEGA Station type into your Internet Browser the URL shortcut ➡ **radio.surf/music**

To inquire about purchasing a Limited Edition NFT of this portrait type into your Internet Browser the URL shortcut ➡ **myartnft.shop/johnnycash**

To view all available NFTs type into your Internet Browser the URL shortcut ➡ **myartnft.shop/all**

# Johnny Mathis

(Net worth: $400 Million)(Total Records Sold: 350+ Million)
(Genre: Pop , Jazz , Crooner)(Height: 5' - 7")

John Royce Mathis (born September 30, 1935) is an American singer-songwriter of popular music. Starting his career with singles of standard music, he became highly popular as an album artist, with several dozen of his albums achieving gold or platinum status and 73 making the Billboard charts to date. Mathis has received the Grammy Lifetime Achievement Award and has been inducted into the Grammy Hall of Fame for three separate recordings.

Although frequently described as a romantic singer, his discography includes traditional pop, Brazilian and Spanish music, soul, rhythm and blues, show tunes, Tin Pan Alley, soft rock, blues, country music, and even a few disco songs for his album Mathis Magic in 1979. Mathis has also recorded six albums of Christmas music. In a 1968 interview, Mathis cited Lena Horne, Nat King Cole, and Bing Crosby among his musical influences.

Mathis was born in Gilmer, Texas, on September 30, 1935, the fourth of seven children of Clem Mathis and Mildred Boyd, both domestic cooks. The family moved to San Francisco, California, settling on 32nd Avenue in the Richmond District, where Mathis grew up. His father, a singer and pianist, had worked in vaudeville, and when he saw his son's talent, he bought an old upright piano for $25 (US$363 in 2019 dollars) and encouraged him. Mathis began learning songs and routines from his father; his parents also ran his fan club. His first song was "My Blue Heaven". Mathis started singing and dancing for visitors at home, at school, and at church functions. Mathis is of African-American and Native American heritage.

When he was 13, voice teacher Connie Cox accepted him as her student in exchange for work around her house. Mathis studied with Cox for six years, learning vocal scales and exercises, voice production, classical and operatic singing. The first band he sang with was formed by his high school friend Merl Saunders. Mathis eulogized Saunders at his funeral in 2008, thanking him for giving Mathis his first chance as a singer.

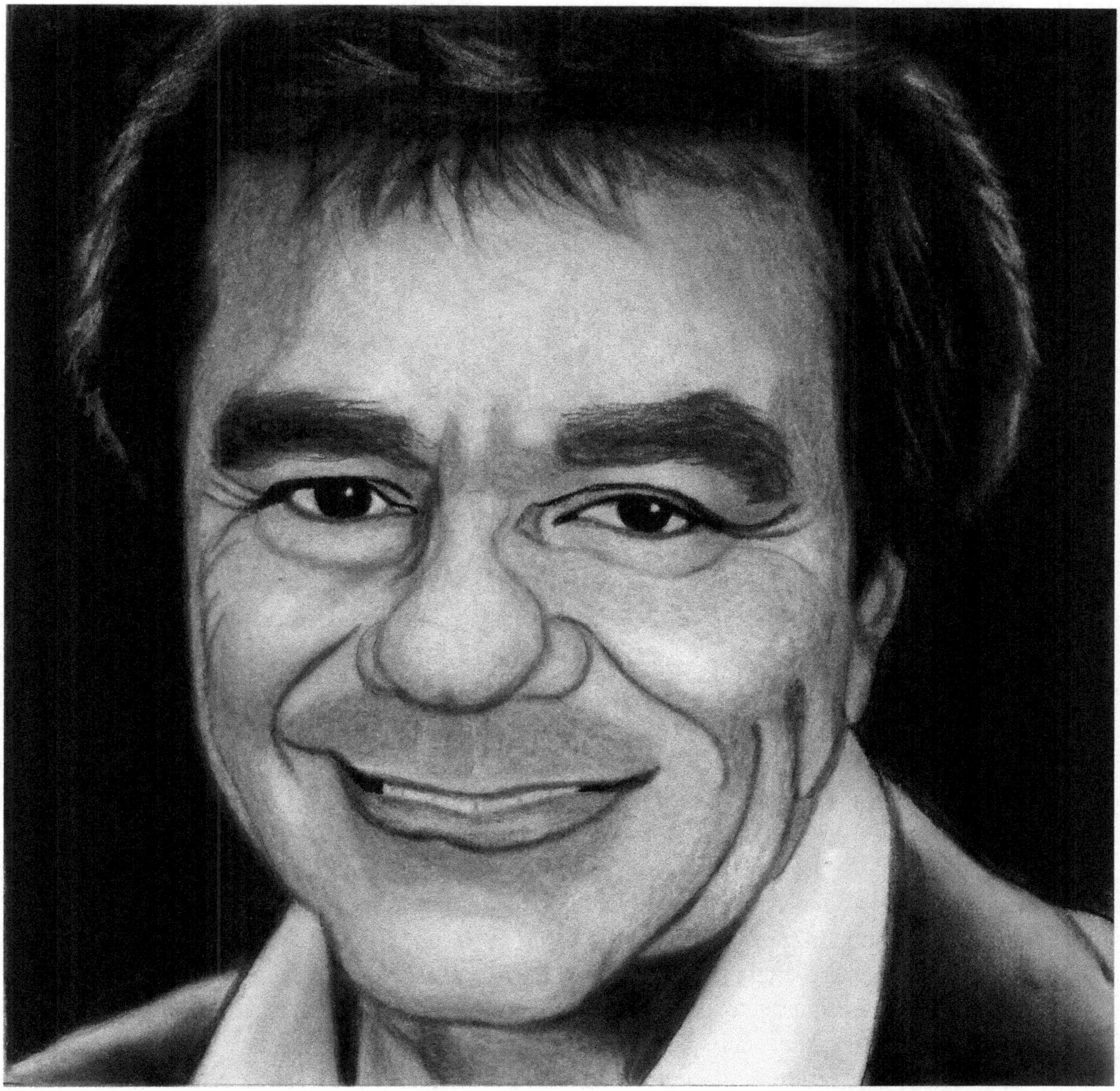

To view how this drawing was masterfully created or to purchase a Limited Edition Framed Artwork of Johnny Mathis type into your Internet Browser the URL shortcut ➡ **myportrait.art/johnnymathis**

To listen to his Greatest Songs type into your Internet Browser the URL shortcut ➡ **radio.surf/johnnymathis**

To view all channels on THE FACE OF MUSIC Internet Radio MEGA Station type into your Internet Browser the URL shortcut ➡ **radio.surf/music**

To inquire about purchasing a Limited Edtion NFT of this portrait type into your Internet Browser the URL shortcut ➡ **myartnft.shop/johnnymathis**

To view all available NFTs type into your Internet Browser the URL shortcut ➡ **myartnft.shop/all**

# Joni Mitchell

(Net worth: $100 Million)(Total Records Sold: 350+ Million)
(Genre: Pop , Jazz , Rock , Folk)(Height: 5' - 6")

Roberta Joan "Joni" Mitchell (born November 7, 1943) is a Canadian singer-songwriter. Drawing from folk, pop, rock, classical, and jazz, Mitchell's songs often reflect on social and philosophical ideals as well as her feelings about romance, womanhood, disillusionment, and joy. She has received many accolades, including nine Grammy Awards and induction into the Rock and Roll Hall of Fame in 1997. Rolling Stone called her "one of the greatest songwriters ever", and AllMusic has stated, "When the dust settles, Joni Mitchell may stand as the most important and influential female recording artist of the late 20th century".

Mitchell began singing in small nightclubs in Saskatoon, Saskatchewan, and throughout western Canada, before moving on to the night clubs of Toronto, Ontario. In 1965, she moved to the United States and began touring. Some of her original songs ("Urge for Going", "Chelsea Morning", "Both Sides, Now", "The Circle Game") were covered by other folk singers, allowing her to sign with Reprise Records and record her debut album, Song to a Seagull, in 1968. Settling in Southern California, Mitchell, with popular songs like "Big Yellow Taxi" and "Woodstock", helped define an era and a generation. Her 1971 album Blue is often cited as one of the best albums of all time; it was rated the 30th best album ever made in Rolling Stone's 2003 list of the "500 Greatest Albums of All Time", rising to No. 3 in the 2020 edition. In 2000, The New York Times chose Blue as one of the 25 albums that represented "turning points and pinnacles in 20th-century popular music".

In 2017, NPR ranked Blue number 1 on a list of Greatest Albums Made By Women. Mitchell's fifth album, For the Roses, was released in 1972. She then switched labels and began exploring more jazz-influenced melodic ideas, by way of lush pop textures, on 1974's Court and Spark, which featured the radio hits "Help Me" and "Free Man in Paris" and became her best-selling album.

Around 1975, Mitchell's vocal range began to shift from mezzo-soprano to more of a wide-ranging contralto. Her distinctive piano and open-tuned guitar compositions also grew more harmonically and rhythmically complex as she explored jazz, melding it with influences of rock and roll, R&B, classical music and non-western beats. In the late 1970s, she began working closely with noted jazz musicians, among them Jaco Pastorius, Wayne Shorter, Herbie Hancock, and Pat Metheny as well as Charles Mingus, who asked her to collaborate on his final recordings. She later turned again toward pop, embraced electronic music, and engaged in political protest. In 2002, she was awarded a Lifetime Achievement Award at the 44th Annual Grammy Awards.

Mitchell is the sole producer credited on most of her albums, including all her work in the 1970s. A blunt critic of the music industry, she quit touring and released her 17th, and reportedly last, album of original songs in 2007. With roots in visual art, Mitchell has designed most of her own album covers. She describes herself as a "painter derailed by circumstance".

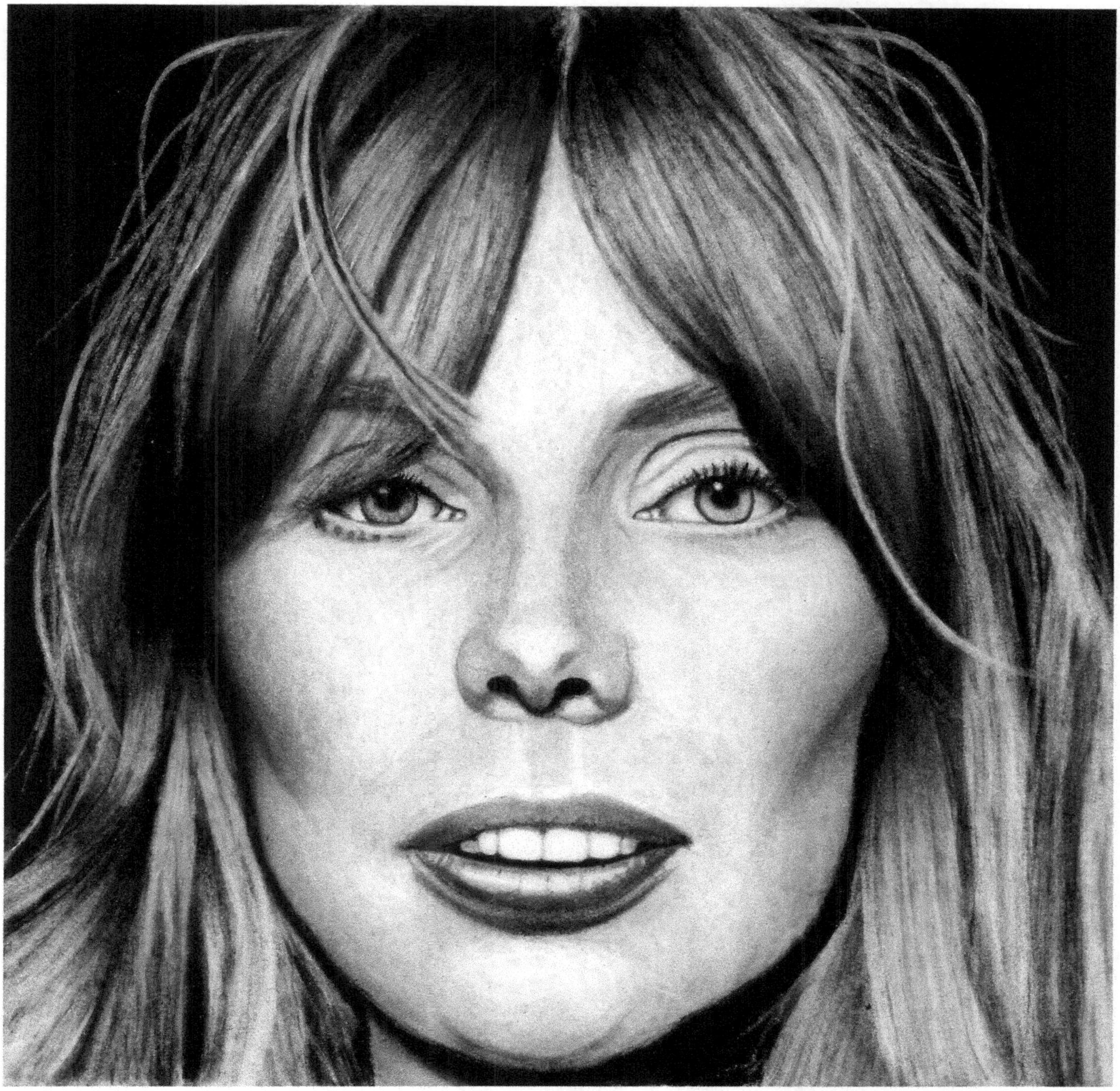

To view how this drawing was masterfully created or to purchase a Limited Edition Framed Artwork of Joni Mitchell type into your Internet Browser the URL shortcut ➡ **myportrait.art/jonimitchell**

To listen to her Greatest Songs type into your Internet Browser the URL shortcut ➡ **radio.surf/jonimitchell**

To view all channels on THE FACE OF MUSIC Internet Radio MEGA Station type into your Internet Browser the URL shortcut ➡ **radio.surf/music**

To inquire about purchasing a Limited Edtion NFT of this portrait type into your Internet Browser the URL shortcut ➡ **myartnft.shop/jonimitchell**

To view all available NFTs type into your Internet Browser the URL shortcut ➡ **myartnft.shop/all**

# Journey

(Total Records Sold: 80+ Million) (Genre: Classic Rock)

Journey is an American rock band formed in San Francisco in 1973, composed of former members of Santana and Frumious Bandersnatch.

Journey had their biggest commercial success between 1978 and 1987, when Steve Perry was lead vocalist; they released a series of hit songs, including "Don't Stop Believin'" (1981), which in 2009 became the top-selling track in iTunes history among songs not released in the 21st century. Escape, Journey's seventh and most successful album, reached No. 1 on the Billboard 200 and yielded another of their most popular singles, "Open Arms". The 1983 follow-up album, Frontiers, was almost as successful in the United States, reaching No. 2 and spawning several successful singles; it broadened the band's appeal in the United Kingdom, where it reached No. 6 on the UK Albums Chart. Journey enjoyed a successful reunion in the mid-1990s and have since regrouped twice; first with Steve Augeri from 1998-2006, then with Arnel Pineda from 2007 to the present.

According to the Recording Industry Association of America, Journey has sold 48 million albums in the U.S., making them the 25th best-selling band. Their worldwide sales have reached over 80 million records globally, making them one of the world's best-selling bands of all time. A 2005 USA Today opinion poll named Journey the fifth-best U.S rock band in history. Their songs have become arena rock staples and are still played on rock radio stations across the world. Journey ranks No. 96 on VH1's 100 Greatest Artists of All Time.

Journey was inducted into the Rock and Roll Hall of Fame with the class of 2017. Inductees included lead singer Steve Perry, guitarist Neal Schon, keyboardists Jonathan Cain and Gregg Rolie, bassist Ross Valory, and drummers Aynsley Dunbar and Steve Smith.

# Steve Perry

(Net Worth: $60 Million)(Height: 5' - 7")

Stephen Ray Perry (born January 22, 1949) is an American singer and songwriter. He is best known as the lead singer of the rock band Journey during their most commercially successful periods from 1977 to 1987, and again from 1995 to 1998. Perry also had a successful solo career between the mid-1980s and mid-1990s, made sporadic appearances in the 2000s, and returned to music full-time in 2018.

Perry's singing voice has garnered acclaim from prominent musical peers and publications; he has been dubbed "The Voice", a moniker originally coined by Jon Bon Jovi. Ranked No. 76 on Rolling Stone's "100 Greatest Singers of All Time", Perry was inducted into the Rock and Roll Hall of Fame as a member of Journey on April 7, 2017.

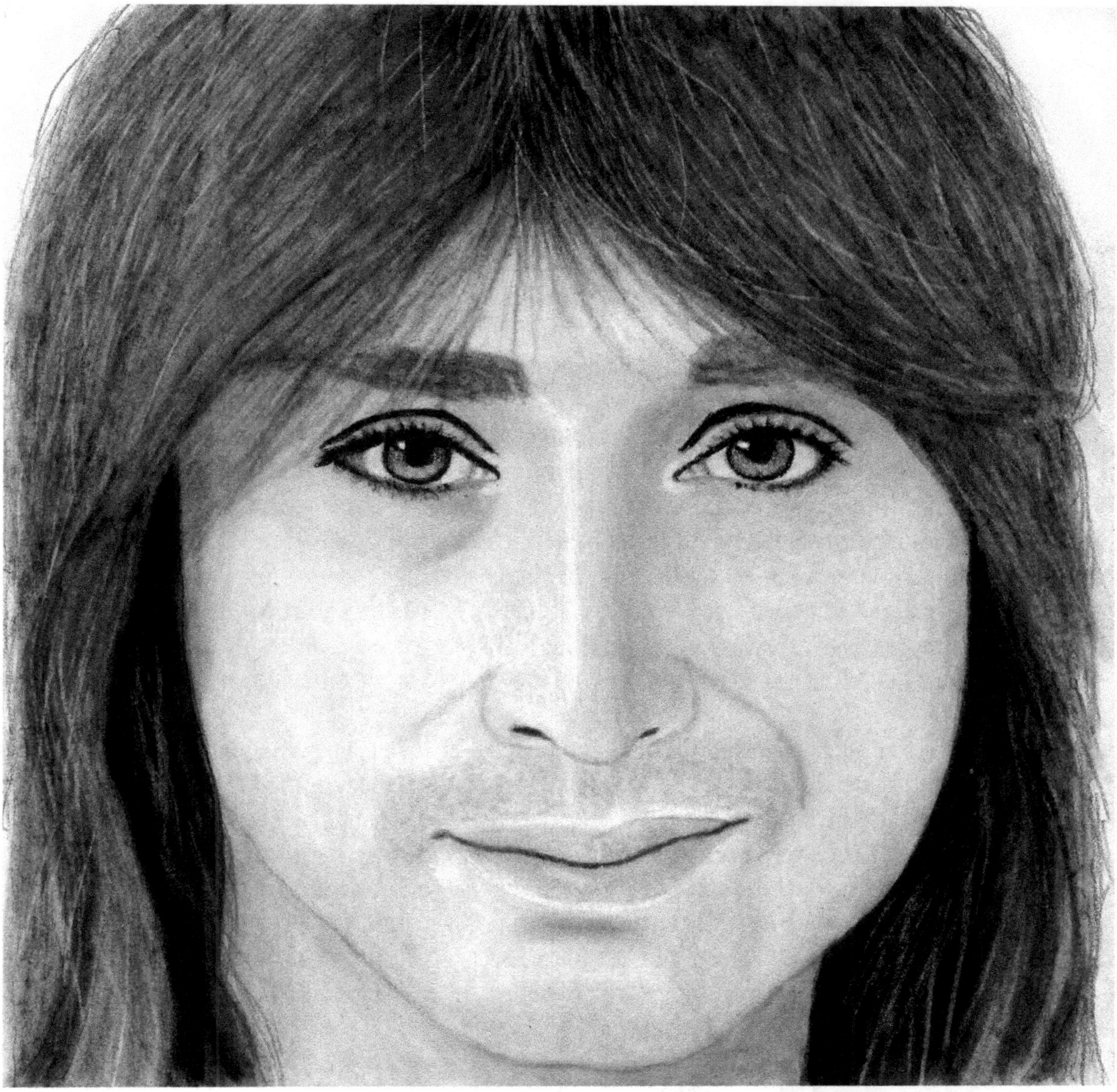

To view how this drawing was masterfully created or to purchase a Limited Edition Framed Artwork of Steve Perry type into your Internet Browser the URL shortcut ➡ **myportrait.art/steveperry**

To listen to their Greatest Songs type into your Internet Browser the URL shortcut ➡ **radio.surf/journey**

To view all channels on THE FACE OF MUSIC Internet Radio MEGA Station type into your Internet Browser the URL shortcut ➡ **radio.surf/music**

To inquire about purchasing a Limited Edtion NFT of this portrait type into your Internet Browser the URL shortcut ➡ **myartnft.shop/steveperry**

To view all available NFTs type into your Internet Browser the URL shortcut ➡ **myartnft.shop/all**

# Judas Priest

(Total Records Sold: 50+ Million) (Genre: Heavy Metal)

Judas Priest are an English heavy metal band formed in Birmingham in 1969. They have sold over 50 million copies of their albums, and are frequently ranked as one of the greatest metal bands of all time. Despite an innovative and pioneering body of work in the latter half of the 1970s, the band had struggled with indifferent record production and a lack of major commercial success until 1980, when they rose to commercial success with the album British Steel.

The band's membership has seen much turnover, including a revolving cast of drummers in the 1970s and the departure of singer Rob Halford in 1992. The American singer Tim "Ripper" Owens replaced Halford in 1996 and recorded two albums with Judas Priest, before Halford returned to the band in 2003. The current line-up consists of Halford, guitarists Glenn Tipton and Richie Faulkner, bassist Ian Hill and drummer Scott Travis. The band's best-selling album is 1982's Screaming for Vengeance, with their most commercially successful line-up featuring Hill, Halford, Tipton, guitarist K. K. Downing, and drummer Dave Holland. Tipton and Hill are the only two members of the band to appear on every album.

Halford's operatic vocal style and the twin guitar sound of Downing and Tipton have been a major influence on heavy metal bands. Judas Priest's image of leather, spikes, and other taboo articles of clothing were widely influential during the glam metal era of the 1980s. The Guardian referred to British Steel as the record that defines heavy metal. Despite a decline in exposure during the mid 1990s, the band has once again seen a resurgence, including worldwide tours, being inaugural inductees into the VH1 Rock Honors in 2006, receiving a Grammy Award for Best Metal Performance in 2010, and having their songs featured in video games such as Guitar Hero and the Rock Band series. Judas Priest was nominated for the Rock and Roll Hall of Fame 2020 class, but did not get in.

# Rob Halford

(Net Worth: $50 Million)(Height: 5' - 11")

Robert John Arthur Halford (born 25 August 1951) is an English singer and songwriter. He is best known as the lead vocalist of the heavy metal band Judas Priest, which was formed in 1969 and has received accolades such as the 2010 Grammy Award for Best Metal Performance. He has been noted for his powerful, wide-ranging voice and trademark leather-and-studs image, both of which have become iconic in heavy metal. He has also been involved with several side projects, including Fight, Two, and Halford.

AllMusic said of Halford, "There have been few vocalists in the history of heavy metal whose singing style has been as influential and instantly recognizable... able to effortlessly alternate between a throaty growl and an ear-splitting falsetto." He was ranked at No. 33 on the list of greatest voices in rock by Planet Rock listeners in 2009. He has also been nicknamed "Metal God" by fans.

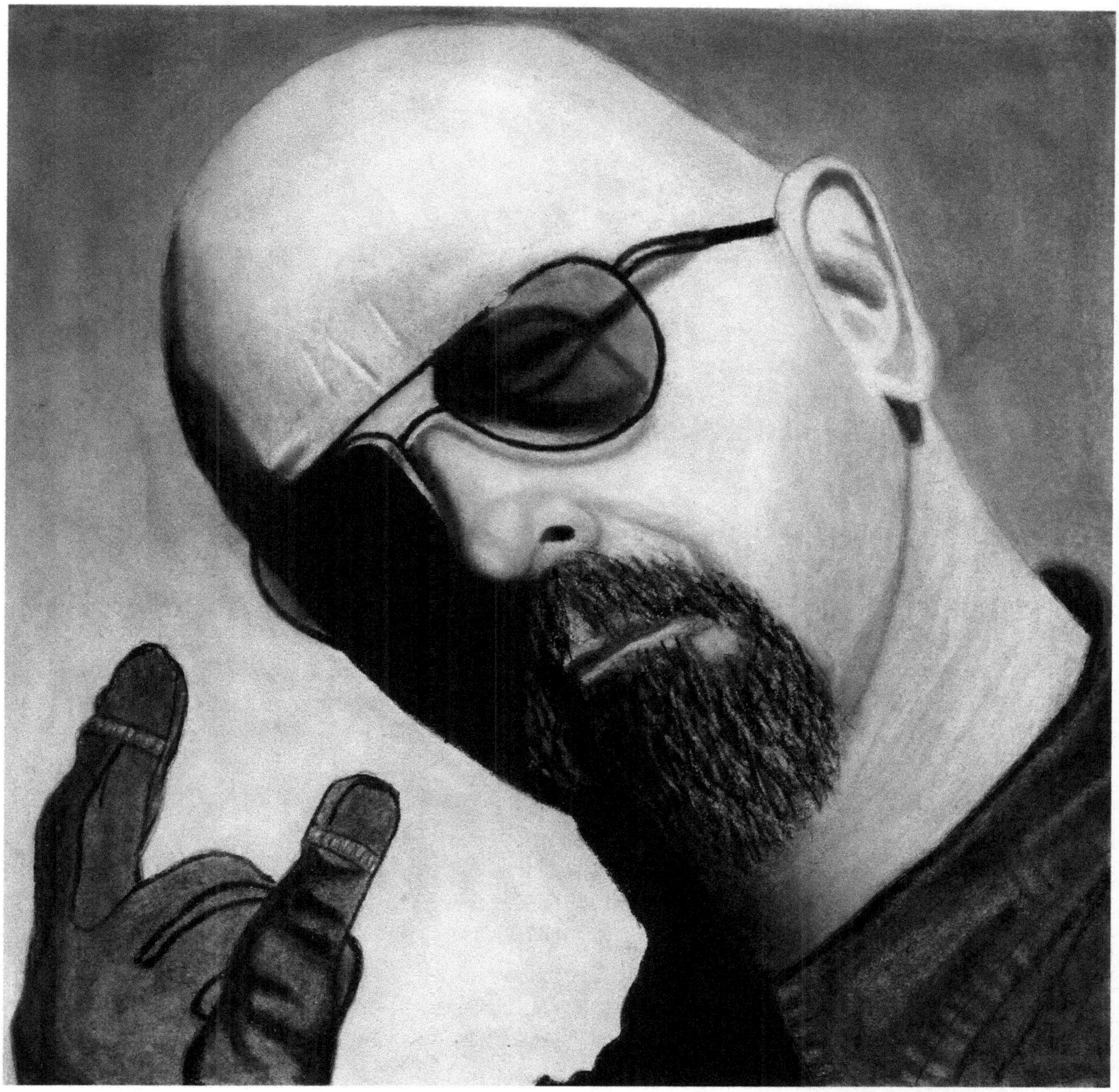

To view how this drawing was masterfully created or to purchase a Limited Edition Framed Artwork of Rob Halford type into your Internet Browser the URL shortcut ➡ **myportrait.art/robhalford**

To listen to their Greatest Songs type into your Internet Browser the URL shortcut ➡ **radio.surf/judaspriest**

To view all channels on THE FACE OF MUSIC Internet Radio MEGA Station type into your Internet Browser the URL shortcut ➡ **radio.surf/music**

To inquire about purchasing a Limited Edtion NFT of this portrait type into your Internet Browser the URL shortcut ➡ **myartnft.shop/robhalford**

To view all available NFTs type into your Internet Browser the URL shortcut ➡ **myartnft.shop/all**

# Judy Garland

(Net worth: $40 Thousand)(Total Records Sold: Millions)
(Genre: Pop)(Height: 4' - 11 1/2")

Judy Garland (born Frances Ethel Gumm; June 10, 1922 – June 22, 1969) was an American actress, singer, vaudevillian, and dancer. With a career spanning 45 years, she attained international stardom as an actress in both musical and dramatic roles, as a recording artist, and on the concert stage. Renowned for her versatility, she received an Academy Juvenile Award, a Golden Globe Award, and a Special Tony Award. Garland was the first woman to win the Grammy Award for Album of the Year, which she won for her 1961 live recording titled Judy at Carnegie Hall.

Garland began performing in vaudeville as a child with her two older sisters and was later signed to Metro-Goldwyn-Mayer as a teenager. She appeared in more than two dozen films for MGM and is remembered for portraying Dorothy Gale in The Wizard of Oz (1939). Garland was a frequent on-screen partner of both Mickey Rooney and Gene Kelly and regularly collaborated with director and second husband Vincente Minnelli. Other film appearances during this period include roles in Meet Me in St. Louis (1944), The Harvey Girls (1946), Easter Parade (1948), and Summer Stock (1950). Garland was released from MGM in 1950, after 15 years with the studio, amid a series of personal struggles that prevented her from fulfilling the terms of her contract.

Although her film career became intermittent thereafter, two of Garland's most critically acclaimed roles came later in her career: she received a nomination for the Academy Award for Best Actress for her performance in A Star Is Born (1954) and a nomination for Best Supporting Actress for her performance in Judgment at Nuremberg (1961). She also made record-breaking concert appearances, released eight studio albums, and hosted her own Emmy-nominated television series, The Judy Garland Show (1963–1964). At age 39, Garland became the youngest and first female recipient of the Cecil B. DeMille Award for lifetime achievement in the film industry. In 1997, Garland was posthumously awarded the Grammy Lifetime Achievement Award. Several of her recordings have been inducted into the Grammy Hall of Fame, and in 1999, the American Film Institute ranked her as the eighth-greatest female screen legend of classic Hollywood cinema.

Garland struggled in her personal life from an early age. The pressures of early stardom affected her physical and mental health from the time she was a teenager; her self-image was influenced by constant criticism from film executives who believed that she was physically unattractive and who manipulated her onscreen physical appearance. Throughout her adulthood she was plagued by alcohol and substance abuse, as well as financial instability, often owing hundreds of thousands of dollars in back taxes. Her lifelong struggle with substance abuse ultimately led to her death in London from an accidental barbiturate overdose at age 47.

Garland was born Frances Ethel Gumm on 10 June 1922, in Grand Rapids, Minnesota. She was the youngest child of Ethel Marion (née Milne; 1893–1953) and Francis Avent "Frank" Gumm (1886–1935). Her parents were vaudevillians who settled in Grand Rapids to run a movie theater that featured vaudeville acts. She was of Irish, English, Scottish, and French Huguenot ancestry, named after both of her parents and baptized at a local Episcopal church.

"Baby" (as she was called by her parents and sisters) shared her family's flair for song and dance. Her first appearance came at the age of two, when she joined her elder sisters Mary Jane "Suzy/Suzanne" Gumm and Dorothy Virginia "Jimmie" Gumm on the stage of her father's movie theater during a Christmas show and sang a chorus of "Jingle Bells". The Gumm Sisters performed there for the next few years, accompanied by their mother on piano

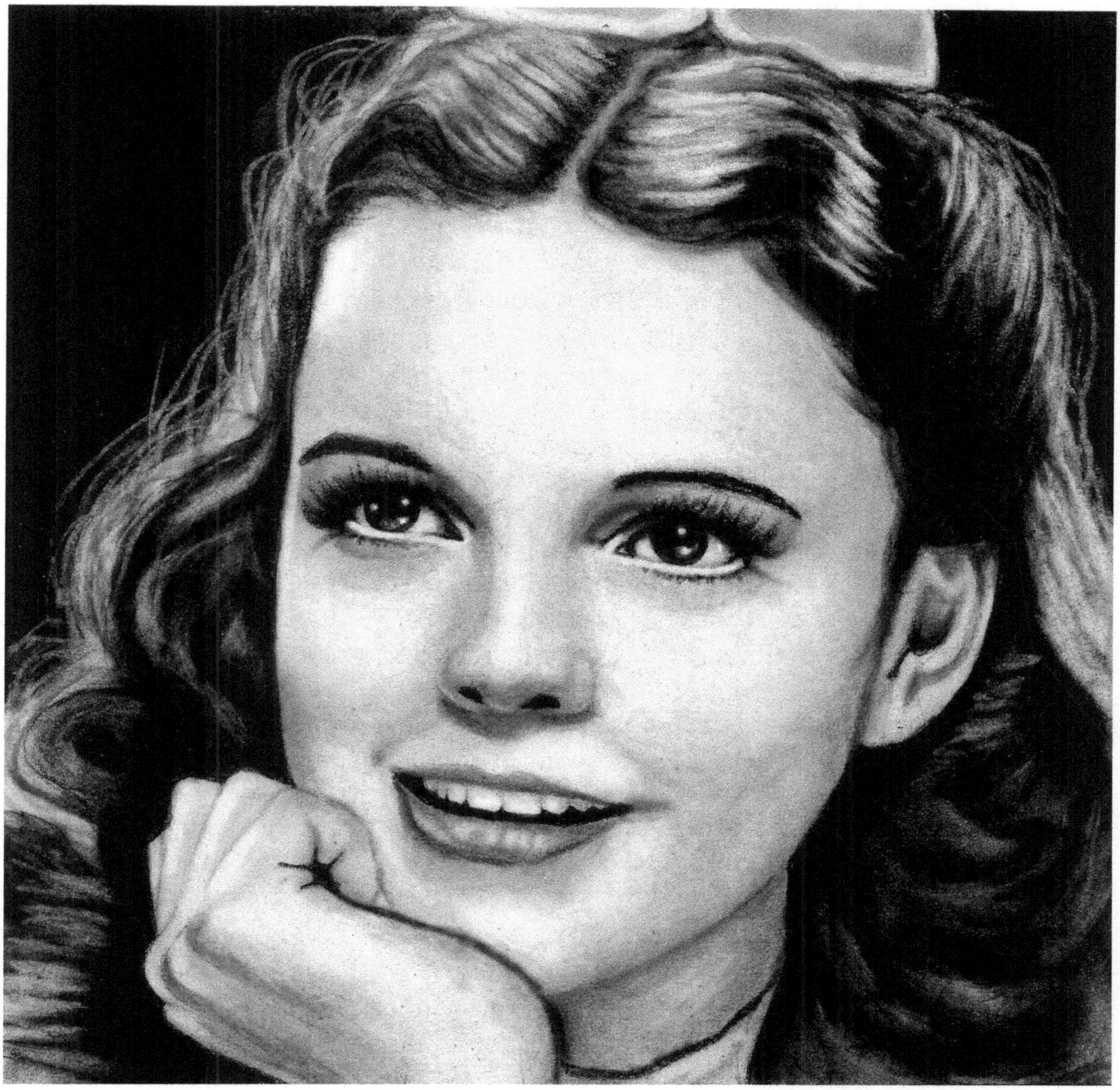

To view how this drawing was masterfully created or to purchase a Limited Edition Framed Artwork of Judy Garland type into your Internet Browser the URL shortcut ➡ **myportrait.art/judygarland**

To listen to her Greatest Songs type into your Internet Browser the URL shortcut ➡ **radio.surf/judygarland**

To view all channels on THE FACE OF MUSIC Internet Radio MEGA Station type into your Internet Browser the URL shortcut ➡ **radio.surf/music**

To inquire about purchasing a Limited Edtion NFT of this portrait type into your Internet Browser the URL shortcut ➡ **myartnft.shop/judygarland**

To view all available NFTs type into your Internet Browser the URL shortcut ➡ **myartnft.shop/all**

# Julio Iglesias

(Net worth: $600 Million)(Total Records Sold: 100 Million)
(Genre: Latin Pop , Dance Pop , Adult Contemporary)(Height: 6' - 1")

Julio José Iglesias (born 23 September 1943) is a Spanish singer, songwriter and former professional footballer. Iglesias is recognized as the most commercially successful continental European singer in the world and one of the top record sellers in music history, having sold more than 100 million records worldwide in 14 languages. It is estimated that during his career he has performed in more than 5000 concerts, for over 60 million people in five continents. In April 2013, Iglesias was inducted into the Latin Songwriters Hall of Fame.

In 1983, Iglesias was celebrated as having recorded songs in the most languages in the world, and in 2013 for being the artist in Latin music with the most records sold in history. In April 2013 in Beijing, he was honoured as the most popular international artist in China. In Brazil, France, Italy and elsewhere, Iglesias is the most successful foreign record seller, while in his home country, Spain, he has sold the most records in history, with 23 million records.

During his career, Iglesias has won many awards in the music industry, including the Grammy, Latin Grammy, World Music Award, Billboard Music Award, American Music Award and Lo Nuestro Award. He has been awarded the Gold Medal for Merit in the Fine Arts of Spain and the Legion of Honour of France. UNICEF named him Special Ambassador for the Performing Arts in 1989. He has had a star on the Hollywood Walk of Fame since 1985.

Iglesias was born in Madrid to Julio Iglesias Sr., a medical doctor from Ourense who became one of the youngest gynecologists in the country, and María del Rosario de la Cueva y Perignat. His paternal grandparents, Manuela Puga Noguerol and Ulpiano Iglesias Sarria, were of Galician ancestry. His maternal grandparents were José de la Cueva y Orejuela (1887–1955) and Dolores de Perignat y Ruiz de Benavides, who was a native of Guayama, Puerto Rico.

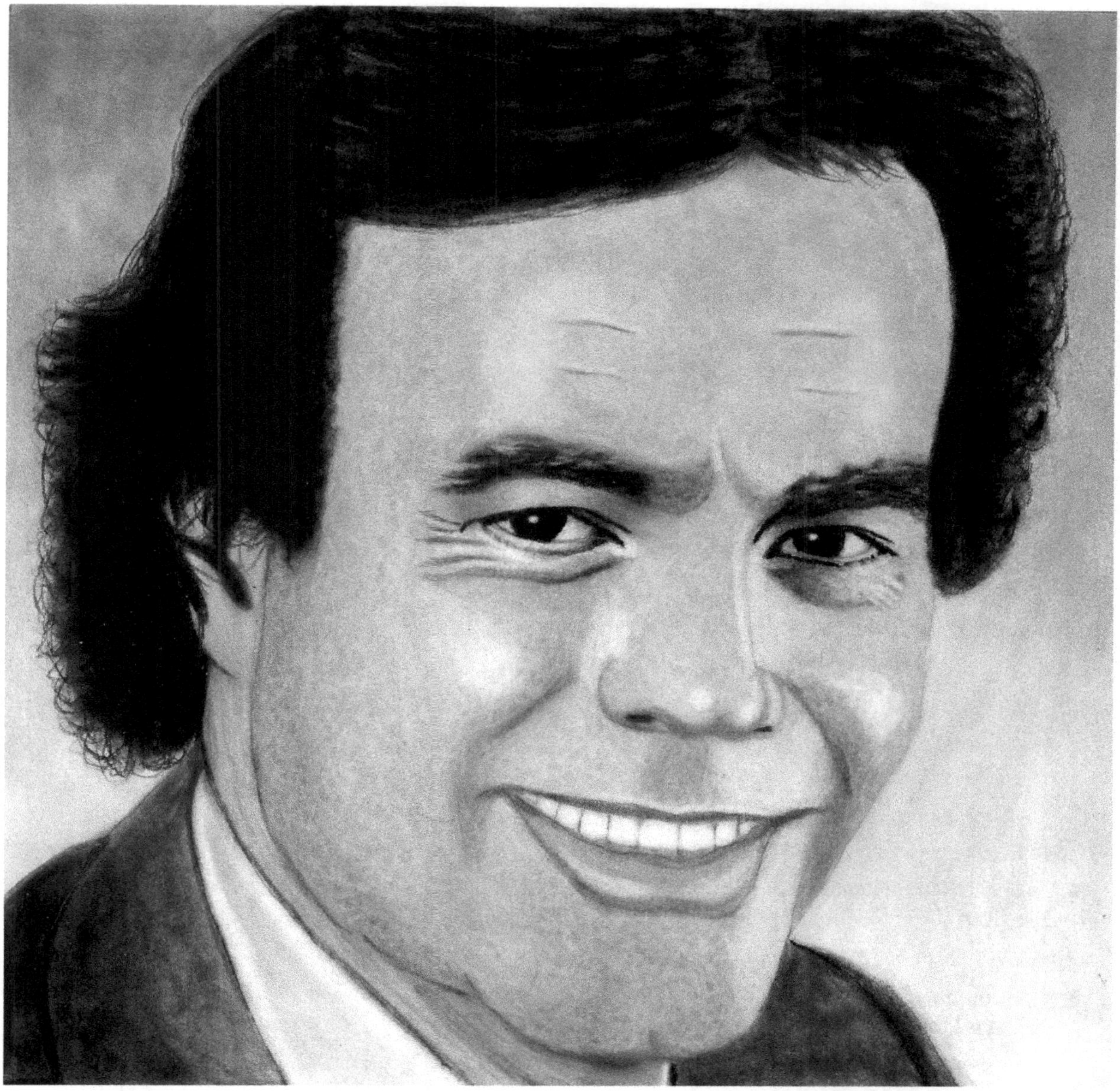

To view how this drawing was masterfully created or to purchase a Limited Edition Framed Artwork of Julio Iglesias Ocasek type into your Internet Browser the URL shortcut ➡ **myportrait.art/julioiglesias**

To listen to his Greatest Songs type into your Internet Browser the URL shortcut ➡ **radio.surf/julioiglesias**

To view all channels on THE FACE OF MUSIC Internet Radio MEGA Station type into your Internet Browser the URL shortcut ➡ **radio.surf/music**

To inquire about purchasing a Limited Edition NFT of this portrait type into your Internet Browser the URL shortcut ➡ **myartnft.shop/julioiglesias**

To view all available NFTs type into your Internet Browser the URL shortcut ➡ **myartnft.shop/all**

# Kanye West

(Net worth: $1.8 Billion)(Total Records Sold: 160 Million)
(Genre: Hip-Hop , Rap)(Height: 5' - 8")

Kanye Omari West (born June 8, 1977) is an American rapper, record producer, fashion designer, and politician. He has been influential in the 21st-century development of mainstream hip hop and popular music in general.

Born in Atlanta and raised in Chicago, West gained notoriety as a producer for Roc-A-Fella Records in the early 2000s, producing singles for several mainstream artists. Intent on pursuing a solo career as a rapper, West released his debut album The College Dropout in 2004 to critical and commercial success, and founded the record label GOOD Music. He experimented with a variety of musical genres on subsequent acclaimed studio albums, including Late Registration (2005), Graduation (2007), and 808s & Heartbreak (2008). Drawing inspiration from maximalism and minimalism, respectively, West's fifth album My Beautiful Dark Twisted Fantasy (2010) and sixth album Yeezus (2013) were also critical successes. He went on to release The Life of Pablo (2016), Ye (2018), and Jesus Is King (2019). West's discography also includes the full-length collaborations Watch the Throne (2011) and Kids See Ghosts (2018) with Jay-Z and Kid Cudi, respectively.

West's outspoken views and life outside of music have received significant media attention. He has been a frequent source of controversy for his conduct at award shows, on social media, and in other public settings, as well as for his comments on the music and fashion industries, U.S. politics, and race. In 2020, he ran an unsuccessful independent presidential campaign that advocated for a consistent life ethic. His Christian faith, as well as his marriage to television personality Kim Kardashian, have also been a source of media attention. As a fashion designer, he has collaborated with Nike, Louis Vuitton, and A.P.C. on both clothing and footwear, and have most prominently resulted in the Yeezy collaboration with Adidas beginning in 2013. He is the founder and head of the creative content company DONDA.

West is one of the world's best-selling music artists, with more than 20 million albums and 140 million singles sold worldwide. He has won a total of 22 Grammy Awards, making him one of the most awarded artists of all time. Among his other awards are the Billboard Artist Achievement Award, a joint-record three Brit Awards for Best International Male Solo Artist and the Michael Jackson Video Vanguard Award. Six of his albums were included on Rolling Stone's 2020 500 Greatest Albums of All Time list; the same publication named him one of the 100 Greatest Songwriters of All Time. West is the tied holder for the most albums (four) topping the annual Pazz & Jop critic poll. Time magazine named him one of the 100 most influential people in the world in 2005 and 2015.

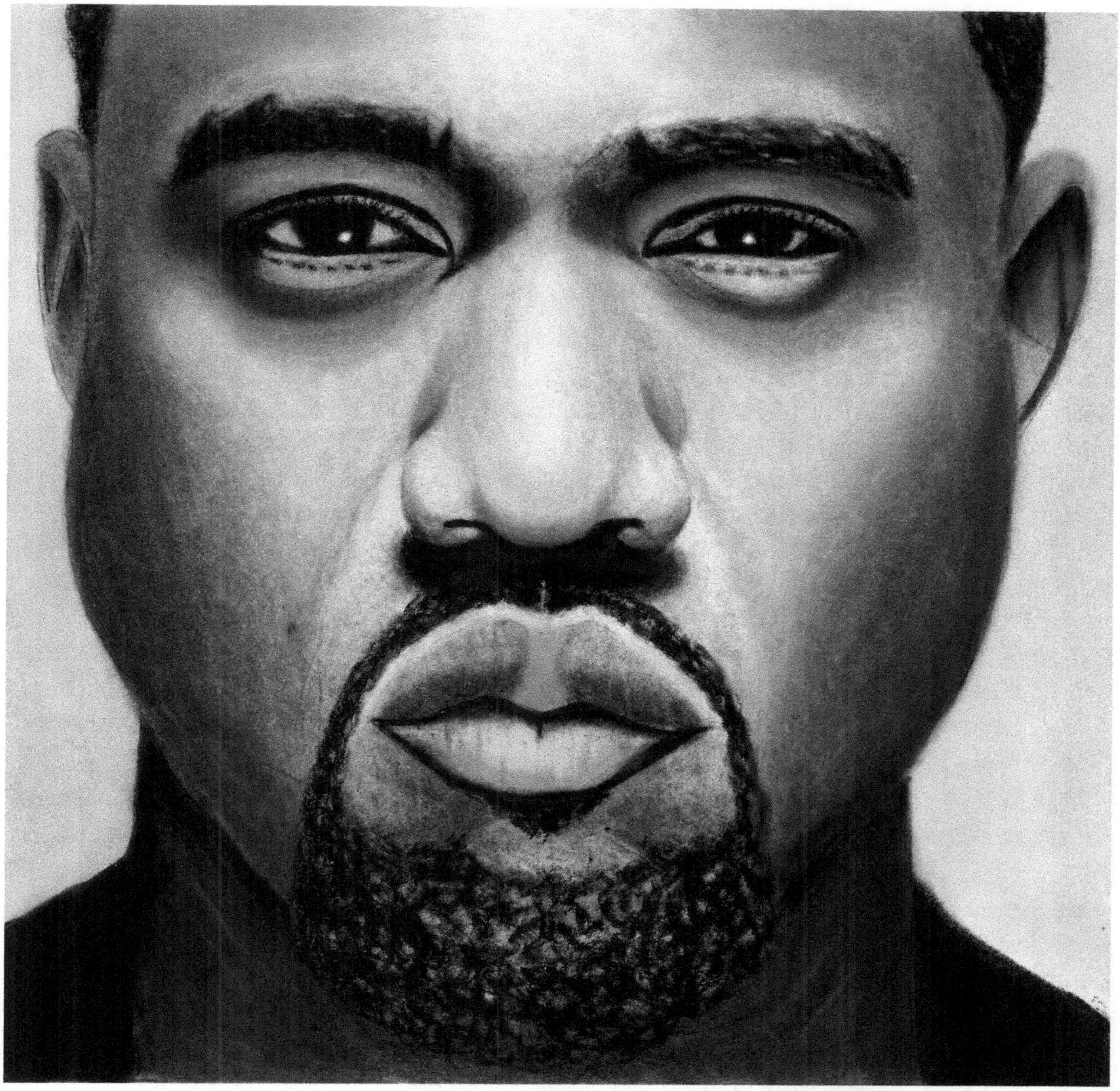

To view how this drawing was masterfully created or to purchase a Limited Edition Framed Artwork of Kanye West type into your Internet Browser the URL shortcut ➡ **myportrait.art/kaynewest**

To listen to his Greatest Songs type into your Internet Browser the URL shortcut ➡ **radio.surf/kaynewest**

To view all channels on THE FACE OF MUSIC Internet Radio MEGA Station type into your Internet Browser the URL shortcut ➡ **radio.surf/music**

To inquire about purchasing a Limited Edition NFT of this portrait type into your Internet Browser the URL shortcut ➡ **myartnft.shop/kaynewest**

To view all available NFTs type into your Internet Browser the URL shortcut ➡ **myartnft.shop/all**

# Kenny Rogers

(Net worth: $250 Million)(Total Records Sold: 100 Million)
(Genre: Country)(Height: 5' - 10 1/2")

Kenneth Ray Rogers (August 21, 1938 – March 20, 2020) was an American singer, songwriter, musician, actor, record producer, and entrepreneur. He was elected to the Country Music Hall of Fame in 2013. Rogers was particularly popular with country audiences but also charted more than 420 hit singles across various genres, topping the country and pop album charts for more than 200 individual weeks in the United States alone. He sold more than 100 million records worldwide during his lifetime, making him one of the best-selling music artists of all time. His fame and career spanned multiple genres: jazz, folk, pop, rock, and country. He remade his career and was one of the most successful cross-over artists of all time.

In the late 1950s, Rogers began his recording career with the Houston-based group the Scholars, who first released "The Poor Little Doggie". After some solo releases, including 1958's "That Crazy Feeling", Rogers then joined a group with the jazz singer Bobby Doyle. In 1966 he became a member of the folk ensemble the New Christy Minstrels, playing double bass and bass guitar as well as singing. In 1967, he and several members of the New Christy Minstrels left to found the group the First Edition, with whom he scored his first major hit, "Just Dropped In (To See What Condition My Condition Was In)", a psychedelic rock song which peaked at number five on the Billboard charts. As Rogers took an increased leadership role in the First Edition following the success of 1969's "Ruby, Don't Take Your Love to Town", the band gradually changed styles to a more country feel. The band broke up in 1975–76, and Rogers embarked on a long and successful solo career, which included several successful collaborations, including duets with singers Dolly Parton and Sheena Easton and a songwriting partnership with Lionel Richie. His signature song, 1978's "The Gambler", was a crossover hit that won him a Grammy Award in 1980 and was selected in 2018 for preservation in the National Recording Registry by the Library of Congress. He developed the Gambler persona into a character for a successful series of television films starting with 1980's Emmy-nominated Kenny Rogers as The Gambler.

Rogers' albums The Gambler and Kenny were featured in the About.com poll of "The 200 Most Influential Country Albums Ever". He was voted the "Favorite Singer of All Time" in a 1986 joint poll by readers of both USA Today and People. He received numerous awards, such as the AMAs, Grammys, ACMs, and CMAs as well as a lifetime achievement award for a career spanning six decades in 2003. Later success included the 2006 album release Water & Bridges, an across-the-board hit that hit the Top 5 in the Billboard Country Albums sales charts, also charting in the Top 15 of the Billboard 200. The first single from the album, "I Can't Unlove You", was also a sizable chart hit. Remaining a popular entertainer around the world, he continued to tour regularly until his retirement in 2017.

Rogers had acting roles in movies and television shows, including the title roles in Kenny Rogers as The Gambler, the MacShayne series for The NBC Mystery Movie, and the 1982 feature film Six Pack. He was a co-founder of the restaurant chain Kenny Rogers Roasters in collaboration with former Kentucky Fried Chicken CEO John Y. Brown Jr. Although the stores closed in the United States, they are still a fixture in Asia.

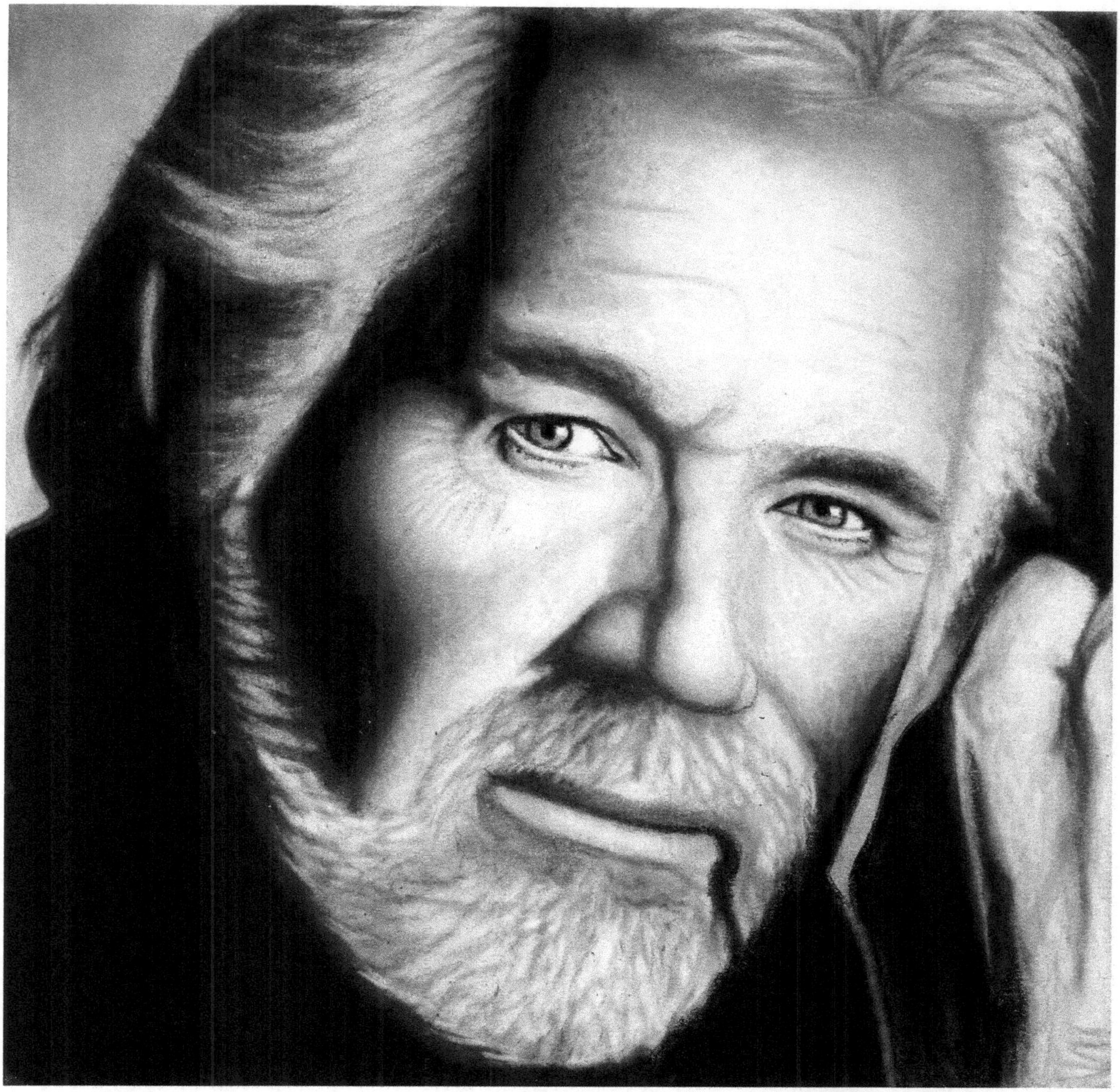

To view how this drawing was masterfully created or to purchase a Limited Edition Framed Artwork of Kenny Rogers type into your Internet Browser the URL shortcut ➡ **myportrait.art/kennyrogers**

To listen to his Greatest Songs type into your Internet Browser the URL shortcut ➡ **radio.surf/kennyrogers**

To view all channels on THE FACE OF MUSIC Internet Radio MEGA Station type into your Internet Browser the URL shortcut ➡ **radio.surf/music**

To inquire about purchasing a Limited Edition NFT of this portrait type into your Internet Browser the URL shortcut ➡ **myartnft.shop/kennyrogers**

To view all available NFTs type into your Internet Browser the URL shortcut ➡ **myartnft.shop/all**

# Kinks, The

(Total Records Sold: 50+ Million) (Genre: Rock , Pop)

The Kinks were an English rock band formed in Muswell Hill, north London, in 1964 by brothers Ray and Dave Davies. They are regarded as one of the most influential rock bands of the 1960s. The band emerged during the height of British rhythm and blues and Merseybeat, and were briefly part of the British Invasion of the United States until their touring ban in 1965 (as a result of constant fighting between the brothers). Their third single, the Ray Davies-penned "You Really Got Me", became an international hit, topping the charts in the United Kingdom and reaching the Top 10 in the United States. Their music was influenced by a wide range of genres, including American R&B and rock and roll initially, and later adopting British music hall, folk, and country. They gained a reputation for reflecting English culture and lifestyle, fuelled by Ray Davies' wittily observational writing style.Early works included albums such as Face to Face (1966), Something Else (1967), The Kinks Are the Village Green Preservation Society (1968), Arthur (1969), Lola Versus Powerman (1970), and Muswell Hillbillies (1971), along with their accompanying singles. After a fallow period in the mid-1970s, the band experienced a revival during the late 1970s and early 1980s with their albums Sleepwalker (1977), Misfits (1978), Low Budget (1979), Give the People What They Want (1981) and State of Confusion (1983). In addition, groups such as Van Halen, the Jam, the Knack, the Pretenders, The Raincoats and the Fall covered their songs, helping to boost the Kinks' record sales. In the 1990s, Britpop acts such as Blur and Oasis cited the band as a major influence.The Kinks have had five Top 10 singles on the US Billboard chart. Nine of their albums charted in the Top 40. In the UK, they have had seventeen Top 20 singles and five Top 10 albums. Four Kinks albums have been certified gold by the RIAA and the band have sold over 50 million records worldwide. Among numerous honours, they received the Ivor Novello Award for "Outstanding Service to British Music". In 1990, the original four members of The Kinks were inducted into the Rock and Roll Hall of Fame, as well as the UK Music Hall of Fame in November 2005. In 2018, after years of ruling out a reunion due to the brothers' animosity and the difficult relationship between longtime drummer Mick Avory and Dave, Ray and Dave Davies finally announced they were working to reform the Kinks, with Avory also on board. However, comments made by each of the Davies brothers in 2020 and 2021 would indicate that in the years since the initial announcement, little (if any) progress has been made towards an actual Kinks reunion for a new studio band album.

## Ray Davies

(Net Worth: $12 Million)(Height: 5' - 11 3/4")

Sir Raymond Douglas Davies, CBE (born 21 June 1944) is an English singer, songwriter and musician. He was the lead singer, rhythm guitarist and main songwriter for the Kinks, which he led with his younger brother, Dave. He has also acted, directed and produced shows for theatre and television. He is often referred to as "the godfather of Britpop". After the dissolution of the Kinks in 1996, Davies embarked on a solo career.

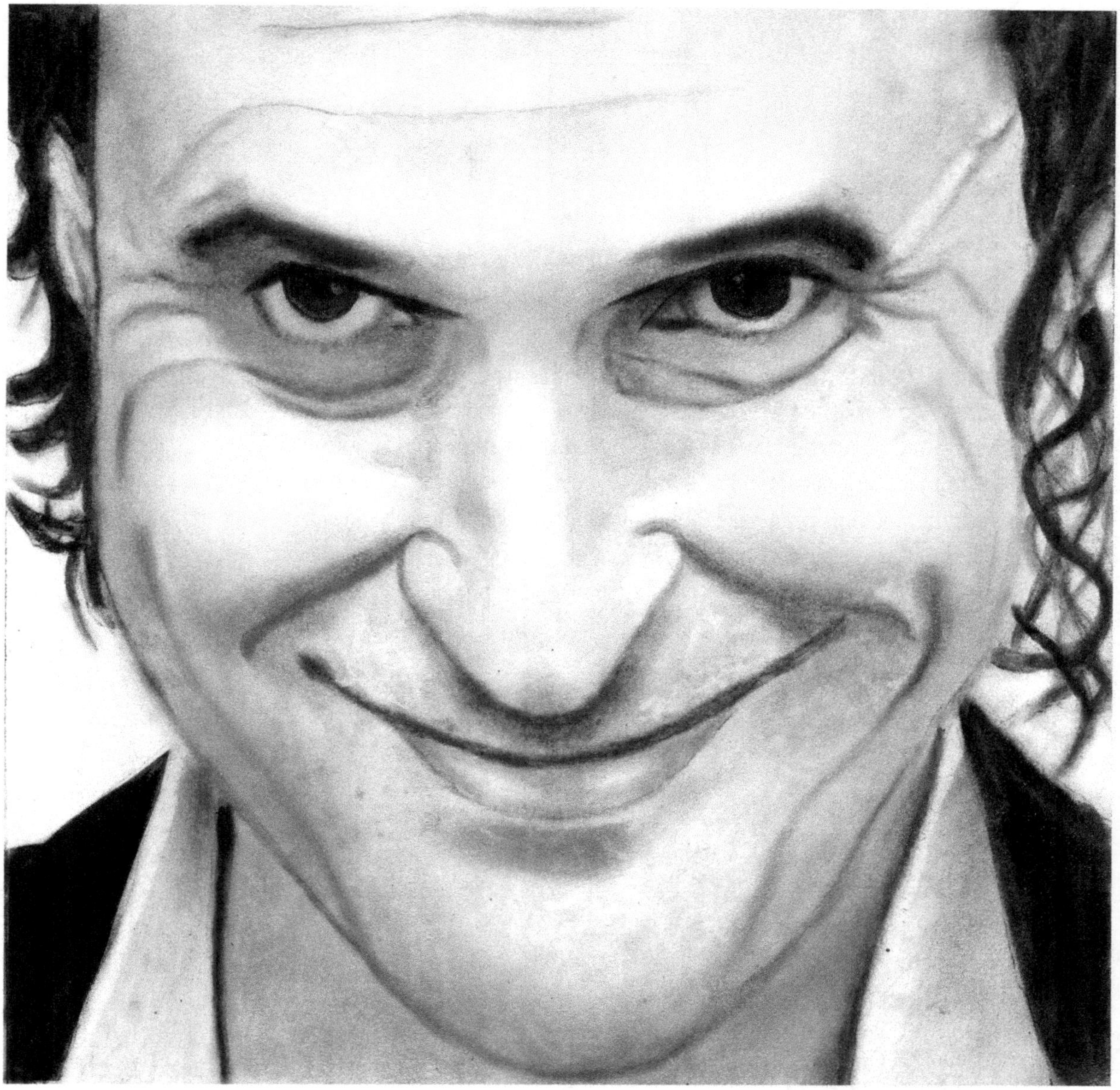

To view how this drawing was masterfully created or to purchase a Limited Edition Framed Artwork of Ray Davies type into your Internet Browser the URL shortcut ➡ **myportrait.art/raydavies**

To listen to their Greatest Songs type into your Internet Browser the URL shortcut ➡ **radio.surf/thekinks**

To view all channels on THE FACE OF MUSIC Internet Radio MEGA Station type into your Internet Browser the URL shortcut ➡ **radio.surf/music**

To inquire about purchasing a Limited Edtion NFT of this portrait type into your Internet Browser the URL shortcut ➡ **myartnft.shop/raydavies**

To view all available NFTs type into your Internet Browser the URL shortcut ➡ **myartnft.shop/all**

# KISS

(Total Records Sold: 100+ Million) (Genre: Hard Rock)

Kiss (often stylized as KISS) is an American rock band formed in New York City in January 1973 by Paul Stanley, Gene Simmons, Ace Frehley, and Peter Criss. Well known for its members' face paint and stage outfits, the group rose to prominence in the mid–late 1970s with its shocking live performances, which featured fire breathing, blood-spitting, smoking guitars, shooting rockets, levitating drum kits, and pyrotechnics. The band has gone through several lineup changes, with Stanley and Simmons being the only members to feature in every lineup. The original and best-known lineup consists of Stanley (vocals and rhythm guitar), Simmons (vocals and bass), Frehley (lead guitar and vocals), and Criss (drums and vocals)

- Continued on Page 357 -.

# Ace Frehley

(Net Worth: $1 Million)(Height: 6' - 0")

Paul Daniel "Ace" Frehley (born April 27, 1951) is an American musician and songwriter best known as the original lead guitarist and co-founding member of the rock band Kiss. He invented the persona of The Spaceman (a.k.a. Space Ace) and played with the group from its inception in 1973 until his departure in 1982. After leaving Kiss, Frehley embarked on a solo career, which was put on hold when he rejoined Kiss in 1996 for a highly successful reunion tour.

Frehley's second tenure with Kiss lasted until 2002, when he left at the conclusion of what was originally purported to be the band's Farewell Tour. His most recent solo album, Origins Vol. 2, was released on September 18, 2020. Guitar World magazine ranked him as the 14th Greatest Metal Guitarist of All Time. Outside Kiss, Frehley had commercial success, with his first solo album going platinum. His first album with his "Frehley's Comet" band was also a big seller. Frehley is noted for his aggressive, atmospheric and melodic guitar playing and is also known for the use of many "special effects" guitars, including a Gibson Les Paul guitar that emits smoke from the neck humbucker pickup and produces spinning pyrotechnics, and a custom Les Paul that emits light based on song tempo.

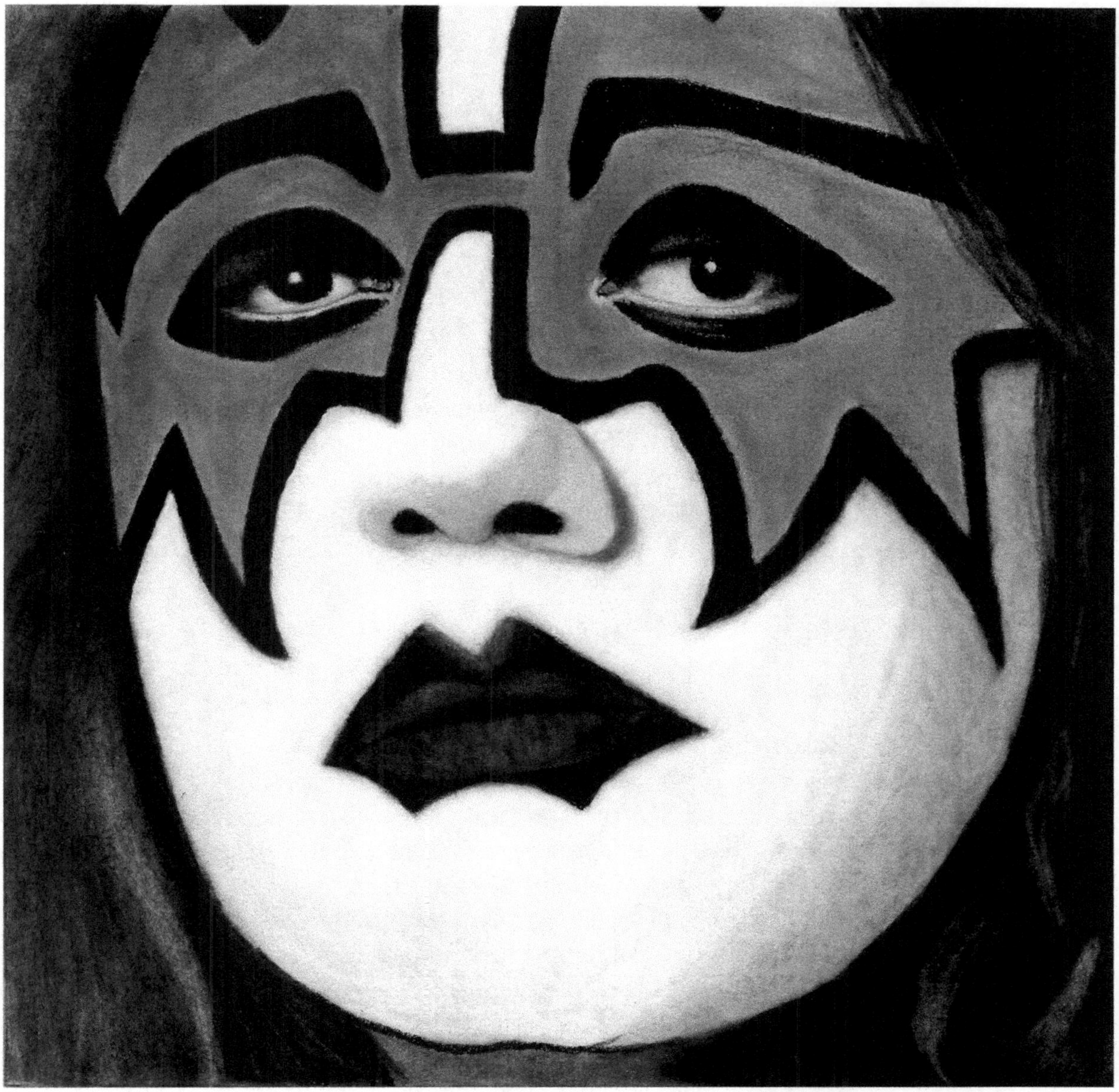

To view how this drawing was masterfully created or to purchase a Limited Edition Framed Artwork of Ace Frehley type into your Internet Browser the URL shortcut ➡ **myportrait.art/acefrehley**

To listen to their Greatest Songs type intc your Internet Browser the URL shortcut ➡ **radio.surf/kiss**

To view all channels on THE FACE OF MUSIC Internet Radio MEGA Station type into your Internet Browser the URL shortcut ➡ **radio.surf/music**

To inquire about purchasing a Limited Edtion NFT of this portrait type into your Internet Browser the URL shortcut ➡ **myartnft.shop/acefrehley**

To view all available NFTs type into your Internet Browser the URL shortcut ➡ **myartnft.shop/all**

# KISS

(Total Records Sold: 100+ Million) (Genre: Hard Rock)

With their make-up and costumes, the band members took on the personae of comic book-style characters: the Starchild (Stanley), the Demon (Simmons), the Spaceman or Space Ace (Frehley), and the Catman (Criss). Due to creative differences, both Criss and Frehley had departed the group by 1982. In 1983, Kiss began performing without makeup and costumes, thus marking the beginning of the band's "unmasked" era that would last for over a decade. The band experienced a commercial resurgence during this era, with the Platinum-certified album Lick It Up successfully introducing them to a new generation of fans, and its music videos received regular airplay on MTV. Eric Carr, who had replaced Criss in 1980, died in 1991 of heart cancer and was replaced by Eric Singer.

- Continued on Page 359 -.

# Gene Simmons

(Net Worth: $400 Million)(Height: 6' - 2")

Gene Klein (born Chaim Witz on August 25, 1949), known professionally as Gene Simmons, is an American musician, singer, and songwriter. Also known by his stage persona The Demon, he is the bassist and co-lead singer of Kiss, the rock band he co-founded with lead singer and rhythm guitarist Paul Stanley in the early 1970s.

Simmons became involved with his first band, Lynx, then renamed the Missing Links, when he was a teenager. Eventually, he disbanded the band to form the Long Island Sounds, the name being a pun on Long Island Sound. While he played in these bands, he worked at odd jobs on the side to make more money, including trading used comic books. Simmons attended Sullivan County Community College in Loch Sheldrake, New York. He joined a new band, Bullfrog Bheer, and the band recorded a demo, "Leeta"; this was later included on the Kiss box set.

Simmons formed the rock band Wicked Lester in the early 1970s with Stanley Eisen (now known as Paul Stanley) and recorded one album, which was never released. Dissatisfied with Wicked Lester's sound and look, Simmons and Stanley attempted to fire their band members; they were met with resistance, and they quit Wicked Lester, walking away from their record deal with Epic Records. They decided to form the "ultimate rock band", and started looking for a drummer. Simmons and Stanley found an ad placed by George Peter John Criscuola (known as Peter Criss) who was playing clubs in Brooklyn at the time; they joined and started out as a trio.

During this time, Criss and Simmons also appeared on an unreleased album by Captain Sanity together with members from Criss' previous band Chelsea. Paul Frehley (better known as Ace Frehley) responded to an ad they put in The Village Voice for a lead guitar player, and soon joined them. Kiss released their self-titled debut album in February 1974. Stanley took on the role of lead performer on stage, while Simmons became the driving force behind what became an extensive Kiss merchandising franchise. The eye section of his "Demon" makeup with Kiss came from the wing design of comic book character Black Bolt.

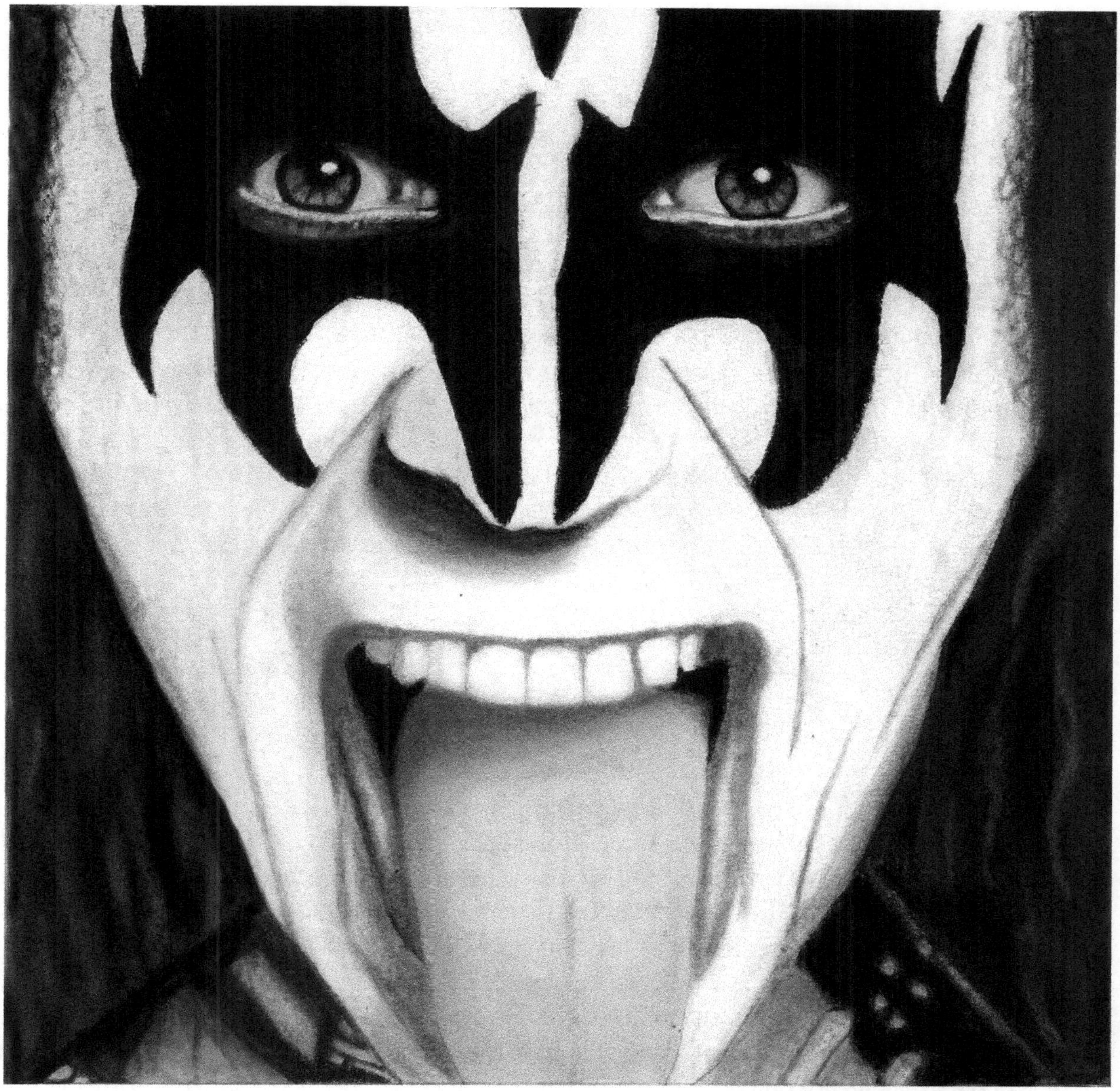

To view how this drawing was masterfully created or to purchase a Limited Edition Framed Artwork of Gene Simmons type into your Internet Browser the URL shortcut ➡ **myportrait.art/genesimmons**

To listen to their Greatest Songs type into your Internet Browser the URL shortcut ➡ **radio.surf/kiss**

To view all channels on THE FACE OF MUSIC Internet Radio MEGA Station type into your Internet Browser the URL shortcut ➡ **radio.surf/music**

To inquire about purchasing a Limited Edtion NFT of this portrait type into your Internet Browser the URL shortcut ➡ **myartnft.shop/genesimmons**

To view all available NFTs type into your Internet Browser the URL shortcut ➡ **myartnft.shop/all**

# KISS

(Total Records Sold: 100+ Million) (Genre: Hard Rock)

In response to a wave of Kiss nostalgia in the mid-1990s, the original lineup re-united in 1996, which also saw the return of its makeup and stage costumes. The resulting reunion tour was highly successful, grossing $143.7 million, making it the band's most successful tour to date. Criss and Frehley subsequently left the band again, and have been replaced by Singer and Tommy Thayer. The band has continued with its original stage makeup, with Singer and Thayer using the original Catman and Spaceman makeup, respectively. In September 2018, Kiss announced that, after 45 years of recording and performing, it would be embarking on its ongoing final tour, the End of the Road World Tour, which started in January 2019 and is currently set to conclude in 2022.

- Continued on Page 361 -.

# Paul Stanley

(Net Worth: $200 Million)(Height: 5' - 11")

Paul Stanley (born January 20, 1952 as Stanley Bert Eisen) is an American musician, singer, and songwriter, best known for being the co-founder, frontman, rhythm guitarist and co-lead vocalist of the rock band Kiss. He is the writer or co-writer of many of the band's most popular songs. Stanley established the Starchild character for his Kiss persona.

Hit Parader ranked him 18th on their list of the Top 100 Metal Vocalists of All Time. A Gibson.com readers' poll also named him 13th on their list of Top 25 Frontmen.

Stanley Bert Eisen was born January 20, 1952, in upper Manhattan, New York City, near 211th St. and Broadway; the Inwood neighborhood near Inwood Hill Park. Both of his parents are Jewish. He was the second of two children; his older sister Julia was born two years earlier. Their mother came from a family that fled Nazi Germany to Amsterdam, Netherlands, and then to New York City. His father's parents were from Poland. Stanley was raised Jewish, although he did not consider his family very observant and did not celebrate his bar mitzvah. His parents listened to classical music and light opera; Stanley was greatly moved by Beethoven's works.

Stanley's right ear was misshapen from a birth defect called microtia until having reconstructive surgery at the age of 30; he was unable to hear on that side, he found it difficult to determine the direction of a sound, and he could not understand speech in a noisy environment. Attending PS 98, he was taunted by other children for his deformed ear.

Despite his hearing problem, Stanley enjoyed listening to music, and he watched American Bandstand on television. His favorite musical artists included Eddie Cochran, Dion and the Belmonts, Jerry Lee Lewis and Little Richard. Stanley learned to sing harmony with his family, and he was given a child's guitar at age seven.

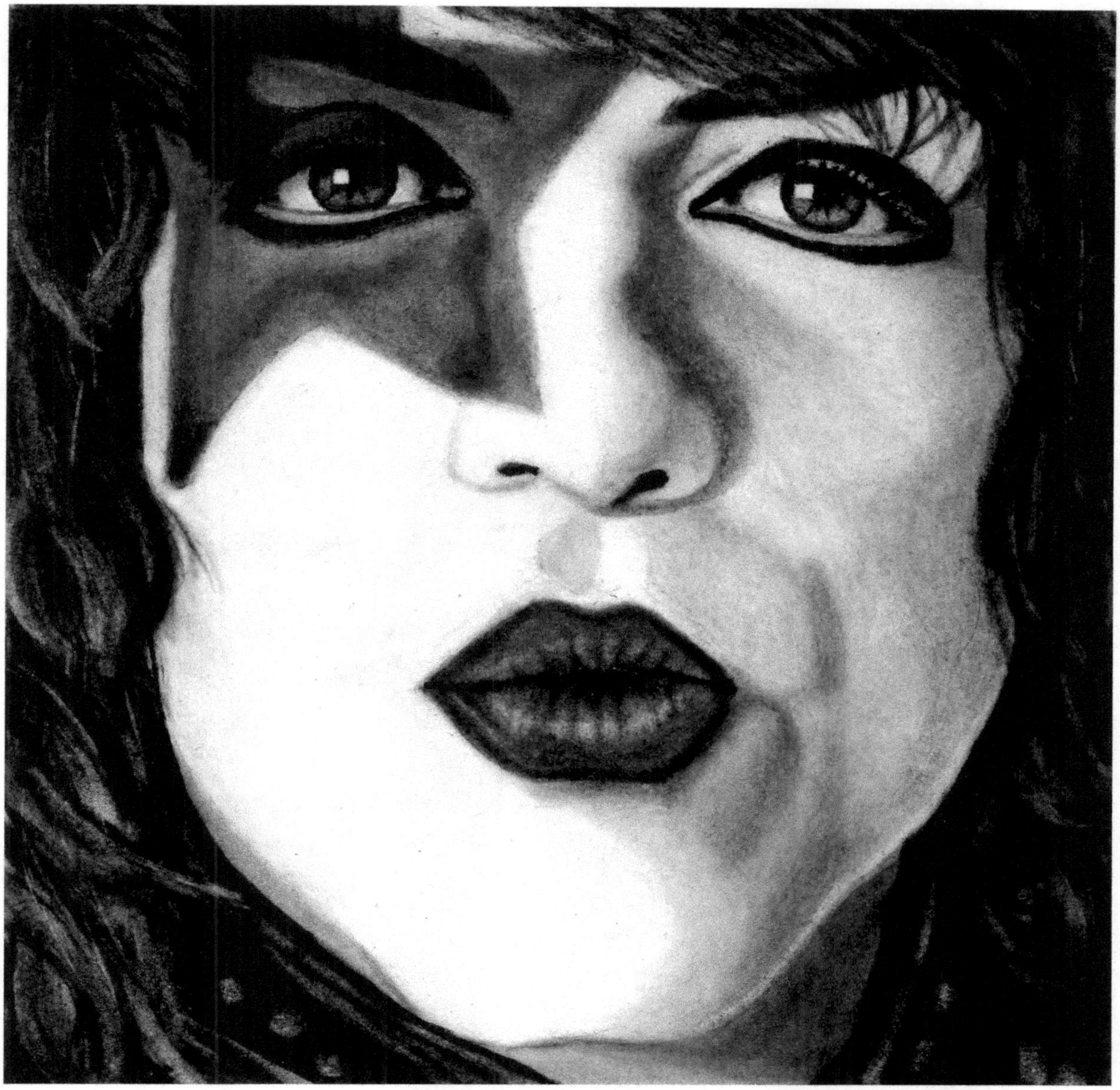

To view how this drawing was masterfully created or to purchase a Limited Edition Framed Artwork of Paul Stanley type into your Internet Browser the URL shortcut ➡ **myportrait.art/paulstanley**

To listen to their Greatest Songs type into your Internet Browser the URL shortcut ➡ **radio.surf/kiss**

To view all channels on THE FACE OF MUSIC Internet Radio MEGA Station type into your Internet Browser the URL shortcut ➡ **radio.surf/music**

To inquire about purchasing a Limited Edition NFT of this portrait type into your Internet Browser the URL shortcut ➡ **myartnft.shop/paulstanley**

To view all available NFTs type into your Internet Browser the URL shortcut ➡ **myartnft.shop/all**

# KISS

(Total Records Sold: 100+ Million) (Genre: Hard Rock)
Kiss is regarded as one of the most influential bands of all time, as well as one of the best-selling bands of all time, having sold more than 100 million records worldwide, including 21 million RIAA-certified albums. Kiss also holds the title as America's No. 1 Gold record award-winning group of all time, having earned 30 Gold albums. Kiss has 14 Platinum albums, with three albums being multi-Platinum. On April 10, 2014, the four original members of Kiss were inducted into the Rock and Roll Hall of Fame. Kiss was ranked by MTV as the ninth "Greatest Metal Band of All Time", and placed tenth on VH1's "100 Greatest Artists of Hard Rock" list, as well as being ranked as the third "Best Metal and Hard Rock Live Band of All Time" by Loudwire magazine.

# Peter Criss

(Net Worth: $3 Million)(Height: 5' - 9")
George Peter John Criscuola (born December 20, 1945), better known by his stage name Peter Criss, is an American retired musician and actor, best known as a co-founder, original drummer, and vocalist of the hard rock band Kiss. Criss established the Catman character for his Kiss persona. Criss possesses a powerful, raspy voice. In 2014, he was inducted into the Rock and Roll Hall of Fame as a member of Kiss.

Criss was born in Brooklyn, New York, the oldest of five children of Loretta and Joseph Criscuola. His father's family came from Scafati, Salerno, Italy. Criss grew up in the Williamsburg section of Brooklyn and was a childhood friend of Jerry Nolan, who would later find success as the drummer of the New York Dolls.

Criss was an avid art student and a swing aficionado. While playing with bandleader Joey Greco, Criss ended up studying under his idol, Gene Krupa, at the Metropole Club in New York.

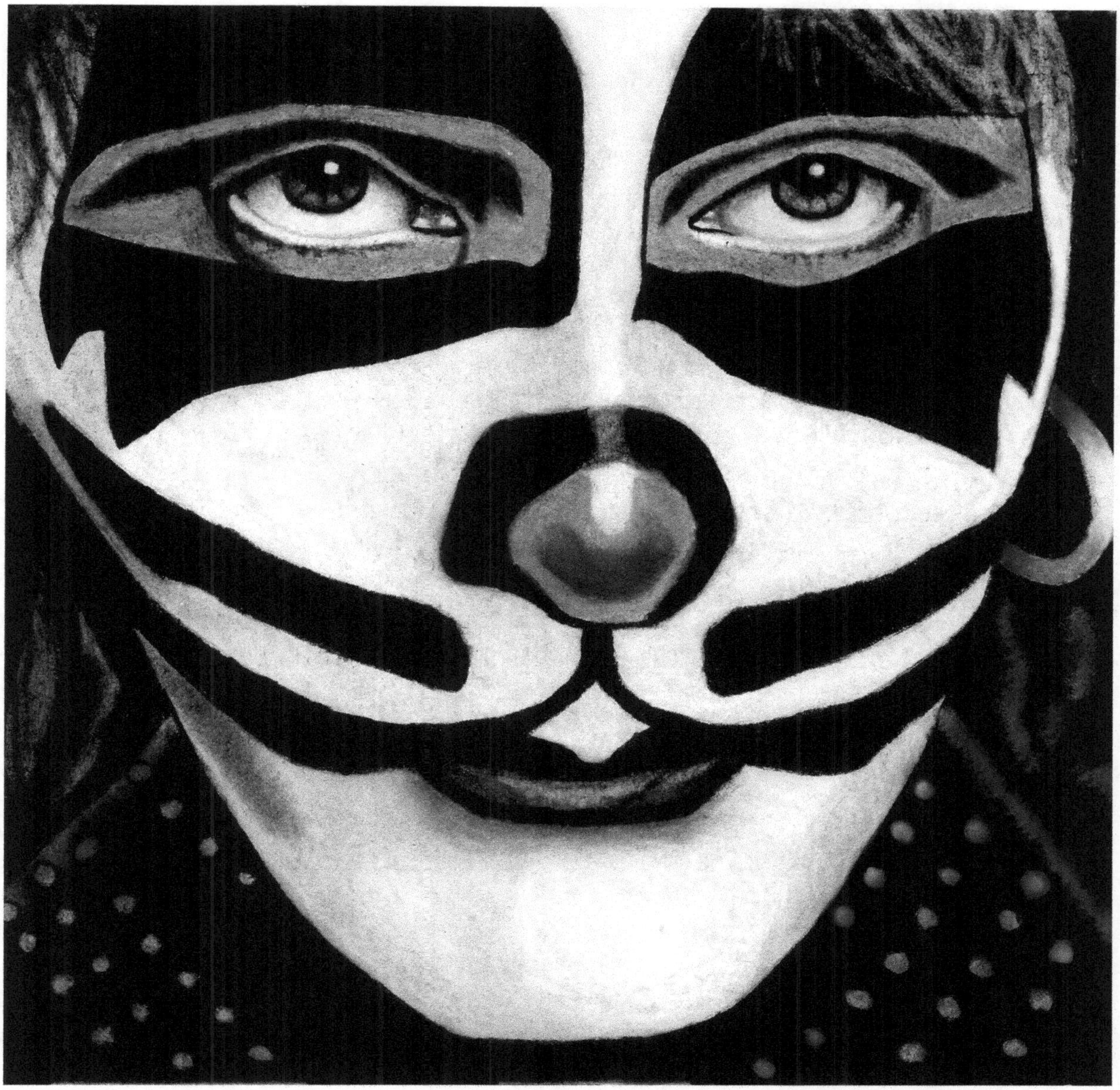

To view how this drawing was masterfully created or to purchase a Limited Edition Framed Artwork of Peter Criss type into your Internet Browser the URL shortcut ➡ **myportrait.art/petercriss**

To listen to their Greatest Songs type into your Internet Browser the URL shortcut ➡ **radio.surf/kiss**

To view all channels on THE FACE OF MUSIC Internet Radio MEGA Station type into your Internet Browser the URL shortcut ➡ **radio.surf/music**

To inquire about purchasing a Limited Edtion NFT of this portrait type into your Internet Browser the URL shortcut ➡ **myartnft.shop/petercriss**

To view all available NFTs type into your Internet Browser the URL shortcut ➡ **myartnft.shop/all**

# Kool & the Gang

(Total Records Sold: 70 Million) (Genre: R&B , Funk , Jazz , Disco , Soul)

Kool & the Gang is an American band formed in Jersey City, New Jersey, in 1964 by brothers Robert "Kool" Bell and Ronald Bell, with Dennis "D.T." Thomas, Robert "Spike" Mickens, Charles Smith, George Brown, and Ricky West. They have undergone numerous changes in personnel and have explored many musical styles throughout their history, including jazz, soul, funk, rock, and pop music. After settling on their name following several changes, the group signed to De-Lite Records and released their debut album, Kool and the Gang (1970).

The band's first taste of success came with the release of their fourth album Wild and Peaceful (1973), which contained the US top-ten singles "Jungle Boogie" and "Hollywood Swinging". Kool & the Gang subsequently entered a period of decline before they reached a second commercial peak between 1979 and 1986 following their partnership with Brazilian musician/producer Eumir Deodato and the addition of singer James "J.T." Taylor to the line-up. Their most successful albums of this period include Ladies' Night (1979), Celebrate! (1980), and Emergency (1984), their highest selling album with two million copies sold in the US. Their hit singles during this period included "Ladies' Night", the US number one "Celebration", "Get Down on It", "Joanna", "Misled", and "Cherish". The band continues to perform worldwide, including as support for Van Halen in 2012 and their fiftieth-anniversary tour in 2014. Kool & the Gang have won numerous awards, including two Grammy Awards, seven American Music Awards, and, in 2006, a Music Business Association Chairman's Award for artistic achievement. As well the band has been inducted into the New Jersey Hall of Fame and been bestowed with a Mobo Award for Outstanding Achievement, the Soul Train Legend Award, the Marian Anderson Award and a star on the Hollywood Walk of Fame. During 2018, the Bells, Brown, and Taylor were also inducted into the Songwriters Hall of Fame. Their discography includes 23 studio albums and almost 70 singles. They have sold 7.5 million and 4.5 million RIAA-certified albums and singles, respectively, in the US. Worldwide, they have sold 70 million albums

# J. T. Taylor

(Net Worth: $6 Million)(Height: 5' - 10")

James "J.T." Taylor (born August 16, 1953, Laurens, South Carolina) is an American singer and actor best known as the former lead singer of the R&B/funk band, Kool & the Gang. Before his rise to fame, Taylor was a teacher and amateur night club singer having first joined a band at the age of 13. He joined Kool & the Gang in 1978 and became the band's lead singer in 1979.

During the 1990s, Taylor began his acting career in earnest appearing in the 1992 Hollywood film The Mambo Kings, and the long-running Broadway musical Raisin.

To view how this drawing was masterfully created or to purchase a Limited Edition Framed Artwork of J. T. Taylor type into your Internet Browser the URL shortcut ➡ **myportrait.art/jttaylor**

To listen to their Greatest Songs type into your Internet Browser the URL shortcut ➡ **radio.surf/koolandthegang**

To view all channels on THE FACE OF MUSIC Internet Radio MEGA Station type into your Internet Browser the URL shortcut ➡ **radio.surf/music**

To inquire about purchasing a Limited Edtion NFT of this portrait type into your Internet Browser the URL shortcut ➡ **myartnft.shop/jttaylor**

To view all available NFTs type into your Internet Browser the URL shortcut ➡ **myartnft.shop/all**

# Korn

(Total Records Sold: 40+ Million) (Genre: Nu Metal)

Korn (stylized as KoЯn) is an American nu metal band from Bakersfield, California, formed in 1993. The band is notable for pioneering the nu metal genre and bringing it into the mainstream. Originally formed in 1993 by three members of the band L.A.P.D., Korn's current lineup features founding members James "Munky" Shaffer (rhythm guitar), Reginald "Fieldy" Arvizu (bass), Brian "Head" Welch (lead guitar, backing vocals), and Jonathan Davis (lead vocals, bagpipes), with the addition of Ray Luzier (drums) in 2007, replacing the band's first drummer, David Silveria. Korn made a demo tape, Neidermayer's Mind, in 1993, which was distributed free to record companies and on request to members of the public. Their debut album, Korn, was released in 1994, followed by Life Is Peachy in 1996. The band first experienced mainstream success with Follow the Leader (1998) and Issues (1999), both of which debuted at number one on the Billboard 200. The band's mainstream success continued with Untouchables (2002), Take a Look in the Mirror (2003) and See You on the Other Side (2005).

A compilation album, Greatest Hits Vol. 1, was released in 2004, spanning a decade of singles and concluding the band's recording contract with Immortal Records and Epic Records. They signed to Virgin Records, releasing See You on the Other Side in 2005, and an untitled album in 2007. Korn's other recent albums, Korn III: Remember Who You Are (2010) and The Path of Totality (2011), were released via Roadrunner Records, The Paradigm Shift (2013) being released via Prospect Park and Caroline Records. The Serenity of Suffering, saw their return to Roadrunner Records. Their latest album, The Nothing, was released on September 13, 2019.

As of 2018, Korn had sold more than 40 million records worldwide. Twelve of the band's official releases have peaked in the top ten of the Billboard 200, eight of which have peaked in the top five. Seven official releases are certified platinum by the Recording Industry Association of America (RIAA), two are certified double platinum, one is certified triple platinum, one is certified five times platinum and two are certified Gold. Korn has released seven video albums and thirty-nine music videos. The band has released forty-one singles, twenty-eight of which have charted. Korn has earned two Grammy Awards out of eight nominations and two MTV Video Music Awards out of eleven nominations.

# Johnathan Davis

(Net Worth: $50 Million)(Height: 6' - 2")

Jonathan Howsmon Davis (born January 18, 1971), also known as JD, JDevil, or J Devil, is an American singer, songwriter, and musician. He is best known as the lead vocalist and frontman of nu metal band Korn, who are considered the pioneering act of the nu metal genre. Davis' distinctive personality and Korn's music influenced a generation of musicians and performers who have come after them.

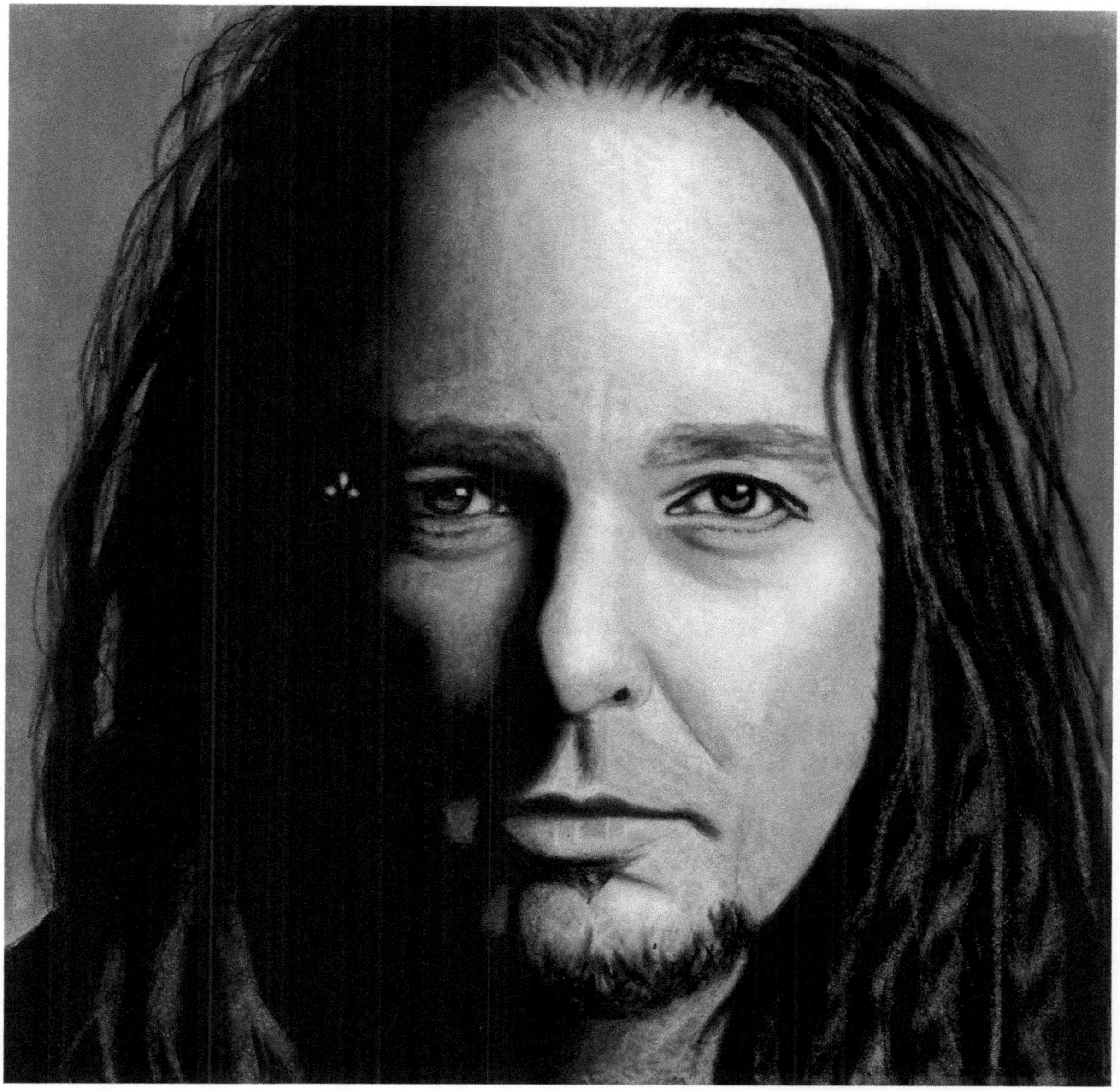

To view how this drawing was masterfully created or to purchase a Limited Edition Framed Artwork of Johnathan Davis type into your Internet Browser the URL shortcut ➡ **myportrait.art/johnathandavis**

To listen to their Greatest Songs type into your Internet Browser the URL shortcut ➡ **radio.surf/korn**

To view all channels on THE FACE OF MUSIC Internet Radio MEGA Station type into your Internet Browser the URL shortcut ➡ **radio.surf/music**

To inquire about purchasing a Limited Edtion NFT of this portrait type into your Internet Browser the URL shortcut ➡ **myartnft.shop/johnathandavis**

To view all available NFTs type into your Internet Browser the URL shortcut ➡ **myartnft.shop/all**

# KRS-One

(Net worth: $6 Million)(Total Albums Sold: Millions)
(Genre: HipHop , Rap)(Height: 6' - 3")

Lawrence "Kris" Parker (born August 20, 1965), better known by his stage names KRS-One , an abbreviation of Knowledge Reigning Supreme Over Nearly Everyone, and Teacha, is an American rapper and occasional producer from Bronx, New York. He rose to prominence as part of the hip hop music group Boogie Down Productions, which he formed with DJ Scott La Rock in the mid-1980s. KRS-One is best known for his top hits, "Sound of da Police", "Love's Gonna Get'cha (Material Love)", and "My Philosophy", among others. Boogie Down Productions received numerous awards and critical acclaim in their early years. Following the release of the group's debut album, Criminal Minded, fellow artist Scott La Rock was shot and killed, but KRS-One continued the group, effectively as a solo project. He began releasing records under his own name in 1993. He is politically active, having started the Stop the Violence Movement after Scott's death. He's also a vegan activist, expressed in songs such as "Beef". He is widely considered an influence to many hip hop artists, including 2Pac and Eminem.

Lawrence Parker was born in the New York City borough of The Bronx in 1965 to an American mother. His father is of to be from the island of Jamaican decent and his step-father was also Jamaican. At age 16, he left home to become an MC, and began living at a homeless shelter in the South Bronx where he was dubbed "Krishna" by the residents due to his curiosity in the Hare Krishna spirituality of some of the anti-poverty workers. During his stay at the community shelter he encountered youth counselor Scott Sterling and there began a DJ/MC relationship. He also engaged in the street art activity graffiti under the alias KRS-One (Knowledge Reigns Supreme Over Nearly Everyone). Together he and Sterling, a.k.a. DJ Scott La Rock, created Boogie Down Productions, releasing their debut album, Criminal Minded, in 1987.

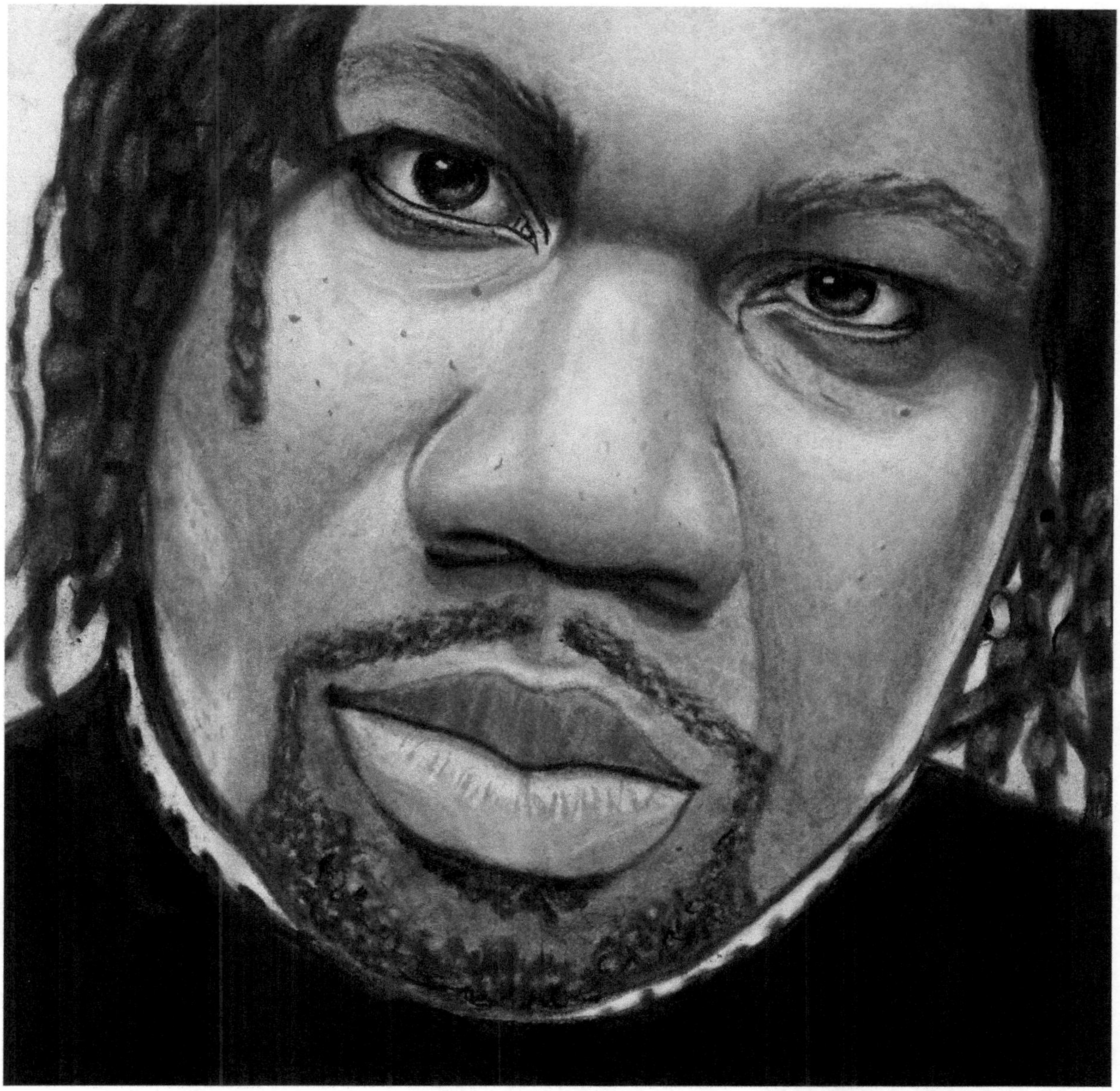

To view how this drawing was masterfully created or to purchase a Limited Edition Framed Artwork of KRS-One type into your Internet Browser the URL shortcut ➡ **myportrait.art/krsone**

To listen to his Greatest Songs type into your Internet Browser the URL shortcut ➡ **radio.surf/krsone**

To view all channels on THE FACE OF MUSIC Internet Radio MEGA Station type into your Internet Browser the URL shortcut ➡ **radio.surf/music**

To inquire about purchasing a Limited Edition NFT of this portrait type into your Internet Browser the URL shortcut ➡ **myartnft.shop/krsone**

To view all available NFTs type into your Internet Browser the URL shortcut ➡ **myartnft.shop/all**

# Led Zeppelin

(Total Records Sold: 200+ Million) (Genre: Hard Rock)

Led Zeppelin were an English rock band formed in London in 1968. The group consisted of vocalist Robert Plant, guitarist Jimmy Page, bassist/keyboardist John Paul Jones, and drummer John Bonham. With a heavy, guitar-driven sound, they are cited as one of the progenitors of hard rock and heavy metal, although their style drew from a variety of influences, including blues and folk music. Led Zeppelin have been credited as significantly impacting the nature of the music industry, particularly in the development of album-oriented rock (AOR) and stadium rock. Many critics consider Led Zeppelin one of the most successful, innovative and influential rock groups in history.

Page wrote most of Led Zeppelin's music, particularly early in their career, while Plant wrote most of the lyrics. Jones's keyboard-based compositions later became central to their music, which featured increasing experimentation. The latter half of their career saw a series of record-breaking tours that earned the group a reputation for excess and debauchery. Although they remained commercially and critically successful, their touring and output, which included Presence (1976) and In Through the Out Door (1979), grew limited, and the group disbanded following Bonham's death in 1980. Since then the surviving former members sporadically collaborated and participated in one-off reunions. The most successful of these was the 2007 Ahmet Ertegun Tribute Concert in London, with Bonham's son Jason Bonham on drums.

Led Zeppelin are one of the best-selling music artists of all time; various sources estimate the group's record sales at 200 to 300 million units worldwide. With RIAA-certified sales of 111.5 million units, they are the third-best-selling band and fifth-best-selling act in the US. They achieved eight consecutive UK number-one albums and six number-one albums on the US Billboard 200, with five of their albums certified Diamond in the US. Rolling Stone magazine described them as "the heaviest band of all time", "the biggest band of the Seventies", and "unquestionably one of the most enduring bands in rock history". They were inducted into the Rock and Roll Hall of Fame in 1995; the museum's biography of the band states that they were "as influential" during the 1970s as the Beatles were during the 1960s.

# Robert Plant

(Net Worth: $200 Million)(Height: 5' - 11")

Robert Anthony Plant (born 20 August 1948) is an English singer, songwriter and musician, best known as the lead singer and lyricist of the English rock band Led Zeppelin.

A powerful and wide vocal range (particularly evident in his high-registered vocals) has given Plant a successful singing career spanning over 50 years. In 2008, Rolling Stone editors ranked him number 15 on their list of the 100 best singers of all time. In 2011, Rolling Stone readers ranked Plant the greatest of all lead singers. In 2006, Hit Parader magazine named Plant the "Greatest Metal Vocalist of All Time". In 2009, Plant was voted "the greatest voice in rock" in a poll conducted by Planet Rock.

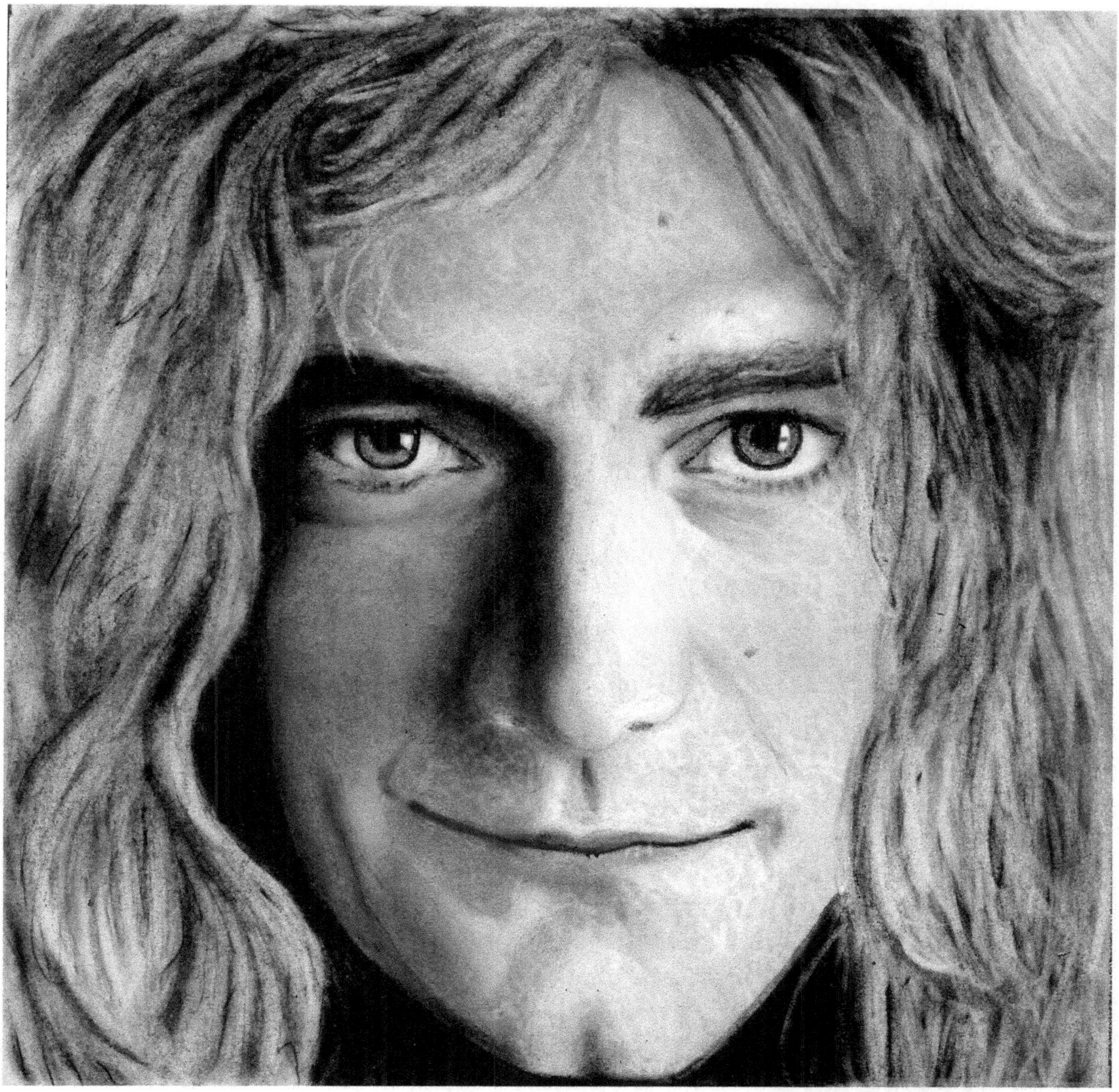

To view how this drawing was masterfully created or to purchase a Limited Edition Framed Artwork of Robert Plant type into your Internet Browser the URL shortcut ➡ **myportrait.art/robertplant**

To listen to their Greatest Songs type into your Internet Browser the URL shortcut ➡ **radio.surf/ledzeppelin**

To view all channels on THE FACE OF MUSIC Internet Radio MEGA Station type into your Internet Browser the URL shortcut ➡ **radio.surf/music**

To inquire about purchasing a Limited Edtion NFT of this portrait type into your Internet Browser the URL shortcut ➡ **myartnft.shop/robertplant**

To view all available NFTs type into your Internet Browser the URL shortcut ➡ **myartnft.shop/all**

# Lenny Kravitz

(Net worth: $80 Million)(Total Albums Sold: 40+ Million)

(Genre: Rock , Progressive Soul)(Height: 5' - 8 1/2")

Leonard Albert Kravitz (born May 26, 1964) is an American singer, songwriter, musician, record producer, and actor. His style incorporates elements of rock, blues, soul, R&B, funk, jazz, reggae, hard rock, psychedelic, pop, folk, and ballads.

Kravitz won the Grammy Award for Best Male Rock Vocal Performance four years in a row from 1999 to 2002, breaking the record for most wins in that category and setting the record for most consecutive wins in one category by a male. He has been nominated for and won other awards, including American Music Awards, MTV Video Music Awards, Radio Music Awards, Brit Awards, and Blockbuster Entertainment Awards. He was also ranked at No. 93 on VH1's "100 Greatest Artists of Hard Rock". He was made an Officer of the Ordre des Arts et des Lettres in 2011, and has played Cinna in the Hunger Games film series. In his career, Kravitz has sold over 40 million albums worldwide.

Leonard Albert Kravitz was born in Manhattan, the only child of actress Roxie Roker (1929–1995) and NBC television news producer Sy Kravitz (fr) (1924–2005). His mother came from a Christian family of African-American and Bahamian descent. His father descended from Ukrainian Jews, with one of his great-grandfathers hailing from Kyiv. Through his mother, Kravitz is a second cousin of television weather presenter Al Roker as their grandfathers were brothers. During his early years, Kravitz did not grow up in a religious environment. After a spiritual experience when he was 13, he started attending church and later became a non-denominational Christian. Kravitz's father was a Green Beret and his uncle, Leonard M. Kravitz, was a Private First Class. Kravitz would be named after Leonard M, who was killed in action in the Korean War at the age of 19 while defending against a Chinese attack, saving most of his platoon in the process. Leonard M. was posthumously awarded the Distinguished Service Cross but was denied the Medal of Honor. In 2014, he received the Medal of Honor in a ceremony that awarded it to 24 servicemen who were passed over because of their ethnicity or religion. Kravitz grew up spending weekdays on the Upper East Side of Manhattan with his parents, attending P.S. 6 for elementary school, and spending weekends at his grandmother Bessie's house in the Bedford-Stuyvesant neighborhood of Brooklyn.

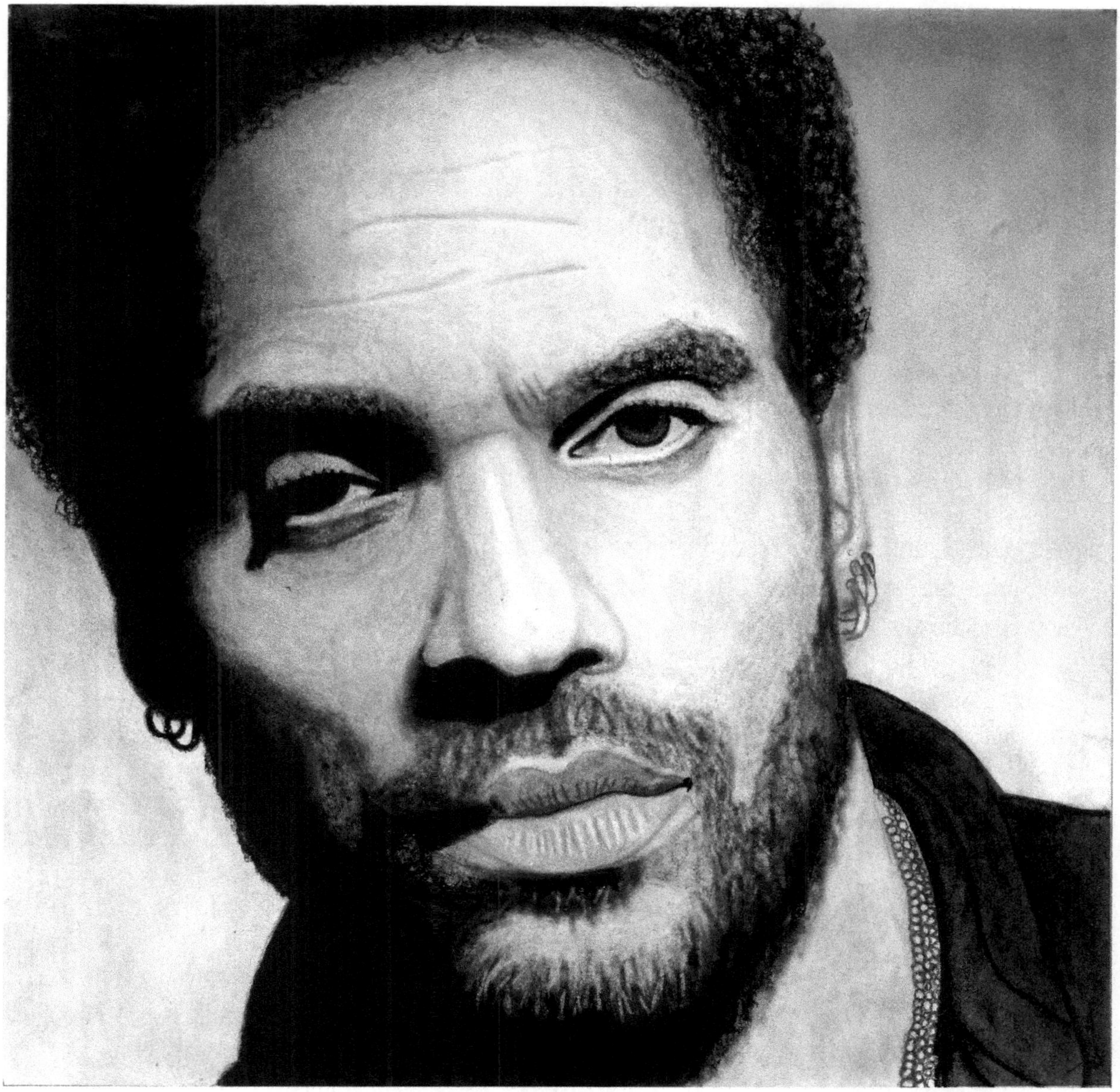

To view how this drawing was masterfully created or to purchase a Limited Edition Framed Artwork of Lenny Kravitz type into your Internet Browser the URL shortcut ➡ **myportrait.art/lennykravitz**

To listen to his Greatest Songs type into your Internet Browser the URL shortcut ➡ **radio.surf/lennykravitz**

To view all channels on THE FACE OF MUSIC Internet Radio MEGA Station type into your Internet Browser the URL shortcut ➡ **radio.surf/music**

To inquire about purchasing a Limited Edition NFT of this portrait type into your Internet Browser the URL shortcut ➡ **myartnft.shop/lennykravitz**

To view all available NFTs type into your Internet Browser the URL shortcut ➡ **myartnft.shop/all**

# Leonard Cohen

(Net worth: $10 Million)(Total Records Sold: Millions)
(Genre: Soft Rock , Folk)(Height: 5' - 9")

Leonard Norman Cohen (September 21, 1934 – November 7, 2016) was a Canadian singer-songwriter, poet, and novelist. His work explored religion, politics, isolation, depression, sexuality, loss, death and romantic relationships. Cohen was inducted into the Canadian Music Hall of Fame, the Canadian Songwriters Hall of Fame, and the Rock and Roll Hall of Fame. He was invested as a Companion of the Order of Canada, the nation's highest civilian honour. In 2011, Cohen received one of the Prince of Asturias Awards for literature and the ninth Glenn Gould Prize.

Cohen pursued a career as a poet and novelist during the 1950s and early 1960s, and did not begin a music career until 1967 at the age of 33. His first album, Songs of Leonard Cohen (1967), was followed by three more albums of folk music: Songs from a Room (1969), Songs of Love and Hate (1971) and New Skin for the Old Ceremony (1974). His 1977 record Death of a Ladies' Man, co-written and produced by Phil Spector, was a move away from Cohen's previous minimalist sound. In 1979, Cohen returned with the more traditional Recent Songs, which blended his acoustic style with jazz, East Asian, and Mediterranean influences. Cohen's most famous song, "Hallelujah", was first released on his studio album Various Positions in 1984. I'm Your Man in 1988 marked Cohen's turn to synthesized productions. In 1992, Cohen released its follow-up, The Future, which had dark lyrics and references to political and social unrest.

Cohen returned to music in 2001 with the release of Ten New Songs, which was a major hit in Canada and Europe. His 11th album, Dear Heather, followed in 2004. Following a successful string of tours between 2008 and 2013, Cohen released three albums in the final four years of his life: Old Ideas (2012), Popular Problems (2014) and You Want It Darker (2016), the last of which was released three weeks before his death. A posthumous album titled Thanks for the Dance was released in November 2019, his fifteenth and final studio album.

Leonard Cohen was born in the Montreal suburb of Westmount, Quebec on September 21, 1934. His Lithuanian-born mother, Marsha ("Masha") Klonitsky (1905–1978), was the daughter of a Talmudic writer, Rabbi Solomon Klonitsky-Kline, and emigrated to Canada in 1927. His paternal grandfather, whose family had moved from Poland to Canada, was Lyon Cohen, the founding president of the Canadian Jewish Congress. His parents gave him the Jewish name Eliezer, which means 'God is help'. His father, Nathan Bernard Cohen (1891–1944), who owned a substantial clothing store, died when Cohen was nine years old. The family observed Orthodox Judaism, and belonged to Congregation Shaar Hashomayim, to which Cohen retained connections for the rest of his life. On the topic of being a kohen, Cohen told Richard Goldstein in 1967, "I had a very Messianic childhood. I was told I was a descendant of Aaron, the high priest."

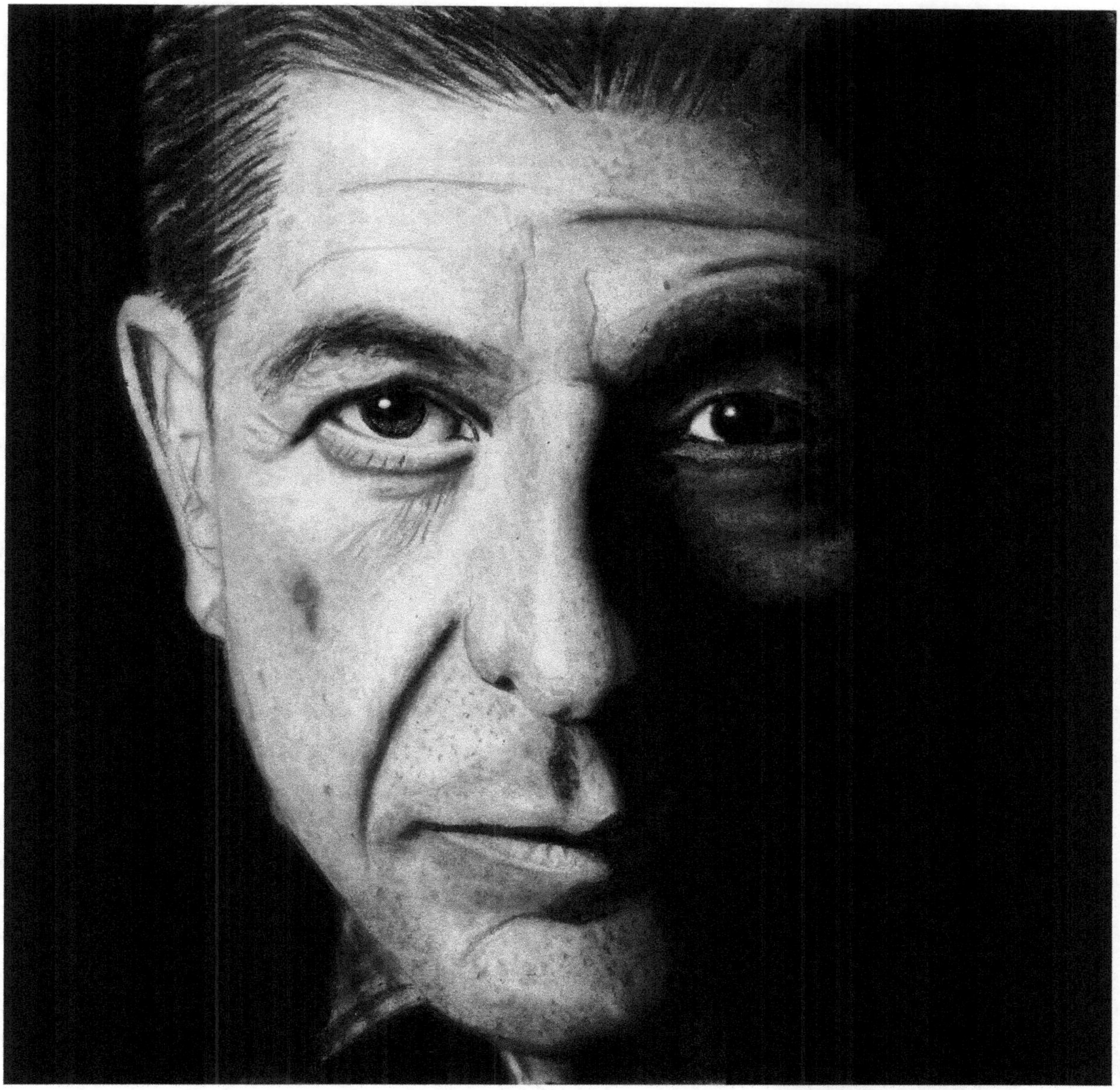

To view how this drawing was masterfully created or to purchase a Limited Edition Framed Artwork of Leonard Cohen type into your Internet Browser the URL shortcut ➡ **myportrait.art/leonardcohen**

To listen to his Greatest Songs type into your Internet Browser the URL shortcut
➡ **radio.surf/leonardcohen**

To view all channels on THE FACE OF MUSIC Internet Radio MEGA Station type into your Internet Browser the URL shortcut ➡ **radio.surf/music**

To inquire about purchasing a Limited Edtion NFT of this portrait type into your Internet Browser the URL shortcut ➡ **myartnft.shop/leonardcohen**

To view all available NFTs type into your Internet Browser the URL shortcut ➡ **myartnft.shop/all**

# Liberace

(Net worth: $115 Million)(Total Records Sold: Millions)
(Genre: Cocktail / Lounge)(Height: 5' - 9 1/2")

Władziu Valentino Liberace (May 16, 1919 – February 4, 1987) was an American pianist, singer and actor. A child prodigy born in Wisconsin to parents of Italian and Polish origin, Liberace enjoyed a career spanning four decades of concerts, recordings, television, motion pictures, and endorsements. At the height of his fame, from the 1950s to the 1970s, Liberace was the highest-paid entertainer in the world, with established concert residencies in Las Vegas, and an international touring schedule. Liberace embraced a lifestyle of flamboyant excess both on and off stage, acquiring the nickname "Mr. Showmanship".

Władziu Valentino Liberace (known as "Lee" to his friends and "Walter" to family) was born in West Allis, Wisconsin, on May 16, 1919. His father, Salvatore ("Sam") Liberace (December 9, 1885 – April 1, 1977), was an immigrant from Formia in the Lazio region of central Italy. His mother, Franciszka Zuchowska (August 31, 1892 – November 1, 1980), was Polish. Liberace had an identical twin who died at birth. He had three surviving siblings: a brother George (who was a violinist), a sister Angelina, and younger brother Rudy (Rudolph Valentino Liberace, named after the actor due to his mother's interest in show business).

Liberace's father played the French horn in bands and movie theaters but often worked as a factory worker or laborer. While Sam encouraged music in his family, his wife, Frances (despite having been a concert pianist before her marriage), believed music lessons and a record player to be unaffordable luxuries. This caused family disputes. Liberace later stated, "My dad's love and respect for music created in him a deep determination to give as his legacy to the world, a family of musicians dedicated to the advancement of the art."

Liberace began playing the piano at age four. While Sam took his children to concerts to further expose them to music, he was also a taskmaster demanding high standards from the children in both practice and performance. Liberace's prodigious talent was evident from his early years. By age seven, he was capable of memorizing difficult pieces. He studied the technique of the Polish pianist Ignacy Paderewski. At age eight, he met Paderewski backstage after a concert at the Pabst Theater in Milwaukee. "I was intoxicated by the joy I got from the great virtuoso's playing. My dreams were filled with fantasies of following his footsteps...Inspired and fired with ambition, I began to practice with a fervor that made my previous interest in the piano look like neglect." Paderewski later became a family friend.

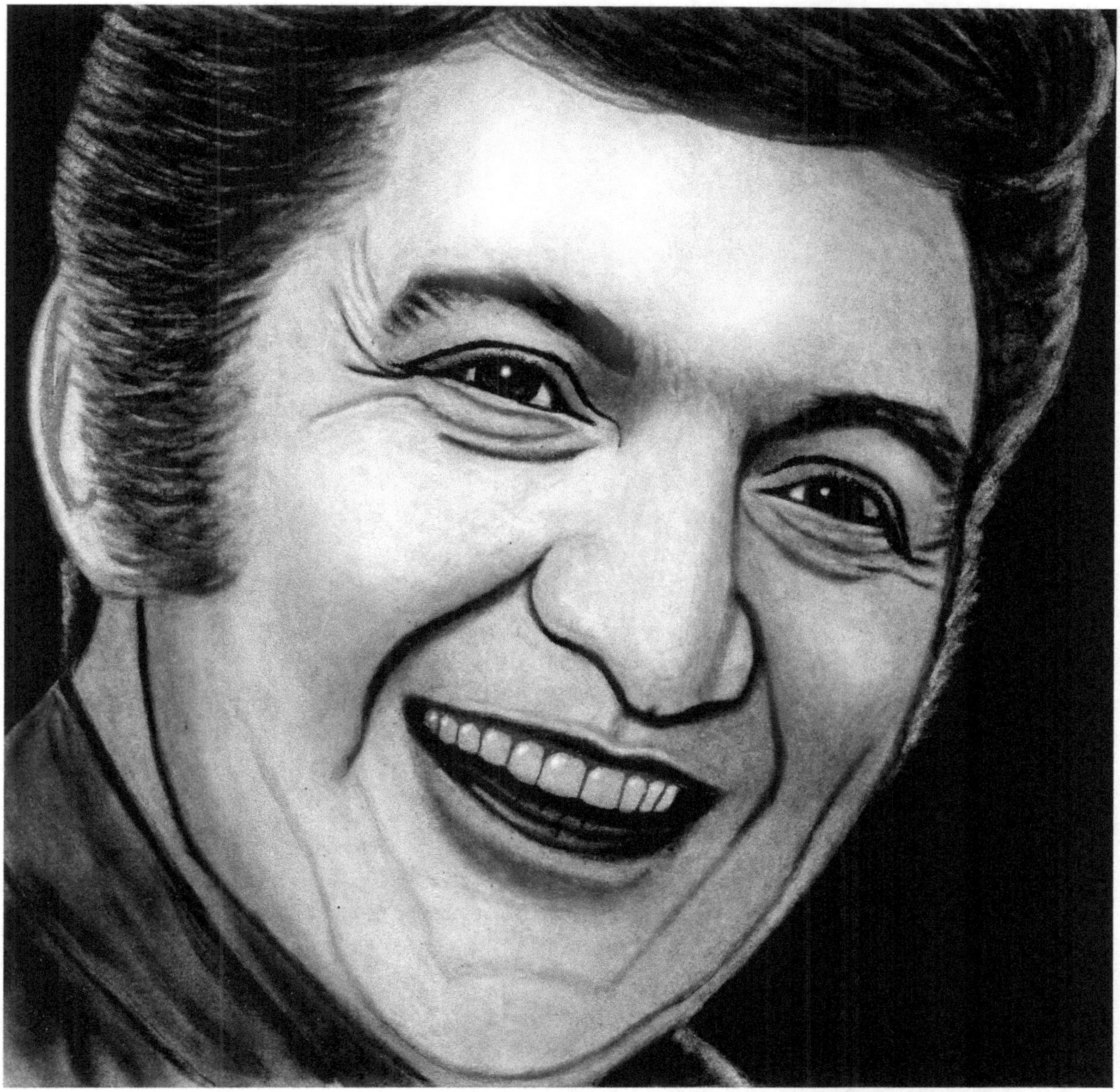

To view how this drawing was masterfully created or to purchase a Limited Edition Framed Artwork of Liberace type into your Internet Browser the URL shortcut ➡ **myportrait.art/liberace**

To listen to his Greatest Music type into your Internet Browser the URL shortcut ➡ **radio.surf/liberace**

To view all channels on THE FACE OF MUSIC Internet Radio MEGA Station type into your Internet Browser the URL shortcut ➡ **radio.surf/music**

To inquire about purchasing a Limited Edition NFT of this portrait type into your Internet Browser the URL shortcut ➡ **myartnft.shop/liberace**

To view all available NFTs type into your Internet Browser the URL shortcut ➡ **myartnft.shop/all**

# Lil Wayne

(Net worth: $150 Million)(Total Records Sold: 120+ Million)
(Genre: Hip-Hop / Rap)(Height: 5' - 5")

Dwayne Michael Carter Jr. (born September 27, 1982), known professionally as Lil Wayne, is an American rapper, singer, songwriter, record executive, entrepreneur, and actor. He is regarded by many contemporaries as one of the most influential hip hop artists of his generation, and often cited as one of the greatest rappers of all time. His career began in 1995, at the age of 12, when he was signed by rapper Birdman, joining Cash Money Records as the youngest member of the label. For many years, Lil Wayne was the flagship artist of Cash Money Records, before ending his association with the company in June 2018.

In 1995, Wayne was put in a duo with label-mate B.G., at that time known as Lil Doogie, and they recorded an album, True Story, released that year, although Wayne (who was at that time known as Baby D) only appeared on three tracks. Wayne soon joined the southern hip hop group Hot Boys, with Cash Money label-mates Juvenile and Turk, as well as Lil Doogie, who had also by this time changed his stage name, to B.G., in 1997; they released their debut album Get It How U Live! in October that year. The Hot Boys became popular following the release of the album Guerrilla Warfare (1999) and the song "Bling Bling".

Lil Wayne's solo debut album Tha Block Is Hot (1999) was his solo breakthrough, and he reached higher popularity with his fourth album Tha Carter (2004) and fifth album Tha Carter II (2005), as well as several mixtapes and collaborations throughout 2006 and 2007. He gained more prominence within the music industry with his sixth album Tha Carter III (2008), with first-week sales of over one million copies in the US. The album won the Grammy Award for Best Rap Album and included successful singles "Lollipop", "A Milli" and "Got Money". Wayne's rock-influenced album titled Rebirth was released in 2010. In March 2010, Lil Wayne began serving an 8-month jail sentence in New York after being convicted of criminal possession of a weapon stemming from an incident in July 2007. His eighth studio album I Am Not a Human Being (2010) was released during his incarceration, while his 2011 album Tha Carter IV was released following his release. Tha Carter IV sold 964,000 copies in its first week in the United States.

His twelfth studio album Tha Carter V was released in 2018 after multiple delays. Wayne's thirteenth album, Funeral, was released in early 2020.

Lil Wayne has sold over 120 million records worldwide, including more than 20 million albums and 70 million digital tracks in the United States, making him one of the world's best-selling music artists. He has won five Grammy Awards, 11 BET Awards, four Billboard Music Awards, two MTV Video Music Awards and eight NAACP Image Awards. On September 27, 2012, he became the first male artist to surpass Elvis Presley with the most entries on the Billboard Hot 100, with 109 songs. Lil Wayne also currently serves as the chief executive officer (CEO) of his own label, Young Money Entertainment.

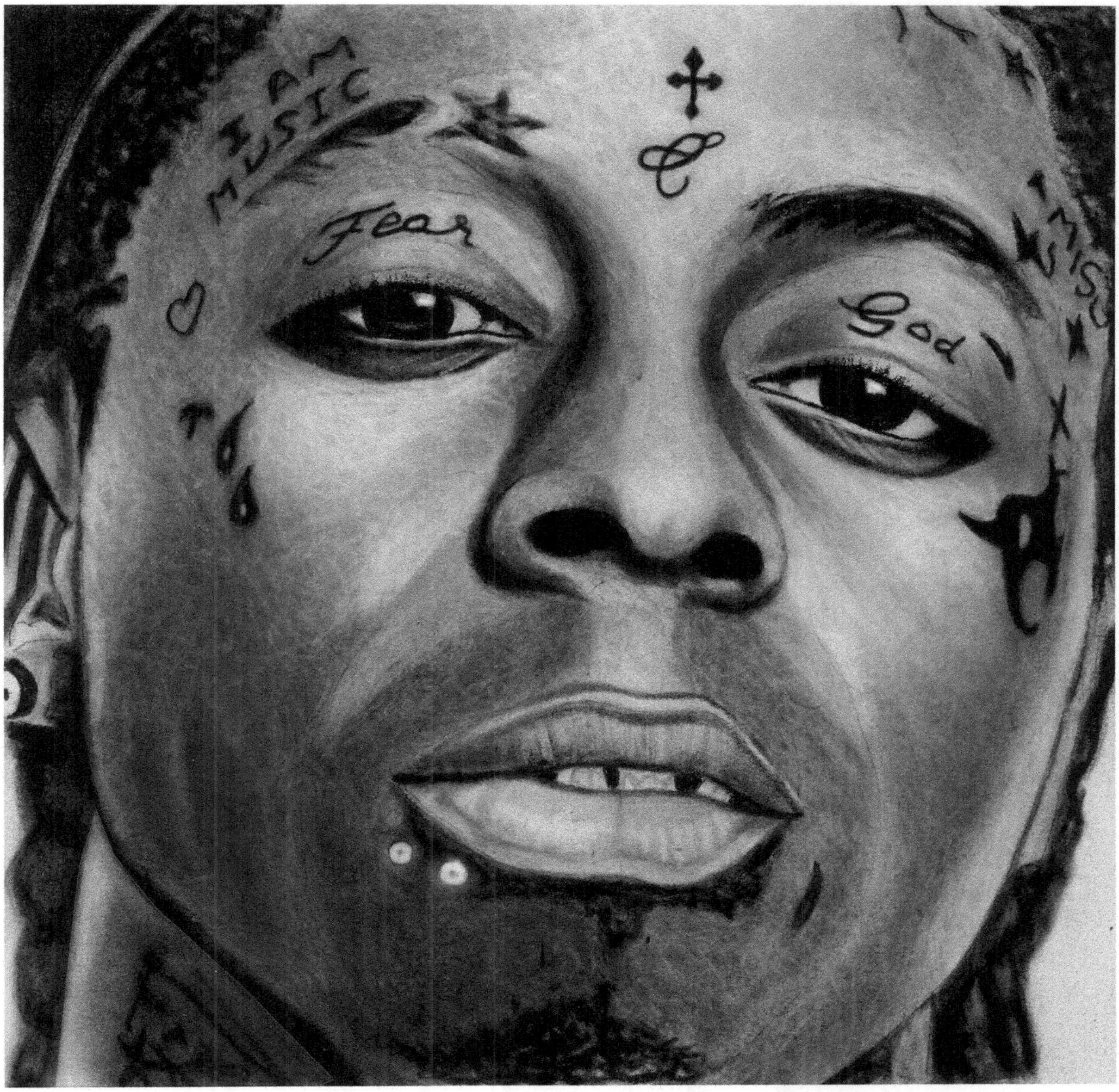


To view how this drawing was masterfully created or to purchase a Limited Edition Framed Artwork of Lil Wayne type into your Internet Browser the URL shortcut ➡ **myportrait.art/lilwayne**

To listen to his Greatest Songs type into your Internet Browser the URL shortcut ➡ **radio.surf/lilwayne**

To view all channels on THE FACE OF MUSIC Internet Radio MEGA Station type into your Internet Browser the URL shortcut ➡ **radio.surf/music**

To inquire about purchasing a Limited Edtion NFT of this portrait type into your Internet Browser the URL shortcut ➡ **myartnft.shop/lilwayne**

To view all available NFTs type into your Internet Browser the URL shortcut ➡ **myartnft.shop/all**

# Limp Bizkit

(Total Records Sold: 40 Million) (Genre: Nu Metal , Rap Rock , Rap Metal)
Limp Bizkit is an American rap rock band from Jacksonville, Florida. Its lineup consists of Fred Durst (lead vocals), Sam Rivers (bass, backing vocals), John Otto (drums, percussion), DJ Lethal (turntables), and Wes Borland (guitars, vocals). The band's music is marked by Durst's angry vocal delivery and Borland's sonic experimentation. Borland's elaborate visual appearance, which includes face and body paint, masks and uniforms, also plays a large role in Limp Bizkit's live shows. The band has been nominated for three Grammy Awards, sold 40 million records worldwide, and won several other awards.Formed in 1994, Limp Bizkit became popular playing in the Jacksonville underground music scene in the late 1990s, and signed with Flip Records, a subsidiary of Interscope, which released the band's debut album, Three Dollar Bill, Y'all (1997). The band achieved mainstream success with its second and third studio albums, Significant Other (1999) and Chocolate Starfish and the Hot Dog Flavored Water (2000), although this success was marred by a series of controversies surrounding its performances at Woodstock '99 and the 2001 Big Day Out festival.

Borland left the group in 2001, but Durst, Rivers, Otto and Lethal continued to record and tour with guitarist Mike Smith. Following the release of its album Results May Vary (2003), Borland rejoined the band and recorded The Unquestionable Truth (Part 1) (2005) with Durst, Rivers, Lethal and drummer Sammy Siegler before entering a hiatus. In 2009, the band reunited with Borland playing guitar and began touring, culminating with the recording of the album Gold Cobra (2011), after which it left Interscope and later signed with Cash Money Records; DJ Lethal quit the band soon afterward, returning in 2018. As of November 2018 the band was still recording its sixth studio album, Stampede of the Disco Elephants.

# Fred Durst

(Net Worth: $20 Million)(Height: 5' - 7 1/2")
William Frederick Durst (born Frederick Allen Mayne III; August 20, 1974) is an American rapper, singer, songwriter, actor, and film director. He is best known as the frontman and lyricist of the nu metal band Limp Bizkit, formed in 1994, with whom he has released six studio albums.

Since 2006, Durst has worked on independent films. He co-starred in Population 436, and made his directorial debut in 2007, with The Education of Charlie Banks. He followed with The Longshots in 2008. His latest film, The Fanatic, came out in 2019.Durst was born Frederick Allen Mayne III in Jacksonville, Florida but soon moved to Orlando and then a farm in Cherryville, North Carolina at one year old. In the fifth grade, he moved to Gastonia, North Carolina where he would later graduate high school. He was raised Wiccan. At the age of 12, Durst took an interest in breakdancing, hip hop, punk rock and heavy metal. He began to rap, skate, beatbox and DJ. Leaving the Navy after just two years (1988–1990), Durst moved back to Jacksonville with his father where he worked as a landscaper and a tattoo artist while developing an idea for a band that combined elements of rock and hip-hop.

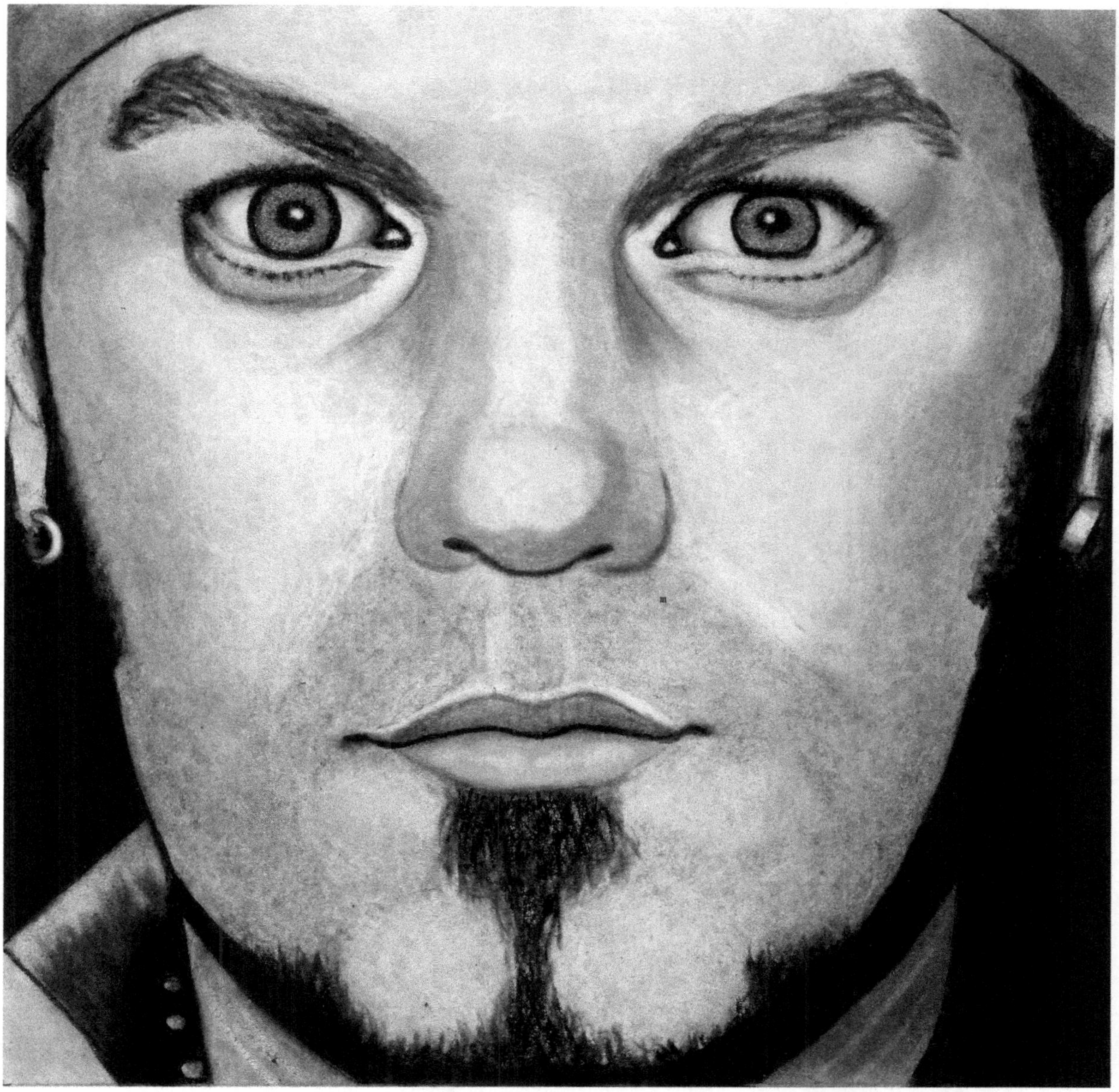

To view how this drawing was masterfully created or to purchase a Limited Edition Framed Artwork of Fred Durst type into your Internet Browser the URL shortcut ➡ **myportrait.art/freddurst**

To listen to their Greatest Songs type into your Internet Browser the URL shortcut ➡ **radio.surf/limpbizkit**

To view all channels on THE FACE OF MUSIC Internet Radio MEGA Station type into your Internet Browser the URL shortcut ➡ **radio.surf/music**

To inquire about purchasing a Limited Edition NFT of this portrait type into your Internet Browser the URL shortcut ➡ **myartnft.shop/freddurst**

To view all available NFTs type into your Internet Browser the URL shortcut ➡ **myartnft.shop/all**

# Linda Ronstadt

(Net worth: $130 Million)(Total Records Sold: 100+ Million)
(Genre: Rock, Country, Light Opera, and Latin)(Height: 5' - 2")

Linda Maria Ronstadt (born July 15, 1946) is a retired American singer who performed and recorded in diverse genres including rock, country, light opera, and Latin. She has earned 10 Grammy Awards, three American Music Awards, two Academy of Country Music awards, an Emmy Award, and an ALMA Award. Many of her albums have been certified gold, platinum or multiplatinum in the United States and internationally. She has also earned nominations for a Tony Award and a Golden Globe award. She was awarded the Latin Grammy Lifetime Achievement Award by the Latin Recording Academy in 2011 and also awarded the Grammy Lifetime Achievement Award by the Recording Academy in 2016. She was inducted into the Rock and Roll Hall of Fame in April 2014. On July 28, 2014, she was awarded the National Medal of Arts and Humanities. In 2019, she received a star jointly with Dolly Parton and Emmylou Harris on the Hollywood Walk of Fame for their work as the group Trio. Ronstadt was among five honorees who received the 2019 Kennedy Center Honors for lifetime artistic achievements.

Ronstadt has released 24 studio albums and 15 compilation or greatest hits albums. She charted 38 US Billboard Hot 100 singles. Twenty-one of those singles reached the top 40, ten reached the top 10, and one reached number one ("You're No Good"). Her success however did not translate across the Atlantic to the UK. Although Ronstadt's duets, "Somewhere Out There" with James Ingram and "Don't Know Much" with Aaron Neville, peaked at numbers 8 and 2 respectively in 1987 and 1989, the single "Blue Bayou" was her only solo single to reach the UK Top 40. She has charted 36 albums, ten top-10 albums, and three number 1 albums on the US Billboard Pop Album Chart.

Ronstadt has collaborated with artists in diverse genres, including Bette Midler, Billy Eckstine, Frank Zappa, Carla Bley (Escalator Over the Hill), Rosemary Clooney, Flaco Jiménez, Philip Glass, Warren Zevon, Emmylou Harris, Gram Parsons, Dolly Parton, Neil Young, Paul Simon, Earl Scruggs, Johnny Cash, and Nelson Riddle. She has lent her voice to over 120 albums and has sold more than 100 million records, making her one of the world's best-selling artists of all time. Christopher Loudon, of Jazz Times, wrote in 2004 that Ronstadt is "blessed with arguably the most sterling set of pipes of her generation."

Ronstadt reduced her activity after 2000 when she felt her singing voice deteriorating, releasing her last full-length album in 2004 and performing her last live concert in 2009. She announced her retirement in 2011 and revealed shortly afterwards that she is no longer able to sing as a result of a degenerative condition later determined to be progressive supranuclear palsy. Since then, Ronstadt has continued to make public appearances, going on a number of public speaking tours in the 2010s. She published an autobiography, Simple Dreams: A Musical Memoir, in September 2013. A documentary based on her memoirs, Linda Ronstadt: The Sound of My Voice, was released in 2019.

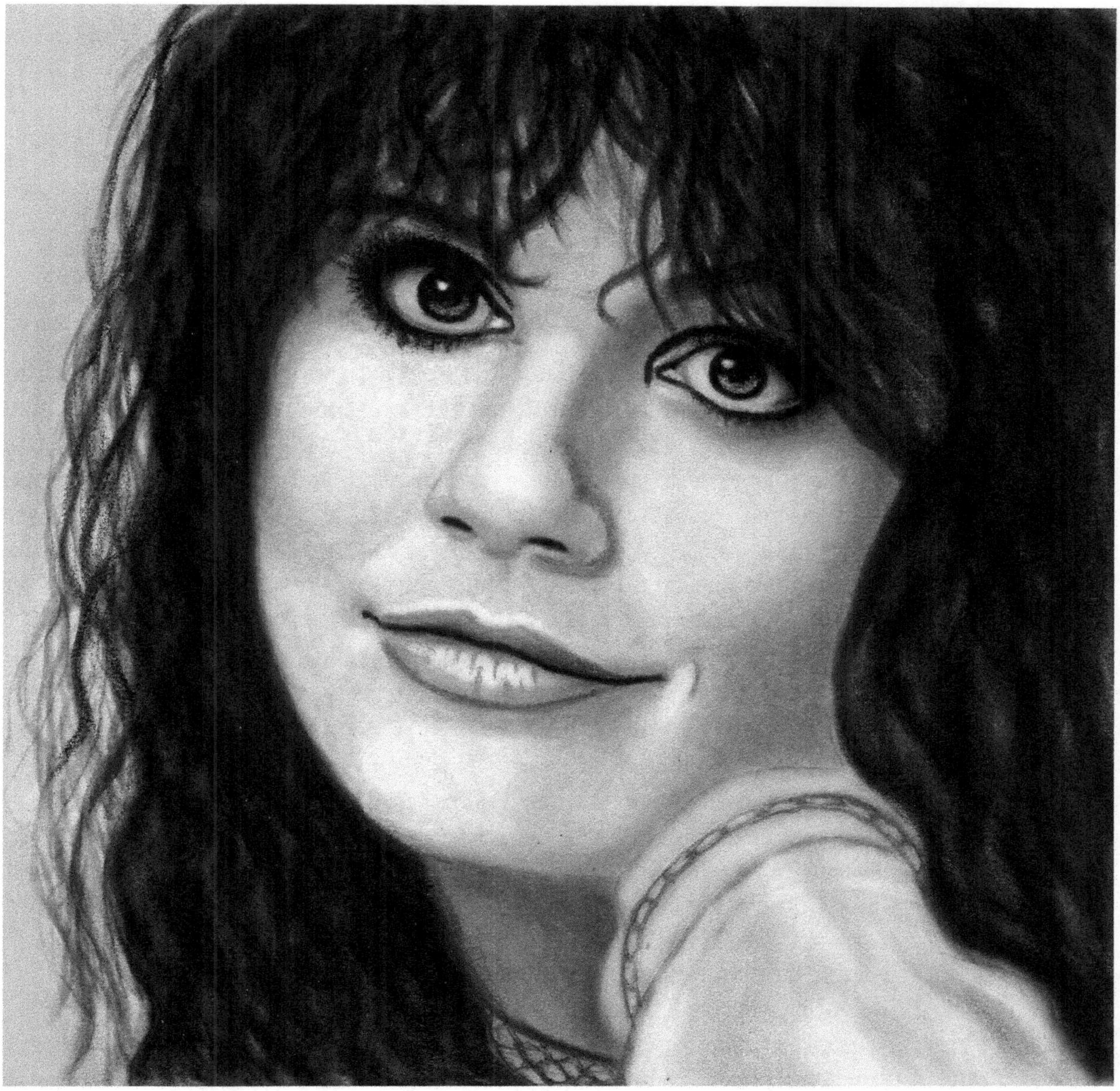

To view how this drawing was masterfully created or to purchase a Limited Edition Framed Artwork of Linda Ronstadt type into your Internet Browser the URL shortcut ➡ **myportrait.art/lindaronstadt**

To listen to her Greatest Songs type into your Internet Browser the URL shortcut ➡ **radio.surf/lindaronstadt**

To view all channels on THE FACE OF MUSIC Internet Radio MEGA Station type into your Internet Browser the URL shortcut ➡ **radio.surf/music**

To inquire about purchasing a Limited Edtion NFT of this portrait type into your Internet Browser the URL shortcut ➡ **myartnft.shop/lindaronstadt**

To view all available NFTs type into your Internet Browser the URL shortcut ➡ **myartnft.shop/all**

# Little Richard

(Net worth: $40 Million)(Total Records Sold: 32+ Million)
(Genre: Rock & Roll , R&B , Gospel , Soul)(Height: 5' - 10")

Richard Wayne Penniman (December 5, 1932 – May 9, 2020), known as Little Richard, was an American musician, singer, and songwriter. He was an influential figure in popular music and culture for seven decades. Nicknamed "The Innovator, The Originator, and The Architect of Rock and Roll," Richard's most celebrated work dates from the mid-1950s, when his charismatic showmanship and dynamic music, characterized by frenetic piano playing, pounding back beat and raspy shouted vocals, laid the foundation for rock and roll. Richard's innovative emotive vocalizations and uptempo rhythmic music also played a key role in the formation of other popular music genres, including soul and funk. He influenced numerous singers and musicians across musical genres from rock to hip hop; his music helped shape rhythm and blues for generations.

"Tutti Frutti" (1955), one of Richard's signature songs, became an instant hit, crossing over to the pop charts in both the United States and overseas in the United Kingdom. His next hit single, "Long Tall Sally" (1956), hit No. 1 on the Billboard Rhythm and Blues Best-Sellers chart, followed by a rapid succession of fifteen more in less than three years. His performances during this period resulted in integration between White Americans and African Americans in his audience. In 1962, during a five-year period in which Richard abandoned rock and roll music for born again Christianity, concert promoter Don Arden persuaded him to tour Europe. During this time, the Beatles opened for Richard on some tour dates. Richard advised the Beatles on how to perform his songs and taught the band's member Paul McCartney his distinctive vocalizations.

Richard is cited as one of the first crossover black artists, reaching audiences of all races. His music and concerts broke the color line, drawing blacks and whites together despite attempts to sustain segregation. Many of his contemporaries, including Elvis Presley, Buddy Holly, Bill Haley, Jerry Lee Lewis, the Everly Brothers, Gene Vincent and Eddie Cochran, recorded covers of his works. Taken by his music and style, and personally covering four of Richard's songs on his own two breakthrough albums in 1956, Presley told Richard in 1969 that his music was an inspiration to him and that he was "the greatest." Richard was honored by many institutions. He was inducted into the Rock and Roll Hall of Fame as part of its first group of inductees in 1986. He was also inducted into the Songwriters Hall of Fame. He was the recipient of a Lifetime Achievement Award from the Recording Academy and a Lifetime Achievement Award from the Rhythm and Blues Foundation. In 2015, Richard received a Rhapsody & Rhythm Award from the National Museum of African American Music for his key role in the formation of popular music genres and helping to bring an end to the racial divide on the music charts and in concert in the mid-1950s changing American culture significantly. "Tutti Frutti" was included in the National Recording Registry of the Library of Congress in 2010, which stated that his "unique vocalizing over the irresistible beat announced a new era in music."

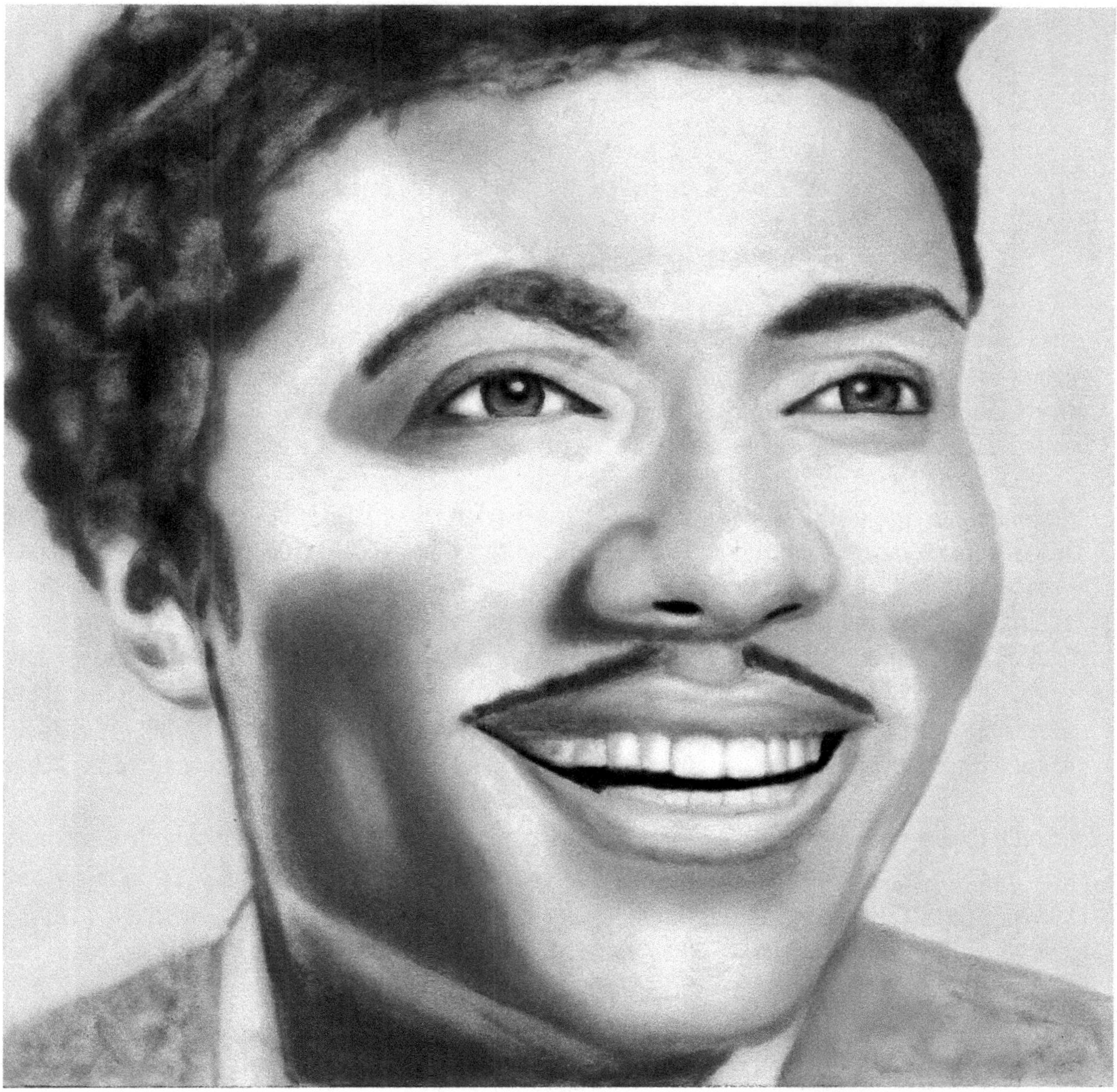

To view how this drawing was masterfully created or to purchase a Limited Edition Framed Artwork of Little Richard type into your Internet Browser the URL shortcut ➡ **myportrait.art/littlerichard**

To listen to his Greatest Songs type into your Internet Browser the URL shortcut ➡ **radio.surf/littlerichard**

To view all channels on THE FACE OF MUSIC Internet Radio MEGA Station type into your Internet Browser the URL shortcut ➡ **radio.surf/music**

To inquire about purchasing a Limited Edtion NFT of this portrait type into your Internet Browser the URL shortcut ➡ **myartnft.shop/littlerichard**

To view all available NFTs type into your Internet Browser the URL shortcut ➡ **myartnft.shop/all**

# Liza Minnelli

(Net worth: $50 Million)(Total Records Sold: Millions)
(Genre: Musical Theatre , Vocal, Disco)(Height: 5' - 3")

Liza May Minnelli (born March 12, 1946) is an American actress, dancer, and singer. She is best known for her performance in Cabaret (1972), the film Arthur (1981), several hit albums and many other film and television appearances. She is famous for her stage presence and her powerful alto singing voice. She is the daughter of actress and singer Judy Garland and director Vincente Minnelli. Liza Minnelli is a Knight of the French Legion of Honour.

Seeking theatrical work, Minnelli moved to New York City in 1961, where she began her career as a musical theatre actress, nightclub performer and traditional pop music artist. She made her professional stage debut in the 1963 Off-Broadway revival of Best Foot Forward and won a Tony Award for starring in Flora the Red Menace in 1965, which marked the start of her lifelong collaboration with John Kander and Fred Ebb. They wrote, produced or directed many of Minnelli's future stage acts and TV shows and helped create her stage persona of a stylized survivor, including her career-defining performances of anthems of survival ("New York, New York", "Cabaret" and "Maybe This Time"). Along with her roles on stage and screen, this persona and her style of performance added to Minnelli's status as an enduring gay icon.

Critically lauded for her early non-musical screen performances—especially in The Sterile Cuckoo (1969) which earned her an Academy Award nomination for Best Actress—Minnelli rose to international stardom, starring in Cabaret and in the Emmy Award–winning TV special Liza with a Z (1972). On 22 June 1969, she lost her mother, Judy Garland, who was 47 at her death. Most of her following films —including Lucky Lady (1975), New York, New York (1977), Rent-a-Cop (1988), and Stepping Out (1991)—were panned by the critics and bombed at the box office, and she had no more major movie hits except Arthur (1981). She returned to Broadway on a number of occasions, including The Act (1977) for which she earned a second Tony Award, The Rink (1984) and Liza's at The Palace.... (2008), worked on various television formats and has predominantly focused on music hall and nightclub performances since the late 1970s. Her concert performances at Carnegie Hall in 1979 and 1987, and at Radio City Music Hall in 1991 and 1992 are recognized among her most successful. From 1988 to 1990, she toured with Frank Sinatra and Sammy Davis Jr. in Frank, Liza & Sammy: The Ultimate Event.

While Minnelli is known for her renditions of American standards, her early-1960s pop singles were produced to attract a young audience. Her albums from 1968 to 1977 contained contemporary singer-songwriter material. In 1989, she ventured into the contemporary pop scene by collaborating with the Pet Shop Boys on the album Results. After a hiatus due to serious health problems, Minnelli returned to the concert stage in 2002 with Liza's Back and was a guest star in the sitcom Arrested Development between 2003 and 2013. Since the 2010s, she has avoided huge concert performances in favor of small retrospective performances.

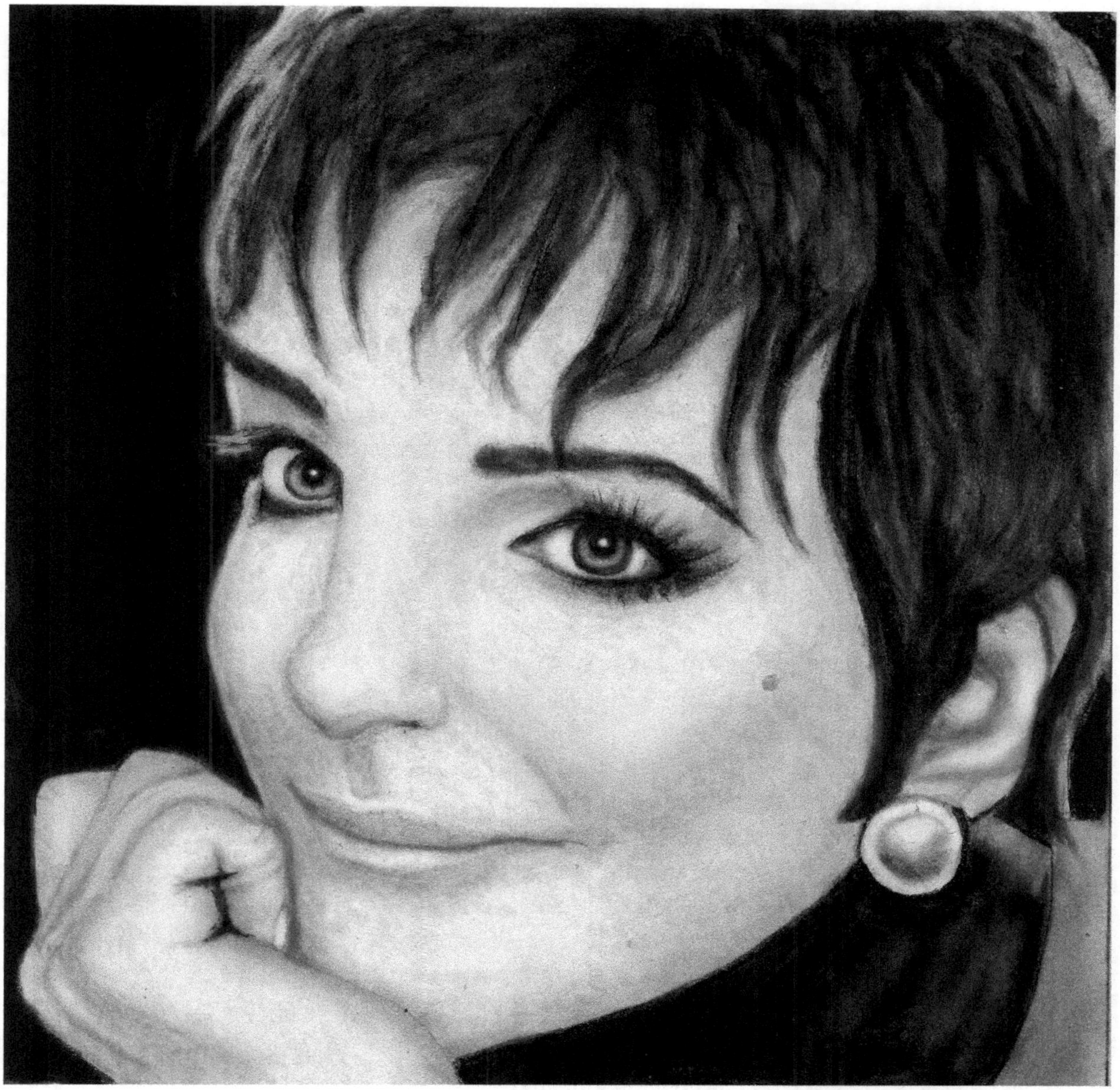

To view how this drawing was masterfully created or to purchase a Limited Edition Framed Artwork of Liza Minnelli type into your Internet Browser the URL shortcut ➡ **myportrait.art/lizaminnelli**

To listen to her Greatest Songs type into ycur Internet Browser the URL shortcut ➡ **radio.surf/lizaminnelli**

To view all channels on THE FACE OF MUSIC Internet Radio MEGA Station type into your Internet Browser the URL shortcut ➡ **radio.surf/music**

To inquire about purchasing a Limited Edtion NFT of this portrait type into your Internet Browser the URL shortcut ➡ **myartnft.shop/lizaminnelli**

To view all available NFTs type into your Internet Browser the URL shortcut ➡ **myartnft.shop/all**

# LL Cool J

(Net worth: $120 Million)(Total Albums Sold: 13.5 Million)
(Genre: Hip-Hop)(Height: 6' - 1 1/4")

James Todd Smith (born January 14, 1968), better known by his stage name LL Cool J (short for Ladies Love Cool James), is an American rapper, record producer, actor, and entrepreneur from Queens, New York. With the breakthrough success of his hit single "I Need a Beat" and the Radio LP, LL Cool J became an early hip-hop act to achieve mainstream success along with Kurtis Blow and Run-DMC.

LL Cool J has released 13 studio albums and two greatest hits compilations. His twelfth album Exit 13 (2008), was his last for his long-tenured deal with Def Jam Recordings. LL Cool J has appeared in numerous films, including In Too Deep, Any Given Sunday, Deep Blue Sea, S.W.A.T., Mindhunters, and Edison. He currently plays NCIS Special Agent Sam Hanna in the CBS crime drama television series NCIS: Los Angeles. LL Cool J also is the host of Lip Sync Battle on Paramount Network. A two-time Grammy Award winner, LL Cool J is known for hip hop hits such as "Going Back to Cali", "I'm Bad", "The Boomin' System", "Rock the Bells", and "Mama Said Knock You Out", as well as R&B hits such as "Doin' It", "I Need Love", "All I Have", "Around the Way Girl" and "Hey Lover". In 2010, VH1 placed him on their "100 Greatest Artists Of All Time" list. In 2017, LL Cool J became the first rapper to receive the Kennedy Center Honors.

LL Cool J's 1987's album "Bigger and Deffer", which was produced by DJ Pooh and the L.A. Posse. This stands as one of his biggest-selling career albums, having sold in excess of two million copies in the United States alone. It spent 11 weeks at No. 1 on Billboard's R&B albums chart. It also reached No. 3 on the Billboard's Pop albums chart. The album featured the singles "I'm Bad", the revolutionary "I Need Love" - LL's first #1 R&B and Top 40 hit, "Bristol Hotel", and "Go Cut Creator Go". While Bigger and Deffer, which was a big success, was produced by the L.A. Posse (at the time consisting of Dwayne Simon, Darryl Pierce and, according to himself the most important for crafting the sound of the LP, Bobby "Bobcat" Ervin), Dwayne Simon was the only one left willing to work on producing LL Cool J's third album Walking with a Panther. Released in 1989, the album was a commercial success, with several charting singles ("Going Back to Cali," "I'm That Type of Guy," "Jingling Baby," "Big Ole Butt," and "One Shot at Love"). Despite commercial appeal, the album was often criticized by the hip-hop community as being too commercial and materialistic, and for focusing too much on love ballads. As a result, his audience base began to decline due to the album's bold commercial and pop aspirations. According to Billboard, the album peaked at No. 6 on the Billboard 200 and was LL Cool J's second #1 R&B Album where it spent four weeks.

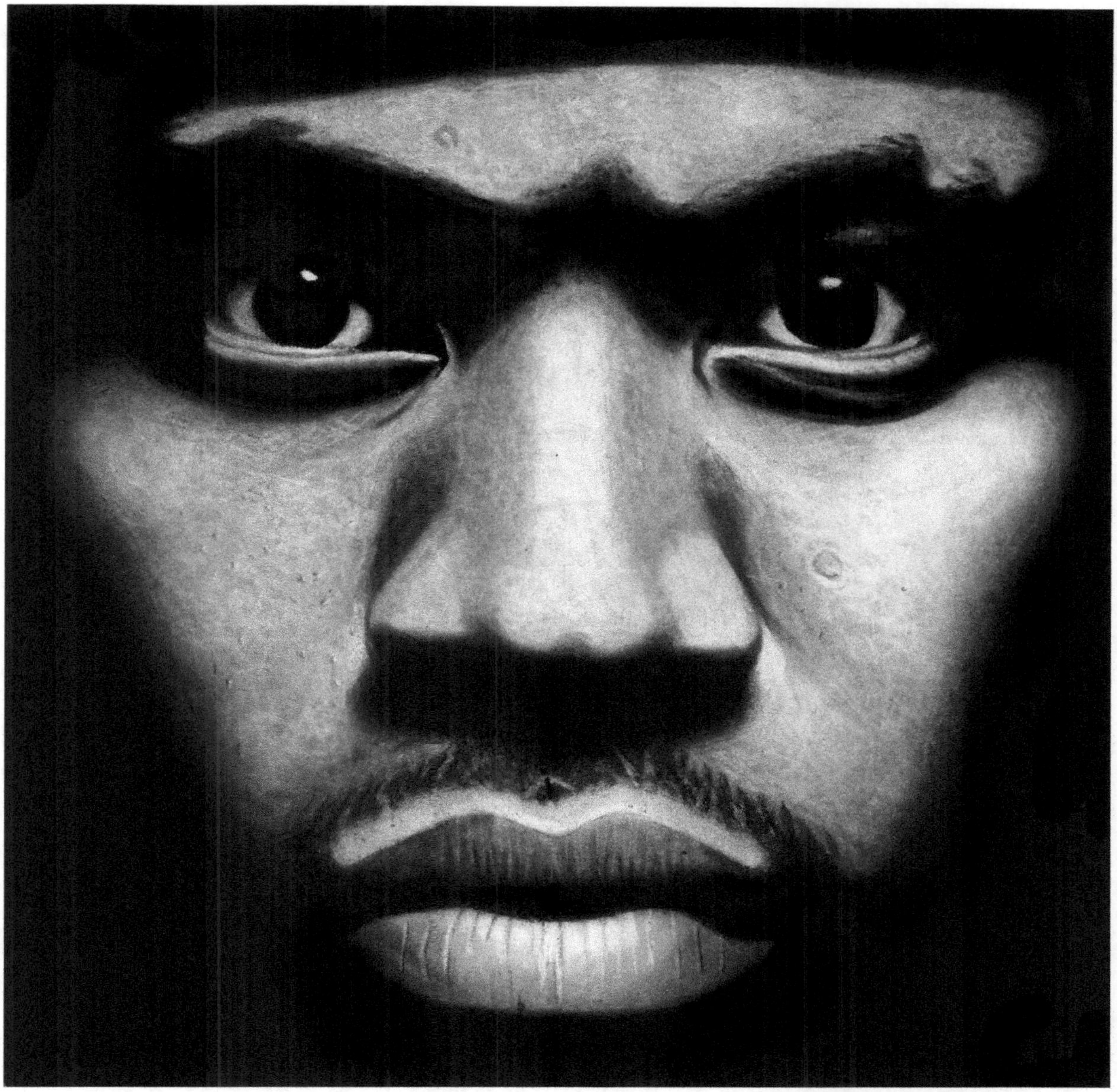

To view how this drawing was masterfully created or to purchase a Limited Edition Framed Artwork of LL Cool J type into your Internet Browser the URL shortcut ➡ **myportrait.art/llcoolj**

To listen to his Greatest Songs type into ycur Internet Browser the URL shortcut ➡ **radio.surf/llcoolj**

To view all channels on THE FACE OF MUSIC Internet Radio MEGA Station type into your Internet Browser the URL shortcut ➡ **radio.surf/music**

To inquire about purchasing a Limited Edtion NFT of this portrait type into your Internet Browser the URL shortcut ➡ **myartnft.shop/llcoolj**

To view all available NFTs type into your Internet Browser the URL shortcut ➡ **myartnft.shop/all**

# Loretta Lynn

(Net worth: $65 Million)(Total Albums Sold: 45+ Million)
(Genre: Country)(Height: 5' - 2")

Loretta Lynn (née Webb: April 14, 1932) is an American singer-songwriter. In a career which spans six decades in country music, Lynn has released multiple gold albums. She is famous for hits such as "You Ain't Woman Enough (To Take My Man)", "Don't Come Home A-Drinkin' (With Lovin' on Your Mind)", "One's on the Way", "Fist City" and "Coal Miner's Daughter" along with the 1980 biographical film of the same name.

Lynn has received numerous awards and other accolades for her groundbreaking role in country music, including awards from both the Country Music Association and Academy of Country Music as a duet partner and an individual artist. She has been nominated 18 times for a GRAMMY Award, and has won 3 times. Lynn is the most awarded female country recording artist and the only female ACM Artist of the Decade (1970s). Lynn has scored 24 No. 1 hit singles and 11 number one albums. She ended nearly 50 years of touring on the road after she suffered a stroke in 2017 and then broke her hip in 2018.

Lynn began singing in local clubs in the late 1950s. She later formed her own band, the Trailblazers, which included her brother Jay Lee Webb. Lynn won a wristwatch in a televised talent contest in Tacoma, Washington, hosted by Buck Owens. Lynn's performance was seen by Canadian Norm Burley of Zero Records, who co-founded the record company after hearing Loretta sing.

Zero Records president, Canadian Don Grashey, arranged a recording session in Hollywood, where four of Lynn's compositions were recorded, including "I'm A Honky Tonk Girl", "Whispering Sea", "Heartache Meet Mister Blues", and "New Rainbow". Her first release featured "Whispering Sea" and "I'm a Honky Tonk Girl". Lynn signed her first contract on February 2, 1960, with Zero. Her album was recorded at United Western Recorders in Hollywood, engineered by Don Blake and produced by Grashey. Musicians who played on the songs were steel guitar player Speedy West, fiddler Harold Hensely, guitarist Roy Lanham, Al Williams on bass, and Muddy Berry on drums. Lynn commented on the different sound of her first record: "Well, there is a West Coast sound that is definitely not the same as the Nashville sound ... It was a shuffle with a West Coast beat".

The Lynns toured the country to promote the release to country stations, while Grashey and Del Roy took the music to KFOX in Long Beach, California. When the Lynns reached Nashville, the song was a hit, climbing to No. 14 on Billboard's Country and Western chart, and Lynn began cutting demo records for the Wilburn Brothers Publishing Company. Through the Wilburns, she secured a contract with Decca Records. The first Loretta Lynn Fan Club formed in November 1960. By the end of the year, Billboard magazine listed Lynn as the No. 4 Most Promising Country Female Artist.

Lynn's relationship with the Wilburn Brothers and her appearances on the Grand Ole Opry, beginning in 1960, helped Lynn become the No. 1 female recording artist in country music. Her contract with the Wilburn Brothers gave them the publishing rights to her material. She unsuccessfully fought the Wilburn Brothers for 30 years to regain the publishing rights to her songs after ending her business relationship with them. Lynn stopped writing music in the 1970s because of the contracts. Lynn joined the Grand Ole Opry on September 25, 1962.

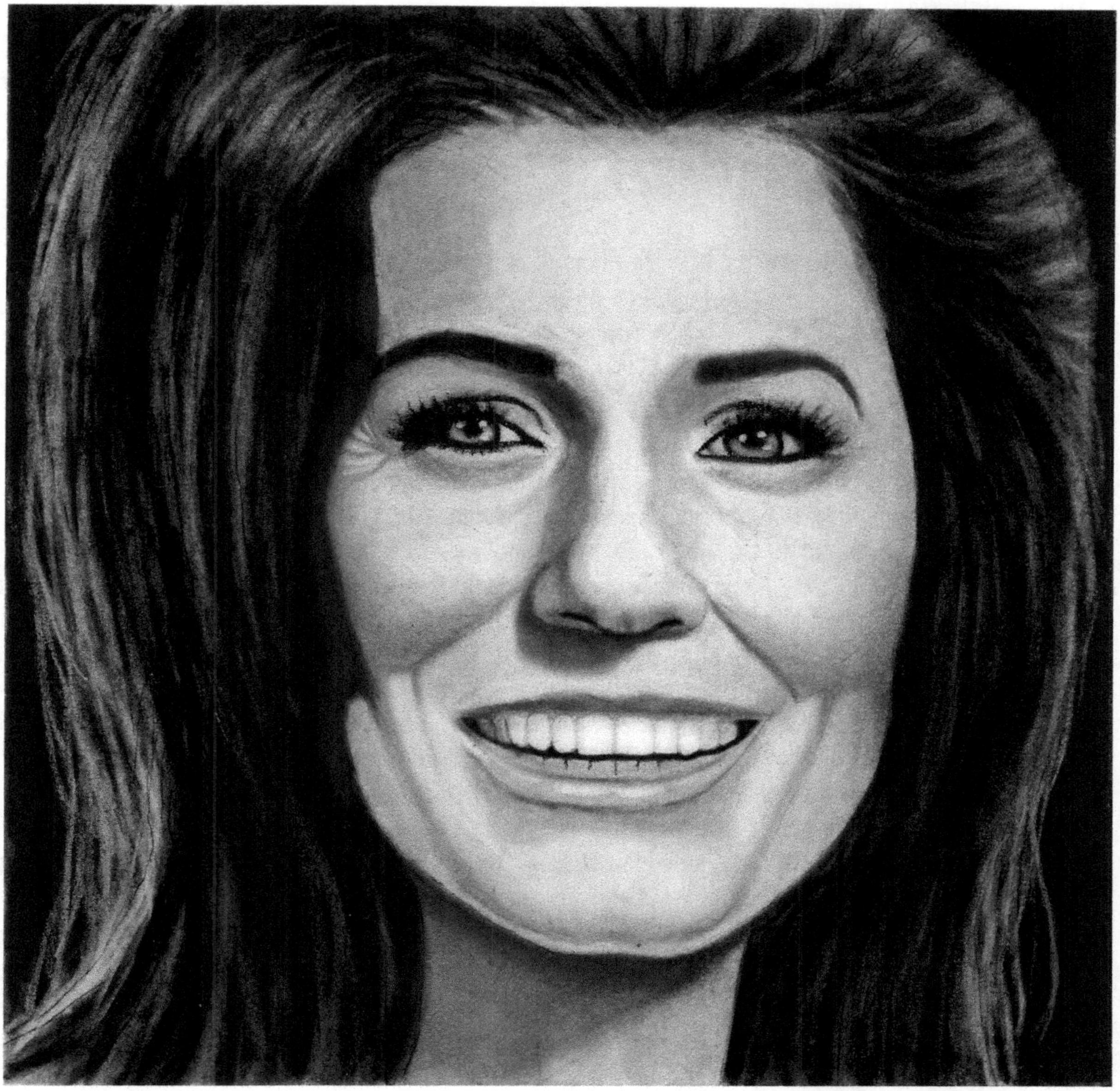

To view how this drawing was masterfully created or to purchase a Limited Edition Framed Artwork of Loretta Lynn type into your Internet Browser the URL shortcut ➡ **myportrait.art/lorettalynn**

To listen to her Greatest Songs type into your Internet Browser the URL shortcut ➡ **radio.surf/lorettalynn**

To view all channels on THE FACE OF MUSIC Internet Radio MEGA Station type into your Internet Browser the URL shortcut ➡ **radio.surf/music**

To inquire about purchasing a Limited Edtion NFT of this portrait type into your Internet Browser the URL shortcut ➡ **myartnft.shop/lorettalynn**

To view all available NFTs type into your Internet Browser the URL shortcut ➡ **myartnft.shop/all**

# Louis Armstrong

(Net worth: $10 Million)(Total Albums Sold: Millions)
(Genre: Jazz , Swing)(Height: 5' - 5 3/4")

Louis Daniel Armstrong (August 4, 1901 – July 6, 1971), nicknamed "Satchmo", "Satch", and "Pops", was an American trumpeter, composer, vocalist, and actor who was among the most influential figures in jazz. His career spanned five decades and different eras in the history of jazz.

Armstrong was born and raised in New Orleans. Coming to prominence in the 1920s as an inventive trumpet and cornet player, Armstrong was a foundational influence in jazz, shifting the focus of the music from collective improvisation to solo performance. Around 1922, he followed his mentor, Joe "King" Oliver, to Chicago to play in the Creole Jazz Band. In Chicago, he spent time with other popular jazz musicians, reconnecting with his friend Bix Beiderbecke and spending time with Hoagy Carmichael and Lil Hardin. He earned a reputation at "cutting contests" and his fame reached band leader Fletcher Henderson. Henderson persuaded Armstrong to come to New York City, where he became a featured and musically influential band soloist and recording artist. Hardin became Armstrong's second wife and they returned to Chicago to play together and then he began to form his own "Hot" jazz bands. After years of touring, he settled in Queens, and by the 1950s, he was a national musical icon, assisted in part, by his appearances on radio and in film and television, in addition to his concerts.

With his instantly recognizable rich, gravelly voice, Armstrong was also an influential singer and skillful improviser, bending the lyrics and melody of a song. He was also skilled at scat singing. Armstrong is renowned for his charismatic stage presence and voice as well as his trumpet playing. By the end of Armstrong's life, his influence had spread to popular music in general. Armstrong was one of the first popular African-American entertainers to "cross over" to wide popularity with white (and international) audiences. He rarely publicly politicized his race, to the dismay of fellow African Americans, but took a well-publicized stand for desegregation in the Little Rock crisis. He was able to access the upper echelons of American society at a time when this was difficult for black men.

Armstrong appeared in films such as High Society (1956) alongside Bing Crosby, Grace Kelly, and Frank Sinatra, and Hello, Dolly! (1969) starring Barbra Streisand. He received many accolades including three Grammy Award nominations and a win for his vocal performance of Hello, Dolly! in 1964. In 2017, he was posthumously inducted into the Rhythm & Blues Hall of Fame.

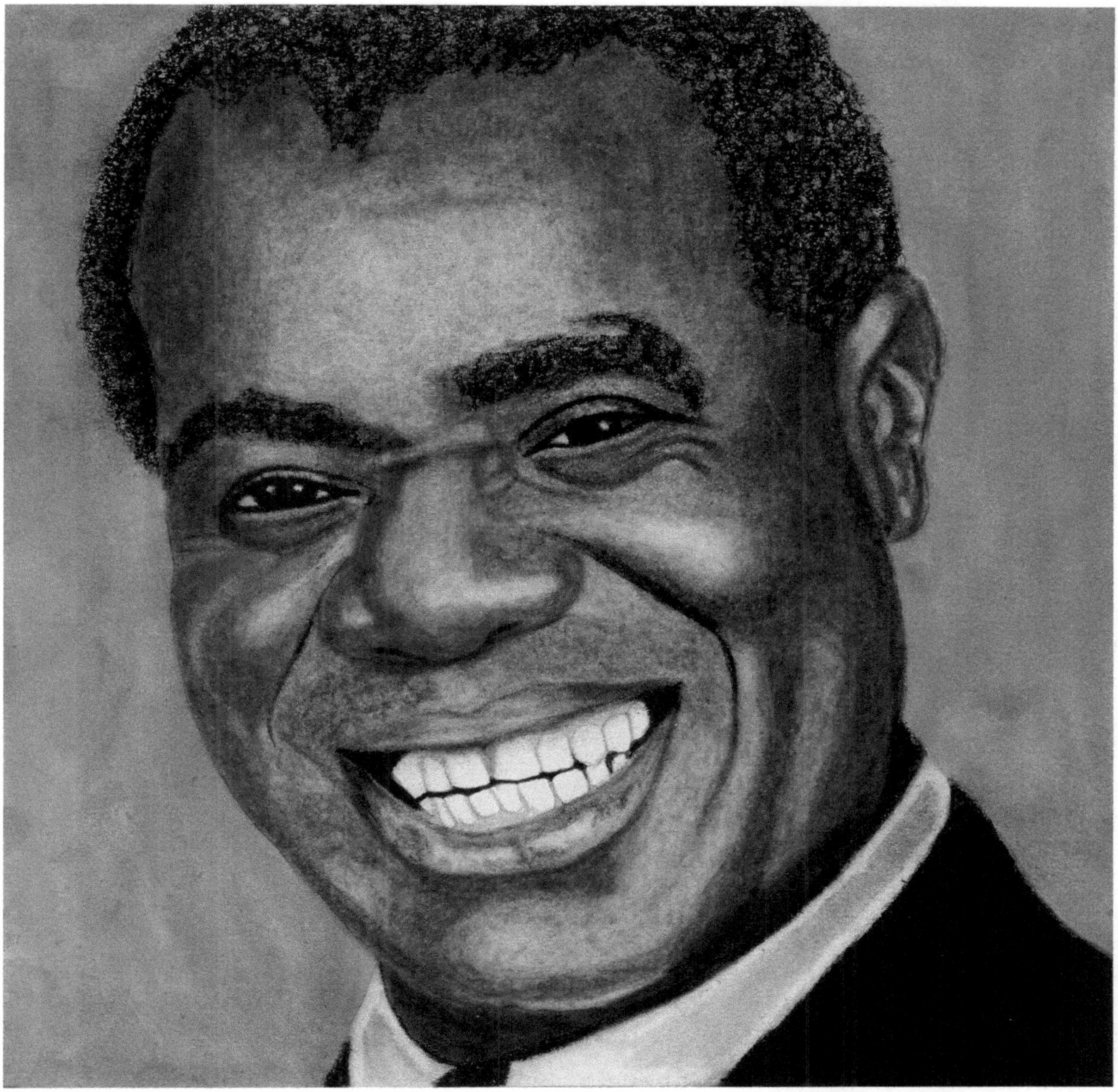

To view how this drawing was masterfully created or to purchase a Limited Edition Framed Artwork of Louis Armstrong type into your Internet Browser the URL shortcut ➡ **myportrait.art/louisarmstrong**

To listen to his Greatest Songs type into your Internet Browser the URL shortcut
➡ **radio.surf/louisarmstrong**

To view all channels on THE FACE OF MUSIC Internet Radio MEGA Station type into your Internet Browser the URL shortcut ➡ **radio.surf/music**

To inquire about purchasing a Limited Edtion NFT of this portrait type into your Internet Browser the URL shortcut ➡ **myartnft.shop/louisarmstrong**

To view all available NFTs type into your Internet Browser the URL shortcut ➡ **myartnft.shop/all**

# Lovin' Spoonful, The

(Total Records Sold: Millions) (Genre: Pop , Folk Rock)

The Lovin' Spoonful is an American rock band which was popular during the mid- to late-1960s. Founded in New York City in 1965 by lead singer/songwriter John Sebastian and guitarist Zal Yanovsky, it is best known for a number of hits which include "Summer in the City", "Do You Believe In Magic", "Did You Ever Have to Make Up Your Mind?", and "Daydream". The band was inducted into the Rock and Roll Hall of Fame in 2000.

The band worked with producer Erik Jacobsen to release their first single on July 20, 1965, "Do You Believe in Magic", written by Sebastian. Additionally, they wrote their own material (aside from a few covers, mostly on their first album), including "Younger Girl" (which missed the Hot 100), which was a hit for The Critters in mid-1966."Do You Believe in Magic" reached #9 on the Hot 100, and the band followed it up with a series of hit singles and albums throughout 1965 and 1966, all produced by Jacobsen. The Lovin' Spoonful became known for such folk-flavored pop hits as "You Didn't Have to Be So Nice", which reached #10, and "Daydream", which went to #2. Other hits included "Did You Ever Have to Make Up Your Mind?" (another #2 hit) and "Summer in the City", their only song to reach #1 on the Hot 100 (August 13–27, 1966). Later that year, the #10 hit "Rain on the Roof" and the #8 hit "Nashville Cats" (which went on to become a staple in the concerts of bluegrass legend Del McCoury) completed the group's first seven consecutive Hot 100 hits to reach that chart's top 10. The only other 1960s act to achieve that feat is Gary Lewis & the Playboys.The Lovin' Spoonful was one of the most successful pop/rock groups to have jug band and folk roots, and nearly half the songs on their first album were modernized versions of blues standards. Their popularity revived interest in the form, and many subsequent jug bands cite them as an inspiration. The rest of their albums featured mostly original songs, but their jug band roots showed up again and again, particularly in "Daydream" and the lesser-known "Money" (which reached only #48, in 1968), featuring a typewriter as percussion.Lovin' Spoonful members termed their approach "good-time music". In the liner notes of "Do You Believe in Magic," Zal Yanovsky said that he "became a convert to Reddy Kilowatt because it's loud, and people dance to it, and it's loud." Soon-to-be members of the psychedelic rock band the Grateful Dead were part of the West Coast acoustic folk music scene when the Lovin' Spoonful came to town on tour. They credited the Lovin' Spoonful concert as a fateful experience, after which they decided to leave the folk scene and "go electric".

# John Sebastian

(Net Worth: $6 Million)

John Benson Sebastian (born March 17, 1944) is an American singer/songwriter, guitarist, harmonicist, and autoharpist. He is best known as a founder of The Lovin' Spoonful, as well as his impromptu appearance at the Woodstock festival in 1969 and a US No. 1 hit in 1976, "Welcome Back".

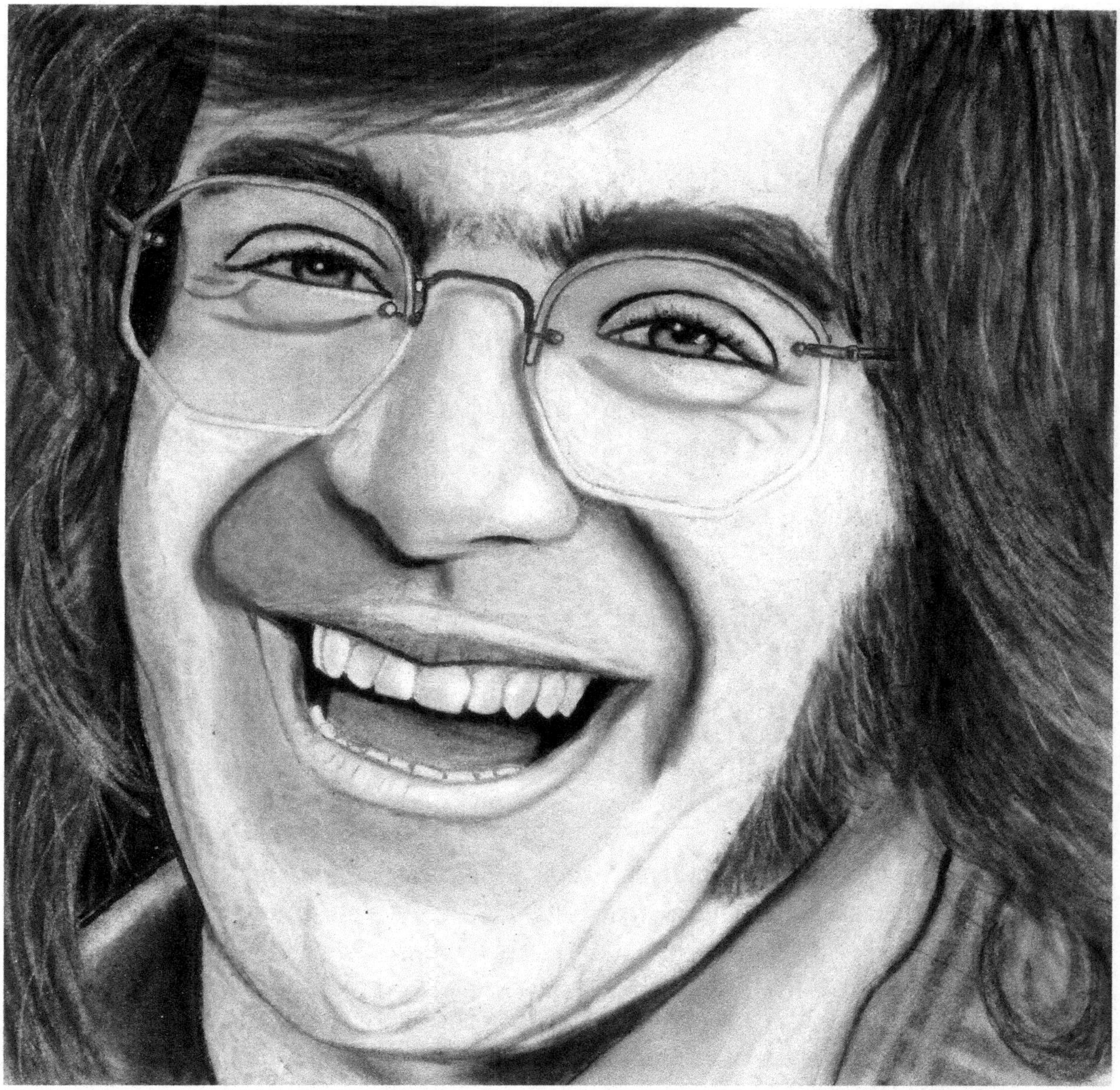

To view how this drawing was masterfully created or to purchase a Limited Edition Framed Artwork of John Sebastian type into your Internet Browser the URL shortcut ➡ **myportrait.art/johnsebastian**

To listen to their Greatest Songs type into your Internet Browser the URL shortcut ➡ **radio.surf/thelovinspooful**

To view all channels on THE FACE OF MUSIC Internet Radio MEGA Station type into your Internet Browser the URL shortcut ➡ **radio.surf/music**

To inquire about purchasing a Limited Edtion NFT of this portrait type into your Internet Browser the URL shortcut ➡ **myartnft.shop/johnsebastian**

To view all available NFTs type into your Internet Browser the URL shortcut ➡ **myartnft.shop/all**

# Ludacris

(Net worth: $25 Million)(Total Records Sold: 24 Million)
(Genre: Hip-Hop)(Height: 5' - 8")

Christopher Brian Bridges (born September 11, 1977), known professionally as Ludacris (is an American rapper and actor. After forming his own label, Disturbing tha Peace in the late 1990s, Ludacris later signed with Def Jam South and would go on to become one of the first Dirty South rappers to achieve mainstream success with his subsequent releases. For his music, Ludacris has won an MTV Video Music Award and three Grammy Awards.

Born in Champaign, Illinois, Ludacris moved to Atlanta at age nine, where he first began rapping. After a brief stint as a DJ, he independently released his first album Incognegro in 1999 to limited success, but achieved national attention the following year with his major label debut, Back for the First Time, which contained the hit singles "Southern Hospitality" and "What's Your Fantasy". In 2001, he released Word of Mouf, followed by Chicken-n-Beer in 2003 and The Red Light District in 2004, all of which were certified multi-platinum by the Recording Industry Association of America (RIAA). He took a more serious approach with his next two albums, Release Therapy (2006), and Theater of the Mind (2008). His next record, Battle of the Sexes, was released in 2010 and featured a return to the more lighthearted tone of his previous albums. His most recent effort, Ludaversal, was released on March 31, 2015.

As an actor, Ludacris is best known for his role as Tej Parker in The Fast and the Furious film series, with his first appearance in the franchise coming in 2002. His other notable roles include Crash (2004), Gamer (2009), and New Year's Eve (2011). For his performances as Parker, Ludacris has won both a Screen Actors Guild Award and a Critic's Choice Award.

Christopher Brian Bridges was born in Champaign, Illinois, the only child of Roberta Shields and Wayne Brian Bridges. He later moved to the Chicago area, where he attended Emerson Middle School in Oak Park. He then moved to Centreville, Virginia and attended Centreville High School for one year. He attended Banneker High School in Atlanta, Georgia and graduated in 1995. From 1998 to 1999, he studied music management at Georgia State University. Bridges is of African American, English, and Native American ancestry. He is a distant cousin of late comedian Richard Pryor. Bridges wrote his first rap song at age nine when moving to Atlanta, and joined an amateur rap group three years later.

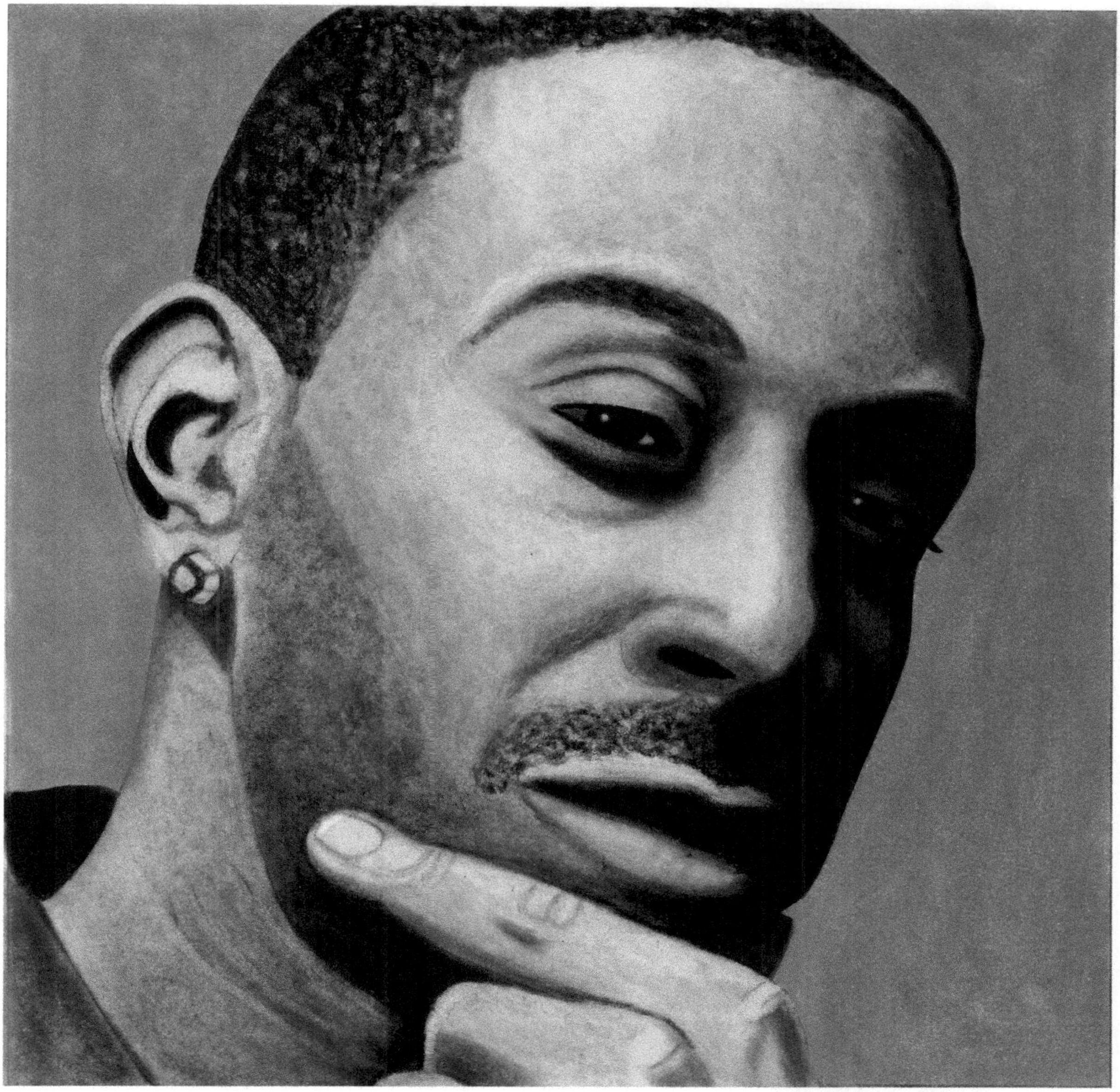

To view how this drawing was masterfully created or to purchase a Limited Edition Framed Artwork of Ludacris type into your Internet Browser the URL shortcut ➡ **myportrait.art/ludacris**

To listen to their Greatest Songs type into your Internet Browser the URL shortcut ➡ **radio.surf/ludacris**

To view all channels on THE FACE OF MUSIC Internet Radio MEGA Station type into your Internet Browser the URL shortcut ➡ **radio.surf/music**

To inquire about purchasing a Limited Edtion NFT of this portrait type into your Internet Browser the URL shortcut ➡ **myartnft.shop/ludacris**

To view all available NFTs type into your Internet Browser the URL shortcut ➡ **myartnft.shop/all**

# Lynyrd Skynyrd

(Total Albums Sold: 28 Million) (Genre: Classic Rock)

Lynyrd Skynyrd ( LEH-ərd SKIN-ərd) is an American rock band formed in Jacksonville, Florida. The group originally formed as My Backyard in 1964 and comprised Ronnie Van Zant (lead vocalist), Gary Rossington (guitar), Allen Collins (guitar), Larry Junstrom (bass guitar) and Bob Burns (drums). The band spent five years touring small venues under various names and with several lineup changes before deciding on "Lynyrd Skynyrd" in 1969. The band released their first album in 1973, having settled on a lineup that included bassist Leon Wilkeson, keyboardist Billy Powell and guitarist Ed King. Burns left and was replaced by Artimus Pyle in 1974. King left in 1975 and was replaced by Steve Gaines in 1976. At the height of their fame in the 1970s, the band popularized the Southern rock genre with songs such as "Sweet Home Alabama" and "Free Bird". After releasing five studio albums and one live album, the band's career was abruptly halted by tragedy on October 20, 1977,

when their chartered airplane crashed, killing Van Zant, Gaines, and backup singer Cassie Gaines, and seriously injuring the rest of the band.

Lynyrd Skynyrd reformed in 1987 for a reunion tour with Ronnie's brother Johnny Van Zant as lead vocalist. They continue to tour and record with co-founder Rossington (the band's sole continuous member), Johnny Van Zant, and Rickey Medlocke, who first wrote and recorded with the band from 1971 to 1972 before his return in 1996. In January 2018, Lynyrd Skynyrd announced its farewell tour, and continue touring as of October 2019. Members are also working on their fifteenth album. In 2004, Rolling Stone magazine ranked Lynyrd Skynyrd No. 95 on their list of the "100 Greatest Artists of All Time". Lynyrd Skynyrd was inducted into the Rock and Roll Hall of Fame on March 13, 2006. To date, the band has sold more than 28 million records in the United States.

# Ronnie Van Zant

(Net Worth: $2 Million)(Height: 5' - 7")

Ronald Wayne Van Zant (January 15, 1948 – October 20, 1977) was an American musician known as the lead vocalist, primary lyricist, and founding member of the Southern rock band Lynyrd Skynyrd. He was the older brother of two other rock vocalists: current Lynyrd Skynyrd lead vocalist Johnny Van Zant and Donnie Van Zant, the founder and vocalist of 38 Special. He was the father of Tammy Van Zant and Melody Van Zant.

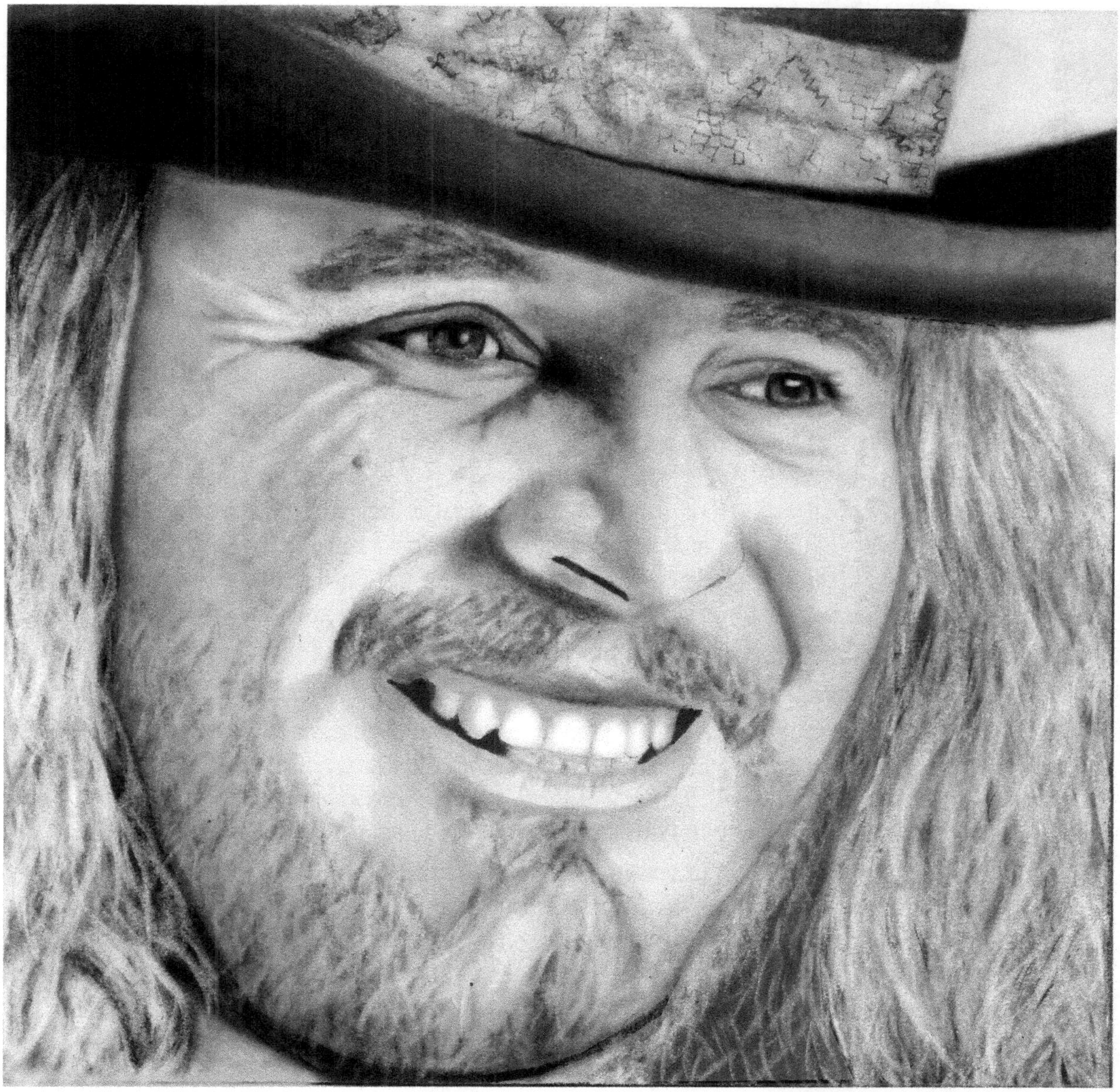

To view how this drawing was masterfully created or to purchase a Limited Edition Framed Artwork of Ronnie Van Zant type into your Internet Browser the URL shortcut ➡ **myportrait.art/ronnievanzant**

To listen to their Greatest Songs type into your Internet Browser the URL shortcut
➡ **radio.surf/lynyrdskynyrd**

To view all channels on THE FACE OF MUSIC Internet Radio MEGA Station type into your Internet Browser the URL shortcut ➡ **radio.surf/music**

To inquire about purchasing a Limited Edtion NFT of this portrait type into your Internet Browser the URL shortcut ➡ **myartnft.shop/ronnievanzant**

To view all available NFTs type into your Internet Browser the URL shortcut ➡ **myartnft.shop/all**

# Madonna

(Net worth: $800 Million)(Total Records Sold: 300+Million)
(Genre: Pop , Dance)(Height: 5' - 5")

Madonna Louise Ciccone (born August 16, 1958) is an American singer, songwriter, and actress. Referred to as the "Queen of Pop", she is regarded as one of the most significant figures in popular culture. Madonna is noted for her continual reinvention and versatility in music production, songwriting, and visual presentation. She is also known for pushing the boundaries of artistic expression in mainstream music while remaining completely in charge of every aspect of her career. Her works, which incorporate social, political, sexual, and religious themes, have generated both critical acclaim and controversy. Madonna is often cited as an influence by other artists.

Born and raised in Michigan, Madonna moved to New York City in 1978 to pursue a career in modern dance. After performing as a drummer, guitarist, and vocalist in the rock bands Breakfast Club and Emmy, she rose to solo stardom with her debut studio album, Madonna (1983). She followed it with a series of successful albums, including all-time bestsellers Like a Virgin (1984) and True Blue (1986) as well as Grammy Award winners Ray of Light (1998) and Confessions on a Dance Floor (2005). Madonna has amassed many number-one singles throughout her career, including "Like a Virgin", "La Isla Bonita", "Like a Prayer", "Vogue", "Take a Bow", "Frozen", "Music", "Hung Up", and "4 Minutes".Madonna's popularity was enhanced by roles in films such as Desperately Seeking Susan (1985), Dick Tracy (1990), A League of Their Own (1992), and Evita (1996). While Evita won her a Golden Globe Award for Best Actress, many of her other films received poor reviews. As a businesswoman, Madonna founded the company Maverick in 1992; it included Maverick Records, one of the most successful artist-run labels in history. Her other ventures include fashion brands, children's books, health clubs, and filmmaking. She contributes to various charities, having founded the Ray of Light Foundation in 1998 and Raising Malawi in 2006.With sales of over 300 million records worldwide, Madonna is certified as the best-selling female recording artist of all time by Guinness World Records. She is the most successful solo artist in the history of the U.S. Billboard Hot 100 chart and holds the record for the most number-one singles by a female artist in Australia, Canada, Italy, Spain, and the United Kingdom. With a revenue of U.S. $1.5 billion from her concert tickets, she remains the highest-grossing solo touring artist of all time. Madonna was inducted into the Rock and Roll Hall of Fame in 2008, her first year of eligibility. She was ranked as the greatest woman in music by VH1 in 2012, and as the greatest music video artist of all time by Billboard in 2020. Rolling Stone also listed Madonna among the 100 Greatest Artists of All Time and the 100 Greatest Songwriters of All Time.Madonna Louise Ciccone was born on August 16, 1958, in Bay City, Michigan, to Catholic parents Madonna Louise (née Fortin) and Silvio Anthony "Tony" Ciccone. Her father's parents were Italian emigrants from Pacentro while her mother was of French-Canadian descent. Tony Ciccone worked as an engineer designer for Chrysler and General Motors. Since Madonna had the same name as her mother, family members called her "Little Nonnie". She later adopted Veronica as a confirmation name when she was confirmed in the Catholic Church in 1966. Madonna was raised in the Detroit suburbs of Pontiac and Avon Township (now Rochester Hills), alongide her two older brothers, Anthony and Martin, and three younger siblings, Paula, Christopher, and Melanie.

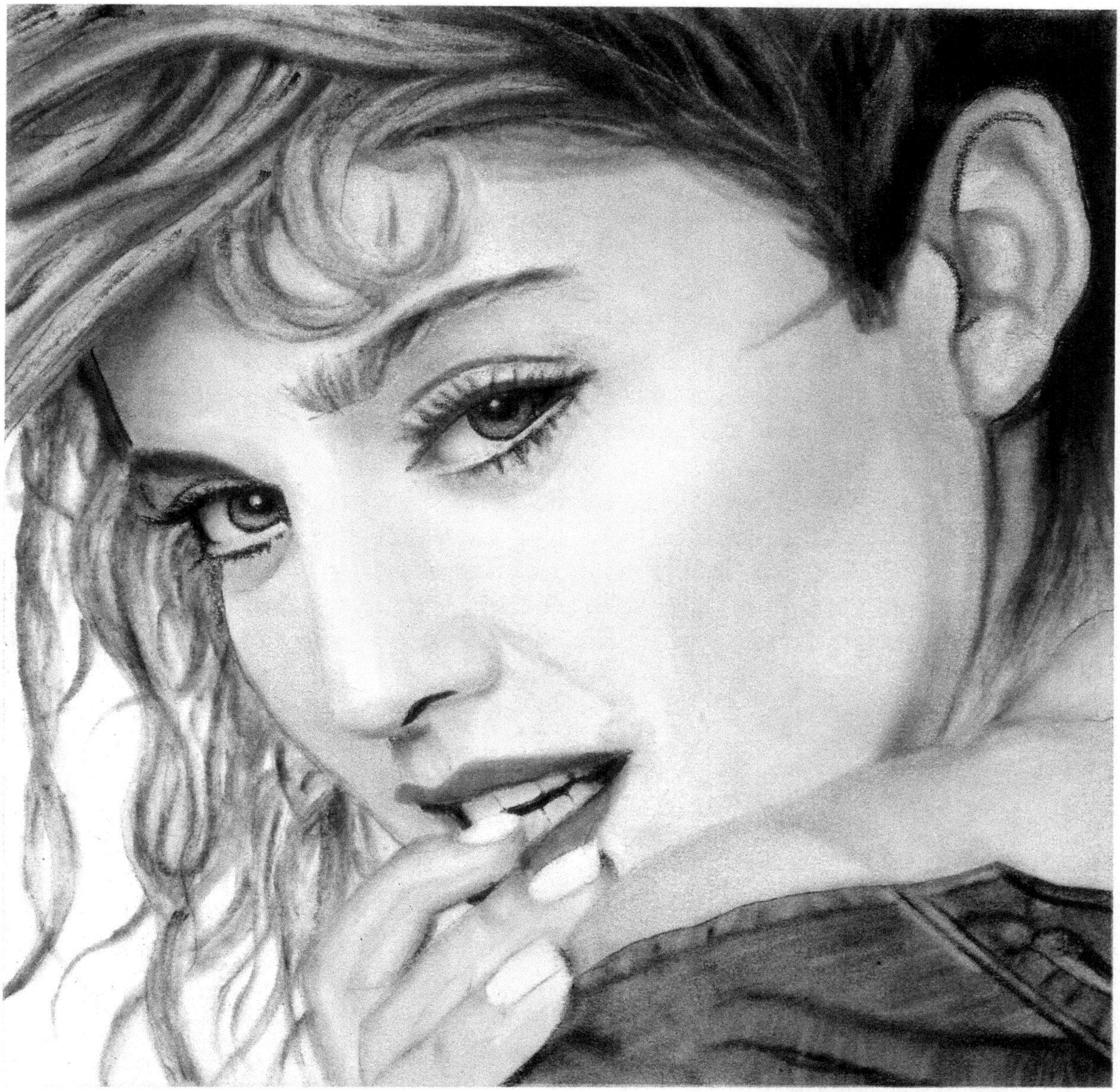

To view how this drawing was masterfully created or to purchase a Limited Edition Framed Artwork of Madonna type into your Internet Browser the URL shortcut ➡ **myportrait.art/madonna**

To listen to her Greatest Songs type into your Internet Browser the URL shortcut ➡ **radio.surf/madonna**

To view all channels on THE FACE OF MUSIC Internet Radio MEGA Station type into your Internet Browser the URL shortcut ➡ **radio.surf/music**

To inquire about purchasing a Limited Edtion NFT of this portrait type into your Internet Browser the URL shortcut ➡ **myartnft.shop/madonna**

To view all available NFTs type into your Internet Browser the URL shortcut ➡ **myartnft.shop/all**

# Mamas & the Papas, The

(Total Records Sold: 40 Million) (Genre: Folk Rock , Psychedelic Pop , Sunshine Pop)
The Mamas & the Papas were an American folk rock vocal group formed in Los Angeles, California which recorded and performed from 1965 to 1968. The group was a defining force in the music scene of the counterculture of the 1960s. The group was composed of John Phillips, Denny Doherty, Cass Elliot, and Michelle Phillips. Their sound was based on vocal harmonies arranged by John Phillips, the songwriter, musician, and leader of the group, who adapted folk to the new beat style of the early 1960s.
The Mamas & the Papas released five studio albums and 17 singles over four years, six of which made the Billboard top 10, and have sold close to 40 million records worldwide. The band was inducted into the Rock and Roll Hall of Fame in 1998 for its contributions to the music industry. The band reunited briefly to record the album People Like Us in 1971 but had ceased touring and performing by that time. Some of their most popular singles include "California Dreamin'", "Monday, Monday", and "Creeque Alley".

# Michelle Phillips

(Net Worth: $10 Million)(Height: 5' - 7")
Michelle Phillips (born Holly Michelle Gilliam; June 4, 1944) is an American singer, songwriter, actress, and former model. She rose to fame as a vocalist in the musical quartet the Mamas and the Papas in the mid-1960s. Her voice was described by Time magazine as the "purest soprano in pop music." She later established a successful career as an actress in film and television in the 1970s. Phillips is the last surviving original member of the Mamas and the Papas.
A native of Long Beach, California, she spent her early life in Los Angeles and Mexico City, raised by her widowed father. While working as a model in San Francisco, she met and married John Phillips in 1962 and went on to co-found the vocal group the Mamas and the Papas in 1965. The band rose to fame with their popular singles "California Dreamin'" and "Creeque Alley", both of which she co-wrote. They released five studio albums before their dissolution in 1970. With John Phillips, she gave birth to a daughter, singer Chynna Phillips.
After the breakup of the Mamas and the Papas and her divorce from John Phillips, she transitioned into acting, appearing in a supporting part in The Last Movie (1971) before being cast as Billie Frechette in the critically acclaimed crime biopic Dillinger (1973), for which she was nominated for a Golden Globe Award for Most Promising Newcomer. In 1974, she had lead roles in two television films: the crime feature The Death Squad, and the teen drama The California Kid, in the latter of which she starred opposite Martin Sheen. She went on to appear in a number of films throughout the remainder of the 1970s, including Ken Russell's Valentino (1977), playing Natacha Rambova, and the thriller Bloodline (1979). She released her only solo album, Victim of Romance, in 1977.

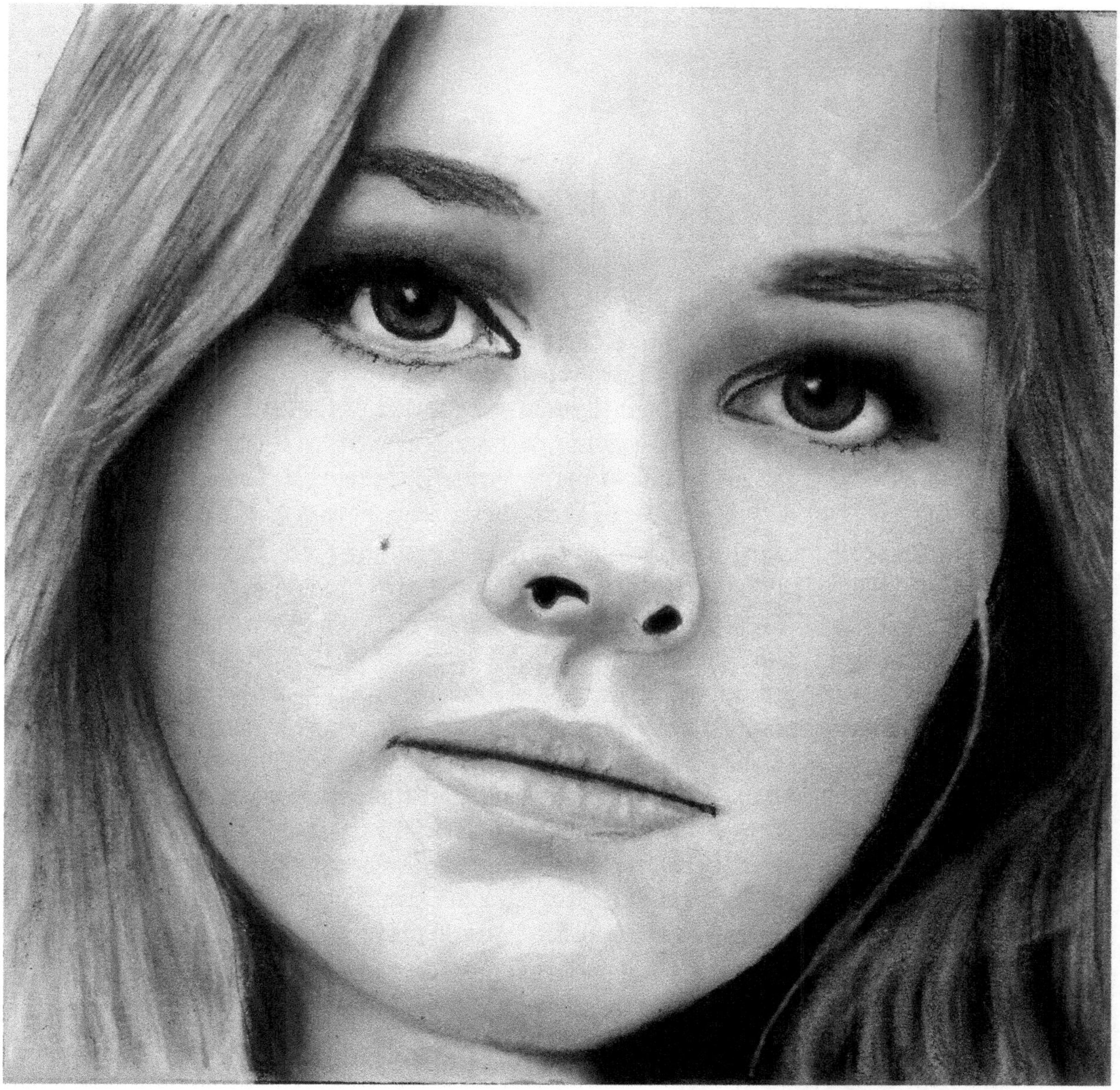

To view how this drawing was masterfully created or to purchase a Limited Edition Framed Artwork of Michelle Phillips type into your Internet Browser the URL shortcut ➡ **myportrait.art/michellephillips**

To listen to their Greatest Songs type into your Internet Browser the URL shortcut
➡ **radio.surf/themamasandthepapas**

To view all channels on THE FACE OF MUSIC Internet Radio MEGA Station type into your Internet Browser the URL shortcut ➡ **radio.surf/music**

To inquire about purchasing a Limited Edtion NFT of this portrait type into your Internet Browser the URL shortcut ➡ **myartnft.shop/michellephillips**

To view all available NFTs type into your Internet Browser the URL shortcut ➡ **myartnft.shop/all**

# Maria Callas

(Net worth: $1 Million)(Total Records Sold: Millions)
(Genre: Classical)(Height: 5' - 8 1/2")

Maria Callas Commendatore OMRI (December 2, 1923 – September 16, 1977) was an American-born Greek soprano.

She was one of the most renowned and influential opera singers of the 20th century. Many critics praised her bel canto technique, wide-ranging voice and dramatic interpretations. Her repertoire ranged from classical opera seria to the bel canto operas of Donizetti, Bellini and Rossini and, further, to the works of Verdi and Puccini; and, in her early career, to the music dramas of Wagner. Her musical and dramatic talents led to her being hailed as La Divina ("the Divine one").

Born in Manhattan, New York City, to Greek immigrant parents, she was raised by an overbearing mother who had wanted a son. Maria received her musical education in Greece at age 13 and later established her career in Italy. Forced to deal with the exigencies of 1940s wartime poverty and with near-sightedness that left her nearly blind onstage, she endured struggles and scandal over the course of her career. She notably underwent a mid-career weight loss, which might have contributed to her vocal decline and the premature end of her career.

The press exulted in publicizing Callas's temperamental behavior, her supposed rivalry with Renata Tebaldi and her love affair with Greek shipping tycoon Aristotle Onassis. Although her dramatic life and personal tragedy have often overshadowed Callas the artist in the popular press, her artistic achievements were such that Leonard Bernstein called her "the Bible of opera" and her influence so enduring that, in 2006, Opera News wrote of her: "Nearly thirty years after her death, she's still the definition of the diva as artist—and still one of classical music's best-selling vocalists."

Callas spent her last years living largely in isolation in Paris and died of a heart attack at age 53 on September 16, 1977.

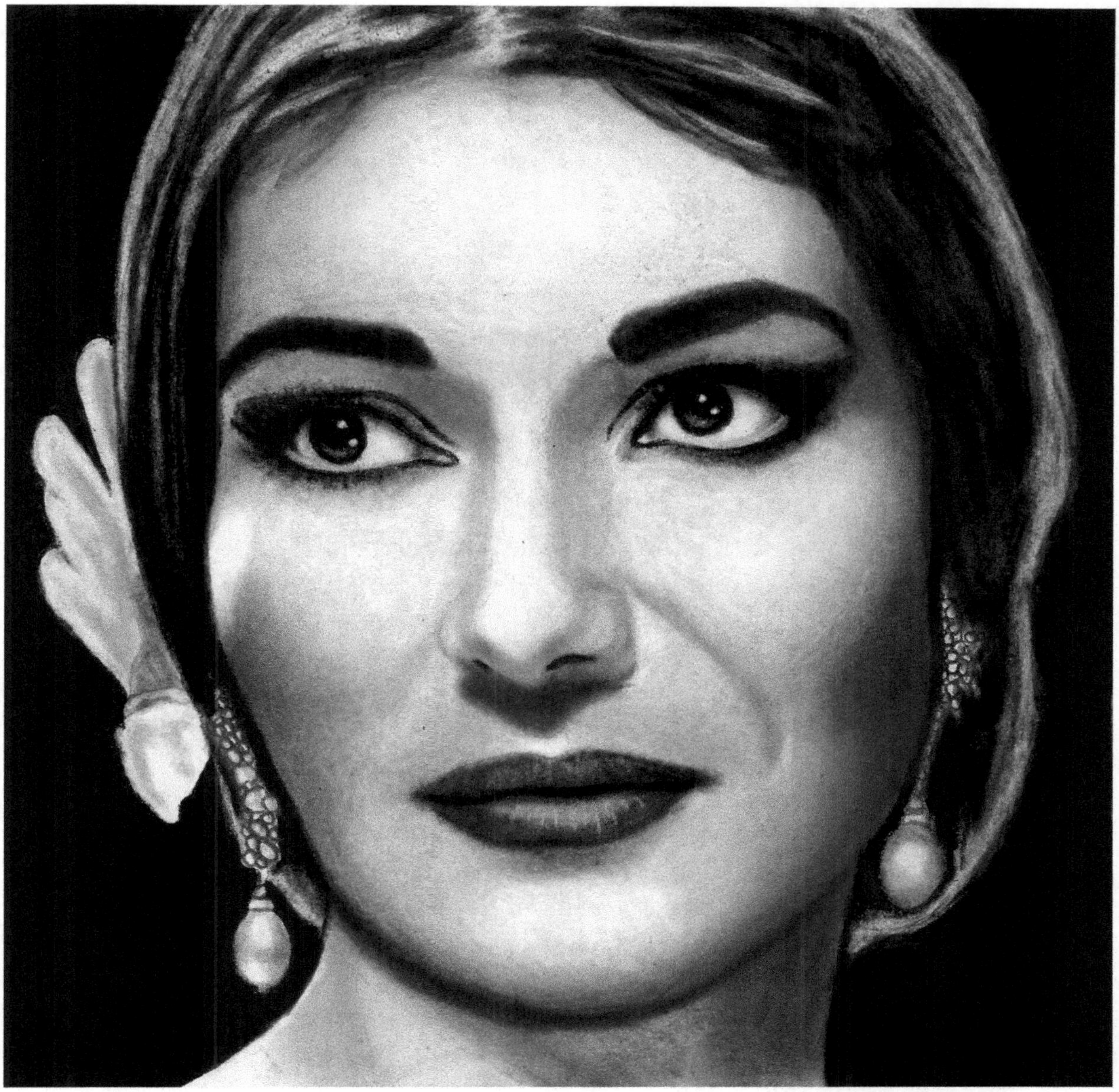

To view how this drawing was masterfully created or to purchase a Limited Edition Framed Artwork of Maria Callas type into your Internet Browser the URL shortcut ➡ **myportrait.art/mariacallas**

To listen to her Greatest Songs type into your Internet Browser the URL shortcut ➡ **radio.surf/mariacallas**

To view all channels on THE FACE OF MUSIC Internet Radio MEGA Station type into your Internet Browser the URL shortcut ➡ **radio.surf/music**

To inquire about purchasing a Limited Edition NFT of this portrait type into your Internet Browser the URL shortcut ➡ **myartnft.shop/mariacallas**

To view all available NFTs type into your Internet Browser the URL shortcut ➡ **myartnft.shop/all**

# Mariah Carey

(Net worth: $320 Million)(Total Records Sold: 200+ Million)
(Genre: R&B, Pop, Hip-Hop, Soul)(Height: 5' - 7")

Mariah Carey (born March 27, 1969) is an American singer-songwriter, record producer, and actress. Known for her five-octave vocal range, melismatic singing style, and signature use of the whistle register, she is referred to as the "Songbird Supreme" and the "Queen of Christmas". She rose to fame in 1990 with her eponymous debut album, released under the guidance of Columbia Records executive Tommy Mottola, who married her three years later. Carey is the first artist in history to have their first five singles reach number one on the Billboard Hot 100, from "Vision of Love" to "Emotions".

She achieved worldwide success with follow-up albums Music Box (1993), Merry Christmas (1994), and Daydream (1995). These albums spawned some of Carey's most successful singles, including "Hero", "Without You", "All I Want for Christmas Is You", "Fantasy", "Always Be My Baby", as well as "One Sweet Day", which topped the US Billboard Hot 100 decade-end chart (1990s). After separating from Mottola, Carey adopted a new image and incorporated more elements of hip hop into her music with the release of Butterfly (1997). Billboard named her the country's most successful artist of the 1990s, while the World Music Awards honored her as the world's best-selling music artist of the 1990s and the best-selling pop female artist of the millennium.

After eleven consecutive years charting a U.S. number-one single, Carey parted ways with Columbia in 2001 and signed a $100 million recording contract with Virgin Records in April of that year. However, following her highly publicized physical and emotional breakdown, as well as the critical and commercial failure of her film Glitter (2001) and its accompanying soundtrack, her contract was bought out for $28 million by Virgin and she signed with Island Records the following year. After a relatively unsuccessful period, she returned to the top of music charts with The Emancipation of Mimi (2005), the world's second-best-selling album of 2005. Its second single, "We Belong Together", topped the US Billboard Hot 100 decade-end chart (2000s). Her performance in the 2009 film Precious won her the Breakthrough Actress Performance Award at the Palm Springs International Film Festival. Carey's subsequent ventures included serving as a judge on American Idol, starring in the docu-series Mariah's World, and appearing in the films The Butler (2013), A Christmas Melody (2015), and The Lego Batman Movie (2017).With sales of over 200 million records worldwide, she is one of the best-selling music artists of all time. Carey has amassed an extensive catalog, with nineteen of her songs topping the Billboard Hot 100, and holds the record for the most number-one singles by a solo artist, a female songwriter, and a female producer. According to the Recording Industry Association of America (RIAA), she is the highest-certified female artist in the United States, with 68.5 million certified album units tying with Barbra Streisand. In 2012, she was ranked second on VH1's list of the 100 Greatest Women in Music. In 2019, Billboard named her the all-time top female artist in the United States, based on both album and song chart performances. Aside from her commercial accomplishments, Carey has won five Grammy Awards, nineteen World Music Awards, ten American Music Awards, and fifteen Billboard Music Awards. An inductee of the Songwriters Hall of Fame, she is noted for inspiring other artists in pop and contemporary R&B music.

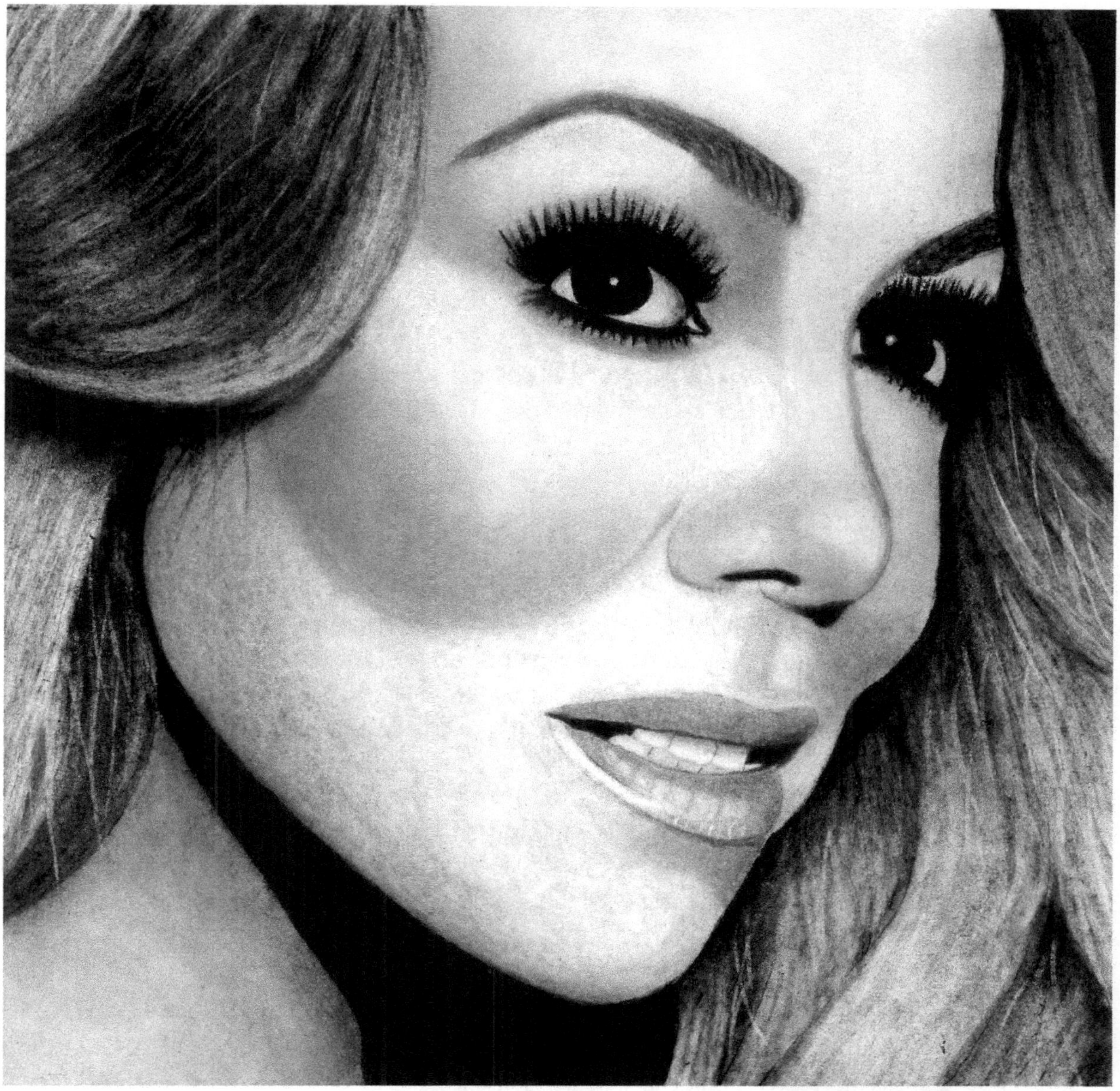

To view how this drawing was masterfully created or to purchase a Limited Edition Framed Artwork of Mariah Carey type into your Internet Browser the URL shortcut ➡ **myportrait.art/mariahcarey**

To listen to her Greatest Songs type into your Internet Browser the URL shortcut ➡ **radio.surf/mariahcarey**

To view all channels on THE FACE OF MUSIC Internet Radio MEGA Station type into your Internet Browser the URL shortcut ➡ **radio.surf/music**

To inquire about purchasing a Limited Edition NFT of this portrait type into your Internet Browser the URL shortcut ➡ **myartnft.shop/mariahcarey**

To view all available NFTs type into your Internet Browser the URL shortcut ➡ **myartnft.shop/all**

# Marvin Gaye

(Net worth: $5 Million)(Total Records Sold: Millions)
(Genre: Classic Soul)(Height: 6' - 0"`)

Marvin Gaye (born Marvin Pentz Gay Jr.; April 2, 1939 – April 1, 1984) was an American singer, songwriter, and record producer. He helped to shape the sound of Motown in the 1960s, first as an in-house session player and later as a solo artist with a string of hits, earning him the nicknames "Prince of Motown" and "Prince of Soul".

Gaye's Motown hits include "Ain't That Peculiar", "How Sweet It Is (To Be Loved By You)", and "I Heard It Through the Grapevine". Gaye also recorded duets with Mary Wells, Kim Weston, Tammi Terrell, and Diana Ross. During the 1970s, Gaye recorded the albums What's Going On and Let's Get It On and became one of the first artists in Motown to break away from the reins of a production company. His later recordings influenced several contemporary R&B subgenres, such as quiet storm and neo soul. He was a tax exile in Europe in the early 1980s; he released "Sexual Healing" the 1982 hit which won his first two Grammy Awards on the album Midnight Love. Gaye's last televised appearances were at the 1983 NBA All-Star Game, where he sang "The Star-Spangled Banner"; Motown 25: Yesterday, Today, Forever; and Soul Train.

On April 1, 1984, the day before his 45th birthday, Gaye was shot dead by his father, Marvin Gay Sr. at their house in West Adams, Los Angeles, after an argument. Many institutions have posthumously bestowed Gaye with awards and other honors including the Grammy Lifetime Achievement Award, and inductions into the Rhythm and Blues Music Hall of Fame, the Songwriters Hall of Fame, and the Rock and Roll Hall of Fame.

Gaye was born Marvin Pentz Gay Jr. on April 2, 1939, at Freedman's Hospital in Washington, D.C., to church minister Marvin Gay Sr. and domestic worker Alberta Gay (née Cooper). His first home was in a public housing project, the Fairfax Apartments (now demolished) at 1617 1st Street SW in the Southwest Waterfront neighborhood. Although one of the city's oldest neighborhoods, with many elegant Federal-style homes, Southwest was primarily a vast slum. Most buildings were small, in extensive disrepair, and lacked both electricity and running water. The alleys were full of one- and two-story shacks, and nearly every dwelling was overcrowded. Gaye and his friends nicknamed the area "Simple City", owing to its being "half-city, half country".

Gaye intervened in a fight between his parents on the afternoon of April 1, 1984, in the family house in the West Adams district of Los Angeles, and he became involved in a physical altercation with his father, Marvin Gay Sr. who shot Gaye twice, once in the chest, piercing his heart, and then into Gaye's shoulder. The shooting took place in Gaye's bedroom at 12:38 p.m. The first shot proved fatal. Gaye was pronounced dead at 1:01 p.m. after his body arrived at California Hospital Medical Center, one day short of his 45th birthday.

After Gaye's funeral, his body was cremated at Forest Lawn Memorial Park-Hollywood Hills; his ashes were scattered into the Pacific Ocean. Gay Sr. was initially charged with first degree murder, but the charges were reduced to voluntary manslaughter following a diagnosis of a brain tumor. He was given a suspended six-year sentence and probation. He died at a nursing home in 1998.

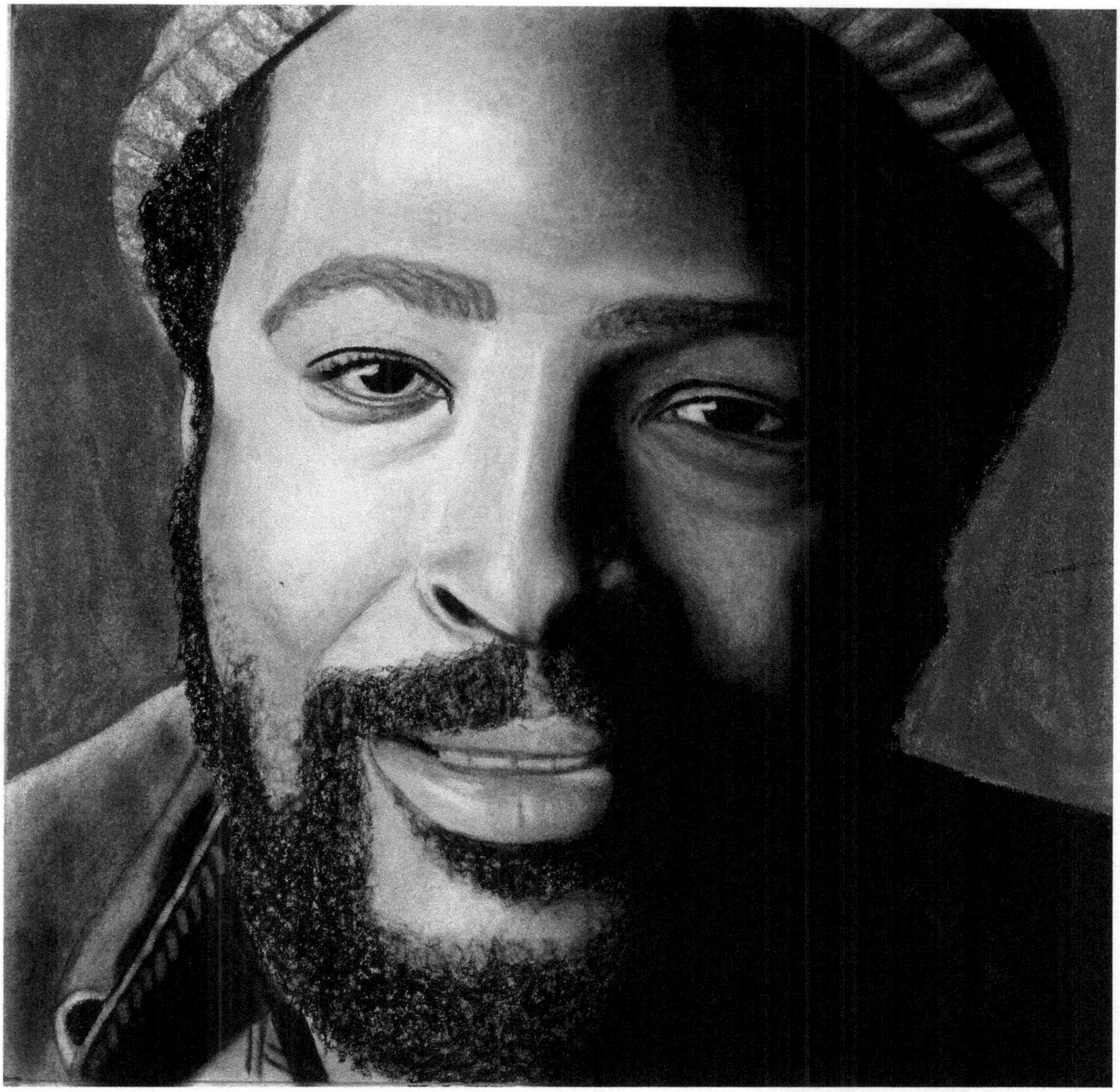

To view how this drawing was masterfully created or to purchase a Limited Edition Framed Artwork of Marvin Gaye type into your Internet Browser the URL shortcut ➡ **myportrait.art/marvingaye**

To listen to his Greatest Songs type into your Internet Browser the URL shortcut ➡ **radio.surf/marvingaye**

To view all channels on THE FACE OF MUSIC Internet Radio MEGA Station type into your Internet Browser the URL shortcut ➡ **radio.surf/music**

To inquire about purchasing a Limited Edtion NFT of this portrait type into your Internet Browser the URL shortcut ➡ **myartnft.shop/marvingaye**

To view all available NFTs type into your Internet Browser the URL shortcut ➡ **myartnft.shop/all**

# Meat Loaf

(Net worth: $25 Million)(Total Records Sold: 80+ Million)
(Genre: Classic Rock)(Height: 5' - 10")

Michael Lee Aday (born Marvin Lee Aday, September 27, 1947), better known as Meat Loaf, is an American singer and actor. He is noted for his powerful, wide-ranging voice and theatrical live shows. His Bat Out of Hell trilogy—Bat Out of Hell, Bat Out of Hell II: Back into Hell, and Bat Out of Hell III: The Monster Is Loose—has sold more than 50 million albums worldwide. More than four decades after its release, the first album still sells an estimated 200,000 copies annually and stayed on the charts for over nine years, making it one of the best-selling albums in history.

After the commercial success of Bat Out of Hell and Bat Out of Hell II: Back Into Hell, and earning a Grammy Award for Best Solo Rock Vocal Performance for the song "I'd Do Anything for Love", Meat Loaf nevertheless experienced some difficulty establishing a steady career within the United States. This did not stop him from becoming one of the best-selling music artists of all time, with worldwide sales of more than 80 million records. The key to this success was his retention of iconic status and popularity in Europe, especially the United Kingdom, where he received the 1994 Brit Award for best-selling album and single, appeared in the 1997 film Spice World, and ranks 23rd for the number of weeks spent on the UK charts, as of 2006. He ranks 96th on VH1's "100 Greatest Artists of Hard Rock".

Sometimes credited as Meat Loaf Aday, he has also appeared in over 50 movies and television shows, sometimes as himself or as characters resembling his stage persona. His most notable film roles include Eddie in The Rocky Horror Picture Show (1975), and Robert "Bob" Paulson in Fight Club (1999). His early stage work included dual roles in the original cast of The Rocky Horror Show, and he was also in the musical Hair, both on- and off-Broadway.

Michael Lee Aday was born Marvin Lee Aday in Dallas, Texas on September 27, 1947, the only child of Wilma Artie (née Hukel), a school teacher and member of the Vo-di-o-do Girls gospel quartet, and Orvis Wesley Aday, a former police officer who went into business selling a homemade cough remedy with his wife and a friend under the name of the Griffin Grocery Company. His father was an alcoholic who would go on drinking binges for days at a time, which started when he was medically discharged from the U.S. Army during World War II after being hit with shrapnel from a mortar. Aday accompanied his mother in driving around all the bars in Dallas to look for his father, and often stayed with his grandmother.

In 1965, Aday graduated from Thomas Jefferson High School, having already started his acting career via school productions such as Where's Charley? and The Music Man. After attending college at Lubbock Christian College, he transferred to North Texas State University (now the University of North Texas). After he received his inheritance from his mother's death, he rented an apartment in Dallas and isolated himself for three and a half months until a friend found him. A short time later, he went to the airport and caught the next flight to Los Angeles.

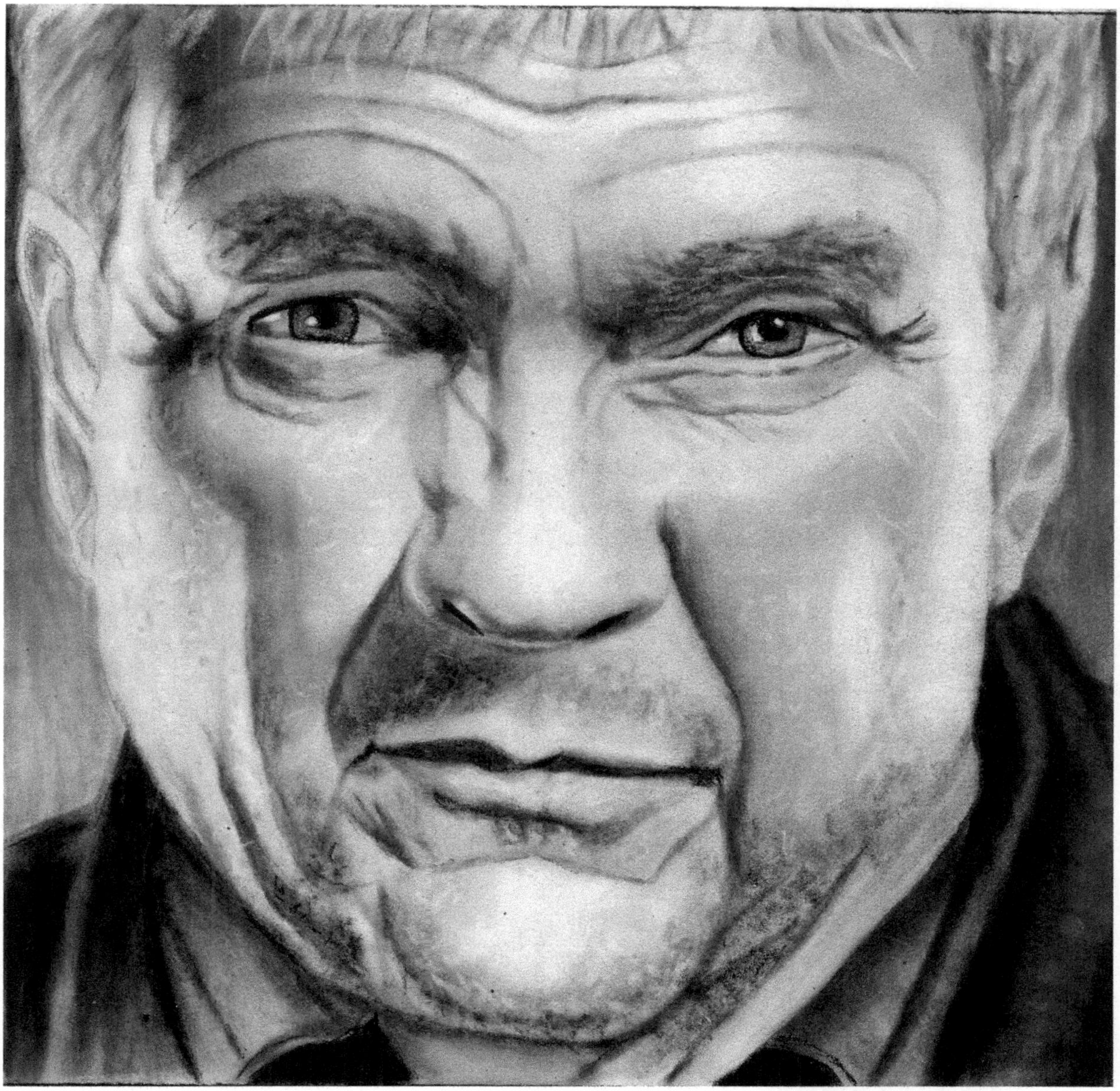

To view how this drawing was masterfully created or to purchase a Limited Edition Framed Artwork of Meat Loaf type into your Internet Browser the URL shortcut ➡ **myportrait.art/meatloaf**

To listen to his Greatest Songs type into your Internet Browser the URL shortcut ➡ **radio.surf/meatloaf**

To view all channels on THE FACE OF MUSIC Internet Radio MEGA Station type into your Internet Browser the URL shortcut ➡ **radio.surf/music**

To inquire about purchasing a Limited Edtion NFT of this portrait type into your Internet Browser the URL shortcut ➡ **myartnft.shop/meatloaf**

To view all available NFTs type into your Internet Browser the URL shortcut ➡ **myartnft.shop/all**

# Megadeth

(Total Records Sold: 38 Million) (Genre: Thrash Metal , Speed Metal)

Megadeth is an American heavy metal band formed in Los Angeles in 1983 by guitarist Dave Mustaine and bassist David Ellefson. Along with Metallica, Anthrax, and Slayer, Megadeth is one of the "big four" of American thrash metal, responsible for its development and popularization. Their music features complex arrangements and fast rhythm sections, and lyrical themes of death, war, politics, personal relationships and religion.

In 1985, Megadeth released its debut album, Killing Is My Business... and Business Is Good!, on the independent record label Combat Records, to moderate success. It caught the attention of bigger labels, which led to Megadeth signing with Capitol Records. Their first major-label album, Peace Sells... but Who's Buying?, was released in 1986 and was a major hit with the underground metal scene. Band members' substance abuse issues and personal disputes brought Megadeth negative publicity during this period.

After the lineup stabilized, Megadeth released a number of platinum-selling albums, including Rust in Peace (1990) and Countdown to Extinction (1992). These albums, along with worldwide tours, brought them public recognition. The band temporarily disbanded in 2002 when Mustaine suffered an arm injury and re-established in 2004 without bassist Ellefson, who had taken legal action against Mustaine. Ellefson settled out of court and rejoined in 2010. Megadeth has hosted its own music festival, Gigantour, several times since July 2005.

Megadeth has sold 38 million records worldwide, earned platinum certification in the United States for six of its fifteen studio albums, and received twelve Grammy nominations. Megadeth won its first Grammy Award in 2017 for the song "Dystopia" in the Best Metal Performance category. The band's mascot, Vic Rattlehead, regularly appears on album artwork and live shows. The group has drawn controversy for its music and lyrics, including album bans and canceled concerts; MTV refused to play two of the band's music videos that the network considered to condone suicide.

# Dave Mustaine

(Net Worth: $18 Million)(Height: 6' - 0")

David Scott Mustaine (born September 13, 1961) is an American musician best known as the co-founder, vocalist, rhythm and lead guitarist, and primary songwriter of thrash metal band Megadeth. Prior to forming Megadeth, Mustaine was the original lead guitarist of thrash metal band Metallica.

Mustaine was born in La Mesa, California, to parents Emily (née David) and John Mustaine. His father was of French, German, Irish and Finnish descent, while his mother was of German-Jewish descent. The Mustaine family were Jehovah's Witnesses.

Mustaine holds black belts in taekwondo and Ukidokan karate. In 2007, he was made a Goodwill Ambassador of the World by the World Taekwondo Federation. Mustaine also started Brazilian Jiu-Jitsu and as of January 2021, was awarded the rank of Purple Belt in the art.

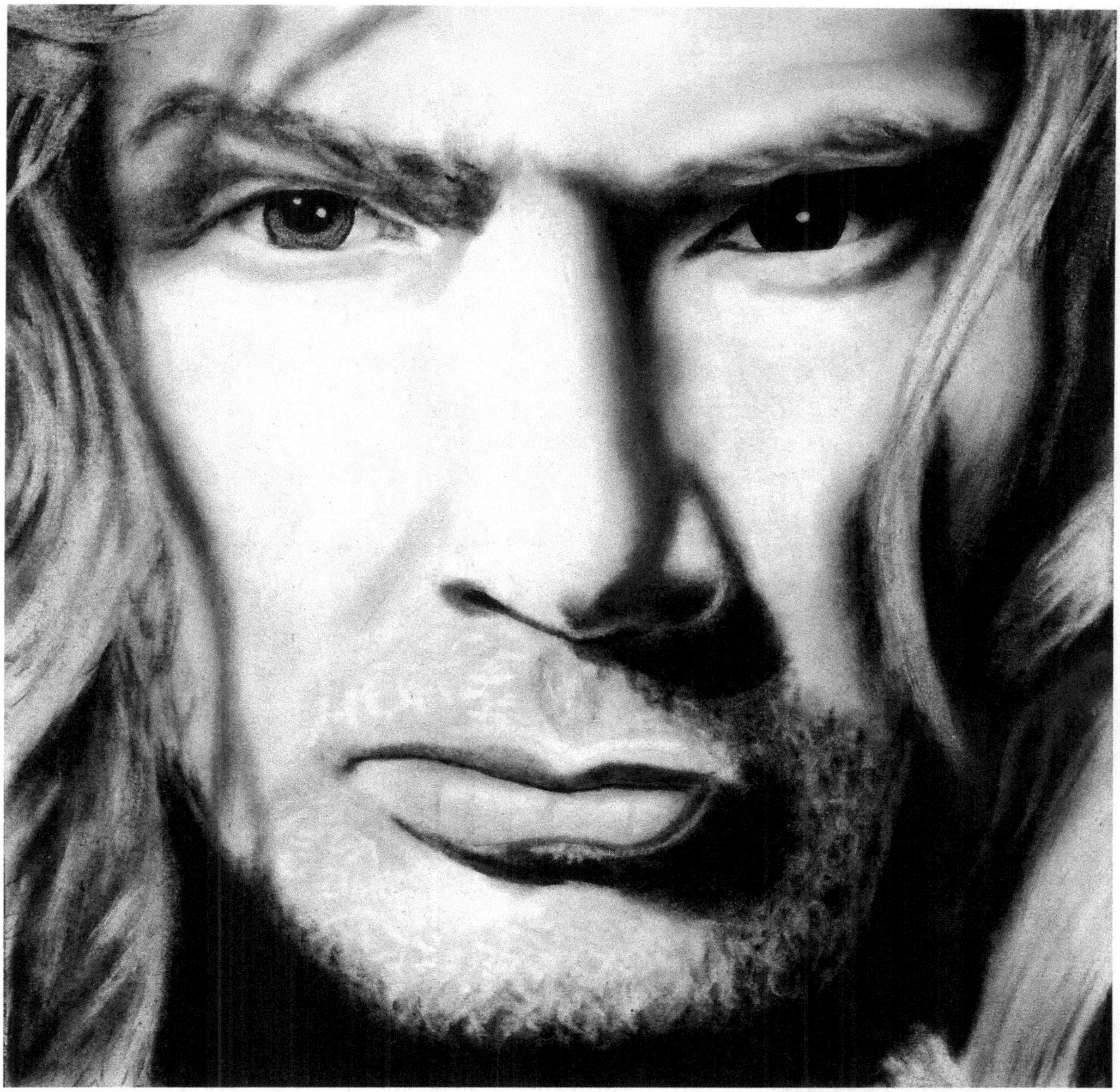

To view how this drawing was masterfully created or to purchase a Limited Edition Framed Artwork of Dave Mustaine type into your Internet Browser the URL shortcut ➡ **myportrait.art/davemustaine**

To listen to their Greatest Songs type into your Internet Browser the URL shortcut ➡ **radio.surf/megadeth**

To view all channels on THE FACE OF MUSIC Internet Radio MEGA Station type into your Internet Browser the URL shortcut ➡ **radio.surf/music**

To inquire about purchasing a Limited Edition NFT of this portrait type into your Internet Browser the URL shortcut ➡ **myartnft.shop/davemustaine**

To view all available NFTs type into your Internet Browser the URL shortcut ➡ **myartnft.shop/all**

# Merle Haggard

(Net worth: $40 Million)(Total Records Sold: Multi-Millions)
(Genre: Country)(Height: 5' - 9")

Merle Ronald Haggard (April 6, 1937 – April 6, 2016) was an American country singer, songwriter, guitarist, and fiddler.

Haggard was born in Oildale, California, during the Great Depression. His childhood was troubled after the death of his father, and he was incarcerated several times in his youth. After being released from San Quentin State Prison in 1960, he managed to turn his life around and launch a successful country music career. He gained popularity with his songs about the working class that occasionally contained conformist and jingoistic themes contrary to the prevailing anti-Vietnam War sentiment of much popular music of the time. Between the 1960s and the 1980s, he had 38 number-one hits on the US country charts, several of which also made the Billboard all-genre singles chart. Haggard continued to release successful albums into the 2000s.

He received many honors and awards for his music, including a Kennedy Center Honor (2010), a Grammy Lifetime Achievement Award (2006), a BMI Icon Award (2006), and induction into the Nashville Songwriters Hall of Fame (1977), Country Music Hall of Fame (1994) and Oklahoma Music Hall of Fame (1997). He died on April 6, 2016—his 79th birthday—at his ranch in Shasta County, California, having recently suffered from double pneumonia.

Haggard's parents were Flossie Mae (née Harp; 1902–1984) and James Francis Haggard (1899–1946). The family moved to California from their home in Checotah, Oklahoma, during the Great Depression, after their barn burned in 1934.

They settled with their two elder children, James 'Lowell' (1922–1996) and Lillian, in an apartment in Bakersfield, while James started working for the Santa Fe Railroad. A woman who owned a boxcar placed in Oildale, a nearby town, asked Haggard's father about the possibility of converting it into a house. He remodeled the boxcar, and soon after moved in, also purchasing the lot, where Merle Ronald Haggard was born on April 6, 1937. The property was eventually expanded by building a bathroom, a second bedroom, a kitchen, and a breakfast nook in the adjacent lot.

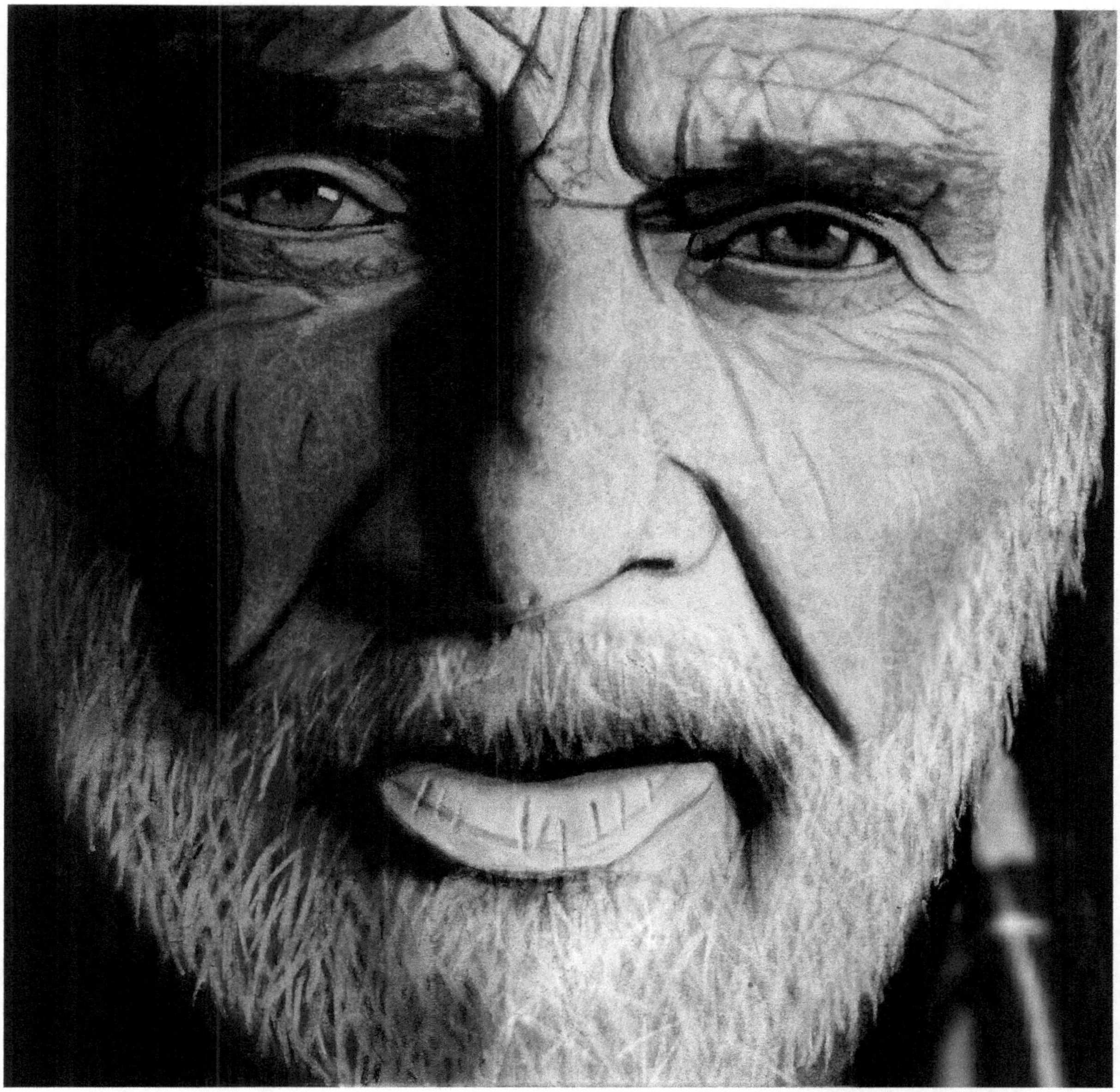

To view how this drawing was masterfully created or to purchase a Limited Edition Framed Artwork of Merle Haggard type into your Internet Browser the URL shortcut ➡ **myportrait.art/merlehaggard**

To listen to his Greatest Songs type into your Internet Browser the URL shortcut
➡ **radio.surf/merlehaggard**

To view all channels on THE FACE OF MUSIC Internet Radio MEGA Station type into your Internet Browser the URL shortcut ➡ **radio.surf/music**

To inquire about purchasing a Limited Edtion NFT of this portrait type into your Internet Browser the URL shortcut ➡ **myartnft.shop/merlehaggard**

To view all available NFTs type into your Internet Browser the URL shortcut ➡ **myartnft.shop/all**

# Metallica

(Total Albums Sold: 125 Million) (Genre: Thrash Metal , Speed Metal)

Metallica is an American heavy metal band. The band was formed in 1981 in Los Angeles by vocalist/ guitarist James Hetfield and drummer Lars Ulrich, and has been based in San Francisco for most of its career. The band's fast tempos, instrumentals and aggressive musicianship made them one of the founding "big four" bands of thrash metal, alongside Megadeth, Anthrax and Slayer. Metallica's current lineup comprises founding members and primary songwriters Hetfield and Ulrich, longtime lead guitarist Kirk Hammett, and bassist Robert Trujillo. Guitarist Dave Mustaine (who went on to form Megadeth after being fired from the band) and bassists Ron McGovney, Cliff Burton (who died in a bus accident in Sweden in 1986) and Jason Newsted are former members of the band.Metallica earned a growing fan base in the underground music community and won critical acclaim with its first five albums. The band's third album, Master of Puppets (1986), was described as one of the heaviest and most influential thrash metal albums. Its eponymous fifth album, Metallica (1991), the band's first to root predominantly in heavy metal, appealed to a more mainstream audience, achieving substantial commercial success and selling over 16 million copies in the United States to date, making it the best-selling album of the SoundScan era. After experimenting with different genres and directions in subsequent releases, the band returned to its thrash metal roots with the release of its ninth album, Death Magnetic (2008), which drew similar praise to that of the band's earlier albums.In 2000, Metallica led the case against the peer-to-peer file sharing service Napster, in which the band and several other artists filed lawsuits against the service for sharing their copyright-protected material without consent; after reaching a settlement, Napster became a pay-to-use service in 2003. Metallica was the subject of the acclaimed 2004 documentary film Metallica: Some Kind of Monster, which documented the troubled production of the band's eighth album, St. Anger (2003), and the internal struggles within the band at the time. In 2009, Metallica was inducted into the Rock and Roll Hall of Fame. The band wrote the screenplay for and starred in the 2013 IMAX concert film Metallica: Through the Never, in which the band performed live against a fictional thriller storyline.Metallica has released ten studio albums, four live albums, a cover album, five extended plays, 37 singles and 39 music videos. The band has won nine Grammy Awards from 23 nominations, and its last six studio albums (beginning with Metallica) have consecutively debuted at number one on the Billboard 200. Metallica ranks as one of the most commercially successful bands of all time, having sold over 125 million albums worldwide as of 2018. Metallica has been listed as one of the greatest artists of all time by magazines such as Rolling Stone, which ranked them at no. 61 on its 100 Greatest Artists of All Time list. As of 2017, Metallica is the third best-selling music artist since Nielsen SoundScan began tracking sales in 1991 selling a total of 58 million albums in the United States.

# James Hetfield

(Net Worth: $300 Million)(Height: 6' - 1 1/4")

James Alan Hetfield (born August 3, 1963) is an American musician and songwriter, best known as the co-founder, lead vocalist, rhythm guitarist and primary songwriter for heavy metal band Metallica.

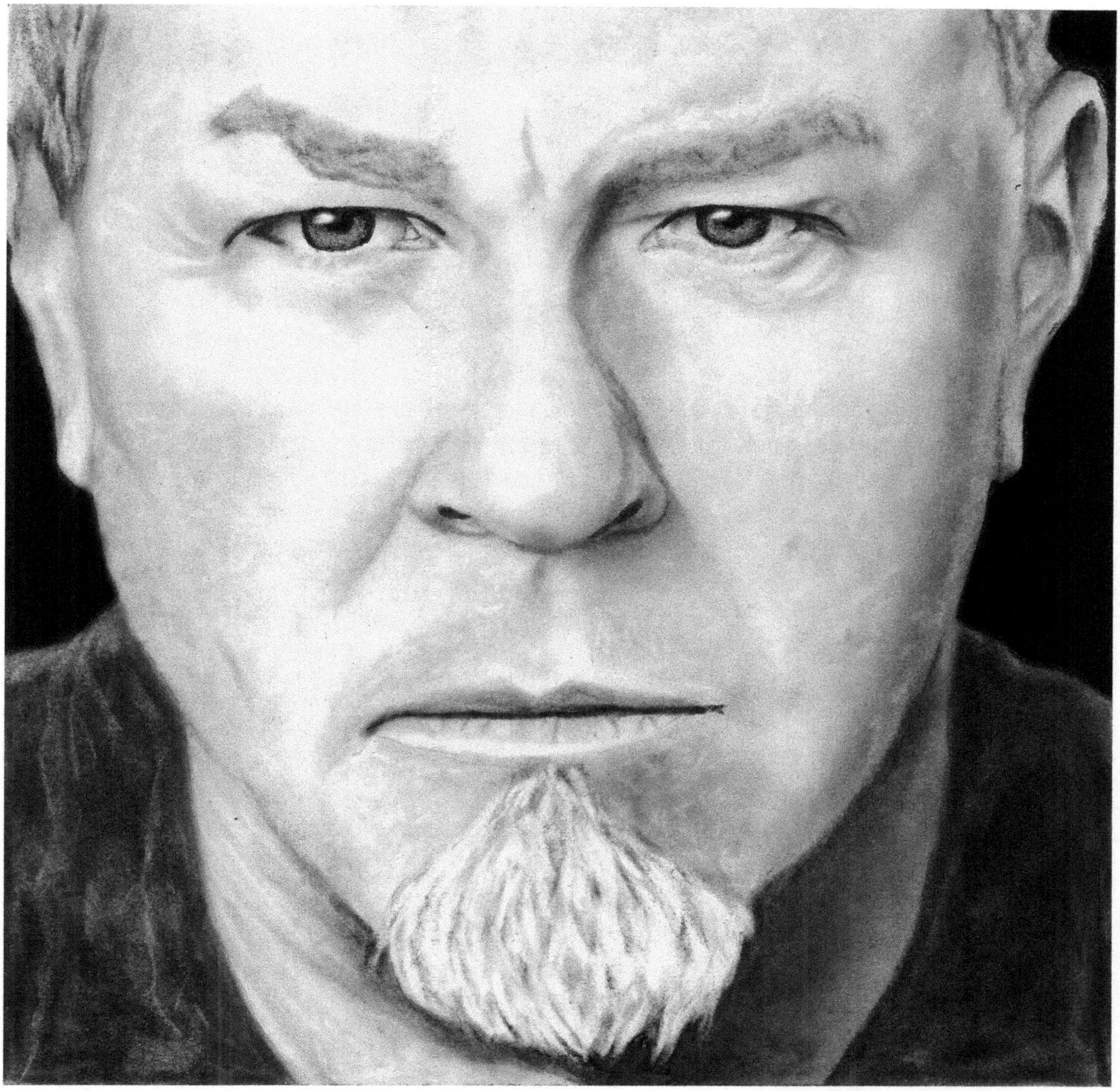

To view how this drawing was masterfully created or to purchase a Limited Edition Framed Artwork of James Hetfield type into your Internet Browser the URL shortcut ➡ **myportrait.art/jameshetfield**

To listen to their Greatest Songs type into your Internet Browser the URL shortcut ➡ **radio.surf/metallica**

To view all channels on THE FACE OF MUSIC Internet Radio MEGA Station type into your Internet Browser the URL shortcut ➡ **radio.surf/music**

To inquire about purchasing a Limited Edition NFT of this portrait type into your Internet Browser the URL shortcut ➡ **myartnft.shop/jameshetfield**

To view all available NFTs type into your Internet Browser the URL shortcut ➡ **myartnft.shop/all**

# Michael Jackson

(Net worth: $500 Million)(Total Records Sold: 350 Million)
(Genre: Pop , Soul , Funk , R&B , Disco)(Height: 5' - 10")

Michael Joseph Jackson ( August 29, 1958 – June 25, 2009) was an American singer, songwriter, and dancer. Dubbed the "King of Pop", he is regarded as one of the most significant cultural figures of the 20th century. Through stage and video performances, he popularized complicated dance moves such as the moonwalk, to which he gave the name, and the robot. His sound and style have influenced artists of various genres, and his contributions to music, dance, and fashion, along with his publicized personal life, made him a global figure in popular culture.

The eighth child of the Jackson family, Jackson made his professional debut in 1964 with his elder brothers Jackie, Tito, Jermaine, and Marlon as a member of the Jackson 5. Jackson began his solo career in 1971 while at Motown Records, and rose to solo stardom with his 1979 album Off the Wall during the peak of the disco era. By the early 1980s, Jackson was a dominant figure in popular music. His music videos, including those for "Beat It", "Billie Jean", and "Thriller" from his 1982 album Thriller, are credited with breaking racial barriers and transforming the medium into an art form and promotional tool. He helped propel the success of MTV and continued to innovate with videos on the albums Bad (1987), Dangerous (1991), and HIStory: Past, Present and Future, Book I (1995). From the late 1980s, Jackson became a figure of controversy and speculation due to his changing appearance, relationships, behavior and lifestyle.

In 1993, he was accused of sexually abusing the child of a family friend. The lawsuit was settled out of civil court, and Jackson was not indicted due to lack of evidence. In 2005, he was tried and acquitted of further child sexual abuse allegations and several other charges. In 2009, while preparing for a series of comeback concerts, This Is It, Jackson died from an overdose of propofol administered by his personal physician, Conrad Murray, who was subsequently convicted of involuntary manslaughter.

Jackson is the most awarded artist in the history of popular music and one of the best-selling music artists of all time, with estimated sales of over 350 million records worldwide. Thriller is the best-selling album of all time, while Bad was the first album to produce five Billboard Hot 100 number-one singles. Jackson had 13 Billboard Hot 100 number-one singles, more than any other male artist in the Hot 100 era, and was the first artist to have a top ten single in the Billboard Hot 100 in five different decades. He received 15 Grammy Awards, six Brit Awards, a Golden Globe Award, and 39 Guinness World Records, including the "Most Successful Entertainer of All Time". Jackson's inductions include the Rock and Roll Hall of Fame twice, the Vocal Group Hall of Fame, the Songwriters Hall of Fame, the Dance Hall of Fame (the only recording artist to be inducted), and the Rhythm and Blues Music Hall of Fame. In 2016, his estate earned $825 million, the highest yearly amount for a celebrity ever recorded by Forbes.

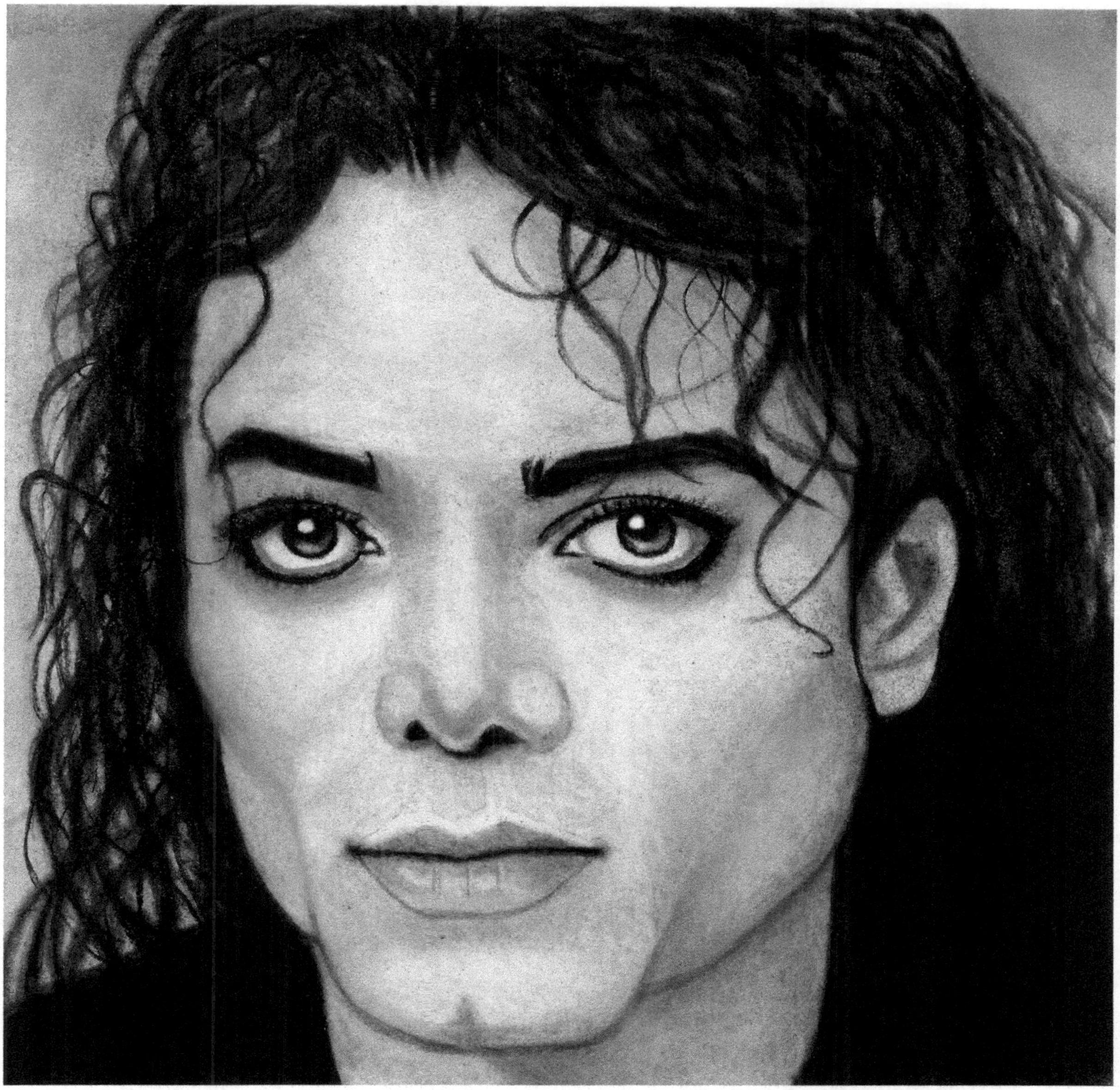

To view how this drawing was masterfully created or to purchase a Limited Edition Framed Artwork of Michael Jackson type into your Internet Browser the URL shortcut ➡ **myportrait.art/michaeljackson**

To listen to his Greatest Songs type into your Internet Browser the URL shortcut
➡ **radio.surf/michaeljackson**

To view all channels on THE FACE OF MUSIC Internet Radio MEGA Station type into your Internet Browser the URL shortcut ➡ **radio.surf/music**

To inquire about purchasing a Limited Edtion NFT of this portrait type into your Internet Browser the URL shortcut ➡ **myartnft.shop/michaeljackson**

To view all available NFTs type into your Internet Browser the URL shortcut ➡ **myartnft.shop/all**

# Miracles, The

(Total Records Sold: Millions) (Genre: R&B, Doo-Wop, Rock & Roll, Soul, Funk, Disco)

The Miracles (also known as Smokey Robinson and the Miracles from 1965 to 1972) were an American rhythm and blues vocal group that was the first successful recording act for Berry Gordy's Motown Records, and one of the most important and influential groups in pop, rock and roll, soul and R&B music history.Referred to as Motown's "soul supergroup", the Miracles recorded 26 Top 40 Pop hits, sixteen of which reached the Billboard Top 20, seven top 10 singles, and a number one single ("The Tears of a Clown") while the Robinsons and Tarplin were members. Following the departure of Tarplin and the Robinsons, the rest of the group continued with singer Billy Griffin and managed by Martin Pichinson who helped rebuild the Miracles, they scored two final top 20 singles, "Do It Baby" and "Love Machine", a second No. 1 hit, which topped the charts before the group departed for Columbia Records in 1977, recording as a quintet with Billy's brother Donald Griffin replacing Marv Tarplin, where after a few releases, they disbanded in 1978. In all, the group had over fifty charted hits by the time they disbanded.On the R&B charts, the Miracles scored 26 Top 10 Billboard R&B hits, with 4 R&B No. 1's, and 11 U.S. R&B Top 10 Albums, including 2-No.1's. Bobby Rogers and Ronald White revived the group as a touring ensemble sporadically during the 1980s and again in the 1990s. Following White's death in 1995, Rogers continued to tour with different members until he was forced into retirement due to health issues in 2011, dying less than two years later.The Miracles have been awarded many top music industry honors over the years. In 1997, the group received the Pioneer Award at the Rhythm and Blues Foundation for their musical achievements. Four years later, in 2001, they were inducted to the Vocal Group Hall of Fame. In 2004, they were ranked No. 32 on the Rolling Stone magazine's list of The 100 Greatest Artists of All Time, retaining that same position seven years later, in 2011. Four of their hit songs were inducted into the Grammy Hall of Fame (The most of any Motown group). In 2009, the group received a star on the Hollywood Walk of Fame. Throughout their careers, the Miracles were also enshrined with honors for their songwriting by both BMI and ASCAP. In 2008, Billboard listed them at No. 61 on their 100 most successful Billboard artists ever list. After much controversy, the Miracles were inducted to the Rock and Roll Hall of Fame in 2012.

# Smokey Robinson

(Net Worth: $150 Million)(Height: 5' - 10 1/2")

William "Smokey" Robinson Jr. (born February 19, 1940) is an American singer, songwriter, record producer, and former record executive. Robinson was the founder and front man of the Motown vocal group the Miracles, for which he was also chief songwriter and producer. He led the group from its 1955 origins as "the Five Chimes" until 1972, when he announced his retirement from the group to focus on his role as Motown's vice president. However, Robinson returned to the music industry as a solo artist the following year. After the sale of Motown Records in 1988, Robinson left the company in 1990.

Robinson was inducted into the Rock and Roll Hall of Fame in 1987, and was awarded the 2016 Library of Congress Gershwin Prize for his lifetime contributions to popular music.

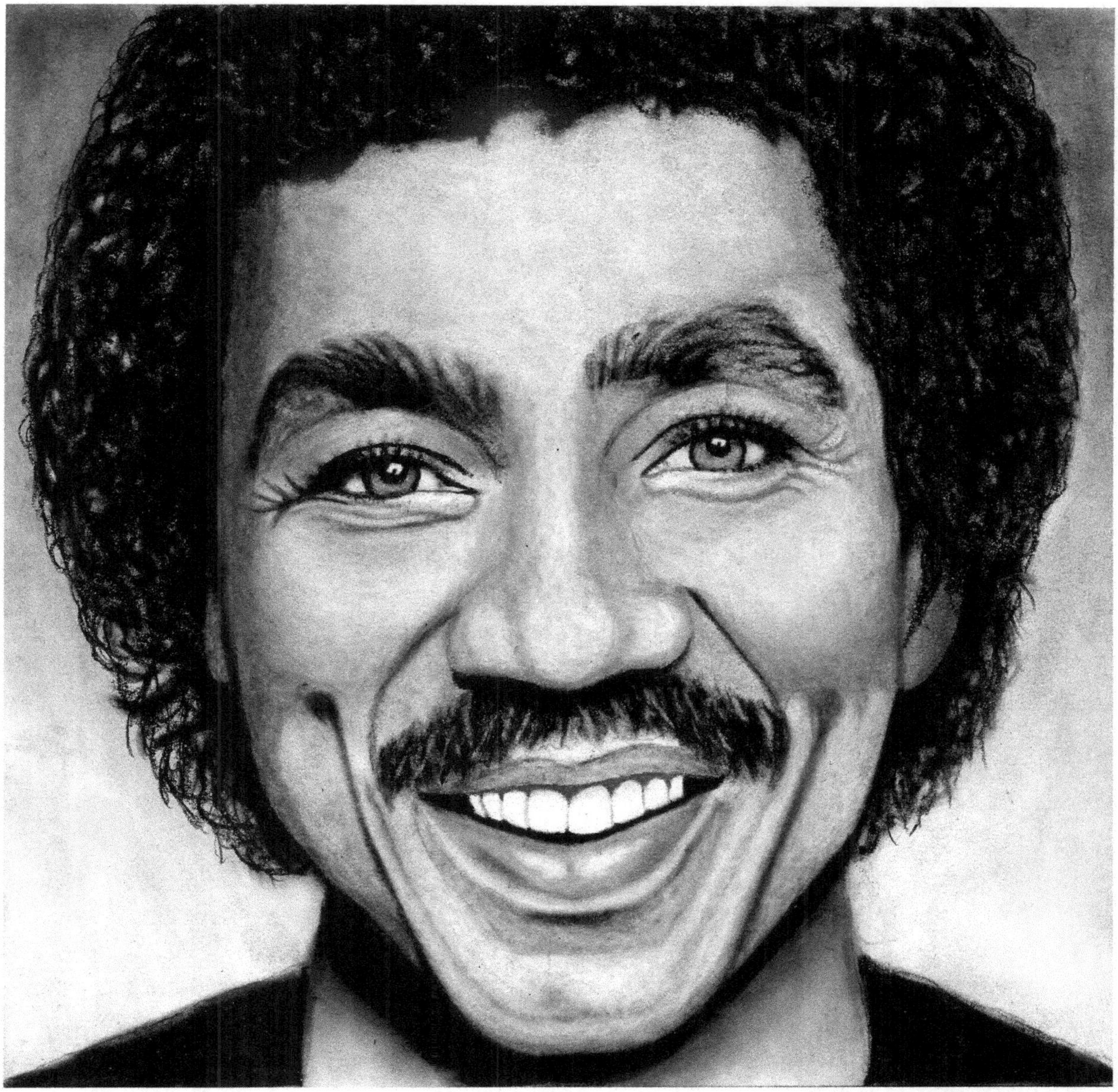

To view how this drawing was masterfully created or to purchase a Limited Edition Framed Artwork of Smokey Robinson type into your Internet Browser the URL shortcut ➡ **myportrait.art/smokeyrobinson**

To listen to their Greatest Songs type into your Internet Browser the URL shortcut ➡ **radio.surf/themiracles**

To view all channels on THE FACE OF MUSIC Internet Radio MEGA Station type into your Internet Browser the URL shortcut ➡ **radio.surf/music**

To inquire about purchasing a Limited Edtion NFT of this portrait type into your Internet Browser the URL shortcut ➡ **myartnft.shop/smokeyrobinson**

To view all available NFTs type into your Internet Browser the URL shortcut ➡ **myartnft.shop/all**

# Monkees, The

(Total Records Sold: 75+ Million) (Genre: Pop , Rock)

The Monkees are an American rock and pop band originally active between 1966 and 1971, with reunion albums and tours in the decades that followed. Their original line-up consisted of the American actor/musicians Micky Dolenz, Michael Nesmith and Peter Tork with English actor/singer Davy Jones. The group was conceived in 1965 by television producers Bob Rafelson and Bert Schneider specifically for the situation comedy series The Monkees, which aired from 1966 to 1968. The band's music was initially supervised by record producer Don Kirshner, backed by the songwriting duo of Tommy Boyce and Bobby Hart.The four actor/musicians were initially allowed only limited roles in the recording studio for the first few months of their five-year career as "the Monkees". This was due in part to the amount of time required to film the television series. Nonetheless, Nesmith composed and produced some songs from the beginning, and Tork contributed limited guitar work on the sessions produced by Nesmith. All four contributed lead vocals to various tracks. They eventually fought for the right to collectively supervise all musical output under the band's name, acting as actors, musicians, singers, songwriters, and producers.Following the television show's cancellation in 1968, the Monkees continued to record music until 1971, after which the group broke up. A revival of interest in the television show came in 1986, which led to a series of reunion tours and new records. The group has reunited and toured several times since then with different line-ups (but always containing Micky Dolenz and at least one of the other original members) and with varying degrees of success. Jones died in February 2012 and Tork died in February 2019. Dolenz and Nesmith remain active members of the group.Dolenz described The Monkees as initially being "a TV show about an imaginary band... that wanted to be the Beatles that was never successful". Ironically, the success of the show led to the actor-musicians becoming one of the most successful bands of the 1960s. The Monkees have sold more than 75 million records worldwide making them one of the biggest-selling groups of all time with international hits, including "Last Train to Clarksville", "I'm a Believer", "Pleasant Valley Sunday", and "Daydream Believer". Newspapers and magazines reported that the Monkees outsold the Beatles and the Rolling Stones combined in 1967, but Nesmith admitted in his autobiography Infinite Tuesday that it was a lie that he told a reporter.

# Davy Jones

(Net Worth: $5 Million)(Height: 5' - 3")

David Thomas Jones (30 December 1945 – 29 February 2012) was an English musician, singer, actor and businessman, best known as a member of the band the Monkees, and for starring in the TV series of the same name.His acting credits include a Tony-nominated performance as the Artful Dodger in the original London and Broadway productions of Oliver! as well as a guest star role in a hallmark episode of The Brady Bunch television show and later reprised parody film: Love, American Style; and My Two Dads. Jones was considered a teen idol.

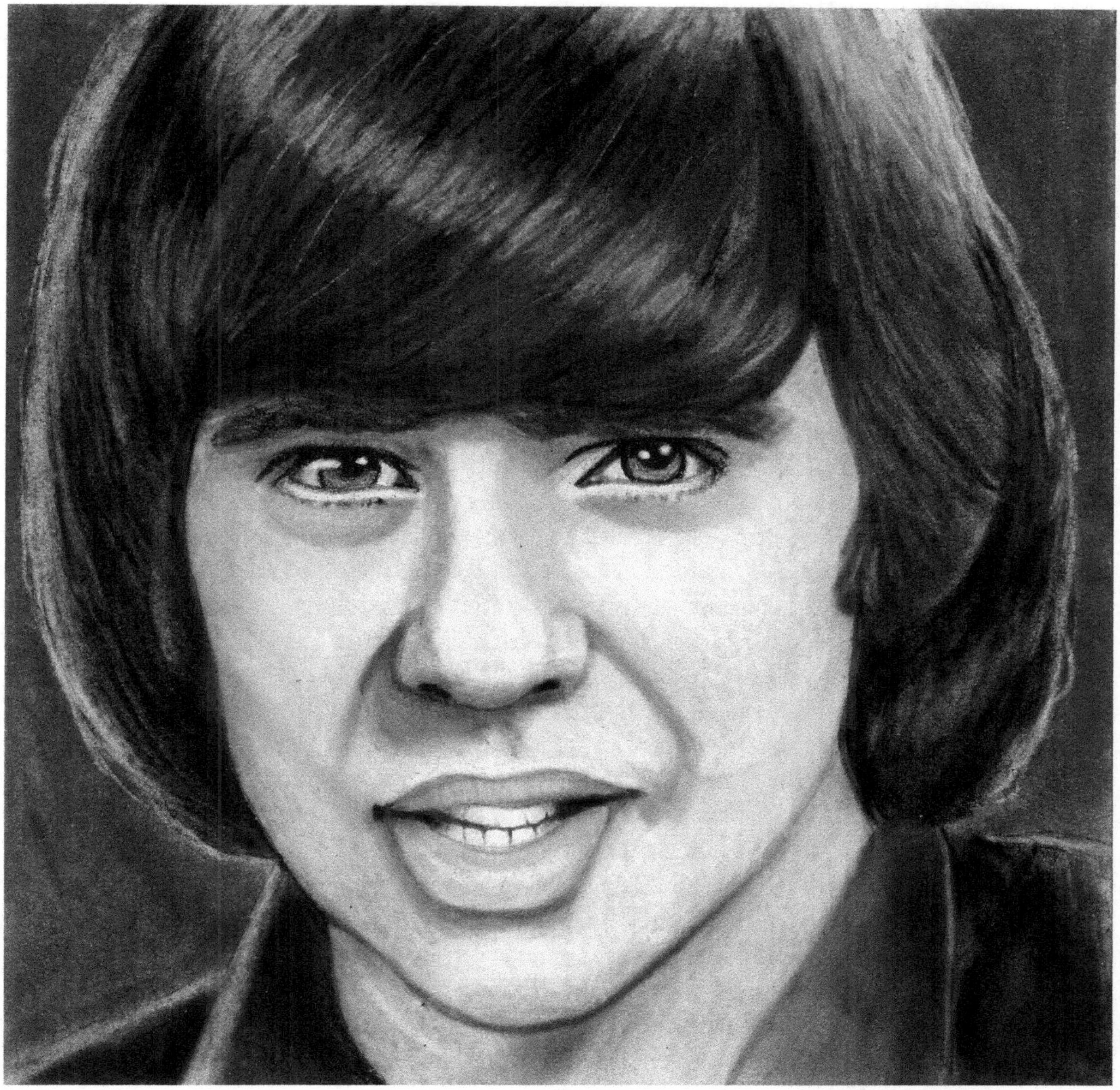

To view how this drawing was masterfully created or to purchase a Limited Edition Framed Artwork of Davy Jones type into your Internet Browser the URL shortcut ➡ **myportrait.art/davyjones**

To listen to their Greatest Songs type into your Internet Browser the URL shortcut ➡ **radio.surf/themonkees**

To view all channels on THE FACE OF MUSIC Internet Radio MEGA Station type into your Internet Browser the URL shortcut ➡ **radio.surf/music**

To inquire about purchasing a Limited Edtion NFT of this portrait type into your Internet Browser the URL shortcut ➡ **myartnft.shop/davyjones**

To view all available NFTs type into your Internet Browser the URL shortcut ➡ **myartnft.shop/all**

# Moody Blues, The

(Total Records Sold: 70+ Million) (Genre: Progressive Rock , Psychedelic Rock)

The Moody Blues are a rock band formed in Birmingham, England, in 1964, initially consisting of keyboardist Mike Pinder, multi-instrumentalist Ray Thomas, guitarist Denny Laine, drummer Graeme Edge, and bassist Clint Warwick. The group came to prominence playing rhythm and blues music. They made some changes in musicians but settled on a line-up of Pinder, Thomas, Edge, guitarist Justin Hayward, and bassist John Lodge, who stayed together for most of the band's "classic era" into the early 1970s.

Their second album, Days of Future Passed, which was released in 1967, was a fusion of rock with classical music which established the band as pioneers in the development of art rock and progressive rock. It has been described as a "landmark" and "one of the first successful concept albums". The group toured extensively through the early 1970s, then took an extended hiatus from 1974 until 1977. Founder Mike Pinder left the group a year after they re-formed and was replaced by Swiss keyboardist Patrick Moraz in 1978. In the following decade they took on a more synth-pop sound and produced The Other Side of Life in 1986, which made them the first act to earn each of its first three top 10 singles in the United States in a different decade. Health troubles led to a diminished role for founder Ray Thomas throughout the 1980s, though his musical contributions rebounded after Moraz departed in 1991. Thomas retired from the band in 2002.

The band's last album was the Christmas album December (2003), after which they eschewed recording any further albums. However, they continued to tour throughout the first decade of the 2000s and still reunite periodically for events, one-off concerts, short tours and cruises.

The Moody Blues' most successful singles include "Go Now", "Nights in White Satin", "Tuesday Afternoon", "Question", "Gemini Dream", "The Voice" and "Your Wildest Dreams". The band has sold 70 million albums worldwide, which includes 18 platinum and gold LPs. They were inducted into the Rock and Roll Hall of Fame in 2018.

# Justin Hayward

(Net Worth: $10 Million)(Height: 6' - 1 1/2")

Justin David Hayward (born 14 October 1946, in Swindon, Wiltshire) is an English musician best known as songwriter, lead singer, and guitarist of the rock band The Moody Blues. Hayward became the group's principal lead guitarist and vocalist over the 1967–1974 period, and the most prolific songwriter and composer of several international hit singles for the band.

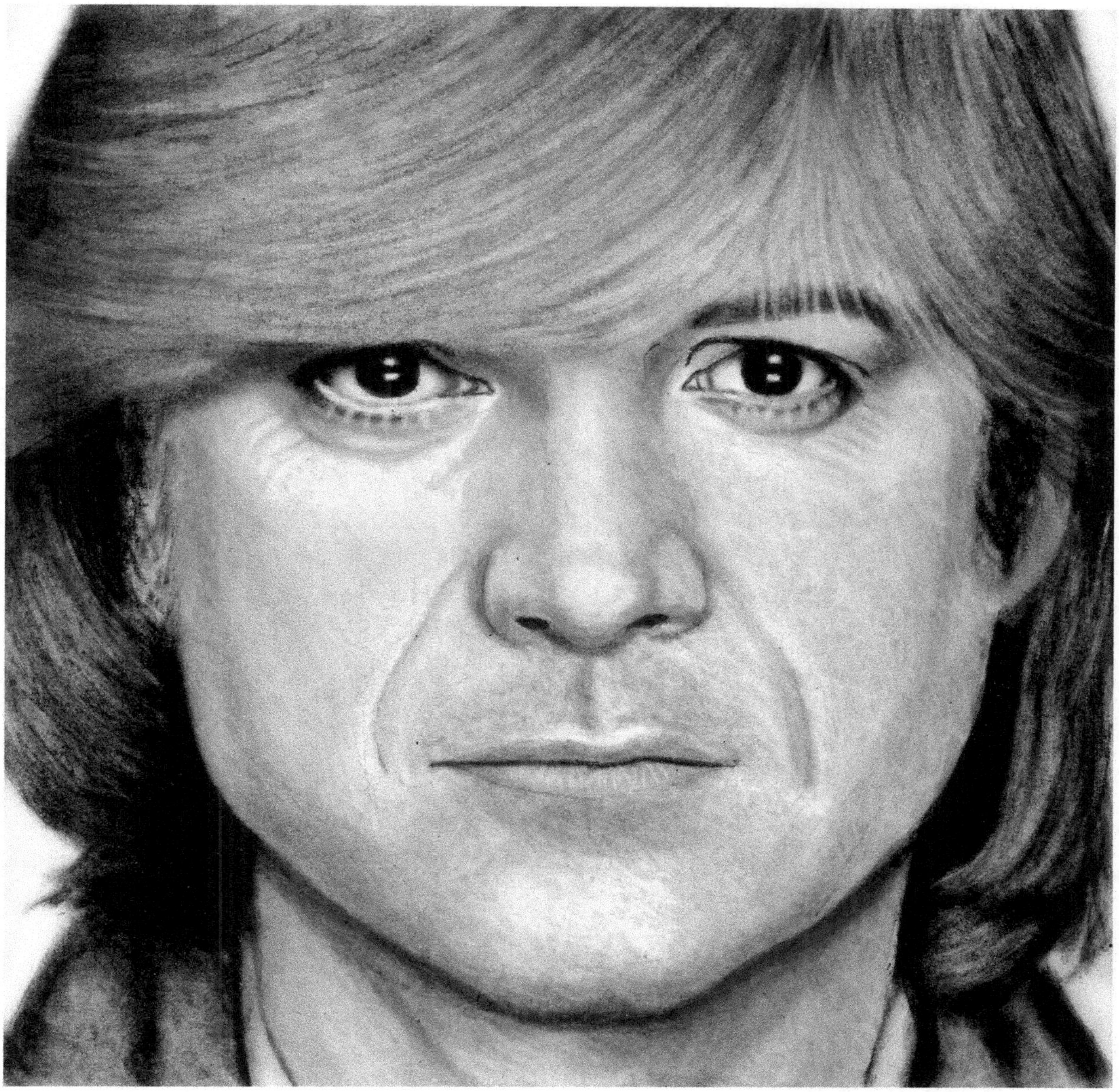

To view how this drawing was masterfully created or to purchase a Limited Edition Framed Artwork of Justin Hayward type into your Internet Browser the URL shortcut ➡ **myportrait.art/justinhayward**

To listen to their Greatest Songs type into your Internet Browser the URL shortcut
➡ **radio.surf/themoodyblues**

To view all channels on THE FACE OF MUSIC Internet Radio MEGA Station type into your Internet Browser the URL shortcut ➡ **radio.surf/music**

To inquire about purchasing a Limited Edition NFT of this portrait type into your Internet Browser the URL shortcut ➡ **myartnft.shop/justinhayward**

To view all available NFTs type into your Internet Browser the URL shortcut ➡ **myartnft.shop/all**

# Mötley Crue

(Total Albums Sold: 100+ Million) (Genre: Hard Rock , Glam Metal)

Mötley Crüe is an American heavy metal band formed in Los Angeles in 1981. The group was founded by bassist Nikki Sixx, drummer Tommy Lee, lead guitarist Mick Mars and lead singer Vince Neil. Mötley Crüe has sold over 100 million albums worldwide. They have also achieved seven platinum or multi-platinum certifications, nine Top 10 albums on the Billboard 200 chart (including 1989's Dr. Feelgood, which is Mötley Crüe's only album to reach number one), twenty-two Top 40 mainstream rock hits, and six Top 20 pop singles. The band experienced several short-term lineup changes in the 1990s and 2000s; these included the introduction of vocalist John Corabi (who was Neil's replacement from 1992 to 1996) and drummers Randy Castillo and Samantha Maloney, both of whom filled in for Lee following his departure from Mötley Crüe in 1999; he returned to the band in 2004.

The members of Mötley Crüe have often been noted for their hedonistic lifestyles and the androgynous personae they maintained. Following the hard rock and heavy metal origins on the band's first two albums, Too Fast for Love (1981) and Shout at the Devil (1983), the release of its third album Theatre of Pain (1985) saw Mötley Crüe joining the first wave of glam metal. The band has also been known for their elaborate live performances, which features flame thrower guitars, roller coaster drum kits, and heavy use of pyrotechnics (including lighting Nikki on fire). Mötley Crüe's most recent studio album, Saints of Los Angeles, was released on June 24, 2008. What was planned to be the band's final show took place on New Year's Eve, December 31, 2015. The concert was filmed for a theatrical and Blu-ray release in 2016. After two-and-a-half years of inactivity, Neil announced in September 2018 that Mötley Crüe had reunited and was working on new material. On March 22, 2019, the band released four new songs on the soundtrack for its Netflix biopic The Dirt, based on the band's New York Times best-selling autobiography. The soundtrack went to Number 1 on the iTunes All Genres Album Chart, Number 3 on Billboard Top Album and Digital Album sales chart, Number 10 on Billboard Top 200, and Top 10 worldwide. The autobiography returned to New York Times Best Seller list at number 6 on Nonfiction Print and number 8 on Nonfiction Combined Print & E-Book.

# Vince Neil

(Net Worth: $50 Million)(Height: 5' - 9")

Vincent Neil Wharton (born February 8, 1961) is an American musician. He is best known as the lead vocalist of heavy metal band Mötley Crüe, but he has also released material as a solo artist.

Neil was born in Hollywood, California to Shirley (née Ortiz) and Clois "Odie" Wharton. He has Mexican ancestry on his mother's side and Native American ancestry on his father's. During the 1960s, his family moved around Southern California from Inglewood to Watts, before finally settling in Glendora, attending Sunflower Intermediate School and later Royal Oak High School. As well as having an interest in music while a teenager, Neil was also interested in surfing, basketball, baseball, football and wrestling.

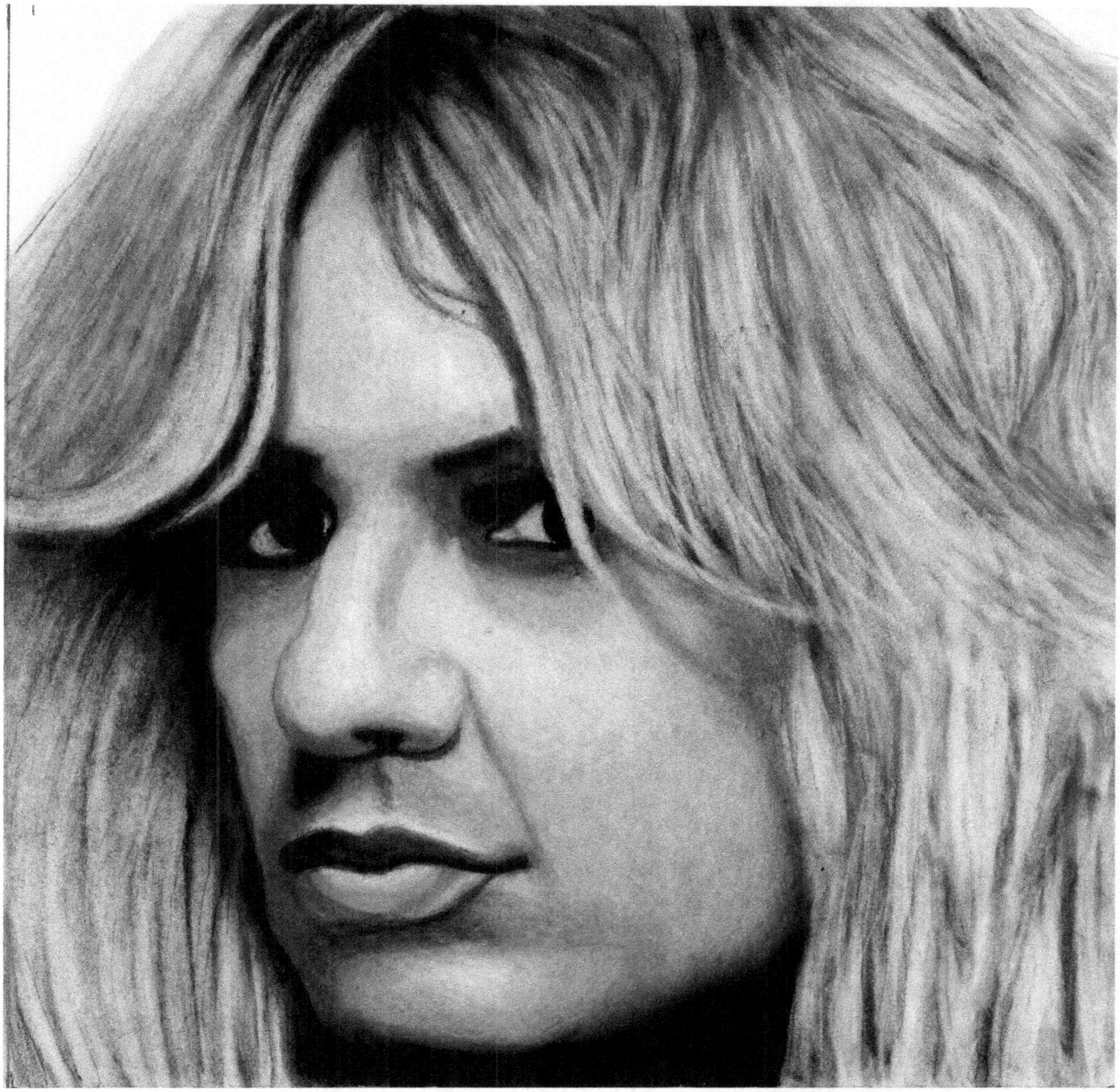

To view how this drawing was masterfully created or to purchase a Limited Edition Framed Artwork of Vince Neil type into your Internet Browser the URL shortcut ➡ **myportrait.art/vinceneil**

To listen to their Greatest Songs type into your Internet Browser the URL shortcut ➡ **radio.surf/motleycrue**

To view all channels on THE FACE OF MUSIC Internet Radio MEGA Station type into your Internet Browser the URL shortcut ➡ **radio.surf/music**

To inquire about purchasing a Limited Edtion NFT of this portrait type into your Internet Browser the URL shortcut ➡ **myartnft.shop/vinceneil**

To view all available NFTs type into your Internet Browser the URL shortcut ➡ **myartnft.shop/all**

# Motörhead

(Total Albums Sold: 15+ Million)

(Genre: Heavy Metal , Hard Rock , Speed Metal , Rock & Roll)

Motörhead were an English rock band formed in June 1975 by bassist, singer, and songwriter Ian "Lemmy" Kilmister (who was the sole constant member), guitarist Larry Wallis and drummer Lucas Fox. The band are often considered a precursor to the new wave of British heavy metal, which re-energised heavy metal in the late 1970s and early 1980s. Though several guitarists and drummers have played in Motörhead, most of their best-selling albums and singles feature the work of Phil "Philthy Animal" Taylor on drums and "Fast" Eddie Clarke on guitars.

Motörhead released 22 studio albums, 10 live recordings, 12 compilation albums, and five EPs over a career spanning 40 years. Usually a power trio, they had particular success in the early 1980s with several successful singles in the UK Top 40 chart. The albums Overkill, Bomber, Ace of Spades, and particularly the live album No Sleep 'til Hammersmith cemented Motörhead's reputation as a top-tier rock band. The band are ranked number 26 on VH1's 100 Greatest Artists of Hard Rock. As of 2016, they have sold more than 15 million albums worldwide.

Most often classified as heavy metal, Motörhead has been credited with being part of and influencing numerous musical scenes, thrash metal and speed metal especially. Lemmy, however, always insisted that they were a rock and roll band. He said that they had more in common with punk bands, but with their own unique sound, Motörhead is embraced in both punk and metal scenes. Their lyrics typically covered such topics as war, good versus evil, abuse of power, promiscuous sex, substance abuse, and, most famously, gambling, the latter theme being the focus of their hit song "Ace of Spades".

Lemmy died on 28 December 2015 from cardiac arrhythmia and congestive heart failure, after being diagnosed with prostate cancer. The day after his death, drummer Mikkey Dee and guitarist Phil Campbell both confirmed that Motörhead had disbanded. By 2018, all three members of Motörhead's classic lineup (Lemmy, Taylor and Clarke) had died.

# Lemmy Kilmister

(Net Worth: $1 Million)(Height: 5' - 10")

Ian Fraser Kilmister (24 December 1945 – 28 December 2015), better known as Lemmy, was a British singer, songwriter, and musician. He is best known as the founder, lead singer, bassist, primary songwriter and only continuous member of the British rock band Motörhead.

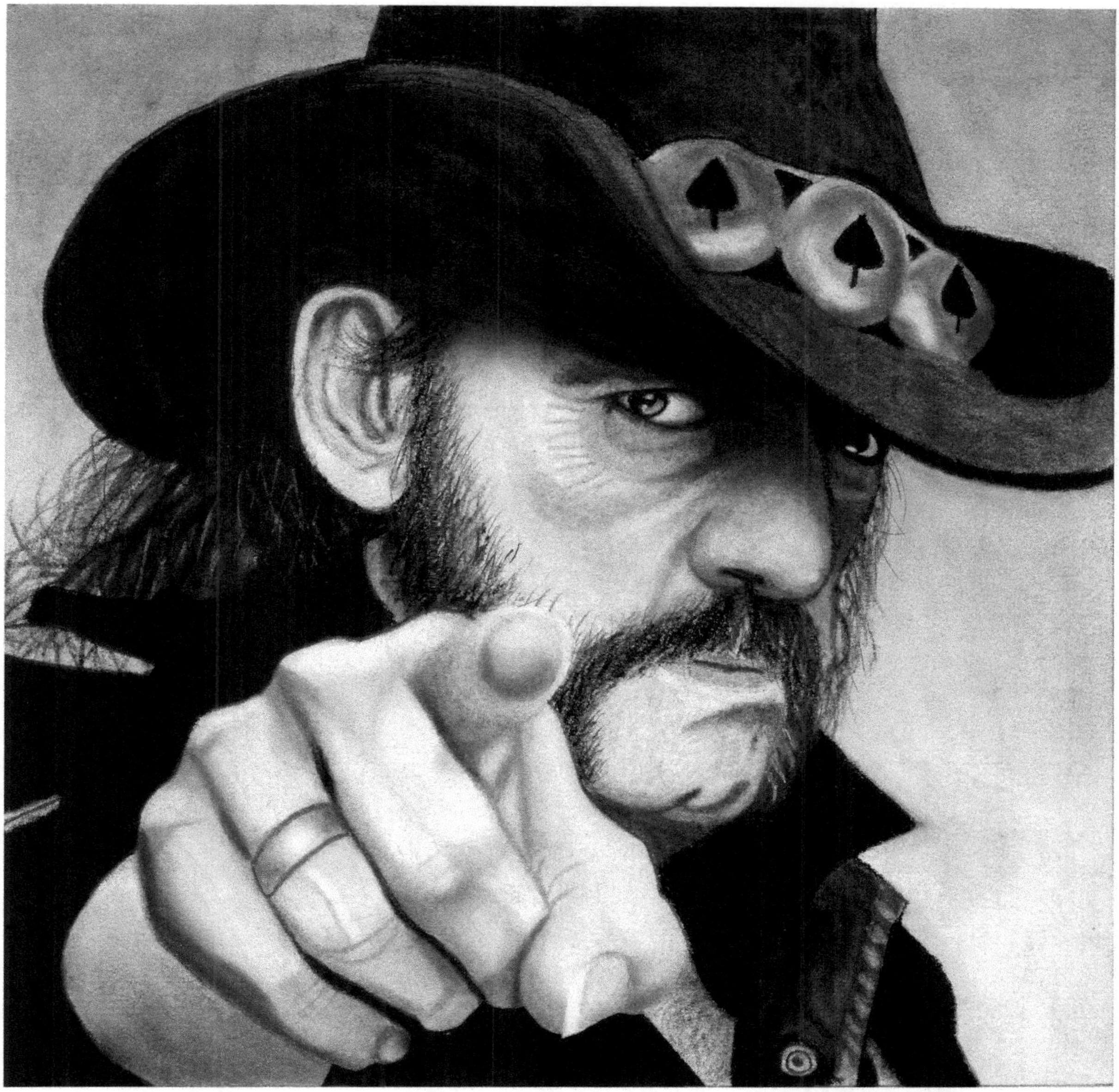

To view how this drawing was masterfully created or to purchase a Limited Edition Framed Artwork of Lemmy Kilmister type into your Internet Browser the URL shortcut ➡ **myportrait.art/lemmykilmister**

To listen to their Greatest Songs type into your Internet Browser the URL shortcut ➡ **radio.surf/motorhead**

To view all channels on THE FACE OF MUSIC Internet Radio MEGA Station type into your Internet Browser the URL shortcut ➡ **radio.surf/music**

To inquire about purchasing a Limited Edtion NFT of this portrait type into your Internet Browser the URL shortcut ➡ **myartnft.shop/lemmykilmister**

To view all available NFTs type into your Internet Browser the URL shortcut ➡ **myartnft.shop/all**

# Muddy Waters

(Net worth: $5 Million)(Total Records Sold: Millions)
(Genre: Blues)(Height: 5' - 10")

McKinley Morganfield (April 4, 1913 – April 30, 1983), known professionally as Muddy Waters, was an American blues singer-songwriter and musician who was an important figure in the post-war blues scene, and is often cited as the "father of modern Chicago blues". His style of playing has been described as "raining down Delta beatitude".

Muddy Waters grew up on Stovall Plantation near Clarksdale, Mississippi, and by age 17 was playing the guitar and the harmonica, emulating the local blues artists Son House and Robert Johnson. He was recorded in Mississippi by Alan Lomax for the Library of Congress in 1941. In 1943, he moved to Chicago to become a full-time professional musician. In 1946, he recorded his first records for Columbia Records and then for Aristocrat Records, a newly formed label run by the brothers Leonard and Phil Chess.

In the early 1950s, Muddy Waters and his band—Little Walter Jacobs on harmonica, Jimmy Rogers on guitar, Elga Edmonds (also known as Elgin Evans) on drums and Otis Spann on piano—recorded several blues classics, some with the bassist and songwriter Willie Dixon. These songs included "Hoochie Coochie Man", "I Just Want to Make Love to You" and "I'm Ready". In 1958, he traveled to England, laying the foundations of the resurgence of interest in the blues there. His performance at the Newport Jazz Festival in 1960 was recorded and released as his first live album, At Newport 1960. Muddy Waters' music has influenced various American music genres, including rock and roll and rock music.Muddy Waters's place and date of birth are not conclusively known. He stated that he was born in Rolling Fork, Mississippi, in 1915, but other evidence suggests that he was born in Jug's Corner, in neighboring Issaquena County, in 1913. In the 1930s and 1940s, before his rise to fame, the year of his birth was reported as 1913 on his marriage license, recording notes, and musicians' union card. A 1955 interview in the Chicago Defender is the earliest in which he stated 1915 as the year of his birth, and he continued to say this in interviews from that point onward. The 1920 census lists him as five years old as of March 6, 1920, suggesting that his birth year may have been 1914. The Social Security Death Index, relying on the Social Security card application submitted after his move to Chicago in the mid-1940s, lists him as being born April 4, 1913. His gravestone gives his birth year as 1915.

His grandmother, Della Grant, raised him after his mother died shortly after his birth. Grant gave him the nickname "Muddy" at an early age because he loved to play in the muddy water of nearby Deer Creek. "Waters" was added years later, as he began to play harmonica and perform locally in his early teens. The remains of the cabin on Stovall Plantation where he lived in his youth are now at the Delta Blues Museum in Clarksdale, Mississippi.He had his first introduction to music in church: "I used to belong to church. I was a good Baptist, singing in the church. So I got all of my good moaning and trembling going on for me right out of church," he recalled. By the time he was 17, he had purchased his first guitar. "I sold the last horse that we had. Made about fifteen dollars for him, gave my grandmother seven dollars and fifty cents, I kept seven-fifty and paid about two-fifty for that guitar. It was a Stella. The people ordered them from Sears-Roebuck in Chicago." He started playing his songs in joints near his hometown, mostly on a plantation owned by Colonel William Howard Stovall.

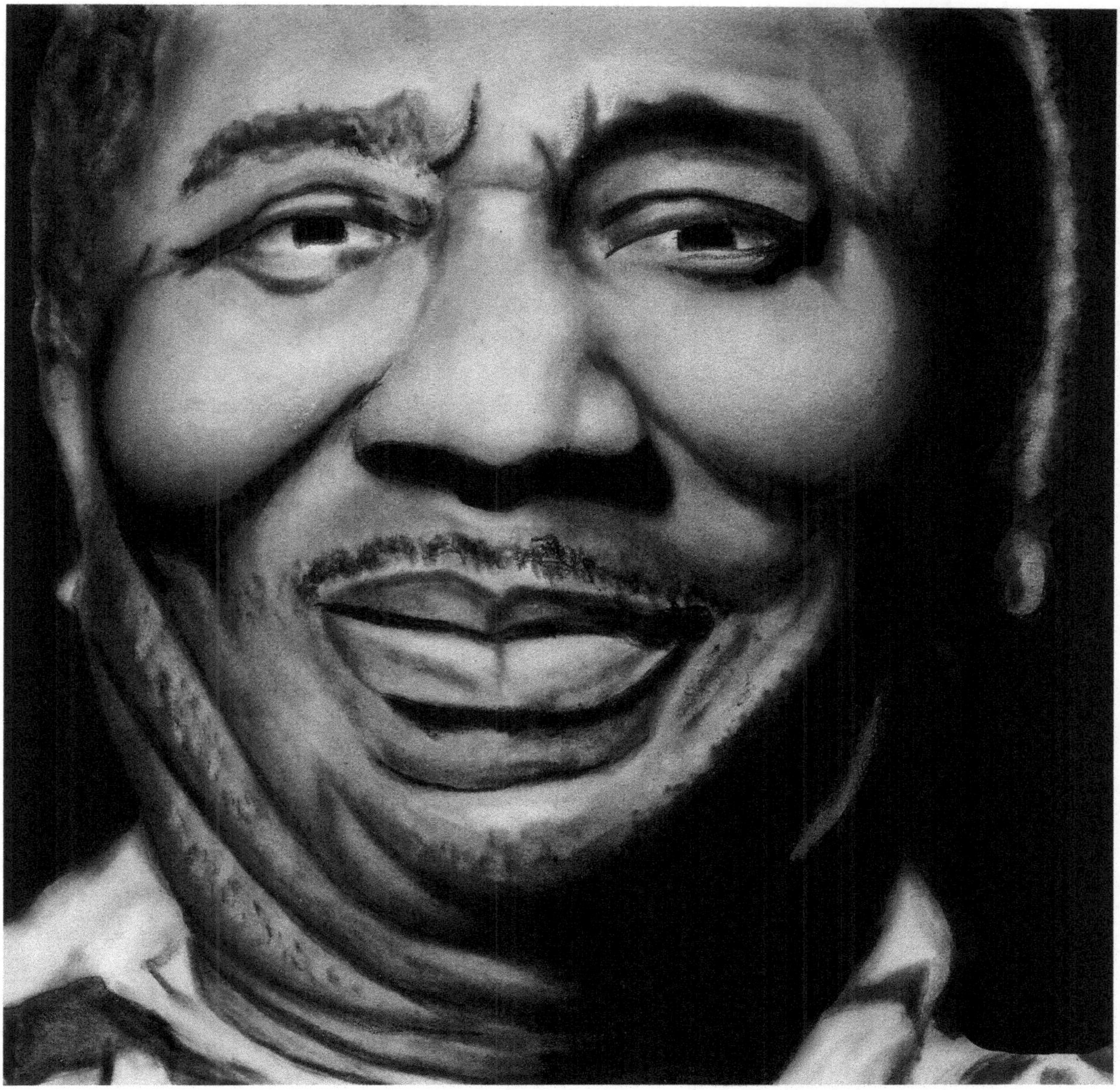

To view how this drawing was masterfully created or to purchase a Limited Edition Framed Artwork of Muddy Waters type into your Internet Browser the URL shortcut ➡ **myportrait.art/muddywaters**

To listen to his Greatest Songs type into your Internet Browser the URL shortcut ➡ **radio.surf/muddywaters**

To view all channels on THE FACE OF MUSIC Internet Radio MEGA Station type into your Internet Browser the URL shortcut ➡ **radio.surf/music**

To inquire about purchasing a Limited Edtion NFT of this portrait type into your Internet Browser the URL shortcut ➡ **myartnft.shop/muddywaters**

To view all available NFTs type into your Internet Browser the URL shortcut ➡ **myartnft.shop/all**

# N.W.A.

(Total Albums Sold: 3+ Million)(Genre: West Coast Hip-Hop , Gangsta Rap)

N.W.A (an abbreviation for Niggaz Wit Attitudes) was an American hip hop group from Compton, California. Its members were among the earliest and most significant popularizers and controversial figures of the gangsta rap subgenre, and the group is widely considered one of the greatest and most influential groups in the history of hip hop music. Active from 1987 to 1991, the rap group endured controversy owing to its music's explicit lyrics which many viewed as being misogynist, as well as to its glorification of drugs and crime. The group was subsequently banned from many mainstream American radio stations. In spite of this, the group has sold over 10 million units in the United States alone. Drawing on its members' own experiences of racism and excessive policing, the group made inherently political music. The group's members were known for their deep hatred of the police system, which has sparked much controversy over the years.

- Continued on Page 433 -.

# Dr. Dre

(Net Worth: $800 Million)(Height: 6' - 1/4")

Andre Romelle Young (born February 18, 1965), known professionally as Dr. Dre, is an American rapper, record producer, audio engineer, record executive, and entrepreneur. He is the founder and CEO of Aftermath Entertainment and Beats Electronics, and was previously co-owner and President of Death Row Records. Dr. Dre began his career as a member of the World Class Wreckin' Cru in 1985 and later found fame with the gangsta rap group N.W.A. The group popularized explicit lyrics in hip hop to detail the violence of street life. During the early 1990s, Dre was credited as a key figure in the crafting and popularization of West Coast G-funk, a subgenre of hip hop characterized by a synthesizer foundation and slow, heavy beats. Dre's solo debut studio album The Chronic (1992), released under Death Row Records, made him one of the best-selling American music artists of 1993. It earned him a Grammy Award for Best Rap Solo Performance for the single "Let Me Ride", as well as several accolades for the single "Nuthin' but a 'G' Thang". That year, he produced Death Row labelmate Snoop Doggy Dogg's debut album Doggystyle and mentored producers such as his step-brother Warren G (leading to the multi-platinum debut Regulate...G Funk Era in 1994) and Snoop Dogg's cousin Daz Dillinger (leading to the double-platinum debut Dogg Food by Tha Dogg Pound in 1995). In 1996, Dr. Dre left Death Row Records to establish his own label, Aftermath Entertainment. He produced a compilation album, Dr. Dre Presents the Aftermath, in 1996, and released a solo album, 2001, in 1999. During the 2000s, Dre focused on producing other artists, occasionally contributing vocals. He signed Eminem in 1998 and 50 Cent in 2002, and co-produced their albums. He has produced albums for and overseen the careers of many other rappers, including 2Pac, the D.O.C., Snoop Dogg, Xzibit, Knoc-turn'al, the Game, Kendrick Lamar, and Anderson Paak. Dre has also had acting roles in movies such as Set It Off, The Wash and Training Day. He has won six Grammy Awards, including Producer of the Year, Non-Classical. Rolling Stone ranked him number 56 on the list of 100 Greatest Artists of All Time. He was the second-richest figure in hip hop as of 2018 with an estimated net worth of $800 million.

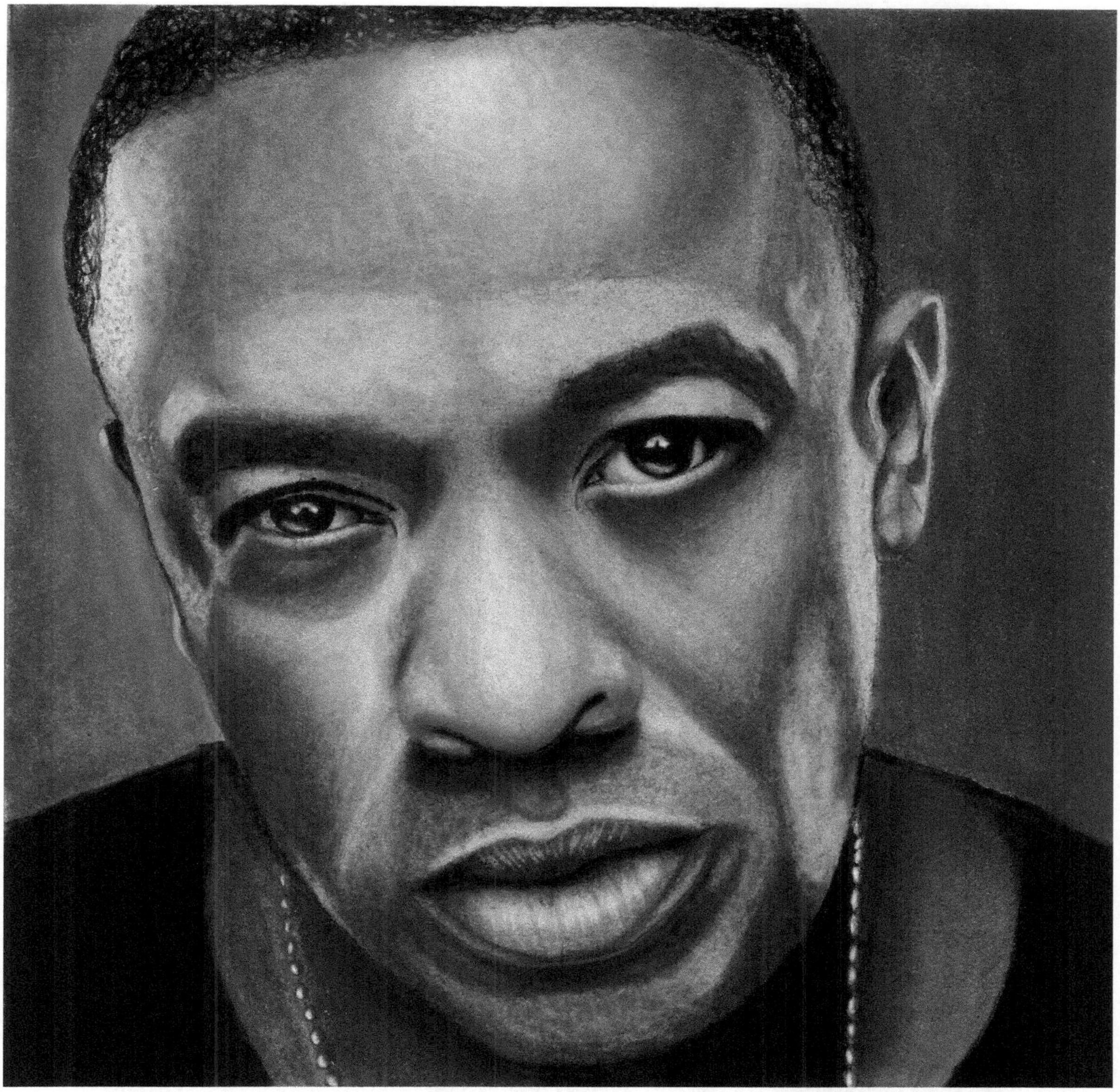

To view how this drawing was masterfully created or to purchase a Limited Edition Framed Artwork of Dr. Dre type into your Internet Broser the URL shortcut ➡ **myportrait.art/drdre**

To listen to N.W.A.'s Greatest Songs type into your Internet Browser the URL shortcut ➡ **radio.surf/nwa**

To listen to Dr. Dre's Greatest Songs type into your Internet Browser the URL shortcut ➡ **radio.surf/drdre**

To view all channels on THE FACE OF MUSIC Internet Radion MEGA Station type into your Internet Browser the URL shortcut ➡ **radio.surf/music**

To inquire about purchasing a Limited Ection NFT of this portrait type into your Internet Browser the URL shortcut ➡ **myartnft.shop/drdre**

To view all available NFTs type into your Internet Browser the URL shortcut ➡ **myartnft.shop/all**

# N.W.A.

(Total Albums Sold: 3+ Million)(Genre: West Coast Hip-Hop , Gangsta Rap)

The original lineup, formed in early 1987, consisted of Arabian Prince, Dr. Dre, Eazy-E, and Ice Cube, with DJ Yella and MC Ren joining later that year. They released their first compilation album as a group in 1987 called N.W.A. and the Posse, which peaked at No. 39 on Billboard magazine's Top R&B/Hip-Hop Albums chart. Arabian Prince left shortly after the release of N.W.A's debut studio album Straight Outta Compton in 1988, with Ice Cube following suit in December 1989. Eazy-E, Ice Cube, MC Ren and Dr. Dre would later become platinum-selling solo artists in their own right in the 1990s. The group's debut album marked the beginning of the new gangsta rap era as the production and social commentary in their lyrics were revolutionary within the genre. N.W.A's second studio album, Niggaz4Life, was the first hardcore rap album to reach number one on the Billboard 200 sales charts. Rolling Stone ranked N.W.A at number 83 on its list of the "100 Greatest Artists of All Time". In 2016, the group was inducted into the Rock and Roll Hall of Fame, following three previous nominations.

- Continued on Page 435 -

# Eazy-E

(Net Worth: $8 Million)(Height: 5' - 2 1/2")

Eric Lynn Wright (September 7, 1964 – March 26, 1995), known professionally as Eazy-E, was an American rapper, songwriter, record producer, and entrepreneur who propelled West Coast rap and gangsta rap by leading the group N.W.A and its label, Ruthless Records, pushing the boundaries of lyrical content.

Born and raised in Compton, California, Wright had several legal troubles before founding Ruthless in 1987. After a short solo career with frequent collaboration with Ice Cube and Dr. Dre, they joined, forming N.W.A, later that year.

N.W.A's debut studio album, Straight Outta Compton, was released in 1988. Controversial upon release, it is now ranked among the greatest and most influential albums. The group released its third and final studio album, Niggaz4Life, in 1991, and soon after disbanded.

During N.W.A's splintering, largely by disputes over money, Eazy-E became embroiled in bitter rivalries with Ice Cube and Dr. Dre, who had departed for solo careers in 1989 and 1991, respectively. Resuming his solo career, Eazy-E released two EPs. Yet he remained more significant behind the scenes, signing and nationally debuting the rap group Bone Thugs-N-Harmony from 1993 to 1994.

In 1995, Eazy-E was suddenly hospitalized and diagnosed with AIDS and died due to its complications. He is often referred to as the "godfather of gangsta rap".

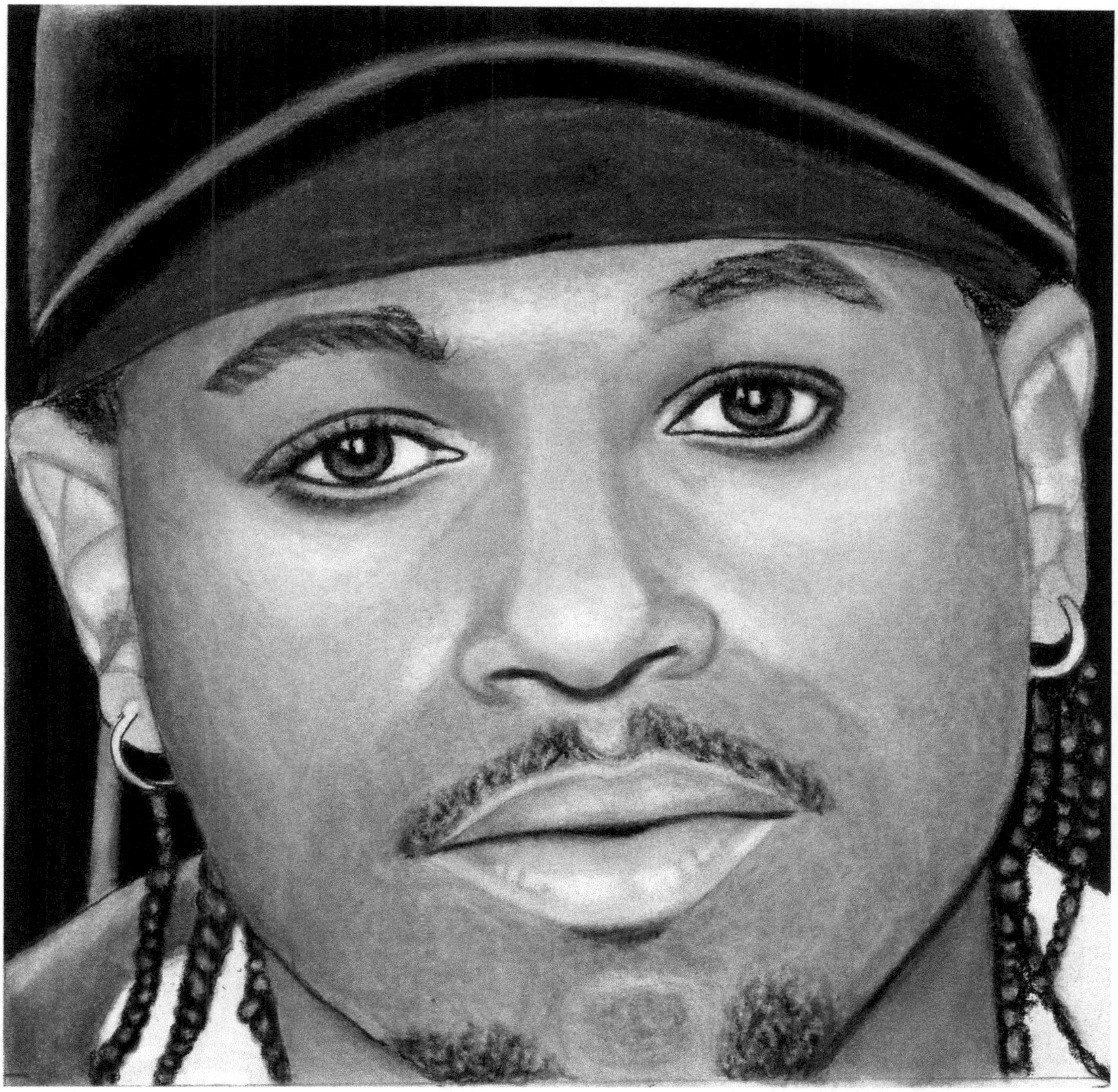

To view how this drawing was masterfully created or to purchase a Limited Edition Framed Artwork of Easy - E type into your Internet Broser the URL shortcut ➡ **myportrait.art/eazye**

To listen to N.W.A.'s Greatest Songs type into your Internet Browser the URL shortcut ➡ **radio.surf/nwa**

To listen to Easy - E's Greatest Songs type into your Internet Browser the URL shortcut ➡ **radio.surf/eazye**

To view all channels on THE FACE OF MUSIC Internet Radion MEGA Station type into your Internet Browser the URL shortcut ➡ **radio.surf/music**

To inquire about purchasing a Limited Edtion NFT of this portrait type into your Internet Browser the URL shortcut ➡ **myartnft.shop/eazye**

To view all available NFTs type into your Internet Browser the URL shortcut ➡ **myartnft.shop/all**

# N.W.A.

(Total Albums Sold: 3+ Million)(Genre: West Coast Hip-Hop , Gangsta Rap)

N.W.A was assembled by Compton-based Eazy-E, who co-founded Ruthless Records with Jerry Heller. Eazy-E sought an introduction to Steve Yano. Although Yano initially rebuffed him, he was impressed by Eazy-E's persistence, and arranged a meeting with Dr. Dre. Initially, N.W.A consisted of Eazy-E and Dr. Dre. Together with fellow producer Arabian Prince, Ice Cube was added to the roster after he had started out as a rapper for the group C.I.A. Dre would later bring DJ Yella on board as well. Dre and Yella were both formerly members of the World Class Wreckin' Cru as DJs and producers. Ruthless released the single "Panic Zone" in 1987 with Macola Records, which was later included on the compilation album N.W.A. and the Posse. N.W.A was still in its developing stages, and is only credited on three of the eleven tracks, notably the uncharacteristic record "Panic Zone", "8-Ball", and "Dopeman", which marked the first collaboration of Arabian Prince, DJ Yella, Dr. Dre, and Ice Cube. Mexican rapper Krazy-Dee co-wrote "Panic Zone", which was originally called "Hispanic Zone", but the title was later changed when Dr. Dre advised Krazy-Dee that the word "hispanic" would hinder sales. Also included was Eazy-E's solo track "Boyz-n-the-Hood".

# Ice Cube

(Net Worth: $160 Million)(Height: 5' - 7")

O'Shea Jackson (born June 15, 1969), better known by his stage name Ice Cube, is an American rapper, actor, and filmmaker. His lyrics on N.W.A's 1988 album Straight Outta Compton contributed to gangsta rap's widespread popularity, and his political rap solo albums of 1990 and 1991 were critically and commercially successful. He has also had an active film career since the early 1990s. A native of Los Angeles, Jackson formed his first rap group, called C.I.A., in 1986. In 1987, with Eazy-E and Dr. Dre, he formed the pioneering gangsta rap group N.W.A. As its lead rapper, he wrote some of Dre's and most of Eazy's lyrics on Straight Outta Compton, a landmark album that shaped West Coast hip hop's early identity and helped differentiate it from East Coast rap. N.W.A was also known for their violent lyrics, threatening to attack abusive police and innocent civilians alike, which stirred controversy. After a monetary dispute over the group's management by Eazy-E and Jerry Heller, Cube left N.W.A in late 1989, teaming with New York artists and launching a solo rap career. His first two solo albums, AmeriKKKa's Most Wanted (1990) and Death Certificate (1991), were critically acclaimed.Ice Cube entered cinema by playing Doughboy in director John Singleton's feature debut Boyz n the Hood, a 1991 drama named after a 1987 rap song that Cube wrote. Cube also cowrote and starred in the 1995 comedy film Friday; "coarse and ribald", it premised a successful franchise and reshaped his persona into a friendly movie star. His directorial debut was the 1998 film The Player's Club. By 2020, his acting roles included about 40 films, among them the 1999 war comedy Three Kings, family comedies like the Barbershop series, and buddy cop comedies 21 Jump Street, 22 Jump Street, and Ride Along. He was an executive producer of many of these films, as well as of the 2015 biopic Straight Outta Compton.

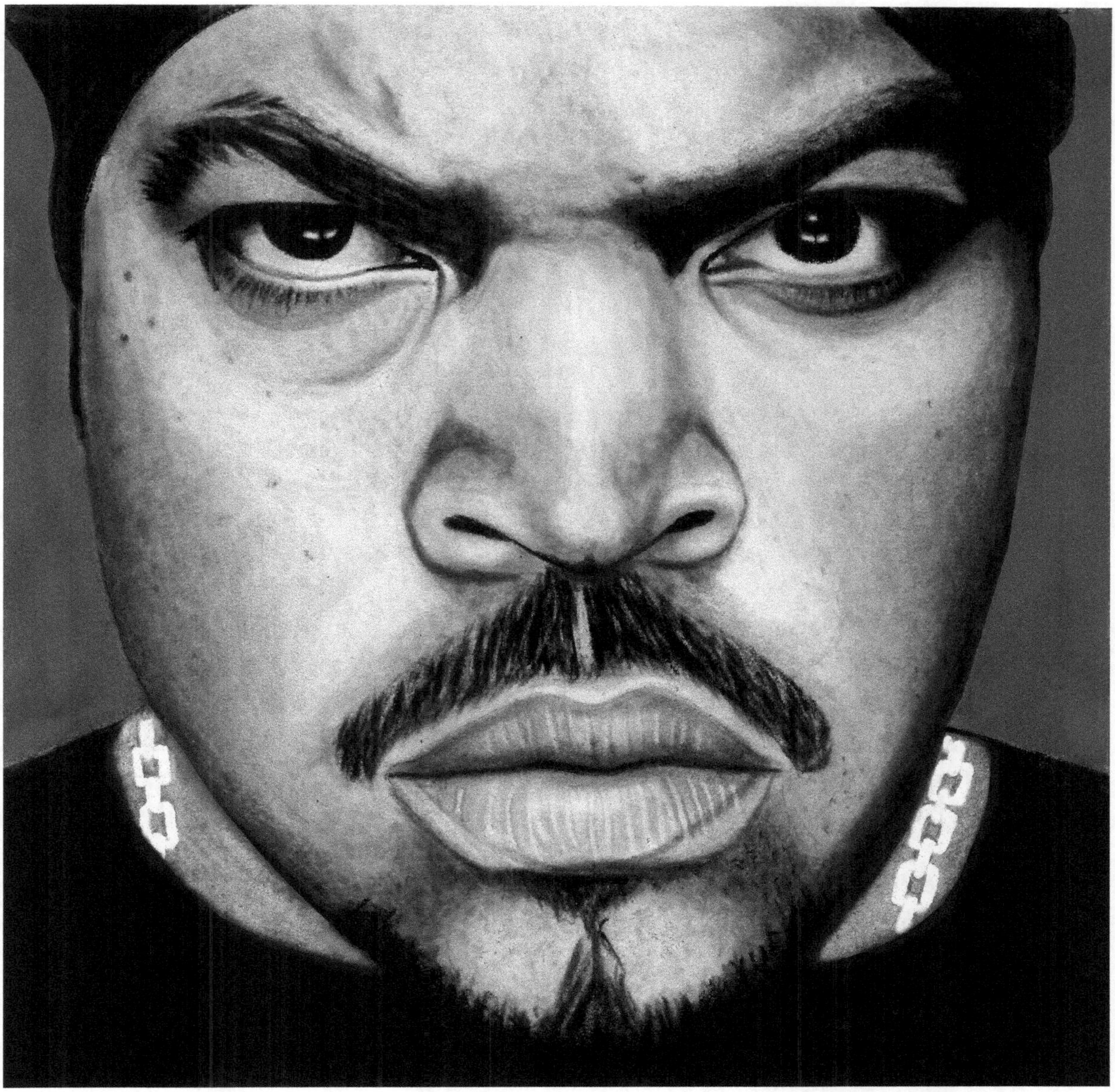

To view how this drawing was masterfully created or to purchase a Limited Edition Framed Artwork of Ice Cube type into your Internet Broser the URL shortcut ➡ **myportrait.art/icecube**

To listen to N.W.A.'s Greatest Songs type into your Internet Browser the URL shortcut ➡ **radio.surf/nwa**

To listen to Ice Cube's Greatest Songs type into your Internet Browser the URL shortcut ➡ **radio.surf/icecube**

To view all channels on THE FACE OF MUSIC Internet Radion MEGA Station type into your Internet Browser the URL shortcut ➡ **radio.surf/music**

To inquire about purchasing a Limited Edtion NFT of this portrait type into your Internet Browser the URL shortcut ➡ **myartnft.shop/icecube**

To view all available NFTs type into your Internet Browser the URL shortcut ➡ **myartnft.shop/all**

# Nas

(Net worth: $70 Million)(Total Records Sold: 15+ Million)
(Genre: East Coast Hip-Hop , Jazz Rap , Gangsta Rap)(Height: 5' - 9")

Nasir bin Olu Dara Jones (born September 14, 1973), better known by his stage name Nas (/nɑːz/), is an American rapper, songwriter, and entrepreneur. Rooted in the New York rap scene, he is regarded as one of the greatest rappers of all-time. Nas has released twelve studio albums since 1994, seven of which are certified platinum and multi-platinum in the U.S.

The son of jazz musician Olu Dara, Jones's musical career began in 1989 as he adopted the moniker of "Nasty Nas" and recorded demos for Large Professor. He was a featured artist on Main Source's "Live at the Barbeque" (1991), also produced by Large Professor. Nas's debut album Illmatic (1994) received universal acclaim upon release, and is considered to be one the greatest hip hop albums of all-time; in 2021, the album was inducted into the Library of Congress's National Recording Registry. His second album It Was Written (1996) debuted atop the Billboard 200 and charted for four consecutive weeks; the album, along with its single "If I Ruled the World (Imagine That)" (featuring Lauryn Hill), catapulted Nas into international success. Nas's albums I Am (1998) and Nastradamus (1999) were criticized as inconsistent and too commercially-oriented, and critics and fans feared that his output was declining in quality.

From 2001 to 2005, Nas was involved in a highly publicized feud with Jay-Z, popularized by the diss track "Ether". It was this feud, along with Nas's albums Stillmatic (2001), God's Son (2002), and the double album Street's Disciple (2004), that helped restore his critical standing. After quashing the feud, Nas signed to Jay-Z's Def Jam Recordings in 2006 and went in a more provocative, politicized direction with the albums Hip Hop Is Dead (2006) and his untitled 9th studio album (2008). In 2010, Nas released Distant Relatives, a collaboration album with Damian Marley, donating all royalties to charities active in Africa. His 11th studio album, Life Is Good (2012), was nominated for Best Rap Album at the 55th Annual Grammy Awards. After receiving thirteen nominations, his 13th studio album, King's Disease (2020), won him his first Grammy for Best Rap Album at the 63rd Annual Grammy Awards.

In 2006, MTV ranked Nas fifth on their list of "The Greatest MCs of All Time". In 2012, The Source ranked him second on their list of the "Top 50 Lyricists of All Time". In 2013, Nas was ranked 4th on MTV's "Hottest MCs in the Game" list. About.com ranked him first on their list of the "50 Greatest MCs of All Time" in 2014, and a year later, Nas was featured on the "10 Best Rappers of All Time" list by Billboard. He is also an entrepreneur through his own record label; he serves as associate publisher of Mass Appeal magazine and the co-founder of Mass Appeal Records.

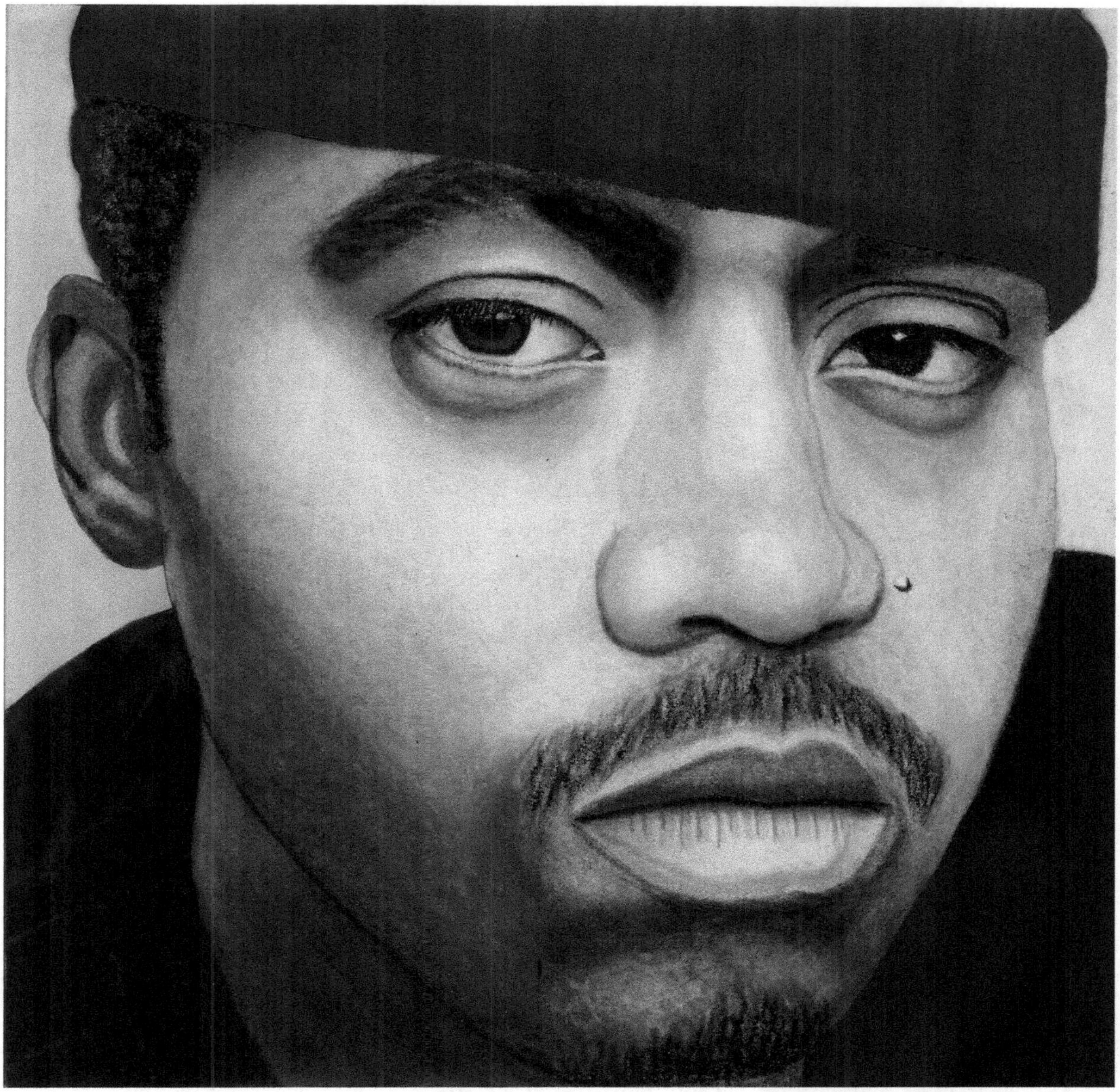

To view how this drawing was masterfully created or to purchase a Limited Edition Framed Artwork of Nas type into your Internet Browser the URL shortcut ➡ **myportrait.art/nas**

To listen to his Greatest Songs type into your Internet Browser the URL shortcut ➡ **radio.surf/nas**

To view all channels on THE FACE OF MUSIC Internet Radio MEGA Station type into your Internet Browser the URL shortcut ➡ **radio.surf/music**

To inquire about purchasing a Limited Edtion NFT of this portrait type into your Internet Browser the URL shortcut ➡ **myartnft.shop/nas**

To view all available NFTs type into your Internet Browser the URL shortcut ➡ **myartnft.shop/all**

# Nat King Cole

(Net worth: $27 Million)(Total Records Sold: 50 Million)
(Genre: R&B , Jazz)(Height: 6' - 1/4")

Nathaniel Adams Coles (March 17, 1919 – February 15, 1965), known professionally as Nat King Cole, was an American singer, jazz pianist, and actor. He recorded over 100 songs that became hits on the pop charts. His trio was the model for small jazz ensembles that followed. Cole also acted in films and on television and performed on Broadway. He was the first African-American man to host an American television series. He was the father of singer-songwriter Natalie Cole (1950–2015).

Nathaniel Adams Coles was born in Montgomery, Alabama, on March 17, 1919. He had three brothers: Eddie (1910–1970), Ike (1927–2001), and Freddy (1931–2020), and a half-sister, Joyce Coles. Each of the Cole brothers pursued careers in music. When Nat King Cole was four years old, the family moved to Chicago, Illinois, where his father, Edward Coles, became a Baptist minister.

Cole learned to play the organ from his mother, Perlina Coles, the church organist. His first performance was "Yes! We Have No Bananas" at the age of four. He began formal lessons at 12, learning jazz, gospel, and classical music on piano "from Johann Sebastian Bach to Sergei Rachmaninoff." As a youth, he joined the news delivery boys' "Bud Billiken Club" band for The Chicago Defender.

The Cole family moved to the Bronzeville neighborhood of Chicago, where he attended Wendell Phillips Academy High School, the school Sam Cooke attended a few years later. He participated in Walter Dyett's music program at DuSable High School. He would sneak out of the house to visit clubs, sitting outside to hear Louis Armstrong, Earl Hines, and Jimmie Noone.

When he was 15, Cole dropped out of high school to pursue a music career. After his brother Eddie, a bassist, came home from touring with Noble Sissle, they formed a sextet and recorded two singles for Decca in 1936 as Eddie Cole's Swingsters. They performed in a revival of the musical Shuffle Along. Nat Cole went on tour with the musical. In 1937, he married Nadine Robinson, who was a member of the cast. After the show ended in Los Angeles, Cole and Nadine settled there while he looked for work. He led a big band, then found work playing piano in nightclubs. When a club owner asked him to form a band, he hired bassist Wesley Prince and guitarist Oscar Moore. They called themselves the King Cole Swingsters after the nursery rhyme in which "Old King Cole was a merry old soul." They changed their name to the King Cole Trio before making radio transcriptions and recording for small labels.

Cole recorded "Sweet Lorraine" in 1940, and it became his first hit. According to legend, his career as a vocalist started when a drunken bar patron demanded that he sing the song. Cole said that this fabricated story sounded good, so he didn't argue with it. In fact, there was a customer one night who demanded that he sing, but because it was a song Cole didn't know, he sang "Sweet Lorraine" instead. As people heard Cole's vocal talent, they requested more vocal songs, and he obliged.

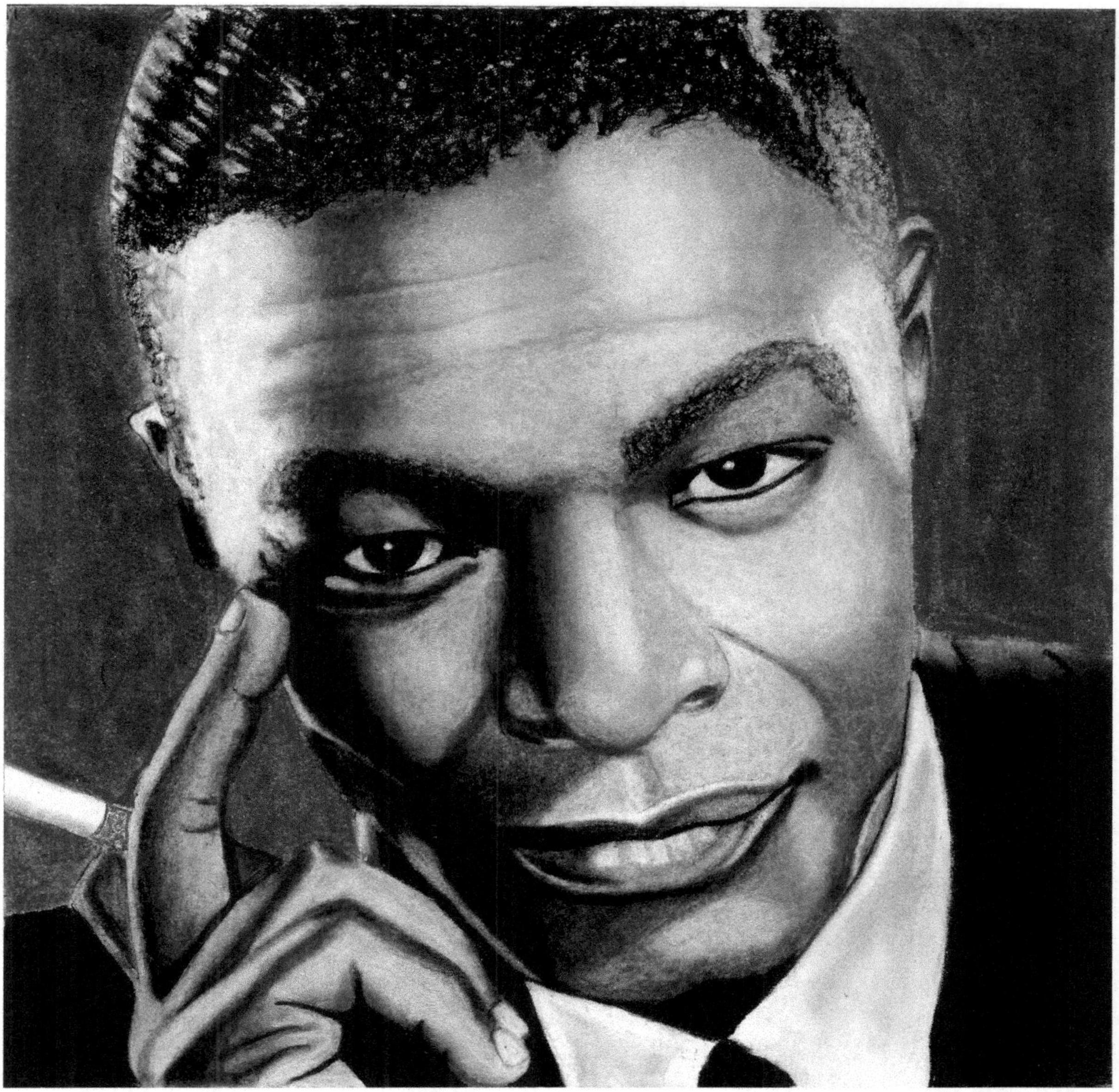

To view how this drawing was masterfully created or to purchase a Limited Edition Framed Artwork of Nat King Cole type into your Internet Browser the URL shortcut ➡ **myportrait.art/natkingcole**

To listen to his Greatest Songs type into your Internet Browser the URL shortcut ➡ **radio.surf/natkingcole**

To view all channels on THE FACE OF MUSIC Internet Radio MEGA Station type into your Internet Browser the URL shortcut ➡ **radio.surf/music**

To inquire about purchasing a Limited Edtion NFT of this portrait type into your Internet Browser the URL shortcut ➡ **myartnft.shop/natkingcole**

To view all available NFTs type into your Internet Browser the URL shortcut ➡ **myartnft.shop/all**

# Neil Diamond

(Net worth: $200 Million)(Total Records Sold: 100+ Million)
(Genre: Pop , Rock , Soft Rock , Folk , Country)(Height: 6' - 0")

Neil Leslie Diamond (born January 24, 1941) is an American singer-songwriter and actor. He has sold more than 100 million records worldwide, making him one of the best-selling musicians of all time. He has had ten No. 1 singles on the Hot 100 and Adult Contemporary charts: "Cracklin' Rosie", "Song Sung Blue", "Longfellow Serenade", "I've Been This Way Before", "If You Know What I Mean", "Desirée", "You Don't Bring Me Flowers", "America", "Yesterday's Songs", and "Heartlight". 38 songs by Diamond have featured in the Top 10 on the Billboard Adult Contemporary charts.

Diamond was inducted into the Songwriters Hall of Fame in 1984 and into the Rock and Roll Hall of Fame in 2011, and he received the Sammy Cahn Lifetime Achievement Award in 2000. In 2011, he was an honoree at the Kennedy Center Honors, and he received the Grammy Lifetime Achievement Award in 2018.

In 2019, his 1969 signature song "Sweet Caroline" was selected by the Library of Congress for preservation in the National Recording Registry for being "culturally, historically, or aesthetically significant".

Diamond was born in Brooklyn, New York, to a Jewish family descended from Russian and Polish immigrants. His parents were Rose (née Rapoport) and Akeeba "Kieve" Diamond, a dry-goods merchant. He grew up in several homes in Brooklyn, having also spent four years in Cheyenne, Wyoming, where his father was stationed in the army. In Brooklyn he attended Erasmus Hall High School and was a member of the Freshman Chorus and Choral Club, along with classmate Barbra Streisand::155 Diamond recalled they were not close friends at the time: "We were two poor kids in Brooklyn. We hung out in the front of Erasmus High and smoked cigarettes." After his family moved, he then attended Abraham Lincoln High School, and was a member of the fencing team. Also on the team was his best friend, future Olympic fencer Herb Cohen.

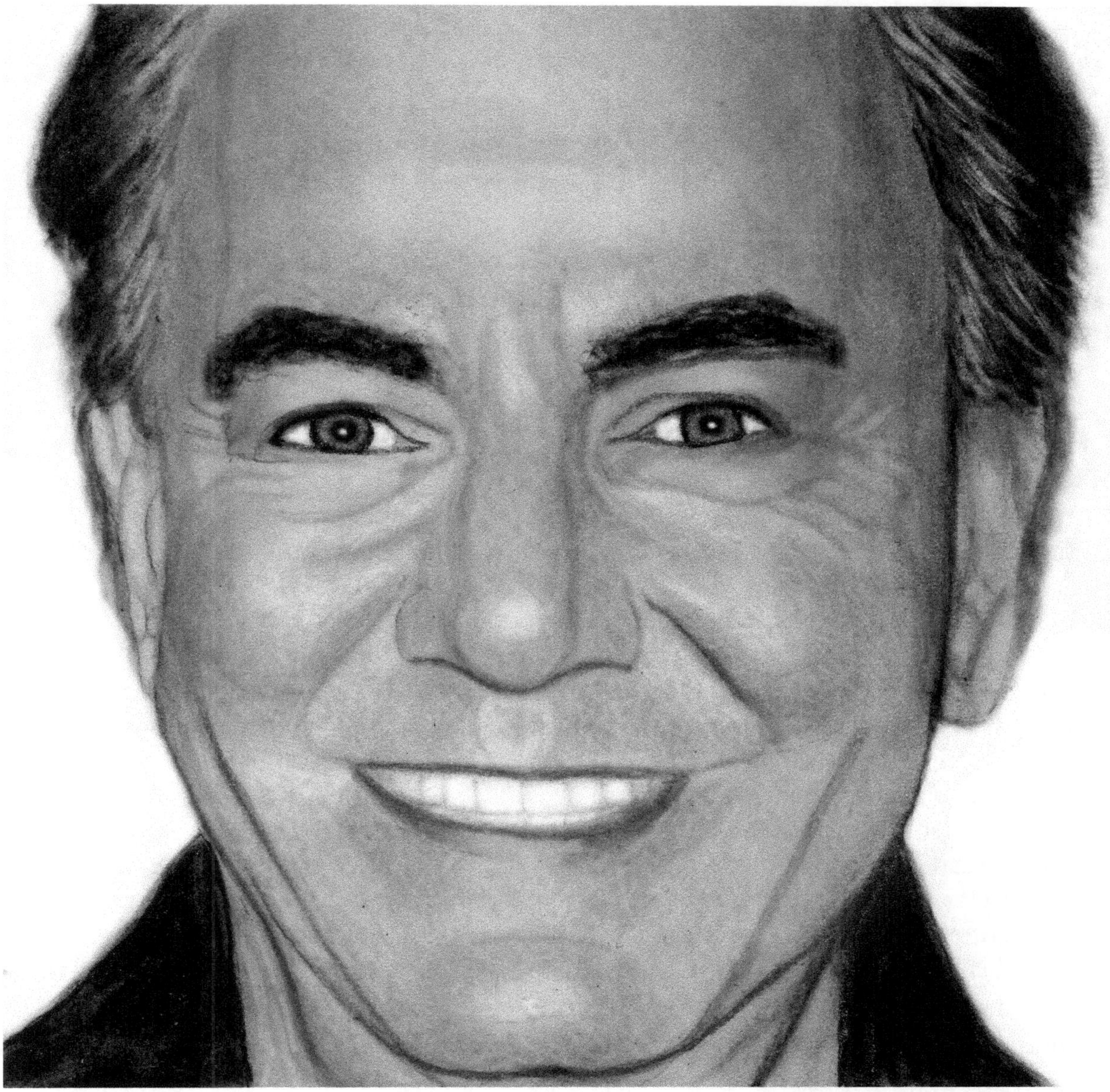

To view how this drawing was masterfully created or to purchase a Limited Edition Framed Artwork of Neil Diamond type into your Internet Browser the URL shortcut ➡ **myportrait.art/neildiamond**

To listen to his Greatest Songs type into your Internet Browser the URL shortcut ➡ **radio.surf/neildiamond**

To view all channels on THE FACE OF MUSIC Internet Radio MEGA Station type into your Internet Browser the URL shortcut ➡ **radio.surf/music**

To inquire about purchasing a Limited Edition NFT of this portrait type into your Internet Browser the URL shortcut ➡ **myartnft.shop/neildiamond**

To view all available NFTs type into your Internet Browser the URL shortcut ➡ **myartnft.shop/all**

# Neil Sedaka

(Net worth: $100 Million)(Total Records Sold: 40 Million)
(Genre: Pop , Rock)(Height: 5' - 5")

Neil Sedaka (/sɛdækə/ born March 13, 1939) is an American pop singer, pianist, composer and record producer. Since his music career began in 1957 as a short-lived founding member of the Tokens, he has sold millions of records as a performer and has written or co-written over 500 songs for himself and others, collaborating mostly with lyricists Howard "Howie" Greenfield and Phil Cody.

His first single for RCA Victor, "The Diary", was inspired by Connie Francis, one of Sedaka and Greenfield's most important clients, while the three were taking a temporary break during their idea-making for a new song. Francis was writing in her diary, Sedaka asked if he could read it, and Connie said no. After Little Anthony and the Imperials passed on the song, Sedaka recorded it himself, and his debut single hit the Top 15 on the Billboard Hot 100, peaking at No. 14 in 1958.

His second single, a novelty tune titled "I Go Ape", just missed the Top 40, peaking at No. 42 but it became a more successful single in the United Kingdom with a No. 9. The third single, "Crying My Heart Out for You", was a commercial failure, missing the Hot 100 entirely, peaking at No. 111 but it reached No. 6 on the pop charts in Italy. RCA Victor had lost money on "I Go Ape" and "Crying My Heart Out For You" and was ready to drop Sedaka from their label; Sedaka feared he was headed for one-hit wonder status. Sedaka and his manager, Al Nevins, persuaded the RCA executives to give him one more chance.Sedaka then bought the three biggest hit singles of the time and listened to them repeatedly, studying the song structure, chord progressions, lyrics and harmonies before writing his next songs. "Oh! Carol" delivered Sedaka his first domestic Top 10 hit, reaching No. 9 on the Hot 100 in 1959 and going to No. 1 on the Italian pop charts in 1960, giving Sedaka his first No. 1 ranking. In the UK, the song spent a total of 17 weeks in the top 40, peaking at No. 3 (4 weeks). In addition, the B-side, "One Way Ticket", reached No. 1 on the pop charts in Japan. Sedaka had dated Carole King when he was still at high school, which gave him the idea to use her name in the song. Gerry Goffin – King's husband – took the tune, and wrote the playful response "Oh! Neil", which King recorded and released as an unsuccessful single the same year. Thus, this was the only time the melody of the song was used by a popular artist and a future sensation around the same time.After establishing himself in 1958, Sedaka wrote many more hits from 1960 to 1962. His flow of Top 30 hits during this period included: "Stairway to Heaven" (No. 9, 1960); "You Mean Everything to Me" (No. 17, 1960); "Run, Samson, Run" (No. 27, 1960); "Calendar Girl" (No. 4, 1961; also reached No. 1 on the Japanese and Canadian pop charts); "Little Devil" (No. 11, 1961); "Happy Birthday Sweet Sixteen" (No. 6, 1961); his signature song, "Breaking Up Is Hard To Do" (No. 1, two weeks: August 11 and 18, 1962); and "Next Door to an Angel" (No. 5, 1962). Singles not making the Top 30 during this period included "Sweet Little You" (No. 59, 1961) and "King of Clowns" (No. 45, 1962). RCA Victor issued four LPs of his works in the United States and Great Britain during this period, and also produced Scopitone and Cinebox videos of "Calendar Girl" in 1961, "Breaking Up Is Hard To Do" in 1962, and "The Dreamer" in 1963. His second LP was instead an album mostly of old standards. He made regular appearances on such TV programs as American Bandstand and Shindig! during this period.

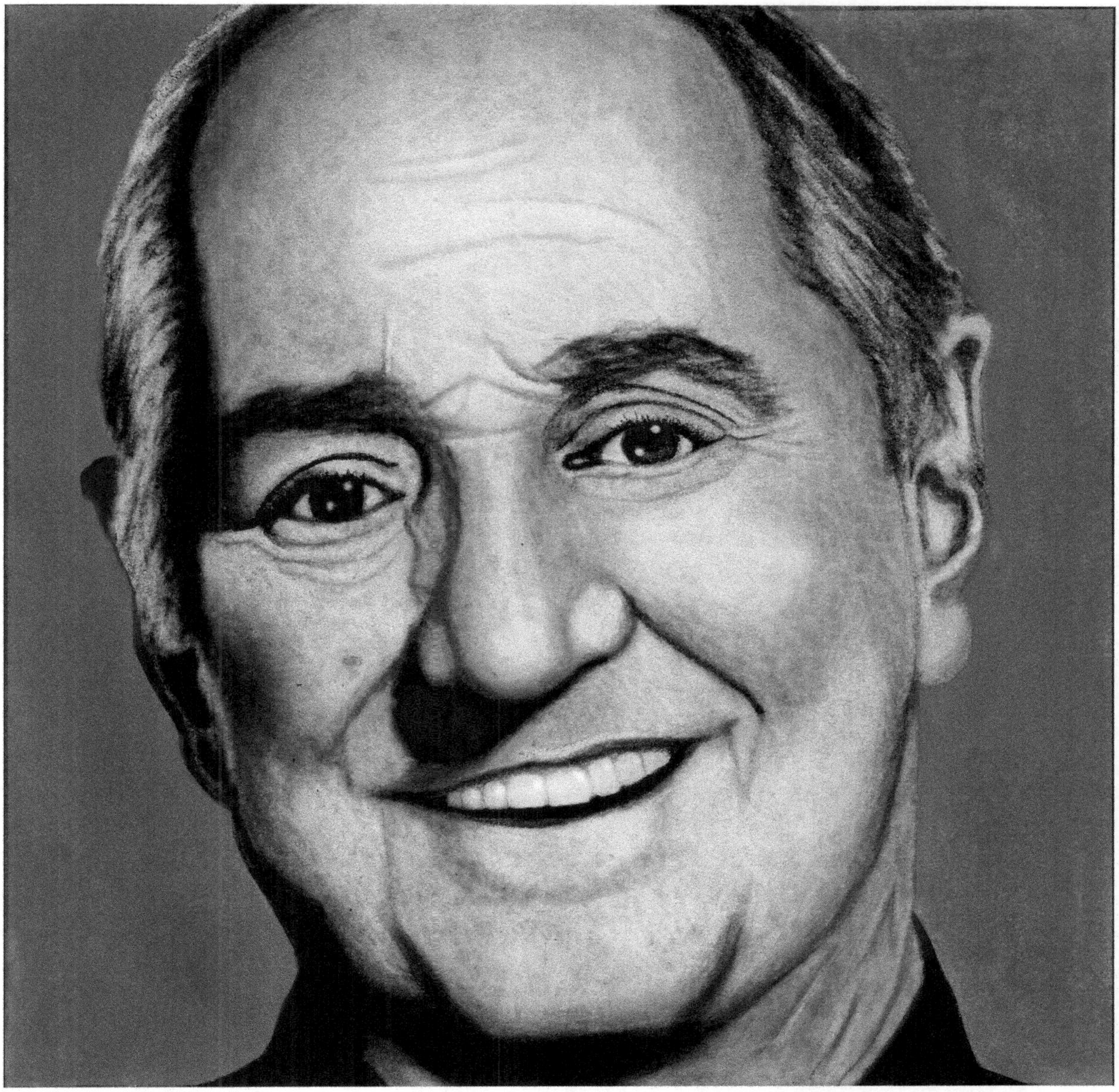

To view how this drawing was masterfully created or to purchase a Limited Edition Framed Artwork of Neil Sedaka type into your Internet Browser the URL shortcut ➡ **myportrait.art/neilsedaka**

To listen to his Greatest Songs type into your Internet Browser the URL shortcut ➡ **radio.surf/neilsedaka**

To view all channels on THE FACE OF MUSIC Internet Radio MEGA Station type into your Internet Browser the URL shortcut ➡ **radio.surf/music**

To inquire about purchasing a Limited Edtion NFT of this portrait type into your Internet Browser the URL shortcut ➡ **myartnft.shop/neilsedaka**

To view all available NFTs type into your Internet Browser the URL shortcut ➡ **myartnft.shop/all**

# Neil Young

(Net worth: $200 Million)(Total Records Sold: Multi-Millions)

(Genre: Rock, Folk Rock, Hard Rock, Country Rock, Psychedelic Rock, Blues Rock)(Height: 6' - 0")

Neil Percival Young OC OM (born November 12, 1945) is a Canadian-American singer-songwriter, musician, and activist. After embarking on a music career in the 1960s, he moved to Los Angeles, joining Buffalo Springfield with Stephen Stills, Richie Furay and others. Since the beginning of his solo career with his backing band Crazy Horse, Young has released many critically acclaimed and important albums, such as After the Gold Rush, Everybody Knows This Is Nowhere, and Harvest.

Young has received several Grammy and Juno Awards. The Rock and Roll Hall of Fame inducted him twice: in 1995 as a solo artist and in 1997 as a member of Buffalo Springfield. In 2000, Rolling Stone named Young the 34th greatest rock 'n roll artist. His guitar work, deeply personal lyrics and signature tenor singing voice define his long career. He also plays piano and harmonica on many albums, which frequently combine folk, rock, country and other musical styles. His often distorted electric guitar playing, especially with Crazy Horse, earned him the nickname "Godfather of Grunge" and led to his 1995 album Mirror Ball with Pearl Jam. More recently he has been backed by Promise of the Real. His 21 albums and singles have been certified Gold and Platinum in U.S by RIAA certification.Young directed (or co-directed) films using the pseudonym Bernard Shakey, including Journey Through the Past (1973), Rust Never Sleeps (1979), Human Highway (1982), Greendale (2003), and CSNY/Déjà Vu (2008). He also contributed to the soundtracks of the films Philadelphia (1993) and Dead Man (1995).Young has lived in California since the 1960s but retains Canadian citizenship. He was awarded the Order of Manitoba on July 14, 2006, and was made an Officer of the Order of Canada on December 30, 2009. He became a United States citizen, taking dual citizenship, on January 22, 2020.Neil Young was born on November 12, 1945, in Toronto, Canada. His father, Scott Alexander Young (1918–2005), was a journalist and sportswriter who also wrote fiction. His mother, Edna Blow Ragland "Rassy" Young (1918–1990) was a member of the Daughters of the American Revolution. Although Canadian, his mother had American and French ancestry. Young's parents married in 1940 in Winnipeg, Manitoba, and their first son, Robert "Bob" Young, was born in 1942.Shortly after Young's birth in 1945, his family moved to rural Omemee, Ontario, which Young later described fondly as a "sleepy little place". Young suffered from polio in 1952 during the last major outbreak of the disease in Ontario After his recovery, the Young family vacationed in Florida. During that period, Young briefly attended Faulkner Elementary School in New Smyrna Beach, Florida. In 1952, upon returning to Canada, Young moved from Omemee to Winnipeg for a year, before relocating to Toronto (1957–1960) and Pickering (1956). While in Toronto, Young attended the high school Lawrence Park Collegiate Institute. He was a freshman at the school in 1959.During the mid-1950s, Young listened to rock 'n roll, rockabilly, doo-wop, R&B, country, and western pop. He idolized Elvis Presley and later referred to him in a number of his songs. Other early musical influences included Link Wray, Jimmy Gilmer and the Fireballs, The Ventures, Cliff Richard and the Shadows, Chuck Berry, Hank Marvin, Little Richard, Fats Domino, The Chantels, The Monotones, Ronnie Self, the Fleetwoods, Jerry Lee Lewis, Johnny Cash, Roy Orbison and Gogi Grant.

In January of 2021 Hipgnosis Songs Fund purchased 50 percent of the rights to Neil Young's entire back catalog in a deal that's said to be worth $150 million, the BBC reports. There are nearly 1,200 entries in the prolific Young's cache of songs.

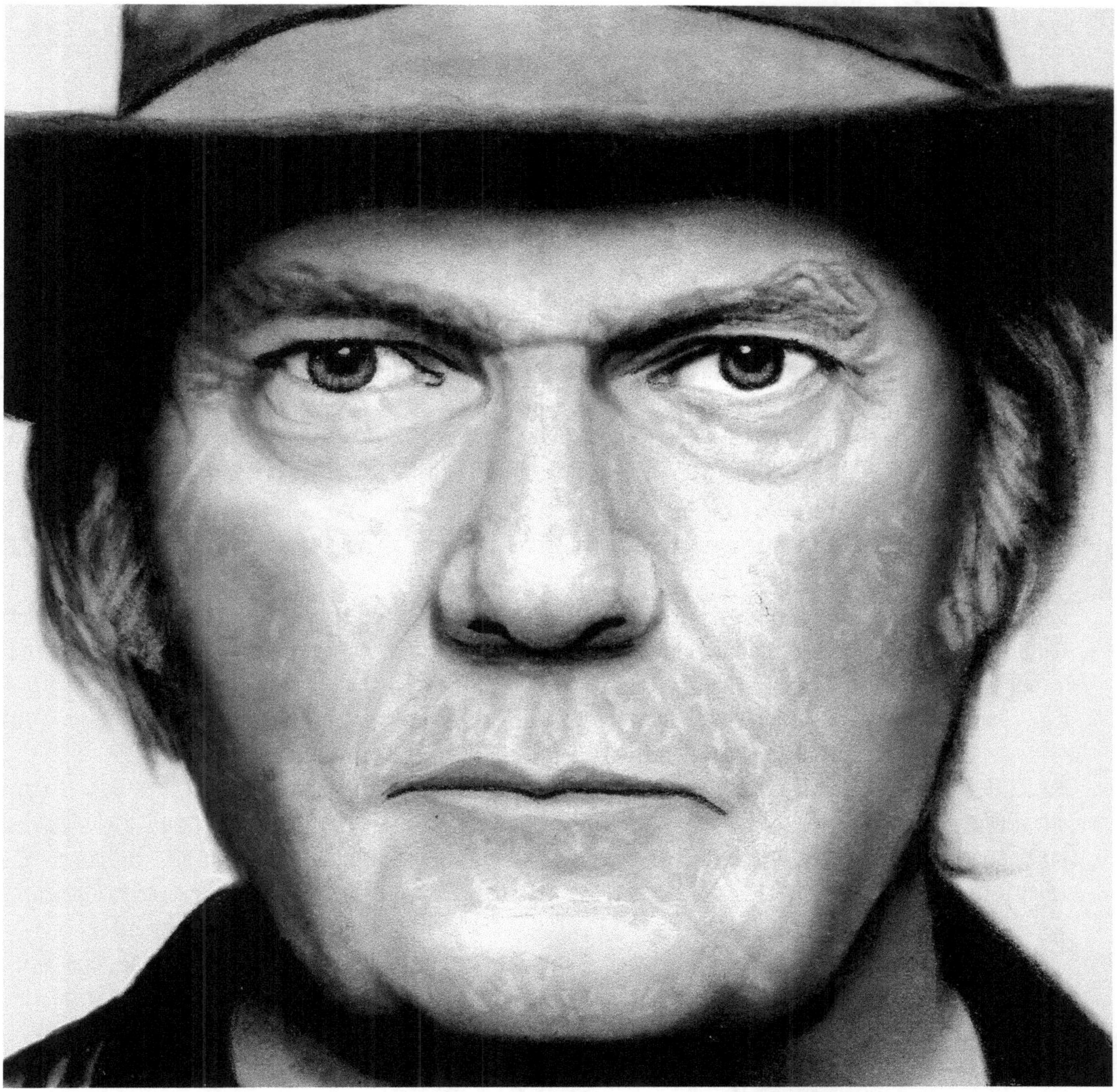

To view how this drawing was masterfully created or to purchase a Limited Edition Framed Artwork of Neil Young type into your Internet Browser the URL shortcut ➡ **myportrait.art/neilyoung**

To listen to his Greatest Songs type into your Internet Browser the URL shortcut ➡ **radio.surf/neilyoung**

To view all channels on THE FACE OF MUSIC Internet Radio MEGA Station type into your Internet Browser the URL shortcut ➡ **radio.surf/music**

To inquire about purchasing a Limited Edtion NFT of this portrait type into your Internet Browser the URL shortcut ➡ **myartnft.shop/neilyoung**

To view all available NFTs type into your Internet Browser the URL shortcut ➡ **myartnft.shop/all**

# Nickelback

(Total Albums Sold: 50 Million)(Genre: Hard Rock , Pop Rock)

Nickelback is a Canadian rock band formed in 1995 in Hanna, Alberta. It is composed of guitarist and lead vocalist Chad Kroeger, guitarist, keyboardist and backing vocalist Ryan Peake, bassist Mike Kroeger, and drummer Daniel Adair. It went through several drummer changes between 1995 and 2005, achieving its current lineup when Adair replaced Ryan Vikedal.

Nickelback is one of the most commercially successful Canadian rock bands, having sold more than 50 million albums worldwide. In 2009, Billboard ranked it the most successful rock group of that decade: "How You Remind Me" was the best-selling rock song and the fourth-best overall. The band ranked at No. 7 on the Billboard top artist of the decade list, with four albums among the publication's top albums of the decade.

The band signed with Roadrunner Records in 1999 and re-released its once-independent album The State. This album was commercially successful, as was its follow-up, Silver Side Up, in 2001. The band then released its biggest hit, "How You Remind Me", a No. 1 on the Billboard and Canadian Singles Charts. The fourth album, The Long Road, was released in 2003 and spawned five singles, including Canadian No. 1 "Someday", which also reached No. 7 on the Billboard Hot 100.

In 2005, the band's best-selling album to date, All the Right Reasons, produced three top-ten and five top-twenty singles on the Billboard Hot 100, including "Photograph", "Far Away", and "Rockstar". Dark Horse sold well in 2008, producing eight singles, one cracking the top ten on the Billboard Hot 100 and two in the top twenty. In 2011, the seventh album, Here and Now, topped the charts. The eighth, No Fixed Address, was released in 2014, followed by Feed the Machine in 2017.

Nickelback is based in Vancouver, British Columbia. It originally published through EMI Canada, before signing a global distribution deal with Roadrunner Records. For Here and Now, it left EMI Canada for Universal Music Canada.

# Chad Kroeger

(Net Worth: $80 Million)(Height: 6' - 1")

Chad Robert Kroeger (born November 15, 1974) is a Canadian singer, songwriter, musician, and producer. He is best known as the lead vocalist and guitarist of rock band Nickelback. In addition to his work with Nickelback, Kroeger has been involved with a variety of collaborations, appearing as a guest musician in several songs and has contributed in both production and songwriting. He has co-written several songs for other artists and films.

Kroeger was born Chad Robert Turton in Hanna, Alberta. His maternal grandfather, politician Henry Kroeger, was born in Moscow to a Mennonite family of German descent. After his father left the family when he was two, he started going by his mother's maiden name of Kroeger. He learned to play the guitar at age 13.

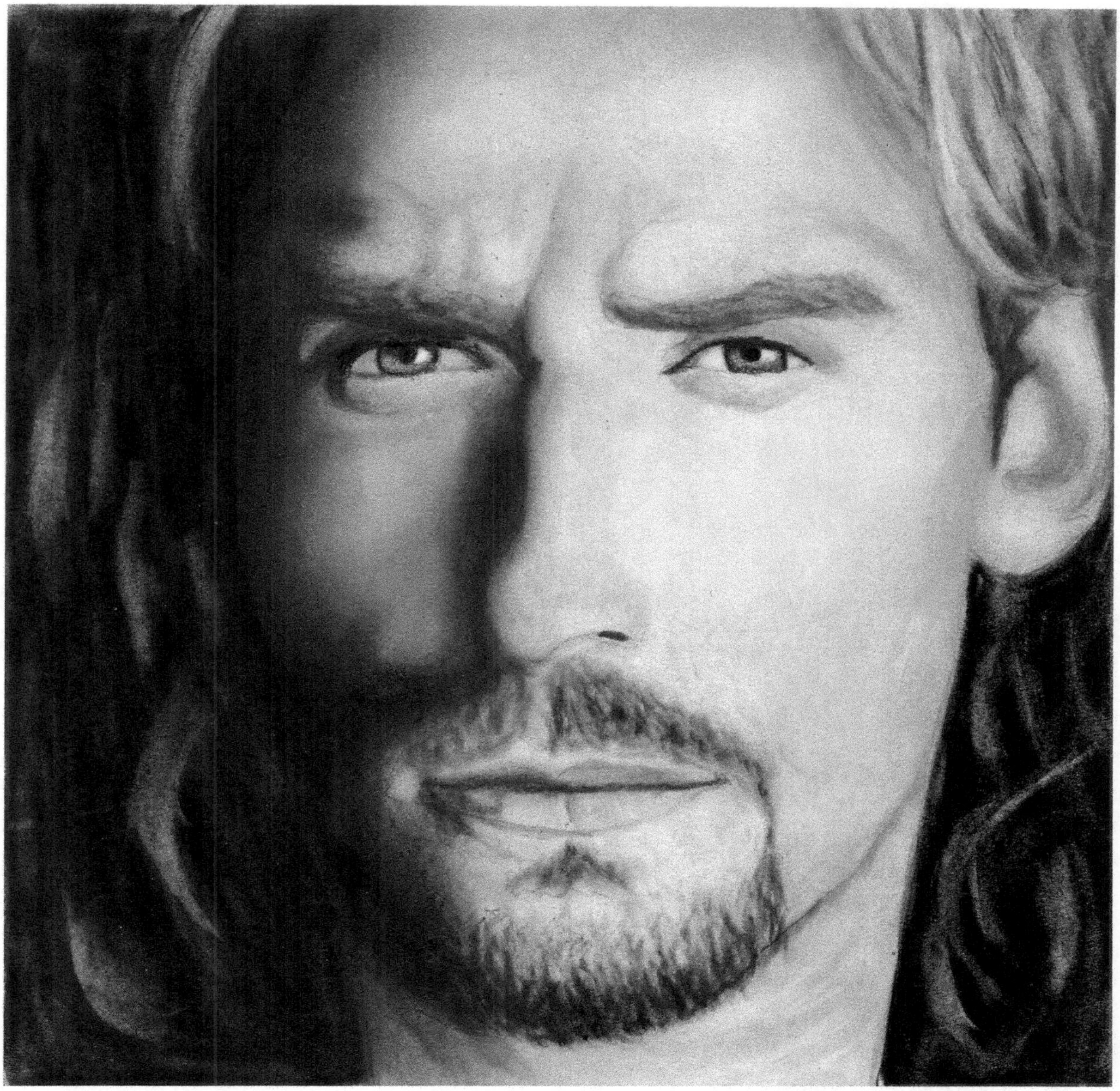

To view how this drawing was masterfully created or to purchase a Limited Edition Framed Artwork of Chad kroeger type into your Internet Browser the URL shortcut ➡ **myportrait.art/chadkroeger**

To listen to their Greatest Songs type into your Internet Browser the URL shortcut ➡ **radio.surf/nickelback**

To view all channels on THE FACE OF MUSIC Internet Radio MEGA Station type into your Internet Browser the URL shortcut ➡ **radio.surf/music**

To inquire about purchasing a Limited Edtion NFT of this portrait type into your Internet Browser the URL shortcut ➡ **myartnft.shop/chadkroeger**

To view all available NFTs type into your Internet Browser the URL shortcut ➡ **myartnft.shop/all**

# Nine Inch Nails

(Total Albums Sold: 20+ Million)(Genre: Industrial Rock)

Nine Inch Nails, commonly abbreviated as NIN and stylized as NIИ, is an American Industrial Rock band formed in 1988 in Cleveland, Ohio. Singer, songwriter, multi-instrumentalist, and producer Trent Reznor was the only permanent member of the band until the official addition of English musician Atticus Ross in 2016. The band's debut album, Pretty Hate Machine (1989), was released via TVT Records. After feuding with TVT about how to promote the album, Reznor signed with Interscope Records and released the EP Broken (1992). The following Nine Inch Nails albums, The Downward Spiral (1994) and The Fragile (1999), were released to critical acclaim and commercial success. Following a hiatus, Nine Inch Nails resumed touring in 2005 and released their fourth album, With Teeth (2005). Following the release of Year Zero (2007), Reznor left Interscope after a feud. Nine Inch Nails continued touring and independently released Ghosts I–IV (2008) and The Slip (2008) before a second hiatus. Their eighth album, Hesitation Marks (2013), was followed by a trilogy consisting of the EPs Not the Actual Events (2016) and Add Violence (2017) and their ninth album Bad Witch (2018). In 2020, Nine Inch Nails released two further installments in the Ghosts series, Ghosts V: Together and Ghosts VI: Locusts.When touring, Reznor typically assembles a live band to perform with him under the Nine Inch Nails name. Not including sporadic band hiatuses, this live band has varied over the decades, with the most recent lineup consisting of Robin Finck (who initially joined in 1994), Alessandro Cortini (who initially joined in 2005), and Ilan Rubin (who initially joined in 2009) alongside Reznor and Ross. The band's concerts are noted for their extensive use of thematic visual elements, complex special effects, and elaborate lighting; songs are often rearranged to fit any given performance, and melodies or lyrics of songs that are not scheduled to be performed are sometimes assimilated into other songs.++Nine Inch Nails has sold over 20 million records and have been nominated for 13 Grammy Awards, winning for the songs "Wish" in 1992 and "Happiness in Slavery" in 1996. Time magazine named Reznor one of its most influential people in 1997, while Spin magazine once described him as "the most vital artist in music". In 2004, Rolling Stone placed Nine Inch Nails at No. 94 on its list of the 100 greatest artists of all time. Nine Inch Nails were nominated for induction into the Rock and Roll Hall of Fame in 2014, their first year of eligibility; they were nominated again in 2015 and 2020, with the latter resulting in an induction.

# Trent Reznor

(Net Worth: $80 Million)(Height: 5' - 7")

Michael Trent Reznor (born May 17, 1965) is an American musician, singer, songwriter, record producer, and composer. Reznor serves as the lead vocalist, multi-instrumentalist, and principal songwriter of the Industrial Rock band Nine Inch Nails, which he founded in 1988 and of which he was the sole official member until 2016.

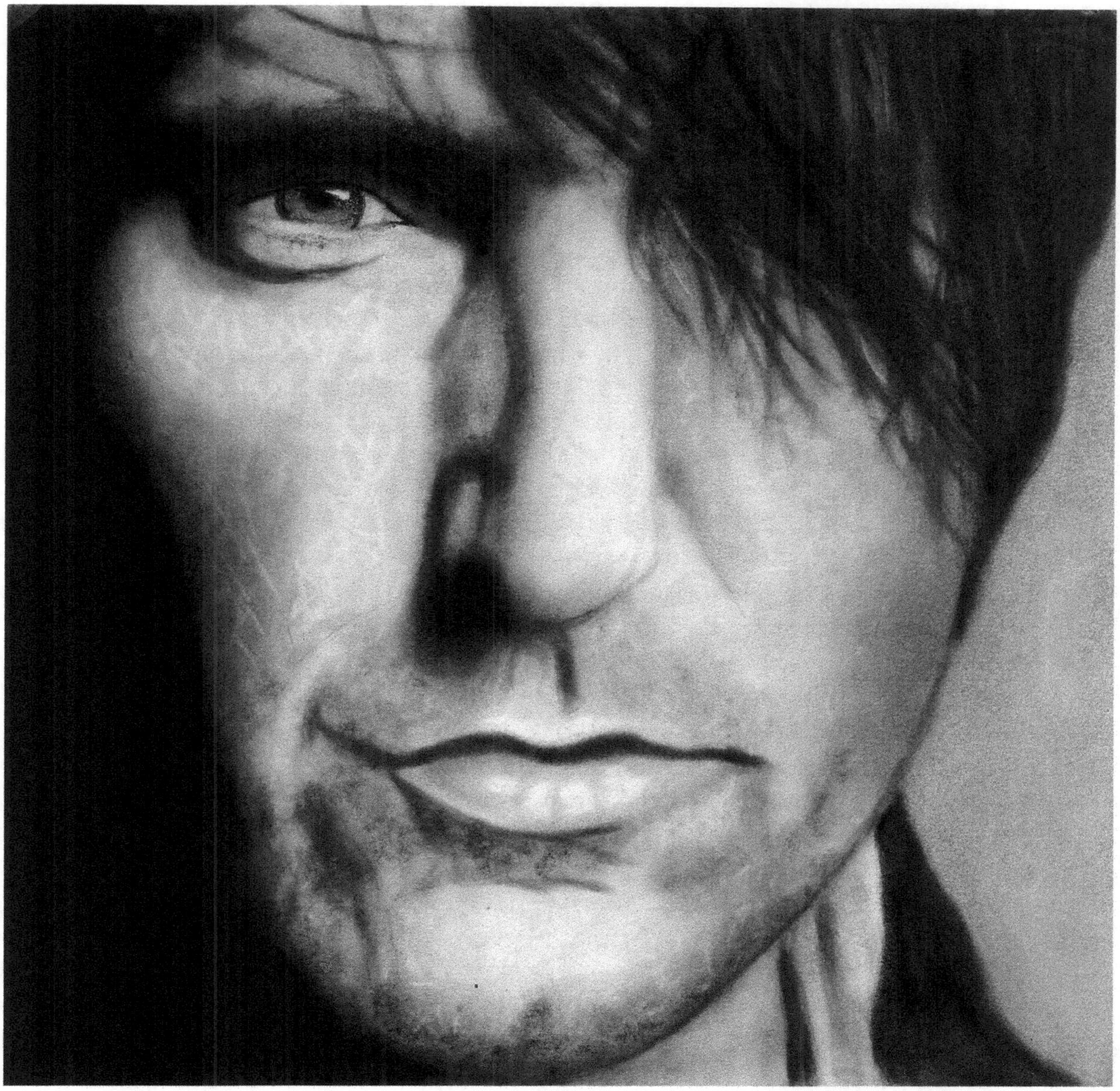

To view how this drawing was masterfully created or to purchase a Limited Edition Framed Artwork of Trent Reznor type into your Internet Browser the URL shortcut ➡ **myportrait.art/trentreznor**

To listen to their Greatest Songs type into your Internet Browser the URL shortcut ➡ **radio.surf/nineinchnails**

To view all channels on THE FACE OF MUSIC Internet Radio MEGA Station type into your Internet Browser the URL shortcut ➡ **radio.surf/music**

To inquire about purchasing a Limited Edtion NFT of this portrait type into your Internet Browser the URL shortcut ➡ **myartnft.shop/trentreznor**

To view all available NFTs type into your Internet Browser the URL shortcut ➡ **myartnft.shop/all**

# Nirvana

(Total Albums Sold: 75+ Million)(Genre: Grunge, Alternative Rock)

Nirvana was an American rock band formed in Aberdeen, Washington in 1987. Founded by lead singer-songwriter and guitarist Kurt Cobain and bassist Krist Novoselic, the band went through a succession of drummers before recruiting Dave Grohl in 1990. Nirvana's success popularized alternative rock, and they were often referenced as the figurehead band of Generation X. Their music maintains a popular following and continues to influence modern rock and roll culture.

In the late 1980s, Nirvana established itself as part of the Seattle grunge scene, releasing its first album, Bleach, for the independent record label Sub Pop in 1989. They developed a sound that relied on dynamic contrasts, often between quiet verses and loud, heavy choruses. After signing to major label DGC Records in 1991, Nirvana found unexpected mainstream success with "Smells Like Teen Spirit", the first single from their landmark second album Nevermind (1991). A cultural phenomenon of the 1990s, Nevermind was certified Diamond by the RIAA and is credited for ending the dominance of hair metal.

Characterized by their punk aesthetic, Nirvana's fusion of pop melodies with noise, combined with their themes of abjection and social alienation, brought them global popularity. Following extensive tours and the 1992 compilation album Incesticide and EP Hormoaning, the band released their abrasive and less mainstream sounding third studio album, In Utero (1993). The album topped both the US and UK album charts, and was acclaimed by critics. Nirvana disbanded following Cobain's suicide in April 1994. Various posthumous releases have been overseen by Novoselic, Grohl, and Cobain's widow Courtney Love. The posthumous live album MTV Unplugged in New York (1994) won Best Alternative Music Performance at the 1996 Grammy Awards.By 2009, Nirvana record sales were over 75 million worldwide, making them one of the best-selling bands of all time. During their three years as a mainstream act, Nirvana received an American Music Award, Brit Award and Grammy Award, as well as seven MTV Video Music Awards and two NME Awards. They achieved five number-one hits on the Billboard Alternative Songs chart and four number-one albums on the Billboard 200. In 2004, Rolling Stone named Nirvana among the 100 greatest artists of all time. They were inducted into the Rock and Roll Hall of Fame in their first year of eligibility in 2014.

# Kurt Cobain

(Net Worth: $50 Million)(Height: 5' - 9")

Kurt Donald Cobain (February 20, 1967 – April 5, 1994) was an American singer-songwriter and musician, best known as the guitarist, primary songwriter and frontman of the rock band Nirvana. Through his angst-fueled songwriting and anti-establishment persona, Cobain's compositions widened the thematic conventions of mainstream rock music. He was often heralded as a spokesman of Generation X and is considered to be one of the most influential musicians in the history of alternative rock.During the last years of his life, Cobain struggled with heroin addiction and chronic health problems such as depression. He also struggled with the personal and professional pressures of fame, as well as his marriage to musician Courtney Love. In March 1994, Cobain overdosed on a combination of champagne and Rohypnol, and subsequently entered an intervention and underwent a detox program. On April 8, 1994, Cobain was found dead at his home in Seattle at the age of 27; police concluded he had died on April 5 from a self-inflicted shotgun wound to the head.

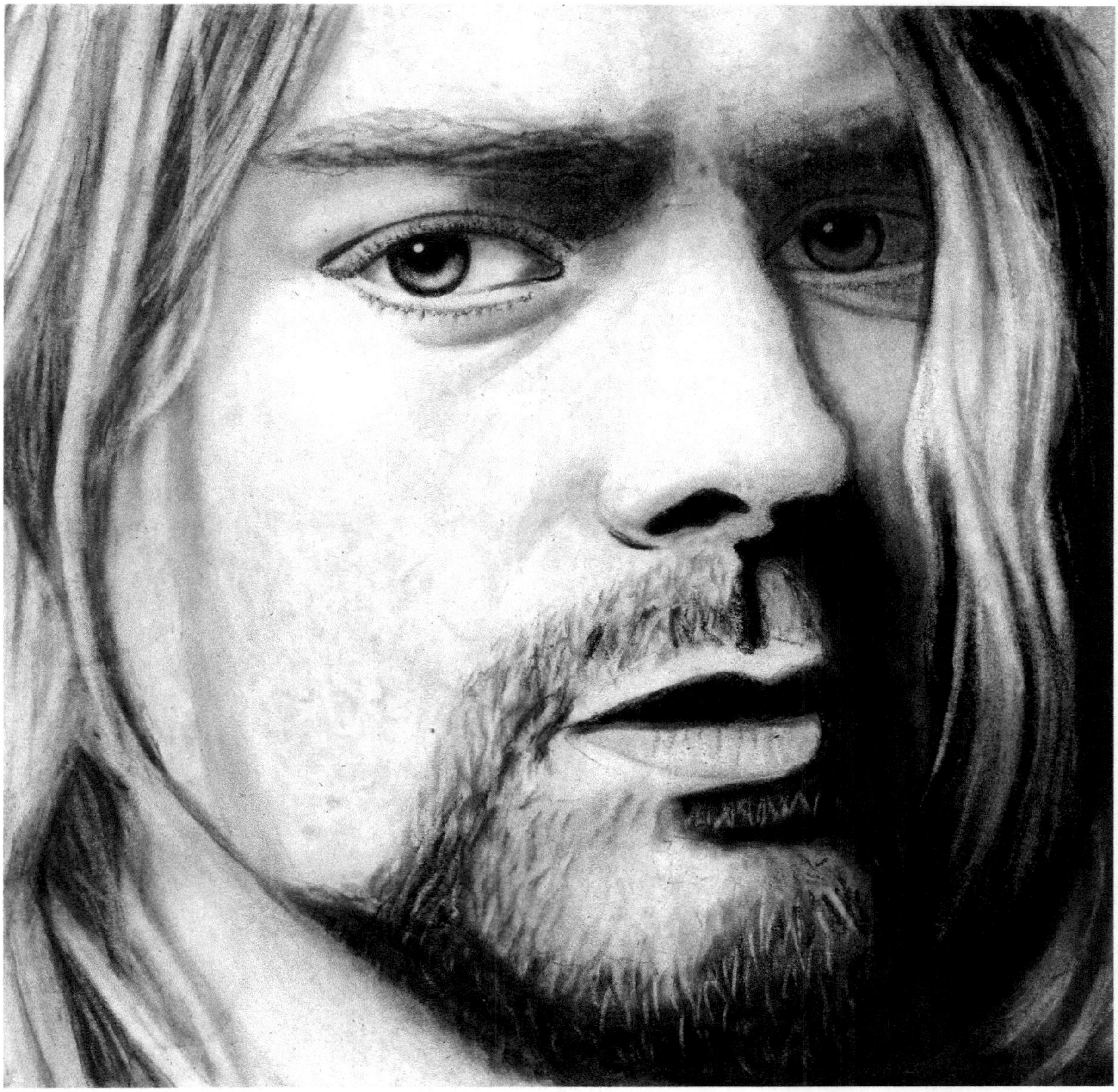

To view how this drawing was masterfully created or to purchase a Limited Edition Framed Artwork of Kurt Cobain type into your Internet Browser the URL shortcut ➡ **myportrait.art/kurtcobain**

To listen to their Greatest Songs type into your Internet Browser the URL shortcut ➡ **radio.surf/nirvana**

To view all channels on THE FACE OF MUSIC Internet Radio MEGA Station type into your Internet Browser the URL shortcut ➡ **radio.surf/music**

To inquire about purchasing a Limited Edition NFT of this portrait type into your Internet Browser the URL shortcut ➡ **myartnft.shop/kurtcobain**

To view all available NFTs type into your Internet Browser the URL shortcut ➡ **myartnft.shop/all**

# No Doubt

(Total Records Sold: 33+ Million)(Genre: Pop Rock, Ska Punk)

No Doubt is an American rock band from Anaheim, California, formed in 1986. The band consists of vocalist Gwen Stefani, guitarist Tom Dumont, bassist Tony Kanal, and drummer Adrian Young. Since the mid-1990s, they have been supported by trombonist and keyboardist Gabrial McNair and trumpeter and keyboardist Stephen Bradley in live performances.

Though their 1992 eponymous debut album failed to make an impact, its ska punk-inspired follow-up The Beacon Street Collection sold over 100,000 copies in 1995, over triple that of its predecessor. The band's diamond-certified album Tragic Kingdom (1995) benefited from the resurgence of third-wave ska in the 1990s, and "Don't Speak", the third single from the album, set a record when it spent 16 weeks at the number one spot on the Billboard Hot 100 Airplay chart. "Just a Girl", co-written by Stefani, was described as "the most popular cut on the CD".

The group's next album, Return of Saturn (2000), despite its Top 40 hit single "Simple Kind of Life", did not match the success of their previous album, but received critical praise and was nominated for Best Rock Album at the 43rd Grammy Awards. Fifteen months later, the band reappeared with the album Rock Steady (2001), which incorporated reggae and dancehall music into their work. The album was primarily recorded in Jamaica and featured collaborations with Jamaican artists Bounty Killer, Sly and Robbie, and Lady Saw. The album produced two Grammy-winning singles, "Hey Baby" and "Underneath It All". "Hella Good" was also nominated for a Grammy award. On November 22, 2002, No Doubt received the Key to the City of Anaheim, given by the Mayor of Anaheim, Tom Daly, in Disneyland during the band's appearance on 'Breakfast with Kevin and Bean' (KROQ-FM) where they performed five songs. After a 2004 tour the band embarked on solo projects, with Stefani releasing two successful solo albums Love. Angel. Music. Baby. (2004) and The Sweet Escape (2006), while Tom Dumont released his own solo music project, Invincible Overlord. In 2008, the band resumed working slowly on their sixth and latest effort, titled Push and Shove (2012), and released their single "Settle Down". They have sold over 33 million records worldwide.

# Gwen Stefani

(Net Worth: $150 Million)(Height: 5' - 6")

Gwen Renée Stefani (born October 3, 1969) is an American singer and songwriter. She is a co-founder, lead vocalist, and the primary songwriter of the band No Doubt, whose singles include "Just a Girl", "Spiderwebs", and "Don't Speak", from their 1995 breakthrough studio album Tragic Kingdom, as well as "Hey Baby" and "It's My Life" from later albums.

During the band's hiatus, Stefani embarked on a solo pop career in 2004 by releasing her debut studio album Love. Angel. Music. Baby. Inspired by pop music from the 1980s, the album was a critical and commercial success. It spawned six singles, including "What You Waiting For?", "Rich Girl", "Hollaback Girl", and "Cool" Stefani has won three Grammy Awards. As a solo artist, she has received an American Music Award, Brit Award, World Music Award, and two Billboard Music Awards. ..

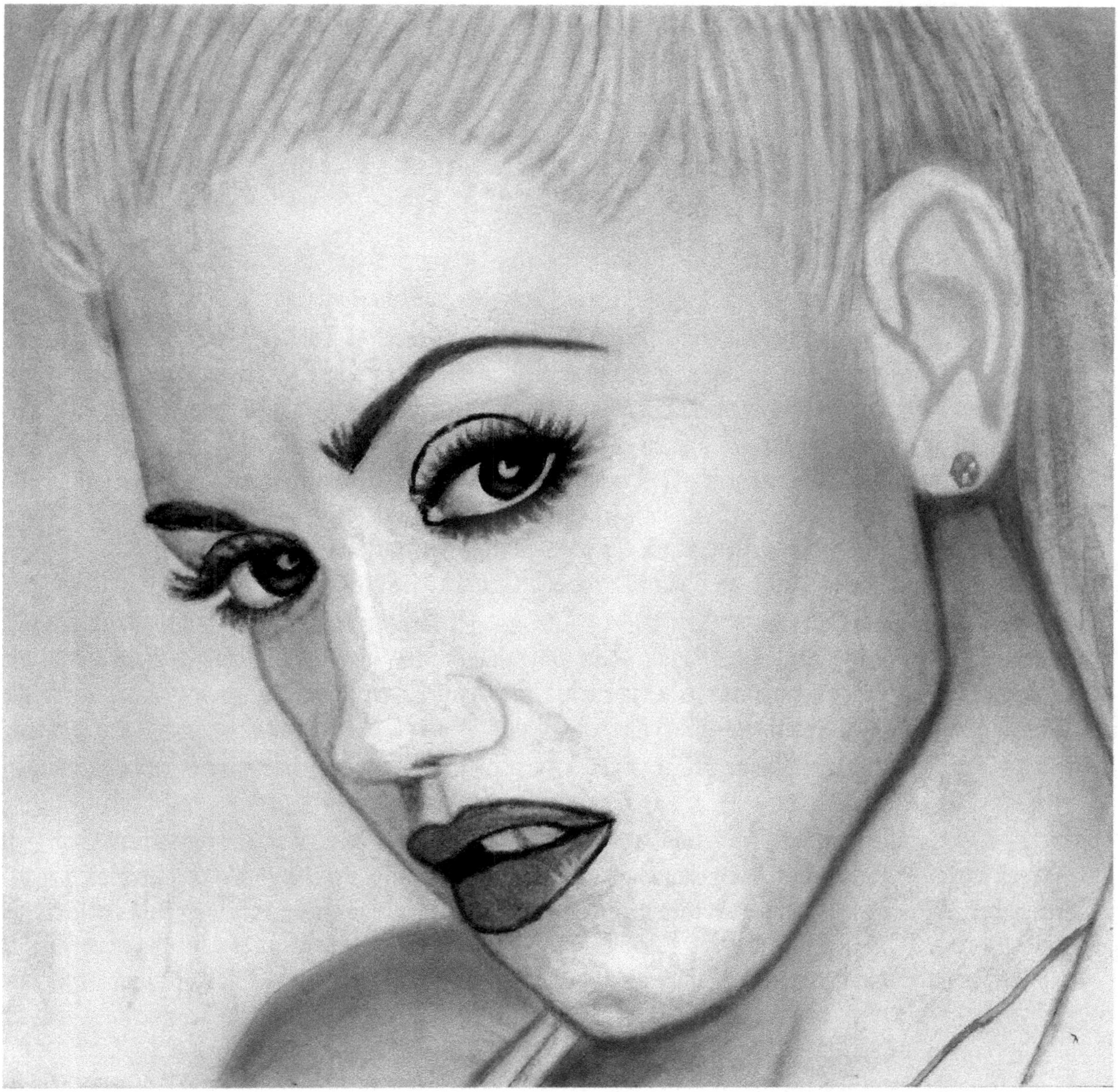

To view how this drawing was masterfully created or to purchase a Limited Edition Framed Artwork of Gwen Stefani type into your Internet Browser the URL shortcut ➡ **myportrait.art/gwenstafani**

To listen to their Greatest Songs type into your Internet Browser the URL shortcut ➡ **radio.surf/nodoubt**

To view all channels on THE FACE OF MUSIC Internet Radio MEGA Station type into your Internet Browser the URL shortcut ➡ **radio.surf/music**

To inquire about purchasing a Limited Edtion NFT of this portrait type into your Internet Browser the URL shortcut ➡ **myartnft.shop/gwenstafani**

To view all available NFTs type into your Internet Browser the URL shortcut ➡ **myartnft.shop/all**

# Notorious B.I.G. , The

(Net worth: $10 Million)(Total Albums Sold: 21 Million)
(Genre: Gangsta Rap , East Coast Hip-Hop)(Height: 6' - 2")

Christopher George Latore Wallace (May 21, 1972 – March 9, 1997), better known by his stage names The Notorious B.I.G., Biggie Smalls, or simply Biggie, was an American rapper and songwriter. Rooted in the New York rap scene and gangsta rap traditions, he is widely considered one of the greatest rappers of all time. Wallace became known for his distinctive laidback lyrical delivery, offsetting the lyrics' often grim content. His music was often semi-autobiographical, telling of hardship and criminality, but also of debauchery and celebration.

Born and raised in Brooklyn, New York City, Wallace signed to Sean "Puffy" Combs' label Bad Boy Records as it launched in 1993, and gained exposure through features on several other artists' singles that year. His debut album Ready to Die (1994) was met with widespread critical acclaim, and included his signature songs "Juicy" and "Big Poppa". The album made him the central figure in East Coast hip hop, and restored New York's visibility at a time when the West Coast hip hop scene was dominating hip hop music. Wallace was awarded the 1995 Billboard Music Awards' Rapper of the Year. The following year, he led his protégé group Junior M.A.F.I.A., a team of himself and longtime friends, including Lil' Kim, to chart success.

During 1996, while recording his second album, Wallace became ensnarled in the escalating East Coast–West Coast hip hop feud. Following Tupac Shakur's death in a drive-by shooting in Las Vegas in September 1996, speculations of involvement by criminal elements orbiting the Bad Boy circle circulated. On March 9, 1997, while visiting Los Angeles, Wallace was murdered in a drive-by shooting. The assailant remains unidentified. Wallace's second album Life After Death, a double album, was released two weeks later. It reached number one on the Billboard 200, and eventually achieved a Diamond certification in the US.

With two more posthumous albums released, Wallace has certified sales of over 28 million copies in the United States, including 21 million albums. Rolling Stone has called him the "greatest rapper that ever lived," and Billboard named him the greatest rapper of all time. The Source magazine named him the greatest rapper of all time in its 150th issue. In 2006, MTV ranked him at No. 3 on their list of The Greatest MCs of All Time, calling him possibly "the most skillful ever on the mic". In 2020, he was inducted into the Rock and Roll Hall of Fame..

Died March 9 1997, Los Angeles, California, U.S.,Drive-by shooting homicide.

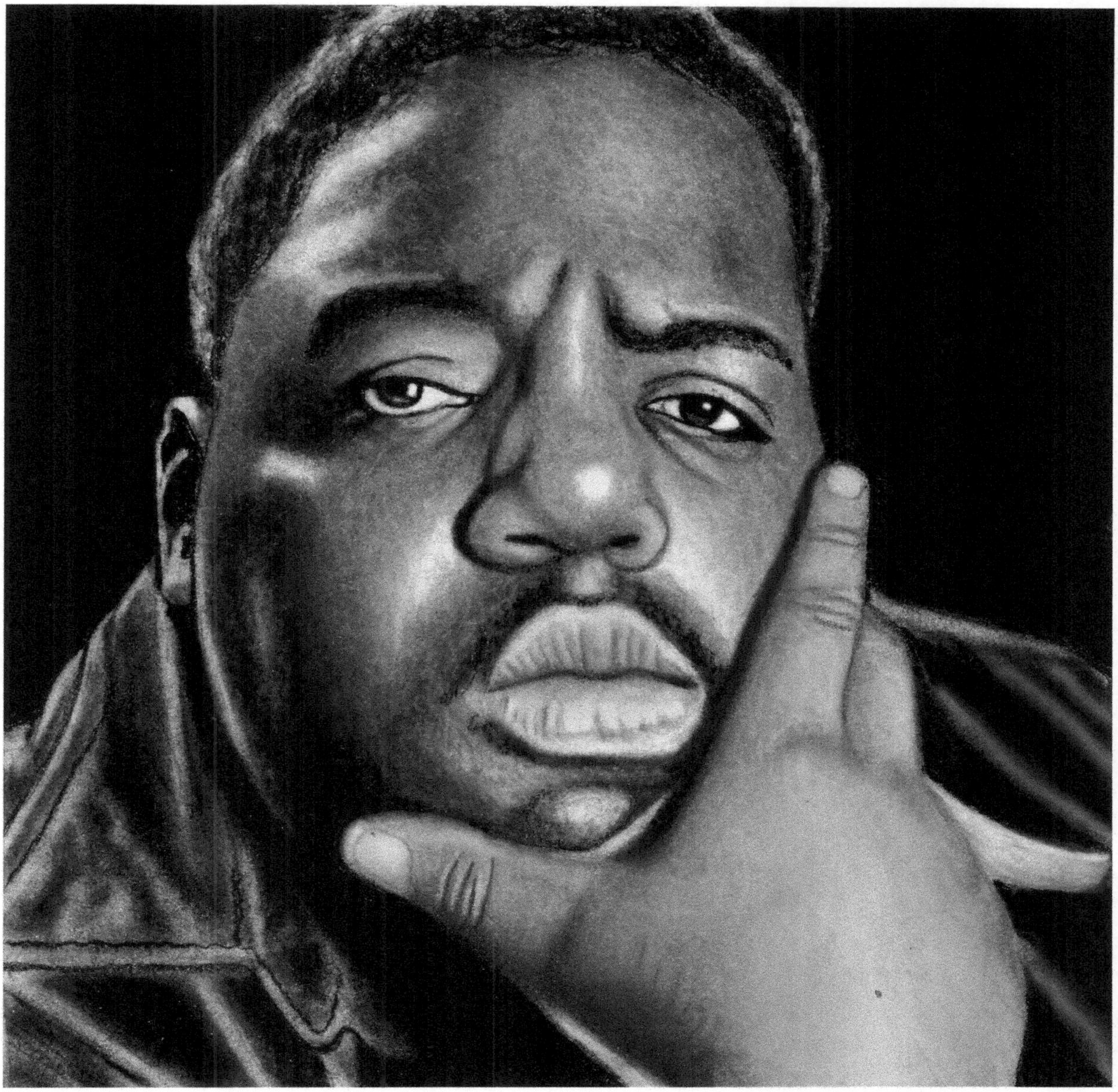

To view how this drawing was masterfully created or to purchase a Limited Edition Framed Artwork of The Notorious BIG type into your Internet Browser the URL shortcut ➡ **myportrait.art/thenotoriousbig**

To listen to his Greatest Songs type into your Internet Browser the URL shortcut
➡ **radio.surf/thenotoriousbig**

To view all channels on THE FACE OF MUSIC Internet Radio MEGA Station type into your Internet Browser the URL shortcut ➡ **radio.surf/music**

To inquire about purchasing a Limited Edtion NFT of this portrait type into your Internet Browser the URL shortcut ➡ **myartnft.shop/thenotoriousbig**

To view all available NFTs type into your Internet Browser the URL shortcut ➡ **myartnft.shop/all**

# Oasis

(Total Records Sold: 75+ Million)(Genre: Pop ,Rock)

Oasis were an English rock band formed in Manchester in 1991. Developed from an earlier group, the Rain, the band originally consisted of Liam Gallagher (lead vocals, tambourine), Paul Arthurs (guitar), Paul McGuigan (bass guitar), and Tony McCarroll (drums). Upon returning from working as a roadie for Inspiral Carpets, Liam's older brother Noel (lead guitar, vocals) joined as a fifth member, finalising the band's core line-up. During the course of their existence, they had various line-up changes, though the Gallagher brothers remained as the staple members.Oasis signed to independent record label Creation Records in 1993 and released their record-setting debut album Definitely Maybe (1994). The following year they recorded (What's the Story) Morning Glory? (1995) with drummer Alan White, in the midst of a chart rivalry with Britpop peers Blur. Spending ten weeks at number one on the UK Albums Chart, (What's the Story) Morning Glory? was also an international chart success, and became one of the best-selling albums of all time. In addition, it stands as the fifth best-selling album in the UK, and the biggest-selling album in the UK of the 1990s. The Gallagher brothers featured regularly in tabloid newspapers for their disputes and wild lifestyles. In 1996, Oasis performed two nights at Knebworth for an audience of 125,000 each night, the largest outdoor concerts in UK history at the time. In 1997, Oasis released their third album, Be Here Now; becoming the fastest-selling album in UK chart history. However, its popularity declined quickly.McGuigan and Arthurs left in 1999 as Oasis released Standing on the Shoulder of Giants (2000). They were replaced by former Heavy Stereo guitarist Gem Archer and former Ride guitarist Andy Bell. White departed in 2004, replaced by Zak Starkey and later Chris Sharrock as touring members. Oasis released three more studio albums, Heathen Chemistry (2002), Don't Believe The Truth (2005) and Dig Out Your Soul (2008). The group abruptly disbanded after the departure of Noel in August 2009. As of 2009, Oasis have sold over 75 million records worldwide, making them one of the best-selling bands of all time. They are among the most successful acts on the UK Singles Chart and Albums Chart, with eight UK number-one singles and eight UK number-one albums. The band also achieved three platinum albums in the US. They won 17 NME Awards, nine Q Awards, four MTV Europe Music Awards and six Brit Awards, including one in 2007 for Outstanding Contribution to Music and one for the "Best Album of the Last 30 Years" (for (What's the Story) Morning Glory?). They were nominated for two Grammy Awards.

# Liam Gallagher

(Net Worth: $60 Million)(Height: 5' - 10")

William John Paul Gallagher (born 21 September 1972) is an English singer and songwriter. He achieved fame as the lead singer of the rock band Oasis from 1991 to 2009, and later fronted the rock band Beady Eye from 2009 to 2014, before starting a solo career in 2017.One of the most recognisable figures in music, Gallagher is noted for his distinctive singing style and his outspoken, brash, and abrasive personality. His attitude during Oasis' commercial peak in the mid-1990s garnered much attention from the British tabloids, which often ran stories concerning his drug use and destructive behaviour. In March 2010, he was voted the greatest frontman of all time in a reader poll by Q magazine. In 2019, he received the MTV Europe Music Award for "Rock Icon".

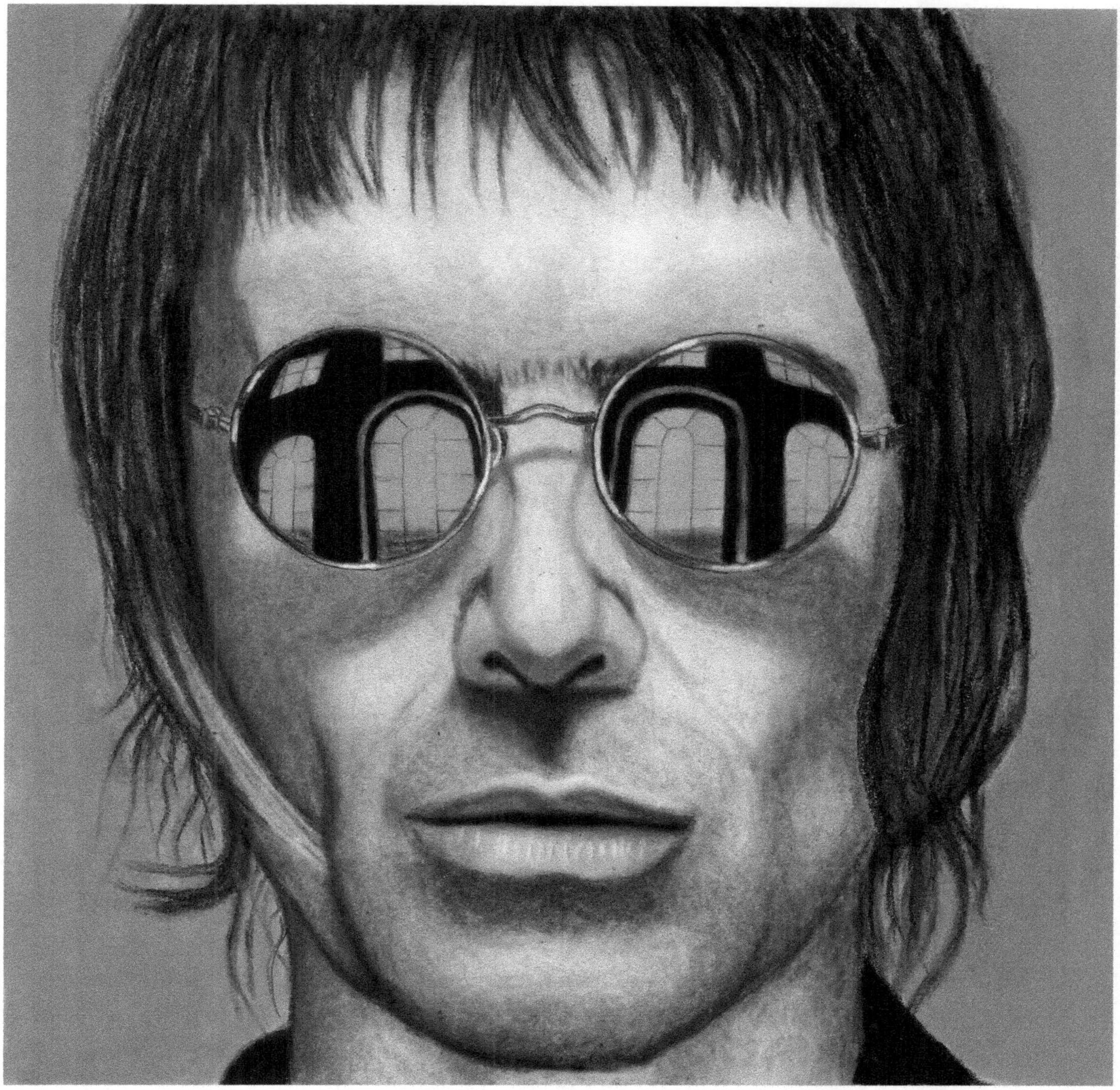

To view how this drawing was masterfully created or to purchase a Limited Edition Framed Artwork of Liam Gallgher type into your Internet Browser the URL shortcut ➡ **myportrait.art/liamgallagher**

To listen to their Greatest Songs type into your Internet Browser the URL shortcut ➡ **radio.surf/oasis**

To view all channels on THE FACE OF MUSIC Internet Radio MEGA Station type into your Internet Browser the URL shortcut ➡ **radio.surf/music**

To inquire about purchasing a Limited Edtion NFT of this portrait type into your Internet Browser the URL shortcut ➡ **myartnft.shop/liamgallagher**

To view all available NFTs type into your Internet Browser the URL shortcut ➡ **myartnft.shop/all**

# Olivia Newton-John

(Net worth: $40 Million)(Total Albums Sold: 120 Million)
(Genre: Pop , Dance Pop)(Height: 5' - 6")

Dame Olivia Newton-John (born 26 September 1948) is a British-Australian singer, songwriter, actress, entrepreneur and activist. She is a four-time Grammy Award winner whose chart career includes five US number ones and another ten Top Tens on Billboard's Hot 100, and two Billboard 200 number-one albums: If You Love Me, Let Me Know (1974) and Have You Never Been Mellow (1975). Eleven of her singles (including two Platinum) and 14 of her albums (including two Platinum and four 2× Platinum) have been certified Gold by the Recording Industry Association of America (RIAA). She has sold an estimated 120 million records worldwide, making her one of the best-selling music artists of all time.

In 1978, she starred in the musical film Grease, whose soundtrack remains one of the most successful in history. It features two major hit duets with co-star John Travolta: "You're the One That I Want" – which ranks as one of the best-selling singles of all time – and "Summer Nights". Her signature solo recordings include the Record of the Year Grammy winner "I Honestly Love You" (1974) and "Physical" (1981) – Billboard's top Hot 100 single of the 1980s – plus her cover of "If Not for You" (1971), "Let Me Be There" (1973), "If You Love Me (Let Me Know)" (1974), "Have You Never Been Mellow" (1975), "Sam" (1977), "Hopelessly Devoted to You" (also from Grease), "A Little More Love" (1978), "Heart Attack" (1982) and, from the 1980 film Xanadu, "Magic" and "Xanadu" (with Electric Light Orchestra).

Newton-John has been a long-time activist for environmental and animal rights issues. She has been an advocate for health awareness, becoming involved with various charities, health products and fundraising efforts. Her business interests have included launching several product lines for Koala Blue and co-owning the Gaia Retreat & Spa in Australia.

Newton-John was born on 26 September 1948 in Cambridge, United Kingdom, to the Welshman Brinley "Bryn" Newton-John (1914–1992) and Irene Helene (née Born; 1914–2003). Her Jewish maternal grandfather, the Nobel Prize-winning physicist Max Born, fled with his family to Britain from Germany before World War II to escape the Nazi regime. Newton-John's maternal grandmother was of paternal Jewish ancestry as well; through her, she is a third cousin of comedian Ben Elton. Her maternal great-grandfather was the jurist Victor Ehrenberg and her matrilineal great-grandmother's father was the jurist Rudolf von Ihering.

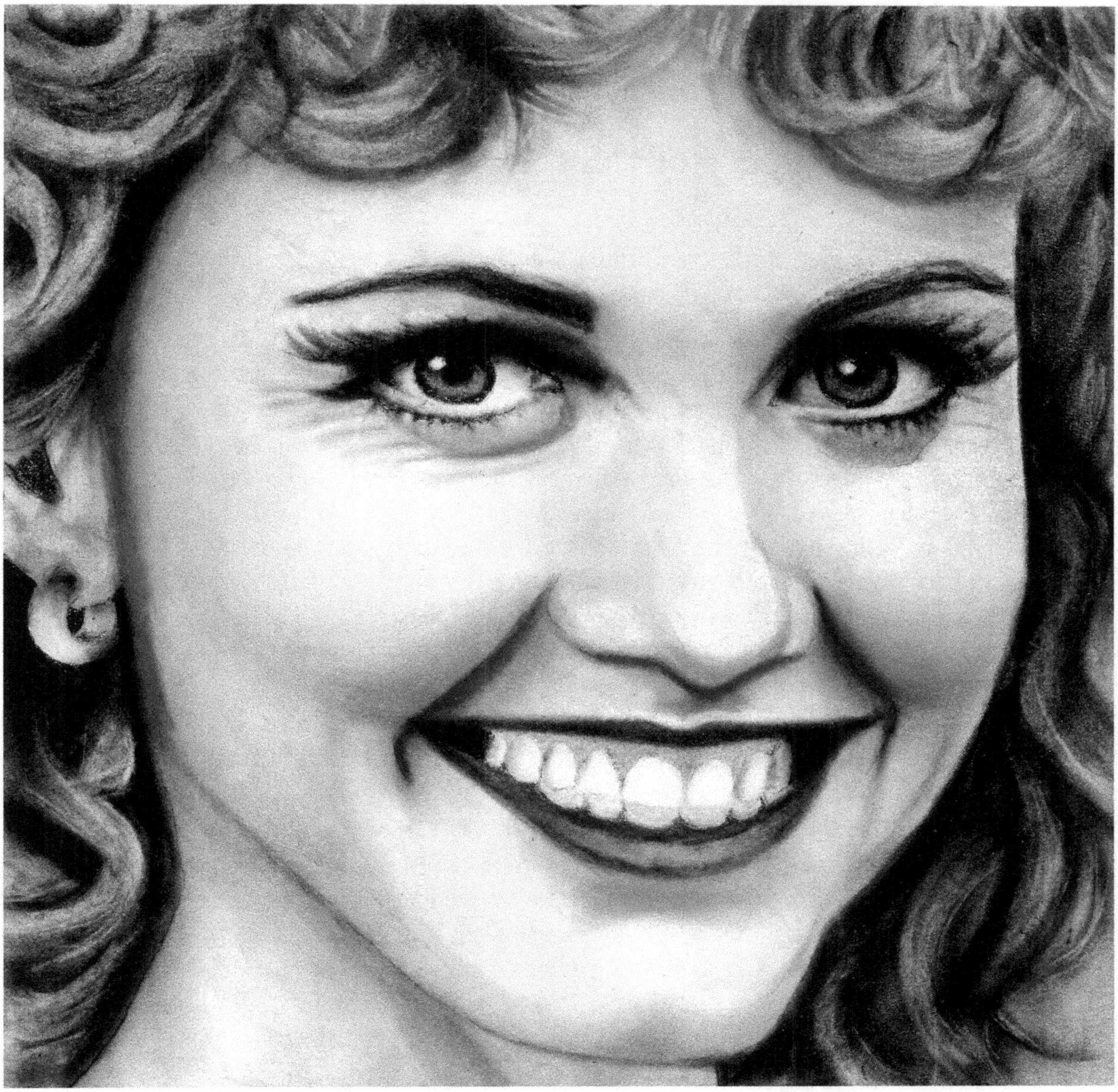

To view how this drawing was masterfully created or to purchase a Limited Edition Framed Artwork of Olivia Newton-John type into your Internet Browser the URL shortcut ➡ **myportrait.art/olivanewtonjohn**

To listen to her Greatest Songs type into your Internet Browser the URL shortcut
➡ **radio.surf/olivanewtonjohn**

To view all channels on THE FACE OF MUSIC Internet Radio MEGA Station type into your Internet Browser the URL shortcut ➡ **radio.surf/music**

To inquire about purchasing a Limited Edtion NFT of this portrait type into your Internet Browser the URL shortcut ➡ **myartnft.shop/olivanewtonjohn**

To view all available NFTs type into your Internet Browser the URL shortcut ➡ **myartnft.shop/all**

# Otis Redding

(Net worth: $10 Million)(Total Records Sold: Millions)
(Genre: Soul , R&B)(Height: 6' - 0")

Otis Ray Redding Jr. (September 9, 1941 – December 10, 1967) was an American singer and songwriter. He is considered one of the greatest singers in the history of American popular music and a seminal artist in soul music and rhythm and blues. Redding's style of singing gained inspiration from the gospel music that preceded the genre. His singing style influenced many other soul artists of the 1960s. Redding was born in Dawson, Georgia, and at the age of 2, moved to Macon, Georgia. Redding quit school at age 15 to support his family, working with Little Richard's backing band, the Upsetters, and by performing in talent shows at the historic Douglass Theatre in Macon. In 1958, he joined Johnny Jenkins's band, the Pinetoppers, with whom he toured the Southern states as a singer and driver. An unscheduled appearance on a Stax recording session led to a contract and his first single, "These Arms of Mine", in 1962.

Stax released Redding's debut album, Pain in My Heart, two years later. Initially popular mainly with African-Americans, Redding later reached a wider American pop music audience. Along with his group, he first played small shows in the American South. He later performed at the popular Los Angeles night club Whisky a Go Go and toured Europe, performing in London, Paris and other major cities. He also performed at the Monterey Pop Festival in 1967.

Shortly before his death in a plane crash, Redding wrote and recorded his iconic "(Sittin' On) The Dock of the Bay" with Steve Cropper. The song became the first posthumous number-one record on both the Billboard Hot 100 and R&B charts. The album The Dock of the Bay was the first posthumous album to reach number one on the UK Albums Chart. Redding's premature death devastated Stax. Already on the verge of bankruptcy, the label soon discovered that the Atco division of Atlantic Records owned the rights to his entire song catalog.

Redding received many posthumous accolades, including two Grammy Awards, the Grammy Lifetime Achievement Award and induction into the Rock and Roll Hall of Fame, the Black Music & Entertainment Walk of Fame, and the Songwriters Hall of Fame. In addition to "(Sittin' On) The Dock of the Bay," "Respect" and "Try a Little Tenderness" are among his best-known songs.

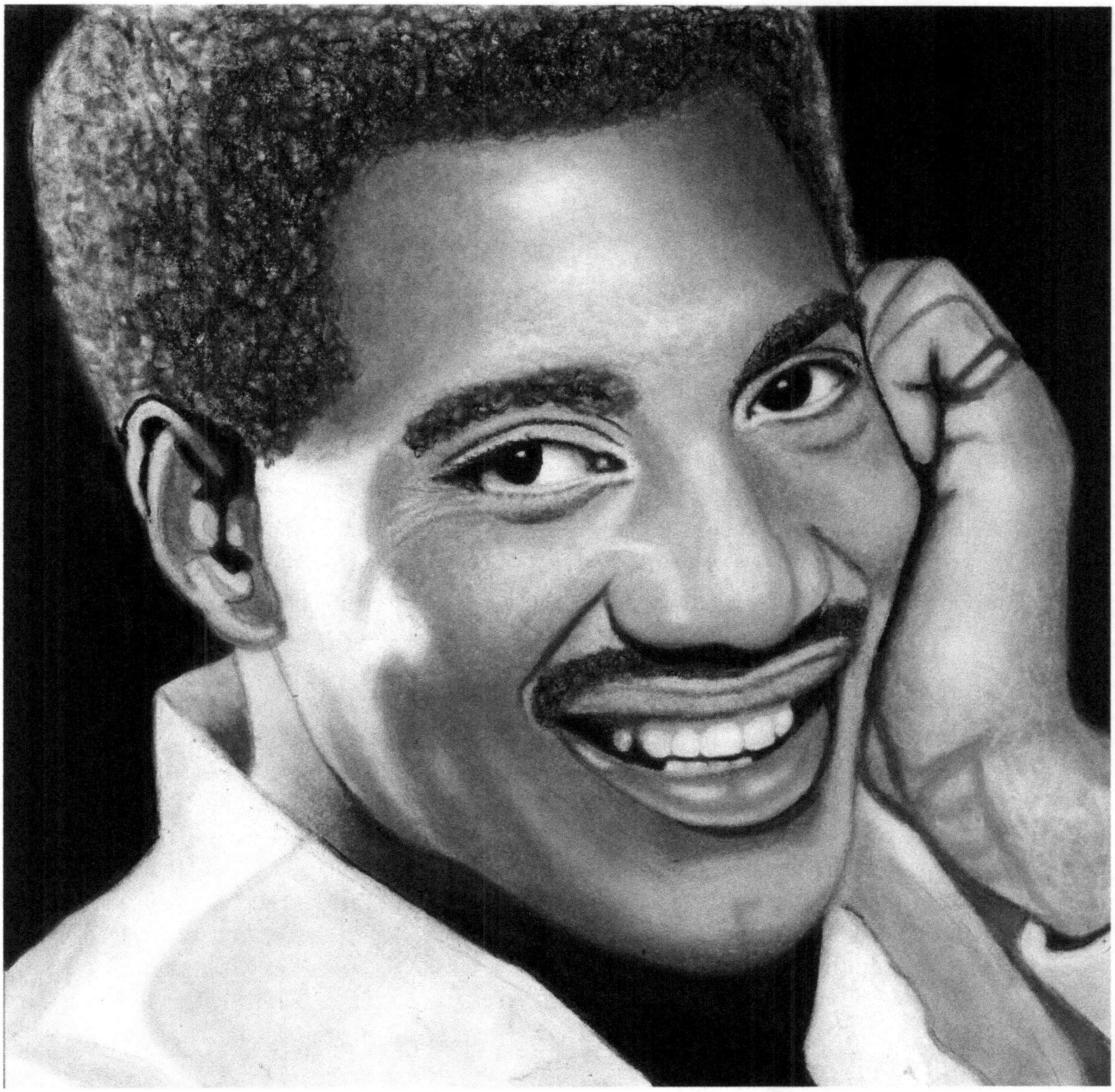

To view how this drawing was masterfully created or to purchase a Limited Edition Framed Artwork of Otis Redding type into your Internet Browser the URL shortcut ➡ **myportrait.art/otisredding**

To listen to his Greatest Songs type into your Internet Browser the URL shortcut ➡ **radio.surf/otisredding**

To view all channels on THE FACE OF MUSIC Internet Radio MEGA Station type into your Internet Browser the URL shortcut ➡ **radio.surf/music**

To inquire about purchasing a Limited Edtion NFT of this portrait type into your Internet Browser the URL shortcut ➡ **myartnft.shop/otisredding**

To view all available NFTs type into your Internet Browser the URL shortcut ➡ **myartnft.shop/all**

# Outkast

(Total Records Sold: 25+ Million)(Genre: Southern Hip-Hop, Rap)

Outkast (sometimes written as OutKast) is an American hip hop duo formed in 1992 in East Point, Georgia, consisting of Atlanta-based rappers André "3000" Benjamin (formerly known as Dré) and Antwan "Big Boi" Patton. Widely recognized for their intricate lyricism, memorable melodies and positive messages, OutKast is often regarded as one of the greatest and most influential hip hop acts of all time. The duo achieved both critical acclaim and commercial success from the mid-1990s to the early 2000s, helping to popularize Southern hip hop while experimenting with diverse genres such as funk, psychedelia, jazz, and techno. Benjamin and Patton formed the group as high school students in 1992. Outkast released their debut album Southernplayalisticadillacmuzik in 1994, which gained popularity after the single "Player's Ball" reached number one on the Billboard Hot Rap Tracks chart. With successive releases including ATLiens (1996) and Aquemini (1998), the duo further developed their sound, experimenting with a variety of styles and achieving commercial success. In 2000, Outkast released the critically acclaimed Stankonia, which included the singles "Ms. Jackson" and "B.O.B."

In September 2003, the duo released the double album Speakerboxxx/The Love Below, which featured the number one singles "Hey Ya!" and "The Way You Move." The album won the Grammy Award for Album of the Year and was certified Diamond by the Recording Industry Association of America. Outkast next released the soundtrack for the 2006 musical film Idlewild, which they also starred in. In 2007, the duo went on hiatus and both members have since pursued solo careers. In 2014, Outkast reunited to celebrate their 20th anniversary by performing at more than 40 festivals worldwide, beginning at the Coachella Festival in April. The duo is one of the most successful hip hop groups of all time, having received six Grammy Awards. Rolling Stone ranked them No. 7 on its list of the 20 Greatest Duos of All Time. Between six studio albums and a greatest hits release, Outkast has sold over 25 million records. Meanwhile, they have garnered widespread critical acclaim, with publications such as Rolling Stone and Pitchfork Media listing albums such as Aquemini and Stankonia among the best of their era.

# André 3000

(Net Worth: $45 Million)(Height: 5' - 10")

André Lauren Benjamin (born May 27, 1975), better known as André 3000, is an American rapper, singer, songwriter, actor, and producer. He is best known for being a part of southern hip hop duo Outkast alongside fellow rapper Big Boi. Many publications, such as Billboard and Showbiz Cheatsheet have listed André 3000 as one of the top 10 rappers of all time. As an actor, Benjamin has made appearances in several films and television series, including Families, The Shield, Be Cool, Revolver, Semi-Pro, Four Brothers, and in the lead role of Jimi Hendrix in All Is by My Side. He currently plays Fredwynn on the AMC anthology series, Dispatches from Elsewhere.In addition to music and acting, he has also been an entrepreneur and an advocate for animal rights. In the spring of 2008, he launched a clothing line called Benjamin Bixby. He is also known for his work on the Cartoon Network animated series Class of 3000, which aired from 2006 to 2008. In 2013, Complex included Benjamin on its list of the 10 best rappers of the 2000s. In 2015, Billboard included Benjamin on its list of the 10 Greatest Rappers of All Time.

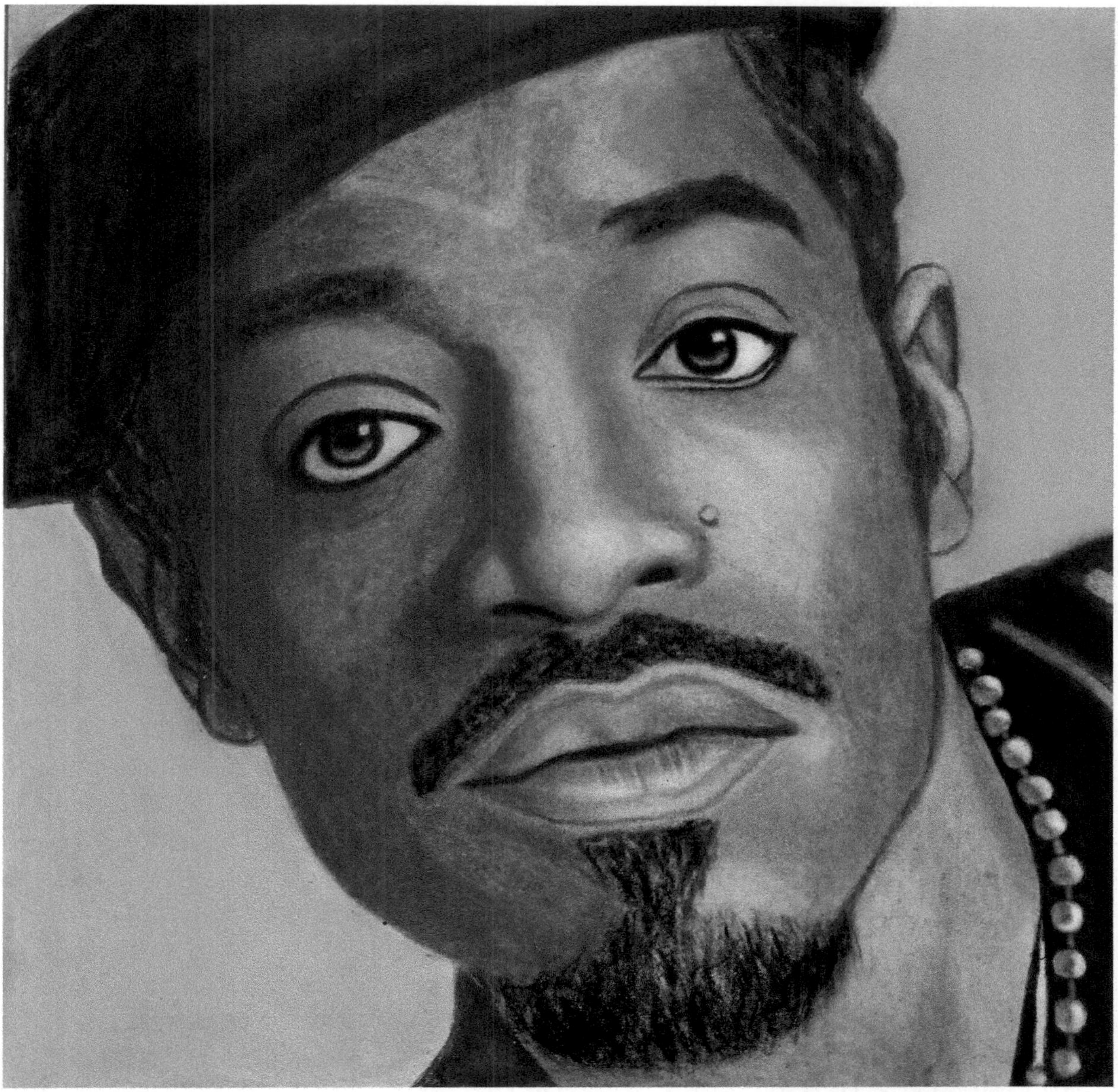

To view how this drawing was masterfully created or to purchase a Limited Edition Framed Artwork of Andre 3000 type into your Internet Browser the URL shortcut ➡ **myportrait.art/andre3000**

To listen to their Greatest Songs type into your Internet Browser the URL shortcut ➡ **radio.surf/outkast**

To view all channels on THE FACE OF MUSIC Internet Radio MEGA Station type into your Internet Browser the URL shortcut ➡ **radio.surf/music**

To inquire about purchasing a Limited Edtion NFT of this portrait type into your Internet Browser the URL shortcut ➡ **myartnft.shop/andre3000**

To view all available NFTs type into your Internet Browser the URL shortcut ➡ **myartnft.shop/all**

# Pantera

(Total Records Sold: 40 Million)(Genre: Heavy Metal, Thrash Metal)

Pantera (Spanish/Portuguese for "Panther") was an American heavy metal band from Arlington, Texas, formed in 1981. The group's best-known lineup consisted of the Abbott brothers—drummer Vinnie Paul and guitarist Dimebag Darrell—along with vocalist Phil Anselmo and bassist Rex Brown. In addition to their development and popularization of the groove metal subgenre, Pantera is credited (along with others, such as Testament, Sepultura and Machine Head) for being part of the second wave of thrash metal scene from the late 1980s to early-to-mid 1990s. Pantera is regarded as one of the most successful and influential bands in heavy metal history, having sold around 40 million records worldwide, and being nominated four times at the Grammys. Having started as a glam metal band, Pantera released three albums in the mid-1980s with lead vocalist Terry Glaze (Metal Magic, Projects in the Jungle, and I Am the Night). Looking for a new and heavier sound, Pantera hired Anselmo in late 1986 and released Power Metal in 1988. They secured a record deal with major label Atco the following year. Their fifth album, 1990's Cowboys from Hell, popularized the groove metal genre, while its 1992 follow-up Vulgar Display of Power achieved an even heavier sound. Far Beyond Driven (1994) debuted at number one on the Billboard 200. Tensions began to surface among the band members when Anselmo became addicted to heroin in 1995; he almost died from an overdose in 1996. These tensions resulted in the recording sessions for The Great Southern Trendkill (1996) being held separately. The ongoing tension lasted for another seven years, during which only one studio album, Reinventing the Steel (2000), was recorded. Pantera went on hiatus in 2001 but was disbanded by the Abbott brothers in 2003 amid communication problems and their conclusion that Anselmo would not return to the band. The Abbott brothers went on to form Damageplan while Anselmo continued to work on several side projects, including Down, which Brown joined as well. On December 8, 2004, Dimebag Darrell was shot and killed on stage by a mentally unstable fan during a Damageplan concert in Columbus, Ohio. Vinnie Paul went on to form Hellyeah after his brother's death, and died of heart failure in 2018, leaving Brown and Anselmo as the only surviving members of the band's best-known lineup.

# Phil Anselmo

(Net Worth: $6 Million)(Height: 6' - 0")

Philip Hansen Anselmo (born June 30, 1968) is an American heavy metal musician best known as the vocalist for Pantera, Down, and Superjoint Ritual, amongst other musical projects. He is the owner of Housecore Records. Anselmo is regarded as one of the greatest frontmen in metal history, known for being particularly animated and donning a machismo attitude that became emblematic of the general theme of Pantera. Earlier in his career with the band, Anselmo took considerable inspiration from heavy metal vocalists such as Rob Halford, singing in full head voice. However, he later became recognized for introducing a more guttural approach to the vocals.

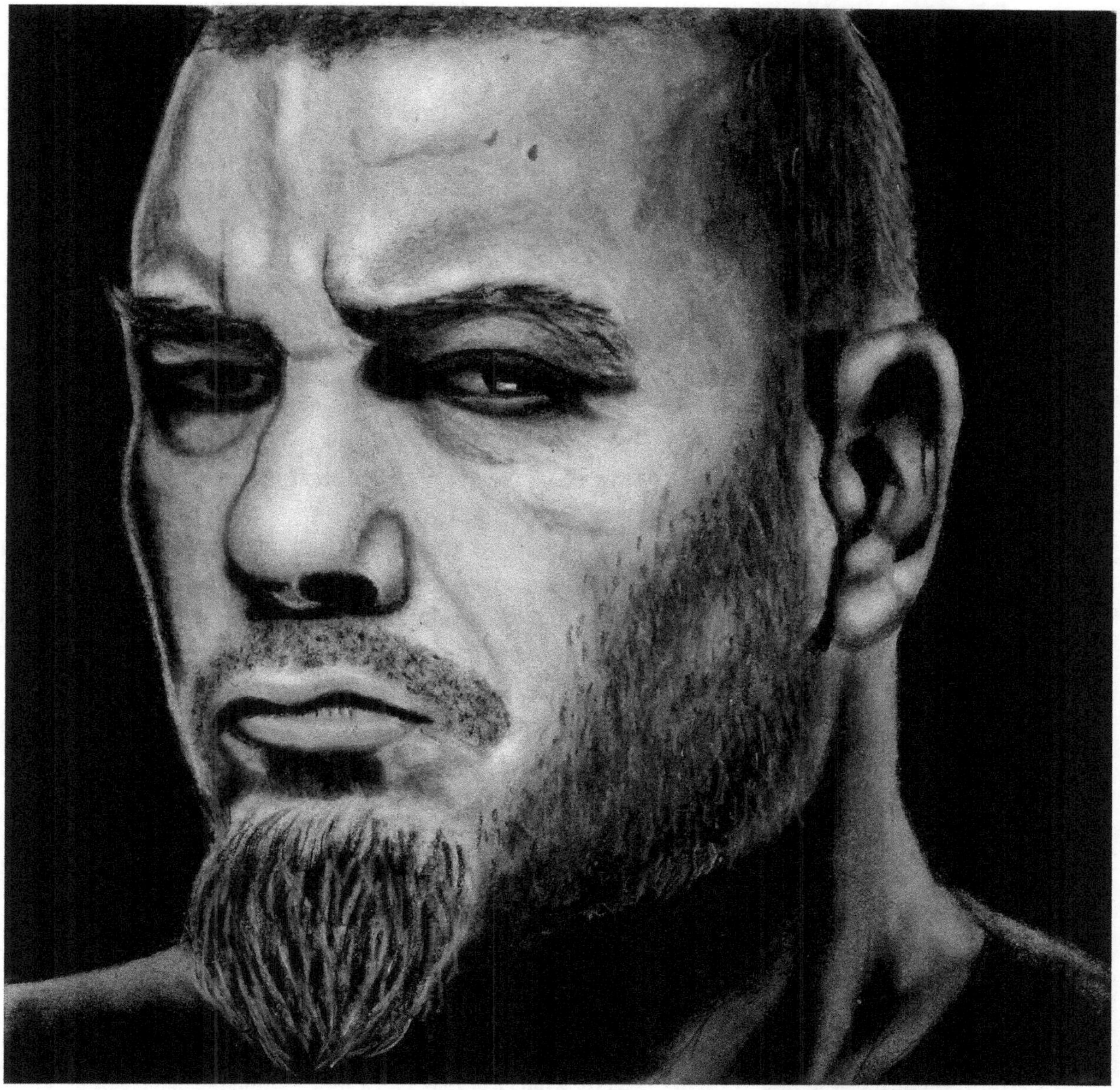

To view how this drawing was masterfully created or to purchase a Limited Edition Framed Artwork of Phil Anselmo type into your Internet Browser the URL shortcut ➡ **myportrait.art/philanselmo**

To listen to their Greatest Songs type into your Internet Browser the URL shortcut ➡ **radio.surf/pantera**

To view all channels on THE FACE OF MUSIC Internet Radio MEGA Station type into your Internet Browser the URL shortcut ➡ **radio.surf/music**

To inquire about purchasing a Limited Edtion NFT of this portrait type into your Internet Browser the URL shortcut ➡ **myartnft.shop/philanselmo**

To view all available NFTs type into your Internet Browser the URL shortcut ➡ **myartnft.shop/all**

# Pat Benatar

(Net worth: $40 Million)(Total Records Sold: 17+ Million)
(Genre: Classic Rock)(Height: 5' - 0")

Patricia Mae Andrzejewski (born January 10, 1953), known professionally as Pat Benatar, is an American rock singer-songwriter and four-time Grammy Award winner. In the United States, she has had two multi-Platinum albums, five Platinum albums, and 15 Billboard Top 40 singles, while in Canada she had eight straight Platinum albums.

Benatar's 1979 debut album, In the Heat of the Night, was her breakthrough in North America, especially in Canada where it reached number 3 on the album chart. Two singles from it were hits: "Heartbreaker" and "We Live for Love", the latter written by her lead guitarist and future husband, Neil Giraldo. Benatar's second album, 1981's Crimes of Passion, was her most successful work, peaking at number 2 in North America and France, being certified 4x and 5x Platinum in the US and Canada, respectively. Its single "Hit Me with Your Best Shot" reached the Top 10 in the US and Canada and is considered to be her best-known song. Benatar's third album, Precious Time (1981) was another success, topping the US Album Chart and becoming her first Top 10 album in Australia. Its single "Fire and Ice" charted highly in the US and Canada. Her next release, Get Nervous (1982), sold less well than her previous two albums, but did include the North American hit "Shadows of the Night".

Benatar's sound began to move towards more atmospheric pop in 1983. The single "Love Is a Battlefield" (1983) was her biggest hit in most countries, including reaching number 1 in the Netherlands, Australia and on the US Rock Tracks chart, and number 5 on the US Hot 100. The live album it came from, Live from Earth, was her biggest seller in Australia, Germany and the Netherlands. In 1984, Benatar released Tropico and its lead single "We Belong", which reached the Top 10 in several countries, including number 5 on the US Hot 100.

Benatar's 1985 album, Seven the Hard Way, sold less well but it yielded two singles harking back to the rock vein: "Invincible", a Top 10 hit in North America, and "Sex as a Weapon". Her follow-up, Wide Awake in Dreamland (1988), marked a resurgence in sales in Canada and Australia, and was her biggest hit in the UK. Its rocker, "All Fired Up", was a significant hit in Canada, Australia and the US. Benatar released four additional albums between 1991 and 2003 and was nominated for induction into the Rock and Roll Hall of Fame

Pat Benatar was born Patricia Mae Andrzejewski on January 10, 1953, in Greenpoint, Brooklyn, New York City. Her mother, Mildred (née Knapp) (1928–2016), was a beautician, and her father, Andrew (Andrzej) Andrzejewski (1926–2009), was a sheet-metal worker. Her father was of Polish descent and her mother was of German, English, and Irish ancestry. Her family moved to North Hamilton Avenue in Lindenhurst, New York, a village in the Long Island town of Babylon

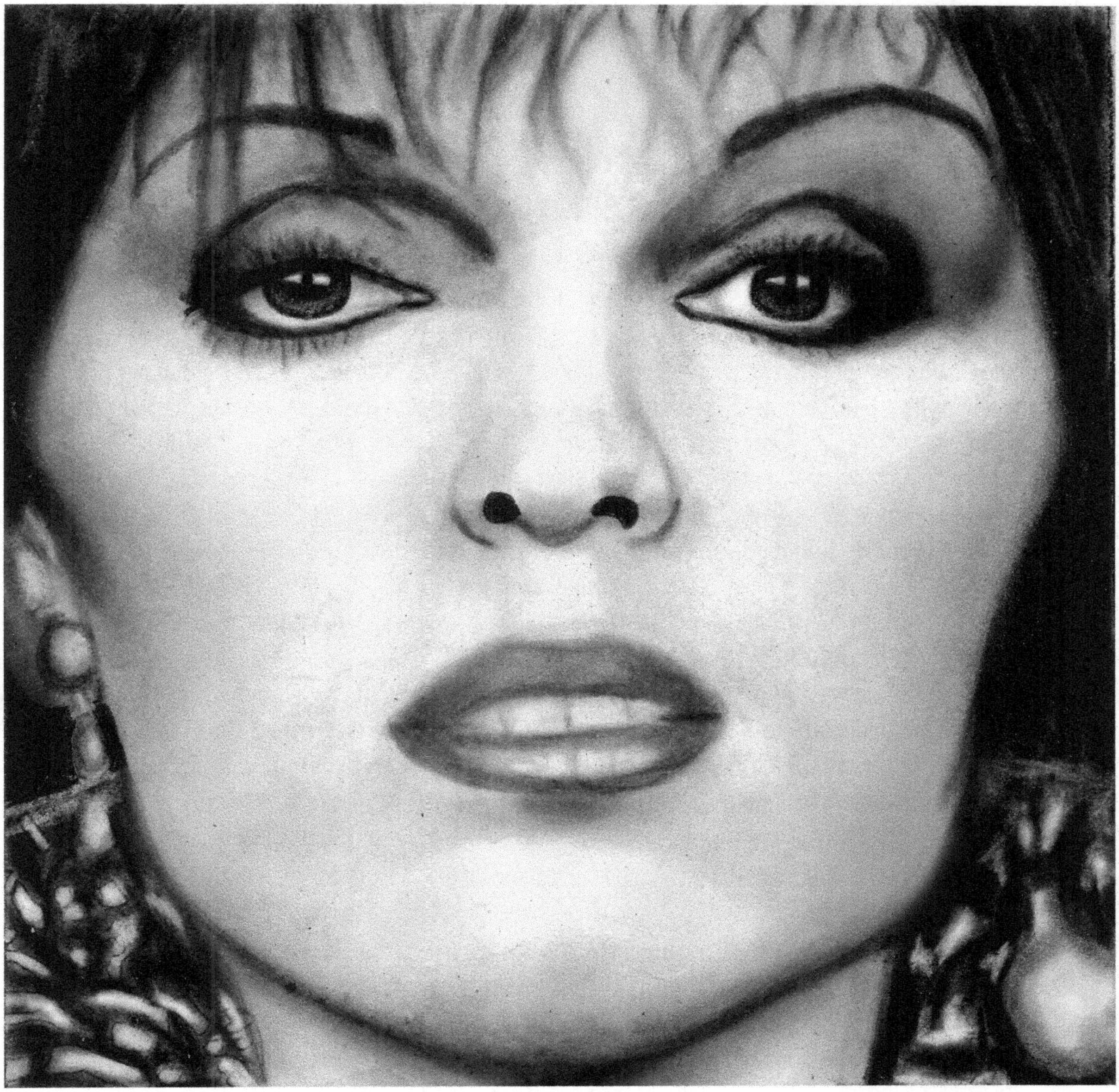

To view how this drawing was masterfully created or to purchase a Limited Edition Framed Artwork of Pat Benatar type into your Internet Browser the URL shortcut ➡ **myportrait.art/patbenatar**

To listen to her Greatest Songs type into your Internet Browser the URL shortcut ➡ **radio.surf/patbenatar**

To view all channels on THE FACE OF MUSIC Internet Radio MEGA Station type into your Internet Browser the URL shortcut ➡ **radio.surf/music**

To inquire about purchasing a Limited Edtion NFT of this portrait type into your Internet Browser the URL shortcut ➡ **myartnft.shop/patbenatar**

To view all available NFTs type into your Internet Browser the URL shortcut ➡ **myartnft.shop/all**

# Pat Boone

(Net worth: $50 Million)(Total Records Sold: 45+ Million)
(Genre: Traditional Pop, Country, Gospel, Vocal Jazz)(Height: 5' - 9 3/4")

Patrick Charles Eugene Boone (born June 1, 1934) is an American singer, composer, actor, writer, television personality, motivational speaker, and spokesman. He was a successful pop singer in the United States during the 1950s and early 1960s. He sold more than 45 million records, had 38 Top 40 hits, and appeared in more than 12 Hollywood films.

According to Billboard, Boone was the second-biggest charting artist of the late 1950s, behind only Elvis Presley, and was ranked at No. 9 in its listing of the Top 100 Top 40 Artists 1955–1995. Until the 2010s, Boone held the Billboard record for spending 220 consecutive weeks on the charts with one or more songs each week.

At the age of 23, he began hosting a half-hour ABC variety television series, The Pat Boone Chevy Showroom, which aired for 115 episodes (1957–1960). Many musical performers, including Edie Adams, Andy Williams, Pearl Bailey, and Johnny Mathis, made appearances on the show. His cover versions of rhythm and blues hits had a noticeable effect on the development of the broad popularity of rock and roll. Elvis Presley was the opening act for a 1955 Pat Boone show in Brooklyn, Ohio.

As an author, Boone had a number-one bestseller in the 1950s (Twixt Twelve and Twenty, Prentice-Hall). In the 1960s, he focused on gospel music and is a member of the Gospel Music Hall of Fame. He continues to perform and speak as a motivational speaker, a television personality, and a conservative political commentator.

Boone was born on June 1, 1934, in Jacksonville, Florida, the son of Margaret Virginia (née Pritchard) and Archie Altman Boone. He was raised in Nashville, Tennessee, where his family moved when he was two years old. Boone attended and graduated in 1952 from David Lipscomb High School in Nashville. His younger brother, whose professional name is Nick Todd, was also a pop singer in the 1950s and is now a church music leader.

Boone's handprints and shoe prints in front of The Great Movie Ride at Disney World's Disney's Hollywood Studios

In a 2007 interview on The 700 Club, Boone claimed that he is the great-great-great-great grandson of the American pioneer Daniel Boone.

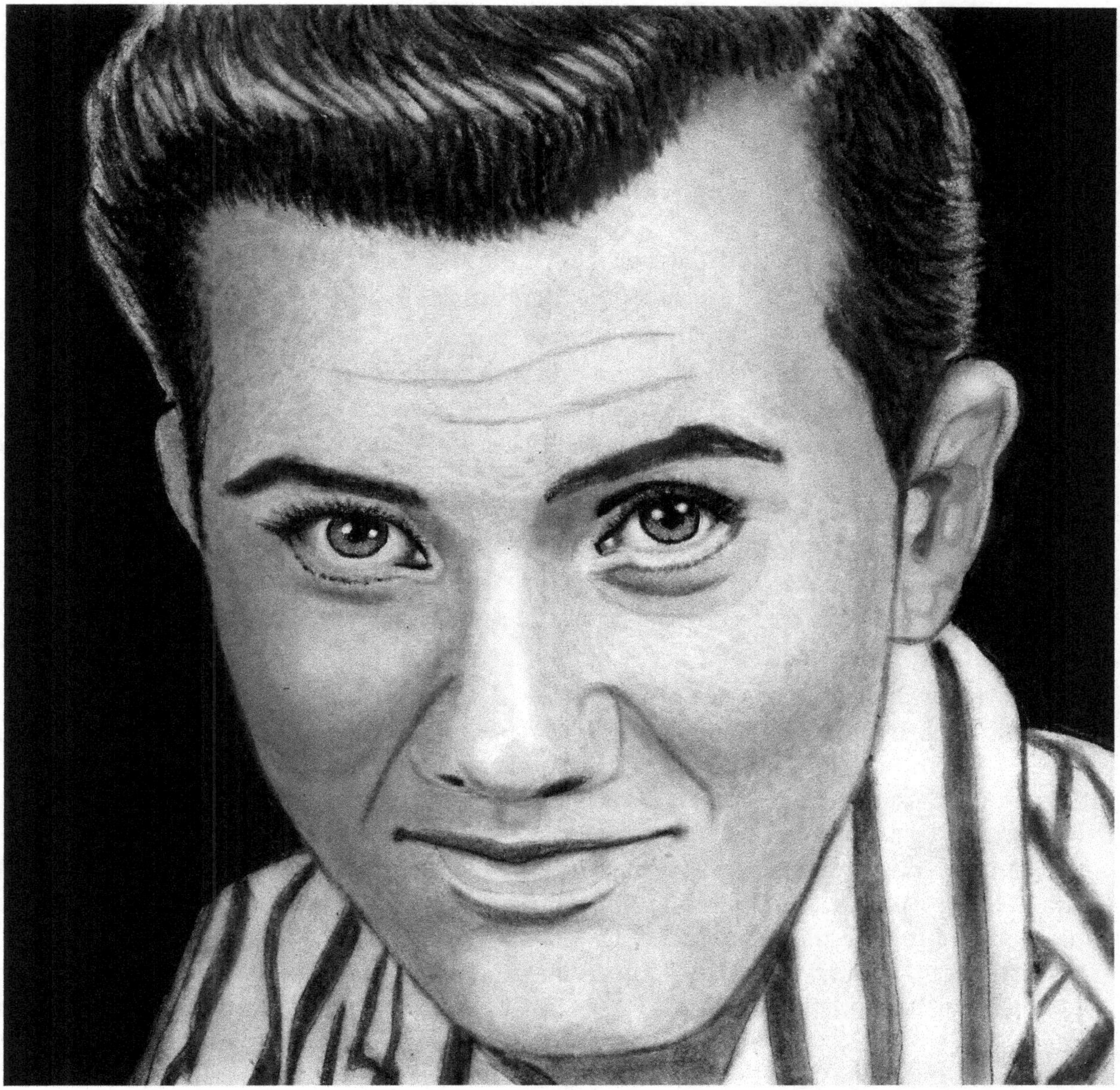

To view how this drawing was masterfully created or to purchase a Limited Edition Framed Artwork of Pat Boone type into your Internet Browser the URL shortcut ➡ **myportrait.art/patboone**

To listen to his Greatest Songs type into your Internet Browser the URL shortcut ➡ **radio.surf/patboone**

To view all channels on THE FACE OF MUSIC Internet Radio MEGA Station type into your Internet Browser the URL shortcut ➡ **radio.surf/music**

To inquire about purchasing a Limited Edition NFT of this portrait type into your Internet Browser the URL shortcut ➡ **myartnft.shop/patboone**

To view all available NFTs type into your Internet Browser the URL shortcut ➡ **myartnft.shop/all**

# Patsy Cline

(Net worth: $10 Million)(Total Records Sold: Multi-Millions)
(Genre: Country)(Height: 5' - 5")

Patsy Cline (born Virginia Patterson Hensley; September 8, 1932 – March 5, 1963) was an American singer. She is considered one of the most influential vocalists of the 20th century and was one of the first country music artists to successfully cross over into pop music. Cline had several major hits during her eight-year recording career, including two number-one hits on the Billboard Hot Country and Western Sides chart.

Cline's first professional performances began at the local WINC radio station when she was fifteen. In the early 1950s, Cline began appearing in a local band led by performer Bill Peer. Various local appearances led to featured performances on Connie B. Gay's Town and Country television broadcasts. It also led to the signing of her first recording contract with the Four Star label in 1954. She had minor success with her earliest Four Star singles including "A Church, a Courtroom, Then Goodbye" (1955) and "I've Loved and Lost Again" (1956). In 1957 however, Cline made her first national television appearance on Arthur Godfrey's Talent Scouts. After performing "Walkin' After Midnight", the single would become her first major hit on both the country and pop charts.

Cline's further singles with Four Star Records were unsuccessful, although she continued performing and recording. After marrying in 1957 and giving birth in 1958, she moved to Nashville, Tennessee, to further her career. Working with new manager Randy Hughes, Cline would become a member of the Grand Ole Opry and then move to Decca Records in 1960. Under the direction of producer Owen Bradley, her musical sound shifted and she achieved consistent success. The 1961 single "I Fall to Pieces" would become her first to top the Billboard country chart. As the song became a hit, Cline was severely injured in an automobile accident, which caused her to spend a month in the hospital. After recovering, her next single release "Crazy" would also become a major hit.

Between 1962 and 1963, Cline had hits with "She's Got You", "When I Get Through with You", "So Wrong" and "Leavin' on Your Mind". She also toured and headlined shows with more frequency. In March 1963, Cline appeared at a benefit show in Kansas City, Kansas. To return home, she boarded a plane along with country performers Cowboy Copas, Hawkshaw Hawkins and manager Randy Hughes. Upon hitting rough weather, the plane crashed outside of Camden, Tennessee, killing all those on board. Since her death, Cline has been cited as one of the most celebrated, respected and influential performers of the 20th century. Her music has influenced performers of various styles and genres. She has also been seen as a forerunner for women in country music, being among the first to sell records and headline concerts. In 1973, she became the first female performer to be inducted into the Country Music Hall of Fame. In the 1980s, Cline's posthumous successes continued in the mass media. She was portrayed twice in major motion pictures, including the 1985 biopic Sweet Dreams starring Jessica Lange. Several documentaries and stage shows were released during this time, including the 1988 musical Always...Patsy Cline. A 1991 box set of her recordings was issued that received critical acclaim. Her greatest hits album sold over 10 million copies in 2005. In 2011, Cline's childhood home was restored as a museum for visitors and fans to tour.

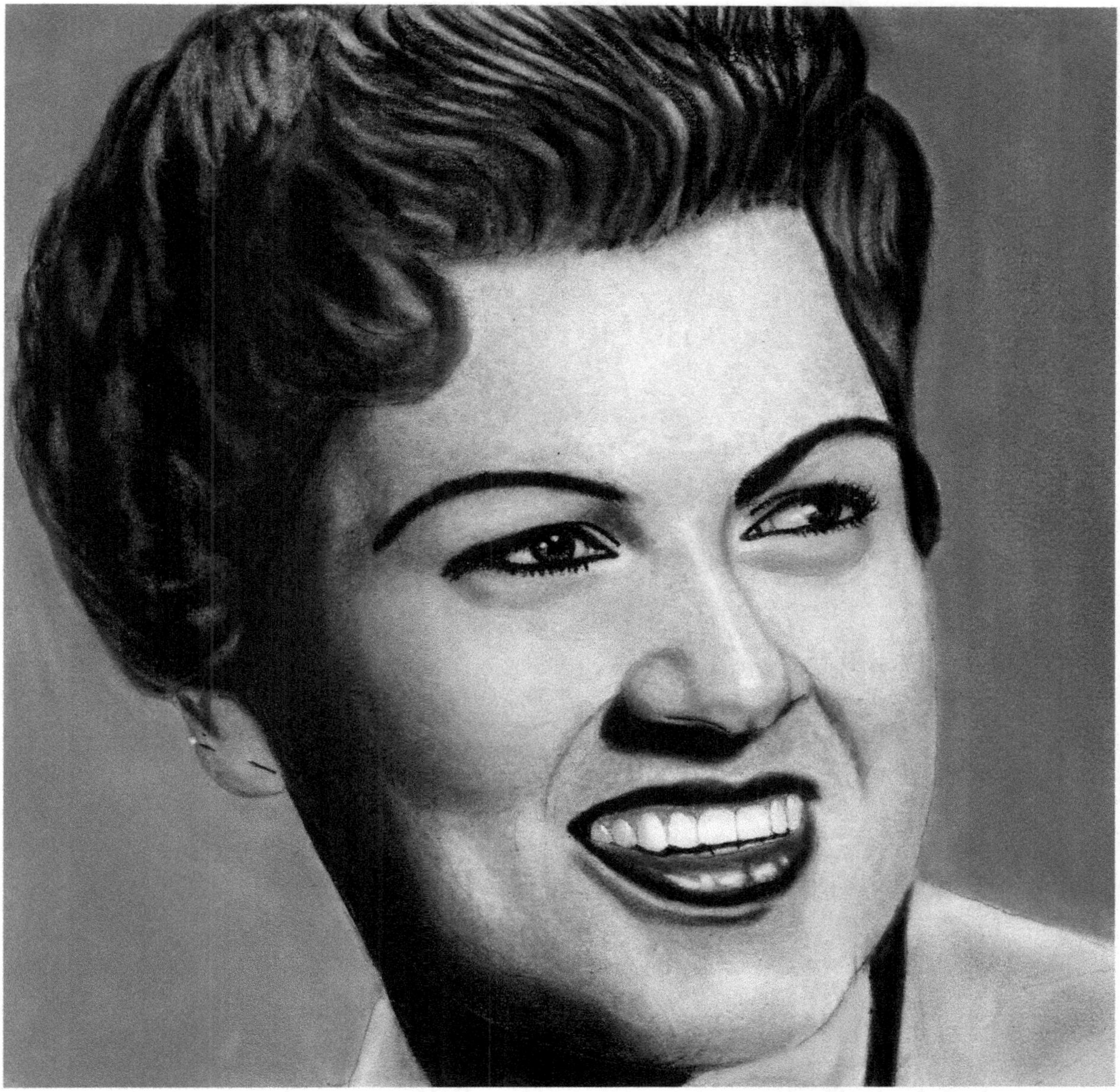

To view how this drawing was masterfully created or to purchase a Limited Edition Framed Artwork of Patsy Cline type into your Internet Browser the URL shortcut ➡ **myportrait.art/patsycline**

To listen to her Greatest Songs type into your Internet Browser the URL shortcut ➡ **radio.surf/patsycline**

To view all channels on THE FACE OF MUSIC Internet Radio MEGA Station type into your Internet Browser the URL shortcut ➡ **radio.surf/music**

To inquire about purchasing a Limited Edtion NFT of this portrait type into your Internet Browser the URL shortcut ➡ **myartnft.shop/patsycline**

To view all available NFTs type into your Internet Browser the URL shortcut ➡ **myartnft.shop/all**

# Paul Anka

(Net worth: $80 Million)(Total Records Sold: Multi-Millions)
(Genre: Pop, Soft Rock, Jazz, Doo-Wop, Rock & Roll, Swing)(Height: 5' - 5")

Paul Albert Anka OC (born July 30, 1941) is a Canadian-American singer, songwriter, and actor. Anka became famous with hit songs like "Diana", "Lonely Boy", "Put Your Head on My Shoulder", and "(You're) Having My Baby". He wrote such well-known music as the theme for The Tonight Show Starring Johnny Carson and one of Tom Jones' biggest hits "She's a Lady". He also wrote the English lyrics to Claude François and Jacques Revaux's music for Frank Sinatra's signature song, "My Way", which has been recorded by many, including Elvis Presley. Two songs he co-wrote with Michael Jackson, "This Is It" (originally titled "I Never Heard") and "Love Never Felt So Good", became posthumous hits for Jackson.

The song "Diana" brought Anka stardom as it went to No. 1 on the Canadian and US music charts. "Diana" is one of the best selling singles ever by a Canadian recording artist.

Paul Anka's talent included the theme for The Tonight Show Starring Johnny Carson (reworked in 1962 from a song Anka wrote earlier called "Toot Sweet"; it had been rewritten with lyrics and recorded by Annette Funicello in 1959 as "It's Really Love"). He wrote "Teddy" – a Top 20 hit for Connie Francis in 1960. Anka wrote the English lyrics to "My Way", Frank Sinatra's signature song (originally the French song "Comme d'habitude"). In the 1960s, Anka began acting in motion pictures as well as writing songs for them, most notably the theme for the hit film The Longest Day (which also was the official march of the Canadian Airborne Regiment), in which he made a cameo appearance as a US Army Ranger. For his film work he wrote and recorded one of his greatest hits "Lonely Boy". He also wrote and recorded "My Home Town", which was a No. 8 pop hit for him the same year. He then went on to become one of the first pop singers to perform at the Las Vegas casinos. In 1960, he appeared twice as himself in NBC's short-lived crime drama Dan Raven.

In 1963, Anka purchased the rights and ownership of his ABC-Paramount catalog in 1963 and re-recorded his earlier hits for RCA Victor, which he had joined in 1960. Like most American recording artists of the mid 1960s, Anka's career was derailed by the British Invasion. By the end of the decade, he focused mainly on adult contemporary and big-band standards and began appearing regularly in Las Vegas. In the early 1970s, Anka signed with Buddah Records, releasing two albums, the self-titled Paul Anka and Jubilation. The former, first released in 1971, included the track "She's a Lady", a song Anka composed that would become the biggest hit for Welsh singer Tom Jones that same year. Anka's version failed to become a chart success.

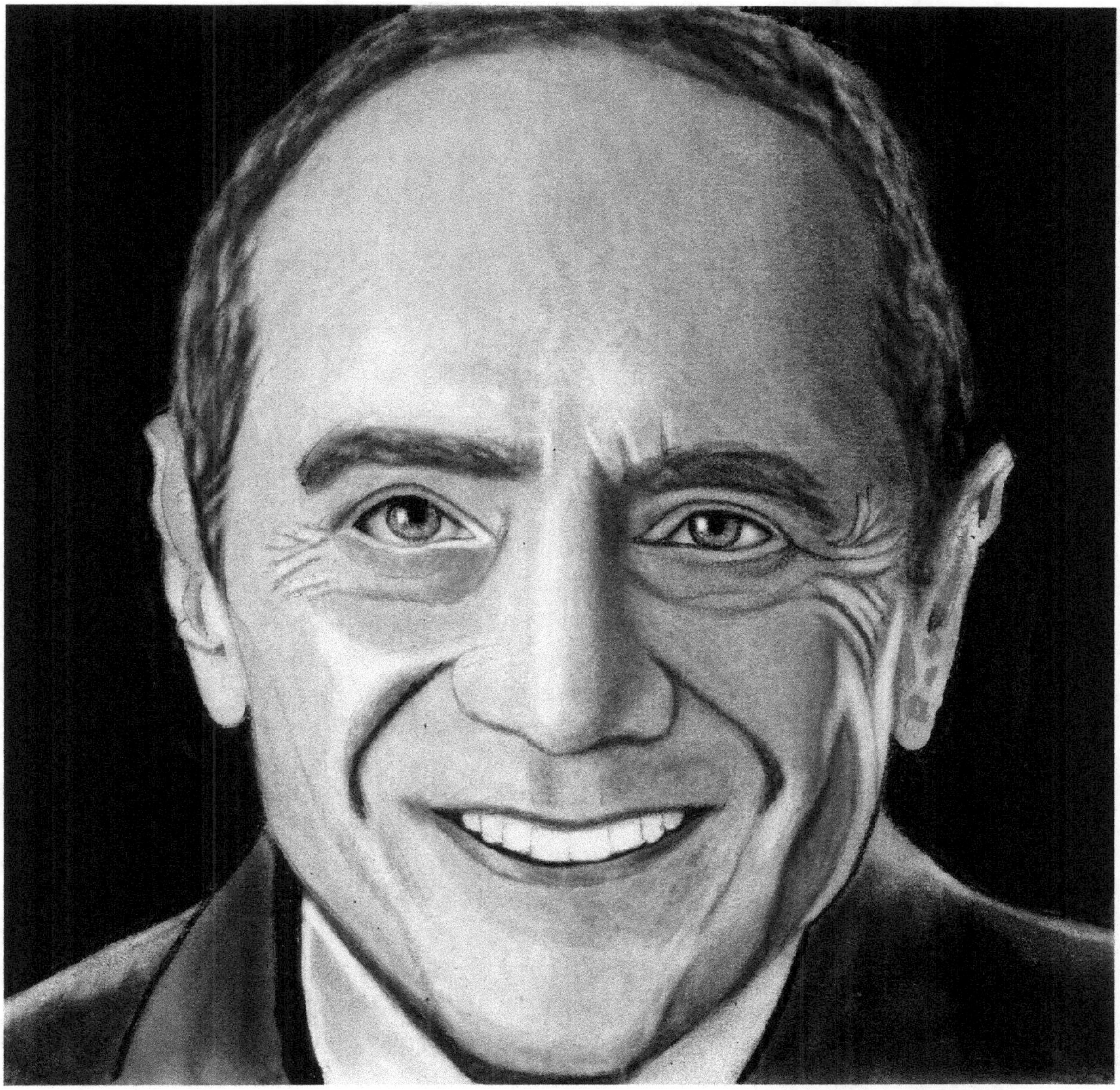

To view how this drawing was masterfully created or to purchase a Limited Edition Framed Artwork of Paul Anka type into your Internet Browser the URL shortcut ➡ **myportrait.art/paulanka**

To listen to his Greatest Songs type into your Internet Browser the URL shortcut ➡ **radio.surf/paulanka**

To view all channels on THE FACE OF MUSIC Internet Radio MEGA Station type into your Internet Browser the URL shortcut ➡ **radio.surf/music**

To inquire about purchasing a Limited Edtion NFT of this portrait type into your Internet Browser the URL shortcut ➡ **myartnft.shop/paulanka**

To view all available NFTs type into your Internet Browser the URL shortcut ➡ **myartnft.shop/all**

# Pavarotti

(Net worth: $250 Million)(Total Records Sold: 100+ Million)
(Genre: Operatic)(Height: 6' - 2")

Luciano Pavarotti Cavaliere di Gran Croce (12 October 1935 – 6 September 2007) was an Italian operatic tenor who during the late part of his career crossed over into popular music, eventually becoming one of the most acclaimed and loved tenors of all time. He made numerous recordings of complete operas and individual arias, gaining worldwide fame for the quality of his tone, and eventually established himself as one of the finest tenors of the 20th century, achieving the honorific title "King of the High Cs".

As one of the Three Tenors, who performed their first concert during the 1990 FIFA World Cup before a global audience, Pavarotti became well known for his televised concerts and media appearances. From the beginning of his professional career as a tenor in 1961 in Italy to his final performance of "Nessun dorma" at the 2006 Winter Olympics in Turin, Pavarotti was at his best in bel canto operas, pre-Aida Verdi roles, and Puccini works such as La bohème, Tosca, Turandot and Madama Butterfly. He sold over 100 million records, and the first Three Tenors recording became the best-selling classical album of all time. Pavarotti was also noted for his charity work on behalf of refugees and the Red Cross, amongst others. He died from pancreatic cancer on 6 September 2007.

Luciano Pavarotti was born in 1935 on the outskirts of Modena in Northern Italy, the son of Fernando Pavarotti, a baker and amateur tenor, and Adele Venturi, a cigar factory worker. Although he spoke fondly of his childhood, the family had little money; its four members were crowded into a two-room apartment. According to Pavarotti, his father had a fine tenor voice but rejected the possibility of a singing career because of nervousness. World War II forced the family out of the city in 1943. For the following year they rented a single room from a farmer in the neighbouring countryside, where the young Pavarotti developed an interest in farming.

After abandoning the dream of becoming a football goalkeeper, Pavarotti spent seven years in vocal training. Pavarotti's earliest musical influences were his father's recordings, most of them featuring the popular tenors of the day—Beniamino Gigli, Giovanni Martinelli, Tito Schipa, and Enrico Caruso. Pavarotti's favourite tenor and idol was Giuseppe Di Stefano and he was also deeply influenced by Mario Lanza, saying: "In my teens I used to go to Mario Lanza movies and then come home and imitate him in the mirror". At around the age of nine he began singing with his father in a small local church choir.

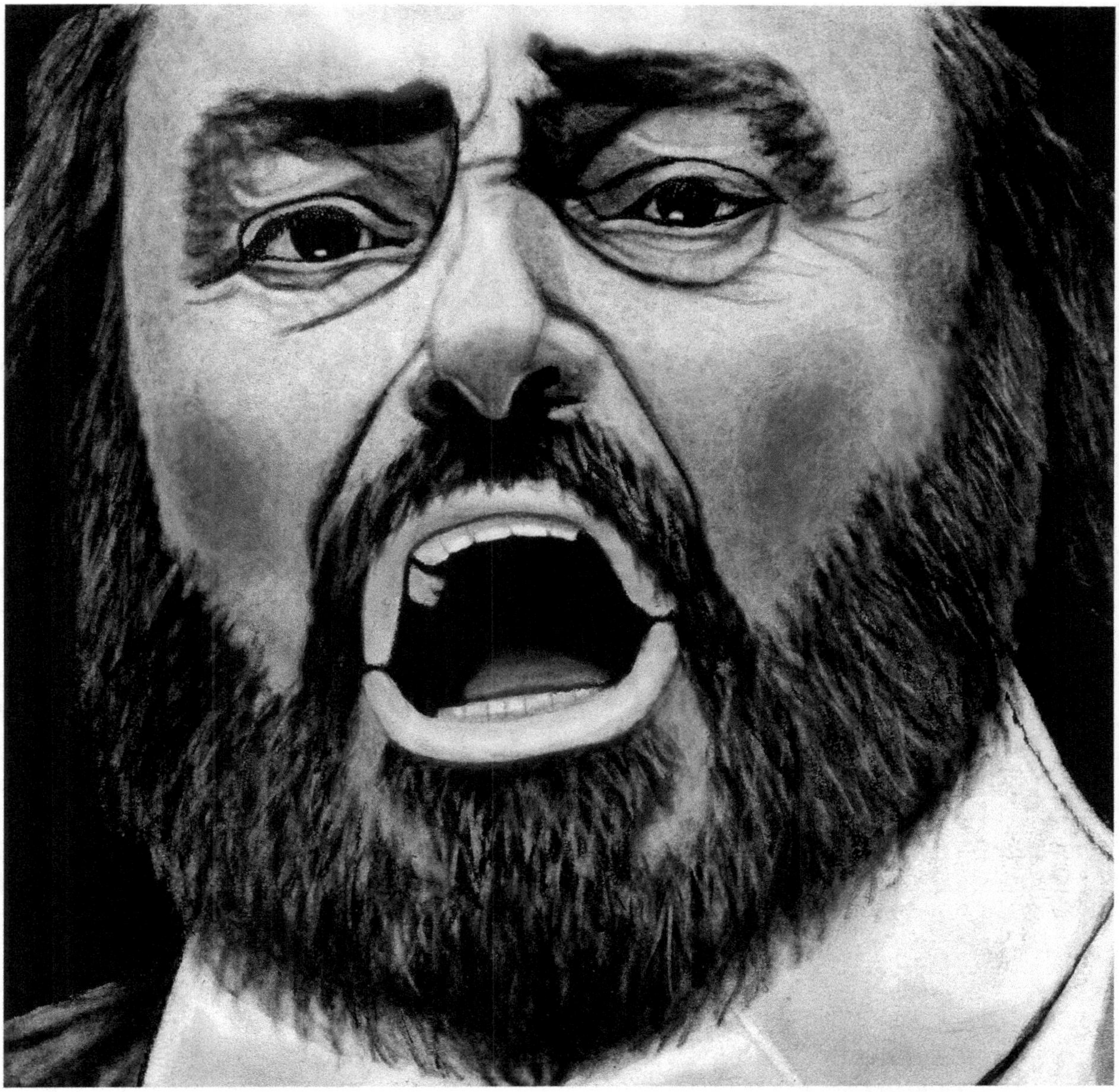

To view how this drawing was masterfully created or to purchase a Limited Edition Framed Artwork of Pavarotti type into your Internet Browser the URL shortcut ➡ **myportrait.art/pavarotti**

To listen to his Greatest Songs type into your Internet Browser the URL shortcut ➡ **radio.surf/pavarotti**

To view all channels on THE FACE OF MUSIC Internet Radio MEGA Station type into your Internet Browser the URL shortcut ➡ **radio.surf/music**

To inquire about purchasing a Limited Edtion NFT of this portrait type into your Internet Browser the URL shortcut ➡ **myartnft.shop/pavarotti**

To view all available NFTs type into your Internet Browser the URL shortcut ➡ **myartnft.shop/all**

# Pearl Jam

(Total Records Sold: 85 Million)(Genre: Alternative Rock , Grunge , Hard Rock)

Pearl Jam is an American rock band formed in Seattle, Washington, in 1990. The band's line up consists of founding members Jeff Ament (bass guitar), Stone Gossard (rhythm guitar), Mike McCready (lead guitar), and Eddie Vedder (lead vocals, guitar), as well as Matt Cameron (drums), who joined in 1998. Keyboardist Boom Gaspar has also been a touring/session member with the band since 2002. Drummers Jack Irons, Dave Krusen, Matt Chamberlain, and Dave Abbruzzese are former members of the band. Pearl Jam outsold many of their contemporary alternative rock bands from the early 1990s, and are considered one of the most influential bands of the decade, being dubbed as "the most popular American rock & roll band of the '90s".Formed after the demise of Gossard and Ament's previous band, Mother Love Bone, Pearl Jam broke into the mainstream with their debut album, Ten, in 1991. Ten stayed on the Billboard 200 chart for nearly five years, and has gone on to become one of the highest-selling rock records ever, going 13x platinum in the United States. Released in 1993, Pearl Jam's second album, Vs., sold over 950,000 copies in its first week of release, setting the record for most copies of an album sold in its first week of release at the time. Their third album, Vitalogy (1994), became the second-fastest-selling CD in history at the time, with more than 877,000 units sold in its first week.One of the key bands in the grunge movement of the early 1990s, Pearl Jam's members often shunned popular music industry practices such as making music videos or participating in interviews. The band also sued Ticketmaster, claiming it had monopolized the concert-ticket market. In 2006, Rolling Stone described the band as having "spent much of the past decade deliberately tearing apart their own fame."Pearl Jam had sold more than 85 million albums worldwide by 2018, including nearly 32 million albums in the United States by 2012, making them one of the best-selling bands of all time. Pearl Jam was inducted into the Rock and Roll Hall of Fame in 2017 in its first year of eligibility. They were ranked at No. 8 in a reader poll by Rolling Stone magazine in its "Top Ten Live Acts of All Time" issue. Throughout its career, the band has also promoted wider social and political issues, from pro-choice sentiments to opposition to George W. Bush's presidency. Vedder acts as the band's spokesman on these issues.

# Eddie Vedder

(Net Worth: $100 Million)(Height: 5' - 7")

Eddie Vedder (born Edward Louis Severson III; December 23, 1964) is an American singer, musician and songwriter, best known as the lead vocalist, one of three guitarists, and the primary lyricist of the American Alternative Rock band Pearl Jam. He also appeared as a guest vocalist in Temple of the Dog, the one-off tribute band dedicated to the late singer Andrew Wood.

Vedder is known for his powerful baritone vocals. He was ranked at number 7 on a list of "Best Lead Singers of All Time", based on a readers' poll compiled by Rolling Stone.r

In 2007, Vedder released his first solo album as a soundtrack for the film Into the Wild (2007). His second album Ukulele Songs and a live DVD titled Water on the Road were released in 2011. In 2017, Vedder was inducted into the Rock and Roll Hall of Fame as a member of Pearl Jam.

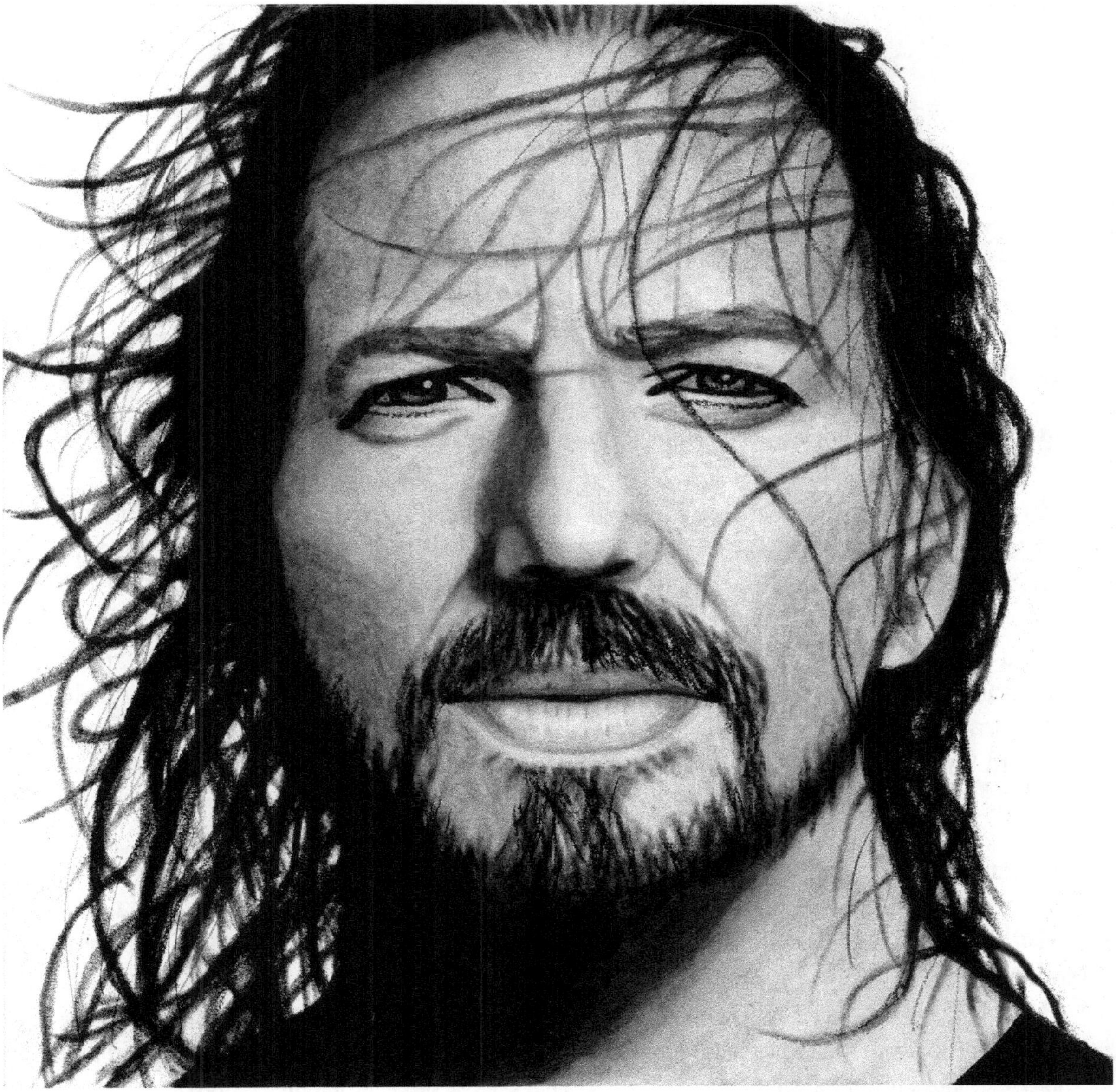

To view how this drawing was masterfully created or to purchase a Limited Edition Framed Artwork of Eddie Vedder type into your Internet Browser the URL shortcut ➡ **myportrait.art/eddievedder**

To listen to their Greatest Songs type into your Internet Browser the URL shortcut ➡ **radio.surf/pearljam**

To view all channels on THE FACE OF MUSIC Internet Radio MEGA Station type into your Internet Browser the URL shortcut ➡ **radio.surf/music**

To inquire about purchasing a Limited Edtion NFT of this portrait type into your Internet Browser the URL shortcut ➡ **myartnft.shop/eddievedder**

To view all available NFTs type into your Internet Browser the URL shortcut ➡ **myartnft.shop/all**

# Perry Como

(Net worth: $40 Million)(Total Records Sold: Multi-Millions)
(Genre: Voval Pop , East Listening)(Height: 5' - 6")

Pierino Ronald "Perry" Como (May 18, 1912 – May 12, 2001) was an Italian-American singer, actor and television personality. During a career spanning more than half a century, he recorded exclusively for RCA Victor for 44 years, after signing with the label in 1943.

He recorded primarily vocal pop and was renowned for recordings in the intimate, easy-listening genre pioneered by multi-media star Bing Crosby.

"Mr. C.", as he was nicknamed, sold millions of records and pioneered a weekly musical variety television show. His weekly television shows and seasonal specials were broadcast throughout the world. In the official RCA Records Billboard magazine memorial, his life was summed up in these few words: "50 years of music and a life well lived. An example to all."

Como received five Emmys from 1955 to 1959, a Christopher Award (1956) and shared a Peabody Award with good friend Jackie Gleason in 1956. He was inducted into the Academy of Television Arts & Sciences Hall of Fame in 1990 and received a Kennedy Center Honor in 1987. Posthumously, Como received the Grammy Lifetime Achievement Award in 2002 and was inducted into the Long Island Music Hall of Fame in 2006. He has the distinction of having three stars on the Hollywood Walk of Fame for his work in radio, television, and music.

Como was born in Canonsburg, Pennsylvania, about 20 miles (32 km) southwest of Pittsburgh. He was the seventh of ten children and the first American-born child of Pietro Como and Lucia Travaglini, who both immigrated to the US in 1910 from the Abruzzese town of Palena, Italy. He did not begin speaking English until he entered school, since the Comos spoke Italian at home. The family had a second-hand organ his father had bought for $3; as soon as Como was able to toddle, he would head to the instrument, pump the bellows, and play music he had heard by ear. Pietro, a mill hand and an amateur baritone, had all his children attend music lessons even if he could barely afford them. In a rare 1957 interview, Como's mother, Lucia, described how her young son also took on other jobs to pay for more music lessons; Como learned to play many different instruments, but never had a voice lesson. He showed more musical talent in his teenage years as a trombone player in the town's brass band, playing guitar, singing at weddings, and as an organist at church. Como was a member of the Canonsburg Italian Band along with the father of singer Bobby Vinton, bandleader Stan Vinton, who was often a customer at his barber shop..

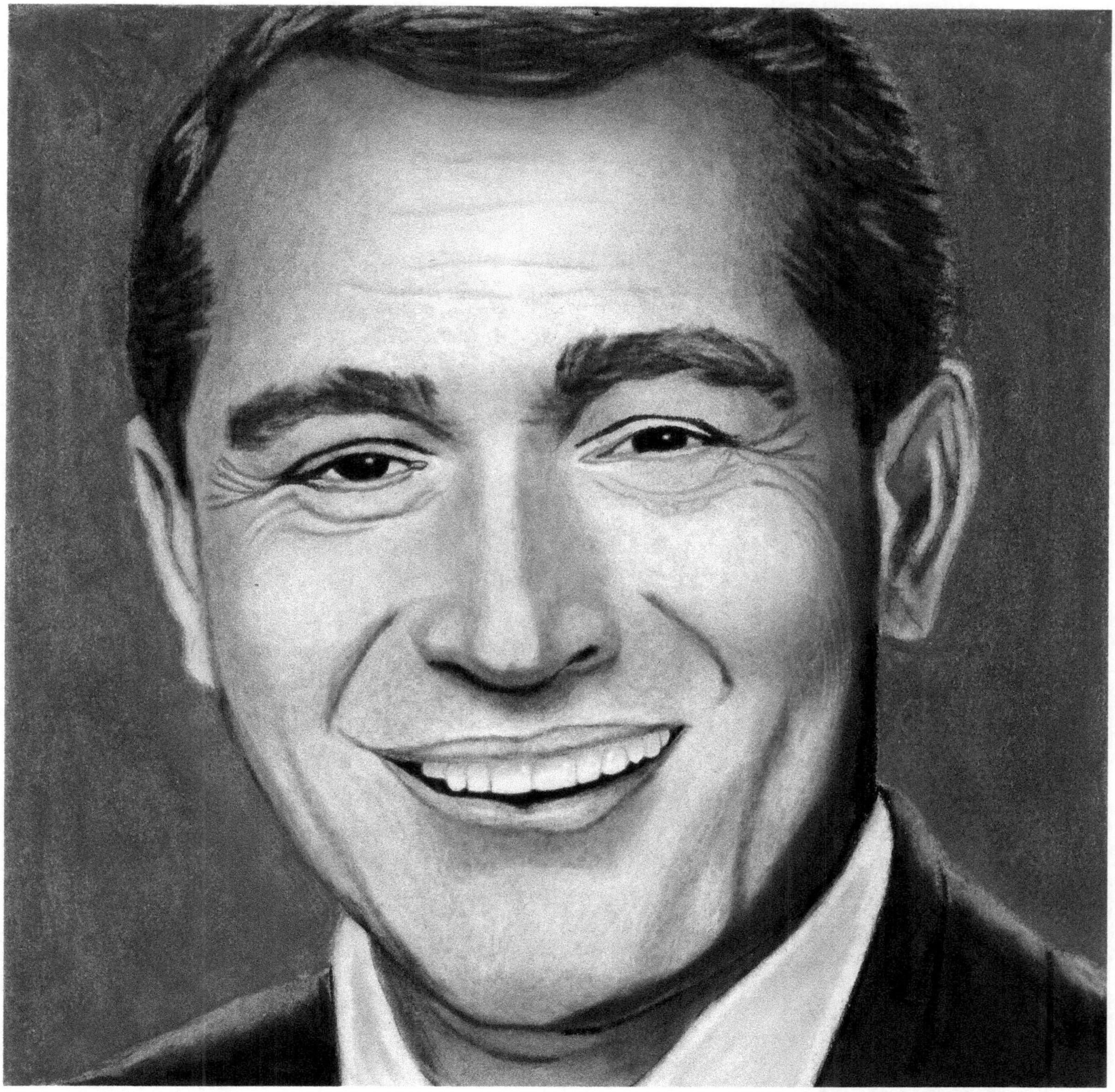

To view how this drawing was masterfully created or to purchase a Limited Edition Framed Artwork of Perry Como type into your Internet Browser the URL shortcut ➡ **myportrait.art/perrycomo**

To listen to his Greatest Songs type into your Internet Browser the URL shortcut ➡ **radio.surf/perrycomo**

To view all channels on THE FACE OF MUSIC Internet Radio MEGA Station type into your Internet Browser the URL shortcut ➡ **radio.surf/music**

To inquire about purchasing a Limited Edtion NFT of this portrait type into your Internet Browser the URL shortcut ➡ **myartnft.shop/perrycomo**

To view all available NFTs type into your Internet Browser the URL shortcut ➡ **myartnft.shop/all**

# Peter Frampton

(Net worth: $30 Million)(Total Records Sold: Multi-Millions)
(Genre: Classic Rock)(Height: 5' - 8")

Peter Kenneth Frampton (born 22 April 1950) is an English rock musician, singer, songwriter, and producer. He was previously associated with the bands Humble Pie and the Herd. As a solo artist, Frampton released several albums including his international breakthrough album, the live release Frampton Comes Alive!. The album sold more than eight million copies in the United States and spawned several hit singles. Since then he has released several other albums. He has also worked with Ringo Starr, the Who's John Entwistle, David Bowie and both Matt Cameron and Mike McCready from Pearl Jam, among others.

Frampton is best known for such hits as "Show Me the Way," "Baby, I Love Your Way," "Do You Feel Like We Do," and "I'm in You," which remain staples on classic rock radio. He has also appeared as himself in television shows such as The Simpsons, Family Guy, and Madam Secretary. Frampton is known for his work as a guitar player, particularly with a talk box and his tenor voice.

Peter Kenneth Frampton was born to Owen and Peggy (née ffitch) Frampton in Beckenham, Kent, UK. He attended Bromley Technical High School, at which his father, Owen Frampton, was a teacher and the head of the Art department. He first became interested in music when he was seven years old. Having discovered his grandmother's banjolele in the attic, he taught himself to play it, going on to later teach himself how to play guitar and piano as well. At the age of eight, he began taking classical music lessons.

His early influences were Cliff Richard & the Shadows (featuring guitarist Hank Marvin) and American rockers Buddy Holly and Eddie Cochran and later the Ventures, Jimi Hendrix and the Beatles. His father introduced him to the recordings of Belgian gypsy jazz guitarist Django Reinhardt. Peter Frampton had little commercial success with his early albums. This changed with Frampton's best-selling live album, Frampton Comes Alive!, in 1976, from which "Baby, I Love Your Way," "Show Me the Way," and an edited version of "Do You Feel Like We Do," were hit singles. The latter two tracks also featured his use of the talk box guitar effect. The album was recorded in 1975, mainly at the Winterland Ballroom in San Francisco, California, where Humble Pie had previously enjoyed a good following. Frampton had a new line-up, with Americans Bob Mayo on keyboards and rhythm guitar and Stanley Sheldon on bass. Wills had been sacked by Frampton at the end of 1974, and Bown had left on the eve of Frampton Comes Alive, to return to England and new fame with Status Quo. Frampton Comes Alive was released in early January, debuting on the charts on 14 February at number 191. The album was on the Billboard 200 for 97 weeks, of which 55 were in the top 40, of which 10 were at the top. The album beat, among others, Fleetwood Mac's Fleetwood Mac to become the top selling album of 1976, and it was also the 14th best seller of 1977. With sales of eight million copies it became the biggest selling live album, although with others subsequently selling more it is now the fourth biggest. Frampton Comes Alive! has been certified as eight times platinum. The album won Frampton a Juno Award in 1977.

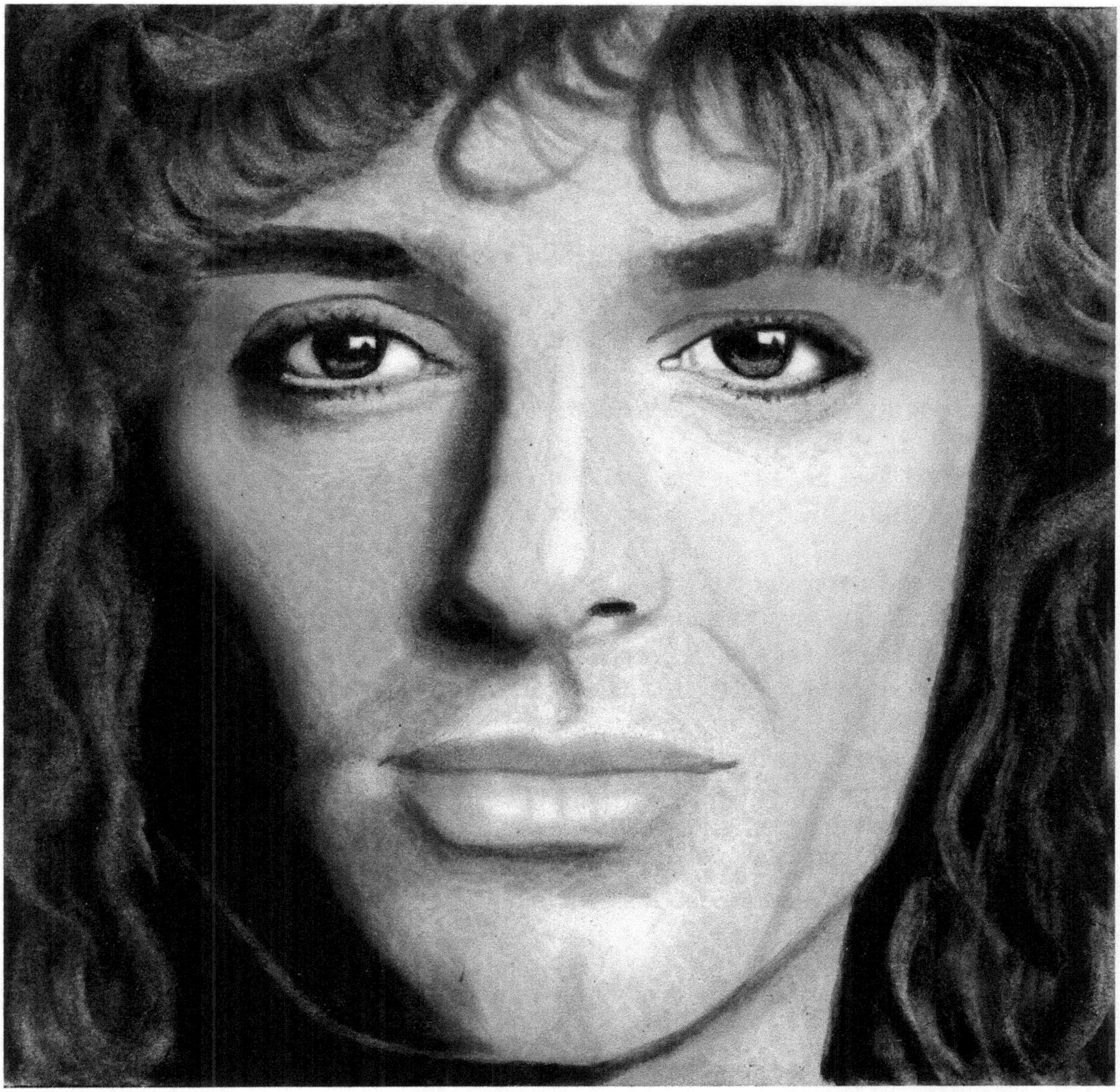

To view how this drawing was masterfully created or to purchase a Limited Edition Framed Artwork of Peter Frampton type into your Internet Browser the URL shortcut ➡ **myportrait.art/peterframpton**

To listen to his Greatest Songs type into your Internet Browser the URL shortcut
➡ **radio.surf/peterframpton**

To view all channels on THE FACE OF MUSIC Internet Radio MEGA Station type into your Internet Browser the URL shortcut ➡ **radio.surf/music**

To inquire about purchasing a Limited Edtion NFT of this portrait type into your Internet Browser the URL shortcut ➡ **myartnft.shop/peterframpton**

To view all available NFTs type into your Internet Browser the URL shortcut ➡ **myartnft.shop/all**

# Peter Gabriel

(Net worth: $95 Million)(Total Albums Sold: 23 Million)
(Genre: Progressive Rock)(Height: 5' - 11")

Peter Brian Gabriel (born 13 February 1950) is an English musician, singer, songwriter, record producer and activist. He rose to fame as the original lead singer of the progressive rock band Genesis. After leaving Genesis in 1975, he launched a successful solo career with "Solsbury Hill" as his first single. His 1986 album, So, is his best-selling release and is certified triple platinum in the UK and five times platinum in the U.S. The album's most successful single, "Sledgehammer", won a record nine MTV Awards at the 1987 MTV Video Music Awards and, according to a report in 2011, it was MTV's most played music video of all time.

Gabriel has been a champion of world music for much of his career. He co-founded the WOMAD festival in 1982. He has continued to focus on producing and promoting world music through his Real World Records label. He has also pioneered digital distribution methods for music, co-founding OD2, one of the first online music download services. Gabriel has also been involved in numerous humanitarian efforts. In 1980, he released the anti-apartheid single "Biko". He has participated in several human rights benefit concerts, including Amnesty International's Human Rights Now! tour in 1988, and co-founded the Witness human rights organisation in 1992. Gabriel developed The Elders with Richard Branson, which was launched by Nelson Mandela in 2007.

Gabriel has won three Brit Awards—winning Best British Male in 1987, six Grammy Awards, thirteen MTV Video Music Awards, the first Pioneer Award at the BT Digital Music Awards, the Q magazine Lifetime Achievement, the Ivor Novello Award for Lifetime Achievement, and the Polar Music Prize. He was made a BMI Icon at the 57th annual BMI London Awards for his "influence on generations of music makers". In recognition of his many years of human rights activism, he received the Man of Peace award from the Nobel Peace Prize laureates in 2006, and Time magazine named him one of the 100 most influential people in the world in 2008. AllMusic has described Gabriel as "one of rock's most ambitious, innovative musicians, as well as one of its most political". He was inducted into the Rock and Roll Hall of Fame as a member of Genesis in 2010, followed by his induction as a solo artist in 2014. In March 2015, he was awarded an honorary doctorate from the University of South Australia in recognition of his achievements in music.

Peter Brian Gabriel was born on 13 February 1950 in Chobham, Surrey. He was raised in a middle-class family in Coxhill, a Victorian manor situated on Deep Pool Farm just outside Chobham. His father, Ralph Parton Gabriel (1912–2012), was an electrical engineer and his mother, Edith Irene Gabriel (née Allen), was from a musical family. His great-great-great-uncle, Sir Thomas Gabriel, 1st Baronet, was Lord Mayor of London from 1866 to 1877. Gabriel attended Cable House, a private primary school in Woking, Surrey, followed by St Andrews Preparatory School for Boys in Horsell, Surrey. During his time at the latter, his teachers noticed his singing talent, but he opted for piano lessons from his mother and developed an interest in drumming. At age 10, he purchased a floor tom-tom.

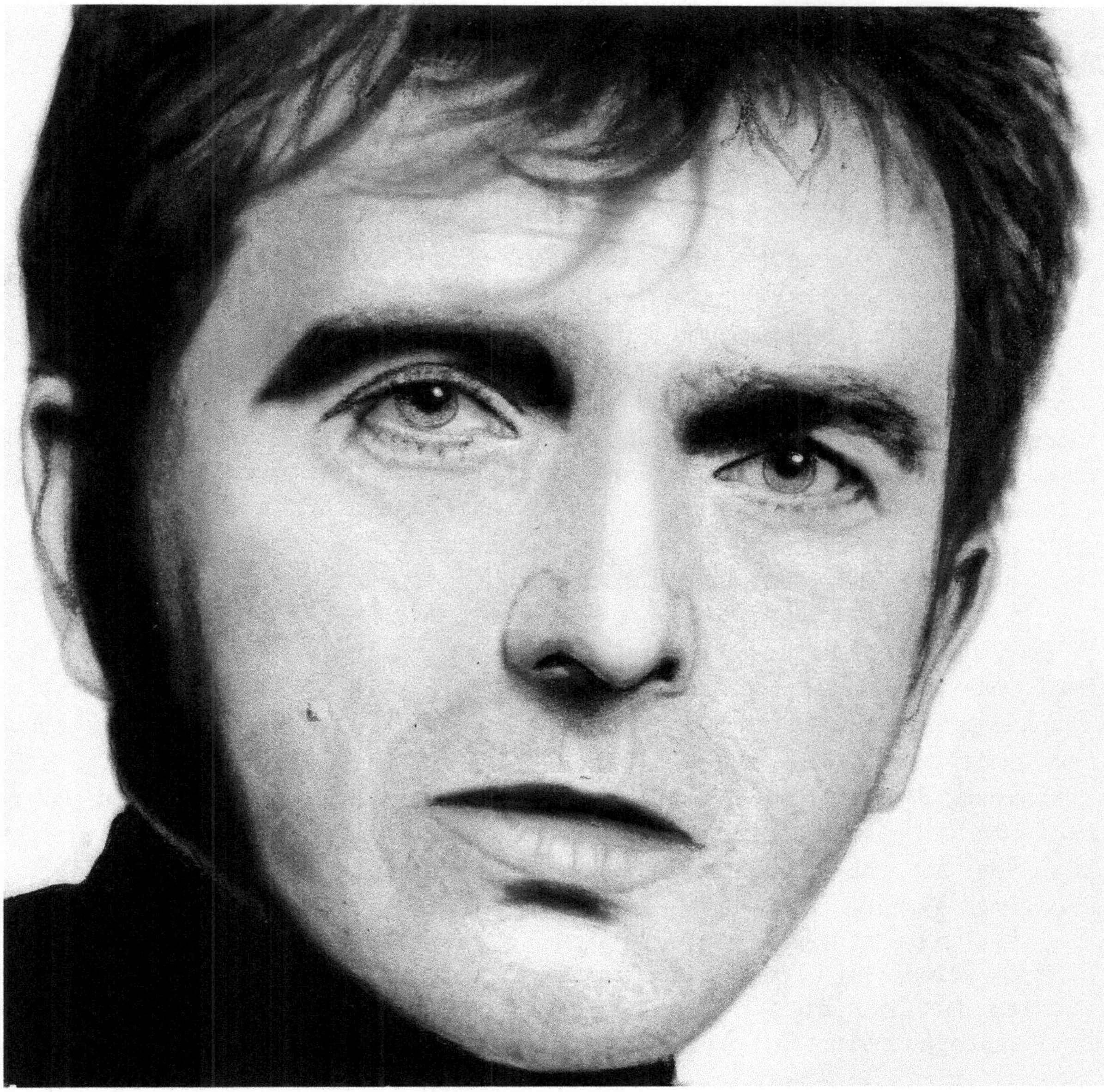

To view how this drawing was masterfully created or to purchase a Limited Edition Framed Artwork of Peter Gabriel type into your Internet Browser the URL shortcut ➡ **myportrait.art/petergabriel**

To listen to his Greatest Songs type into your Internet Browser the URL shortcut ➡ **radio.surf/petergabriel**

To view all channels on THE FACE OF MUSIC Internet Radio MEGA Station type into your Internet Browser the URL shortcut ➡ **radio.surf/music**

To inquire about purchasing a Limited Edition NFT of this portrait type into your Internet Browser the URL shortcut ➡ **myartnft.shop/petergabriel**

To view all available NFTs type into your Internet Browser the URL shortcut ➡ **myartnft.shop/all**

# Pink

(Net worth: $200 Million)(Total Records Sold: 90+ Million)
(Genre: Pop , Pop Rock , R&B)(Height: 5' - 4")

Alecia Beth Moore (born September 8, 1979), known professionally as Pink (stylized as P!nk), is an American singer and songwriter. She was originally a member of the girl group Choice. In 1995, LaFace Records saw potential in Pink and offered her a solo recording contract. Her R&B-influenced debut studio album Can't Take Me Home (2000) was certified double-platinum in the United States and spawned two Billboard Hot 100 top-ten songs: "There You Go" and "Most Girls". She gained further recognition with the collaborative single "Lady Marmalade" from the Moulin Rouge! soundtrack, which topped many charts worldwide. Refocusing her sound to pop rock with her second studio album Missundaztood (2001), the album sold more than 13 million copies worldwide and yielded the international number-one songs "Get the Party Started", "Don't Let Me Get Me", and "Just Like a Pill".

While Pink's third studio album, Try This (2003), sold significantly less than her previous work, it earned her the Grammy Award for Best Female Rock Vocal Performance. She returned to the top of record charts with her fourth and fifth studio albums, I'm Not Dead (2006) and Funhouse (2008), which spawned the top-ten entries "Who Knew" and "U + Ur Hand", as well as the number-one single "So What". Pink's sixth studio album, The Truth About Love (2012), was her first Billboard 200 number-one album and spawned her fourth US number-one single, "Just Give Me a Reason". In 2014, Pink recorded a collaborative album, Rose Ave., with Canadian musician Dallas Green under a folk music duo named You+Me. Her next studio albums, Beautiful Trauma (2017) and Hurts 2B Human (2019), both debuted at atop the Billboard 200 chart, with the former becoming the world's third best-selling album of the year.

Noted for her distinctive raspy voice and acrobatic stage presence, Pink has sold over 90 million records worldwide as of 2020, making her one of the world's best-selling music artists. Her career accolades include three Grammy Awards, two Brit Awards, a Daytime Emmy Award and seven MTV Video Music Awards, including the Michael Jackson Video Vanguard Award. In 2009, Billboard named Pink the Pop Songs Artist of the Decade. Pink was also the second most-played female solo artist in the United Kingdom during the 2000s decade, behind only Madonna. VH1 ranked her at number ten on their list of the 100 Greatest Women in Music, while Billboard awarded her the Woman of the Year award in 2013. At the 63rd annual BMI Pop Awards, she received the BMI President's Award for "her outstanding achievement in songwriting and global impact on pop culture and the entertainment industry."

Alecia Beth Moore was born on September 8, 1979, in Doylestown, Pennsylvania, to emergency room nurse Judith "Judy" Moore (née Kugel) and insurance salesman James "Jim" Moore. She has described herself as an "Irish-German-Lithuanian-Jew",and self-identifies as Jewish. Although a healthy baby at birth, she quickly developed asthma that plagued her through her early years. When Pink was a toddler, her parents began having marital problems and divorced before she was 10.

Pink was trained as a competitive gymnast between the ages 4 and 12. She developed her voice early in life. She attended Central Bucks High School West. In high school, Pink joined her first band, Middleground, but it disbanded upon losing a Battle of the Bands competition. As a teenager, she wrote lyrics as an outlet for her feelings, and her mother commented, "Her initial writings were always very introspective. Some of it was very black, and very deep, almost worrisome."

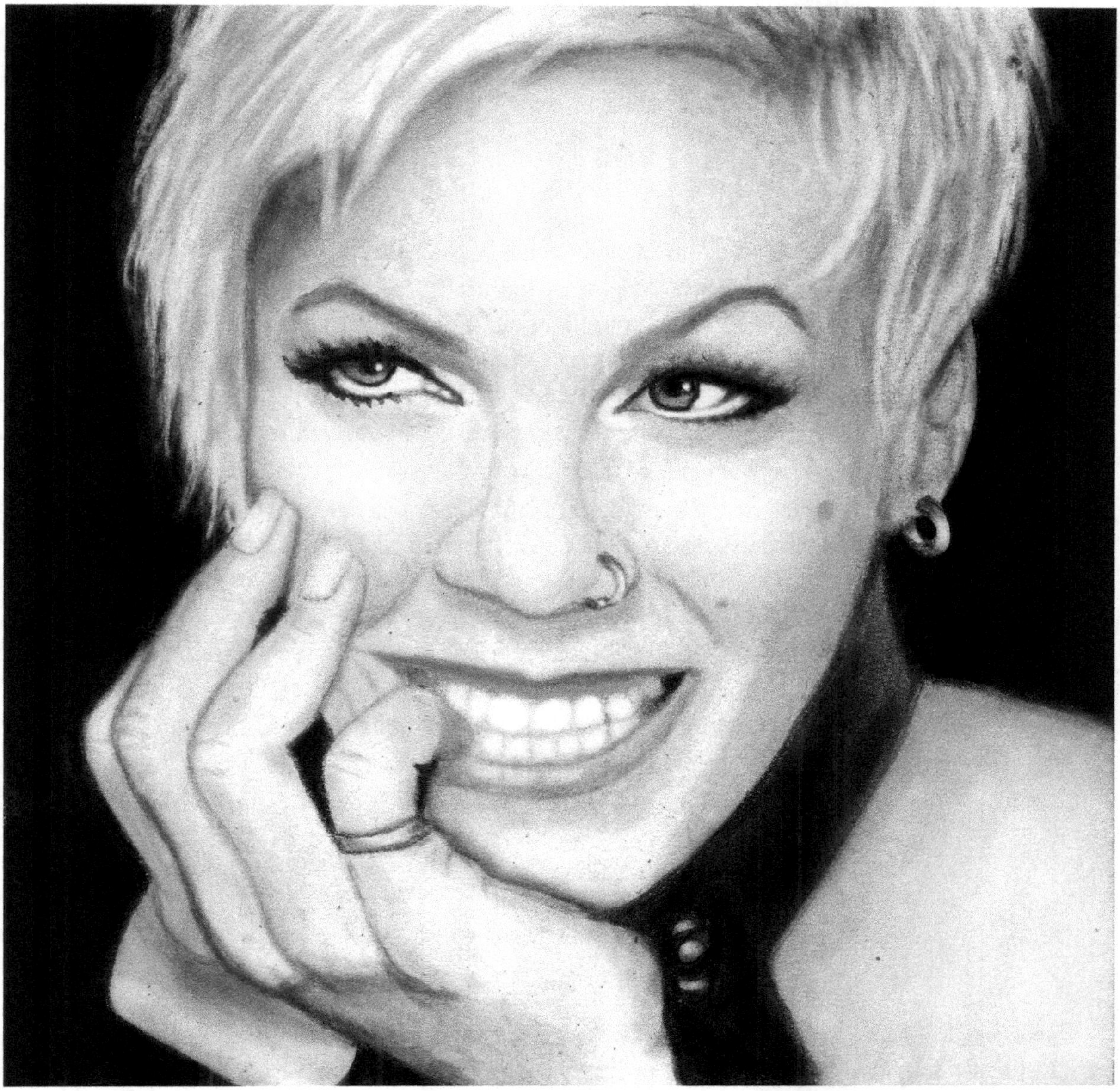

To view how this drawing was masterfully created or to purchase a Limited Edition Framed Artwork of Pink type into your Internet Browser the URL shortcut ➡ **myportrait.art/pink**

To listen to her Greatest Songs type into your Internet Browser the URL shortcut ➡ **radio.surf/pink**

To view all channels on THE FACE OF MUSIC Internet Radio MEGA Station type into your Internet Browser the URL shortcut ➡ **radio.surf/music**

To inquire about purchasing a Limited Edtion NFT of this portrait type into your Internet Browser the URL shortcut ➡ **myartnft.shop/pink**

To view all available NFTs type into your Internet Browser the URL shortcut ➡ **myartnft.shop/all**

# Pink Floyd

(Total Records Sold: 250+ Million)

(Genre: Progressive Rock, Experimental Rock, Psychedelic Rock)

Pink Floyd were an English rock band formed in London in 1965. Gaining an early following as one of the first British psychedelic groups, they were distinguished for their extended compositions, sonic experimentation, philosophical lyrics and elaborate live shows, and became a leading band of the progressive rock genre.Pink Floyd were founded by students Syd Barrett (guitar, lead vocals), Nick Mason (drums), Roger Waters (bass guitar, vocals), and Richard Wright (keyboards, vocals). Under Barrett's leadership, they released two charting singles and a successful debut album, The Piper at the Gates of Dawn (1967).

Guitarist and vocalist David Gilmour joined in December 1967; Barrett left in April 1968 due to deteriorating mental health. Waters became the primary lyricist and thematic leader, devising the concepts behind the band's peak of critical and commercial success with the albums The Dark Side of the Moon (1973), Wish You Were Here (1975), Animals (1977), and The Wall (1979). The musical film based on The Wall, Pink Floyd – The Wall (1982), won two BAFTA Awards.

Following personal tensions, Wright left Pink Floyd in 1979, followed by Waters in 1985. Gilmour and Mason continued as Pink Floyd, rejoined later by Wright. The band produced two more albums—

- Continued on Page 489 -

# David Gilmour

(Net Worth: $180 Million)(Height: 6' - 0")

David Jon Gilmour (born 6 March 1946) is an English musician who was a member of rock band Pink Floyd. He joined as guitarist and co-lead vocalist in 1968 shortly before the departure of founder member Syd Barrett. Pink Floyd achieved international success with the concept albums The Dark Side of the Moon (1973), Wish You Were Here (1975), Animals (1977), and The Wall (1979). By the early 1980s, they had become one of the highest-selling and most acclaimed acts in music history; by 2012. Following the departure of Roger Waters in 1985, Pink Floyd continued under Gilmour's leadership and released three more studio albums.

Gilmour has produced a variety of artists, such as the Dream Academy, and has released four solo studio albums: David Gilmour, About Face, On an Island, and Rattle That Lock. He is also credited for bringing singer-songwriter Kate Bush to public attention. As a member of Pink Floyd, he was inducted into the US Rock and Roll Hall of Fame in 1996, and the UK Music Hall of Fame in 2005. In 2003, Gilmour was made a Commander of the Order of the British Empire (CBE). He was awarded with the Outstanding Contribution title at the 2008 Q Awards. In 2011, Rolling Stone magazine ranked him number 14 in their list of the greatest guitarists of all time. He was also voted number 36 in the greatest voices in rock by Planet Rock listeners in 2009.

Gilmour has taken part in projects related to issues including animal rights, environmentalism, homelessness, poverty, and human rights. He has married twice and is the father of eight children.

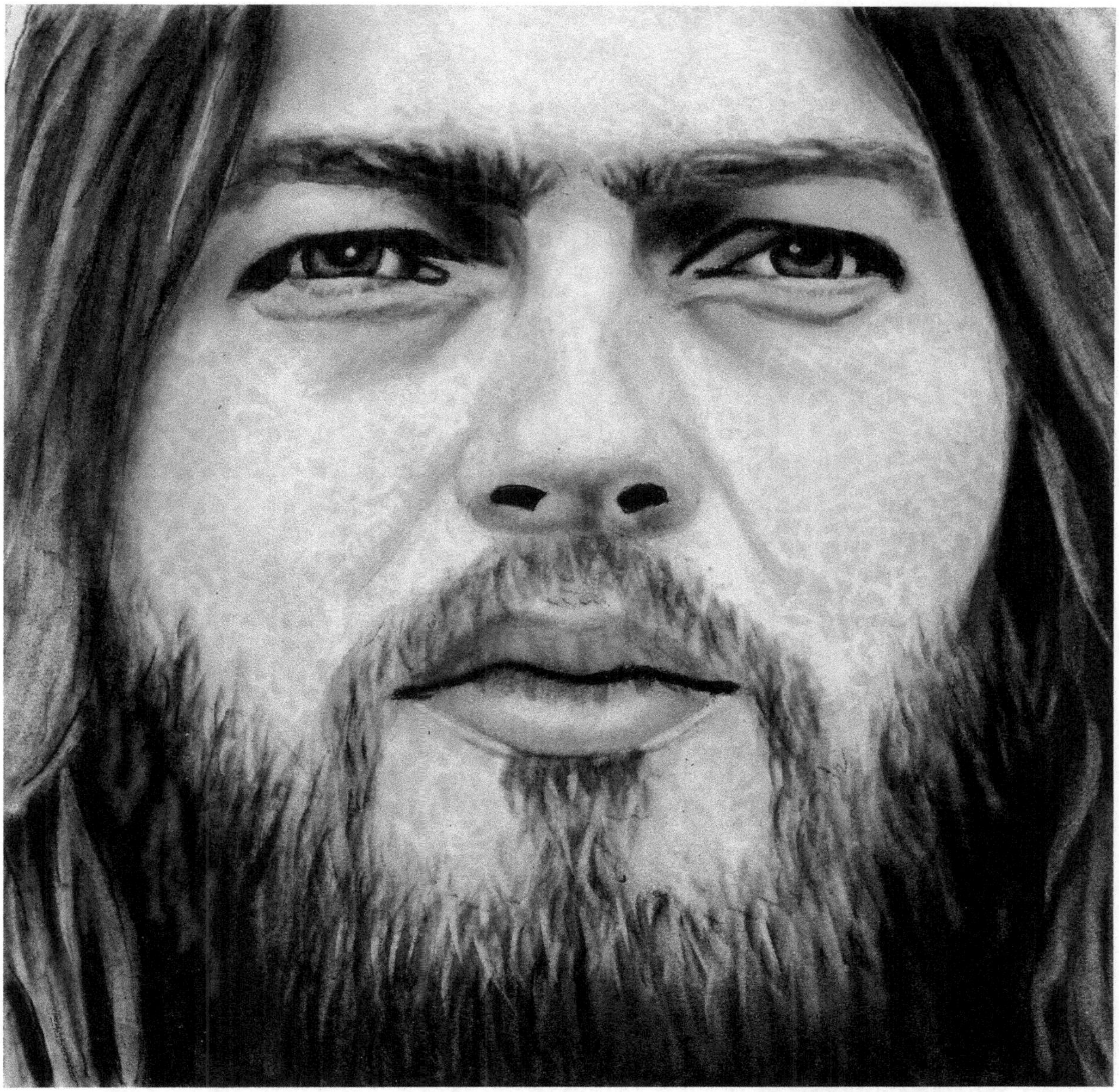

To view how this drawing was masterfully created or to purchase a Limited Edition Framed Artwork of David Gilmour type into your Internet Browser the URL shortcut ➡ **myportrait.art/davidgilmour**

To listen to their Greatest Songs type into your Internet Browser the URL shortcut ➡ **radio.surf/pinkfloyd**

To view all channels on THE FACE OF MUSIC Internet Radio MEGA Station type into your Internet Browser the URL shortcut ➡ **radio.surf/music**

To inquire about purchasing a Limited Edtion NFT of this portrait type into your Internet Browser the URL shortcut ➡ **myartnft.shop/davidgilmour**

To view all available NFTs type into your Internet Browser the URL shortcut ➡ **myartnft.shop/all**

# Pink Floyd

(Total Records Sold: 250+ Million)

(Genre: Progressive Rock , Experimental Rock , Psychedelic Rock)

—A Momentary Lapse of Reason (1987) and The Division Bell (1994)—and toured both albums before entering a long period of inactivity. In 2005, all but Barrett reunited for a one-off performance at the global awareness event Live 8. Barrett died in 2006, and Wright in 2008. The last Pink Floyd studio album, The Endless River (2014), was based on unreleased material from the Division Bell recording sessions.By 2013, Pink Floyd had sold more than 250 million records worldwide, making them one of the best-selling music artists of all time. The Dark Side of the Moon and The Wall are among the best-selling albums of all time, and both have been inducted into the Grammy Hall of Fame. Four of the band's albums topped US or UK record charts, and hit singles produced include "See Emily Play" (1967), "Money" (1973), the three-part composition "Another Brick in the Wall" (1979), "Not Now John" (1983), "On the Turning Away" (1987) and "High Hopes" (1994). The band also composed several film scores. They were inducted into the US Rock and Roll Hall of Fame in 1996 and the UK Music Hall of Fame in 2005. In 2008, King Carl XVI Gustaf of Sweden presented Pink Floyd with the Polar Music Prize for their contribution to modern music.

# Roger Waters

(Net Worth: $310 Million)(Height: 6' -3")

George Roger Waters (born 6 September 1943) is an English songwriter, singer, bassist, and composer. In 1965, he co-founded the progressive rock band Pink Floyd. Waters initially served solely as the bassist, but following the departure of singer-songwriter Syd Barrett in 1968, he also became their lyricist, co-lead vocalist, and conceptual leader.Pink Floyd achieved international success with the concept albums The Dark Side of the Moon (1973), Wish You Were Here (1975), Animals (1977), and The Wall (1979). By the early 1980s, they had become one of the most critically acclaimed and commercially successful groups in popular music. Amid creative differences, Waters left in 1985 and began a legal dispute over the use of the band's name and material. They settled out of court in 1987.Waters' solo work includes the studio albums The Pros and Cons of Hitch Hiking (1984), Radio K.A.O.S. (1987), Amused to Death (1992), and Is This the Life We Really Want? (2017). In 2005, he released Ça Ira, an opera translated from Étienne and Nadine Roda-Gils' libretto about the French Revolution.In 1990, Waters staged one of the largest rock concerts in history, The Wall – Live in Berlin, with an attendance of 450,000. As a member of Pink Floyd, he was inducted into the US Rock and Roll Hall of Fame in 1996 and the UK Music Hall of Fame in 2005. Later that year, he reunited with Pink Floyd bandmates Nick Mason, Richard Wright and David Gilmour for the Live 8 global awareness event, the group's first appearance with Waters since 1981. He has toured extensively as a solo act since 1999; he performed The Dark Side of the Moon in its entirety for his world tour of 2006–2008, and the Wall Live tour of 2010–2013 was the highest-grossing tour by a solo artist at the time.

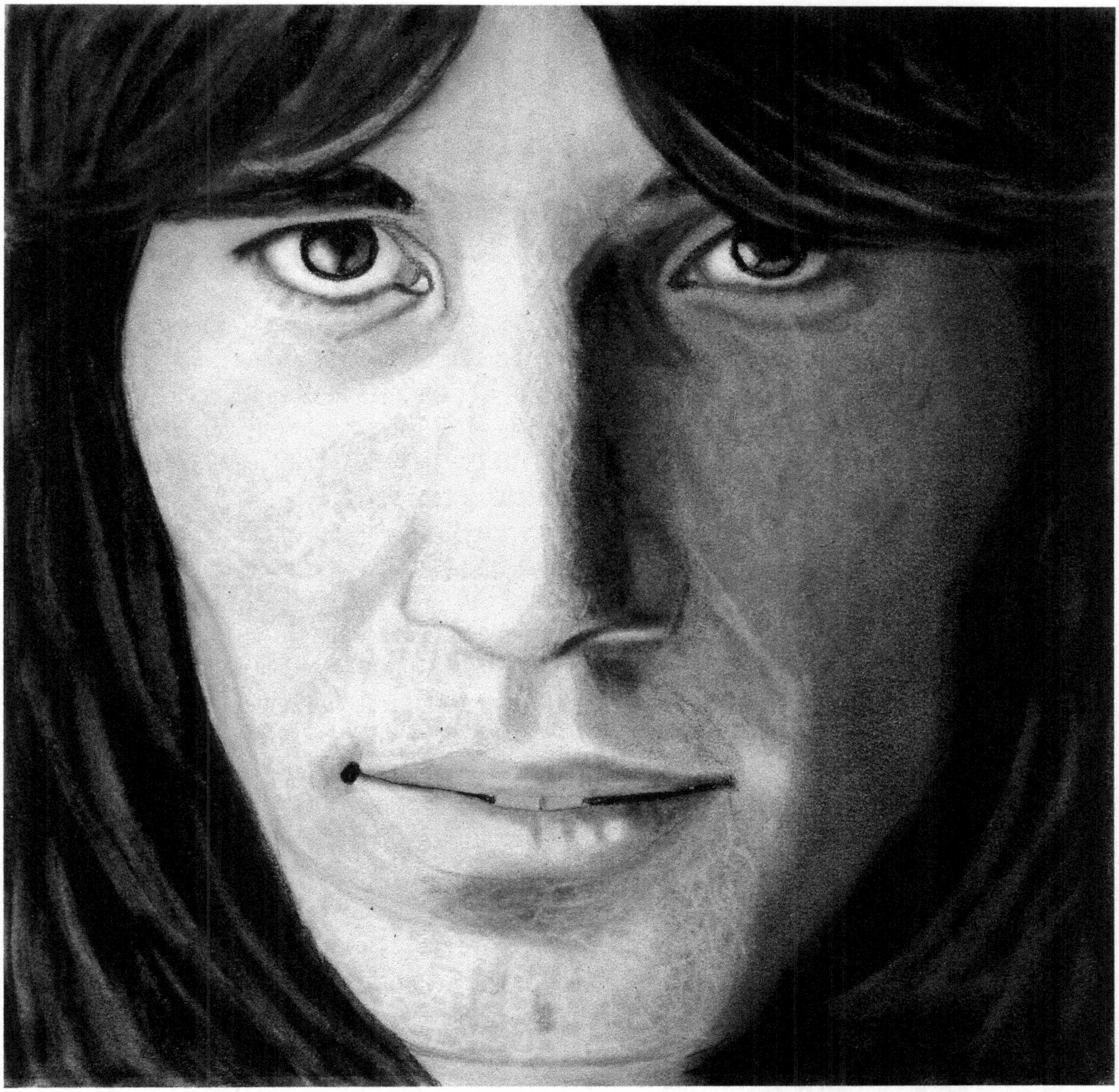

To view how this drawing was masterfully created or to purchase a Limited Edition Framed Artwork of Roger Waters type into your Internet Browser the URL shortcut ➡ **myportrait.art/rogerwaters**

To listen to their Greatest Songs type into your Internet Browser the URL shortcut ➡ **radio.surf/pinkfloyd**

To view all channels on THE FACE OF MUSIC Internet Radio MEGA Station type into your Internet Browser the URL shortcut ➡ **radio.surf/music**

To inquire about purchasing a Limited Edtion NFT of this portrait type into your Internet Browser the URL shortcut ➡ **myartnft.shop/rogerwaters**

To view all available NFTs type into your Internet Browser the URL shortcut ➡ **myartnft.shop/all**

# Platters, The

(Total Records Sold: Multi-Millions)
(Genre: R&B , Soul)

The Platters are an American vocal group formed in 1952. They are one of the most successful vocal groups of the early rock and roll era. Originally, their distinctive sound was a bridge between the pre-rock Tin Pan Alley tradition and the burgeoning new genre. The act has gone through several personnel changes, with one of the most successful incarnations comprising lead tenor Tony Williams, David Lynch, Paul Robi, Herb Reed, and Zola Taylor. The group had 40 charting singles on the Billboard Hot 100 chart between 1955 and 1967, including four number-one hits.

The Platters formed in Los Angeles in 1952 and were initially managed by Federal Records A&R man, Ralph Bass. The original group consisted of founding and naming member, Herb Reed, Alex Hodge, Cornell Gunter and Joe Jefferson.

In June 1953, Gunter left to join The Flairs and was replaced by lead vocalist Tony Williams.

The group was inducted into the Rock and Roll Hall of Fame in 1990 and into the Vocal Group Hall of Fame in its inaugural year of 1998. The Platters were the first rock and roll era group to have a Top Ten album in the United States. They were also the only act to have three songs included on the American Graffiti soundtrack that fueled an oldies revival already underway in the early to mid-1970s: "Smoke Gets in Your Eyes", "The Great Pretender", and "Only You (and You Alone)". The group had four top 100

# Tony Williams

(Net Worth: $5 Million)

Samuel E. "Tony" Williams ( April 5, 1928 – August 14, 1992) was the lead singer of the Platters from 1953 to 1960. Williams was born in Elizabeth, New Jersey, and died in Manhattan of emphysema. He had an older sister, Linda Hayes.

The Platters were discovered and managed by Buck Ram. On the Mercury record label 45 rpm release of the Platters' song, "My Prayer," Williams was listed as Tony Wilson. In a dispute over money, Williams left the Platters to pursue a solo career, and continued to work with Ram.

Williams was elected to the Rock and Roll Hall of Fame as a member of the Platters in 1990. Tony performed with his own, unauthorized version of the Platters, known as the International Platters, featuring his wife Helen Williams. Musical Director William Gulino worked with Tony Williams and the Platters off and on from 1978 to 1992.

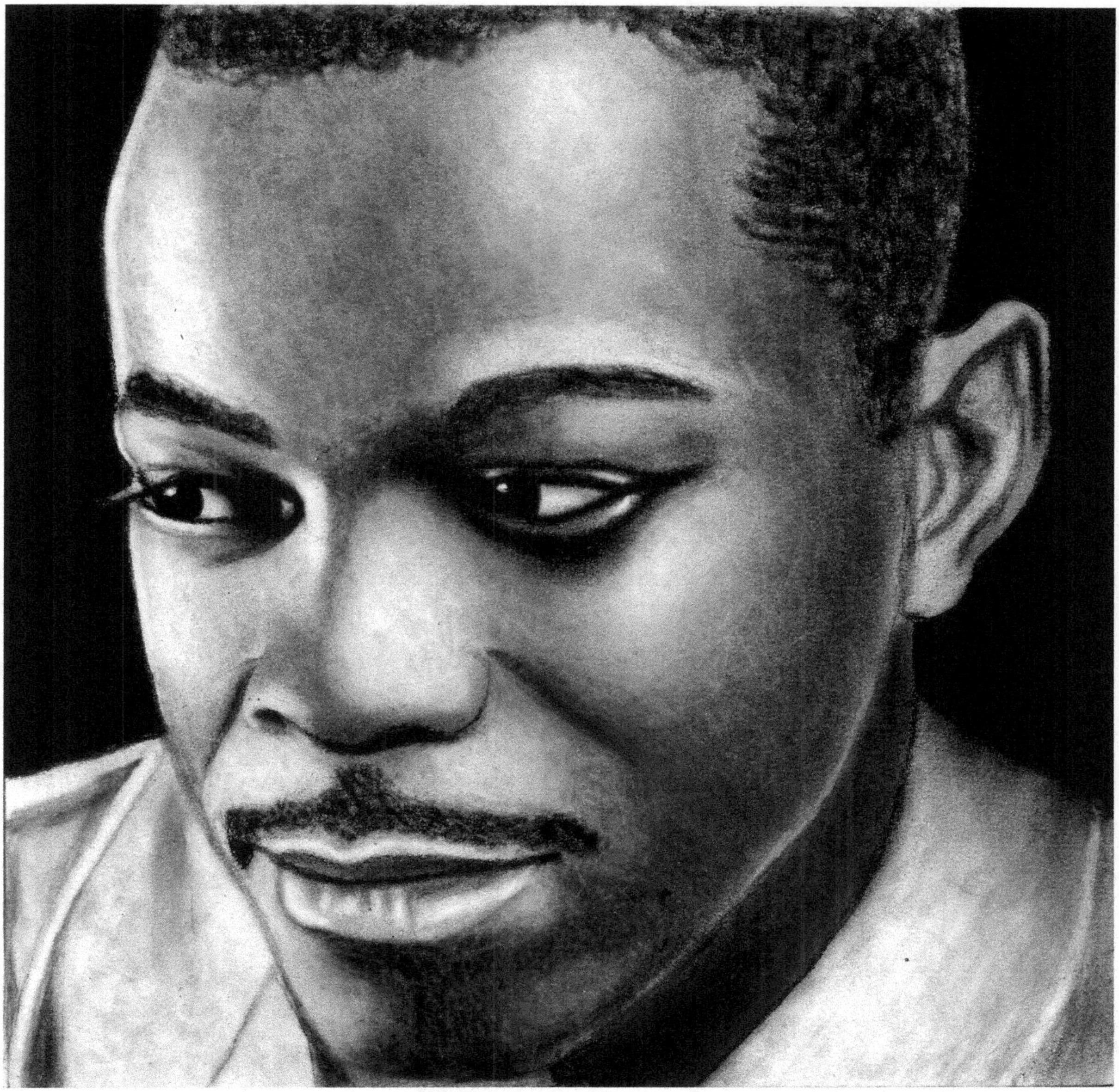

To view how this drawing was masterfully created or to purchase a Limited Edition Framed Artwork of Tony Williams type into your Internet Browser the URL shortcut ➡ **myportrait.art/tonywilliams**

To listen to their Greatest Songs type into your Internet Browser the URL shortcut ➡ **radio.surf/theplatters**

To view all channels on THE FACE OF MUSIC Internet Radio MEGA Station type into your Internet Browser the URL shortcut ➡ **radio.surf/music**

To inquire about purchasing a Limited Edtion NFT of this portrait type into your Internet Browser the URL shortcut ➡ **myartnft.shop/tonywilliams**

To view all available NFTs type into your Internet Browser the URL shortcut ➡ **myartnft.shop/all**

# Poison

(Total Albums Sold: 50+ Million)(Genre: Glam Metal , Hard Rock)

Poison is an American heavy metal/glam metal band which achieved commercial success in the mid-1980s through the mid-1990s and has sold 15 million records in the United States and over 50 million albums worldwide. The band has charted ten singles in the Top 40 of the Billboard Hot 100, including six Top 10 singles and the Hot 100 number-one, "Every Rose Has Its Thorn". The band's breakthrough debut album, the multi-platinum Look What the Cat Dragged In, was released in 1986, followed by Open Up and Say... Ahh!, which was certified 5× platinum in the US. Their third consecutive multi-platinum and best selling album was Flesh & Blood. The most successful incarnation of the band consists of founding members lead singer and rhythm guitarist Bret Michaels, drummer Rikki Rockett, bassist and pianist Bobby Dall and longtime lead guitarist and backing vocalist C.C. DeVille. Former guitarists of the band include: founding member Matt Smith, who left before recording; Richie Kotzen, who appeared on Native Tongue in 1993; and Blues Saraceno who played on Crack a Smile... and More!. C.C. DeVille rejoined in 1996, solidifying the lineup that remains to this day. Since their debut in 1986, they have released seven studio albums, four live albums, five compilation albums, and have issued 28 singles to radio. In 2012 VH1 ranked them at #1 on their list of the "Top 5 Hair Bands of the '80s". compilation albums in the Australian top 100 between 1975 and 1986.

# Bret Michaels

(Net Worth: $16 Million)(Height: 5' - 9")

Bret Michael Sychak (born March 15, 1963), professionally known as Bret Michaels, is an American singer-songwriter, musician, producer, and actor. He gained fame as the frontman of rock band Poison who have sold well over 45 million records worldwide and 15 million records in the United States alone. The band has also charted 10 singles to the Top 40 of the Billboard Hot 100, including six Top 10 singles and a number-one single, "Every Rose Has Its Thorn".

Besides his career as frontman, he has several solo albums to his credit, including the soundtrack album to the 1998 film A Letter from Death Row in which Michaels starred, wrote and directed, and a rock album, Songs of Life, in 2003. Michaels has appeared in several films and TV shows, including as a judge on the talent show Nashville Star which led to his country influenced rock album Freedom of Sound in 2005. He starred in the hit VH1 reality show Rock of Love with Bret Michaels and its sequels, which inspired his successful solo album Rock My World. He was also the winning contestant on NBC's reality show Celebrity Apprentice 3 and also featured in his own reality docu-series Bret Michaels: Life As I Know It, which inspired his highest charting album as a solo artist, Custom Built, reaching No. 1 on Billboard's Hard Rock list. He is also known for hosting on the Travel Channel. In 2006, Hit Parader ranked Michaels at #40 on their list of greatest heavy metal singers of all-time.

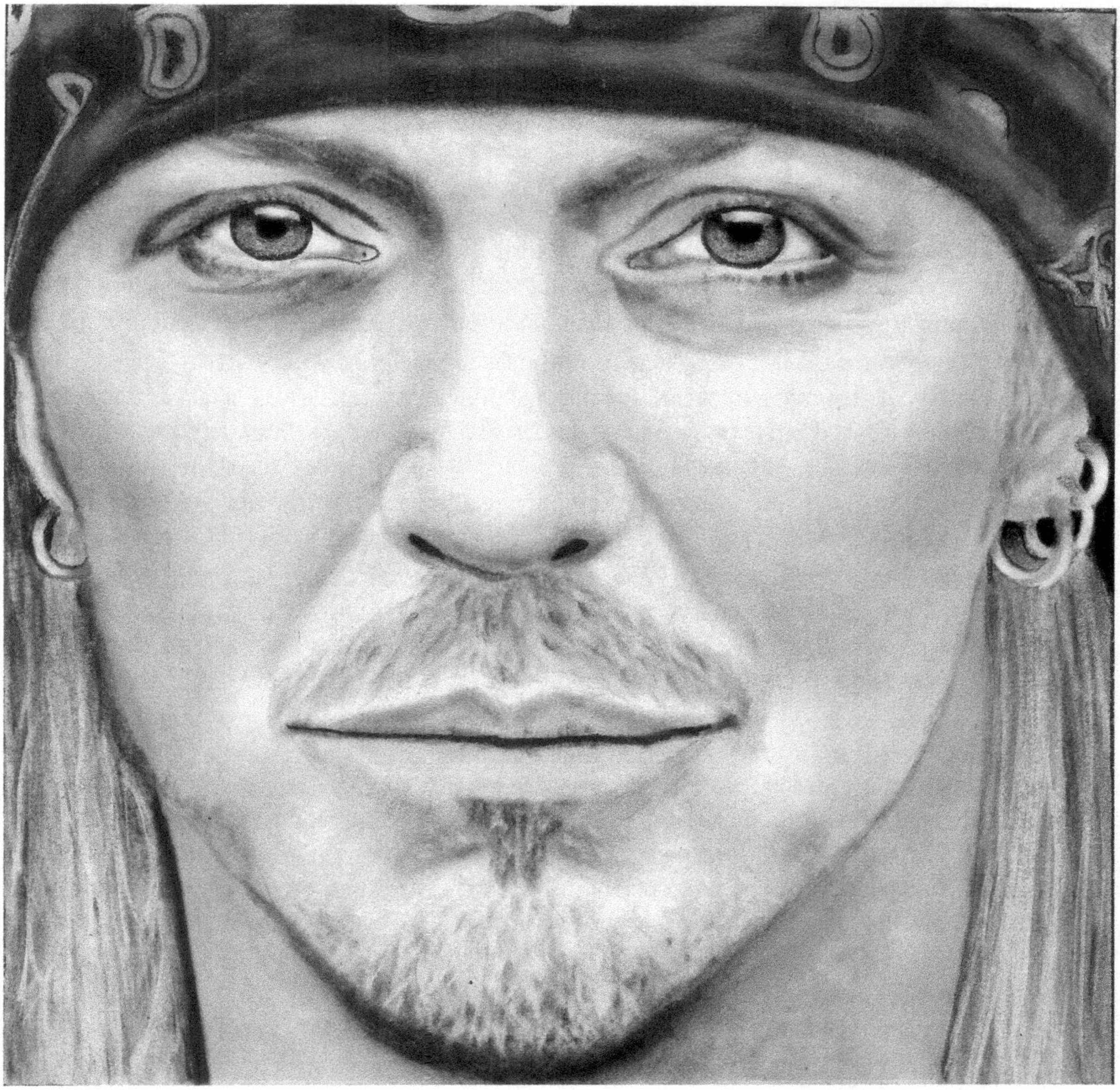

To view how this drawing was masterfully created or to purchase a Limited Edition Framed Artwork of Brey Michaels type into your Internet Browser the URL shortcut ➡ **myportrait.art/bretmichaels**

To listen to their Greatest Songs type into your Internet Browser the URL shortcut ➡ **radio.surf/poison**

To view all channels on THE FACE OF MUSIC Internet Radio MEGA Station type into your Internet Browser the URL shortcut ➡ **radio.surf/music**

To inquire about purchasing a Limited Edtion NFT of this portrait type into your Internet Browser the URL shortcut ➡ **myartnft.shop/bretmichaels**

To view all available NFTs type into your Internet Browser the URL shortcut ➡ **myartnft.shop/all**

# Police, The

(Total Albums Sold: 100+ Million)(Genre: New Wave, Reggae Rock, Pop Rock)

The Police were an English rock band formed in London in 1977. For most of their history the line-up consisted of primary songwriter Sting (lead vocals, bass guitar), Andy Summers (guitar) and Stewart Copeland (drums, percussion). The Police became globally popular in the late 1970s and early 1980s. Emerging in the British new wave scene, they played a style of rock influenced by punk, reggae, and jazz. Their 1978 debut album, Outlandos d'Amour, reached No. 6 on the UK Albums Chart on the strength of the singles "Roxanne" and "Can't Stand Losing You". Their second album, Reggatta de Blanc (1979), became the first of four consecutive No. 1 studio albums in the UK and Australia; its first two singles, "Message in a Bottle" and "Walking on the Moon", became their first UK number ones. Their next two albums, Zenyatta Mondatta (1980) and Ghost in the Machine (1981), led to further critical and commercial success with two songs, "Don't Stand So Close to Me" and "Every Little Thing She Does Is Magic", becoming UK number-one singles and Top 5 hits in other countries; the latter album and single were their breakthrough into the US as both reached the Top 3 there.

Their final studio album, Synchronicity (1983), was No. 1 in the UK, Canada, Australia, Italy and the US selling over 8 million copies in the US. Its lead single, "Every Breath You Take", became their fifth UK number one, and only US number one. During this time, the band were considered one of the leaders of the Second British Invasion of the US; in 1983 Rolling Stone labelled them "the first British New Wave act to break through in America on a grand scale, and possibly the biggest band in the world." The Police disbanded in 1986, but reunited in early 2007 for a one-off world tour that ended in August 2008. They were the world's highest-earning musicians in 2008, due to their reunion tour.

The Police have sold over 75 million records, making them one of the best-selling bands of all time. The band won a number of music awards, including six Grammy Awards, two Brit Awards—winning Best British Group once, and an MTV Video Music Award. In 2003, they were inducted into the Rock and Roll Hall of Fame. Four of their five studio albums appeared on Rolling Stone's list of the "500 Greatest Albums of All Time". The band were included among both Rolling Stone's and VH1's lists of the "100 Greatest Artists of All Time".

# Sting

(Net Worth: $400 Million)(Height: 5' - 11")

Gordon Matthew Thomas Sumner CBE (born 2 October 1951), known professionally as Sting, is an English musician and actor. He was the principal songwriter, lead singer, and bassist for new wave rock band the Police from 1977 to 1984, and launched a solo career in 1985. He has included elements of rock, jazz, reggae, classical, new-age and worldbeat in his music.

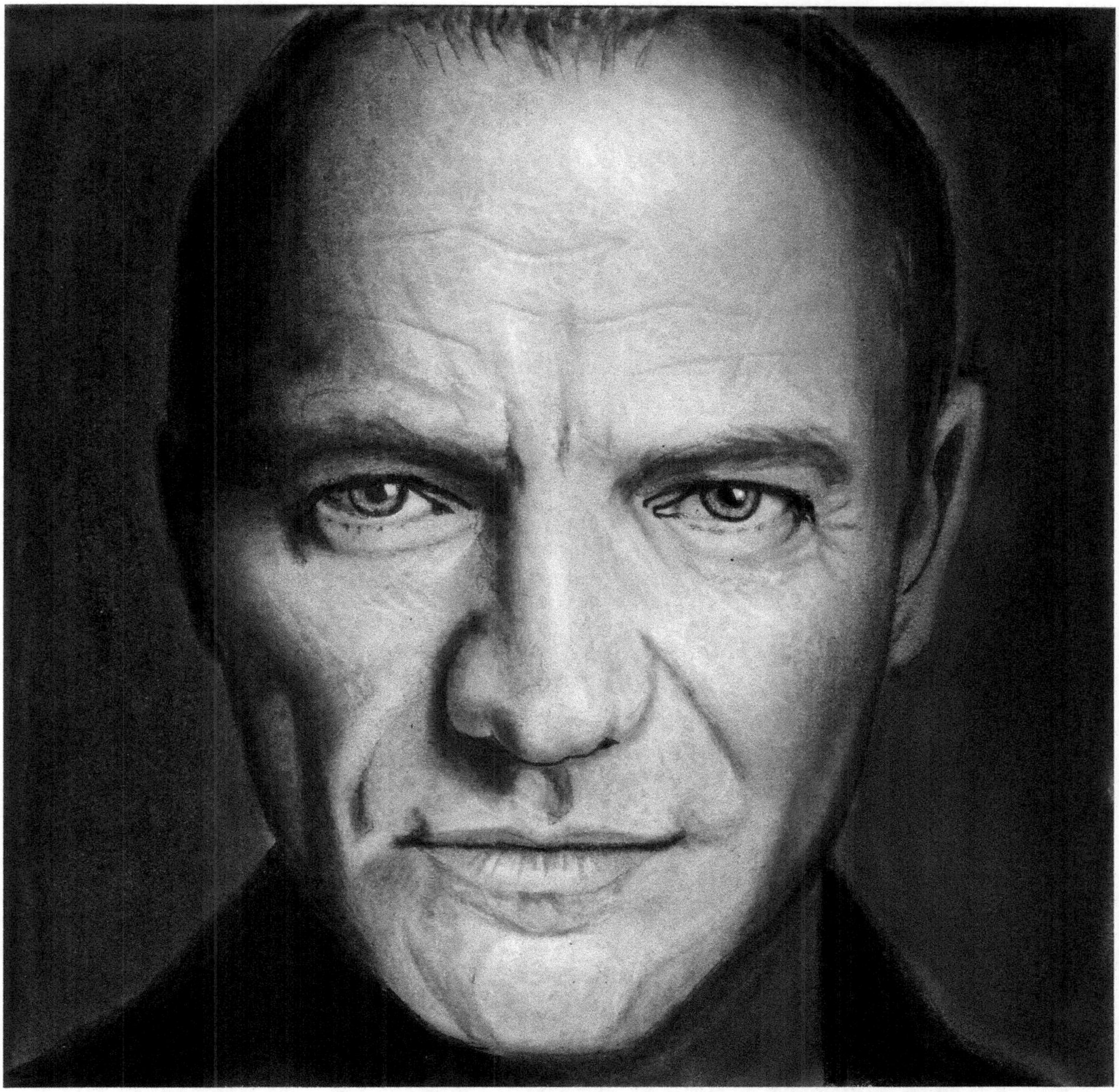

To view how this drawing was masterfully created or to purchase a Limited Edition Framed Artwork of Sting type into your Internet Browser the URL shortcut ➡ **myportrait.art/sting**

To listen to their Greatest Songs type into your Internet Browser the URL shortcut ➡ **radio.surf/thepolice**

To view all channels on THE FACE OF MUSIC Internet Radio MEGA Station type into your Internet Browser the URL shortcut ➡ **radio.surf/music**

To inquire about purchasing a Limited Edtion NFT of this portrait type into your Internet Browser the URL shortcut ➡ **myartnft.shop/sting**

To view all available NFTs type into your Internet Browser the URL shortcut ➡ **myartnft.shop/all**

# Pretenders, The

(Total Albums Sold: Millions)(Genre: Punk Rock , Alternative Rock , New Wave)

The Pretenders are a British– American rock band formed in March 1978. The original band consisted of founder and main songwriter Chrissie Hynde (lead vocals, rhythm guitar), James Honeyman-Scott (lead guitar, backing vocals, keyboards), Pete Farndon (bass guitar, backing vocals), and Martin Chambers (drums, backing vocals, percussion). Following the deaths of Honeyman-Scott and Farndon in 1982 and 1983, the band experienced numerous personnel changes; Hynde has been the band's only consistent member.

The Pretenders' hit songs include "Kid" (1979), "Brass in Pocket" (1979), "Talk of the Town" (1980), "Message of Love" (1981), "Back on the Chain Gang" (1982), "Middle of the Road" (1983), "2000 Miles" (1983), "Don't Get Me Wrong" (1986), "My Baby" (1986), and "I'll Stand by You" (1994). The band was inducted into the Rock and Roll Hall of Fame in 2005.

# Chrissie Hynde

(Net Worth: $12 Million)(Height: 5' - 6")

Christine Ellen Hynde (born September 7, 1951) is an American singer-songwriter and musician. She is a founding member and the guitarist, lead vocalist, and primary songwriter of the rock band the Pretenders, as well as its only constant member.

Hynde formed the Pretenders in 1978 with Pete Farndon, James Honeyman-Scott and Martin Chambers. She has also released a number of songs with other musicians including Frank Sinatra, Cher and UB40, and she released the solo album Stockholm in 2014. Hynde was inducted into the Rock and Roll Hall of Fame in 2005 as a member of the Pretenders. She performed at Live Aid in 1985..

In 1978, Hynde made a demo tape and gave it to Dave Hill, owner of the label Real Records. Hill stepped in to manage her career, and began by paying off the back rent owed on her rehearsal room in Covent Garden, London. Hill also advised Hynde to take her time and get a band together. In the spring of 1978, Hynde met bass guitarist Pete Farndon and they selected a band consisting of James Honeyman-Scott (guitar, vocals, keyboards), and Martin Chambers (drums, vocals, percussion). The name "The Pretenders" was inspired by the Sam Cooke version of the Platters' 1955 R&B hit "The Great Pretender".

They recorded a demo tape (including "Precious", "The Wait" and a Kinks cover, "Stop Your Sobbing"), handed it to Hynde's friend Nick Lowe, produced a single ("Stop Your Sobbing"/"The Wait") and performed their first gig at a club in Paris. The single was released in January 1979 and hit No. 33 in the UK. A second single "Kid" followed to similar success in July 1979. In November 1979 the Pretenders released their first signature single "Brass In Pocket" in the UK, which hit UK number 1 on January 19, 1980 the same date as their eponymous first album. Both went on to similar chart success worldwide.

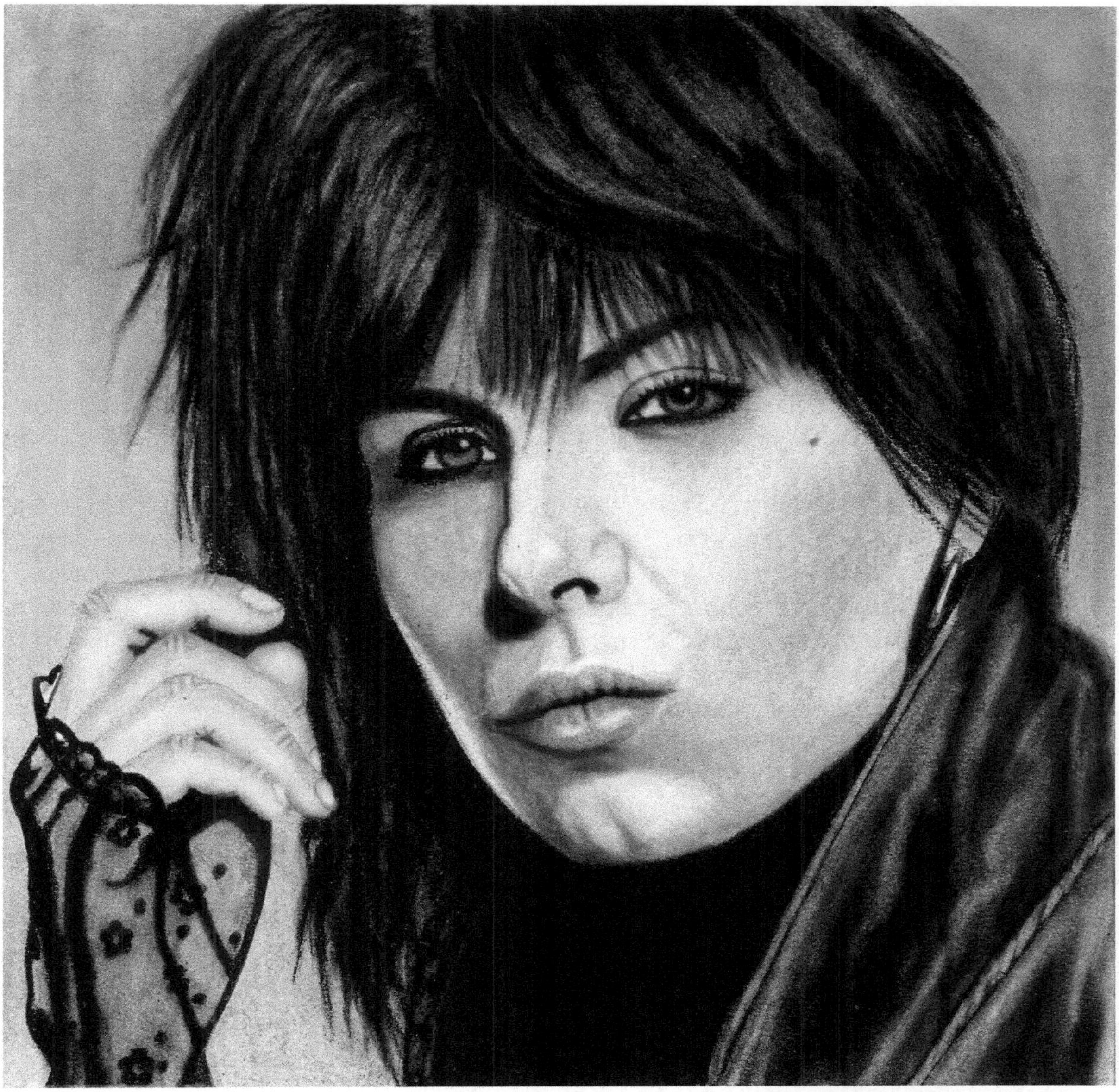

To view how this drawing was masterfully created or to purchase a Limited Edition Framed Artwork of Chrissie Hynde type into your Internet Browser the URL shortcut ➡ **myportrait.art/chrissiehynde**

To listen to their Greatest Songs type into your Internet Browser the URL shortcut
➡ **radio.surf/thepretenders**

To view all channels on THE FACE OF MUSIC Internet Radio MEGA Station type into your Internet Browser the URL shortcut ➡ **radio.surf/music**

To inquire about purchasing a Limited Edtion NFT of this portrait type into your Internet Browser the URL shortcut ➡ **myartnft.shop/chrissiehynde**

To view all available NFTs type into your Internet Browser the URL shortcut ➡ **myartnft.shop/all**

# Prince

(Net worth: $300 Million)(Total Records Sold: 150+ Million)
(Genre: R&B, Funk, Rock, Minneapolis Sound, Soul, Progressive Soul)(Height: 5' - 2")

Prince Rogers Nelson (June 7, 1958 – April 21, 2016), mononymously known as Prince, was an American singer-songwriter, multi-instrumentalist, record producer, dancer, actor, and director. He is widely regarded as one of the greatest musicians of his generation. Considered a guitar virtuoso, he was well known for his eclectic work across multiple genres, flamboyant and androgynous persona, and wide vocal range which included a far-reaching falsetto and high-pitched screams.

Prince's innovative music integrated a wide variety of styles, including funk, R&B, Latin, rock, new wave, classical, soul, synth-pop, psychedelia, pop, jazz, and hip hop. He pioneered the Minneapolis sound, a funk rock subgenre that emerged in the late 1970s. He was also known for his prolific output, releasing 39 albums during his life, with a vast array of unreleased projects left in a vault at his home after his death; it is believed that the vault contains dozens of fully produced albums and over 50 music videos that have never been released, along with various other media. He released hundreds of songs both under his own name and multiple pseudonyms during his life, as well as writing songs that were made famous by other musicians, such as "Nothing Compares 2 U" and "Manic Monday". Estimates of the complete number of songs written by Prince range anywhere from 500 to well over 1,000.

Born and raised in Minneapolis, Minnesota, Prince signed a recording contract with Warner Bros. Records at the age of 19. Prince went on to achieve critical success with the innovative albums Dirty Mind (1980), Controversy (1981), and 1999 (1982). His sixth album, Purple Rain (1984), was recorded with his backup band the Revolution, and was the soundtrack to his film acting debut of the same name. Purple Rain spent six consecutive months atop the Billboard 200. Prince won the Academy Award for Best Original Song Score. After disbanding the Revolution, Prince went on to achieve continued critical success with Sign o' the Times (1987). In the midst of a contractual dispute with Warner Bros in 1993, he changed his stage name to the unpronounceable symbol Logo. Hollow circle above downward arrow crossed with a curlicued horn-shaped symbol and then a short bar (known to fans as the "Love Symbol"), and was sometimes referred to as The Artist Formerly Known as Prince or TAFKAP, or simply the Artist. He signed with Arista Records in 1998 and began referring to himself by his own name again in 2000. After returning to mainstream prominence following a performance at the Grammy Awards ceremony in 2004, he scored six US top ten albums over the following decade. Joni Mitchell said of Prince, "He's driven like an artist. His motivations are growth and experimentation as opposed to formula and hits."

In mid-life, Prince reportedly experienced considerable pain from injuries to his body (mainly hips) sustained through his dynamic stage performances (which included leaping off speaker stacks in high heels), and was sometimes seen using a cane. In April 2016, at the age of 57, Prince died of an accidental fentanyl overdose at his Paisley Park home and recording studio in Chanhassen, Minnesota. Prince sold over 150 million records worldwide, ranking him among the best-selling music artists of all time. His awards included the Grammy President's Merit Award, the American Music Awards for Achievement and of Merit, the Billboard Icon Award, an Academy Award and a Golden Globe Award. He was inducted into the Rock and Roll Hall of Fame in 2004, the UK Music Hall of Fame in 2006, and the Rhythm and Blues Music Hall of Fame in 2016.

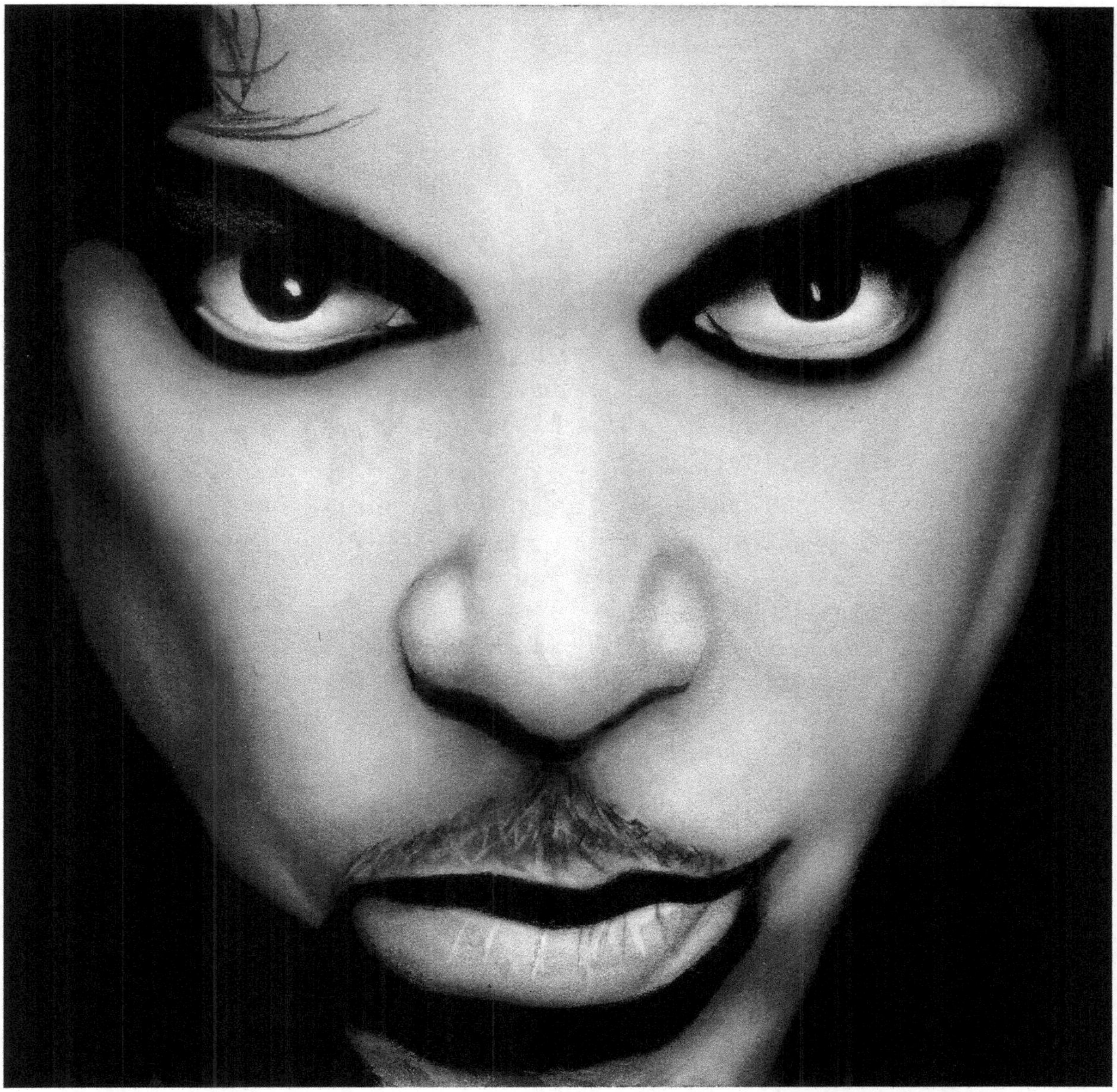

To view how this drawing was masterfully created or to purchase a Limited Edition Framed Artwork of Prince type into your Internet Browser the URL shortcut ➡ **myportrait.art/prince**

To listen to his Greatest Songs type into your Internet Browser the URL shortcut ➡ **radio.surf/prince**

To view all channels on THE FACE OF MUSIC Internet Radio MEGA Station type into your Internet Browser the URL shortcut ➡ **radio.surf/music**

To inquire about purchasing a Limited Edition NFT of this portrait type into your Internet Browser the URL shortcut ➡ **myartnft.shop/prince**

To view all available NFTs type into your Internet Browser the URL shortcut ➡ **myartnft.shop/all**

# Public Enemy

(Total Albums Sold: 3+ Million)(Genre: East Coast Hip-Hop)

Public Enemy is an American hip hop group formed by Chuck D and Flavor Flav on Long Island, New York, in 1985. The group came to attention for their music with a heavy political message alongside strong criticism of the media of the United States, with many of their works also revolving around frustrations and concerns of the African American community. Public Enemy's debut album, Yo! Bum Rush the Show, was released in 1987 to critical acclaim and their second album, It Takes a Nation of Millions to Hold Us Back (1988), was the first hip hop album to top The Village Voice's Pazz & Jop critics' poll. Their next three albums, Fear of a Black Planet (1990), Apocalypse 91... The Enemy Strikes Black (1991) and Muse Sick-n-Hour Mess Age (1994), were also well received by music critics.

Public Enemy has gone through lineup changes over the years, with Chuck D and Flavor Flav being the only constant members of the group. One of its founding members Professor Griff left in 1989 but rejoined in 1998, though he parted ways with the group again some years later. DJ Lord also joined Public Enemy in 1998 as the replacement of the group's original DJ Terminator X. In 2020, it was announced that Flavor Flav had been fired from the group. His firing was later revealed to be a publicity stunt that was called an April Fools' Day prank. Public Enemy, without Flavor Flav, would also tour and record music under the name of Public Enemy Radio which consists of the lineup of Chuck D, Jahi, DJ Lord and the S1Ws.

Public Enemy's first four albums during the late 1980s and early 1990s were all certified either gold or platinum and were, according to music critic Robert Hilburn in 1998, "the most acclaimed body of work ever by a hip hop act". Critic Stephen Thomas Erlewine called them "the most influential and radical band of their time". They were inducted into Rock and Roll Hall of Fame in 2013. They were honored with the Grammy Lifetime Achievement Award at the 62nd Grammy Awards.

# Chuck D

(Net Worth: $14 Million)(Height: 5' - 9")

Carlton Douglas Ridenhour (born August 1, 1960), known professionally as Chuck D, is an American rapper, author, and producer. As the leader of the rap group Public Enemy, which he co-founded in 1985 with Flavor Flav, Chuck D helped create politically and socially conscious hip hop music in the mid-1980s. The Source ranked him at No. 12 on their list of the Top 50 Hip-Hop Lyricists of All Time. Ridenhour was born in Queens, New York. He began writing rhymes after the New York City blackout of 1977. After attending W. Tresper Clarke High School, he went to Adelphi University on Long Island to study graphic design, where he met William Drayton (Flavor Flav). He received a B.F.A. from Adelphi in 1984 and later received an honorary doctorate from Adelphi in 2013.

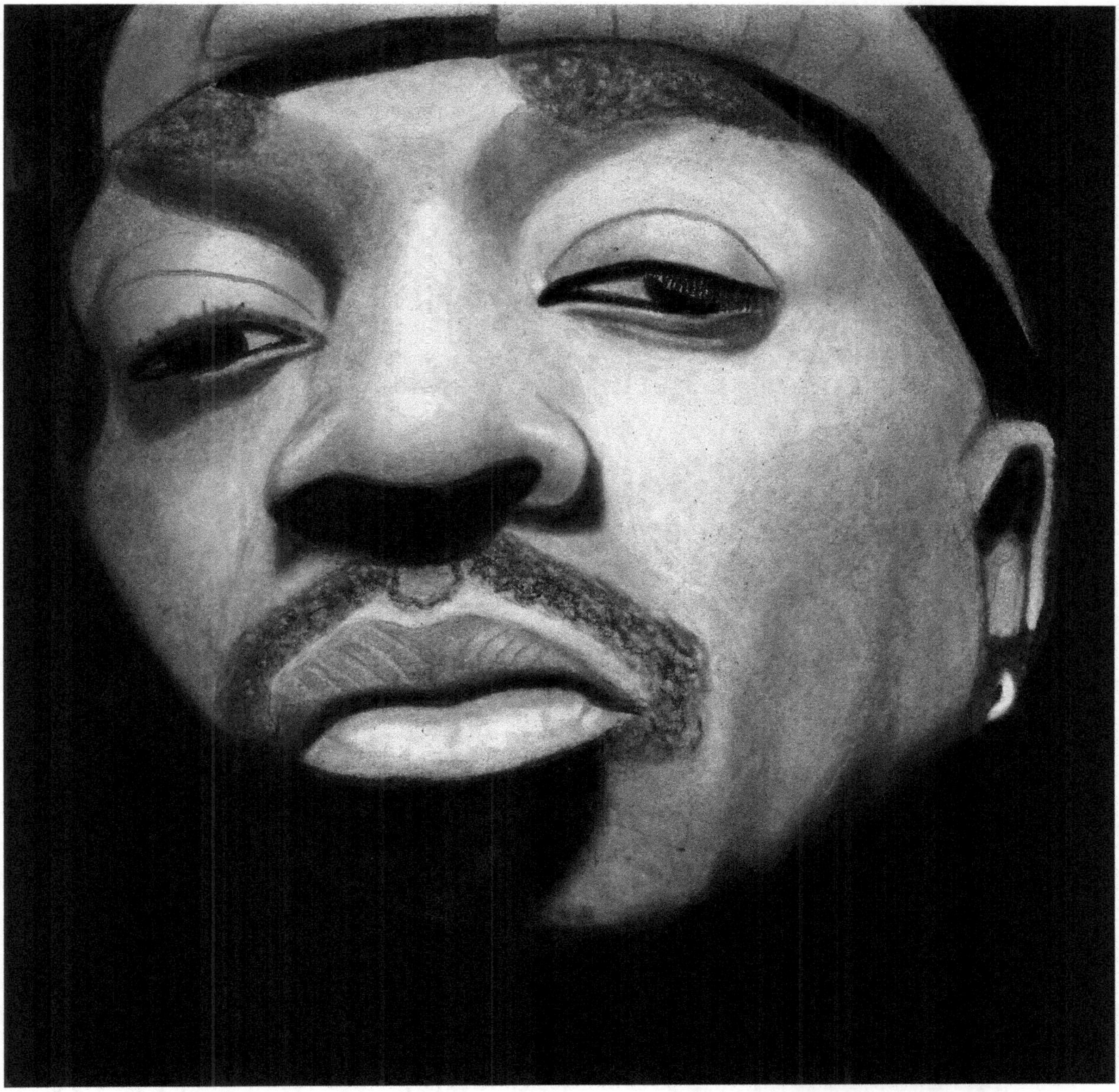

To view how this drawing was masterfully created or to purchase a Limited Edition Framed Artwork of Chuck D type into your Internet Browser the URL shortcut ➡ **myportrait.art/chuckd**

To listen to their Greatest Songs type into your Internet Browser the URL shortcut
➡ **radio.surf/publicenemy**

To view all channels on THE FACE OF MUSIC Internet Radio MEGA Station type into your Internet Browser the URL shortcut ➡ **radio.surf/music**

To inquire about purchasing a Limited Edtion NFT of this portrait type into your Internet Browser the URL shortcut ➡ **myartnft.shop/chuckd**

To view all available NFTs type into your Internet Browser the URL shortcut ➡ **myartnft.shop/all**

# Queen

(Total Records Sold: 300 Million)(Genre: Classic Rock)

Queen are a British rock band formed in London in 1970. Their classic line-up was Freddie Mercury (lead vocals, piano), Brian May (guitar, vocals), Roger Taylor (drums, vocals) and John Deacon (bass). Their earliest works were influenced by progressive rock, hard rock and heavy metal, but the band gradually ventured into more conventional and radio-friendly works by incorporating further styles, such as arena rock and pop rock.Before forming Queen, May and Taylor had played together in the band Smile. Mercury was a fan of Smile and encouraged them to experiment with more elaborate stage and recording techniques. He joined in 1970 and suggested the name "Queen". Deacon was recruited in February 1971, before the band released their eponymous debut album in 1973. Queen first charted in the UK with their second album, Queen II, in 1974. Sheer Heart Attack later that year and A Night at the Opera in 1975 brought them international success. The latter featured "Bohemian Rhapsody", which stayed at number one in the UK for nine weeks and helped popularise the music video format.

The band's 1977 album News of the World contained "We Will Rock You" and "We Are the Champions", which have become anthems at sporting events. By the early 1980s, Queen were one of the biggest stadium rock bands in the world. "Another One Bites the Dust" from The Game (1980) became their best-selling single, while their 1981 compilation album Greatest Hits is the best-selling album in the UK and is certified nine times platinum in the US. Their performance at the 1985 Live Aid concert is ranked among the greatest in rock history by various publications. In August 1986, Mercury gave his last performance with Queen at Knebworth, England. In 1991, he died of bronchopneumonia—a complication of AIDS—and Deacon retired in 1997. Since 2004, May and Taylor have toured under the "Queen +" name with vocalists Paul Rodgers and Adam Lambert.Estimates of Queen's record sales is 300 million records, making them one of the world's best-selling music artists. In 1990, Queen received the Brit Award for Outstanding Contribution to British Music from the British Phonographic Industry. They were inducted into the Rock and Roll Hall of Fame in 2001. Each member has composed hit singles, and all four were inducted into the Songwriters Hall of Fame in 2003. In 2005, Queen received the Ivor Novello Award for Outstanding Song Collection from the British Academy of Songwriters, Composers, and Authors. In 2018, they were presented the Grammy Lifetime Achievement Award.

# Freddie Mercury

(Net Worth: $50 Million)(Height: 5' - 9")

Freddie Mercury (born Farrokh Bulsara; 5 September 1946 – 24 November 1991) was a British singer, songwriter, record producer, and lead vocalist of the rock band Queen. Regarded as one of the greatest singers in the history of rock music, he was known for his flamboyant stage persona and four-octave vocal range. Mercury defied the conventions of a rock frontman, with his highly theatrical style influencing the artistic direction of Queen.On the evening of 24 November 1991, about 24 hours after issuing the statement, Mercury died at the age of 45 at his home in Kensington. The cause of death was bronchial pneumonia resulting from AIDS.

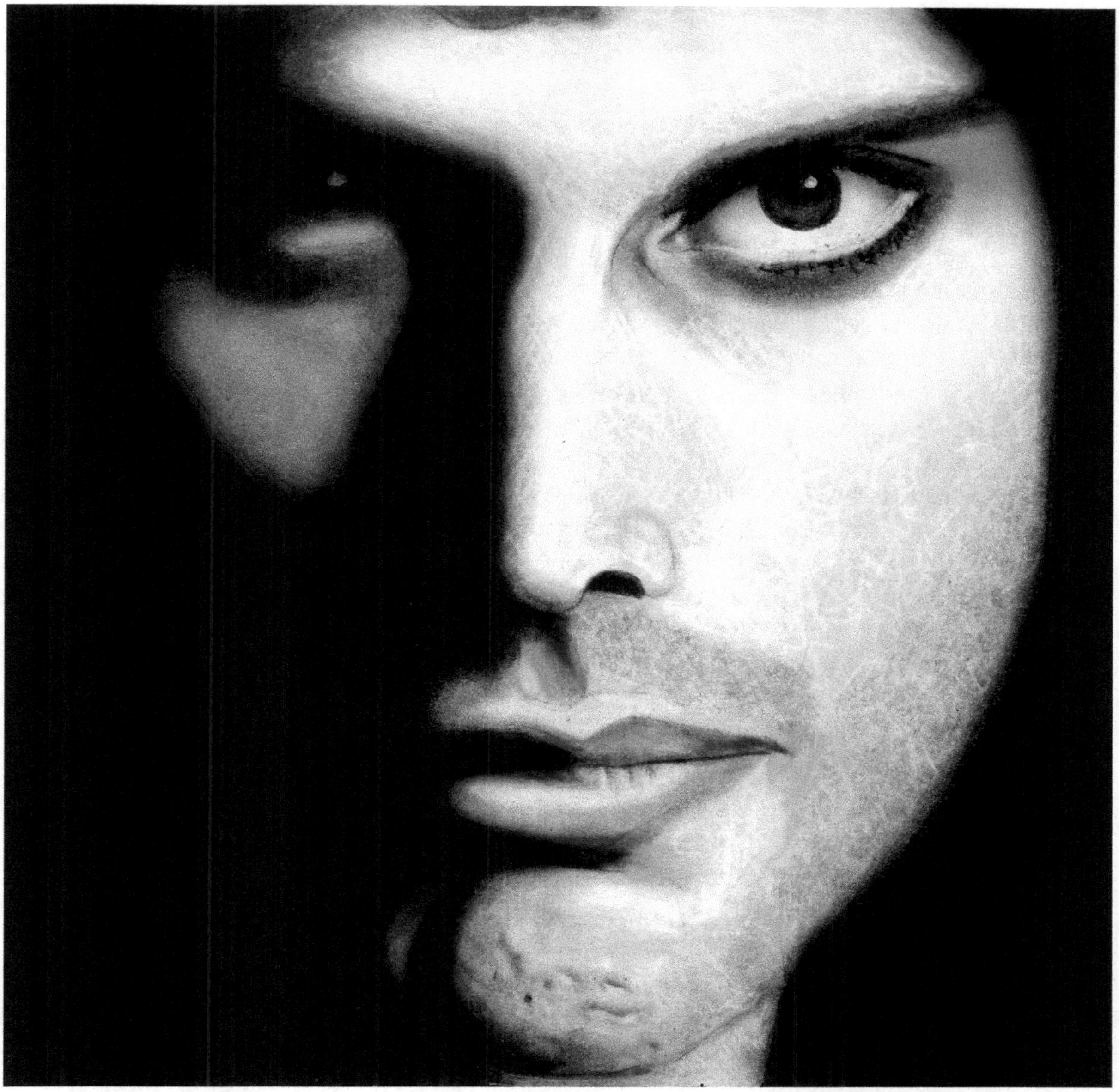

To view how this drawing was masterfully created or to purchase a Limited Edition Framed Artwork of Freddie Mercury type into your Internet Browser the URL shortcut ➡ **myportrait.art/freddiemercury**

To listen to their Greatest Songs type into your Internet Browser the URL shortcut ➡ **radio.surf/queen**

To view all channels on THE FACE OF MUSIC Internet Radio MEGA Station type into your Internet Browser the URL shortcut ➡ **radio.surf/music**

To inquire about purchasing a Limited Edtion NFT of this portrait type into your Internet Browser the URL shortcut ➡ **myartnft.shop/freddiemercury**

To view all available NFTs type into your Internet Browser the URL shortcut ➡ **myartnft.shop/all**

# Queensrÿche

(Total Albums Sold: 20+ Million)(Genre: Progressive Metal)

Queensrÿche is an American heavy metal band. It formed in 1980 in Bellevue, Washington, out of the local band the Mob. The band has released 15 studio albums, one EP, and several DVDs, and continues to tour and record. The original lineup consisted of guitarists Michael Wilton and Chris DeGarmo, drummer Scott Rockenfield, bassist Eddie Jackson, and lead vocalist Geoff Tate.Queensrÿche has sold over 20 million albums worldwide, including over 6 million albums in the United States. They are considered one of the leaders of the progressive metal scene of the mid-to-late 1980s, and often referred to as one of the "Big Three" of the genre, along with Dream Theater and Fates Warning. The band received worldwide acclaim after the release of their 1988 album Operation: Mindcrime, which is often considered one of the greatest heavy metal concept albums of all time. Their follow-up release, Empire, released in 1990, was also very successful and included the hit single "Silent Lucidity". The band has received three Grammy Award nominations for songs from both albums. In 1998, drummer Rockenfield received an individual Grammy nomination.Also in 1998, guitarist and primary songwriter Chris DeGarmo left the band for personal reasons, returning briefly in 2003 to write and record the Tribe album. Over the years, his replacements have been Kelly Gray, Mike Stone, and Parker Lundgren. Following a highly publicized backstage altercation before a show in São Paulo, Brazil, in April 2012, Tate was fired from the band and replaced with then-Crimson Glory singer Todd La Torre. In response to his dismissal, Tate and his wife Susan (who served as the band's manager from 2005 to 2012) filed a lawsuit in a Washington court, claiming that he was wrongfully terminated. The ruling in the preliminary injunction was that both parties were allowed to use the name Queensrÿche until a court ruling or a settlement decided who would get to use the name. A settlement was reached on April 17, 2014, in which founding members Wilton, Rockenfield and Jackson were awarded the rights to the band trademark, continuing to play with the lineup that additionally includes singer La Torre and guitarist Lundgren.During the time, both parties could use the name Queensrÿche, Tate created his own lineup featuring former guitarist Gray and musicians from bands including Blue Öyster Cult, Ozzy Osbourne, Whitesnake, Dio, AC/DC and Quiet Riot. This version of Queensrÿche with Geoff Tate released the album Frequency Unknown on April 23, 2013, while Queensrÿche (with La Torre replacing Tate) released their eponymous album on June 24 and 25, 2013 (European and American release date, respectively). Both bands toured in 2013 and 2014.

# Geoff Tate

(Net Worth: $12 Million)(Height: 5' - 8")

Geoff Tate (born Jeffrey Wayne Tate, January 14, 1959; he later changed his first name to Geoffery or Geoffrey) is an American singer and songwriter. He rose to fame with the progressive metal band Queensrÿche, who had commercial success with their 1988 album Operation: Mindcrime and 1990 album Empire. Tate is ranked fourteenth on Hit Parader's list of the 100 Greatest Metal Vocalists of All Time. He was voted No. 2 on That Metal Show's top 5 hard rock vocalists of the 1980s. In 2012, he won the Vegas Rocks! Magazine Music Award for "Voice in Progressive Heavy Metal". In 2015, he placed ninth on OC Weekly's list of the 10 Best High-Pitched Metal Singers. After his farewell tour as Queensrÿche, he renamed his band Operation: Mindcrime, after the Queensrÿche album of the same name.

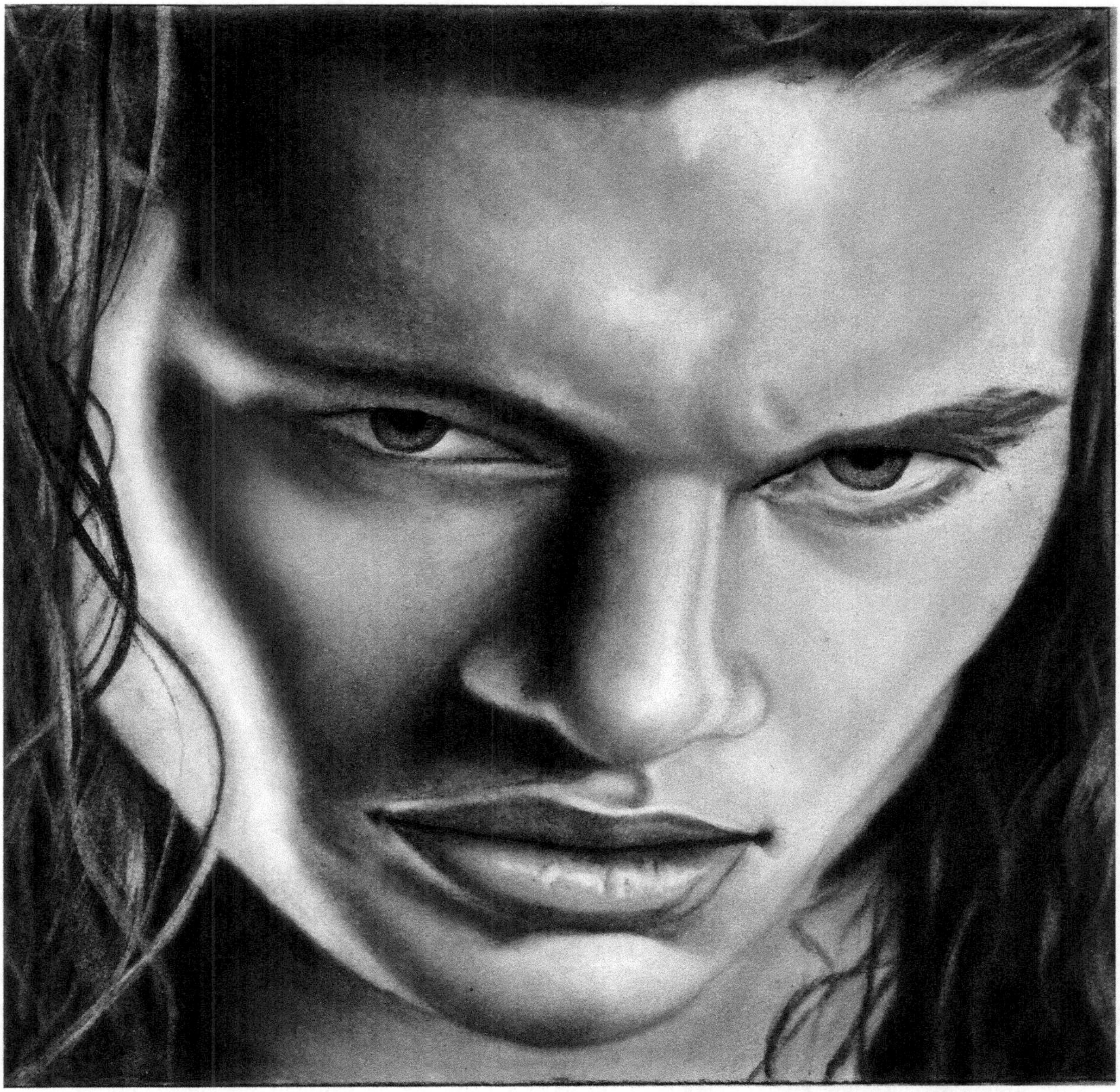

To view how this drawing was masterfully created or to purchase a Limited Edition Framed Artwork of Geoff Tate type into your Internet Browser the URL shortcut ➡ **myportrait.art/geofftate**

To listen to their Greatest Songs type into your Internet Browser the URL shortcut ➡ **radio.surf/queensryche**

To view all channels on THE FACE OF MUSIC Internet Radio MEGA Station type into your Internet Browser the URL shortcut ➡ **radio.surf/music**

To inquire about purchasing a Limited Edtion NFT of this portrait type into your Internet Browser the URL shortcut ➡ **myartnft.shop/geofftate**

To view all available NFTs type into your Internet Browser the URL shortcut ➡ **myartnft.shop/all**

# R.E.M.

(Total Albums Sold: 85+ Million)(Genre: Alternative Rock)

R.E.M. was an American rock band from Athens, Georgia, formed in 1980 by drummer Bill Berry, guitarist Peter Buck, bassist Mike Mills, and lead vocalist Michael Stipe, who were students at the University of Georgia. Liner notes from some of the band's albums list attorney Bertis Downs and manager Jefferson Holt as non-musical members. One of the first alternative rock bands, R.E.M. was noted for Buck's ringing, arpeggiated guitar style; Stipe's distinctive vocal quality, unique stage presence, and obscure lyrics; Mills's melodic bass lines and backing vocals; and Berry's tight, economical drumming style. In the early 1990s, other alternative rock acts such as Nirvana and Pavement viewed R.E.M. as a pioneer of the genre. After Berry left the band in 1997, the band continued its career in the 2000s with mixed critical and commercial success. The band broke up amicably in 2011 with members devoting time to solo projects after having sold more than 85 million albums worldwide and becoming one of the world's best-selling music acts.

# Michael Stipe

(Net Worth: $75 Million)(Height: 5' - 9")

John Michael Stipe (born January 4, 1960) is an American singer-songwriter best known as the lead singer and lyricist of alternative rock band R.E.M.. He is known for his distinctive vocal quality, poetic lyrics and unique stage presence.

Possessing a distinctive voice, Stipe has been noted for the "mumbling" style of his early career. Since the mid-1980s, Stipe sings in "wailing, keening, arching vocal figures" that R.E.M. biographer David Buckley compared to Celtic folk artists and Muslim muezzin. He was in charge of R.E.M.'s visual aspect, often selecting album artwork and directing many of the band's music videos. Outside the music industry, he owns and runs two film production studios, C-00 and Single Cell Pictures.

As a member of R.E.M., Stipe was inducted into the Rock and Roll Hall of Fame in 2007. As a singer-songwriter, Stipe influenced a wide range of artists, including Kurt Cobain of Nirvana and Thom Yorke of Radiohead. Bono of U2 described his voice as "extraordinary", and Yorke told The Guardian that Stipe is his favorite lyricist, saying "I loved the way he would take an emotion and then take a step back from it and in doing so make it so much more powerful."

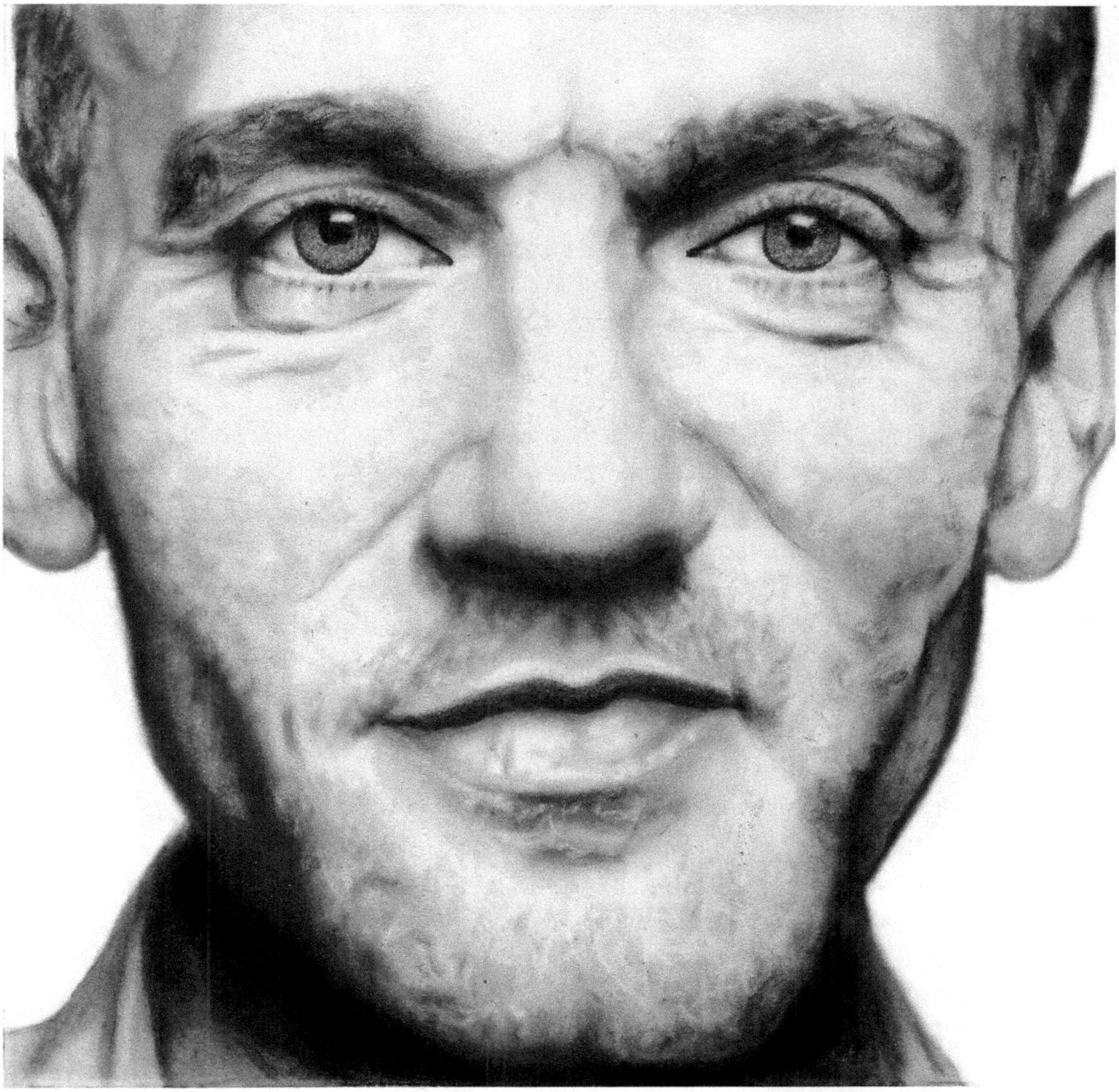

To view how this drawing was masterfully created or to purchase a Limited Edition Framed Artwork of Michael Stipe type into your Internet Browser the URL shortcut ➡ **myportrait.art/michaelstipe**

To listen to their Greatest Songs type into your Internet Browser the URL shortcut ➡ **radio.surf/rem**

To view all channels on THE FACE OF MUSIC Internet Radio MEGA Station type into your Internet Browser the URL shortcut ➡ **radio.surf/music**

To inquire about purchasing a Limited Edtion NFT of this portrait type into your Internet Browser the URL shortcut ➡ **myartnft.shop/michaelstipe**

To view all available NFTs type into your Internet Browser the URL shortcut ➡ **myartnft.shop/all**

# Radiohead

(Total Albums Sold: 30+ Million)(Genre: Alternative Rock)

Radiohead are an English rock band formed in Abingdon, Oxfordshire, in 1985. The band consists of Thom Yorke (vocals, guitar, piano, keyboards), brothers Jonny Greenwood (lead guitar, keyboards, other instruments) and Colin Greenwood (bass), Ed O'Brien (guitar, backing vocals) and Philip Selway (drums, percussion). They have worked with producer Nigel Godrich and cover artist Stanley Donwood since 1994. Radiohead's experimental approach is credited with advancing the sound of alternative rock. After signing to EMI in 1991, Radiohead released their debut single, "Creep", in 1992. It became a worldwide hit after the release of their debut album, Pablo Honey (1993). Their popularity and critical standing rose in the UK with the release of their second album, The Bends (1995). Radiohead's third album, OK Computer (1997), brought them international fame; noted for its complex production and themes of modern alienation, it is acclaimed as a landmark record of the Generation X era. Kid A (2000) marked a dramatic change in style, incorporating influences from electronic music, jazz, classical music and krautrock. Though Kid A divided listeners, it later attracted wide acclaim. It was followed by Amnesiac (2001), recorded in the same sessions.Hail to the Thief (2003), with lyrics inspired by the War on Terror, was Radiohead's final album for EMI. Their subsequent releases have pioneered alternative release platforms such as pay-what-you-want and BitTorrent; Radiohead self-released their seventh album, In Rainbows (2007), as a download for which customers could set their own price, to critical and chart success. Their eighth album, The King of Limbs (2011), an exploration of rhythm, was developed using extensive looping and sampling. A Moon Shaped Pool (2016) prominently featured Jonny Greenwood's orchestral arrangements. Yorke, Jonny Greenwood, Selway, and O'Brien have released solo albums.As of 2011, Radiohead have sold more than 30 million albums worldwide. Their awards include six Grammy Awards and four Ivor Novello Awards. They have achieved seven top 10 hits on the UK Singles Chart: "Creep" (1992), "Street Spirit (Fade Out)" (1996), "Paranoid Android" (1997), "Karma Police" (1998), "No Surprises" (1998), "Pyramid Song" (2001) and "There There" (2003). They have also achieved two top 40 hits on the US Billboard Hot 100. Rolling Stone named Radiohead one of the 100 greatest artists of all time, and Rolling Stone readers voted them the second-best artist of the 2000s. Five Radiohead albums have been included in Rolling Stone's 500 Greatest Albums of All Time lists, and the band are the most nominated act in Mercury Prize history, with five nominations. They were inducted into the Rock and Roll Hall of Fame in 2019.

# Thom Yorke

(Net Worth: $45 Million)(Height: 5' - 5")

Thomas Edward Yorke (born 7 October 1968) is an English musician and the main vocalist and songwriter of the rock band Radiohead. A multi-instrumentalist, he mainly plays guitar and keyboards, and is known for his falsetto.

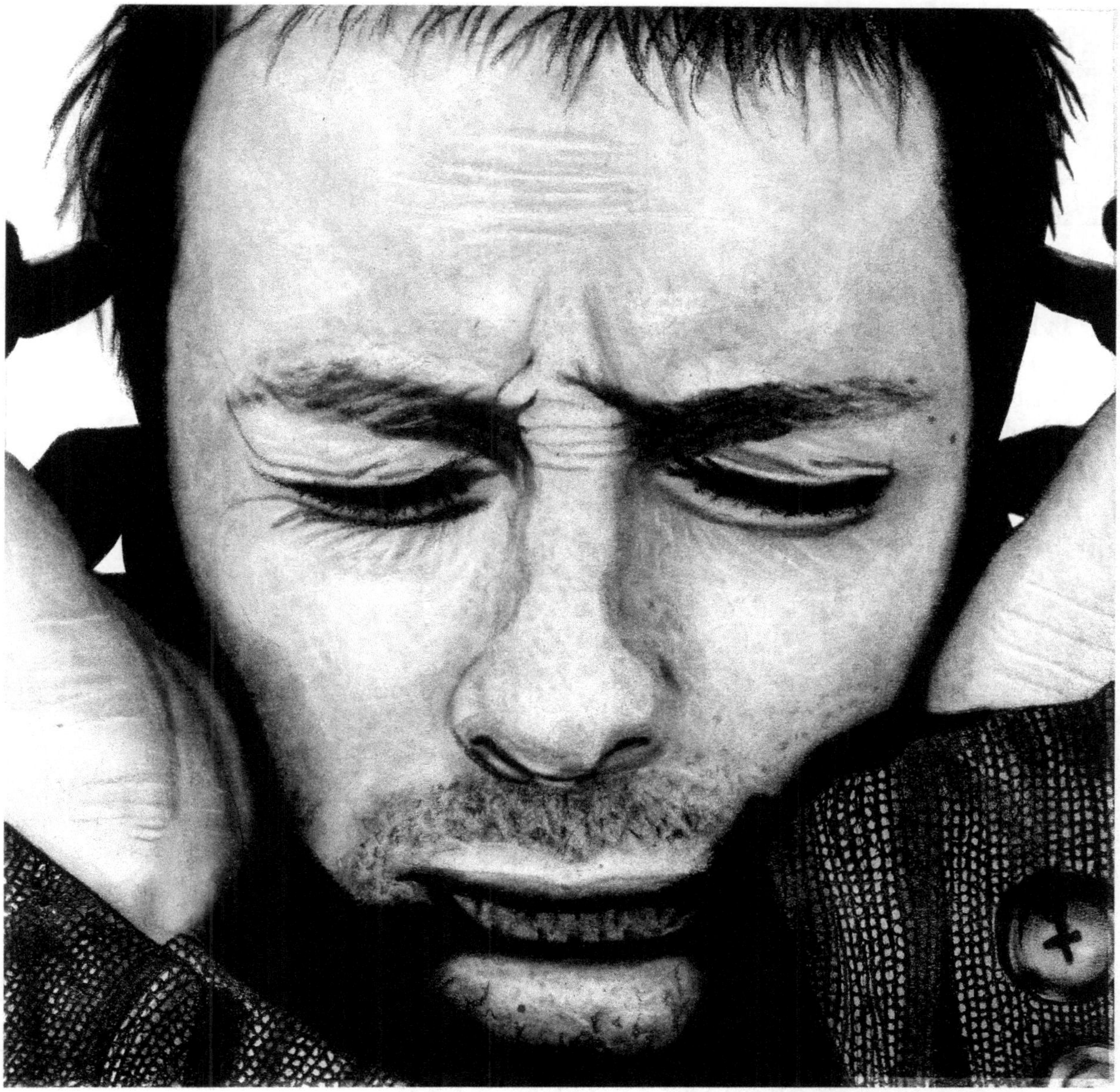

To view how this drawing was masterfully created or to purchase a Limited Edition Framed Artwork of Thom Yorke type into your Internet Browser the URL shortcut ➡ **myportrait.art/thomyorke**

To listen to their Greatest Songs type into your Internet Browser the URL shortcut ➡ **radio.surf/radiohead**

To view all channels on THE FACE OF MUSIC Internet Radio MEGA Station type into your Internet Browser the URL shortcut ➡ **radio.surf/music**

To inquire about purchasing a Limited Edtion NFT of this portrait type into your Internet Browser the URL shortcut ➡ **myartnft.shop/thomyorke**

To view all available NFTs type into your Internet Browser the URL shortcut ➡ **myartnft.shop/all**

# Rage Against the Machine

(Total Albums Sold: 16+ Million)(Genre: Nu Metal)

Rage Against the Machine (often abbreviated as RATM or shortened to Rage) is an American rock band from Los Angeles, California. Formed in 1991, the group consists of vocalist Zack de la Rocha, bassist and backing vocalist Tim Commerford, guitarist Tom Morello, and drummer Brad Wilk. Their songs express revolutionary political views. As of 2010, they have sold over 16 million records worldwide. The band was nominated for induction into the Rock & Roll Hall of Fame in their first year of eligibility in 2017, then again in 2018, 2019, and 2021, though the bids failed.

Rage Against the Machine released its self-titled debut album in 1992 to commercial and critical success, leading to a slot in the 1993 Lollapalooza festival; in 2003, the album was ranked number 368 on Rolling Stone's list of the 500 greatest albums of all time. The follow-up albums, Evil Empire (1996) and The Battle of Los Angeles (1999), were also successful; both albums topped the Billboard 200 chart. During their initial nine-year run, Rage Against the Machine became one of the most popular and influential bands in music history, and had a large influence on the nu metal genre which came to prominence during the second half of the 1990s. They were also ranked No. 33 on VH1's 100 Greatest Artists of Hard Rock.

In 2000, Rage Against the Machine released the cover album Renegades and disbanded after growing creative differences led to De la Rocha's departure. De la Rocha started a low-profile solo career, while the rest of the band formed the rock supergroup Audioslave with Chris Cornell, the former frontman of Soundgarden; Audioslave recorded three albums before disbanding in 2007. The same year, Rage Against the Machine announced a reunion and performed together for the first time in seven years at the Coachella Valley Music and Arts Festival in April 2007. Within the next four years, minus a sabbatical in 2009, the band continued to perform at more live venues and festivals around the world before going on hiatus once again in 2011. In 2016, Morello, Commerford and Wilk formed a new band, Prophets of Rage, with B-Real, Chuck D, and DJ Lord; that band released one EP and one full-length studio album before disbanding in 2019.

# Zack de la Rocha

(Net Worth: $25 Million)(Height: 5' - 10")

Zacharias Manuel de la Rocha (born January 12, 1970) is an American musician, singer, songwriter, rapper, and activist. He is best known as the vocalist and lyricist of rock band Rage Against the Machine. Through both Rage Against the Machine and his activism, de la Rocha promotes left-wing political positions and opposes corporate America, the military-industrial complex and government oppression.

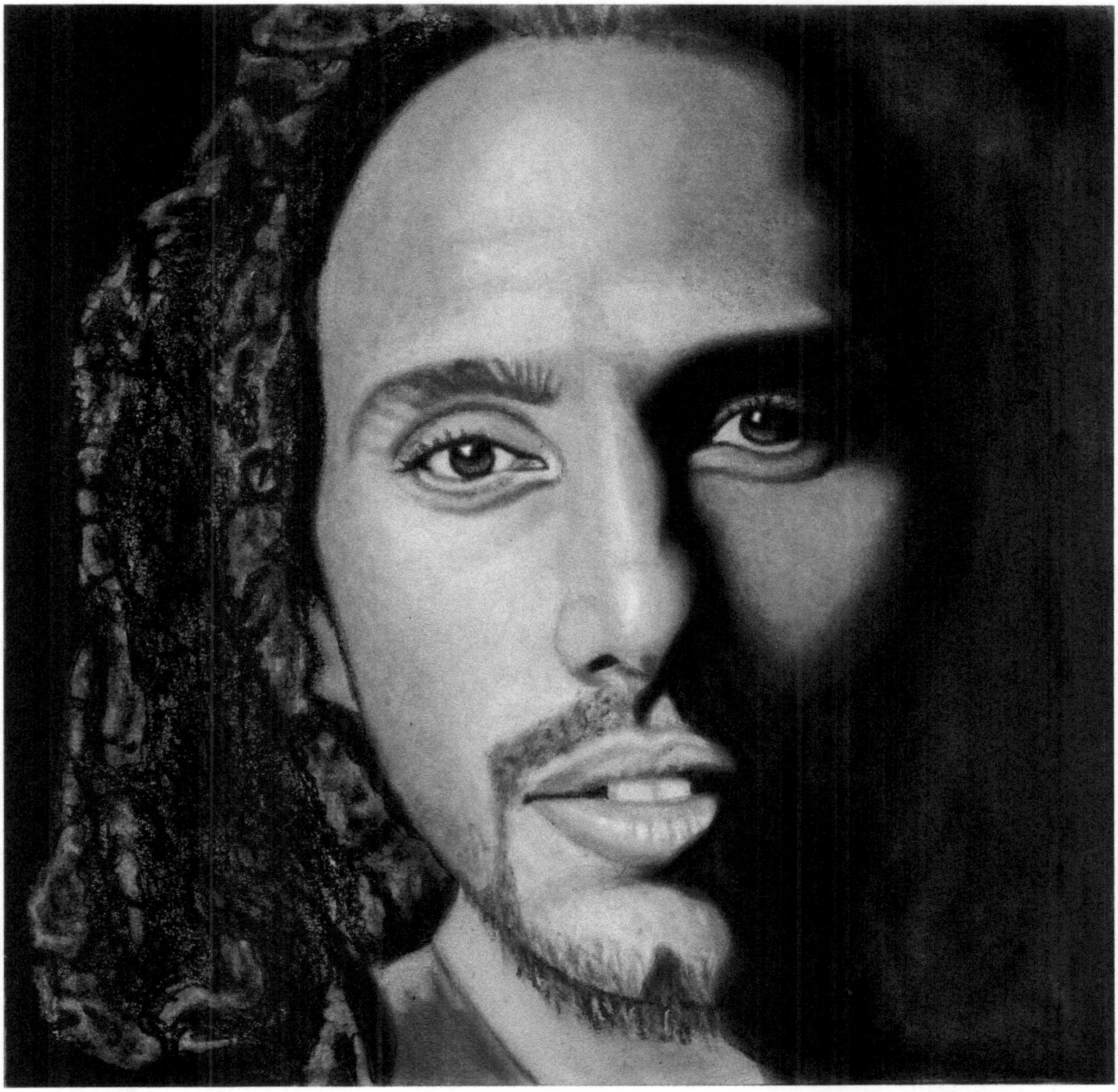

To view how this drawing was masterfully created or to purchase a Limited Edition Framed Artwork of Zack de la Rocha type into your Internet Browser the URL shortcut ➡ **myportrait.art/zackdelarocha**

To listen to their Greatest Songs type intc your Internet Browser the URL shortcut
➡ **radio.surf/rageagainstthemachine**

To view all channels on THE FACE OF MUSIC Internet Radio MEGA Station type into your Internet Browser the URL shortcut ➡ **radio.surf/music**

To inquire about purchasing a Limited Edtion NFT of this portrait type into your Internet Browser the URL shortcut ➡ **myartnft.shop/zackdelarocha**

To view all available NFTs type into your Internet Browser the URL shortcut ➡ **myartnft.shop/all**

# Ramones

(Total Albums Sold: Millions)(Genre: Punk Rock)

The Ramones were an American punk rock band that formed in the New York City neighborhood of Forest Hills, Queens, in 1974. They are often cited as the first true punk rock group. Despite achieving only limited commercial success initially, the band was highly influential in the United States, Argentina, Brazil and most of South America, as well as Europe, including the United Kingdom, the Netherlands, Germany, Sweden and Belgium.

All of the band members adopted pseudonyms ending with the surname "Ramone", although none of them were biologically related; they were inspired by Paul McCartney of the Beatles, who would check into hotels as "Paul Ramon". They performed 2,263 concerts, touring virtually nonstop for 22 years. In 1996, after a tour with the Lollapalooza music festival, the Ramones played a farewell concert in Los Angeles and disbanded. By 2014, all four of the band's original members had died – lead singer Joey Ramone (1951–2001), bassist Dee Dee Ramone (1951–2002), guitarist Johnny Ramone (1948–2004) and drummer Tommy Ramone (1949–2014). The remaining surviving members of the Ramones—bassist C. J. Ramone (who replaced Dee Dee in 1989 and stayed with the band until its dissolution) and drummers Marky Ramone, Richie Ramone and Elvis Ramone—are still musically active.

Recognition of the band's importance built over the years, and they are now mentioned in many assessments of all-time great rock music, such as number 26 in the Rolling Stone magazine list of the "100 Greatest Artists of All Time" and number 17 in VH1's "100 Greatest Artists of Hard Rock". In 2002, the Ramones were ranked the second-greatest band of all time by Spin, trailing only the Beatles. On March 18, 2002, the original four members and Tommy's replacement on drums, Marky Ramone, were inducted into the Rock and Roll Hall of Fame on their first year of eligibility, though Joey had died by then. In 2011, the group was awarded a Grammy Lifetime Achievement Award

# Joey Ramone

(Net Worth: $6 Million)(Height: 6' - 5")

Jeffrey Ross Hyman (May 19, 1951 – April 15, 2001), known professionally as Joey Ramone, was an American musician, singer, composer, and lead vocalist of the punk rock band the Ramones. Joey Ramone's image, voice, and tenure as frontman of the Ramones made him a countercultural icon.

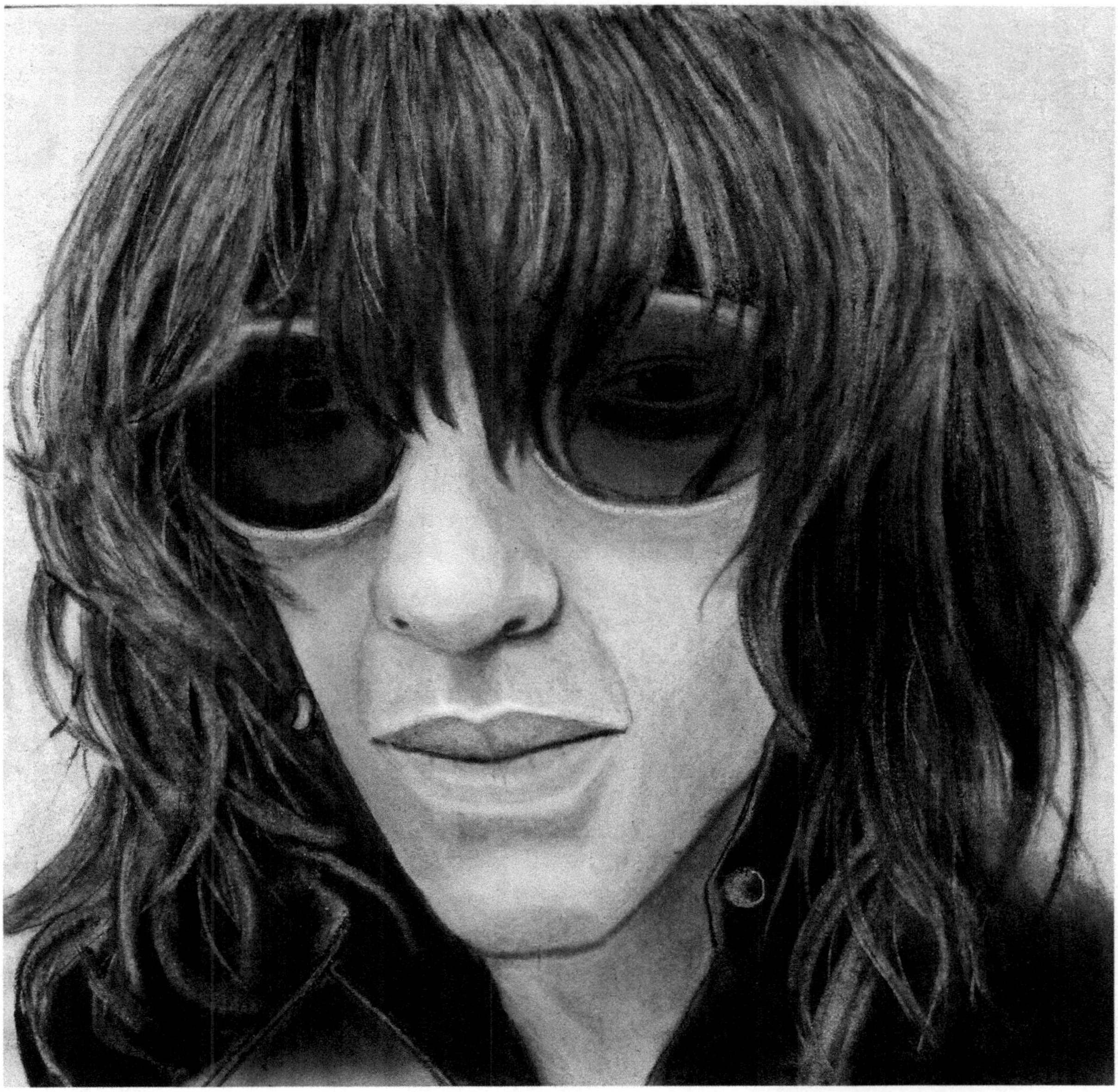

To view how this drawing was masterfully created or to purchase a Limited Edition Framed Artwork of Joey Ramone type into your Internet Browser the URL shortcut ➡ **myportrait.art/joeyramone**

To listen to their Greatest Songs type into your Internet Browser the URL shortcut ➡ **radio.surf/ramones**

To view all channels on THE FACE OF MUSIC Internet Radio MEGA Station type into your Internet Browser the URL shortcut ➡ **radio.surf/music**

To inquire about purchasing a Limited Edtion NFT of this portrait type into your Internet Browser the URL shortcut ➡ **myartnft.shop/joeyramone**

To view all available NFTs type into your Internet Browser the URL shortcut ➡ **myartnft.shop/all**

# Ray Charles

(Net worth: $75 Million)(Total Records Sold: Multi-Millions)
(Genre: R&B, Soul, Blues, Jazz, Gospel)(Height: 5' - 9")

Ray Charles Robinson (September 23, 1930 – June 10, 2004) was an American singer, songwriter, pianist, and composer. Among friends and fellow musicians he preferred being called "Brother Ray". He was often referred to as "The Genius". Charles was blinded during childhood due to glaucoma. Charles pioneered the soul music genre during the 1950s by combining blues, jazz, rhythm and blues, and gospel styles into the music he recorded for Atlantic. He contributed to the integration of country music, rhythm and blues, and pop music during the 1960s with his crossover success on ABC Records, notably with his two Modern Sounds albums. While he was with ABC, Charles became one of the first Black musicians to be granted artistic control by a mainstream record company.

Charles' 1960 hit "Georgia On My Mind" was the first of his three career No. 1 hits on the Billboard Hot 100. His 1962 album Modern Sounds In Country And Western Music became his first album to top the Billboard 200. Charles had multiple singles reach the Top 40 on various Billboard charts: 44 on the US R&B singles chart, 11 on the Hot 100 singles chart, 2 on the Hot Country singles charts. Charles cited Nat King Cole as a primary influence, but his music was also influenced by Louis Jordan and Charles Brown. He had a lifelong friendship and occasional partnership with Quincy Jones. Frank Sinatra called Ray Charles "the only true genius in show business," although Charles downplayed this notion. Billy Joel said, "This may sound like sacrilege, but I think Ray Charles was more important than Elvis Presley".

For his musical contributions, Charles received the Kennedy Center Honors, the National Medal of Arts, and the Polar Music Prize. He won 17 Grammy Awards, including 5 posthumously. Charles was honored with the Grammy Lifetime Achievement Award in 1987, and 10 of his recordings have been inducted into the Grammy Hall of Fame. Rolling Stone ranked Charles No. 10 on their list of the 100 Greatest Artists of All Time, and No. 2 on their list of the 100 Greatest Singers of All Time.

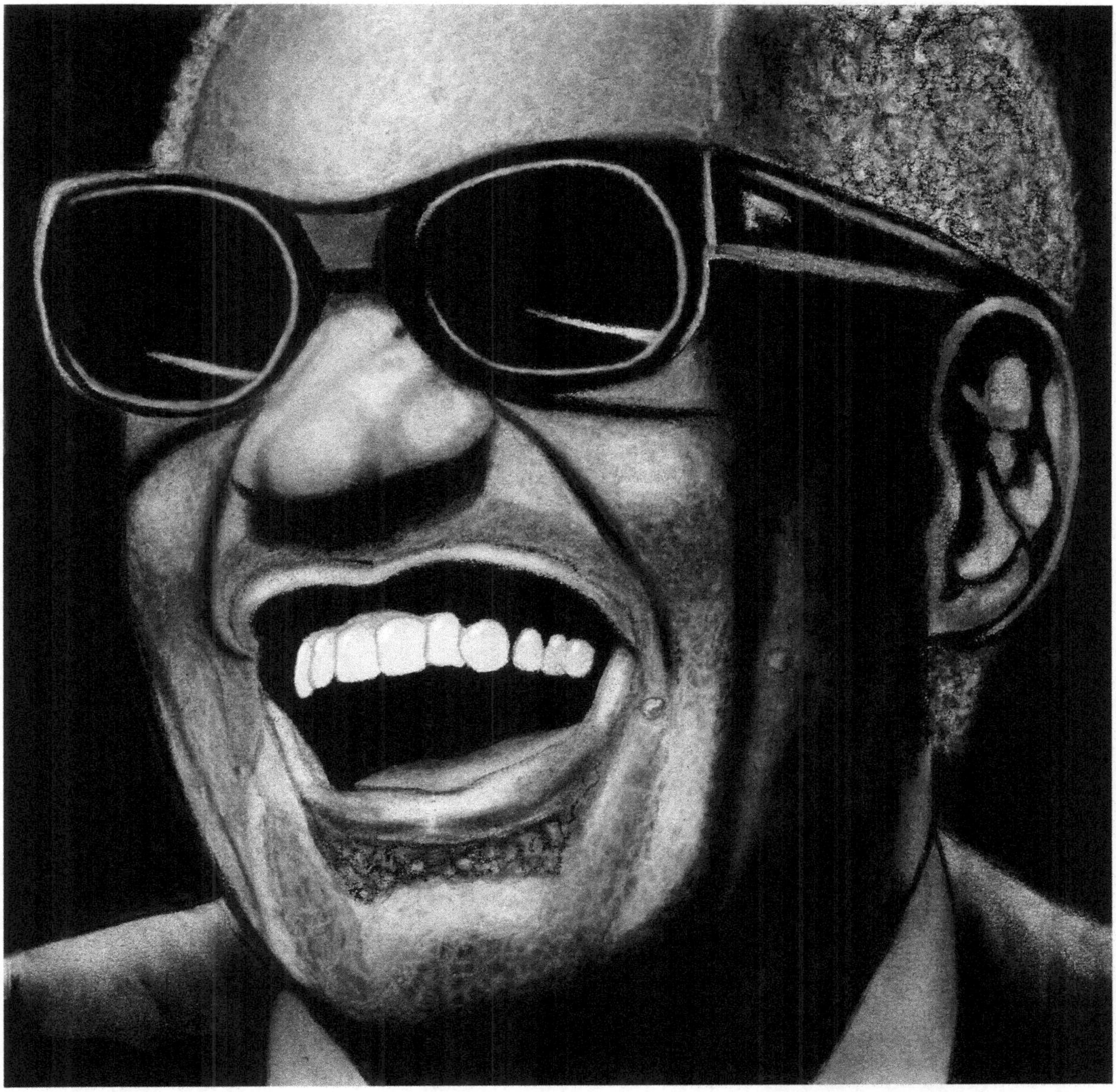

To view how this drawing was masterfully created or to purchase a Limited Edition Framed Artwork of Ray Charles type into your Internet Browser the URL shortcut ➡ **myportrait.art/raycharles**

To listen to his Greatest Songs type into your Internet Browser the URL shortcut ➡ **radio.surf/raycharles**

To view all channels on THE FACE OF MUSIC Internet Radio MEGA Station type into your Internet Browser the URL shortcut ➡ **radio.surf/music**

To inquire about purchasing a Limited Edition NFT of this portrait type into your Internet Browser the URL shortcut ➡ **myartnft.shop/raycharles**

To view all available NFTs type into your Internet Browser the URL shortcut ➡ **myartnft.shop/all**

# Red Hot Chili Peppers

(Total Albums Sold: 80+ Million)(Genre: Funk Rock, Alternative Rock, Rap Rock)

The Red Hot Chili Peppers are an American rock band formed in Los Angeles in 1983. Their music incorporates elements of alternative rock, funk, punk rock and psychedelic rock. The band consists of vocalist Anthony Kiedis, bassist Flea, drummer Chad Smith, and guitarist John Frusciante. With over 80 million records sold worldwide, the Red Hot Chili Peppers are one of the best-selling bands of all time. They are the most successful band in the history of alternative rock, with the records for most number-one singles (13), most cumulative weeks at number one (85) and most top-ten songs (25) on the Billboard Alternative Songs chart. They have won six Grammy Awards, and in 2012 were inducted into the Rock and Roll Hall of Fame.

The Red Hot Chili Peppers were formed in Los Angeles by Kiedis, Flea, guitarist Hillel Slovak and drummer Jack Irons. Because of commitments to other bands, Slovak and Irons did not play on the band's 1984 self-titled debut album, which instead featured guitarist Jack Sherman and drummer Cliff Martinez. Slovak rejoined in time for their second album, Freaky Styley (1985), and Irons rejoined for their third, The Uplift Mofo Party Plan (1987). Slovak died of a drug overdose on June 25, 1988; Irons, devastated, left the band.

With new recruits Frusciante and Smith, the Red Hot Chili Peppers recorded Mother's Milk (1989) and their first major commercial success, Blood Sugar Sex Magik (1991). Frusciante was uncomfortable with their newfound popularity and left abruptly on tour in 1992; he was replaced by Dave Navarro, who appeared on the group's sixth album, One Hot Minute (1995). Although successful, the album failed to match the critical or popular acclaim of its predecessor. Frusciante and Kiedis struggled with drug addiction throughout the 1990s.

In 1998, following Navarro's departure, Frusciante rejoined the band. Their seventh album, Californication (1999), became their biggest commercial success, with 16 million copies sold worldwide. By the Way (2002) and Stadium Arcadium (2006) were also successful; Stadium Arcadium was their first album to reach number one on the Billboard 200 chart. Frusciante left again in 2009 to focus on his solo career; he was replaced by Josh Klinghoffer, who appeared on I'm with You (2011) and The Getaway (2016), before Frusciante rejoined in 2019.

# Anthony Kiedis

(Net Worth: $140 Million)(Height: 5' - 8")

Anthony Kiedis (born November 1, 1962) is an American musician and is a founding member of the rock band Red Hot Chili Peppers. Kiedis and his fellow band members were inducted into the Rock and Roll Hall of Fame in 2012.

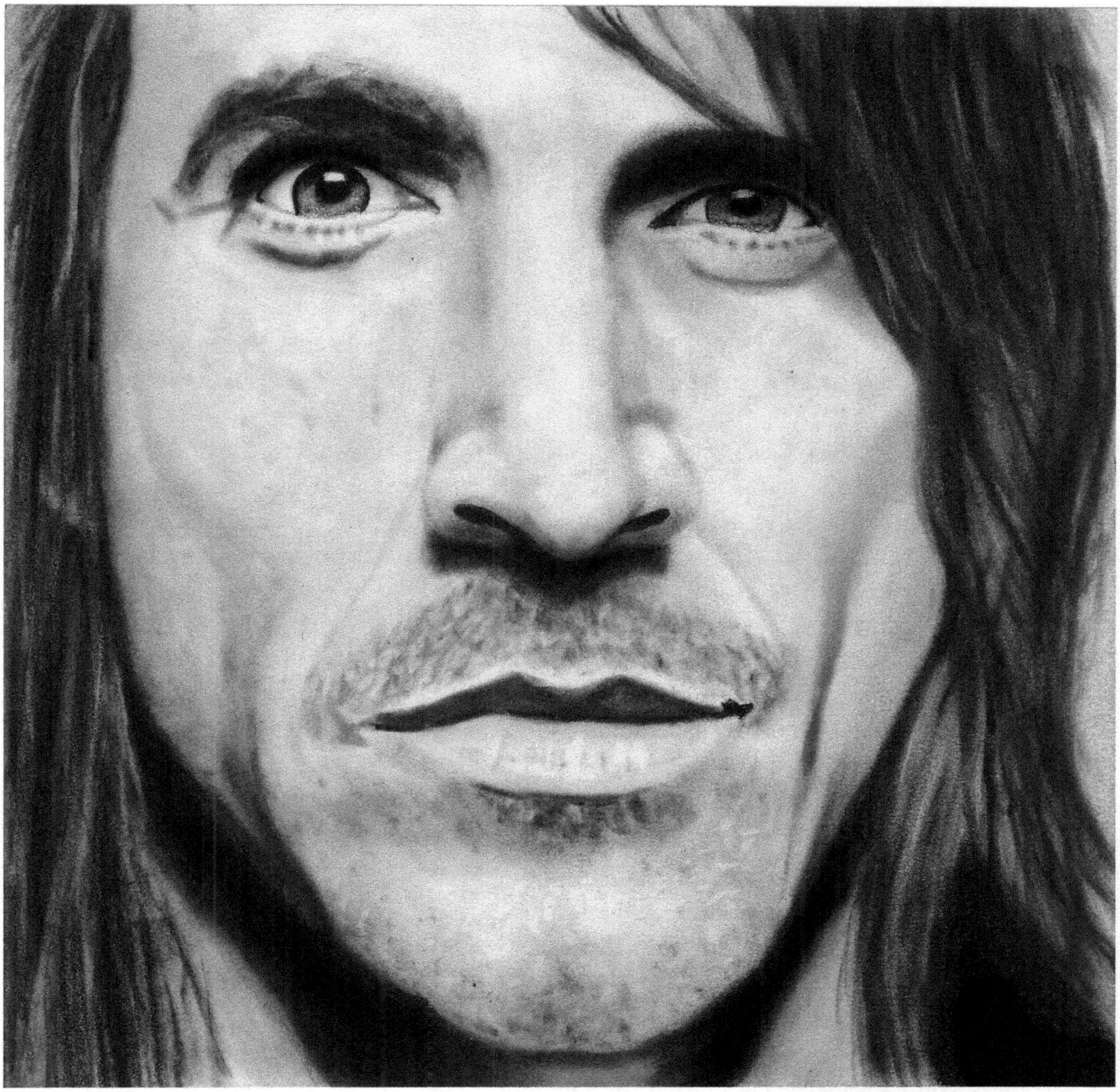

To view how this drawing was masterfully created or to purchase a Limited Edition Framed Artwork of Anthony Kiedis type into your Internet Browser the URL shortcut ➡ **myportrait.art/anthonykiedis**

To listen to their Greatest Songs type into your Internet Browser the URL shortcut ➡ **radio.surf/redhotchilipeppers**

To view all channels on THE FACE OF MUSIC Internet Radio MEGA Station type into your Internet Browser the URL shortcut ➡ **radio.surf/music**

To inquire about purchasing a Limited Edition NFT of this portrait type into your Internet Browser the URL shortcut ➡ **myartnft.shop/anthonykiedis**

To view all available NFTs type into your Internet Browser the URL shortcut ➡ **myartnft.shop/all**

# Redman

(Net worth: $10 Million)(Total Records Sold: 25+ Million)
(Genre: Hip-Hop, Rap)(Height: 6' - 0")

Reginald "Reggie" Noble (born April 17, 1970), better known by his stage name Redman, is an American rapper, DJ, record producer, and actor. He rose to fame in the early 1990s as an artist on the Def Jam label.

He is well known for his collaborations with his close friend Method Man, as one-half of the rap duo Method Man & Redman, including their starring roles in films and sitcoms. He was also a member of the Def Squad in the late 1990s.

In 1990, Redman made his official debut on EPMD's album Business as Usual, appearing on the tracks "Hardcore" and "Brothers on My Jock".

In 1992, Redman released his debut album, Whut? Thee Album, which Allmusic noted for blending "reggae and funk influences" with a "terse, though fluid rap style". The album peaked at number forty-nine on the Billboard 200 and was certified gold. He was named "Rap Artist of the Year" by The Source. Redman followed this up with his 1994 album, Dare Iz a Darkside. The first single, "Rockafella", samples Leon Haywood's "I Want'a Do Something Freaky to You" and George Clinton's "Flash Light", two of the most sampled songs in hip hop. Redman's second album was notable for having most of the tracks produced by the artist himself (later on Redman would let other producers make most of his beats). During this time he used former mentor Erick Sermon to produce his records, including "Pick it up" and "Whatera Man" from Muddy Waters.

In 1992, Redman appeared in A Tribe Called Quest's "Scenario" music video.

Redman released his second studio album, "Dare Iz a Darkside" on November 22, 1994, by Def Jam Recordings. The album debuted at 13 on the US Billboard 200. The album was certified gold by the Recording Industry Association of America. Redman has said that he was on drugs during the recording of the album, and said in 2010 that he doesn't play the album in recent years because it was made during one of the dark times in his life.

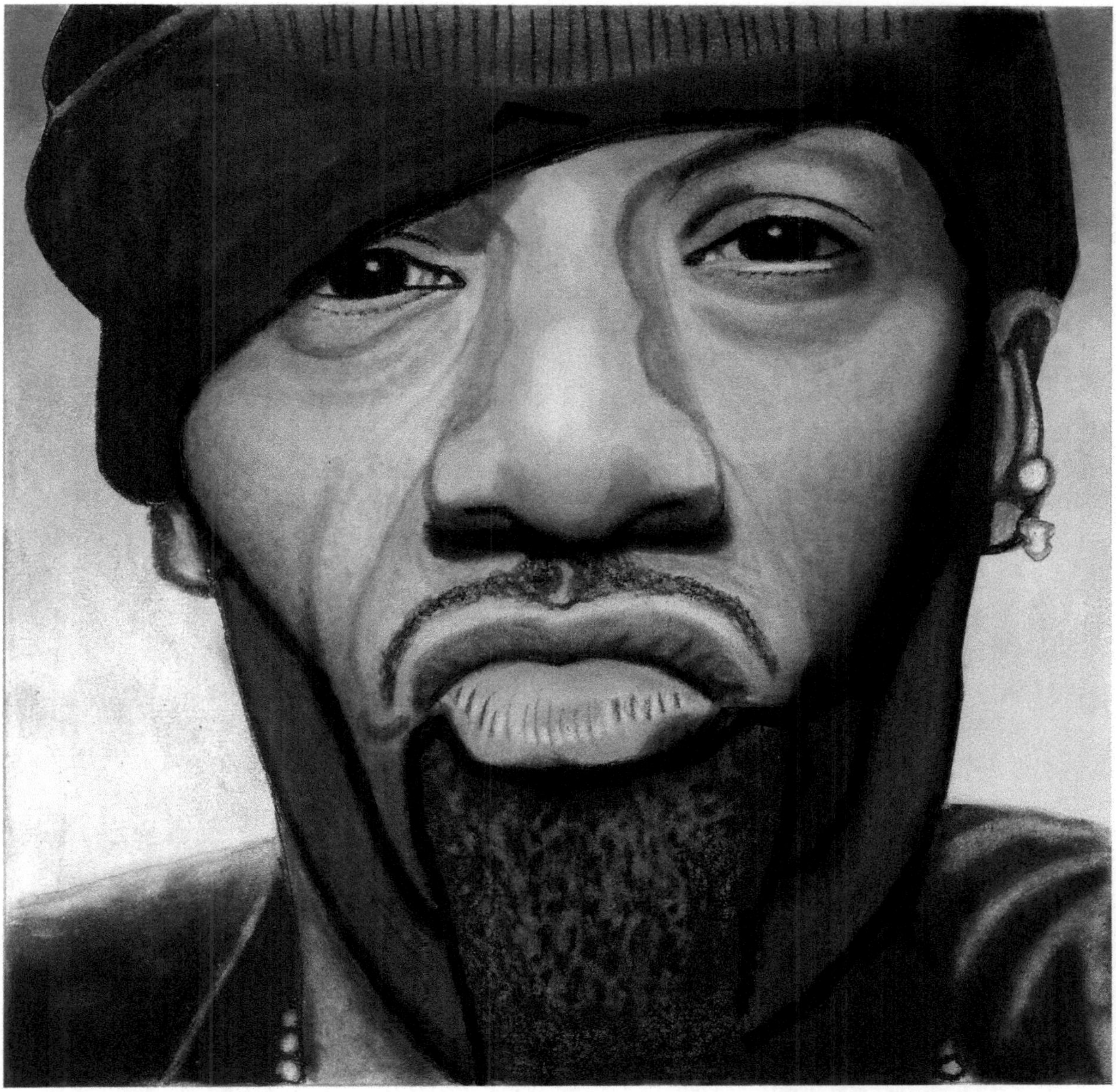

To view how this drawing was masterfully created or to purchase a Limited Edition Framed Artwork of Redmank type into your Internet Browser the URL shortcut ➡ **myportrait.art/redman**

To listen to his Greatest Songs type into your Internet Browser the URL shortcut ➡ **radio.surf/redman**

To view all channels on THE FACE OF MUSIC Internet Radio MEGA Station type into your Internet Browser the URL shortcut ➡ **radio.surf/music**

To inquire about purchasing a Limited Edtion NFT of this portrait type into your Internet Browser the URL shortcut ➡ **myartnft.shop/redman**

To view all available NFTs type into your Internet Browser the URL shortcut ➡ **myartnft.shop/all**

# REO Speedwagon

(Total Albums Sold: 40+ Million)(Genre: Hard Rock, Pop Rock, Soft)

REO Speedwagon (originally stylized as R.E.O. Speedwagon) is an American rock band from Champaign, Illinois. Formed in 1967, the band cultivated a following during the 1970s and achieved significant commercial success throughout the 1980s. The group's best-selling album, Hi Infidelity (1980), contained four US Top 40 hits and sold more than 10 million copies.

Over the course of its career, the band has sold more than 40 million records and has charted 13 Top 40 hits, including the number ones "Keep On Loving You" and "Can't Fight This Feeling". REO Speedwagon's mainstream popularity waned in the late 1980s, but the band remains a popular live act.

On November 21, 1980, Epic released Hi Infidelity, which represented a change in sound, going from hard rock to more pop-oriented material. Hi Infidelity spawned four hit singles written by Richrath and Cronin, including the chart-topping "Keep On Loving You" (Cronin), plus "Take It on the Run" (#5) (Richrath), "In Your Letter" (#20) (Richrath), and "Don't Let Him Go" (#24) (Cronin), and remained on the charts for 65 weeks, 32 of which were spent in the top ten, including 15 weeks atop the Billboard 200. Hi Infidelity sold over 10 million copies.

The band's follow-up album, Good Trouble, was released in June 1982. Although it was not as successful as its predecessor, the album performed moderately well commercially, featuring the hit singles "Keep the Fire Burnin'" (U.S. #7), "Sweet Time" (U.S. #26) and the Album Rock chart hit "The Key."

The band came storming back two years later with Wheels Are Turnin', an album that included the #1 hit single "Can't Fight This Feeling" plus three more hits: "I Do' Wanna Know" (U.S. #29), "One Lonely Night" (U.S. #19), and "Live Every Moment" (U.S. #34).

REO Speedwagon toured the US in 1985, including a sold-out concert in Madison, Wisconsin in May. On July 13, on the way to a show in Milwaukee, the band made a stop in Philadelphia to play at the US leg of Live Aid, which broke a record for number of viewers. They performed "Can't Fight This Feeling" and "Roll With the Changes," which featured members of the Beach Boys, the band members' families, and Paul Shaffer on stage for backing vocals.

# Kevin Cronin

(Net Worth: $25 Million)(Height: 5' - 10")

Kevin Patrick Cronin (born October 6, 1951) is the lead vocalist, rhythm guitarist, and occasional pianist for the American rock band, REO Speedwagon.

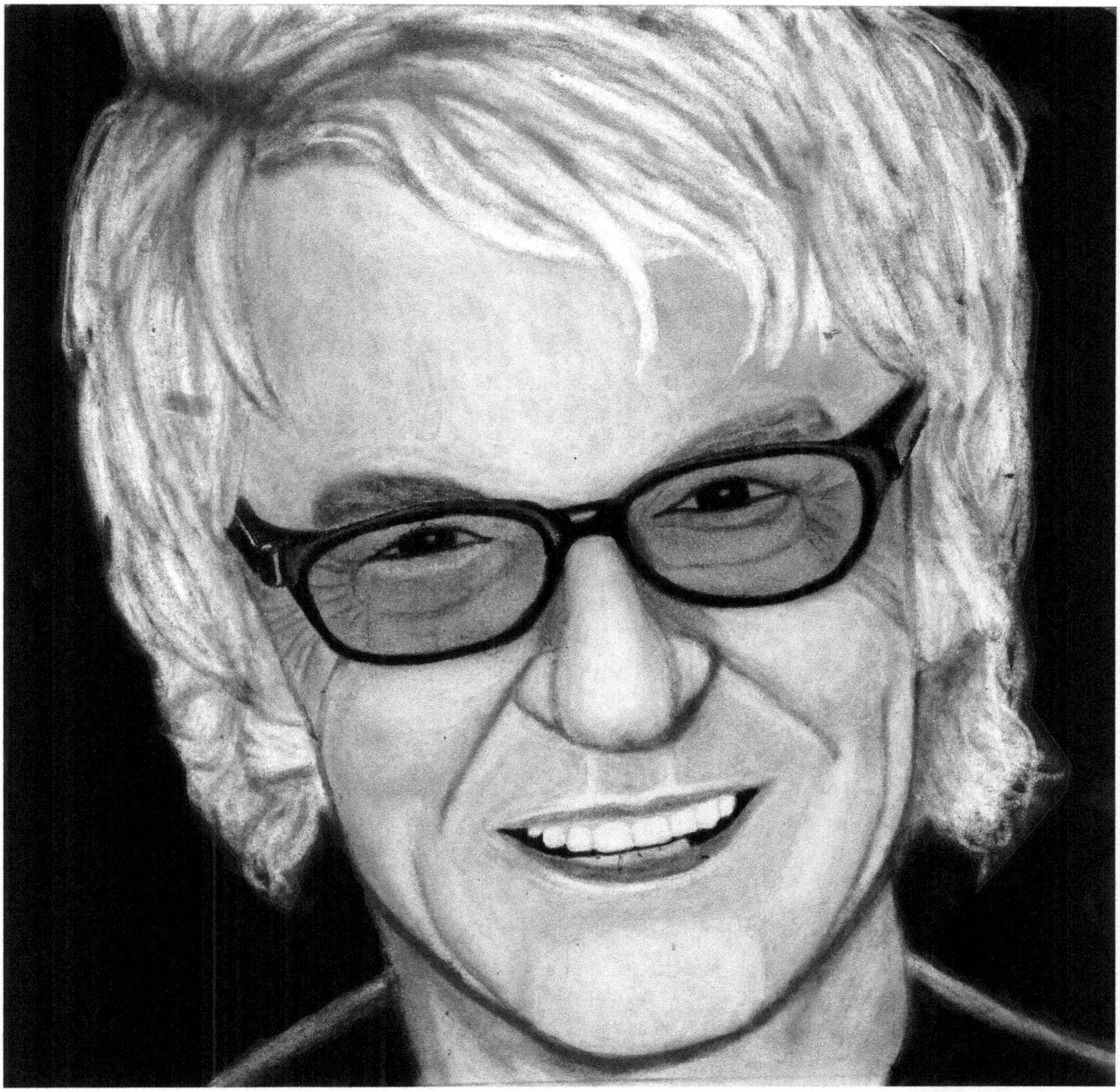

To view how this drawing was masterfully created or to purchase a Limited Edition Framed Artwork of Kevin Cronin type into your Internet Browser the URL shortcut ➡ **myportrait.art/kevincronin**

To listen to their Greatest Songs type into your Internet Browser the URL shortcut
➡ **radio.surf/reospeedwagon**

To view all channels on THE FACE OF MUSIC Internet Radio MEGA Station type into your Internet Browser the URL shortcut ➡ **radio.surf/music**

To inquire about purchasing a Limited Edition NFT of this portrait type into your Internet Browser the URL shortcut ➡ **myartnft.shop/kevincronin**

To view all available NFTs type into your Internet Browser the URL shortcut ➡ **myartnft.shop/all**

# Rick Springfield

(Net worth: $10 Million)(Total Records Sold: Millions)
(Genre: Hard Rock , Pop Rock)(Height: 6' - 1")

Richard Lewis Springthorpe (born 23 August 1949), known professionally as Rick Springfield, is an Australian musician and actor. He was a member of the pop rock group Zoot from 1969 to 1971, then started his solo career with his debut single "Speak to the Sky" reaching the top 10 in Australia in mid-1972, when he moved to the United States. He had a No. 1 hit with "Jessie's Girl" in 1981 in both Australia and the U.S., for which he received the Grammy Award for Best Male Rock Vocal Performance. He followed with four more top 10 U.S. hits: "I've Done Everything for You", "Don't Talk to Strangers", "Affair of the Heart", and "Love Somebody". Springfield's two U.S. top 10 albums are Working Class Dog (1981) and Success Hasn't Spoiled Me Yet (1982).

As an actor, he starred in the television series High Tide, from 1994–97, and has appeared in supporting roles in Ricki and the Flash and True Detective (both 2015). He portrayed Dr. Noah Drake on the daytime drama General Hospital, 1981–83, 2005–08, and 2012, returning in 2013 for the show's 50th anniversary with his son, actor Liam Springthorpe. He played a depraved version of himself in Californication (2009). In 2010, Springfield published his autobiography, Late, Late at Night: A Memoir. In 2016 he starred as Vince Vincente/Lucifer in season 12 of The CW series Supernatural. In 2017, he starred as Pastor Charles in the American Horror Story episode entitled "Winter of Our Discontent".

Rick Springfield was born Richard Lewis Springthorpe on 23 August 1949 in South Wentworthville, an outer western suburb of Sydney. He is the son of Eileen Louise (Evennett) and Norman James Springthorpe, an Australian Army career officer. His maternal grandparents were English. When he was young, he lived at the army camp with his family in Broadmeadows, Victoria, Australia. At 14, he saw the Beatles perform at Festival Hall in Melbourne.

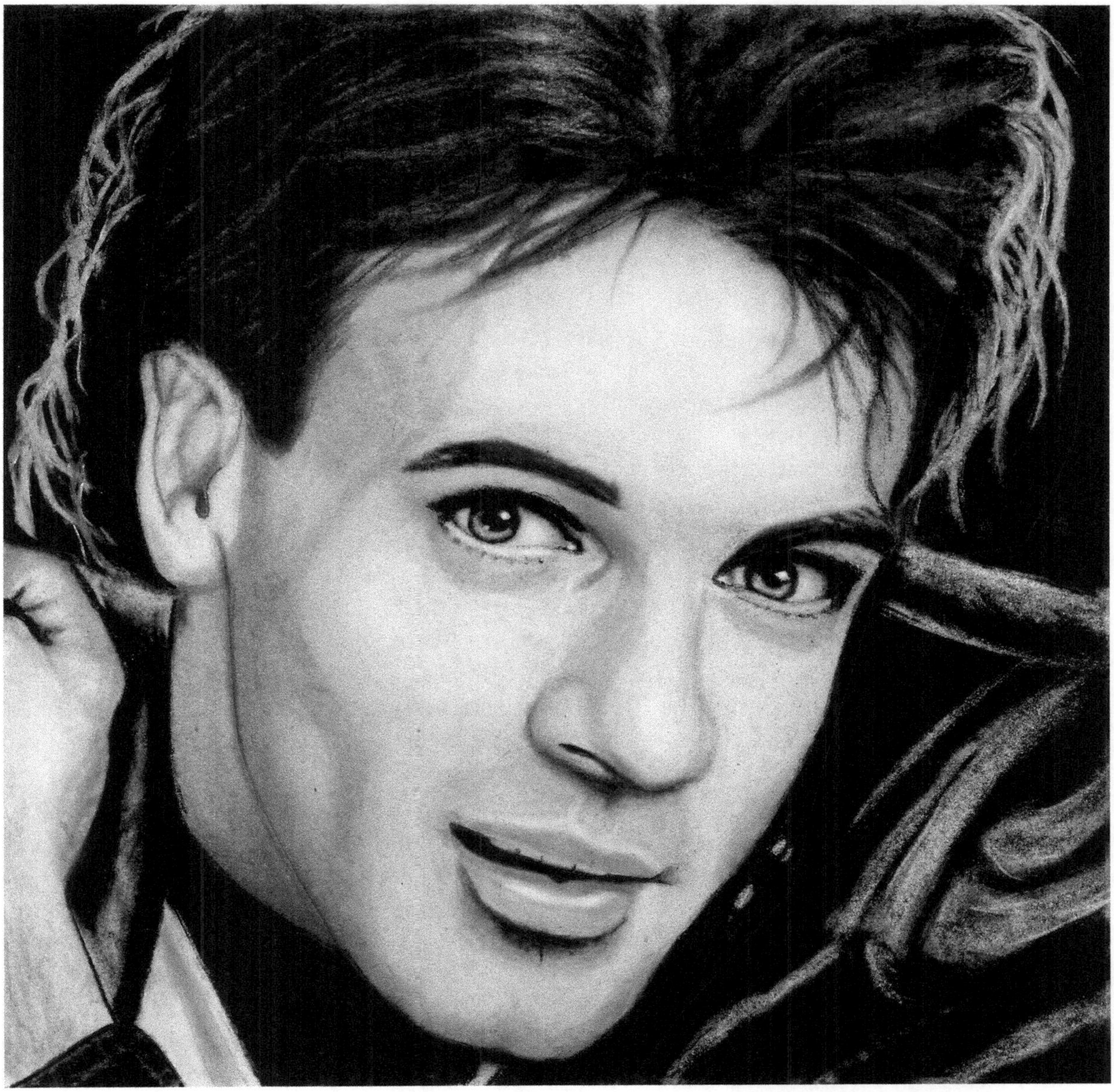

To view how this drawing was masterfully created or to purchase a Limited Edition Framed Artwork of Rick Springfield type into your Internet Browser the URL shortcut ➡ **myportrait.art/rickspringfield**

To listen to his Greatest Songs type into your Internet Browser the URL shortcut ➡ **radio.surf/rickspringfield**

To view all channels on THE FACE OF MUSIC Internet Radio MEGA Station type into your Internet Browser the URL shortcut ➡ **radio.surf/music**

To inquire about purchasing a Limited Edtion NFT of this portrait type into your Internet Browser the URL shortcut ➡ **myartnft.shop/rickspringfield**

To view all available NFTs type into your Internet Browser the URL shortcut ➡ **myartnft.shop/all**

# Ricky Nelson

(Net worth: $500 Thousand)(Total Records Sold: 35+ Million)
(Genre: Rock & Roll, Rockabilly, Pop)(Height: 5' - 11")

Eric Hilliard Nelson (May 8, 1940 – December 31, 1985), known professionally as Ricky Nelson until his 21st birthday when he officially dropped the "y" and simply became Rick Nelson, was an American rock 'n' roll star, pop pioneer, musician, singer-songwriter and actor. From age eight he starred alongside his family in the radio and television series The Adventures of Ozzie and Harriet. In 1957, he began a long and successful career as a popular recording artist. As one of the top "teen idols" of the 1950s, his fame led to a motion picture role co-starring alongside John Wayne and Dean Martin in Howard Hawks's western feature film Rio Bravo (1959). He placed 53 songs on the Billboard Hot 100, and its predecessors, between 1957 and 1973, including "Poor Little Fool" in 1958, which was the first number 1 song on Billboard magazine's then-newly created Hot 100 chart. He recorded 19 additional Top 10 hits and was inducted into the Rock and Roll Hall of Fame on January 21, 1987. In 1996 Nelson was ranked No. 49 on TV Guide's 50 Greatest TV Stars of All Time.

Nelson began his entertainment career in 1949, playing himself in the radio sitcom series, The Adventures of Ozzie and Harriet. In 1952, he appeared in his first feature film, Here Come the Nelsons. In 1957, he recorded his first single, debuted as a singer on the television version of the sitcom, and released the No. 1 album titled Ricky. In 1958, Nelson released his first #1 single, "Poor Little Fool", and in 1959 received a Golden Globe nomination for "Most Promising Male Newcomer" after starring in Rio Bravo. A few films followed, and when the television series was cancelled in 1966, Nelson made occasional appearances as a guest star on various television programs.

Nelson and Sharon Kristin Harmon were married on April 20, 1963, and divorced in December 1982. They had four children: Tracy Kristine, twin sons Gunnar Eric and Matthew Gray, and Sam Hilliard.

In early summer 1957, Ozzie Nelson pulled his son from Verve after disputes about royalties and signed him to a lucrative five-year deal with Imperial Records that gave him approval over song selection, sleeve artwork, and other production details. Ricky's first Imperial single, "Be-Bop Baby", generated 750,000 advance orders, sold over one million copies, and reached No. 3 on the charts. Nelson's first album, Ricky, was released in October 1957 and hit #1 before the end of the year. Following these successes, Nelson was given a more prominent role on the Ozzie and Harriet show and ended every two or three episodes with a musical number.Nelson grew increasingly dissatisfied performing with older jazz and country session musicians, who were openly contemptuous of rock and roll. After his Ohio and Minnesota tours in the summer of 1957, he decided to form his own band with members closer to his age. Eighteen-year-old electric guitarist James Burton was the first signed. Bassist James Kirkland, drummer Richie Frost, and pianist Gene Garf completed the band. Their first recording together was "Believe What You Say". Prior to this, Joe Maphis had been playing the lead guitar part, and played lead on his first hits "Be-Bop Baby", "Stood Up", and "Waitin In School". In 1958, Nelson recorded 17-year-old Sharon Sheeley's "Poor Little Fool" for his second album, Ricky Nelson, released in June 1958. Radio airplay brought the tune notice, and Imperial suggested releasing a single, but Nelson opposed the idea, believing a single would diminish EP sales. When a single was released nonetheless, he exercised his contractual right to approve any artwork and vetoed a picture sleeve. On August 4, 1958, "Poor Little Fool" became the #1 single on Billboard's newly instituted Hot 100 singles chart and sold over two million copies.

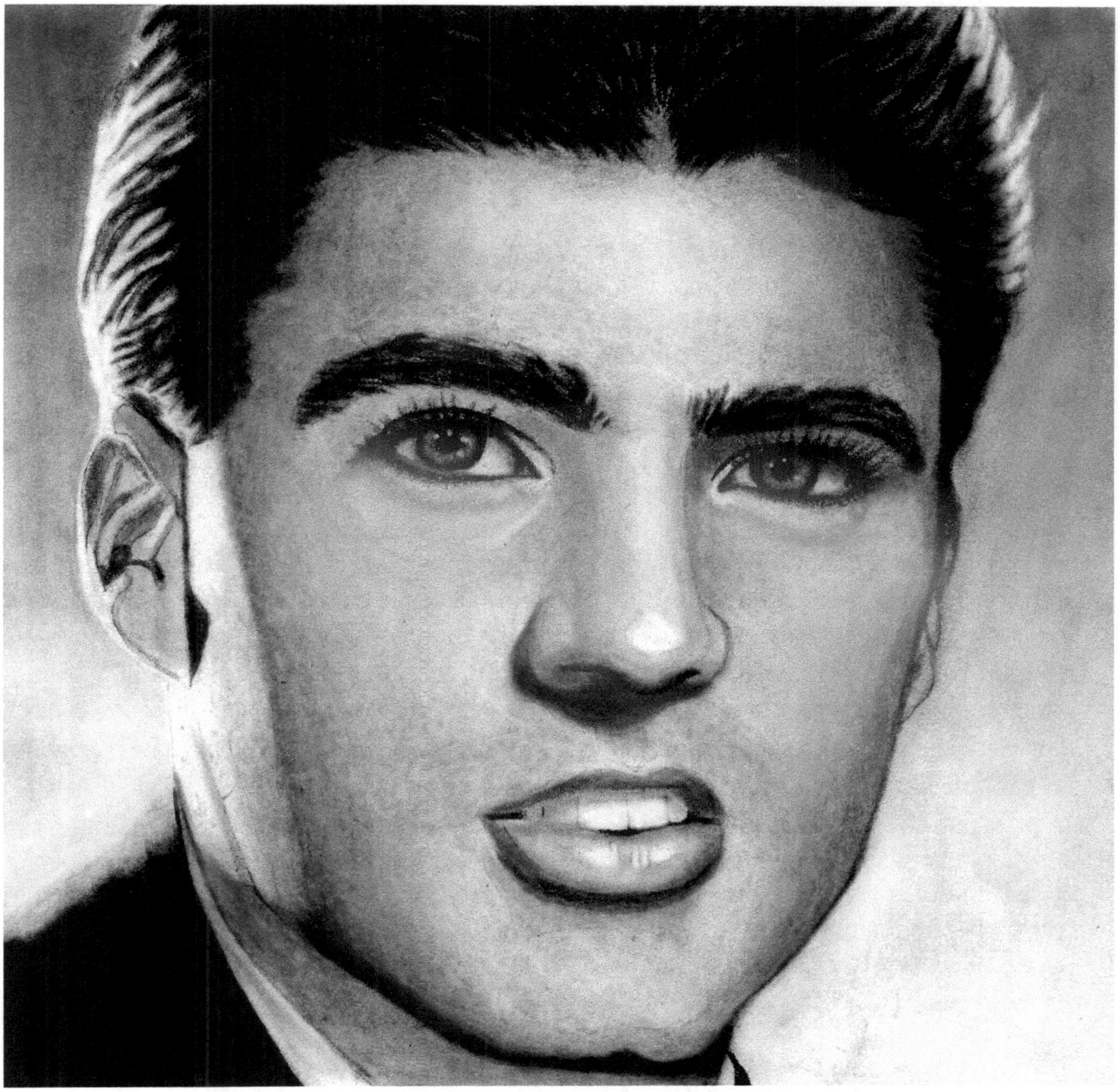

To view how this drawing was masterfully created or to purchase a Limited Edition Framed Artwork of Ricky Nelson type into your Internet Browser the URL shortcut ➡ **myportrait.art/rickynelson**

To listen to his Greatest Songs type into your Internet Browser the URL shortcut ➡ **radio.surf/rickynelson**

To view all channels on THE FACE OF MUSIC Internet Radio MEGA Station type into your Internet Browser the URL shortcut ➡ **radio.surf/music**

To inquire about purchasing a Limited Edtion NFT of this portrait type into your Internet Browser the URL shortcut ➡ **myartnft.shop/rickynelson**

To view all available NFTs type into your Internet Browser the URL shortcut ➡ **myartnft.shop/all**

# Righteous Brothers

(Total Records Sold: Multi-Millions)(Genre: Pop , Soul)

The Righteous Brothers are an American musical duo originally formed by Bill Medley and Bobby Hatfield but now comprising Medley and Bucky Heard. Medley formed the group with Hatfield in 1963. They had first performed together in 1962 in the Los Angeles area as part of a five-member group called the Paramours, and adopted the name The Righteous Brothers when they embarked on their recording career as a duo. Their most active recording period was in the 1960s and '70s, and, after several years inactive as a duo, Hatfield and Medley reunited in 1981 and continued to perform until Hatfield's death in 2003. The music they performed is sometimes dubbed "blue-eyed soul".

Hatfield and Medley had contrasting vocal ranges, which helped them create a distinctive sound as a duet, but also strong vocal talent individually that allowed them to perform as soloists. Medley sang the low parts with his bass-baritone voice, with Hatfield taking the higher-register vocals with his tenor. Following a year-and-a-half of Top 40 non-entries on Billboard's Hot 100, the duo hit big with the late-1964 release of what would become their signature record, "You're Lost That Lovin' Feelin'" – a transatlantic number one produced by Phil Spector, often considered one of his finest works and a landmark recording in popular music. Other notable hits include three US 1965 Top Tens – "Just Once in My Life" and covers of "Unchained Melody" (also a huge hit in 1990) and "Ebb Tide" – and the massive US 1966 number one "(You're My) Soul and Inspiration", plus the 1974 comeback hit "Rock and Roll Heaven". Both Hatfield and Medley also had for a time their own solo careers.

In 2016, Medley re-formed The Righteous Brothers with Bucky Heard and they continue to perform as a duo.The Righteous Brothers were inducted into the Rock and Roll Hall of Fame in 2003. Rolling Stone ranked them no. 16 on its list of the 20 Greatest Duos of All Time.

# Bobby Hatfield

(Net Worth: $45 Million)

Robert Lee Hatfield ( August 10, 1940 – November 5, 2003) was an American singer. With Bill Medley, he was part of the Righteous Brothers. He sang the tenor part for the duo, and sang solo on the group's 1965 recording of "Unchained Melody".

Bobby Hatfield initially was in a group from Anaheim called the Variations. In 1962, Hatfield joined with Medley who was in a group called the Paramours, and formed a five-member group using the same name Paramours. They first performed at a club called John's Black Derby in Santa Ana. Later they performed as a duo and named their singing act The Righteous Brothers. They were often told they sounded like African-American gospel singers and chose the name after black Marines remarked of their singing, "that's righteous, brothers" and called them "righteous brothers". Their first charted single as the Righteous Brothers was "Little Latin Lupe Lu" released under the label Moonglow Records, and they appeared regularly on the television show Shindig! Hatfield also recorded as solo artist with Moonglow and released an uncharted single, "Hot Tamales" / "I Need a Girl".

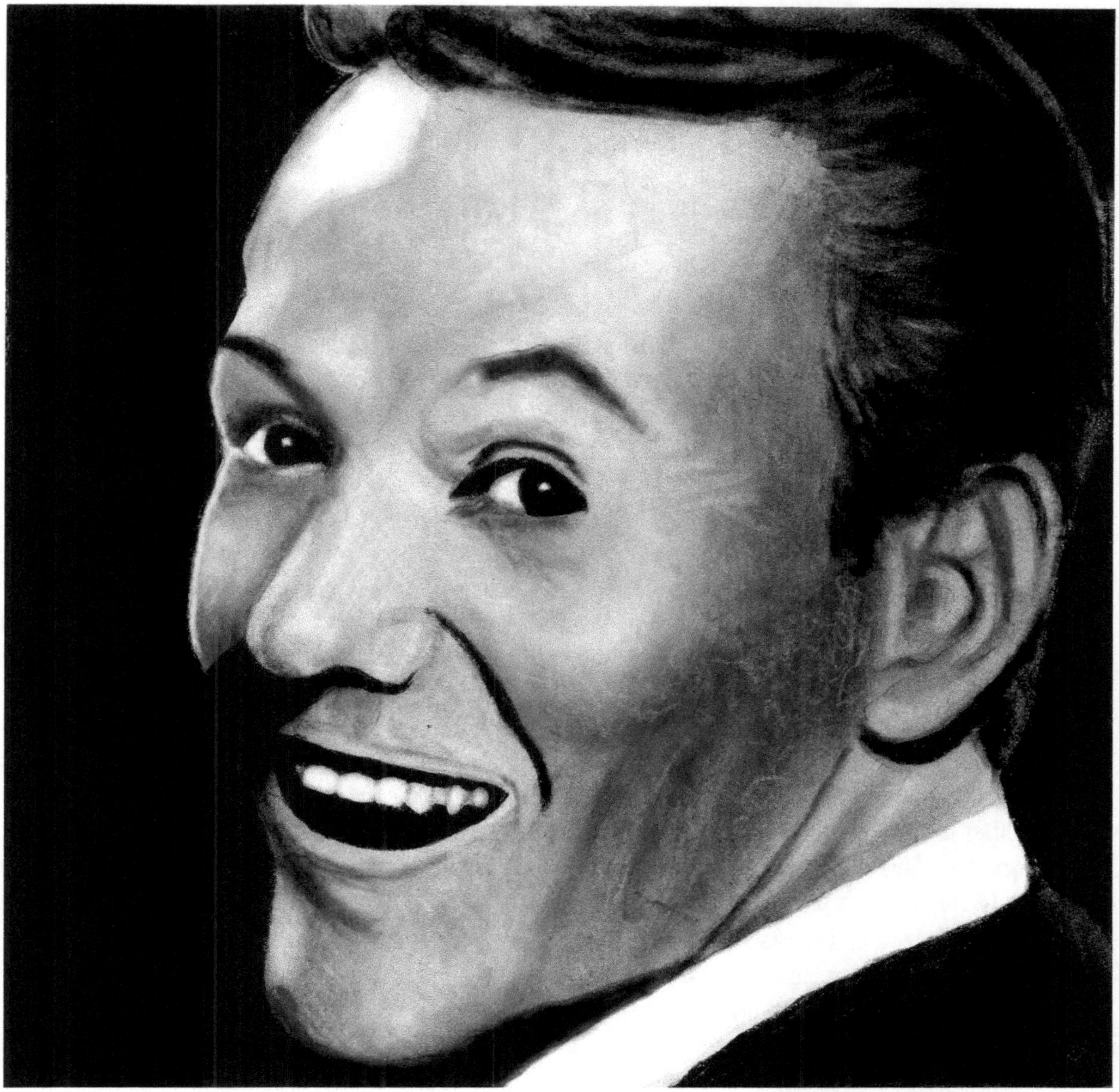

To view how this drawing was masterfully created or to purchase a Limited Edition Framed Artwork of Bobby Hatfield type into your Internet Browser the URL shortcut ➡ **myportrait.art/bobbyhatfield**

To listen to their Greatest Songs type into your Internet Browser the URL shortcut ➡ **radio.surf/righteousbrothers**

To view all channels on THE FACE OF MUSIC Internet Radio MEGA Station type into your Internet Browser the URL shortcut ➡ **radio.surf/music**

To inquire about purchasing a Limited Edition NFT of this portrait type into your Internet Browser the URL shortcut ➡ **myartnft.shop/bobbyhatfield**

To view all available NFTs type into your Internet Browser the URL shortcut ➡ **myartnft.shop/all**

# Robert Palmer

(Net worth: $10 Million)(Total Records Sold: Millions)
(Genre: Rock , Pop)(Height: 5' - 8")

Robert Allen Palmer (19 January 1949 – 26 September 2003) was an English singer-songwriter, musician and record producer. He was known for his powerful, distinctive, gritty and soulful voice, sartorial elegance and for combining soul, jazz, rock, pop, reggae and blues.
Palmer's involvement in the music industry began in the 1960s, covered four decades and included a spell with the band Vinegar Joe. He found success both in his solo career and with the Power Station, and had Top 10 songs in both the United Kingdom and the United States in the 1980s. Three of his hit singles, "I Didn't Mean to Turn You On", "Addicted to Love" and "Simply Irresistible", were accompanied with stylish music videos directed by British fashion photographer Terence Donovan.
Palmer received a number of awards throughout his career, including two Grammy Awards for Best Male Rock Vocal Performance, an MTV Video Music Award and two Brit Award nominations for Best British Male Solo Artist. He died aged 54, following a heart attack on 26 September 2003.
Palmer's father was a British naval intelligence officer stationed in Malta. In 1949, Palmer moved with his family from Batley, where he was born, to Scarborough. Influenced as a child by blues, soul and jazz music on American Forces Radio, Robert Palmer joined his first band, The Mandrakes, at the age of 15 whilst still at Scarborough High School for Boys. His first major break came with the departure of singer Jess Roden from the band The Alan Bown Set in 1969, after which Palmer was invited to London to sing on their single "Gypsy Girl". The vocals for the album The Alan Bown Set!, originally recorded by Roden (and released in the US that way), were re-recorded by Palmer after the success of the single. According to music journalist Paul Lester, Palmer rose from northern clubs in England to become "elegant and sophisticated" and the master of several styles.

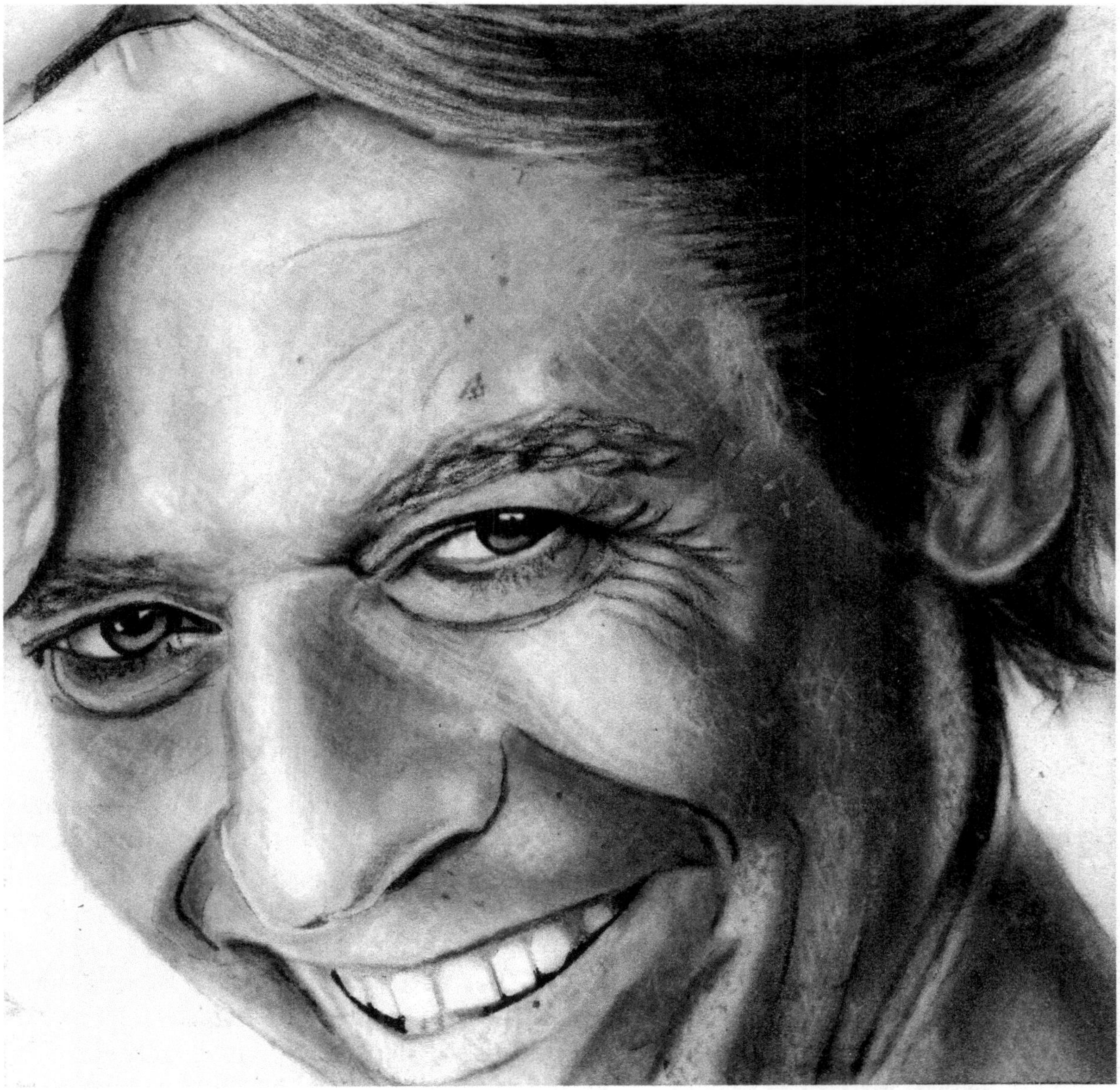

To view how this drawing was masterfully created or to purchase a Limited Edition Framed Artwork of Robert Palmer type into your Internet Browser the URL shortcut ➡ **myportrait.art/robertpalmer**

To listen to his Greatest Songs type into your Internet Browser the URL shortcut
➡ **radio.surf/robertpalmer**

To view all channels on THE FACE OF MUSIC Internet Radio MEGA Station type into your Internet Browser the URL shortcut ➡ **radio.surf/music**

To inquire about purchasing a Limited Edtion NFT of this portrait type into your Internet Browser the URL shortcut ➡ **myartnft.shop/robertpalmer**

To view all available NFTs type into your Internet Browser the URL shortcut ➡ **myartnft.shop/all**

# Rod Stewart

(Net worth: $300 Million)(Total Records Sold: 250+ Million)
(Genre: Rock, Pop, Disco, Soft Rock, Blues Rock, Folk Rock)(Height: 5' - 9")

Sir Roderick David Stewart CBE (born 10 January 1945) is a British rock and pop singer, songwriter, and record producer. Born and raised in London, he is of Scottish and English ancestry. With his distinctive raspy singing voice, Stewart is one of the best-selling music artists of all time, having sold over 250 million records worldwide. He has had 10 number-one albums and 31 top ten singles in the UK, 6 of which reached number one. Stewart has had 16 top ten singles in the US with four reaching number one on the Billboard Hot 100. He was knighted in the 2016 Birthday Honours for services to music and charity.

Stewart's music career began in 1962 when he took up busking with a harmonica. In 1963, he joined The Dimensions as harmonica player and vocalist. In 1964, Stewart joined Long John Baldry and the All Stars before moving to the Jeff Beck Group in 1967. Joining the Faces in 1969, he also maintained a solo career releasing his debut album that same year. Stewart's early albums were a fusion of rock, folk music, soul music, and R&B. His third album, 1971's Every Picture Tells a Story, was his breakthrough, topping the charts in the UK, US, Canada and Australia, as did its ballad "Maggie May". His 1972 follow-up album, Never a Dull Moment, also reached number one in the UK and Australia, while going top three in the US and Canada. Its single, "You Wear It Well", topped the chart in the UK and was a moderate hit elsewhere. After a handful more UK top ten hits, Stewart announced the breakup of the Faces in 1975. His next few singles were ballads with "Sailing", off the 1975 UK and Australian number-one album, Atlantic Crossing, becoming a hit in the UK and the Netherlands (number one), Germany (number four) and other countries, but barely charting in North America. A Night on the Town (1976), his fifth straight chart-topper in the UK, began a three-album run of going number one or top three in North America, the UK and Australia with each release. That album's "Tonight's the Night (Gonna Be Alright)" spent almost two months at number one in the US and Canada, and made the top five in other countries. Foot Loose & Fancy Free (1977) featured the major hit "You're In My Heart (The Final Acclaim)" as well as the rocker "Hot Legs". Blondes Have More Fun (1978) and its disco-tinged "Da Ya Think I'm Sexy" both went to number one in Canada, Australia and the US, with "Da Ya Think I'm Sexy" also hitting number one in the UK and the top ten in other countries. Stewart's albums regularly hit the upper rungs of the charts in the Netherlands throughout the 70s and in Sweden from 1975 onward.

After a disco and new wave period in the late 1970s and early 1980s, Stewart's music turned to a soft rock/middle-of-the-road style, with most of his albums reaching the top ten in the UK, Germany and Sweden, but faring less well in the US. The single "Rhythm of My Heart" was a top five hit in the UK, US and other countries, with its source album, 1991's Vagabond Heart, becoming, at number ten in the US and number two in the UK, his highest charting album in a decade. In 1993, he collaborated with Bryan Adams and Sting on the power ballad "All for Love", which went to number one in many countries. In the early 2000s, he released a series of successful albums interpreting the Great American Songbook. In 2008, Billboard magazine ranked him the 17th most successful artist on the "Billboard Hot 100 All-Time Top Artists". A Grammy and Brit Award recipient, he was voted at No. 33 in Q Magazine's list of the Top 100 Greatest Singers of all time As a solo artist, Stewart was inducted into the US Rock and Roll Hall of Fame in 1994, the UK Music Hall of Fame in 2006, and he was inducted a second time into the US Rock and Roll Hall of Fame in 2012 as a member of Faces.

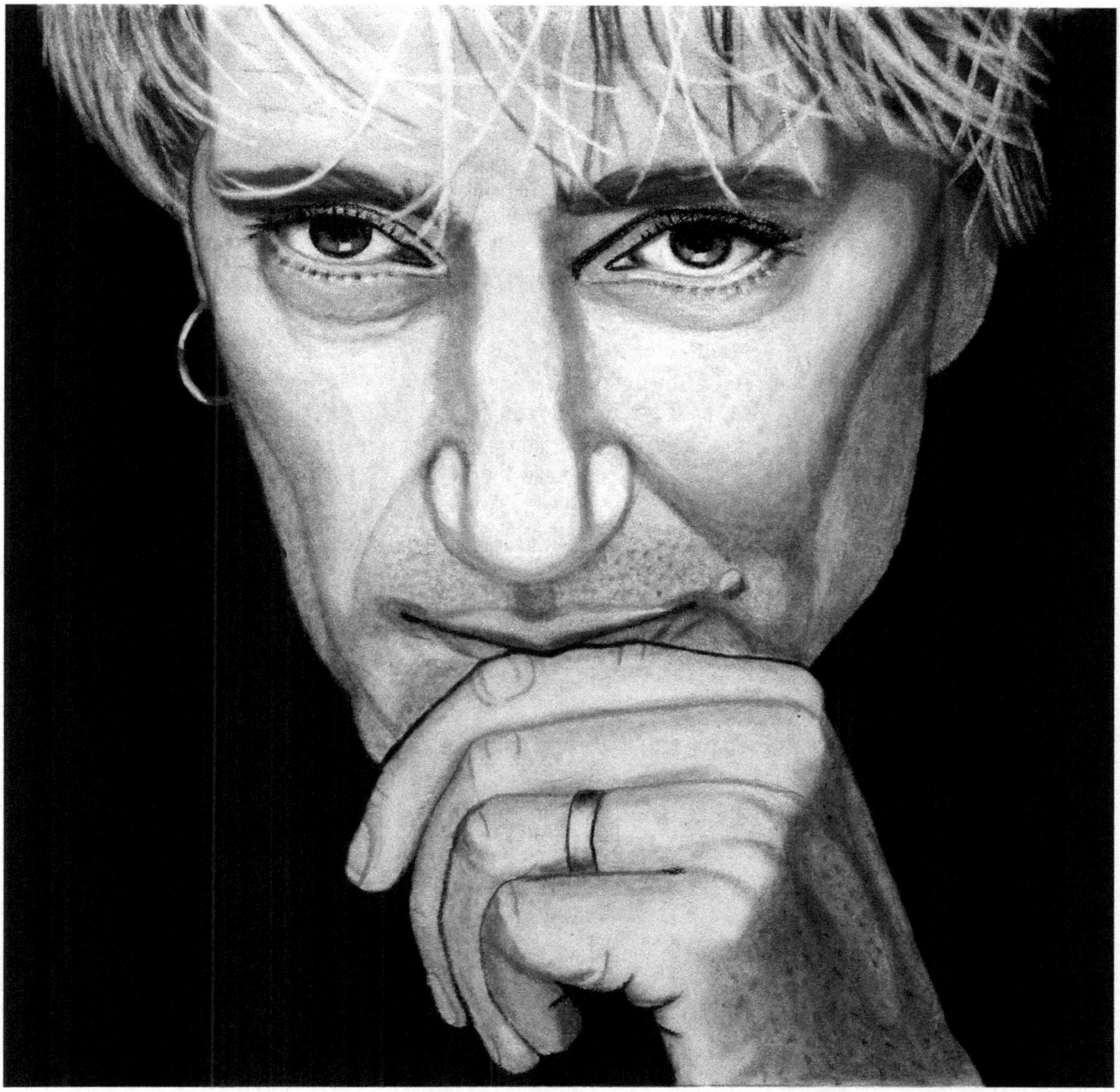

To view how this drawing was masterfully created or to purchase a Limited Edition Framed Artwork of Rod Stewart type into your Internet Browser the URL shortcut ➡ **myportrait.art/rodstewart**

To listen to his Greatest Songs type into your Internet Browser the URL shortcut
➡ **myportrait.art/rodstewart**

To view all channels on THE FACE OF MUSIC Internet Radio MEGA Station type into your Internet Browser the URL shortcut ➡ **radio.surf/music**

To inquire about purchasing a Limited Edtion NFT of this portrait type into your Internet Browser the URL shortcut ➡ **myartnft.shop/rodstewart**

To view all available NFTs type into your Internet Browser the URL shortcut ➡ **myartnft.shop/all**

# Rolling Stones, The

(Total Records Sold: 240 Million)(Genre: Rock, Blues, Hard Rock, Pop, Rock & Roll)
The Rolling Stones are an English rock band formed in London in 1962. Diverging from the pop rock of the early-1960s, the Rolling Stones pioneered the gritty, heavier-driven sound that came to define hard rock, and continued to record and perform for decades.

Their first stable line-up was vocalist Mick Jagger, multi-instrumentalist Brian Jones, guitarist Keith Richards, drummer Charlie Watts, and bassist Bill Wyman. Initially the band performed mostly covers of American blues and R&B songs, and during their formative years Brian Jones was the primary leader: he put the band together, named it, and drove the sound and look of the band. After Andrew Loog Oldham became the group's manager in 1963, he encouraged them to write their own songs. Jagger and Richards became the primary creative force behind the band, alienating Jones, who developed a drug addiction that interfered with his ability to meaningfully contribute. He left the band shortly before his death in 1969, having been replaced by guitarist Mick Taylor, who in turn left in 1974 to be replaced by Ronnie Wood. Since Wyman's departure in 1993, Darryl Jones has served as bassist.

Rooted in blues and early rock and roll, the Rolling Stones started out playing covers and were at the forefront of the British Invasion in 1964, also being identified with the youthful and rebellious counterculture of the 1960s. They then found greater success with their own material as "(I Can't Get No) Satisfaction", "Get Off of My Cloud" and "Paint It Black" became No. 1 hits in the UK, North America, Australia and Europe. Aftermath (1966) – their first entirely original album – is considered the most important of their formative records. In 1967, they had the double-sided hit "Ruby Tuesday"/"Let's Spend the Night Together" and then experimented with psychedelic rock on Their Satanic Majesties Request. They went back to their roots with such hits as "Jumpin' Jack Flash" (1968) and "Honky Tonk Women" (1969), and albums such as Beggars Banquet (1968), featuring "Sympathy for the Devil", and Let It Bleed (1969), featuring "You Can't Always Get What You Want" and "Gimme Shelter". Let It Bleed was the first of five straight No. 1 albums in the UK. In 1969, they were first introduced on stage as 'The Greatest Rock and Roll Band in the World'.The Rolling Stones' estimated record sales of 240 million makes them one of the best-selling music artists of all time. The band has won three Grammy Awards and a Grammy Lifetime Achievement Award. They were inducted into the Rock and Roll Hall of Fame in 1989 and the UK Music Hall of Fame in 2004. In 2008, the Rolling Stones were listed 10th on the Billboard Hot 100 All-Time Top Artists chart, and in 2019 Billboard magazine ranked them second in their list of the "Greatest Artists of All Time" based on US chart success. They are ranked 4th on Rolling Stone's list of the Greatest Artists of All Time.

# Mick Jagger

(Net Worth: $360 Million)(Height: 5' - 10")
Sir Michael Philip Jagger (born 26 July 1943) is an English singer, songwriter, actor, and film producer who has gained worldwide fame as the lead singer and one of the founder members of the Rolling Stones. Jagger's career has spanned over six decades, and he has been described as "one of the most popular and influential frontmen in the history of rock & roll". His distinctive voice and energetic live performances, along with Keith Richards' guitar style, have been the trademark of the Rolling Stones throughout the band's career. Jagger gained press notoriety for his romantic involvements and was often portrayed as a countercultural figure.

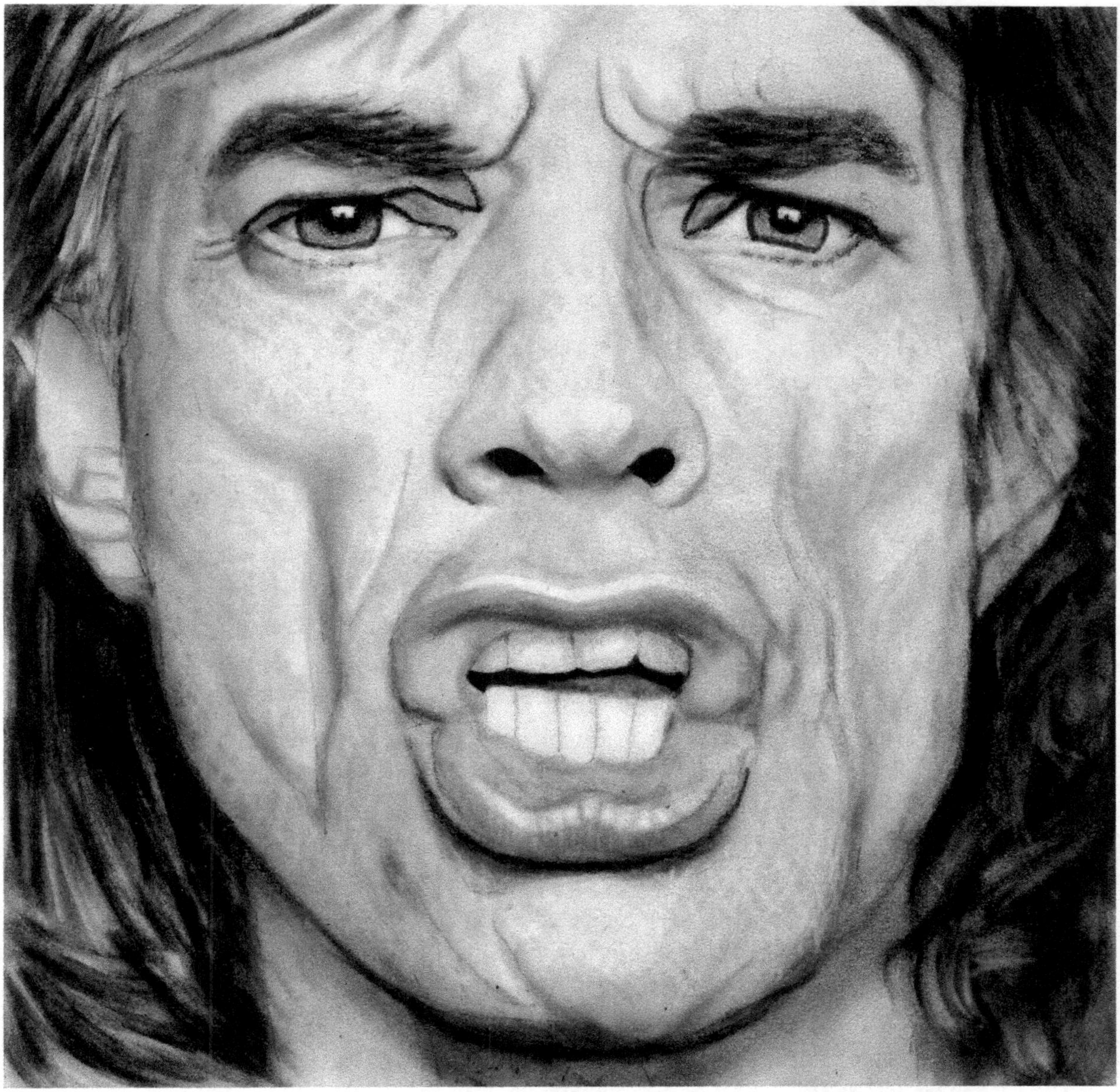

To view how this drawing was masterfully created or to purchase a Limited Edition Framed Artwork of Mick Jagger type into your Internet Browser the URL shortcut ➡ **myportrait.art/mickjagger**

To listen to their Greatest Songs type into your Internet Browser the URL shortcut ➡ **radio.surf/therollingstones**

To view all channels on THE FACE OF MUSIC Internet Radio MEGA Station type into your Internet Browser the URL shortcut ➡ **radio.surf/music**

To inquire about purchasing a Limited Edtion NFT of this portrait type into your Internet Browser the URL shortcut ➡ **myartnft.shop/mickjagger**

To view all available NFTs type into your Internet Browser the URL shortcut ➡ **myartnft.shop/all**

# Roy Orbison

(Net worth: $20 Million)(Total Records Sold: Multi-Millions)
(Genre: Rock, Pop, Rock & Roll, Country, Rockabilly)(Height: 5' - 10")

Roy Kelton Orbison (April 23, 1936 – December 6, 1988) was an American singer, songwriter, and musician known for his impassioned singing style, complex song structures, and dark, emotional ballads. His music was described by critics as operatic, earning him the nicknames "the Caruso of Rock" and "the Big O". Many of Orbison's songs conveyed vulnerability at a time when most male rock-and-roll performers chose to project defiant masculinity. He was known for his shyness and stage fright, which he countered by wearing dark sunglasses.

Orbison began singing in a rockabilly and country-and-western band at high school. He was signed by Sam Phillips of Sun Records in 1956, but enjoyed his greatest success with Monument Records. From 1960 to 1966, 22 of Orbison's singles reached the Billboard Top 40. He wrote or co-wrote almost all of his own Top 10 hits, including "Only the Lonely" (1960), "Running Scared" (1961), "Crying" (1961), "In Dreams" (1963), and "Oh, Pretty Woman" (1964). Beginning in the mid-1960s, Orbison suffered a number of personal tragedies and his career faltered.

Orbison experienced a resurgence in popularity in the 1980s following the success of several cover versions of his songs. In 1988, he co-founded the Traveling Wilburys (a rock supergroup) with George Harrison, Bob Dylan, Tom Petty, and Jeff Lynne. Orbison died of a heart attack in December 1988 at age 52. One month later, his song "You Got It" (1989) was released as a solo single, becoming his first hit to reach the U.S. Top 10 in nearly 25 years.

Orbison's honors include inductions into the Rock and Roll Hall of Fame and Nashville Songwriters Hall of Fame in 1987, the Songwriters Hall of Fame in 1989, and the Musicians Hall of Fame and Museum in 2014. He received a Grammy Lifetime Achievement Award and five other Grammy Awards. Rolling Stone placed him at number 37 on its list of the "Greatest Artists of All Time" and number 13 on its list of the "100 Greatest Singers of All Time". In 2002, Billboard magazine listed him at number 74 on its list of the Top 600 recording artists.

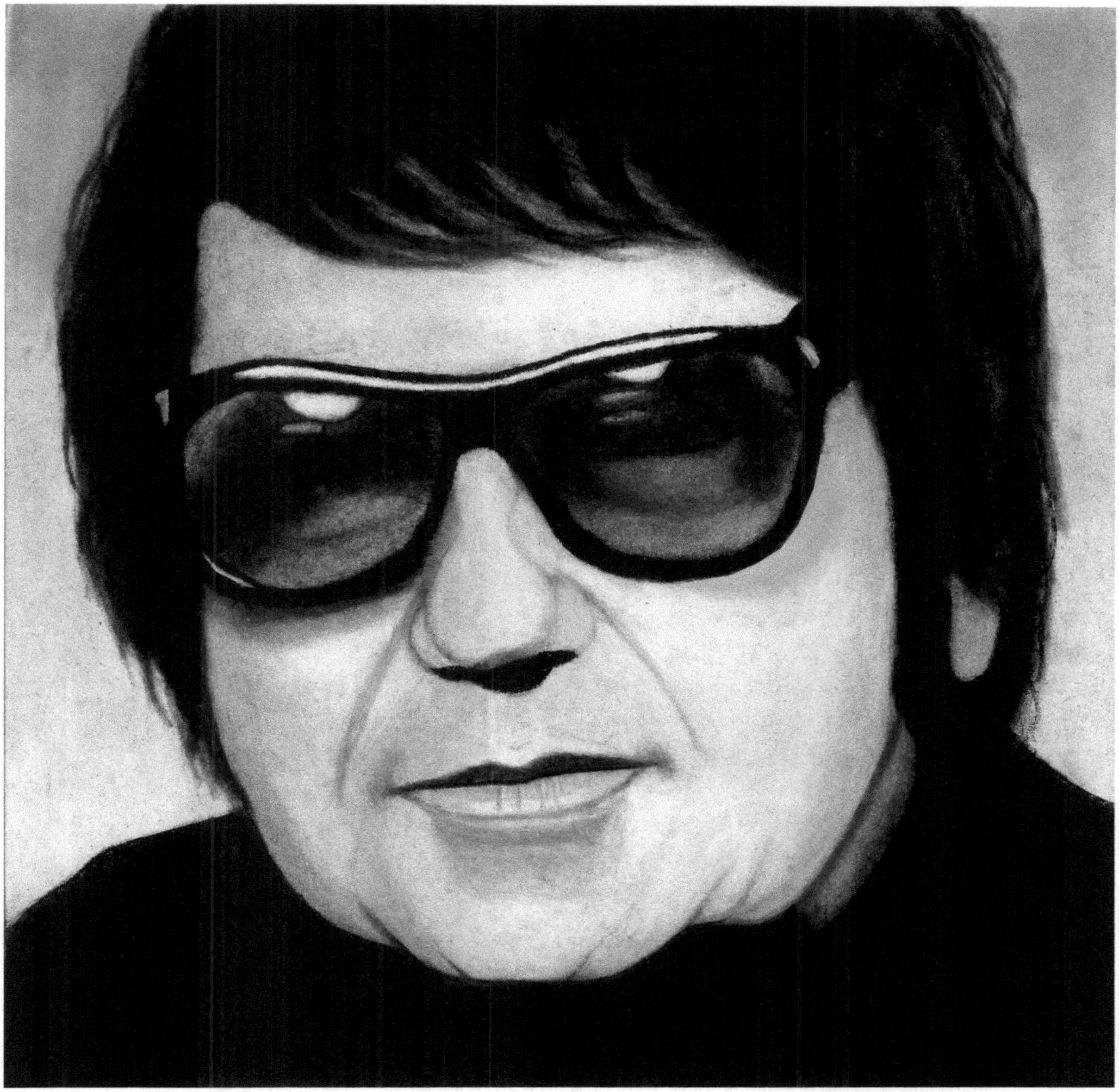

To view how this drawing was masterfully created or to purchase a Limited Edition Framed Artwork of Roy Orbison type into your Internet Browser the URL shortcut ➡ **myportrait.art/royorbison**

To listen to his Greatest Songs type into your Internet Browser the URL shortcut ➡ **radio.surf/royorbison**

To view all channels on THE FACE OF MUSIC Internet Radio MEGA Station type into your Internet Browser the URL shortcut ➡ **radio.surf/music**

To inquire about purchasing a Limited Edtion NFT of this portrait type into your Internet Browser the URL shortcut ➡ **myartnft.shop/royorbison**

To view all available NFTs type into your Internet Browser the URL shortcut ➡ **myartnft.shop/all**

# Run DMC

(Total Records Sold: 15+ Million)(Genre: Hip-Hop , Rap)

Run-DMC (also spelled Run-D.M.C.) was an American hip hop group from Hollis, Queens, New York, founded in 1983 by Joseph Simmons, Darryl McDaniels, and Jason Mizell. Run-DMC is regarded as one of the most influential acts in the history of hip hop culture and one of the most famous hip hop acts of the 1980s. Along with Beastie Boys, LL Cool J and Public Enemy, the group pioneered new school hip hop music. The group was among the first to highlight the importance of the MC and DJ relationship.

With the release Run-D.M.C. (1984), Run-DMC became the first hip hop group to achieve a Gold record. Run-D.M.C. was followed with the certified Platinum record King of Rock (1985), making Run-DMC the first hip hop group to achieve this. Raising Hell (1986) became the first multi-platinum hip hop record. Run-DMC's cover of "Walk This Way", featuring Steven Tyler and Joe Perry, charted higher on the Billboard Hot 100 than Aerosmith's original version, peaking at number four. It became one of the best known songs in both hip hop and rock. Run-DMC was the first hip hop act to have their music videos broadcast on MTV, appear on American Bandstand, be on the cover of Rolling Stone, perform at Live Aid and be nominated for a Grammy Award.

In 2004, Rolling Stone ranked Run-DMC at number 48 in its list of the 100 Greatest Artists of All Time. In 2007, they were named The Greatest Hip Hop Group of All Time by MTV and Greatest Hip Hop Artist of All Time by VH1. In 2009, Run-DMC became the second hip hop group to be inducted into the Rock and Roll Hall of Fame. In 2016, the group received the Grammy Lifetime Achievement Award. In 2018, Raising Hell was inducted into the National Recording Registry by the Library of Congress as being "culturally, historically, or artistically significant".

# Darryl McDaniels

(Net Worth: $45 Million)(Height: 6'-0")

Darryl Matthews McDaniels (born May 31, 1964), better known by his stage name DMC, is an American rapper. He is a founding member of the hip hop group Run-D.M.C., and is considered one of the pioneers of hip hop culture.

McDaniels grew up in Hollis, Queens. He was born to an unwed mother who surrendered him to the New York Foundling home. He was a ward of the Foundling, in foster care, until placed with the McDaniels and eventually adopted by them. He attended Rice High School in Manhattan and later enrolled in St. John's University in Queens.

McDaniels first became interested in hip hop music after listening to recordings of Grandmaster Flash and the Furious Five. In 1978, McDaniels taught himself to DJ in the basement of his parents' home, using turntables and a mixer that he bought with his older brother, Alford, after having a comic book sale in their neighborhood. During this period he adopted the stage name "Grandmaster Get High".

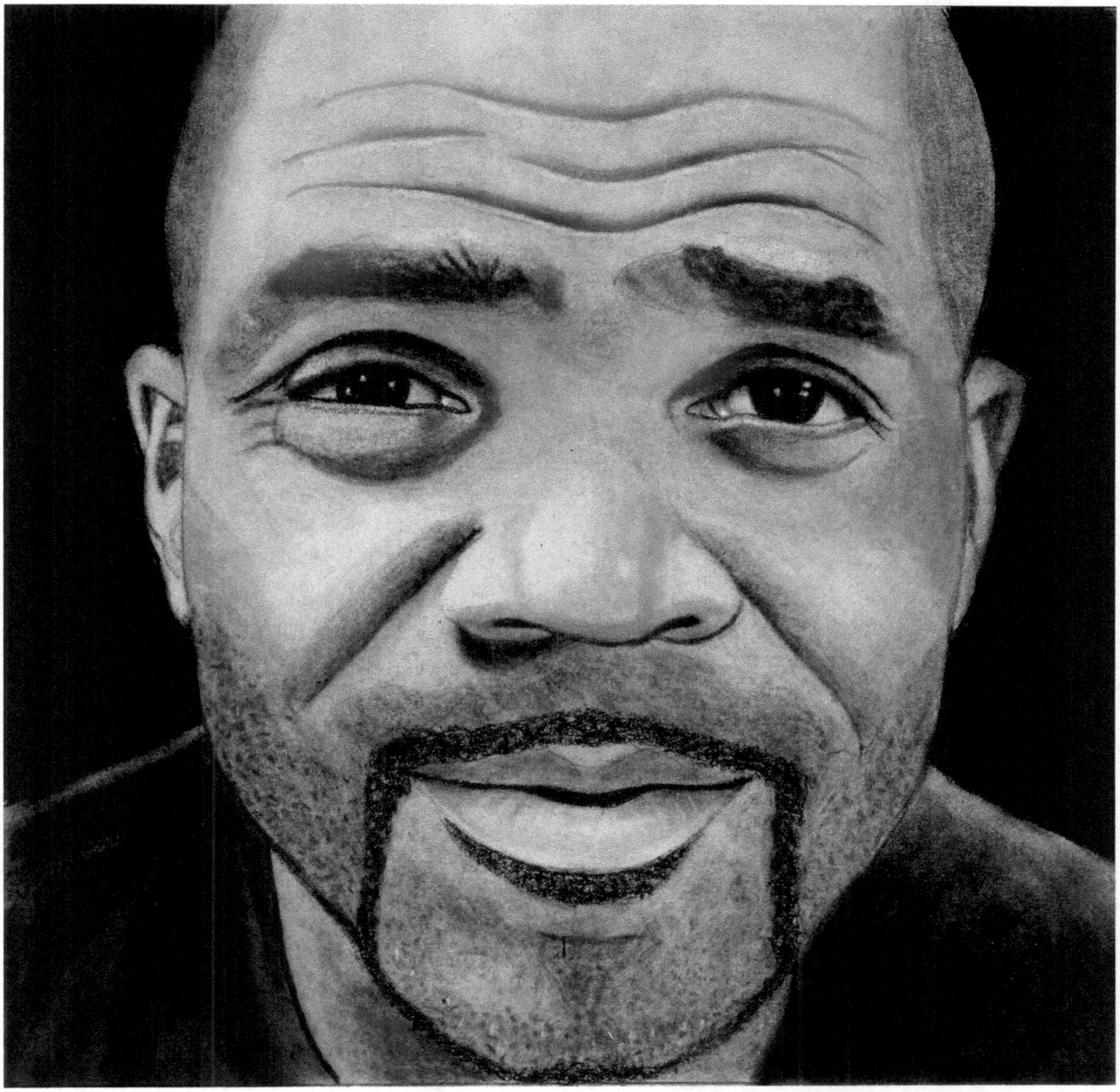

To view how this drawing was masterfully created or to purchase a Limited Edition Framed Artwork of Darly McDaniels type into your Internet Browser the URL shortcut ➡ **myportrait.art/darlymcdaniels**

To listen to their Greatest Songs type into your Internet Browser the URL shortcut ➡ **radio.surf/rundmc**

To view all channels on THE FACE OF MUSIC Internet Radio MEGA Station type into your Internet Browser the URL shortcut ➡ **radio.surf/music**

To inquire about purchasing a Limited Edtion NFT of this portrait type into your Internet Browser the URL shortcut ➡ **myartnft.shop/darlymcdaniels**

To view all available NFTs type into your Internet Browser the URL shortcut ➡ **myartnft.shop/all**

# Rush

(Total Records Sold: 40+Million)(Genre: Classic Rock)

Rush was a Canadian rock band formed in Toronto in 1968, consisting of Geddy Lee (bass, vocals, keyboards, composer), Alex Lifeson (guitars, composer), and Neil Peart (drums, percussion, lyricist). After its formation in 1968, the band went through several configurations before arriving at its classic power trio lineup with the addition of Peart in 1974, who replaced original drummer John Rutsey right after the release of their eponymous debut album, which contained their first highly-regarded song, "Working Man".

After Peart joined the band, Rush achieved commercial success in the 1970s with several albums, including Fly by Night, (1975), 2112 (1976), A Farewell to Kings (1977) and Hemispheres (1978). The band's rise in popularity continued throughout the 1980s and 1990s, with some albums charting highly in both Canada and the US including Permanent Waves (1980), Moving Pictures (1981), Signals (1982) and Counterparts (1993). Rush continued to record and perform until 1997, after which the band entered a four year hiatus due to personal tragedies in Peart's life. The trio regrouped in 2001 and released three more studio albums: Vapor Trails (2002), Snakes & Arrows (2007), and Clockwork Angels (2012). Rush ceased large-scale touring at the end of 2015, and Lifeson announced in January 2018 that the band would not continue. On January 7, 2020, Peart died of glioblastoma, a type of brain cancer at the age of 67.Rush is known for its musicianship, complex compositions, and eclectic lyrical motifs drawing heavily on science fiction, fantasy and philosophy. The band's style changed over the years, from a blues-inspired hard rock beginning, later moving into progressive rock, then a period marked by heavy use of synthesizers, before returning to guitar-driven hard rock since the end of the 1980s. The members of Rush have been acknowledged as some of the most proficient players on their respective instruments, with each winning numerous awards in magazine readers' polls.Rush ranks 88th in the U.S. with sales of 25 million albums and industry sources estimate their total worldwide album sales at over 40 million as of 2005. Rush has been awarded 14 Platinum and 3 multi-Platinum albums in the US plus 17 Platinum albums in Canada. Rush was nominated for seven Grammy Awards, won several Juno Awards, and won an International Achievement Award at the 2009 SOCAN Awards. The band was inducted into the Canadian Music Hall of Fame in 1994 and the Rock and Roll Hall of Fame in 2013

# Geddy Lee

(Net Worth: $40 Million)(Height: 5' - 10")

Geddy Lee Weinrib, OC (born Gary Lee Weinrib; July 29, 1953), known professionally as Geddy Lee, is a Canadian musician, singer, and songwriter. He is best known as the lead vocalist, bassist, and keyboardist for the Canadian rock group Rush. Lee joined what would become Rush in September 1968, at the request of his childhood friend Alex Lifeson, replacing original bassist and frontman Jeff Jones. Lee's solo effort, My Favourite Headache, was released in 2000.An award-winning musician, Lee's style, technique, and skill on the bass have inspired many rock musicians such as Cliff Burton of Metallica, Steve Harris of Iron Maiden, John Myung of Dream Theater, Les Claypool of Primus, and Tim Commerford of Rage Against the Machine and Audioslave. Along with his Rush bandmates – guitarist Alex Lifeson and drummer Neil Peart – Lee was made an Officer of the Order of Canada on May 9, 1996. The trio was the first rock band to be so honoured as a group. In 2013, the group was inducted into the Rock and Roll Hall of Fame after 14 years of eligibility; they were nominated overwhelmingly in the Hall's first selection via fan ballot.

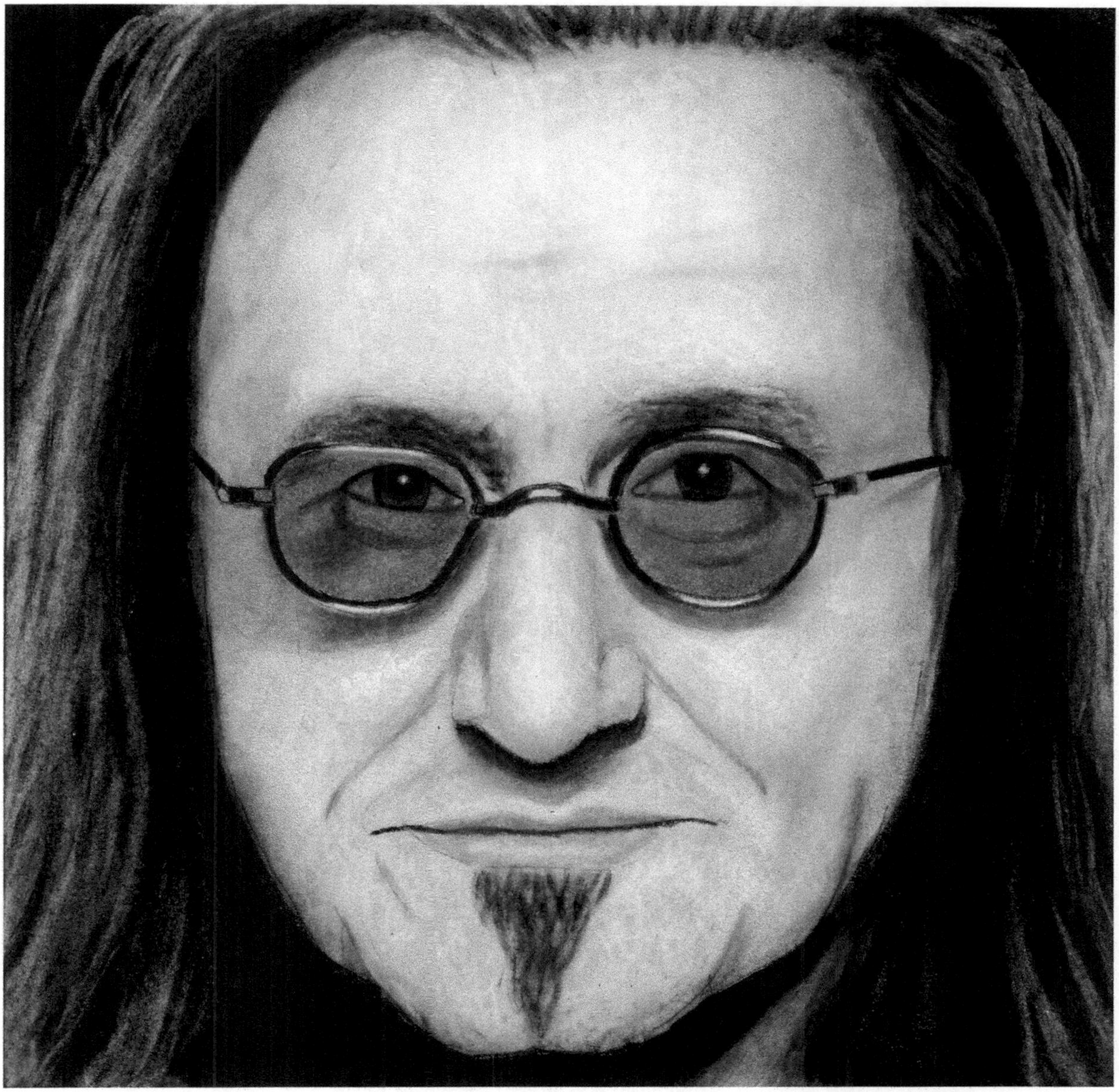

To view how this drawing was masterfully created or to purchase a Limited Edition Framed Artwork of Geddy Lee type into your Internet Browser the URL shortcut ➡ **myportrait.art/geddylee**

To listen to their Greatest Songs type into your Internet Browser the URL shortcut ➡ **radio.surf/rush**

To view all channels on THE FACE OF MUSIC Internet Radio MEGA Station type into your Internet Browser the URL shortcut ➡ **radio.surf/music**

To inquire about purchasing a Limited Edition NFT of this portrait type into your Internet Browser the URL shortcut ➡ **myartnft.shop/geddylee**

To view all available NFTs type into your Internet Browser the URL shortcut ➡ **myartnft.shop/all**

# Sade

(Net worth: $70 Million)(Total Records Sold: 75+Million)
(Genre: Soul , Smooth Jazz)(Height: 5' - 6")

Helen Folasade Adu CBE (born 16 January 1959), known professionally as Sade Adu or simply Sade (shah-DAY), is a Nigerian-born British singer, songwriter, and actress, known as the lead singer of her eponymous band. One of the most successful British female artists in history, she is often recognised as an influence on contemporary music. Her services to music were recognised in the UK with an award of the OBE in 2002, and a CBE in the 2017 Birthday Honours.

Born in Ibadan, Nigeria, and brought up partly in Essex, England, since the age of four, Sade studied at Saint Martin's School of Art in London and gained modest recognition as a fashion designer and part-time model, prior to joining the band Pride in the early 1980s. After gaining attention as a performer, she formed the band Sade, and secured a recording contract with Epic Records in 1983. A year later the band released the album Diamond Life, which became one of the best-selling albums of the era, and the best-selling debut by a British female vocalist. In July 1985, Sade was among the performers at the Live Aid charity concert at Wembley Stadium, and the following year she appeared in the film Absolute Beginners. Following the band's third and fourth albums, Stronger Than Pride (1988) and Love Deluxe (1992), they went on hiatus after the birth of Sade's child, while the singer experienced widespread media coverage for unsubstantiated claims of mental health and addiction issues. After a spell of eight years without an album, the band reunited in 1999, and released Lovers Rock in 2000. The album departed from the jazz-inspired inflections of their previous work, featuring mellower sounds and pop compositions. The band then underwent another hiatus, not producing music for another ten years until the release of Soldier of Love. Following that album's release, the band entered a third period of extended hiatus, and have only released two songs ("Flower of the Universe" for the soundtrack of Disney's A Wrinkle in Time, and "The Big Unknown" as part of the soundtrack for Steve McQueen's film Widows) to date.

Helen Fọláṣadé Adu was born on 16 January 1959 in Ibadan, Oyo State, Nigeria, but is a native of Ekiti State. Her middle name, Folasade, means "wealth confers a crown". Her parents are Adebisi Adu, a Nigerian lecturer in economics of Yoruba background, and Anne Hayes, an English district nurse; they met in London, married in 1955, and moved to Nigeria. When Sade was four years old, her parents separated. Anne Hayes then returned to England, taking Sade and the girl's elder brother Banji with her to live with their grandparents near Colchester, Essex. When Sade was 11 years old, she moved to Holland-on-Sea, Essex, to live with her mother. After completing her education at Clacton County High School and Colchester Institute at the age of 18, she moved to London and studied fashion design at Saint Martin's School of Art..

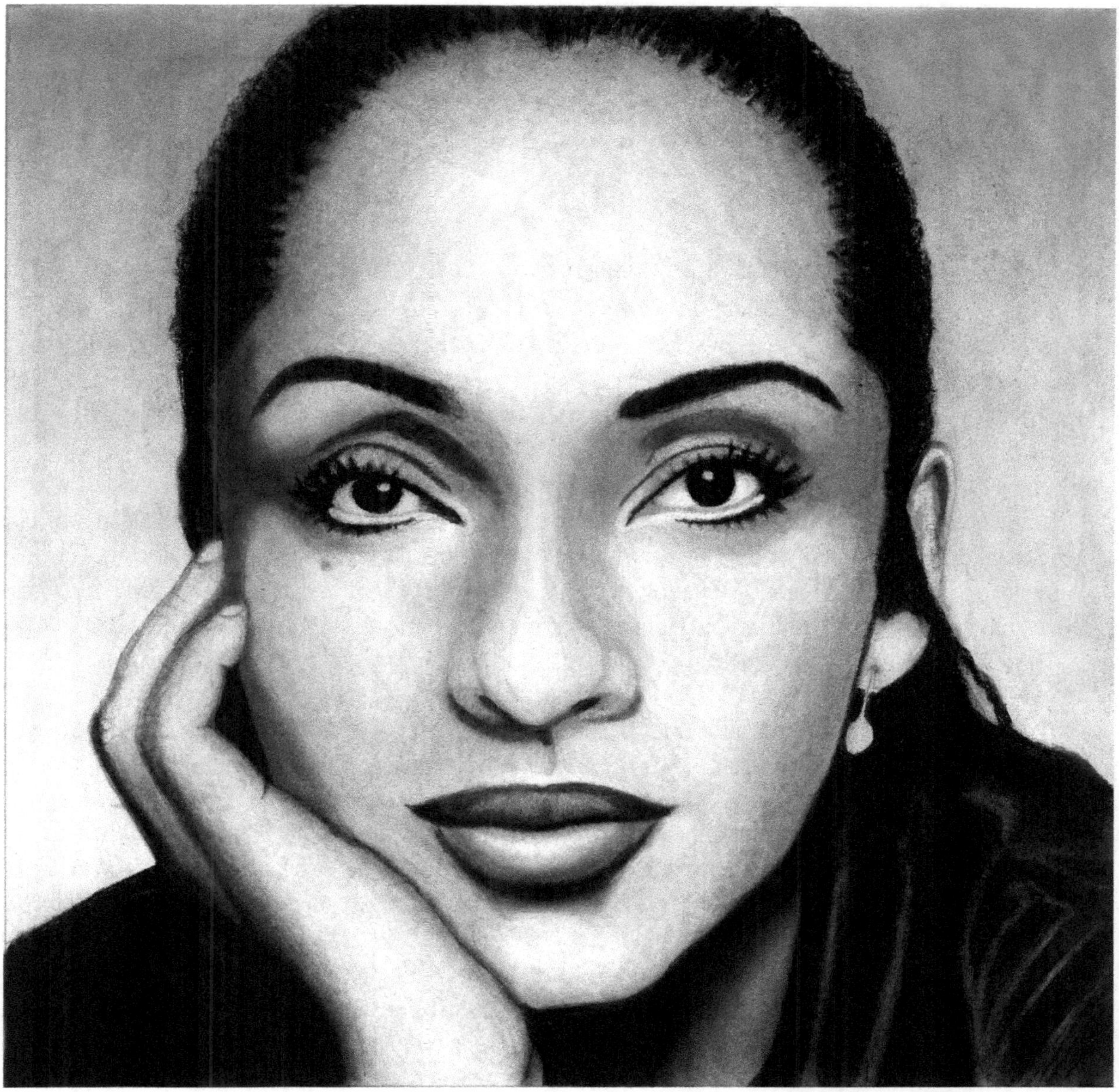

To view how this drawing was masterfully created or to purchase a Limited Edition Framed Artwork of Sade type into your Internet Browser the URL shortcut ➡ **myportrait.art/sade**

To listen to her Greatest Songs type into your Internet Browser the URL shortcut ➡ **radio.surf/sade**

To view all channels on THE FACE OF MUSIC Internet Radio MEGA Station type into your Internet Browser the URL shortcut ➡ **radio.surf/music**

To inquire about purchasing a Limited Edtion NFT of this portrait type into your Internet Browser the URL shortcut ➡ **myartnft.shop/sade**

To view all available NFTs type into your Internet Browser the URL shortcut ➡ **myartnft.shop/all**

# Sam Cooke

(Net worth: $2 Million)(Total Records Sold: Millions)
(Genre: Soul , Gospel , R&B)(Height: 5' - 9")

Samuel Cook (January 22, 1931 – December 11, 1964), known professionally as Sam Cooke, was an American singer, songwriter, and entrepreneur. Considered to be a pioneer and one of the most influential soul artists of all time, Cooke is commonly referred to as the "King of Soul" for his distinctive vocals, notable contributions to the genre and high significance in popular music.

Cooke was born in Mississippi and later relocated to Chicago with his family at a young age, where he began singing as a child and joined the Soul Stirrers as lead singer in the 1950s. Going solo in 1957, Cooke released a string of hit songs, including "You Send Me", "A Change Is Gonna Come", "Cupid", "Wonderful World", "Chain Gang", "Twistin' the Night Away", "Bring It On Home to Me", and "Good Times". During his eight year career, Cooke released 29 singles that charted in the Top 40 of the Billboard Pop Singles chart, as well as 20 singles in the Top Ten of Billboard's Black Singles chart.

In 1964, Cooke was shot and killed by the manager of a motel in Los Angeles. After an inquest and investigation, the courts ruled Cooke's death to be a justifiable homicide; his family has since questioned the circumstances of his death.

Cooke's pioneering contributions to soul music contributed to the rise of Aretha Franklin, Bobby Womack, Al Green, Curtis Mayfield, Stevie Wonder, Marvin Gaye, and Billy Preston, and popularized the work of Otis Redding and James Brown. AllMusic biographer Bruce Eder wrote that Cooke was "the inventor of soul music", and possessed "an incredible natural singing voice and a smooth, effortless delivery that has never been surpassed".

Cooke was also a central part of the Civil Rights Movement, using his influence and popularity with the white and Black population to fight for the cause. He was good friends with boxer Muhammad Ali, activist Malcolm X and football player Jim Brown, who together campaigned for racial equality.

Cooke was born Samuel Cook in Clarksdale, Mississippi, in 1931 (he added the "e" to his last name in 1957 to signify a new start to his life). He was the fifth of eight children of the Rev. Charles Cook, a minister in the Church of Christ (Holiness), and his wife, Annie Mae. One of his younger brothers, L.C. (1932–2017), later became a member of the doo-wop band Johnny Keyes and the Magnificents.

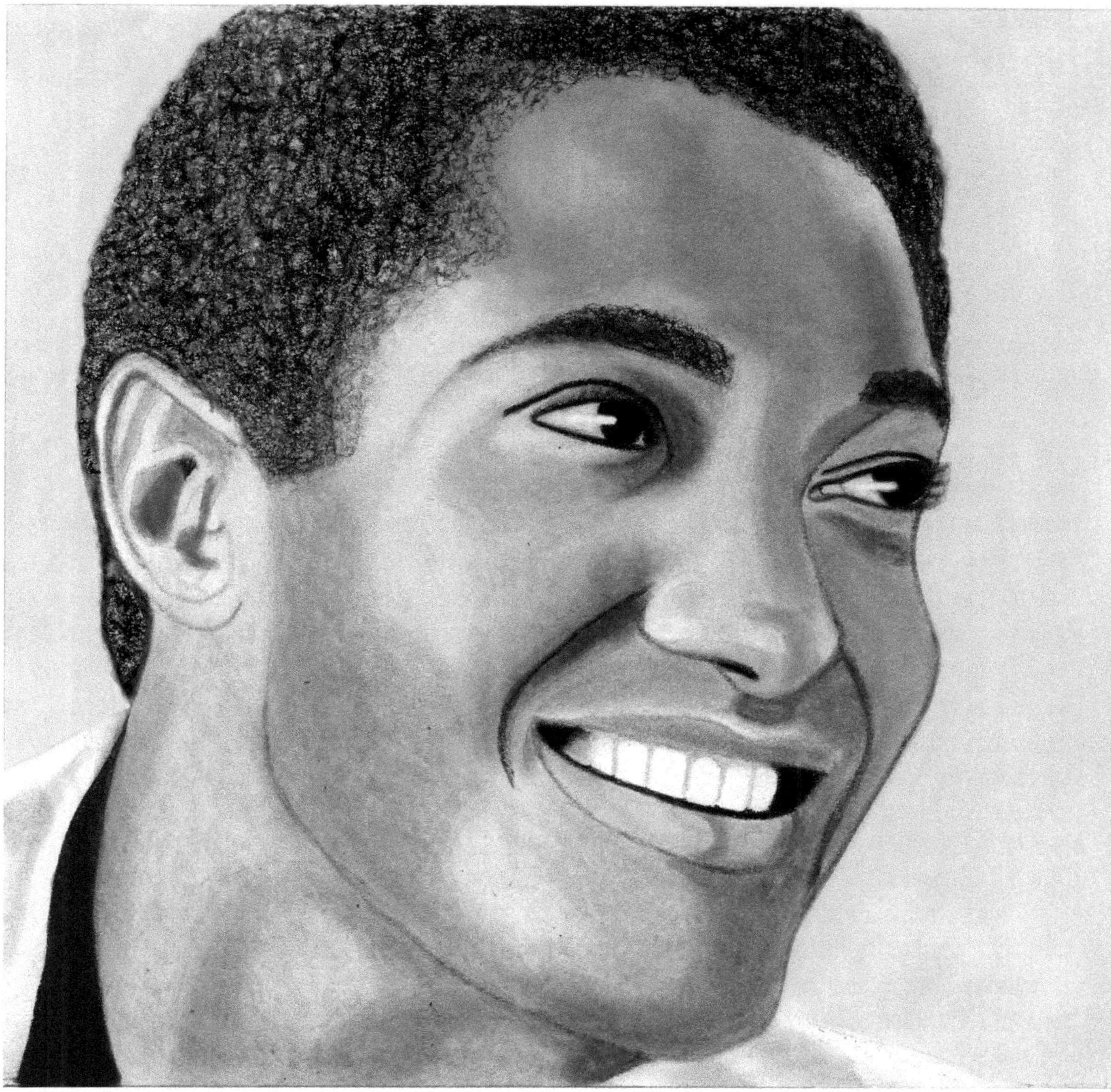

To view how this drawing was masterfully created or to purchase a Limited Edition Framed Artwork of Sam Cooke type into your Internet Browser the URL shortcut ➡ **myportrait.art/samcooke**

To listen to his Greatest Songs type into your Internet Browser the URL shortcut ➡ **radio.surf/samcooke**

To view all channels on THE FACE OF MUSIC Internet Radio MEGA Station type into your Internet Browser the URL shortcut ➡ **radio.surf/music**

To inquire about purchasing a Limited Edtion NFT of this portrait type into your Internet Browser the URL shortcut ➡ **myartnft.shop/samcooke**

To view all available NFTs type into your Internet Browser the URL shortcut ➡ **myartnft.shop/all**

# Sammy Davis Jr.

(Net worth: $5 Million)(Total Records Sold: Millions)
(Genre: Pop, Jazz, Swing, Blues)(Height: 5' - 6")

Samuel George Davis Jr. (December 8, 1925 – May 16, 1990) was an American singer, dancer, actor, vauderillian and comedian whom critic Randy Blaser called "the greatest entertainer ever to grace a stage in these United States".

At age three, Davis began his career in vaudeville with his father Sammy Davis Sr. and the Will Mastin Trio, which toured nationally, and his film career began in 1933. After military service, Davis returned to the trio and became an overnight sensation following a nightclub performance at Ciro's (in West Hollywood) after the 1951 Academy Awards. With the trio, he became a recording artist. In 1954, at the age of 29, he lost his left eye in a car accident. Several years later, he converted to Judaism, finding commonalities between the oppression experienced by African-American and Jewish communities.

After a starring role on Broadway in Mr. Wonderful with Chita Rivera (1956), he returned to the stage in 1964 in a musical adaptation of Clifford Odets' Golden Boy opposite Paula Wayne. Davis was nominated for a Tony Award for his performance and the show was said to have featured the first interracial kiss on Broadway. In 1960, he appeared in the Rat Pack film Ocean's 11. In 1966, he had his own TV variety show, titled The Sammy Davis Jr. Show. While Davis's career slowed in the late 1960s, his biggest hit, "The Candy Man", reached the top of the Billboard Hot 100 in June 1972, and he became a star in Las Vegas, earning him the nickname "Mister Show Business".

Davis's popularity helped break the race barrier of the segregated entertainment industry. He did however have a complex relationship with the black community and drew criticism after publicly supporting President Richard Nixon in 1972. One day on a golf course with Jack Benny, he was asked what his handicap was. "Handicap?" he asked. "Talk about handicap. I'm a one-eyed Negro who's Jewish." This was to become a signature comment, recounted in his autobiography and in many articles.

After reuniting with Frank Sinatra and Dean Martin in 1987, Davis toured with them and Liza Minnelli internationally, before his death in 1990. He died in debt to the Internal Revenue Service, and his estate was the subject of legal battles after the death of his wife. Davis was awarded the Spingarn Medal by the NAACP and was nominated for a Golden Globe Award and an Emmy Award for his television performances. He was a recipient of the Kennedy Center Honors in 1987, and in 2001, he was posthumously awarded the Grammy Lifetime Achievement Award.

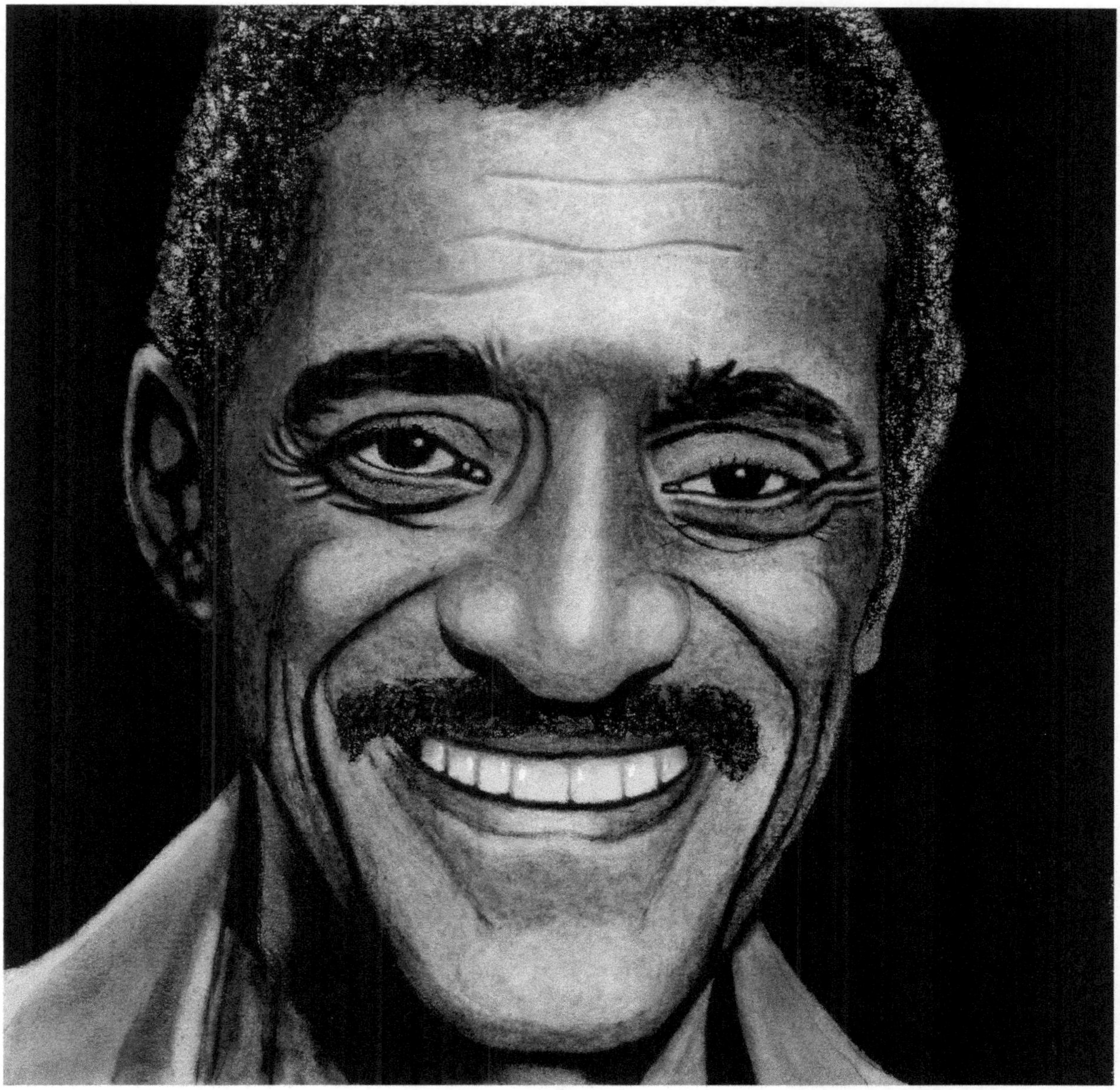

To view how this drawing was masterfully created or to purchase a Limited Edition Framed Artwork of Sammy Davis Jr type into your Internet Browser the URL shortcut ➡ **myportrait.art/sammydavisjr**

To listen to his Greatest Songs type into your Internet Browser the URL shortcut ➡ **radio.surf/sammydavisjr**

To view all channels on THE FACE OF MUSIC Internet Radio MEGA Station type into your Internet Browser the URL shortcut ➡ **radio.surf/music**

To inquire about purchasing a Limited Edtion NFT of this portrait type into your Internet Browser the URL shortcut ➡ **myartnft.shop/sammydavisjr**

To view all available NFTs type into your Internet Browser the URL shortcut ➡ **myartnft.shop/all**

# Santana

(Total Records Sold: 100 Million) (Genre: Latin Rock, Blues Rock, Psychedelic Rock)

Santana is an American rock band formed in San Francisco in 1966 by Mexican-American guitarist and songwriter Carlos Santana. The band has undergone multiple recording and performing line-ups in its history, with Carlos Santana the only consistent member. Santana had early success with their appearance at Woodstock in 1969 and their first three albums, Santana (1969), Abraxas (1970), and Santana III (1971). Other important core members during this period include Gregg Rolie, Michael Carabello, Michael Shrieve, David Brown, and José "Chepito" Areas, forming the "classic" line-up.

Following its initial success Santana experimented with elements of jazz fusion on Caravanserai (1972), Welcome (1973), and Borboletta (1974). Santana reached a new peak of commercial and critical success with Supernatural (1999) and its singles "Smooth", featuring singer Rob Thomas, and "Maria Maria". The album reached No. 1 in eleven countries and sold 12 million copies in the US. In 2014, the "classic" line-up reunited for Santana IV (2016) and the group continue to perform and record.

Santana is one of the best-selling groups of all time with 43.5 million certified albums sold the US and an estimated 100 million sold worldwide. Its discography include 25 studio albums, 14 of which reached the US top 10. In 1998, the line-up of Santana, Rolie, Carabello, Shrieve, Brown, and Areas was inducted into the Rock and Roll Hall of Fame. In 2000, the band won six Grammy Awards in one night, a record tied with Michael Jackson, and three Latin Grammy Awards.

# Carlos Santana

(Net Worth: $80 Million)(Height: 5' - 9")

Carlos Humberto Santana Barragán (born July 20, 1947) is a Mexican and American guitarist who rose to fame in the late 1960s and early 1970s with his band Santana, which pioneered a fusion of rock 'n' roll and Latin American jazz. Its sound featured his melodic, blues-based lines set against Latin and African rhythms played on percussion instruments not generally heard in rock, such as timbales and congas. He experienced a resurgence of popularity and critical acclaim in the late 1990s. In 2015, Rolling Stone magazine listed him at No. 20 on their list of the 100 greatest guitarists. He has received 10 Grammy Awards and three Latin Grammy Awards, and was inducted along with his namesake band into the Rock and Roll Hall of Fame in 1998.

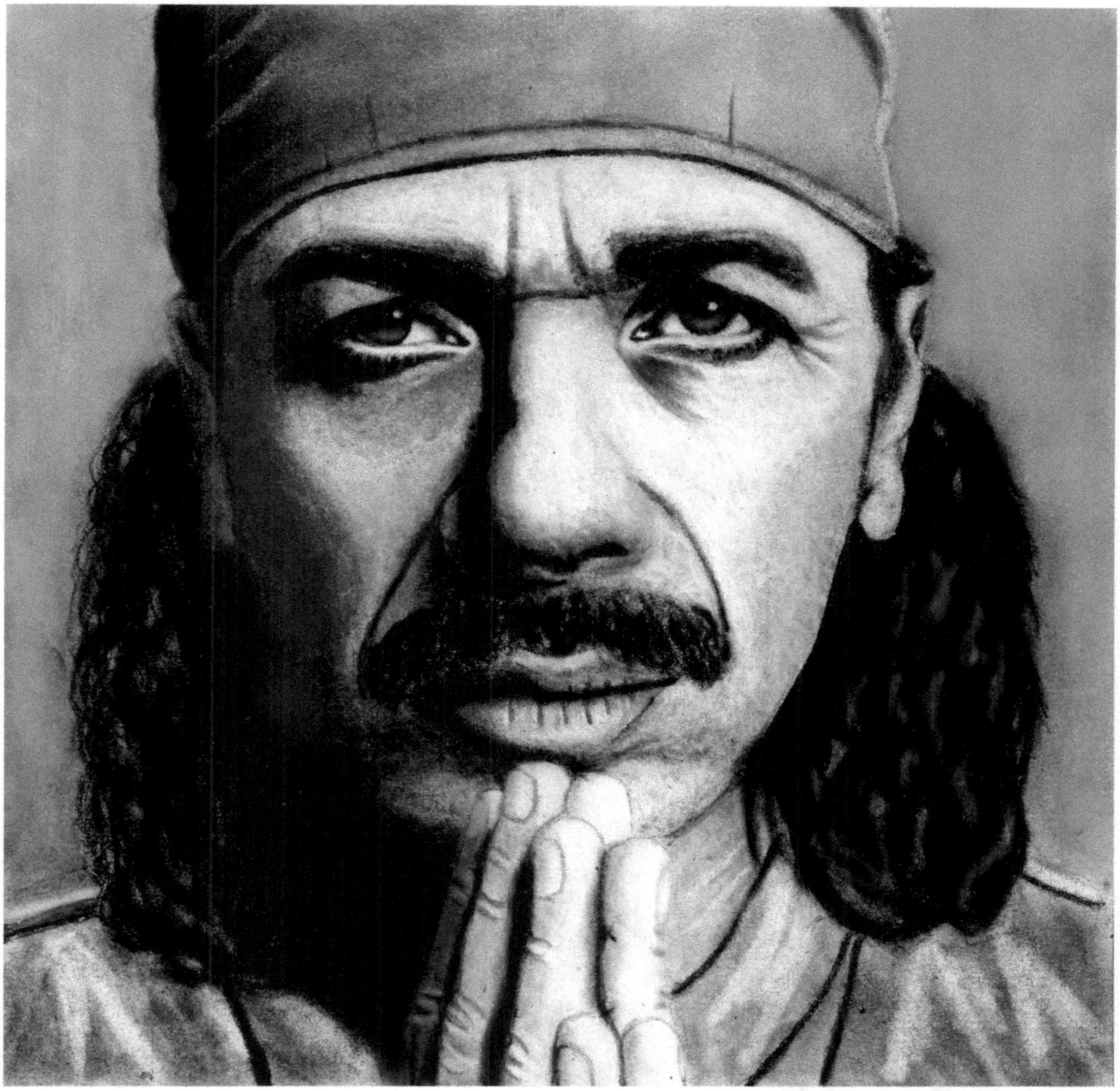

To view how this drawing was masterfully created or to purchase a Limited Edition Framed Artwork of Santana type into your Internet Browser the URL shortcut ➡ **myportrait.art/santana**

To listen to their Greatest Songs type intc your Internet Browser the URL shortcut ➡ **radio.surf/santana**

To view all channels on THE FACE OF MUSIC Internet Radio MEGA Station type into your Internet Browser the URL shortcut ➡ **radio.surf/music**

To inquire about purchasing a Limited Edtion NFT of this portrait type into your Internet Browser the URL shortcut ➡ **myartnft.shop/santana**

To view all available NFTs type into your Internet Browser the URL shortcut ➡ **myartnft.shop/all**

# Scorpions

(Total Records Sold: 110+ Million) (Genre: Hard Rock , Heavy Metal)

The Scorpions are a German heavy metal band formed in 1965 in Hanover by Rudolf Schenker. Since the band's inception, its musical style has ranged from hard rock, heavy metal, and glam metal. The lineup from 1978 to 1992 was the most successful incarnation of the group, and included Klaus Meine (vocals), Rudolf Schenker (rhythm guitar), Matthias Jabs (lead guitar), Francis Buchholz (bass), and Herman Rarebell (drums). The band's only continuous member has been Schenker, although Meine has appeared on all of Scorpions' studio albums, while Jabs has been a consistent member since 1978, and bassist Paweł Mąciwoda and drummer Mikkey Dee have been in the band since 2003 and 2016 respectively.During the mid-1970s, with guitarist Uli Jon Roth part of the line-up, the music of the Scorpions was defined as hard rock. After the departure of Roth in 1978 and short-lived reunion with Schenker's brother Michael, Matthias Jabs joined and, following the guidance of producer Dieter Dierks, the Scorpions changed their sound towards hard rock/heavy metal, mixed with rock power ballads. Throughout the 1980s the group received positive reviews and critical acclaim from music critics, and experienced commercial success with the albums Animal Magnetism (1980), Blackout (1982), Love at First Sting (1984), the live recording World Wide Live (1985), Savage Amusement (1988) and Best of Rockers 'n' Ballads (1989), which is their best-selling compilation album.

Scorpions' eleventh studio album Crazy World (1990) was also well-received, and included the song "Wind of Change", a symbolic anthem of the political changes in Eastern Europe in the late 1980s and early 1990s and the fall of the Berlin Wall. It is one of the best-selling singles in the world with over fourteen million copies sold. Scorpions have sold over 110 million records in total. They have released 18 studio albums, 27 compilation albums and 74 singles. Six of their singles have reached number one on the charts in different countries. Their albums, singles, compilations and video releases have reached gold, platinum and multi-platinum status 200 times in different countries.

Rolling Stone described the Scorpions as "the heroes of heavy metal", and MTV called them "Ambassadors of Rock". The band has influenced a number of acts such as Guns N' Roses, Mötley Crüe, Def Leppard, Metallica, Megadeth, Testament, Skid Row, Cinderella, Doro, Helloween, Hanoi Rocks, and Yngwie Malmsteen. The Scorpions were ranked number 46 on VH1's Greatest Artists of Hard Rock programme, with "Rock You Like a Hurricane" at number 18 on VH1's list of the 100 Greatest Hard Rock Songs. "Still Loving You" ranked 22nd place among the greatest ballads. They have received prestigious awards such as three World Music Awards, a star on the Hollywood Rock wall, and a presence in the permanent exhibition of the Rock and Roll Hall of Fame. In 2015, the group celebrated its 50th anniversary.

# Klaus Meine

(Net Worth: $75 Million)(Height: 5' - 4")

Klaus Meine (born 25 May 1948) is a German vocalist, songwriter and instrumentalist best known as the frontman of the heavy metal band Scorpions.

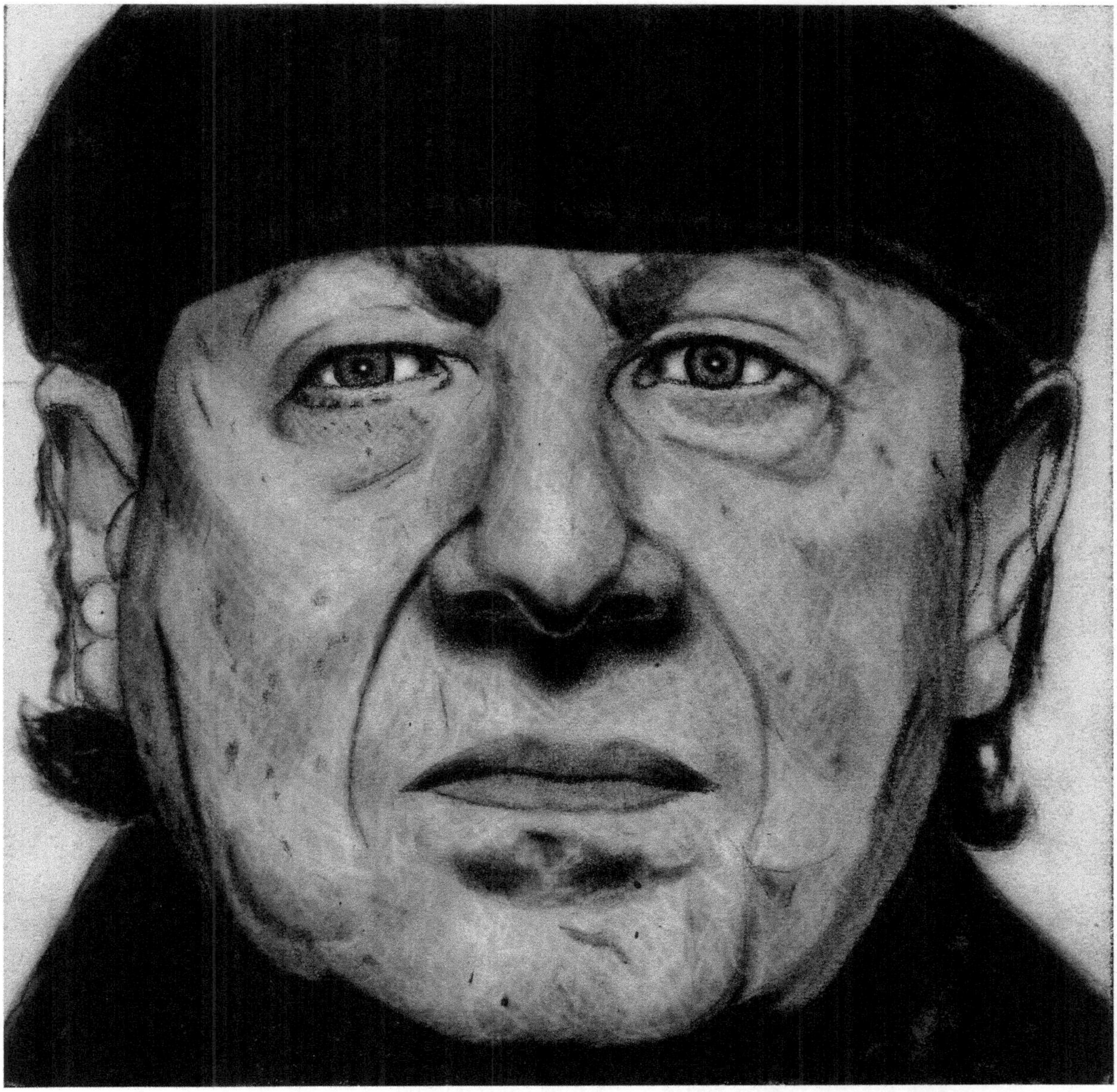

To view how this drawing was masterfully created or to purchase a Limited Edition Framed Artwork of Klaus Meine type into your Internet Browser the URL shortcut ➡ **myportrait.art/klausmeine**

To listen to their Greatest Songs type into your Internet Browser the URL shortcut ➡ **radio.surf/scorpions**

To view all channels on THE FACE OF MUSIC Internet Radio MEGA Station type into your Internet Browser the URL shortcut ➡ **radio.surf/music**

To inquire about purchasing a Limited Edtion NFT of this portrait type into your Internet Browser the URL shortcut ➡ **myartnft.shop/klausmeine**

To view all available NFTs type into your Internet Browser the URL shortcut ➡ **myartnft.shop/all**

# Sean Combs

(Net worth: $740 Million)(Total Records Sold: 12+Million)
(Genre: Hip-Hop , R&B)(Height: 5' - 10")

Sean Love Combs (born Sean John Combs; November 4, 1969), also known by the stage names Puff Daddy, P. Diddy, Puffy, or Diddy, is an American rapper, record producer, record executive, and entrepreneur. Born in New York City and raised in the suburb of Mount Vernon, he worked as a talent director at Uptown Records before founding his own record label, Bad Boy Records in 1993. Since then, Combs has produced and cultivated artists such as The Notorious B.I.G., Mary J. Blige, and Usher. Combs' debut album, No Way Out (1997), has been certified seven times platinum. The album was followed by Forever (1999), The Saga Continues... (2001), and Press Play (2006), all of which were commercially successful. In 2009, Combs formed the musical group Dirty Money and released the critically and commercially successful album Last Train to Paris (2010).

Combs has won three Grammy Awards and two MTV Video Music Awards, and is the producer of MTV's Making the Band.

Sean John Combs was born on November 4, 1969 in Manhattan's Harlem in New York City and was raised in Mount Vernon, New York. His mother, Janice (Smalls), was a model and teacher's assistant and his father, Melvin Earl Combs, served in the U.S. Air Force and was an associate of convicted New York drug dealer Frank Lucas. At age 33, Melvin was shot to death while sitting in his car on Central Park West, when Combs was 2 years old.

Combs graduated from the Roman Catholic Mount Saint Michael Academy in 1987. He played football for the academy and his team won a division title in 1986. Combs said he was given the nickname "Puff" as a child, because he would "huff and puff" when he was angry.

Combs was a business major at Howard University but left after his sophomore year. In 2014, he returned to Howard University to receive an Honorary Doctorate in Humanities and deliver the University's 146th Commencement Address.

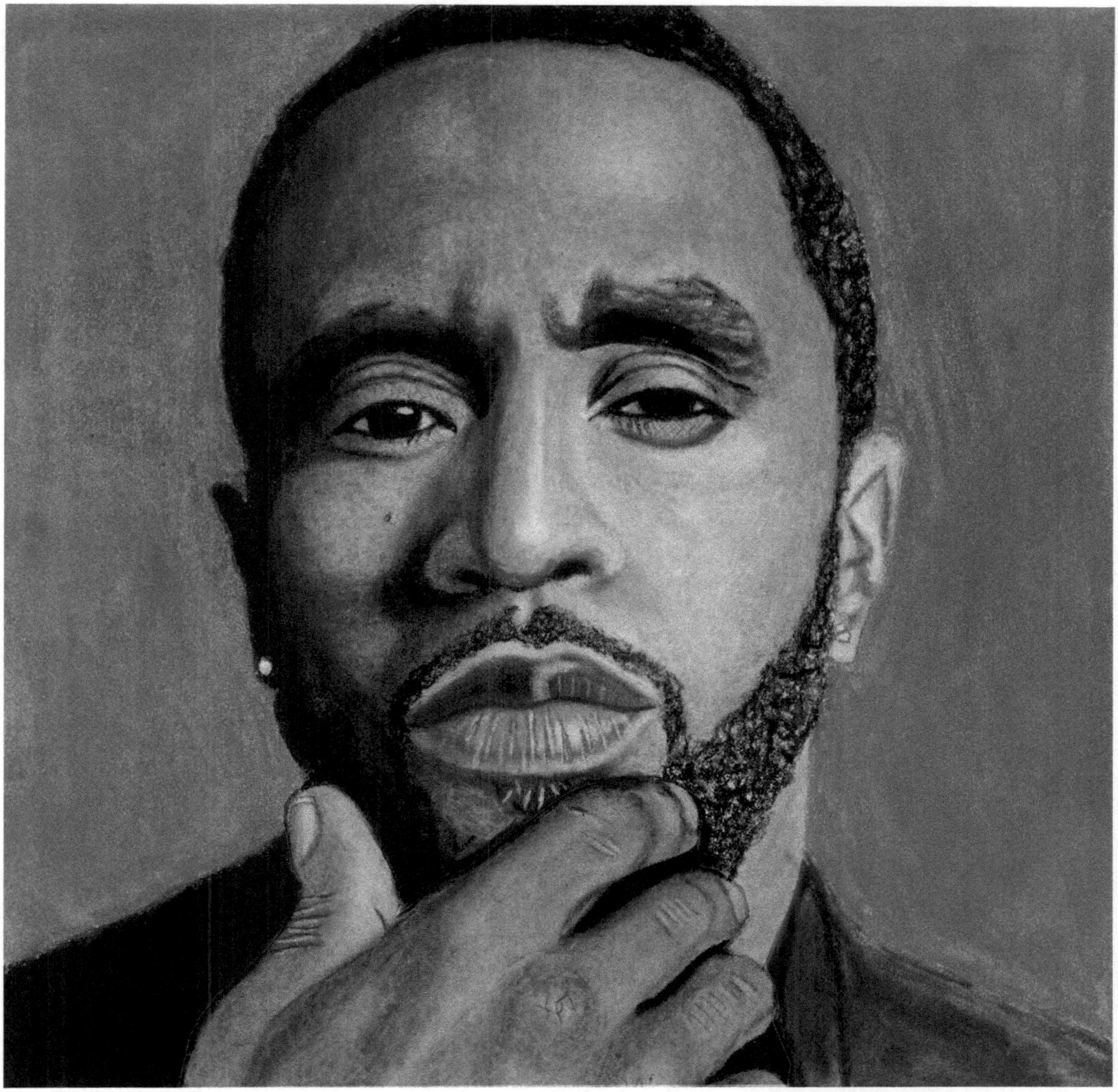

To view how this drawing was masterfully created or to purchase a Limited Edition Framed Artwork of Sean Combs type into your Internet Browser the URL shortcut ➡ **myportrait.art/seancombs**

To listen to their Greatest Songs type into your Internet Browser the URL shortcut ➡ **radio.surf/seancombs**

To view all channels on THE FACE OF MUSIC Internet Radio MEGA Station type into your Internet Browser the URL shortcut ➡ **radio.surf/music**

To inquire about purchasing a Limited Edtion NFT of this portrait type into your Internet Browser the URL shortcut ➡ **myartnft.shop/seancombs**

To view all available NFTs type into your Internet Browser the URL shortcut ➡ **myartnft.shop/all**

# Sex Pistols

(Total Records Sold: Millions) (Genre: Punk Rock)

The Sex Pistols were an English punk rock band that formed in London in 1975. Although their initial career lasted just two and a half years, they are regarded as one of the most groundbreaking acts in the history of popular music. They were responsible for initiating the punk movement in the United Kingdom and inspiring many later punk and alternative rock musicians. Their fashion and hairstyles have been credited as a significant influence on punk image, and they are often associated with anarchism within music.The Sex Pistols originally comprised vocalist John Lydon (known at the time by his stage name "Johnny Rotten"), guitarist Steve Jones, drummer Paul Cook and bassist Glen Matlock. Matlock was replaced by Sid Vicious in early 1977. Under the management of Malcolm McLaren, the band attracted controversies that both captivated and appalled Britain. Through an obscenity-laced television interview in December 1976 and their May 1977 single "God Save the Queen", attacking Britons' social conformity and deference to the Crown, they precipitated the punk rock movement. It was banned not only by the BBC but also by nearly every independent radio station, making it the "most heavily censored record in British history".The band's only album Never Mind the Bollocks, Here's the Sex Pistols (1977)—a UK number one album—is a staple record of punk rock. In January 1978, at the end of their over-hyped and turbulent tour of the United States, Rotten announced the band's break-up. Over the next few months, the three remaining band members recorded songs for McLaren's film version of the Sex Pistols' story, The Great Rock 'n' Roll Swindle. Vicious died of a heroin overdose in February 1979, following his arrest for the alleged murder of his girlfriend, Nancy Spungen. Rotten, Jones, Cook and Matlock reunited for a highly successful concert tour in 1996. Further one-off performances and short tours followed over the next decade.

The Sex Pistols have been recognised as an influence on various genres, including grunge, indie, thrash metal and hip hop. In 2004, Rolling Stone placed them No. 58 on its list of the "100 Greatest Artists of All Time". On 24 February 2006, the Sex Pistols—the four original members plus Vicious—were inducted into the Rock and Roll Hall of Fame, but they refused to attend the ceremony, calling the museum "a piss stain".

# Johnny Rotten

(Net Worth: $1 Million)(Height: 5' - 8")

John Joseph Lydon (born 31 January 1956), also known by his stage name Johnny Rotten, is an English singer and songwriter. He is best known as the lead singer of the late-1970s British punk band the Sex Pistols, which lasted from 1975 until 1978, and again for various revivals during the 1990s and 2000s. He is also the lead singer of post-punk band Public Image Ltd (PiL), which he founded and fronted from 1978 until 1993, and again since 2009.

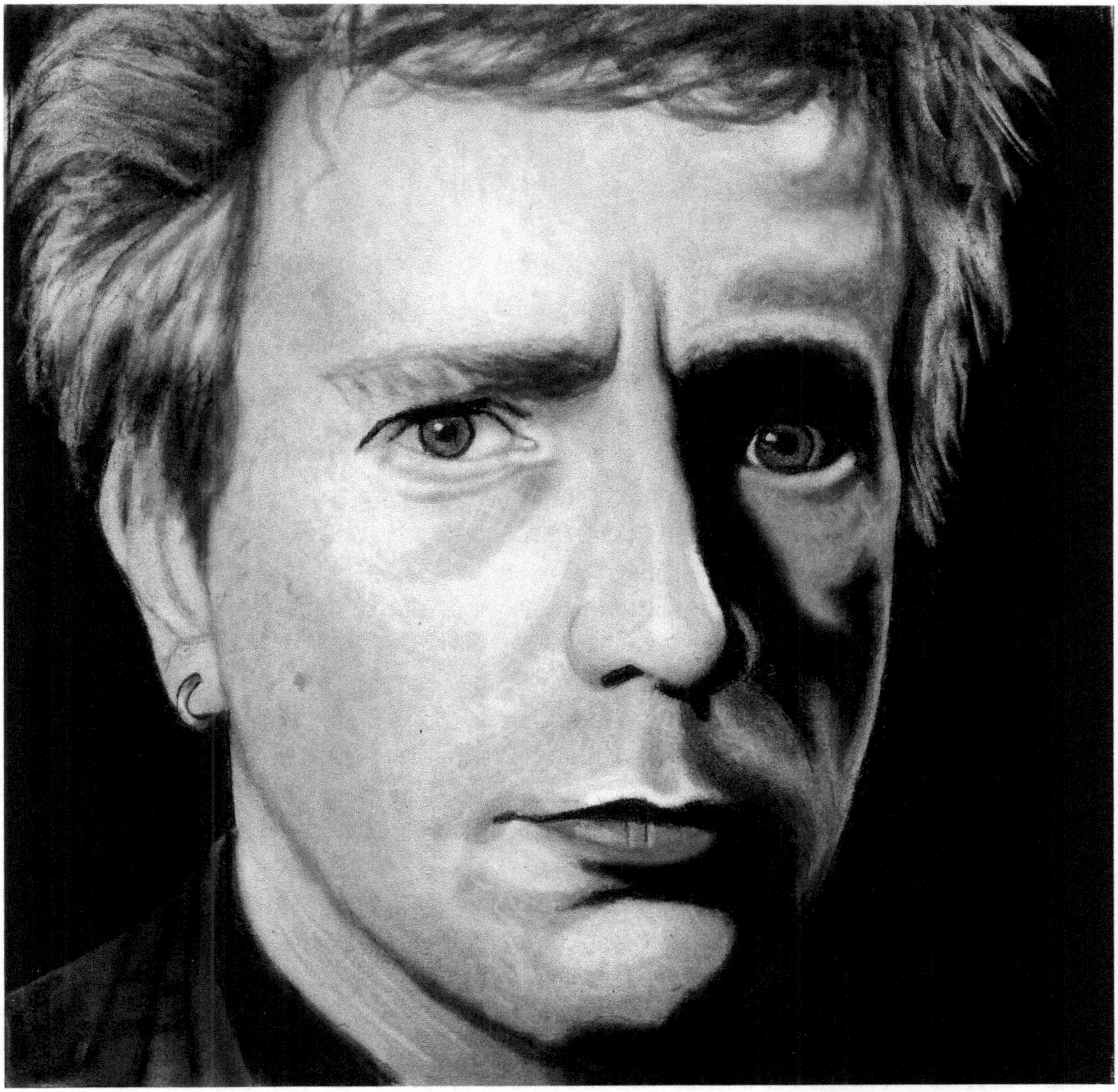

To view how this drawing was masterfully created or to purchase a Limited Edition Framed Artwork of Johnny Rotten type into your Internet Browser the URL shortcut ➡ **myportrait.art/johnnyrotten**

To listen to their Greatest Songs type into your Internet Browser the URL shortcut ➡ **radio.surf/sexpistols**

To view all channels on THE FACE OF MUSIC Internet Radio MEGA Station type into your Internet Browser the URL shortcut ➡ **radio.surf/music**

To inquire about purchasing a Limited Edtion NFT of this portrait type into your Internet Browser the URL shortcut ➡ **myartnft.shop/johnnyrotten**

To view all available NFTs type into your Internet Browser the URL shortcut ➡ **myartnft.shop/all**

# Shakira

(Net worth: $300 Million)(Total Records Sold: 75 Million)
(Genre: Pop , Rock , Latin)(Height: 5' - 2")

Shakira Isabel Mebarak Ripoll (born 2 February 1977) is a Colombian singer and songwriter. Born and raised in Barranquilla, Shakira has been referred to as the Queen of Latin Music and is noted for her versatility in music. She made her recording debut under Sony Music Colombia at the age of 13. Following the commercial failure of her first two albums, Magia (1991) and Peligro (1993), she rose to prominence in Hispanic countries with her next albums, Pies Descalzos (1995) and Dónde Están los Ladrones? (1998). Shakira entered the English-language market with her fifth album, Laundry Service (2001), which sold over 15 million copies worldwide. Buoyed by the international number-one singles "Whenever, Wherever" and "Underneath Your Clothes", the album propelled her reputation as a leading crossover artist.

Her success was further solidified with the Spanish albums Fijación Oral, Vol. 1 (2005), Sale el Sol (2010), and El Dorado (2017), all of which topped the Billboard Top Latin Albums chart and were certified diamante by the Recording Industry Association of America. Meanwhile, her English albums Oral Fixation, Vol. 2 (2005), She Wolf (2009) and Shakira (2014) were all certified gold, platinum, or multi-platinum in various countries worldwide. Some of her songs have charted at number one in multiple countries, including "La Tortura", "Hips Don't Lie", "Beautiful Liar", "Waka Waka (This Time for Africa)", "Loca", and "Chantaje". Shakira served as a coach on two seasons of the American singing competition television series The Voice (2013–2014).

With a catalog of 145 songs, Shakira has sold over 75 million records which have made her the best-selling female Latin artist of all time. Shakira remains one of the world's best-selling music artists. Forbes reported that as of 2018, Shakira has become the female Latin artist who has sold the most albums in history. Shakira has received numerous awards, including three Grammy Awards, twelve Latin Grammy Awards, four MTV Video Music Awards, seven Billboard Music Awards, thirty-nine Billboard Latin Music Awards, six Guinness World Records and a star on the Hollywood Walk of Fame. She was named the Top Female Latin Artist of the Decade by Billboard twice (2000s and 2010s). For her philanthropic work with her Barefoot Foundation and her contributions to music she received the Latin Recording Academy Person of the Year and Harvard Foundation Artist of the Year awards in 2011. She was appointed to the President's Advisory Commission on Educational Excellence for Hispanics in the US in 2011, and Chevalier of the Order of Arts and Letters by the French government in 2012.

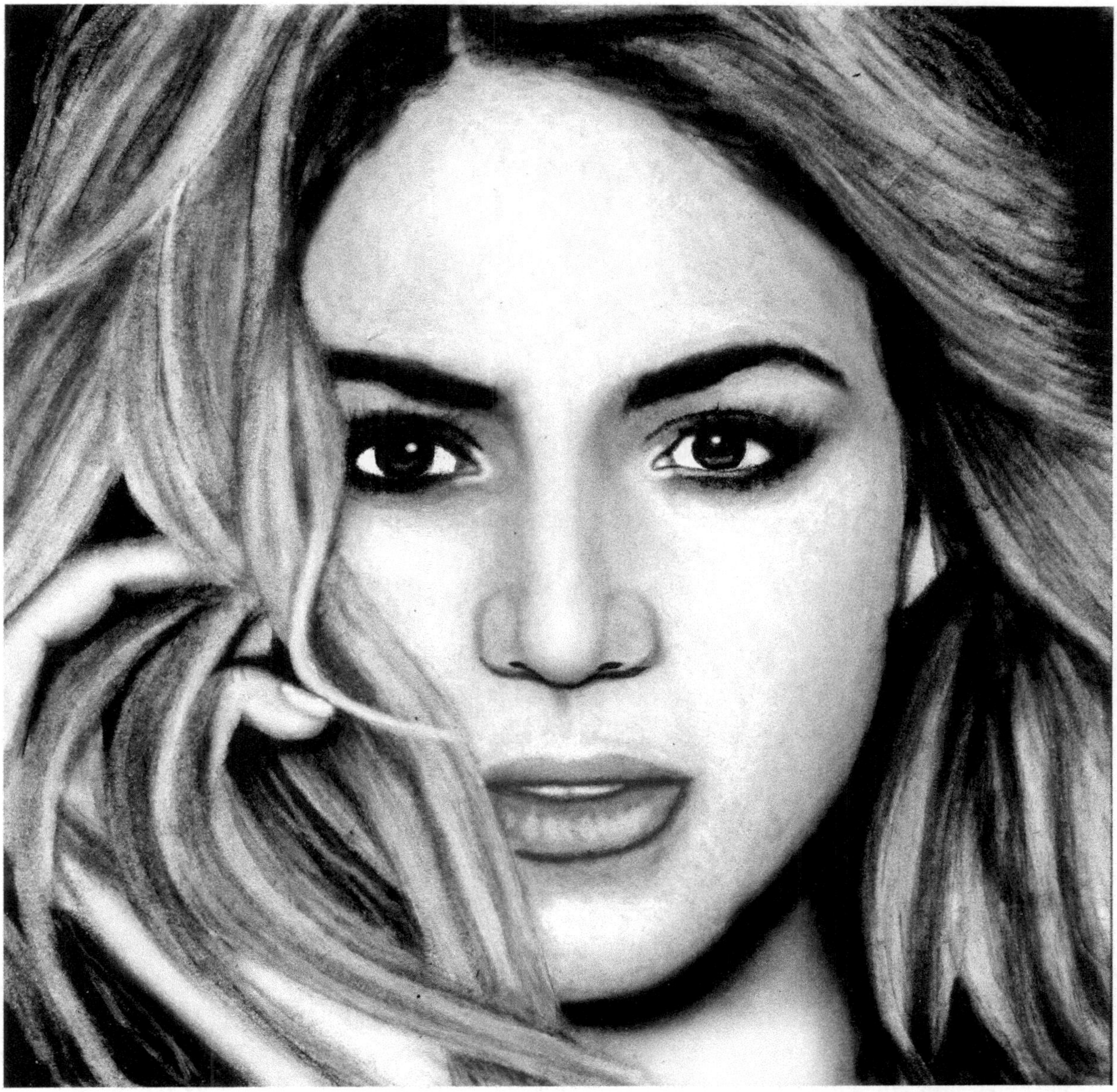

To view how this drawing was masterfully created or to purchase a Limited Edition Framed Artwork of Shakira type into your Internet Browser the URL shortcut ➡ **myportrait.art/shakira**

To listen to her Greatest Songs type into your Internet Browser the URL shortcut ➡ **radio.surf/shakira**

To view all channels on THE FACE OF MUSIC Internet Radio MEGA Station type into your Internet Browser the URL shortcut ➡ **radio.surf/music**

To inquire about purchasing a Limited Edtion NFT of this portrait type into your Internet Browser the URL shortcut ➡ **myartnft.shop/shakira**

To view all available NFTs type into your Internet Browser the URL shortcut ➡ **myartnft.shop/all**

# Shania Twain

(Net worth: $450 Million)(Total Records Sold: 85 Million)
(Genre: Pop , Country Pop , Country)(Height: 5' - 4")

Eilleen "Shania" Twain (born Eilleen Regina Edwards; August 28, 1965) is a Canadian singer and songwriter. She has sold over 100 million records, making her the best-selling female artist in country music history and among the best-selling music artists of all time. Her success garnered her several honorific titles including the "Queen of Country Pop". While Billboard named her as the leader of the '90s country-pop crossover stars.

Raised in Timmins, Ontario, Twain pursued singing and songwriting from a young age before signing with Mercury Nashville Records in the early 1990s. Her self-titled debut studio album was a commercial failure upon release in 1993. After collaborating with producer and later husband Robert John "Mutt" Lange, Twain rose to fame with her second studio album, The Woman in Me (1995), which brought her widespread success. It sold over 20 million copies worldwide, spawned eight singles, including "Any Man of Mine" and earned her a Grammy Award. Her third studio album, Come On Over (1997), became the best-selling studio album by a female act in any genre and the best-selling country album of all time, selling over 40 million copies worldwide. Come On Over produced twelve singles, including "You're Still the One", "From This Moment On", "That Don't Impress Me Much" and "Man! I Feel Like a Woman!" and earned Twain four Grammy Awards. Her fourth studio album, Up! (2002), spawned eight singles, including "I'm Gonna Getcha Good!", "Ka-Ching!" and "Forever and for Always", selling over 20 million copies worldwide, also being certified Diamond in the United States.

In 2004, after releasing her Greatest Hits album, which produced three new singles including "Party for Two", Twain entered a hiatus, revealing years later that diagnoses with Lyme disease and dysphonia led to a severely weakened singing voice. She chronicled her vocal rehabilitation on the OWN miniseries Why Not? with Shania Twain, released her first single in seven years in 2012, "Today Is Your Day", and published an autobiography, From This Moment On. Twain returned to performing the following year with an exclusive concert residency at The Colosseum at Caesars Palace, Shania: Still the One, which ran until 2014. In 2015, she launched the North American Rock This Country Tour, which was billed as her farewell tour. Twain released her first studio album in 15 years in 2017, Now, and embarked on the Now Tour in 2018.

Twain has received five Grammy Awards, a World Music Award, 27 BMI Songwriter Awards, stars on Canada's Walk of Fame and the Hollywood Walk of Fame, and an induction into the Canadian Music Hall of Fame. According to the RIAA she is the only female artist in history to have three (consecutive) albums certified Diamond by the RIAA, and is the sixth best-selling female artist in the United States. Altogether, Twain is ranked as the 10th best-selling artist of the Nielsen SoundScan era. Billboard listed Twain as the 13th Greatest Music Video Female Solo Artist of all time (42nd overall)

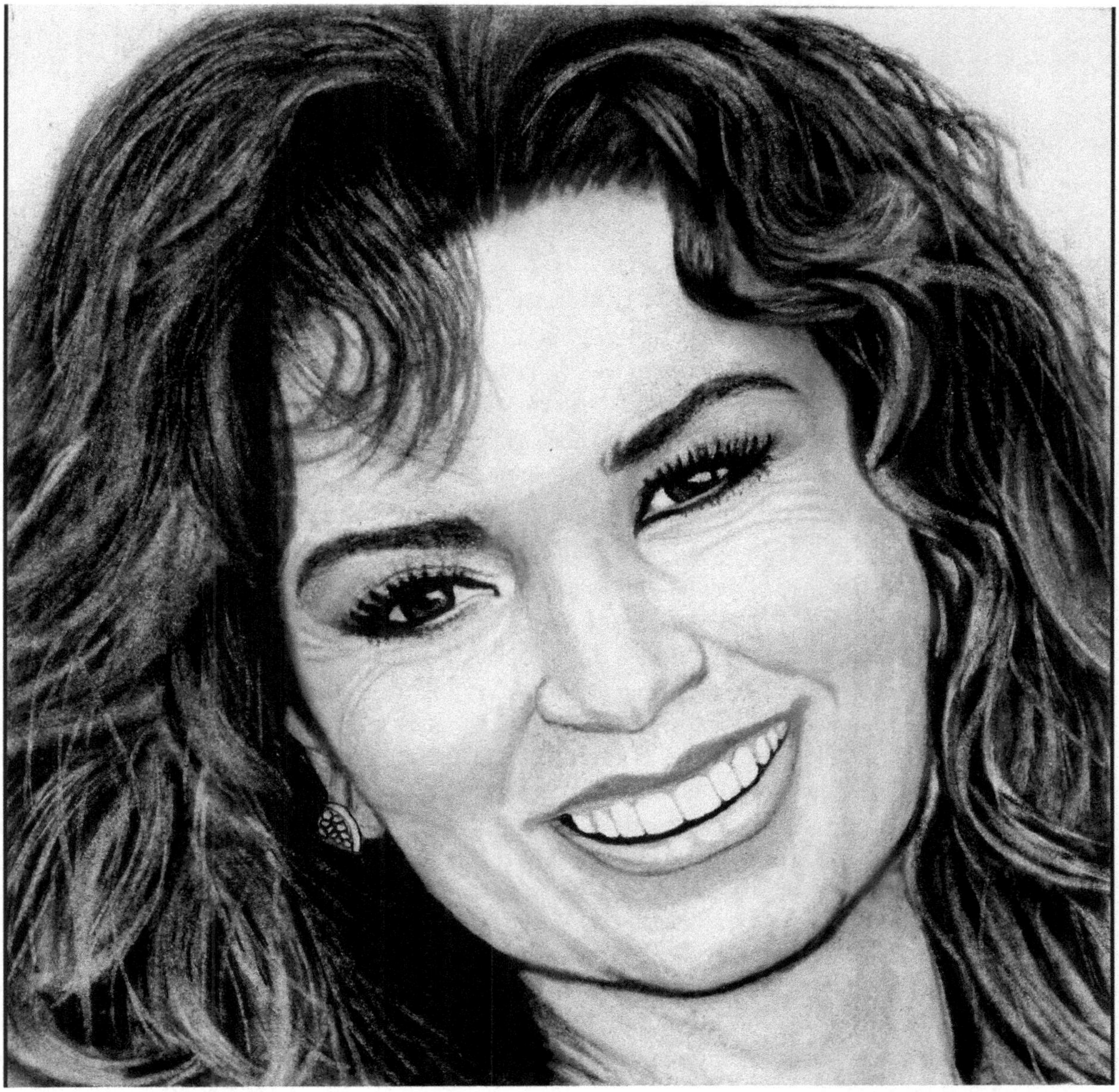

To view how this drawing was masterfully created or to purchase a Limited Edition Framed Artwork of Shania Twain type into your Internet Browser the URL shortcut ➡ **myportrait.art/shaniatwain**

To listen to her Greatest Songs type into your Internet Browser the URL shortcut ➡ **radio.surf/shaniatwain**

To view all channels on THE FACE OF MUSIC Internet Radio MEGA Station type into your Internet Browser the URL shortcut ➡ **radio.surf/music**

To inquire about purchasing a Limited Edtion NFT of this portrait type into your Internet Browser the URL shortcut ➡ **myartnft.shop/shaniatwain**

To view all available NFTs type into your Internet Browser the URL shortcut ➡ **myartnft.shop/all**

# Sheryl Crow

(Net worth: $70 Million)(Total Albums Sold: 50+ Million)
(Genre: Rock , Pop , Country , Folk)(Height: 5' - 3")

Sheryl Suzanne Crow (born February 11, 1962) is an American musician, singer, songwriter, and actress. Her music incorporates elements of pop, rock, country, jazz, and blues. She has released ten studio albums, four compilations, and two live albums, and has contributed to several film soundtracks. Her most popular songs include "All I Wanna Do" (1994), "Strong Enough" (1994), "If It Makes You Happy" (1996), "Everyday Is a Winding Road" (1996), "Tomorrow Never Dies" (1997) (the theme song for the James Bond film of the same name), "My Favorite Mistake" (1998), "Picture" (2002) (duet with rapper Kid Rock) and "Soak Up the Sun" (2002).

Crow has sold more than 50 million albums worldwide, and won nine Grammy Awards (out of 32 nominations) from the National Academy of Recording Arts and Sciences. As an actress, Crow has appeared on various television series including 30 Rock, Cop Rock, GCB Cougar Town, Jon Stewart and Stephen Colbert's Rally to Restore Sanity and/or Fear, One Tree Hill and NCIS: New Orleans.

Crow began dating Kevin Gilbert and joined him in an ad hoc group of musicians known to themselves as the "Tuesday Music Club". The group existed as a casual songwriting collective prior to its association with Crow, but rapidly developed into a vehicle for her debut album after her arrival. Group members Gilbert, David Baerwald, and David Ricketts (both formerly of David & David), Bill Bottrell, Brian MacLeod, and Dan Schwartz share songwriting credits with Crow on her debut album, Tuesday Night Music Club, released in August 1993. Her relationship with Gilbert became acrimonious soon after the album was released, and disputes arose about songwriting credits. Tuesday Night Music Club featured many of the songs written by Crow's friends, including the second single, "Leaving Las Vegas". The album was slow to garner attention, until "All I Wanna Do" became an unexpected smash hit in October 1994. As she later stated in People, she found an old poetry book in a used book store in the Los Angeles area and used a poem as the lyrics of the song. The singles "Strong Enough" and "Can't Cry Anymore" were also released, with the first song ("Strong Enough") charting at No. 5 on Billboard and "Can't Cry Anymore" hitting the Top 40. Tuesday Night Music Club went on to sell more than 7 million copies in the US and UK during the 1990s. The album also won Crow three Grammy Awards in 1995: Record of the Year, Best New Artist and Best Female Vocal Performance.

Crow performed at the 1994 Woodstock Festival, and appeared in the "New Faces" section of Rolling Stone in 1994. She also supplied background vocals to the song "The Garden of Allah" from Don Henley's 1995 album Actual Miles: Henley's Greatest Hits.

In 1996, Crow released her self-titled second album. She produced the album herself and also played a variety of instruments, from various guitars, bass or pedal steel to various organs and piano. The debut single, "If It Makes You Happy", became a radio success and netted her two Grammy awards for Best Female Rock Vocal Performance and Best Rock Album. Other singles included "A Change Would Do You Good", "Home", and "Everyday Is a Winding Road". The album was banned from sale at Wal-Mart, because in the lyrics to "Love Is a Good Thing" Crow says that Wal-Mart sells guns to children. The album also features a protest song called "Redemption Day", which was covered by Johnny Cash on his last album American VI: Ain't No Grave.Crow performed at Another Roadside Attraction in 1997. Also in 1997, Crow contributed the theme song to the James Bond film Tomorrow Never Dies. Her song "Tomorrow Never Dies" was nominated for a Grammy Award and Best Original Song Golden Globe.

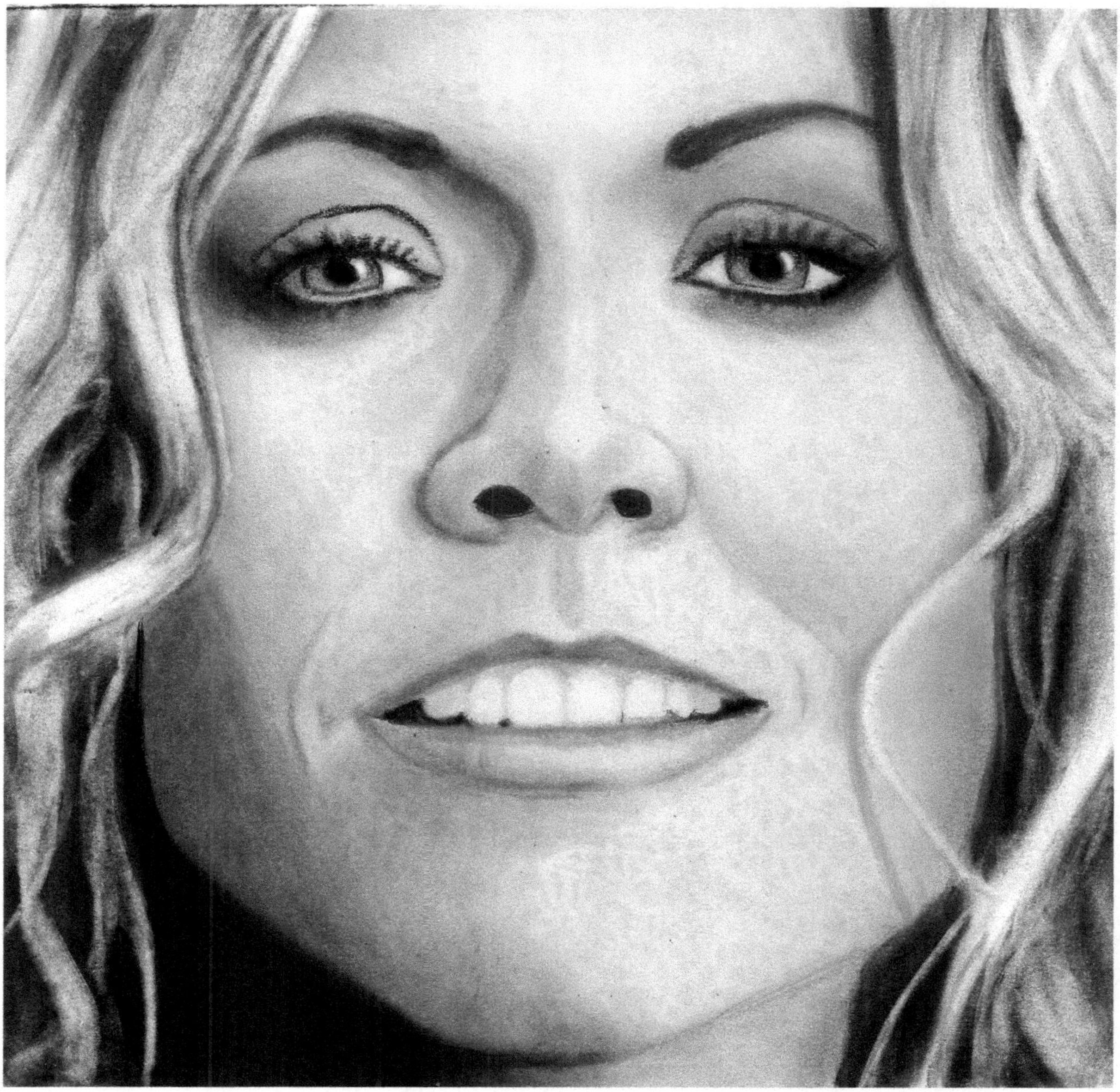

To view how this drawing was masterfully created or to purchase a Limited Edition Framed Artwork of Sheryl Crow type into your Internet Browser the URL shortcut ➡ **myportrait.art/sherylcrow**

To listen to her Greatest Songs type into your Internet Browser the URL shortcut ➡ **radio.surf/sherylcrow**

To view all channels on THE FACE OF MUSIC Internet Radio MEGA Station type into your Internet Browser the URL shortcut ➡ **radio.surf/music**

To inquire about purchasing a Limited Edtion NFT of this portrait type into your Internet Browser the URL shortcut ➡ **myartnft.shop/sherylcrow**

To view all available NFTs type into your Internet Browser the URL shortcut ➡ **myartnft.shop/all**

# Simon & Garfunkel

(Total Records Sold: 100+ Million) (Genre: Folk Rock)

Simon & Garfunkel were an American folk-rock duo consisting of singer-songwriter Paul Simon and singer Art Garfunkel. They were one of the best-selling music groups of the 1960s, and their biggest hits—including "The Sound of Silence" (1965), "Mrs. Robinson" (1968), "The Boxer" (1969), and "Bridge over Troubled Water" (1970)—reached number one on singles charts worldwide. Simon and Garfunkel met in elementary school in Queens, New York, in 1953, where they learned to harmonize together and began writing material. By 1957, under the name Tom & Jerry, the teenagers had their first minor success with "Hey Schoolgirl", a song imitating their idols the Everly Brothers. In 1963, aware of a growing public interest in folk music, they regrouped and were signed to Columbia Records as Simon & Garfunkel. Their debut, Wednesday Morning, 3 A.M., sold poorly, and they once again disbanded; Simon returned to a solo career, this time in England. In June 1965, a new version of "The Sound of Silence" overdubbed with electric guitar and drums became a major U.S. AM radio hit, reaching number one on the Billboard Hot 100. The duo reunited to release a second studio album, Sounds of Silence, and tour colleges nationwide. On their third release, Parsley, Sage, Rosemary and Thyme (1966), the duo assumed more creative control. Their music was featured in the 1967 film The Graduate, giving them further exposure. Their next album Bookends (1968) topped the Billboard 200 chart and included the number-one single "Mrs. Robinson" from the film.

- Continued on Page 563 -.

# Art Garfunkel

(Net Worth: $95 Million)(Height: 6' - 0")

Arthur Ira Garfunkel (born November 5, 1941) is an American singer, poet, and actor. He is best known for his partnership with Paul Simon in the folk rock duo Simon & Garfunkel. Highlights of Garfunkel's solo music career include a top 10 hit, three top 20 hits, six top 40 hits, 14 Adult Contemporary top 30 singles, five Adult Contemporary number ones, two UK number ones and a People's Choice Award. Through his solo and collaborative work, Garfunkel has earned eight Grammys, including a Lifetime Achievement Award. In 1990, he and Simon were inducted into the Rock and Roll Hall of Fame. In 2008, Garfunkel was ranked 86th in Rolling Stone magazine's list of the 100 Greatest Singers of All Time.

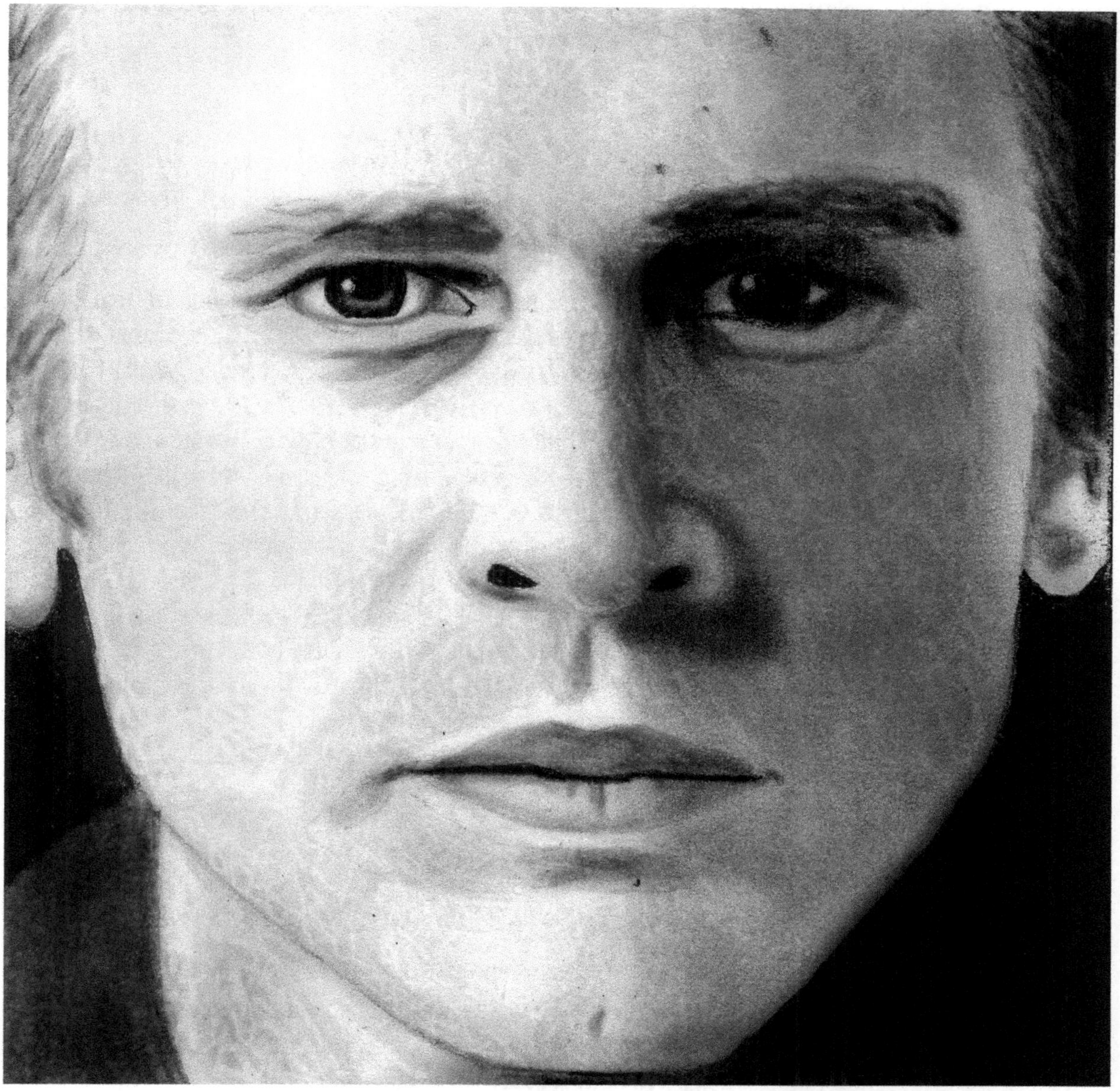

To view how this drawing was masterfully created or to purchase a Limited Edition Framed Artwork of Art Garfunkel type into your Internet Browser the URL shortcut ➡ **myportrait.art/artgarfunkel**

To listen to their Greatest Songs type into your Internet Browser the URL shortcut
➡ **radio.surf/simonandgarfunkel**

To view all channels on THE FACE OF MUSIC Internet Radio MEGA Station type into your Internet Browser the URL shortcut ➡ **radio.surf/music**

To inquire about purchasing a Limited Edtion NFT of this portrait type into your Internet Browser the URL shortcut ➡ **myartnft.shop/artgarfunkel**

To view all available NFTs type into your Internet Browser the URL shortcut ➡ **myartnft.shop/all**

# Simon & Garfunkel

(Total Records Sold: 100+Million) (Genre: Folk Rock)

The duo's often rocky relationship led to artistic disagreements and their breakup in 1970. Their final studio album, Bridge over Troubled Water, was released in January of that year, becoming their most successful release and one of the world's best-selling albums. After their breakup, Simon released a number of acclaimed albums, including 1986's Graceland. Garfunkel released solo hits such as "All I Know" and briefly pursued an acting career, with leading roles in two Mike Nichols films, Catch-22 and Carnal Knowledge, and in Nicolas Roeg's 1980 Bad Timing. The duo have reunited several times, most famously in 1981 for The Concert in Central Park, which attracted more than 500,000 people, one of the largest concert attendances in history.

Simon & Garfunkel won 10 Grammy Awards and were inducted into the Rock and Roll Hall of Fame in 1990. Rolling Stone ranked them number 3 on its list of the 20 Greatest Duos of All Time. Richie Unterberger described them as "the most successful folk-rock duo of the 1960s" and one of the most popular artists from the decade. They are among the best-selling music artists, having sold more than 100 million records. Bridge over Troubled Water is ranked at number 172 on Rolling Stone's 500 Greatest Albums of All Time.

# Paul Simon

(Net Worth: $150 Million)(Height: 5' - 3")

Paul Frederic Simon (born October 13, 1941) is an American musician, singer, songwriter and actor. Simon's musical career has spanned over six decades. He is widely regarded as one of the best songwriters in popular music history.

Simon formed the duo Simon & Garfunkel with his schoolfriend Art Garfunkel in 1956. They released five studio albums and became one of the most acclaimed groups of the 1960s. Simon composed nearly all of their songs, including "The Sound of Silence", "Mrs. Robinson", "America", "Bridge over Troubled Water", and "The Boxer".

After Simon & Garfunkel split in 1970, Simon recorded three acclaimed albums over the following five years, all of which charted in the top 5 on the Billboard 200. His 1972 self-titled album contained the hit songs "Mother and Child Reunion" and "Me and Julio Down by the Schoolyard". The 1975 album Still Crazy After All These Years, which featured guest vocals from Garfunkel, was his first number-one solo album, and featured the number 1 hit single "50 Ways to Leave Your Lover", among other top-40 songs such as "Still Crazy After All These Years", "Gone at Last", and "My Little Town".

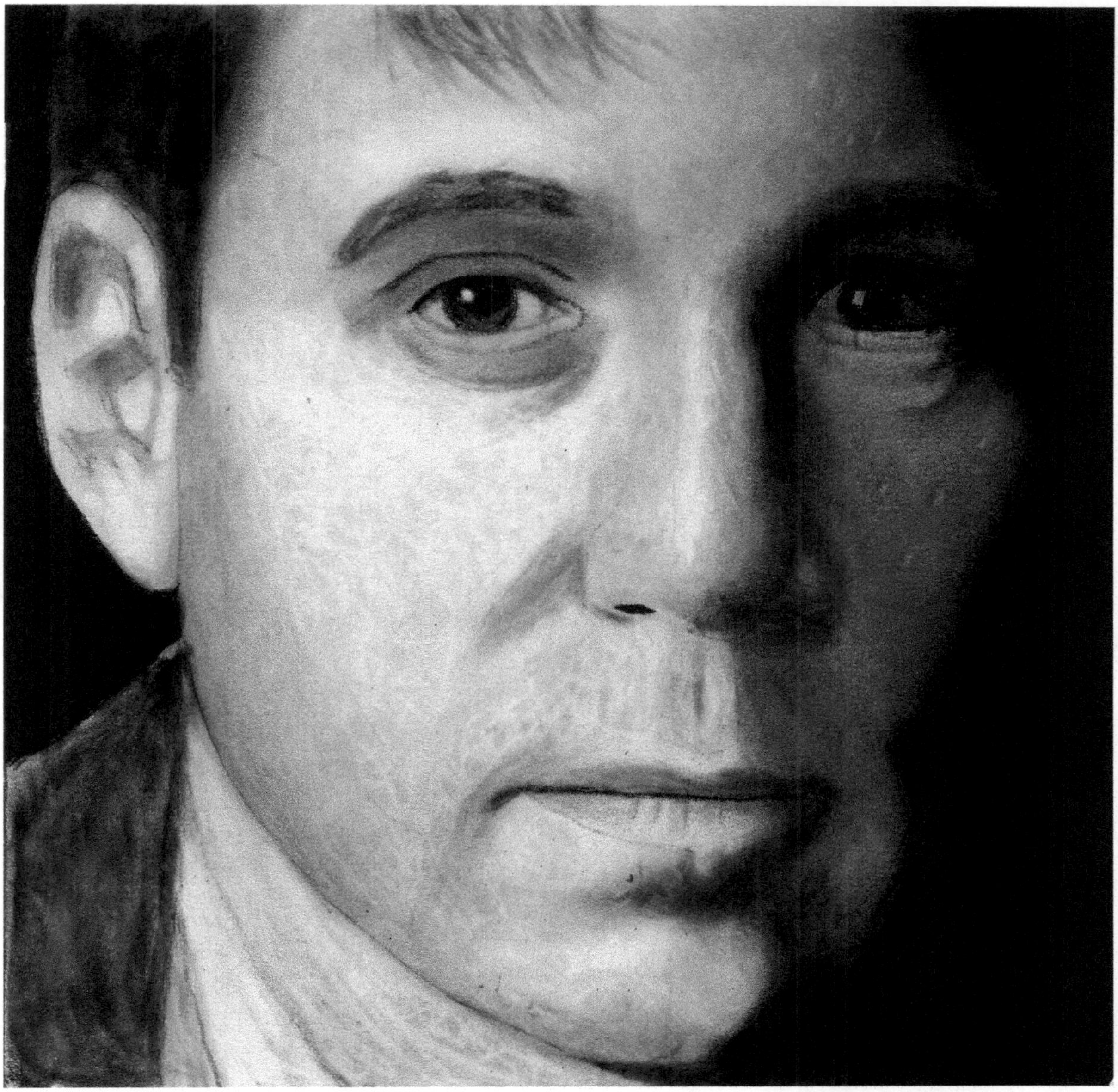

To view how this drawing was masterfully created or to purchase a Limited Edition Framed Artwork of Paul Simon type into your Internet Browser the URL shortcut ➡ **myportrait.art/paulsimon**

To listen to their Greatest Songs type into your Internet Browser the URL shortcut
➡ **radio.surf/simonandgarfunkel**

To view all channels on THE FACE OF MUSIC Internet Radio MEGA Station type into your Internet Browser the URL shortcut ➡ **radio.surf/music**

To inquire about purchasing a Limited Edtion NFT of this portrait type into your Internet Browser the URL shortcut ➡ **myartnft.shop/paulsimon**

To view all available NFTs type into your Internet Browser the URL shortcut ➡ **myartnft.shop/all**

# Skid Row

(Total Albums Sold: 20 Million) (Genre: Heavy Metal , Hard Rock)

Skid Row is an American rock band, formed in 1986 in Toms River, New Jersey. Their current lineup comprises bassist Rachel Bolan, guitarists Dave Sabo and Scotti Hill, drummer Rob Hammersmith and vocalist ZP Theart. The group achieved commercial success in the late 1980s and early 1990s, with its first two albums Skid Row (1989) and Slave to the Grind (1991) certified multi-platinum, the latter of which reached number one on the Billboard 200. Those two albums also produced some of Skid Row's most popular hits, both in and outside of the United States, such as "Youth Gone Wild", "18 and Life", "I Remember You", "Monkey Business", "Slave to the Grind", "Wasted Time" and "In a Darkened Room". The band's third album Subhuman Race (1995) was also critically acclaimed, but failed to repeat the success of its predecessors. During this period, the band consisted of Bolan, Sabo, Hill, drummer Rob Affuso and frontman Sebastian Bach. The band had sold 20 million albums worldwide by the end of 1996.

After replacing Bach with Johnny Solinger and Affuso with Phil Varone in 1999, Skid Row released Thickskin (2003) and Revolutions per Minute (2006), both of which garnered mixed reception. In April 2015, Skid Row announced that they had parted ways with Solinger, and replaced him with former TNT singer Tony Harnell. Eight months later, however, Harnell left the band. In January 2017, former DragonForce vocalist ZP Theart was named the official lead singer after spending a year as a touring member of the group.

# Sebastian Bach

(Net Worth: $10 Million)(Height: 6' - 3")

Sebastian Philip Bierk (born April 3, 1968), known professionally as Sebastian Bach, is a Canadian singer and songwriter who achieved mainstream success as the frontman of heavy metal band Skid Row from 1987 to 1996. He continues a solo career, acted on Broadway and has made appearances in film and television such as Trailer Park Boys and Gilmore Girls.

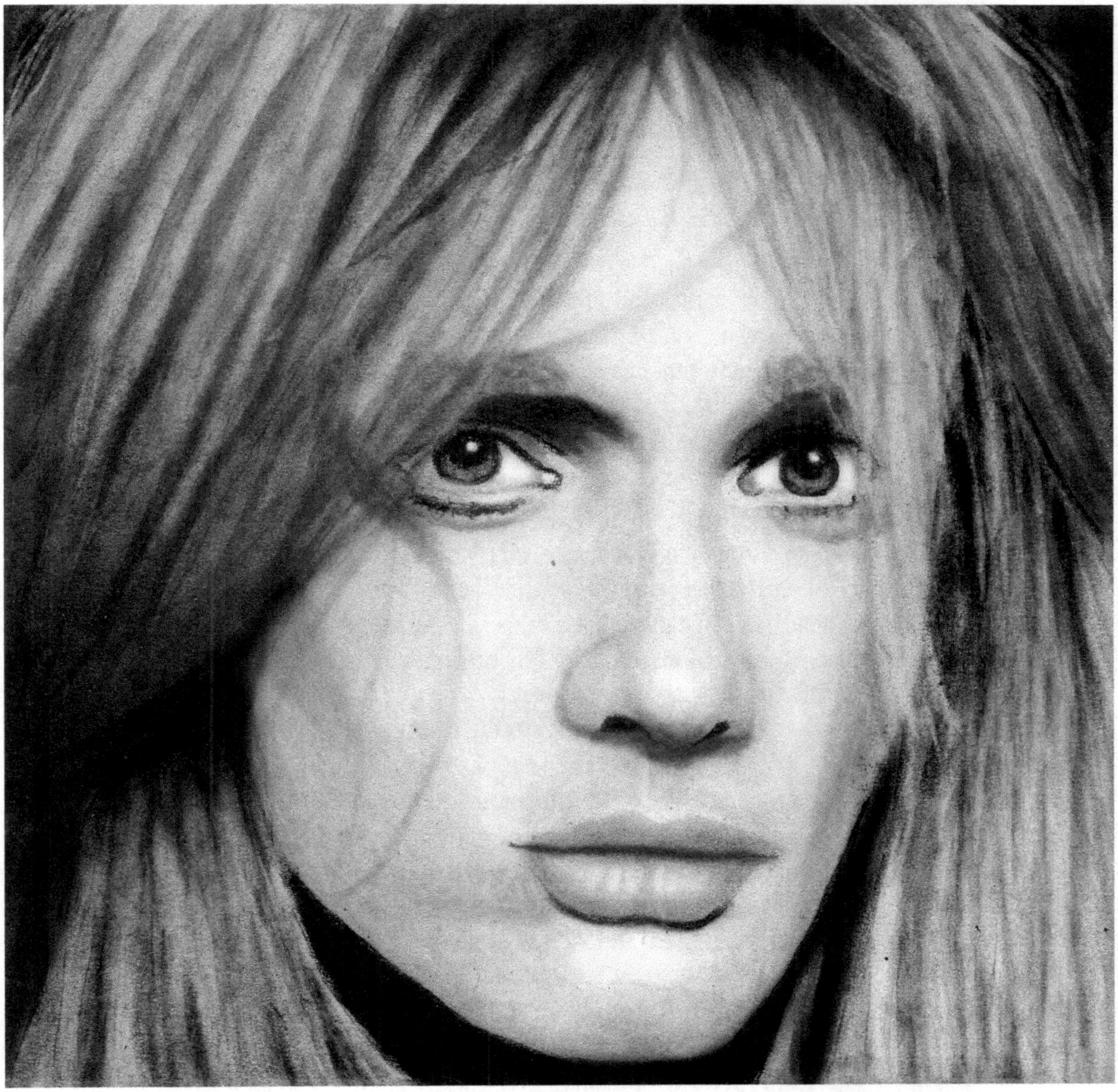

To view how this drawing was masterfully created or to purchase a Limited Edition Framed Artwork of Sabastian Bach type into your Internet Browser the URL shortcut ➡ **myportrait.art/sabastianbach**

To listen to their Greatest Songs type into your Internet Browser the URL shortcut ➡ **radio.surf/skidrow**

To view all channels on THE FACE OF MUSIC Internet Radio MEGA Station type into your Internet Browser the URL shortcut ➡ **radio.surf/music**

To inquire about purchasing a Limited Edtion NFT of this portrait type into your Internet Browser the URL shortcut ➡ **myartnft.shop/sabastianbach**

To view all available NFTs type into your Internet Browser the URL shortcut ➡ **myartnft.shop/all**

# Slayer

(Total Albums Sold: 20+Million) (Genre: Thrash Metal)

Slayer was an American thrash metal band from Huntington Park, California. The band was formed in 1981 by guitarists Kerry King and Jeff Hanneman, drummer Dave Lombardo, and bassist and vocalist Tom Araya. Slayer's fast and aggressive musical style made them one of the "big four" bands of thrash metal, alongside Metallica, Megadeth, and Anthrax. Slayer's final lineup comprised King, Araya, drummer Paul Bostaph (who replaced Lombardo in 1992 and again in 2013) and guitarist Gary Holt (who replaced Hanneman in 2011). Drummer Jon Dette was also a member of the band. In the original lineup, King, Hanneman and Araya contributed to the band's lyrics, and all of the band's music was written by King and Hanneman. The band's lyrics and album art, which cover topics such as murder, serial killers, torture, genocide, politics, human subject research, organized crime, secret societies, mythology, occultism, Satanism, hate crimes, terrorism, religion or antireligion, Nazism, fascism, racism, xenophobia, war and prison, have generated album bans, delays, lawsuits and criticism from religious groups and factions of the general public. However, its music has been highly influential, often being cited by many bands as an influence musically, visually and lyrically; the band's third album, Reign in Blood (1986), has been described as one of the heaviest and most influential thrash metal albums.

Slayer released twelve studio albums, two live albums, a box set, six music videos, two extended plays and a cover album. Four of the band's studio albums have received gold certification in the United States. Slayer sold 5 million copies in the United States from 1991 to 2013, according to Nielsen SoundScan, and over 20 million worldwide. The band has received five Grammy Award nominations, winning one in 2007 for the song "Eyes of the Insane" and one in 2008 for the song "Final Six", both of which were from the album Christ Illusion (2006). After more than three decades of recording and performing, Slayer announced in January 2018 that it would embark on a farewell tour, which took place from May 2018 to November 2019, after which the band disbanded.

# Tom Araya

(Net Worth: $14 Million)(Height: 5' - 10")

Tomás Enrique Araya Díaz (born June 6, 1961) is a Chilean-American musician, best known as the vocalist and bassist of American thrash metal band Slayer. Araya is ranked fifty-eighth by Hit Parader on their list of the 100 Greatest Metal Vocalists of All Time.

Araya was employed as a respiratory therapist in the early 1980s and used his earnings to finance Slayer's debut album Show No Mercy. Much of Araya's lyrical content is about serial killers, a subject he finds interesting; his first credited lyrical contribution was the vampire-themed track "At Dawn They Sleep" from 1985's Hell Awaits.

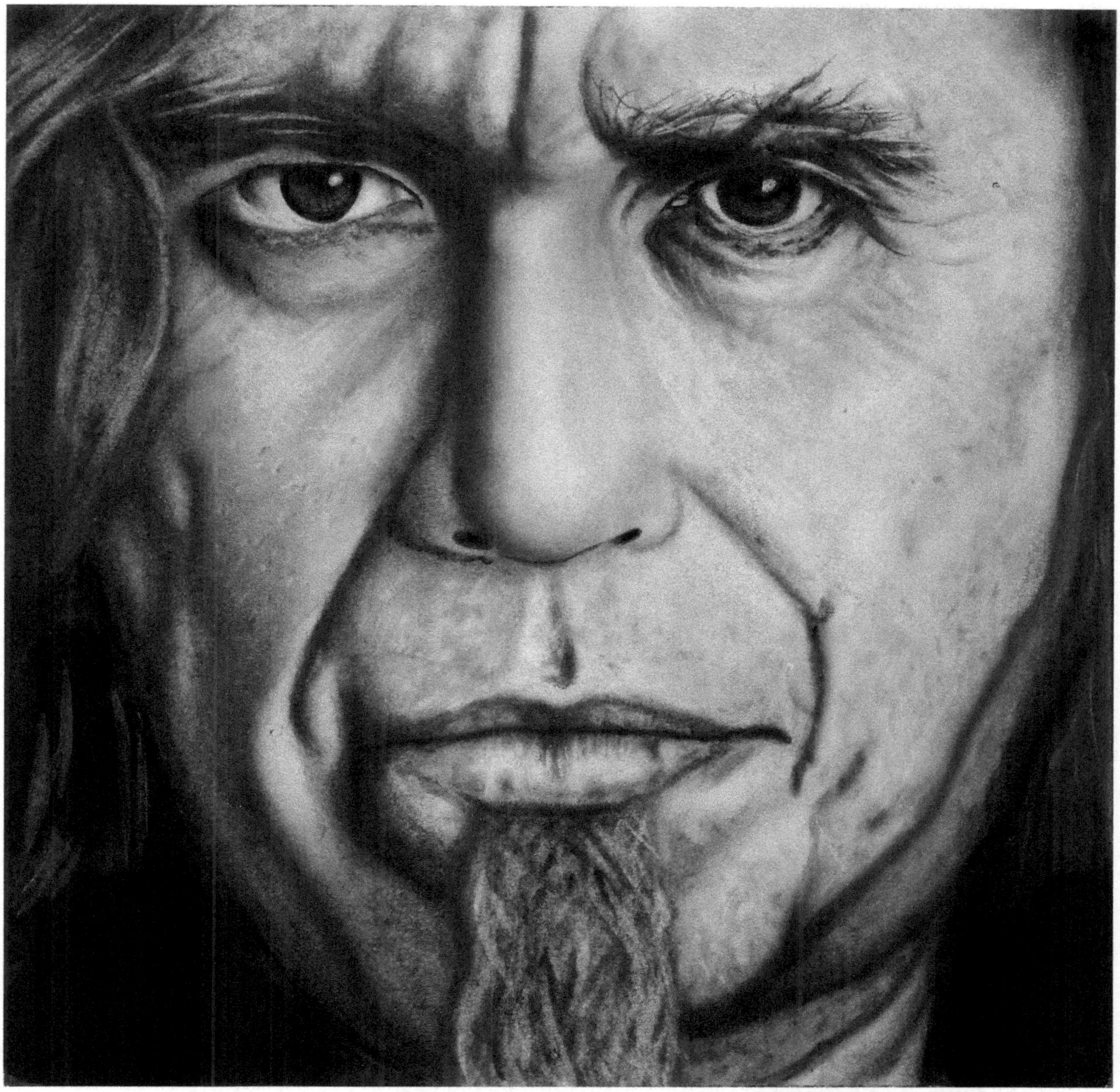

To view how this drawing was masterfully created or to purchase a Limited Edition Framed Artwork of Tom Araya type into your Internet Browser the URL shortcut ➡ **myportrait.art/tomaraya**

To listen to their Greatest Songs type into your Internet Browser the URL shortcut ➡ **radio.surf/slayer**

To view all channels on THE FACE OF MUSIC Internet Radio MEGA Station type into your Internet Browser the URL shortcut ➡ **radio.surf/music**

To inquire about purchasing a Limited Edtion NFT of this portrait type into your Internet Browser the URL shortcut ➡ **myartnft.shop/tomaraya**

To view all available NFTs type into your Internet Browser the URL shortcut ➡ **myartnft.shop/all**

# Slick Rick

(Net worth: $1 Million)(Total Albums Sold: Millions)
(Genre: Hip-Hop)(Height: 5' - 6")

Richard Martin Lloyd Walters (born January 14, 1965), better known as Slick Rick, is an English-American rapper and record producer.

He rose to prominence with Doug E. Fresh & the Get Fresh Crew in the mid-1980s. Their songs "The Show" and "La Di Da Di" are considered early hip hop classics. "La Di Da Di" is one of the most sampled songs in history.

In 1986, Slick Rick became the third artist signed to Def Jam Records. He has released four albums: The Great Adventures of Slick Rick (1988), The Ruler's Back (1991), Behind Bars (1994) and The Art of Storytelling (1999). His music has been sampled and interpolated over 1,000 times, in dozens of songs by artists, including Eminem, Beyoncé, Mariah Carey, the Beastie Boys, TLC, Nas, Miley Cyrus, Kanye West, Black Star, The Notorious B.I.G., Snoop Dogg, MC Ren, Montell Jordan and Color Me Badd. In the process, Slick Rick has become one of the most-sampled hip-hop artists ever. Many of these songs based on Slick Rick samples went on to become hit singles.

Slick Rick has been a VH-1 Hip Hop Honors honoree, and About.com ranked him No. 12 on their list of the Top 50 MCs of Our Time, while The Source ranked him No. 15 on their list of the Top 50 Lyricists of All Time. He has acted and cameo-ed in 10 movies and videos.

His career began in 1985; Walters first gained success in the rap industry after joining Doug E. Fresh's Get Fresh Crew, using the stage name MC Ricky D. He was featured on the single "The Show" and its even more popular B-side, "La Di Da Di", which featured Walters' rapping over Doug E. Fresh's beatbox. Both tracks gained some mainstream attention, they appeared on Top of the Pops and Soul Train with the Get Fresh Crew. Reflecting on the double-sided gem in Rolling Stone magazine, Roots drummer and Tonight Show bandleader Ahmir "Questlove" Thompson said, "Point blank: Slick Rick's voice was the most beautiful thing to happen to hip-hop culture. Rick is full of punchlines, wit, melody, cool cadence, confidence and style. He is the blueprint."

In 1986, Slick Rick joined Russell Simmons's Rush Artist Management and became the third artist signed to Def Jam Records, the leading rap/hip-hop label at the time. Collaborating with his friend, DJ Vance Wright, Walters produced his solo debut, The Great Adventures of Slick Rick, which came out in 1988 on Def Jam. The album was very successful, reaching the No. 1 spot on Billboard's R&B/Hip-Hop chart. It also featured three charting singles: "Children's Story", "Hey Young World", and "Teenage Love". The release is known for its storytelling and vocal characterizations. "With the combination of Rick's Dick Van Dyke-on-dope accent and his unique narrative style, the record was an instant classic," wrote critic Matt Weiner. "Each of Rick's songs was an amusing, enthralling story that lasted from the first groove to the last."

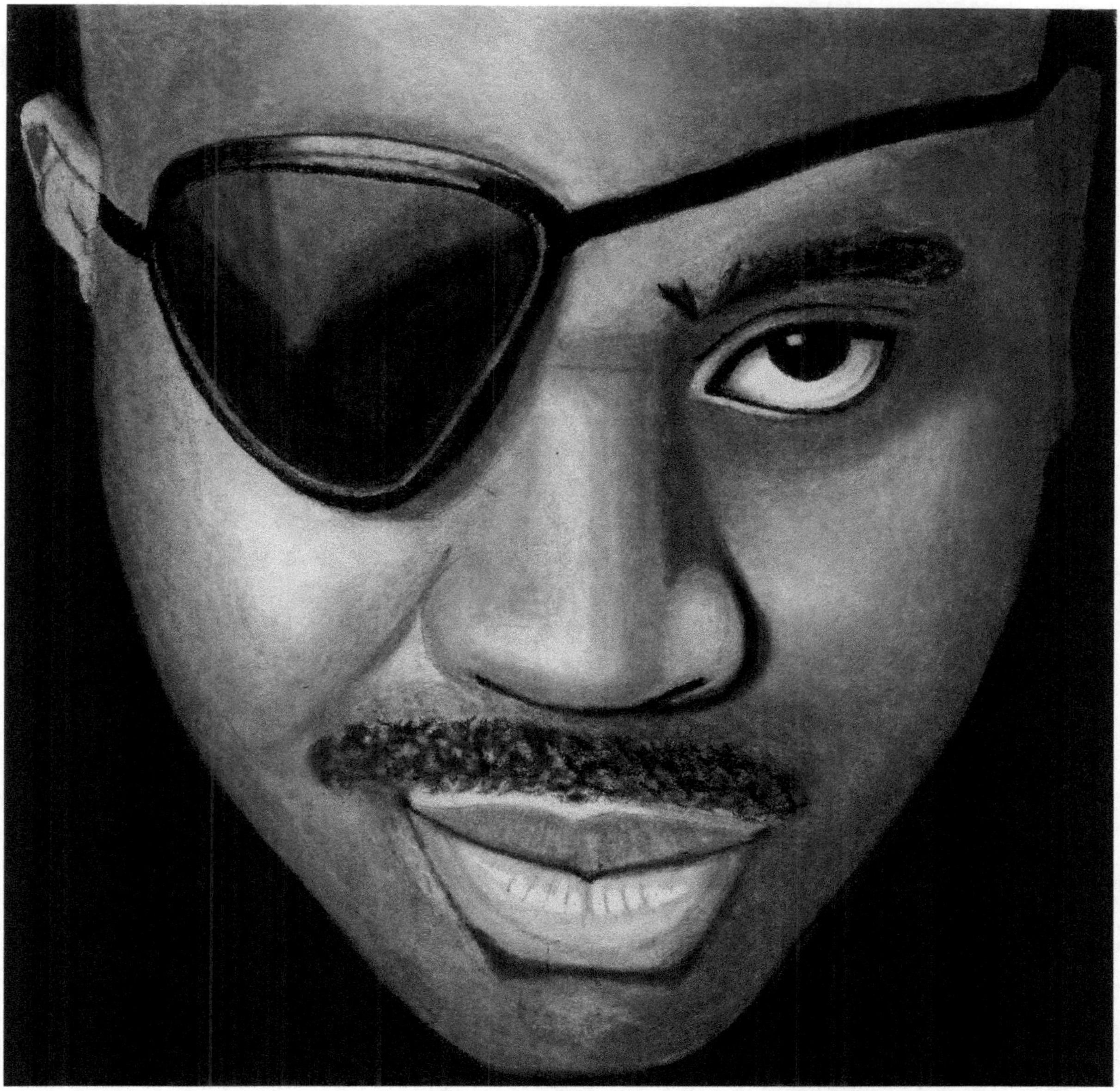

To view how this drawing was masterfully created or to purchase a Limited Edition Framed Artwork of Slick Rick type into your Internet Browser the URL shortcut ➡ **myportrait.art/slickrick**

To listen to his Greatest Songs type into your Internet Browser the URL shortcut ➡ **radio.surf/slickrick**

To view all channels on THE FACE OF MUSIC Internet Radio MEGA Station type into your Internet Browser the URL shortcut ➡ **radio.surf/music**

To inquire about purchasing a Limited Edtion NFT of this portrait type into your Internet Browser the URL shortcut ➡ **myartnft.shop/slickrick**

To view all available NFTs type into your Internet Browser the URL shortcut ➡ **myartnft.shop/all**

# Slim Whitman

(Net worth: $50 Million)(Total Records Sold: 70 Million)
(Genre: Country & Western , Folk)(Height: 6' - 3")

Ottis Dewey Whitman Jr. (January 20, 1923 – June 19, 2013), professionally known by the stage name Slim Whitman, was an American country music singer-songwriter and guitarist known for his yodeling abilities and his smooth, high, three-octave-range falsetto in a style christened as "countrypolitan". He personally stated that he had sold in excess of 120 million records, although the recorded sales figures give 70 million, during a career that spanned over seven decades, and consisted of a prolific output of over 100 albums and around 500 recorded songs, that not only consisted of country music, but also of contemporary gospel, Broadway show tunes, love songs and standards. In the 1950s, Whitman toured with Elvis Presley as the opening act. In the 1990s and 2000s a new generation was exposed to Whitman through his songs featured in the film Mars Attacks!; his famed "Indian Love Call" would kill the invading Martians every time the record was played and his rendition of "I Remember You" was heard in Rob Zombie's House of 1000 Corpses.

Whitman was a self-taught left-handed guitarist, though he was right-handed. He had lost almost all of the second finger on his left hand in an accident while working at a meat packing plant. He worked odd jobs at a Tampa shipyard while developing a musical career, eventually performing with bands such as the Variety Rhythm Boys and the Light Crust Doughboys. He was briefly nicknamed The Smiling Starduster after a stint with a group called The Stardusters. Whitman's first big break came when talent manager "Colonel" Tom Parker heard him singing on the radio and offered to represent him. After signing with RCA Records, he was billed as "the cowboy singer Slim Whitman", after Canadian singer Wilf Carter, who was known in the United States as Montana Slim. Whitman released his first single in 1948, "I'm Casting My Lasso Towards The Sky", complete with yodel. He toured and sang in a variety of venues, including the radio show Louisiana Hayride.

At first he was unable to make a living from music, and kept a part-time job at a post office. That changed in the early 1950s after he recorded a version of the Bob Nolan hit "Love Song of the Waterfall", which made it into the country music top ten. His next single, "Indian Love Call", taken from the light operetta Rose-Marie, was even more successful, reaching number two in the country music charts and appearing in the US pop music chart's top ten.

A yodeller, Whitman avoided country music's "down on yer luck, buried in booze" songs, preferring instead to sing laid-back romantic melodies about simple life and love. Critics dubbed his style "countrypolitan," owing to its fusion of country music and a more sophisticated crooning vocal style. Although he recorded many country and western tunes, including hits "Tumbling Tumbleweeds", "Singing Hills", and "The Cattle Call", love and romance songs like "Serenade", "Something Beautiful (to remember)", and "Keep It a Secret" figured prominently in his repertoire.

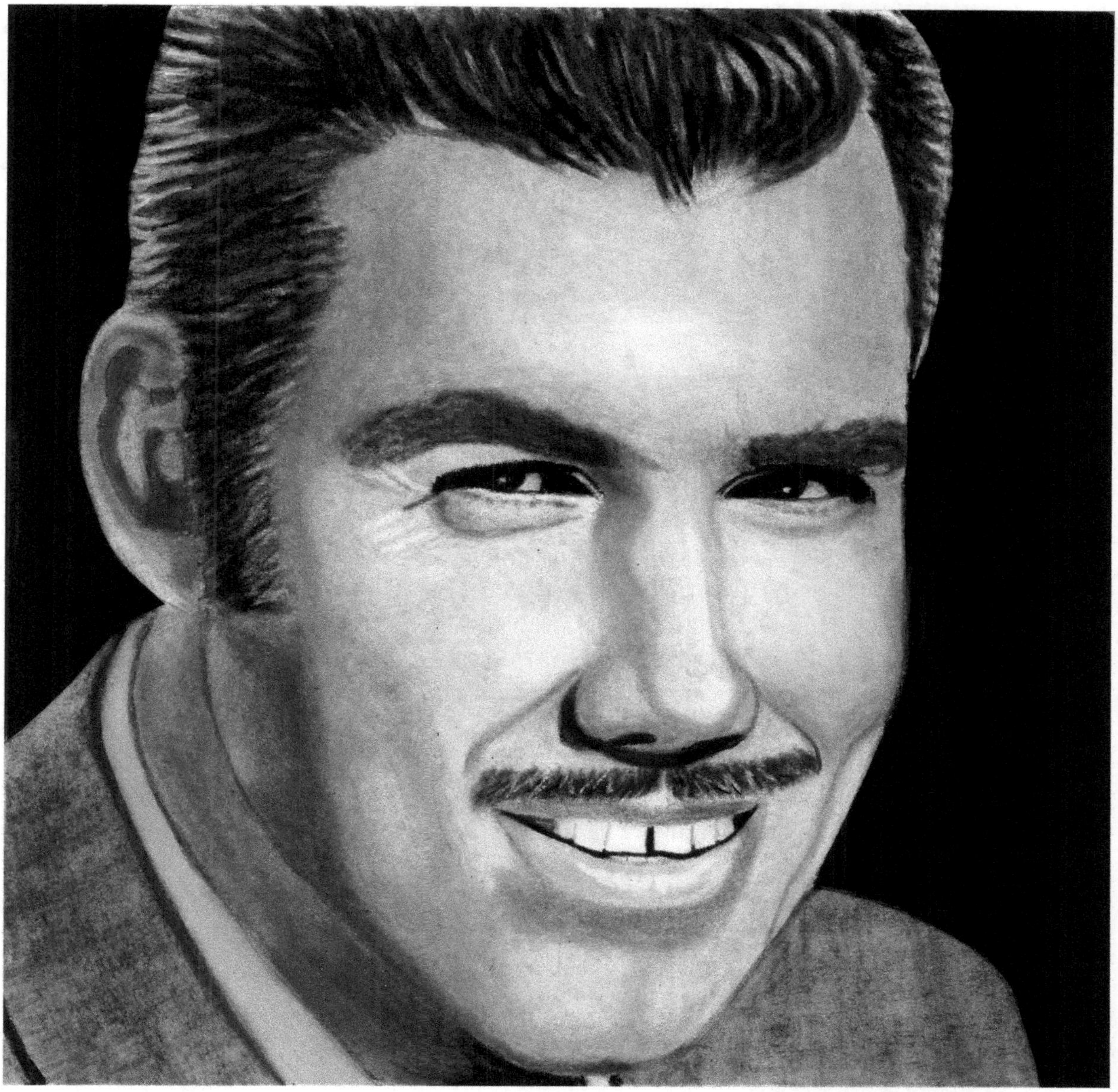

To view how this drawing was masterfully created or to purchase a Limited Edition Framed Artwork of Slim Whitman type into your Internet Browser the URL shortcut ➡ **myportrait.art/slimwhitman**

To listen to his Greatest Songs type into your Internet Browser the URL shortcut ➡ **radio.surf/slimwhitman**

To view all channels on THE FACE OF MUSIC Internet Radio MEGA Station type into your Internet Browser the URL shortcut ➡ **radio.surf/music**

To inquire about purchasing a Limited Edtion NFT of this portrait type into your Internet Browser the URL shortcut ➡ **myartnft.shop/slimwhitman**

To view all available NFTs type into your Internet Browser the URL shortcut ➡ **myartnft.shop/all**

# Smashing Pumpkins, The

(Total Albums Sold: 30 Million) (Genre: Alternative Rock)

The Smashing Pumpkins are an American alternative rock band from Chicago. Formed in 1988 by frontman Billy Corgan (lead vocals, guitar), D'arcy Wretzky (bass), James Iha (guitar), and Jimmy Chamberlin (drums), the band has undergone many line-up changes. The current lineup features Corgan, Chamberlin, Iha and guitarist Jeff Schroeder.

Disavowing the punk rock roots of many of their alt-rock contemporaries, they have a diverse, densely layered, and guitar-heavy sound, containing elements of gothic rock, heavy metal, dream pop, psychedelic rock, progressive rock, shoegazing, and, in later recordings, electronica. Corgan is the group's primary songwriter; his musical ambitions and cathartic lyrics have shaped the band's albums and songs, which have been described as "anguished, bruised reports from Billy Corgan's nightmare-land".

The Smashing Pumpkins broke into the musical mainstream with their second album, 1993's Siamese Dream. The group built its audience with extensive touring and their 1995 follow-up, the double album Mellon Collie and the Infinite Sadness, debuted at number one on the Billboard 200 album chart. With 30 million albums sold worldwide, the Smashing Pumpkins were one of the most commercially successful and critically acclaimed bands of the 1990s. However, internal fighting, drug use, and diminishing record sales led to a 2000 break-up.

In 2006, Corgan and Chamberlin reconvened to record a new Smashing Pumpkins album, Zeitgeist. After touring throughout 2007 and 2008 with a lineup including new guitarist Jeff Schroeder, Chamberlin left the band in early 2009. Later that year, Corgan began a new recording series with a rotating lineup of musicians entitled Teargarden by Kaleidyscope, which encompassed the release of stand-alone singles, compilation EP releases, and two full albums that also fell under the project's scope —Oceania in 2012 and Monuments to an Elegy in 2014. Chamberlin and Iha officially rejoined the band in February 2018. The reunited lineup released the album Shiny and Oh So Bright, Vol. 1 / LP: No Past. No Future. No Sun. in November 2018 and Cyr in November 2020.

# Billy Corgan

(Net Worth: $60 Million)(Height: 6' - 3")

William Patrick Corgan (March 17, 1967) is an American musician, singer, songwriter, and professional wrestling promoter. He is best known as the lead singer, primary songwriter, guitarist, and only permanent member of the rock band the Smashing Pumpkins. He is currently the owner and promoter of the National Wrestling Alliance (NWA).

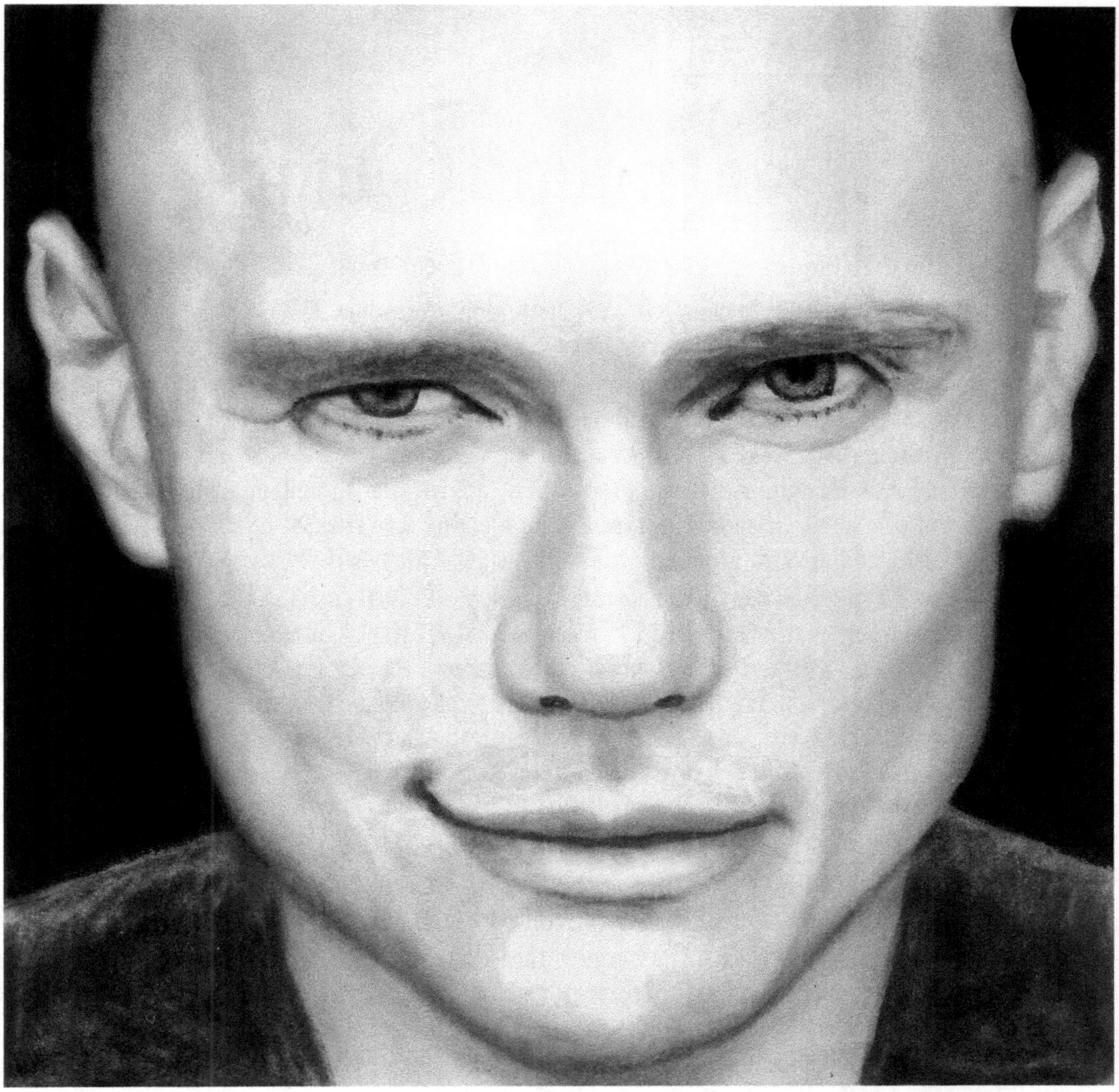

To view how this drawing was masterfully created or to purchase a Limited Edition Framed Artwork of Billy Corgan type into your Internet Browser the URL shortcut ➡ **myportrait.art/billycorgan**

To listen to their Greatest Songs type into your Internet Browser the URL shortcut ➡ **radio.surf/thesmashingpumpkins**

To view all channels on THE FACE OF MUSIC Internet Radio MEGA Station type into your Internet Browser the URL shortcut ➡ **radio.surf/music**

To inquire about purchasing a Limited Edtion NFT of this portrait type into your Internet Browser the URL shortcut ➡ **myartnft.shop/billycorgan**

To view all available NFTs type into your Internet Browser the URL shortcut ➡ **myartnft.shop/all**

# Snoop Dogg

(Net worth: $150 Million)(Total Albums Sold: 37 Million)
(Genre: Hip-Hop , Funk , Gangsta Rap , Reggae)(Height: 6' - 4")

Calvin Cordozar Broadus Jr. (born October 20, 1971), known professionally as Snoop Dogg (previously Snoop Doggy Dogg and briefly Snoop Lion), is an American rapper, singer, songwriter, actor, record producer, media personality, and businessman. His fame dates to 1992 when he featured on Dr. Dre's debut solo single, "Deep Cover," and then on Dre's debut solo album, The Chronic. Snoop has since sold over 23 million albums in the United States and 35 million albums worldwide.

Snoop's debut solo album, Doggystyle, produced by Dr. Dre, was released by Death Row Records in November 1993, and debuted at number one on the popular albums chart, the Billboard 200, and on Billboard's Top R&B/Hip-Hop Albums chart. Selling 800,000 copies in its first week, Doggystyle was certified quadruple-platinum in 1994 and bore several hit singles, including "What's My Name?" and "Gin & Juice." In 1994, Death Row Records released a soundtrack, by Snoop, for the short film Murder Was the Case, starring Snoop. In 1996, his second album, Tha Doggfather, also debuted at number one on both charts, with "Snoop's Upside Ya Head" as the lead single. The next year, the album was certified double-platinum.

After leaving Death Row Records in January 1998, Snoop signed with No Limit Records, releasing three Snoop albums: Da Game is to Be Sold, Not to Be Told (1998), No Limit Top Dogg (1999), and Tha Last Meal (2000). In 2002, he signed with Priority/Capitol/EMI Records, releasing Paid tha Cost to Be da Boss. In 2004, he signed to Geffen Records, releasing his next three albums: R&G (Rhythm & Gangsta): The Masterpiece, then Tha Blue Carpet Treatment, and Ego Trippin'. Priority Records released his album Malice 'n Wonderland during 2009, followed by Doggumentary during 2011. Snoop Dogg has starred in motion pictures and hosted several television shows, including Doggy Fizzle Televizzle, Snoop Dogg's Father Hood, and Dogg After Dark. He also coaches a youth football league and high-school football team. In September 2009, EMI hired him as the chairman of a reactivated Priority Records.

In 2012, after a trip to Jamaica, Snoop announced a conversion to Rastafari and a new alias, Snoop Lion. As Snoop Lion he released a reggae album, Reincarnated, and a documentary film of the same name, about his Jamaican experience, in early 2013. His 13th studio album, Bush, was released in May 2015 and marked a return of the Snoop Dogg name. His 14th solo studio album, Coolaid, was released in July 2016. Snoop has 17 Grammy nominations without a win. In March 2016, the night before WrestleMania 32 in Arlington, Texas, he was inducted into the celebrity wing of the WWE Hall of Fame, having made several appearances for the company, including as master of ceremonies during a match at WrestleMania XXIV. In 2018, Snoop announced that he was "a born-again Christian" and released his first gospel album Bible of Love. On November 19, 2018, Snoop Dogg was given a star on the Hollywood Walk of Fame. He released his seventeenth solo album, I Wanna Thank Me, in 2019

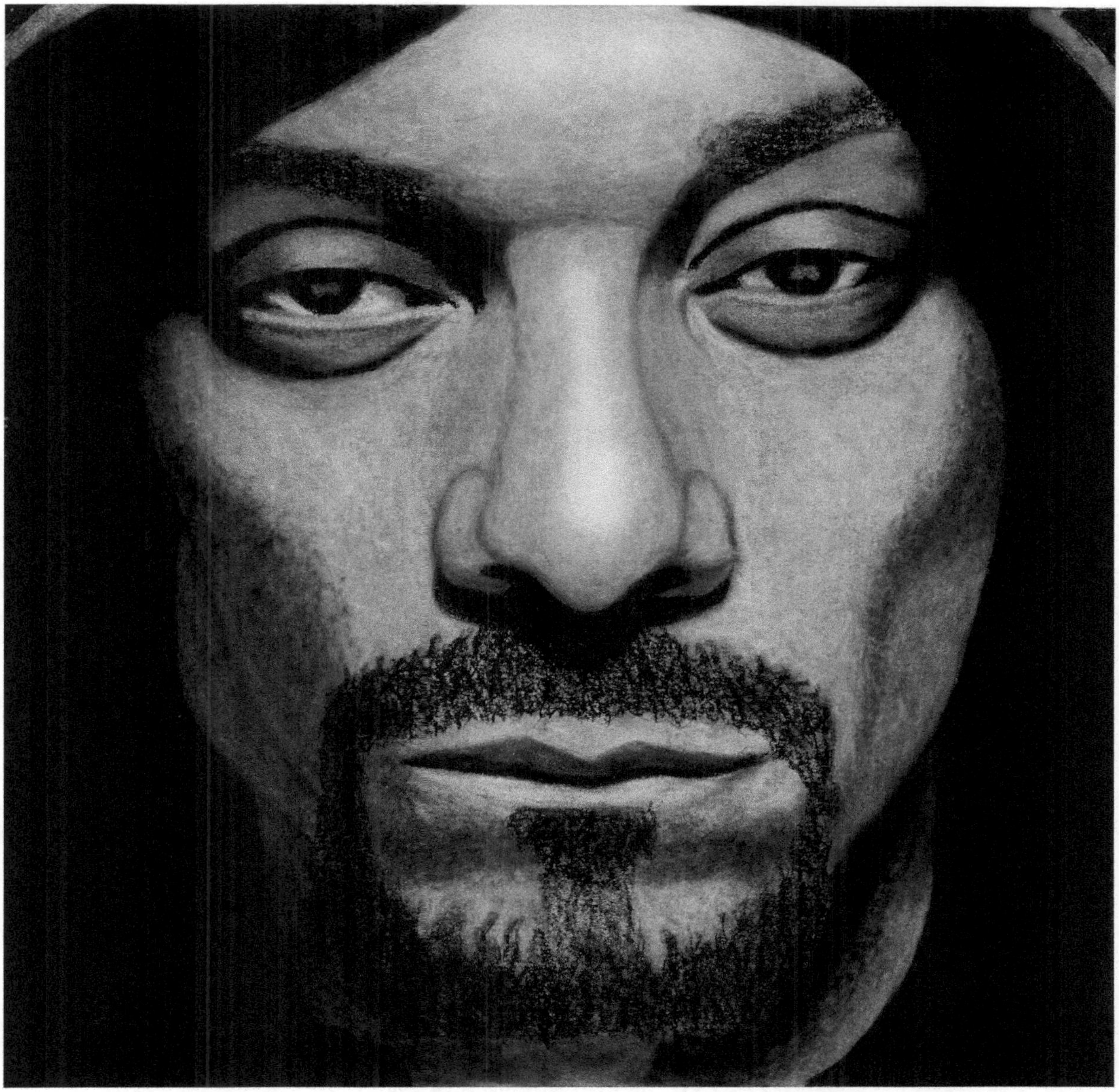

To view how this drawing was masterfully created or to purchase a Limited Edition Framed Artwork of Snoop Dogg type into your Internet Browser the URL shortcut ➡ **myportrait.art/snoopdogg**

To listen to his Greatest Songs type into your Internet Browser the URL shortcut ➡ **radio.surf/snoopdogg**

To view all channels on THE FACE OF MUSIC Internet Radio MEGA Station type into your Internet Browser the URL shortcut ➡ **radio.surf/music**

To inquire about purchasing a Limited Edtion NFT of this portrait type into your Internet Browser the URL shortcut ➡ **myartnft.shop/snoopdogg**

To view all available NFTs type into your Internet Browser the URL shortcut ➡ **myartnft.shop/all**

# Soundgarden

(Total Records Sold: 25 Million) (Genre: Grunge , Alternative Rock)

Soundgarden was an American rock band formed in Seattle, Washington, in 1984 by singer and rhythm guitarist Chris Cornell, lead guitarist Kim Thayil (both of whom are the only members to appear in every incarnation of the band), and bassist Hiro Yamamoto. Matt Cameron became the band's full-time drummer in 1986, while bassist Ben Shepherd became a permanent replacement for Yamamoto in 1990. The band dissolved in 1997 and re-formed in 2010. Following Cornell's death in 2017 and a year of uncertainty of the band's future, Thayil declared in October 2018 that the band was finished; they did, however, reunite in January 2019 for a one-off concert in tribute to Cornell.

Soundgarden was one of the seminal creators of grunge, a style of alternative rock that developed in Seattle, and was the first of a number of grunge bands to sign to the record label Sub Pop. Soundgarden was also one of the first grunge bands to sign to a major label (A&M Records in 1989), though they did not achieve commercial success until they popularized the genre in the early 1990s with Seattle contemporaries Alice in Chains, Pearl Jam, and Nirvana.Soundgarden achieved its biggest success with the 1994 album Superunknown, which debuted at number one on the Billboard 200 and yielded the Grammy Award-winning singles "Spoonman" and "Black Hole Sun". In 1997, the band broke up due to internal strife over its creative direction and exhaustion from touring. After more than a decade of working on projects and other bands, Soundgarden reunited in 2010, and Republic Records released their sixth and final studio album, King Animal, two years later. As of 2012, Soundgarden sold more than 10.5 million records in the United States, and an estimated 25 million worldwide. VH1 ranked Soundgarden at number 14 in their special 100 Greatest Artists of Hard Rock.

# Chris Cornell

(Net Worth: $40 Million)(Height: 6' - 2")

Christopher John Cornell (July 20, 1964 – May 18, 2017) was an American singer, songwriter, and musician best known as the lead vocalist and rhythm guitarist for the rock bands Soundgarden and Audioslave. He also had a solo career and contributed to soundtracks. Cornell was also the founder and frontman of Temple of the Dog, a one-off tribute band dedicated to his late friend Andrew Wood.Cornell is considered one of the key figures of the 1990s grunge movement, and is well known for his extensive catalog as a songwriter, his nearly four-octave vocal range, and his powerful vocal belting technique. He released four solo studio albums, Euphoria Morning (1999), Carry On (2007), Scream (2009), and Higher Truth (2015); the live album Songbook (2011); and two compilations, The Roads We Choose (2007) and Chris Cornell (2018), the latter released posthumously. He received a Golden Globe Award nomination for his song "The Keeper", which appeared in the 2011 film Machine Gun Preacher, and co-wrote and performed "You Know My Name", the theme song to the 2006 James Bond film Casino Royale. His last solo release before his death was the charity single "The Promise", written for the ending credits for the 2016 film of the same name.Cornell struggled with depression for most of his life. He was found dead in his Detroit hotel room in the early hours of May 18, 2017, after performing at a Soundgarden concert an hour earlier at the Fox Theatre. His death was ruled a suicide by hanging.

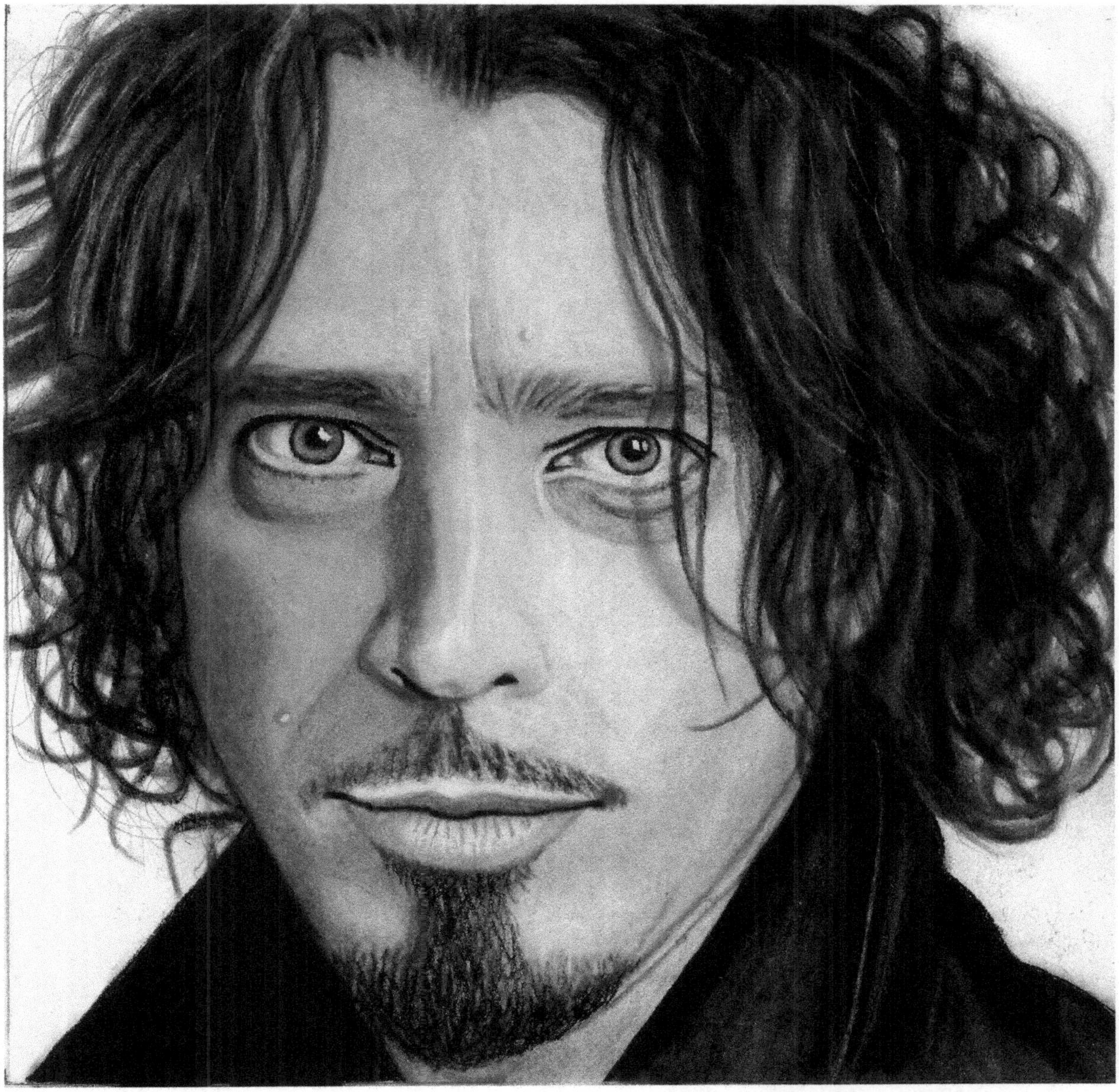

To view how this drawing was masterfully created or to purchase a Limited Edition Framed Artwork of Chris Cornell type into your Internet Browser the URL shortcut ➡ **myportrait.art/chriscornell**

To listen to their Greatest Songs type into ycur Internet Browser the URL shortcut ➡ **radio.surf/soundgarden**

To view all channels on THE FACE OF MUSIC Internet Radio MEGA Station type into your Internet Browser the URL shortcut ➡ **radio.surf/music**

To inquire about purchasing a Limited Edtion NFT of this portrait type into your Internet Browser the URL shortcut ➡ **myartnft.shop/chriscornell**

To view all available NFTs type into your Internet Browser the URL shortcut ➡ **myartnft.shop/all**

# Steely Dan

(Total Records Sold: 40+Million) (Genre: Jazz Rock , Soft Rock , Pop Rock)

Steely Dan is an American rock band founded in 1971 by core members Walter Becker (guitars, bass, backing vocals) and Donald Fagen (keyboards, lead vocals). Blending elements of rock, jazz, latin music, R&B, blues and sophisticated studio production with cryptic and ironic lyrics, the band enjoyed critical and commercial success starting from the early 1970s until breaking up in 1981. Initially the band had a core lineup, but in 1974, Becker and Fagen retired the band from live performances altogether to become a studio-only band, opting to record with a revolving cast of session musicians. Rolling Stone has called them "the perfect musical antiheroes for the Seventies".

After the group disbanded in 1981, Becker and Fagen were less active throughout most of the next decade, though a cult following remained devoted to the group. Since reuniting in 1993, Steely Dan has toured steadily and released two albums of new material, the first of which, Two Against Nature, earned a Grammy Award for Album of the Year. They have sold more than 40 million albums worldwide and were inducted into the Rock and Roll Hall of Fame in March 2001. VH1 ranked Steely Dan at No. 82 on their list of the 100 Greatest Musical Artists of All Time. Rolling Stone ranked them No. 15 on its list of the 20 Greatest Duos of All Time. Founding member Walter Becker died on September 3, 2017, leaving Fagen as the sole official member.

# Donald Fagen

(Net Worth: $50 Million)(Height: 5' - 8")

Donald Jay Fagen (born January 10, 1948) is an American musician best known as the co-founder, lead singer, co-songwriter, and keyboardist of the band Steely Dan, formed in the early 1970s. He has also released four albums as a solo artist and in 2001 was inducted into the Rock and Roll Hall of Fame. The 2017 death of Steely Dan's co-founder Walter Becker left Fagen as the only remaining original member.

Donald Fagen met Walter Becker in a coffee house at Bard College in 1967. They began to form Steely Dan in the summer of 1970, after a Village Voice ad for a bassist and keyboard player with jazz chops was placed by guitarist Denny Dias, which was answered by Fagen and Becker. Dias was immediately impressed by the pair's abilities, and particularly by the fact that they already had a whole stack of original material. The group's first lineup was assembled in December 1971 in Los Angeles, where Becker and Fagen had relocated to work as staff songwriters for ABC/Dunhill. Becker and Fagen formed the core of the band and wrote all the songs, with Becker on bass, and later lead guitar, and Fagen on keyboards and vocals.

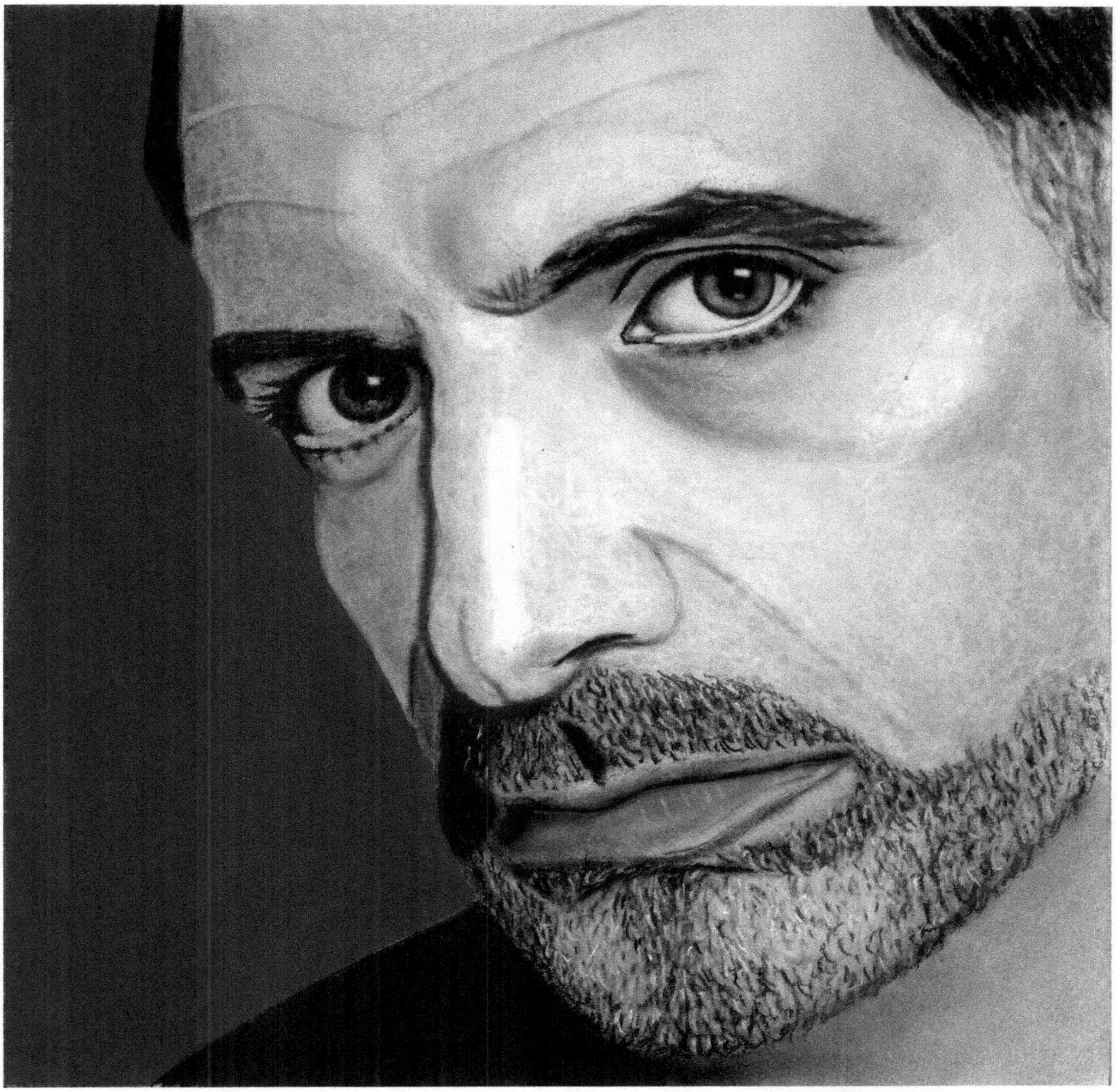

To view how this drawing was masterfully created or to purchase a Limited Edition Framed Artwork of Donald Fagen type into your Internet Browser the URL shortcut ➡ **myportrait.art/donaldfagen**

To listen to their Greatest Songs type into your Internet Browser the URL shortcut ➡ **radio.surf/steelydan**

To view all channels on THE FACE OF MUSIC Internet Radio MEGA Station type into your Internet Browser the URL shortcut ➡ **radio.surf/music**

To inquire about purchasing a Limited Edtion NFT of this portrait type into your Internet Browser the URL shortcut ➡ **myartnft.shop/donaldfagen**

To view all available NFTs type into your Internet Browser the URL shortcut ➡ **myartnft.shop/all**

# Steppenwolf

(Total Records Sold: 25+Million) (Genre: Psychedelic Rock , Hard Rock , Blues Rock)

Steppenwolf was a Canadian-American rock band, prominent from 1968 to 1972. The group was formed in late 1967 in Los Angeles by lead singer John Kay, keyboardist Goldy McJohn, and drummer Jerry Edmonton, all formerly of the Canadian band the Sparrows. Guitarist Michael Monarch and bass guitarist Rushton Moreve were recruited via notices placed in Los Angeles-area record and musical instrument stores.

Steppenwolf sold over 25 million records worldwide, released seven gold albums and one platinum album, and had 13 Billboard Hot 100 singles, of which seven were Top 40 hits, including three top 10 successes: "Born to Be Wild", "Magic Carpet Ride", and "Rock Me". Steppenwolf enjoyed worldwide success from 1968 to 1972, but clashing personalities led to the end of the core lineup. Today, John Kay is the only original member, having been the lead singer since 1967. The band was called John Kay & Steppenwolf from 1980 to 2018.

In 2016, The Rock and Roll Hall of Fame saw fit to nominate them for induction in 2017. Although they fell short of enough votes to qualify for induction that year, in 2018 The Rock and Roll Hall of Fame selected one of their biggest singles - 1968's "Born to Be Wild" - as one of the first five singles that shaped rock and roll to be inducted into the hall in its history.

In late 1967, Gabriel Mekler urged Kay to re-form the Sparrows and suggested the name change to Steppenwolf, inspired by Hermann Hesse's 1927 novel of the same name. Steppenwolf's first two singles were "A Girl I Knew" and "Sookie Sookie". The band finally rocketed to worldwide fame after their third single, "Born to Be Wild", was released in 1968, as well as their version of Hoyt Axton's "The Pusher". Both of these tunes were used prominently in the 1969 counterculture cult film Easy Rider (both titles originally had been released on the band's debut album). In the movie, "The Pusher" accompanies a drug deal, and Peter Fonda stuffing dollar bills into his Stars and Stripes-clad fuel tank, after which "Born to Be Wild" is heard in the opening credits, with Fonda and Dennis Hopper riding their Harley choppers through the America of the late 1960s. The song, which has been closely associated with motorcycles ever since, introduced to rock lyrics the signature term "heavy metal" (though not about a kind of music, but about a motorcycle: "I like smoke and lightning, heavy metal thunder, racin' with the wind...").

# John Kay

(Net Worth: $6 Million)(Height: 5' - 10")

John Kay (born Joachim Fritz Krauledat, 12 April 1944) is a German-born Canadian rock singer, songwriter, and guitarist known as the frontman of Steppenwolf.

In 2004, although he never became a Canadian citizen, Kay was inducted into Canada's Walk of Fame in recognition of the beginning of his musical career in Toronto. Kay was present at the induction ceremony in Toronto and reiterated his strong affection for Canada.

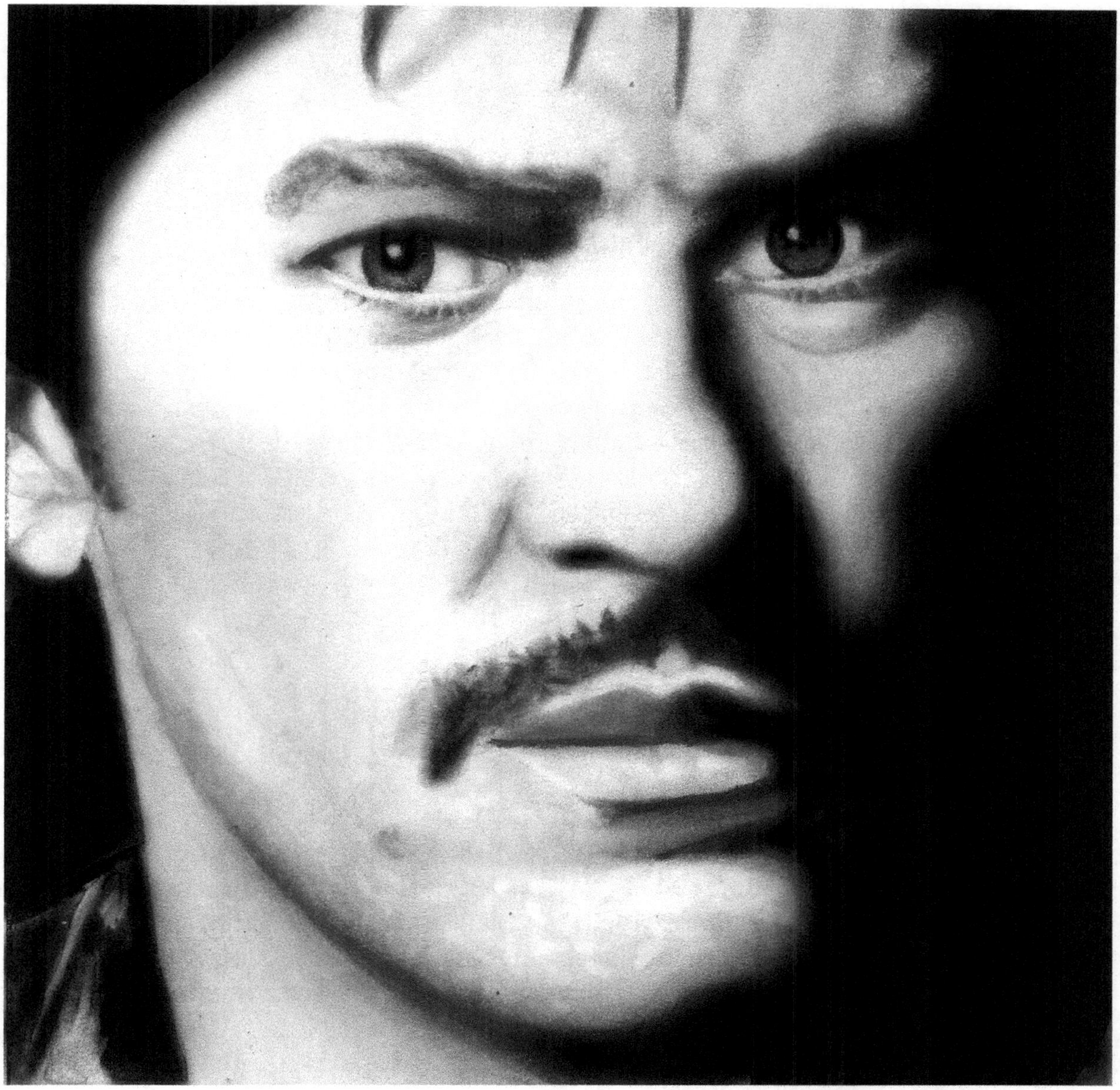

To view how this drawing was masterfully created or to purchase a Limited Edition Framed Artwork of John Kay type into your Internet Browser the URL shortcut ➡ **myportrait.art/johnkay**

To listen to their Greatest Songs type into your Internet Browser the URL shortcut ➡ **radio.surf/steppenwolf**

To view all channels on THE FACE OF MUSIC Internet Radio MEGA Station type into your Internet Browser the URL shortcut ➡ **radio.surf/music**

To inquire about purchasing a Limited Edtion NFT of this portrait type into your Internet Browser the URL shortcut ➡ **myartnft.shop/johnkay**

To view all available NFTs type into your Internet Browser the URL shortcut ➡ **myartnft.shop/all**

# Steve Miller Band

(Total Records Sold: 50+ Million) (Genre: Classic Rock)

The Steve Miller Band is an American rock band formed in 1966 in San Francisco, California. The band is led by Steve Miller on guitar and lead vocals. The group had a string of mid- to late-1970s hit singles that are staples of classic rock radio, as well as several earlier psychedelic rock albums. Miller left his first band to move to San Francisco and form the Steve Miller Blues Band. Shortly after Harvey Kornspan negotiated the band's contract with Capitol Records in 1967, the band shortened its name to the Steve Miller Band. In February 1968, the band recorded its debut album, Children of the Future. It went on to produce the albums Sailor, Brave New World, Your Saving Grace, Number 5, Rock Love, Fly Like an Eagle, Book of Dreams, among others. The band's Greatest Hits 1974–78, released in 1978, sold over 13 million copies. In 2016, Steve Miller was inducted as a solo artist in the Rock and Roll Hall of Fame.

# Steve Miller

(Net Worth: $60 Million)(Height: 6' - 2")

Steven Haworth Miller (born October 5, 1943) is an American guitarist, singer and songwriter, known as leader of the Steve Miller Band. He began his career in blues and blues rock and evolved to a more pop-oriented sound during the mid-1970s through the early 1980s, releasing popular singles and albums. Miller was inducted into the Rock and Roll Hall of Fame in 2016.

Born in Milwaukee, Wisconsin, Miller received his first exposure to music from his mother, Bertha, whom he described as a remarkable jazz-influenced singer, and his physician father, George, known as "Sonny" who, in addition to his profession as a pathologist, was a jazz enthusiast and an accomplished amateur recording engineer. Guitar virtuoso Les Paul and his musical partner Mary Ford were regular visitors at the Miller house. The Millers were best man and matron of honor at the December 1949 Paul/Ford wedding. Paul became Steve's godfather. Les Paul heard Steve, who was six, on a wire recording made by Dr. Miller, "banging away" on a guitar given to him by his uncle, Dr. K. Dale Atterbury. Paul encouraged Miller to continue with his interest in the guitar... and "perhaps he will be something one day."

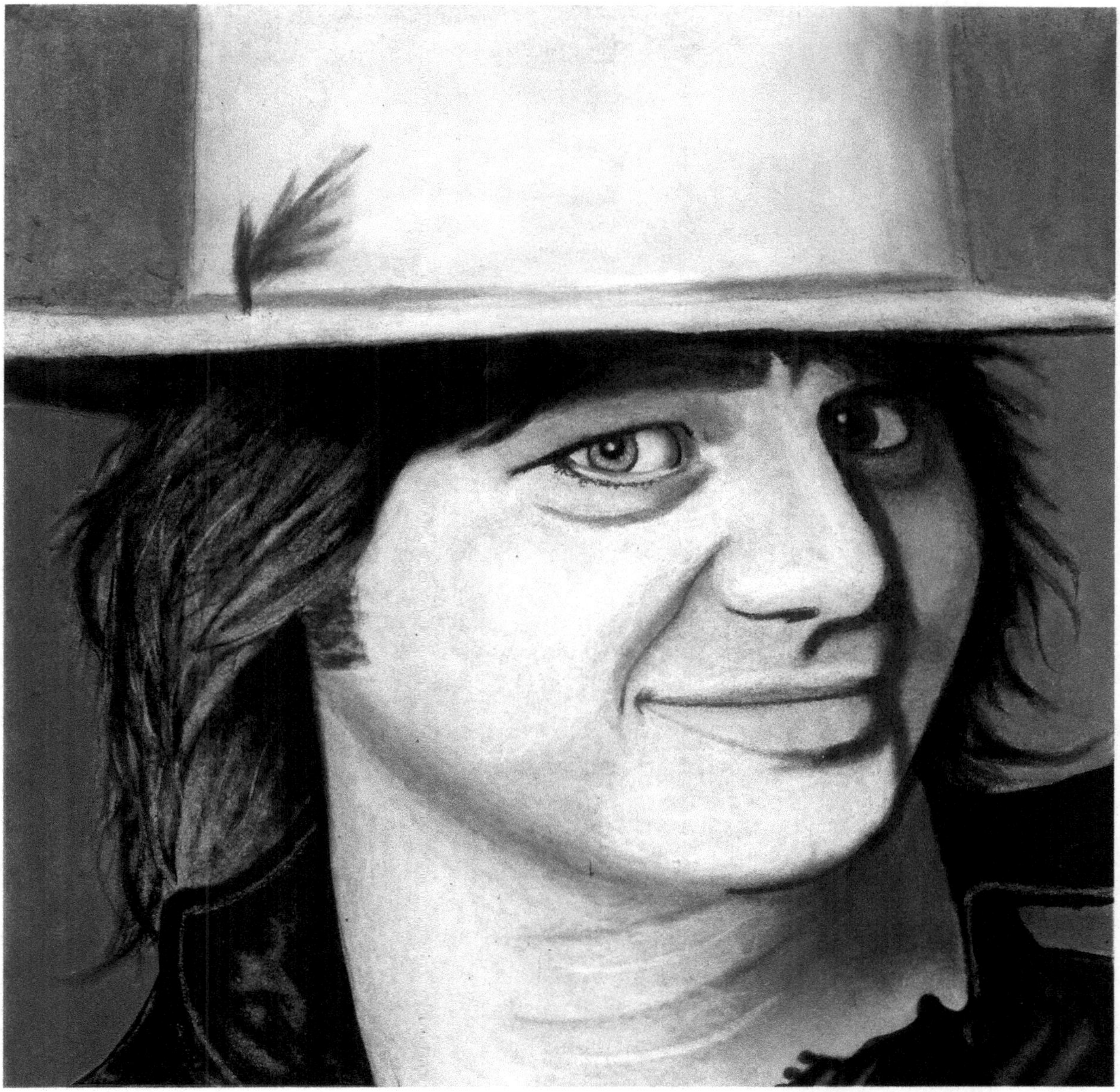

To view how this drawing was masterfully created or to purchase a Limited Edition Framed Artwork of Steve Miller type into your Internet Browser the URL shortcut ➡ **myportrait.art/stevemiller**

To listen to their Greatest Songs type into your Internet Browser the URL shortcut ➡ **radio.surf/stevemillerband**

To view all channels on THE FACE OF MUSIC Internet Radio MEGA Station type into your Internet Browser the URL shortcut ➡ **radio.surf/music**

To inquire about purchasing a Limited Edtion NFT of this portrait type into your Internet Browser the URL shortcut ➡ **myartnft.shop/stevemiller**

To view all available NFTs type into your Internet Browser the URL shortcut ➡ **myartnft.shop/all**

# Stevie Ray Vaughan

(Net worth: $8 Million)(Total Albums Sold: 15 Million)
(Genre: Blues Rock)(Height: 5' - 4")

Stephen Ray Vaughan (October 3, 1954 – August 27, 1990) was an American musician, singer, songwriter, and record producer, best known as the guitarist and frontman of the blues rock band Double Trouble. Although his mainstream career only spanned seven years, he is considered to be one of the most iconic and influential musicians in the history of blues music, and one of the greatest guitarists of all time. Born and raised in Dallas, Texas, Vaughan began playing guitar at age seven, initially inspired by his elder brother Jimmie Vaughan. In 1972, he dropped out of high school and moved to Austin, where he began to gain a following after playing gigs on the local club circuit. Vaughan formed the band Double Trouble in 1978 and established it as part of the Austin music scene, which soon became one of the most popular acts in Texas. He performed at the Montreux Jazz Festival in 1982 where David Bowie saw him play and contacted him for a studio gig, resulting in Stevie playing his blues guitar on the album Let's Dance (1983) before being discovered by John Hammond, who interested major label Epic Records in signing them to a record deal. Within months, Vaughan achieved mainstream success with Double Trouble for the critically acclaimed debut album Texas Flood. With a series of successful network television appearances and extensive concert tours, he became the leading figure in the blues revival of the 1980s. Playing his guitar behind his back or plucking the strings with his teeth like Jimi Hendrix did, he earned unprecedented stardom in Europe which later resulted in breakthroughs for guitar players like Robert Cray, Jeff Healey, Robben Ford and Walter Trout, amongst others.

During the majority of his life, Vaughan struggled with drug and alcohol addiction. He also struggled with the personal and professional pressures of fame, and his marriage to Lenora "Lenny" Bailey. He successfully completed rehabilitation and began touring again with Double Trouble in November 1986. His fourth and final studio album In Step reached number 33 in the United States in 1989; it was one of Vaughan's most critically and commercially successful releases and included his only number-one hit "Crossfire". He became one of the world's most highly demanded blues performers, and he headlined Madison Square Garden in 1989 and the Beale Street Music Festival in 1990.

On August 27, 1990, Vaughan and four others were killed in a helicopter crash in East Troy, Wisconsin, after performing with Double Trouble at Alpine Valley Music Theatre. An investigation concluded that the cause was pilot error and Vaughan's family later filed a wrongful death lawsuit against Omniflight Helicopters, which was settled out of court. Vaughan's music continued to achieve commercial success with several posthumous releases and has sold over 15 million albums in the United States alone. In 2003, David Fricke of Rolling Stone ranked him the seventh greatest guitarist of all time. Vaughan was posthumously inducted into the Rock and Roll Hall of Fame in 2015, along with Double Trouble bandmates Chris Layton, Tommy Shannon, and Reese Wynans.

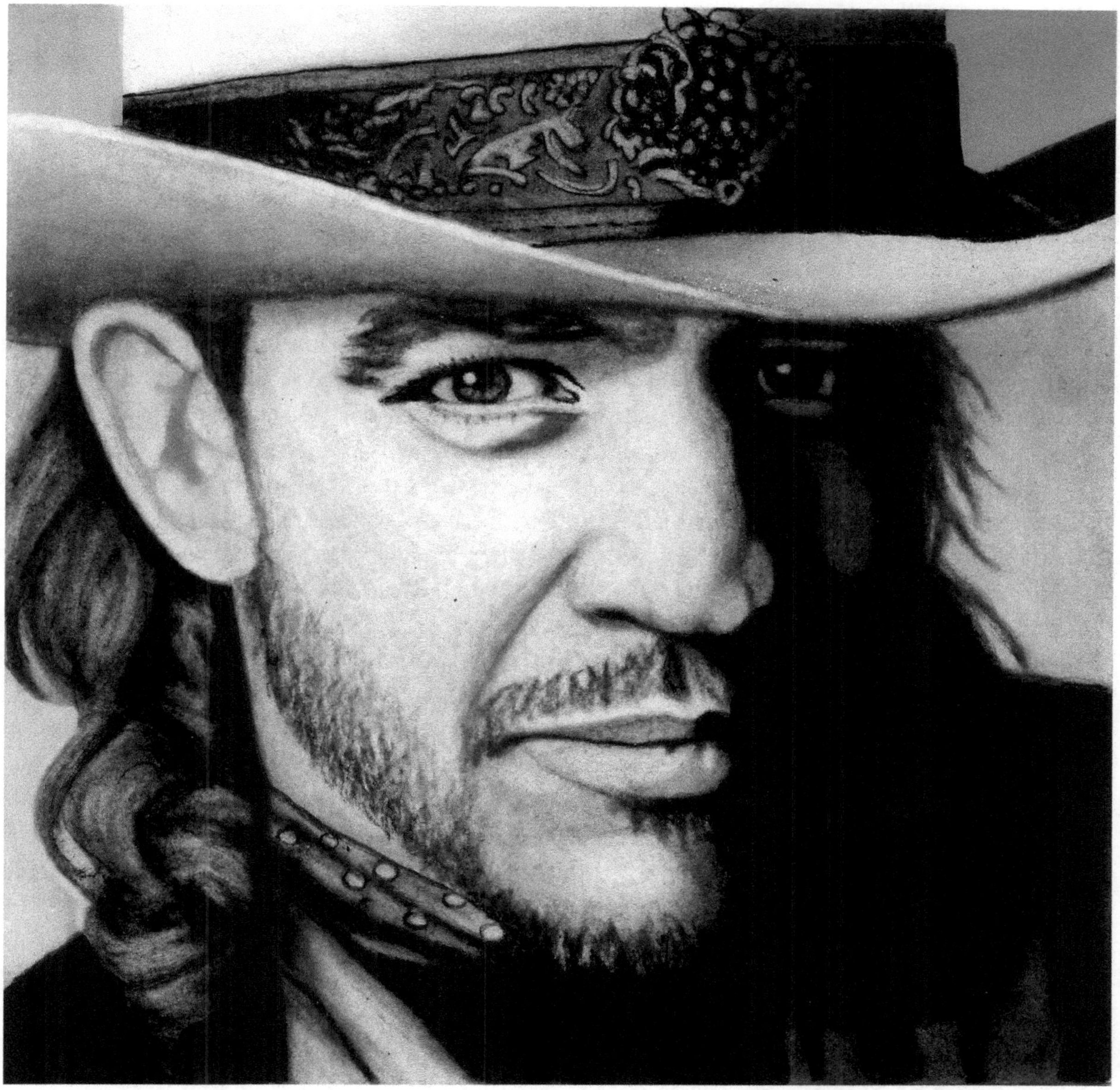

To view how this drawing was masterfully created or to purchase a Limited Edition Framed Artwork of Stevie Ray Vaughan type into your Internet Browser the URL shortcut ➡ **myportrait.art/stevierayvaughan**

To listen to his Greatest Songs type into your Internet Browser the URL shortcut
➡ **radio.surf/stevierayvaughan**

To view all channels on THE FACE OF MUSIC Internet Radio MEGA Station type into your Internet Browser the URL shortcut ➡ **radio.surf/music**

To inquire about purchasing a Limited Edtion NFT of this portrait type into your Internet Browser the URL shortcut ➡ **myartnft.shop/stevierayvaughan**

To view all available NFTs type into your Internet Browser the URL shortcut ➡ **myartnft.shop/all**

# Stevie Wonder

(Net worth: $110 Million)(Total Records Sold: 100+ Million)
(Genre: R&B, Pop, Soul, Gospel, Funk, Jazz)(Height: 6' - 0")

Stevland Hardaway Morris (born May 13, 1950), known professionally as Stevie Wonder, is an American singer, songwriter, musician and record producer. A prominent figure in popular music during the second half of the 20th century, Wonder is one of the most successful songwriters and musicians. A virtual one-man band, his use of synthesizers and further electronic musical instruments during the 1970s reshaped the conventions of R&B. He also helped drive the genre into the album era, crafting his LPs as cohesive, consistent socially conscious statements with complex compositions. Wonder is often hailed as a "genius", and has been credited as a pioneer and influence to musicians of various genres including rhythm and blues, pop, soul, gospel, funk, and jazz.

Blind since shortly after his birth, Wonder was a child prodigy known as Little Stevie Wonder, leading him to sign with Motown's Tamla label at the age of 11. In 1963, the single "Fingertips" was a number-one hit on the Billboard Hot 100 when Wonder was 13, making him the youngest artist ever to top the chart. Wonder's critical success was at its peak in the 1970s. His "classic period" began in 1972 with the releases of Music of My Mind and Talking Book, the latter featuring "Superstition", which is one of the most distinctive and famous examples of the sound of the Hohner Clavinet keyboard. His works Innervisions (1973), Fulfillingness' First Finale (1974) and Songs in the Key of Life (1976) all won the Grammy Award for Album of the Year, making him the tied-record holder for the most Album of the Year wins, with three. He is also the only artist to have won the award with three consecutive album releases.

Wonder's "classic period", which culminated in 1976, was marked by his funky keyboard style, personal control of production, and use of integrated series of songs to make concept albums. In 1979, Wonder used Computer Music Inc.'s early music sampler, the Melodian, on his soundtrack album Stevie Wonder's Journey Through "The Secret Life of Plants". This was his first digital recording and one of the earliest popular albums to use the technology, which Wonder used for all subsequent recordings. The pioneering stylistics of Wonder's 1970s albums are widely regarded as having influenced the shape of pop music in the following decade.

Wonder has sold over 100 million records worldwide, making him one of the best-selling music artists of all time. He has won 22 Grammy Awards. He was the first Motown artist and second African-American musician to win an Academy Award for Best Original Song, for the 1984 film The Woman in Red. Wonder has been inducted into the Rhythm and Blues Music Hall of Fame, Rock and Roll Hall of Fame and Songwriters Hall of Fame, and has received a star on the Hollywood Walk of Fame. He is also noted for his work as an activist for political causes, including his 1980 campaign to make Martin Luther King Jr.'s birthday a federal holiday in the United States. In 2009, he was named a United Nations Messenger of Peace. In 2014, he was honored with the Presidential Medal of Freedom.

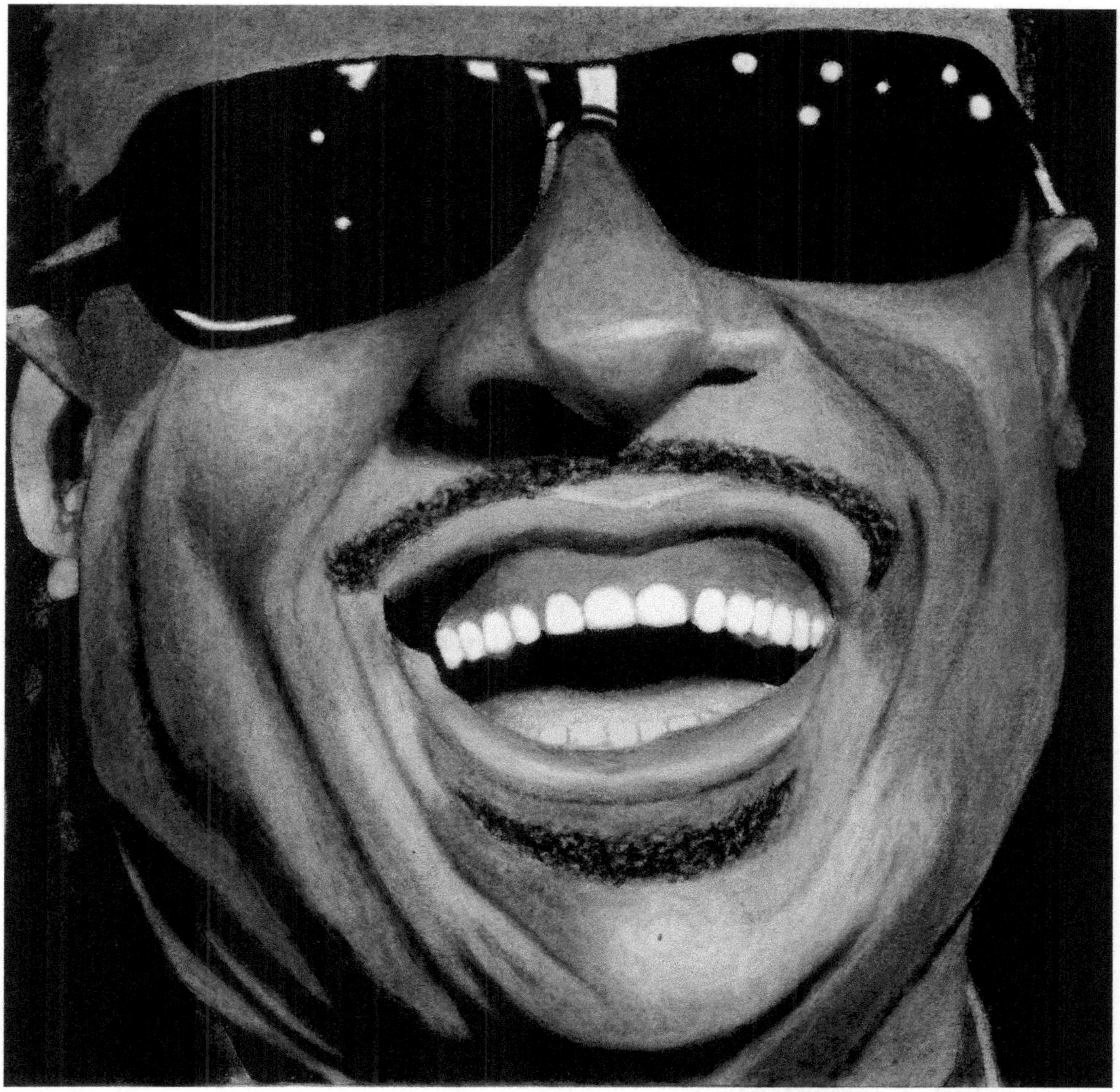

To view how this drawing was masterfully created or to purchase a Limited Edition Framed Artwork of Stevie Wonder type into your Internet Browser the URL shortcut ➡ **myportrait.art/steviewonder**

To listen to his Greatest Songs type into your Internet Browser the URL shortcut
➡ **radio.surf/steviewonder**

To view all channels on THE FACE OF MUSIC Internet Radio MEGA Station type into your Internet Browser the URL shortcut ➡ **radio.surf/music**

To inquire about purchasing a Limited Edtion NFT of this portrait type into your Internet Browser the URL shortcut ➡ **myartnft.shop/steviewonder**

To view all available NFTs type into your Internet Browser the URL shortcut ➡ **myartnft.shop/all**

# Styx

(Total Records Sold: 54+ Million) (Genre: Classic Rock)

Styx is an American rock band from Chicago that formed in 1972 and is best known for melding hard rock guitar balanced with acoustic guitar, synthesizers mixed with acoustic piano, upbeat tracks with power ballads, and incorporating elements of international musical theatre. The band established itself with a progressive rock sound in the 1970s, and began to incorporate pop rock and soft rock elements in the 1980s.Beginning with Styx in 1972, the band usually released an album a year. Styx II (1973) had the sleeper hit, "Lady," a power ballad which reached No. 6 in the US helping the album make the Top 20. "Lady" was also a Top 20 hit in Canada, Australia and New Zealand. Equinox (1975) and Crystal Ball (1976) reached the US Top 70 with the first featuring "Lorelei," a No. 6 hit in Canada, while the second marked the addition of Tommy Shaw to the band.Styx's commercial breakthrough in North America came with The Grand Illusion (1977), which peaked at No. 6 in both the US and Canada, and became the first of four straight triple-platinum albums in the US for Styx. It featured the single, "Come Sail Away," a Top 10 hit in both countries. The band's follow-up, Pieces of Eight (1978), was another No. 6 hit in the US but at No. 3, peaked higher in Canada due to a Top 10 hit, "Renegade," and a Top 20 song, "Blue Collar Man (Long Nights)," there (both went Top 30 in US). In 1979, Styx's Cornerstone went to No. 2 in both countries on the strength of the cross-border No. 1 hit ballad "Babe." The album became their breakthrough album in Australia and New Zealand, reaching the Top 20, with "Babe" peaking at No. 3. "Babe" was a No. 6 hit in the UK, their first and only Top 40 hit there, leading Cornerstone to be their first album to chart (No. 36) there.In 1981, Styx's Paradise Theatre was a No. 1 album in the US and Canada, while also reaching the Top 10 in Scandinavia and the UK (their biggest album there) and the Top 30 in Australia and New Zealand. "The Best of Times" off the album reached No. 1 in Canada, No. 3 in the US (Billboard), No. 1 on the US CHR chart (Radio and Records), and the Top 30 in some other countries, while "Too Much Time on My Hands" was also a Top 10 hit in North America. Kilroy Was Here (1983) was Styx's last major hit album, reaching the Top 3 in North America and the Top 10 in Scandinavia, although it was less successful elsewhere. Its lead single, "Mr. Roboto," became Styx's third chart-topper in Canada, was a No. 3 hit in the US and was their biggest hit in Germany (No. 8). After a seven-year break, Styx returned with Edge of the Century (1990), which reached No. 63 in the US with its single, Show Me the Way, becoming a Top 3 hit in North America in early 1991 (Billboard).Overall, Styx had eight songs that hit the Top 10 on the US Billboard Hot 100, as well as 16 Top 40 singles. Seven of their eight Top 10 singles were written and sung by founding member and lead singer Dennis DeYoung, who has not been part of the band since 1999.

# Dennis DeYoung

(Net Worth: $25 Million)(Height: 6' - 0")

Dennis DeYoung (born February 18, 1947) is an American singer-songwriter, musician and producer. He is a founding member of the rock band Styx as primary lead vocalist and keyboardist, a tenure that lasted from 1970 until June 1999.

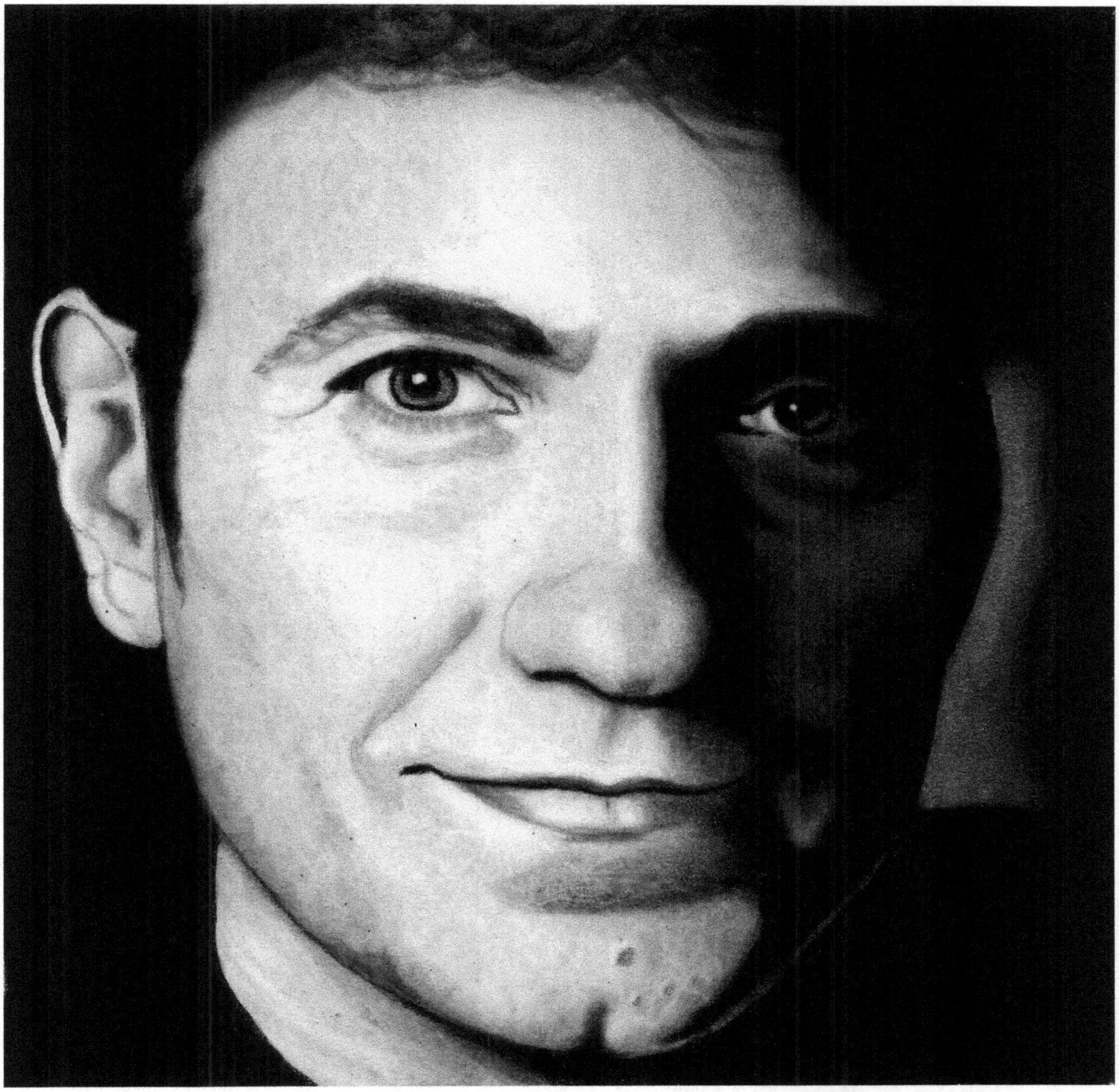

To view how this drawing was masterfully created or to purchase a Limited Edition Framed Artwork of Dennis DeYoung type into your Internet Browser the URL shortcut ➡ **myportrait.art/dennisdeyoung**

To listen to their Greatest Songs type intc your Internet Browser the URL shortcut ➡ **radio.surf/styx**

To view all channels on THE FACE OF MUSIC Internet Radio MEGA Station type into your Internet Browser the URL shortcut ➡ **radio.surf/music**

To inquire about purchasing a Limited Edtion NFT of this portrait type into your Internet Browser the URL shortcut ➡ **myartnft.shop/dennisdeyoung**

To view all available NFTs type into your Internet Browser the URL shortcut ➡ **myartnft.shop/all**

# Supertramp

(Total Albums Sold: 60+ Million) (Genre: Progressive Rock , Soft Rock)

Supertramp were an English rock band formed in London, England in 1970. Marked by the individual songwriting of founders Roger Hodgson (vocals, keyboards, and guitars) and Rick Davies (vocals and keyboards), they are distinguished for blending progressive rock and pop styles as well as for a sound that relied heavily on Wurlitzer electric piano. The group's line-up changed numerous times throughout their career, with Davies being the only consistent member throughout the decades. Other longtime members included bassist Dougie Thomson, drummer Bob Siebenberg, and saxophonist John Helliwell. The band were initially a full-fledged prog-rock group, but starting with their third album Crime of the Century (1974), they began moving towards a more pop-oriented sound. They reached their commercial peak with 1979's Breakfast in America, which yielded the international top 10 singles "The Logical Song", "Breakfast in America", "Goodbye Stranger", and "Take the Long Way Home". Their other top 40 hits included "Dreamer" (1974), "Give a Little Bit", (1977) and "It's Raining Again" (1982). In 1983, Hodgson left the group to pursue a solo career. Davies took over as the band's sole leader until 1988, after which they disbanded and periodically reformed in various configurations.

As of 2007, Supertramp album sales exceeded 60 million. They attained significant popularity in North America, Europe, South Africa, and Australia. Their highest sales levels were in Canada, where they had two diamond-certified (ten-times platinum) albums (Crime of the Century and Breakfast in America), and their only number 1 singles anywhere ("The Logical Song" and "Dreamer").

# Roger Hodgson

(Net Worth: $10 Million)(Height: 5' - 11")

Charles Roger Pomfret Hodgson (born 21 March 1950) is an English musician, singer and songwriter, best known as the former co-frontman and founding member of progressive rock band Supertramp. Hodgson composed and sang the majority of the band's hits such as "Dreamer", "Give a Little Bit", "Take the Long Way Home", "The Logical Song", "It's Raining Again", and "Breakfast in America".

Hodgson left Supertramp in 1983 and moved his family away from the Los Angeles music scene to live a simpler lifestyle close to nature and be home with his children as they were growing up. Hodgson returned to touring in 2001. He often writes about spiritual and philosophical topics, and his lyrics have been described as personal and meaningful.

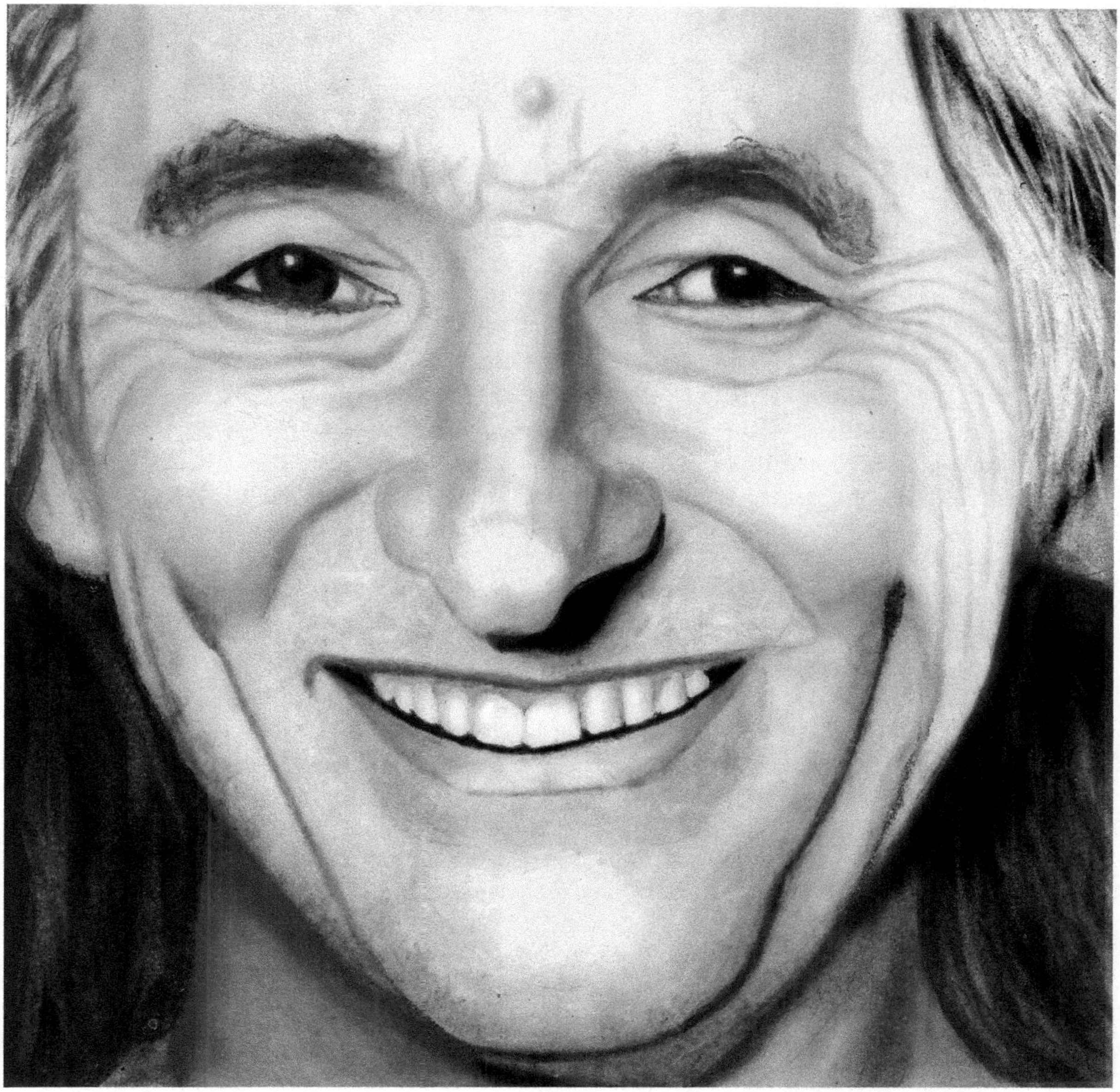

To view how this drawing was masterfully created or to purchase a Limited Edition Framed Artwork of Roger Hodgson type into your Internet Browser the URL shortcut ➡ **myportrait.art/rogerhodgson**

To listen to their Greatest Songs type into your Internet Browser the URL shortcut ➡ **radio.surf/supertramp**

To view all channels on THE FACE OF MUSIC Internet Radio MEGA Station type into your Internet Browser the URL shortcut ➡ **radio.surf/music**

To inquire about purchasing a Limited Edtion NFT of this portrait type into your Internet Browser the URL shortcut ➡ **myartnft.shop/rogerhodgson**

To view all available NFTs type into your Internet Browser the URL shortcut ➡ **myartnft.shop/all**

# Supremes, The

(Total Records Sold: 100+ Million) (Genre: R&B, Soul, Pop, Doo-Wop, Dissco)

The Supremes were an American female singing group and a premier act of Motown Records during the 1960s. Founded as The Primettes in Detroit, Michigan, in 1959, the Supremes were the most commercially successful of Motown's acts and the most successful American vocal group, with 12 number one singles on the Billboard Hot 100. Most of these hits were written and produced by Motown's main songwriting and production team, Holland–Dozier–Holland. At their peak in the mid-1960s, the Supremes rivaled the Beatles in worldwide popularity, and it is said that their breakthrough made it possible for future African American R&B and soul musicians to find mainstream success. Billboard ranked The Supremes as the 16th greatest Hot 100 artist of all time.

Florence Ballard, Mary Wilson, Diana Ross, and Betty McGlown, the original group, were all from the Brewster-Douglass public housing project in Detroit. They formed the Primettes as the sister act to the Primes (with Paul Williams and Eddie Kendricks, who went on to form the Temptations). Barbara Martin replaced McGlown in 1960, and the group signed with Motown the following year as The Supremes. Martin left the act in early 1962, and Ross, Ballard, and Wilson carried on as a trio.

During the mid-1960s, the Supremes achieved mainstream success with Ross as lead singer and Holland-Dozier-Holland as its songwriting and production team. In 1967, Motown president Berry Gordy renamed the group Diana Ross & the Supremes, and replaced Ballard with Cindy Birdsong. In 1970, Ross left to pursue a solo career and was replaced by Jean Terrell and the group reverted to being The Supremes again. During the mid-1970s, the lineup changed with Lynda Laurence, Scherrie Payne and Susaye Greene joining until, after 18 years, the group disbanded in 1977.

# Diana Ross

(Net Worth: $250 Million)(Height: 5' - 5")

Diana Ernestine Earle Ross (born March 26, 1944) is an American singer and actress. Born and raised in Detroit, Michigan, she rose to fame as the lead singer of the vocal group The Supremes, who became Motown's most successful act during the 1960s and one of the world's best-selling girl groups of all time.

Following departure from the Supremes in 1970, Ross embarked on a highly successful, globally ground-breaking solo career in music, television, film and stage.

Ross was named the "Female Entertainer of the Century" by Billboard in 1976. She is the only female artist to have number-one singles on the Billboard Hot 100 as a solo artist, as the other half of a duet, as a member of a trio, and as an ensemble member. Billboard ranked her as 28th greatest Hot 100 artist of all time. Ross ranks among the Top 5 artists on the Billboard Hot 100 singles chart from 1955 to 2018 when combining her solo and Supremes' hits. She had a top 10 UK hit in every one of the last five decades, and sang lead on a top 75 hit single at least once every year from 1964 to 1996 in the UK, a period of 33 consecutive years and a record for any performer. In 1988, Ross was inducted to the Rock and Roll Hall of Fame as a member of the Supremes. Guinness Book of World Records recognized her success in the United States and United Kingdom for having more hits than any female artist in the charts, with a career total of 70 hit singles with her work with the Supremes and as a solo artist. She was the recipient of the Kennedy Center Honors in 2007, the Grammy Lifetime Achievement Award in 2012, and the Presidential Medal of Freedom in 2016.

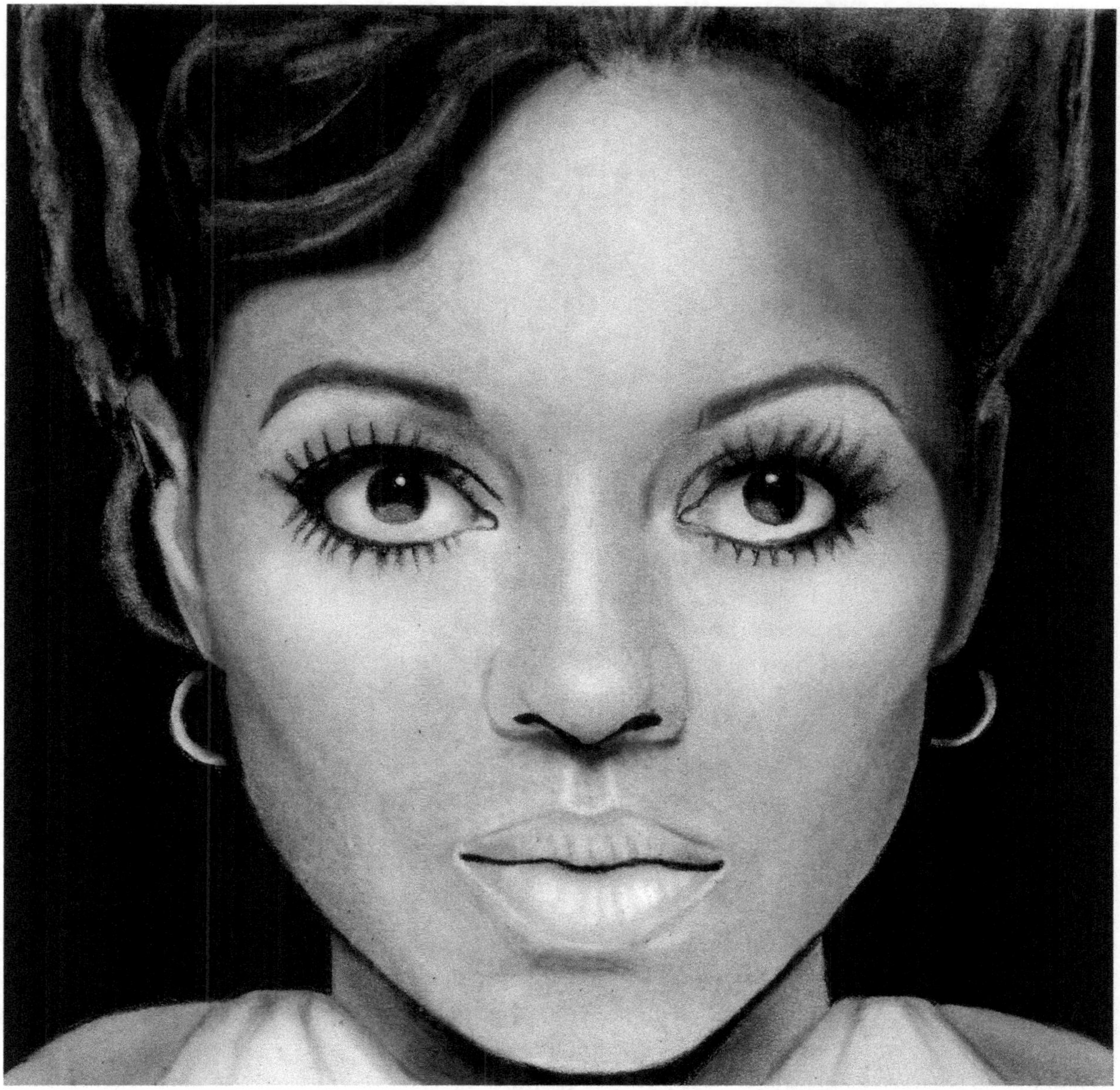

To view how this drawing was masterfully created or to purchase a Limited Edition Framed Artwork of Diana Ross type into your Internet Browser the URL shortcut ➡ **myportrait.art/dianaross**

To listen to their Greatest Songs type into your Internet Browser the URL shortcut
➡ **http://www.radio.surf/thesupremes**

To view all channels on THE FACE OF MUSIC Internet Radio MEGA Station type into your Internet Browser the URL shortcut ➡ **radio.surf/music**

To inquire about purchasing a Limited Edtion NFT of this portrait type into your Internet Browser the URL shortcut ➡ **myartnft.shop/dianaross**

To view all available NFTs type into your Internet Browser the URL shortcut ➡ **myartnft.shop/all**

# System of a Down

(Total Records Sold: 40+ Million) (Genre: Nu Metal , Heavy Metal)

System of a Down is an Armenian-American heavy metal band formed in Glendale, California, in 1994. It currently consists of members Serj Tankian (lead vocals, keyboards), Daron Malakian (guitar, vocals), Shavo Odadjian (bass, backing vocals), and John Dolmayan (drums), who replaced original drummer Andy Khachaturian in 1997.

The band achieved commercial success with the release of five studio albums, three of which debuted at number one on the US Billboard 200. System of a Down has been nominated for four Grammy Awards and their song "B.Y.O.B." won a Grammy Award for Best Hard Rock Performance in 2006. The band went on hiatus in 2006 and reunited in 2010. Other than two new songs in 2020 ("Protect the Land" and "Genocidal Humanoidz"), System of a Down has not released a full-length record since the Mezmerize and Hypnotize albums in 2005. The band has sold over 40 million records worldwide, while two of their singles "Aerials" and "Hypnotize" reached number one on Billboard's Alternative Songs chart.

# Serj Tankian

(Net Worth: $20 Million)(Height: 5' - 10")

Serj Tankian (born August 21, 1967) is an Armenian-American singer, musician, songwriter, record producer, political activist and trained opera singer. He is best known as the lead vocalist, primary lyricist, keyboardist, and occasional rhythm guitarist of heavy metal band System of a Down, which was formed in 1994.

Tankian is regarded as one of the best vocalists in heavy metal, with praise given to his unusual delivery and his wide vocal range. In 2006, he was ranked No. 26 on the Hit Parader list of "Top 100 Heavy Metal Vocalists". A study conducted by VVN Music found that Tankian possesses a high and diverse vocal range of 4.2 octaves. In 2002, he co-founded the non-profit political activism organization Axis of Justice, alongside guitarist and fellow activist Tom Morello. In 2011, he was awarded the Armenian Prime Minister's Medal for his contributions to the recognition of the Armenian Genocide and the advancement of music.

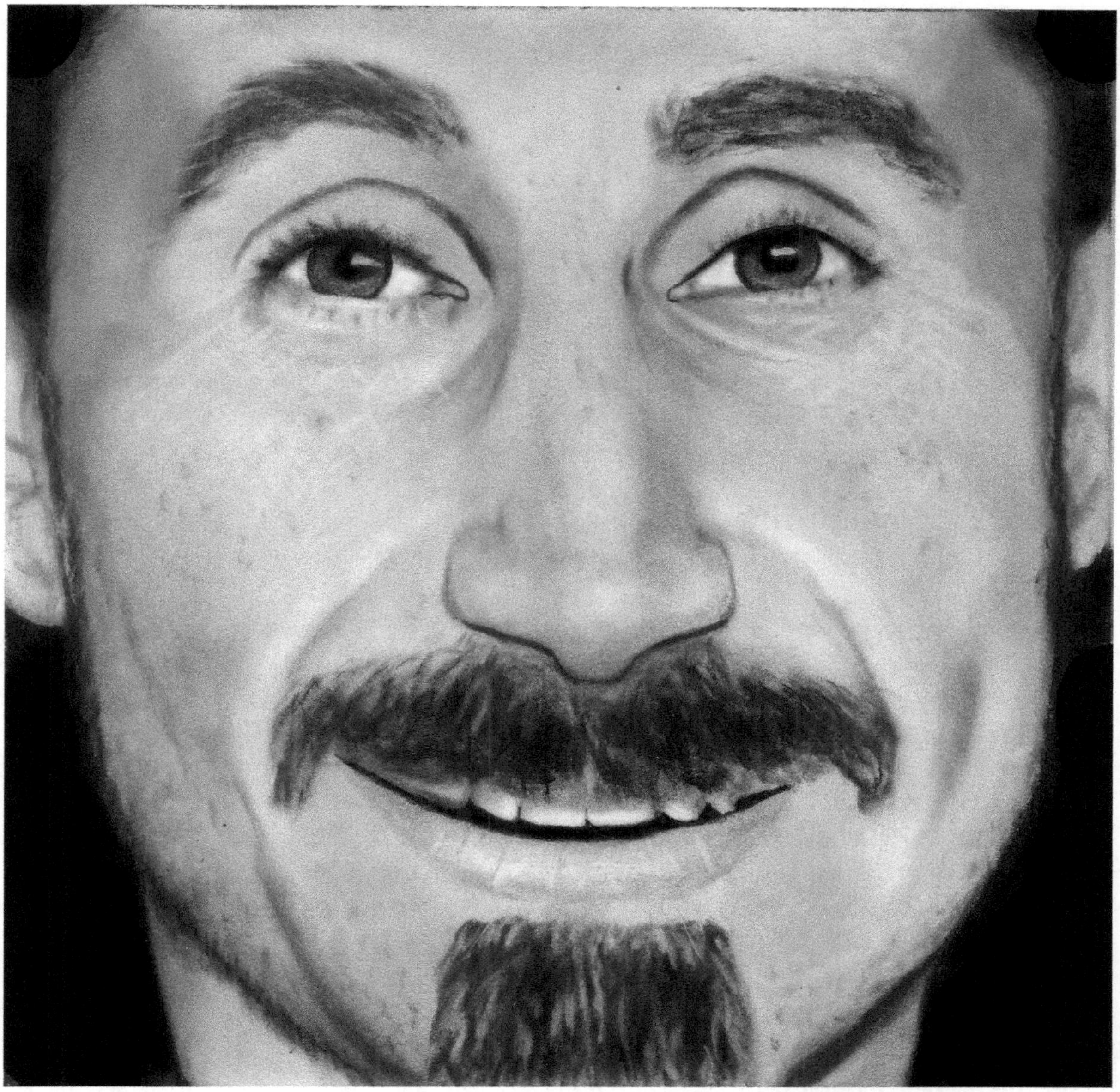

To view how this drawing was masterfully created or to purchase a Limited Edition Framed Artwork of Serj Tankian type into your Internet Browser the URL shortcut ➡ **myportrait.art/serjtankian**

To listen to their Greatest Songs type into your Internet Browser the URL shortcut ➡ **radio.surf/systemofadown**

To view all channels on THE FACE OF MUSIC Internet Radio MEGA Station type into your Internet Browser the URL shortcut ➡ **radio.surf/music**

To inquire about purchasing a Limited Edtion NFT of this portrait type into your Internet Browser the URL shortcut ➡ **myartnft.shop/serjtankian**

To view all available NFTs type into your Internet Browser the URL shortcut ➡ **myartnft.shop/all**

# T.I.

(Net worth: $50 Million)(Total Albums Sold: Millions)
(Genre: Hip-Hop , Rap)(Height: 5' - 8")

Clifford Joseph Harris Jr. (born September 25, 1980), better known by the stage names T.I. and Tip (often stylized as TIP or T.I.P.), is an American rapper, singer, songwriter, actor, record producer, and entrepreneur. He signed his first major-label record deal in 1999 with Arista subsidiary LaFace. In 2001, he formed the southern hip hop group P$C, alongside his longtime friends and fellow Atlanta-based rappers Big Kuntry King, Mac Boney, AK and C-Rod. Upon being released from Arista, Harris signed to Atlantic and subsequently became the co-chief executive officer (CEO) of his own label imprint, Grand Hustle Records, which he launched in 2003. Harris is also known as one of the pioneers of the hip hop subgenre trap music, along with fellow Atlanta-based rappers Jeezy and Gucci Mane.Harris, a three time Grammy Award winner, has released 11 studio albums, with seven of them reaching the top five of the US Billboard 200 chart. Throughout his career, Harris has also released several highly successful singles, including Billboard Hot 100 number one hits "Whatever You Like" and "Live Your Life", the latter replaced the former atop the chart and helped Harris join a select group of artists to replace themselves at number one and simultaneously occupy the top two positions. Harris began to gain major recognition in 2003 following his first high-profile feature on fellow Atlanta-based rapper Bone Crusher's single "Never Scared". Harris earned more prominence with the release of Trap Muzik (2003), which includes the Top 40 songs "Rubber Band Man" and "Let's Get Away". The following year, Harris appeared on Destiny's Child's international hit "Soldier" alongside Lil Wayne, and capitalized on it with the release of his Urban Legend (2004) album. His subsequent albums, King and T.I. vs. T.I.P., generated high record sales and were supported by popular singles, such as "What You Know" and "Big Shit Poppin' (Do It)", respectively.Harris' sixth album, Paper Trail (2008), became his most successful project, with the album being certified gold for first-week sales of over 500,000 copies in the United States, additionally making it his third consecutive number one album. In 2013, Harris was featured on Robin Thicke's single "Blurred Lines" alongside Pharrell Williams, which peaked at number one on several major music charts. In November 2013, Harris announced that he had signed with Columbia Records after his 10-year contract with Atlantic came to an end. He released his Columbia debut Paperwork, in October 2014. In February 2016, Harris signed a distribution deal with Roc Nation and later another deal with Epic Records in September 2018. The former served as a means to release his political Us or Else EP series, while the latter released his long-delayed tenth album Dime Trap, in October of that year.Harris has served two terms in county jail, twice for probation violations and a federal prison bid for a U.S federal weapons charge. While serving 11 months in prison, he released his seventh studio album No Mercy (2010). Harris has also had a successful acting career, starring in the films ATL, Takers, Get Hard, Identity Thief, and in the Marvel Cinematic Universe films Ant-Man and its sequel. He is also a published author of two novels, Power & Beauty (2011) and Trouble & Triumph (2012), both of which were released to moderate success. Harris has also starred in the American reality television series T.I.'s Road to Redemption, T.I. & Tiny: The Family Hustle, and The Grand Hustle. In 2009, Billboard ranked him as the 27th best artist of the 2000s decade.

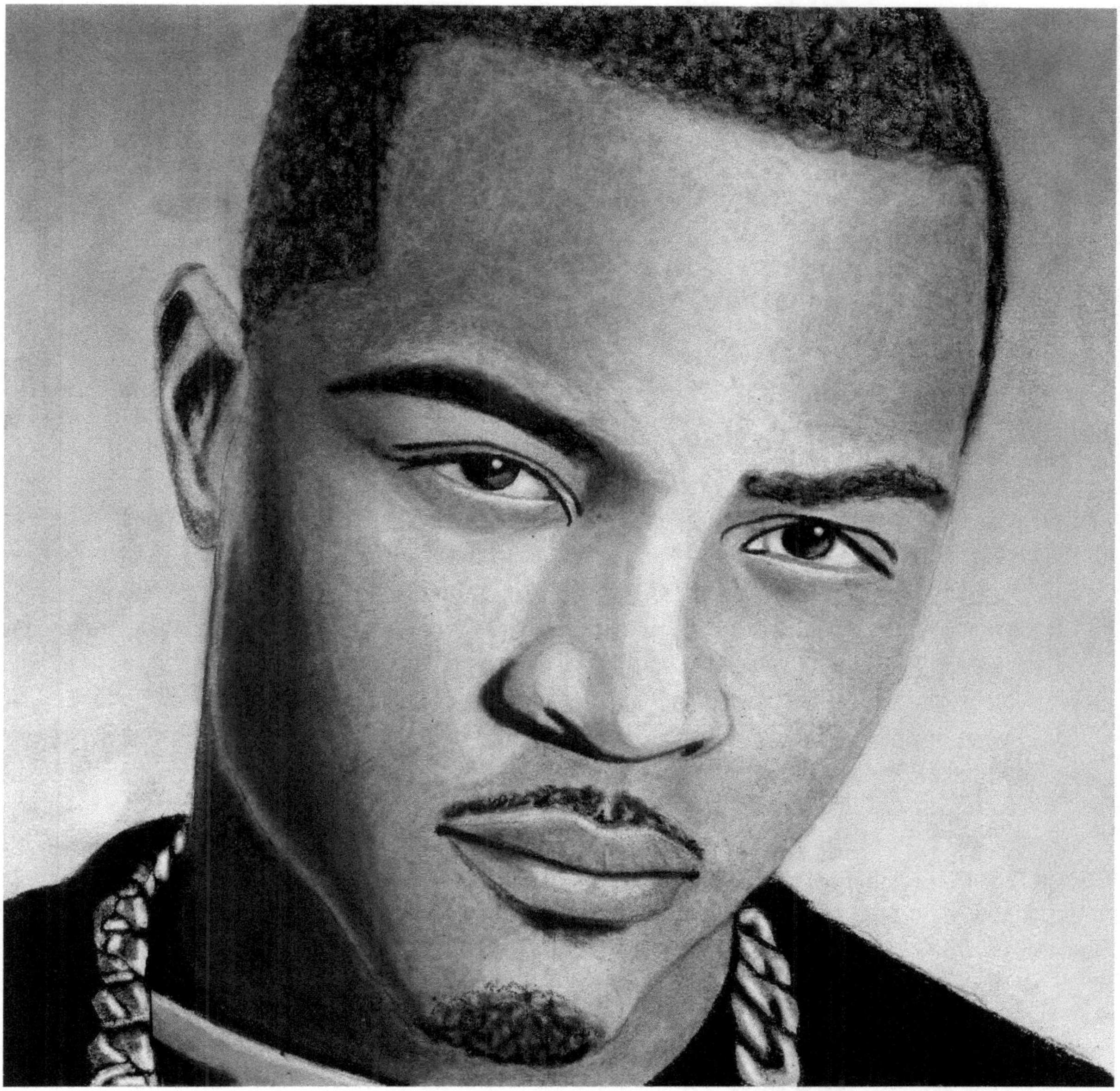

To view how this drawing was masterfully created or to purchase a Limited Edition Framed Artwork of T I type into your Internet Browser the URL shortcut ➡ **myportrait.art/ti**

To listen to his Greatest Songs type into your Internet Browser the URL shortcut ➡ **radio.surf/ti**

To view all channels on THE FACE OF MUSIC Internet Radio MEGA Station type into your Internet Browser the URL shortcut ➡ **radio.surf/music**

To inquire about purchasing a Limited Edtion NFT of this portrait type into your Internet Browser the URL shortcut ➡ **myartnft.shop/ti**

To view all available NFTs type into your Internet Browser the URL shortcut ➡ **myartnft.shop/all**

# Talking Heads

(Total Records Sold: Millions) (Genre: New Wave , Art Pop)

The Talking Heads were an American rock band formed in 1975 in New York City and active until 1991. The band was composed of David Byrne (lead vocals, guitar), Chris Frantz (drums), Tina Weymouth (bass), and Jerry Harrison (keyboards, guitar). Described as "one of the most critically acclaimed bands of the '80s", the group helped to pioneer new wave music by integrating elements of punk, art rock, funk, and world music with avant-garde sensibilities and an anxious, clean-cut image. Former art school students who became involved in the 1970s New York punk scene, Talking Heads released their 1977 debut album, Talking Heads: 77, to positive reviews. They collaborated with producer Brian Eno on a trio of experimental and critically acclaimed releases: More Songs About Buildings and Food (1978), Fear of Music (1979), and Remain in Light (1980). After a hiatus, Talking Heads hit their commercial peak in 1983 with the U.S. Top 10 hit "Burning Down the House" from the album Speaking in Tongues and released the concert film Stop Making Sense, directed by Jonathan Demme. They released several more albums, including their best-selling LP Little Creatures (1985), before disbanding in 1991. Without Byrne, the other band members performed under the name Shrunken Heads, and released an album, No Talking, Just Head, as the Heads in 1996.

In 2002, the Talking Heads were inducted into the Rock and Roll Hall of Fame. Four of their albums appear in Rolling Stone's list of the 500 Greatest Albums of All Time, and three of their songs ("Psycho Killer", "Life During Wartime", and "Once in a Lifetime") were included among the Rock and Roll Hall of Fame's 500 Songs That Shaped Rock and Roll. Talking Heads were also number 64 on VH1's list of the "100 Greatest Artists of All Time". In the 2011 update of Rolling Stone's "100 Greatest Artists of All Time", they were ranked number 100.

# David Byrne

(Net Worth: $40 Million)(Height: 6' - 0")

David Byrne (born 14 May 1952) is a Scottish-American singer, songwriter, record producer, actor, writer, music theorist, and filmmaker, who was a founding member and the principal songwriter, lead singer, and guitarist of the American new wave band Talking Heads.

Byrne has released solo recordings and worked with various media including film, photography, opera, fiction, and non-fiction. He has received Academy, Grammy, and Golden Globe Awards, and he is an inductee to the Rock and Roll Hall of Fame as part of Talking Heads.

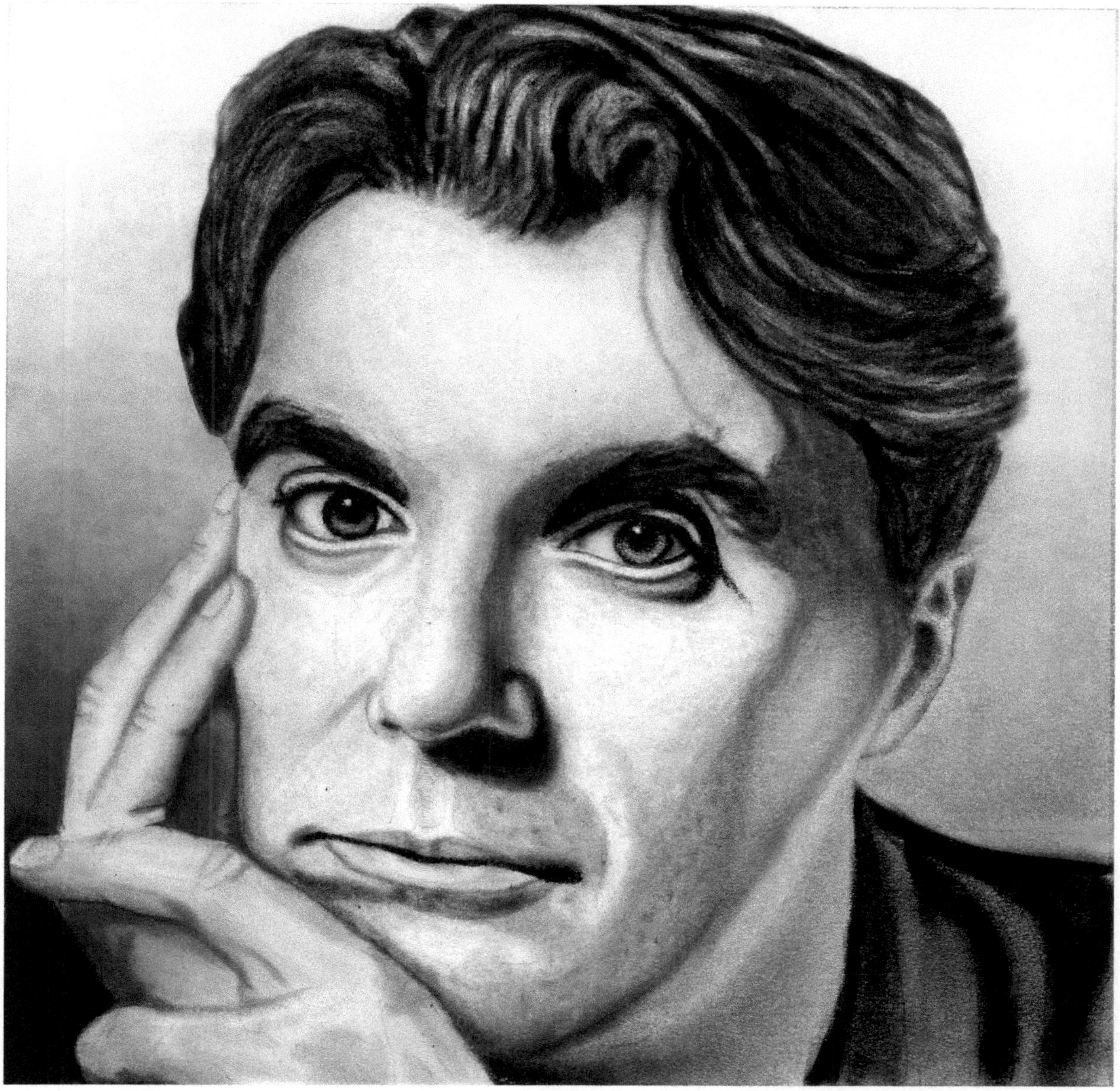

To view how this drawing was masterfully created or to purchase a Limited Edition Framed Artwork of David Byrne type into your Internet Browser the URL shortcut ➡ **myportrait.art/davidbyrne**

To listen to their Greatest Songs type into your Internet Browser the URL shortcut
➡ **radio.surf/talkingheads**

To view all channels on THE FACE OF MUSIC Internet Radio MEGA Station type into your Internet Browser the URL shortcut ➡ **radio.surf/music**

To inquire about purchasing a Limited Edtion NFT of this portrait type into your Internet Browser the URL shortcut ➡ **myartnft.shop/davidbyrne**

To view all available NFTs type into your Internet Browser the URL shortcut ➡ **myartnft.shop/all**

# Tammy Wynette

(Net worth: $900 Thousand)(Total Albums Sold: Millions)
(Genre: Country)(Height: 5' - 2")

Tammy Wynette (born Virginia Wynette Pugh; May 5, 1942 – April 6, 1998) was an American country music singer-songwriter and musician and was one of country music's best-known artists and biggest-selling female singers.Wynette was called the "First Lady of Country Music", and her best-known song, "Stand by Your Man", is one of the best-selling hit singles by a woman in the history of country music. Many of her hits dealt with themes of loneliness, divorce, and the difficulties of life and relationships. During the late 1960s and early 1970s, Wynette charted 20 number-one songs on the Billboard Country Chart. Along with Loretta Lynn, Lynn Anderson, and Dolly Parton, she is credited with having defined the role of women in country music during the 1970s.Wynette's marriage to country music singer George Jones in 1969 created a country music "couple", following the earlier success of Johnny Cash and June Carter Cash. Though they divorced in 1975, the couple recorded a sequence of albums and singles together that hit the charts throughout the 1970s and early 1980s.While working as a hairdresser in Midfield, Alabama, in 1965, Wynette sang on the Country Boy Eddie Show on WBRC-TV in Birmingham, which led to performances with country music star Porter Wagoner. In 1966, she moved with her three daughters (Gwen, Tina, and Jackie) from Birmingham to Nashville, Tennessee, in hopes of landing a recording deal. After being turned down repeatedly she auditioned for Epic Records producer Billy Sherrill. Initially reluctant to sign her, Sherrill found himself in need of a singer for a tune written by Bobby Austin and Johnny Paycheck, "Apartment No. 9". Upon hearing Wynette's version he was impressed and put her under contract.Once she was signed to Epic, Sherrill suggested she change her name to make more of an impression. According to her 1979 memoir, Stand by Your Man, during their meeting, Wynette was wearing her long, blonde hair in a ponytail, and Sherrill noted that she reminded him of Debbie Reynolds in the film Tammy and the Bachelor. He suggested "Tammy" as a possible name, so she became Tammy Wynette.Her first single, "Apartment No. 9" , was released in December 1966, and just missed the top 40 on the Country charts, peaking at number 44. It was followed by "Your Good Girl's Gonna Go Bad", which became a big hit, peaking at number three. The song launched a string of top-ten hits that ran through the end of the 1970s, interrupted only by three singles that didn't crack the Top Ten. After "Your Good Girl's Gonna Go Bad" was a success, "My Elusive Dreams", a duet with David Houston, became her first number one in the summer of 1967, followed by "I Don't Wanna Play House" later that year. "I Don't Wanna Play House" won Wynette a Grammy award in 1967 for Best Female Country Vocal Performance, one of two wins for Wynette in that category.During 1968 and 1969, Wynette had five number-one hits – "Take Me to Your World", "D-I-V-O-R-C-E", "Stand by Your Man" (all 1968), "Singing My Song", and "The Ways to Love a Man" (both 1969). "Stand by Your Man" was reportedly written in the Epic studio in just 15 minutes by Billy Sherrill and Wynette, and was released at a time when the women's-rights movement was beginning to stir in the U.S. The message in the song stated a woman should stay with her man, despite his faults and shortcomings. It stirred up controversy and was criticized initially, and it became a lightning rod for feminists. Nevertheless, the song became very successful, reaching the top spot on the Country charts, and was also a top-20 pop hit, peaking at number 19 on the Billboard pop charts in 1968, Wynette's only top-40 hit as a solo artist on the pop charts. In 1969, Wynette won the Grammy award for Best Female Country Vocal Performance for "Stand by Your Man", which is now, according to critics, considered a "classic" or country music "standard". She earned a gold record (awarded for albums selling in excess of 500,000 copies) for Tammy's Greatest Hits which was certified in 1970 by the RIAA. The album was awarded platinum record status (awarded for albums selling in excess of 1,000,000 copies) in June 1989. In 1970, director Bob Rafelson used a number of her songs in the soundtrack of his 1970 film Five Easy Pieces.

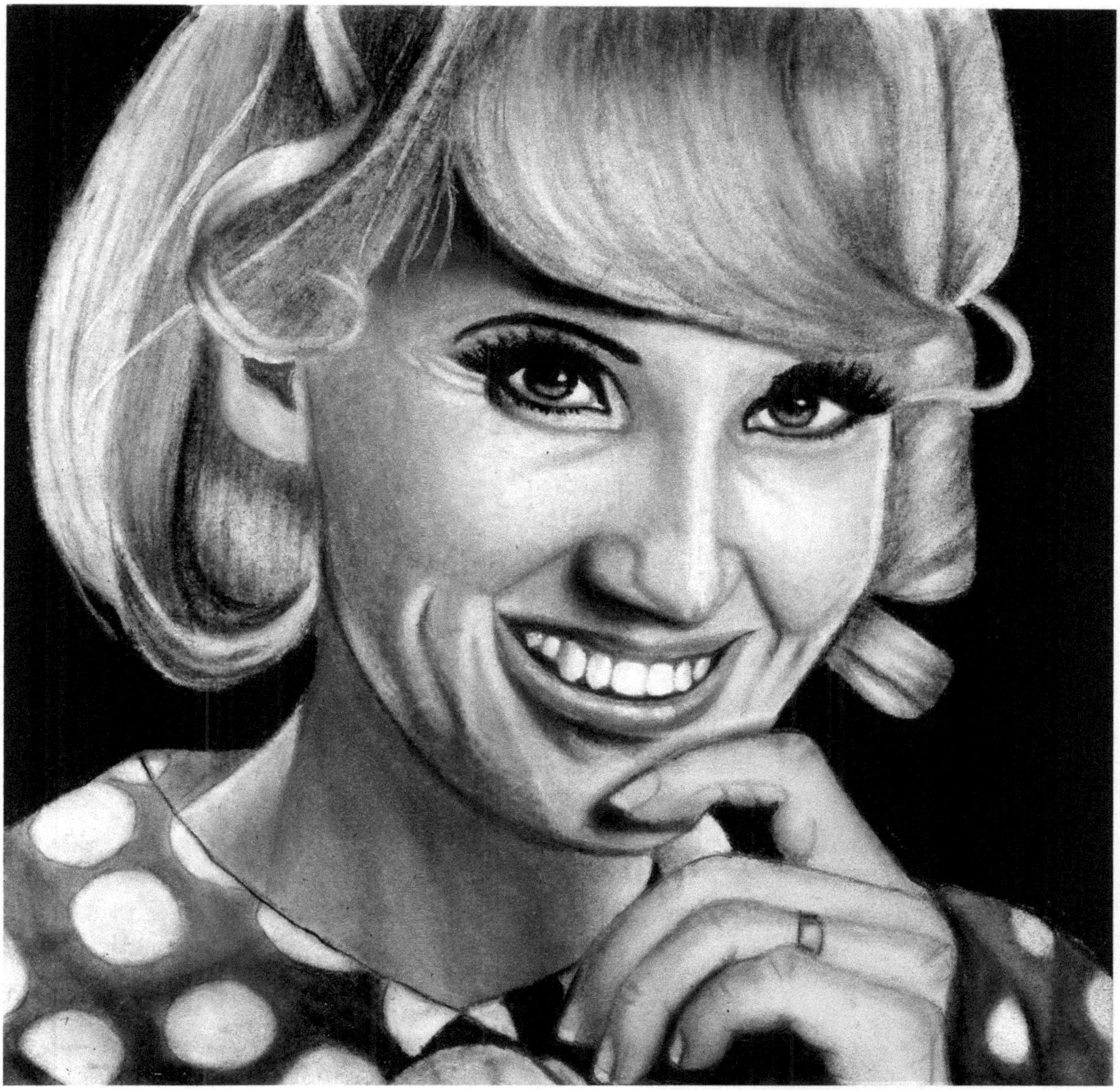

To view how this drawing was masterfully created or to purchase a Limited Edition Framed Artwork of Tammy Wynette type into your Internet Browser the URL shortcut ➡ **myportrait.art/tammywynette**

To listen to her Greatest Songs type into your Internet Browser the URL shortcut
➡ **radio.surf/tammywynette**

To view all channels on THE FACE OF MUSIC Internet Radio MEGA Station type into your Internet Browser the URL shortcut ➡ **radio.surf/music**

To inquire about purchasing a Limited Edtion NFT of this portrait type into your Internet Browser the URL shortcut ➡ **myartnft.shop/tammywynette**

To view all available NFTs type into your Internet Browser the URL shortcut ➡ **myartnft.shop/all**

# Ted Nugent

(Net worth: $20 Million)(Total Albums Sold: Millions)
(Genre: Hard Rock)(Height: 5' - 11")

Theodore Anthony Nugent (born December 13, 1948) is an American singer-songwriter, guitarist, and pro-gun political activist. He initially gained fame as the lead guitarist of The Amboy Dukes, a band formed in 1963 that played psychedelic rock and hard rock. After dissolving the band, he embarked on a solo career. Nugent is known for his Gibson Byrdland, his bluesy and frenzied guitar playing and his energetic live shows. Despite possessing a distinctive, wide-ranging singing voice, Nugent recorded and toured with other singers during much of his early solo career, including Derek St. Holmes, Brian Howe, and Meat Loaf, only taking on full lead vocal duties later on. In the late 1980s and early 1990s, he was part of the supergroup Damn Yankees.

In later years, Nugent has drawn attention for his outspoken conservative political views, as well as his strident advocacy of hunting and gun ownership rights. He is a board member of the National Rifle Association and a strong supporter of the Republican Party. He has made a number of controversial and threatening statements against advocates of gun control; in one case, the Secret Service investigated him based on comments about President Barack Obama.

Nugent dropped the Amboy Dukes band name for good in 1975, and signed to Epic Records. Derek St. Holmes (guitar, vocals), Rob Grange (bass) and Clifford Davies (drums) were the primary additional band members for his 1970s multi-platinum albums: Ted Nugent (1975), Free-for-All (1976) and Cat Scratch Fever (1977). These albums produced the popular radio anthems "Hey Baby", "Stranglehold", "Dog Eat Dog", and "Cat Scratch Fever". Despite most of the songwriting credits being listed as solely Nugent, St. Holmes claims they were co-written by the whole band, and that Nugent took sole credit as a way to not pay them royalties.

It was during these three years that Nugent emerged as a guitar hero to hard rock fans, many of whom were unaware of his lengthy apprenticeship with the Amboy Dukes. This band lineup toured extensively, also releasing the multi-platinum live album Double Live Gonzo! (1978), until its breakup in 1978 when St. Holmes and Grange departed. St. Holmes was replaced by Charlie Huhn and Grange by Dave Kiswiney. Davies left around 1982 after staying on to record Weekend Warriors (1978), State of Shock (1979), Scream Dream (1980) and Intensities in 10 Cities (1981). The "Intensities in 10 Cities" album includes the controversial song "Jailbait".

On July 8, 1979, Ted was on the rock radio program King Biscuit Flower Hour. This was the original broadcast of Ted's performance of Live at Hammersmith '79 which had been recorded during the second set of a night at London's Hammersmith Odeon in 1979. An album of this program was released in 1997.

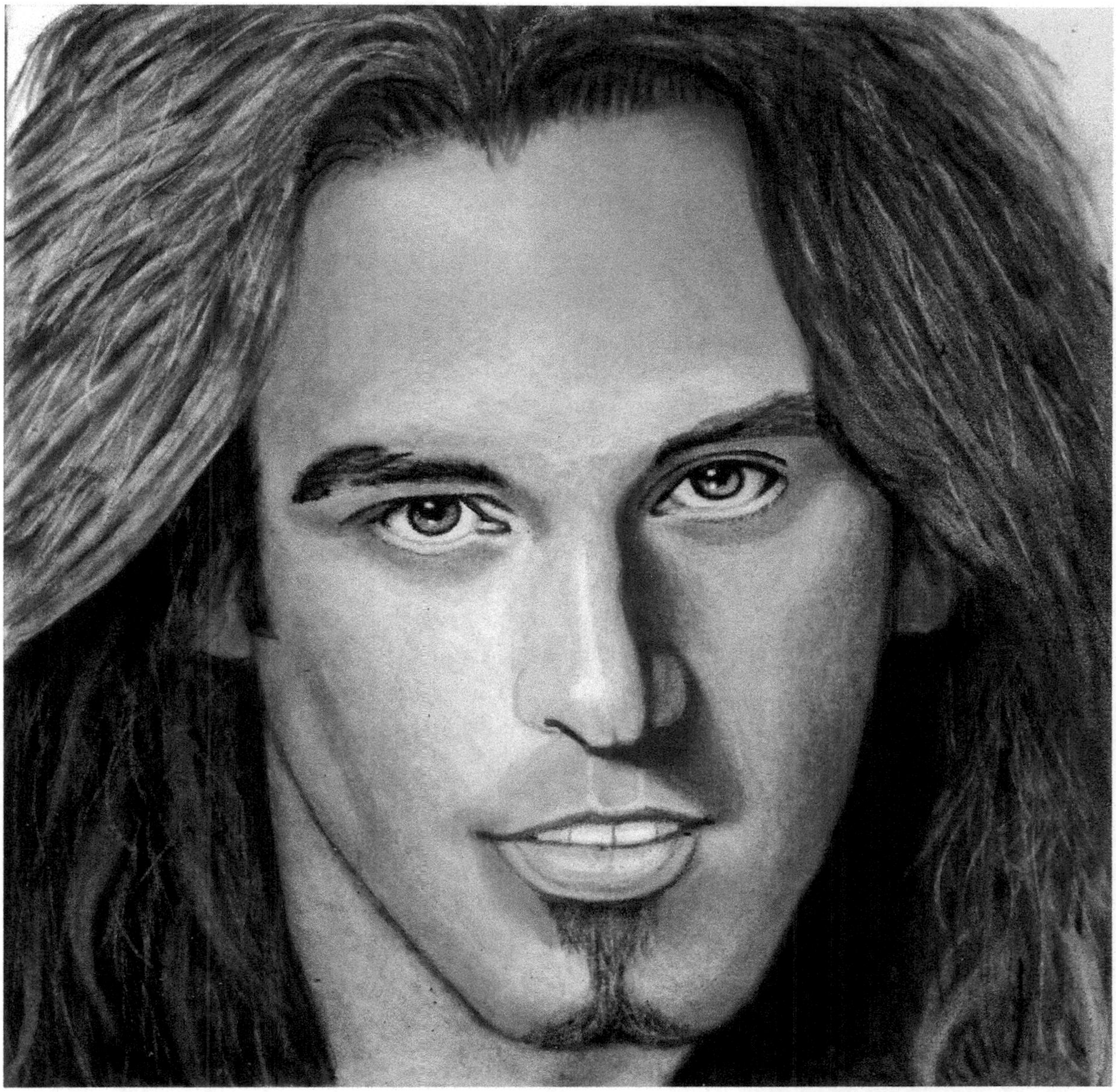

To view how this drawing was masterfully created or to purchase a Limited Edition Framed Artwork of Ted Nugent type into your Internet Browser the URL shortcut ➡ **myportrait.art/tednugent**

To listen to his Greatest Songs type into your Internet Browser the URL shortcut ➡ **radio.surf/tednugent**

To view all channels on THE FACE OF MUSIC Internet Radio MEGA Station type into your Internet Browser the URL shortcut ➡ **radio.surf/music**

To inquire about purchasing a Limited Edtion NFT of this portrait type into your Internet Browser the URL shortcut ➡ **myartnft.shop/tednugent**

To view all available NFTs type into your Internet Browser the URL shortcut ➡ **myartnft.shop/all**

# Temptations, The

(Total Albums Sold: 22 Million) (Genre: R&B , Soul , Funk)

The Temptations are an American vocal group from Detroit, Michigan, who released a series of successful singles and albums with Motown Records during the 1960s and 1970s. The group's work with producer Norman Whitfield, beginning with the Top 10 hit single "Cloud Nine" in October 1968, pioneered psychedelic soul, and was significant in the evolution of R&B and soul music. The band members are known for their choreography, distinct harmonies, and dress style. Having sold tens of millions of albums, the Temptations are among the most successful groups in popular music. Featuring five male vocalists and dancers (save for brief periods with fewer or more members), the group formed in 1960 in Detroit under the name the Elgins. The founding members came from two rival Detroit vocal groups: Otis Williams, Elbridge "Al" Bryant, and Melvin Franklin of Otis Williams & the Distants, and Eddie Kendricks and Paul Williams of the Primes. In 1964, Bryant was replaced by David Ruffin, who was the lead vocalist on a number of the group's biggest hits, including "My Girl" (1964), "Ain't Too Proud to Beg" (1966), and "I Wish It Would Rain" (1967). Ruffin was replaced in 1968 by Dennis Edwards, with whom the group continued to record hit records such as "Cloud Nine" (1969) and "Ball of Confusion (That's What the World Is Today)" (1970). The group's lineup has changed frequently since the departures of Kendricks and Paul Williams from the act in 1971. Later members of the group have included singers such as Richard Street, Damon Harris, Ron Tyson, and Ali-Ollie Woodson, with whom the group scored a late-period hit in 1984 with "Treat Her Like a Lady".Over the course of their career, the Temptations released four Billboard Hot 100 number-one singles and fourteen R&B number-one singles. Their music has earned three Grammy Awards. The Temptations were the first Motown recording act to win a Grammy Award – for "Cloud Nine" in 1969 – and in 2013 received the Grammy Lifetime Achievement Award. Six of the Temptations (Edwards, Franklin, Kendricks, Ruffin, Otis Williams and Paul Williams) were inducted into the Rock and Roll Hall of Fame in 1989. Three classic Temptations songs, "My Girl", "Just My Imagination (Running Away with Me)", and "Papa Was a Rollin' Stone", are among The Rock and Roll Hall of Fame's 500 Songs that Shaped Rock and Roll. The Temptations were ranked at number 68 on Rolling Stone magazine's list of the 100 Greatest Artists of all time.

# Dennis Edwards

(Net Worth: $5 Million)(Height: 6' - 4")

Dennis Edwards Jr. (February 3, 1943 – February 1, 2018) was an American soul and R&B singer who was best known as the frontman in The Temptations, on Motown Records. Edwards joined the Temptations in 1968, replacing David Ruffin and sang with the group from 1968 to 1976, 1980 to 1984 and 1987 to 1989. In the mid-1980s, he attempted a solo career, scoring a hit in 1984 with "Don't Look Any Further" (featuring Siedah Garrett). Until his death, Edwards was the lead singer of The Temptations Review, a Temptations splinter group.

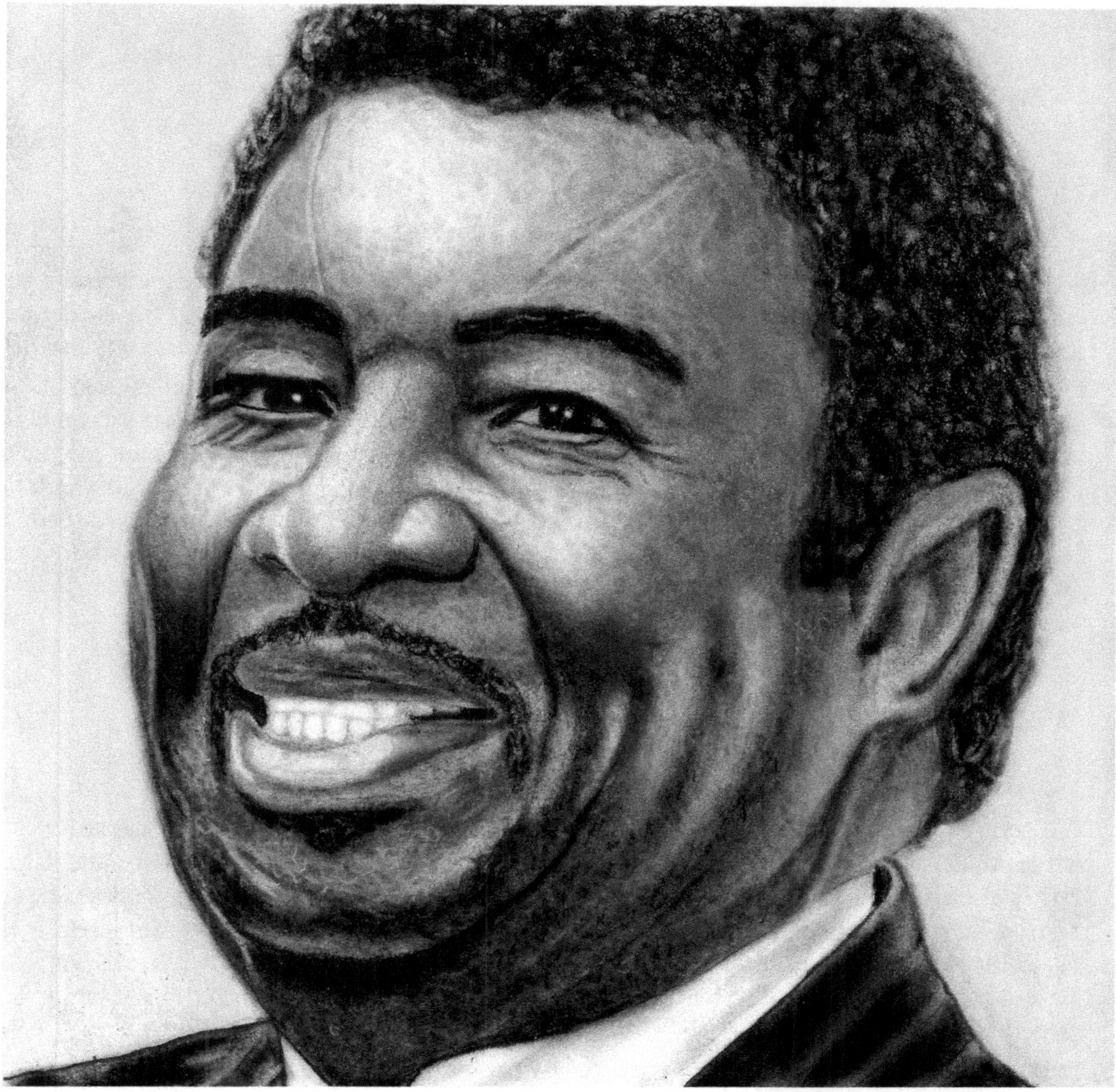

To view how this drawing was masterfully created or to purchase a Limited Edition Framed Artwork of Dennis Edwards type into your Internet Browser the URL shortcut ➡ **myportrait.art/dennisedwards**

To listen to their Greatest Songs type into your Internet Browser the URL shortcut
➡ **radio.surf/thetemptations**

To view all channels on THE FACE OF MUSIC Internet Radio MEGA Station type into your Internet Browser the URL shortcut ➡ **radio.surf/music**

To inquire about purchasing a Limited Edtion NFT of this portrait type into your Internet Browser the URL shortcut ➡ **myartnft.shop/dennisedwards**

To view all available NFTs type into your Internet Browser the URL shortcut ➡ **myartnft.shop/all**

# Them

(Total Albums Sold: Millions) (Genre: Rock)

Them were a rock group formed in Belfast, Northern Ireland, in April 1964, most prominently known for the rock standard "Gloria" and launching singer Van Morrison's musical career. The original five-member band consisted of Morrison, Alan Henderson, Ronnie Milling, Billy Harrison and Eric Wrixon.Them scored two UK hits in 1965 with "Baby, Please Don't Go" (UK No. 10) and "Here Comes the Night" (UK No. 2; Ireland No. 2). The latter song and "Mystic Eyes" were Top 40 hits in the U.S.Morrison quit the band in 1966 and went on to a successful career as a solo artist. Despite their relatively few hit singles, the Belfast group had considerable influence on other bands, such as the Doors.The band's 1964 recording of "Gloria" was inducted into the Grammy Hall of Fame in 1999. It was rated at No.69 on Dave Marsh's 1989 book, The Heart of Rock and Soul, The 1001 Greatest Singles Ever and "Mystic Eyes" was rated at No458. "Gloria" was listed at No.208 on the 2004 Rolling Stone magazine's feature, The 500 Greatest Songs of All Time.

# Van Morrison

(Net Worth: $90 Million)(Height: 5' - 4")

Sir George Ivan Morrison (born 31 August 1945) is a Northern Irish singer-songwriter, instrumentalist and record producer. His professional career began as a teenager in the late 1950s, playing a variety of instruments including guitar, harmonica, keyboards and saxophone for various Irish showbands, covering the popular hits of that time. Known as "Van the Man" to his fans, he rose to prominence in the mid-1960s as the lead singer of the Northern Irish R&B and rock band Them, with whom he recorded the garage band classic "Gloria". His solo career began in 1967, under the pop-hit orientated guidance of Bert Berns with the release of the hit single "Brown Eyed Girl". After Berns's death, Warner Bros. Records bought out his contract and allowed him three sessions to record Astral Weeks (1968). Though this album eventually garnered praise, it was initially a poor seller.Morrison has a reputation for being at once stubborn, idiosyncratic, and 'sublime.' His live performances have been described as 'transcendental' and 'inspired.' Some of his recordings, such as the studio albums Astral Weeks and Moondance, and the live album It's Too Late to Stop Now, are highly acclaimed. His albums have performed well in Ireland and the UK, with more than 40 hitting the UK top 40. He has scored 18 top 40 albums in the US, 12 of them between 1997 and 2017.Moondance (1970) established Morrison as a major artist, and he built on his reputation throughout the 1970s with a series of acclaimed albums and live performances. He continues to record and tour, producing albums and live performances, and sometimes collaborating with other artists, such as Georgie Fame and The Chieftains.Much of Morrison's music is structured around the conventions of soul music and R&B. An equal part of his catalogue consists of lengthy, spiritually inspired musical journeys that show the influence of Celtic tradition, jazz and stream-of-consciousness narrative, such as the album Astral Weeks. The two strains together are sometimes referred to as "Celtic soul".He has received two Grammy Awards, the 1994 Brit Award for Outstanding Contribution to Music, the 2017 Americana Music Lifetime Achievement Award for Songwriting and has been inducted into both the Rock and Roll Hall of Fame and the Songwriters Hall of Fame. In 2016, he was knighted for services to the music industry and to tourism in Northern Ireland.

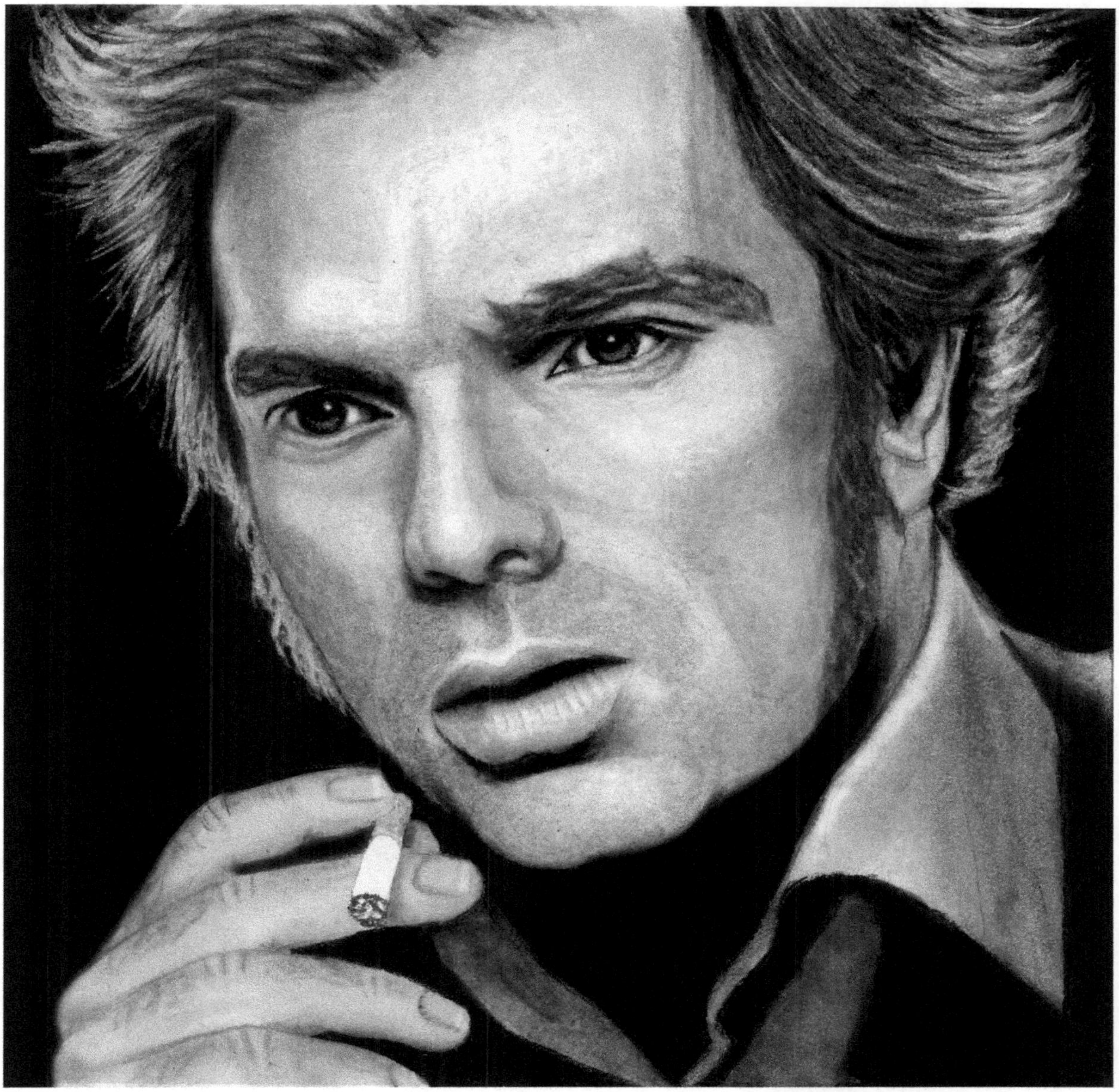

To view how this drawing was masterfully created or to purchase a Limited Edition Framed Artwork of Van Morrison type into your Internet Browser the URL shortcut ➡ **myportrait.art/vanmorrison**

To listen to their Greatest Songs type into your Internet Browser the URL shortcut ➡ **radio.surf/them**

To view all channels on THE FACE OF MUSIC Internet Radio MEGA Station type into your Internet Browser the URL shortcut ➡ **radio.surf/music**

To inquire about purchasing a Limited Edtion NFT of this portrait type into your Internet Browser the URL shortcut ➡ **myartnft.shop/vanmorrison**

To view all available NFTs type into your Internet Browser the URL shortcut ➡ **myartnft.shop/all**

# Tim McGraw

(Net worth: $85 Million)(Total Records Sold: 80+Million)
(Genre: Country)(Height: 5' - 9")

Samuel Timothy McGraw (born May 1, 1967) is an American singer, actor, guitarist, and record producer. McGraw has released 15 studio albums (11 for Curb Records, three for Big Machine Records and one for Arista Nashville). 10 of those albums have reached number one on the Top Country Albums charts, with his 1994 breakthrough album Not a Moment Too Soon being the top country album of 1994. All of these albums have produced 65 singles, 25 of which have reached number one on the Hot Country Songs or Country Airplay charts. Three of these singles – "It's Your Love", "Just to See You Smile", and "Live Like You Were Dying" – were respectively the top country songs of 1997, 1998, and 2004 according to Billboard Year-End. He has also won three Grammy Awards, 14 Academy of Country Music awards, 11 Country Music Association (CMA) awards, 10 American Music Awards, and three People's Choice Awards. His Soul2Soul II Tour, which was done in partnership with his wife, Faith Hill, is one of the highest-grossing tours in country music history, and one of the top five among all genres of music. He has sold more than 80 million records worldwide, making him one of the best-selling music artists of all time.

McGraw has ventured into acting, with supporting roles in The Blind Side (with Sandra Bullock), Friday Night Lights, The Kingdom, Tomorrowland, and Four Christmases (with Vince Vaughn and Reese Witherspoon), and The Shack, and lead roles in Flicka (2006) and Country Strong (2010). He was a minority owner of the Arena Football League's Nashville Kats.

In acknowledgement of his grandfather's Italian heritage, McGraw was honored by the National Italian American Foundation (NIAF) in 2004, receiving the NIAF Special Achievement Award in Music during the Foundation's 29th Anniversary Gala.

He has been married to singer Faith Hill since 1996, and is a son of former MLB pitcher Tug McGraw.Samuel Timothy McGraw was born in Start, Louisiana, the only child of Elizabeth "Betty" Ann D'Agostino, a waitress from Jacksonville, Florida, and Frank Edwin "Tug" McGraw Jr., a pitcher for the minor league Jacksonville Suns and future star pitcher for the New York Mets and the Philadelphia Phillies. McGraw is of Italian and Irish descent on his mother's side, and has Irish, English, Scottish, Swiss, Dutch, Czech, and German ancestry on his father's side. In 1966, D'Agostino was a student at Terry Parker High School. She lived in the same apartment building as Tug McGraw, who was playing baseball for Jacksonville. When she became pregnant with McGraw as a teen, D'Agostino's parents sent her to Louisiana to live with relatives. Through his father, McGraw has two half-brothers, Mark and Matthew, and a half-sister named Cari.

During college, McGraw learned to play guitar, and would frequently perform and sing for money. He has claimed his roommates often hid the guitar because he was so bad. McGraw followed his mother when she returned to Jacksonville, Florida, in 1987. After the move, he attended Florida Community College at Jacksonville for one term, and occasionally sat in with local bands. In 1989, on the day his hero Keith Whitley died, McGraw dropped out of college to head to Nashville and pursue a musical career.

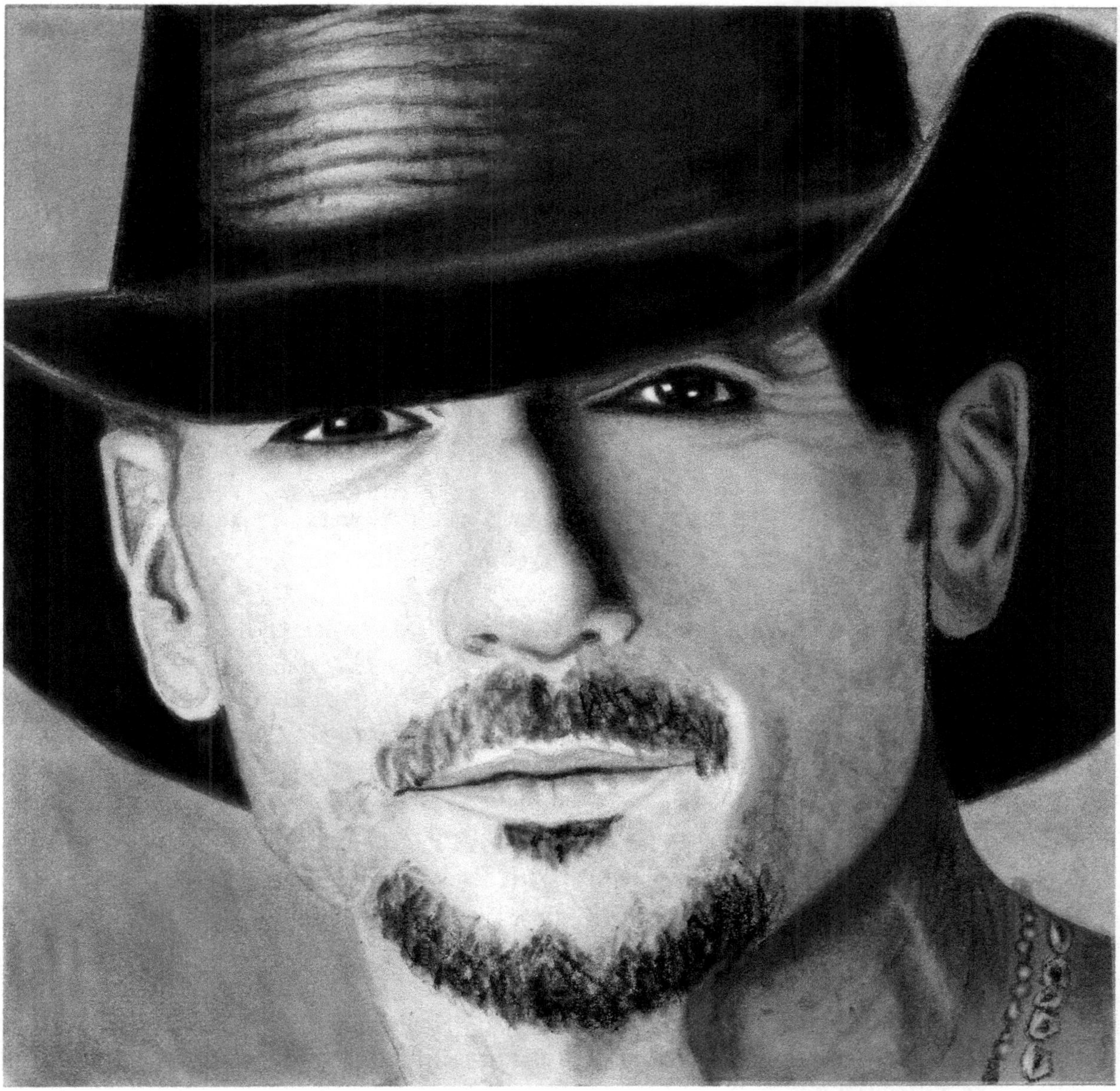

To view how this drawing was masterfully created or to purchase a Limited Edition Framed Artwork of Tim McGraw type into your Internet Browser the URL shortcut ➡ **myportrait.art/timmcgraw**

To listen to his Greatest Songs type into ycur Internet Browser the URL shortcut ➡ **radio.surf/timmcgraw**

To view all channels on THE FACE OF MUSIC Internet Radio MEGA Station type into your Internet Browser the URL shortcut ➡ **radio.surf/music**

To inquire about purchasing a Limited Edtion NFT of this portrait type into your Internet Browser the URL shortcut ➡ **myartnft.shop/timmcgraw**

To view all available NFTs type into your Internet Browser the URL shortcut ➡ **myartnft.shop/all**

# Tina Turner

(Net worth: $250 Million)(Total Records Sold: 100+Million)
(Genre: Rock , R&B , Soul , Pop)(Height: 5' - 4")

Tina Turner (born Anna Mae Bullock; November 26, 1939) is an American-born singer, songwriter, and actress. Widely referred to as the "Queen of Rock 'n' Roll", she rose to prominence as the lead singer of Ike & Tina Turner before launching a successful career as a solo performer.

Turner began her career with Ike Turner's Kings of Rhythm in 1957. Under the name Little Ann she appeared on her first record, "Boxtop", in 1958. In 1960, she was introduced as Tina Turner with the hit single "A Fool in Love". The duo went on to become "one of the most formidable live acts in history". They released hits such as "It's Gonna Work Out Fine", "River Deep – Mountain High", the Grammy-winning "Proud Mary", and "Nutbush City Limits" before disbanding in 1976.

In the 1980s, Turner launched "one of the greatest comebacks in music history". Her 1984 multi-platinum album, Private Dancer contained her hit song "What's Love Got to Do with It", which won the Grammy Award for Record of the Year, and it became her first and only No.1 on the Billboard Hot 100. At age 44, she was the oldest female solo artist to top the Hot 100. Her chart success continued with "Better Be Good to Me", "Private Dancer", "We Don't Need Another Hero (Thunderdome)", "Typical Male", "The Best", "I Don't Wanna Fight", and "GoldenEye". During her Break Every Rule World Tour in 1988, she set a then-Guinness World Record for the largest paying audience (180,000) for a solo performer. Turner also acted in the films Tommy (1975), Mad Max Beyond Thunderdome (1985), and Last Action Hero (1993). In 1993, What's Love Got to Do with It, a biopic adapted from her autobiography I, Tina: My Life Story, was released. In 2009, Turner retired after completing her Tina!: 50th Anniversary Tour, which is one of the highest-grossing tours of all time. Having sold over 100 million records, Turner is one of the best-selling recording artists of all time. She has received 12 Grammy Awards, which include eight competitive awards, three Grammy Hall of Fame awards, and a Grammy Lifetime Achievement Award. She was the first black artist and first female to be on the cover of Rolling Stone. Rolling Stone ranked her among the 100 Greatest Artists of All Time and the 100 Greatest Singers of All Time. She has a star on the Hollywood Walk of Fame and the St. Louis Walk of Fame. She was inducted into the Rock and Roll Hall of Fame with Ike Turner in 1991, and is a 2005 recipient of the Kennedy Center Honors. A resident of Küsnacht since 1994, she relinquished her American citizenship after obtaining Swiss citizenship in 2013.

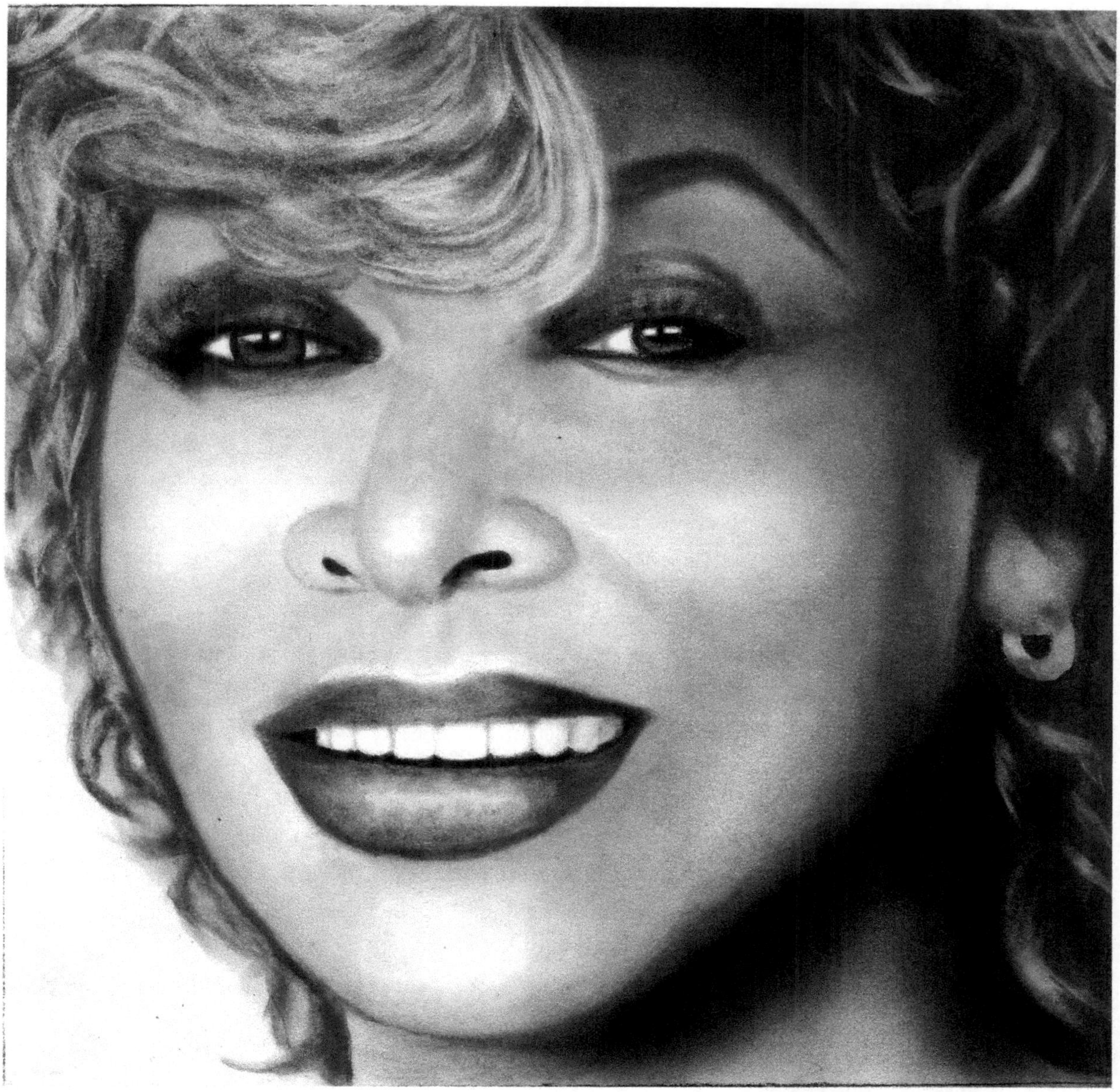

To view how this drawing was masterfully created or to purchase a Limited Edition Framed Artwork of Tina Turner type into your Internet Browser the URL shortcut ➡ **myportrait.art/tinaturner**

To listen to their Greatest Songs type into your Internet Browser the URL shortcut ➡ **radio.surf/tinaturner**

To view all channels on THE FACE OF MUSIC Internet Radio MEGA Station type into your Internet Browser the URL shortcut ➡ **radio.surf/music**

To inquire about purchasing a Limited Edtion NFT of this portrait type into your Internet Browser the URL shortcut ➡ **myartnft.shop/tinaturner**

To view all available NFTs type into your Internet Browser the URL shortcut ➡ **myartnft.shop/all**

# Tom Jones

(Net worth: $250 Million)(Total Records Sold: 100+Million)
(Genre: R&B, Soul, Country, Gospel)(Height: 5' - 10")

Sir Thomas John Woodward (born 7 June 1940), known professionally as Tom Jones, is a Welsh singer. His career began with a string of top-ten hits in the mid-1960s. He has toured regularly, with appearances in Las Vegas (1967–2011). Jones's voice has been described by Stephen Thomas Erlewine of AllMusic as a "full-throated, robust baritone".

His performing range has included pop, R&B, show tunes, country, dance, soul and gospel. In 2008, the New York Times called Jones a musical "shape shifter", who could "slide from soulful rasp to pop croon, with a voice as husky as it was pretty". Jones has sold over 100 million records, with 36 Top 40 hits in the UK and 19 in the US, including "It's Not Unusual", "What's New Pussycat?", the theme song for the 1965 James Bond film Thunderball, "Green, Green Grass of Home", "Delilah", "She's a Lady", "Kiss" and "Sex Bomb".

Jones has also occasionally dabbled in acting, first making his acting debut playing the lead role in the 1979 television film Pleasure Cove. He also appeared as himself in Tim Burton's 1996 film Mars Attacks!. In 1970 he received a Golden Globe Award for Best Actor – Television Series Musical or Comedy nomination for hosting the television series This Is Tom Jones. In 2012, he played his first dramatic acting role in an episode of Playhouse Presents. Jones received a Grammy Award for Best New Artist in 1966, an MTV Video Music Award in 1989, as well as two Brit Awards: Best British Male in 2000 and the Outstanding Contribution to Music award in 2003. Jones was appointed Officer of the Order of the British Empire (OBE) in 1998 and knighted by Queen Elizabeth II for services to music in 2005. Jones experienced a resurgence in notability in the 2010s due to his coaching role on the television talent show The Voice UK from 2012 (with the exception of 2016).

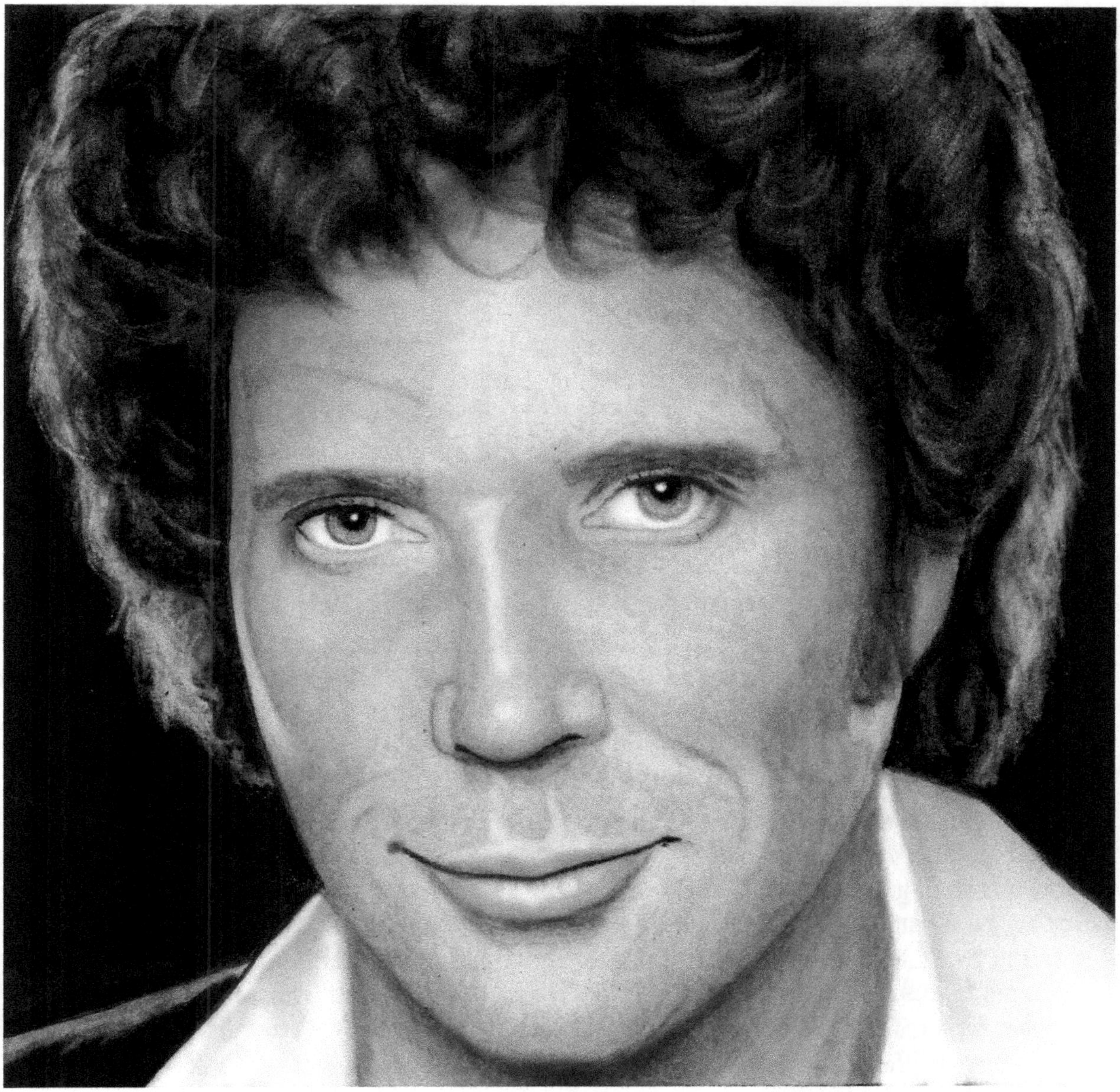

To view how this drawing was masterfully created or to purchase a Limited Edition Framed Artwork of Tom Jones type into your Internet Browser the URL shortcut ➡ **myportrait.art/tomjones**

To listen to his Greatest Songs type into your Internet Browser the URL shortcut ➡ **radio.surf/tomjones**

To view all channels on THE FACE OF MUSIC Internet Radio MEGA Station type into your Internet Browser the URL shortcut ➡ **radio.surf/music**

To inquire about purchasing a Limited Edtion NFT of this portrait type into your Internet Browser the URL shortcut ➡ **myartnft.shop/tomjones**

To view all available NFTs type into your Internet Browser the URL shortcut ➡ **myartnft.shop/all**

# Tom Petty

(Net worth: $95 Million)(Total Records Sold: 80+Million)
(Genre: Classic Rock)(Height: 5' - 9")

Thomas Earl Petty (October 20, 1950 – October 2, 2017) was an American singer, songwriter, musician, record producer, and actor. He was the lead vocalist and guitarist of Tom Petty and the Heartbreakers, formed in 1976. He previously led the band Mudcrutch, and was also a member of the late 1980s supergroup the Traveling Wilburys.

Petty recorded a number of hit singles with the Heartbreakers and as a solo artist. His hit singles with the Heartbreakers include "Don't Do Me Like That" (1979), "Refugee" (1980), "The Waiting" (1981), "Don't Come Around Here No More" (1985) and "Learning to Fly" (1991). Petty's hit singles as a solo act include "I Won't Back Down" (1989), "Free Fallin'" (1989), and "You Don't Know How It Feels" (1994). In his career, he sold more than 80 million records worldwide, making him one of the best-selling music artists of all time. Petty and the Heartbreakers were inducted into the Rock and Roll Hall of Fame in 2002.

Petty died of an accidental drug overdose on October 2, 2017, one week after the end of the Heartbreakers' 40th Anniversary Tour.

Petty was born October 20, 1950, in Gainesville, Florida, the first of two sons of Kitty (Katherine) Petty, a local tax office worker, and Earl Petty, who was a traveling salesman. He had a brother, Bruce, who was seven years younger. His interest in rock and roll music began at age ten when he met Elvis Presley. In the summer of 1961, his uncle was working on the set of Presley's film Follow That Dream, in nearby Ocala, and invited Petty to watch the shoot. He instantly became a Presley fan, and when he returned that Saturday, he was greeted by his friend Keith Harben, and soon traded his Wham-O slingshot for a collection of Elvis 45's. Of that meeting with Presley, Petty said, "Elvis glowed." In a 2006 interview, Petty said he knew he wanted to be in a band the moment he saw the Beatles on The Ed Sullivan Show.

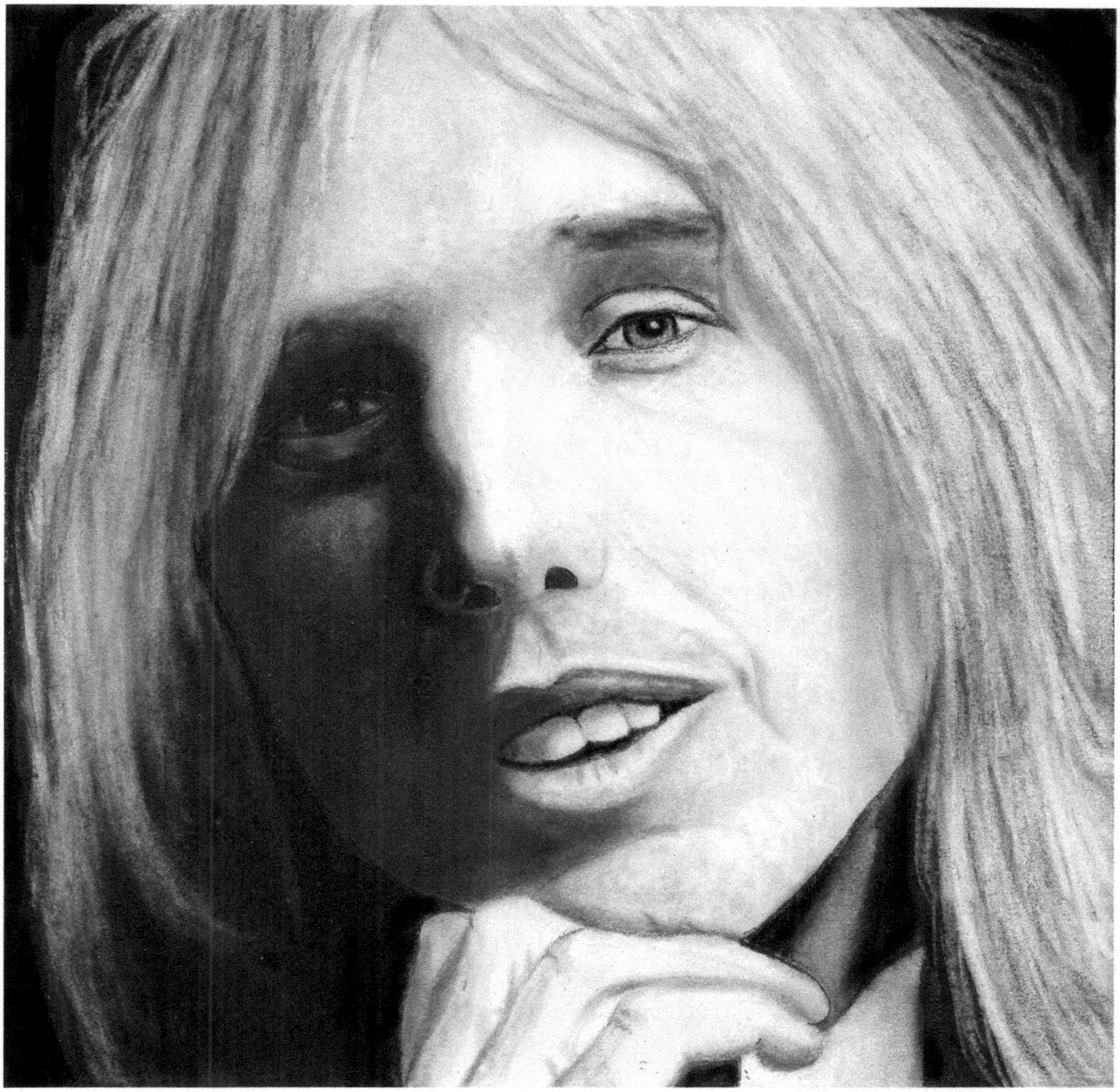

To view how this drawing was masterfully created or to purchase a Limited Edition Framed Artwork of Tom Petty type into your Internet Browser the URL shortcut ➡ **myportrait.art/tompetty**

To listen to his Greatest Songs type into your Internet Browser the URL shortcut ➡ **radio.surf/tompetty**

To view all channels on THE FACE OF MUSIC Internet Radio MEGA Station type into your Internet Browser the URL shortcut ➡ **radio.surf/music**

To inquire about purchasing a Limited Edtion NFT of this portrait type into your Internet Browser the URL shortcut ➡ **myartnft.shop/tompetty**

To view all available NFTs type into your Internet Browser the URL shortcut ➡ **myartnft.shop/all**

# Tony Bennett

(Net worth: $200 Million)(Total Records Sold: 50+Million)
(Genre: Swing, Jazz, Crooner)(Height: 5' - 5")

Anthony Dominick Benedetto (born August 3, 1926), known professionally as Tony Bennett, is an American singer of traditional pop standards, big band, show tunes, and jazz. He is also a painter, having created works under his birth name that are on permanent public display in several institutions. He is the founder of the Frank Sinatra School of the Arts in Astoria, Queens, New York.

Born and raised in Astoria and Pyrites, New York to an Italian-American family, Bennett began singing at an early age. He fought in the final stages of World War II as a U.S. Army infantryman in the European Theater. Afterward, he developed his singing technique, signed with Columbia Records and had his first number-one popular song with "Because of You" in 1951. Several top hits such as "Rags to Riches" followed in early 1953. He then refined his approach to encompass jazz singing. He reached an artistic peak in the late 1950s with albums such as The Beat of My Heart and Basie Swings, Bennett Sings. In 1962, Bennett recorded his signature song, "I Left My Heart in San Francisco". His career and personal life experienced an extended downturn during the height of the rock music era. Bennett staged a comeback in the late 1980s and 1990s, putting out gold record albums again and expanding his reach to the MTV generation while keeping his musical style intact. He remains a popular and critically praised recording artist and concert performer to date. His work includes a collaboration with Lady Gaga having toured and released an album together, Cheek to Cheek (2014), for which they won the Grammy Award for Best Traditional Pop Vocal Album.

He has won 19 Grammy Awards (including a Lifetime Achievement Award, presented in 2001) and two Primetime Emmy Awards, and was named an NEA Jazz Master and a Kennedy Center Honoree. Bennett has sold over 50 million records worldwide.

In February 2021, it was revealed that Bennett was diagnosed with Alzheimer's disease in 2016. Due to the slow progression of his illness, he has continued to record, tour, and perform

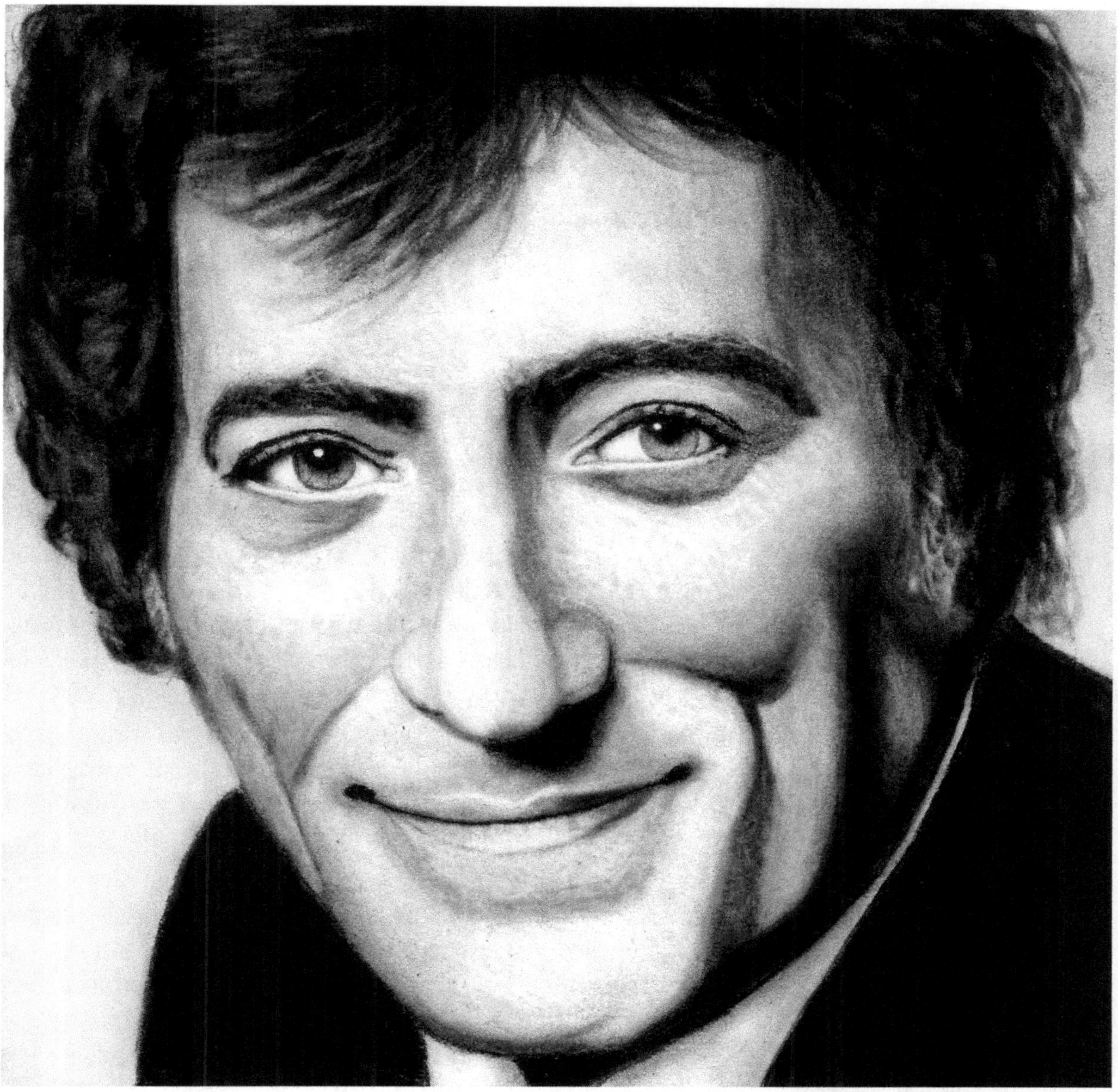

To view how this drawing was masterfully created or to purchase a Limited Edition Framed Artwork of Tony Bennett type into your Internet Browser the URL shortcut ➡ **myportrait.art/tonybennett**

To listen to his Greatest Songs type into your Internet Browser the URL shortcut ➡ **radio.surf/tonybennett**

To view all channels on THE FACE OF MUSIC Internet Radio MEGA Station type into your Internet Browser the URL shortcut ➡ **radio.surf/music**

To inquire about purchasing a Limited Edtion NFT of this portrait type into your Internet Browser the URL shortcut ➡ **myartnft.shop/tonybennett**

To view all available NFTs type into your Internet Browser the URL shortcut ➡ **myartnft.shop/all**

# Tupac

(Net worth: $200 Thousand)(Total Records Sold: 75+Million)
(Genre: West Coast Hip-Hop)(Height: 5' - 9")

Tupac Amaru Shakur (born Lesane Parish Crooks, June 16, 1971 – September 13, 1996), better known by his stage name 2Pac and by his alias Makaveli, was an American rapper and actor. He is widely considered to be one of the most influential rappers of all time. Much of Shakur's work has been noted for addressing contemporary social issues that plagued inner cities, and he has often been considered a symbol of activism against inequality.

Shakur was born in Manhattan, a borough of New York City, but relocated to Baltimore, Maryland in 1984 and then the San Francisco Bay Area in 1988. He moved to Los Angeles in 1993 to further pursue his music career. By the time he released his debut album 2Pacalypse Now in 1991, he had become a central figure in West Coast hip hop, introducing social issues to the genre at a time when gangsta rap was dominant in the mainstream. Shakur achieved further critical and commercial success with his follow-up albums Strictly 4 My N.I.G.G.A.Z... (1993) and Me Against the World (1995).

In 1995, Shakur served eight months in prison on sexual assault charges, but was released after agreeing to sign with Suge Knight's label Death Row Records in exchange for Knight posting his bail. Following his release, Shakur became heavily involved in the growing East Coast–West Coast hip hop rivalry. His double-disc album All Eyez on Me (1996) was certified Diamond by the RIAA. On September 7, 1996, Shakur was shot four times by an unknown assailant in a drive-by shooting in Las Vegas, Nevada; he died six days later and the gunman was never captured. Shakur's friend-turned-rival, The Notorious B.I.G., was at first considered a suspect due to the pair's public feud, but was also murdered in another drive-by shooting six months later. Five more albums have been released since Shakur's death, all of which have been certified platinum in the United States.

Shakur is one of the best-selling music artists of all time, having sold over 75 million records worldwide. In 2002, he was inducted into the Hip-Hop Hall of Fame. In 2017, he was inducted into the Rock and Roll Hall of Fame in his first year of eligibility. Rolling Stone named Shakur in its list of the 100 Greatest Artists of All Time. Outside music, Shakur also found considerable success as an actor, with his starring roles as Bishop in Juice (1992), Lucky in Poetic Justice (1993) where he starred alongside Janet Jackson, Ezekiel in Gridlock'd (1997), and Jake in Gang Related (1997), all of which garnered praise from critics.

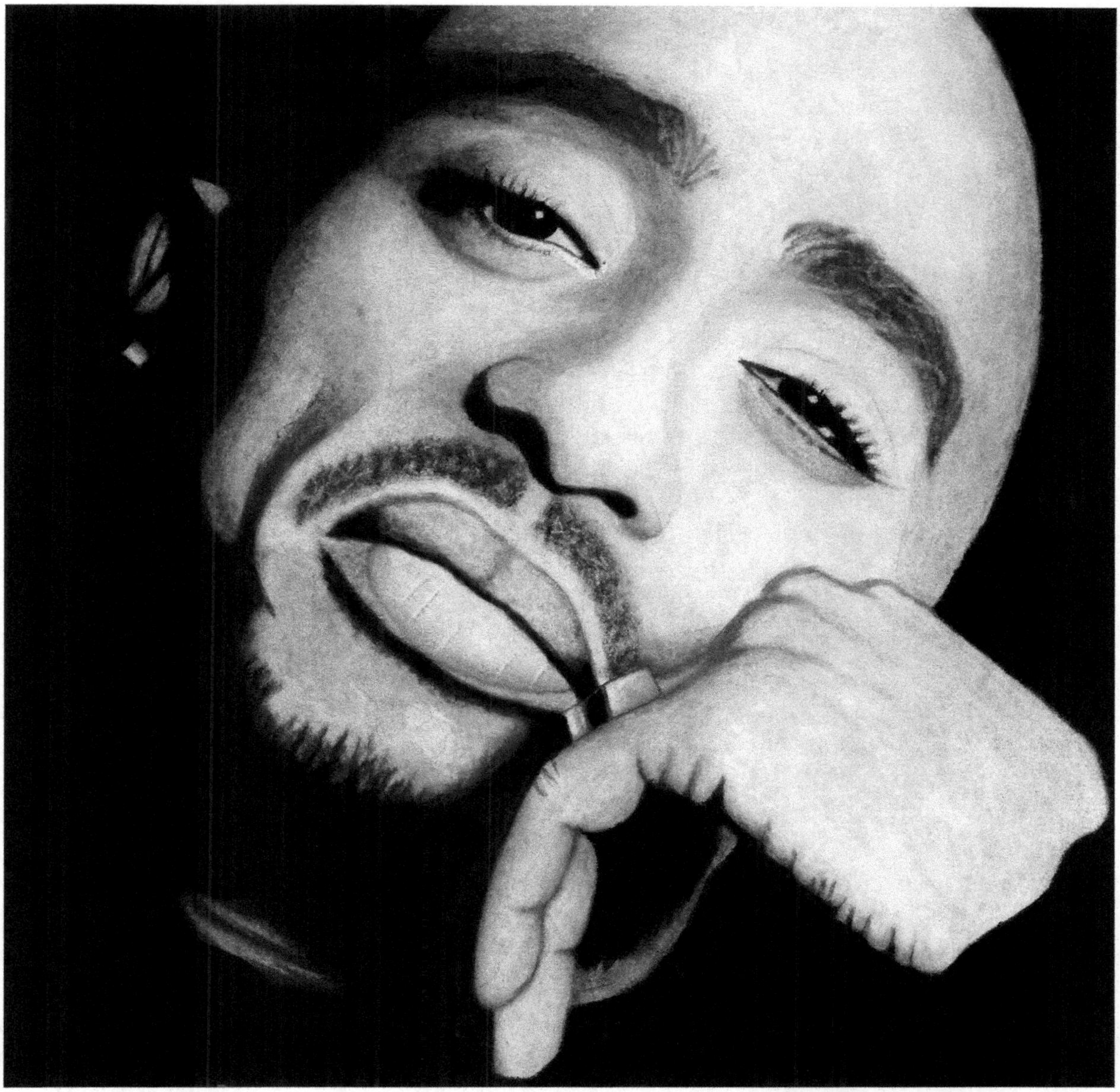

To view how this drawing was masterfully created or to purchase a Limited Edition Framed Artwork of Tupac type into your Internet Browser the URL shortcut ➡ **myportrait.art/tupac**

To listen to his Greatest Songs type into your Internet Browser the URL shortcut ➡ **radio.surf/tupac**

To view all channels on THE FACE OF MUSIC Internet Radio MEGA Station type into your Internet Browser the URL shortcut ➡ **radio.surf/music**

To inquire about purchasing a Limited Edtion NFT of this portrait type into your Internet Browser the URL shortcut ➡ **myartnft.shop/tupac**

To view all available NFTs type into your Internet Browser the URL shortcut ➡ **myartnft.shop/all**

# U2

(Total Records Sold: 150+ Million) (Genre: Rock , Pop)

U2 are an Irish rock band from Dublin, formed in 1976. The group consists of Bono (lead vocals and rhythm guitar), the Edge (lead guitar, keyboards, and backing vocals), Adam Clayton (bass guitar), and Larry Mullen Jr. (drums and percussion). Initially rooted in post-punk, U2's musical style has evolved throughout their career, yet has maintained an anthemic quality built on Bono's expressive vocals and the Edge's chiming, effects-based guitar sounds. Their lyrics, often embellished with spiritual imagery, focus on personal and sociopolitical themes. Popular for their live performances, the group have staged several ambitious and elaborate tours over their career.The band was formed when the members were teenaged pupils of Mount Temple Comprehensive School and had limited musical proficiency. Within four years, they signed with Island Records and released their debut album, Boy (1980). Subsequent work such as their first UK number-one album, War (1983), and the singles "Sunday Bloody Sunday" and "Pride (In the Name of Love)" helped establish U2's reputation as a politically and socially conscious group. By the mid-1980s, they had become renowned globally for their live act, highlighted by their performance at Live Aid in 1985. The group's fifth album, The Joshua Tree (1987), made them international superstars and was their greatest critical and commercial success. Topping music charts around the world, it produced their only number-one singles in the US to date: "With or Without You" and "I Still Haven't Found What I'm Looking For".Facing creative stagnation and a backlash to their documentary/ double album, Rattle and Hum (1988), U2 reinvented themselves in the 1990s. Beginning with their acclaimed seventh album, Achtung Baby (1991), and the multimedia-intensive Zoo TV Tour, the band pursued a new musical direction influenced by alternative rock, electronic dance music, and industrial music, and they embraced a more ironic, flippant image. This experimentation continued through their ninth album, Pop (1997), and the PopMart Tour, which were mixed successes. U2 regained critical and commercial favour with the records All That You Can't Leave Behind (2000) and How to Dismantle an Atomic Bomb (2004), which established a more conventional, mainstream sound for the group. Their U2 360° Tour of 2009–2011 set records for the highest-attended and highest-grossing concert tour, both of which were surpassed in 2019. The group most recently released the companion albums Songs of Innocence (2014) and Songs of Experience (2017), the former of which received criticism for its pervasive, no-cost release through the iTunes Store.U2 have released 14 studio albums and are one of the world's best-selling music artists, having sold an estimated 150–170 million records worldwide. They have won 22 Grammy Awards, more than any other band, and in 2005, they were inducted into the Rock and Roll Hall of Fame in their first year of eligibility. Rolling Stone ranked U2 at number 22 on its list of the "100 Greatest Artists of All Time". Throughout their career, as a band and as individuals, they have campaigned for human rights and social justice causes, including Amnesty International, Jubilee 2000, the ONE/DATA campaigns, Product Red, War Child, and Music Rising.

# Bono

(Net Worth: $700 Million)(Height: 5' - 6")

Paul David Hewson (born 10 May 1960), known by his stage name Bono , is an Irish singer-songwriter, activist, philanthropist, venture capitalist, businessman, and actor. He is best known as the lead vocalist and primary lyricist of rock band U2.

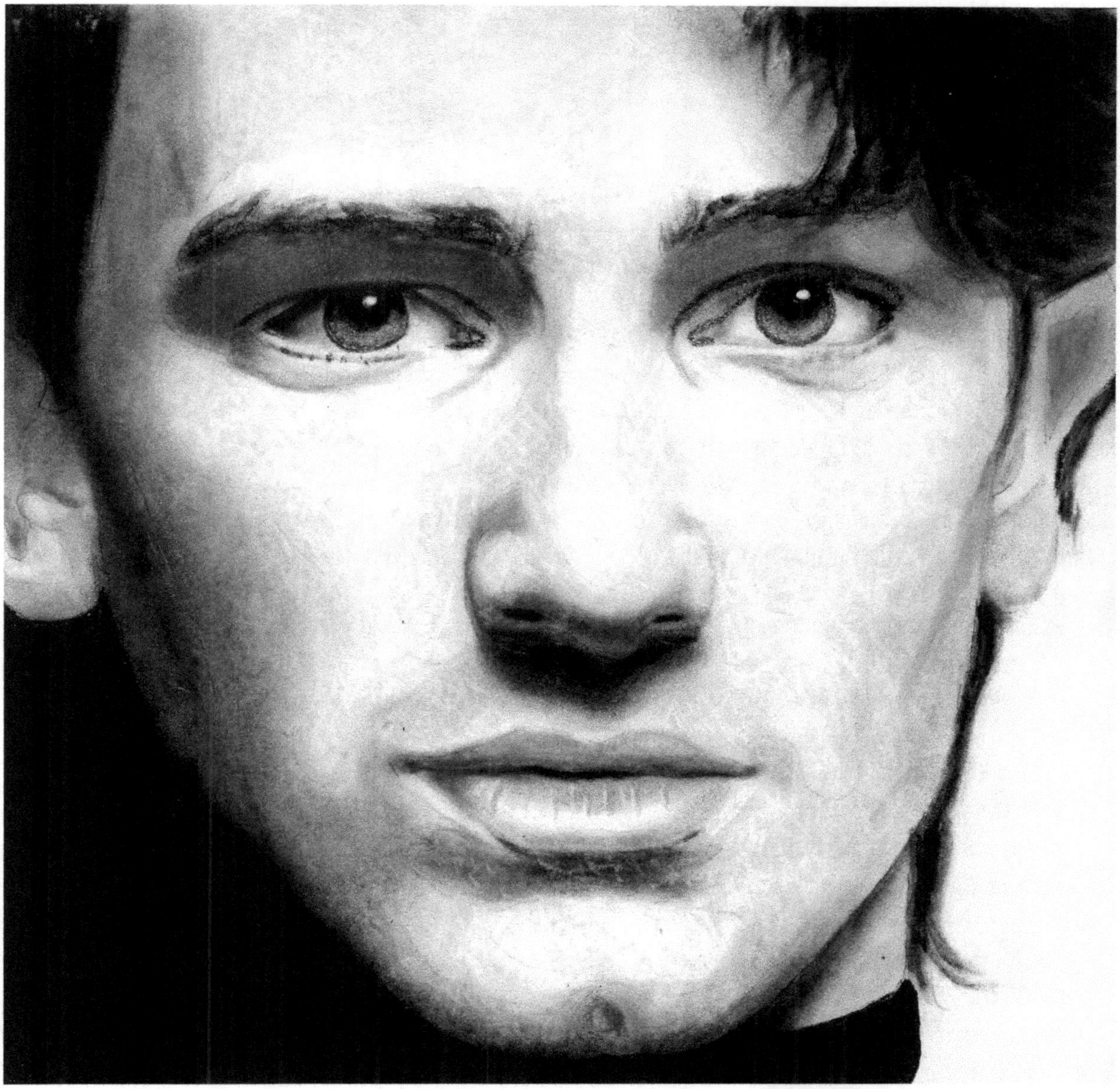

To view how this drawing was masterfully created or to purchase a Limited Edition Framed Artwork of Bono type into your Internet Browser the URL shortcut ➡ **myportrait.art/bono**

To listen to their Greatest Songs type into your Internet Browser the URL shortcut ➡ **radio.surf/u2**

To view all channels on THE FACE OF MUSIC Internet Radio MEGA Station type into your Internet Browser the URL shortcut ➡ **radio.surf/music**

To inquire about purchasing a Limited Edtion NFT of this portrait type into your Internet Browser the URL shortcut ➡ **myartnft.shop/bono**

To view all available NFTs type into your Internet Browser the URL shortcut ➡ **myartnft.shop/all**

# Usher

(Net worth: $180 Million)(Total Records Sold: 80 Million)
(Genre: R&B , Pop , Hip-Hop)(Height: 5' - 8")

Usher Raymond IV (born October 14, 1978) is an American singer, songwriter, actor, businessman, and dancer. He was born in Dallas, Texas, but raised in Chattanooga, Tennessee, until moving to Atlanta, Georgia. At the age of 12, his mother put him in local singing competitions before catching the attention of a music A&R from LaFace Records. He released his self-titled debut album Usher (1994), and rose to fame in the late 1990s with the release of his second album My Way (1997). It spawned his first U.S. Billboard Hot 100 number-one single "Nice & Slow", and the top-two singles "You Make Me Wanna..." and "My Way". His third album, 8701 (2001), produced the number-one singles "U Remind Me" and "U Got It Bad", as well as the top-three single "U Don't Have to Call". It sold eight million copies worldwide and won his first two Grammy Awards as Best Male R&B Vocal Performance in 2002 and 2003. Confessions (2004) established him as one of the best-selling musical artists of the 2000s decade, containing four consecutive Billboard Hot 100 number-one singles—"Yeah!" (featuring Lil Jon and Ludacris), "Burn", "Confessions Part II", and "My Boo" (with Alicia Keys)—and the top-ten "Caught Up". It sold over 20 million copies worldwide and was certified Diamond by the RIAA. After splitting from his manager and mother in 2007, he released the albums Here I Stand (2008) and Raymond v. Raymond (2010), both of which debuted atop of the Billboard 200 chart and respectively produced the number-one singles "Love in This Club" (featuring Young Jeezy) and "OMG" (featuring will.i.am). The EP Versus produced the top-five single "DJ Got Us Fallin' in Love" (featuring Pitbull) before the release of the top-fifteen single "More". Looking 4 Myself (2012) also debuted atop the Billboard 200 chart with the top-ten single "Scream". The R&B ballads "There Goes My Baby" and "Climax" received Grammy Awards in 2011 and 2013. "I Don't Mind" (featuring Juicy J) also reached the top-fifteen in 2014, while Hard II Love (2016) peaked at five on the Billboard 200 chart. In 2018, he released A, a collaborative album with record producer Zaytoven.

Usher has sold 23.8 million albums and 38.2 million digital songs in the United States. Internationally, he has sold 80 million records worldwide, making him one of the best-selling music artists of all time. At the end of 2009, Billboard named him the second most successful artist of the 2000s decade, the number-one Hot 100 artist of the 2000s decade, and ranked Confessions as the top solo album of the 2000s decade. In 2010, Billboard placed him at number 6 on their list of Top 50 R&B/Hip-Hop Artists of the Past 25 Years. In 2019, Billboard also placed him at number 14 on their "Greatest of All Time Hot 100 Artists" list. Usher has earned 9 number-one singles. Considered an icon and sex symbol, he has had TV and film appearances and seen inductions into the Georgia Music Hall of Fame and Hollywood Walk of Fame. Usher has won numerous awards and accolades including eight Grammy Awards, 34 ASCAP Awards, nine Soul Train Music Awards, and eight American Music Awards. With 18 awards, Usher is the fifth-most awarded artist at the Billboard Music Awards. He owns the record label Raymond-Braun Media Group (RBMG), a joint venture with talent manager Scooter Braun that includes Canadian singer Justin Bieber. Alongside a successful music career, Usher is also acclaimed for involvement in humanitarian causes and is the founder of Usher's New Look foundation.

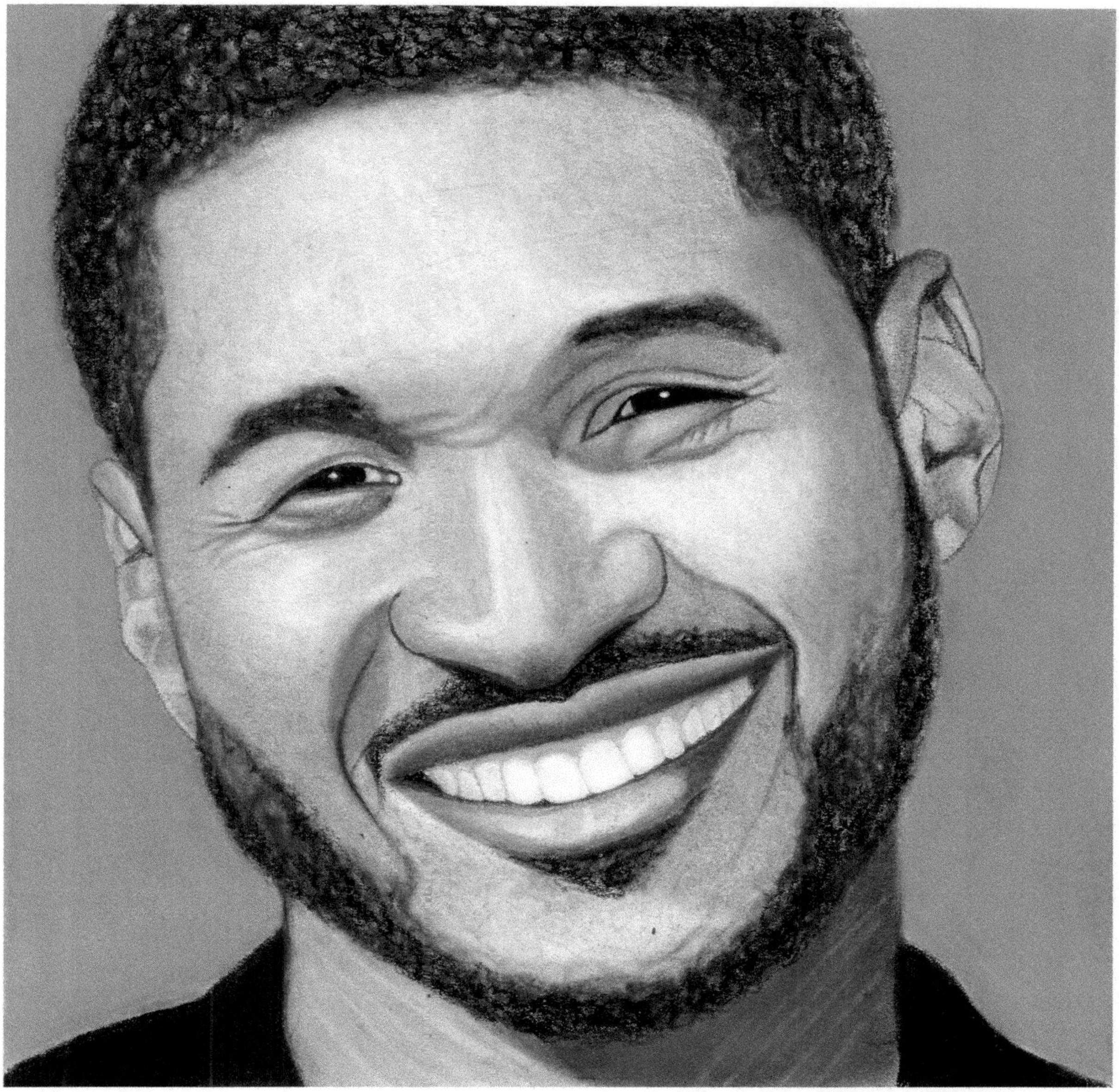

To view how this drawing was masterfully created or to purchase a Limited Edition Framed Artwork of Usher type into your Internet Browser the URL shortcut ➡ **myportrait.art/usher**

To listen to his Greatest Songs type into your Internet Browser the URL shortcut ➡ **radio.surf/usher**

To view all channels on THE FACE OF MUSIC Internet Radio MEGA Station type into your Internet Browser the URL shortcut ➡ **radio.surf/music**

To inquire about purchasing a Limited Edtion NFT of this portrait type into your Internet Browser the URL shortcut ➡ **myartnft.shop/usher**

To view all available NFTs type into your Internet Browser the URL shortcut ➡ **myartnft.shop/all**

# Van Halen

(Total Albums Sold: 80 Million) (Genre: Hard Rock)

Van Halen was an American rock band formed in Pasadena, California in 1974. Credited with "restoring hard rock to the forefront of the music scene", Van Halen was known for its energetic live shows and for the virtuosic talent of its prodigy lead-guitarist, Eddie Van Halen. The band was inducted into the Rock and Roll Hall of Fame in 2007.From 1974 until 1985, Van Halen consisted of Eddie Van Halen; Eddie's brother, drummer Alex Van Halen; energetic vocalist David Lee Roth; and bassist/vocalist Michael Anthony. Upon its release in 1978, the band's self-titled debut album reached No. 19 on the Billboard pop music charts and would sell over 10 million copies in the U.S. By 1982, the band released four more albums (Van Halen II, Women and Children First, Fair Warning, and Diver Down), all of which have since been certified multi-platinum. By the early 1980s, Van Halen was one of the most successful rock acts of the day. The album 1984 was a commercial success with U.S. sales of 10 million copies and four hit singles; its lead single, "Jump", was the band's only U.S. number one single.In 1985, Roth left the band to embark on a solo career and was replaced by former Montrose lead vocalist Sammy Hagar. With Hagar, the group released four U.S. number-one, multi-platinum albums over the course of 11 years (5150 in 1986, OU812 in 1988, For Unlawful Carnal Knowledge in 1991, and Balance in 1995). Hagar left the band in 1996 shortly before the release of the band's first greatest hits collection, Best Of – Volume I. Former Extreme frontman Gary Cherone replaced Hagar and recorded the commercially unsuccessful album Van Halen III with the band in 1998, before parting ways in 1999. Van Halen then went on hiatus until reuniting with Hagar in 2003 for a worldwide tour in 2004 and the double-disc greatest hits collection The Best of Both Worlds. Hagar again left Van Halen in 2005. In 2006 Roth returned, but Anthony was replaced on bass guitar by Wolfgang Van Halen, Eddie's son. In 2012, the band released their final studio album A Different Kind of Truth, which was commercially and critically successful; it was also Van Halen's only album with Roth in 28 years and the only one to feature Wolfgang. As of March 2019, Van Halen is 20th on the RIAA list of best-selling artists in the United States; the band has sold 56 million albums in the States and more than 80 million worldwide, making them one of the best-selling groups of all time. As of 2007, Van Halen is one of only five rock bands with two studio albums to sell more than 10 million copies in the United States and is tied for the most multi-platinum albums by an American band. Additionally, Van Halen has charted 13 number-one hits on Billboard's Mainstream Rock chart. VH1 ranked the band seventh on a list of the top 100 Hard Rock artists of all time.On October 6, 2020, Eddie died from cancer, which he was initially diagnosed with in 2001. Wolfgang subsequently confirmed a month after his father's death that Van Halen had disbanded.

# David Lee Roth

(Net Worth: $150 Million)(Height: 6' - 0")

David Lee Roth (born October 10, 1954) is an American rock musician, singer, songwriter, and former radio personality. He is best known as the lead singer of hard rock band Van Halen.

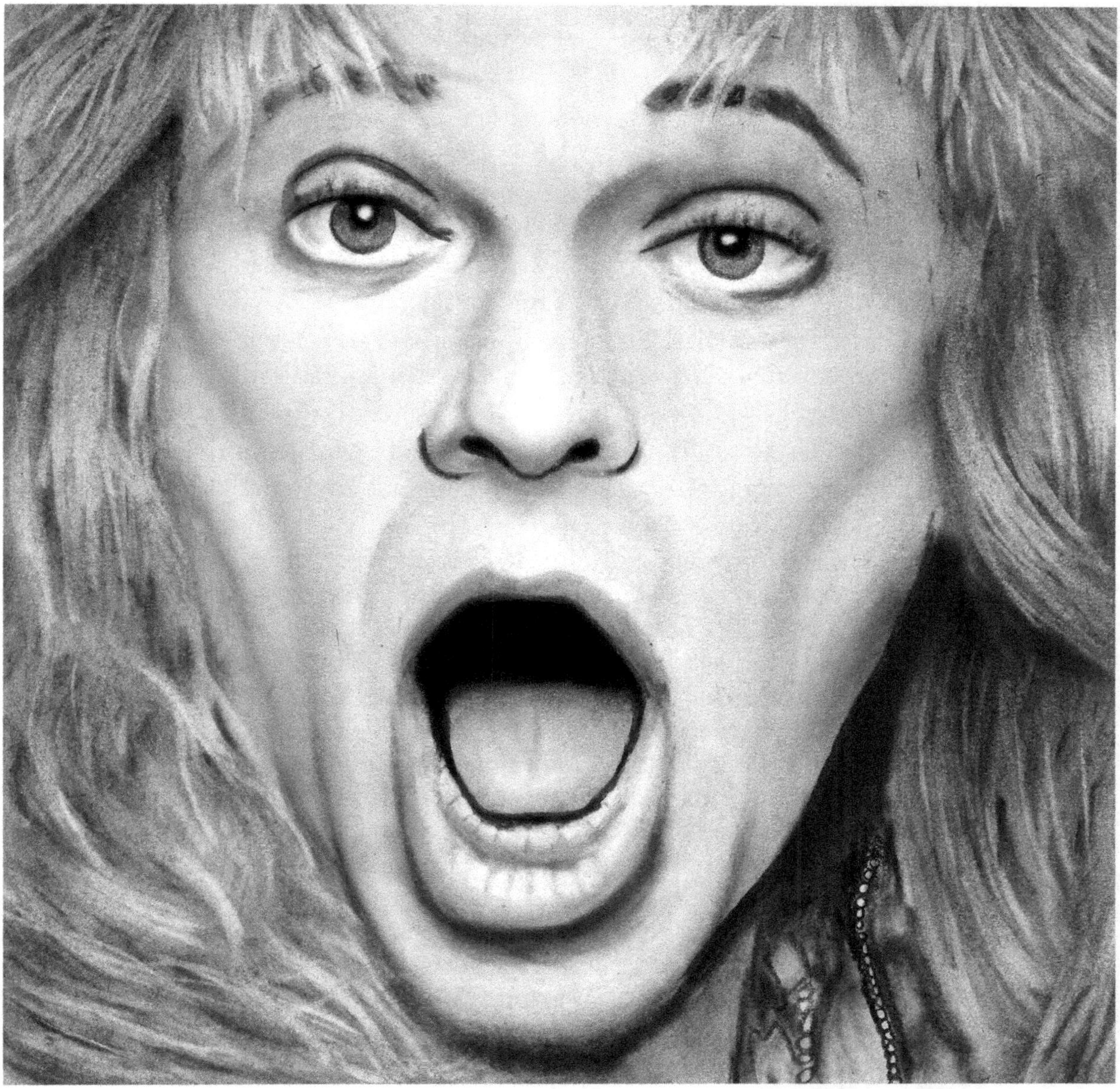

To view how this drawing was masterfully created or to purchase a Limited Edition Framed Artwork of David Lee Roth type into your Internet Browser the URL shortcut ➡ **myportrait.art/davidleeroth**

To listen to their Greatest Songs type into your Internet Browser the URL shortcut ➡ **radio.surf/vanhalen**

To view all channels on THE FACE OF MUSIC Internet Radio MEGA Station type into your Internet Browser the URL shortcut ➡ **radio.surf/music**

To inquire about purchasing a Limited Edtion NFT of this portrait type into your Internet Browser the URL shortcut ➡ **myartnft.shop/davidleeroth**

To view all available NFTs type into your Internet Browser the URL shortcut ➡ **myartnft.shop/all**

# Wayne Newton

(Net worth: $50 Million)(Total Records Sold: Millions)
(Genre: Jazz , Pop)(Height: 6' - 1")

Carson Wayne Newton (born April 3, 1942) is an American singer and actor. One of the best-known entertainers in Las Vegas, Nevada, he is known by the nicknames The Midnight Idol, Mr. Las Vegas and Mr. Entertainment. His well known songs include 1972's "Daddy, Don't You Walk So Fast" (his biggest hit, peaking at No. 4 on the Hot 100), "Years" (1980), and his vocal version of "Red Roses for a Blue Lady" (1965). His signature song "Danke Schoen" (1963) was notably used in the score for Ferris Bueller's Day Off (1986).

Many prominent entertainment icons such as Lucille Ball, Bobby Darin, Danny Thomas, George Burns, and Jack Benny lent Newton their support. In particular, Benny hired Newton as an opening act for his show. After his job with Benny ended, Newton was offered a job to open for another comic at the Flamingo Hotel, but Newton asked for, and was given, a headline act. In 1972 his recording of "Daddy, Don't You Walk So Fast" sold over one million copies and was awarded a gold disc by the R.I.A.A. in July 1972. The song peaked at number 1 in Australia in June 1972, while the album of the same name peaked at number 25 on the album charts. Influential music director Rosalie Trombley of Canadian station CKLW "The Big 8" radio in the Detroit-Windsor area decided to add the record to her radio station to embarrass her ex-husband, who wasn't faithful about seeing his children, as Trombley explained in the documentary Radio Revolution: The Rise and Fall of the Big 8. The record topped the Canadian charts. From Detroit, "Daddy Don't You Walk So Fast" took off and broke nationwide.

Newton's "distinctive high-pitched voice stayed with him as he progressed from teen singer to Las Vegas legend," although his voice did lower somewhat in the 1970s and 1980s.

From 1980 through 1982, The Beach Boys and The Grass Roots performed Independence Day concerts on the National Mall in Washington, D.C., attracting large crowds. However, in April 1983, James G. Watt, President Ronald Reagan's Secretary of the Interior, banned Independence Day concerts on the Mall by such groups. Watt said that "rock bands" that had performed on the Mall on Independence Day in 1981 and 1982 had encouraged drug use and alcoholism and had attracted "the wrong element", who would mug individuals and families attending any similar events in the future. Watt then announced that Newton, a friend and supporter of President Reagan and a contributor to Republican Party political campaigns, would perform at the Mall's 1983 Independence Day celebration. Newton entered the Independence Day stage on the Mall on July 4, 1983, to mostly cheering members of the audience, but some members booed.

On May 23, 1989, Newton's live stage show was broadcast as a pay-per-view event called Wayne Newton Live in Concert. Newton did not perform his trademark songs "Danke Schoen" or "Red Roses for a Blue Lady". However, he closed the show with a special finale of "MacArthur Park", which culminated with an onstage rainfall.

On December 12, 1992, Newton hit #1 on the Cashbox Pop and Country charts with an Elvis Presley-inspired song, "The Letter". Controversy swirled around this chart feat, as "The Letter" did not chart at all on Billboard Magazine's authoritative Hot 100 chart, Adult Contemporary chart or "Bubbling Under" chart. It did not make the Radio and Records magazine chart either. This marked the first and only time in history that a record hit #1 on the Cashbox Top 100 chart, yet failed even to chart on Billboard's Hot 100.

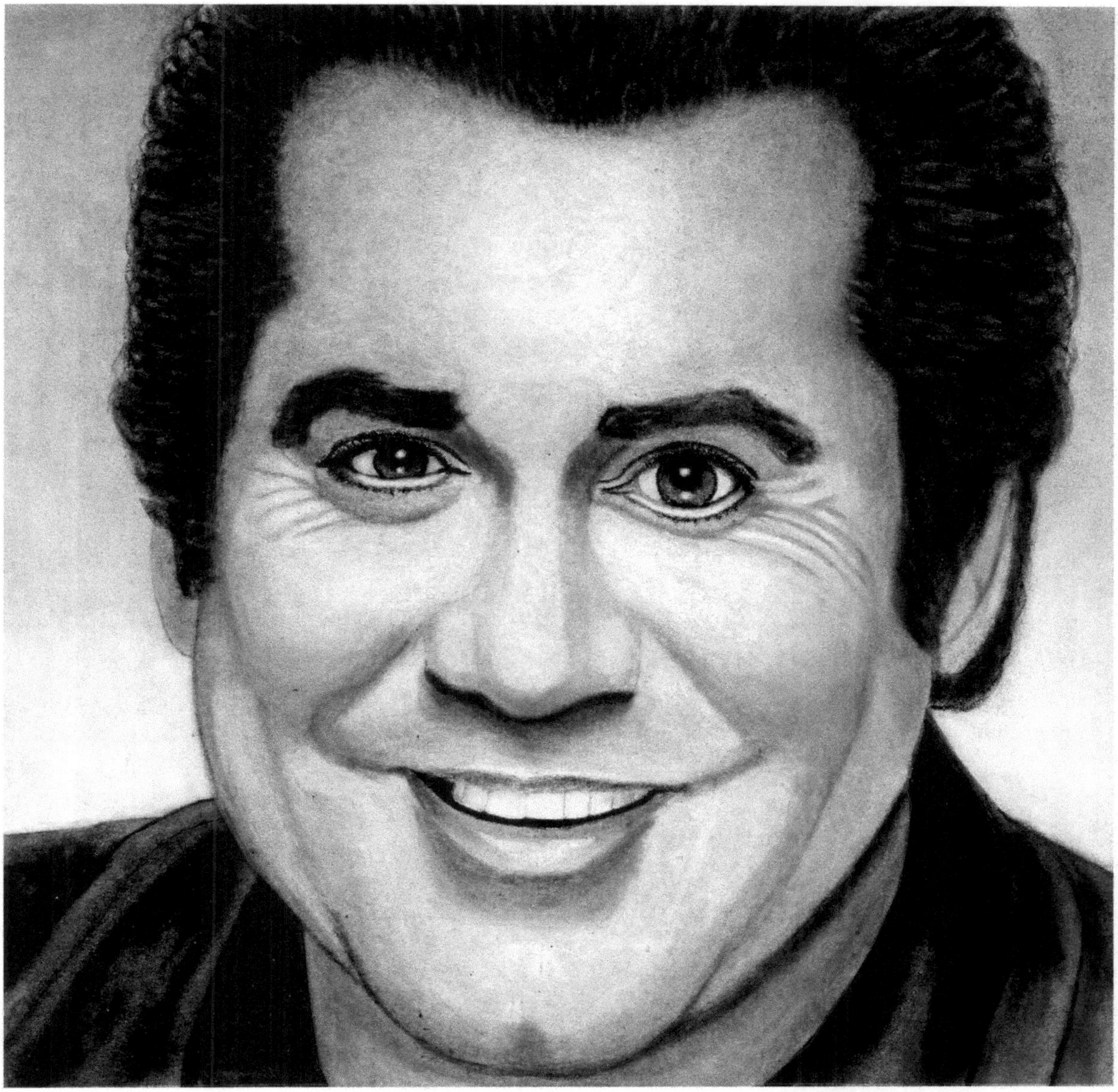

To view how this drawing was masterfully created or to purchase a Limited Edition Framed Artwork of Wayne Newton type into your Internet Browser the URL shortcut ➡ **myportrait.art/waynenewton**

To listen to his Greatest Songs type into your Internet Browser the URL shortcut
➡ **radio.surf/waynenewton**

To view all channels on THE FACE OF MUSIC Internet Radio MEGA Station type into your Internet Browser the URL shortcut ➡ **radio.surf/music**

To inquire about purchasing a Limited Edtion NFT of this portrait type into your Internet Browser the URL shortcut ➡ **myartnft.shop/waynenewton**

To view all available NFTs type into your Internet Browser the URL shortcut ➡ **myartnft.shop/all**

# White Zombie

(Total Albums Sold: Millions) (Genre: Heavy Metal)

White Zombie was an American heavy metal band that formed in 1985. Based in New York City, White Zombie was originally a noise rock band, and was known for its later heavy metal-oriented sound. Their best-known songs include "Thunder Kiss '65", "Black Sunshine" and "More Human than Human". The group officially disbanded in 1998. In 2000, White Zombie was included on VH1's 100 Greatest Artists of Hard Rock, ranking at No. 56.

White Zombie was co-founded by Rob Zombie, after coming up with the band idea in 1985 while attending Parsons School of Design in his junior year. Zombie's girlfriend at the time, Sean Yseult, was the other co-founder. She had been playing the Farfisa keyboard in the band LIFE with Ivan de Prume, but the band soon broke up. Ena Kostabi owned a recording studio, which he would rent out to different bands. When he met Yseult, she asked if he could teach her to play bass. They then recruited Peter Landau to play drums and began to write and record songs. White Zombie's first release, Gods on Voodoo Moon, was an EP and was recorded on October 18, 1985. It was released under the band's own label Silent Explosion, under which they would release most of their early work. Only 300 copies were pressed, of which only 100 were sold; the band members still retain possession of the remaining 200.

# Rob Zombie

(Net Worth: $50 Million)(Height: 5' -10")

Robert Bartleh Cummings (born January 12, 1965), known professionally as Rob Zombie, is an American singer, songwriter, filmmaker, and voice actor. He is a founding member of the heavy metal band White Zombie, releasing four studio albums with the band. He is the older brother of Spider One, the lead vocalist of the industrial metal band Powerman 5000.

Zombie's first solo effort was a 1996 song titled "Hands of Death (Burn Baby Burn)", written and performed with Alice Cooper. It went on to receive a nomination for Best Metal Performance at the 39th Annual Grammy Awards. In 1997, he began working on his debut solo studio album, Hellbilly Deluxe, which was released in August 1998. A month later, Zombie officially disbanded White Zombie. Hellbilly Deluxe went on to sell over three million copies worldwide and spawned three singles. Zombie directed the horror film House of 1000 Corpses in 2000, though the controversial project was not released until 2003. His second studio album, The Sinister Urge (2001), became his second platinum album in the U.S.

Since the beginning of his music career, Zombie's music and lyrics have featured notable horror and sci-fi themes. His live shows have been praised for their elaborate shock rock theatricality. Since beginning his solo career, Zombie has sold an estimated fifteen million albums worldwide.

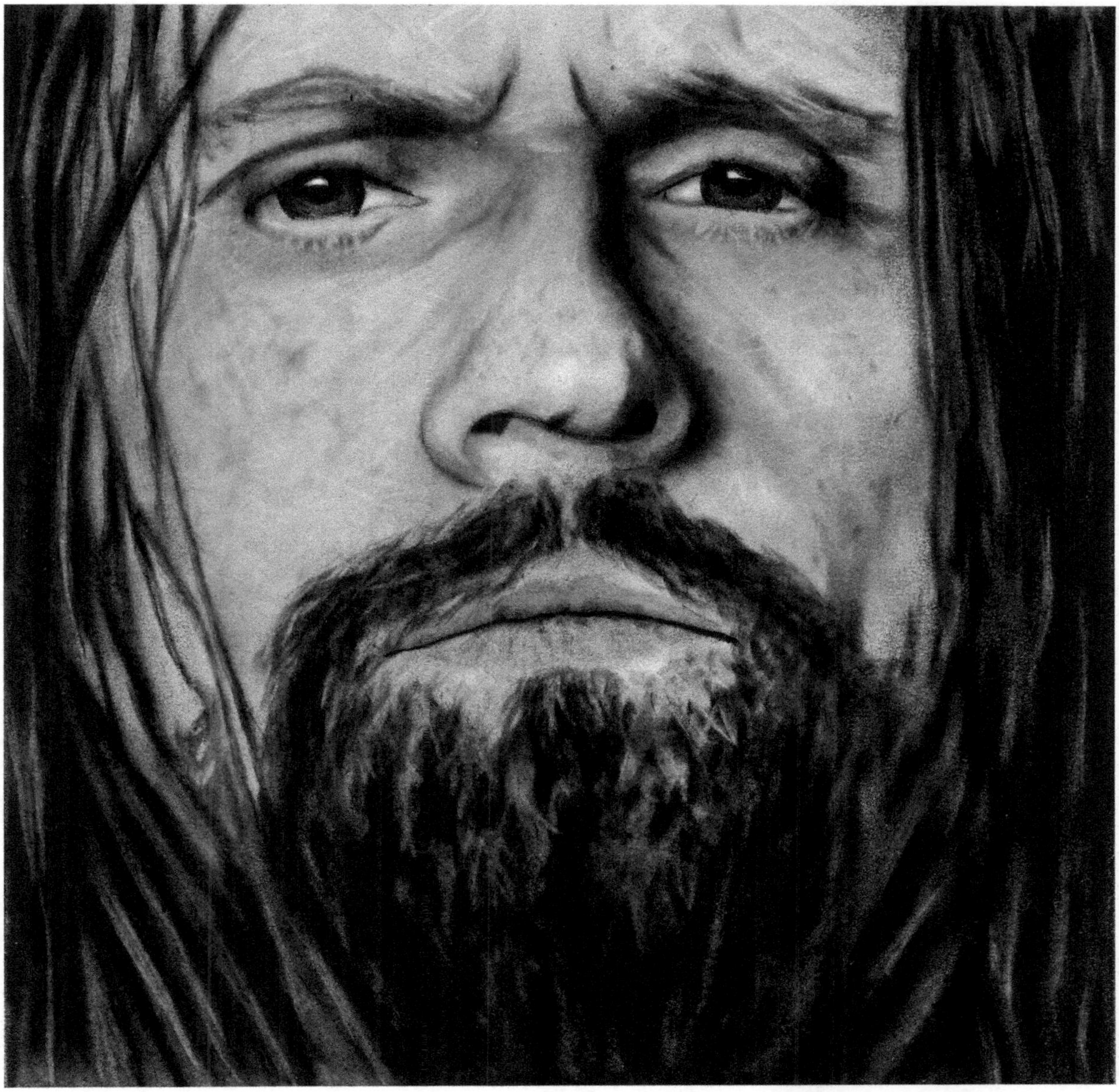

To view how this drawing was masterfully created or to purchase a Limited Edition Framed Artwork of Rob Zombie type into your Internet Browser the URL shortcut ➡ **myportrait.art/robzombie**

To listen to their Greatest Songs type into your Internet Browser the URL shortcut
➡ **radio.surf/whitezombie**

To view all channels on THE FACE OF MUSIC Internet Radio MEGA Station type into your Internet Browser the URL shortcut ➡ **radio.surf/music**

To inquire about purchasing a Limited Edtion NFT of this portrait type into your Internet Browser the URL shortcut ➡ **myartnft.shop/robzombie**

To view all available NFTs type into your Internet Browser the URL shortcut ➡ **myartnft.shop/all**

# Whitesnake

(Total Albums Sold: Multi-Millions) (Genre: Hard Rock)

Whitesnake are a hard rock band formed in England in 1978. The group was originally put together as the backing band for singer David Coverdale, who had recently left Deep Purple. Though the band quickly developed into their own entity, Coverdale is the only constant member throughout their history. Whitesnake enjoyed much success in the UK, Europe and Japan through their early years. The albums Ready an' Willing, Come an' Get It and Saints & Sinners all reached the top ten on the UK Albums Chart. By the mid-1980s, however, Coverdale had set his sights on breaking through in North America, where Whitesnake remained largely unknown. With the backing of American label Geffen Records, Whitesnake released their self-titled album in 1987, which proved to be their biggest success to date, selling over eight million copies in the US and spawning the hit singles "Here I Go Again" and "Is This Love". Whitesnake also adopted a more contemporary look, akin to the Los Angeles glam metal scene. After releasing Slip of the Tongue in 1989, Coverdale decided to put Whitesnake on hold to take a break from the music industry. Aside from a few short-lived reunions in the 1990s, the band remained mostly inactive until 2003, when Coverdale put together a new line-up to celebrate Whitesnake's 25th anniversary. Since then Whitesnake have released four more studio albums and toured extensively around the world.

Whitesnake's early sound has been characterized by critics as blues rock, but they slowly began moving toward a more commercially accessible hard rock style. Themes such as love and sex are common in Whitesnake's lyrics, which have also been criticized for their excessive use of sexual innuendos and double entendres. Whitesnake have been nominated for several awards during their career, including Best British Group at the 1988 Brit Awards. They have also been featured on lists of the greatest hard rock bands of all time by several media outlets, while their songs and albums have appeared on many "best of" lists by outlets, such as VH1 and Rolling Stone.

# David Coverdale

(Net Worth: $18 Million)(Height: 5' -10")

David Coverdale (born 22 September 1951) is an English rock singer-songwriter best known for his work with Whitesnake, a hard rock band he founded in 1978. Before Whitesnake, Coverdale was the lead singer of Deep Purple from 1973 to 1976, after which he established his solo career. A collaboration with Jimmy Page resulted in a 1993 album that was certified Platinum. In 2016, Coverdale was inducted into the Rock and Roll Hall of Fame as a member of Deep Purple, giving one of the band's induction speeches. Coverdale is known in particular for his powerful blues-tinged voice.

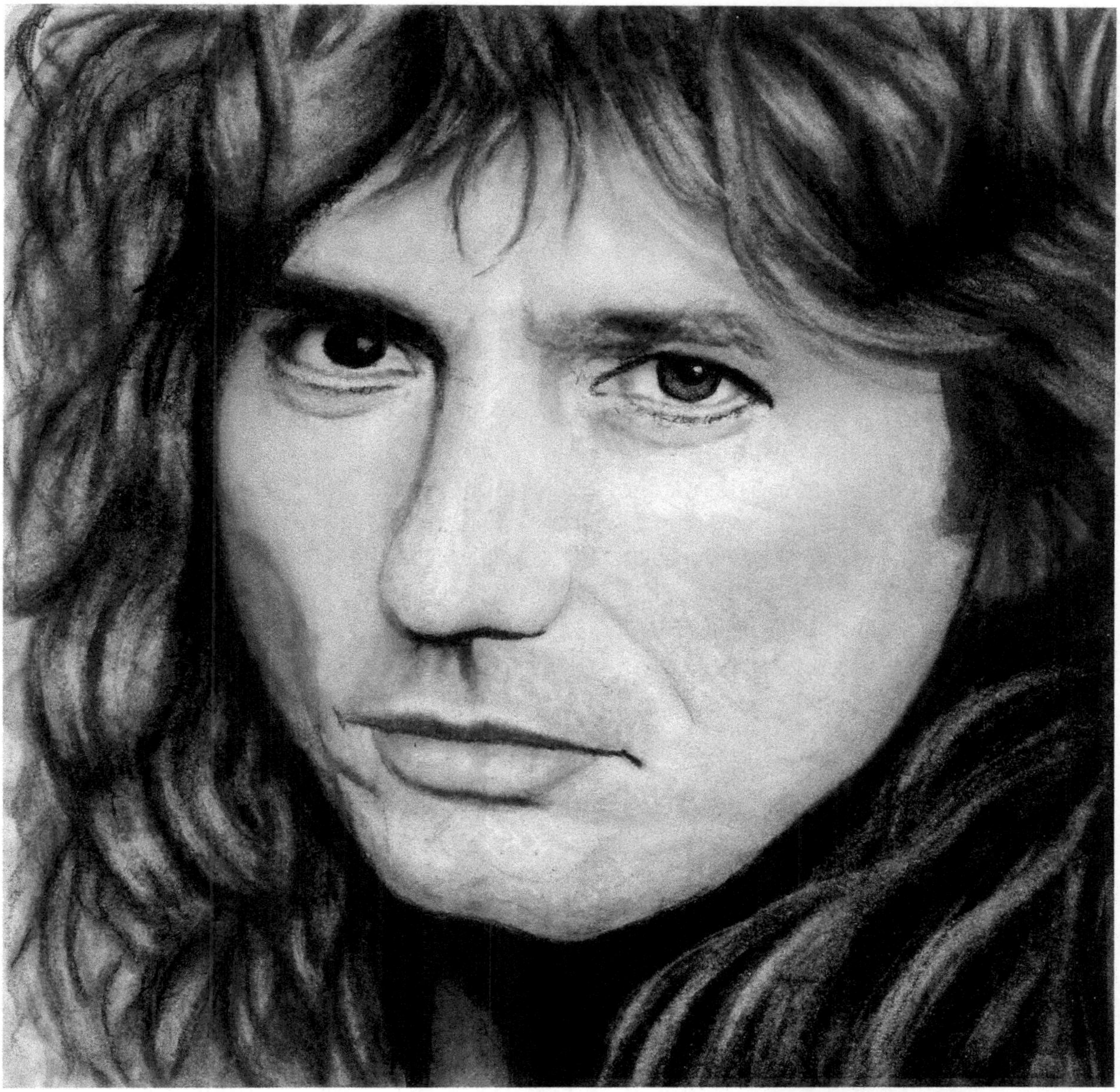

To view how this drawing was masterfully created or to purchase a Limited Edition Framed Artwork of David Coverdale type into your Internet Browser the URL shortcut ➡ **myportrait.art/davidcoverdale**

To listen to their Greatest Songs type into your Internet Browser the URL shortcut ➡ **radio.surf/whitesnake**

To view all channels on THE FACE OF MUSIC Internet Radio MEGA Station type into your Internet Browser the URL shortcut ➡ **radio.surf/music**

To inquire about purchasing a Limited Edtion NFT of this portrait type into your Internet Browser the URL shortcut ➡ **myartnft.shop/davidcoverdale**

To view all available NFTs type into your Internet Browser the URL shortcut ➡ **myartnft.shop/all**

# Whitney Houston

(Net worth: Negative $20 Million)(Total Records Sold: 200+Million)
(Genre: R&B , Pop , Dance , Soul , Gospel)(Height: 5' - 7 1/2")

Whitney Elizabeth Houston ( August 9, 1963 – February 11, 2012) was an American singer and actress. She is one of the best-selling recording artists of all time, with sales of over 200 million records worldwide. Houston released seven studio albums and two soundtrack albums, all of which have been certified diamond, multi-platinum, platinum, or gold by the Recording Industry Association of America (RIAA). Her crossover appeal on the popular music charts as well as her prominence on MTV influenced several African-American female artists.

Houston began singing in church as a child and became a background vocalist while in high school. With the guidance of Arista Records chairman Clive Davis, she signed to the label at age 19. Her first two studio albums, Whitney Houston (1985) and Whitney (1987), both peaked at number one on the Billboard 200 and are among the best-selling albums of all time. She is the only artist to have seven consecutive number-one singles on the US Billboard Hot 100 chart, from "Saving All My Love for You" in 1985 to "Where Do Broken Hearts Go" in 1988.

Houston's third studio album, I'm Your Baby Tonight (1990), yielded two Billboard Hot 100 number-one singles, "I'm Your Baby Tonight" and "All the Man That I Need", and was certified quintuple platinum by RIAA. Houston made her acting debut with the romantic thriller film The Bodyguard (1992). She recorded six songs for the film's soundtrack, including "I Will Always Love You", which won the Grammy Award for Record of the Year and became the best-selling physical single by a female in music history. It won the Grammy Award for Album of the Year and remains the best-selling soundtrack album of all time. Houston starred and recorded soundtracks for two other high-profile films, Waiting to Exhale (1995) and The Preacher's Wife (1996), with the latter's soundtrack being the best-selling gospel album of all time.

Following the critical and commercial success of My Love Is Your Love (1998), Houston renewed her contract with Arista for $100 million. However, her personal struggles began overshadowing her career, and the album Just Whitney (2002) received mixed reviews. Her drug use and a tumultuous marriage to singer Bobby Brown received widespread media coverage. After a six-year break from recording, Houston returned to the top of the Billboard 200 chart with her final studio album, I Look to You (2009). On February 11, 2012, Houston was found dead at the Beverly Hilton in Beverly Hills, California. The coroner's report showed that she had accidentally drowned in the bathtub, with heart disease and cocaine use as contributing factors. News of her death coincided with the 2012 Grammy Awards and was featured prominently in international media. Houston was inducted into the Rock and Roll Hall of Fame in 2020.

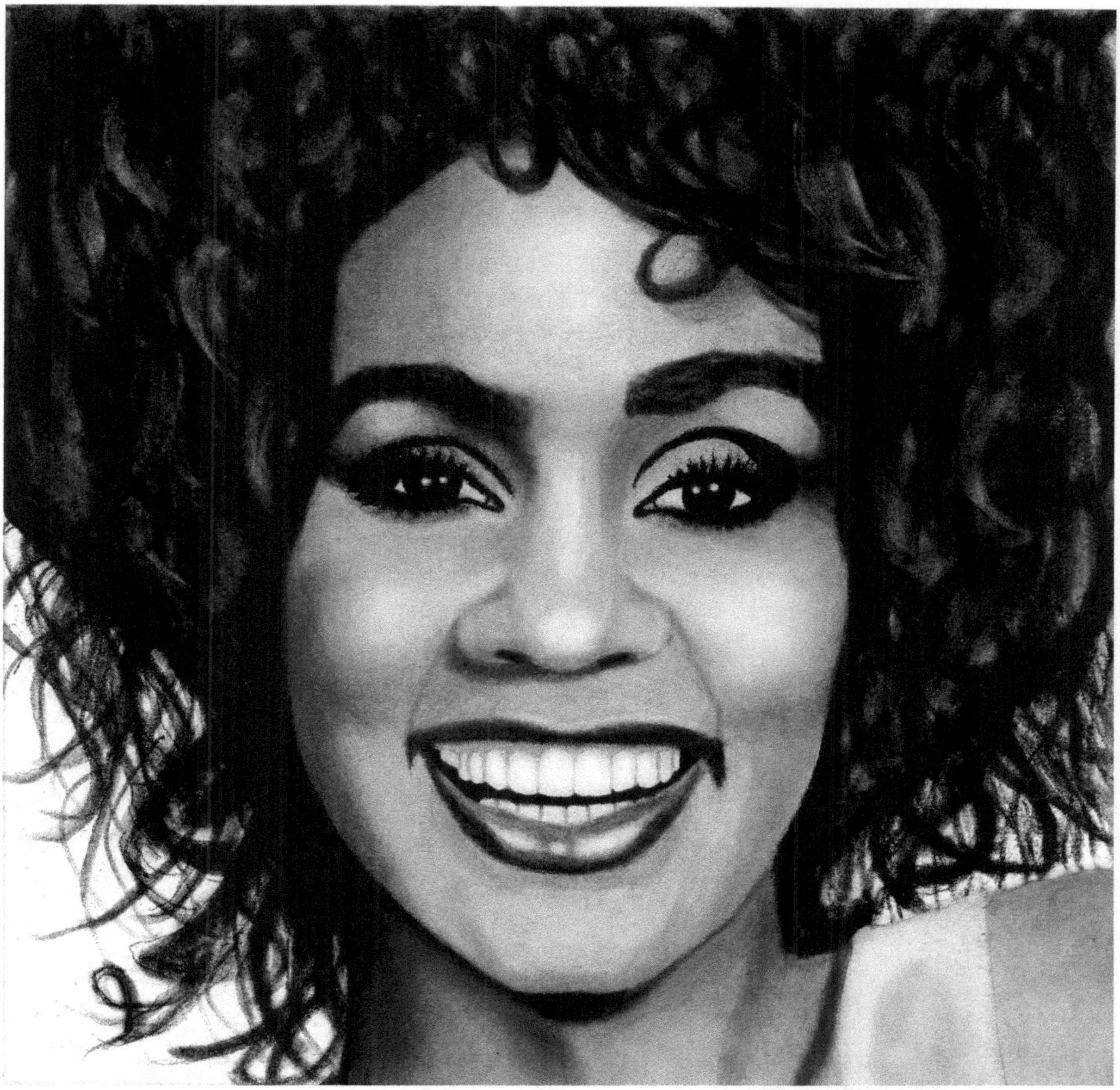

To view how this drawing was masterfully created or to purchase a Limited Edition Framed Artwork of Whitney Houston type into your Internet Browser the URL shortcut ➡ **myportrait.art/whitneyhouston**

To listen to her Greatest Songs type into your Internet Browser the URL shortcut
➡ **radio.surf/whitneyhouston**

To view all channels on THE FACE OF MUSIC Internet Radio MEGA Station type into your Internet Browser the URL shortcut ➡ **radio.surf/music**

To inquire about purchasing a Limited Edtion NFT of this portrait type into your Internet Browser the URL shortcut ➡ **myartnft.shop/whitneyhouston**

To view all available NFTs type into your Internet Browser the URL shortcut ➡ **myartnft.shop/all**

# Who, The

(Total Records Sold: 100+Million) (Genre: Classic Rock)

The Who are an English rock band formed in London in 1964. Their classic lineup consisted of lead singer Roger Daltrey, guitarist and singer Pete Townshend, bass guitarist and singer John Entwistle, and drummer Keith Moon. They are considered one of the most influential rock bands of the 20th century and have sold over 100 million records worldwide. Their contributions to rock music include the development of the Marshall stack, large PA systems, the use of the synthesizer, Entwistle and Moon's influential playing styles, Townshend's feedback and power chord guitar technique, and the development of the rock opera. They are cited as an influence by many hard rock, punk rock and mod bands, and their songs still receive regular exposure.

The Who developed from an earlier group, the Detours, and established themselves as part of the pop art and mod movements, featuring auto-destructive art by destroying guitars and drums on stage. Their first single as the Who, "I Can't Explain" (1965), reached the UK top ten, and was followed by a string of hit singles including "My Generation" (1965), "Substitute" (1966) and "Happy Jack" (1966). In 1967, they performed at the Monterey Pop Festival and released "I Can See for Miles", their only US top ten single. The group's 1969 concept album Tommy included the single "Pinball Wizard" and was a critical and commercial success.

# Roger Daltrey

(Net Worth: $90 Million)(Height: 5' -5 1/2")

Roger Harry Daltrey CBE (born 1 March 1944) is an English singer, occasional songwriter, actor and film producer. He is a co-founder and the lead singer of the rock band the Who.

Daltrey received a Lifetime achievement award from the British Phonographic Industry in 1988, and from the Grammy Foundation in 2001. He was inducted into the Rock and Roll Hall of Fame in 1990, and the UK Music Hall of Fame in 2005. He and Pete Townshend received Kennedy Center Honors in 2008 and The George and Ira Gershwin Award for Lifetime Musical Achievement at UCLA on 21 May 2016. Daltrey has also been an actor and film producer, with roles in films, theatre, and television. Planet Rock listeners voted him rock's fifth-greatest voice in 2009, and he was ranked number 61 on Rolling Stone's list of the 100 greatest singers of all time in 2010.

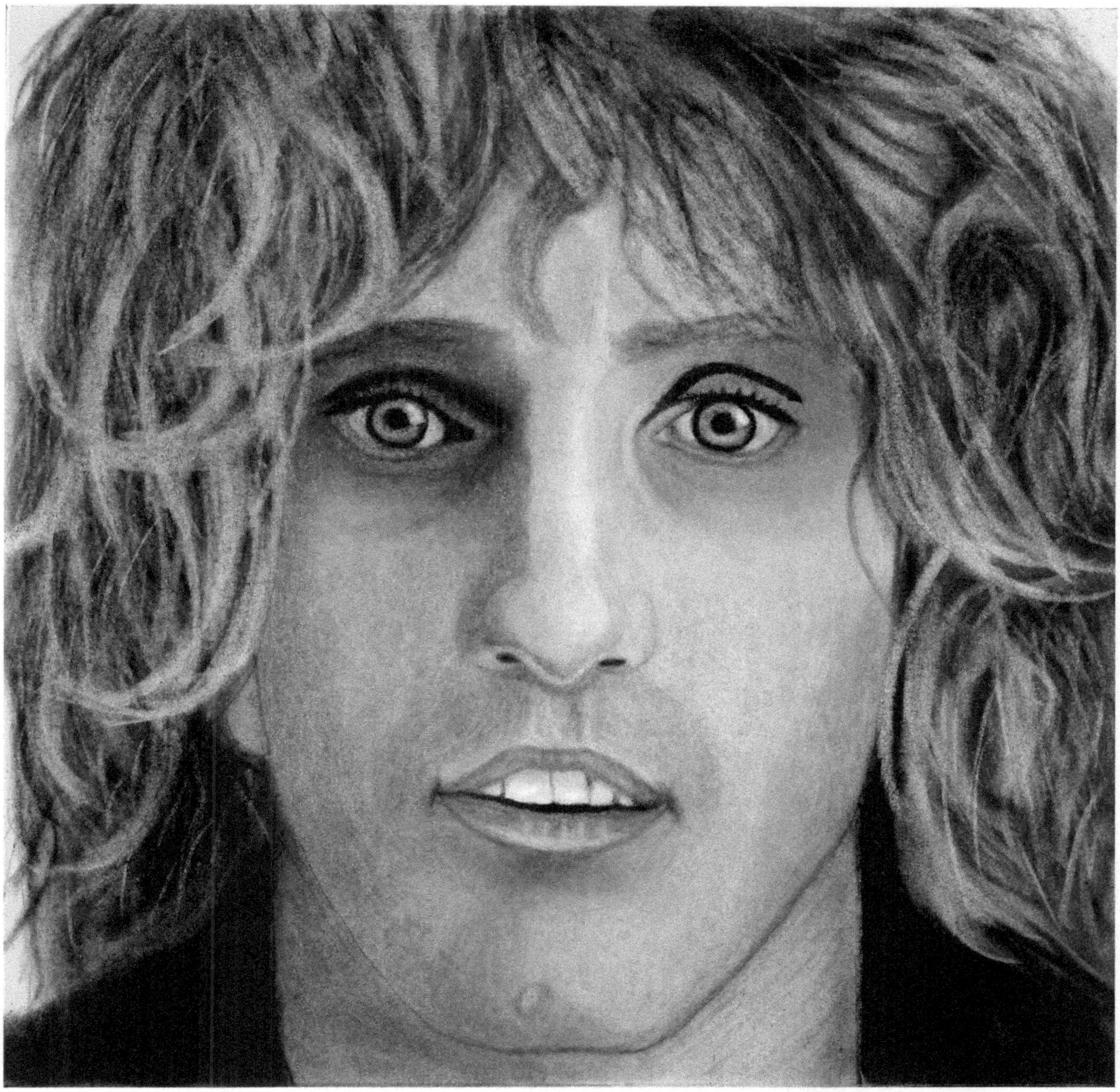

To view how this drawing was masterfully created or to purchase a Limited Edition Framed Artwork of Roger Daltrey type into your Internet Browser the URL shortcut ➡ **myportrait.art/rogerdaltrey**

To listen to their Greatest Songs type intc your Internet Browser the URL shortcut ➡ **radio.surf/thewho**

To view all channels on THE FACE OF MUSIC Internet Radio MEGA Station type into your Internet Browser the URL shortcut ➡ **radio.surf/music**

To inquire about purchasing a Limited Edtion NFT of this portrait type into your Internet Browser the URL shortcut ➡ **myartnft.shop/rogerdaltrey**

To view all available NFTs type into your Internet Browser the URL shortcut ➡ **myartnft.shop/all**

# Willie Nelson

(Net worth: $25 Million)(Total Albums Sold: 40+Million)
(Genre: Country)(Height: 5' - 6")

Willie Hugh Nelson (born April 29, 1933) is an American musician, actor, and activist. The critical success of the album Shotgun Willie (1973), combined with the critical and commercial success of Red Headed Stranger (1975) and Stardust (1978), made Nelson one of the most recognized artists in country music. He was one of the main figures of outlaw country, a subgenre of country music that developed in the late 1960s as a reaction to the conservative restrictions of the Nashville sound. Nelson has acted in over 30 films, co-authored several books, and has been involved in activism for the use of biofuels and the legalization of marijuana.

Born during the Great Depression and raised by his grandparents, Nelson wrote his first song at age seven and joined his first band at ten. During high school, he toured locally with the Bohemian Polka as their lead singer and guitar player. After graduating from high school in 1950, he joined the U.S. Air Force but was later discharged due to back problems. After his return, Nelson attended Baylor University for two years but dropped out because he was succeeding in music. During this time, he worked as a disc jockey in Texas radio stations and a singer in honky-tonks. Nelson moved to Vancouver, Washington, where he wrote "Family Bible" and recorded the song "Lumberjack" in 1956. He also worked as a disc jockey at various radio stations in Vancouver and nearby Portland, Oregon. In 1958, he moved to Houston, Texas, after signing a contract with D Records. He sang at the Esquire Ballroom weekly and he worked as a disc jockey. During that time, he wrote songs that would become country standards, including "Funny How Time Slips Away", "Hello Walls", "Pretty Paper", and "Crazy". In 1960 he moved to Nashville, Tennessee, and later signed a publishing contract with Pamper Music which allowed him to join Ray Price's band as a bassist. In 1962, he recorded his first album, ...And Then I Wrote. Due to this success, Nelson signed in 1964 with RCA Victor and joined the Grand Ole Opry the following year. After mid-chart hits in the late 1960s and the early 1970s, Nelson retired in 1972 and moved to Austin, Texas. The ongoing music scene of Austin motivated Nelson to return from retirement, performing frequently at the Armadillo World Headquarters.In 1973, after signing with Atlantic Records, Nelson turned to outlaw country, including albums such as Shotgun Willie and Phases and Stages. In 1975, he switched to Columbia Records, where he recorded the critically acclaimed album Red Headed Stranger. The same year, he recorded another outlaw country album, Wanted! The Outlaws, along with Waylon Jennings, Jessi Colter, and Tompall Glaser. During the mid-1980s, while creating hit albums like Honeysuckle Rose and recording hit songs like "On the Road Again", "To All the Girls I've Loved Before", and "Pancho and Lefty", he joined the country supergroup The Highwaymen, along with fellow singers Johnny Cash, Waylon Jennings, and Kris Kristofferson.In 1990, Nelson's assets were seized by the Internal Revenue Service, which claimed that he owed $32 million. The difficulty of paying his outstanding debt was aggravated by weak investments he had made during the 1980s. In 1992, Nelson released The IRS Tapes: Who'll Buy My Memories?; the profits of the double album—destined to the IRS—and the auction of Nelson's assets cleared his debt. During the 1990s and 2000s, Nelson continued touring extensively, and released albums every year. Reviews ranged from positive to mixed. He explored genres such as reggae, blues, jazz, and folk.

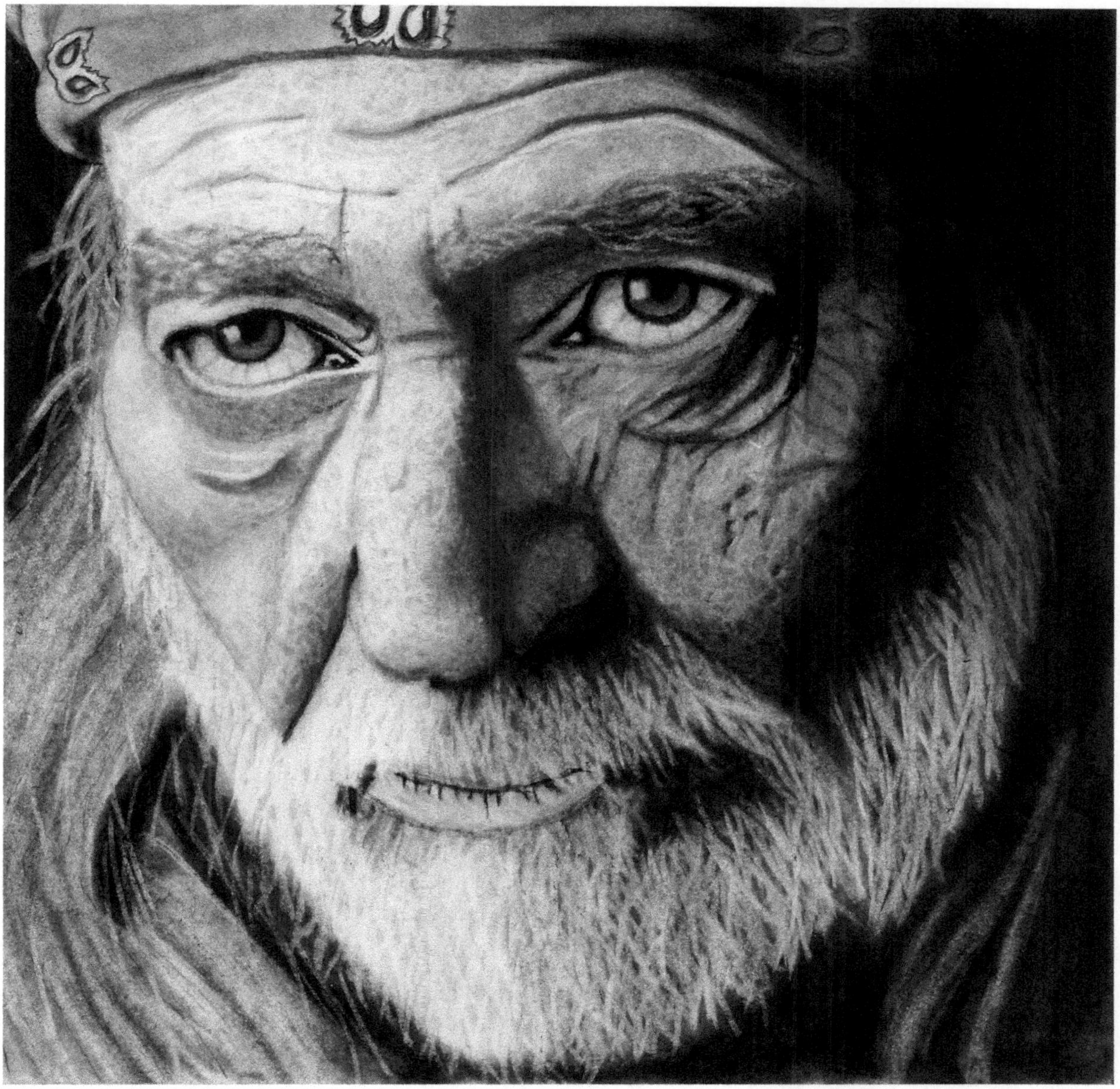

To view how this drawing was masterfully created or to purchase a Limited Edition Framed Artwork of Willie Nelson type into your Internet Browser the URL shortcut ➡ **myportrait.art/willienelson**

To listen to his Greatest Songs type into your Internet Browser the URL shortcut ➡ **radio.surf/willienelson**

To view all channels on THE FACE OF MUSIC Internet Radio MEGA Station type into your Internet Browser the URL shortcut ➡ **radio.surf/music**

To inquire about purchasing a Limited Edtion NFT of this portrait type into your Internet Browser the URL shortcut ➡ **myartnft.shop/willienelson**

To view all available NFTs type into your Internet Browser the URL shortcut ➡ **myartnft.shop/all**

# Wilson Pickett

(Net worth: $1/2 Million)(Total Albums Sold: Millions)
(Genre: R&B , Soul)(Height: 5' - 8")

Wilson Pickett (March 18, 1941 – January 19, 2006) was an American singer and songwriter. A major figure in the development of American soul music, Pickett recorded over 50 songs which made the US R&B charts, many of which crossed over to the Billboard Hot 100. Among his best-known hits are "In the Midnight Hour" (which he co-wrote), "Land of 1,000 Dances", "Mustang Sally", and "Funky Broadway".

Pickett was inducted into the Rock and Roll Hall of Fame in 1991, in recognition of his impact on songwriting and recording.

Pickett's Atlantic career began with the self-produced single, "I'm Gonna Cry". Looking to boost Pickett's chart chances, Atlantic paired him with record producer Bert Berns and established songwriters Barry Mann and Cynthia Weil. With this team, Pickett recorded "Come Home Baby," a duet with singer Tami Lynn, but this single failed to chart.

Pickett's breakthrough came at Stax Records' studio in Memphis, Tennessee, where he recorded his third Atlantic single, "In the Midnight Hour" (1965). This song was Pickett's first big hit, peaking at #1 R&B, #21 pop (US), and #12 (UK). It sold over one million copies, and was awarded a gold disc. It garnered Pickett his first Grammy nomination for Best Rhythm & Blues Recording at the 8th Annual Grammy Awards.

The genesis of "In the Midnight Hour" was a recording session on May 12, 1965, at which Wexler worked out a powerful rhythm track with studio musicians Steve Cropper and Al Jackson of the Stax Records house band, including bassist Donald "Duck" Dunn. (Stax keyboard player Booker T. Jones, who usually played with Dunn, Cropper and Jackson as Booker T. & the M.G.'s, did not play on the studio sessions with Pickett.) Wexler said to Cropper and Jackson, "Why don't you pick up on this thing here?" He performed a dance step. Cropper explained in an interview that Wexler told them that "this was the way the kids were dancing; they were putting the accent on two. Basically, we'd been one-beat-accenters with an afterbeat; it was like 'boom dah,' but here was a thing that went 'um-chaw,' just the reverse as far as the accent goes."

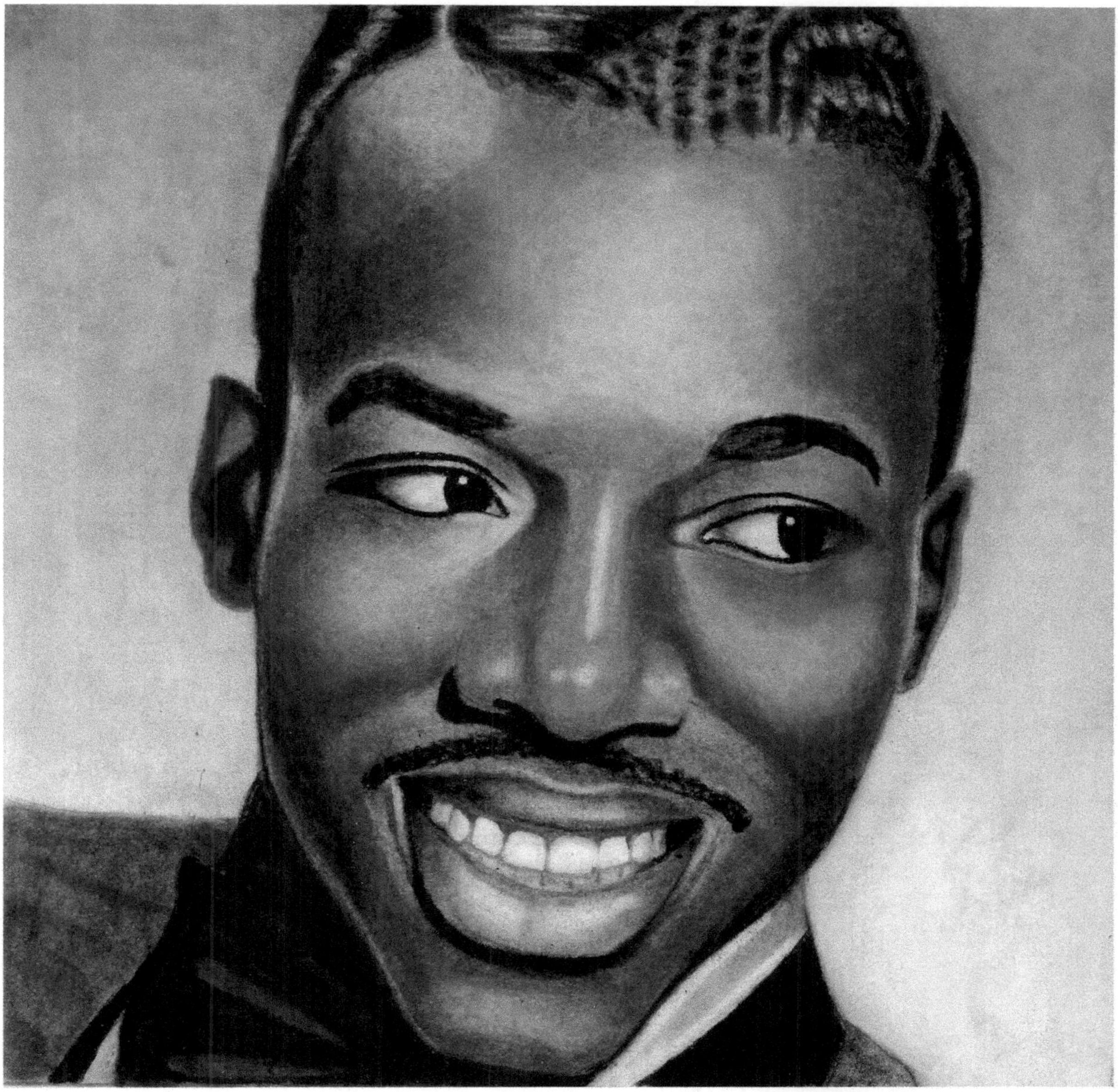

To view how this drawing was masterfully created or to purchase a Limited Edition Framed Artwork of Wilson Pickett type into your Internet Browser the URL shortcut ➡ **myportrait.art/wilsonpickett**

To listen to his Greatest Songs type into your Internet Browser the URL shortcut ➡ **radio.surf/wilsonpickett**

To view all channels on THE FACE OF MUSIC Internet Radio MEGA Station type into your Internet Browser the URL shortcut ➡ **radio.surf/music**

To inquire about purchasing a Limited Edtion NFT of this portrait type into your Internet Browser the URL shortcut ➡ **myartnft.shop/wilsonpickett**

To view all available NFTs type into your Internet Browser the URL shortcut ➡ **myartnft.shop/all**

# Wu-Tang Clan

(Total Records Sold: 40 Million) (Genre: East Coast Hip-Hop, Hardcore Hip-Hop)

Wu-Tang Clan is an American hip hop group formed in Staten Island, New York City in 1992. Its original members include RZA, GZA, Ol' Dirty Bastard, Method Man, Raekwon, Ghostface Killah, Inspectah Deck, U-God, and Masta Killa. Close affiliate Cappadonna later became an official member. Wu-Tang Clan are regarded as a highly influential group in hip hop, helping to popularize and develop the East Coast hip hop and hardcore hip hop styles.

After signing to Steve Rifkind's label Loud Records in 1992, Wu-Tang Clan released their debut album, Enter the Wu-Tang (36 Chambers), in 1993; it received widespread critical acclaim and has since been consistently rated as one of the greatest hip hop albums of all time. Members of the group released solo albums between 1994 and 1996. In 1997, the group released their second album, Wu-Tang Forever. It debuted atop the Billboard 200 and was nominated for Best Rap Album at the 1998 Grammy Awards. The group later released the albums The W (2000), Iron Flag (2001), 8 Diagrams (2007) and A Better Tomorrow (2014), to less popularity. The only copy of their seventh album, Once Upon a Time in Shaolin (2015), was bought for $2 million by hedge fund manager Martin Shkreli. The group's eighth album, The Saga Continues, was released in 2017.

Wu-Tang Clan has introduced and launched the careers of a number of affiliated artists and groups, collectively known as the Wu-Tang Killa Bees. In 2008, About ranked Wu-Tang Clan "the No. 1 greatest hip hop group of all time". Kris Ex of Rolling Stone called Wu-Tang Clan "the best rap group ever". In 2004, NME hailed them as one of the most influential groups of the last ten years.

# Method Man

(Net Worth: $14 Million)(Height: 6' - 3")

Clifford Smith Jr. (born March 2, 1971), better known by his stage name Method Man, is an American rapper, songwriter, record producer and actor. He is known as a member of the East Coast hip hop collective Wu-Tang Clan. He is also one half of the hip hop duo Method Man & Redman. He took his stage name from the 1979 film Method Man. In 1996, Smith won a Grammy Award for Best Rap Performance by a Duo or Group, for "I'll Be There for You/You're All I Need to Get By", featuring American R&B singer Mary J. Blige, whom he currently stars with in Power Book II: Ghost, a spin-off of its original show Power.

Smith has appeared in films such as 187 (1997), Belly (1998), How High (2001), Garden State (2004), The Wackness (2008), Venom (2005), Red Tails (2012), Keanu (2016), and The Cobbler (2014). On television, he and frequent collaborator, fellow East Coast rapper Redman, co-starred on the short-lived Fox sitcom Method & Red. He has also had recurring roles in three HBO series, as Tug Daniels in Oz, Melvin "Cheese" Wagstaff in The Wire, and Rodney in The Deuce. Method Man also appears in the TBS comedy The Last O.G..

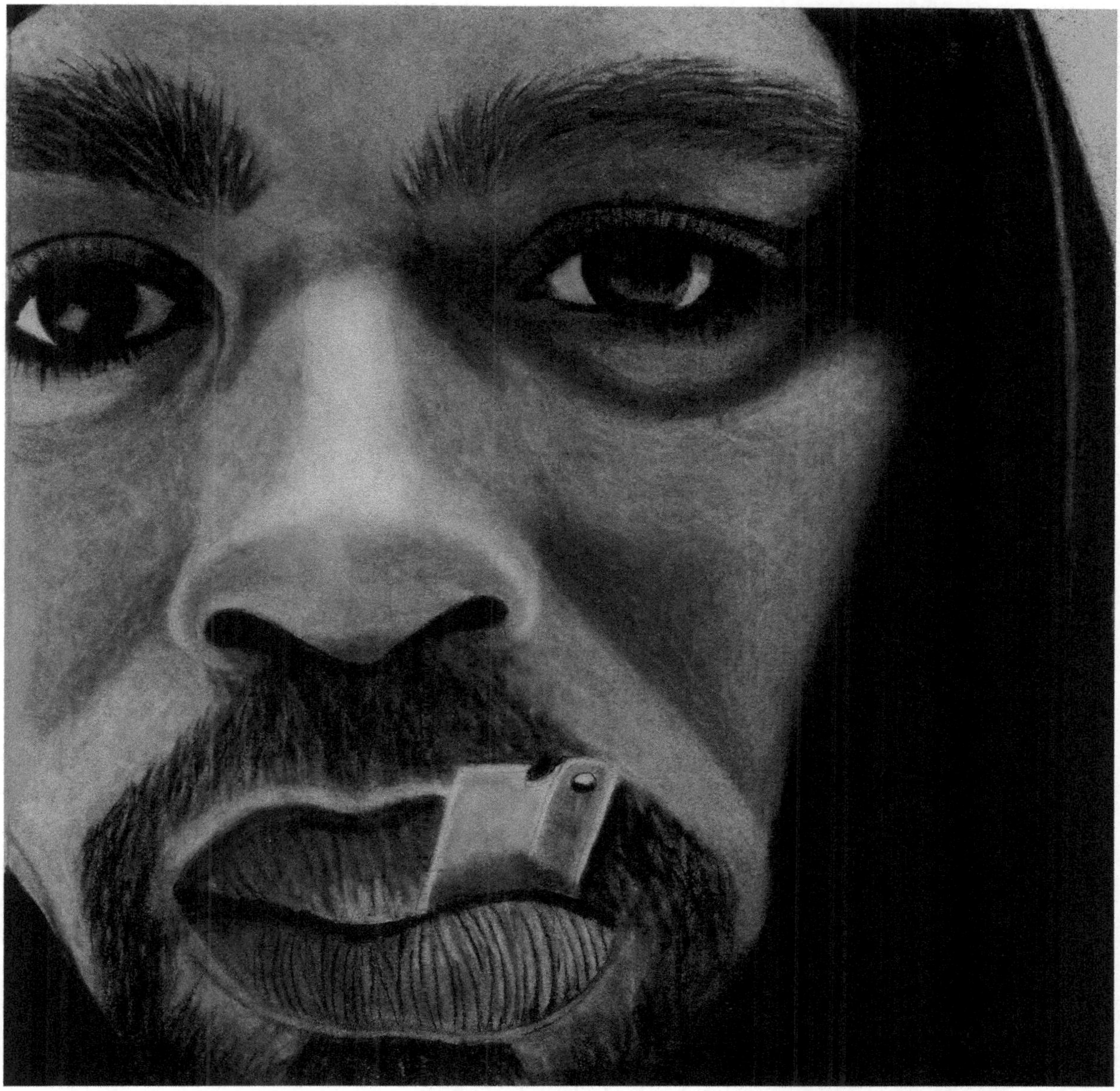

To view how this drawing was masterfully created or to purchase a Limited Edition Framed Artwork of Method Man type into your Internet Browser the URL shortcut ➡ **myportrait.art/methodman**

To listen to their Greatest Songs type into your Internet Browser the URL shortcut ➡ **radio.surf/wutangclan**

To view all channels on THE FACE OF MUSIC Internet Radio MEGA Station type

To inquire about purchasing a Limited Edtion NFT of this portrait type into your Internet Browser the URL shortcut ➡ **myartnft.shop/methodman**

To view all available NFTs type into your Internet Browser the URL shortcut ➡ **myartnft.shop/all**

# Yardbirds, The

(Total Records Sold: Millions) (Genre: Psychedelic Rock , Blues Rock , R&B)

The Yardbirds are an English rock band, formed in London in 1963. The band's core lineup featured vocalist and harmonica player Keith Relf, drummer Jim McCarty, rhythm guitarist/bassist Chris Dreja and bassist/producer Paul Samwell-Smith. The band is known for starting the careers of three of rock's most famous guitarists, Eric Clapton, Jimmy Page, and Jeff Beck, all of whom ranked in the top five of Rolling Stone magazine's list of 100 greatest guitarists. The band had a string of hits throughout the mid-1960s, including "For Your Love", "Heart Full of Soul", "Shapes of Things", and "Over Under Sideways Down".

Originally a blues-based band noted for their signature "rave-up" instrumental breaks, the Yardbirds broadened their range into pop, pioneering psychedelic rock and early hard rock; and contributed to many electric guitar innovations of the mid-1960s. Some rock critics and historians also cite their influence on the later punk rock, progressive rock, and heavy metal trends. Following the band's split in 1968, Relf and McCarty formed Renaissance and guitarist Jimmy Page formed Led Zeppelin - the latter of which was initially intended as a direct successor to the Yardbirds.

The band was inducted into the Rock and Roll Hall of Fame in 1992. They were included at number 89 in Rolling Stone's list of the "100 Greatest Artists of All Time", and ranked number 37 on VH1's 100 Greatest Artists of Hard Rock.

The Yardbirds reformed in the 1990s, featuring drummer Jim McCarty and rhythm guitarist/bassist Chris Dreja as the only original members of the band. Dreja left the band in 2012, leaving McCarty as the sole original member of the band present in the lineup.

## Keith Relf

(Net Worth: $5 Million)

William Keith Relf (22 March 1943 – 12 May 1976) was an English musician, best known as the lead vocalist and harmonica player for the Yardbirds.

Relf started playing in bands around the summer of 1956 as a singer, guitarist, and harmonica player. His blues harp and vocals were as key to the Yardbirds' sound and success as were the group's three superstar lead guitarists Eric Clapton, Jeff Beck, and Jimmy Page.

Relf co-wrote many of the original Yardbirds songs ("Shapes of Things", "I Ain't Done Wrong", "Over Under Sideways Down", "Happenings Ten Years Time Ago"), later showing a leaning towards acoustic/folk music as the sixties unfolded ("Only the Black Rose"). He also sang an early version of "Dazed and Confused" in live Yardbirds concerts, after hearing musician Jake Holmes perform the song, which was later recorded by the band's successor group Led Zeppelin.

Relf died in the basement of his home in 1976 at age 33 from electrocution while playing an electric guitar.

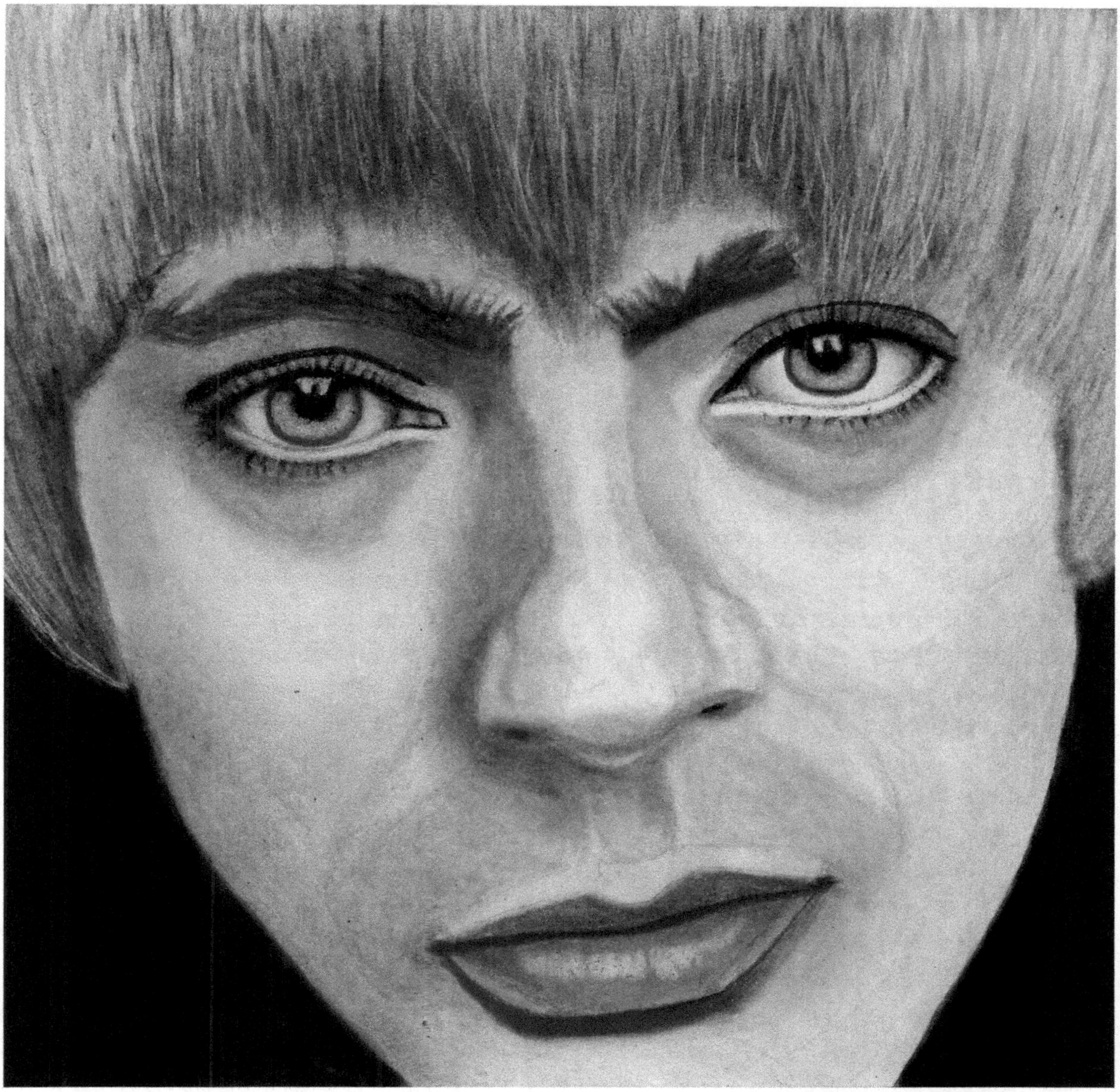

To view how this drawing was masterfully created or to purchase a Limited Edition Framed Artwork of Keith Relf type into your Internet Browser the URL shortcut ➡ **myportrait.art/keithrelf**

To listen to their Greatest Songs type into your Internet Browser the URL shortcut ➡ **radio.surf/theyardbirds**

To view all channels on THE FACE OF MUSIC Internet Radio MEGA Station type into your Internet Browser the URL shortcut ➡ **radio.surf/music**

To inquire about purchasing a Limited Edtion NFT of this portrait type into your Internet Browser the URL shortcut ➡ **myartnft.shop/keithrelf**

To view all available NFTs type into your Internet Browser the URL shortcut ➡ **myartnft.shop/all**

# Yes

(Total Records Sold: 13.5+ Million) (Genre: Progressive Rock , Art Rock)

Yes are an English progressive rock band formed in London in 1968 by singer Jon Anderson, bassist Chris Squire, guitarist Peter Banks, keyboardist Tony Kaye, and drummer Bill Bruford. The band has undergone numerous formations throughout its history; nineteen musicians have been full-time members. Since June 2015, it has consisted of guitarist Steve Howe, drummer Alan White, keyboardist Geoff Downes, singer Jon Davison, and bassist Billy Sherwood. Yes have explored several musical styles over the years, and are most notably regarded as progressive rock pioneers.

Yes began performing original songs and rearranged covers of rock, pop, blues and jazz songs, as evident on their first two albums. A change of direction in 1970 led to a series of successful progressive rock albums until their disbanding in 1981, their most successful being The Yes Album (1971), Fragile (1971) and Close to the Edge (1972). Yes toured as a major rock act that earned the band a reputation for their elaborate stage sets, light displays, and album covers designed by Roger Dean. The success of "Roundabout", the single from Fragile, cemented their popularity across the decade and beyond. In 1983, Yes reformed with a new line-up that included Trevor Rabin and a more commercial and pop-oriented musical direction. The result was 90125 (1983), their highest-selling album, which contained the U.S. number-one single "Owner of a Lonely Heart". From 1990 to 1992, Yes were an eight-member formation after they merged with Anderson Bruford Wakeman Howe for Union (1991) and its tour. Since 1994, Yes have released albums with varied levels of success and completed tours from 1994 to 2004. After a four-year hiatus, they resumed touring in 2008 and continue to release albums; their most recent is Heaven & Earth (2014). In 2016, a new group of former Yes members began touring and named themselves Yes Featuring Jon Anderson, Trevor Rabin, Rick Wakeman.

Yes are one of the most successful, influential, and longest-lasting progressive rock bands. They have sold 13.5 million RIAA-certified albums in the US. In 1985, they won a Grammy Award for Best Rock Instrumental Performance with "Cinema", and received five Grammy nominations between 1985 and 1992. They were ranked No. 94 on VH1's 100 Greatest Artists of Hard Rock. Yes have headlined annual progressive rock-themed cruises since 2013 named Cruise to the Edge. Their discography spans 21 studio albums. In April 2017, Yes were inducted into the Rock and Roll Hall of Fame, which chose to induct current and former members Anderson, Squire, Bruford, Kaye, Howe, Wakeman, White and Rabin.

## Jon Anderson

(Net Worth: $12 Million) (Height: 5' - 5")

John Roy Anderson (born 25 October 1944), known professionally as Jon Anderson, is an English-American singer and songwriter best known as the former lead singer of the progressive rock band Yes, which he formed in 1968 with bassist Chris Squire. He was a member of the band across three tenures until 2008. Anderson was also a member of Yes Featuring Jon Anderson, Trevor Rabin, Rick Wakeman.

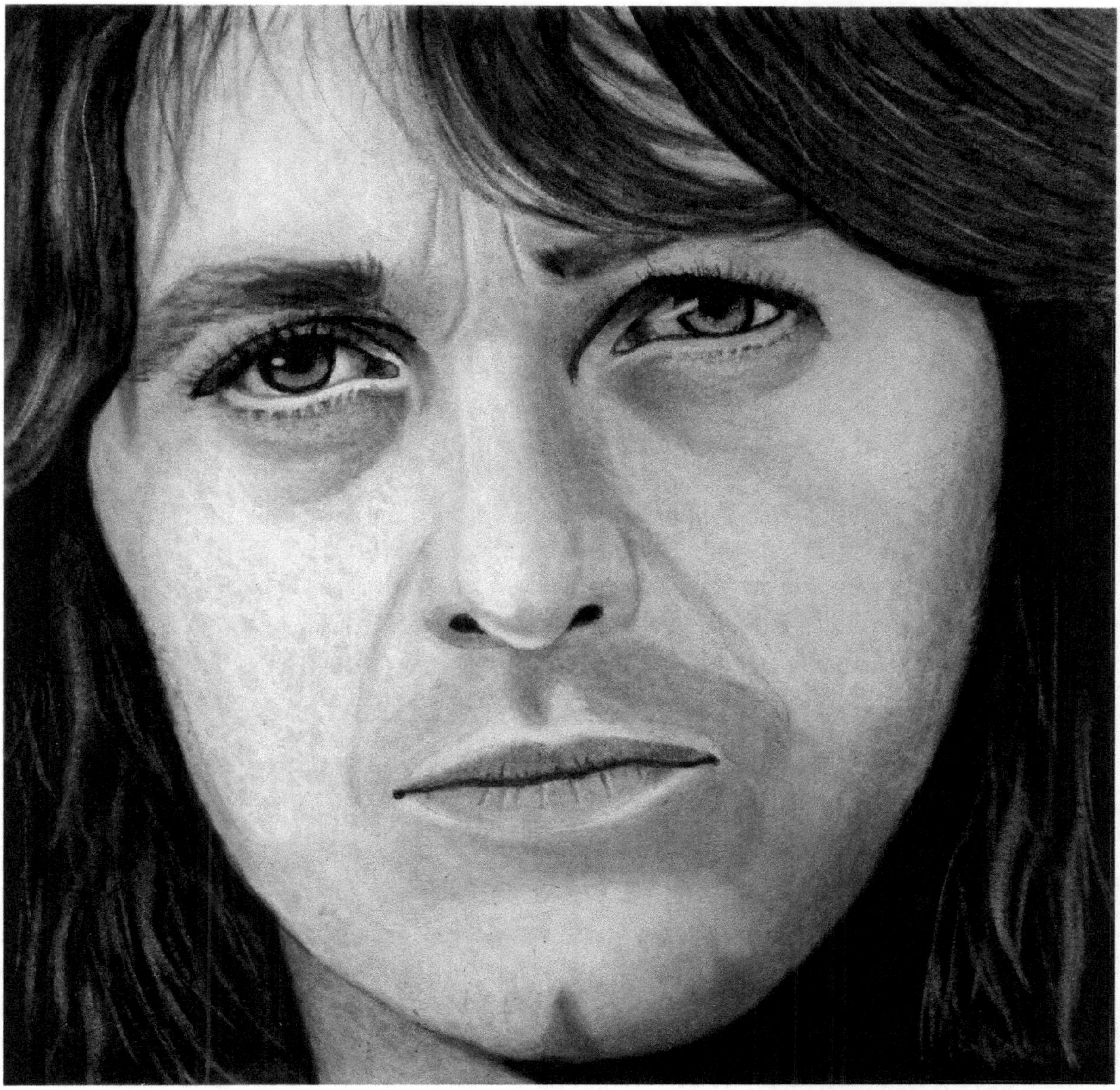

To view how this drawing was masterfully created or to purchase a Limited Edition Framed Artwork of Jon Anderson type into your Internet Browser the URL shortcut ➡ **myportrait.art/jonanderson**

To listen to their Greatest Songs type into your Internet Browser the URL shortcut ➡ **radio.surf/yes**

To view all channels on THE FACE OF MUSIC Internet Radio MEGA Station type into your Internet Browser the URL shortcut ➡ **radio.surf/music**

To inquire about purchasing a Limited Edtion NFT of this portrait type into your Internet Browser the URL shortcut ➡ **myartnft.shop/jonanderson**

To view all available NFTs type into your Internet Browser the URL shortcut ➡ **myartnft.shop/all**

# Zombies, The

(Total Records Sold: Millions) (Genre: Rock , Psychedelic Pop)

The Zombies are an English rock band formed in 1960 in St Albans and led by keyboardist and vocalist Rod Argent and vocalist Colin Blunstone. The group scored a British and American hit in 1964 with "She's Not There". In the US two further singles—"Tell Her No" in 1965 and "Time of the Season" in 1968—were also successful. Their 1968 album Odessey and Oracle is ranked number 100 on Rolling Stone's list of the 500 Greatest Albums of All Time. The Zombies were inducted into the Rock and Roll Hall of Fame in 2019.

Three members of the band, Rod Argent, Paul Atkinson, and Hugh Grundy, first came together to jam in 1961 in St Albans, Hertfordshire, England. Argent wanted to form a band and initially asked his elder cousin Jim Rodford to join as a bassist. Rodford was in a successful local band, the Bluetones, at the time and so declined, but he offered to help Argent (Rodford would later join in 2004 when the band reformed). Colin Blunstone and Paul Arnold joined the other three to form the band in April 1962, while all five members were at school.

# Colin Blunstone

(Net Worth: $3 Million) (Height: 6' - 1 1/2")

Colin Edward Michael Blunstone (born 24 June 1945) is an English singer, songwriter and musician. In a career spanning more than 50 years, Blunstone came to prominence in the mid 1960s as the lead singer of the English rock band the Zombies, which released four singles that entered the Top 75 charts in the United States during the 1960s, including "She's Not There", "Tell Her No", "She's Coming Home", and "Time of the Season". Blunstone began his solo career in 1969, releasing three singles under a pseudonym of Neil MacArthur. Since then, he has released ten studio albums and one live album under his real name. His solo hits include "She's Not There", "Say You Don't Mind", "I Don't Believe in Miracles", "How Could We Dare to Be Wrong", "What Becomes of the Brokenhearted", and "The Tracks of My Tears". In 2019, Blunstone was inducted into the Rock and Roll Hall of Fame as part of The Zombies.

He is also known for his participation on various albums with the Alan Parsons Project, as he sang their song "Old and Wise" which became famous with Blunstone's vocals.

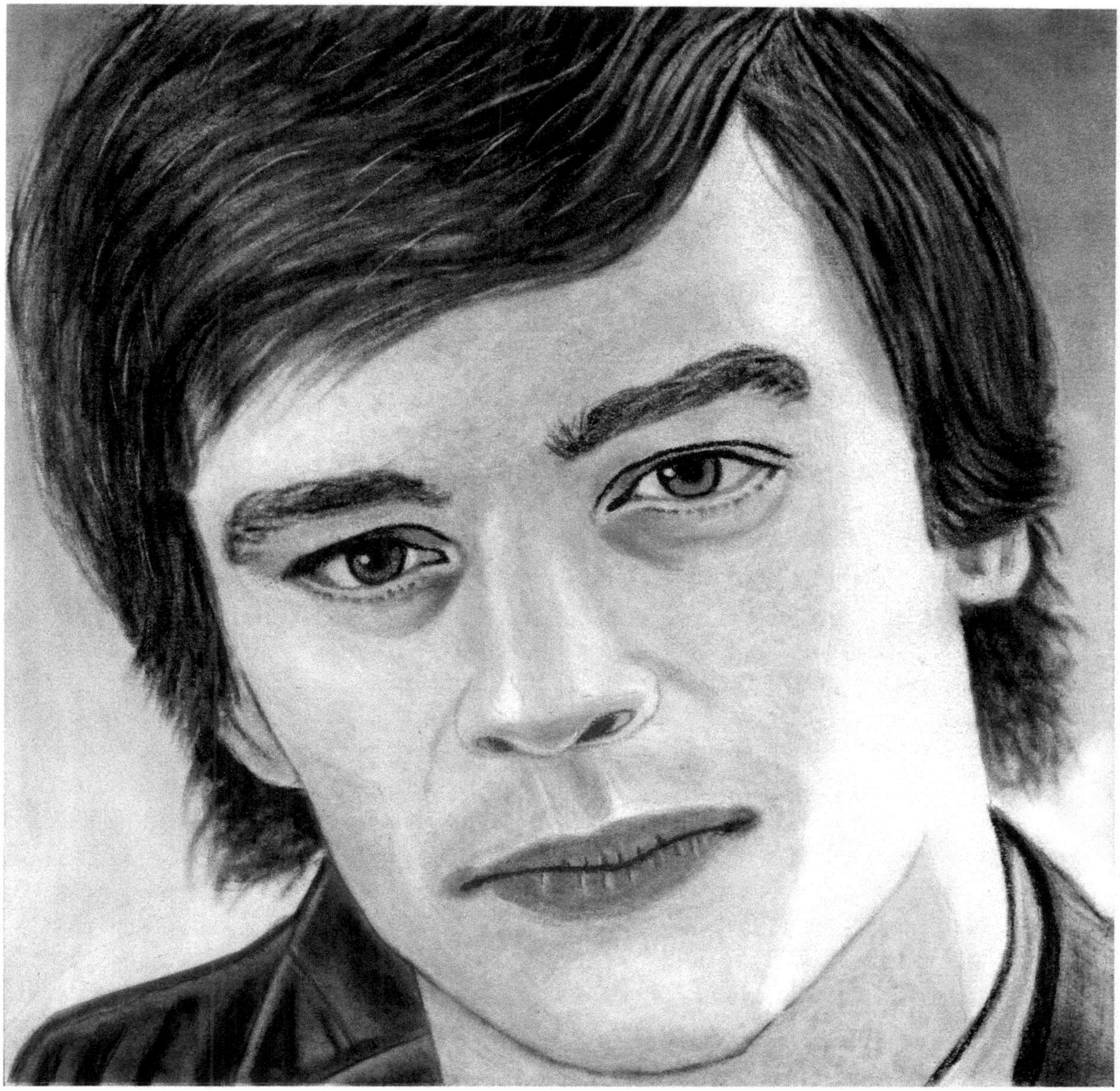

To view how this drawing was masterfully created or to purchase a Limited Edition Framed Artwork of Colin Blunstone type into your Internet Browser the URL shortcut ➡ **myportrait.art/colinblunstone**

To listen to their Greatest Songs type into your Internet Browser the URL shortcut ➡ **radio.surf/thezombies**

To view all channels on THE FACE OF MUSIC Internet Radio MEGA Station type into your Internet Browser the URL shortcut ➡ **radio.surf/music**

To inquire about purchasing a Limited Edtion NFT of this portrait type into your Internet Browser the URL shortcut ➡ **myartnft.shop/colinblunstone**

To view all available NFTs type into your Internet Browser the URL shortcut ➡ **myartnft.shop/all**

# ZZ Top

(Total Albums Sold: 50 Million) (Genre: Classic Rock)

ZZ Top is an American rock band formed in 1969 in Houston, Texas. The group consists of founder Billy Gibbons (vocals, guitar), Dusty Hill (vocals, bass), and Frank Beard (drums). Initially rooted in blues, the band's style has evolved throughout their career, with a signature sound based on Gibbons' blues guitar style and the rhythm section of Hill and Beard. Their lyrics, often embellished with sexual innuendo, focus on their Texas roots and sense of humor. Popular for their live performances and the identical physical appearances of Gibbons and Hill—who are rarely seen without their long beards, sunglasses, and Stetson hats—the group has staged several elaborate tours.

ZZ Top formed after the demise of Moving Sidewalks, Gibbons' previous band. Within a year, they signed with London Records and released ZZ Top's First Album (1971). Subsequent releases, such as their first top-ten album Tres Hombres (1973) and the singles "La Grange" and "Tush", gained extensive radio airplay. By the mid-1970s, they had become renowned in North America for their live act, highlighted by their performances during the Worldwide Texas Tour from 1976 to 1977, which was a critical and commercial success.Following a two-year break in response to creative stagnation and exhaustion, ZZ Top reinvented themselves in the late 1970s with a new musical direction and their now-famous public image. Beginning with their albums Degüello (1979) and El Loco (1981), they experimented with instruments including clarinets, saxophones, and synthesizers. They established a more mainstream sound and gained international favor with the records Eliminator (1983) and Afterburner (1985), which integrated influences from new wave, punk, and dance-rock. The popularity of their music videos, including those for "Gimme All Your Lovin'", "Sharp Dressed Man", and "Legs", helped propel them onto the television channel MTV and made them one of the more prominent artists in 1980s pop culture. Their Afterburner Tour set records for the highest-attended and highest-grossing concert tour of 1986. After additional acclaim with the release of their 10th album Recycler (1990) and its accompanying tour, their experimentation continued with mixed successes on the albums Antenna (1994), Rhythmeen (1996), XXX (1999), and Mescalero (2003). The group most recently released La Futura (2012) and Goin' 50 (2019), the latter of which is a compilation album commemorating the band's 50th anniversary.ZZ Top has released 15 studio albums and sold an estimated 50 million albums worldwide. They have won three MTV Video Music Awards, and in 2004, they were inducted into the Rock and Roll Hall of Fame. Rolling Stone ranked Gibbons number 32 on its list of the "100 Greatest Guitarists of All Time". Throughout their career, as a band and as individuals, they have supported several campaigns and charities, including Childline, St. Jude Children's Research Hospital, and a fundraiser for the Delta Blues Museum.

# Billy Gibbons

(Net Worth: $60 Million) (Height: 5' - 11")

William Frederick Gibbons (born December 16, 1949) is an American musician, singer, songwriter, record producer, and actor, best known as the guitarist and primary lead vocalist of American rock band ZZ Top.

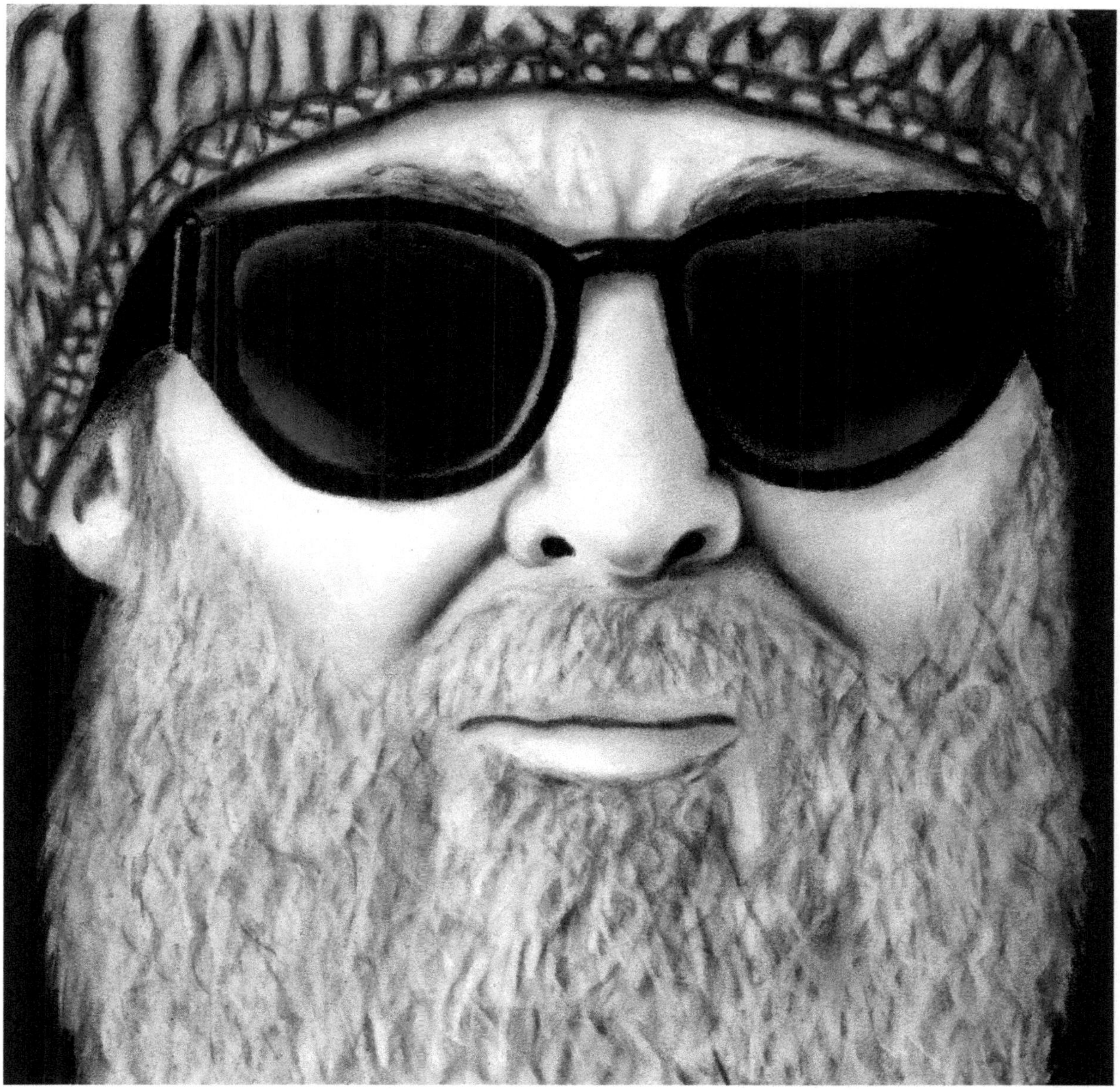

To view how this drawing was masterfully created or to purchase a Limited Edition Framed Artwork of Billy Gibbons type into your Internet Browser the URL shortcut ➡ **myportrait.art/billygibbons**

To listen to their Greatest Songs type into your Internet Browser the URL shortcut ➡ **radio.surf/zztop**

To view all channels on THE FACE OF MUSIC Internet Radio MEGA Station type into your Internet Browser the URL shortcut ➡ **radio.surf/music**

To inquire about purchasing a Limited Edtion NFT of this portrait type into your Internet Browser the URL shortcut ➡ **myartnft.shop/billygibbons**

To view all available NFTs type into your Internet Browser the URL shortcut ➡ **myartnft.shop/all**

# Poems
by
David S. Thompson

# The Phoenix

With my heart
full of bold

To rise above
all that seams

To my being
not of dreams

To be with soul
may I only know

With these thoughts
to the end

May I only shine
God be it...
Once again...

David S. Thompson

# Summer Breese

Sitting here breathing...
Breathing summer breese...
Dark death to no one ...to no one can see
I am a man..I am strong
To no thoughts may I be wrong!!...???
People run because they are frighten
To a government that only will tighten???
Predicting death to follow....
As we all wait in wallow
Only the weak left to die
From lines of death they wait to buy
As the wealth being given out as all to borrow
Leaves us with but with no tomorrow
No money for the eye to see
As our time has left us be
The banks left to way
To no money that will be of pay
As our buildings left to crumble
Waiting streets will a rumble
As war lords will arise
To pointing fingers they will size
To the fleeing people will all plee
Oh Genocide....Oh Genocide...let us be
Oh god please... take us away. ..so far..so far away.....

David S. Thompson

# *To The Gates Of Hell*

*The walls and roof is all I see...*
*Oh Lucifer please...please take me as I be*
*Anywhere I not fear...anywhere but here*
*To the hell you have brought*
*I try not to think a single thought*
*As I can't see past my eyes*
*To my mind I forever demise*
*No one can give a dam of how I be*
*To nothing they can ever see*
*How can anyone imagine this*
*That sent me to this abyss*
*WHY..WHY..do you keep me*
*Is from nothing I can't see*
*To only scream from my mind*
*Just to nothing can anyone find*
*To how far can you see*
*When you know nothing can of be*
*Oh darkness take me from this light*
*There is nothing left...left to fight*
*As I fade again into the night*
*To find the same hell...I just can't fight*
*To Heaven or Hell please just take*
*To my last words I will make*
*I tried. ..I tried as I fell*
*With all roads leading to hell*
*Oh peace ..oh peace. ...*
*To my fellow man*
*Please find peace when ever you can*
*With failing hands I can only pass*
*The torch of hope may forever you may last.*

***David S. Thompson***

My thoughts while being bedridden for 4 years.

# Fear Not

Fear is their only game
with no one left to a blame
to the pedicle they will sit
with many voices they'll commit
to those that brought us to this grieve
to no one in their path they will leave
as they will slither and snake
to their truth they will make
to his licence that came with birth
to leave us Nothing. ..but nothing of worth
To his mind... he has shut the door
To nothing of money... will be a allure
To the Goliaths he will treat
To our paying times... will meet their feet
As he passes on the wealth
To his pointed finger will find in stealth
An enigma wrapped in fortune and fame
To others they only see your shameful blame
As you play with madness..
To leave us nothing but deep in sadness
As hell fire raises to his eyes
All left to wonder from shallow cries
As if life was but fairy tales
To coffins filled full... of the gravest of nails
To a world only left to return....
To leave his thoughts....
but only ... but only to burn

David S. Thompson

# Satins Smile

Shine you sun
Please shine through
But to nothing
we would knew
To shine on us all
we are but nothing but tall
Nothing to divide us
Nothing at all
Together we stand
Divided we will fall…..
To stick a cunning knife
Into our Country's only life
To the people will divide
Nowhere left to hide
You may laugh
I may cry...
To your reasons why
One death is of sorrow
To a million you will of borrow
Has the weak become the soldiers
To a life of no tomorrow's
Their Living is only for dying
Their Dying is brought of you
As your Dreams goes to nightmares
As your Nightmares goes to hell
Hell goes to Satin
To the last screaming souls yell

David S. Thompson

# Hurt

My closest of friend
Why do you must befriend
When I'm down and out
You showed how to be without
When i have lost a love
You should me how to be above
When i cant find a way
You point me in your given way
I'm amazed in how you guide
As there is nothing left to hide
I listen to you when a don't won't to hear
Then you turn dark skies into the shine of clear
When my state of mind
is nothing left to find
You send me through the forever grind
You drag my heart
Until i find i new of start
You always remember and never forget
To climb above i will get
Try as you may you can not break
A shattered heart you may make
Oh Hurt… my closest of friends
Please never leave me....
Never again....

David S. Thompson

# Innocence

Long… long time ago
I used to be a friend
A friend to happiness and good times I would send
I had no judgement to all I would meet
To all thoughts I would keep
Why could I not see
The smiling faces from under to of be
With bellows and all a good day
We are with you they would say
But come of judgement not to did I see
Where oh where did friends all of did of leave
Not from the days did I see
Why oh lord can this be
As they turned my face from front to back
Only did I see their attack
You...you... never my friends
To your only gains you would pretend
Never never again...
Listen to my wisp of words...
Only if you can....
Now to know from these only thoughts
To my life I'll always be ...
to rise above
for all to see....

David S. Thompson

# BIOGRAPHIES OF DAVID S. THOMPSON

To view this Biography type into you Internet Browser the short cut -> myportrait.art/bio1

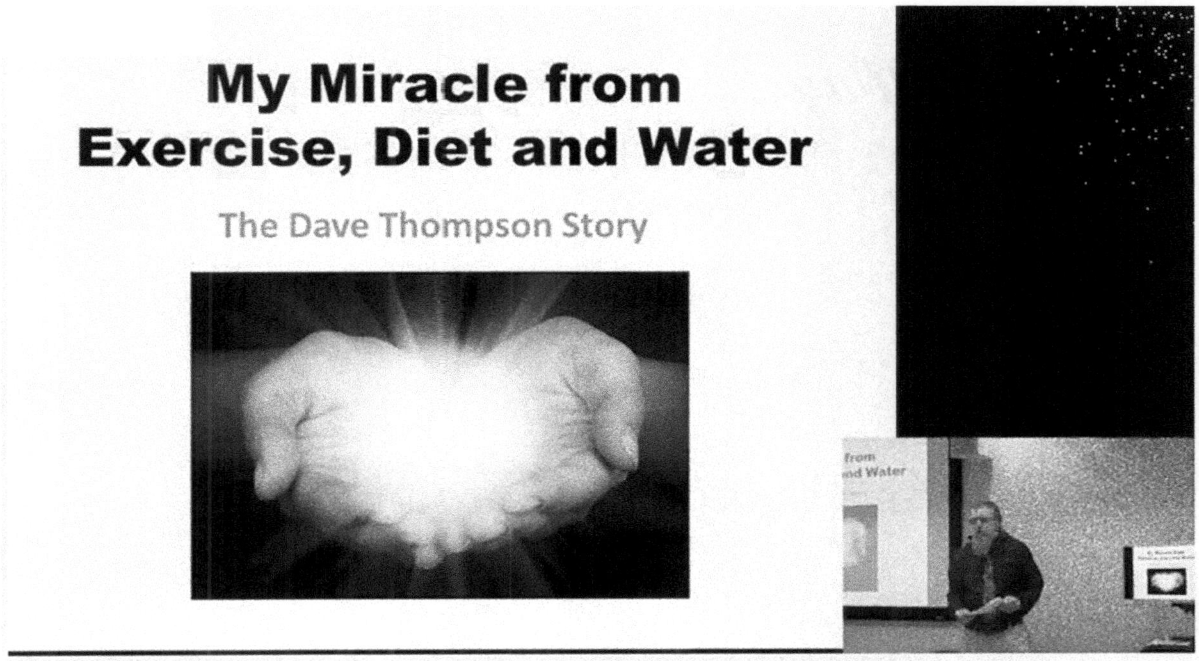


The Dave Thompson Story: My Miracle from Exercise, Diet and Water

December 9, 2016

This was my presentation to an audience of Kitchener/Waterloo Canada Resident doctors which I talk about my deepest darkest times and powered only by shear will was I able to take back control of my life and overcome most all that ailed me medically and mentally. To those who watch this video I hope you can take something from it.

**To view this Biography type into you Internet Browser the short cut -> myportrait.art/bio2**

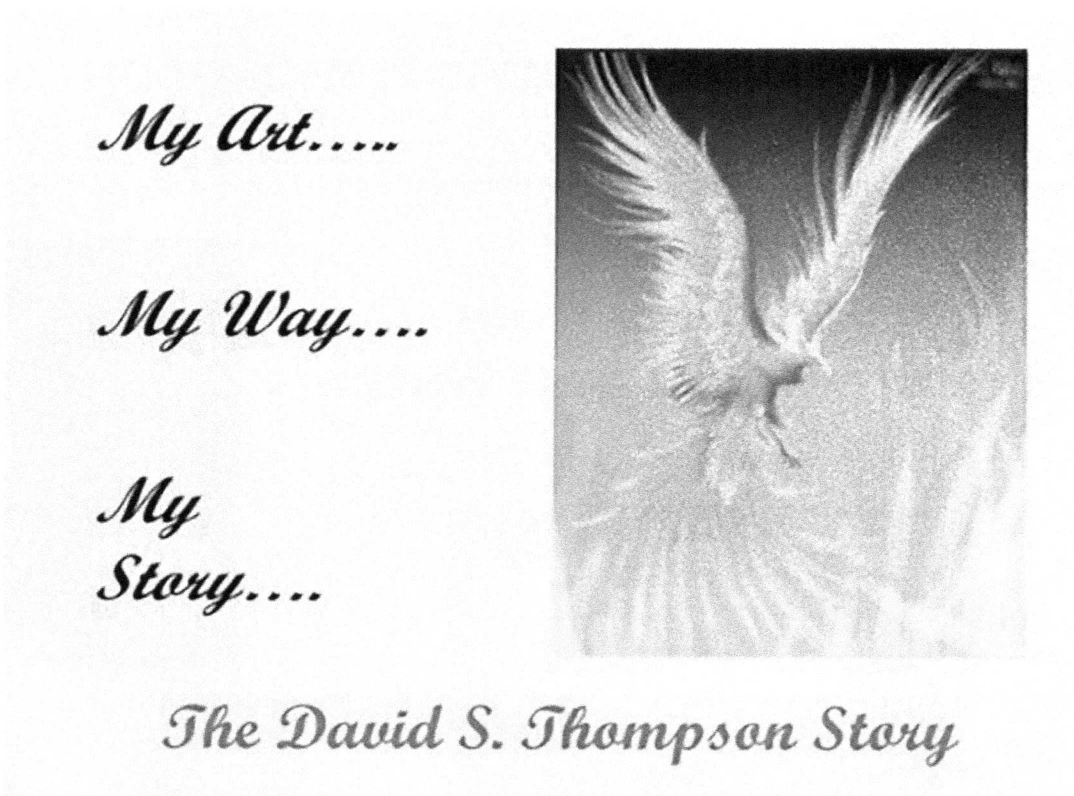


June 28, 2018

This was my Powerpoint presentation to Kitchener-Waterloo Canada city officials and honored guests at their yearly function about how art was able to guide me through my deepest and darkest days of depression, hopelessness and total loss of self worth. Mid way through my speech I must admit I thought to myself "what am I'm doing up here...nobody cares about my stupid story ...I'm just making a fool of myself". Then at the end when I said "Thank you"..I walked of the podium with my head down looking at the floor saying to myself "that was terrible". ..and then in a fraction of a second something happened I'll remember and cherish forever.. I heard clapping and cheers and when I looked up I saw them all standing clapping and cheering me on. It was absolutely the most amazing feeling I've ever had. I hope somehow now that I can give hope to the hopeless .... courage to the meekly depressed and a fighting spirit to go through the toughest of times and to show that yes...IT CAN BE DONE.

# ART SHOWS

Toronto Ontario Canada 2016

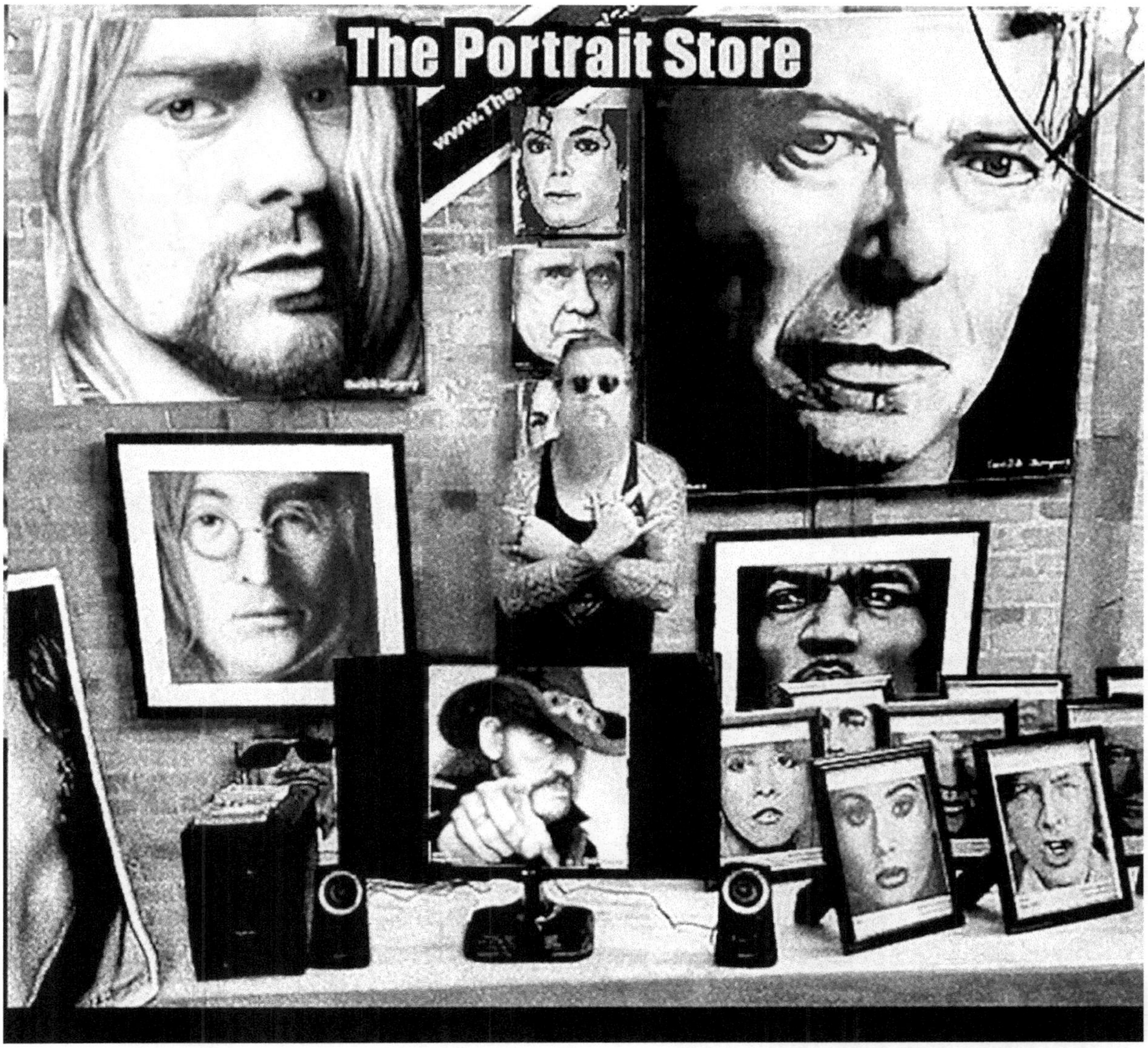

Kitchener Ontario Canada 2018 – Freeport Hospital

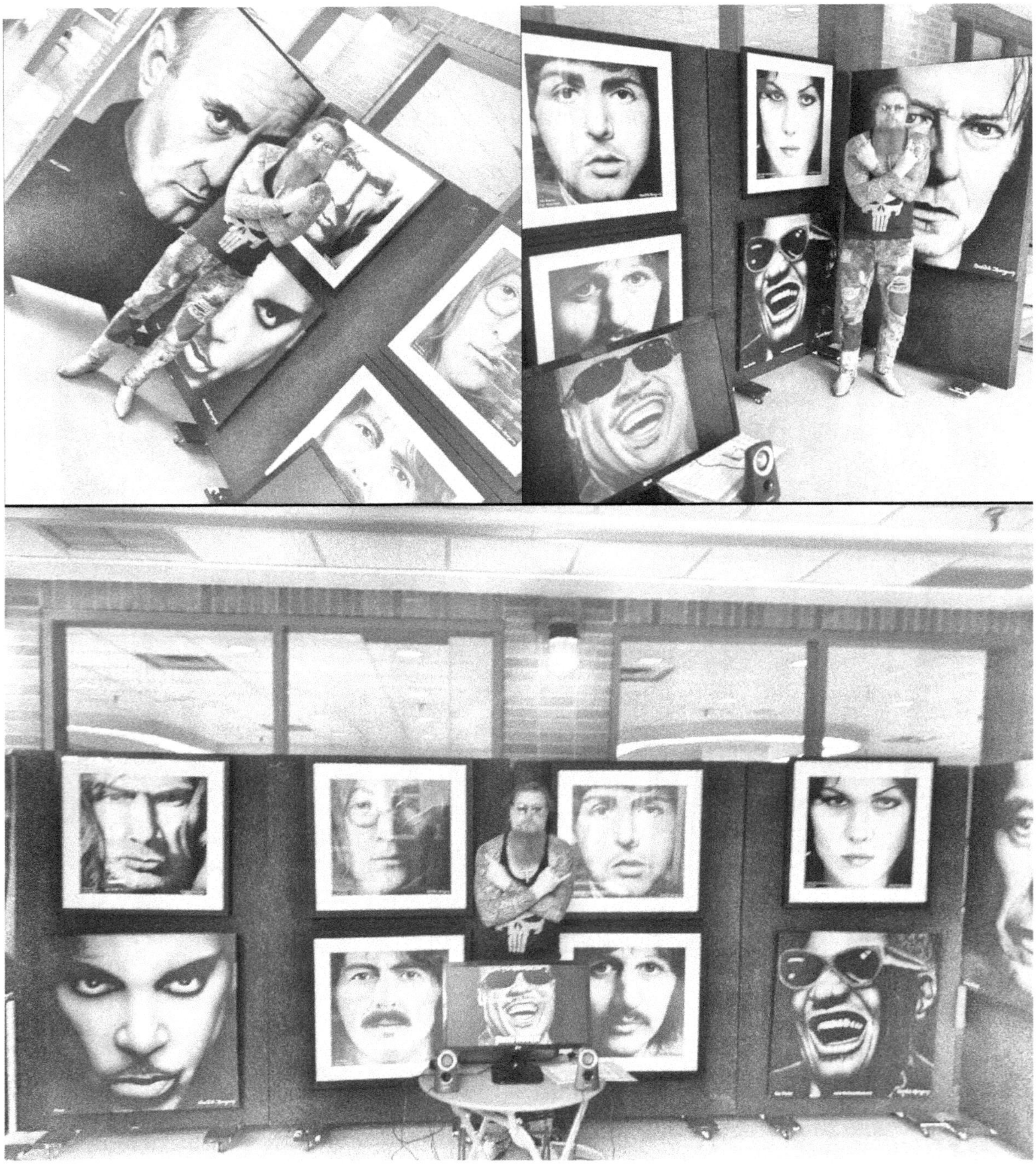

# INDEX

## D



## E



## F

## L



## M



## N



## O



## P

## Q



## R



## S



## T

## U



## V



## W



## Y



## Z

CPSIA information can be obtained
at www.ICGtesting.com
Printed in the USA
LVHW061121151121
703259LV00032B/386

9 780228 849391